MOVIES

GENERAL EDITOR
CHRIS FUJIWARA

MOVIES

CASSELL
ILLUSTRATED

A CASSELL BOOK

An Hachette Livre UK Company

First published in the UK 2007 by
Cassell Illustrated, a division of
Octopus Publishing Group Ltd.
2-4 Heron Quays,
London E14 4JP

Text, design and layout © 2007 Octopus Publishing Group Ltd.

A CIP catalogue record for this book is available from the
British Library.

ISBN-13: 978-1-84403590-8 (UK Edition)
ISBN-10: 1-84403-590-5 (UK Edition)

Distributed in the United States and Canada by
Sterling Publishing Co., Inc
387 Park Avenue South, New York, NY 10016-8810

ISBN-13: 978-1-84403604-2 (U.S. Edition)
ISBN-10: 1-84403-604-9 (U.S. Edition)

10 9 8 7 6 5 4 3 2 1

Commissioning Editor: Laura Price
Editor: Toby Nuttall
Designer: John Round

Printed in China

4/08
Bet

CONTENTS

CONTRIBUTORS

Geoff Andrew is Head of Film Programme at London's National Film Theatre and Contributing Editor to *Time Out London*. He has written a number of books on film, including studies of Nicholas Ray and the US "indie" filmmakers of the 1980s and '90s, and monographs on Kiarostami's *10* and Kieslowski's Three Colours Trilogy. In 2007, he delivered a lecture at the National Gallery on the subject of "Velazquez and the Cinema."

Sonia Benjamin is currently pursuing a Ph.D. in Film and Media Studies at the School of Oriental and African Studies (SOAS), London. Her dissertation, "The Cinema of Small Things: Malayalam Cinema in Globalised India," looks at the struggle of Malayalam cinema to find a new identity in the last decade.

Paolo Bertolin is an Italian film critic and journalist, regularly contributing to *Il Manifesto* and *Cineforum*. His writings in English include contributions to the *Korea Times*, *Senses of Cinema*, *Cinemaya*, *Ekran*, and Koreanfilm.org.

Fred Camper is a longtime writer and lecturer on film and art who lives in Chicago. He has published on film in *Film Culture*, *Artforum*, the *Chicago Reader*, and many other periodicals, and has taught at several colleges and universities. He is also an artist. His website is http://www.fredcamper.com.

Tim Cavanaugh is an editor at the *Los Angeles Times*. He has been an editor and reporter at *Reason* and Suck.com, and his work has appeared in the *Washington Post*, the *Boston Globe*, the *San Francisco Chronicle*, the *Beirut Daily Star*, *Wired*, *Newsday*, *Salon*, and many other publications.

Paolo Cherchi Usai, film curator, critic, and writer, is director of the National Film and Sound Archive of Australia and co-founder of the Pordenone Silent Film Festival and of the L. Jeffrey Selznick School of Film Preservation at George Eastman House in Rochester, New York. Among his books are *Silent Cinema: An Introduction* and *The Death of Cinema*. He is the author of the experimental silent feature *Passio*, a visual meditation on the challenges and limits of film preservation.

Antoine Coppola is a writer, professor, film director, film critic, and adviser to film festivals. His books include *Asian Cinema*, *Le Cinéma de Guy Debord*, *Image and Power*, and *South Korean Cinema*. He has directed several documentaries and feature films, including *Cruel Tales of De Sade* and *The Communards*.

Jean-Pierre Coursodon was born in Paris in 1935 and has lived in the United States since 1965. He is the author or co-author of a dozen books on American film, including *Buster Keaton*, *American Directors*, and *50 ans de cinéma américain* (co-written with Bertrand Tavernier). He has translated into French several biographies of American film directors, as well as Michael Powell's two-volume autobiography.

Mark Cousins is a filmmaker, author, and festival director. His last book, *The Story of Film*, was published in ten languages, including Mandarin. His last documentary was made with Abbas Kiarostami. His last festival, Cinema China, covering eight decades of Chinese film history, played in 20 UK cities.

Nick Deocampo is a prize-winning Filipino filmmaker and author. He has written several essays and books on Filipino and Asian cinemas. His latest publications include *Cine: Spanish Infuences on Early Cinema in the Philippines* and *Lost Films of Asia*.

Rashmi Doraiswamy is Professor (Central Asia) at the Academy of Third World Studies, University of Jamia Millia Islamia, New Delhi. She has written and lectured widely on cinema, literature and culture. She won the National Award for Best Film Critic in 1995.

Rachel Dwyer is Reader in Indian Studies and Cinema at SOAS, University of London. Her books include *Yash Chopra, Cinema India* (co-authored with Divia Patel), *100 Bollywood Films*, and *Filming the Gods*.

David Ehrenstein has been writing about film and the arts for upwards of 40 years. His essays have appeared in *Film Culture*, *Film Quarterly*, *Film Comment*, *Cahiers du cinéma*, *Positif*, and *Sight & Sound*. His books include *The Scorsese Picture* and *Open Secret: Gay Hollywood 1928-2000*.

Jean-Michel Frodon is the editorial director of *Cahiers du cinéma* and the author of several books on cinema.

Chris Fujiwara is the author of *Jacques Tourneur: The Cinema of Nightfall* and the editor of *Undercurrent* (http://www.fipresci.org/undercurrent). He has written extensively on film for many newspapers, magazines, and anthologies. His book on Otto Preminger is forthcoming from Faber & Faber. His website is http://www.insanemute.com.

Meenu Gaur is a Felix scholar and doctoral candidate in the Centre for Film and Media Studies, SOAS, University of London. She is also an independent documentary filmmaker and co-founder of the SOAS-based independent research collective, Sacred Media Cow (http://www.sacredmediacow.com).

Aaron Gerow is assistant professor of Japanese cinema at Yale University. He has published numerous articles in multiple languages on Japanese film and popular culture and has books forthcoming on *A Page of Madness* and silent-era Japanese film culture. His book on Kitano Takeshi was recently published by the BFI.

Violet Glaze is a film writer based in Baltimore. She teaches film history at Maryland Institute College of Art and contributes regularly to many print and online publications. Her three favorite movies of all time are *Taxi Driver*, *Sherlock Jr.*, and *The Empire Strikes Back*. Her work can be found at http://www.violetglaze.com.

Joshua Glenn is a Boston-based writer, editor, and independent scholar. He was formerly editor and publisher of Hermenaut and associate editor of the *Boston Globe*'s "Ideas" section.

Barry Keith Grant is Professor of Film and Popular Culture at Brock University in Ontario, Canada. He is the author of numerous books, most recently *Film Genre: Iconography and Ideology* (Wallflower Press). He edits film books for Wayne State University Press and Blackwell Publishing, and served as Editor-in-Chief of the *Schirmer Encyclopedia of Film*.

A. S. Hamrah is a writer and semiotic brand analyst living in Brooklyn, New York.

James Harvey is the author of *Romantic Comedy in Hollywood: from Lubitsch to Sturges* (Knopf) and *Movie Love in the Fifties* (Knopf) – both currently available in paperback from Da Capo Press – and has contributed to many periodicals, including the *New York Review of Books* and *Film Comment*. He's currently working on a book on star presence which will be published by Faber and Faber.

Bruce Hodsdon, who is currently at the State Library of Queensland, has been employed in film programming and curatorial work for more than 30 years.

Christoph Huber is film and music critic for the Austrian daily *Die Presse*, is European editor of *Cinema Scope* magazine, and writes the program notes for the Austrian Filmmuseum. He has contributed to several books and numerous publications on cinema.

Dina Iordanova is Chair of Film Studies and Director of the Centre for Film Studies at the University of St. Andrews. Her expertise is mostly in East European and Balkan cinema; she has published extensively also on international and transnational film art and industry and on film festivals.

Robert Keser teaches film at National-Louis University in Chicago. He is Associate Editor of *Bright Lights Film Journal* and also writes regularly for *Senses of Cinema* and *Slant*.

Stuart Klawans has been the film critic of the *Nation* since 1988. He is the author of *Film Follies: The Cinema Out of Order* and *Left in the Dark: Film Reviews and Essays, 1988-2001*.

Frank Lafond teaches film studies at the Faculté Libre des Lettres et Sciences Humaines de Lille (France). He has written extensively on film for a variety of publications. His most recent book is *Jacques Tourneur, les figures de la peur*.

Dennis Lim is the Editorial Director at the Museum of the Moving Image and the editor of the Museum's website, Moving Image Source. His work appears in the *New York Times* and the *Los Angeles Times*, and he is a contributing editor to *Cinema Scope*. Formerly the film editor of the *Village Voice*, he is the editor of the *Village Voice Film Guide* and the author of a forthcoming book on David Lynch.

Blake Lucas is a writer and film critic living in Los Angeles. Some of his writing on cinema may be found in the anthologies *The Western Reader*, *The Film Comedy Reader*, and *The Science Fiction Film Reader*, and in *The Film Journal* online, as well as in over 100 individual essays on films, filmmakers, film history and film theory in *Magill's Survey of Cinema* and *Magill's Cinema Annuals*. His e-mail address is lukethedealer@juno.com.

Miguel Marías, born in Madrid in 1947, is an economist who has written on film since 1966. The director of the Spanish Film Archive from 1986 to 1988, he is the author of books on Manuel Mur Oti and Leo McCarey.

Steven Marsh teaches film, Spanish and comparative literature at the University of South Carolina. He is the author of *Popular Spanish Film Under Franco: Comedy and the Weakening of the State* (Palgrave) and one of the writers of the forthcoming collaborative volume *Cinema and the Mediation of*

Everyday Life: An Oral History of Cinema Going in 1940s and 1950s Spain. He is co-editor of the anthology *Gender and Spanish Cinema* (Berg).

Adrian Martin is Senior Research Fellow in Film and Television Studies, Monash University (Melbourne). He is the author of *Once Upon a Time in America* (BFI) and *The Mad Max Movies* (Currency), and co-editor of *Movie Mutations* (BFI) and *Rouge* (http://www.rouge.com.au).

Michael T. Martin is director of the Black Film Center/Archives and professor of African American and African Diaspora Studies at Indiana University, Bloomington. He is the editor/co-editor of *Redress for Historical Injustices in the United States: Slavery, Jim Crow, and Their Legacies* (Duke University Press), *Studies of Development and Change in the Modern World* (Oxford University Press), *Cinemas of the Black Diaspora* (Wayne State University Press), and *New Latin American Cinema* (Wayne State University Press). He directed an award-winning feature documentary on *Nicaragua, In the Absence of Peace*.

Travis Miles is a semi-professional writer, film programmer, and lecturer, and has been consistently sustained by the films he sees and the people with whom he sees them. He is currently languishing in Los Angeles.

Gino Moliterno teaches Film Studies at the Australian National University.

Hassan Abd. Muthalib is a self-taught film director, animator, and writer. His writings on film and animation appear in local and international publications. He is presently researching early Malaysian cinema.

Kim Newman is an award-winning novelist, critic, and broadcaster. His non-fiction books include *Nightmare Movies*, *Ghastly Beyond Belief* (with Neil Gaiman), *Horror: 100 Best Books* (with Stephen Jones), *The BFI Companion to Horror*, *Millennium Movies*, and BFI Classics studies of *Cat People* and *Doctor Who*. He has also written numerous works of fiction. He is a contributing editor to *Sight & Sound* and *Empire* magazines. His official website, *Dr Shade's Laboratory*, can be found at http://www.johnnyalucard.com.

Geoffrey O'Brien is Editor in Chief of the Library of America. His most recent books are *Sonata for Jukebox: An Autobiography of My Ears* and *Red Sky Café*.

Darcy Paquet is the founder of Koreanfilm.org and also serves as the Korea correspondent for *Variety*. He has been living in Seoul since 1997.

James Parker is a writer living in Brookline, Massachusetts. He has been a contributing editor to the *Idler* and *Hermenaut*. He is the author of *Turned On*, an unauthorized biography of Henry Rollins. He currently writes a pop culture column for the *Boston Globe*'s Ideas section and a reality TV column for the *Boston Phoenix*.

Fernando Martín Peña is a film archivist and historian. He has been the artistic director of the Buenos Aires International Festival of Independent Cinema since 2005 and is the author of several books on film.

Andrew Pike is an Australian film historian and documentary filmmaker. He co-authored the book *Australian Film 1900 to 1977* (Oxford University Press), a basic reference work on

Australian cinema history. He is currently President of the Friends of the National Film and Sound Archive and has served on the Archive's Council.

Jerry Pinto is a poet, journalist and anthologist who lives in Mumbai and writes about popular Hindi cinema, among other things. He is the author of *Helen – The Life and Times of an H-Bomb* (Penguin).

Dana Polan is a Professor of Cinema Studies at New York University. His most recent book is *Scenes of Instruction: The Beginnings of the U. S. Study of Film* (University of California Press). He is at work on a monograph on Julia Child's French Chef TV show.

Murray Pomerance is Professor in the Department of Sociology at Ryerson University and the author of *Johnny Depp Starts Here*, *An Eye for Hitchcock*, *Magia d'Amore*, and *Savage Time*. He has edited numerous anthologies, including *City That Never Sleeps: New York and the Filmic Imagination* and *American Cinema of the 1950s: Themes and Variations*. He is editor of the "Horizons of Cinema" series at SUNY Press and co-editor of the "Screen Decades" and "Star Decades" series at Rutgers University Press.

Richard Porton is an editor of *Cineaste* and the author of *Film and the Anarchist Imagination* (Verso).

Nandini Ramnath is a Bombay-based journalist who specializes in cinema.

Maithili Rao is a Bombay-based film critic and writer. She has contributed to all the leading Indian papers and magazines, such as the *Hindu*, *Frontline*, *Man's World*, *Outlook*, *Screen*, *Times of India*, and *South Asian Cinema*, as well as *Film Comment*, *International Film Guide*, and festival publications.

Bérénice Reynaud teaches in the School of Film/Video and in the School of Critical Studies at CalArts. She has written extensively on film for numerous publications, has curated many film and video exhibitions and retrospectives, and is the author of *Nouvelles Chines, nouveaux cinemas* (Cahiers du cinéma) and *Hou Hsiao-hsien's "A City of Sadness"* (BFI). She is currently working on a book on sexual politics in the Chinese Martial Arts movie.

Gregg Rickman is the editor of *The Science Fiction Film Reader* and *The Comedy Film Reader* and the co-editor (with Jim Kitses) of *The Western Reader*. He lives in Berkeley, California with his wife and cat.

Jonathan Rosenbaum is a film critic for the *Chicago Reader*. His books include *Discovering Orson Welles*, *Essential Cinema*, *Movie Mutations* (co-edited with Adrian Martin), *Abbas Kiarostami* (with Mehrnaz Saeed-Vafa), *Dead Man*, *Movie Wars*, *Movies as Politics*, *Greed*, *Placing Movies*, *Film: The Front Line 1983*, *Midnight Movies* (with J. Hoberman), and *Moving Places*.

Dan Sallitt is a filmmaker and film writer living in New York. He was the film critic for the *Los Angeles Reader*, and his writings have appeared in the *Chicago Reader*, *Slate*, *Wide Angle*, *Senses of Cinema*, the *Nashville Scene*, the *Minneapolis City Pages*, and other venues. His films include *Honeymoon* (1998) and *All the Ships at Sea* (2004).

Matt Zoller Seitz is a film critic for the *New York Times* and the editor and publisher of the movie and TV criticism website *The House Next Door*. Formerly film critic for the *New York Press*, he has also written for many other publications. He is currently completing a screenplay based on a lurid pulp thriller, writing a critical book on the films of Wes Anderson, and directing a

science fiction epic starring puppets and stuffed animals, co-written with his nine-year-old daughter, Hannah.

Michael Sicinski is a frequent contributor to *Cineaste* and *Cinema Scope*. He also maintains *The Academic Hack*, a film review website.

David Sterritt is chairman of the National Society of Film Critics, past chairman of the New York Film Critics Circle and the Columbia University Seminar on Cinema and Interdisciplinary Interpretetion, and professor emeritus of theater and film at Long Island University. His writing has appeared in *Cahiers du cinéma*, the *New York Times*, and many other publications, and until retirement he was film critic of the *Christian Science Monitor* for more than 35 years. His most recent book is *Guiltless Pleasures: A David Sterritt Film Reader*.

Brad Stevens is the author of *Monte Hellman: His Life and Films* (McFarland) and *Abel Ferrara: The Moral Vision* (FAB Press). He has contributed to *Sight & Sound*, *Cineaction*, *Film International*, *Trafic*, *The Dark Side*, and *Video Watchdog*, as well as the websites *Senses of Cinema* and *Screening the Past*. He lives in the UK.

David Stratton was director of the Sydney Film Festival from 1966 to 1983 and film reviewer for *Variety* from 1984 to 2003. He has been film reviewer for the *Australian* since 1990. He is the host of *At the Movies* for ABC-TV in Australia and a Lecturer in Film History in the Continuing Education Programme at the University of Sydney. He is the author of *The Last New Wave: The Australian Film Revival* and *The Avocado Plantation: Boom and Bust in the Australian Film Industry*.

Aruna Vasudev is the founder/editor of *Osian's-Cinemaya, The Asian Film Quarterly*; the founder/director of

Osian's-Cinefan, the Asian Film Festival; and president of NETPAC (Network for the Promotion of Asian Cinema). An author and critic, she has a Ph.D. in cinema from the University of Paris.

Noel Vera is a regular film critic for *Businessworld*, a Manila-based weekly, and a correspondent for *BigO Magazine* (Singapore) and *Cinemaya* (New Delhi). His book *Critic After Dark, a Review of Philippine Cinema* is available from BigO Books in Singapore (http://www.bigozine2.com/theshop/books/NVcritic.html).

Valentina Vitali teaches comparative film theory at the Centre for Media Research, University of Ulster, where she obtained a Ph.D. for a thesis on cultural modernisation and Hindi cinema. She is co-editor, with Paul Willemen, of *Theorising National Cinema* (BFI). Her essays have appeared in the journals *boundary 2*, *Inter-Asia Cultural Studies*, *Kinema*, *Framework*, *Women: a Cultural Review*, and *Journal of Asian Studies*, and in *Hong Kong Connections: Transnational Imagination in Action Cinema* (edited by M. Morris and S. Chan).

Al Weisel is the co-author of *Live Fast, Die Young: The Wild Ride of Making Rebel Without a Cause* and has written for such publications as *Rolling Stone*, *Spin*, *Tracks*, *George*, *Travel & Leisure*, *Out*, the *Washington Post*, *Time Out New York*, the *Bulletin (Australia)*, *New York Newsday*, and *US Magazine*, where he was a contributing editor. He lives in New York City.

Opposite *Chimes at Midnight*

INTRODUCTION

Opposite **Harold Lloyd**

A book that celebrates 1000 defining moments of cinema demands two introductory remarks. The first, a disclaimer, can be got out of the way quickly. This book is in no way intended to represent "the greatest" or "most important" moments in cinema – as if there existed some way to determine objectively what these were. Instead, the book is designed to highlight film scenes, or events in the history of cinema, that the contributors (who include film critics, film historians, writers in other fields, and academics) regard as profound, essential, illuminating, or significant.

The second remark is really a set of questions that need much lengthier consideration than I can provide in this introduction – that need a book, in fact (and it might as well be this one). What is a moment? How do we recognize it, and how do we determine the points where it can be taken out of the flow of a film? Once extracted, can it stand for the film as a whole, or does it become a mini-film of its own? Is there a special relationship between the moment and cinema? Is cinema, perhaps, a technology for gathering and preserving moments?

At every page of this book the reader will meet different criteria for choosing moments and different reasons to appreciate them. As general editor I deliberately avoided imposing a narrow definition of what constitutes a key moment and instead invited each contributor to bring to the book his or her sense of what's most valuable in cinema. The aim of this strategy was not to deny the validity of a more theoretical approach, or to say meekly that cinema is "more than the sum of its parts," but to bring into play a variety of positions. Just as the people sleeping on Tokyo trains in *Sans soleil* dream together the "ultimate film" (as Dennis Lim writes in his entry here on Chris Marker's masterpiece), so this book might be read as a collective dream of film.

What makes a moment? "An ideal combination of style, story, and feeling" (David Sterritt on *Barry Lyndon*). The power to evoke overwhelming emotion (Fred Camper on *The Satin Slipper*) or to represent "the highest expression of joy in the movies" (Miguel Marías on *Singin' in the Rain*). An evocative snatch of dialogue (*Fellini's Casanova*). The exhaustive use of a fetishized location, such as a parking garage (*Diva*). The way someone runs (*The Last of the Mohicans*). A moment might be great because of a performance (Agnes Moorehead's in *The Magnificent Ambersons*, Chhabi Biswas's in *The Music Room*, Isabelle Huppert's in *The Piano Teacher*), a gesture (*Rio Bravo*, *L'Avventura*, *7 Women*), or a camera movement (*Day of Wrath*, *Notorious*, *Silver Lode*). Maybe it's a memorable speech – and "Key Speeches," starting with Al Jolson's remarks to the audience in *The Jazz Singer*, get their own running category in this book. Another subcategory includes a few of the many "Key Persons" who might have been picked for their momentous contributions to cinema.

A moment can represent the whole of cinema (Adrian Martin on *L'Enfant secret*: "we feel the cinema being born, and even dying") or play with, and reveal in a new light, the material properties of film (*La Flamme*). Or break – and thus reveal – convention through a "mistake" (*Dogtown and Z-Boys*). Or make us question what we see and hear (*Close Up*). The moment can be the event that threatens the loss of all moments (Paolo Cherchi Usai on "the death of cinema"). It can call cinema itself – as institution and as practice – into question and "make the very exercises of making and seeing films seem vaguely pointless" (Tim Cavanaugh on *Fitzcarraldo*), or it can collect moments from other films in order to show that "cinema is dead" (Antoine Coppola on *In girum imus nocte consumimur igni*).

11

A moment can be one brief shot (*La Jetée*) or an elaborate section of a film (*Psycho*). In his entry on *Love Streams*, Adrian Martin alludes to the difficulty of selecting a single moment from a film in which "incidents overlap and blur." I've stretched the definition of a moment to allow whole films to be included – films that call a halt to the normal traffic of cinema, demanding to be treated as moments apart. How can one scene stand for a 15½ hour film (*Berlin Alexanderplatz*)? Or even a 4-minute film, if it happens to show "nothing less than the entire world in flux," as Christoph Huber writes of *37/78 Tree Again*? These and other films are themselves moments, and are so treated here.

There are as many reasons for picking moments as there are ways of enjoying films, Gregg Rickman reminds us in his entry on Thora Birch in *Ghost World* dancing to a tune from the Bollywood musical *Gumnaam*. By the way, many moments in this book are musical ones, from Hollywood classics like *Gold Diggers of 1935* and *The Band Wagon* to Russia's *By the Bluest of Seas*, India's *Mahal*, Italy's *8½*, Britain's *Trainspotting*, Iran's *Offside*, France's *Wild Innocence*, and Mali's *Bamako*. The geographical range of this list raises another point: just as many points of view on cinema are represented here, so are many filmmaking regions, and the reader will find American and Western European dominance increasingly disputed in these pages as the decades move on.

You'll probably find some of your own key moments here, and you'll inevitably miss some others. If some scenes are included that could hardly have been left out, such as Kong on the Empire State Building or Janet Leigh in the shower, some well-known scenes are skipped in favor of others less familiar. Apart from a handful of exceptions where a film is represented by both a scene and a historical event, I stuck to a rule of one entry per film. The absence of the crop-dusting scene in *North by Northwest* may surprise some, but the great auction scene from that film is here (as is, by the way,

Vincent Gallo's attempt in *Arizona Dream* to recreate the action highlight of Hitchcock's classic).

Some of the most memorable cinematic moments are endings. Whenever an entry might give away so much about the plot of a film as to endanger the pleasure of a viewer who hasn't yet seen it, we've labeled the entry a "Spoiler."

When I solicited proposals for the big list of 1000, many scenes turned up again and again on different writers' lists: the last sequence of *Eclipse*, the camera going through the hotel-room window in *The Passenger*, Mr. Sophistication's rendition of "I Can't Give You Anything but Love" in *The Killing of a Chinese Bookie*, the subjective funeral sequence in *Vampyr*, the first appearance of Buddy Love in *The Nutty Professor*. Pleasing hints of an unforeseen coherence emerged in the spontaneous cross-references between different writers' entries. Miguel Marías compares a scene in *The Dream of Light* to the scene of James Stewart and Richard Widmark talking by the river in *Two Rode Together* – the subject of a piece by Geoffrey O'Brien. There are entries on both the murder of Pier Paolo Pasolini and the scene in *Caro Diario* in which Nanni Moretti visits the site where it happened, on both Eisenstein's Odessa Steps sequence and Brian De Palma's homage to it in *The Untouchables*. Several writers independently express the opinion that everything worth doing in cinema can be done without computer-generated imagery – a view from which at least one other writer (Violet Glaze on *The Matrix*) strongly dissents.

For a compendium of 1000 short pieces written by 62 people of various professions, nationalities, and interests, who were all given almost free rein (apart from space limits) regarding what to write about and how to write about it, this book reveals, I think, as many continuities as discontinuities. It's a network of visions and preoccupations, an anthology of cinephilic passions, a casual encyclopedia of cinematic events. I hope it will be enjoyed as such.

Chris Fujiwara

Opposite *The Crowd*

Key Event
The death of cinema

A frightening short by Paolo Lipari, *Due dollari al chilo* (2000), shows how film prints are destroyed after their commercial distribution. The stuff dreams are made of is converted into low-cost fuel for industrial plants and raw material for benches, combs, eyeglass frames and clothing. The phenomenon is not new: cinema was killed at its birth, when exhibitors could purchase films and dispose them after use; at the dawn of sound, when producers threw away their silent films; with the introduction of safety stock, when nitrate became a liability; it is still going on today, in developing countries where prints are melting at high temperature and humidity levels. Cinema isn't the only victim: over 95% of the motion pictures produced each year will no longer be extant within twelve months, regardless of their media. To be sure, the percentage is lower in Europe and North America, thus supporting the old dictum that history is written by the winners. As in matters of climate change and religious

fundamentalism, humankind does not react to processes; we need catastrophes to wake up. Stewart Brand wrote that "the great creator is the great eraser"; the intentional obliteration of what we see is proving his point. Are we ready to think about the demise of digital? Not right now, as this technology is on the rise, but a healthy society should be prepared for that as well. I'm not afraid of the death of cinema; what I'm terrified about is our indifference towards its life.
Paolo Cherchi Usai

Date 1895

Why It's Key Film should have its biological life.

Key Event **First show of Lumière films for paying customers**

By late 1894 or early 1895, the brothers Auguste and Louis Lumière, manufacturers of photographic products based in Lyon, had devised an apparatus capable of both photographing motion on film stock and projecting the result on a screen (their patent #245.032 for the invention is dated February 13, 1895). In March and April 1895 they introduced their "Cinématographe" to groups of industrialists and scientists in Paris, showing the one film they had been able to shoot to date: *Workers Leaving the Lumière Factory*. By early June they had made seven or eight more one-minute films (they called them "views") which they showed at a photographers' convention in Lyon, then later in the year to professional and scientific groups in Paris and Brussels.

The showings had aroused enormous interest among specialists. The next step was to introduce the new wonder to the general public. The brothers' father found a mostly unused room, called the "Salon indien," in the basement of the Grand Café on 14 Boulevard des

Capucines, almost next door to the Opéra (the room could seat about a hundred people and was reached by walking down a spiral staircase). The Grand Café owner leased the premises for a year for a daily rent of 30 francs. Although the three or four evening shows of that historical Saturday, December 28, brought in a mere 35 francs, not covering expenses (each showing lasted half an hour for an admission price of one franc) business rapidly picked up, and soon long lines of eager spectators stretched along the boulevard. The first program included ten "views" under the general title of "*Sujets actuels*," among which were the famed *L'Arroseur arrosé* ("The Waterer Watered," listed as "*Le Jardinier*") and the first or second version of *Workers Leaving the Factory* (listed as "*La Sortie de l'Usine Lumière à Lyon*"). The success was such that in April 1896 the brothers rented a new, larger venue a few hundred yards from the Grand Café and called it "Cinéma Lumière."
Jean-Pierre Coursodon

Date December 28, 1895

Why It's Key This legendary premiere marks the birth of cinema as entertainment and of motion-picture exhibition as a business.

Opposite The Lumière brothers

Key Film
Arrival of a Train at La Ciotat Station

Auguste and Louis Lumière are commonly considered the first documentary filmmakers, and, with *Arrival of a Train at La Ciotat Station*, they seem to offer one of their typical slices of life: they show us a steam train arriving at a station and its alighting passengers. This short film is particularly interesting for the depth of field produced by a framing that gives the impression that the train is moving toward the spectators (and thus out of the picture) – an impression that makes it impossible to separate the film from an important date in cinema history.

Arrival of a Train at La Ciotat Station was among the films shown at the very first public screening that took place in the Salon Indien of the Grand Café in Paris, on 28 December 1895. According to an extremely persistent legend, the onwards movement of the locomotive provoked an all-too-real feeling of fear: allegedly, spectators stood up, jumped, moved back their seats in great haste, etc. However, this so-called wave of panic prompted by the film's projection is, to say the least, unconfirmed. Although a few testimonies corroborate this founding myth, it is nowadays an acknowledged fact that the audience's reaction has been largely exaggerated. It still remains the first experience of fear in front of a movie. At least two versions of this film were shot by the Lumière brothers, with a probable intention of improving its efficiency – an intention that marks the boundary of their documentary practice.

Frank Lafond

Date 1895

Nationality France

Directors Auguste and Louis Lumière

Original Title *L'Arrivée d'un train en gare de La Ciotat*

Why It's Key It's the first experience of fear at the movies.

Opposite *Arrival of a Train at La Ciotat Station*

Key Event
Méliès discovers stop motion

Georges Méliès's rudimentary first camera was prone to jamming – a defect that, he recalled, "produced an unexpected effect one day when I was prosaically photographing the Place de l'Opéra. It took a minute to unblock the film and get the camera going again. During this minute, passers-by, buses, cars had changed their places, of course. In projecting the film, joined together again at the point where the break had occurred, I suddenly saw a Madeleine-Bastille bus change into a hearse, and men change into women." Méliès had stumbled upon a new and crucial trick, the first intentional application of which was his *Escamotage d'une dame au théâtre Robert-Houdin* (*The Vanishing Lady*) in October 1896.

An accident of cinema had enabled Méliès to discover discontinuity within the apparent continuity of normal experience. It was a lesson that many filmmakers would take to heart throughout the long tradition of stop-motion animation, represented most gloriously by Willis O'Brien (*The Lost World* [1925], *King Kong* [1933]) and Ray Harryhausen (*The Beast from 20,000 Fathoms* [1953], *Jason and the Argonauts* [1963]). Though in recent years stop motion has been widely replaced by CGI, and though the naïve enjoy gloating over the presumed deficiencies of special effects of the past, it can be argued that special effects have never been about the illusion of reality so much as they've been about the liberation of a concealed reality by the mechanism of cinema. In this domain, the work of Méliès, O'Brien, and Harryhausen remains unsurpassable.

Chris Fujiwara

Date 1896

Why It's Key An accident was at the origin of the development of special effects in cinema.

Key Event
The first public film exhibition in Asia

The show held on July 7, 1896, at Watson's Hotel in Bombay appears to mark the advent of cinema in Asia, barely six months after the Lumière brothers first showed their films to the public in Paris. Maurice Sestier was the Lumière agent who organized the pioneering exhibition in Bombay. Sestier's initial show consisted of early Lumière titles like *Arrival of a Train at La Ciotat Station* and *Workers Leaving the Factory*. *The Times of India* described the show as "living photographic pictures in life-sized reproductions," while the program was billed as "the marvel of the century, the wonder of the world." Initial showings stirred enough excitement that, starting the following week, the Novelty Theater showed the films continuously, until interest began to wane in the following month.

An imported technology, cinema spread quickly to Asia's other colonial communities. It initially thrived in coastal cities like Shanghai, Hong Kong, Manila, Sugbu (now Cebu), Tokyo, Bangkok, Singapore, Malacca, Seoul, Batavia (now Jakarta), Formosa (now Taiwan), and Ceylon (now Sri Lanka). Film became a lasting legacy left behind by the Western colonial powers that once divided and ruled Asia. In the mid-20th-century, those independent countries that had strong film cultures defined their national identities through their cinemas, and these national cinemas have given the region its now-vibrant film culture.

Nick Deocampo

Date July 7, 1896

Why It's Key The arrival of film in Asia helped shape the identity and culture of people in the region.

Key Event
The world's first film archive

In 1897, Robert William Paul donated several of his films to the British Museum, hoping that the venerable institution would begin acquiring reproductions of notable events in the form of moving images. The museum didn't know what to do with the new objects, so there never was a second donation; the first film archive was an enigma even for its owners. Other attempts followed between 1910 and 1912 in Denmark and Sweden, but there is a certain degree of poignancy in the British precedent: there are now hundreds of film archives all over the world, and yet their status is as fragile today as it was in the late nineteenth century. Regrettably, the motion picture heritage is not seen as so vital to society as other forms of cultural expression such as books, paintings, or theatre. It is at the mercy of commercial pressures, often incorporated within industry bodies; quick and instant access to the collections is taken for granted, to the detriment of long-term conservation strategies.

Archival holdings are being called "content", in the mistaken assumption that reproduction equals preservation; corporate firms see them as an easy source of revenue; by and large, the public doesn't care, as it is believed that a 1940 film available digitally is restored somewhere anyhow. It will take time before existing organizations dealing with the past of the moving image will be allowed to treat history in its own terms. Strange as it may seem, the first film archive has yet to exist.

Paolo Cherchi Usai

Date 1897

Why It's Key It was an unfulfilled promise of historical awareness.

Key Film
The Brahmin and the Butterfly

Films made before 1906 are often categorized as "cinema of attractions," a mode of narration based on a single event of curious, spectacular, or otherwise remarkable nature: the grimaces of a man who is suffering indigestion, a boy wreaking havoc in a bakery, the ethereal apotheosis of a *féerie*. Taken at face value, *The Brahmin and the Butterfly* perfectly fits the latter category: it's a two-minute scene, apparently a single shot (there are in fact some optical tricks that required in-camera editing), very much like hundreds of exotic visions of an imaginary East as seen through the eyes of a turn-of-the-century conjuror. The difference lies in the chain of events depicted in Méliès' beautifully hand-colored oriental garden: a Brahmin summons a very large caterpillar with his magic flute, then puts it in a cocoon, thus giving life to a gorgeous female butterfly. Entranced by her beauty, the Brahmin wraps her in a striped cloth. The butterfly turns into a ravishing Hindu princess; overwhelmed with joy, the

man declares his unrequited love to the beautiful lady. After having rebuffed his courtship, the woman puts her foot over the head of the adoring man, who is suddenly transformed into a crawling caterpillar, very much like the one at the beginning of the film.

Talk about fatal (cinema of) "attractions"! In little more than a hundred seconds, Méliès has given us the most concise, poignant and sardonic story of *amour fou* in the history of early cinema.

Paolo Cherchi Usai

Date 1901

Nationality France

Director Georges Méliès

Cast Georges Méliès

Original Title *La Chrysalide et le Papillon*

Why It's Key The shortest "fatal attraction" of early cinema is also the meanest.

Key Person **Edwin S. Porter**
The Life of an American Fireman

The basic grammar of film can be traced to a handful of visionary pioneers. Prominent among them is Pennsylvania-born Edwin S. Porter, a jack-of-all-trades in turn-of-the-20th-century America who is credited as the first filmmaker to assemble disparate individual shots into a continuous sequence of parallel actions. In 1896, he went to work for the company marketing Thomas A. Edison's then-novel Vitascope. Porter subsequently teamed with Edison in New York, first as a machinist, then as a projectionist, finally as a filmmaker. In 1903, Porter married stock footage of horse-drawn fire engines leaving a station house to staged sequences of firemen saving a woman from a burning house. Cross-cutting shots of the rescue taken inside and outside the building, the six-minute film creates, for the first time, the illusion of linear continuity. Subsequent to *The Life of an American Fireman*, Porter made more than 50 films, including *The Great Train Robbery* (also 1903), widely

considered to be his most historically important. In 1908, he directed *Rescued from an Eagle's Nest*, which starred a struggling young actor and future film director named David Wark Griffith. Porter lost his fortune in the 1929 stock market crash and died in obscurity. Though controversy exists as to the precise sequencing of his original cut of *The Life of an American Fireman*, there's little doubt of the influence it, and he, had on the nascent art form.

David Stratton

Date 1903

Nationality USA

Director Edwin S. Porter

Why It's Key This was probably the first film to edit single shots together to form a narrative story.

Key Scene **The outlaw firing at the camera**
The Great Train Robbery

Regarded as the first western in cinema history, *The Great Train Robbery* tells the story of four bandits who rob a train before being hunted down and killed by a posse. Central to the film is an increased impression of reality that manifests itself in many different ways. Whereas in Auguste and Louis Lumière's *Arrival of a Train at La Ciotat Station* (1895), a locomotive moves toward the spectators and threatens to break the screen boundaries, here, the leader of the bandits (Barnes) looks directly at the camera lens and empties his revolver point blank at the audience. According to the company's catalogue, this disturbing shot could be placed at the beginning or at the end of the picture: as the first image of the subject, it could be an easy – although abrupt – way to introduce the main character, used as an epilogue, it takes a moment out of the narrative, and its unusual size (a medium close-up) establishes a strong and sudden contrast with all the previous sequences, filmed in more common medium or long shots. In either case, it brings realism to the movie through the intensification of the spectators' identification with the unfortunate victims of the robbery. By destroying any distance between the audience and the events, both the Lumière brothers' and Porter's films aimed at inducing a feeling of fear, if not a startling effect. However, only this shot of *The Great Train Robbery*, which has often been imitated since, remains truly effective for the more sophisticated modern audience.

Frank Lafond

Date 1903

Nationality USA

Director Edwin S. Porter

Cast Justus D. Barnes

Why It's Key It's one of the best known shots in primitive cinema.

Opposite *The Great Train Robbery*

Key Event
Alfred Hitchcock sent to prison

Although he generally preferred not to discuss his childhood, Alfred Hitchcock repeated one anecdote so often he could probably have related it in his sleep: "When I was no more than six years of age, I did something that my father considered worthy of reprimand. He sent me to the local police station with a note. The officer on duty read it and locked me in a jail cell for five minutes, saying, 'This is what we do to naughty boys.'" This version of the story (quoted in Donald Spoto's *The Dark Side of Genius*) dates from 1979, but when François Truffaut interviewed Hitchcock 17 years earlier, it was already familiar enough to be recited as a kind of duet by both men. Yet when Truffaut asked "Why were you being punished?", Hitchcock could only reply "I haven't the faintest idea." Though Hitchcock might have long since forgotten whether his youthful incarceration was memory or fantasy, he certainly saw it as "explaining" his subsequent interest in crime and punishment. But Hitchcock's insistence that he did not know what "crime" he had committed also connects with his films' frequent emphasis on unjust punishments: Richard Hannay in *The 39 Steps* (1935) plunged into a nightmare for showing casual sexual interest; Guy Haines in *Strangers on a Train* (1951) punished for desiring the death of his wife; Manny Balestrero in *The Wrong Man* (1956) persecuted by a Kafkaesque justice system; and, crucially, Marion Crane in *Psycho* (1960) murdered after deciding to return the money she stole from her employer – surely among the most unjust punishments in cinema history. Much as it may have been intended to discourage further speculation, the prison story, whether true or not, suggests just how personal Hitchcock's work really was.

Brad Stevens

Date Circa 1905

Why It's Key This anecdote connects with several aspects of Hitchcock's work.

Key Event **Premiere of, arguably, the world's first dramatic feature film**

On December 26, 1906, *The Story of the Kelly Gang* opened at the Athenaeum Hall in Melbourne, Australia, advertised proudly as 4,000 feet in length (running about an hour) – certainly the longest film then made by the fledgling Australian film industry, and much longer than "feature" films then being made in the UK and the USA. Accompanied by an orchestra, sound effects, and a narrator, it was enormously popular, and within weeks "additional scenes" were being promoted and multiple copies were screening around the country. In 1907 it screened in England, billed as "the longest film ever made." Whatever the accuracy of its claim to be a world first, it was certainly the first statement on film of what had become, ever since the capture and hanging of the real Ned Kelly in 1880, one of the iconic stories of Australian popular culture. The Kelly gang were notorious "bushrangers" or outlaws who became folk heroes for their defiance of authority and for their daring raids. Their story was told many times on film, as it was on stage and in print, song, and art.

In the film, Kelly was played by Frank Mills, a Canadian actor. A family of highly successful theatre entrepreneurs – John, Nevin, and Charles Tait – were primarily responsible for the film, and they and other members of the large Tait family played some of the supporting roles. Collaborating with the Taits were Millard Johnson and William Gibson, two chemists who had become interested in film and, like the Taits, were actively showing film programmes to large crowds in Melbourne. Only fragments of *The Story of the Kelly Gang* survive today.

Andrew Pike

Date December 26, 1906
Nationality Australia
Director Charles Tait
Cast Frank Mills, Elizabeth Tait, John Tait
Why It's Key Released in 1906, *The Story of the Kelly Gang* was the longest narrative drama then seen in Australia and quite possibly in the world.

Key Event **D. W. Griffith starts directing at Biograph**

It was as a none-too-successful actor and would-be writer that D. W. Griffith approached the New York production house, The American Mutoscope & Biograph Co., with some story ideas. His interest and initiative were noticed when he was on the set as an actor, and when the house director fell ill, Griffith was offered the job. It seems that Griffith was reluctant to take on the role, as he felt that if he failed it might jeopardize his employment as a writer and actor. Billy Bitzer, one of the two cameramen then working at Biograph, gave him some coaching in direction. From the available synopses, Griffith chose *The Adventures of Dollie* as his first film, as it could be filmed on location away from the eyes of his bosses. The success of his initial ventures led to Griffith's becoming the studio's principal producer-director until his departure in 1913.

The remarkable survival of around 450 short films, almost Griffith's entire output at Biograph (1908-1913), provides an invaluable marker for the transition from early cinema to Hollywood. Griffith was not alone in adapting existing filmic devices to the demands of storytelling in this important transitional period. It is evident in his Biograph films, however, that he was in the forefront of breaking up film narrative into an ever increasing number of shots and deploying cross-cutting for suspense, to contrast ways of life, or to make moral points. Overcoming his initial doubts about the cultural and artistic worth of the cinema, Griffith combined increasingly imaginative shot selection and an eye for composition and location with intensity of characterization and performance. He also played a central role in the transformation of acting from histrionic to more realistic styles.

Bruce Hodsdon

Date June 18, 1908
Why It's Key Griffith's assumption of the role of director positioned him to play a major role in the shaping of the American cinema.

Opposite D.W Griffith

Key Film
A Trip to Davy Jones' Locker

On December 16, 1934, the Film Society of London organized a screening of John Grierson's *The Song of Ceylon*, accompanied by a group of Soviet documentaries. An unidentified French *féerie* (we know only its English release title) was also there, promoted as an example of "colour being applied direct on to the positive film." The nitrate copy eventually went to the British Film Institute, where I viewed it more than half a century later on a rewind bench. I had already seen hundreds of films from the same period, but this one was different. It was a sensual epiphany. Blue, yellow, red tinting and toning were still leaping from the emulsion; splashes of other stenciled colors exploded in consecutive images until they filled the entire frame. It felt as if the aniline pigments were asking to be fondled as soon as they reached the screen. Instinctively, I took the nitrate print in my hands: I was seeing with my fingertips, I was touching with my eyes. In short, I was witnessing the proof that some

time in the early 1910s cinema was more of a multisensory experience than it is today. I have seen modern copies of that film, and the magic was gone. I don't know if the original still exists. It may now be a dormant body, still recalling the time when its skin was fresh and fragrant and beautiful. Or it may be gone forever, in which case it will remain beautiful for as long as I can project it in my mind.

Paolo Cherchi Usai

Date 1910

Nationality France

Director unknown

Cast unknown

Why It's Key It proves that cinema involves more than seeing and hearing.

Key Scene **The final shot**
The Land Beyond the Sunset

Long before the introduction of censorship, silent cinema was quite cautious in all matters related to the representation of violence. Ellipses and abstractions were the norm; depictions of cruelty were tolerated in non-fiction – especially in relation to subjects dealing with the animal world – but were strictly forbidden elsewhere. *The Land Beyond the Sunset* is no exception; the film was produced as a promotional short for the New York Fresh Air Fund, a charitable organization which is still active today. The subject matter of this unknown masterpiece is a blend of stark social realism and medieval fairy tale: a poor boy sells newspapers on the streets, is mistreated by his mother and finds relief with an excursion to the countryside. In the course of the picnic, the boy socializes with other children and listens to the story of an enchanted world where the film's main character sees himself as a prince threatened by a witch (his real-life mother), is saved by a young woman with a magic wand, and is

taken by boat to the land of eternal happiness. The storyteller closes his book and tells the children that it's time to go back to the city; however, the boy has no such intention. Left alone, he decides to recreate the fairy tale and join the idealized world he had just heard about. There's a boat on the shore. He pushes it, jumps onboard, and drifts towards the horizon in the sunset. His farewell to life is an astonishing one-minute shot where the suicide of a child becomes an object of pure poetry.

Paolo Cherchi Usai

Date 1912

Nationality USA

Director Harold Shaw

Cast Mrs. William Bechtel, Martin Fuller

Why It's Key Social realism is transfigured into poetry.

Key Event
Introduction of panchromatic film

In 1912, French producer Léon Gaumont asked Kodak to devise a new kind of film stock for the color process he was developing, Chronochrome. What he needed was an emulsion sensitive to the entire spectrum of visible radiations. Until then, filmmakers were using orthochromatic film, which required a relatively modest amount of light but was fully sensitive only to certain colors (violet, blue), partially "blind" to yellow and green, and could not capture red objects at all (lipstick and red roses would appear as black spots on the screen): set designers were thus forced to paint their sets accordingly. Panchromatic stock was the solution to the problem. An almost infinite range of grey was now within cameramen's reach, therefore allowing directors such as Josef von Sternberg to become masters of chiaroscuro. One drawback of panchromatic film was that it required much stronger lights on the set (studios quickly took care of that); another one was that the distinctive look of orthochromatic film was lost forever. Those who have seen the original print of a film made before the mid-1920s – when panchromatic stock became the standard in film production – describe it as the equivalent of looking at an alpine landscape against a clear blue sky, with the profile of the mountain peaks leaping out with extreme sharpness. Viewers of the 1922 feature *The Headless Horseman* (the first feature film entirely made with the new emulsion) didn't mind the difference. Such is the history of visual perception: major changes often go unnoticed.

Paolo Cherchi Usai

Date 1912

Why It's Key It changed the way we perceive moving images.

Key Scene **Max Linder's dog calls him on the phone** *Max and His Dog*

Though everybody regards Max Linder as the first great comedy actor, I feel that he tends to be a little overlooked as an innovative director. Yet there are many proofs of Linder's visual inventiveness throughout his great body of work. Take for example *Max and His Dog* (which also happens to be one of his most misogynistic films). Right after her marriage to Max, his wife begins an affair with a former suitor. Suspecting something, Max orders his dog to keep an eye on his wife while he goes to work. As soon as a lover comes in, the dog goes to the bedroom to verify the situation and then, quite amazingly, goes to the phone and calls Max. While the audience is still taking in the surprise of the dog's action, Max receives the call in his office, and then the screen gets split in three parts: on the left side, we see Max with the phone in his hand; in the right side, there's the dog barking the news to Max; and in the middle section, there's a very busy Paris street that represents the distance between them. So Max goes back to his house, surprises the lovers and shows them the way out. The closing shot has Max and his dog happily sharing lunch.

Fernando Martín Peña

Date 1912

Nationality France

Director Max Linder

Cast Linder

Original Title *Max et son chien Dick*

Why It's Key It's a great example of Linder's visual inventiveness.

Key Scene **The last intitle**
Cabiria

The name of Gabriele D'Annunzio has often been associated with Pastrone's dazzling historical epic in dismissive terms. As the story goes, the director lured the greedy Italian poet with a hefty check of 50,000 Liras – a huge sum for the time – in exchange for his agreement to appear as the "author" of the film. The marketing stunt was a stroke of genius at a time when cinema was being regarded with contempt by highbrow intellectuals. In practice, D'Annunzio's contribution to *Cabiria* was nothing more than a first draft of the intertitles, plus some suggestions regarding the characters' names. Over the years, it became clear that the film was the result of Pastrone's vision and that D'Annunzio's main contribution was largely of a symbolic nature: after all, what is striking about *Cabiria* is its camerawork rather than its flamboyant titles, often so convoluted than even an Italian reader has to read them twice in order to make sense out of them. Nevertheless, some intertitles can still be seen as beautiful poems in miniature. The last one is striking for its compelling ambiguity: "I was not defeated by wars," it more or less says, "but by a new force that throws darts for the eyes." Commentators have understood these lines as a celebration of love (the ending shows Cabiria embracing her hero), but it would be equally plausible to interpret them as a metaphor for cinema itself. I'd like to think that both readings may be correct, and that the poet and the filmmaker wrote them together.

Paolo Cherchi Usai

Date 1914

Nationality Italy

Director Giovanni Pastrone

Cast Lydia Quaranta, Umberto Mozzato

Why It's Key D'Annunzio was more than just the film's nominal writer.

Key Scene **The origins of the slave trade**
The Birth of a Nation

Time has not been kind to the first masterpiece of American cinema. *The Birth of a Nation* is begrudgingly recognized as a key moment in the evolution of film as art, and yet it is impossible to separate its innovative style from the inflammatory racial issues it depicts. It makes no sense to say that it is a great film despite its content: form and thought are too deeply intertwined to allow a purely formalist or political interpretation. In light of other films where Griffith deals with history and race (namely *The Escape*, a disturbing defense of eugenics as a tool for social reform), it is easy to understand why he was so adamant in his protest against all forms of cultural censorship. From his perspective, he was simply telling an uncomfortable truth, the tragedy of the Reconstruction era after the devastating years of the Civil War. The first shot of the film makes his point clear: the deportation of African slaves to America was the original sin, and the Puritan settlers of the Northern states were responsible for it. In his view, the war those states waged against the Confederates was an act of hypocrisy, all the more appalling in that it divided a nation with the pretext of defending egalitarian values which the Unionists were the first to deny as former slave traders. Few films have been more extensively discussed than *The Birth of a Nation*, but the essence of Griffith's populist ideology is still awaiting proper consideration.

Paolo Cherchi Usai

Date 1915

Nationality USA

Director D. W. Griffith

Why It's Key It reveals the core of Griffith's political thought.

Opposite *The Birth of a Nation*

Key Scene **The fatal braid**
Daydreams

The year 1989 was a time of glasnost in cinema history as well as in Eastern European politics. Russian films made before the 1917 revolution had become *terra incognita* since the early days of the Soviet Union: they were not necessarily lost, but their aesthetics were inevitably identified with bourgeois culture, thus condemning them to oblivion. There was also a good excuse for this: constructivist cinema is based on aggressive editing and visual dynamism; Tsarist cinema is resolutely slow, relying upon a leisurely alternation of very long shots and intertitles. Slow does not mean tedious, though, as demonstrated by the films of Evgeni Bauer, now widely regarded as a one of the greatest directors of his time. *Daydreams* is arguably the best illustration of his style, blessed by an astounding mastery of depth of field, dramatic lighting, and beautiful tracking shots at a time when camera movements were not common at all. For the modern viewer, though, the film is first of all a tale of the uncanny: a man (Vyrubov) desperate since the death of his wife keeps her long braid as a cherished memento. He then falls for an actress (Chernobaeva) who resembles his defunct spouse (here's another *Vertigo* for you), only to discover that she is a deceitful, shallow creature. In an outburst of rage, the man strangles his lover with the braid that belonged to his true love. Necrophilia, mysticism, and abstraction converge in the final shot, worthy of the eeriest gothic tale.

Paolo Cherchi Usai

Date 1915

Nationality Russia

Director Evgeni Bauer

Cast Aleksandr Vyrubov, N. Chernobaeva

Original Title *Grezy*

Why It's Key Russian cinema before the Soviet era is a revelation.

Key Scene **The branding iron**
The Cheat

No scene aroused more furor during the silent era than the sight of an elegant young Asian man (Hayakawa) taking a white-hot iron and branding the shoulder of the Caucasian heroine (Ward), who has just repelled his sexual assault. She is a stockbroker's spendthrift wife who, entrusted with safekeeping $10,000 in charity funds, squanders the money in a thoughtless stock market investment. He is a wealthy ivory merchant who lends her the cash to cover her crime, with the clear intention of erotic payback. Audiences flocked to the melodrama less for the intense acting or DeMille's remarkable visual evocation of emotional hysteria, and much more to enjoy the forbidden frissons of repressed desire and the matinee-idol charisma of the Japanese star. The very same year that Griffith's *The Birth of a Nation* exposed and exacerbated America's black/white racial divisions, DeMille's depiction of an angry crowd out for the Asian's hide incurred considerable outrage from the Japanese-American community, who forced the studio to identify the character as Burmese in later reissues. Surprisingly, rather than reducing Hayakawa to a "yellow peril" villain, the metaphoric rape scene actually turned him into one of Hollywood's highest paid stars. He then started producing his own Asian-themed movies, and repeated his *Cheat* role decades later in Marcel L'Herbier's 1937 French remake, *Forfaiture*, this time as a Mongolian. The longevity of Hayakawa's career, capped by a Best Supporting Actor Oscar for *The Bridge on the River Kwai* in 1957, proved the enduring attraction of the "bad boy" in cinema.

Robert Keser

Date 1915

Nationality USA

Director Cecil B. DeMille

Cast Sessue Hayakawa, Fannie Ward

Why It's Key It established the "bad boy's" appeal among moviegoers.

Key Scene **Burning down the town**
Hell's Hinges

It is a town "unworthy of the soil on which it stands," a town that wants to remain godless. A minister (Jack Standing) arrives to bring religion but proves unequal to the task: in a few days he winds up drunk in the arms of a prostitute, and later he becames a violent alcoholic. As usual in his films, William S. Hart plays a baddie who converts for the love of a woman, in this case the minister's sister (Clara Williams). He helps her carry on the work that the minister neglects and, as a little congregation forms, they begin to build a church. But when Hart rides away on some errand, a mob puts a torch in the drunken minister's hand and makes him lead the burning of the church. There's some shooting, and the minister gets killed.

Then comes the key moment of the film. When Hart returns, he finds the church in flames and the woman he loves crying beside her brother's dead body. That does it. Like a proto-Schwarzenegger, Hart says, more or less, "I'll be back" and single-handedly burns up the whole town to kingdom come. There are impressive shots of Hart walking quietly out of town, surrounded by flames, heavy smoke, and people running wild to save themselves from his wrath.

Everyone in the story is wholly evil or wholly good. Only the minister and Hart experience some change, but they seem to cancel each other, as one degrades and the other upgrades in a sort of counterbalance. So when Hart burns the town down, he's not just avenging the killing of the minister for the sake of the girl he loves, and he's not just avenging the burning of the church for the sake of the good people who built it. He's performing something of a Biblical feat: a one-horseman apocalypse.
Fernando Martín Peña

Date 1916

Nationality USA

Director Charles Swickard

Cast William S. Hart

Why It's Key Most of the surviving westerns of William S. Hart are wonderful, but this one is special – not just because of this key scene, but because of the epic scale the film achieves through its deliberate Manicheanism.

Key Scene **Gassing the upper class**
Les Vampires

The fifth episode of the mysterious saga alternates scenes of people returning to consciousness and people losing it. The thief Moréno (Herrmann), arch rival of the Vampires' criminal gang, swallows what appears to be a suicide pill. Reporter Philippe Guerande (Mathé), conked by the Vampires, awakens in a basket tumbling down a long flight of stairs. Most memorably, the Grand Vampire (Aymé) and Irma Vep (Musidora) disguise themselves as a baron and his niece to host a society ball where they gas dozens of rich people, taking their jewels and fat wallets when they succumb.

Feuillade's camera dollies past the hands of party guests clawing to escape the sealed room. The Vampires, silhouettes framed in doorways, led by Irma in her skintight black suit, descend on the sleeping guests like the gas or like dreams. This French serial introduced the supervillain and the sexy accomplice who wear disguises and turn the devices of modernity against the people they were invented to help. It made criminal anarchy and terror into entertainment, which Feuillade made into art.

Feuillade filmed his exteriors in Paris locations that the First World War had emptied of people. The idea that places and objects recorded by the movie camera shimmer with life and might be trying to tell us something dates from encounters with Feuillade's crime serials. "It is in *Les Vampires* that one must look for the great reality of our century – they are beyond fashion and beyond taste," wrote the surrealists Aragon and Breton.
A. S. Hamrah

Date 1916

Nationality France

Director Louis Feuillade

Cast Musidora, Jean Aymé, Fernand Herrmann, Édouard Mathé, Marcel Lévesque

Why It's Key Feuillade's serial is "beyond fashion and beyond taste."

Key Scene **Love's struggle throughout the ages** *Intolerance*

Hurt by the racially-charged controversy surrounding his 1915 Civil-War saga *The Birth of a Nation*, director D.W. Griffith decided to face his detractors squarely. He'd already completed a modestly-budgeted contemporary melodrama called *The Mother and the Law*, in which a falsely accused young man faces the gallows. Inspired by what he perceived as the intolerance of his critics, Griffith quickly wrote three additional stories involving Christ's passion, the French slaughter of the Huguenots, and Cyrus the Persian's vanquishing of ancient Babylon. Fourteen months and some two million 1916 dollars later – 20 times the cost of *Nation* – Griffith had an eight-hour rough cut that intertwined the four stories to imaginative and thrilling effect. Though the film was eventually pared down to between three and three-and-a-half hours (various versions have surfaced), the undisturbed power of the final sequence comes from the breathless way in which the wife and governor converge on the scene of the hanging, Christ approaches Calvary, a Mountain Girl races to warn Babylon, and the Huguenots are defeated. As Griffith described the crosscutting to one interviewer, "they mingle in one mighty river of expression." *Intolerance* was a failure at the box office, baffling audiences of the day with its scope and complexity. The experience drove Griffith to the brink of financial ruin. His subsequent career, while vigorous and peripatetic, yielded nothing as magisterial as *Intolerance*.
David Stratton

Date 1916

Nationality USA

Director D.W. Griffith

Cast Lillian Gish, Robert Harron, Mae Marsh, Constance Talmadge, Bessie Love, Seena Owen, Alfred Paget, Eugene Pallette

Why It's Key Among cinema's earliest and most ambitious epics, a prolonged and impassioned meditation on the dangers of the title's sentiment.

Opposite *The Birth of a Nation*

Key Scene **The unborn lovers** *The Blue Bird*

Film buffs are familiar with Jacques Tourneur, author of the cult movie *Cat People* (1942); fewer are aware that he was the son of French-born director Maurice Tourneur, the great pictorialist of silent cinema. In 1918 he introduced a new style of filmmaking – based on the art of pantomime – in *Prunella* and *The Blue Bird*. Both films were outstanding achievements but failed at the boxoffice, partly because of their highly stylized Art Deco set design. Even by today's standards these films (only a long fragment of *Prunella* survives) are beautiful to watch but not easy to engage with at a dramatic level.

For all its abstraction, Tourneur's adaptation of the famous Maeterlinck play could be seen as an early version of *The Wizard of Oz*. One moment in particular makes it hard to keep the eyes dry. Mytyl (Bell) and Tyltyl (MacDougall) have reached the Land of the Unborn, where hundreds of babies are expecting a big vessel to take them to their parents. Only a few of them are allowed to board at each dispatch. Two children are seen in a tender embrace: they are the Lovers. As fate would have it, only one is chosen to be born; the other has to stay a bit longer. "Tell me how to find you!", he implores while leaving. "I shall be the saddest thing on Earth; you will know me by that," she replies. The scene ends with a shot of the girl, alone in the empty hall, waiting to join her beloved.
Paolo Cherchi Usai

Date 1918

Nationality USA

Director Maurice Tourneur

Cast Tula Bell, Robin MacDougall, Edwin E. Reed, Emma Lowry

Why It's Key It's a triumph of Art Deco and a moving love scene.

Key Scene **The lovers' embrace in the storm** *The Outlaw and His Wife*

Together with Mauritz Stiller, Victor Sjöström is unanimously acknowledged as one of the masters of Swedish cinema in the silent era. The subtlety of his characterizations and the role of landscape in the unfolding of his stories have secured him a place in the pantheon of cinema as an art. To me, however, Sjöström's greatest achievement is his ability to expose the darkest aspects of the human psyche. An accomplished theatre actor, he proved with his controversial début feature *Ingeborg Holm* (1913) how complex emotions could be evoked within the framework of social realism. The urge to conceal unrequited passion through mean behavior – pretending to hate because love hurts too much – is one of the most difficult feelings to convey with any sense of authenticity; Sjöström does so in the last moments of this drama of *amour maudit*. A widow (Erastoff) falls in love with an escaped convict (Sjöström) and flees with him in the mountains. Passion can't endure the hardships for too long: things become sour between the couple, so sour that they can't sit together in the same room without scorching each other; their quarrels and recriminations are an uncomfortable, at times excruciating sight.

As a storm erupts outside their cabin during the night, she has had enough of her partner and leaves. It is at this point that the man discovers again his true feelings towards her, and goes searching for her in the blizzard. The next shot shows them the following morning, both dead, their bodies frozen in the snow, embraced together.

Paolo Cherchi Usai

Date 1918

Nationality Sweden

Director Victor Sjöström

Cast Victor Sjöström, Edith Erastoff

Original Title *Berg-Ejvind och hans hustru*

Why It's Key Nature resurrects through death a love turned sour.

Key Scene **Salome's dance in the kitchen** *The Cook*

One of the greatest injustices in cinema history is the fate of Roscoe "Fatty" Arbuckle, a master of silent comedy whose career was virtually put to an end in the 1920s after the scandal provoked by an unfounded allegation of sexual abuse (Mabel Normand, another talented comedian who teamed with Arbuckle in a number of inspired slapstick shorts, was also the victim of this early example of blacklisting in Hollywood). *The Cook* not only demonstrates Arbuckle's creativity; it also shows how much Buster Keaton owes to him. This two-reeler survives in incomplete form, but the many gags squeezed within a few minutes of running time are more than enough to prove the point. Buster is the waiter in the Bull Pup Café, a joint whose kitchen is managed by Arbuckle with a great deal of nonchalance: in an interval between orders, he decides to stage an improvised version of the Salome story by dressing up like the biblical character – well, so to speak. First, he puts a colander on his head; then he applies frying pans and other kitchen supplies around his apron and over his chest in order to recreate the perverse heroine's dance in costume. John the Baptist's head, by the way, is a big cauliflower brought on a plate by a faithful servant. As a final touch, Arbuckle takes a string of sausages and puts one end of it under his kitchenware bra, patiently waiting for the "snake" to bite. Wait a minute: was it Salome, or Cleopatra? Never mind.

Paolo Cherchi Usai

Date 1918

Nationality USA

Director Roscoe Arbuckle

Cast Buster Keaton, Roscoe Arbuckle, Al St. John

Why It's Key Keaton learned his craft with Arbuckle.

Key Scene **Trapped in the closet** *Broken Blossoms*

Lucy Burrows (Gish) has never known kindness. Her heartless father (Crisp) has beaten her for the slightest transgression for so long that she can't remember how to smile. But the gentle Buddhist missionary Cheng Huan (Caucasian actor Richard Barthelmess in restrained yellowface) sees great beauty and tenderness in the bedraggled waif and chastely nurses her back to health in his humble attic loft. When Lucy's father finds out his daughter is rooming with a "dirty chink," he goes on a rampage, tearing apart Cheng Huan's room and dragging his daughter back to their decrepit flat. Lucy knows this time his rage is murderous and begs him not to kill her. She flings herself into a claustrophobic closet and shuts the door. Gish's performance in *Broken Blossoms* is exceptionally sensitive, possibly the high point of an already stellar and multi-decade career. Her Lucy is delineated with small and pointed touches, as when she desperately tries to smile by pushing up the corners of her mouth in a detached and grotesque facsimile of joy. But the closet scene is her finest moment. As Lucy's father attacks the door with an axe, Lucy clutches at her doll, gnaws on her fingers like an animal in a trap, and, spinning irrationally in terror, scrabbles at the walls for some secret exit as death closes in. The audience bleeds with pity for Lucy, the broken blossom – her only crime was turning towards compassion like a flower following the sun.

Violet Glaze

Date 1919

Nationality USA

Director D.W. Griffith

Cast Lillian Gish, Donald Crisp, Richard Barthelmess

Why It's Key Lillian Gish's depiction of terror is a high water mark in her career.

1910–1919

33

Key Scene **Love at first sight for the Bloke** *The Sentimental Bloke*

The poet C. J. Dennis wrote a book-length verse narrative called *The Sentimental Bloke* in 1915. With its colloquial Australian language and self-deprecating humor, it became an instant best-seller and remains popular to this day. In Longford's film, Dennis appears briefly as himself to introduce the story of the Bloke and his love for his "ideal tart," Doreen. The Bloke is a street "larrikin" – constantly in trouble with alcohol, gambling and the police. One day in the Wolloomooloo market in Sydney, he meets Doreen, a woman of modest aspiration to culture and refinement, and falls instantly in love. The story of their romance is told with an affecting naturalism and was retold in several later films as well as a successful stage musical. Longford and his creative partner, Lottie Lyell, were key figures in Australian silent cinema, before Lyell's untimely death at the age of 35 in 1925. Together they made many films (starting in 1911 with *The Fatal Wedding*). Their work in *The Sentimental Bloke* is distinguished by its use of real locations in the streets of working-class inner-city areas of Sydney, and a strong sense of naturalism in the performances. Lyell herself played Doreen, and the Bloke was played by Arthur Tauchert, a prolific vaudeville performer making his first major film debut. He later played the Bloke in two sequels by Longford and Lyell. *The Sentimental Bloke* was released in October 1919 and quickly established itself as an enduring favourite of Australian audiences. It also played profitably in England, but attempts to adapt its intertitles to American slang for release in the USA proved futile. The film was re-released in a restored version by the National Film and Sound Archive of Australia in 2005.

Andrew Pike

Date 1919

Nationality Australia

Director Raymond Longford

Cast Arthur Tauchert, Lottie Lyell, Gilbert Emery

Why it's Key This is the starting point for a romance that became one of the best-loved stories in Australian popular culture.

Key Event
United Artists founded

On February 5, Charlie Chaplin, Mary Pickford, Douglas Fairbanks, D.W. Griffith, and William S. Hart signed a contract that brought United Artists into being. In the early days of cinema, moguls had been leery of even giving credit to screen actors, but public demand and commercial necessity had led to the invention of the movie star, and four of these five were now the biggest stars in the industry. Griffith, a director, was scarcely less famous. The declared aim of UA was to work outside the already-established studio system, which the founders felt tended "to force upon the theatre-going public mediocre productions and machine-made entertainment." The principals, who were all working under various other non-exclusive contracts, committed to making films for the company and would receive a lion's share of any profits rather than the straight salaries they took down elsewhere. Hart soon dropped out, and the other artists didn't quite deliver. As with several subsequent attempts

(e.g.: "First Artists," established by Steve McQueen, Sidney Poitier, Paul Newman, and Barbra Streisand in the 1970s) by creatives to found their own studios (caricatured as "the lunatics taking over the asylum"), there was a tendency for the likes of Chaplin and Griffith to use their UA deals to make non-commercial personal projects that other, harder-headed studios wouldn't finance while continuing to compete with themselves by shooting crowd-pleasers on their old studio deals. Though the original artists lost control of the company before the end of the 1920s, UA remained in business for 60 years before being bought by MGM, in the wake of the disaster of *Heaven's Gate* (1980). When Steven Spielberg, David Geffen, and Jeffrey Katzenberg founded DreamWorks SKG in 1996, they took care not to use the word "artists" in the company name.
Kim Newman

Date February 5, 1919

Why It's Key This was the first serious attempt by the "talent" to build their own dream factory.

Opposite United Artists

34

Key Film
The Cabinet of Dr. Caligari

In the small North German town of Holstenwall, a series of murders seems to point to a somnambulist, Cesare (Veidt), and his bitter handler, Dr. Caligari (Krauss). These events are related by Francis (Feher), who may or may not be telling a true story. Director Wiene assumed control from Fritz Lang, whose addition of the Francis framing device significantly transformed an anti-authoritarian tale into a more startling genre piece. From the early scenes of the film, it's clear Holstenwall is an odd place, full of impossibly jumbled buildings, forced perspectives, stark black-and-white contrasts, and heavily made-up citizenry. The film's Expressionistic style drew inspiration from German theater of the period, but, as with many innovations, its real root cause was money: seized by the economic recession that followed World War I, the production didn't have enough of it to build "real" sets. Those designed and painted by Hermann Warm, Walter Röhrig, and Walter Reimann perfectly approximated

the deranged nature of the proceedings. The flowers of Expressionism bloomed quickly: Paul Wegener and Carl Boese made *The Golem* the same year, and other early examples of the movement included Fritz Lang's *Der müde Tod* (*Destiny*; 1921), F. W. Murnau's *Nosferatu* (1922), and Paul Leni's *Waxworks* (1924). In the next two decades, geopolitical turmoil would force German film artists to America, where Expressionism became a major influence on film noir.
David Stratton

Date 1919

Nationality Germany

Director Robert Wiene

Cast Werner Krauss, Conrad Veidt, Friedrich Feher, Lil Dagover

Original Title *Das Cabinet des Dr. Caligari* (later *Das Kabinett des Dr. Caligari*)

Why It's Key The birth of German Expressionism in cinema.

Key Scene **Sequestered society women break free and run amok** *Tih Minh*

Think about a dozen or so ladies in the respectable society of the Côte d'Azur, clad in white. They've all been kidnapped and drugged senseless by a band of nefarious villains, who sequester them in Nice's opulent Villa Lucile, which is bugged with hidden microphones. Suddenly, the women break free from their captivity and run outdoors, into the warm Mediterranean sunlight. Imagine them fluttering around a formal garden like butterflies or drifting handkerchiefs as they suddenly taste and enjoy their freedom.

Better yet, don't think at all, but dream a little instead. It's hard to believe that Louis Feuillade and his resourceful cast and crew were doing anything but playing out giddy fantasies of their own, never mind what they meant.

Tih Minh (1919) isn't the most celebrated of the wonderful Feuillade serials, each of which run between five and seven hours. *Fantômas* (1914), *Les Vampires* (1916), and *Judex* (1917), all released by now on DVD,

are better known. But *Tih Minh*, as Gilbert Adair points out, is undoubtedly "the greatest, which is to say, the weirdest, most uncanny, most dreamlike."

What is it about? The title heroine is the Vietnamese fiancée of adventurer Jacques d'Athys, who, on a mission in India, comes into possession of a sacred book containing the secret of a fabulous treasure. The three scheming villains kidnap the fiancée and drug her into amnesia in order to persuade d'Athys to relinquish the book, and those society women are likewise victims of the same criminal modus operandi.
Jonathan Rosenbaum

Date 1919

Nationality France

Director Louis Feuillade

Cast uncredited

Why It's Key It's pre-Surrealist visual poetry about respectable perversity and lyrical hysteria.

Key Scene **The image of untroubled young love returned** *True Heart Susie*

Long overshadowed by his epic, spectacular films, Griffith's pastoral romances show better his more subtle qualities, and they reach a heartbreaking apex in this gentle but piercing melodrama, which further refines the qualities of another of his masterpieces, *A Romance of Happy Valley*, released earlier the same year and also starring Gish and Harron. Here the two play young country sweethearts, Susie and William, innocent in experience but not in complexity of feeling, whose paths start to separate after she (without his knowledge) sells her pet cow so he can go to college; he returns a minister and then is enticed into marriage by a faster city girl, Bettina (Clarine Seymour). William quickly becomes as unhappy as the quietly suffering Susie, but this being a movie, the contrived death of Bettina finally reunites them, and a beautiful title – "And we may believe they walk again as they did long years ago" – precedes a final long shot of the two wandering down a country road together. Griffith daringly

foregrounds the formal quality of this reversal, ready as he always was to let a shot stand alone in privileged time and space. This final shot is plainly not of the characters in the present of the ending, but as they were at the beginning – in the period of their almost-kiss, before the later reveries and yearnings and regrets took away the youthful love they were never fully to know. It is a moment we never actually saw, simply one in which "we may believe." So art returns the truth, nearer to the heart's desire.
Blake Lucas

Date 1919

Nationality USA

Director D. W. Griffith

Cast Lillian Gish, Robert Harron

Why It's Key Griffith here creates his most indelible image, in a model of his long practiced gift for abstracting a privileged moment from the narrative it appears to serve and giving it its own emotional life.

Key Event
The Kuleshov Effect

Soviet director and theoretician Lev Kuleshov devised an experiment at his State Film School workshop around 1920 to gauge audiences' reactions to paired images. Taking a close-up of pre-revolutionary matinee idol Ivan Mozhukin staring without expression, Kuleshov intercut this with shots of a bowl of soup, a woman in a coffin, and a child with a toy (differing accounts also mention a shot of an open cell door). When shown to the public, this juxtaposition reportedly caused viewers to read an appropriate emotion (hunger, sorrow, and paternal love, respectively) into the actor's impassive expression, each spectator thus becoming a storyteller by inferring a cause-effect narrative connection between two unrelated shots. Thus, rather than passively absorbing images, spectators seemed to participate significantly in creating meaning – implying a fundamental interactivity of the film medium. Now considered a foundational principle of cinema, this discovery provided theoretical underpinning for Soviet montage-based filmmaking, demonstrating that the content of individual shots is less significant than their sequencing. In fact, Kuleshov (who introduced the word "montage") concluded that editing changes the meaning of any shot, thus implying the primacy of director over actor. As the Kuleshov Effect holds that an actor's moment-to-moment performance choices remain subordinate to context, it also suggests that understated acting may heighten the emotion conveyed to the audience. Recent attempts to duplicate the experiment among modern viewers more attuned to complex visual stimuli have tended to disprove the original findings, yet Kuleshov's principle still exerts the powerful pull of intuitive truth.
Robert Keser

Date Circa 1920

Why It's Key This discovery suggested the primacy of editing in the film medium and formed the basis for Soviet montage theory.

Key Film
The High Sign

The last few Arbuckle shorts with Keaton showed the marked influence of the latter's subtle comic invention, but the degree of accomplishment in *The High Sign* is truly impressive. Keaton imitates no one, is not tentative or in search of his persona. The film brims over with often nonsensical, borderline-surrealistic gags and situations that already define the Keaton *modus operandi*. Most remarkable perhaps is Keaton's sense of structure, his intricate construction of gags and motifs echoing each other from one sequence, even one reel, to the next. The film's climax is a jaw-dropping chase throughout four rooms on two floors of a house that, toward the end, is seen with the front wall removed, so that we can follow the lightning-fast action without a cut.

Neither Keaton nor anybody else has clearly explained why he was dissatisfied with the film (after making it in early 1920, he demanded that it be shelved, and it was not released until April 1921, by which time Keaton had made his mark with such outstanding shorts as *One Week* and *Neighbors*), or why he might have been right to be. The claim, from Rudy Blesh to Marion Meade (the first and third Keaton biographers), that the film was "too much like an Arbuckle comedy" is absurd: *The High Sign* is light years away from anything Arbuckle ever did (with the possible exception of a couple of Keaton-flavored late Arbuckle shorts, notably the 1919 *Backstage*). In a 1954 interview, Keaton described a gag from the film that didn't bring a laugh at a preview; when rediscovered Keaton shorts were shown to modern audiences in 1970, the gag in question invariably got one of the biggest laughs of the entire film – proof enough that Keaton had been amazingly ahead of his time.
Jean-Pierre Coursodon

Date 1921

Nationality USA

Directors Buster Keaton, Eddie Cline

Cast Buster Keaton, Al St. John

Why It's Key Keaton's first solo short after an apprenticeship in a series of Fatty Arbuckle comedies, this film shows stunningly original comic invention and mastery of the medium.

Key Event
The death of Virginia Rappé

On Labor Day, starlet Virginia Rappé – whose roles were mostly uncredited, but included "Pretty Lady in Car" in *His Wedding Night* (1917) – went to a party thrown by popular comedian Roscoe "Fatty" Arbuckle at the Saint Francis Hotel in San Francisco. The next day she collapsed in the lobby. On September 9, she died of peritonitis – a complication from a ruptured bladder. It now seems certain that Rappé died because of a botched abortion performed before she attended the party, but rumours soon circulated that Arbuckle was involved, specifically that the jovial fat man had raped the girl with a broken bottle. Arbuckle instantly became a box-office pariah and was tried three times for manslaughter. Eventual acquittal did not repair his shattered career. This was the first major Hollywood scandal, and lurid details of the wild behavior of film folk (during Prohibition, simply holding a boozy party was shocking enough) were hashed and rehashed in the yellow press, which hypocritically criticized screen idols for their misbehavior while gloating over (and, indeed, inventing) many of their outrages against common decency. The furore set the pattern for Hollywood scandals to come, including Errol Flynn's statutory rape prosecution and the O. J. Simpson murder trial, and founded three industries – the muckraking showbiz scandal sheet, the high-profile celebrity trial, and (perhaps most lastingly) film censorship in America. In the wake of Rappé's death, there was a feeling in the country that "something ought to be done" about that hotbed of sin and vice, Hollywood. Since it was impractical to police the private lives of the stars, what was done was that former postmaster Will H. Hays was appointed the first Director of the Motion Picture Producers and Distributors Association of America. He set about establishing a restrictive code of practices ("the Hays Code"), which fully came into force in 1934 and eliminated much "adult" material from American movies for decades to come.
Kim Newman

Date September 9, 1921

Why It's Key Besides ruining a major screen career, this accident brought the attentions of the censorious down on sinful Hollywood.

Opposite Virginia Rappé

Key Scene **The episode with the armless veteran** *Foolish Wives*

We're in Monte Carlo shortly after the end of World War I, where veterans on crutches and kids playing soldiers form an essential part of the background. Karamzin (Stroheim), a counterfeiter pretending to be a count, dressed to the nines in a military uniform, has been flirting with Mrs. Hughes (Miss Dupont), a wealthy American, on the terrace of a swank hotel. He even bribes a bellboy into paging him in order to impress her. When a stolid man nearby neglects to pick up the book she accidentally drops, we assume that this incidental character is around merely to indicate the kind of courtesy she's accustomed to receiving, and to provide Karamzin with an opportunity to display his own gallantry by picking up the book and taking it over to her.

The second time this man appears, he neglects to pick up her dropped purse in an elevator, and we imagine him to be some sort of running gag. Then, when we subsequently discover he's armless from the war, we're brought up short, made to feel guilty, and moved to pity. But as Mrs. Hughes – who feels guilty herself for having leapt to the wrong conclusion – proceeds to fondle and caress one of this veteran's armless sleeves, pity quickly turns into disquieting morbidity, and what we've previously been led to ignore we're now obliged to dwell upon. In a brief instant that illuminates the rest of the film, comedy turns into tragedy and the tragedy becomes a fetish.
Jonathan Rosenbaum

Date 1922

Nationality USA

Director Erich von Stroheim

Actors Erich von Stroheim, Miss Dupont (Patsie Hannon)

Why it's Key Stroheim moves from comedy to pity to morbidity as he introduces and brings back a minor character.

Key Scene **Jump for the demon**
Witchcraft through the Ages

A monk is seated at a desk, writing. It is dark; he sits with his back to the camera and occupies the lower half of the frame. Suddenly, a demon comes out from behind the desk, and it is impossible not to jump in your seat, just as the poor monk does. Extremely simple, the scene is staged exactly as in a modern horror film.

That's one of the many great moments of *Witchcraft through the Ages*, a unique film for its boldness in dealing with its taboo subject, for its amazing visual inventiveness, and also for its complex structure that combines various narrative levels: there are facts exposed as in a traditional documentary, scenes with actors that are supposed to be accurate recreations of documented practices, and visual renderings of dreams and fantasies. The director himself appears at the beginning and addresses his audience through intertitles, as if the whole film was a lecture that he has prepared on the subject of witchcraft. Incidentally, he also plays the demon.

Never an easy film to see, until in the late sixties a print appeared that replaced most of the intertitles with a voice-over narration by William Burroughs (bringing up to date the documentary form that Christensen wanted), *Witchcraft through the Ages* was often banned and cut, mostly because of Christensen's deeply anticlerical views. As if it weren't enough to depict a monk chasing a woman (and getting her), the horrors of the Inquisition, the masochistic pleasures of a young priest, and nuns desecrating holy images and shrines, Christensen suggests at the end of the film that psychoanalysis could cure those poor souls that suffer because of their "fear of the devil". Which is to say "fear of God".

Fernando Martín Peña

Date 1922

Nationality Denmark

Director Benjamin Christensen

Cast Benjamin Christensen

Original Title *Häxan*

Why It's Key It's probably the earliest frightening moment of cinema that still works with an audience.

Opposite *Witchcraft through the Ages*

Key Film
Nanook of the North

Flaherty got the idea to make a film of Inuit life while working as an explorer for a railway company in northern Quebec in the 1910s. The Inuit were called Eskimos then. A fur company set him up with movie equipment, but he rejected his initial efforts as amateurish and lost other attempts in a fire. Working slowly in the cold of the "illimitable spaces which top the world," aided by the Inuit who appeared in his film as versions of themselves, Flaherty finished his work, which he conceived as a story film as much as an ethnographic record, and released it to theaters. It succeeded and made Nanook the Eskimo a household word; the man who played him died of starvation "in the actual Arctic" six months after the film came out.

Nanook enters our consciousness from within the white of the frame. He pushes himself out from inside an igloo he has just built. The film ends in a nighttime so real it's like science-fiction. We leave Nanook as he falls asleep.

Almost ninety years after its release, *Nanook of the North* is still controversial; Flaherty is taken to task for not making a "real" documentary. It is a harsh writer indeed who would criticize the scene – a remarkable scene about sound in a silent movie – in which a white trader plays a gramophone and Nanook takes off the record and bites it. Who hasn't loved a record so much they wanted to bite it?

A. S. Hamrah

Date 1922

Nationality USA

Director Robert Flaherty

Cast Allakariallak, Nyla, Cunayou, Allegoo, Allee

Why It's Key The documentary is born – with *Nanook*, Flaherty created the non-fiction film.

Key Scene **The power of the vampire's shadow** *Nosferatu*

Most movie vampires, from Bela Lugosi to Christopher Lee to even Tom Cruise and Brad Pitt in *Interview With the Vampire* (1994) depend on charisma to enthrall their prey. So it's all the more frightening to see beautiful women crumple in somnambulistic ecstasy at the approach of the grotesque and shriveled Nosferatu (Schreck). He'd be laughable if he weren't so disquieting, with his misshapen posture and hairless skull and hollow eyes staring in impolite attention out at the warm-blooded world. When he goes after Ellen (Schröder) in her bedroom, there's something even more unsettling about the way we see only his hunched shadow creep up the stairs. This vampire doesn't have to turn into a bat to traverse long distances – he can go anywhere there's light and shade, into any room containing a crack wide enough to accommodate a sliver of darkness. She jumps in terror at the nameless, bodiless thing scratching at the door with its attenuated talons, like every unidentifiable silhouette that thwarted our childhood sleep. She cowers onto her bed, chest heaving in hyperventilating panic, but the ominous shadow of the monster's claw crawls up her white nightgown and closes in a fist at her heart. Aside from being a gorgeously expressionistic way to depict the vampire's conquest, there's a little wink in F. W. Murnau's metaphor. Film's just light and dark, after all. Those in the audience frightened by this scene now share Ellen's knowledge of what it's like to be menaced by a shadow.

Violet Glaze

Date 1922

Nationality Germany

Director F. W. Murnau

Cast Max Schreck, Greta Schröder

Original Title *Nosferatu, eine Symphonie des Grauens*

Why It's Key Murnau terrorizes the audience the same way Nosferatu charms his victims.

Key Event **Erich von Stroheim sacked by Irving Thalberg**

On October 6, 1922, six weeks into shooting of *Merry-Go-Round*, director Erich von Stroheim – famous for bringing films in over budget and months past the original completion date – was summoned to the office of Irving Thalberg, Universal Pictures' 22-year-old Head of Production, and fired. Thalberg gave von Stroheim a letter setting out the reasons for this dismissal, including "totally inexcusable and repeated acts of insubordination …, extravagant ideas which you have been unwilling to sacrifice in the slightest particular, repeated and unnecessary delays occasioned by your attitude in arguing against practically every instruction that had been given to you in good faith, and your apparent idea that you are greater and more powerful than the organization that employs you." Compliant journeyman Rupert Julian replaced von Stroheim on set, and the picture was finished. Within a year, Thalberg and von Stroheim were at MGM and clashing again over *Greed*.

In the early years of cinema, the director was all-powerful, and the martinet von Stroheim came to epitomize the idea of director as visionary artist and near-insane perfectionist (dressing extras in monogrammed period underwear which would never be seen on screen). When Thalberg sacked von Stroheim, he essentially invented the modern power structure of the movies – in which the front office held the purse strings and the true creator (as hyphenates like Howard Hawks and Alfred Hitchcock recognized) was the producer. Von Stroheim's films remain works of genius, even in the cut-down forms ultimately released, but his need to humiliate and discomfort the studios by spending their money on films that couldn't turn a profit even if they were hits or turning in ten-hour cuts that could never be released was ultimately self-defeating and justified draconian treatment of far more reasonable directors. After von Stroheim slunk off the Universal lot, directors became hired hands.

Kim Newman

Date October 6, 1922

Why It's Key This was the moment when the studio executive ascended above the director in the Hollywood power structure.

Key Scene **The cradle in the dining room**
Sylvester

It's New Year's Eve: people dressed up for a party are flocking to a lavish restaurant. The clients of a more modest joint are also waiting for their midnight toasts and dances. Behind the doors of the tavern, a smiling woman is preparing the table while her husband is serving drinks at the bar. A baby (whom we never see) is sleeping in his cradle. All seems to go well, until the silhouette of an old lady is seen outside the window. It is the husband's mother, who would like to join for the evening. The wife no longer smiles. This is the premise of *Sylvester*, a family drama conceived like a thriller: why is the wife so upset? And why is the mother acting in such a protective way towards his son? Within minutes, a clash of personalities unfolds with the violence of an Euripides tragedy, all the more devastating in that it is not accompanied by a single line of dialogue. There are no intertitles in Lupu-Pick's *kammerspiel*, one of the most disturbing works of German silent cinema. They are not necessary, as it

soon becomes clear that the two women of the film hate each other. It would be unfair to reveal too much of the plot; suffice it to say that the husband dies at midnight, thus leaving the two vengeful women alone in the room. Well, almost alone. A chilling shot brings us closer to the cradle: the baby could be the next victim.
Paolo Cherchi Usai

Date 1923

Nationality Germany

Director Lupu-Pick

Cast Eugen Klöpfer, Edith Posca, Frida Richard

Why It's Key *Kammerspiel* is treated like a Greek tragedy.

Key Scene **The human fly**
Safety Last!

The reputation of silent comedian Harold Lloyd has not survived in the way that those of his contemporaries Keaton and Chaplin have; while they are hailed as great artists and innovators, Lloyd (who devised his vehicles, but seldom directed or wrote them – missing out on the auteur acclaim he deserves) is remembered for only one thing: climbing a building in his vehicle *Safety Last!* Nevertheless, Lloyd's bespectacled, straw-hatted sharpie was a key screen character of the 1920s, more comfortable with gag-filled action than with the sentiment and cerebration that crept into his rivals' oeuvres. The *Safety Last!* scene is a riff on a 1920s craze for public stunts, especially involving then-new urban high-rises – the joke being that the professional Human Fly (Bill Strother) whom department-store publicist Lloyd has hired for a stunt has to flee from the cops, and the intrepid, inexperienced, terrified-of-heights hero has to step in and clamber up the outside of the

skyscraping building, braving all manner of comical perils from a mouse down the trousers through pecking birds and a mad dog to a clock that comes away from the wall when Lloyd puts all his weight on one of the hands. Excerpted in many compilations of the highlights of silent comedy, the scene has been often referenced in other pictures. In the 1960s, a best-selling poster preserved the moment on a thousand student dorm walls.
Kim Newman

Date 1923

Nationality USA

Directors Fred C. Newmeyer, Sam Taylor

Cast Harold Lloyd

Why It's Key Over 80 years on, Harold Lloyd dangling from the clock is still one of the cinema's Top Ten iconic images.

Key Event
The cutting of *Greed*

In the early 1920s, actor-turned-director Erich von Stroheim was one of the few filmmakers whose celebrity rivaled that of any living star. Born to working class Austrian Jews, he devised a pseudo-Prussian background, complete with the prefix "von," and a cartoonishly dictatorial persona, with adopted monocle and riding crop. But his pioneering dramatic features, including *Foolish Wives* (1922) and *Merry-Go-Round* (1923), eclipsed his eccentric behavior, even though the former film was gutted by its studio, and he was fired from the latter. Von Stroheim's fifth and most ambitious effort, *Greed* – a Gold Rush-era love triangle revolving around the disputed ownership of a lottery ticket, based on Frank Norris' bestselling novel *McTeague* – was his Waterloo. To releasing studio MGM's chagrin, he spent $750,000 shooting the entire novel, in actual San Francisco and Death Valley locations specified in the the text. The result was a cynical, grim, nine-hour-plus movie; MGM screened it once to satisfy von Stroheim's contract, then ordered him to cut and cut and cut it, then shut him out and cut it some more, then melted down the excised footage to recover the silver nitrate in its film stock. The end product ran about two hours. Von Stroheim never recovered his power and prestige and was later seen in the 1950 Hollywood satire *Sunset Blvd.*, playing a parody of himself. In 1999, Turner Classic Movies and film archivist Rick Schmidlin used still photos and other placeholding material to reconstruct a four-and-a-half-hour cut that von Stroheim had begged MGM to let him release in two parts.
Matt Zoller Seitz

Date 1924

Why It's Key It was the first in a long line of productions ÷ including Orson Welles's *The Magnificent Ambersons*, Sam Peckinpah's Major Dundee, and Michael Cimino's *Heaven's Gate* – in which a visionary auteur bucked his studio bosses and saw his would-be masterpiece butchered.

Key Film **The water-hose attack**
Strike

In this exuberant film debut, the ambitious 26-year old Eisenstein justified Lenin's visionary policy of funding cinema as a crucial tool for both public education and social agitation. Armed with geometric expertise from his engineering studies, Eisenstein joined the Constructivist era's fascination with dynamic movement to the ideological commitment to a collective protagonist. He used the story of a 1912 strike in a locomotive factory to teach techniques for recognizing spies and provocateurs, withstanding the psychological toll of a long-term strike, and resisting concessions. To the horizontal narrative that pitted heroic workers against cartoonish capitalists, the director added a kind of vertical dimension that experimented with form, depicting an event from multiple angles at a speed close to simultaneity, achieving what has been called a "cubist" montage. Boldly violating rules for matching movement to direction, and freely using unmotivated extreme angles, Eisenstein challenged Hollywood's seamless concealment of edits, introducing shock juxtapositions to jolt audiences out of their habits of perception. *Strike*'s most dazzling illustration of filmmaking less for storytelling than for aesthetic purposes comes just before the finale. In a four-minute sequence, police wield powerful water hoses to battle strikers. Two, then four, and then six jets of water arc and curve and cross, their force blasting the hapless workers. By devising a contrapuntal montage of rhythmic movements and spatial dynamics that economically underscore the tragedy, Eisenstein shows how the water blasts entrap the crowd, long shots giving way to closeups on individual faces, ending in an abstract blur of cascading water. Cinema had to absorb Eisenstein's new concept of montage, though its formalism would spell trouble for the director throughout Stalin's quarter-century rule.
Robert Keser

Date 1924

Nationality USSR

Director Sergei Eisenstein

Cast The Proletcult Collective

Original Title *Stachka*

Why It's Key This film introduced the "montage of shocks," using editing for purely aesthetic purposes.

Opposite Movie poster for *Strike* (*Stachka*)

Key Scene **Round and round we go**
The Last Laugh

This film follows upheavals in the career of an aging hotel doorman (Jannings). The doorman has come to be attached to his position in a prestigious hotel, to his glorious uniform with its long coat and shiny brass buttons, and to the sense of purpose and dignity that comes with long employment in a role that provides status and meaning. What he has not banked on are the forces of modernity, even though, in the form of bustling traffic and a flood of strangers, they confront him every day. The management has deemed him too old and incompetent and has made arrangements for him to be replaced by a younger man; there is a position for him downstairs, as the men's toilet attendant.

Symbolizing the tenuousness of occupational position and psychological balance in such a precarious environment is a gleaming glass revolving door, through which the doorman pushes his way blithely at the start of the film. The door is as if invisible to him; but *not to us*. Too soon, we come to understand that not only passage in and out of the hotel is revolutionary, but so is all experience in an age of pervasive change. The doorman walking out at a critical moment fails to see his replacement walking in at the same moment. The film constructs all of this man's experience as a kind of "revolving door" through life, where, without any apparent effort, he is suddenly heading in the wrong direction, suddenly spinning, and where the gap between out and in, yesterday and tomorrow, is simply, almost magically, erased.

Murray Pomerance

Date 1924

Nationality Germany

Director F. W. Murnau

Cast Emil Jannings

Original Title *Der letzte Mann*

Why It's Key This moment shows the centrality of modern life in cinema.

Key Scene **The projectionist enters the film** *Sherlock Jr.*

By 1923, Buster Keaton was perhaps the most physically adroit film star in the still-new Hollywood. His third feature under the Keaton Productions banner was *Sherlock Jr.*, a typically clockwork-paced flight of fancy about a young movie projectionist falsely accused of theft by his girlfriend's father. In an early, fast-paced sequence lasting some three to four minutes, Keaton's character escapes from his sleeping body in the projection booth, walks up the aisle of the crowded theater, leaps over the piano, and enters the film as it is being shown. A giddily rapid series of cuts finds him, in order, surrounded by the characters in a drawing room, on the front porch of a house, in a garden, on a busy street, atop a cliff, amongst lions, between cactus and a speeding train, on an ocean rock, in a snow bank, and then back in the garden. It's a bravura sequence that taps into the fluidity of film editing and its unlimited ability to link disparate images into a cohesive whole. Representing the admiration of the European avant-garde intelligentsia, René Clair compared the film to Luigi Pirandello's *Six Characters in Search of an Author*. Some 60 years later, Woody Allen affectionately borrowed the central conceit of *Sherlock Jr.* for his own, excellent *The Purple Rose of Cairo*.

David Stratton

Date 1924

Nationality USA

Director Buster Keaton

Cast Buster Keaton

Why It's Key Cinema's greatest physical performer, Keaton is also a director with a visionary understanding of the relationship between film and fantasy.

Key Scene **The chariot race**
Ben-Hur

The newly formed Metro-Goldwyn-Mayer invested all its cash in this adaptation of Lew Wallace's bestseller, spending $6 million to make this the silent era's most expensive production – no mean feat when profligate Hollywood was elaborately reconstructing everything from Babylon (D. W. Griffith's *Intolerance* [1916]) to Monte Carlo (Erich von Stroheim's *Foolish Wives* [1922]). Action specialist Eason was commissioned to re-conceive the stage adaptation's chariot-race centerpiece (which featured horses on treadmills) on cinema's grandest scale. With 42 cameras (more than had ever been used before on a single production) stationed on towers and cranes and dug in to the track, the 12-minute film-within-a-film captured extraordinary footage of sheer pulse-pounding dynamism. While "all Antioch" arrives to fill the giant colosseum, trumpets flourish as the long-simmering resentment between the race-baiting Messala (Bushman) and the proud Jew, Ben-Hur

(Novarro), turns into a rivalry unto death. Soon the furious action cuts between horses' hooves thundering and manes streaming, as chariots careen vertiginously around sharp corners and riders tumble into the dust, until Messala perishes in a final collision of beasts and vehicles, and the hero rides through a triumphal shower of rose petals. Future filmmakers took notes for their own self-contained displays of fast-moving spectacle and kinetic excitement, in films as varied as Sergei Eisenstein's *Alexander Nevsky* (1937), George Lucas's *Star Wars* (1977), Zhang Yimou's *Hero* (2002), and, not least, William Wyler's 1959 *Ben-Hur* remake, in which once again a second-unit director (Andrew Marton) worked independently on the chariot race, which matched the original's thrills.

Robert Keser

Date 1925

Nationality USA

Director Fred Niblo (and B. Reeves Eason)

Cast Ramon Novarro, Francis X. Bushman

Why It's Key This is the prototype of all "thrill ride" sequences.

Key Person
Buster Keaton *Go West*

A man in Western gear, a scarf, and a flat hat peers around a corner. He leans forward. The wind blows his hat off. In a single motion he grabs the hat and replaces it on his head.

Here in the space of a few seconds is the genius of Buster Keaton. This is far from the most spectacular stunt Keaton ever performed, but like the riding of a fence in *Cops* (1922), or the sliding into the shot on his ear in *Steamboat Bill, Jr.* (1928), it demonstrates Keaton's absolute and utter control of his body.

Only his arm moves. The way Keaton's arm seems to have a life of its own, anticipating the loss of his hat and recapturing it before the rest of Keaton's body notices the loss, is the essence of his comedy.

On the screen the gag seems spontaneous. It looks like Buster's hat flew off during a shot and the camera happened to catch its trajectory. Here in another nutshell is Keaton's genius as a director, making the remarkable seem ordinary and thus all the

more remarkable. The film's narrative at this point is not about Keaton's virtuosity – it's about Keaton's character looking after the cow he's attached to and protecting. A close examination of the scene, however, finds Keaton bracing his arm on his leg as he prepares to lean forward, into the path of we can presume to be a wind machine. He's prepared himself for the stunt. Genius takes work, and careful preparation. Another lesson from Keaton.

Gregg Rickman

Date 1925

Nationality USA

Director Buster Keaton

Cast Buster Keaton

Why It's Key A seemingly casual gag sums up the comedian's brilliance.

Key Scene **Odessa Steps sequence**
Battleship Potemkin

The "Odessa Steps" sequence of Sergei Eisenstein's *Battleship Potemkin*, based on actual events in 1905, is commonly regarded as one of the greatest in all of cinema. With frenzied editing combined with a masterly control of mise en scène, Eisenstein manipulates real space and time through the plastic elements of the film medium to create an unforgettable drama of helpless victims crushed by State oppression.

The people of Odessa are standing on the city steps, celebrating their solidarity with the sailors of the battleship in the harbor, who have mutinied because of oppressive conditions onboard, when a detachment of Cossacks suddenly appears and opens fire on the assembled throng without provocation. As the massacre unfolds, Eisenstein individualizes many of the people in the crowd – even a bourgeois who mocks their revolutionary fervor – but presents the Cossacks as a faceless, anonymous group signified metonymically by their boots and rifles. They march in unison mechanically and mercilessly, while the people of Odessa flee in all directions, individuals responding differently to the same threat. Eisenstein deftly manipulates the graphic composition, shot scale, and movement within the frame of each image to clash with the others. The director was perfectly aware of the propaganda potential of the film medium, and viewers cannot help identifying with the people against the barbaric Cossacks when watching this scene. The sequence is a perfect illustration of Eisenstein's dictum that "montage is conflict," here achieved on both the level of form and content simultaneously.
Barry Keith Grant

Date 1925

Nationality USSR

Director Sergei Eisenstein

Original Title *Bronenosets Potyomkin*

Why It's Key The textbook example of Eisenstein's theories of montage, this famous scene has been widely imitated and endlessly discussed.

Opposite Movie poster for *Battleship Potemkin* (*Bronenosets Potyomkin*)

Key Scene **The dance of the rolls**
The Gold Rush

The dance of the rolls occurs in a film, *The Gold Rush*, that Theodore Huff, writing in 1951, would call "probably Chaplin's most celebrated picture." Now that Chaplin no longer commands a popular audience, *The Gold Rush*, though still a classic, is probably known to fewer viewers than have seen Chaplin's *City Lights* (1931), *Modern Times* (1936), or *The Great Dictator* (1940), and among Chaplin connoisseurs, it seems to arouse less enthusiasm than *Monsieur Verdoux* (1947), *Limelight* (1952), or *A King in New York* (1957). Perhaps *The Gold Rush* should now be classed among films deserving rediscovery. The same could be said of this scene, also once much celebrated, which sums up so many of Chaplin's essential qualities: his interest in dream and fantasy (in the narrative, the scene is a dream the Chaplin character has while waiting for his guests to come to his New Year's Eve party), his love of improvisation and ingenuity (as a tribute to his guests, Charlie entertains them with what he calls "the Oceana Roll" by impaling two bread rolls with forks and manipulating them over the surface of a table as if the forks were legs and the rolls feet), the tremendous concentration of his face (the humor of the dance comes not just from his deftness with his hands, but also from the grace of his features), the pathos (the triumph of the dance dissolves when Charlie wakes up to confront the certainty that his guests will not come). This small and charming scene can still delight viewers, as long as it's not made to weigh down on them with its "classic" status.
Chris Fujiwara

Date 1925

Nationality USA

Director Charles Chaplin

Cast Charles Chaplin

Why It's Key Famous as it is, it can still be rediscovered.

Key Scene **The unmasking**
The Phantom of the Opera

Erik (Chaney), the masked Phantom, has abducted his soprano protégée Christine (Philbin) and spirited her away to his lair underneath the Paris Opera House. As he pounds a huge pipe organ, serenading her with his own composition "Don Juan Triumphant," the girl timidly creeps up behind the mystery man and – with some trepidation – reaches around to rip away his mask. Controversy persists as to whether the credited director (Rupert Julian) or the star himself was responsible for the staging of the great unmasking scene from *The Phantom of the Opera*, but it is one of the cinema's most magnificent "reveals." It manages a double shock: since the scene is photographed face-on, the audience has a privileged look at Chaney's still-startling skull-faced make-up job, alive with rage as Christine cowers behind him; then, Erik turns to the horror-struck girl, and we cut to her subjective point-of-view, which goes out of focus as the Phantom looms over her. "Feast your eyes," rants the Phantom in an intertitle, "gloat your soul upon my accursed ugliness!" Chaney, who famously designed and applied his own make-up, took his inspiration (unlike every subsequent screen Phantom) directly from Gaston Leroux's novel. "His eyes are so deep you can hardly see the fixed pupils. You just see two big black holes, as in a dead man's skull. His skin, which is stretched across his bones like a drum head, is not white but a nasty yellow. His nose is so little worth talking about that you can't see it sideface; the absence of a nose is a horrible thing to look at." Publicity materials at the time held back the look of the unmasked Phantom, which was reputedly shocking enough to cause many faintings among the original audiences.
Kim Newman

Date 1925

Nationality USA

Director Rupert Julian

Cast Lon Chaney, Mary Philbin

Why It's Key This is still unequaled as a shock "reveal" of the monster.

Opposite *Phantom of the Opera*

1920–1929

Key Scene **The farewell scene**
The Big Parade

Our visual memory is full of farewell scenes, both in fiction and in real life. It all boils down to three eternal questions: remember how happy we were together? Do you really know what you mean to me? Will I see you again, and if I do, will you still be mine? There seems to be a profound affinity between cinema and the experience of leaving or being left: we revive memories, we seize the fugitive moment, we try to get prepared to deal with longing and desire. A great film can indeed prove that the art of seeing and the art of living have a common ground; that's why the love stories told by King Vidor have such a uniquely deep resonance. *The Big Parade* makes the point with breathtaking candor. John Gilbert is a soldier leaving for the front, Renée Adorée is the beloved who is about to be left behind. He's on a truck with other soldiers, she's watching the convoy leave her village. She knew it was bound to happen, but now that it's happening she just can't stand it: she does not want him to go away. So she runs towards her man, desperately trying to reach him once more, to tell him that her heart is breaking. We can't hear her scream, but her pain reaches us loud and clear. She can't run fast enough; as she falls on the ground while the convoy disappears on the horizon, her desperate sobs have become ours.
Paolo Cherchi Usai

Date 1925

Nationality USA

Director King Vidor

Cast John Gilbert, Renée Adorée

Why It's Key The agony of separation becomes a palpable truth.

Key Scene **A car behaves like a chicken**
Egged On

The Cinémathèque de Toulouse was the first to rediscover the genius of Charley Bowers, a master of Surrealism who probably never saw a piece of Surrealist art before making his rural slapstick comedies in which pieces of metal scraps eat ostriches, eggs generate adult chicken, and Scotland Yard is a lawn with detectives wearing kilts, grazing the field with their magnifying lenses. By the time Joseph Losey asked him to assist in the making of a short film, Bowers was already a forgotten name: very little remained of the flamboyant Arcimboldo-style creations he produced between 1926 and 1930. A dozen titles have now resurfaced in film archives; *Egged On* is arguably the best of the crop. "You see, my friend," Charley explains, "Mother Nature never considered the advantages of less fragile eggs. Anyone who invents a way to make unbreakable eggs will become rich." "Why don't you invent a machine to pay your rent?", says the landlady, but Charley has better plans. After having tried to haul a sample of eggs in his car (all get smashed), he manages to find more specimens for his experiment and gives them shelter in the car's radiator, with unexpected results: thanks to the heat of the motor, the eggs open up and become tiny cars running around a much satisfied four-wheel mother hen. Aside from the technical wizardry in animating real objects, this unforgettable gag points to Bowers's *idée fixe*, the transmutation of the natural world into technological dreams. No wonder André Breton raved about Bowers.
Paolo Cherchi Usai

Date 1926
Nationality USA
Director Charley Bowers and Harold L. Muller
Cast Charley Bowers
Why It's Key Slapstick comedy meets Surrealism.

Key Event **The immolation of Australian cinema's history**

It is said that, at a conference of archivists, the celebrated French curator Dominique Païni solemnly announced: "85% of films from the early years of cinema are lost." But then he added an optimistic twist: "85% of films are not worth preserving anyway!" The American entrepreneur Norman Dawn may have shared this sentiment. *For the Term of His Natural Life*, shot in Australia in 1926, was the third adaptation of Marcus Clarke's novel of prison life. It was filmed in Sydney and in Tasmania's Port Arthur – a haunted spot in Australian history, more recently the site of a horrendous mass murder. As a foreign interloper – who had been handed this project after local pioneer Raymond Longford was forced off it – Dawn had to bear being called, in the press, a "party to the slaughtering" of Australia's young, struggling film industry. It seems he took these words to heart. For a spectacular scene of a ship catching fire, Dawn, well-known for his ingenuity with special effects, devised a particular treat: he combined 25 pounds of dynamite with two tons of assembled nitrate film soaked in crude oil. Thus, for this one scene in a film, prints of reportedly hundreds of previous movies – some now completely lost – were sacrificed. And it would not be the last time: Ken G. Hall, another local legend, repeated the trick for *The Squatter's Daughter* in 1933. Little wonder that contemporary archivists take these tales as allegories of the cinema industry's bad-faith relation to its own history.
Adrian Martin

Date 1926
Why It's Key Hundreds of films were sacrificed for the shooting of a single scene.

Key Scene **On a park bench, an old man gives a girl some bread** *Ménilmontant*

A very hungry girl (Sibirskaïa) sits on a park bench. She is alone and does not have a place to go. An old man is sitting on the same bench, eating. The man barely looks at her, but he quietly handles her some of his bread. He doesn't try to admonish her, doesn't ask her to explain her situation, and doesn't invade her feelings in any way. He just helps. And just from the way he does it we can imagine a whole life of hardship for that character, who never again appears the film.

Part of the deep emotional effect of the scene stems from a mise en scène that carefully avoids conventional sentimentality, though the whole film's plot is basically melodramatic: two country sisters lose their parents in a crime of passion, move to the big city, and, at different moments, fall prey to the same man, who seduces and then abandons them. Working exclusively in visual terms, without intertitles of any kind, director Kirsanoff manages to flesh out that basic story with all kinds of subtleties of characterization, mood, and

context. He even finds a few opportunities, particularly when dealing with time ellipses, to try some effects suggestive of avant-garde films. The film is also an astonishing example of rapid cutting techniques, which prefigure the work of many contemporary directors.

Ménilmontant is just one of many silent French films that 40 years ago were regular staples in film societies but now are not so readily available and which nobody writes about, like Germaine Dulac's *The Smiling Madame Beudet* (1922) or Jacques Feyder's *Crainquebille* (1922). Not to speak of Abel Gance's whole silent oeuvre or some true oddities like Ivan Mozhukhin's *The Burning Brazier* (1923). It is a pity that – besides the paralyzing rigors of the conventional film market – we usually submit to following "trends" in something as vast and happily unpredictable as film history.

Fernando Martín Peña

Date 1926

Nationality France

Director Dimitri Kirsanoff

Cast Nadia Sibirskaïa

Why It's Key It's a deeply moving scene in an exceptional and now almost forgotten film.

Key Scene **The "affair"** *Mighty like a Moose*

C harley Chase and Vivien Oakland are husband and wife. From the beginning it is obvious that they have married because they were rejected by everybody else: he has "teeth like a walrus," and she has a preposterous nose. One day, separately, they decide to undergo plastic surgery. When the operations are over, they meet on the street, fail to recognize each other, and carry on what they both think is an illicit affair. He invites her to a party, she accepts, and they both go back by separate ways to their home in order to get dressed. At the house, they try to hide from each other to conceal their facial changes, so there follows a carefully choreographed series of encounters in which one of them always has his or her face covered in some way. After they get properly dressed, they go out by different doors, meet again some blocks away, and go to the party, still convinced that they are going to cheat on each other.

This is certainly one of the most perfectly constructed comedies of all time and a good piece of evidence for arguing that Charley Chase and Leo McCarey invented the situation comedy (probably with some help by Max Linder). With minor changes, the basic plot of the film could be used in any modern TV sitcom without losing any of its comedy value.

Fernando Martín Peña

Date 1926

Nationality USA

Director Leo McCarey

Cast Charley Chase, Vivien Oakland.

Why It's Key Charley Chase and Leo McCarey invented the situation comedy.

Key Event
The death of Rudolf Valentino

Rudolf Valentino's death was not glamorous. "*The Sheik*" should have succumbed to a saber duel, a bullfighting mishap, a firing squad execution. But the undignified malady that did him in at the age of 31 – fatal peritonitis precipitated by a bleeding ulcer – was enough to send cataclysmic ripples through the moviegoing public. "Women are not in love with me," Valentino astutely once acknowledged, "but with the picture of me on the screen. I am merely the canvas on which women paint their dreams." Something in the public imagination went unhinged when the receptacle for all that longing disappeared. An estimated 100,000 people mobbed Valentino's wake, their hysterical surge towards the entrance quickly devolving into a crushing riot. Rumors spread of suicide attempts by grief-stricken fans. Actress Pola Negri sent 4,000 roses to the viewing, an overwrought gesture that still seemed insufficient. Nowadays, so many actors – James Dean, Marilyn Monroe, Bruce Lee, River Phoenix – have died while still shimmering with vitality and charisma that the slight perfume of necrophilia is expected to flavor any continued cult following. But the bereft crowds mobbing New York streets in the hours after their idol's death had no precedent for how to behave. The rules of media celebrity were still being written. The shockwave of Valentino's death demonstrated that star power was like nuclear power: it could light the world when harnessed safely by the Hollywood machine – but when accidental calamity unleashed its hot reactor core, no one was safe.

Violet Glaze

Date August 23, 1926

Why It's Key Celebrity worship first reveals its dark side in the aftermath of sudden tragedy.

Opposite Valentino in a classic pose

Key Scene **The opening sequence**
A Page of Madness

Torrential rain beats down on a street at night. A car arrives, and a figure steps out. Such is the "narrative" in the first 50 or so shots of Teinosuke Kinugasa's *A Page of Madness*, but it is largely irrelevant: we never find out who this person is or the reason for the visit. What matters is the rhythmic montage of rain, tires, stairs, a telephone pole, windows, and lightning, combined through cuts, double exposures, and even upside-down images. Such experimental film technique is partially motivated by the revelation that this is a mental hospital, as the film begins, in the next hundred shots, to implicate the viewer in the delusions of a dancing inmate, combining wild body movements with synesthetic evocations of music into a culminating flurry of shots of only one frame apiece. Although influenced by French Impressionist film, the entire sequence was praised by Japanese critics as surpassing the best of contemporary European cinema, even if some complained about the film's other melodramatic segments. Kinugasa, however, did not take the film with him when he traveled to Europe in 1928, and *A Page of Madness* was long thought lost until the director found a print in his storehouse in 1971. Its subsequent re-release, albeit in a version shorter than the 1926 original, has only increased the film's avant-garde reputation. One only wonders what the reaction would have been if Europeans had viewed the opening sequence of *A Page of Madness* in 1928.

Aaron Gerow

Date 1926

Nationality Japan

Director Teinosuke Kinugasa

Cast Masao Inoue, Eiko Minami

Original Title *Kurutta ichipeiji* (aka *Kurutta ippeiji*)

Why It's Key This scene is an exemplar of experimental form in silent narrative cinema.

Key Speech **"You ain't heard nothin' yet!"**
The Jazz Singer

The Jazz Singer was not the first motion picture with sound. Edison's original demonstration of the movies synchronized pictures with gramophone records, and there had been many similar experiments throughout the cinema's first decades. Nay-sayers and conservatives within the established film industry saw these as the equivalent of the 3-D crazes that came later or brief fads like Odorama, and when Warner Bros. decided to try out a synchronized sound process (which involved wedding soundtrack to image on a single film strip), the studio didn't think it would change forever the way movies were made and shown. *The Jazz Singer* isn't even an "all-talking, all-singing" picture, but a silent that was supposed to burst into sound whenever Al Jolson's character got up on stage to sing. The historic moment came almost by accident, as the irrepressible entertainer improvised a few words of preamble before launching into his first big number. "Wait a minute, wait a minute, you ain't heard nothin'

yet! Wait a minute, I tell ya! You ain't heard nothin'! You wanna hear 'Toot Toot Tootsie'? All right, hold on, hold on ... Lou, listen. Play 'Toot Toot Tootsie,' three chorus, you understand. In the third chorus, I whistle. Now give it to 'em hard and heavy, go right ahead." With those few words, Jolson killed silent films – "they are doing away with the greatest boon that has ever been offered to the deaf," carped critic E. V. Lucas – and made the musical a major movie genre.

Kim Newman

Date 1927

Nationality USA

Director Michael Curtiz

Cast Al Jolson

Why It's Key Even if it weren't an important historical turning point, it would still be an exciting speech: the brash, confident voice of urban, 20th-century melting-pot America telling audiences that the future was already here and would be consistently astonishing.

Opposite *The Jazz Singer*

Key Scene **The cab ride**
Springtime Saps

The catalogue of the legendary retrospective held at the 1994 Pordenone Silent Film Festival devoted to American slapstick lists 1,674 actors and actresses who contributed to the humblest and most creative form of art in silent cinema. The majority of them are footnotes of film history, hundreds of unknown silent clowns who have been condemned to oblivion after a brief flirtation with popularity. Snub Pollard is much more than a footnote (his rowdy gags often verge on the ethereal), and yet the first reel of *Springtime Saps* is so unremarkable that it would barely fall within the radar of the most dedicated specialist. Be patient, as the second part has a surprise to share. Snub is driving a taxi; inside, his partner is engaged in a casual conversation with a young lady who sells women's stockings. Her suitcase includes two false legs, which she uses to display the latest novelties in intimate apparel. As she makes her sales pitch, one of the legs leans out of the cab's left window; she pulls the other

one and sticks it out the opposite window. While the camera alternates shots from within and in front of the taxi, the lady rotates the artificial legs in order to better display her product. Your imagination can do the rest. Vulgarity – the main ingredient of genuine slapstick – is elevated here to the sublime. If film censors sat in front of this short and then gave their approval to it, they must have been sleeping.

Paolo Cherchi Usai

Date 1927

Nationality USA

Director Les Goodwins

Cast Snub Pollard

Why It's Key Vulgarity can be sublime.

Key Scene **Wood on the tracks**
The General

In the first shot, the camera is on the railroad tracks, right in front of the action: Keaton is cleaning the railroad of various obstacles (boxes, barrels, big pieces of wood) that were placed there by the enemy. He does so by running ahead of his engine, which he has set up to advance slowly. Then, one big piece of wood gets stuck in the tracks, and Keaton needs some time to take it off. He succeeds just in time and ends up seated on the front bumper of the machine, holding the piece of wood with both hands. In the second shot, the camera travels parallel to Keaton's engine as he tries to balance on the bumper, holding the piece of wood. In the third shot, with the camera again in front of the engine but now tracking back, a second piece of wood is revealed in the path of the engine. After a moment of suspense, Keaton throws the first piece of wood right onto the end of the second piece, causing it to leap off the tracks at a perfect 180-degree angle.

As a performer, Keaton is often praised for his stunts, which were certainly amazing, but it was in this type of gag, subtler but more physically demanding, that his unique talents were truly revealed. As a director, he was unsurpassed when he dealt with his own material: the three shots perfectly establish the situation and build to its climax. The three of them are essential for the scene, and it is impossible to imagine any better way of shooting it. The scene covers many significant levels of Keaton's work: it's about obstacles that keep coming and must be overcome by sheer resourcefulness; it works with objects handled in unexpected ways; it deals with physics and Keaton's lifelong need to move forward; it has the poetic sense of a perfectly choreographed dance. And, above all, it makes us laugh.

Fernando Martín Peña

Date 1927

Nationality USA

Directors Buster Keaton, Clyde Bruckman

Cast Buster Keaton

Why It's Key This is a good example of Keaton's style as a performer, director, and comedy mastermind.

Key Person **Laurel and Hardy**
The Battle of the Century

Although they appeared in no less than 14 Hal Roach two-reelers released in 1927, it was only after about ten of those that Laurel and Hardy became an actual team – and were billed as such. (*Hats Off*, *The Second Hundred Years*, and *Putting Pants on Philip*, all 1927, have been variously identified as the first "official" Laurel and Hardy comedy.) *The Battle of the Century*, a short famous mainly for its climactic cream-pie fight, features the familiar couple, with self-important, long-suffering Hardy perpetually frustrated by Laurel's blunders, yet they still don't have their personalities and relationship to each other entirely set. Hardy's key mannerisms (such as the camera stare) are missing, and his acting, although comically exaggerated, remains basically straight: as the trainer of Stan's hapless prizefighter, he comes across as Laurel's straight man (most of Laurel's key mannerisms are in place, though). The two are not yet called Stan and Ollie (or, as Ollie will often introduce the

duo later, "Mr. Laurel and Mr. Hardy"): Stan is "Canvasback Clump" (aka "the human mop") while Hardy is simply introduced as his manager. In later films, such a business relationship between the two will no longer be necessary: they'll just be together as a team, forever inseparable no matter what.

More typical of the team than the boxing match is a fine routine at the end of reel one (it has disappeared, but a script of it and some stills do survive) in which Stan, trying to use a fountain pen, keeps squirting ink in Ollie's face. But the highlight is of course the pie-throwing orgy, orchestrated and choreographed in typical L&H style as each pie thrown hits an unintended target, and more and more throwers and victims get into the game.

Jean-Pierre Coursodon

Date 1927

Nationality USA

Director Clyde Bruckman

Why It's Key This is one of the best Laurel and Hardy comedy shorts, and one of the first in which their respective personalities are firmly established.

Opposite **Laurel and Hardy**

Key Scene **The triptych sequence**
Napoleon

An unexpected effect of cinema's first appearance in Russia was the audience reaction to the flickering image on the screen. People felt anguished as they saw people walk past the camera and disappear into nothingness. What happened to them? It was like death by projection. Such a response should not be taken lightly. Why is the image rectangular and not, say, circular? Why should the edges of the frame be so sharp? What defines the boundaries of vision, and what is their meaning? Filmmakers and theatre owners tried all sorts of solutions: build giant screens (Imax), double the size of the frame (70mm), make the image look wider (CinemaScope) or so large that you have to turn your head to see it all (Grimoin-Sanson's Cinéorama, a 360-degree projection that failed at the 1900 Paris Exhibition). Abel Gance's Polyvision is another attempt to achieve this utopia of human vision; it would have been forgotten like many others if it weren't for two things: first, the triptych effect erupts on the screen from a single, standard image, as if we were under the effect of a very powerful anamorphic drug; second, the expanded view is not so much the result of an overstretched screen as of an avalanche of mental associations, flashing simultaneously before our eyes: Napoléon (Dieudonné), his armies, his beloved Joséphine (Manès), an eagle with open wings. Cinema is not just bigger than life; it can break its limits, thus defying the death so much feared by the Moscow viewers of 1896.

Paolo Cherchi Usai

Date 1927

Nationality France

Director Abel Gance

Cast Albert Dieudonné, Gina Manès, Wladimir Roudenko

Original Title *Napoléon vu par Abel Gance*

Why It's Key You can't restrain creativity in a frame.

Key Scene **Freder catches his father with the False Maria** *Metropolis*

SPOILER

Few canonical films are as allegorically frontloaded as *Metropolis*, the ur-text for cinema's ongoing fascination with visionary dystopia. Many scholars, most recently Tom Gunning, have discussed in detail the ways in which Lang and screenwriter Thea von Harbou interweave political, sociological, technological, and psychoanalytical themes, resulting in a film that is as endlessly compelling as it is ideologically incoherent. In the scene in question, the Oedipal conflict that has undergirded *Metropolis*'s hesitant critique of power suddenly breaks open like a collapsed dam. But what's more, Lang uses non-objective visual forms to inscribe this breakdown directly onto the surface of the film itself.

As Freder (Fröhlich) opens the door and finds his father (Abel) in the arms of the robotic double of Maria (Helm), the woman he loves, the space around Freder goes black. His image is first replaced and then supplemented by bursting circles of pure white light. Jagged starbursts appear to be scratched directly on the negative. The faces of all three principals are surrounded by whirling kaleidoscopic superimpositions. Keep in mind, the techniques Lang uses in this scene were not exactly new. Early modernist experiments in abstract cinema by Fischinger, Léger, and Man Ray were already in full swing by 1927, as were the experimental narrative works by the so-called French Impressionist filmmakers. But few of these films had the same degree of cultural impact *Metropolis* did, and as a result Freder's Cubist hissy fit represents a cinematic landmark. For about one minute, *Metropolis* is a fully avant-garde film.

Michael Sicinski

Date 1927

Nationality Germany

Director Fritz Lang

Cast Gustav Fröhlich, Brigitte Helm, Alfred Abel

Why It's Key Lang's representation of an Oedipal breakdown is also a key early example of the intersection between narrative and avant-garde cinemas.

Key Scene **The full-moon tracking shot**
Sunrise

In this famous and profound shot, the magnetic attractions of sexuality and modernity appear as two related paths. One is that of a farmer (O'Brien) walking at night across a field near his home toward a rendezvous with his mistress, a visitor from the city (Livingstone). His journey is doubled – it might be better to say raised to a higher power – by the unearthly fluidity of Murnau's camera, which first follows him, then tracks alongside him (as his winding route diverges sharply from the camera's), and then faces him before pivoting around and losing his figure to approach (through tree branches that magically part) the woman who is waiting for him. This very fluidity makes it clear – as does the full moon that looms in the top left of the composition at the start of the shot, reappearing at the end of it to illuminate the chic, black-clad woman – that the man's trajectory is a symbolic configuration of forces that transcend the human and that he has abdicated free will to become

their vehicle. The shot is as much a protest against this enslavement as it is a glorification of it. In this internal tension and in the overwhelming beauty of Murnau's shot, we can find a definition of mise en scène.
Chris Fujiwara

Date 1927

Nationality USA

Director F. W. Murnau

Cast George O'Brien, Margaret Livingstone

Why It's Key This camera movement provides a definition of mise en scène.

Key Scene **Alonzo's mad laughter**
The Unknown

Nanon (Crawford) is extremely beautiful and desirable. However, she has a problem: she says she can't stand men's hands because "all my life men have tried to put their beastly hands on me… to paw over me." Alonzo (Chaney) listens very carefully and meditates about this. He has seen her violently rejecting Malabar (Kerry), a suitor who tried to touch her. Alonzo loves Nanon, and it is a question of how far he's willing to go for that love.

One day he goes away and has both his arms amputated to become Nanon's ideal. However, when he comes back to her, he finds her in the strong arms of Malabar. "Remember how I used to be afraid of his hands?", she says. Of course he remembers. Then she adds: "I am not any more. I love them now." As she makes Malabar caress her, Alonzo understands and begins to laugh, until his whole body collapses.

This is probably the best film ever made about the tragedy of unrequited love. The plot, of course, is a little

more complicated: Alonzo has a criminal past, there's a revenge attempt, and everything happens in the world of the circus, so the film has a borderline quality from the start. However, its moral is universal: *la donna è mobile*: woman is fickle.
Fernando Martín Peña

Date 1927

Nationality USA

Director Tod Browning

Cast Lon Chaney, Joan Crawford, Norman Kerry

Why It's Key It's a moment of black irony from a great film on unrequited love.

Key Scene **The dinner**
Pass the Gravy

Max Davidson deserves a place in cinema history for at least two reasons: first, he was the one who in 1907 persuaded a struggling theater actor named D.W. Griffith to earn some extra money by playing small parts at the Biograph Company in New York (Griffith reciprocated in 1916 by giving him a small part as a kindly tenant in the modern episode of *Intolerance*); second, he made about 30 short comedies between 1923 and 1929, in which his Jewish-style humor brought slapstick to the pinnacle of its achievements. *Pass the Gravy* has now earned a place in the pantheon of the best short film comedies ever made, partly because of Leo McCarey's clockwork script. The story revolves around Brigham, an award-winning rooster owned by Max's neighbor. It's time to celebrate with a dinner at Max's. Instead of buying a chicken with the money given to him, his hapless son (O'Donnell) brings Brigham to the table in the form of roasted dinner. As soon as the boy notices the identification ring around the victim's leg, he tries to inform his father of the terrible mistake he made. Brigham's owner is the guest of honor, so the culprit can only use sign language, in the hope Dad will understand. Well, he won't. The ensuing gag – extended over several minutes of uproarious suspense – is handled through a brilliant use of silence as an expressive device, a supreme demonstration of what cinema could achieve, not despite but thanks to the absence of a soundtrack.

Paolo Cherchi Usai

Date 1928

Nationality USA

Director Fred L. Guiol

Cast Max Davidson, Spec O'Donnell

Why It's Key The absence of sound is part of the gag.

Key Person **Charlie Chaplin**
The Tramp goes on alone *The Circus*

Rich in both comic invention and tender sentiment, *The Circus* is a beautifully shaped masterpiece of comedy centered on the familiar figure of the Tramp (Chaplin), who inadvertently becomes star of a circus as a clown, only to have his heart broken when the equestrienne he befriends, protects, and loves (Merna Kennedy) winds up in love with a high-wire man (Harry Crocker). At the end, he chooses to let the circus go on without him. He sits sadly on a box in the outline of a circle where the circus had been, looks at a torn paper with a star on it, crumples up the paper and kicks it behind his back, and walks off into the distance as the image irises out. This brief final scene crystallizes all that is great about Chaplin – for it is not only entirely his creation but is only about him, from the moment the circus wagons roll away behind him through the dust in long shot, their motion less riveting than his still dark figure as he watches their departure. No one within the film sees the Tramp's exquisitely performed final gesture within the abandoned circle, but in solitude he is not less "the funny man" the circus audiences had earlier clamored for, nor less the touching man, the resilient man, the poetic man. As Chaplin the filmmaker perceives him, he is all these things, an eternal figure. That takes a strong ego, but Chaplin the artist justifies that view, behind the camera and before it.

Blake Lucas

Date 1928

Nationality USA

Director Charlie Chaplin

Cast Charlie Chaplin

Why It's Key Chaplin's genius is distilled in an ending at once simple and sublime.

Opposite **Charlie Chaplin**

Key Scene **Keaton shares a dressing room with another man** *The Cameraman*

B uster Keaton's favorite kind of gag was big, genuine, and dangerous. Whether centered on a runaway steam engine in *The General* (1927), the breakaway façade of a house rigged to crash down around his ears in *Steamboat Bill, Jr.* (1928), the accelerating avalanche in *Seven Chances* (1925), or the riptide current of a very real waterfall in *Our Hospitality* (1923), Keaton's humorous stunts usually involved tremendous risk of genuine bodily harm. But the comedic daredevil-cum-director could also play his wit close to the vest, as demonstrated by the small-scale changing-room scene in *The Cameraman* (1928). Buster snags a booth in the crowded locker room of a public swimming pool when he's interrupted by a beefy lout (Brophy) who wants the room for himself. An overhead shot describes the veal crate of a space the two men must share, and while Buster gamely tries to negotiate a compromise, pretty soon he's bullied into a corner, receives an elbow in the sternum, tangles himself in

the other man's suspenders, and, in bending over to remove his sock garters, somehow ends up on his nemesis's shoulders – all capped by the hysterical visual punchline of Buster exiting the dressing room in an old-fashioned bathing costume sized for a much bigger man. *The Cameraman* was the first film Keaton made under an ill-starred deal with MGM, and the last that shows his genius in top form. In this scene, Buster proves he's still the master of absurdity writ large and small.
Violet Glaze

Date 1928

Nationality USA

Director Edward Sedgwick, Buster Keaton

Cast Buster Keaton, Marceline Day, Edward Brophy

Why It's Key Buster Keaton proves he's just as adept at pocket-sized jokes as he is at large-scale stunts.

Key Scene **The office building** *The Crowd*

A t the very cusp of the Great Depression, this unflinching depiction of a struggling American Everyman lost in the impersonal metropolis foreshadowed the economic realities to come and would inspire later neorealist works, including Roberto Rossellini's *Open City* (1945) and Vittorio De Sica's *The Bicycle Thief* (1948). The most elaborate and widely remarked shot in *The Crowd* was not realist at all but spectacularly stylized. To illustrate the odds against his luckless protagonist, "one of the seven million that believe New York depends on them," Vidor positions his camera for a curbside look at a towering skyscraper but then sends it upward to scale the building until it reaches an upper window. With a quick dissolve, the camera moves inside, hovering high above an apparently endless room crossed by diagonal rows of desks where insurance company clerks busily work, all moving to the same rhythm, their faces swallowed in the dehumanizing mass. Speeding along a ceiling track,

the camera finally descends to desk #137, locating the hero in the midst of white-collar anonymity. But he's not doing his work; he's watching the clock (quitting time approaches) and pondering his entry in a get-rich-quick contest to name a new motor fuel – actions that indicate both his time-serving estrangement from the workplace and his unrealistic ambition. The geometric set design of this sequence, which was immediately recognized as a classic, embodied corporate depersonalization and was explicitly referenced for the same reason in Billy Wilder's *The Apartment* (1960).
Robert Keser

Date 1928

Nationality USA

Director King Vidor

Cast James Murray

Why It's Key It's a definitive image of mass depersonalization.

Opposite **Still from** *The Crowd*

SPOILER

Key Person **Jules Furthman**
The Docks of New York

Not a lot is known about Jules Furthman. He was a Chicago newspaperman who got to Hollywood about ten years before Ben Hecht did and also wrote for von Sternberg and Hawks. Leigh Brackett, who wrote scripts with him even though she was 30 years his junior, said he was the kind of writer who didn't like to write things down. He wrote over a hundred films, the first in 1915, the last in 1959 (*Rio Bravo*, with Brackett). In his Hawks biography, Todd McCarthy describes Furthman as cantankerous and quotes Hawks as saying only he, von Sternberg, and Victor Fleming would work with him, because "he was such a mean guy we thought he was great."

Furthman specialized in unclassy tales of redemption in tawdry settings featuring charming semi-brutal men and glamorous women, who were a little ruined, people in trouble who rise to the occasion against their instincts. His women could be Dietrich or Bacall, his men Bogart or John Wayne. In *The Docks of New York*, George Bancroft's stoker and Betty Compson's Mae are primitive versions, violent, romantic, and drunk. The originals, concocted out of who knows who or what, lived in Furthman's head. Certain gestures of theirs cross between the films of the directors Furthman worked with, gestures that must be attributable to him. They can be seen in everything Furthman worked on: *China Seas* (1935), a Clark Gable movie directed by Tay Garnett, plays like knock-off von Sternberg or Hawks wafting over MGM.
A. S. Hamrah

Date 1928

Nationality USA

Director Josef von Sternberg

Cast George Bancroft, Betty Compson

Why It's Key Did Furthman create the modern movie character?

Key Scene **The phonograph record**
Lonesome

Paul Fejos is one of the most intriguing and underrated personalities of the late silent period. After having made a number of films in his native Hungary, he moved to the United States and made a short film – *The Last Moment* (1928), the portrait of a man who is about to commit suicide – which was hailed by Chaplin as a masterpiece (no print is extant). That was the beginning of a strange, erratic career: his frustration with the studio system was reciprocated by Hollywood, who forced him back to Europe at the dawn of the sound era. After a few films in France (*Fantômas* [1932]) and Hungary (*Mary, A Hungarian Legend* [1932], another overlooked gem), he bade farewell to commercial production and became a notable director of ethnographic films. In a way, *Lonesome* could fit into this category: it's the simple love story of two lonely people in the big city. The two protagonists casually meet on their way to Coney Island, fall deeply in love, then lose each other during a thunderstorm. They only know each other's first names, and didn't think about exchanging addresses. Have they lost their golden chance? Romance suddenly becomes a thriller, whose solution lies in a phonograph record played in the man's modest apartment. "I'll be loving you always," says the song; its notes provide the film with a *coup de théâtre* of arresting simplicity. Can't tell you what it is: to see is to believe. Thanks to that song, our lovers will no longer be lonesome.
Paolo Cherchi Usai

Date 1928

Nationality USA

Director Paul Fejos

Cast Barbara Kent, Glenn Tryon

Why It's Key A silent film uses sound to bring a romance to its happy ending.

Key Scene **The hero's bath is prepared**
Spies

It's a brief montage of four shots, sandwiched in the middle of a sequence packed with action and intrigue, offering us an elliptical breather in the midst of Lang's most suspenseful thriller. Two hands emerge from the foreground in close-up to turn on a bathtub's spigots; a hand places a fresh bar of soap in the soap dish; a fresh towel is draped over the towel rack; and a fancy thermometer is dipped in the tub's water by the same hand, pulled out so the temperature can be checked, then set afloat while bath salts are sprinkled in the water.

From the sleeve of a striped jacket, we know the hands belong to the hero's valet (Hörbiger), dutifully preparing his master's bath. Just before, the hero (Willy Fritsch) – a detective identified in the credits as "No. 326," disguised as a filthy tramp – has returned to his hotel suite via roof and fire escape, only to be greeted by a sexy spy (Gerda Maurus) who's just shot a man in the next room who she claims was attacking her and

has run to 326's room for refuge. In fact, this is a seductive ruse; she's been sent by the villain to 326's room to find information about a secret treaty, and just after the bath montage, we see her find and steal a document from his desk while he's still bathing and dressing. So the hero's bath is never shown or depicted, yet Lang evokes it vividly and even luxuriously through the elaborate way his servant prepares it.

Jonathan Rosenbaum

Date 1928
Nationality Germany
Director Fritz Lang
Cast Paul Hörbiger
Original Title *Spione*
Why It's Key It's a calm oasis of peace and luxury in the midst of a tight, sinister thriller.

1920–1929

67

Key Scene **The white horse**
The Wind

It all started in December 1918, with D.W. Griffith's *Broken Blossoms*. Lillian Gish was shooting the scene where Lucy is hiding in a closet while her adoptive father is smashing the door with an axe: Lillian's screams were so loud and desperate that a crowd gathered outside the studio, and Griffith's collaborators had to go out and reassure everyone that it was only a movie being filmed. The director was speechless. "My God," he is reported as having said, "why didn't you tell me you were going to do *that*?" A decade later, Swedish émigré Victor Sjöström shot a similar sequence in a cabin shattered by a sandstorm while Gish is looking out of the window: the corpse of the man who raped her and whom she killed is being slowly unearthed by the raging wind. Sjöström made the actress scream again in fear, but this time her mouth is hidden by the window frame; all we see is her hallucinating eyes, the mirrors of a mind on the brink of madness. We don't need to hear the deafening noise of

the storm that seems about to break the cabin into shreds – it is all in Lillian's petrified stare. And then, like a frightening ghost, the White Horse appears. It is in fact the negative image of a huge stallion, rushing towards the camera against a black background. Reality is no longer enough to convey terror; this archetypal image of primeval, overwhelming power becomes its sexual symbol.

Paolo Cherchi Usai

Date 1928
Nationality USA
Director Victor Sjöström
Cast Lillian Gish
Why It's Key Gish surpasses herself in an overpowering vision of sexual fear.

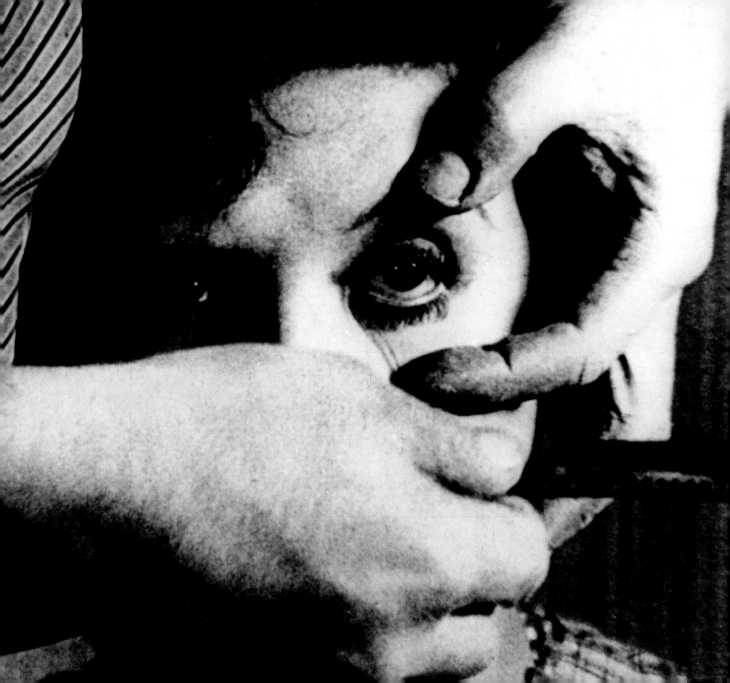

Key Scene **The missing scenes**
The River

We are not keen to talk about film as art. We don't like to admit it, but we should know that this is, to a great extent, wishful thinking. For the vast majority of people "art" is a painting, a classic novel, a symphony, a statue, an ancient temple; not cinema. Films are called "movies", "pictures," "flicks," and behind the familiar terms there is often a hint of condescension. Ask someone about, say, *The Wizard of Oz*. If she or he knows about it, the likely answer will be "oh, that's an old movie," and maybe adding that it's also a great one. We don't say, "oh, it's an old painting" when we mention a work of Cézanne, do we?

A case in point is Borzage's *The River*. It is a work of supreme, timeless beauty, but it's not recognized as such by a larger public – even by cinephiles – because fifty minutes of film are all that's left. *The River* is only a long fragment, and cinema aficionados hate fragments so much they don't use the word "restoration" at all if the whole thing isn't there to view.

If the same criterion was applied to the other arts, the Victory of Samothrace would be buried in the basement of the Louvre; the Colosseum would be ignored by all; there would be no interest in the poetry of ancient Greece; no orchestra would perform Schubert's Tenth Symphony. *The River* is cinema's Venus de Milo.

Paolo Cherchi Usai

Date 1929

Nationality USA

Director Frank Borzage

Cast Charles Farrell, Mary Duncan

Why It's Key Film fragments can be as beautiful as director's cuts.

Key Scene **A slice of eye**
Un chien andalou

At the very beginning of Luis Buñuel's first film, the eye of a young woman is sliced by a recently sharpened razor blade. A close-up of her face is followed by an extreme close-up that shows every detail of the action. Between these two images, the shot of an horizontal cloud floating across the middle of a full moon produces a visual rhyme and lets us hope that the worst will be spared us. It's not: the eye is slit open, and the shot's size has a strong impact on the spectator, especially at the film's start. Here (as well as later, when we will be offered a severed hand and rotting donkeys), *Un chien andalou* qualifies as a gore film, even though the scene lacks realism, since the victim doesn't move back at the sight of the blade and the special effect is quite obvious – it's easy enough to see that the head of a calf was used by the filmmaker. The image is disturbing, however, voluntarily shocking; with the vitreous humor that oozes out of the eye, the director, who manipulates the razor in person, wants to

let us see what's really inside human beings: urges, passion, and desires. The slicing can also be interpreted as a call to contemplate the world in a different light, to see other things. In any case, this visual assault brilliantly expresses the theoretical perspective of the Surrealist revolution while simultaneously applying it. Above all it reminds us that we have to keep an eye… wide open!

Frank Lafond

Date 1929

Nationality France

Director Luis Buñuel

Cast Simone Mareuil, Luis Buñuel

Why It's Key It's one of the most provocative moments in cinema.

Opposite *Un Chien Andalou*

Key Scene **The horse ride near the end**
Arsenal

There's Soviet cinema of the '20s – all that rush, that movie adrenalin, that Utopianism – and then there's the Ukrainian, Blakean Dovzhenko. This, his fifth film, is in one sense about the emergence of pan-Ukrainian politics after World War I, and the lead up to a disastrous strike in Kiev. But it's not about the official version of these events. Whereas Eisenstein was sometimes ideologically shrill, and Pudovkin was always ideologically shrill, Dovzhenko looked too closely, and responded to the landscape too intimately, to conform completely to the Soviet song and dance. So his film starts in stillness: "There was a mother." Women stand motionlessly. "There was a war." We see silent, dead villages like de Chirico paintings. A horse talks. A buried soldier makes a joke. The war is absurd. Perhaps Dovzhenko saw Fernand Léger's *Ballet Mécanique* in Paris, but he certainly felt the tragedy of war, and filmed it.

Arsenal's one sequence that is full of Soviet fervor and speed, the famous horse ride towards the end of this film, brings tears to the eyes: A soldier is dying. He wants to be buried at home, so a horse races through a wintry landscape, with him in tow. So full of speed and hope is the scene that modern viewers half expect the horse to take off into the sky like the boys on the bikes in *E.T.*, but here is Dovzhenko's *coup de foudre*: As all this happens, the soldier's mother stands beside his open grave waiting for him. There's nothing more moving in Soviet cinema of the 1920s.

Mark Cousins

Date 1929

Nationality USSR

Director Aleksandr Dovzhenko

Why It's Key This is one of the most moving and exciting scenes in revolutionary Soviet cinema.

Key Event **Two Best Picture Oscars presented**

The first awards ceremony hosted by the Academy of Motion Picture Arts and Sciences concluded with the presentation of *two* Best Picture Oscars. The record books usually list William Wellman's spectacular WWI aviation epic *Wings* (1928) as the first Best Picture winner. Actually, it took home a statuette for "Best Picture, Production," while F. W. Murnau's *Sunrise* (1928) was recognized as "Best Picture, Unique and Artistic Production." The original intention was to honor both mainstream, audience-friendly "big pictures" *and* the innovative, experimental, limited-appeal films the Academy believed important to the development of the cinema as an art *and* entertainment medium. In 1930, the Academy decided to award only one Best Picture Oscar: by giving the statuette to MGM's musical *The Broadway Melody* (1929), the voters clearly indicated the "Best Picture, Unique and Artistic Production" category had been abolished, as does the tradition that the "Best Picture" award is collected by the producer of

the winning film (it could also be classed as a "Best Producer" honor). The backroom decision, made while the Academy and its annual awards were new, undoubtedly eliminated confusion about which Best Picture was best, but in favoring the followers of Wellman over the heirs of Murnau, the Academy sent a message that Oscar was in the business of honoring Hollywood's own rather than bestowing awards on pretentious foreigners. Ever since, the Best Picture award has tended to favor solidly middlebrow, technically competent films rather than groundbreaking cinema – *How Green Was My Valley* over *Citizen Kane*, *Oliver!* over *2001: A Space Odyssey*. A fascinating parlor game might be to imagine that the set-up of 1929 continued – which films, down through the years, would have been nominated for and won subsequent "Best Picture, Unique and Artistic Production" Oscars?

Kim Newman

Date May 16, 1929

Why It's Key Once, briefly, the Academy made a distinction between artistic achievement and middlebrow success.

Opposite *Sunrise*

Key Scene **The city comes to life**
Man with a Movie Camera

Bourgeois people arrive in a cinema. The seats tilt down of their own accord. The orchestra begins to play. A film begins. We see a city. It is extraordinarily still and empty. The streets are deserted. People sleep on park benches. A woman snoozes in her bed. A banner flutters in the breeze. Pigeons fly, but, apart from that, stasis. Then a man arrives. He carries a camera. With his arrival comes some movement. The snoozing woman turns over. More pigeons fly. She starts to wake. Glimpses of her naked body. The moving hand of the bench sleeper. The cameraman drives away. The speed of the cutting increases. We sense a rhythm, a train-like rhythm. We see a train hurtling along a track. A man has got his ankle caught in the track! The train is closer, closer! We are under the train! A crescendo! The day has begun.

Nearly eight decades after it was made, *Man with a Movie Camera* still feels like it has an outboard engine attached. Its director's nom de cinéma, Dziga

Vertov, means spinning top, and his film feels like one. The Soviet Union in the '20s was perhaps the movie think tank, and the utopian belief that movies helped fuel a new, better society energized everyone working in film. Soviet films can seem ideologically shrill, but to witness the sheer cinematic joy of this one is to feel that film has never been as good.

Mark Cousins

Date 1929

Nationality USSR

Director Dziga Vertov

Original Title *Chelovek s kino-apparatom*

Why It's Key In this scene from the greatest work of experimental documentary in cinema, a camera seems to raise a city from the dead.

Key Person **Brigitte Helm**
The Wonderful Lies of Nina Petrowna

Brigitte Helm had a face that honored Louis Delluc's somewhat mystical definition of "*fotogénie*": her moral qualities showed when she reflected the light through the lens. With that face came the slim body of a dancer, which in her case was flexible to the point of outrageousness. Discovered by Fritz Lang for *Metropolis*, she became a star and appeared in a handful of films, most of them difficult to find but always rewarding. She tended to drive the men in her films crazy with lust (as in *Alraune* or *L'Argent*), and she produced a similar effect on her audiences. Argentine critic and scriptwriter Ulyses Petit de Murat, who was famous for his pompous and puritan style, wrote in 1930 a long, almost surrealistic poem about her, devoted to describing every curve in her body, which he obviously was unable to get out his mind at night.

In spite of the visual elegance that director Hanns Schwarz managed to achieve, *Nina Petrowna* is a film that has only Brigitte Helm as a raison d'être. Of course,

by 1929 that was reason enough. In the film she's married to an officer she does not love and falls for a younger one. Alone with the young officer for the first time, she openly tries to spend the night with him, but he acts timidly. At one point she throws herself backwards on her bed and gives him a look that encompasses every sin of the flesh performed throughout the history of mankind. The man is paralysed. She understands his reaction, retreats, and begins to devise a more subtle strategy. Even a femme fatale knows when she's gone too far.

Fernando Martín Peña

Date 1929

Nationality Germany

Director Hanns Schwarz

Cast Brigitte Helm

Original Title *Die Wunderbare Lüge der Nina Petrowna*

Why It's Key "Beautiful" is not a good word to define her screen presence. "Ravishing" or perhaps even "alluring," though commonplace, seem more appropriate.

1920–1929

72

Key Film
L'Age d'or

The first, and arguably the only truly surrealist feature film ever made (its running time is 67 minutes, as opposed to the seven minutes of Buñuel's acclaimed 1928 *Un chien andalou*), *L'Age d'or* remains as radically and aggressively revolutionary today as it was back in 1930 when it created an unprecedented scandal that resulted in its banning by the Paris chief of police and the impounding of all the prints.

An avant-garde film if there ever was one, *L'Age d'or* deliberately eschewed all the "experimental" stylistic flourishes that characterized the 1920s French avant-garde as well as most avant-garde films of later decades. Indeed, it provocatively opens with a straight documentary on scorpions. A pseudo-narrative, the film gleefully challenges or disregards all the most basic storytelling rules and conventions and deals with space and time in blithely irrational fashion. Throughout, Buñuel's unadorned, thoroughly "realistic" camera style enhances the staggering outlandishness of the images

he conjures up: skeletons of mitred archbishops, lovers wallowing in the mud as they attempt to copulate, a cow sprawled on a young woman's bed, a horse-drawn cart driven through an elegant drawing-room, a Christ-like rapist emerging from a Sadian chateau…

Described by its auteur as being "against everything," *L'Age d'or* throws a wry, anarchic gaze on religion, the family, the homeland, the ruling classes, all the bourgeois values, and all the social strictures and conventions that frustrate self-expression and particularly love and desire – Buñuel called it "*un film d'amour fou*." One of the very first sound films made in France, *L'Age d'or* used music, sounds and occasional speech in a highly creative and original fashion.

The film's career was as unique as its content. It remained banned in France until 1981 and was never shown publicly (except for screenings at the Cinémathèque française) for half a century.
Jean-Pierre Coursodon

Date 1930

Nationality France

Director Luis Buñuel

Cast Gaston Modot, Lya Lys

Why It's Key Few films can be described as thoroughly unique, and none has greater claim to uniqueness than this one.

Key Scene **A kulak claims the land as his** *Earth*

SPOILER

This final scene takes place just as the funeral of Vasyl, the slain Bolshevik, evolves into a fervent demonstration extolling the Communism for which young Vasyl died. Even Vasyl's father, who had up to this point been skeptical about Communism's plan to collectivize the farmlands, joins the struggle. But the kulaks, the landowning peasant class from whom the farms are being expropriated, are going down swinging. Khoma Bilokon (Masokha), the eldest son of the area's dominant kulak family, has already committed murder, having shot Vasyl in the back. Khoma confesses, but *Earth* is not a crime procedural, and Dovzhenko's final scene is both politically sharp and poetically evocative.

Using an odd form of cross-cutting that makes Khoma's spatial relationship to the funeral extremely ambiguous, Dovzhenko moves us between the guilty individual and the burgeoning collective, the past and the future. Khoma shouts out to the mourners that he shot Vasyl, in the back, under cover of night. The crowd

completely ignores him. Hysterical, Khoma exclaims that the land belongs to him, and he even goes so far as to plant his head in the dirt and run in circles. However, both within the diegetic world of the film and within Dovzhenko's cinematic syntax, Khoma and the kulak class are marginal, almost nonexistent. Although this image is compromised by the truth Dovzhenko cannot depict – that of Stalin's mass extermination of the kulaks – its representation of what it feels like when history passes you by remains unequalled.
Michael Sicinski

Date 1930

Nationality USSR

Director Aleksandr Dovzhenko

Cast Pyotr Masokha

Original Title *Zemlya*

Why It's Key The great film poet of Soviet silent cinema finds the ideal cinematic language to depict the shrinking influence of one class and the ascendancy of another.

Key Event
Eisenstein goes to Hollywood

After *The Battleship Potemkin*'s worldwide success in 1925, the Soviet government sent its star director on a tour of European capitals to study the new sound process, though armed with only US$25 of foreign currency. In Paris, the young formalist director accepted a six-month contract with Paramount (Hollywood's most sophisticated and continental studio), to develop and direct films in the movie capital. Preceded by Lubitsch, Sjöström, and Murnau, who had all achieved artistic and/or financial success in the capitalist mecca, Eisenstein foresaw alternating projects between Moscow and Hollywood. During his five-month tenure in California, he was photographed with Mickey Mouse, feted by Charlie Chaplin, and consulted by D. W. Griffith, but Paramount rejected Eisenstein's first scenario, for *Sutter's Gold*, about the destructive effects of the 1849 California gold rush. Ordering their resident Russian to undertake *An American Tragedy*, the studio executives envisaged

Theodore Dreiser's social critique as a love story sans "side issues" like class distinctions and economic injustices (George Stevens would faithfully deliver such a version of the novel with *A Place in the Sun* [1951]), but Eisenstein confounded expectations with his disdain for professional actors and his insistent focus on indicting capitalism and America's reverence for legalisms.

As a right-wing campaign sought to deport Paramount's "Jewish Bolshevik," Paramount put aside its yearning for artistic respectability and chose to draw a firm line between commercial concerns and progressive art, annulling Eisenstein's contract while forcing a reluctant Josef von Sternberg to film the project with a different script. The hapless Eisenstein then headed south for a disastrous sojourn in Mexico and ultimate condemnation upon his return to Russia.
Robert Keser

Date 1930

Why It's Key Commerce and formalist art forever diverged in Hollywood.

Key Scene **The kiss and the flower**
Morocco

The dreamscape Morocco created by Sternberg is vividly real on its own terms, so attentive is he to sets and decor, play of light and sound, and pacing of the action, richly providing an atmosphere in which behavior always breathes with intriguing nuance. The early nightclub scene in which all important characters are present, and in which Amy Jolly (Dietrich) and legionnaire Tom Brown (Cooper) first see each other and interact, is emblematic and justifiably famous, especially for the unusual erotic exchange that occurs, in which conventional sexual roles are thrown to the wayside by these two bold characters. Amy performs her first song dressed as a man (tuxedo and top hat) and caps her performance by asking a beautiful woman (Compton) for a flower, kissing her on the lips as she takes it, then tossing it to Tom. A conspicuous fade in the middle of the long sequence follows, after which Amy comes back in changed costume; when she reappears, Tom's first gesture is to put the flower

behind his ear, deliberately feminizing himself. These gestures are only external signs of a dissatisfaction that both feel with male and female personas, which they can play well but need to test if they are to connect more richly to each other, with all true feelings and vulnerability exposed; they are rhyming gestures, which elegantly foreshadow everything that will happen in their relationship. Through that relationship, Sternberg movingly unsettles notions of masculinity and femininity in a way that still seems modern.
Blake Lucas

Date 1930

Nationality USA

Director Josef von Sternberg

Cast Gary Cooper, Marlene Dietrich, Adolphe Menjou, Paul Porcasi, Ullrich Haupt, Eve Southern, Juliette Compton

Why It's Key An exotic melodrama provides an expressive frame for a sexual statement as charming as it is challenging.

Opposite *Morocco*

Key Scene **Two gunshots interrupt the lake party** *An American Tragedy*

Sergei Eisenstein, replaced by Josef von Sternberg as director of Dreiser's *An American Tragedy*, dismissed the finished project: "Sternberg confined his attention to the studio's wishes – and filmed a straight detective case." Few judgments have stood the test of time so poorly. Sternberg was one generation ahead of his time in his willingness to substitute his own otherworldly, meditative perspective for the pleasures of entertainment cinema. The film's central scene, best known for its early use of offscreen sound, shows how confidently and inobtrusively Sternberg deployed sound effects, even in the early talkies. The police who are pursuing hapless protagonist Clyde Griffiths (Holmes) have arranged to move in on their quarry at the sound of two gunshots. Meanwhile, Clyde and his upper-class beloved, Sondra Finchley (Dee), are in the midst of a summertime idyll, drifting slowly in a rowboat toward the lakeside dock party of their friends. Sternberg keeps the slow-moving boat in the middle of a long

shot, so that we see the partying, ukelele-playing youths, some of them in other boats, glide into the frame, one at a time or in small groups, with sound obviously recorded live, so that small lip movements register on the soundtrack. Then the gunshots echo over the lake: Clyde and the partygoers react in confusion, though they don't know that the shots spell Clyde's doom. The boat continues its inevitable glide through the middle of the party, and the camera continues its graceful following pan through a world suddenly turned ominous.

Dan Sallitt

Date 1931

Nationality USA

Director Josef von Sternberg

Cast Phillips Holmes, Frances Dee

Why It's Key At a time when other directors were still experimenting with synchronized sound, this scene shows Sternberg in effortless command of the new medium.

Key Scene **The last scene** *City Lights*

Film is a confrontation between two moments: the moment of the viewer and the moment of what is seen. The genius of Chaplin in the last scene of *City Lights* is to find an image for this confrontation and place it within the film itself. "The Tramp" (Chaplin), just out of prison and more down and out than ever, gets free of some teenage boys who have been tormenting him on the street. As he turns, he sees "the Girl" (Cherrill) selling flowers in an area recessed from the sidewalk: a witness to the Tramp's discomfiture, she has been laughing at him behind his back – unaware that he is the benefactor who funded the operation that has enabled her to see. He is overjoyed to see her and that the operation has been successful, but, ashamed of his own appearance, he backs away from her when she approaches him with a flower and a coin. She presses the coin into his hand anyway and, from the feel of his skin, realizes who he is. For those who have watched this film repeatedly, the ensuing

intertitles (resisting the pressure of talkies, Chaplin gave his film a synchronized score and a few sound effects, but no recorded dialogue) are as rooted in the memory as human voices would have been: "You?" she asks. He nods shyly, and, after a moment, points to his own eyes: "You can see now?" She looks at him. "Yes, I can see now." The film fades to black on a closeup of him looking at her, smiling but still torn, apparently, between joy and a state of terrible tension and uncertainty. It's one of those scenes that seem to dismiss all commentary – so exquisite that merely recalling it is enough to bring tears; yet it's also a moment of inexhaustible profundity and a reflection by a great film director on his art.

Chris Fujiwara

Date 1931

Nationality USA

Director Charles Chaplin

Cast Charles Chaplin, Virginia Cherrill

Why It's Key It's one of the most sublime, and most definitive, moments in cinema.

Key Person **Peter Lorre**
The mass murderer defends himself *M*

M is a paradigm of societal dissection, revealing the importance of social class, occupational position, power, and desperation in modern life, and the transcendent importance of justice when they evaporate. Kidnapper and killer of little Elsie Beckmann, the serial murderer Beckert (Lorre) antagonizes both the police and the criminal underworld of a great city. But the thieves get him first. A young pickpocket having chalked an "M" on the back of his shoulder, he has been dragged into a warehouse for his "trial," where bowler-hatted Schränker (Gründgens) leans over a table to snap out a prosecution for these horrible murders. With his performance in this scene, Lorre established not only a career for himself but an iconographic portrait of evil as banal and diseased.

He glares with his enormous eyes, whimpers, meows like a cat in a corner, spieling to his interlocutor and the underworld jury how dark, dank forces overwhelm him, attack him, transform him, and move him to action. It is not his fault. He is better than these criminals, who are "proud of breaking safes or cheating at cards" and is in fact a perfectly law-abiding citizen until these dark forces drown him. Only a kangaroo court could suggest he is truly, deeply perverse. "Kill him! Crush him!", the crowd cries, but the police intervene just in time.

What echoes long after Lorre's desperate, sweaty, pallid, bug-eyed face is gone: the police invocation which began the hunt. "Any man on the street could be the guilty one." He is any one of us, then, overwhelmed and influenced (as perhaps we are by this film).
Murray Pomerance

Date 1931

Nationality Germany

Director Fritz Lang

Cast Peter Lorre, Gustaf Gründgens

Original Title *M – Eine Stadt sucht einen Mörder*

Why It's Key This scene marks the high point of Peter Lorre's stunning, career-making performance.

Key Speech **The card game**
Marius

Playwright Marcel Pagnol was the first show-business personality in France to enthusiastically embrace talking pictures, which were generally viewed with suspicion or scorn in both theater and movie circles. Although he didn't direct the first two entries of his Marseille trilogy (*Marius* is masterfully directed by Alexander Korda with little of the clumsiness that marred most early sound pictures), the films are thoroughly his.

Pagnol was a master of popular Southern language, and much of the charm of his plays and films comes from his deft use of the Marseille accent, whose particular pronunciation, inflections, and lilt ("a kind of little music," in Pagnol's words) make it thoroughly different from other French accents (one minor character in the trilogy, Monsieur Brun, is originally from Lyon, and his alien-sounding tone and pitch are used for comic contrast with the way the locals speak). The Marseille accent (only slightly exaggerated in the films for theatrical effect) is to the ordinary way of speaking of the Paris metropolitan area what an Irish brogue is to the King's English.

The card-game scene (which is really a sequence in two scenes and a coda – four players, then three, then two) became particularly popular in France: through the thirties and forties and beyond, most French people could quote several of its lines, some of which became catchphrases. It is a set piece for the thinly-disguised attempts at cheating by César (Raimu) in the first section, and a comical altercation with the ferryboat captain Escartefigue (Dullac) in the second, with the latter's immortal line: "*La marine française, elle te dit merde*" ("The French Navy tells you to go to hell") – which of course must be spoken with the proper accent to acquire all its flavor.
Jean-Pierre Coursodon

Date 1931

Nationality France

Director Alexander Korda

Cast Raimu, Fernand Charpin, Paul Dullac, Robert Vattier

Why It's Key It's become, at least in France, the most famous scene in Pagnol's oeuvre, and it shows Raimu and the rest at their comical best.

Key Film
Night Nurse

The vastly exaggerated history of Will Hays and his Hollywood Production Code has recently been more about hipster self-congratulation and the market for "Forbidden Hollywood" chestnuts than about fair-minded history. Made vulnerable by a First Amendment-trashing 1915 U.S. Supreme Court decision, the major studios understandably saw self-censorship as a means of self-preservation and adopted the Production Code in 1930, but it took four years to establish a mechanism of enforcement. Various films have emerged as holy relics of the period, among them *Scarface* (1932) and *Tarzan and His Mate* (1934), the first movie to feel the Code's bite. But Barbara Stanwyck is Forbidden Hollywood's secular saint, having caused bulging eyeballs with this film and the superhumanly licentious *Baby Face* (1933).

Baby Face's merry amorality and racial daring make it worthy of its own study, but *Night Nurse* has a remarkably feminist texture. The "pre-Code" demands are satisfied by an apparent requirement that Stanwyck change into or out of her nurse's uniform every ten minutes or so. (Blondell performs sassy-best-friend duties as fellow nurse "Maloney.") The absurd plot has Stanwyck discover an improbable slow-poison scheme against a pair of rich children in her care, hatched by Gable's bullying chauffeur villain. The catch is that her efforts to expose the plot bring her up against the iron wall of the patriarchy – skeptical authorities, a crooked doctor, Gable in jodhpurs. Ben Lyon's jaunty bootlegger is the only man worth trusting. *Night Nurse* may lack the erotic flights of more celebrated pre-Code works, but it hints at the kind of truly subversive art that self-censorship obviated. It's also a crucial text for anybody who considers him- or herself a devoted Stanwyckian (and who doesn't?).

Tim Cavanaugh

Date 1931

Nationality USA

Director William A. Wellman

Cast Barbara Stanwyck, Ben Lyon, Joan Blondell, Clark Gable, Blanche Friderici, Charles Winninger, Vera Lewis, Walter McGrail

Why It's Key Barbara Stanwyck singlehandedly justified the Production Code.

Key Speech **"I… am… Dracula"**
Dracula

"I… am … Dracula." In Tod Browning's *Dracula*, the first great talking horror film, Bela Lugosi's Count makes a grand entrance at the top of a cobweb-curtained staircase, immaculately clad in evening clothes and a black cape. He introduces himself, enunciating every word so that it gains several extra syllables, eyes glowing like neon when the pinlight spots hit them properly, and drips courtesy and menace in equal parts. The nervous Renfield (Frye), an estate agent summoned to Castle Dracula, is suitably impressed – and doomed. The speech comes directly from Bram Stoker's novel and the Broadway play in which Lugosi had first taken the role. At that time, the Hungarian émigré's command of English was still shaky, so he had to learn his lines phonetically, adding to the curiousness of his cadences. Others (Christopher Lee, Jack Palance, Louis Jourdan, Frank Langella, Gary Oldman) have played the role and been required to put their own spin on the line – but, three-quarters of a century on, Lugosi is still the default Dracula. Whenever a comedian tries to "do Drac," he copies Lugosi's clothes, gestures, and accent.

Kim Newman

Date 1931

Nationality USA

Director Tod Browning

Cast Bela Lugosi, Dwight Frye

Why It's Key Because Lugosi remains the definitive Dracula.

Opposite *Dracula*

Key Scene **An old man closes a hatchway and cuts a rope** *Tabu*

Supple in its light poetry but ultimately devastatingly brutal in its fatalism, *Tabu* tells of two Polynesian lovers. The girl (Chevalier) has been declared an inviolable virgin; the boy (Matahi) kidnaps her; they are pursued by a tribal elder (Hitu), who we know will hunt them down. In the midst of scenes full of organic life and compositions that are more organic than geometrical, the prow of Hitu's boat suddenly intrudes into the frame from offscreen at one moment; at another, his shadow cuts a severe diagonal line across the land. These moments of offscreen entry enlist offscreen space in the service of Murnau's tragic point: that wherever the lovers flee, they will be pursued; what is "after" them is ultimately a force larger than anything that can be contained in the film's composition. All of these moments reach their horrible fulfillment when Hitu takes the girl away in his boat by moonlight. As her pursuing lover approaches, swimming impossibly fast, Hitu closes the cover to her cabin in a brief linear motion. Then he cuts the rope that the boy grabs onto. These two brutal lateral movements literally sever the lovers from each other in space, walling off the space they had brought to life, in their scenes together, for much of the film.

Fred Camper

Date 1931

Nationality USA

Director F. W. Murnau

Cast Matahi, Anne Chevalier, Hitu

Why It's Key Murnau's fatalism is at its most overpowering in this, his greatest film, expressed by objects that cross the frame more than once to end with the devastating closure of the final movements.

Key Scene **The "other woman" communes with her dead lover** *Back Street*

Ray (Dunne) and Walter (John) meet and have a brief romance in turn-of-the-century Cincinnati just before his marriage. They meet again five years later in New York, and Ray becomes his mistress for 25 years. Stylistically and philosophically, Stahl is (along with, in a different way, Borzage) the opposite of Sirk, believing in the authenticity of human connections, and he frames the scenes of Ray and Walter, the film's emotional core, in ways that connect them. Whether the camera is following them at a dance, or showing them together surrounded by swirling snow, or filming them in near-silhouette as they meet clandestinely framed against the sea, the implication is always: no barriers – and that's underlined by a brief quarrel in which the camera keeps them apart. When Walter is stricken by a stroke, he asks his son to dial her. He can say only her name before he dies, but there's an amazing feeling of emotion being transparently transmitted through the wires – so much so that it "converts" Walter's son, who previously hated Ray. In the film's concluding scene, Stahl intercuts between Ray and a head-on view of Walter's portrait, and the feeling of direct connection is even more affecting – real love has perhaps never been so movingly rendered in a Hollywood film. Similar portraits function in the opposite sense in Sirk, reducing characters to objects; here, Walter is so totally present for Ray that his image occasions a fantasy in which time is reversed and she and Walter can marry.

Fred Camper

Date 1932

Nationality USA

Director John M. Stahl

Cast Irene Dunne, John Boles.

Why It's Key It's one of cinema's great versions of the power of love to transcend social barriers, time, and even death.

Key Scene *"Hot Voodoo"*
Blonde Venus

Twenty-three minutes into *Blonde Venus*, a jazz band starts playing desultory drumbeats as chorus girls in blackface and war paint dance with spears and shields, leading a chained gorilla down from the nightclub stage. After parading through the audience, the ape pulls off a glove to reveal a dazzling white hand covered with glinting bracelets, then the other glove, and then the head, as Marlene Dietrich emerges in one of cinema's greatest entrances: the ravishing beauty concealed within the beast, hirsute virility shed for teasing female eroticism. Donning a platinum-blonde afro wig, she surveys the patrons with hooded eyes and teeth agleam in a sardonic smile, letting her gorilla suit slide to the floor. Intercut with shots of her wealthy suitor (Grant), bewitched by the show, she stands and throatily sings "Hot voodoo, burn my clothes, I want to start dancing just wearing a smile." Within the maternal-melodrama surroundings of the plot of *Blonde Venus* – in which the heroine relinquishes the ostensible joys of housekeeping and raising her beloved moppet (Dickie Jones) to toil in spangles under Broadway's hot lights, all to fund medical treatment for her ailing husband (Herbert Marshall), a victim of radium poisoning – this expressively lit tour-de-force number makes an unlikely but potent illustration of the heroine's perverse self-sacrifice. Sternberg pushes the genre's conventions to the farthest limits, as his star keeps reinventing herself in every variety of womanhood available in Hollywood at the time: devoted mother, cabaret star, drunken whore. Nowhere does the film confound conventional morality more than in the five minutes of erotically charged glamor of "Hot Voodoo."
Robert Keser

Date 1932

Nationality USA

Director Josef von Sternberg

Cast Marlene Dietrich, Cary Grant

Why It's Key Among the greatest entrances in all film, this moment signals the intention to subvert conventional morality.

Key Scene **The movie show at the boss's house** *I Was Born, But…*

It is a surprise, perhaps, to turn the clock back to aggressive Japan in the 1930s, to a silent film directed by cinema's great master of resignation, and find a movie so full of playfulness and joy, but that's the case with *I Was Born, But…* Long before his main melody became the sadness of time passing, Ozu, who was 29 when he made this, his 23rd film, was influenced by the American comedies of Harold Lloyd.

His subject here is suburban Japan and the family of a salaryman, Yoshi (Saito). His sons, brilliantly played by Sugawara and Aoki, think they are the toughest boys on the block, but their hard faces mask the minds of young children. One day they go to the house of their father's boss (Sakamoto), who shows an amateur movie in which their dad clowns for and kowtows to his employer. They are shocked and embarrassed that their father debases himself in this way. They cannot accept his subservience at work, and, as they feel this demeans them too, go on hunger strike. The stand-off continues for some time, but then, in signature Ozu scenes, fades as they come to accept that the adult world is hierarchical and that very few people can be at the top. Thematically rich and freshly acted, *I Was Born, But…* is also the first of Ozu's surviving films to deploy the director's stylistic panoply that would lead him to be acclaimed as one of the world's greatest filmmakers.
Mark Cousins

Date 1932

Nationality Japan

Director Yasujiro Ozu

Cast Tatsuo Saito, Takeshi Sakamoto, Hideo Sugawara, Tomio Aoki (Tokkan Kozo)

Original Title *Umarete wa mita keredo*

Why It's Key This scene is the thematic turning point in one of the greatest films ever made.

Key Scene **An old peasant proudly refusing to work** *Ivan*

The standard Western line on postrevolutionary Soviet cinema is that it's politically correct to a fault. But considering the trouble Ukrainian master Alexander Dovzhenko got himself into – especially with *Earth* and *Ivan*, two of his greatest works – this cliché has to be revised. The latter, his first sound film, celebrates the construction of a huge dam on the Dnieper River that we never see in any finished state. One of the three characters in the film named Ivan has an illiterate father named Stepan Iosovich Guba (Shkurat), a peasant who unapologetically refuses to join in the work and laughs derisively at those who do.

He's first seen grasping and sniffing a daisy while scoffing at the very notion of going to work; his gutteral, diabolical laughter almost makes him seem like a predatory animal. But he's the comic relief, a little bit like Walter Brennan's Stumpy in *Rio Bravo*, and it's clear that Dovzhenko can't get enough of him, even after his son denounces him at a public meeting and he proudly replies, "I am a unique individual."

While countless others are viewed from heroic low angles working on the dam construction, we see him fishing, framed at eye level. Nearly all his appearances in the film are hilarious solo performances, including the scene when he picks up his paycheck. At a key moment, he shows the camera first his profile, then the back of his neck before proceeding to ridicule his comrades by marching around in stiff formation. In short, he's irresistible.

Jonathan Rosenbaum

Date 1932

Nationality USSR

Director Alexander Dovzhenko

Cast Stepan Shkurat

Why It's Key In a film exalting collective work, here's an appreciation of an old coot who refuses to join in.

Key Speech **"Dirty, slimy freaks"** *Freaks*

What is the 'turning point' that contemporary screenwriters love to extol? It is the moment in a plot when all the tables are turned – when a major reversal of the established elements swings the narrative onto a new, more intense plateau. One of cinema's greatest turning points occurs in *Freaks*. In a circus troupe, the strong-man, Hercules (Victor), and the trapeze-woman, Cleopatra (Baclanova), decide to fleece the gullible dwarf, Hans (Earles). Cleopatra seduces and marries Hans – and then sets about slowly poisoning him. Her true self was already evident to everyone but Hans at the moment of the wedding when she exclaimed: "Dirty, slimy freaks!" But, in a later scene where she goes about preparing the poison, and other circus performers spy through the window, Hans, alone, finally acknowledges what's really going on. He alters his facial expression into a hard countenance and repeats those three little, atrocious words: "Dirty, slimy freaks." It is a superb announcement of intended revenge; but there is also a broader thematic context for this turning point in *Freaks*. The film begins with a reassuring, almost paradisal idyll, as a passerby observes the freaks gamboling in a field and compares them to innocent little children. This is a bold ruse on Browning's part, for the film leads us inexorably to the startled recognition of the passionate, fully adult humanity of these freaks – in the end, reducing the morally ugly creatures who wronged them to an even lower rung of sub-human existence.

Adrian Martin

Date 1932

Nationality USA

Director Tod Browning

Cast Harry Earles, Olga Baclanova, Henry Victor

Why It's Key It's one of the greatest turning points in cinema.

Opposite *Freaks*

Key Event **Shiro Kido tells Mikio Naruse he doesn't need another Ozu**

Only one of the first 16 films Mikio Naruse made survives. It's called *Flunky, Work Hard!* After ten years at Shochiku, after being passed over for Heinosuke Gosho and Yasujiro Ozu, who'd started in the film industry after him, in 1930 Naruse finally got to direct a film. He had to shoot it non-stop in 36 hours. When he finished he collapsed.

According to Audie Bock's book *Japanese Film Directors*, in the early '30s Naruse was making the equivalent of $360 a month as a salaried director at Shochiku and living in a rented room over a sushi place. He got meal tickets from the studio he traded for cigarettes, choosing to eat alone in cheap bars. One film he made was shelved because studio boss Shiro Kido thought it was too much like Ozu. Kido kept Naruse on, but in 1932 he took him aside and explained that Shochiku didn't need two Ozus. While he was at it Kido threw in that Naruse shouldn't imitate Hiroshi Shimizu, Gosho, or Yasujiro Shimazu, either.

Today it's hard to believe this happened. Imitations of hit films are exactly what producers want. Kido's insult forced Naruse to look for stories in the harsh world where he was eating lunch. The name of the film Naruse was working on when he had his conversation with Kido? *Be Great!* For the next 35 years Naruse made films "with the thought that the word we live in betrays us," poignant films that stand on their own next to the best ones made anywhere.
A. S. Hamrah

Date 1932

Why It's Key An admonishing producer forced Naruse to be himself.

Key Scene **The cocktail glasses break**
One Way Passage

SPOILER

This sure-fire tearjerker (from an Oscar-winning story) opens in a teeming Hong Kong bar, where two strangers, Dan (Powell) and Joan (Francis), bump into each other over shared "Paradise" cocktails. When they finish, he impulsively breaks his cocktail glass on the counter, so she breaks hers as well and crosses the stems on the bar. Meeting again on a trans-Pacific ship to San Francisco (on the high seas, where all are free to tipple regardless of the US Prohibition, still in force), they become lovers but conceal their secrets: she suffers from a fatal heart condition, while he faces certain hanging for murder. When she collapses during a romantic Honolulu stopover, he sacrifices his chance to escape to get help for her. Director Garnett finesses a remarkable love scene in which neither Dan nor Joan can bear to acknowledge the truth, and when the ship docks and they must separate, the doomed lovers continue the charade, vowing to do the impossible: to meet on New Year's Eve at a Mexican bar in Agua

Caliente. Inevitably, neither shows up, yet two cocktail glasses break of their own accord on the bar, their stems crossed in a mystical reenactment of the lovers' promise, with a romantic logic never questioned by the movie. Garnett thus brought to talkies the silent-film trope of Love transcending Death (repeated in Edmund Goulding's 1940 remake, *Till We Meet Again*) and provided the model for future distinctive tokens of emotional commitment, such as the ceremony of lighting two cigarettes in Irving Rapper's *Now, Voyager* (1942) and the lovers' involvement in their signature song in Michael Curtiz's *Casablanca* (1942).
Robert Keser

Date 1932

Nationality USA

Director Tay Garnett

Cast William Powell, Kay Francis

Why It's Key This moment provides the model for the private tokens of lovers in romantic melodramas.

Key Person **Ben Hecht**
The machine gun spits *Scarface*

SPOILER

Among other things, Ben Hecht was a Chicago newspaperman, a playwright, author of maybe the funniest American novel, recipient of the call-to-Hollywood telegram from Herman J. Mankiewicz that read "millions to be grabbed out here and your only competition is idiots," and screenwriter of the original *Scarface*.

Hecht arrived in Hollywood at the end of the silent era. He wrote Sternberg's *Underworld*, the first gangster picture, then worked on 13 dozen other movies, often without credit.

He told *Scarface* producer Howard Hughes he could double the body count of any previous gangster film and write one twice as good, then worked out a payment arrangement designed to add to his image as a hired gun. Hughes had to pay him a thousand dollars in cash every night at 6 until he finished the first draft. He finished in 11 days. He wrote the final draft with Hawks on a train to New York on their way to test Muni for the title part, Tony Camonte.

Hecht defines the writer-producer relationship in a speech Camonte makes to his boss. "There's only one thing that gets orders and gives orders, and this is it," Camonte says, indicating his machine gun. "That's how I got the South Side for you and that's how I'm gonna get the North Side for you. It's a little typewriter, right? I'm gonna write my name all over this town with it, in big letters. Get outta my way, I'm gonna spit!" he yells, and starts firing.

A. S. Hamrah

Date 1932

Nationality USA

Director Howard Hawks

Cast Paul Muni

Why It's Key Hecht's bold screenplay made Hawks's film the best of the '30s gangster cycle.

Key Scene **Alone in the train, Shanghai Lily looks up at the light** *Shanghai Express*

In the fourth of her seven films with Sternberg, Dietrich plays Shanghai Lily, a notorious "coaster" who becomes reunited with her old lover (Clive Brook) aboard the title train as it is commandeered by a sadistic rebel leader (Warner Oland). "You are in China, now, sir, where time and life have no value," claims the latter, announcing a possible interpretation of Sternberg's style, here at its most hieratic: the narrative evaporates amid hallucinatory interruptions, lingering dissolves, slow line readings, and the furious and languorous patterns of light and dark in which the director (aided by cinematographer Lee Garmes) places his actors.

In this scene, alarmed over the unknown fate of her missing lover, Lily returns alone to her train compartment and closes the door, before which she remains standing. Her eyes shift upward toward the overhead light. Maybe she's looking for something, some reassurance, even God (since the dialogue has contained some discussion of faith and prayer). But the way Dietrich – visibly "directed," here, as she is so often in Sternberg's films – moves her eyes discourages any interpretation driven by the narrative or by her character's putative feelings and impulses. She does it vacantly and automatically, so that the shot as a whole carries a meaning of something like hopelessness, but something, too, beyond hopelessness: we contemplate a luminous being who has moved beyond despair and beyond faith.

Chris Fujiwara

Date 1932

Nationality USA

Director Josef von Sternberg

Cast Marlene Dietrich

Why It's Key Marlene Dietrich perfectly inhabits Josef von Sternberg's invented world of light and shadow.

Key Film
Trouble in Paradise

"I came here to rob you but unfortunately I fell in love with you," confesses gentleman thief Gaston (elegantly tailored Marshall, his voice purring like a Rolls Royce engine), neatly capsulizing the plot for his employer, the sensationally available widow Mariette (bejeweled and befeathered Francis). He hides his romantic involvement from Lily (giddy Hopkins), his partner in crime and love, while Parisian café society drolly muses on the situation ("She says he's her secretary. And he says he's her secretary. Maybe I'm wrong. Maybe he *is* her secretary"). To the seductive strains of a romantic tango, this glittering prototype for the sophisticated romantic comedy dares to propose pickpocketing as a kind of foreplay and theft as a form of possession akin to sexual conquest. Lubitsch glides his unpredictable plot as if on casters, always provocatively evasive about exactly who beds whom and when (the butler remains perpetually baffled: no one stays in his or her assigned bedroom). With its

liberating playfulness, his celebrated "Lubitsch touch" takes the sting out of the crime and any residual banality from the romance. The film's exuberant impetuosity (Lily has to sit on her hands to stop herself from pilfering Mariette's nearby jewelbox) would inspire the capricious flights of screwball comedy of Leo McCarey's *The Awful Truth* (1937), Howard Hawks's *Bringing Up Baby* (1938) and Mitchell Leisen's *Midnight* (1939), not to mention Billy Wilder's *Some Like It Hot* (1959). With a plot that models sex sans marriage and robbery without consequences, the film was reliably condemned by the Roman Catholic Legion of Decency and banned by the Nazis; neither Lubitsch nor his critics realized they were living in pre-Code freedom.
Robert Keser

Date 1932

Nationality USA

Director Ernst Lubitsch

Cast Herbert Marshall, Kay Francis, Miriam Hopkins

Why It's Key Lubitsch perfects the comedy of manners.

Key Scene **The coffin point of view**
Vampyr

Taking the vampire-tale template for his oblique tenth feature (and first sound film), Dreyer sought to evoke dread by joining shadowy German-Expressionist lighting to a French-Surrealist eruption of unconscious imagery. His restlessly mobile camera, disorienting light changes, and inexplicable effects destabilize the viewer's perceptions. Doors fly open without help, a river reflects figures with no counterparts on land, and sounds arise without sources. The hero peers into windows as he wanders entranced through this inchoate dreamscape until, thanks to double exposures, he and his own shadow separate and move apart in cinematic mitosis. Now transparent, he peers into an open coffin and sees his own body supine and covered with flowers. An intensely unnerving five-minute sequence follows, in which we are sealed inside the coffin and watch through the glass-windowed lid as a workman screws it shut, and a vampire lights a candle and stares at us. Intercut with

closeups of the corpse's face, the disturbing subjective camera view shifts as the coffin is borne outside, with trees streaming overhead and walls moving past – a view disturbingly like what an infant sees from its mother's arms. Thus the voyeur witnesses his own funeral, as if punished for looking, and the audience shares the claustrophobia. Subsequent corpse's eye-view sequences in Roger Corman's *The Premature Burial* (1962), Ken Russell's *Mahler* (1974), and even the Pet Shop Boys' music video *Videography* (1991) all bow to *Vampyr*.
Robert Keser

Date 1932

Nationality France/Germany

Director Carl Theodor Dreyer

Cast Julian West (Baron Nicholas de Gunzberg), Sybille Schmitz

Why It's Key This scene pushes the subjective camera to a new depth of psychological horror.

Key Film *Liebelei*
A sleigh ride in eternity

There is no more beautiful love story in cinema than *Liebelei* – joyful then sad, graceful then severe, and finally elevating an intense yet fleeting romance so that it resonates beyond its own end. Ophuls was understandably rapt by Old World ambiance (even if turn-of-the-century Vienna comes in for criticism here for its rigid, destructive social codes). Other masterpieces of his made in different times and places, especially *Letter from an Unknown Woman* (1948) and *Madame De...* (1953), share the visual atmosphere and the music (especially the waltzes) of this one. They also share duels, but with a difference: here, if Fritz (Liebeneiner) survived, he and Christine (Schneider) would be together with no barriers to an untroubled future. And that is key to the heartbreak that befalls them and their equally attractive friends, Mitzi (Ullrich) and Theo (Eichberger) – the more lighthearted of the two couples (though deceptively so, given their ultimate bearing and actions). The film is marked by a moment

of supreme happiness that consecrates the idea of how much life can offer: Christine and Fritz's sleigh ride through a wintry landscape. It is to this that Ophuls returns at the end, when they are both dead, in a reprise of that scene's slow final track through a snow-covered graveyard; only now, though the sleigh bells can still be heard, the sleigh itself is gone, and there is only what the lovers had spoken of – eternity. In so exquisitely placing earthly experience within a deeper sense of time and space, Ophuls makes it even more affecting while also suffusing it with a serene philosophical perspective.

Blake Lucas

Date 1933

Nationality Germany

Director Max Ophuls

Cast Magda Schneider, Wolfgang Liebeneiner, Luise Ullrich, Willi Eichberger, Paul Horbiger, Gustaf Gründgens, Olga Tschechowa

Why It's Key The artistry and sensibility of Max Ophuls lift a tragic love story to another plane.

Key Scene **The ending**
Only Yesterday

SPOILER

Actor-turned-director John M. Stahl is probably best remembered for the sublime Technicolored melodramatics of *Leave Her to Heaven* (1945), but he also made the original versions of such enduring melodramas as *Back Street* (1932), *Imitation of Life* (1934), and *Magnificent Obsession* (1935). In the middle of this rich period comes *Only Yesterday*, which has a plot startlingly similar to that of *Letter from an Unknown Woman* (1948), though it's based not on the Stefan Zweig story but on a novel by Frederick Lewis Allen. Wiped out by the 1929 Stock Market crash, banker James Emerson (Boles) is about to end his life when curiosity forces him to open a letter from an unknown, dying, woman. Unfolding flashbacks depict the one-night stand Emerson spent with Mary Lane (Margaret Sullavan) on the eve of his departure for the Great War; nine months later she gives birth to Jim Jr. After the war she's unable to contact her lover, and when they do meet he doesn't recognize her. Having

read her letter he rushes to the address she has given him, too late. But he meets 11-year-old Jim (Butler), who is wearing a military school uniform. In a scene of exquisite tenderness, he tries to get to know the grieving boy, who has no idea who this strange man is. On learning he's a good shot, he offers to take him hunting. "With you?" asks the boy, surprised. "Why not, Jimmy? I'm your father." "My father?" says Jim with a tremor in his voice, and the film ends abruptly there, concluding perhaps the most beautifully directed scene in Stahl's impressive oeuvre.

David Stratton

Date 1933

Nationality USA

Director John M. Stahl

Cast John Boles, Jimmy Butler

Why It's Key A powerfully emotional conclusion to a neglected film.

Key Event **Goebbels asks Fritz Lang to head German film industry**

In March 1933, shortly after Hitler took office, Joseph Goebbels took the direction of the newly-founded Ministry of Propaganda. Fritz Lang's latest film, *The Testament of Dr. Mabuse*, which should have had its premiere in March, was banned by the censorship office of the Ministry. Shortly after (some say late March, others early April), Goebbels allegedly summoned Lang to his office, apologized for the banning, told Lang that both he and Hitler were great fans of his films, and invited him to head a new agency supervising German film production.

In many interviews, Lang described his meeting with Goebbels in dramatic, even melodramatic terms (the details very precise but often changing) and insisted that on the very night following their encounter, he gathered a few belongings and took a train to Paris, with no intention of ever returning. However, Lang's passport, which was acquired by the Berlin Kinemathek after his death, shows no customs stamp to France between February and June 23, 1933. Moreover, the passport indicates that after that date, he returned several times to Berlin, leaving Germany for good only on July 31 (after he was invited to work in Paris by the producer Erich Pommer). Lang knew how to tell a good story, and it remains unclear whether the legendary meeting with Goebbels actually occurred or is pure or part fiction.

Jean-Pierre Coursodon

Date March 1933

Why It's Key At this moment, Germany's most prestigious film director decided to flee the Nazi regime.

Opposite Fritz Lang

Key Scene **The fall before "Shanghai Lil"** *Footlight Parade*

When the advent of talking pictures threatens to put him out of work, theatrical producer Chester Kent (Cagney) fights back by assembling touring units to put on live musical "prologues" as added attractions in movie theaters. Kent's whole life is a race against time – something superbly captured by Lloyd Bacon's deft pacing of the film's non-musical sequences. At the climax of the film, Kent appears in danger of losing the race: the curtain has already risen for the scheduled start of the show, and everything's ready except the leading man, whom Kent finds in his dressing room drunk and with a bad case of stage fright. Kent drags him out; the two men struggle, reaching the top of a spiral staircase over the stage. A cut elides the result of the struggle, and one of the two men – we aren't shown his face – tumbles down the staircase. (This cut marks the dividing line not just between backstage and on-stage but also, presumably, between the contributions of Bacon and co-director Busby Berkeley.)

The orchestra conductor stops the music and peers querulously from his pit. At the foot of the spiral stairs, the fallen man's hand gives an impatient signal. Reassured, the conductor leads the orchestra through the prelude to "Shanghai Lil," the climactic production number of *Footlight Parade*. It was, of course, Chester who fell down the stairs and who now must play the lead role – which, being a former hoofer himself, and being Cagney, he does to idiosyncratic perfection.

The dreadful pause before the fallen man restarts the orchestra and rises to become part of the scene is a thrilling moment of cinema. Confusion, the reign of brute accident, the maws of disaster all appear before us – to be magically waved away by Chester's hand signal. The show goes on.

Chris Fujiwara

Date 1933

Nationality USA

Directors Busby Berkeley, Lloyd Bacon

Cast James Cagney

Why It's Key A thrilling moment of uncertainty marks the dividing line between the backstage world and the world of theatrical (and cinematic) illusion.

Key Scene **Which apartment is yours?**
Sons of the Desert (aka *Fraternally Yours*)

Thin and fragile Brit Stan Laurel, who came to America in the same English music-hall troupe as Charlie Chaplin, first met American character heavy Oliver Hardy in 1927, when the two worked for legendary comedy producer Hal Roach. Of the 106 films in which they eventually appeared together – a partnership encouraged by no less a comic genius than Leo McCarey – a few stand as enduring collaborations of character, timing, and comedic nuance. Chief among their handful of feature-length works is 1933's *Sons of the Desert* (*Fraternally Yours* in England), in which the boys must create an elaborate set of fictions to escape their wives and travel to the annual meeting of the titular men's lodge. Laurel, the genius behind most of their best routines, always tried to include some comedic business involving the boys in a doorway, such as the calamitous entrance into Billy Gilbert's house in their Oscar-winning 1932 short *The Music Box*. Here, it's an early scene establishing their domestic situations: though they live in attached, seemingly identical apartments side-by-side, one nameplate says "Mr. and Mrs. Stan Laurel," while the other proclaims "Oliver Hardy and wife." When the men return home from the first lodge meeting, an intricately blocked sequence of misunderstandings and double-backs establishes the power structure between the friends and among their wives. Modest but telling, it underscores their appeal as the most successful comic duo in movie history.

David Stratton

Date 1933

Nationality USA

Director William A. Seiter

Cast Stan Laurel, Oliver Hardy, Mae Busch, Dorothy Christy

Why It's Key It's a telling scene from what is easily the best feature in the long and fruitful career of beloved comedy duo Mr. Laurel and Mr. Hardy.

Opposite Laurel and Hardy

Key Scene **The final shot**
Queen Christina

SPOILER

Rouben Mamoulian, like his contemporary at Paramount, Josef von Sternberg, was an experimenter who was constantly looking for ways to visualise the sometimes banal narratives he tackled, and, like Sternberg, his career in film ended far too soon. Greta Garbo, at the height of her powers, requested that he direct her in *Queen Christina*, the sombre story of the Swedish queen who discovers love for the first time in the arms of the Spanish Ambassador (John Gilbert), abdicates the throne for him, and then loses him when he is killed in a duel as their ship is about to embark. In interviews and in conversation, Mamoulian often talked about the film's celebrated final shot, in which, after her lover's death, the Queen turns her back on Sweden and stands alone at the prow of the ship taking her to Spain. First there was the requirement to develop a new lens that would allow the camera to move in from a full shot to a huge close-up, cutting off Garbo's chin and the top of her forehead, so that the audience could look deep into those luminous eyes. But most important was his instruction to his actor to become a *tabula rasa*, to turn her face into a blank page on which the audience could read whatever it wanted. Garbo was ordered to think of nothing at all, and not to blink (though she does, twice). It's one of the cinema's most memorable final scenes.

David Stratton

Date 1933

Nationality USA

Director Rouben Mamoulian

Cast Greta Garbo

Why It's Key A great actor and a great director show that they can be eloquent without the use of dialogue.

Key Scene **Solidaric Utopia**
Sonnenstrahl

Paul Fejos is one of the great mystery men of cinema. Important parts of his oeuvre are missing, including all his early Hungarian works, his subsequent independent US debut *The Last Moment*, hailed as a masterpiece back in 1928, and some of the career-capping ethnographic films shot in Africa, Asia, and South America a dozen years later. (He spent the two decades till his death in 1963 teaching as an anthropologist.) The remains suggest an occasionally erratic, but extraordinary filmmaker – indeed, Fejos's 1929 Hollywood advent *Lonesome* has been compared to Murnau's *Sunrise* for its supreme silent-era poetry. After less satisfying experiences, Fejos rejected Hollywood and left a cross-continent trail of very diverse European features. The secret masterpiece was the one closest to *Lonesome*: *Sonnenstrahl* recombines city symphony, love story, fairy tale aspects, and pronounced social interests, as two unemployed, suicidal people accidentally meet and find in each other the strength to start anew. Finally, another blow of fate strikes, but they are saved by the solidarity of the other workers in their apartment house: money rains into the courtyard. The setting is representative, a real building from the era of "Red Vienna," the strong socialist movement soon to be overrun by dictatorship; the film itself like that movement's last manifesto (in hindsight: its memento). Yet the happy ending of *Sonnenstrahl* derives its extraordinary power not just from nostalgia or the near-magical circumstances: It's the realization that solidarity is a concept neither the movies nor real-life politics have much use for anymore.

Christoph Huber

Date 1933

Nationality Austria

Director Paul Fejos

Cast Gustav Fröhlich, Annabella

Why It's Key It's the culmination of mysterious director Paul Fejos's secret masterpiece – and the filmic legacy of Vienna's socialist movement.

Key Person **Mae West**
I'm No Angel

At once a down-to-earth daughter of the people and a fearless empowered woman, free to indulge her own libidinal energies, Mae West's unique onscreen persona reached a peak of refinement in her third feature, *I'm No Angel*. The statuesque blonde siren controlled her image as no female player had before, by virtue of writing both story and screenplay to showcase her own performance. As the carnival sideshow dancer Tira, she cheerfully models her hourglass-figure-hugging sequined gowns, while unapologetically asserting a woman's right to utilize the male population. Opposing contemporary society's judgmental condemnation of "gold diggers," she slides up the class ladder from carny grifters to society swells ("silk hats," in her vernacular), alert to the economic reality that only with a millionaire's resources can she permanently surmount her lowly origins. When lawyers try to besmirch her reputation by enumerating her many gentleman friends, she argues: "Why shouldn't I know guys? I travel from coast to coast. A dame like me can't make trips without meeting some of the male population." Warming to the task, she takes charge of the courtroom, sashaying past the all-male jury and flirting shamelessly with the judge, and then demolishes her chief adversary's lies herself. The result was her greatest hit, credited with saving Paramount's fortunes by luring Depression-era ticket-buyers back into the theatres. According to a smiling exhibitor, "Church people clamor for clean pictures, but they all come out to see Mae West." At least they did until the Hays Office amassed enough power to crack down on her innuendo-rich comedy.

Robert Keser

Date 1933

Nationality USA

Director Wesley Ruggles

Cast Mae West, Cary Grant

Why It's Key Mae West reaches her peak.

Opposite **Poster for *I'm No Angel***

MAE WEST

"I'm No Angel"

WITH

CARY GRANT

DIRECTED BY WESLEY RUGGLES

Key Scene **The waterlilies sequence**
Daybreak

Since the golden age of silents, the influence of Hollywood on Chinese cinema has been profound. Production values were remarkably high; acting style was quite sophisticated (as testified by the performances of Ruan Lingyu, a major star of the time), and the atmosphere of Fox studios is palpable in a number of interior set designs. *Daybreak* is a lavish *mélo* with political undertones – one could see it as a propaganda film, a celebration of nationalist China – and strong echoes from *Seventh Heaven* (1927): the vertical tracking shot cutting across the staircase of an apartment building directly quotes Frank Borzage. Melodrama means exaggeration, and contemporary critics had some qualms about the heroine's defiant smile in front of a firing squad at the end of the film. An earlier sequence, however, remains indelibly imprinted in the memory of the viewer for its plaintive tones: it's the moment when the character played by Li Lili – a country girl who went to the big city to become a prostitute-spy – goes back to her shabby lodging at the end of the day. Her country fiancé had given her a necklace of waterlilies; the memento is under the pillow of the bed where the girl is now daydreaming of her lost love. A flashback shows her with her man on a boat gliding across waterlilies, gently embraced by water and sky, in the remote haven of a benevolent nature. A dissolve brings us back to the girl holding the waterlilies necklace. It's almost dark. She is quietly weeping.
Paolo Cherchi Usai

Date 1933

Nationality China

Director Sun Yu

Cast Gao Zhanfei, Li Lili, Ye Juanjuan

Original Title *Tianming*

Why It's Key A chant of lost love is heard across a pond.

Key Scene **Mirror image**
Duck Soup

At the behest of rich matron Mrs. Teasdale (Margaret Dumont), the bankrupt and politically unstable country of Fredonia hires a new leader, Rufus T. Firefly (Groucho Marx). Complicating matters are two bumbling spies from neighboring Sylvania, Pinky (Harpo Marx) and Chicolini (Chico Marx). Thus begins one of the most anarchic anti-war, anti-government, and anti-authority comedies ever made. In the frenetic course of the proceedings, Firefly and Pinky find themselves in matching nightshirts and caps, with the latter doing a frantic mirror-image impression of the former to escape detection. *Duck Soup* is often cited as among the most irreverent anti-war comedies ever made, a claim deflated by Groucho's assertion that they were "just four Jews trying to get a laugh." Maybe so, but the film was reportedly banned in Italy by Benito Mussolini – who thought it was about him. The quartet's last film for Paramount before their lavish but spotty run at MGM, *Duck Soup* is all Marx Brothers all the time, and thus their strongest and most vibrant showcase.

The mirror gag had many variations then and since, having been used previously by Charlie Chaplin in *The Floorwalker* (1917) and Max Linder in *Seven Years Bad Luck* (1921), with a variation on the theme providing a visual highpoint in Roman Polanski's *The Fearless Vampire Killers* (1966). Harpo even encored it with Lucille Ball on her American TV program in 1951. But none of these top this inspired bit of nonsense, which Roger Ebert has cited as "one of the gems of the first century of film."
David Stratton

Date 1933

Nationality USA

Director Leo McCarey

Cast Groucho Marx, Harpo Marx, Chico Marx

Why It's Key Silent comedy lives on in the talkies.

Opposite **Poster for *Duck Soup***

Key Scene **On top of the world**
King Kong

He stands atop the world's tallest man-made structure with the same fierce pride, the same compelling dignity, as at the top of his high mountain crag on Skull Island. Kong, the great ape, king of the mysterious jungle, awarded the delectable Ann Darrow (Wray) as living sacrifice by a horde of frenzied natives, seizing her and carrying her off to his lonely aerie, attacked and captured by cupidinous American businessmen-adventurers, bound and transported across the sea, hoisted, shackled, humiliated as a showman's freak in the limelight of gaudy Broadway, can hold in his wrath no longer and breaks free. Pandemonium. He rampages through the theater, into the streets, trampling cars and pedestrians in his fury. From her apartment he withdraws the sleeping Ann, then climbs with her to the highest place he can find.

Now he is at once an ultimate cinematic icon and a cluster of brilliant contradictions, the huge wild ape crowning the elegantly architected skyscraper, the innocent beast beset by a squadron of fighter planes from all directions, the dark primordial soul surveying the always shifting, always glittering modern world. We look up at him, we look down upon him; we swoop into his field of vision and his gargantuan reach (one of the planes he seizes as though it were a mere dragonfly); we precipitously dangle with Ann in his giant, tender hand. Finally the bullets find their mark and the spirit goes out of him, he seems to sigh with the sadness of a deity before leaning, collapsing, putting her gently down, then dropping off into space, hero of a neo-Rousseauan epic on the follies of greed, civilization, advancement. The beauty that killed this beast is not Ann but the extravagant, raw, magnificent art of the cinema.
Murray Pomerance

Date 1933

Nationality USA

Directors Merian C. Cooper, Ernest B. Schoedsack

Cast Fay Wray

Why It's Key It's one of the great iconic moments of Hollywood cinema.

Opposite *King Kong*

Key Scene **Pillow fight**
Zero for Conduct

Jean Vigo's enormously influential film, a semi-autobiographical account (peppered with famously surreal touches) of the director's unhappy sojourn at a dreary French boarding school, synthesizes lyricism and revolutionary fervor with astonishing flair. Vigo's anarchist background fuels anti-authoritarian jabs at autocratic teachers and repressive pedagogy.

The famous pillow fight embodies Vigo's anti-authoritarian stance with poetic precision. Tabard (de Bédarieux), a sensitive boy who many critics assume is Vigo's alter ego, instigates the playful warfare. Tabard's relatively innocuous horseplay defuses his rage towards a lascivious science teacher while anticipating the actual insurrection that concludes the film. As conceived by Vigo, however, the pillow fight is far more than a glimpse of bored schoolchildren "letting off steam." The mock-crucifixion of a particularly odious teacher, Pète Sec (le Flon), and the transformation of what Gavin Millar labels the transformation of "the severe box of a dormitory into a magical snow-flecked landscape" can be viewed as a powerful antidote to the conformity imposed upon hapless students everywhere and a vision of ecstasy that provides the young rebels with an exhilarating taste of freedom. Although the slow-motion pillow fracas recalls a similar sequence in Abel Gance's *Napoleon*, Vigo's fusion of poetic frisson and revolutionary ardor is completely *sui generis*.
Richard Porton

Date 1933

Nationality France

Director Jean Vigo

Cast Jean Dasté, Louis Lefebvre, Gilbert Pruchon, Coco Golstein, Gérard de Bédarieux, Robert le Flon

Original Title *Zéro de conduite*

Why It's Key A poetic interlude in Vigo's celebrated film exemplifies this influential director's radical vision.

Key Scene **The beds scene**
L'Atalante

Vigo's single full-length feature is one of the greatest movies ever made, magnificent in many respects. Cheaply made, it's richly rewarding; profoundly poetic, it's also rooted in the kind of social authenticity later taken up by the Italian neorealists; combining genres while refusing to be constricted to any one, it's suspenseful, subversive, anarchic, deeply moral, funny, moving, chastening, uplifting… and, despite its narrative and visual chastity, one of the most genuinely erotic movies in the history of cinema.

The key scene occurs after the skipper of a Seine barge (Dasté) has seemingly abandoned or been abandoned by his recent bride (Parlo), an innocent village girl who, against his wishes, decided to windowshop the fabled delights of Paris. Truth to tell, they don't really want to be apart; it's just anger, born of the difficulties of marital compromise, that has separated them, but he's sleeping alone in the bridal bed on their barge while she's taken refuge in a faintly seedy Parisian hotel. Alone, apart, they dream of each other… and Vigo intercuts between their feverish, fumbling reveries, to the (a)rousing strains of Maurice Jaubert's rightly rhapsodic score, to create one of the subtlest yet most suggestively lyrical accounts of human desire committed to celluloid. The lovers aren't even in the same physical space; yet the physicality of their longing is marvellously evident not only in the actors' rapt gestures but in Vigo's rhythmic montage, which fully grasps that beauty – and absolutely everything that that entails – is in the eye of the beholder.
Geoff Andrew

Date 1934

Nationality France

Director Jean Vigo

Cast Jean Dasté, Dita Parlo

Why It's Key Sex has always been a staple of cinema, but few filmmakers have grasped the simple truth that desire is primarily a matter of imagination. Vigo got it right – and how.

Key Scene **Walk through the mausoleum**
The Black Cat

Ulmer, a former assistant of Murnau, showed his fidelity to Murnau's values in his own work. No clearer example exists than a scene from *The Black Cat*, one of the great stylistic triumphs to come from Hollywood. Dr. Vitus Werdegast (Lugosi) has come to the Central European home of architect Hjalmar Poelzig (Karloff), bent on revenge for a wartime betrayal by the latter that resulted in Werdegast's being taken prisoner by the Russians. Poelzig also took advantage of Werdegast's incarceration to steal the latter's wife. But Poelzig claims that the woman is dead, and he has the proof: her perfectly preserved corpse upright in a glass case in his basement. Werdegast threatens to kill Poelzig but, terrified by the sudden apparition of a black cat, is unable to carry out his threat. Poelzig walks him back through the basement toward the staircase exit and talks to him soothingly. As he does so, the camera, assuming a quasi-subjective position, tracks forward. Poelzig asks, "Of what use are all these melodramatic gestures?", and the stark decor, suddenly foregrounded by the slow camera movement, helps effect the very dedramatization his voice calls for. Poelzig announces that both of the two men, having suffered soul death during the war only to have their bodies survive, are now "the living dead" – and the gliding camera movement, disembodied yet also anchored to the movement of the characters, reflects that condition while letting the viewer imaginatively share in it.
Chris Fujiwara

Date 1934

Nationality USA

Director Edgar G. Ulmer

Cast Boris Karloff, Bela Lugosi

Why It's Key Camera movement, decor, and the human voice create a moment of psychological horror.

Key Scene **The boy discovers the shark**
Man of Aran

There are dozens of books written about Flaherty in general and this wonderful film in particular. It's well known that most of *Man of Aran* is a poetic fake. Flaherty wanted to show man's struggle with nature and decided to present life in the Aran Islands as it was half a century before the filming. Flaherty got one of the most impressive scenes in his career by staging the hunting of sharks – which were supposedly needed to provide oil for the lamps, though in fact by 1934 the Aran Islands already had electricity and nobody remembered how sharks were hunted.

However, there are in the film some precious moments of truth, and most of them involve a boy (Dirrane). When he is seen fishing at the cliff, he's only doing for the camera the same thing that he did every day. There is a chilling moment when, strolling very close to the water, he discovers there a great shark with its terrifying mouth wide open. The power of that moment comes not only from the image of the shark,

but especially from the fact that the music score suddenly comes to a stop. It is a quite modern effect and a very strange artistic decision by Flaherty, considering that he had no previous experience with sound and that the rest of the film is literally flooded with music.

Fernando Martín Peña

Date 1934

Nationality UK

Director Robert Flaherty

Cast Michael Dirrane

Why It's Key A moment of truth in the middle of a largely staged documentary, this scene creates a strikingly modern effect.

Key Scene **Committing the crime**
The Crime of Monsieur Lange

Scripted by Jacques Prévert during the heyday of the Popular Front, Renoir's delightful fable celebrates the rise of a Parisian publishing collective after the reported death of the staff's lecherous, callously exploitative boss Batala (Berry). When he emerges from hiding disguised as a priest, having heard of their success with cowboy serials penned by dreamy innocent Lange (Lefevre), and tells the author he's resuming control, the disgusted Lange decides the boss is better off dead after all....

For all its narrative contrivance, Renoir ensures the sequence's credibility through a mix of supremely naturalistic performances – gloriously evident at a boozy celebration held by the workers in a downstairs room in the courtyard that is the film's main location – and carefully calibrated drama, as when Lange, leaving the festivities to write upstairs, finds Batala unexpectedly back in the land of the living and displaying no remorse for his many sins. Indeed, the

embodiment of unbridled capitalist arrogance, he boasts he'll reap all the profits while reserving the right to fire his entire staff. Cutting between the pair's confrontation and a drunken concierge (Lévesque) tidying up downstairs, Renoir builds suspense until Batala descends himself and starts trying to seduce old flame Valentine (Florelle), now in love with Lange, who – observed from outside in one of Renoir's long, elegant crane shots – leaves the office, descends the stairs, and crosses the yard to shoot Batala in the belly. The lovers take flight, leaving the concierge yelling for a priest to provide last rites for the victim – still garbed as a priest. Both the irony and the sense of poetic justice are deliciously acute.

Geoff Andrew

Date 1935

Nationality France

Director Jean Renoir

Cast René Lefevre, Jules Berry, Florelle, Marcel Lévesque

Original Title *Le Crime de Monsieur Lange*

Why It's Key Unobtrusively virtuoso camerawork seamlessly blends boisterous comedy with politically resonant drama to memorably stirring effect.

Key Scene **The wedding ceremony**
The Scarlet Empress

The last great movie released during the pre-Code era, and the sixth of Sternberg's seven feature films built around Dietrich, this sardonic comedy of Catherine the Great's ascension to power mocks Hollywood's conventional groveling toward royalty, recounting the worldly education of the guileless girl-child. Her romantic ideals cannot withstand the stale protocol, rank hypocrisy and greed, and preening sexual vulgarity of the imperial Russian court. Amidst the suffocating décor with doors so monumental that it takes six women to push them open and threatening furniture depicting gargoyles writhing in agony, the frightened girl must learn that she has "weapons more powerful than any political machine." Her wedding poises Catherine at the brink of achieving the erotic potency that will make her "the Messalina of the North," though with no help from her grinning halfwit bridegroom (Jaffe). Interrupting the nuptial preparations, Empress Elizabeth (Dresser) reminds Catherine of her "brood mare" duties, and

Sternberg counterpoints the matriarch's coarse behavior with an exquisite multi-layered composition, the star's face reflected in multiple mirrors while handmaidens raise diaphanous fabrics, and dark figures rise to obscure the foreground for enhanced depth. The marriage ceremony itself proceeds in 29 shots, a grand *tableau vivant* of head-spinning claustrophobia as the camera sweeps diagonally above bearded Orthodox clerics and massed candles and crucifixes; then, as the husband's glowering mistress (Stevens) and the wife's prospective lover (Lodge) watch, the couple move through clouds of incense; Dietrich's face appears trapped motionless behind textures, her breathing animating a candle flame that dances just beyond her veil, as each feverish screen-filling close-up is held longer than the last. Amidst the stupefying artificiality, her breath flickers with life: Sternberg's lesson in visualizing the ethereal with material means.

Robert Keser

Date 1934

Nationality USA

Director Josef von Sternberg

Cast Marlene Dietrich, Sam Jaffe, Louise Dresser, John Lodge, Ruthelma Stevens

Why It's Key It's the apotheosis of Sternberg's unique visual textures.

1930–1939

101

Key Scene **The Walls of Jericho**
It Happened One Night

Ten years after Harry Cohn founded Columbia Pictures in 1924, the studio had an unexpected smash with the genre template *It Happened One Night*. Cohn was a master penny-pincher who specialized in borrowing disgruntled stars from other studios, finding the perfect alignment in Paramount's Claudette Colbert as a bratty socialite on the run and MGM's Clark Gable as the hard-nosed reporter who agrees to help her for the story but inevitably falls in love. Frank Capra's no-frills direction meshes perfectly with Robert Riskin's rat-a-tat script, traits the two would subsequently hone with *Mr. Deeds Goes to Town* (1936), *Lost Horizon* (1937), *You Can't Take It with You* (1938), and *Meet John Doe* (1941). In an early scene, hot stuff for the day, Colbert and Gable must share a rural motel room. He uses a blanket he dubs "The Walls of Jericho" to block their views of each other, and she realises they're still strangers: "You've got a name," she asks, "haven't you?" "Yeah, I got a name. Peter Warne." "Peter Warne.

I don't like it." "Don't let it bother you. You're giving it back to me in the morning." "Pleased to meet you, Mr. Warne." And then, Riskin's risqué kicker: "The pleasure is all mine, Mrs. Warne." Is there any doubt this wall, built of blankets or inhibitions, will come tumblin' down? *It Happened One Night* was the first of three films to date to win all top-five Oscars: production, director, actor, actress, and screenplay. The others? *One Flew Over the Cuckoo's Nest* (1975) and *The Silence of the Lambs* (1991).

David Stratton

Date 1934

Nationality USA

Director Frank Capra

Cast Clark Gable, Claudette Colbert

Why It's Key It's the most legendary scene from the original Hollywood romantic comedy – ageless.

Opposite *It Happened One Night*

Key Person **Ruan Lingyu**
The Goddess

Who were the greatest actors of the 1930s? James Cagney? Jean Gabin? Ozu's Takeshi Sakamoto? Charles Laughton? Mizoguchi's Kakuko Mori? Katharine Hepburn? One name unlikely to be mentioned these days is the astonishing Ruan Lingyu, often called the Chinese Greta Garbo. Born in Shanghai in 1910, Ruan made her first film in 1927. Four years later, in *The Peach Girl* (1931), she began to evince the subtle sadness that fitted so well with the realism in Chinese cinema at the time. *Small Toys* (1933) used her role to debate the role of women in society. In *The Goddess* (1934), playing the first sympathetic prostitute in the history of cinema, there is a famous moment when she looks toward the ceiling. It's a look that, almost everywhere in the world, means "help me, God" – and here she needs help. Her child needs feeding. She is very poor. The hooded look in her eyes and her slumped body language are remarkably modern. In *New Women* (1935), she played an actress

and screenwriter who committed suicide after being hounded by the press. The prurient Shanghai tabloids of the time attacked the film and Ruan herself because they took *New Women* as an attack on them and because there was gossip about Ruan's liberated love life. Her response was tragic. She herself took an overdose of barbiturates and died in 1935. Her funeral procession was three miles long. Three women committed suicide at it. The *New York Times'* front page called it "the most spectacular funeral of the century," nine years after Rudolph Valentino's. Today, Ruan appears in almost no film encyclopaedias. Maggie Cheung played her, beautifully, in Stanley Kwan's *Centre Stage* (1992). Ruan's naturalism in this scene in *The Goddess* predated the Method by more than two decades.

Mark Cousins

Date 1934

Nationality China

Director Wu Yonggang

Cast Ruan Lingyu

Original Title *Shen nu*

Why It's Key This scene is perhaps the most famous moment in realist Chinese cinema of the 1930s, and the great Ruan Lingyu suits it magnificently.

Key Scene **"The Lullaby of Broadway"**
Gold Diggers of 1935

Busby Berkeley's art is made for anthologies: it's an art of detachable pleasures and isolated scenes, as, perhaps, no film illustrates more paradigmatically than *Gold Diggers of 1935*. This film has, to be sure, a plot, but one so pointless that it seems to vanish, leaving no trace, even as the film unspools. The only reason for *Gold Diggers of 1935* to exist is the free-wheeling mastery of choreography, camerawork, and editing that Berkeley displays in his production numbers, the most stunning of which, "The Lullaby of Broadway," is one of the peaks of Hollywood filmmaking.

This totally self-contained film-within-a-film concerns the last night on Earth of a high-living "Broadway baby" (Shaw). Her fatal frolic at a ritzy nightclub is the occasion for some characteristic Berkeley pyrotechnics involving a legion of tap dancers on a vast tiered set, but the highpoint of the sequence is its beginning. As Shaw sings "The Lullaby of Broadway," the camera cranes slowly and from very far

away toward her white face, hovering in a sea of black. Finally in closeup, the face dissolves into an aerial view of the island of Manhattan. The sequence becomes more concrete as Berkeley details a typical morning in the city, zeroing in on the Shaw character's exhausted return home to a walk-up apartment as the rest of New York is starting its day. In these hard-bitten and leisurely shots, and in the bewildering contrast they make with the club sequence that ensues, Berkeley created an enduring cinematic representation of the Depression.

Chris Fujiwara

Date 1935

Nationality USA

Director Busby Berkeley

Cast Winifred Shaw, Dick Powell

Why It's Key This famous sequence marks Busby Berkeley's summit.

Opposite *Gold Diggers of 1935*

Key Scene **A blind man enters a general store** *It's a Gift*

There isn't a better illustration of unsparing Fields comedy than this portrait of Mr. Muckle, a hostile, uncontrollable blind man. While scrambling to fill an obstreperous customer's order for "ten pounds of kumquats," Fields notices that outside a black-clad figure in sunglasses is making a beeline for his store carrying a cane. Fields immediately stops what he's doing, points, and yells "Open the door for Mr. Muckle!"

Already something has been set in motion that has happened before and is too late to stop. Suddenly Muckle is upon Fields and us and the world. He crashes his cane through the store's glass door, points out that "you got that door closed again," and falls into a stack of boxes. To add to the scene's audacity, Fields tries to placate and console this intractable old man, who is also partially deaf and has to be shouted at through an ear trumpet, by calling him "honey" and "dear." When he hands Muckle the five-cent pack of gum he came in for,

the blind man refuses to "lug that with me" and insists it be delivered.

Here Fields sets up his world, where slow-moving forces of mulish humanity become like the objects (light bulbs, coconuts, ice picks) they use to bedevil him. For Fields, Depression-era America was a combination of *The Grapes of Wrath* ("Shades of Bacchus!" he exclaims at one point) and *L'Age d'or*, with all the frustrating sadness and bitter absurdity that coupling implies.
A. S. Hamrah

Date 1934

Nationality USA

Director Norman Z. McLeod

Cast W. C. Fields, Charles Sellon

Why It's Key Fields presents the human condition.

Opposite *It's a Gift*

Key Film
Becky Sharp

Littérateurs dropped their monocles at Hollywood's impudent stripping-down of *Vanity Fair*, Thackeray's classic panorama of social climbing. Despite the film's many witty nuances and the brilliant chattering of Miriam Hopkins in the title role, the real point was to display the new technology of three-strip Technicolor, finally perfected after 20 years of experimentation. The old processes, which registered only variations of red and green, gave way here to brilliantly distinct new shades of buttercup yellow, burnt orange, and Wedgwood blue, as well as a more natural skin tone. Dr. Herbert and Natalie Kalmus controlled the patents and the camera equipment of the Technicolor Corporation, enforcing their aesthetic of deep focus, razor-sharp definition, and ultrabright colors via high-key lighting (Hollywood veterans complained that the Kalmuses even demanded full illumination beneath a sofa). In *Becky Sharp*'s Brussels ball sequence, set within sight of Waterloo on the eve

of the decisive battle, all the possibilities of the full color spectrum blossom when Mamoulian lets cannon shots blow open the windows, turning waltzing to pandemonium. Audaciously extinguishing the lights, he works in delicate half-lit shadows, introducing muted hues never before captured onscreen, while the players become elements in patterns of color and movement, pastel ball gowns succeeded by soldiers' scarlet capes streaming and gold helmets gleaming in lantern-light. The film's retinal extravagance and theatrical vigor made a good advertisement for Technicolor, but the Kalmus-dominated process remained expensive, so widespread adoption of color came only in the 1950s with the invention of the more economical Eastmancolor.
Robert Keser

Date 1935

Nationality USA

Director Rouben Mamoulian

Cast Miriam Hopkins

Why It's Key It was the first feature film to showcase the range of the new three-strip Technicolor process.

Key Event
"Sticks Nix Hick Pix"

On July 17, 1935, *Variety*, the showbiz trade paper, ran the front page headline "Sticks Nix Hick Pix" over an interview with midwestern exhibitor Joe Kinsky who, among other things, noted that supposedly upscale films like *The Barretts of Wimpole Street* performed well in Illinois, Omaha, and Nebraska and "farmers are not interested in farming pictures" (though he made an exception for *State Fair*). On the scale of things, the story, by Hollywood correspondent George McCall, was fairly minor, but the headline – purportedly coined by New York editor Abel Green – came to epitomise the sharp, punchy, slangy, frankly urban (non-sticks) tone of *Variety* in particular and show business in general. In the movie *Yankee Doodle Dandy* (1942), James Cagney's George M. Cohan reads the headline and spins it off into a patter song. The wordplay is immortal, but the sentiment isn't a hard and fast rule – subsequent

hick pix and TV shows ("skeins" in Varietyspeak), from *The Grapes of Wrath* to *The Waltons*, have achieved considerable success ("clicked"), especially with rural audiences ("the sticks").

Kim Newman

Date July 17, 1935

Why It's Key This showbiz insider sentence entered the language.

Key Scene **Hannay hides out at the crofter's cottage** *The 39 Steps*

Master of suspense Hitchcock has long been famous for building dramatic tension, but not for making us feel deeply for his characters; moreover, his technically more sophisticated Hollywood films have often overshadowed the earlier, lower-budget British fare. This adaptation of John Buchan's novel – alongside *The Lady Vanishes* (1938), the best of his British movies – is also the warmest film in the director's long and prolific career.

From the moment hero-on-the-run Richard Hannay (Donat) meets crofter John (Laurie), negotiates a deal for dinner and a bed, and makes an innocent gaff by assuming Margaret (Ashcroft) is his daughter – 'Ma wife!' comes the curt response – it's clear the wanted man isn't very welcome as far as his host's concerned. The young mistress of the house, however, is both curious about his city life and generous enough to believe he's innocent of a murder reported in the papers. She even wakes him when the police

arrive, warning of her husband's likely treachery and giving Hannay his overcoat; "He'll pray at me, but no more," she says bravely (and, as it later transpires, erroneously) when the fugitive voices concern at the possible consequences. Though brief, the scene so deftly depicts the growing confidentiality between the younger characters that we really come to feel for Margaret, shut away in this remote place with her penny-pinching, untrusting, and too-old husband; despite her claim to the contrary, we know she'll suffer more than blows, as is shown by her desolate expression as she pensively closes the door behind the departing Hannay. A brief dream of adventure has ended…

Geoff Andrew

Date 1935

Nationality UK

Director Alfred Hitchcock

Cast Robert Donat, Peggy Ashcroft, John Laurie

Why It's Key Taut suspense from Hitch, of course, but also, more atypically, one of his most warmly human and emotionally affecting scenes.

Key Scene **The broken watches**
Tit for Tat

A housewife (Mae Busch) helps Oliver Hardy out of her bedroom, where he has fallen after a series of mishaps. On his way out, Hardy says to her, in apology, one of the most *risqué* lines in comedy cinema: "I've never been in that position." Her husband (Hall) arrives just in time to hear the line, so it means war. In Laurel and Hardy's world, "war" often takes the form of a most disciplined exchange of property damage and personal humiliation (their film *Big Business* [1929] is an unsurpassed masterpiece in that respect).

However, there's a sublime moment in *Tit for Tat* that implies, if possible, an almost surreal evolution of the same process. Hall goes to their shop and patiently destroys five or six watches that they have for sale. Dutifully awaiting their turn, Laurel and Hardy let him complete the destruction of their property, observing each step with little reaction and an almost scientific detachment. After he finishes, they proceed to examine the damage. Then, Laurel picks a wheel from the wreckage and makes it spin like a child's toy. And instead of returning it to the pile of rubbish, he decides to keep it in his pocket. He obviously intends to play with it later on.

It is an exquisite digression, one that gets to the core of the characters they played ever since they found each other.
Fernando Martín Peña

Date 1935

Nationality USA

Director Charley Rogers

Cast Stan Laurel, Oliver Hardy, Charlie Hall

Why It's Key An advanced stage of the battle structure typical of Laurel and Hardy films gives rise to a sublime digression.

Key Scene **Hitler arrives by plane**
Triumph of the Will

In this "documentary" of a Nazi Party rally, a rally actually staged for the making of the film, Riefenstahl begins with shots of clouds from a plane. The film's most awe-inspiringly beautiful images, they show giant, towering forms fringed with sunlight; even here, the way that objects are equated with power makes their beauty, to anyone who would question power worship, troubling. The city of Nuremburg, an ancient center of German culture, appears through the clouds, and the plane's shadow traverses a line of buildings and a street – individual power imposing itself on the town and on history. Then Hitler emerges from the plane, a revolting moment that also causes one to question how much less revolting it would have been if the subject was, say, Roosevelt. To what extent is power worship itself wrong, and to what extent is the decision to worship evil ideas the real issue? Riefenstahl cuts between masses of hands raised in the Hitler salute and Hitler's raised hand alone answering them as he rides into town, thus differentiating Hitler from all others, the masses from the single figure they all worship, a motif continued for the rest of the film. The camera rotates around Hitler during his speeches, giving a sense that the world revolves around him, an honor denied the other Nazis who speak. When Hitler is not in the frame, the subject matter is most often endlessly repeating objects: soldiers marching past, or long rows of Nazi flags. That the film's showings in Germany were often accompanied by beatings of Jews forced to attend only confirms the awful ideology it espouses: that individuals should subjugate their wills to a single "great leader" – and an evil one at that.
Fred Camper

Date 1935

Nationality Germany

Director Leni Riefenstahl

Cast Adolf Hitler

Original Title *Triumph des Willens*

Why It's Key Riefenstahl finds a cinematic form for the worship of a single man, and for the worship of power, raising many questions, not the least about film and evil.

Key Scene **The creation of the bride**
Bride of Frankenstein

With a budget twice the size of the original's US$200,000 and a darkly funny script that buttresses genuinely unsettling genre elements with a strong homosexual subtext, the lavishly baroque *Bride of Frankenstein* is generally acknowledged as the smartest and most subversive entry in the golden age of horror films produced by Universal Pictures. Much of the credit belongs to British director James Whale (1896-1957), a gay sophisticate who had followed 1931's *Frankenstein* with *The Old Dark House* (1932) and *The Invisible Man* (1933). Working from a campy script by John Balderston, Whale refined and deepened the moral complexity inherent in the tale, leavening this with the often batty antics of mad doctor Pretorius (Ernst Thesiger) and coating everything with a strong visual dose of German Expressionism and Franz Waxman's influential score. So, too, Boris Karloff's playing of the Monster is more measured and compassionate than in the first *Frankenstein*,

presenting a creature at least as frightened and confused as actually dangerous. Nowhere is this more obvious than in the film's frenzied climax, in which the titular mate (Elsa Lanchester, who also plays *Frankenstein* author Mary Wollstonecraft Shelley in a preface added by Whale to deflect Production Code meddling) is animated in a fast-paced sequence of odd angles and humming machinery. "It's alive!" crows Dr. Frankenstein (Clive), speaking as much of his hideous creation as of the energy and wit of this singular achievement, the thinking person's monster movie.
David Stratton

Date 1935

Nationality USA

Director James Whale

Cast Boris Karloff, Colin Clive, Ernest Thesiger, Elsa Lanchester

Why It's Key This scene caps an audacious blend of horror and horror spoof.

Opposite *Bride of Frankenstein*

Key Scene **The final separation**
Wife, Be like a Rose!

SPOILER

The film concerns the efforts of Kimiko (Chiba) to reunite her estranged parents. She has managed to coax her father (Maruyama) back to Tokyo from the mountain village where he has been living with his mistress and her young children. But he's uncomfortable in the presence of his mild, intellectual, repressed wife, Etsuko (Ito), and decides to return to the country. The final sequence lays out, in a rush of short shots, each character's realization of and coming-to-terms with the inevitability of the family's separation. Naruse transforms the simple domestic space into a complex zone of criss-crossing confrontations and solitary discoveries: the space itself becomes, not merely the place where the crisis occurs, but the formal embodiment of the crisis. The father leaves before the mother can be urged out of her study to say goodbye to him. Then, over and over, Naruse intercuts a shot that tracks back from the devastated, weeping Etsuko with a shot that tracks in on Kimiko as she looks

at her mother. Kimiko says simply, "Mother, you've lost," and it's up to us to put together, mentally, the meaning of the scene that Naruse has shattered into so many fragments. Freezing Kimiko's vision in time, the volley of complementary shots suggests that the moment of separation will be repeated again and again in the women's memories.
Chris Fujiwara

Date 1935

Nationality Japan

Director Mikio Naruse

Cast Sachiko Chiba, Tomoko Ito, Sadao Maruyama, Kamatari Fujiwara, Heihachiro Okawa

Original Title *Tsuma yo bara no you ni*

Why It's Key This swift and furiously concentrated sequence is one of the most intense studies of domestic collapse in cinema.

Key Scene **Dance celebrates a return to life**
By the Bluest of Seas

By the Bluest of Seas is a movie loved by filmmakers, such as Otar Iosseliani: "Anything is possible at any moment of this film." Some 50 years after seeing it, Jean-Luc Godard remembered a particular scene in a way that is wonky, but profoundly true to the spirit of Barnet: "A woman dies, they bury her, and suddenly she returns among the living. They look at her and say: 'What are you doing here? You're dead!' And then they start dancing. Why do they dance? It doesn't matter; there is nothing to understand." Actually, it's the woman (Elena Kouzmina as Misha) – presumed drowned at sea – who returns to her pals at the kolkhoz, as they hold a mournful wake for her; and it's she who asks, "Who's dead?", only to receive the delightful answer from one of her two handsome suitors: "You!" But what truly matters is the dancing that instantly breaks out and envelops the room: nutty, athletic, scarcely containable in the frame. It envelops Barnet's cinematic language, too: the camera movements, the editing of image and sound, catch the spark. Godard opposed the free flux of Barnet's film to the "grim imperative" to dance in Hollywood musicals: "no longer happiness, only neurosis." But there is no need to damn the Americans in order to laud the Russian: Barnet, who seemed able to insert song and dance into any story (no matter how dramatic or tragic), simply rejoiced in the opportunity to transform and reinvent physical gesture, the figure in motion.
Adrian Martin

Date 1936

Nationality USSR

Director Boris Barnet

Cast Elena Kouzmina

Original Title *U samogo sinyego morya*

Why It's Key Barnet rejoices in the figure in free motion

Key Scene **Island epilogue**
A Day in the Country

So much hesitation, yearning, maybe-it'll-happen-maybe-it-won't tension fills up the immortal seconds near the end of *A Day in the Country* – itself a poignantly uncompleted work, and yet such a perfectly formed piece of crystal. The camera tracks with Henri (Darnoux) but can hardly frame him or keep him in its path as he rushes, slows, stops, as if to take refuge behind a small, hanging tree branch. There is a whip-movement of the camera that finds, with his gaze and yet not in it, his former lover of a single day, Henriette (Bataille). She turns, sees him, tentatively moves forward, with the camera accompanying her. Then Renoir changes tack, abandons the roving camera, and employs shot/reverse-shot cutting between the faces, first in close-up, then over-the-shoulder framings in quick succession. Their dialogue is heavy with what can never be, but equally the lost possibility that they can never forget. It ends with both of them exiting the frame, and the solitary gesture of Henri smoking and lighting a cigarette against a heavily blurred background, as Joseph Kosma's searing music swells. The content is heartbreaking enough, but it is what art historians call the "formal pathos" of the scene that clinches its immense emotion. Through all the movements (of the camera, bodies, eyes, cuts, of nature itself) that connect and disconnect this pair, a philosophical mystery is posed and exquisitely explored: how can we ever know, at any moment, the forces that will draw us together, or tear us apart?
Adrian Martin

Date 1936

Nationality France

Director Jean Renoir

Cast Georges Darnoux, Sylvia Bataille

Original Title *Partie de campagne*

Why It's Key This moment of immense pathos probes a profound philosophical mystery.

Key Event **The foundation of the Cinémathèque française**

Ernest Lindgren in the UK, Jacques Ledoux in Belgium, Iris Barry in the U.S. and Henri Langlois in France are among the founding fathers of film archives. They all shaped the art and science of collecting, preserving, and making available the moving image heritage for posterity at a time when cinema was regarded as a minor form of expression. The name of Henri Langlois is the only one familiar to the literate cinephile. Why? He wasn't the only one to promote the cause of film preservation. Filmmaker Georges Franju, film historian Jean Mitry, and Langlois are responsible for the birth of the Cinémathèque française in 1936; only the name of Langlois is now identified with the venerable institution in Paris. Why? There are many answers to these questions, but one stands out: Langlois had an uncanny talent for turning his passion into a *cause célèbre*. His genius for agitprop helped shape the *Nouvelle vague* movement and even influenced the course of the students'

protests in 1968. His connoisseurship of film earned him the attention of Iris Barry at the Museum of Modern Art, thus forging an enduring institutional bond. The way he amassed (and concealed) film prints is the stuff legends are made of. His notion of preservation was cavalier; he was possessive about the collection; his idiosyncrasies won him staunch supporters and bitter enemies. Still, no film archive ever came as close to the status of a cultural icon as the Cinémathèque française. There is a moral lesson in this.
Paolo Cherchi Usai

Date 1936

Why It's Key Preserving film became a cultural phenomenon.

Key Scene **"Never Gonna Dance"** *Swing Time*

Swing Time is a special film for many reasons, not the least being the original songs composed by Jerome Kern (composer of *Show Boat*) with lyrics by Dorothy Fields, including the Oscar-winning "The Way You Look Tonight." The comedy involving Astaire and Rogers and supporting actors Victor Moore, Helen Broderick, and Eric Blore is perfectly handled. But the climactic number, "Never Gonna Dance," is the biggest reward, and it has nothing to do with the comedy that drives the film's storyline. Instead, the song is the basis for a dramatic dance duet for Astaire and Rogers, dancing alone in a deserted nightclub. Behind the dancers is a double staircase leading up to another dance floor. As the dancers move together to Kern's beautiful melody, the camera does not simply record the dance: it gracefully moves with the dancers, back and forth, side to side, tracking and panning as they move. Then, in one of the greatest of all magic moments in cinema, the

dancers ascend the staircase, and the camera swoops up with them – an electrifying synergy of dance and camera movement. David Abel was the cinematographer, and his collaboration with director George Stevens makes this one of the best moments in the whole Astaire-Rogers oeuvre. Rarely did the directors of their musicals display such sensitivity to the movement of their dancing, or aspire to enhance it with such smoothly complementary camera movements. Legend has it that "Never Gonna Dance" took 40 takes to film, but what we see on screen is covered in only two shots: it's a seamless blending of faultless dancing and faultless camerawork.
Andrew Pike

Date 1936

Nationality USA

Director George Stevens

Cast Fred Astaire, Ginger Rogers

Why It's Key Here is one of the best dramatic dances performed by Astaire and Rogers, magnificently filmed by director George Stevens.

Key Scene **A movie projector is used to show the truth** *Fury*

For his first American film, Fritz Lang took on a very American subject – lynching. Joe (Spencer Tracy), a young man who has done well enough to marry by starting a gas station with his brothers, drives to another state to marry his fiancée (Sylvia Sidney), when he is wrongly arrested on suspicion of kidnapping. Before he can be exonerated, the town goes mad; failing to break into his cell, they burn down the jail.

Miraculously escaping, he hides out during the trial in the hope that his would-be lynchers will be executed for murder. The townspeople perjure themselves at length about each other's whereabouts, which is part of what makes the subsequent introduction of the movie projector so stunning. Suddenly we are seeing scenes of cruelty we had not seen during the actual lynching. Cinema here functions as an expander of eyesight, as a truth teller. It also functions as an intervening system beyond the will or consciousness of a single human. In this sense, it 'rhymes' with similar

moments of both truth and evil. As the lynch mob approaches the jail, for example, a high-angle camera movement in on the front of the building looks like a point-of-view shot but could not be from any one person's perspective, rendering the mob truly "beyond human." During the trial, Joe is seen in his hideout predicting the action and rejoicing, a Dr. Mabuse figure who seems to be manipulating the main action from afar. And at the end, when Joe decides to do the right thing, his march into the courtroom stops one of the defendants (Cabot) in his tracks, another case of some external element intervening on the action. Society is envisioned as a mechanism over which individuals can have very limited control.

Fred Camper

Date 1936

Nationality USA

Director Fritz Lang

Cast Walter Abel, Bruce Cabot

Why It's Key This great plot point connects with the film's whole system, which expands the frameworks of control or knowledge beyond individual characters to larger social mechanisms.

1930–1939

113

Key Scene **The spirit of the machine** *Modern Times*

Henry Ford revealed his assembly line in 1913; Charlie Chaplin revealed his in this film. A huge factory, dynamos and levers, pistons and dials everywhere, and all controlled by managers at the behest of a magnate sitting calmly in his office and watching by remote television. A principal feature is the conveyor belt, manned by, among other sad menials, The Tramp (Chaplin). He stands in overalls while widgets whiz past him, reaching out to adjust a bolt on two of them at a time with a wrench in each hand. Twist . . . retract . . . twist . . . retract . . . twist. His head beginning to swim, his eyeballs to rotate, our hero presses on, dedicated to serving his master and to the slim shreds of nobility woven into his job. But the owner is hardly satisfied to make profit when even more profit is possible. He gives the signal and the conveyor belt is speeded up. Twist, retract, twist, retract. And up and up. Twistretracttwistretracttwist. The object being manufactured is beyond this worker's

ken; his actions are purely mechanical, not only imitations of the shifts and metrical thrusts of the machines around him but, finally, machine movements in fact. He has become a part of the great machine, his body devoted and submissive to the ceaseless cycle of urgency, requirement, and satisfaction that is mechanized life.

A bell sounds and he can take a break for lunch. He sits with his bowl of steamy soup, twitching to the rhythm of the machine. As he tries to drink, the soup scatters over his neighbor and the floor. He is ashamed of his lack of control and in this modesty, this hesitation, rests the trace of his humanity.

Murray Pomerance

Date 1936

Nationality USA

Director Charles Chaplin

Cast Charles Chaplin

Why It's Key It epitomizes Chaplin's screen performance, and cinematic performance in general.

Opposite *Modern Times*

Key Scene **Who gets the dog?**
The Awful Truth

Near the start of *The Awful Truth* McCarey cuts to an insert of a toy Jerry Warriner (Grant) shows his dog, Mr. Smith (Asta, of the *Thin Man* movies). It's a tennis-size ball in the form of a Chihuahua's head with poppy eyes. Breaking into a scene that way was unusual in a Hollywood film then, but the ball gets a closeup all its own. Jerry's wife, Lucy (Dunne) throws it for Mr. Smith, who chases it.

Jerry and Lucy have decided to separate. In the next scene, divorce proceedings are ending, but the matter of who will get custody of Mr. Smith isn't settled. The judge (Stanton) orders the fox terrier into court. "Custody of the dog will depend on his own desires," he tells the couple. "Will you each call the dog?"

Jerry and Lucy position Mr. Smith between them, imploring him with here-boys and clapping. Jerry seems to be winning, so Lucy surreptitiously nods the doghead toy at Mr. Smith. He jumps in her lap.

Case closed. Now we see why McCarey highlighted the toy earlier.

Jerry and Lucy compete for Mr. Smith's attention the way Grant and Dunne compete for ours. They are so captivating that without realizing it we willingly put ourselves in the position of a dog choosing between masters. McCarey's doggie reaction shots aren't too cute; Mr. Smith doesn't cock his head or whine. He's a sober audience conned by a little trick Lucy uses to make him love her more.

A. S. Hamrah

Date 1937

Nationality USA

Director Leo McCarey

Cast Cary Grant, Irene Dunne, Asta, Paul Stanton

Why It's Key A dog's choice shows how actors compete for our affection.

114

Key Scene **News from the front**
Grand Illusion

Englishmen in drag singing "It's a Long Way to Tipperary" is not exactly what you'd expect in a French prisoner-of-war film, but this famous scene from Renoir's *Grand Illusion* achieves a resolute toughness that explains its classic status. The film breathes where other prison-camp movies stifle.

The scene begins in full-on goofiness during a prisoners' variety show. A tuxedoed prisoner named Cartier (Carette), a music-hall comic in civilian life, leads a troupe of English officers dressed as showgirls. Their performance erases the difference between the prisoners and their German guards by reminding them of the world they've left behind for the Great War's mud: the city life of women and music. As Cartier good-naturedly thumbs his nose at a guard, Renoir cuts to French prisoners Maréchal (Gabin) and Rosenthal (Dalio) backstage reading a newspaper. Maréchal takes the stage: "Stop! Stop! We've retaken Douaumont!"

One of the Englishmen removes his wig and requests that the band play the "Marseillaise." He begins to sing in his lipstick and off-the-shoulder dress. The camera pans past the musicians, including a trumpet player who rolls his eyes upward like he's trying to remember the song. Maréchal and Rosenthal, in black sweaters, look down toward the German guards. The camera follows, crossing a pillar to find the audience of prisoners on their feet, singing the anthem sternly but almost placidly. Unstructured, amateurish nonsense coalesces into meaning and beauty. The variety show's foolishness doesn't just stand in for the civilization the war leaves behind; it becomes its living proof.

A. S. Hamrah

Date 1937

Nationality France

Director Jean Renoir

Cast Jean Gabin, Marcel Dalio, Julien Carette

Original Title *La grande illusion*

Why It's Key In the midst of war, harmless antics can become a defiant stand.

Key Scene **The elderly couple say goodbye**
Make Way for Tomorrow

Pa and Ma, played by Moore and Bondi, have been married for a very long time. Now they're elderly, in financial distress, and facing the loss of their home. Their grown-up children decide they'll have to take the old folks in, but since nobody's willing to shelter both of them, the aging couple will have to stay in different households. Problems arise: The senior citizens are set in their ways, and while their offspring have good intentions, they're pursuing independent lives that don't allow much leeway for other people's quirks.

In the end it seems the parents will be separated for keeps, and from the rest of their family to boot. They say goodbye at the train station, speaking what will probably be the last words they'll ever exchange face to face. And the superbly nuanced screenplay is smart enough to make their little speeches as ordinary as they might be in real life: Statements like "It's been nice knowing you" are hardly the best memorials for a lifetime of love and togetherness, but it's the best these common folks can manage. At least their clichés don't interfere with the little dignity they have left.

Pa's train pulls out of the station, its movement subtly destabilizing the frame, as Ma watches in hapless, helpless dismay. Their kids don't feel good about all this, but hey, there's just so much they can do. Hollywood has never produced a truer take on the state of the modern American family.

David Sterritt

Date 1937

Nationality USA

Director Leo McCarey

Cast Victor Moore, Beulah Bondi

Why It's Key The conclusion of this unique comedy-drama caps what may be the most skeptical take on the American family to emerge from a Hollywood studio.

Key Scene **Yasubei's run towards the duel**
Takadanobaba Duel

Yasubei Nakayama (Bando), a masterless samurai who loves to drink and fight, is inebriated when he returns home one day to find a letter from his uncle Kayono, who had visited hoping for help in a duel against 18 men. Realizing the dire situation, Yasubei runs towards Takadanobaba. Normally, this dash would be presented in a few shots, or perhaps in parallel editing, but filmmakers in prewar Japan often showed off their directorial skill through what David Bordwell calls "flourishes," moments of stylistic excess that can be pleasurable in themselves, apart from their narrative function. One can debate how much these represented a different norm from Hollywood cinema, but Yasubei's run to the duel is one of the more delicious flourishes in Japanese film. A camera looking up at a raised road captures Yasubei and his neighbors running in a series of pans, first in long, last in medium shot. Not one, not two, but 35, all from the same camera position. It may seem like Yasubei is running over the same road, but the slight differences, coupled with the increased tempo in cutting, convey the urgency of his run and delight us with the filmmaker's stylistic audacity. It prepares us for the ensuing duel, one of the best in Japanese cinema, which itself is filmed like a dance. Hiroshi Inagaki was a master of montage, as his *The Life of Matsu the Untamed* (1943) shows, but these scenes surely come from Masahiro Makino, one of the maestros of cinematic tempo.

Aaron Gerow

Date 1937

Nationality Japan

Directors Masahiro Makino and Hiroshi Inagaki

Cast Tsumasaburo Bando

Original Title *Chikemuri Takadanobaba* (later re-released as *Ketto Takadanobaba*)

Why It's Key This is a strong example of the bravura cinematic flourishes of prewar Japanese film.

Key Scene "Rocky Dies Yellow"
Angels With Dirty Faces

SPOILER

The night before he's due to die in the electric chair, gangster Rocky Sullivan (Cagney) is visited by boyhood friend Father Jerry (O'Brien). Rocky has been convicted of the murder of a no-good, double-crossing rat (Humphrey Bogart) and is unrepentant. He promises to die the way he lived, defiantly spitting in the eye of authority, refusing to give witnesses the satisfaction of seeing him break. But Father Jerry reminds Rocky that if the slum-born teenagers who idolize him grow up to be just like him, they're likely to wind up on death row too. Rocky seems not to take this on board but, the next morning, as he is led from his cell to the chair, he cracks up – though a wink to the priest lets us know it's all an act – and has to be dragged screaming to his death. The newspaper headline cries "Rocky Dies Yellow," and, disappointed that this tough guy has proved a coward, Soapy (Billy Halop), Bim (Leo Gorcey), Patsy (Gabriel Dell), Crab (Huntz Hall), and the gang resolve to spend more time at the church-sponsored youth club preparing for honest toil than at the pool hall learning how to be flashy hoods. No one in the movies died better deaths than Cagney – a mummy delivered to his mother in *The Public Enemy* (1931), shot down on the church steps in *The Roaring Twenties* (1939), detonated atop a gasholder in *White Heat* (1949) – and this is his most elaborate, unusual exit. When he admits "I ain't so tough" as the gutshot Public Enemy, he proves he is man enough to recognize his frailty; Rocky's coward act makes him a genuine martyr, commemorated in a eulogy by the only man who knows how brave and self-sacrificing a murderer he is.

Kim Newman

Date 1938

Nationality USA

Director Michael Curtiz

Cast James Cagney, Pat O'Brien

Why It's Key It's still shocking – Cagney's screams sound so *real* – and yet a great Hollywood-schmaltz moment.

Opposite *Angels With Dirty Faces*

116

Key Event
"Box Office Poison" publicity

The Independent Exhibitors of America stunned Hollywood by placing this widely-discussed ad in movie trade papers dismissing eight notable stars as "box office deterrents." Following this public humiliation, most of those named retooled their images and achieved major artistic and popular successes within a year. Both Greta Garbo and Marlene Dietrich immediately rebounded with more user-friendly personas in two notable hits, Garbo as the Soviet commissar who melts under the ravishments of Paris in Ernst Lubitsch's *Ninotchka* (1939) and Dietrich as the feisty, brawling dance-hall floozie in George Marshall's *Destry Rides Again* (1939). Switching to a bad-girl role in George Cukor's *The Women* (1939), Joan Crawford won plaudits and soon reinvented herself at Warners, crowning her career with the iconic *Mildred Pierce*, directed by Michael Curtiz, in 1945. Katharine Hepburn retreated to Broadway, commissioning playwright Philip Barry to craft a showcase to soften and humanize her perceived abrasiveness and unseemly independence, an exercise that resulted in her greatest personal hit, first onstage and then (under Cukor's direction) onscreen, *The Philadelphia Story* (1940). Fred Astaire suffered dwindling budgets until he announced his retirement from the screen, only to be lured back for another decade of top-flight musicals, capped by Vincente Minnelli's classic *The Band Wagon* (1953). However, neither Kay Francis nor Mae West would recapture her film audience, while Edward Arnold forsook leading roles to settle into character parts.

Robert Keser

Date May 3, 1938

Why It's Key This infamous attack seemed to spell doom for eight stars' careers – a perception that most of the stars managed to refute.

Key Event **Joris Ivens gives a camera to the Yan'an Film Group**

In 1938, documentarist Joris Ivens, cinematographer John Ferno (who, the previous year, had shot Ivens's Spanish Civil War film, *The Spanish Earth*), and photographer Robert Capa went to Hankou, China, to make a film on the Sino-Japanese war. Despite constant interference from representatives of Chiang Kai-shek's Nationalist government, Ivens managed to film some battle footage. However, Ivens was prevented from completing a planned journey to the Communist base area Yan'an, where the documentarist hoped to film Mao Zedong's army. Back in Hankou, Ivens managed to elude the Nationalist minions who were keeping tabs on him and handed off his Bell & Howell Eyemo 35mm camera and some film stock to Communist cinematographer Wu Yinxian, who had shot the well-known Shanghai production *Street Angel* (1937). Though Ivens was disappointed in the footage he brought back from China to the U.S. (editor Helene Van Dongen shaped the footage into *The 400 Million*,

which was released in 1939), the camera he left behind became a precious tool for the Yan'an Film Group, enabling Wu and other filmmakers to shoot documentary footage of the Communists' resistance against Japan.
Chris Fujiwara

Date July 1938

Why It's Key Ivens's gift, evidence of a great filmmaker's idealism and perseverance, is also a symbol of cinematic solidarity.

Key Scene **The battle on the ice**
Alexander Nevsky

Although analyzed as something of a mathematical exercise by Eisenstein in his book *The Film Sense*, the battle on the ice has enormous visceral impact and stands as one of the director's most gripping achievements. As the film announces in an intertitle, the battle took place on 5 April 1242 on a frozen lake, between Russian patriots led by Prince Nevsky (Cherkasov) and invading German forces. The Germans, depersonalized in their uniform of white capes and helmets, are ultimately outflanked and defeated by the Russian hordes after a long battle – which lasts for some 30 minutes in the film. With every visual detail carefully controlled by Eisenstein, the battle was shot during a heat wave on a field covered in fake snow, with filters to make the cloudy sky look wintry. The sequence alternates between natural sound and music – some of which was composed by Prokofiev after the sequence was edited, and some edited to a pre-recorded music track. Eisenstein described at length

how Prokofiev responded to the "music" inherent in the visual dynamics, especially in the suspenseful moments before the fighting actually commenced, with the orchestra mixing sinister rumbling with dramatic staccato outbursts while the troops assemble. It's a masterful collaboration between composer and filmmaker, enriching a sequence that has influenced countless filmmakers since. The film, and especially the battle sequence, restored Eisenstein to favor in the Soviet film industry and in Stalin's eyes. Prokofiev subsequently adapted his score into a magnificent orchestral suite that is still a staple of classical symphonic orchestras in Russia and the West.
Andrew Pike

Date 1938

Nationality USSR

Director Sergei Eisenstein

Cast Nikolai Cherkasov

Original Title *Aleksandr Nevskiy*

Why It's Key This scene is a famous highlight of the superb collaboration between director Eisenstein and composer Prokofiev.

Opposite *Alexander Nevsky*

Key Scene **The song at the railroad dance**
La Bête humaine (*The Human Beast*)

As clear-eyed as anyone about life, love, and the complexities of people, Renoir transfigures Zola while providing one of the most beautiful moments, aesthetically and emotionally, in all cinema. Railroad engineer Jacques Lantier (Gabin) and Séverine (Simon) became lovers after the murder of a man by her husband, Roubaud (Fernand Ledoux), but she broke it off when Jacques proved unable to kill Roubaud and so set her free. At a railroad dance, Jacques and Séverine dance to the tune of an old popular song, and later he comes to her apartment and there, unexpectedly, strangles her. Renoir cuts at the moment of murder back to the dance hall, where a singer sings the same song, "Le petit cœur de Ninon," then cuts back to the murder scene, the song continuing over at the same volume, as we see both Severine's lifeless body and Jacques's look of desolation in the mirror. The effect is ineffable. The sentiment of the song and the lilting music transform the cinematic narrative, as Renoir brings to perfection an idea he had first tried out in *La Chienne* (1931). Instead of the response of pity and terror traditionally associated with a tragic catharsis, Renoir provokes a nostalgia for the most simple and prosaic moments of happiness that cut through the gloom of human existence, even for these ill-fated characters. Far from diminishing the tragedy, this generous and loving perspective enhances it.

Blake Lucas

Date 1938

Nationality France

Director Jean Renoir

Cast Jean Gabin, Simone Simon

Why It's Key The sensibility of Jean Renoir takes Émile Zola's novel to another level, profound in its embracing vision of life, in a justly famous sequence that juxtaposes an old popular song with a tragic murder scene.

120

Key Scene **The ending**
Masseurs and a Woman

Set at a hot-spring resort, this delicate masterpiece probes, in short vignettes dispersed in an almost plotless manner, the mystery surrounding a beautiful Tokyo woman (Takamine) who becomes suspected of a series of thefts at the inn where she is staying. Shimizu uses the figures of itinerant blind masseurs – their senses of touch, smell, and intuition sharpened by sightlessness – as manifestations of something intangible floating in the beautiful space of the film – its airy, leisurely, but nervous and excited quality. The whole film is astonishing in its freshness and its devotion to mood, but the ending is particularly remarkable. It begins with a long shot of a street in daylight, small groups of people walking, carrying umbrellas. The heroine boards the cart that will take her away from the resort and the people who have befriended her – among them, a little boy and one of the masseurs, Toku (Tokudaiji), who has become fascinated with her. As the cart leaves, the heroine looks out the window and tells the servants from the inn to say goodbye to the boy for her. Toku, in a kind of daze, runs a little way after the cart, then stops. Here Shimizu cuts to what can only be interpreted as a paradoxical subjective shot from the blind man's "point of view," a handheld shot that moves forward jerkily and turns a bend in the road to catch sight of the cart again before it disappears. The unexpected insertion of this radical shot heightens the scene's enormous sense of rupture and loss.

Chris Fujiwara

Date 1938

Nationality Japan

Director Hiroshi Shimizu

Cast Mieko Takamine, Shin Tokudaiji

Original Title *Anma to onna*

Why It's Key This amazing scene, with its paradoxical point-of-view shot, closes the film with an acute feeling of loss.

Key Event **First meeting between Michael Powell and Emeric Pressburger**

It happened in the office of London Film's head, Alexander Korda, at Denham. Korda had assigned Emeric Pressburger, a fellow Hungarian, to write yet another treatment for *The Spy in Black*, which was to be a vehicle for actor Conrad Veidt. Director Michael Powell happened to be present when Pressburger presented his ideas. Powell and Korda were enthusiastic, and Korda immediately assigned the pair to what was to be their first collaboration.

This collaboration resulted in 18 feature films on which both men, or Powell alone, are credited as director. In the sense that conventional narrative provided the pretext rather than the *raison d'être*, the majority of their films could be described as experimental, even oppositional. The pair nevertheless had access to substantial resources within the industry and made films that were popular with audiences – if not always with a British critical establishment wedded to a certain concept of realism. Often seen at the time as eccentric, their hybrids of disparate genres and styles have become an inspiration to many, including Martin Scorsese and Francis Ford Coppola.

Their productions were driven by Powell's creative passion and his ability to assemble and orchestrate the skills of a range of exceptional talent and by Pressburger's complex imagination as a writer. The Archers, as they called their production company, was a collaboration in the fullest sense of the word, not a "partnership" (which might suggest a division of functions), but a true synthesis of kindred spirits.
Bruce Hodsdon

Date Late July 1938

Why it's Key This is the beginning of what still remains the most significant creative collaboration in British cinema history.

Key Scene **Tycoon meets jobless working girl in Central Park Zoo** *5th Ave Girl*

Mostly remembered for *My Man Godfrey* (1936) and *Stage Door* (1937), La Cava directed (and often co-wrote, uncredited) a number of other highly original comedies, like this one. The film's premise is quite similar to *My Man Godfrey*'s: working-class victim of Great Depression penetrates wealthy New York family and changes its life and outlooks. In the opening scene, the owner of Amalgamated Pump (Connolly) is informed by his associates that the company is on the brink of bankrupcy. Despondent, he goes back home to his Fifth Avenue mansion, but although it's his birthday, neither his wife (who spends most of her time with a gigolo) nor his spoiled-rotten children are around. His butler suggests a walk in the park, as it's a nice early-spring day. So the tycoon walks over to the Central Park Zoo and finds himself watching the seals in-between a loquacious know-it-all gentleman and a tight-lipped young woman with a knack for quietly deadpan cynical repartee. She moves to a bench to eat her apple, and the industrialist engages her in a conversation. He (feeding the pigeons): "Friendly little fellows!" She (matter-of-factly): "They're just hungry." He: "You're on a diet?" She: "Yes, but against my will" (it transpires that she is out of work and has only five dollars left). "I could jump in the seals' pool, maybe someone would throw me a fish." Connolly introduces himself. He: "Have you heard of Amalgamated Pump?" She: "What kind of pump?" He invites her to dinner in a fancy restaurant.

This is the most innocent and charming pickup scene on record, with La Cava unobtrusively framing the unlikely couple in long two-shots, and Rogers superbly underplaying, with a world-weary, slightly squinting gaze into the camera.
Jean-Pierre Coursodon

Date 1939

Nationality USA

Director Gregory La Cava

Cast Ginger Rogers, Walter Connolly

Why It's Key This scene shows La Cava's sly sense of humor at its best.

Key Scene **"Over the Rainbow"**
The Wizard of Oz

When MGM's super-production of *The Wizard of Oz* was first previewed, there was a general sense at the studio that the film was way too long – it swiftly lost a whole number ("The Jitterbug") and a couple of dances/reprises (which is why it's a rare musical in which all the songs are front-loaded in the first half of the film). MGM executives at first insisted Judy Garland's "Over the Rainbow" go. They felt audiences would be impatient to get out of black and white Kansas and into the colors of Oz, and that (per "Sticks Nix Hick Pix") no one went to the movies to look at a girl sing in a farmyard. Wiser heads prevailed, and the most achingly lovely song performance in Hollywood history remained in the picture.

"Over the Rainbow" went on to win the Best Original Song Oscar for Harold Arlen and E.Y. Harburg and remained Garland's signature tune for the rest of her career. Without "Over the Rainbow," *The Wizard of Oz* would be just a madcap fantasy comedy; with it, the film is a multi-leveled masterpiece as melancholy as it is joyous.

Kim Newman

Date 1939

Nationality USA

Director King Vidor (uncredited; Victor Fleming, the credited director, had already been reassigned to *Gone with the Wind* when this scene was shot)

Cast Judy Garland

Why It's Key This is one of the greatest song performances in the history of cinema.

Opposite *The Wizard of Oz*

Key Scene **Among the wounded**
Gone With the Wind

For a big picture that covers decades of the Civil War and the Reconstruction era, *Gone With the Wind* is surprisingly short on spectacle. Margaret Mitchell's plot is more concerned with the romantic travails of Scarlett, Rhett, and the rest than the big battles or even the sweep of history. Indeed, outside of the famous burning of Atlanta, it's a film where much of the "action" – Leslie Howard's night-riding raids with the Ku Klux Klan, even the deaths of major characters – takes place off-screen. Nevertheless, it persists in the memory as a "big" picture as much as a "long" one – almost entirely because of a single crane shot orchestrated by special effects man William Cameron Menzies and devised (without credit) by producer's assistant Val Lewton (later of RKO horror film fame). Scarlett O'Hara (Leigh) searches for Dr. Meade (Harry Davenport) among a crowd of 16,000 wounded Confederate soldiers, and realises (as do we) the extent of the suffering caused by the war she has previously taken almost lightly. Eight hundred extras, augmented by 800 dummies, are on screen as the camera pulls back and up to take in an acre of open-air hospital from a godlike vantage. When *Gone With the Wind* was re-released in the 1950s in a "widescreen" version, there were actually fewer wounded men on display – the top and bottom of the standard-frame original were trimmed in order to make the film bigger lengthwise.

Kim Newman

Date 1939

Nationality USA

Director Victor Fleming

Cast Vivien Leigh

Why It's Key It still conveys the dreadful price paid by common soldiers in wartime.

Key Speech **The filibuster**
Mr. Smith Goes to Washington

The filibuster at the end of *Mr. Smith Goes to Washington* not only defined James Stewart's screen persona; it helped define how Americans would see themselves – and be seen by others – in the postwar era. His Mr. Smith is the quintessential American hero: boyish and energetic, naïve and idealistic. An innocent thrust into politics by a corrupt political machine that thinks he will be easy to manipulate, he is nearly destroyed as he fights what seems to be a losing battle. At the time of its release, many attacked the film as unpatriotic for its depiction of rampant corruption in Washington, and though Frank Capra's films are now often dismissed by many critics as corny and overly simplistic, those critics fail to see how subversive and dark his portrayals of American life are. As the patron saint of lost causes, Stewart, his boyish face covered with a mossy growth of beard and his voice shredded to a rasp (Stewart reportedly had a doctor treat his vocal chords with dichloride of mercury), embodies the homegrown myth that anyone has the power to transform the world around him. There is something almost frighteningly crazed about his desperation as his ideals confront reality, which would be pushed further in *It's a Wonderful Life* (1946) in his mad dash around Pottersville. In Stewart's eyes we can see reflected the zeal of the true believer – a zeal that would lead to such future American debacles as Vietnam and Iraq.

Al Weisel

Date 1939

Nationality USA

Director Frank Capra

Cast James Stewart

Why It's Key In his crazed, desperate zeal, James Stewart's Mr. Smith represented the dark side of American idealism.

1930–1939

Opposite *Mr. Smith Goes to Washington*

125

Key Speech **The hat in the window**
Ninotchka

SPOILER

In 1939 Shirley Temple, age 11, was tops at the box office. Glamorous stars like Greta Garbo were considered unwholesome. The year before, *The Hollywood Reporter* had declared her "box office poison." But Garbo laughed in *Ninotchka*, and America went through a spell of adulthood that lasted until *Gone with the Wind* came out – about two months.

We meet Nina Ivanovna Yakushova (Garbo), special envoy from Moscow, on a Paris train platform. She wears a plain suit, a hat with the brim down, and men's shoes. When a porter (Davis) explains it's his business to carry her bags, she tells him, "That's no business. That's *social injustice*." Three comrades (Bressart, Ruman, and Granach) take her to her hotel room, passing a fancy hat shop in the lobby. She looks in the window: "What is that?" "A woman's hat," answers one of the Russians. "How can such a civilization survive which permits their women to put things like that on their heads? It won't be long now, comrades," she says, raising an eyebrow at the doomed frivolity of the capitalist West.

Lubitsch predicts the history of communism in the story of this hat. Ninotchka shakes her head at it a second time before we meet it again as she takes it out of a locked drawer to wear on a date with a handsome Frenchman (Douglas). This is the cinema's lightest and sharpest appraisal of communism. Only Lubitsch would have the nonchalance to reject it for making an omelet fall.

A. S. Hamrah

Date 1939

Nationality USA

Director Ernst Lubitsch

Cast Greta Garbo, Melvyn Douglas, Felix Bressart, Sig Ruman, Alexander Granach, George Davis

Why It's Key Garbo scoffs.

Key Scene "The Kid" takes off
Only Angels Have Wings

Hawks is rightly famous for serio-comic genre gems that deploy a closed male group to probe notions of professionalism, courage, honor, and responsibility. This movie about a motley crew of expat American fliers regularly risking their lives over the Andes is one of the most enduringly enjoyable, despite the near-risible costume – broad-brimmed white hat, bullet-belt, and armpit-hugging slacks – paraded by Geoff Carter (Grant), the forever beleaguered but stoic freight-airline boss holding things together notwithstanding fragile crates, terrible weather, ailing pilots, and a couple of doting dames. Given his need to keep his partner Dutchy (Sig Ruman) in business and his own fingers from getting romantically burnt – those chorus girls! – nothing can dent Carter's cynical facade…

Except there's best friend "the Kid" (Mitchell), almost as devoted to the perilous pleasures of aviation as he is to Geoff, and therefore knocked sideways when failing sight grounds him. A final flight results in a broken neck; bluntly/gently told how things stand by Geoff, the Kid tells him all other witnesses to his imminent demise must leave the hangar; Poppa Carter fixes that, offers a last drag on a cigarette, and discreetly departs, knowing how important it is to undertake a solo flight without observers… Hawks never overplays the metaphor, but intuitively grasps the effectiveness of subdued performance, lighting, music and terse dialogue in supplying a subtext that is at once deeply touching and, in its own way, existentially profound. (An earlier scene, centred on the line "Who's Joe?" and the eating of spare steak cooked for a dead pilot, is nearly as affecting, but not quite.)

Geoff Andrew

Date 1939
Nationality USA
Director Howard Hawks
Cast Cary Grant, Thomas Mitchell, Jean Arthur
Why It's Key Laconic understatement guarantees emotional and philosophical depth to a rousing aerial adventure that might otherwise seem absurdly romantic.

126

Key Speech "Everyone has his reasons"
Rules of the Game

The fact that Octave, the character who proclaims early in Renoir's classic that "everyone has his reasons," is played by the director himself has doubtless led to the somewhat misleading assumption that this sentiment represents the director's credo. Commentators frequently divorce Octave's assertion from its narrative context and point to it as a concise summation of what is often labeled – somewhat amorphously – as Renoir's "humanism." To start with, it's easy to forget the longer version of this musing by this philosophical outsider: "the terrible thing about this world is that everyone has his reasons." In addition, this *bon mot* is not uttered from a completely detached perspective – it is partially Octave's ruse to convince his friend Robert (Dalio) to invite Octave's aviator pal (and Robert's wife's lover) to his country estate. This adulterous interlude takes on ominous consequences by the end of Renoir's melancholy comedy. A seemingly light-hearted tale inspired by Alfred de Musset begins to resemble a socially conscious warning about the reactionary frivolity of the idle rich at a time when France found itself on the verge of war. In truth, however, the magnanimous observation that "everyone has its reasons" exemplifies the "rich ambiguity" Robin Wood locates in a film that can be viewed as, alternately, a "virulent social satire" or a straightforward reflection of the director's admission that he loved his characters and "would have loved to live in that world." If we consider Octave's speech as a corollary to the internal "tensions" Wood analyzes, it can be deemed both heartfelt and aligned with a distinctively Renoiresque "humanism"– as well as an ironic commentary on the self-absorption and pettiness of his shallow, if occasionally endearing, protagonists.

Richard Porton

Date 1939
Nationality France
Director Jean Renoir
Cast Marcel Dalio, Jean Renoir
Original Title *La règle du jeu*
Why It's Key The most frequently cited speech from Renoir's masterpiece provides a concise summation of its narrative and thematic intricacies.

Key Scene **The last of Eddie**
The Roaring Twenties

In the last scene of *The Roaring Twenties*, when ex-bootlegger Eddie Bartlett (Cagney) has just given up the ghost, his long time friend Panama Smith (George) declares to the police officer who questions her, "He used to be a big shot." Like the controversial gangster films of the early thirties such as William Wellman's *The Public Enemy* (1931), which made Cagney famous, Raoul Walsh's picture offers a rise-and-fall narrative that suggests a parody of Horatio Alger's novels. However, unlike the earlier films, *The Roaring Twenties* presents a fall that doesn't coincide with the moment of death. If Eddie has become a nobody after the 1929 crash and the loss of his love, if he is gunned down in the middle of the street, his death isn't entirely wretched. Eddie seems to be redeemed by the self-sacrifice he has just committed (he has killed an ex-associate in order to help the woman he loved), and the last shots of the film introduce a religious dimension. Not only does the gangster collapse on the steps leading to a church in the pure white snow of New Year's Eve (and not in the gutter like his cinematic predecessors), but he is shown as a Christ-like figure: Panama takes him on her lap, and the couple form a Pietà. On the other hand, it could be argued that, since Cagney's character doesn't succeed in entering the sacred place, he is stopped on his way to redemption. Either way, it's a good example of Hollywood tempering the gangster genre with a resort to moral values.

Frank Lafond

Date 1939

Nationality USA

Director Raoul Walsh

Cast James Cagney, Gladys George

Why It's Key It's one of the most memorable endings in cinema history.

Key Scene **The Ann Rutledge scene**
Young Mr. Lincoln

The scene opens with Lincoln (Fonda) sitting beneath a tree in a bucolic setting, reading Blackstone's *Commentaries on the Laws of England*, a basic text published in the 1750s (Abe got it from a barrelful of old books a family of pioneers gave him in payment). Lincoln reads aloud passages, then Ann Rutledge (Moore) appears. As they walk along the river, their conversation about Lincoln's readings and interests (poetry, Shakespeare, the law…) grows romantic when he tells her how beautiful she looks…. Before she leaves, she encourages him to become a lawyer. Lincoln, now alone, throws a stone in the river.

The gesture, dramatically and diegetically pointless, even "meaningless," becomes meaningful as the ripples in the water dissolve into a shot of ice floes on the same river, connoting the passing of time. Indeed, this second scene by the river makes it possible to grasp the full meaning and importance of the encounter with Ann. For we discover that Ann has died, and Lincoln has brought some flowers to her grave, which – improbably but most romantically – happens to be located at the very same place where they had first met. The protagonist's soliloquy on the grave of the dear departed – a standard Ford scene, used earlier in *Judge Priest* (1934) and later again in *She Wore a Yellow Ribbon* (1949) – ends with his decision (playfully disguised as a tossup) to follow Ann's advice and practice law. Their encounter and Lincoln's destiny are thus indissolubly linked.

Jean-Pierre Coursodon

Date 1939

Nationality USA

Director John Ford

Cast Henry Fonda, Pauline Moore

Why It's Key This is a crucial moment in both the Lincoln legend and Ford's version of it, bringing together closely related themes: Lincoln's first (and, supposedly, only true) love and his love for the law, in the context of his love of nature.

Key Film *The Shop Around the Corner*
"Ochi chornie" cigarette boxes

The classic American cinema had depth and charm, and in some special cases it had both. *The Shop Around the Corner* shows this in every way but perhaps especially in the way comedy and drama so perfectly dovetail within a tightly-knit narrative. The whole film involves the Budapest shop Matuschek and Company and the interaction of the people who work there, and most of the story plays fluidly within the interiors of the shop. Within this framework, Lubitsch and his great screenwriter Samson Raphaelson develop the delightful tension of the main romance between Alfred (Stewart) and Klara (Sullavan) against the betrayal of the owner Matuschek (Morgan) by his never-seen wife. These threads are tied together most brilliantly in the cigarette boxes that play the tune "Ochi chornie" – Klara gets a job by selling one in her first, very amusing scene, but no others sell even on markdown, and late in the film, when Vadas (Schildkraut) is revealed to be Mrs. Matuschek's

seducer, Alfred (who had been wrongly suspected) pushes him against the boxes, which all fall to the floor with him and begin playing the tune in a momentarily striking, delicate disharmony, allowing the soundtrack along with the image to punctuate this turning point with stunning effect. The comic touch of the boxes has become, without the least show of effort, the film's most dramatic one as well, while also underscoring the subtly musical quality of the whole.
Blake Lucas

Date 1940

Nationality USA

Director Ernst Lubitsch

Cast Margaret Sullavan, James Stewart, Frank Morgan, Joseph Schildkraut, Felix Bressart, Sara Haden, Inez Courtney, William Tracy, Charles Smith

Why It's Key Lubitsch and company provide the model for playing in complementary registers throughout a film, always keeping comedy and drama in perfect balance.

Key Scene **The arrest of Earl Williams**
His Girl Friday

We're in the press room of the Criminal Courts building of a major American city. Newspaper editor Walter Burns (Grant) and his ace reporter, Hildy Johnson (Russell), have just had an exclusive fall in their lap: convicted murderer Earl Williams (Qualen), after escaping from death row, has picked the press room to hide in; Burns gives Earl a hand by hiding him in a rolltop desk. Soon the police and some other reporters converge on the room, and during a heated confrontation, Burns inadvertently gives the game away by banging his fist on the desk – whereupon, in response to what he thinks is the signal Burns and he have prearranged, Earl bangs back from the inside. The police draw their guns, the reporters phone-in tense blow-by-blows to their editorial desks – and the series of short shots culminates when the desk opens up to reveal the listless, confused Earl (a "mock turtle," Burns called him earlier) saying: "Go ahead, shoot me."

In the middle of this fast-paced comedy about sharpies, Hawks gives the figure of the bewildered outsider Earl a measure of discreet pathos and the rare tribute of a forward tracking shot (when the desk is opened). This great scene also contains a magnificent, thrown-away, typically Hawksian shot in which two other outsiders, Hildy's unwanted fiance (Bellamy) and the latter's indignant mother (Kruger), are ejected for good from both the scene and the narrative by a door that shuts them away from the camera just as they are reunited in the corridor.
Chris Fujiwara

Date 1940

Nationality USA

Director Howard Hawks

Cast Cary Grant, Rosalind Russell, John Qualen, Gene Lockhart, Porter Hall, Roscoe Karns, Frank Jenks, Regis Toomey, Cliff Edwards, Ralph Bellamy, Alma Kruger

Why It's Key It's Hawks at his most laconic and most eloquent.

Opposite *His Girl Friday*

Key Person **Bugs Bunny**
A Wild Hare

A rabbit often referred to – for punning purposes – as a hare in the titles of the Warner Bros. cartoons in which he starred, Bugs Bunny is the most charismatic and beloved character in the entire animated universe. Although he had made earlier appearances in the Porky Pig vehicle *Porky's Hare Hunt* (1938), in *Hare-um Scare-um* (1939), both by Ben Hardaway, and, just a few months before the release of *A Wild Hare*, in Charles M. Jones's *Elmer's Candid Camera* (the first pairing of Bugs with the most inept wabbit hunter in the world, although in that one Elmer was only shooting pictures), Bugs acquired his final personality and style in Avery's Oscar-nominated entry. Hardaway's Bugs was more aggressive and mischievous than the one most viewers are familiar with, not unlike Woody Woodpecker (another Hardaway creation). Jones's version provides the evolutionary link between Hardaway's Bugs and Avery's. Credit where credit is due: Avery even gives his own variation on the scene from *Elmer's Candid Camera* in which Bugs, pretending to be dying, does a takeoff on classic movie death scenes.

Avery's Bugs is the epitome of cool, a master of sly irony and false innocence. He is so laid back in *A Wild Hare* that he obligingly gives Elmer tips on how best to shoot him dead. Elmer is so clueless that although he is hunting rabbit he doesn't know what a rabbit looks like, and Bugs has to describe it to him, finally revealing: "Confidentially, I am a rabbit!" Clearly, Bugs knows that he has nothing to fear from this "screwy guy."

Jean-Pierre Coursodon

Date 1940

Nationality USA

Director Fred (Tex) Avery

Cast Bugs Bunny, Elmer Fudd

Why It's Key Jerry Beck and Will Friedwald said it best in their *Guide to the Warner Bros. Cartoons*: "The classic cartoon that solidified the personalities of Bugs Bunny and Elmer Fudd and became the blueprint for their future encounters." Better yet, the film contains the first utterance of the famous line: "What's Up, Doc?"

Key Scene **Objects and shadows express transcendent vision** *The Mortal Storm*

SPOILER

Near the end of this early and brave engagement with Nazism, Eric (Stack), a young man who had become a Nazi, returns to the family home. He has realized, finally, the error of his ways, and as he walks through the house alone, the camera pans the objects there to come to rest on each's shadow, as we hear the memories summoned up by each object on the sound track. This scene is a key not only to the film but to Borzage's whole vision. Our attachment to specific objects and specific symbols is a sign of an excess of ego; for Borzage, truth can only be found when we leave materiality behind. It is only in the shadows of things, which stand here for the traces they leave in our memories, their spiritual essences, that we can find understanding. The young Eric, who had instead been attached to the rules of the party and the symbol of the swastika, now finally sees past the material world, to the way shadows, much more than physical objects or appearances, can evoke the essences of others. This long take also seems to take apart some of the film's earlier geographical conceits – looking across the mountains to trap a fleeing woman – by suggesting that such crudely physical notions, while they may lead to physical death, tell us nothing. When Eric leaves, the film ends with a sublime dissolve, in which the footprints his feet have left in the snow leading up to the front door seem to become covered over, a reference to the way nature and time obliterate individual identity – while leaving unseeable spiritual essences, the shadows, in our hearts.

Fred Camper

Date 1940

Nationality USA

Director Frank Borzage

Cast Robert Stack

Why It's Key Borzage invokes his belief in the transcendent power of the spirit in the face of the brutal physicality of Nazism.

Key Scene **The end credits**
Citizen Kane

"I've got his trunk all packed. I've had it packed for a week now." One of the first lines we hear in the end-credits sequence of *Citizen Kane* is a callback to the moment it was first uttered. Like the other callbacks in this grand finale – designed as kind of curtain-call-cum-introduction to the film's cast, "The Mercury Players" – it has both a particular purpose and a special poignancy. *Citizen Kane* is in many ways a series of inventories – a feature-length stock-taking of a man's life. The "News on the March" newsreel is the first of these, and subsequent interviews made with the people who knew Kane either well (Joseph Cotten's Jed Leland, Dorothy Comingore's Susan Alexander) or not at all (Paul Stewart's Raymond the butler, George Coulouris's Mr. Thatcher) fill in the blanks. Supposedly we're looking for the meaning of "Rosebud," Kane's dying word. And we learn it has a connection to his childhood and his mother – thus the special poignancy of Moorehead's delivery. But in the end it's the

uncomprehending Thatcher who speaks both for Kane and his creator, Welles, with the film's *real* last line: "I think it would be fun to run a newspaper!" It was the encyclopedic nature of the film that doubtless impressed Jorge Luis Borges, who called *Kane* a film that "teems with multiplicity and incongruity." And never more so than in its final moments.

David Ehrenstein

Date 1941

Nationality USA

Director Orson Welles

Cast Joseph Cotten, Dorothy Comingore, Agnes Moorehead, Ruth Warrick, Ray Collins, Erskine Sanford, Everett Sloane, William Alland, Paul Stewart, George Coulouris

Why It's Key The true end of *Kane*, this final accounting of the story reconfigures the cinema itself as a *catalogue raisonné*.

Key Scene **The film screening**
Sullivan's Travels

Sturges's celebrated satire of Hollywood mores mixes genres with astonishing finesse: rollicking screwball comedy, social commentary, and melodramatic pathos all coalesce in one of the most entertaining films of the Forties. The cockeyed journey Hollywood director John L. Sullivan (McCrea) makes before arriving, as a member of a chain gang, at a black church's movie screening constitutes a gently satiric indictment of guilty limousine liberals. Disgusted with making escapist comedies, Sullivan impersonates a hobo and, through a case of mistaken identity, is accused of murder and ends up on a prison farm in the Deep South. The uproarious laughter inspired by the church screening of a cartoon convinces him that commercial entertainment can allow the poor and oppressed to forget their misery for a short period and should not be condemned as empty frivolity.

It almost goes without saying that Sulllivan's epiphany spawned a host of contradictory interpretations – many of them quite critical of Sturges

and his presumed artistic and political agenda. For some critics, the pro-Hollywood message promoted by the chain gang screening is nothing more than a director justifying his own work while dismissing socially conscious movies such as *I Am a Fugitive From a Chain Gang* (1932) and *The Grapes of Wrath* (1940). Others view this scene's implications as straightforwardly conservative – and it is true that the film appeared on *National Review*'s 1996 list of the "100 Best Conservative Movies." Yet categorizing Sturges's stance as unabashedly conservative is surely simplistic. While he is loath to condemn Hollywood entertainment with moralistic bromides, the scenes he includes in the film *leading up* to the chain gang screening are actually examples of the socially conscious filmmaking he appears to sneer at subsequently. The film *in toto* is an example of both the "deep dish" filmmaking it lampoons and a superb diversion.

Richard Porton

Date 1941

Nationality USA

Director Preston Sturges

Cast Joel McCrea

Why It's Key One of the most famous scenes in Sturges's beloved comedy reveals myriad political ambiguities.

Key Scene **Eve reveals her "past"**
The Lady Eve

Jean Harrington (Stanwyck), glamorous con artist, grabs the attention of Charles Pike (Fonda), bashful heir to an ale fortune, by sticking out a luscious leg and tripping him. Many plot twists later, she's furious with him and planning a complicated revenge: She'll snare him all over again, masquerading as an English aristocrat named Eve, and when he's fallen head over heels, she'll mercilessly burst his romantic bubble. The scheme proceeds, and soon they're newlyweds starting their honeymoon on a speeding train. So she springs the trap, letting slip a not-so-casual remark that prompts a question from Charles, which leads to another "casual" remark, and another question, and… all calculated to reveal an astonishing number of affairs "Eve" racked up before Charles met her. Charles forgives her indiscretions, of course, and forgives them again and again – but the lady's past grows more unsavory by the second, and eventually he just can't take it anymore. Leaving the train at a tiny whistle stop in the pouring rain, he steps into the muddy mess underfoot and slides full-length into the muck – a rueful echo of the tumble he took over Jean's shapely leg, and one of the most poignant pratfalls ever filmed.

Comedy took a major turn in the 1940s, using dialogue in ways more sophisticated than most filmmakers could manage in the 1930s, when sound cinema was still new. Sturges was a leader in this happy development, and no movie better shows why than *The Lady Eve*.

David Sterritt

Date 1941

Nationality USA

Director Preston Sturges

Cast Barbara Stanwyck, Henry Fonda

Why It's Key Combining uproarious humor with genuine pathos, this bittersweet scene crystallizes Sturges's brilliance as a screenwriter and director, and thus the finest qualities of Hollywood comedy in the 1940s.

Opposite *The Lady Eve*

Key Event **Japanese government declares "not one foot of film for the industry"**

It was a hot, humid day when Ryuzo Kawamo, chief of Section Five in the Information Bureau, told the heads of the major studios that the government had not one foot of film left to give the private industry. Japan was already at war in China and was almost totally reliant on foreign film stock, but this declaration was more a threat than a statement of fact. The government had decided to take advantage of its authority under various statutes, especially the Film Law of 1939, and use its control over raw materials to force a reorganization of the industry and establish state authority over film. By September, an agreement was ironed out between bureaucrats and the industry to institute limits on the number and length of films that could be made and reduce the number of fiction-film studios from ten to three, and the number of other producers from several hundred to one. It was easier to manage the content of films if the industry was leaner and producing fewer films, but bureaucrats were also aiming to modernize a business that was known for its inefficiencies and over-production. The effects of this reorganization would continue even after the war, as it forged a film industry that would shape the golden age of Japanese cinema in the 1950s, especially creating a new studio, Daiei, that would produce the films – such as Akira Kurosawa's *Rashomon* (1950) and Kenji Mizoguchi's *Ugetsu* (1953) – that established Japan's presence on the global film scene.

Aaron Gerow

Date August 16, 1941

Why It's Key This move increased government control over film and transformed the movie industry.

Key Scene **The opening sequence**
Hellzapoppin'

A crude, raucous, yet strangely arresting attempt at giving a filmic equivalent to a Broadway hit that was intent on erasing the boundary between stage and audience, *Hellzapoppin'* comes across as a dizzying Russian-dolls game of film-within-film-within-film in which the action keeps spilling into the movie theatre and engaging the spectators. Auto-referential to the hilt and diegetically mind-boggling, the opening sequence takes us from a projection booth into the projected film (dancing girls suddenly slide down into "Hell" as the credits roll) which is itself about the filming of *Hellzapoppin'*: in a slapstick Dante's inferno where taxicabs explode and devils spit-roast pretty girls over a blazing fire, Olsen and Johnson, the creators and stars of the Broadway show, barge in and wreak havoc until the director pointedly complains that nothing going on makes any sense. An argument among the two stars, the director, and the screenwriter ensues. Unintentionally auto-critical (since his remark actually points to one of the film's weaknesses), the director reminds the comics that you must have a love story in a Hollywood movie. The writer starts telling the plot. The director tacks an eight-by-ten glossy on a wall: it's a still of the action he is planning to shoot. The still becomes animated, and here are Olsen and Johnson in a truck delivering props for a stage show (*Hellzapoppin'*, of course). "What are we doing there?" asks Olsen, pointing at himself on the wall. The characters on the wall start talking with the ones in the studio, explaining the plot. Then we enter the picture and the story proper… such as it is.

Jean-Pierre Coursodon

Date 1941

Nationality USA

Director H.C. Potter

Cast Ole Olsen, Chic Johnson, Martha Raye

Why It's Key It's the ultimate in self-referential shenanigans.

Key Scene **The dead stay alive in memory**
How Green Was My Valley

SPOILER

Towards the ending of this elegiac chronicle of how a formerly green Welsh valley turned black before the coal mines became unprofitable and were shut down, the invisible protagonist, Huw Morgan (the voice of Pichel as a man, represented by McDowall as a child, in the flashback), takes his leave from it and recalls the gradual disintegration of his family. There's an accident at the mine shaft. Huw's mother (Allgood) has a set face, fearing the worst, which is about to happen: Huw reaches his trapped father (Crisp) only to see him expire. The lift unearths the corpses and a few haggard survivors. It is a moment which, in another director's hands, would have been only very sad. With Ford, however, the sadness of an unhappy ending is more poignant still, because there is something in him that does not accept death as final. "Men like my father cannot die…," claims the older Huw, now leaving his home village for good – "How green was my valley then!", while the main characters of the film reappear at their moments of joy, youth and happiness, now gone overseas or dead but kept alive in his recollections. That's why Ford's characters go to graveyards and talk to their departed.

Miguel Marías

Date 1941

Nationality USA

Director John Ford

Cast Roddy McDowall, Donald Crisp, Walter Pidgeon, Sara Allgood, Rhys Williams, Barry Fitzgerald, Maureen O'Hara, Anna Lee, Irving Pichel (voice)

Why It's Key This scene, so characteristically John Ford's, embodies this filmmaker's unequalled ability to preserve the past and find in memories a sort of vindication of the defeated.

Key Speech **"Open up the door, Schnitzel!"**
Blitz Wolf

One of the great pleasures of Hollywood's studio system was an alchemy that allowed for telling stories in a compact manner. In these days of overinflated cinematic output, even the most humble average-to-good 1930s Warner Bros. programmer seems to zip by with a density, wit, and pace that suggest a 70-minute-demonstration of some forgotten, mysterious science. Yet it would look unwieldy compared to your average Warners cartoon. On the basis of compression and speed, the short, anarchic, surreal Looney Tunes animations may be the greatest achievement in 20th-century cinema, both epic catalogue and knowing parody of film's possibilities at the height of the studio era. Key Warners cartoonist Tex Avery left for MGM in 1942, but he certainly wasn't softened by higher budgets: his work there rivals his best at his old studio, as is sufficiently proven by his debut, *Blitz Wolf*, alone. *Three Little Pigs* with Adolf Hitler in the guise of

Avery's preferred lead – the howling wolf, it seems to contain everything and its opposite in nine minutes, including Avery's reliably relentless and reckless punning (the wolf arrives in a car labelled "Der Fewer, Der Better"). Indeed, the opening anti-disclaimer about intended similarities with "that *!!&% jerk Hitler" is immediately followed by a disclaimer about the picture's fictitious car tires. There are even subtitles when the wolf threatens to huff and puff in hilariously garbled German – but they are unnecessary, thanks to the wolf's accented, but perfectly clear enunciation: "Open up the door, Schnitzel!"
Christoph Huber

Date 1942

Nationality USA

Director Tex Avery

Why It's Key When key cartoonist Tex Avery left Warner Bros. for MGM, he sure didn't slow down on gags – down to the last subtitle.

Key Scene **The cornered pheasant's death**
Bambi

SPOILER

Judging from the clips that pop up in "favorite moments" retrospectives, *Bambi* is remembered as an intravenous saccharine drip of a film, 70 minutes of near-lethal neoteny punctuated with wobbly fauns on ice, sassy bunnies, and "Oh, that's all right – he can call me Flower . . . if he *wants* to." But it isn't fair to dismiss Bambi as a pasteurized retread of nature's tooth and claw. When the adolescent Bambi (voiced by Hardie Albright) fights a rival buck for the right to mate with pretty doe Faline (Cammie King), the scene is rendered in dramatic scarlets and cobalt blues, implied sex and violence merging in expressionistic strokes. (Are there any other characters in the Disney pantheon who go through puberty, getting – quite literally in Bambi's case – horny?) Those who explicitly describe the murder of Bambi's mother are confusing her restrained off-screen demise with the holocaustic siege on the forest by hunters, dogs, and fire at the movie's end. The terror and helplessness of the animals are encapsulated in a

brief scene of three pheasants cowering in the tall grass. "He's coming closer!" one whispers hoarsely. "Be calm, don't get excited," another pleads. "Don't fly. Whatever you do, don't fly!" But the desperate pheasant does fly, essentially choosing death in the kind of Faustian bind unseen in children's films. We're not even spared the sight of her suddenly lifeless body tumbling to the ground. Anyone who describes the sentimentalizing of nature as "bambification" only proves they haven't seen the film.
Violet Glaze

Date 1942

Nationality USA

Director David Hand

Cast Peter Behn, Stan Alexander, Donnie Dunagan, Paula Winslow, Thelma Hubbard

Why It's Key It highlights the emotional depth of a movie commonly regarded as just cute.

Key Scene **The bus**
Cat People

In one of the stand-out sequences of *Cat People*, Alice (Randolph) walks through Central Park and becomes spooked. Irena (Simone Simon), jealous of Alice's closeness with her husband, is in pursuit – and might well transform into a murderous black leopard. The punchline of this masterfully orchestrated crescendo of suspense comes when Alice leaves the park for the safety of the street – a sudden hissing noise and a shape lurching into frame. The hiss isn't the cat creature, but the air-brakes of a prosaic New York City bus, and there's no menace behind the scare. The tactic of building up tension, then paying off with an unexpected jolt that makes the on-screen characters (and the audience) jump, had been used before in horror films (in Tod Browning's *Mark of the Vampire* [1935], for instance), but producer Val Lewton and director Jacques Tourneur made a habit of it. When the trick was used in later Lewton productions (a snorting horse in *The Body Snatcher* [1945]), he referred to it as a "bus," and the usage has entered the filmmaking lexicon. John Carpenter's *Halloween* (1976) is almost entirely structured around "buses" (the broken pipe that breaks a window, etc). Seemingly every stalk-and-slash picture is obliged to include a bit in which a girl creeping terrified through the dark is given a fright (ironically, given the narrative circumstances of *Cat People*) by a harmless but hissy cat before the knife-wielding killer pounces for real.

Kim Newman

Date 1942

Nationality USA

Director Jacques Tourneur

Cast Jane Randolph

Why It's Key Not only did this moment make audiences jump in 1942, but it gave a name to a tactic still in use in horror.

Key Person **James Agee starts writing a film column for *The Nation***

By the time James Agee's first film column for *The Nation* appeared on December 26, 1942, he had already been reviewing movies for a year at *Time*. Yet, despite *The Nation*'s much smaller readership, Agee's reputation as the preeminent film critic of the 1940s was cemented at the left-wing journal of opinion, despite his ability to reach millions at Henry Luce's mass-circulation newsweekly. Whereas snappy, often glib prose was required of *Time*'s staff writers, *The Nation*'s literary editor, Margaret Marshall, allowed Agee to submit meditative, in-depth columns that would never have passed muster at Luce's magazine.

Agee's first *Nation* column is marked by his usual blend of idiosyncratic critical judgments and subtle aesthetic ruminations. Proclaiming himself an "amateur," the fledgling movie critic admits to not having seen William Wyler's *Mrs. Miniver*, one of the successes of the year that was just about to end, and that, for him, Chaplin's 1925 *The Gold Rush* was the best film he saw in 1942. These throwaway comments are a mere prelude to the crux of the column: a contemplative consideration of the nature of movie "kitsch" triggered by a consideration of Noël Coward and David Lean's wartime drama, *In Which We Serve*. Phillip Lopate describes Agee's prose as "syntactically complex, baroque in diction," and the digression on Coward – praised for possessing a "dancer's delight in form" but damned for capitulating to facile "effects" – is characteristically nuanced. The Popular Front political outlook that led Agee to praise films such as Rossellini's *Rome Open City* (1945) and John Huston's *The Battle of San Pietro* (1945) is absent in this debut column. But the moral seriousness and openness to many varieties of cinematic experience that would mark his brief career as a film critic are unquestionably evident.

Richard Porton

Date December 26, 1942

Why it's Key Agee's column in *The Nation* helped to cement his reputation as one of America's most respected film critics.

Opposite James Agee

Key Scene **John L. Sullivan crashes Jim Corbett's victory party** *Gentleman Jim*

In 1892, boxing great John L. Sullivan (Bond), heavyweight champion of the world, has agreed to defend his title against "Gentleman Jim" Corbett (Flynn), who acquired his sobriquet for bringing dandy-esque manners, youthful charm, and intense discipline to a sport known for the free-style brawling of which Sullivan is the icon. Against odds, Corbett beats the heavier Sullivan by a knockout in the 21st round. As Corbett celebrates his victory in his hotel suite with a high-spirited crowd, Sullivan, in formal dress, enters unexpectedly. The once-boisterous giant is deferential and sober, maybe still stunned. The room goes quiet as Sullivan greets Corbett with a simple "Hello, Jim." Sensitive to the older man's trauma, Corbett delivers a gracious, sincere encomium, declaring himself glad that his opponent tonight wasn't the Sullivan of 10 years ago. Appreciative, Sullivan responds in kind, praising Corbett's speed and acknowledging that hard as it is to lose, "it's a lot tougher to be a good winner." Corbett concludes: "I hope that when my time comes, I can go out with my head just as high as yours. There'll never be another John L. Sullivan."

This touching scene is flawlessly acted. Losing their usual outgoing self-confidence, both Flynn and Bond appear as men of action who, suddenly aware of themselves as actors in a tragic ritual, acquire unaccustomed eloquence and gravity. Surrounded by a hushed crowd, the two speak quietly, as if their words, so charged with history, were for each other only. In his slow approach across the room and his final shrinking withdrawal, Sullivan appears in a mirror on the wall behind Corbett. The mirror registers the fact that this defeated champion is an image of the future of all young heroes – a future that this film (which ends ebulliently) will not directly show.
Chris Fujiwara

Date 1942

Nationality USA

Director Raoul Walsh

Cast Errol Flynn, Ward Bond

Why It's Key Amid spirited celebration, Raoul Walsh stages a quiet confrontation between two men who have just shared a historical turning point.

139

Key Event **RKO cuts *The Magnificent Ambersons***

In the spring of 1942 when Orson Welles was in South America making *It's All True* at RKO's behest, the studio previewed *The Magnificent Ambersons* after a showing of *The Fleet's In*, a musical comedy. Kids in the audience who had come to see Betty Hutton sing and dance hooted Welles's bittersweet masterpiece and wrote they didn't like it on preview cards. An RKO producer sent Welles a mewling telegram right away: "Never in all my experience in the industry have I taken so much punishment or suffered as I did at the Pomona preview."

RKO removed over 50 minutes of Welles's cut and threw away the negative. In Welles's absence the producers demanded that editor Robert Wise and the Mercury unit shoot a couple of new scenes to patch up what was missing and tack them to the end of the film. The studio released *The Magnificent Ambersons* in July 1942 with a running time of 88 minutes – there's something insulting about that number, like a full 90 minutes wouldn't have left enough room for *Mexican Spitfire Sees a Ghost*, the movie RKO tied to *The Magnificent Ambersons* before they dumped it into theaters.

The butchering of *The Magnificent Ambersons* is indefensible, yet Welles critics have been making excuses for it for years. Significantly, it happened during wartime, when hysteria becomes internalized and can leach into anything. "There aren't any times but new times," says the automobile inventor Joseph Cotten plays in the film. Editing by preview card is still with us. This was its low point, the most final cut in film history.
A. S. Hamrah

Date Spring 1942

Why It's Key The studio's decision meant Welles's original would never be seen.

Opposite *The Magnificent Ambersons*

Key Person **Agnes Moorehead** Aunt Fanny's breakdown *The Magnificent Ambersons*

Mutilated after Welles's cut was deemed too long and dark, his second feature remains a masterpiece, with only a few later re-cut or re-shot scenes weakening an ambitious, subtle account of a wealthy dynasty's demise due to an inabilty to handle the transition from 19th-century feudalism to the industrialised progress of the 20th century. Nostalgic for quieter times while aware of the inequalities and hardships of the past, the film moves elegantly from one superb set piece to another: an opening narration on changing styles, a ballroom scene, a dinner-table rumination on the automobile delivered by Eugene (Joseph Cotten), an old family friend who grasps the seismic changes affecting American society, and a kitchen conversation in which Fanny (Moorehead) tells snobbish, headstrong nephew George (Holt) of local gossip regarding the attention Eugene's paying to George's widowed mother, Isabel (Dolores Costello).

The last is a paradigm of deftly nuanced writing and acting, but doesn't have the emotional force of a later encounter after several Ambersons – Isabel included – have died. Aunt and nephew, alone in an echoing mansion, have fallen on hard times. Distraught, Fanny sinks to the floor as she tearfully relates her forlorn attempts to save money; when George tells her not to sit against the boiler, she wails, "It's not hot, it's *cold*," explaining the heating's been cut off. As delivered by Moorehead, those five words encompass an astonishing range of emotions: panic, despair, rage, guilt, grief, even a blackly comic sense of life's cruel ironies. Her work here is as memorably good as anything committed to film by a Hollywood actress.
Geoff Andrew

Date 1942

Nationality USA

Director Orson Welles

Cast Agnes Moorehead, Tim Holt

Why It's Key Peerless acting from Moorehead makes for a scene imbued with an emotional range and intensity virtually unmatched in Hollywood studio fare.

Key Scene **The camera, panning away from Anne, tracks after her** *Day of Wrath*

The time and place are Denmark in 1623, when people still believed in witches – or Denmark in 1943, during the height of the Nazi occupation, when Jews were being deported and Carl Dreyer was shooting this masterpiece. Although he later disavowed any intention of commenting on the present, it's difficult to avoid the parallels whereby apparent demons are identified, tracked down, captured, and finally burned.

Anne (Movin), the sexy young heroine, married to a pastor who's much older than her, is walking across the rectory to the room where an old woman who's accused of being a witch is being interrogated by her husband. Anne's own mother was burned as a witch, and it would appear that she's both attracted to and repelled by the notion that she might actually be a witch herself – a notion she eventually comes to believe by the film's conclusion. Whether this is a film about repression and paranoia or one about

how witches are produced, it solicits our identification as well as our detachment.

Dreyer invented a very sensual form of camera movement in which the camera glides on unseen tracks in one direction while it pans in another direction. It's this complex and hypnotic movement that accompanies Anne as she crosses the rectory, drawn forward and then momentarily retreating, burning with fear as well as curiosity as the camera, moving both towards and away from her, conveys her passionate ambivalence. And the melodramatic music that follows her passage starkly conveys the same principle of attraction-repulsion.
Jonathan Rosenbaum

Date 1943

Nationality Denmark

Director Carl Dreyer

Cast Lisbeth Movin

Original Title *Vredens dag*

Why it's Key Dreyer uses a camera movement he invented to express a complex, conflicted emotion.

Key Scene **The opening sequence**
The Gang's All Here

As the film opens, the camera tracks in toward the face of a singer (singing "Brazil"), the rest of his body engulfed in black. We slowly come to a close-up for one chorus of the song, then the camera pulls back, glides down and out of the black screen to the hull of a docked ship (the S.S. Brazil), and performs a complex maneuver following a group of disembarking passengers, then a stevedore, then the merchandise being unloaded, including a huge bundle of fruit that becomes a close-up filling the screen. We are about two minutes and 14 seconds into the sequence, and the close-up allows for a smooth, invisible cut (the first one) to – Carmen Miranda, whose fruit-laden hat echoes the bundle of fruit above her head.

Carmen gives her own rendition of "Brazil," at the end of which a marching band enters to the strains of "Hail to the Chief," followed by a limousine carrying an official, who gives Carmen the keys of the city ("Got any coffee on you?" he asks her). At this point the camera pulls back to reveal that the entire scene has been performed on the stage of a nightclub. Camera tracks back to Carmen, who launches into the second song of the sequence, "You Discover that You're in New York," during which the first real cut occurs, at 3'16". For a second chorus of the song, the camera, in a high-angle shot, follows Miranda, who walks off stage and into the nightclub; the camera pans and tracks over seven elegant black-clad women, each of whom sings four lines of the song. The camera follows Carmen and the women back to the stage for a finale at about 5'55". WOW!

Jean-Pierre Coursodon

Date 1943

Nationality USA

Director Busby Berkeley

Cast Alice Faye, Carmen Miranda

Why It's Key Hitchcock's ten-minute takes in *Rope* or Welles's opening crane shot in *Touch of Evil* are deservedly famous, but few have commented on this earlier *tour de force*: an amazingly complex, six-minute-long production number.

Key Scene **Teresa walks home at night in a Mexican border town** *The Leopard Man*

A five-minute sequence occurring only eight minutes into a 66-minute feature, this sequence terrifies, above all, because of the way it prods our imagination. The story has just strangely shifted focus from a nightclub dancer in a border town – who unwittingly caused a rival's rented leopard to break loose – to Teresa (Landry), a teenage neighbor whose house she passes.

Sent out by her mother (Lawson) to buy corn meal for her father's tortillas, Teresa doesn't want to go because of the escaped leopard, but her unsympathetic mother dismisses her fears even after her kid brother (Bobby Spindola) teases her about them. Her mother even locks the front door after her, saying she can't return without the corn meal. But the nearest shop she visits is already closed, so she has to walk across the dark, wind-swept town, dodging tumbleweeds that suddenly sweep past her, to a larger store, where the shopkeeper (Charles Lung) remembers her as a girl afraid of the dark. Then, on her way home, our dread is stoked by the sound of dripping water and a pair of shining eyes under a railway trestle, then by the sudden scream of a train speeding past, and finally by close-ups of the snarling leopard. She flees, and when we next hear her hammering on the door of her home, pleading for her mother to open it, the lock jams, and we hear rather than see what ensues – until a trickle of blood appears under the door. Imagining the awfulness rather than seeing it only makes it more upsetting.

Jonathan Rosenbaum

Date 1943

Nationality USA

Director Jacques Tourneur

Actors Margaret Landry, Kate Lawson

Why it's Key It's the most terrifying sequence in Val Lewton's oeuvre.

Key Scene **The first appearance of the missing Jacqueline** *The Seventh Victim*

This is not the only Val Lewton production to begin from a particular narrative template of crossed trajectories and comparative character-types: as in *I Walked with a Zombie* (1943), we have a fresh-faced, innocent girl (Kim Hunter as Mary) in the process of discovering (not without disillusionment) her identity in a forbidding adult world; and a "lost" girl (Jean Brooks as Jacqueline) who has suffered some nameless trauma and experienced virtual imprisonment at the hands of shadowy conspirators. Whether it is Jacques Tourneur at the helm (as in *Zombie*) or Mark Robson (as here), the enigmatic, unsettling world-view of Lewton remains constant: his films, with their highbrow literary quotations, references to history and myth, and inspired atmospherics, derive their energy and mystery from the constant interchange between life-forces and death-forces. Thirty-one minutes into *The Seventh Victim*, we get our first glimpse of the missing Jacqueline. Standing in a doorway, not saying a word,

she steps forward, puts a finger to her lips to forbid speech, becomes apprehensive about something off-screen, then quickly shuts the door, blotting out her image. A second later, as Mary gives chase, she appears to have evaporated; it will be another 23 minutes before we see her again. Jacqueline is the modern screen heroine *par excellence*: her being seems co-substantial with the cuts, fades, and flickerings of the cinematic machine. Appropriately, *The Seventh Victim* would later influence Jacques Rivette, whose *Story of Marie and Julien* (2003) recreates the spooky "suicide room" kept by a similarly lost girl.
Adrian Martin

Date 1943

Nationality USA

Director Mark Robson

Cast Kim Hunter, Jean Brooks

Why It's Key The fleeting presence of this mysterious figure makes her the modern screen heroine *par excellence*.

Key Speech **The last line** *Casablanca*

On an airfield in North Africa, after Rick (Bogart) has persuaded Ilsa (Ingrid Bergman) to fly off to safety with Victor (Paul Henried), his life seems over, and he's dead inside. He has given up the love of his life for the greater good, lost his business and position in Casablanca (selling Rick's Café Américain to Signor Ferrari, along with his sidekick Sam and a parcel of supporting characters), and – by shooting dead Major Strasser (Conrad Veidt) – undoubtedly landed himself on the Axis's list of to-be-executed troublemakers. To Rick's rescue comes Captain Renault (Rains), the corrupt police chief, who covers for Rick's crime ("round up the usual suspects"), symbolically tosses a non-product-placement bottle of Vichy water in the trash, and proposes that the two former-cynics-now-revealed-as-sentimental-patriots join the Free French to fight the Nazis. Upon reflection, Rick agrees and the pair walk off into the foggy night

(fog? In Morocco?) to an unknown, but presumably legendary future. The last line takes the sting off what might be a downbeat, sentimental wartime sacrifice ending. "Louis, I think this is the beginning of a beautiful friendship."
Kim Newman

Date 1943

Nationality USA

Director Michael Curtiz

Cast Humphrey Bogart, Claude Rains

Why It's Key Like all great endings, it's also a beginning – of a story we can only imagine.

142

SPOILER

Opposite *Casablanca*

Key Speech **"Are they human, or are they fat, wheezing animals?"** *Shadow of a Doubt*

*S*hadow of a Doubt is a brilliantly misnamed movie. From the first scene the audience knows for certain that Joseph Cotten is the serial killer of rich hags known to the papers and the cops as the "Merry Widow Murderer." The only question is how long it will take for Teresa Wright, as Cotten's namesake and favorite niece, to catch on. She has plenty of warning: police officers pursuing Cotten move in on Wright's family of by-the-numbers lovable eccentrics by posing as magazine editors doing a spread on a typical American family, and soon let her know their real intention. Wright herself immediately recognizes that something is a little off with her uncle.

But it is Cotten who works hardest to clear up the mystery, caressing Thornton Wilder's energetically cynical and misanthropic dialogue in a perverse effort to win over Wright. In his keynote speech, he denounces "Middle-aged widows, husbands dead, husbands who've spent their lives making fortunes, working and working, and then they die and leave their money to their wives, their silly wives... You see them in the best hotels every day by the thousands, drinking the money, eating the money... smelling of money... horrible, faded, fat, greedy women."

There's both a confession and a come-on in this obsessive misogyny. He's not just explaining his loathing of women, but sending a coded message to the ever-perky Wright: *but you're different*. And he's right! Teresa Wright is different, and her willingness to keep an open mind about her creepy uncle isn't a mark of gullibility but of an exalted soul. *Shadow of a Doubt*'s inverted mystery setup – later fully exploited in *Columbo* and the *NBC Mystery Movie* – makes the killer the focus of audience sympathy, and the uncertain pursuer a sort of superego for that sympathy.
Tim Cavanaugh

Date 1943

Nationality USA

Director Alfred Hitchcock

Cast Teresa Wright, Joseph Cotten

Why It's Key It created the template for non-suspense suspense.

Key Scene **Ida Lupino's song and dance routine** *Thank Your Lucky Stars*

*T*hank Your Lucky Stars was a wartime morale booster from Warner Bros., featuring a large cast of the studio's stars performing items for a charity show. Ida Lupino teams up with Olivia de Havilland and George Tobias for an upbeat swing number, "The Dreamer" (music by Arthur Schwartz and lyrics by Frank Loesser). It's a nonsense song lacking a strong melody, but Lupino projects real charisma throughout. Both de Havilland and Lupino are costumed in zany, child-like outfits – all pinafores and outsized bows – and their dance routine involves a lot of clowning with their straight man, Tobias. Best known by this time as a dramatic actress, especially for *High Sierra* (1941), Lupino went on to direct sardonic "*noir*" thrillers like *The Hitch-hiker* (1953) and bleak dramas like *The Bigamist* (1953). In this comic scene from *Thank Your Lucky Stars*, a certain sang-froid creeps through in her relaxed gum-chewing deadpan style that contrasts strongly with the effort and exaggeration of de Havilland. Lupino seems perfectly at home with singing, dancing, and slapstick. It's one of the few highlights in an otherwise dull compendium of star turns, and it reveals an aspect of Lupino's considerable talent that was rarely exploited by the studios.
Andrew Pike

Date 1943

Nationality USA

Director David Butler

Cast Ida Lupino, Olivia de Havilland, George Tobias

Why it's Key This is a rare scene of comedy and music for a great "*film noir*" actress and director.

Key Scene **The end – the mass production of war planes** *An American Romance*

Steve (Donlevy) immigrates to the U.S. just before 1900, and walks from New York to the Minnesota iron mines to find employment. He's curious, and asks the local schoolteacher how the ore he mines is made into steel. She refers him to an encyclopedia – and then has to teach him to read. Soon after, he peruses a steam shovel manual on lunch break and figures out how to operate it. A line can be drawn from these early learning scenes to the first scenes of steel making, after the ambitious Steve moves to work in a mill and learn the process, and then to the scenes in which, purchasing a new car that's unreliable, he takes it apart, reassembles it as a more reliable model, and co-founds a car company with his friend Howard (Abel), soon employing one of his sons, Teddy (McNally). With war imminent, they accept a government contract to manufacture planes. The final aircraft-making scene is a visual poem in which aircraft parts moving within the frame and camera movements criss-cross the screen in multiple directions to give a sense of parts coming together to make a larger and larger whole, climaxing in the the long line of planes that, after the assembly scenes, is seen to start up and fly off. A single insert of the trio recalls their importance in the process, and the final shot looking directly upward shows a huge formation of planes flying at several levels of depth. Through composition and editing Vidor achieves an extraordinary physical intensity: each of the objects radiates power, and the process of their assemblage seems to be multiplying, rather than adding, individual forces to make something much bigger.
Fred Camper

Date 1944

Nationality USA

Director King Vidor

Cast Brian Donlevy, Walter Abel, Stephen McNally

Why It's Key A scene that to some eyes might seem to be just war propaganda – which it can also serve as – is, in the context of the whole film, about both the industrialization of America and the process of learning to master the physical world.

Key Scene **The falcon and the Spitfire** *A Canterbury Tale*

Michael Powell and Emeric Pressburger's *A Canterbury Tale* opens with a quote from Chaucer, an illuminated manuscript, and a group of mediaeval pilgrims on a road through the Kentish countryside, heading for Canterbury, as if this is going to be a pageant-like costume romp. In close-up, a hood is taken off a falcon, and the bird soars into the skies, watched by a noble falconer (Sadler). In a match-cut that skips 600 years, the falcon seems to become a Spitfire, and we return to Sadler's face looking up, only now he is wearing a 1944-vintage British soldier's tin hat, and we realize that this will be a contemporary-set film suffused with the history and culture of this rolling landscape. The effect is as astonishing as the very similar match cut between falling bone and orbital-weapons platform Stanley Kubrick stages in *2001: A Space Odyssey* (1968).
Kim Newman

Date 1944

Nationality UK

Directors Michael Powell, Emeric Pressburger

Cast James Sadler

Why It's Key It may be the single greatest cut in the history of film.

Key Person **Deanna Durbin**
"Liebestod" *Christmas Holiday*

This is the movie that Deanna Durbin never made: her fans wanted to forget it, and even retrospectives of her career now routinely leave it out. It was also her biggest box-office hit: everyone wanted to see it at the time, though no one seemed to like it (except her – it was reportedly her favorite). The New York Times called it "grotesque," as if "a sweet schoolgirl" had been made to play "a Sadie Thompson." Durbin as Abigail Martin is something like that schoolgirl – in screenwriter Herman Mankiewicz's Kane-like maze of flashbacks – for half the movie. But as Jackie Lamont in the other half she is a whore, albeit a singing one, in an upscale dive called the Maison Lafitte.

Siodmak not only transforms his star but his improbable material as well, principally by centering less on the dramatic action than on the variegated pieces of music that the characters either hear or perform, ranging from a Wagner concert to a Catholic High Mass to Tin Pan Alley. Durbin – who is wonderful – sings Berlin's "Always" twice, first as Abigail, then later as Jackie, the first time meltingly, at the parlor piano with her husband, the second time bluesily, in front of the Lafitte's combo. With them she also does Frank Loesser's "Spring Will Be a Little Late This Year" (written for the movie) in a deadpan style that seems less like a raised voice than a raised eyebrow. But it's Wagner's "Liebestod" that ends the movie – which turns out in the end to be less about doomed love than about the way a great piece of music, whether you're making it or listening to it, can somehow transfigure even bummers like that.
James Harvey

Date 1944
Nationality USA
Director Robert Siodmak
Cast Deanna Durbin, Gene Kelly
Why It's Key Siodmak's most neglected *film noir* is also his boldest and most brilliant one.

Key Scene **The return**
Laura

SPOILER

In the most famous scene of *Laura*, the title character (Tierney) returns to her apartment before the amazed eyes of the police lieutenant (Andrews) who's been investigating her supposed murder. Though Preminger might seem, to unsympathetic viewers, the most prosaic, least romantic of directors, special circumstances give this scene an oneiric charge that made it a prized moment among French Surrealists. It's a rainy night; Lt. MacPherson, alone in Laura's apartment, has been drinking and has fallen asleep beneath her portrait on the wall. He is in love with her, though he knows her only through others' recollections, through the decor of her apartment, her clothes, her perfume, her favorite song left on the phonograph (David Raksin's enchanted title tune). When Laura walks in, it's as if MacPherson's desire for her has called her into being. It could be a dream (American film scholar Kristin Thompson devoted a famous essay to interpreting *Laura* as if this sequence – and everything that follows it – were the lieutenant's dream).

Yet the scene is far from an unbridled moment of cinematic *amour fou*. MacPherson and Laura never touch. The scene is played as much from Laura's point of view as from MacPherson's: Preminger invites us to share her astonishment at finding a stranger in her home, no less than his at seeing her alive. Above all, the scene is played as if from the point of view of the space itself, which seems to widen (the camera tracking back from MacPherson sleeping under the portrait) and breathe (for a suspenseful moment the soundtrack contains almost nothing but a clock ticking) as it stands waiting for its mistress's return.
Chris Fujiwara

Date 1944
Nationality USA
Director Otto Preminger
Cast Dana Andrews, Gene Tierney
Why It's Key Preminger's *mise en scène* makes this miraculous scene memorable.

Opposite *Laura*

Key Film *Jammin' the Blues*
The best jazz film ever made

Jazz parallels cinema as an art form to emerge and mature in the 20th century, but the music – at its best magisterial and irreplaceable – has rarely been well served in films. There's plenty of footage of performance, much of it directed with something approaching indifference (at best), while biographies tend to homogenize the music itself, and fiction often portrays jazz musicians as inhabitants of sad, shadowy worlds. The ten-minute short *Jammin' the Blues* is the most glowing of all exceptions, a work of art, filmed with the resources of a major studio, featuring a racially integrated group of first-rate musicians – including one of the greatest of all jazzmen, tenor saxophonist Young – playing in an undiluted way in a true representation of the music, as it was in that time but timeless as well. Beginning with a shot of Young's porkpie hat and then gracefully booming down to his face as he begins to play his solo on a slow blues against a black background with a filigree of cigarette smoke, Mili inventively varies compositons and camera angles with comparable brilliance throughout, briefly going to white background as vocalist Bryant sings the middle selection, the standard "On the Sunny Side of the Street," then bringing in some jitterbugging dancers and matching the hard-swinging verve of the final fast blues with a flow of bold, adventurous images, as Young and trumpeter Edison are joined as principal soloists by guitarist Kessel and a second tenor, the brash and extroverted Jacquet, who brings the film to an exciting close.

Blake Lucas

Date 1944

Nationality USA

Director Gjon Mili

Cast Lester Young, Red Callender, Harry Edison, Marlowe Morris, Sidney Catlett, Barney Kessel, Jo Jones, John Simmons, Illinois Jacquet, Marie Bryant

Why It's Key The beauty of jazz for once finds a match in the beauty of film, in a souvenir of musicians in top form, which has only become more precious with the passage of time.

Opposite *Jammin' the Blues*

148

Key Scene **The Halloween sequence**
Meet Me in St. Louis

In his third feature (and first in Technicolor), Minnelli came into full mastery of his art in his evocation of life in turn-of-the-century St. Louis, based on the reminiscences by writer Sally Benson of her own family, but also resonating against Minnelli's own Midwest childhood. This is especially true of a sequence dear to his heart, the nocturnal Halloween adventure of Tootie Smith (O'Brien), an intense and imaginative child, who gives herself totally to the fantasy of "killing" Mr. Braukoff, most feared man in the neighborhood, with a handful of flour. Though Minnelli loves all the characters of this glowing ensemble piece, he plainly has special affection for Tootie, in whom one sees so many great Minnelli characters to come, living their lives subjectively and creatively, imaginative even to the point of hysteria (though Tootie's family is a safe haven in which to indulge her morbid fantasies). Venturing fearfully out with her older sister Agnes (Carroll), making that long walk alone to the Braukoffs' in artfully lit forward tracking shot, or looking rapturous as the other children finally acknowledge her as "the most horrible," she seems to be an artist waiting to emerge. Visually and dramatically, Minnelli's handling of the sequence matches his affection – yet, ironically, it was almost cut from the film. We may thank the benevolent gods that sometimes watch over Hollywood that this did not occur, for the film and for the confidence with which Minnelli would go on to carve out one of cinema's great bodies of work.

Blake Lucas

Date 1944

Nationality USA

Director Vincente Minnelli

Cast Margaret O'Brien, Joan Carroll, Darryl Hickman

Why It's Key In a celebrated sequence of the masterpiece that established him, Vincente Minnelli gives the full measure of creativity to a first portrait of the kind of character who most has his heart.

Key Film *The Miracle of Morgan's Creek*
A grand finale

SPOILER

Made at the height of World War II in 1942, though censorship issues delayed its release until 1944, this merry farce pushed all available limits with its bare-faced spoof of American sacred cows, including motherhood, patriotism, and small-town morality. Unable to show a pregnant woman, or even to utter the word "pregnant," Sturges found a way to cap his comedy in which a small-town girl's overly enthusiastic send-off for combat-bound soldiers results in an unremembered conception and a very public motherhood. For maximal subversion, the birth takes place on Christmas Day, as nurses and doctors bustle in and out of the delivery room, first announcing "it's a boy!", then returning to cry "twins!", then several more trips until a nurse cries "Six! All boys!" This finale, in which the new mother (Hutton) shows her newborn sextuplets, succeeded in steamrolling over Production Code restrictions and Hays Office objections with sheer numbers. One infant of dubious legitimacy would have been completely unacceptable, but six (one more than the celebrity Dionne quintuplets) constituted an outrageous *reductio ad absurdum* that stymied the censors. Furthermore, for patriotic punch, Hitler is shown reacting with a tantrum as he "demands a recount." In preparing the production, Sturges masterfully manipulated the Code enforcers by showing them only individual scenes from the script, thus giving them all the trees while withholding the forest – a strategy that James Agee celebrated in his famous quip that the Hays Office had been "raped in its sleep."

Robert Keser

Date 1944

Nationality USA

Director Preston Sturges

Cast Betty Hutton

Why It's Key Fertility is used to pacify bluenoses.

Opposite *The Miracle of Morgan's Creek*

Key Scene **Troubling dream**
The Woman in the Window

SPOILER

It's based on a novel that ends with the protagonist's suicide, unacceptable to Hollywood in 1944, so Lang contrived to end *The Woman in the Window* in a dream instead.

Richard Wanley (Robinson), a professor of criminal psychology with a wife and two children, has a problem. After Wanley kills a man (Loft) in the apartment of a woman (Joan Bennett) he barely knows, he's embroiled in a blackmail scheme from which he can't escape. Desperate, this middle-class everyman drinks poison, then takes a seat next to a table holding photographs of his family. As he loses consciousness the phone on the table rings – it's a call exonerating him. He doesn't answer it. The clock behind him chimes. The camera dollies in for a closeup – Wanley is dead. Then a hand enters the frame and shakes his shoulder: "It's 10:30, Professor Wanley."

Wanley wakes up. He's in his club, not at home. The camera pulls back. Without a cut Lang has changed the set and Wanley's outfit. The glass in his hand is no longer poison but brandy. Wanley stands, finishes his drink and exits. The people he meets on his way out – the hatcheck guy, the doorman – are the villains from his dream.

Lang acknowledged "it was only a dream" endings were old hat. Yet this well-executed ending adds something that would not have been there had Wanley killed himself. The dream ending is a negation that moves the film back into real life.

A. S. Hamrah

Date 1944

Nationality USA

Director Fritz Lang

Cast Edward G. Robinson, Arthur Loft, Dan Duryea

Why It's Key Lang turns a problem ending into an asset.

Key Person **Barbara Stanwyck**
Her first appearance *Double Indemnity*

The entrance of the femme fatale in a *film noir* is always a key moment, and *Double Indemnity*, one of the finest entries in the cycle, does not depart from this rule. When insurance agent Walter Neff (MacMurray) paid one of his customers a routine visit on a sunny afternoon, he wasn't prepared to meet Phyllis Dietrichson (Stanwyck). More than its famous counterparts, such as the first appearance of Lana Turner in Tay Garnett's *The Postman Always Rings Twice* (1946), the whole scene foregrounds her sexuality and establishes a tension between the two characters. Standing at the top of the stairs, covered only by a towel, she seems unattainable and dominates the aroused visitor – a meaningful *mise en scène* absent from James Cain's novel. And then she comes downstairs. Her commonness is emphasized by her obviously phony blonde wig and the anklet bracelet with her name engraved on it that keeps drawing attention to her legs. If Stanwyck wasn't the most gorgeous actress of its time, she was one of the most talented, and she manages to convincingly portray her character as both cold and engaging. While the two banter rather innocently and use dialogues full of double meanings and metaphors – a trademark of *film noir* – the suburban mermaid already shows her manipulative nature, although only the spectator becomes aware of it. From this point, however, the insurance man dreams only of one thing: getting closer and closer to this unusual customer. Unfortunately for him, his wish will soon come true.

Frank Lafond

Date 1944

Nationality USA

Director Billy Wilder

Cast Barbara Stanwyck, Fred MacMurray

Why It's Key This moment is a great example of *film noir*'s construction of femininity and a highlight in Barbara Stanwyck's career.

Key Speech **"All you have to do is whistle"**
To Have and Have Not

Martinique during World War II. Times are tough, so cynical boatman Harry Morgan (Bogart) is forced to abandon his neutrality and work for the Resistance. One of the movement's sympathisers is Marie Browning (Bacall), a trumpet-voiced chanteuse in the local nightclub.

The situation is pure Bogart: a selfish man forced by circumstances to commit to a cause. Bacall, in her first film, was a revelation. An 18-year-old spotted on the cover of a magazine by Hawks's wife, Slim, Bacall was so nervous that she tensed her neck muscles and dropped her chin in what would become known as "the look." The scene in question, in which Browning flirts with Morgan with the famous lines – "You know how to whistle, don't you, Steve? You just put your lips together and blow" – resonates for various reasons. Hawks liked his female characters to be masculine, hence the insolence in the dialogue and Bacall's husky delivery. The screenplay is co-credited to novelist William Faulkner, but these lines (Bacall disclosed in an interview) were penned by Jules Furthman, who had written for the equally insolent, masculine Marlene Dietrich. The Morgan-Browning relationship echoed that of Hawks and his wife, and, as if to emphasize the fact, Bacall's nickname in the picture was Slim. Bacall and Bogart fell in love on set, married the following year, and become one of the great postwar Hollywood couples. Such was their chemistry here that they were paired again in *The Big Sleep* (1946), *Dark Passage* (1947), and *Key Largo* (1948). The storyline was echoed in real life when political fence-sitter Bogart was converted to the Democratic, anti-HUAC cause by his wife. Most significantly of all, perhaps, this scene launched one of the most distinctive women in cinema. Bacall says she copied her onscreen confidence from Katharine Hepburn, but, for half a century, she has made it her own.

Mark Cousins

Date 1944

Nationality USA

Director Howard Hawks

Cast Lauren Bacall, Humphrey Bogart

Why It's Key It's an iconic moment in the depiction of gender relations in Hollywood cinema.

Opposite *To Have and Have Not*

Key Scene **The last seats on the last plane**
They Were Expendable

It's 1942, the U.S. has had its ass kicked by the Japanese in the Philippines, and General MacArthur, after being evacuated to safety, has made his famous promise: "I shall return." Some other key personnel have been chosen to be shipped out on the last plane to Australia. The plane holds 30 passengers. Our heroes, PT-boat mavericks Brickley (Montgomery) and Ryan (Wayne), are numbers 27 and 28 on the list. Their two ensigns are assigned numbers 29 and 30, but when the plane is ready to leave and the ensigns still haven't shown up, their places are given to the first men on the waiting list, "Ohio" (Heydt), a hospital-ward chum of Ryan's, and one Morton (Ames). The airplane door is closed, the propellers turn: suddenly there is a knock, and the hatch is reopened: the two ensigns have turned up, and Ohio and Morton must give up their seats. The two men rise as the ensigns (Thompson, Mitchell) materialize before them – younger than the men they are displacing, and their

sweating faces showing their obliviousness to the fact that fortune has just caused impersonal military procedure to take the form of the most personal exchange possible: because the ensigns will live, Ohio and Morton will die. Of course, none of this is expressed overtly: in fact, the force of the scene lies in the refusal of the two doomed men to let their faces betray any sadness or any acknowledgment of the cruel trick fate has played on them.
Chris Fujiwara

Date 1945

Nationality USA

Director John Ford

Cast Robert Montgomery, John Wayne, Leon Ames, Louis Jean Heydt, Marshall Thompson, Cameron Mitchell

Why It's Key Ford pays unobtrusive tribute to the nobility of unprotesting sacrifice.

154

Key Scene **Ivan and the masses**
Ivan the Terrible, Part I

In the final sequence of the first part of Sergei M. Eisenstein's *Ivan the Terrible* – a monstrous, angular masterpiece that can be seen simultaneously as a blistering and remarkably courageous parody of Josef Stalin, an apologia for the same demagogue, a troubled self-portrait, and the greatest Flash Gordon serial ever made – the title hero has just abdicated his throne and gone to live in a monastery. An endless procession of people is seen approaching from a distance to persuade him to return to power, and Ivan goes out to see them – not to greet them, for he's plainly too godlike for that, but at least to take note of them. He strikes a series of almost mystical poses in which he appears to be both listening and brooding while the zig-zag shape of his arm and scepter uncannily "rhymes" with the snaking line of the distant crowd behind him.

As Russian historian Joan Neuberger notes, this scene is one of several showing us how Eisenstein's

view of the masses, the heroes of his silent classics *Potemkin* and *October*, has darkened considerably so that they now seem to yearn for subjugation rather than freedom. "The magnificent shot compositions of the finale emphasize the enormous power of the tsar and the minuscule insignificance of the people.... He becomes a detached, impersonal, symbolic figure, an abstraction, the embodiment of the Great Russian State." And paradoxically, Eisenstein is twisting tyrannically the shapes of both Nikolai Cherkasov and the crowd into mirroring pretzels in order to make his point.
Jonathan Rosenbaum

Date 1945

Nationality USSR

Director Sergei M. Eisenstein

Cast Nikolai Cherkasov

Original Title *Ivan Grozny I*

Why It's Key The master of Russian cinema subjugates the former ruler of Russia *and* the Russian people.

Key Film
Kolberg

In its twelfth and final year, Nazi Propaganda Minister Goebbels marshaled all the resources of the "Thousand Year Reich" to produce *Kolberg*, the costliest German production in history, a mammoth Agfacolor folly that consciously tried to challenge Hollywood spectacles like *Gone With the Wind*. Ignoring the 1807 defeat of the Baltic city's Prussian population by Napoleon's troops, the screenplay substitutes a timely patriotic myth of Teutons resisting invasion, neatly dramatizing the eleventh-hour Nazi call for "total war." With location filming taking place under the direst circumstances as Allied armies surrounded Germany, battle scenes employed over 180,000 extras, among them soldiers and sailors diverted from the war effort, whose reassignment spared them almost certain death or at least capture. Meanwhile, munitions makers manufactured thousands of rounds of dummy bullets, and transport trains carried vats of salt to simulate snow. Director Harlan staged spectacular battles that evoked the intended grandeur, but the government mandated radical cuts of war atrocity scenes deemed too demoralizing for public consumption. The result left continuity gaps that court incoherence, though for a thundering epic, *Kolberg* clearly exudes an astonishing air of grim finality. A dual premiere was scheduled for January 30, 1945, in Berlin (with the Red Army a day's march away) and in Kolberg's historic fortress (now completely blocked, so that the Luftwaffe had to parachute the film cans in). Given the societal breakdown, with cinemas out of commission throughout the country, the concluding irony was that *Kolberg*'s cast vastly outnumbered its viewers.
Robert Keser

Date 1945
Nationality Germany
Director Veit Harlan
Cast Heinrich George, Kristina Söderbaum
Why It's Key Nazi film production self-destructs.

Key Scene **If looks could drown**
Leave Her to Heaven

SPOILER

Regarded as one of the rare examples of *film noir* shot in color, Stahl's film offers a surprising murder scene taking place on a bright sunny day. Obsessed by her husband, Ellen Berent (Tierney) is so little able to stand any obstacle to her love that, nearly halfway through *Leave Her to Heaven*, she even lets her crippled brother-in-law, Danny (Hickman), with whom she has been forced to share her husband's attentions, drown in the quiet waters of a mountain lake. The isolation and the Eden-like beauty of the country setting are shown off by extreme long shots that alternate with closer images of the two characters. While Danny swims and then briefly struggles in the water, Ellen, who is following him from a distance in a small boat, barely moves. The almost heart-shaped sunglasses worn by Gene Tierney strengthen the inscrutability of her perfect face by preventing us from reading her thoughts, but, when she finally takes them off, we see two harsh eyes that keep staring at the lake without any sign of pity. The whole scene is strangely peaceful, and nothing, except the heroine's implicit resentment, emerges to change its tone: there is no music, the dialogue is trivial (although Ellen's voice, little by little, becomes devoid of any expression), and Danny doesn't even have the time to scream before disappearing under the surface. In fact, Ellen simply kills the boy by her complete inaction. In Otto Preminger's *Laura* (1944), Tierney portrayed a complex character; here, she simply becomes calm, cold, transparent, beautiful, and dangerous as the lake itself.
Frank Lafond

Date 1945
Nationality USA
Director John M. Stahl
Cast Gene Tierney, Darryl Hickman
Why It's Key Gene Tierney has never been more dangerously angelic.

Key Event **Publication of Bazin's "The Ontology of the Photographic Image"**

The anthology *Les Problèmes de la peinture*, edited by art critic Gaston Diehl, contained essays on painting by luminaries like Cocteau, Dufy, Bonnard, Braque, Matisse…and the then-somewhat-less-celebrated André Bazin, a 27-year-old who was active in the Paris ciné-club scene. "The Ontology of the Photographic Image" barely touched on the cinema as such: it concerned itself with the impact of the invention of photography, "clearly the most important event in the history of plastic arts." Years later, after Bazin had become the editor of *Cahiers du cinéma*, died of leukemia at age 40, and been compiled into anthologies of his own, it became clear that "Ontology" was the first link in a chain of ideas that revolutionized film criticism. Proposing that painting and sculpture originate in the age-old desire to preserve the dead, and that photography is the culmination of this urge toward representation, Bazin makes audacious claims for photographic realism: "(The image) proceeds, by

virtue of its genesis, from the ontology of the model: it *is* the model." In an era when cinema was still valued for the techniques that distinguish it from the older arts – the more strenuously the better, it often seemed – Bazin was laying the basis for an approach to film founded on the image's intrinsic relationship to time and space, an approach that would become so influential that Andrew Sarris could later write, "Bazin is as central a figure in film aesthetics as Freud is in psychology."

Dan Sallitt

Date 1945

Why It's Key It marks, arguably, the beginning of modern film criticism.

Key Scene **The shooting of Pina**
Rome Open City

SPOILER

In the midst of all the upheaval of the war, finally some light and hope: Pina (Magnani), an already widowed mother, and Francesco (Grandjacquet) are today getting married. But Francesco's best man, Giorgio (Pagliero), is one of the leaders of the Resistance movement and, as he and Francesco dress for the wedding, Pina bursts in to warn that Germans and Fascists have surrounded the building. Lined up with everyone else outside, Pina attempts to comfort another woman while also contending with the leering advances of an SS guard. Slapping away his roving hand, she notices in terror that Francesco and Giorgio are being loaded onto a truck. Screaming out Francesco's name, she breaks through the cordon and runs after the truck as it is driven away. We see her from Francesco's point of view as she continues to chase the truck, gesturing and repeatedly calling out his name. Then, an abrupt burst of machine-gun fire –

and she's dead. The camera frames her lying in the street, legs slightly exposed, wedding garter in view.

This is undoubtedly one of the most iconic sequences in cinema history, condensing into a few moments of screen time and several indelible images both the inscrutability of fate and the senseless suffering inflicted by war on ordinary people. Pina was originally meant to die by being shot in the middle of the crowd. The idea of having her shot while chasing the truck came to the screenwriter, Sergio Amidei, late one night when he saw Magnani, after a dreadful fight between her and her current lover, chase after the car in which the latter was being driven away.

Gino Moliterno

Date 1945

Nationality Italy

Director Roberto Rossellini

Cast Aldo Fabrizi, Anna Magnani, Francesco Grandjacquet, Marcello Pagliero

Original Title *Roma città aperta*

Why It's Key This crucial sequence divides the film in two – just as the film itself marks a turning point in film history.

Opposite *Rome Open City*

Key Scene **The husband returns**
Scarlet Street

Imposing painted portraits – usually of the dear departed – have often figured in the domestic settings of movies, from American romances and mystery-thrillers of the '40s to Alain Resnais's *Cœurs* (2006). But few are more imposing than that of the beefy, well-decorated cop Homer Higgins (Kemper), the previous husband of Adele (Ivan), looking down from the wall upon his rather emasculated successor, Chris Cross (Robinson), in *Scarlet Street*. That is, until an unexpected plot move, which must count among the most outrageous in cinema history. Chris – who has guiltily got himself into a spiral of illicit wrongdoing for the sake of the prostitute with whom he is besotted, Kitty (Joan Bennett) – is informed, in his cage-like office, that a detective awaits him in the street. A pudgy, sniffling, rather vulgar chap with an eye-patch approaches: it is Homer, back from the dead! In a bar, this once-honored individual reveals his backstory, and what a laconic, truly Langian dance with destiny

it is: feeling suicidal after various corrupt schemes unravelled, he jumped into the river to save a woman … and ended up, his hand on her purse full of money, aboard a "banana boat to Honduras." In this pitilessly ironic tale of the treacherous logic of appearances – where daily reality is subject to what Pascal Bonitzer identified as Lang's penchant for "wigs, untinted mirrors, false identities, 'unbelievable truths,' various masks" – the grandly-named Homer will find himself, in turn, unmanned by the deadly duplicity of how things seem.

Adrian Martin

Date 1945

Nationality USA

Director Fritz Lang

Cast Edward G. Robinson, Charles Kemper, Rosalind Ivan

Why It's Key Once again, Lang exposes the treacherous logic of appearances.

Key Scene **Twilight for Monty Beragon**
Mildred Pierce

Mildred Pierce is the ultimate Los Angeles story, yet it's built on an aphorism more suited to San Francisco, or even Sacramento: that in a gold rush it's the seller of shovels who thrives. Joan Crawford as James M. Cain's titular heroine scales the ladder of wealth in Southern California's dizzying economy, but only as a hardworking entrepreneur, a Glendale housewife who gets lucky with a chain of stylish diners. Everywhere, Mildred is reminded of the class and breeding that the culture pretends are not for sale: her spoiled, pompous elder daughter (Ann Blyth) parley-voos to humiliate her (the amiable younger daughter [Jo Ann Marlowe] dies of an advanced case of plot convenience); her deadbeat first husband (Bruce Bennett) turns everything he touches to dust.

But it's her second, classier paramour who brings on Mildred's downfall. Zachary Scott's Monty Beragon, the scuzzbucket scion of some depleted Pasadena clan, defines all that Mildred lacks in two words: "pride and a

name." Then he proves it by screwing the pretentious daughter (named "Veda," in a witty nod to the new age faiths L.A. was growing even in the '40s). Cain stages it all as unrelieved humiliation, but the movie gives Mildred an instant of transcendence. In one of her attempts to break up with Monty, Mildred delivers with a boss's ruthless perfection: Monty isn't just being dumped, he's being fired; and when he makes an unkind reference to the smell of grease that surrounds her, he gets the unrebuttable rebuttal: "You don't shrink away from a fifty-dollar bill because it smells of grease."

Curtiz and a writing squad that reportedly included William Faulkner have even greater shames in store for the heroine, including a grafted-in murder that makes the movie even bleaker than the book. But in this early version of what we now recognize as the you-go-girl scene, *Mildred Pierce* lays bare the fictions of class and tradition.

Tim Cavanaugh

Date 1945

Nationality USA

Director Michael Curtiz

Cast Joan Crawford, Zachary Scott

Why It's Key In the midst of humiliation, this scene gives the heroine a moment of transcendence.

Opposite *Mildred Pierce*

Key Scene **The camera pans the room in a great vision of madness** *Detour*

Al Roberts (Neal), a man hitchhiking from New York to Los Angeles to join his girlfriend, accepts a ride from a man who then dies, and, afraid he'll be blamed, he hides the body and takes the car. Then he picks up a young woman (Savage) who guesses some of what happened and holds him hostage to her wishes. ("There's a cute little gas chamber waiting for you, Roberts, and I hear extradition to Arizona is a cinch.") There's a foreboding shot of the woman asleep in head-on profile, her head producing a curiously dissociated feel that recalls the oversized coffee-cup of the opening (the film is told in one large flashback). Near the film's end, in a quarrel, she locks herself in a room threatening to turn Roberts in. He pulls on the phone cord to stop her, and then discovers that he's strangled her. This occasions one of the greatest visions of madness in film history, a slow pan in which the objects in the room come in and out of focus, completely disorienting the space, evoking the mad

delirium of the moment and the event, and answering the hints of dissociation dropped earlier. Objects are now unmoored from meaning and function, and space has become an out-of-time, disconnected blur in which the moments of clarity – the moments when the objects come into focus – seem more terrible for their precision, their reminders of the "real" world with its names and logic and laws and prisons – than the longer moments of foggy blur.
Fred Camper

Date 1945

Nationality USA

Director Edgar G. Ulmer

Cast Tom Neal, Ann Savage

Why It's Key Hollywood cinema, known for its focus on action, here offers one of cinema's most poetic, and authentic, visions of a dissociative madness, in which ordinary objects lose their meanings.

Opposite *Detour*

Key Event *Film noir* **discovered by the French**

As a genre, *film noir* was not invented but discovered. The directors, writers, and actors mostly thought they were making detective stories, crime melodramas, gangster pictures, or psychological thrillers. During World War II, American films were, of course, not screened in occupied or Vichy France – so immediate-postwar cinemas were full of five years' worth of Hollywood pictures, including *Citizen Kane* (1941), *The Maltese Falcon* (1941), *Double Indemnity* (1944), *Laura* (1944), and *Scarlet Street* (1945). French cinéastes recognised that a style had evolved, combining American hard-boiled writing with European Expressionist cinematography, and compared these films – and many, many others – with the *Série Noire* paperbacks, popular issues of books by Dashiell Hammett, Raymond Chandler, James M. Cain, and company. It seems that Nino Frank was the first writer to use the term *"film noir"* in print, in 1946 (in an article in the August 28 issue of *L'Ecran français*), but it truly

entered the critical lexicon in 1955 (when the cycle of films was just about petering out) with the publication of Raymond Borde and Etienne Chaumeton's book *Panorama du film noir américain*. In English, key articles popularising the term came from Charles Higham and Joel Greenberg (*Hollywood in the Forties* [1968]), Raymond Durgnat ("The Family Tree of Film Noir" [1970]), and Paul Schrader ("Notes on Film Noir" [1972]). When he wrote *Taxi Driver* (1976), Schrader was probably the first filmmaker to set out deliberately to make a *film noir*.
Kim Newman

Date August 28, 1946

Why It's Key It took an outsider view to see what had been plainly in sight for years – that a new genre had been born.

Key Person **Erich Wolfgang Korngold**
The cello concerto *Deception*

Warner Bros. was famous in the '40s for its movies involving classical music and musicians, but in no other WB film was "serious" music more important, more central to the plot than in *Deception*, which revolves around the rehearsals and first public performance of a famous composer's new cello concerto. Alexander Hollenius (Rains), an evil genius (and gourmet extraordinaire) is described by Karel Novak (Henreid), a rising cello player from Europe, as "combining the rhythms of today with the melodies of yesterday" – whatever that may mean. Erich Korngold wears two musical hats here – as the composer of the film's score (unfairly described by one critic as his "loudest, most flamboyant, and least successful") and as composer of Hollenius's concerto, fairly large portions of which are performed in the film. Although it can be heard as Post-Romantic bombast (there is a moment in the concerto where a cello phrase sounds dangerously like "The Flight of the Bumblebee"), the music is efficient, and its flourishes fit well with the story's melodramatic strain (strings, and especially cellos, are prominent in both the score and the concerto).

Korngold uses music deftly for dramatic purposes both in plot moments of tension (e.g., the final confrontation between Davis and Rains, when the music keeps switching from ominous string buildups to complete silence) and during the rehearsal of the concerto, in which Hollenius deliberately upsets Novak, his soloist, by having a short flute section reprised again and again until Novak explodes: "After all, this is not a flute concerto!" Nearly five minutes of the concerto are actually performed on screen.
Jean-Pierre Coursodon

Date 1946

Nationality USA

Director Irving Rapper

Cast Bette Davis, Paul Henreid, Claude Rains

Why It's Key It's a typical Korngold score that additionally gives the composer a chance to write a concerto.

Key Scene **The crane down to the key** *Notorious*

The crane had been among the visionary filmmaker's favorite toys from the earliest years of cinema, but suspense master Alfred Hitchcock's use of it in the Cary Grant-Ingrid Bergman thriller *Notorious* still ranks among its most memorable appearances. The setup finds Grant's CIA agent, Devlin, manipulating Bergman's character, Alicia – a promiscuous, alcoholic socialite whose father was convicted of being a Nazi agent – into marrying an Brazil-based German (Claude Rains), the better to expose a conspiracy to stockpile radioactive material for use in bombs. The famous crane shot occurs during a black-tie party at which Alicia is supposed to use a purloined key to access the wine cellar where the radioactive material is being stored in bottles; it starts high above the party, peering down over a second floor railing at guests, then slowly descends to pick out Alicia, then moves even closer to reveal the key clutched in her hand. In some ways an inversion of the equally famous crane shot in *Gone with the Wind* – which starts close on Scarlett O'Hara at a train station, then rises up to reveal the bodies of hundreds of dead and wounded Confederate soldiers – Hitchcock's camera move goes from scene-setting panorama to plot-and-character-specific detail while subliminally suggesting the psychological pressure bearing down on his heroine. It's a textbook example of style equaling substance.
Matt Zoller Seitz

Date 1946

Nationality USA.

Director Alfred Hitchcock

Cast Ingrid Bergman

Why It's Key It's one of the most memorable, and meaningful, of all camera movements.

Key Scene **The settled present gives way to a vividly evoked past** *Margie*

Margie (Crain) is a girl passing through adolescence, and the film that bears her name is rich in the humor and charm common in treatments of the subject but has much more as well: its vibrant, emotionally intense heroine is seen in long, highly expressive scenes of solitude, and her melancholy bent, in part a response to a troubled relationship with a distant father (Hobart Cavanaugh), makes a compelling dramatic center to a work brought to glowing life in King's realization (with extraordinary use of Technicolor by King and cinematographer Charles Clarke). There are memorable moments throughout, and they are all made possible by the magical transition to flashback at the beginning, as a poised adult Margie shares memories with her daughter (Todd), while a record plays of Rudy Vallee singing "My Time is Your Time" (by Leo Dance and Eric Little). King was a master of these transitions, and it was never more evident: panning over the phonograph, he

displaces Vallee with the same music blaring from a Herbert Hoover campaign truck, while dissolving to the past and moving the camera with the students across the crowded landscape of a wintry campus, then segues to a beautiful long shot of Margie's friend Marybelle (Lawrence), tracking in to her as she sings the song in a quickening rhythm, accompanied by the sound of a boy's ukelele. By the time the camera is at rest on a closer shot of Marybelle and friends, a special ambiance has been imbued in *Margie*, one that will not be lost.

Blake Lucas

Date 1946

Nationality USA

Director Henry King

Cast Jeanne Crain, Barbara Lawrence, Ann Todd

Why It's Key A well-chosen popular song links past with present and an introspective heroine with her more extroverted friend, in one of the most beautiful flashback transitions in the history of the cinema.

Key Event **Opening night of the first international film festival at Cannes**

Nineteen countries banded together to take the first substantial step toward creating a global film culture by organizing the Cannes International Film Festival, still the largest marketplace and most prestigious stop on the exhibition circuit. Earlier attempts begun at Venice in 1932 were fatally co-opted by nationalist political pressures from the fascist regimes of Italy and Germany, tensions coming to a head when the 1938 grand prize to Leni Riefenstahl's *Olympia* caused a walkout by British, French, and American representatives. This scandal provided the impetus for convening a fraternal event "where countries could be assured of total equality and total equity," according to the Cannes festival's first director. Though Hitler's invasion of Poland pre-empted the planned 1939 opening, the festival finally opened properly in 1946, with celebratory fireworks and film-star/soprano Grace Moore singing the "Marseillaise." Even though all films were screened

without subtitles or air-conditioning, and despite a string of mishaps – a government minister absent-mindedly declaring it "the first festival of agriculture," power blackouts disrupting the opening night, and reels of Hitchcock's *Notorious* projected in the wrong order – nothing could dim the event's success, not even the budding Cold War rivalry that was manifested when the Soviets scheduled their major party opposite the screening of an American movie. With a jury composed of one delegate from each participating nation, every country took home at least one of the awards, which included eleven "grand prizes," ten "international grand prizes," and numerous subsidiary awards. Winners ranged from Billy Wilder's *The Lost Weekend* (USA) to Roberto Rossellini's *Rome Open City* (Italy) to Emilio Fernández's *María Candelaria* (Mexico). The modern era of cinematic cross-influences had begun.

Robert Keser

Date September 20, 1946

Why It's Key It marked the birth of a worldwide film culture.

Key Scene **Dr Kotnis decides to practice in China** *The Immortal Journey of Dr Kotnis*

Dr Kotnis (Shantaram) returns from the city to his native Sholapur, having got his medical degree. He meets his parents only to inform them that he has decided to go to China to treat people affected by the war with Japan. Kotnis narrates to his father the impact the call to join the struggle in defense of China had on him. This narration begins in his voice, but other voices take over – those of a nationalist leader and of volunteers opting to go to China. The father, too, listens, as if he can actually hear what his son calls forth from his memory. The rousing speeches, the volunteers reciting their names, the excitement of the crowd are all conveyed through the soundtrack, while the camera covers the differing expressions of father and son. This is a unique "flashback" that is done through sound and in a single take.

The film is based on the life of the real Dr Kotnis. Made in the context of the nationalist movement that was then at its peak, the film is the classic plural text,

having made the British, the nationalists, and the Communists – in fierce political confrontation with one another – happy. For the British and the Communists, the film stood as an effort in the war against fascism, and for the nationalists, it created a self-image of a modern, enlightened community, with progressive ideals, where the individual thinks nothing of sacrificing himself for a greater cause.

Rashmi Doraiswamy

Date 1946

Nationality India

Director V. Shantaram

Cast V. Shantaram

Original Title *Dr Kotnis ki Amar Kahani*

Why It's Key It's an unusual example of a flashback in which the past is conveyed through sound, while the present is shown in a long take.

Key Speech **Free money** *The Best Years of Our Lives*

Ayn Rand, the unhinged goddess of Objectivism, was not wrong when she made plans (subsequently scotched by prudent lawmakers) to denounce William Wyler's beloved returning-veterans hit before the House Un-American Affairs Committee. And this speech, a drunken plea for a massive increase in federally guaranteed loans, is why.

Standing before a banquet of porcine small-town bankers, most of them spawned during the 19th century, Fredric March, playing a rising bank middle manager who has just returned to his job after serving as an Army NCO in the Pacific, uses a war story to condemn the cheapness of the moneymen. If we'd fought like bankers, goes the parable, seeking collateral for every risk and a guarantee on every expenditure, we'd have lost the war. March's vision, of having the bank prove its great "heart" by giving money to every young veteran with a dream and no credit record, is bound up in *bien pensant*, New Deal language, and he

deftly plays against the delivery – rambling, losing the audience, misfiring with his jokes. But at bottom it's a straightforward redistribution-of-wealth argument, in which the prerogatives of the common good are asserted in the baldest terms: If the state can claim the lives (or in the case of disabled co-star Harold Russell, the hands) of its citizens, who are you to try and hang onto your property?

The joke of history is that all that free money March was calling for created one of the greatest booms in the country's history – the suburbanization of America, which is derided by the *bien pensant* classes who now claim there's *too much* easy credit out there. *The Best Years of Our Lives* is nostalgic from first note to last, but it's most interesting in those points (including also a subplot that treats with equanimity a homewrecking scheme by perpetual ingenue Teresa Wright) where it welcomes the chaos, risk, and freedom of the future.

Tim Cavanaugh

Date 1946

Nationality USA

Director William Wyler

Cast Fredric March

Why It's Key Is it socialist propaganda, or the future of America?

Opposite *The Best Years of Our Lives*

Slinky!
Sultry!
Sensational !!!

LAUREN BACALL
AND
HUMPHREY BOGART
IN
"THE BIG SLEEP" 'A'
A WARNER BROS. PICTURE

Key Scene **The finest moment in 1940s movies** *The Big Sleep*

If reverence were an appropriate response to a wise-guy writer like Manny Farber, then he would be among the most revered of film critics – a status that now burdens one of his favorite scenes, in *The Big Sleep*. Playing the role of a private detective, Humphrey Bogart walks across a city street and in so doing glances up at a sign over a bookstore window. This tiny gesture, Farber repeatedly insisted, this flick of the eyes that went unnoticed by most viewers, is the finest moment in 1940s American film.

Farber's detractors argue that Bogart isn't looking at a sign at all. He's reacting on cue to a rumble of thunder, which prepares you for the downpour in the following scene. In fact, we are witnessing nothing more than a detail of directorial carpentry.

But truths are sometimes larger than facts – and Farber's truth lies in the freedom he saw in this moment, the actorly intuition that emerged as if spontaneously and the directorial style that was able to accommodate it. If Bogart glances up at a sign, then there's a world for him to be curious about, and a personality large enough to extend into that world. What Farber valued in *The Big Sleep* – even if it didn't exist – was the humble, undemonstrative act that created this filmed reality.

Because of Farber's high reputation, this specimen of "termite art" (as he called it) is now in danger of being elevated to his category of "white elephant." So maybe it's good that the moment never happened.
Stuart Klawans

Date 1946

Nationality USA

Director Howard Hawks

Cast Humphrey Bogart, Lauren Bacall

Why It's Key In polemics about the deepest values of film, one small gesture in *The Big Sleep* has acquired momunental importance.

Opposite *The Big Sleep*

1940–1949

167

Key Scene **The final scene** *Paisan*

The Po River delta, Italy, 1944. The narrator of Rossellini's six-part film on World War II in Italy introduces the final episode thus: "Behind the lines, Italian partisans and American OSS officers join forces in a struggle which, although not mentioned in the war bulletins, is perhaps even tougher and more desperate." Appropriately, Rossellini's handling of the episode is abrupt, blunt, and almost anonymous. In the last scene, the Germans line up six captured partisans, their hands tied behind them, on the edge of a boat, and push them one by one into the water. On the shore, a captured American officer and a captured British officer, not part of the lineup (since, unlike the Italians, they enjoy the theoretical protection of international law), see what's going on, shout, and start to run toward the boat. A German officer drops his arm, and the two men are gunned down as they run. Then the remaining partisans fall into the water, the waves from the last splash gradually diminish, and the narrator concludes rapidly: "This happened in the winter of 1944. At the beginning of spring, the war was over." These final 40 seconds of *Paisan* constitute one of the most terrible passages of war poetry in cinema, made all the more devastating by the distance of the camera (which renders the people faceless), the swiftness of all the movements, the report-like calmness of the pan with which the camera follows the two men on their impulsive final run.
Chris Fujiwara

Date 1946

Nationality Italy

Director Roberto Rossellini

Cast Dale Edmonds

Original Title *Paisà*

Why It's Key It's one of the bleakest images of war on film.

Key Scene **Gilda sings "Put the Blame on Mame" – twice** *Gilda*

Rita Hayworth ("assisted" by the voice of Anita Ellis) actually sings "Put the Blame on Mame" twice in Charles Vidor's *Gilda*, both performances being preceded by shots of Johnny Farrell (Ford) looking out the window of his office and seeing Gilda (Hayworth) in the nightclub below. Yet aside from their identical introductions, which juxtapose Johnny's elevated position with Gilda's lowly one, these two scenes could not be more different. The first occurs after the club's customers have left. Gilda is discovered singing "Put the Blame on Mame" while seated on a card table, providing her own accompaniment with a guitar. Her audience consists solely of Uncle Pio (Geray), a menial who functions in the film as a Shakespearean clown, delivering acerbic comments on the activities and personalities of his "superiors." Gilda's rendition of the song comes across as sad and genuine, suggesting a shared intimacy with Pio, who, like Gilda herself, is little more than a pawn in a game played by powerful males.

The second version of "Put the Blame on Mame" shows Gilda singing for a large audience: in contrast to that simple white dress of the earlier scene, she is wearing a revealing black outfit, including long gloves which she peels off while dancing in a highly sexual manner, parodically presenting herself as an erotic spectacle for the masculine gaze. The solitary guitar is replaced by a full orchestra, and Gilda's sincere interpretation transformed into a defiantly celebratory one in which she seems to be ironically affirming the existence of a *noir* world where men (dismissively referred to as "boys" in the lyrics) define women as living embodiments of evil.
Brad Stevens

Date 1946

Nationality USA

Director Charles Vidor

Cast Rita Hayworth, Glenn Ford, Steven Geray

Why It's Key These scenes show how a classic *film noir* can provide a critique of that misogyny so frequently imputed to the genre.

Opposite *Gilda*

Key Scene **Introducing Chips Rafferty** *The Overlanders*

Harry Watt, a British director respected for his documentaries and wartime features, was commissioned to make a film about the Australian war effort. After much research, he settled on the story of a gigantic cattle drive that had taken place in 1942 to remove resources from beyond the reach of the Japanese, in the event of an enemy invasion. As part of this "scorched earth" policy, huge herds of cattle were driven 2,000 miles across Australia – a journey taking up to two years. As the central figure in his story, Watt deliberately set out to find a "typical" Australian hero and worked with actor Chips Rafferty to create a figure who defined the unique qualities that Watt discerned in people of the Australian outback. In the opening scenes of the film, Watt and Rafferty brilliantly sketch in the essential elements of the character – both physical characteristics (the long stride, the tipping of the hat, the rolling of the cigarette) but also the disrespect for authority, the stubborn insistence on points of principle,

and the practical "can do" response to any challenge. It's a dense and skilful exposition that, within a few minutes, established the screen persona that Rafferty played for the rest of his career and which became the definition for many Australians of the true Aussie bushman. Previously Rafferty had been a tall, gangling comedian and a supporting actor of no particular note, but with his entrance in *The Overlanders*, his future was set – and a significant contribution was made to the evolution of Australia's national identity.
Andrew Pike

Date 1946

Nationality UK/Australia

Director Harry Watt

Cast Chips Rafferty, Daphne Campbell, Jean Blue

Why it's Key Here is the introduction of a character who became the stereotype of the Australian bushman.

Key Film
It's a Wonderful Life

Capra's variation on *A Christmas Carol* traveled a remarkable arc – one unpredicted by any Ghost of Box-Office Future – starting with modest popularity in 1946 (though the film lost money, thanks to its high production cost), then obsolescence during the 1950s, until repeated television showings in the 1980s enabled its rediscovery as an American classic, while occasioning parodies of the story's angels and family-friendly values. From the time a clerical oversight let the copyright lapse on 6 February 1975, the film never left U.S. TV screens, a seasonal gift to under-resourced television programmers who embraced it as cheap holiday fare. This darkest of Capra's works guides small-town banker George Bailey (Stewart), on the brink of financial ruin and contemplating a Christmas Eve suicide, toward embracing the warmth of his community relationships, especially when small depositors flock together to save his livelihood. By depicting the alternate reality of how the town would look if George had never been born, Capra opts for the sentimental argument, rather than asking what would have changed if George had followed his dream of globetrotting adventure. The film's growing cult stature could not protect it from years of public-domain indignities, including murky prints and colorization, but in 1993 copyright was successfully reasserted based on ownership of the soundtrack, and restored prints are now controlled.

Robert Keser

Date 1946

Nationality USA

Director Frank Capra

Cast James Stewart

Why It's Key This once-forgotten film became a pop-culture phenomenon.

1940–1949

Opposite *It's a Wonderful Life*

Key Scene **Frank Chambers arrives**
The Postman Always Rings Twice

Tay Garnett's film of *The Postman Always Rings Twice* begins with a scene that has no equivalent in James M. Cain's source novel. Frank Chambers (Garfield) is introduced being dropped off outside the Twin Oaks diner by a man with whom he has just hitched a ride. This man, who will shortly be identified as District Attorney Kyle Sackett (Ames), clearly represents those values Frank rejects: he is wearing a hat and tie, whereas Frank is bareheaded and has an open collar. The implication that Frank is a free spirit, breezily dismissing anything which might connect him with bourgeois society, is reinforced by the dialogue:

Sackett: Why do you keep looking for new places, new people, new ideas?
Frank: Well, I never liked any job I ever had, and maybe the next one'll be the one I've always been looking for.

Sackett: Not worried about your future?
Frank: Oh, I got plenty of time for that. Besides, maybe my future starts right now.

Frank is standing outside the car during this conversation, leaning down to address Sackett through the front right window. Garnett's camera, however, is placed inside the car: as Frank delivers his ode to the joys of freedom, he is enclosed on all four sides by that frame within a frame created by the window. Whereas the dialogue and costumes express Frank's ideals, Garnett's *mise en scène* defines these ideals as illusory, anticipating that trap which will soon close around the protagonist and the literal prison he will eventually occupy. There could be no finer example of the way in which style creates meaning in the *film noir*.

Brad Stevens

Date 1946

Nationality USA

Director Tay Garnett

Cast John Garfield, Leon Ames

Why It's Key This scene demonstrates how style creates meaning in a typical *film noir*.

Key Film **Sense-stimulated memories**
Black Narcissus

With its voluptuous color and trompe-l'oeil Himalayas, this classic drama of five British nuns struggling against Nature and their own repressions to establish a mountaintop outpost represents a peak of studio artifice. Notwithstanding these classic elements, in 1947 the film's series of sense-memory flashbacks caused great controversy, though they now look like an enduringly original embodiment of the film's argument for bodily imperatives over spiritual ideals. Unbidden and allusive, these memories arise in the unwilling daydreamer, Sister Clodagh (Kerr). Her heightened senses react to sights and sounds that seduce her from chapel prayers to relive the romantic frustration that drove her to a religious vocation (an objectionable motivation to U.S. censors, who snipped the flashbacks from the original release). One glimpse of brilliant blue sky triggers a memory of a half-forgotten idyll, with a lake's sparkling waves seeming to promise hope for marital fulfillment. Then, a dog's bark prompts a vision of fox-hunting hounds and riders bounding across the Irish landscape, while a mention of emeralds summons up the image of her grandmother's necklace, "for when you marry." Finally, a particular hymn during Christmas services evokes the happiness of caroling with her suitor, but the nun catches herself feeling too much pleasure from the worldly emotions invading her consciousness. "I had forgotten everything until I came here," she later confesses. These poetic jolts, in which psychology keeps the past alive in the present, pointed the way for later explorations of memory by Alain Resnais and Raul Ruiz.

Robert Keser

Date 1947

Nationality UK

Directors Michael Powell and Emeric Pressburger

Cast Deborah Kerr

Why It's Key Memory assumes more psychological import than mere flashbacks.

Key Scene **Sailors appear from nowhere to menace the protagonist** *Fireworks*

In his devastatingly powerful debut, made when he was 17 (Anger made earlier films but does not generally show them), Anger announces his masochistic obsession with the male body. In the key scene, he enters a men's room to be confronted with the groundless and undefined vastness of a city at night. Soon there is a cut to a shot of a group of sailors, head and torsos stunningly lit against a background that's totally black. They slice into the darkness with the same power that they later use to seemingly cut into Anger's flesh. The contrast between their whites and grays and the blackness around them is the key here: it gives them a visionary phallic power that makes the beating they give Anger, playing himself, seem erotic even to one who is not a masochist. Throughout the film, and throughout Anger's work, power resides in light and light contrasts, and this is the earliest source of that motif. That the plot turns ultimately restorative – "the sleeper returns to his bed less empty than before" – does nothing to obviate the sailors' power. Indeed, in the film's system, it is the violence of the sailors' image, and the actual violence that follows, that seem to function as the restorer.

Fred Camper

Date 1947

Nationality USA

Director Kenneth Anger

Cast Kenneth Anger, Bill Seltzer, Gordon Gray

Why It's Key Throughout Kenneth Anger's oeuvre, light is equated with power, and the apparition of the sailors represents the first, and most explicitly phallic, instance of this theme.

Key Scene **The heroine disarms a man intent on murder** *The Man I Love*

Date 1947

Nationality USA

Director Raoul Walsh

Cast Ida Lupino, Don McGuire, Robert Alda

Why It's Key The fervor of Lupino and the abstraction of Walsh combine to create a moment of truth.

SPOILER

In this neglected melodrama, Ida Lupino stars as hardbitten jazz singer Petey Brown, who arrives from New York to visit her siblings in Los Angeles. Her stay is marked by interlocking crises that culminate one night when Gloria (Dolores Moran), a flirtatious married woman who lives across the hall from the family, is hit and killed by a car while on her way home from a tryst with nightclub owner Teresca (Alda). In love with Petey and hoping to use Gloria's death (in which Petey's brother was also involved) to keep her in his clutches, Teresca invites Petey out for a night drive. They leave his office and start to descend the stairs to the garage when Gloria's vengeful husband, Johnny (McGuire), appears at the bottom of the stairs and brandishes a gun, intent on killing Teresca. While Teresca remains frozen in fear, Petey approaches Johnny and stops him halfway up the stairs with a bid to talk some sense into him; when that doesn't work, she disarms him with a karate chop to the wrist, slaps

him back and forth across the face, and, after a few compassionate words with the chastened would-be assassin, sends him home.

The greatness of *The Man I Love* owes equally to Raoul Walsh's ability to configure his characters into an abstract pattern in motion and to the melancholy fervor of Lupino's performance. In this scene, whose moment-of-truth quality is heightened by the geometrical starkness of the set, the absolute conviction Lupino packs into her performance, no less than her unexpected and authoritative use of physical force, makes a resonant statement that caps off this most pro-woman of Warner Bros. films.
Chris Fujiwara

Key Scene **Verdoux attempts to kill Annabella in a rowboat** *Monsieur Verdoux*

Date 1947

Nationality USA

Director Charles Chaplin

Cast Charles Chaplin, Martha Raye

Why It's Key This scene shows how radically Chaplin revised his "Little Tramp" image.

Even today, the idea of "Charlie" Chaplin playing a serial killer seems remarkably audacious: in 1947 it must have come across as nothing short of outrageous. Yet *Monsieur Verdoux*, rather than shy away from the implications of recasting Chaplin's "Little Tramp" as a multiple wife-murderer, constantly reminds us of the comic tradition being traduced. Consider the scene in which Henri Verdoux (Chaplin) sits in a rowboat with Annabella Bonheur (Raye), his latest wife/victim. As Annabella fishes while facing away from him, Verdoux picks up a noose concealed near his feet and prepares to slip it around Annabella's neck. When Annabella unexpectedly turns around, Verdoux attempts to conceal his actions by dropping the noose, crossing his legs, placing his linked hands over his knees, and swaying from left to right with a broad grin on his face. It is precisely the kind of "innocent" gesture we are familiar with from the earlier work of Chaplin, whose Tramp character frequently expressed his

essential goodness by moving and smiling in this way (see, for example, the ending of *City Lights* [1931]). The Tramp was clearly a member of the bourgeoisie fallen on hard times: *Monsieur Verdoux* has him rejoin "respectable" society by liquidating members of the opposite sex, something which Verdoux's opening voiceover reassures us he did "as a strictly business enterprise, to support a home and family." As the courtroom climax suggests, older conceptions of innocence are no longer viable in a world where businessmen thrive by causing death on a massive scale: The Tramp can only survive in this world by becoming a psychopath.
Brad Stevens

Key Scene **Recuperating in Irene's apartment** *Dark Passage*

A dream-like thriller whose atmosphere oscillates between grim melodrama and nothing-is-impossible fairy tale (few movies can boast as many unlikely coincidences), *Dark Passage* is perhaps the least appreciated of the four Bogart-Bacall movies, probably because it eschewed the blatant erotic tension and double-entendre banter of Howard Hawks's earlier *The Big Sleep* and *To Have and Have Not*. In this scene, Vincent Parry (Bogart), an escaped convict who is innocent of the murder for which he was serving a life sentence in San Quentin, has just undergone plastic surgery to change his facial appearance, and he seeks shelter in the apartment of Irene (Bacall), a young woman who picked him up on the road after he escaped. He is weak, his face is entirely wrapped up, he cannot talk and has to be fed through a glass tube. Irene's motherly attention and Vincent's infant-like condition contribute to make the scene a metaphor for gestation and birth, the

cozy apartment a womb-like safe haven before Vincent can be born again: Irene feeds him through a tube that, to pursue the metaphor, may be seen as some kind of umbilical cord, and later, after unwrapping his bandages, she will give him his new identity – a new name.

Jean-Pierre Coursodon

Date 1947

Nationality USA

Director Delmer Daves

Cast Humphrey Bogart, Lauren Bacall, Agnes Moorehead

Why It's Key It's a rare and precious moment of intimacy and tenderness in the history of *film noir* and the joint career of Bogart and Bacall.

Opposite *Dark Passage*

Key Scene **In walked Kathie** *Out of the Past*

"And then I saw her coming out of the sun...." With this line of flashback narration by Jeff Bailey/ex-Jeff Markham (Mitchum), a wonderfully individualized moment marks off this classic *film noir* from all the others. As its action moves to Mexico, settling in Acapulco, Tourneur disdains any showy effect, quickly moving from evocative establishing shots to a few brief, expressive images of Jeff walking toward the Café La Mar Azul, the Ciné Pico behind him, then sitting in the café. Tourneur then cuts between "And then I saw her..." and "...coming out of the sun" as Kathie Moffat (Greer), in white dress and hat, quietly but magically enters in wide shot – in sunlight as the shot begins, moving into shadow, settling into light shade as she reaches the foreground and sits at a table. The same calm in image and sound defines the closer shots that follow, as the two characters meet and talk: even the director's less immediately striking compositions display the same balance, integrity, and

subtle beauty. Beyond this, there is the effect on the narrative. It's not a first meeting of lovers who are destined always to love each other unambiguously, but as much as any such meeting, it casts a spell and remains moving, even when Kathie has long been revealed as treacherous. As a grim end approaches, she evokes her entrance by telling Jeff, "I want to walk out of the sun again and find you waiting." Now there are only shadows. Yet somehow, in our imaginations and the emotions they tap, it is the sunlight that remains

Blake Lucas

Date 1947

Nationality USA

Director Jacques Tourneur

Cast Robert Mitchum, Jane Greer

Why It's Key Exceptional atmospheric and compositional beauty combine with a mature inflection to give poetic power to one of cinema's most memorable characters in her very first moments on screen, with telling effect on the film in which she is a central figure.

Key Scene **The pearl dive**
The Pearl

Perhaps best known outside Mexico for his acting roles in Sam Peckinpah's *The Wild Bunch* (1969) and *Pat Garrett & Billy the Kid* (1973), Emilio Fernández was the William Wyler of Mexican cinema, its deep-space classical master, the central figure in the country's cinematic golden age. Known as "Il Indio" because his mother was Indian, he was imprisoned during the Mexican Revolution, became an actor, and made his directing debut in 1941. When his 1944 film *María Candelaria* won the Grand Prix at Cannes, it put him and Mexican cinema on the map. Such was his fame that John Steinbeck allowed him to film his novel *The Pearl* before it was published. The result, Fernández's ninth film as director, had his name written all over it. As with many of his films, the protagonists of *The Pearl* are indigenous people. Its tragic story, about how a pearl diver (Armendáriz) and his family are ruined after he finds a pearl, has a compassionate New Testament intensity, the wife

(Marqués) frequently filmed as if she were the Virgin Mary. Its photography, by one of the world's greatest DPs, Gabriel Figueroa, uses deep space and chiaroscuro with the brilliance of Gregg Toland, with whom Figueroa worked. Technically, the luminous pearl dive itself matches Hollywood at its very best in this period. The underwater cinematography is breathtaking. Armendariz's dive is full of jeopardy, as the pearl itself is hard to reach. When he does so and finally returns to the surface, Fernandez stages the triumphant sequence with brilliance.

Mark Cousins

Date 1947

Nationality Mexico

Director Emilio Fernández

Cast Pedro Armendáriz, María Elena Marqués

Original Title *La Perla*

Why It's Key It's one of the key moments in Mexican cinema's golden age.

Key Event
The Waldorf meeting

The House Un-American Activities Committee (HUAC) began its investigation into the supposed spread of "Communist subversion" in 1947. By the time a group of studio executives, producers, and representatives from regulatory and employer groups met at New York's Waldorf-Astoria Hotel on November 24-25, 1947, the "Hollywood Ten" – a group of directors and screenwriters who defied Congress by refusing to inform on others (aka "naming names," a ritual of self-abnegation and the title of a book on the Hollywood Blacklist by Victor Navasky) – were in danger of losing their jobs and going to prison.

Wary of Congressional intervention and threats to their industry, the participants in the Waldorf Conference decided to abandon the Ten and capitulate to HUAC's demands to institute a blacklist and, at least implicitly, agree to the committee's desire to monitor so-called "subversive" content in the motion-picture industry. Following the meeting, what has been christened the "Waldorf Statement" proclaimed that "members of the

Association of Motion Picture Producers deplore the action of the ten Hollywood men who have been cited for contempt" and asserted that "we will not knowingly employ a Communist or member of any party or group which advocates the overthrow of the government."

For many radicals, the failure of liberal members of the film industry to defend the rights of leftists – and the Hollywood Ten specifically – was a fateful chapter in the history of the Blacklist. Dore Schary, an RKO executive with well-known liberal views, was attacked for his cowardice by many Hollywood radicals. In Patrick McGilligan and Paul Buhle's *Tender Comrades*, collected interviews with some of the most famous blacklistees, Paul Jarrico, a screenwriter blacklisted in the 1950s, well known for producing the radical classic *Salt of the Earth* (1954), observed that the failure of liberals to support their leftist brethren during the Waldorf Conference insured the staying power of the blacklist.

Richard Porton

Date November 24-25, 1947

Why It's Key This meeting of studio executives and producers sealed the fate of the Hollywood Ten and helped to reinforce the US Congress's assault on "subversion" in the entertainment industry.

Key Event **Publication of "Birth of a New Avant-Garde: The *Caméra-Stylo*"**

On March 30, 1948, *L'Écran français* number 144 published an article by literary critic-turned-cineaste Alexandre Astruc, the 25-year-old son of Parisian journalists, which announced a New Wave in cinema and was a stepping stone towards it. Astruc relied on analogy, comparing a film director to a novelist: the latter's pen became the former's camera-pen. Even the earliest film theorists used such analogies, to elevate cinema into the realm of the other arts, to insist that it was personal and psychological, that it had a duty to render real life honestly. The comparison also implied that cinema had a language of its own. Astruc was not the first to say this, but he wrote in a cinephile country and had the ear of filmmakers, and *L'Écran français* was born in the era of the Resistance, when subjectivity was valued more than mass action. His ideas took hold. François Truffaut built on them six years later in "A Certain Tendency in the French Cinema," the second theoretical essay that paved the way for the French New Wave. The Astruc-Truffaut call to arms, in the spirit of Faulkner and Baudelaire, was compelling, though Truffaut became a literary filmmaker of the type his earlier self might not have admired, and Astruc, who started directing in the year of his famous essay, was one from the start. Perhaps only in the digital age can Astruc's dream of the camera-pen be realized.

Mark Cousins

Date March 30, 1948

Why It's Key Alexandre Astruc's groundbreaking essay challenged the mainstream idea that film is a producer's medium.

Key Scene **Mice fool a cat by switching landscapes** *Mouse Wreckers*

SPOILER

Two mice find their potential new home, one occupied by a cat whose trophy case includes "Best Mouser 1948." Realizing the need for "stragety" to evict it, they proceed to try to drive the cat mad, beginning pranks while it sleeps such as pumping it up with air so that it shoots around when deflating. The cat is driven first to nerve tonic, and then to reading a psychology book, just before the ultimate prank, in which the mice nail all the furniture in its room to the ceiling and attach a ceiling lamp to the floor. On awakening, the confused cat tries to clutch at the ceiling – until, walking into the next room, it discovers the furniture is right side up. The film's greatest moment follows, when the cat looks to one window, and the view outside is of an upside-down landscape, now contradicting the right-side-up furniture – and we see that the mice have placed a painting against the window. The cat looks at another and its landscape is sideways, and the third and last window appears to be underwater – the mice have placed a fish tank against it. Stark raving mad, the cat rushes from the house. As in Jones's work at his best, space, and time, and sometimes language, are used as vehicles of control – to discombobulate the characters, or to assert one's control over the other.

Fred Camper

Date 1948

Nationality USA

Director Chuck Jones

Why It's Key Jones's vision, turning on control of physical space, gains a hilarious and ecstatically disorienting expression here.

Key Speech **"You shoulda let them kill me"**
Red River

Howard Hawks fans like to parrot received wisdom about the director's "ethos of professionalism," pointing out that many of his action-adventure films explore what happens when prickly, talented individualists join forces in a mission impossible. But those of us who have attempted to assemble such groups know how thankless a task it is to keep everyone motivated. An exact contemporary of Hawks's, André Breton, is vilified to this day for his autocratic leadership of the French Surrealists; so why do we find Hawks's group leaders – from Cary Grant in *Only Angels Have Wings* (1939) to John Wayne in *Rio Bravo* (1959) – so sympathetic?

The answer is revealed in *Red River*, in which Thomas Dunson (Wayne) signs up a gang of recalcitrant cowboys – among them his adopted son Matt (Clift), and the gunslinger Cherry Valance (Ireland) – for a near-suicidal cattle drive across the 1,000-mile-long Chisholm Trail. Dunson becomes increasingly tyrannical, and in a climactic scene guns down three men who try to jump ship. Matt prevents the others from retaliating, but takes over the drive, abandoning Dunson. The last thing Dunson says to him? "You shoulda let them kill me." It's impossible to tell, from the look on Wayne's face, whether Dunson is angry with Matt or proud of him – probably both.

The drive succeeds, not because of the ethos of professionalism shared by Matt and Cherry, but because they're more scared of Dunson catching up than they are of the Comanches ahead. This is Hawks's secret: A charismatic leader is a terrifying one.
Joshua Glenn

Date 1948

Nationality USA

Director Howard Hawks

Cast John Wayne, Montgomery Clift, John Ireland

Why It's Key Howard Hawks and John Wayne offer a lesson in leadership.

Opposite *Red River*

Key Scene **The ending**
Force of Evil

There was a velvety hush about the best *films noirs*, something so sotto voce that when the violence finally came, it seemed almost hysterical. Usually the velvet was sexual, but blacklisted director Abraham Polonsky's *Force of Evil* seems to care as much about poetry as sex. Set against a numbers racket, it tells a Cain-and-Abel story about sharky, silver-tongued Joe Morse (Garfield) and his decent, small-time, overweight brother Leo (Thomas Gomez). Joe has his eyes on the big time, the capitalist dream, but his plans will grind people like Leo into the ground. The screenplay, by Polonsky and novelist Ira Wolfert, plays with the fact that each knows this, so the dread builds, but the moral stench is sweetened by scenes of verbal richness rare in American cinema, where Joe woos Doris (Pearson), and she responds with moral acuity. In their sparring they seduce, repeating each other's words again and again. In the film's climax, Joe goes in search of his dead brother, past factories, down past the meat-packing district, down flights of steps, over bollards, and down to the water's edge. Here he finds the body of his brother. Visually, the sequence is a descent into hell. The camera gets there first, and watches as Garfield rushes to get there, too, where he deserves to be.

Because of the shameful HUAC blacklist, this master director would not make his next film for 21 years. *Force of Evil* influenced Martin Scorsese's films *Mean Streets* (1973), *Raging Bull* (1980), and *Goodfellas* (1990). He introduced it to Francis Ford Coppola, Robert De Niro, and Michael Powell. It's not hard to see why.
Mark Cousins

Date 1948

Nationality USA

Director Abraham Polonsky

Cast John Garfield, Beatrice Pearson

Why It's Key This scene demonstrates the visual mastery of one of America's greatest political filmmakers.

Key Scene **Stefan's realisation**
Letter from an Unknown Woman

All dramatists aim for something that sounds simple enough, but is the hardest of all to craft: the invention of plot incidents that are at once *inevitable* – perfectly logical, even predictable – and yet truly, richly *surprising*. In cinema, such narrative gifts are more powerful than in theatre or literature, since we see the fictional world, still calmly unfolding as it should, but also witness the *epiphany* that comes as an emotional surplus. *Letter from an Unknown Woman*, one of cinema's most perfect works, structures itself towards the unveiling of just such an epiphany. It begins with Stefan (Jourdan), a celebrity pianist with a long line of casual lovers, receiving a letter from the "unknown" (because forgotten by him) Lisa (Joan Fontaine), whose life has been tragically shaped by her encounters with him. Her story unfolds in flashback, with minimal reminders of the "framing" situation of Stefan at his desk. But finally, after the long, slow, painful decline of Lisa has been narrated, we return to the letter's recipient: Stefan lifts his head and, accompanied by an intense musical stab of strings, shows us that he is now crying. From everyday indifference to utter absorption: Stefan's path mirrors that of the spectator. But it is made all the more keenly poignant for being cleverly hidden from us, "shuffled under" the unfolding flashback. The device adds surprise to inevitability – who would not be moved to tears by Lisa's tale? – and sharpens the film's affective force: Stefan's "delayed reaction" triggers his own catharsis.

Adrian Martin

Date 1948

Nationality USA

Director Max Ophuls

Cast Louis Jourdan

Why It's Key One of the most perfect of all films culminates in an emotional epiphany.

Key Scene **Antonio and Bruno eat in the restaurant** *The Bicycle Thief* (*Bicycle Thieves*)

It's Sunday, and Antonio (Maggiorani) and his son, Bruno (Staiola), have been scouring the city in a fruitless search for the stolen bicycle that is indispensable for Antonio to hold down his new job as a bill poster. Frustrated and annoyed, Antonio slaps Bruno and goes off to look along the river on his own. Returning to see a number of people rescuing a young boy from the water, Antonio, relieved to see Bruno sitting safely near the bridge, decides to make amends by buying both of them a pizza in a nearby *trattoria*.

The scene in the restaurant that follows – arguably the only reasonably light-hearted scene in the entire film – is more than just one other episode in the day's fruitless search but rather has a complex role to play within the film's overall economy. As the father finally decides to pay more attention to his son's needs than to his own stolen bike, the moment serves to re-establish the bond between the two, which has been fraying as the day has worn on. In asking Bruno to share a glass of wine with him, Antonio is not only attending to the boy's needs but also treating him as an adult, a gesture that will be amply repayed when, at the end of the film, Bruno will offer his disgraced father his own hand. At the same time, the juxtaposition between the poor fare they can hardly afford and the feast being eaten by the rich family at the next table, further underscored by the financial calculations that Antonio asks Bruno to do on paper, reiterates the overwhelming importance of the bicycle for the family's survival, thus contributing to Bruno's understanding of his father's desperate and humiliating attempt to steal a bicycle himself at the end of the film.

Gino Moliterno

Date 1948

Nationality Italy

Director Vittorio De Sica

Cast Lamberto Maggiorani, Enzo Staiola

Original Title *Ladri di biciclette*

Why It's Key The scene re-establishes the close bond between father and son while reiterating what the loss of the bicycle means for the whole family.

Opposite *The Bicycle Thief*

SPOILER

Key Scene **Hall of mirrors**
The Lady from Shanghai

The shattering of ambiguously multiple mirror images in an off-season fairground brings to a climax the continually shifting imagery in this play with *film noir* as dark comedy. The unstable mental state of the hero, sailor Michael O'Hara (Welles), is expressed in physical terms as he tumbles from the *Caligari*-like expressionism of the Crazy House to the fragmented world of the Hall of Mirrors. The final shootout, in which the bullets fired by vicious lawyer Bannister (Everett Sloane) and his conniving wife, Elsa (Hayworth), smash mirror after mirror before finding their targets, illustrates, as J. P. Telotte writes in *Voices in the Dark*, "the destructive circularity desire can unleash."

Welles's demolition of Hayworth's persona in *The Lady from Shanghai* seems more a challenge to the Hollywood convention of the romantic heroine than the reflection of any animosity towards his then-estranged wife. Hayworth appears to have been willingly complicit in this project, apparently having entertained the hope that she would enhance her status as an actress by taking on the role of the femme fatale Elsa against type. The incongruity of Welles's construction and playing of the role of O'Hara as a figure of ingenuous inconsequence is maintained to the end as he stands silhouetted in the background, unmoved by Elsa's pleas for help, only to walk away, diminished by the craning camera, as he tritely concludes that "everybody's somebody's fool."
Bruce Hodsdon

Date 1948

Nationality USA

Director Orson Welles

Cast Orson Welles, Rita Hayworth, Everett Sloane

Why It's Key This must rank as one of the most satisfyingly ambivalent dénouements in the annals of *film noir*, if not in all of classical Hollywood cinema.

Opposite *The Lady from Shanghai*

1940–1949

183

Key Scene **The stairs**
A Hen in the Wind

A Hen in the Wind remains one of the lesser-known works of Japanese master Yasujiro Ozu, but it occupies a crucial position in his body of work. Although often superficially treated as one homogenous, near-perfect block, with the inimitable, slow, harmonious, and more famous late films serving as models for generalizations, Ozu's oeuvre is a lot more variegated, including some remarkably lively silent work (often in genre assignments) and a critical phase of near-silence during the Second World War. Ozu clearly tried to come to grips with the war, and *A Hen in the Wind* was his most overt attempt to do so – maybe that's why the shy director considered it a failure. Yet it's an outstanding film, in which – tellingly – some key elements of Ozu's late style crystallize, so its neglect may have to do with its atypical nature, *A Hen in the Wind* being clearly an "Occupation" film and containing a shocking scene one would not expect from Ozu. The story is about a poor woman (Tanaka) who, waiting for her husband (Sano) to return from the war, must prostitute herself to pay their sick son's hospital bill. When the man returns, he cannot forgive her, and ultimately, he unexpectedly pushes her down the stairs. After lying immobile and distorted for a while, she slowly, painfully climbs back up, and only then he considers reconciliation, by forgetting the past. It may be dubious as an allegory, but then the film's tone certainly does not suggest patriotic reconstruction – rather, human-scale compromise.
Christoph Huber

Date 1948

Nationality Japan

Director Yasujiro Ozu

Cast Kinuyo Tanaka, Shuji Sano

Original Title *Kaze no naka no mendori*

Why It's Key Japanese master Yasujiro Ozu is generally and superficially identified with his refined late style. But his earlier work is full of surprises – including a truly unexpected moment in this unfairly neglected postwar drama.

Key Scene **A late night song**
Jungle Patrol

During World War II, a squadron of eight officers stationed in New Guinea has had the seemingly miraculous good fortune of suffering no fatalities despite long engagement in aerial combat. A USO entertainer, Jean (Miller), unexpectedly arrives by herself, and quickly makes friends with the men in this group. In the evening, she entertains all the soldiers on the base, then has a more intimate late-night interaction with the eight in the makeshift officers club, where she sings them a beautiful song, "Forever and Always" (by Al Rinker and Floyd Huddleston). Leaning against the piano while Johnny (Murphy) plays, there is a communion of her face and voice with the silent faces of the men, as she shares this moment of highest emotion with them, one that suggests that her presence among them and the unusual circumstance they all share do have a special place in the flow of eternity. What this place is, the film never explicitly says, but Newman gives the audience a chance to contemplate it through his feeling for the characters and way of visualizing them. The scene may seem simple, but its idealism is unmistakable in his sensitive hands, and it becomes the film's touchstone. For in it, the director finds in Miller an image off which to play the action that follows the next morning – most of it evoked in sound alone – as the world comes into balance in a way that affirms the mystical quality of this haunting work.
Blake Lucas

Date 1948

Nationality USA

Director Joseph M. Newman

Cast Kristine Miller, Arthur Franz, Ross Ford, Tommy Noonan, Gene Reynolds, Richard Jaeckel, Mickey Knox, Harry Lauter, William Murphy

Why It's Key An intimate war movie, modest in its production but not its vision, fortuitously falls into the hands of Newman, whose sometimes submerged humanism here finds ideal expression.

Key Scene **The death leap**
The Red Shoes

SPOILER

The climactic moment of this matchless drama of the ballet world was the very first scene its young star, Moira Shearer, had shot. Torn between her career as a prima ballerina, under the thumb of all-controlling impresario Lermontov (Walbrook), and the young composer husband (Goring) who loves her but insists she give up her dancing career, Victoria Page (Shearer) runs out of her dressing room, down the stairs of the theater, and onto the terrace of the Monte Carlo hotel that overlooks the railway station. As if to join her husband – and abandon him at the same time – she leaps off the balustrade, to be run over by the oncoming train that has arrived at the station to take him away from her. Devastatingly horrible, yet oddly beautiful, this signal moment can only be followed by another – an ashen-faced Lermontov informing his audience: "Miss Page is unable to dance *The Red Shoes* tonight – or any other night!" In his memoir, *A Life in Movies*, Powell explained it best: "I think the real reason why *The Red Shoes* was such a success was that we had been told for ten years to go out and die for freedom and democracy, for this and for that, and now that the war was over, *The Red Shoes* told us to go out and die for art."
David Ehrenstein

Date 1948

Nationality UK

Directors Michael Powell and Emeric Pressburger

Cast Moira Shearer, Anton Walbrook, Marius Goring

Why It's Key One of the most unforgettable climaxes in cinematic history, the scene shows how death can transcend love and art.

Key Scene **The desiring hand through the broken glass** *Spring in a Small Town*

Quiet panning on a young woman, Yuwen (Wei), as she goes through the garden to the pavilion used as a guest room for Zhishen (Shi), the man she didn't marry when she was 16 and who has turned out to be a friend of her ailing husband. A reverse-angle shot shows Zhishen trying to prevent her from entering. After a couple of back and forth cuts, she's in; he follows her. Cut to the moon.

Yuwen tries to light a candle; Zhishen blows out the match. Insert of the fragrant orchid she gave him. She turns toward him; he carries her in his arms, then puts her down, turns his back to her; the camera follows him. He opens the door, she tries to stop him. Outside, he locks the door. With a small cry of pain, she breaks the glass pane; the camera espouses the movement of her hand in Zhishen's direction, then follows him back as he returns to the door and opens it.

He takes her hand, then crosses the room to his doctor's kit. Cutting to Yuwen, her head lowered in shame, the camera then pans on Zhishen's movements, as he joins her and bandages her hand. She slowly raises her head and turns; they are now framed together. The camera tilts down, he kisses her bandaged hand. Cut to her face, eyes closed. She opens her eyes but does not look at him; he stands up. She has regained her composure and gets up: they are on the same level. She says, coolly: "Thank you."

Bérénice Reynaud

Date 1948

Nationality China

Director Fei Mu

Cast Wei Wei, Shi Yu

Original Title *Xiao cheng zhi chun*

Why It's Key Through gliding camera movements, Fei Mu expresses post-Confucian, repressed passion during the crisis that followed the war, and turns his last film into a masterpiece.

Key Scene **A man compares his feet with his earlier footprints** *Moonrise*

The rural setting of *Moonrise* is enlivened a bit by a local character, Billy Scripture (Morgan), who never speaks. The protagonist, Danny (Clark), usually friendly to him, threatens him once. Near the film's end, Billy is seen trying to fit his feet in the footprints he apparently made in wet cement years ago. This apparently innocuous moment is not only tremendously moving, but carries a real visionary force, because of the way it connects with the style and meaning of the whole film – and of much of Borzage's work. A major theme in *Moonrise* is the power of the past over the present: Danny is haunted by his father's hanging, which occurred in his infancy. This theme is foregrounded many times, from the stunning opening montage to the pan past a doll hanging by Danny's old crib very near the end. What the wise but mute Billy realizes through the mismatch between his feet and their imprint, long before Danny does, is that time is irreversible, that you cannot go back, can never be the person that you once

were – a realization that is a first step toward becoming free of the past. Throughout Borzage's films, objects and shadows – the old room's furniture in *Smilin' Through* (1941), the grandmother's shawl in *I've Always Loved You* (1946) – stand for those aspects of humans that do not reside in the body but represent spirit or soul. Billy's footprints are related to these objects – and his realization that he is changing is what finally helps free Danny, too.

Fred Camper

Date 1948

Nationality USA

Director Frank Borzage

Cast Dane Clark, Harry Morgan

Why It's Key For Borzage, shadows, objects, and other signs of characters evoke the idea of the soul.

Key Scene **The unwanted guest**
The Treasure of the Sierra Madre

"I know what gold can do to men's souls," says crafty old-timer Howard (Walter Huston, father of director John), cautioning his new cohorts, Fred C. Dobbs (Bogart) and Bob Curtin (Holt), about the evils and pitfalls of greed. The three prospectors are in 1920s Mexico searching for the precious metal, and are eventually undone by their own greed – particularly Dobbs, who becomes a raving psychotic by film's end. John Huston, who has a cameo as a white-suited American in the early reels, had been fascinated with reclusive author B. Traven's novel for years. In one particularly tense sequence that plumbs the depths of depravity to which these ill-fated adventurers have already sunk, the distrustful trio is approached at the remote location of their gold mine by another American, Cody (Bennett), a seemingly honest guy who wants a cut of their action. Grudgingly tolerated for a night, he speaks bluntly about their options – kill him, let him go, or make him a partner.

They decide to protect their claim by killing him, but before they can do so, they are interrupted by a bandit attack, during which Cody is killed helping them defend the camp. Later, Dobbs discovers sincere letters to and from his wife: he was on the level, after all.
David Stratton

Date 1948

Nationality USA

Director John Huston

Cast Humphrey Bogart, Walter Huston, Tim Holt, Bruce Bennett

Why It's Key This tense sequence plumbs the depths of depravity to which greed can drive people.

Opposite *The Treasure of the Sierra Madre*

Key Event
The Paramount divestiture decree

Complaints from independent theater exhibitors that the Hollywood studios' chokehold on producing, exhibiting, and distributing films constituted a monopoly that restrained free competition prompted the federal government to file a lawsuit in 1938 called *United States vs. Paramount Pictures, Inc. et al.,* charging the "Big Five" studios (Paramount, MGM, Warners, 20th Century-Fox, and RKO) with violating antitrust statutes. Ten years of industry attempts to foil the antitrust forces with legal appeals, as well as behind-the-scenes political jockeying and proposed concessions, foundered when the U.S. Supreme Court unanimously ruled that all studios had to divest themselves of their nationwide theater chains. Combined with plummeting ticket sales and the growing proliferation of television sets, this ruling, which meant the loss of predictable and guaranteed theatrical income for the studios, started forces that would result in the physical dismantling and sale of studio backlots and warehouses barely a decade later. Ironically, as theater attendance declined throughout the 1950s, it was the motion-picture corporations that ultimately benefited from having sold their aging real-estate holdings, thus passing on the loss to independent theater owners, exactly those that the Paramount decree had intended to protect.
Robert Keser

Date May 3, 1948

Why It's Key It spelled the beginning of the end for Hollywood's studio system.

Key Scene **The end of the couple's journey**
Colorado Territory

In 1941 Walsh directed the classic gangster film *High Sierra* – from a screenplay by John Huston and W. R. Burnett – in which the protagonist (Humphrey Bogart) is shot and killed on a mountain, while the woman who loves him (Ida Lupino) watches helplessly from below. In this Western remake, Walsh had the opportunity (with Edmund H. North and his favorite writing collaborator, John Twist) to reconceive this ending, and in a setting – sacred Indian cliff dwellings of the Southwest – that feels even more eternal. Here, after sympathetic outlaw Wes McQueen (McCrea) is shot, soulmate Colorado Carson (Mayo) is able to run to him, two guns in her hands, and shoot it out with the posse, drawing their fire so that as Wes moves to her side and takes her hand, she too is shot and dies with him. The forceful visual style of Walsh makes this moment a peak of his work, as he tracks in on the pair as they fall, letting the camera come to rest on their joined hands, but beyond its realization, the scene lifts the whole film to an intensely spiritual plane. The final union in death of Wes and Colorado not only gives meaning to their whole lives, both separately and together – she has returned to sources, the land she grew up in, to "live over" the life that had led her low with a new result, while he has "lived over" his outlaw life to finally bring it to rest – but intimates a harmony in time and space that accords to their love a transcendent value and sense of redemption.

Blake Lucas

Date 1949

Nationality USA

Director Raoul Walsh

Cast Joel McCrea, Virginia Mayo

Why It's Key Amid a vast body of work that always favored male-female couples in which the man and the woman are complementary and equally strong, a great American director finds an apotheosis in the most dramatic of all final reunions.

Key Scene **Last night in a Kyoto inn**
Late Spring

Late in Ozu's extremely moving film comes one of the most discussed scenes in cinema. A widowed father (Ryu) and his devoted daughter (Hara) lie side by side in their room at an inn in Kyoto, on the last night of the last trip they will take together. She turns toward him, seemingly about to broach the topic that has been a main theme of the film: her father's supposed intention to remarry (which is actually a ruse to compel his daughter, who would otherwise follow her inclination to stay with him forever, to accept a marriage offer). He is apparently asleep. She looks up, smiling, and Ozu cuts to a shot of another area of the darkened room: a vase in the center of the composition; behind it, a *shoji* (rice paper) screen. Ozu cuts back to the daughter, her eyes still open, her face sad. Then he cuts again to the shot with the vase.

The cutting confronts Setsuko Hara's face with a space that both accommodates and excludes her (a space that is as "full" as it is "empty") and with an image of a devastating sublimity, in whose proximity she can only turn away and stare off into the real indeterminacy that always opens in front of her. The shot is an image of the irremediable, a reminder that, as much as we (like the Hara character) might want it to go on forever, the film is soon going to end, and there is nothing we can do about it.

Chris Fujiwara

Date 1949

Nationality Japan

Director Yasujiro Ozu

Cast Setsuko Hara, Chishu Ryu

Original Title *Banshun*

Why It's Key This famous scene, the subject of many divergent interpretations, offers an image of the sublime and the irremediable.

Key Scene **A strange deposition**
D.O.A.

Some *films noirs* begin after the events they depict, with a voice coming from beyond the grave (Billy Wilder's *Sunset Blvd.* [1950]), others offer an unexpected twist (Otto Preminger's *Laura* [1944]). The first scene of *D.O.A.* manages to combine both approaches in the most striking way. During the opening credits, two long travelling shots follow Frank Bigelow (O'Brien) entering, with determination, a police station and stopping at the Homicide Division. There, he reports a murder, and we finally see his face when he designates as the victim – himself! Although the setting appears rather conventional for the cycle (the night and the contrasted lighting create a menacing surrounding), the scene itself is symptomatic of the fast-paced narrative that will unfold. Maté's film draws its inspiration from Robert Siodmak's German film *Der Mann, der seinen Mörder sucht* (*Looking for His Murderer* [1931]) and relates the investigation that an accountant undertakes when he discovers he has been poisoned by radiation. Thus, *D.O.A.* presents an original variation on the classical structure of detective stories, with Bigelow embodying both the murder victim and the investigator. He is a living/dead character who will stay alive just long enough to tell his story in a desperate attempt to make sense of what has happened to him: as such, he is the typical *noir* anti-hero, doomed from the very beginning. However, the fatalism inherent to the cycle manifests itself in a generic disruption. Needless to say, this shocking beginning was kept for the inferior 1988 remake.

Frank Lafond

Date 1949

Nationality USA

Director Rudolph Maté

Cast Edmond O'Brien

Why It's Key it's a perfect example of *film noir*'s fatalistic and nightmarish narratives.

Key Person **Lata Mangeshkar**
Mahal (*The Palace*)

Mahal is a ghost story and a romance and a murder mystery and several other things thrown in. Hari Shankar (Ashok Kumar) inherits an old house and comes upon the portrait of a young woman (Madhubala) who died in the house. Then Hari Shankar begins to see an apparition – and it's the woman in the portrait.

A huge hit, the film lives through its music, specially the "Aayega Aanewaala" ("He who is destined to arrive will arrive") song, which featured a 19-year-old singer named Lata Mangeshkar. She came from the small state of Goa, south of Mumbai, where her family was of the devadasi caste, which meant they sang and danced in the temples. For the next 50 years, Mangeshkar lent her voice to several generations of Bollywood's heroines. Blessed with perfect pitch and tone, her voice suited the presumptive virgins (heroines, mothers, sisters), while her sister, Asha Bhosle, sang the naughtier numbers for the fallen women (vamps, cabaret dancers, et al.). For a while, Mangeshkar was in the *Guinness Book of World Records* for having sung 30,000 songs, but the number is closer to 6,000. But those are numbers, and they have no bearing on the importance of Mangeshkar to Indian music, to Indian film, and to India in general. Hers is a voice that is now symbolic, much larger than itself. It stands for a certain vision of India, a socialist vision where the farmer and the soldier were upheld over the entrepreneur or the industrialist. It is the voice of a prelapsarian innocence, even though the Mangeshkar monopoly, as the two sisters frightened off all competition for years, is well attested. Even today, when she is sometimes off-key, music directors and audiences refuse to acknowledge that the glory days are gone. "Lata is Lata," they say. Many Indians agree.

Jerry Pinto

Date 1949

Nationality India

Director Kamal Amrohi

Cast Ashok Kumar, Madhubala, Kumar

Why It's Key Singer Lata Mangeshkar scores her first big hit and begins a legendary career as a playback singer.

Key Person **James Cagney**
Buzzsaw in his head *White Heat*

Before *White Heat* no gangster film had featured anybody like Cody Jarrett (Cagney). The film is set in the prewar Warner Bros. tradition but takes place in a postwar world still reeling from Hitler and Hiroshima.

Walsh sets the scene quietly for Cody's possibly epileptic prison breakdown. There is nothing wasteful here. The scene runs exactly three minutes. Three hundred convicts file silently into a mess hall under guard. A whistle blows. Cody sits and notices a new prisoner, a member of a gang that works the same territory he does, and under his breath passes a question about his mother down the line of cons sitting next to him. The camera dollies across the men and back as they whisper the words "she's dead" one after another until the news reaches Cody. We know Cody is neurotically dependent on his mother, but we can't predict his reaction. He slams down his cup, stands on the table, slides himself across it and attacks the guards. They manage to subdue him and

carry him out as he makes animal noises, the only sounds we hear as the other prisoners gape silently. Cagney didn't tell Walsh what he was going to do in this scene, so the extras didn't know either. Their stunned reaction mimics ours.

Cagney's performance is not gratuitous. It is structured, formidable. That Cagney decided *White Heat* was what he should do after 20 years in movies is a testament to his originality.

A. S. Hamrah

Date 1949

Nationality USA

Director Raoul Walsh

Cast James Cagney, Edmond O'Brien, Robert Osterloh, Eddie Foster

Why It's Key Cagney's all-out performance brought new depth to the gangster film in the postwar era even as it undermined the figure of the gangster.

Opposite *White Heat*

1940–1949

191

Key Person **Ida Lupino**
A walk in purgatory *Not Wanted*

Though not credited as the director of *Not Wanted* (she took over for an ill Clifton at the start of production), co-producer and co-scenarist Lupino does have the first credit – "Ida Lupino introduces" – over a brilliant opening shot of Forrest (whose name is the next to appear) as she ascends from the bottom of the frame to the top in fixed shot (until its final seconds), walking quietly up the sidewalk of a city street until the image has become a close-up of her face, a face filled with depths of barely suppressed anguish that are in these first moments a mystery. With this shot, a major directorial voice is born. It is a voice that within this initial work will offer a profound lesson in cinema, for in the final reel, most of this opening shot is replayed – a flashback has ended, and we now know all the reasons why the character, an unwed mother who gave away her baby for adoption, is so desperate. The details of the familiar narrative, however, have not made the image more dramatic, even as they have given it

clear meaning. Its drama was always as pure cinema: the composition of the woman on the street, the movement toward us, the compelling face – a moment complete within itself. It has been noted that Forrest resembles a younger Lupino, but if Lupino was one of Hollywood's most skilled and affecting actresses, she is even more valuable behind the camera, at one not only with a character but with a cinematic world a half-dozen modest but irreplaceable independent films made all her own.

Blake Lucas

Date 1949

Nationality USA

Director Elmer Clifton (and, uncredited, Ida Lupino)

Cast Sally Forrest

Why It's Key In a brilliant and highly individual opening shot an accomplished veteran actress cuts deep with a personal – and for the time uniquely female – directorial vision that would sustain a small but precious group of films.

Key Person **The Road Runner and Wile E. Coyote** *Fast and Furry-ous*

In *Fast and Furry-ous*, the protagonists are introduced under phony "scientific" Latin names (which will vary constantly from one cartoon to the next). The "plot" of this, as well as all the following entries, can be summed up in four words: "Coyote pursues Road Runner." Characterization is minimal in this two-character series. The coyote's sole motivation is to catch and eat the Road Runner. (His single-mindedness, coupled with inexhaustible invention, is a splendid example of overreaching resourcefulness compounded by sustained bad luck.) The Road Runner's sole purpose in life seems to be to dart to and fro at lightning speed in dreamlike, stylized desert landscapes. He never actually arrives at any destination, but just zips through, frustrating his would-be captor. The Road Runner has only one facial expression, a kind of smirk that never vanishes (why should it? He always wins).

Unlike most animals in the Warner cartoon menagerie, these two never speak (although the Coyote proved quite garrulous in *Operation Rabbit*, an atypical episode in which Bugs Bunny exceptionally substituted for the Road Runner). They occasionally address each other and the audience through brief messages scribbled on signposts. In *Fast and Furry-ous*, the nonsensical nature of this mode of communication is underlined in an excellent gag: Coyote puts up a sign reading "School crossing," hoping this will stop the Road Runner (for added realism, he disguises himself as a schoolgirl). Road Runner zips through as usual, ignoring the sign, then comes back, also in girlish garb, and produces a sign reading: "Road Runners can't read!"

Jean-Pierre Coursodon

Date 1949

Nationality USA

Director Charles M. Jones

Cast Road Runner, Wile E. Coyote

Why It's Key The first of some 40 entries in a hugely popular series that lasted until the late sixties, this cartoon introduces the Road Runner (*Accelleratii incredibus*) and the Coyote (*Carnivorous vulgaris*) and their saga of never-ending pursuit.

Key Scene **The camera connects the woman and the couple** *Slattery's Hurricane*

Will Slattery (Widmark) and his girlfriend, Dolores (Lake), run into his old Navy pal Hobbie (John Russell) and Hobbie's wife, Aggie (Darnell), with whom Will once had a passionate affair. Despite Will's friendship with Hobbie, and over the protests of the selfless Dolores, who argues that Will should at least think of his friend, they resume. When Will is belatedly awarded the Navy Cross for World War II heroism, both women attend the ceremony. Even though Dolores had left him, she moves toward him, presumably for congratulations, only to see him kissing Aggie – and collapses. The camera follows Dolores inside her racing ambulance, quickly pulls back, and turns around its front as the ambulance also turns. As the ambulance starts leaving the frame the open convertible carrying Will and Aggie comes into view, replacing it in the image. Though many of De Toth's films have happy endings, the best also have moments of utter hopelessness such as this: the "happy" couple replaces the stricken Dolores in a way so tightly choreographed as to suggest that no one is free, ensnaring the characters in a closing net. This take is also one of those great moments in which a film's style becomes so explicit that it helps one see the whole: from the rain-filled frames of the opening, to many smaller camera movements throughout, to the hurricane flight we see mostly near the end, the images present tightly wound surfaces that deny freedom.

Fred Camper

Date 1949

Nationality USA

Director André De Toth

Cast Richard Widmark, Linda Darnell, Veronica Lake

Why It's Key One of the most spectacular camera movements in all cinema, this isn't simply a bravura effect, but beautifully expresses the entrapping closure of De Toth's universe.

1940–1949

Key Film **Running a house and raising a family** *The Reckless Moment*

When Lucia Harper (Bennett), a California housewife with two children at home and a husband away overseas, finds the body of the boyfriend her teenage daughter has accidentally killed, she proceeds to hide it, lugging it onto a boat and dumping it in the bay. But there are incriminating letters, and a blackmailer who has them, Irishman Martin Donnelly (Mason), who soon has a crush on Lucia as well – unreciprocated ("You shouldn't smoke so much," he tells her – and she smokes even more). There are also a recovered body; a second, more sinister, blackmailer; an innocent party charged; and finally another body to hide. All this without Lucia even being late to family meals, it seems – she is so supremely the mom. But the furtive collaboration – as it turns into – between housewife and crook becomes deep and tangled and tragic.

This is surely one of the most withering and incisive – and heartbreaking – movies ever made about the middle-class family, about its myopia and self-enclosure, about its final loneliness – as sardonic as Buñuel but more delicately inflected, without his jokes or satiric tone (one reason it was unnoticed). In Bennett's wonderful performance, Lucia is something of a monster, driven by impulses she herself hardly understands or recognizes: she is "Running a House" and "Raising a Family," and nothing is beyond her. Except reality. *The Reckless Moment* would be a much less extraordinary movie if this incredible heroine weren't also so humanly attractive – if we didn't understand and sympathize with Donnelly's stricken and adoring eyes when he looks at her. A stunning achievement, unsurpassed in American films generally.
James Harvey

Date 1949

Nationality USA

Director Max Ophuls

Cast James Mason, Joan Bennett

Why It's Key Hardly noticed at the time or even since, this rich and astonishing melodrama was Ophuls's final and greatest American movie.

1940–1949

193

Key Film
Little Rural Riding Hood

Tex Avery directed no less than four thoroughly delirious versions of the Little Red Riding Hood story, all featuring the ever-lustful Wolf: *Little Red Walking Hood* (1938), *Red Hot Riding Hood* (1943), *Swing Shift Cinderella* (1945; this one started with the Wolf chasing a Riding Hood lookalike who stops and drags him back to the title card, showing him he is in the wrong movie; the subsequent action, however, follows very much the same pattern as the other three shorts), and the last and most brilliant entry, in which the Wolf, a country bumpkin with a Goofy kind of voice, burns with desire for a very ugly backwoods Riding Hood who speaks with an impenetrable Appalachian accent. His hot pursuit of her, of course, leads nowhere. In one gag he stands in a doorway to stop her, and she just goes through his body, bisecting it into two flat sections that flap like swinging saloon doors….

A telegram from Wolf's ultra-sophisticated city cousin invites him to see "a real city Riding Hood," and at the sight of the attached picture of the girl in question, Wolf, in the throes of hysterical erotic excitement, starts literally falling apart (head, legs, arms, torso are all shooting off in different directions). Suave City Wolf takes him to a nightclub, where the girl (we have seen her in earlier Avery cartoons) performs an extremely sexy "Oh, Wolfie," throughout which Country Wolf keeps trying to grab her and is repeatedly restrained by his cousin in the most surrealistic and hilarious manner. You may see Country Wolf as the raging Id and City Wolf as the Superego working hard at repressing it – or the whole thing as a metaphor for the tension between the movies' natural tendency toward eroticism and the ever-watchful censors of the Hays Office.
Jean-Pierre Coursodon

Date 1949

Nationality USA

Director Tex Avery

Cast Country Wolf, City Wolf, Country Red, City Red

Why It's Key It's one of the masterpieces of Avery's MGM period, and the culmination of his "Riding Hood" tetralogy.

Key Scene **The Hampton bank robbery**
Gun Crazy

As a *film noir* centred on an outlaw couple, Joseph H. Lewis's *Gun Crazy* offers a variety of aggressions towards society. At one point, Bart Tare (Dall) and Annie Laurie Starr (Cummins) rob a bank in the town of Hampton: Bart goes in while Laurie stays behind the wheel of the getaway car and deals with a policeman, and they quickly escape with the loot. In the script, the sequence required 17 pages (that needed three days of shooting) and took us inside the establishment. Instead, Lewis decided to use a single long take, and, after a test shot in 16mm, he managed to wrap the scene in three hours, giving it a documentary feeling through the almost complete improvisation of dialogue, the absence of music before Bart's return, and the use of real time that enhances suspense. *Gun Crazy* is not the first film to shoot a robbery this way – Nicholas Ray's *They Live by Night* (1949) had already done that before – but what is at stake here greatly differs. Looking over the couple's shoulders and not knowing where they are taking him, the spectator is placed in the back seat of a stolen Cadillac and forced to participate. Thus, when Laurie looks back, checking that they are not followed, she simultaneously thanks their unwilling accomplice: the viewer. The scene also features the mix of violence and eroticism that runs thorough the film, with the two characters dressed as cowboys and behaving as if they were still in the Wild West.

Frank Lafond

Date 1949

Nationality USA

Director Joseph H. Lewis

Cast Peggy Cummins, John Dall

Why It's Key This moment is a great example of B movies' ability to transcend their limitations.

Opposite *Gun Crazy*

Key Scene **"My memoirs"**
Kind Hearts and Coronets

SPOILER

Louis Mazzini (the great Dennis Price), after becoming the Duke of D'Ascoyne by killing several people with prior claims to that title (all played by Alec Guinness), is then – irony of ironies – sentenced to hang for a murder he *didn't* commit. A last-minute bargain with the victim's widow (Greenwood), conducted in veiled terms in the prison visiting room, leads to Louis's last-minute release. Just outside the heavy prison door, Louis, distracted by the cheers of anonymous well-wishers and the presence of two women each of whom expects him to join her, is greeted by a shabby-looking reporter (Lowe) with an offer for the publication of his memoirs. "My memoirs?" he repeats, then repeats the words again, in voice-over, to himself: "My memoirs!" The film cuts to the prison cell he's just vacated, the camera tracking toward the neat pile of papers on which Louis has left the witty account (which has served as the armature for the film's flashback narrative) of all the murders he *did* commit, and for which he'll now be charged and convicted. (Unless he can retrieve the document before it's found and read – a possibility that the film, which ends on this shot, leaves open.) The two lines converging toward the desk – the simple camera movement and the slant of dazzling early-morning sunlight from the cell window – create a chill that stays in the mind.

Chris Fujiwara

Date 1949

Nationality UK

Director Robert Hamer

Cast Dennis Price, Arthur Lowe, Valerie Hobson, Joan Greenwood

Why It's Key One of the most memorable moments in this classic British comedy is its sublime and understated ending.

D. PEDLOW, JR
MANAGER

Key Scene **The ball**
Madame Bovary

A master of both the musical and the melodrama, Vincente Minnelli was also the director who best showed the close kinship between the two genres. (The word "melodrama" means, etymologically, "music" plus "drama," as has often been pointed out.) Minnelli's films are filled with dynamic and visually stunning set pieces of mounting tension and blissful release: his is a cinema of "key moments." Of them, none is more brilliant than the scene in *Madame Bovary* in which provincial doctor Charles Bovary (Heflin) and his beautiful wife, Emma (Jones), attend a ball given by a nobleman (Cavanagh) whose servant Bovary once treated. The scene is structured by the changing styles, tempos, and time signatures of the musical pieces played at the ball (composed by Miklos Rozsa). While Charles, consigned to the billiard room where he is helplessly out of place among the snobbish guests, becomes increasingly drunk, Emma is courted for dance after dance by a succession of admirers.

Finally, though out of breath and protesting her inability to waltz, Emma is claimed as partner by the dashing Rodolphe (Jourdan). They whirl around the ballroom, pursued by Minnelli's tirelessly moving camera. When Emma becomes unable to breathe, her host obligingly and regally orders all the windows smashed. Charles's lurching descent onto the ballroom floor in pursuit of his wife brings the scene to a close that's as cinematically satisfying as it is socially embarrassing.

Chris Fujiwara

Date 1949

Nationality USA

Director Vincente Minnelli

Cast Jennifer Jones, Van Heflin, Louis Jourdan, Paul Cavanagh

Why It's Key Vincente Minnelli is at the peak of his powers in this kinetic sequence.

Opposite *Madame Bovary*

Key Scene **Four rounds**
The Set-Up

M any types of drama have played out in cinematic boxing rings: Cinderella stories where the underdog survives and/or triumphs; parables in which innocence is lost or redeemed; socially conscious tales exposing the capitalist underbelly; one-last-job comeback melodramas. What the movies almost never show is the actual spectacle that brings people out to see a fight: two guys trying to beat each other up over an extended period of time.

The Set-Up's 18-minute centerpiece, a bloody four-round slugfest, comes as close as a dramatic film probably will to documenting that brute struggle. Joseph Moncure March, whose narrative poem formed the kernel of the script, was dismayed to learn that RKO had changed his hero – an aging black puncher with the wonderfully ironic name "Pansy Jones" – into "Stoker Thompson," played by that whitest of white men, Robert Ryan. But it is the gangly trained-boxer Ryan, with his flatfooted, roundhouse-throwing style

and permanent grimace, who persuades the audience that there's a real fight going on.

Shooting mostly from outside the ropes, Wise creates a magnificent illusion: Ryan and California Heavyweight Champion Hal "Baylor" Fieberling seem to be going at it with no direction at all. The few directorial flourishes consist of cuts to hateful, stentorian fans; some ringside narrative business advancing a corny plot twist; and a point-of-view shot revealing the supine Ryan's hazy view of the lights. The rest is struggle: sweat, stumbling, pain, punches that miss or connect. By his own account, Martin Scorsese based his decision to eschew realism in favor of fussy, multilayered camp in *Raging Bull* on one hard fact: *The Set-Up*'s fight sequence couldn't be topped.

Tim Cavanaugh

Date 1949

Nationality USA

Director Robert Wise

Cast Robert Ryan, Hal "Baylor" Fieberling

Why It's Key It's the only time a dramatic film has truly captured the sweet science.

Key Speech "The cuckoo clock"
The Third Man

Out-of-work pulp writer Holly Martins (Cotten) arrives in the chaos of post-World War II Vienna, only to discover that the man who invited him, former school chum Harry Lime (Welles), has been hit and killed by a truck. Or has he? Thus begins this shrewd geopolitical thriller from the pen of Graham Greene, an atmospheric tale of deceit and delusion at the dawn of the Cold War. The deeper Holly digs, the more dirt he uncovers on Harry – who turns out to be an amoral black market racketeer, very much alive and pushing tainted penicillin. Holly and Harry finally meet, atop the Prater amusement park's Riesenrad ferris wheel. Both nervous and cocky, Lime injects strained bonhomie into his justification for profiteering, ending with a classic speech penned by Welles himself: "Don't be so gloomy. After all, it's not that awful. Like the fella says, in Italy for thirty years under the Borgias they had warfare, terror, murder, and bloodshed, but they produced Michelangelo, Leonardo Da Vinci, and the Renaissance.

In Switzerland they had brotherly love – they had five hundred years of democracy and peace, and what did they produce? The cuckoo clock. So long, Holly." The honeyed tones with which Welles delivers this great speech are tinged with menace; the contempt and at the same time the attraction Holly feels for this charming psychopath are shared by the viewer.

David Stratton

Date 1949

Nationality UK

Director Carol Reed

Cast Joseph Cotten, Orson Welles

Why It's Key A taut tale of amoral mystery in post-World War II Vienna features one of Welles's cockiest performances.

Opposite *The Third Man*

1940–1949

198

Key Scene **The mirror**
Orpheus

Jean Cocteau was a poet before he became a filmmaker. Each of the films in his so-called Orphic trilogy is not only about poets and poetry; each is itself a visual poem, burgeoning with enigmatic imagery as ineluctable and as pregnant with meaning as the words in a poem. As much as Cocteau delighted in romanticizing and mythologizing the Poet, he had no romantic illusions about how poetry is created. Just as a poet must concern himself with the mechanics of rhythm and language, Cocteau mastered the grammar of cinema, constructing every special effect with the care of a poet choosing a literary device. *Orpheus*, a modern retelling of the Orpheus myth where death comes in the form of a princess and her gang of leather-clad motorcyclists, depicts the poet (Marais) as a Left Bank existentialist in postwar Paris. After his wife, Eurydice, is taken from him, he enters the underworld through a mirror, which for Cocteau were our windows on mortality: "Look at yourself in a mirror

all your life and you will see death at work," says Heurtebise (Périer), Death's chauffeur, to Orpheus. To depict the poet's crossing through the mirror into the underworld, Cocteau filmed the actor putting his gloved hands into a vat of mercury. His solution to the technological problem of how to visualize the image in his head was a stroke of genius that still looks stunning even today in this age of CGI. Magic, as any poet will tell you, is hard work.

Al Weisel

Date 1950

Nationality France

Director Jean Cocteau

Cast Jean Marais, François Périer

Original Title *Orphée*

Why It's Key It's visual poetry.

Key Scene **Margo's party**
All about Eve

Mankiewicz was rightly famous for his barbed and literate dialogue, but this sardonic, multi-Oscar-winning cautionary tale about the ruthless ambition and intense paranoia infecting the American theatre world found his writing in peak form. About the titular ingenue and purported aficionado (Baxter) strategically securing the affections first of ageing stage star Margo Channing (Davis) and then of the flattered diva's lofty clique, the film revels in bitchy interaction and acerbic observation, the latter proffered first in the narration of cynical critic Addison de Witt (Sanders), which begins with Eve's acceptance of an award and proceeds to explain how she achieved said gong.

The pleasingly peppery flavour really takes hold in a party scene where it's immediately clear Margo reckons Eve – now her live-in amanuensis – is receiving excessive admiration. When writer and occasional beau Bill (Merrill) notes the mood's "very Macbeth-ish," Margo, asked if things might improve, glugs on her champagne before proudly announcing, "Fasten your seat belts, it's going to be a bumpy night." Welcoming de Witt with a suitably withering greeting, she's immediately informed the critic's not entirely unattractive younger companion Miss Casswell (Monroe) is "a graduate of the Copacabana School of Dramatic Art." Margo may be queen here, but Addison's no slouch; introduced to Eve, without so much as a raised eyebrow he brazenly advises his inarticulate (and therefore, in this context, unduly innocent) companion to go off and make an old producer who's present happy. In other words, he's talking pimping and prostitution, a metaphor that informs the entire movie's vision of the theatrical world.

Geoff Andrew

Date 1950

Nationality USA

Director Joseph L. Mankiewicz

Cast Bette Davis, Anne Baxter, George Sanders, Marilyn Monroe, Gary Merrill, Celeste Holm, Gregory Ratoff

Why It's Key Deliciously witty wordplay highlights the constantly theatrical behavior of the Broadway set.

Opposite *All about Eve*

1950–1959

Key Scene **St. Francis sends his followers to "preach peace"** *Flowers of St. Francis*

Rossellini's portrayal of the beginnings of the Franciscan order stresses the monks' childlike innocence. St. Francis (Geraldi) praises "Brother Fire"; Ginepro, one of his followers, keeps giving his tunic away to poor people. In one key scene, Ginepro enters the camp of Nicolaio (Aldo Fabrizi), a tyrant besieging Viterbo. When Ginepro wins him over with his simple expression that contrasts with the tyrant's ego-asserting, bug-eyed attempts to intimidate him, Nicolaio lifts the siege. Rossellini's images all reveal his anti-formalist style, abjuring preconceived compositional ideas or architectures; his compositions seem as open and innocent as the friars themselves. At the film's end, St. Francis commands his followers to spin until they fall from dizziness, and then proceed in the direction that they have fallen – one toward Siena, another toward Florence, another toward Arezzo. Then, in a magnificent high-angled long take, they head off in these and other different directions; first, several exit at the sides; next, two exit toward the camera; finally, as more walk further into the background, the camera pans up to the clouds, and several dissolves offer more clouds. In this long take, Rossellini makes explicit the stylistic conceit of this and virtually all his future films, even illuminating the way he uses the zoom in much later works: his compositions are always constructed to point to the space beyond their borders with a world-embracing hugeness shared by some of his key characters – such as St. Francis.

Fred Camper

Date 1950

Nationality Italy

Director Roberto Rossellini

Cast Brother Nazario Geraldi

Original Title *Francesco giullare di Dio*

Why It's Key In a single image at the end of this film, Rossellini finds a metaphor for the central stylistic trait of most of his work.

Key Film *Los Olvidados*
The return of Buñuel

In 1929, after the Paris theater where it was booked refused to screen it, Buñuel and Salvador Dali's *Un Chien andalou* became a *succès de scandale*. At showings of 1930's *L'Age d'or* angry Parisians threw ink at the screen and yelled "Death to the Jews!" at this film by a Catholic from Spain. A friend of Buñuel's won a lottery, so in 1933 Buñuel made *Las Hurdes*, a documentary about a backward region of Spain promptly banned by the Spanish government. Buñuel left for Hollywood and New York, where he looked on as his erstwhile partner Dali became a celebrity who resembled, according to Max Ernst, "those horrid jellies Americans eat for dessert."

Frustrated, in 1945 Buñuel moved to Mexico. The reputations of his three films grew, but as far as anyone knew he was out of filmmaking. In Mexico he made a couple of low-budget genre films. One flopped, but one did okay and in 1950 Buñuel made *Los Olvidados*, a story of Mexico City street kids that synthesized Val Lewton horror and neorealism – it put the realism back in surrealism, mixing poverty and nightmares. One of the kids in it tosses a raw egg into the camera lens.

Buñuel had stayed true to his vision through bad jobs, short funds, and 17 years of projects that never got off the ground. While *Los Olvidados* met with protest in Mexico, it won two prizes at Cannes and allowed him to make 26 films in the next 26 years.
A. S. Hamrah

Date 1950

Nationality Mexico

Director Luis Buñuel

Cast Alfonso Mejía, Roberto Cobo, Estela Inda

Aka *The Young and the Damned*

Why It's Key After a decade and a half the director of *L'Age d'or* came back to the cinema undiminished.

Key Scene **Karin and the volcano**
Stromboli

Karin (Bergman), who has married a fisherman in order to escape a displaced persons' camp, only to find life with him in his primitive fishing village off the coast of Sicily intolerable, leaves the village on foot, taking the only route available – over a volcanic mountain. On the way, she confronts the terror of Nature, in the form of a volcanic eruption, and breaks down sobbing. In the morning, she wakes amid a scene of calm, to which she responds by exclaiming: "What mystery! What beauty!" When RKO originally released *Stromboli*, a voice-over narration was added at the end to explain that Karin will go back to her husband. Rossellini's version, now generally available, offers no such assurance: we see Karin crying out to God, asking for "strength, understanding, and courage"; the last shot of the film shows birds flying. The ending can be regarded only as a moment of radical indeterminateness. All that can be said positively is that the question of whether or not Karin will go back is transcended. What Rossellini has brought us to, in this extraordinarily moving moment, is a situation in which the protagonist, utterly alone, is also – for the first time – free of all contingency and of all determination by her conditions. To Karin as she is at this point, where we leave her forever, whether she returns or not is irrelevant.
Chris Fujiwara

Date 1950

Nationality Italy

Director Roberto Rossellini

Cast Ingrid Bergman

Original Title *Stromboli terra di Dio*

Why It's Key It's one of the most moving episodes in cinema.

Opposite *Stromboli*

RAGING ISLAND...RAGING PASSIONS!

This is IT!

THE PLACE:

STROMBOLI

THE STAR:

BERGMAN

UNDER

THE INSPIRED DIRECTION OF

ROSSELLINI

Produced and Directed by Roberto Rossellini • Released by RKO Radio Pictures

50 169

Key Speech **The parson reads the imaginary will** *Stars in My Crown*

Stars in My Crown was Jacques Tourneur's favorite among his own films. But he's commonly viewed as a genre director, and if this uncharacteristic and low-budget MGM item about a small-town parson (McCrea) in the post-bellum South belongs to any recognizable genre, it's the inspirational religious picture. Yet Tourneur clearly believed in the audience's imagination and its innate decency more than any religion. And Parson Gray pretending to read the imaginary will of Uncle Famous Prill (Hernandez), a black man who refuses to sell his property, to a band of neo-Klansmen with torches preparing to lynch him, is a beautiful illustration of the wisdom underlying both beliefs. What Gray accomplishes in his performance to the masked men he accomplishes with us as well, because we discover that the will is imaginary only at the scene's end. "You can have him now," Gray says melodramatically, after reaching the end of Prill's thoughtful bequeathments to his neighbors – knowing

or at least hoping that these reminders of Prill's generosity and his many links to this community will ultimately save his life, as it does.

"There's no writing here – this ain't no will," says Gray's adopted son, John (Stockwell), the film's narrator, when he sees the blank pages on the ground. "Yes it is, son – it's the will of God," says Gray, which might be taken as a concession to Tourneur's designated genre. But in fact, it's the collective will and conscience that Tourneur is speaking to, stirring, and celebrating.

Jonathan Rosenbaum

Date 1950

Nationality USA

Director Jacques Tourneur

Actors Joel McCrea, Juano Hernandez, Dean Stockwell

Why It's Key Jacques Tourneur illustrates his credo – that nothing is more powerful than people's imaginations.

1950-1959

205

Key Scene **Break-up** *In a Lonely Place*

In a typical case of tone-deafness, studio publicity described the ending of *In a Lonely Place* when it came out as a "stunning surprise climax." Only in Hollywood could somebody's innocence be touted as shock. But if what they meant was that the climax was emotionally devastating, and that emotional devastation was unexpected in a studio film, they had a point. Inner conflict structures every scene in this film. By its end, everything, even the way Bogart puts down a telephone receiver to make two black holes in the frame, adds to its heartache.

"Can't you relax for a second?", Grahame's Laurel Gray asks Bogart's Dixon Steele. He can't. Steele, a Hollywood screenwriter, exists in the tension between creative work and real life. His fear of being misunderstood and punished for being right plagues him, makes him lash out, and poisons his relationships. We see it happen in wrenching closeups of Laurel's face as she looks at him. In the film's last scene, Ray

keeps subtly emptying the frame until Dix and Laurel break up and disappear, he through an arch that leads to the street, she behind a door she closes.

It's not just the end, but the film's whole last half hour that wrecks you. Ray couples anger to tenderness. Dix beats up a guy, then delivers the film's (maybe any film's) most romantic lines. He describes a "good love scene" to the woman he loves even as she realizes she has to leave him.

A. S. Hamrah

Date 1950

Nationality USA

Director Nicholas Ray

Cast Humphrey Bogart, Gloria Grahame, Frank Lovejoy, Carl Benton Reid

Why It's Key The film's unhappy ending introduced maturity and an adult sadness into its genre.

Opposite *In a Lonely Place*

Key Scene **A visit to the studio**
Sunset Blvd.

Gloria Swanson's Norma Desmond is one of the great characters of the screen. Despotic, infantile, pathetic, yet also bearing all the noble qualities of an age long gone, she lives to stare at private screenings of her silent movies and to call up memories of the day when she was the toast of Hollywood. Her home is a palatial temple to the rococo formalities and extravagances of the 1920s, a stage in which she can pretend to be Chaplin's Tramp or the queen of cinema, in which she can remember the sweet working relationship she had with men like Cecil B. DeMille. Trapped in her domain is Joe Gillis (Holden), a failed screenwriter, whom she has plied with her woebegone script for *Salome*. One day she is informed she has received a telephone call from Paramount. Surely, then, Mr. DeMille wishes to see her about this script!

Chauffeured to the studio in a magnificent touring car, heavily made up and dressed with chic, she gains admittance and is driven to the soundstage where DeMille is shooting. Warning passes from the gate guard to the assistant director to DeMille himself, who interrupts work to come and greet her at the door: "Hello, young fella!" Arm in arm, they walk into the great dark cavern that is the heart of the movies, and the dozens of extras fall into a hush – "That's *Norma Desmond*!" A gaffer on a catwalk calls down, "Miss Desmond, it's me, Hog-Eye!," and turns a spot on her. For a moment, in the magical stream of light, time has stopped, and she is again the silver-screen beauty of yesteryear. Then DeMille calls everyone back to work, dissipating the moment. He has to let her down, though he does it sweetly: it wasn't he but the production chief who phoned, and only to borrow the car. In a breath, the past returns to its proper place, that airless vault in which memory lingers, dries up, disappears.

Murray Pomerance

Date 1950

Nationality USA

Director Billy Wilder

Cast Gloria Swanson, William Holden, Cecil B. DeMille

Why It's Key A moment of supreme pathos graces a supreme film performance.

Key Event **James Stewart cuts the first movie-star back-end deal**

Aw-shucks leading man Stewart was still struggling to reinvent himself after his World War II service when he agreed to star in the western *Winchester '73*, his first project after the genial comedy *Harvey*. The result was a milestone that didn't just signal the start of Stewart's tenure with director Anthony Mann, for whom he'd make four more Westerns, but also the beginning of the studios' decline as power centers and their gradual replacement by movie stars allied with ruthless and well-connected agents. *Winchester '73* is believed to mark the first instance of a matinee idol asking for and receiving a cut of a film's profits before production had even begun. The deal occurred at a transitional time in Hollywood, when the major studios, whose hammerlock on popular consciousness was rattled by the upstart medium of television, were losing control over their once slave-like contract labor pools, and being forced to deal with top actors and directors on a project-to-project basis. The Stewart deal, negotiated by MCA agent and future Hollywood power broker Lew Wasserman, had the star cutting his up-front asking price in exchange for cast approval and a piece of net box-office profits. While some of Stewart's colleagues thought him reckless, his gamble paid off in spades. *Winchester '73* was a hit that netted Stewart more money for one gig – $600,000 – than he'd gotten for his last few pictures combined. After that, the Stewart deal became the template for Hollywood's economy. Hot directors, entrenched producers and popular actors skim a movie's gross box-office take from the first dollar onward; sometimes the percentage deal was in addition to a handsome flat fee. Nowadays, when a film is a smash, the payoff can be mind-boggling: Jack Nicholson, for example, is believed to have grossed $60 million just from his performance as the Joker in Tim Burton's 1989 *Batman*.

Matt Zoller Seitz

Date 1950

Why It's Key This deal set a template for the new Hollywood economy.

Opposite *Winchester '73*

Key Scene **The Chuck-A-Walla-Swing**
Wagon Master

After a long trek to water, the pioneers in a Mormon wagon train, now refreshed and renewed, enjoy a festive evening. Mormons, horse traders (who have signed on as wagon masters), and showfolk picked up along the way all take part in a joyful square dance – "The Chuck-A-Walla-Swing" (composed by Stan Jones, sung by the Sons of the Pioneers). It is in the many songs and dances, possessed of a ritual beauty, that the deepest feelings of a Ford film often begin to take hold, and there is no lovelier example than this one, as a few fleeting minutes see the first real blooming of two romances, moments of charming comedy, and a communal harmony in which past intimations of intolerance dissolve in mutual pleasure. As music is one of the most carefully-wrought tools of Ford's art, so too are the kinds of startling shifts of mood and changes of tone that this sequence displays – for the Cleggs men, a family of unsparing outlaws who have been introduced much earlier (in the opening scene),

arrive out of the darkness just as the exhilaration of the dance is at its height. In a moment, Ford has shown the closeness of the light and the dark, and he will continue to play that counterpoint until the Cleggs perish in violence – he is never so fixed on the drama that lyricism and romance cannot find their own imperishable images. In the end, too, the "Chuck-A-Walla-Swing" returns, magically introducing the reprised moments of a coda as a present square dance cuts to that precious earlier one.
Blake Lucas

Date 1950

Nationality USA

Director John Ford

Cast Ben Johnson, Joanne Dru, Harry Carey, Jr., Ward Bond, Kathleen O'Malley, Ruth Clifford, Alan Mowbray, Charles Kemper

Why It's Key John Ford's gift for imparting the deepest feelings of his films in songs and dances, and the ease with which he shifts moods between light and dark, reach a peak in one of his most wonderful sequences.

Key Scene **"Mem'ry Island"**
Summer Stock

Rehearsal scenes, a staple of "backstage" musicals, are more often than not perturbed by some degree of chaos. Here Charles Walters directs such a scene with both consummate elegance and a sure sense of humor, his staging and camerawork turning a corny song being tentatively essayed by a couple of less-than-stellar performers into a delightful exercise in self-conscious parody.

Performed with no set, no props, no costumes and on a makeshift "stage" (actually a barn) cluttered with paraphernalia and people milling about, the number looks and sounds rather bare, as the couple – Hans Conried as the slumming "name" in the cast, and Gloria DeHaven – sing and "pretend" they're on an exotic island, coached by Gene Kelly, the producer/director/star of the show, who attempts to inject some grace into their stiff performance.

Walters's direction of Kelly's directing of the number is so fluid and witty that it actually negates the clumsiness of the acting, turning it into one of the film's highlights.
Jean-Pierre Coursodon

Date 1950

Nationality USA

Director Charles Walters

Cast Gene Kelly, Hans Conried, Gloria DeHaven

Why It's Key Making fun of movie-musical cliches, Walters masterfully achieves a small musical gem.

Key Film
Awaara (The Vagabond)

During the 1950s and the early 1960s, Indian popular culture exported very well internationally, and Indian musical melodramas attained a dominant presence on the theatrical-exhibition circuit across a range of non-Western territories around the world. One of these films, Raj Kapoor's *Awaara*, an exotic and lavish social drama, may well have been the most successful film of its period within world cinema at large. Such a claim, however, is not supported by hard box-office data (such as we have about Hollywood hits) but only by anecdotal testimonies given unanimously by various international film historians, who talk of the film's huge triumph in areas with wide audiences, like Russia (where the film was seen by a staggering 65 million people just within one year, 1954). No other film of the 1950s was seen in so many countries and was so widely acclaimed. The title song from the film topped charts in many countries, and at least several remakes were made internationally. *Awaara* has enjoyed remarkable longevity and remains a truly enduring global hit.

Recognizing the great reception of Indian film among African, Arab, Russian and East European, Chinese, and Latin American audiences is an important step in the creation of an alternative film geography, one involving forgotten or under-researched aspects of global film circulation and transnational cinematic exchanges.

Dina Iordanova

Date 1951

Nationality India

Director Raj Kapoor

Cast Raj Kapoor, Nargis, Prithviraj Kapoor

Why It's Key Recognizing the neglected evidence of the stupendous international success of Indian cinema helps create a better understanding of the dynamics of exports and influences in world cinema at large.

Key Scene **The dream sequence**
Awaara (The Vagabond)

Awaara, a great success not just in India but in the former Soviet Union and in China, turns on the nature-versus-nurture debate in an Oedipal manner as real life father (Prithviraj Kapoor) and son (Raj Kapoor) play the roles of a judge and his criminal son, Raj, who seeks to avenge his father's injustice to his mother, while falling in love with his father's ward, Rita (Nargis).

The dream/nightmare sequence in *Awaara* is the big "item" of the film, 12 minutes in length, said to have taken three months and cost considerable amounts of money and added at the last minute as a major attraction. Dancers appear amid clouds, presumably heaven, where there are images of gods. Rita sings a love song, "Tere bin aag yeh chaandni" ("Without you this moonlight is like fire"). Raj appears in the torments of hell, singing of his desires for love. As he moves upwards through clouds to the sound of "Om namah Shivaya" ("Homage to Lord Shiva"), Nargis bends down to take him by the hand to lead him to heaven. She sings "Ghar aaya mera pardesi" ("My foreigner has come home"), then climbs the spiral stairs as Raj follows her. They walk along a twisting road, when a giant form of Raj's adopted father appears, holding a knife. Raj plunges back into hell, yelling "Rita"; then he wakes up, shouting, "Mother, save me!"

The sequence condenses the film's themes into a dream about love, religion, women, motherhood, punishment, and crime and shows how the Hindi film enacts these in songs, dances, and the very *mise en scène*.

Rachel Dwyer

Date 1951

Nationality India

Director Raj Kapoor

Cast Raj Kapoor, Nargis, Prithviraj Kapoor

Why It's Key This is one of the greatest "item numbers" in Hindi film, with its remarkable stars, sets, songs, and imagery.

Key Scene **Maddalena cries for help**
Bellissima

When people say that Anna Magnani was a force of nature, they're half right. Like certain other great actors (Albert Finney comes to mind), she seemed to have immediate access to her emotions – all of them, at any time. When you watch her perform, you're never tempted to think about the calibrations of vocal and physical technique, the deliberate accretions of a backstory, or the deployments of sense memory that other actors call upon. Magnani's immediacy appears to be purely spontaneous – but to think so is wrong, as wrong as it would be to mistake Prospero for the tempest.

At one extraordinary moment, though, in the performance that is arguably the greatest of her career, Magnani did let loose an act of unplanned, intuitive genius. It happened at the end of *Bellissima*, in which she played Maddalena, a would-be stage mother from Rome's working class. The scene called for Magnani to sit alone on a bench, letting despair overtake her as she thought about the collapse of Maddalena's schemes and hopes. This, Magnani could do. With that uncanny ability to draw on her emotions, she took herself in a few seconds through every stage of a headstrong, proud, foolish woman's breakdown.

Then, out of her throat, came an unscripted cry: "*Aiuda*!" ("Help!") To whom was Maddalena calling? Nobody, or the whole world. What answer did she expect? None. The most brilliant screenwriters, of whom Luchino Visconti had several, could never have thought up that irrational, perfect outburst. It took a force of nature.

Stuart Klawans

Date 1951

Nationality Italy

Director Luchino Visconti

Cast Anna Magnani

Why It's Key In perhaps her greatest performance, Magnani lives up to her reputation as the screen's most intuitive actress.

1950–1959

210

Key Event **The first issue of *Cahiers du cinéma***

When book reviewers read in Colin MacCabe's biography of Godard that *Cahiers du cinéma* was "the most significant cultural journal of the twentieth century" they couldn't wait to jump on him for laying it on so thick. What do they know? There is film criticism before *Cahiers du cinéma* and film criticism after it. Because of the tremendous impact of the *Nouvelle vague*, which sprang from its pages, there is visual culture (and the analysis of visual culture) before and after *Cahiers du cinéma*, too.

The magazine's presiding figure was André Bazin, a tireless worker in the postwar French ciné-club movement who contributed to the *Revue du cinéma* and other journals. When the *Revue*'s editor died, Jacques Doniol-Valcroze and Bazin found financing and in April 1951 began publishing *Cahiers* in Paris. The magazine hired young writers from ciné-club newsletters, the habitués of the Cinémathèque française who later formed the nucleus of the French New Wave – Eric Rohmer, Jacques Rivette, François Truffaut, Claude Chabrol, and Jean-Luc Godard. They favored Rossellini and Hollywood genre movies over the "quality" they saw stultifying French cinema.

Unlike film critics today, these writers did not complain that they were powerless. They defended the movies they loved and excoriated the ones they hated. For them film criticism was a confrontation, its goal to change how films were viewed and how they were made. The magazine's polarizing "auteur theory" was attacked with the vehemence that heralds artistic breakthrough. By the decade's end the group's first films came out.

A. S. Hamrah

Date April 1951

Why It's Key This magazine's debut marked a permanent change in criticism and filmmaking.

Key Event *Treatise on Slime and Eternity* shown at Cannes

April 1951 marks a crucial event in the history of cinema's avant-garde. And, of all places, at the Cannes Film Festival. A young artist, Isidore Isou, presented his first film, *Treatise on Slime and Eternity*, in a special "sidebar" event. Isou's aesthetic approach, backed up by an elaborate, innovative theoretical philosophy, was named Lettrism, and its chief tool was "chiselling": as far as he was concerned, cinema, like all established art forms, had come to the end of its expansive, "amplic" phase, and was now good only for progressive breaking-down, frame by frame, syllable by syllable, letter by letter. His *Treatise* was a provocation that proceeded by setting up familiar reference points (Paris streets, well-known celebrities including Jean Cocteau) and then hacking them to bits: images flipped upside-down and drawn upon, nonsensical "sound poetry" (a Lettrist specialty) at a complete tangent to the visuals, cavalier evacuation of plot. But Isou's greatest blow against the audience came about by

accident: the lab had not finished putting the visual and aural elements together, so the entire second hour unreeled with sound only, over a black screen. The audience noisily complained, voting with its feet, and the event quickly became known as a mythic *affaire*. The film's final line, a quote from Nietzsche, accurately predicted its own forthcoming legend, as well as the notoriety of its indefatigably experimental maker: "You must have chaos within you to give birth to a dancing star." *Treatise* is dedicated to "Griffith, Chaplin, Clair, von Stroheim, Flaherty, Buñuel, Cocteau."

Adrian Martin

Date April 1951

Why It's Key "You must have chaos within you to give birth to a dancing star."

Key Scene **Sleep**
The River

SPOILER

Renoir's *The River* chooses relaxation, flow, and expansiveness over narrative drive. The logic of this choice becomes poignantly clear during one of the film's greatest lyrical interludes. One afternoon, several members of the household of a British jute-mill-owning family in India take naps. Renoir links the people, who are dispersed in space in various parts of the estate, by dissolving from one to another, and in each shot the camera tracks in or out, so that the sequence as a whole creates the impression of a continuous flow of movement on which the sleepers are carried along together. This flow isn't movement in any direction; it's like breathing, or like a tide wafting in and out (to relate the sequence to the film's overriding water metaphor).

The next scene reveals that while everyone was blissfully asleep, the family's young male child (Foster), defying his elders' repeated warnings not to get too close to a certain tree where a cobra lives, was bitten by the cobra and killed. Eclipsed by the sleepers'

unconsciousness, elided by the flow of Renoir's sequence, the boy's death occurs offscreen and is witnessed by no one except another little boy (Barik), who won't speak about it. Death has struck at a precise moment of time, but for the film this moment can never be known and in a sense never happened – since it occurred during a passage of infinite duration.

Chris Fujiwara

Date 1951

Nationality USA/India

Director Jean Renoir

Cast Patricia Walters, Nora Swinburne, Suprova Mukerjee, Richard R. Foster, Nimai Barik

Why It's Key This superb lyrical interlude poses a paradox about film time.

Key Scene **Recognizing the killer**
The Lost One

German postwar cinema's most deeply felt film is the sole directorial effort of Peter Lorre, who returned some 16 years after he fled from the Nazis, attempting to revive his career at home after it had started to dwindle in his Hollywood exile. Telling the story of a scientist (played by Lorre) whose serial killings were covered up by Hitler's regime to protect secret research, *The Lost One* is a unique kind of bifurcated exorcism: the bitter allegory of German war guilt is unmistakable, but the film also doubles as a tragic tale of Lorre's failed attempts to escape the horror of Hollywood typecasting that was inaugurated by his astonishing breakthrough performance 20 years earlier as the child murderer in Fritz Lang's classic *M*. The antihero of *The Lost One* is a similarly tragic monster. His moment of truth comes in a suspense scene on an empty staircase, when a prostitute stares at his unmistakable features and exclaims "*Totmacher!*" – a memorably awkward German phrasing for killer. No

less memorably awkward and compelling is the film's style, a collision of *M*-era prewar expressionism and postwar naturalism. Released at a time when being not reconciled was not an official option, this uncomfortable masterwork died at the national box-office and is hardly known elsewhere. Tellingly, two most heartfelt homages to it come from the most controversial among Germany's major directors, Romuald Karmakar, who named his 1996 serial killer film *Der Totmacher*, and from Austrian avant-garde master Kurt Kren, who had similarly spent years in U.S. exile, and used another piece of murder-recognition dialogue from *The Lost One* for his 1995 short *tausendjahrekino*.

Christoph Huber

Date 1951

Nationality Germany

Director Peter Lorre

Cast Peter Lorre, Gisela Trowe

Original Title *Der Verlorene*

Why it's Key This moment condenses the tragedy of its star and one-time director, beloved character-acting genius Peter Lorre.

Key Scene **The retrieval of the lighter**
Strangers on a Train

A symbolic object that becomes critical to the plot, the cigarette lighter is introduced a few minutes into this masterful thriller, which preserves the basic premise and gay subtext of the original Patricia Highsmith novel but adds plenty of Hitchcockian variations. Guy (Granger), a tennis pro, finds himself in the same train compartment as Bruno (Walker), an eccentric fan who strikes up an awkwardly intimate conversation. Aware that Guy wants a divorce so that he can marry a senator's daughter, Bruno suggests that they swap murders: Bruno will kill Guy's wife if Guy will kill Bruno's father. Rattled by this proposal, Guy hastily departs, leaving behind his lighter, which Bruno pockets. A gift from his girlfriend, Ann, it bears the inscription "A to G" and is engraved with two crossed tennis rackets – a neat emblem of Bruno's "criss-cross" scheme.

Bruno keeps his half of the perceived bargain and plans to frame Guy by placing the lighter at the scene

of the murder. On his way, though, he drops the lighter down a sewer and has to retrieve it through a grating. At that moment, Guy is playing a tennis match that he must win quickly if he is to stop Bruno.

Hitchcock generates suspense by cross-cutting between both men's desperate exertions: Bruno thrusting his arm deep into the dark storm drain and Guy lunging for every ball on the sunlit court. In this struggle between id and superego, Hitchcock, as usual, complicates the process of audience identification. The viewer roots for the villain to reach the lighter that he needs to incriminate the hero – a response that attests to the superb complexity of Walker's performance and the sly ingenuity of Hitchcock's filmmaking.

Dennis Lim

Date 1951

Nationality USA

Director Alfred Hitchcock

Cast Robert Walker, Farley Granger

Why It's Key This suspenseful scene is a textbook example of Hitchcock's brilliant manipulation of viewer identification.

Opposite *Strangers on a Train*

Key Scene **The killer's "just a kid"** *On Dangerous Ground*

One of the most strikingly beautiful black-and-white films Hollywood ever made, Ray's seminal rogue-cop drama charts the geographical, psychological, and moral odyssey undertaken by lonely, repressed, and brutally efficient officer Jim Wilson (Ryan), from the dark mean streets of a northeastern metropolis to an in many ways wilder, wintry rural community haunted by the (possibly sexual) murder of a young girl. A plot strand centred on the ethically blinkered Wilson's relationship with Mary (Ida Lupino), protective blind sister of immature killer Danny (Williams), has its sticky moments, but Ray keeps things pacy, suspenseful, and mostly unsentimental.

When Wilson and Walter Brent (Bond) – the dead girl's dad, who's forever vowing to forget the law and fill the killer's belly with bullets – pursue the boy up an icy cliff until he slips to his death, it's not only the cop who realizes his vengeful alter ego's gone too far; we also have to reassess any assumptions we've made about a child-murderer. Belatedly, Brent recognizes that his prey – Bernard Herrmann's best score always stresses the chase as an unfairly weighted hunt – was "just a kid" and carries him *pietà*-style over the snow to a nearby hamlet. But by now, as a grieving Mary asks Wilson, "What difference does it make?" Too often the shoot-first-then-ask-questions ethos of traditional American mores makes for mistakes and tragedy. Ray knew how easily the American Dream became a nightmare, and this moment bemoans the prevalence of violent fear, the death of trust and innocence.

Geoff Andrew

Date 1951

Nationality USA

Director Nicholas Ray

Cast Robert Ryan, Ward Bond, Sumner Williams

Why It's Key Lyrical and redemptive, it's a rare example of Hollywood abandoning simplistic notions of "evil" for something more troublingly complex.

Key Event *Rashomon* **wins the Golden Lion at the Venice Film Festival**

In September 1951, Akira Kurosawa's *Rashomon* (1950) was awarded the coveted Golden Lion for best film at the Venice Film Festival and suddenly thrust Japanese cinema into the world spotlight. Little of Japanese cinema had been seen in the West prior to this award, but *Rashomon* went on to travel widely on the strength of its prize and helped to make Kurosawa a familiar name in the West. The film has a bold and unusual structure that challenged many audiences: At its centre is a story of rape and murder that is told four times, each time from a different perspective, by a different participant. The Japanese studio behind the film, Daiei, had little faith in the film and only reluctantly agreed to enter it in the Venice competition. The award came as a shock not only to Daiei but to the Japanese film establishment as well. The Japanese industry responded with a flurry of films intended specifically for what they believed was Western taste, especially "historical" dramas such as the relentlessly exotic *Gate of Hell* (1953; directed by Teinosuke Kinugasa). Kurosawa, however, continued to make his own idiosyncratic films and soon confirmed his reputation worldwide with such masterpieces as *Seven Samurai* (1954) and *Throne of Blood* (1957). Ultimately, the Venice award put Japanese cinema on the map, and films by a range of Japanese directors (Ozu, Mizoguchi, Ichikawa, and others) became regular inclusions in festival programming thereafter.

Andrew Pike

Date September 1951

Why It's Key the award opened the eyes of the West to Japanese cinema.

Opposite *Rashomon*

Key Event
Elia Kazan names names

During part of his time with The Group Theatre in the 1930s, Elia Kazan belonged to The Group's Communist Party unit. By 1952, Kazan had reached the highest success as a director of Broadway plays and, with the release of *A Streetcar Named Desire*, had entered the top tier of Hollywood directors. In testifying about his party activities before the House Committee on Un-American Activities (HUAC) on January 14, Kazan declined to identify other members, although the ritual of denunciation was understood to be a requirement for former Communists who wished to avoid the loss of Hollywood employment. In a second appearance on April 10, Kazan rectified his omission, naming eight members of The Group's Communist Party unit and several other party members, and saying that his reluctance to name names had been "wrong,... because secrecy serves the Communists, and is exactly what they want." On April 12, in a paid advertisement in the *New York Times*, Kazan stated

his reasons for testifying. He said that Communist activities posed a grave threat to the American "way of life" and called the argument that exposing American Communists was an attack on civil liberties "a lie."

Kazan's HUAC testimony and *New York Times* statement earned him the reprobation of many on the Left and made him the ultimate symbol of the "friendly witness." In 1999, the awarding of an honorary Oscar to Kazan for his "lifetime achievement" met with much protest – the scale and vehemence of which, together with the attention it received from news media, proved the enduring significance of the anti-Communist witch hunt in the film industry.

Chris Fujiwara

Date April 10, 1952

Why It's Key Kazan's act made him the definitive embodiment of the Hollywood informer.

Key Speech **The borderline of theatre and life** *The Golden Coach*

At a loss to choose among her love for the stage and three men – Felipe (Campbell), whom she met during her trip from Italy to Peru; the powerful and courteous Viceroy (Lamont), who has promised her a golden coach; and the dashing bullfighter Ramón (Rioli) – the actress Camilla (Magnani) despairs and asks poignantly to the Viceroy (and to herself) why she succeeds on the stage and fails in real life: "Where is truth? Where does the theatre end and life begin?", only to be interrupted by the other two aspiring lovers, who, having hidden in nearby rooms as in a stage play, discover each other and start fighting for real, causing a scandal that will force her to make a final choice.

Near the ending of this most serious of farces (or most joyful of tragedies), Camilla is about to renounce her worldly ambitions and take refuge in the safer, orderly illusion of theatre. The old director of the commedia dell'arte company, Don Antonio (Spadaro), encourages her: "Do not waste your time on the so-

called real life ... Felipe, Ramón or the Viceroy ... do you miss them?" "A little," is Camilla's quiet, melancholy answer, realizing she cannot live on the borderline of both sides, but must choose one and therefore, alas, lose the other. It is always with the utmost simplicity that Renoir reflects on the real dilemmas of life.

Miguel Marías

Date 1952

Nationality France/Italy

Director Jean Renoir

Cast Anna Magnani, Duncan Lamont, Paul Campbell, Riccardo Rioli, Odoardo Spadaro

Original Titles *Le Carrosse d'or/La carrozza d'oro*

Why It's Key This moment proves that artifice and theatre can lead to truth and cinema, but people must take sides.

Key Scene **A spectacular catastrophe**
The Greatest Show on Earth

Sporting spangly garments in lavender, avocado, fuchsia, tangerine, and cornflower blue, brave circus performers struggle against dark forces and the whims of fate to keep putting on their show. This is one of the truly overwhelming Technicolor features of the 1950s, utilizing the Ringling Bros., Barnum and Bailey Circus, real locations, and an all-star cast. Racketeers want to muscle in on the sideshow, and Brad, the circus manager (Heston), is fighting them. As the company moves one night in a long, winding train from one venue to another, the bad guys cause a train wreck, one of the primary early examples of catastrophe cinema. The saturation of colors in early evening, the combination of model shots and live-action footage, and the integration of animals into the scene of destruction make for an optically stunning sequence. Wrecked cars cantilevered at all angles, wounded personnel, survivors racing around panicky and still beautiful in nightclothes, escaped wild beasts prowling among the shattered objects – all of this is elegantly composed and brilliantly choreographed with an eye to action, subplot, innuendo, and dazzling color all at once. The wreck serves as a turning point in the plot, as well. Buttons the clown (Stewart) has been harboring a dark and secret past as a medical practitioner. When he sees his friend Brad severely wounded, possibly dying, he aborts his furtive escape plan and returns to the circus family to reveal his real talents. Perhaps now he will be arrested for the crime he has been hiding, perhaps the show will go on.

Murray Pomerance

Date 1952

Nationality USA

Director Cecil B. DeMille

Cast Charlton Heston, James Stewart

Why It's Key It's an important example of Technicolor screen spectacle.

Key Event **The Supreme Court ruling in the case of *The Miracle***

It is astonishing to note that, until the U.S. Supreme Court's landmark *Miracle* decision, films, unlike literary works, were not deemed worthy of First Amendment protection: movies were implicitly reviled as a glorified fairground attraction and not considered a legitimate art form.

Roberto Rossellini's *The Miracle* (1948), the short feature that led to the Supreme Court ruling, was far from pornographic, and despite the American Catholic Church's outraged response to a film now considered a classic, might actually be categorized as an example of devotional art. Nevertheless, Rossellini's moving fable about a peasant woman (played memorably by Anna Magnani) who is convinced that the drifter who impregnates her is in fact the incarnation of Saint Joseph created an enormous ruckus in post-World War II America. Although *The Miracle* had premiered in Italy in 1948 without a peep from Church authorities, the film's premiere in New York City (where it was included in an omnibus package with two other short features by Renoir and Pagnol), prompted Edward T. McCaffrey, the commissioner of licenses, to condemn the film as "personally and officially blasphemous." While McCaffrey's alliance with the Catholic-dominated Legion of Decency led to some heavy-handed intervention from local censors, New York State courts soon overturned a clearly illegal ban. Besides lending motion pictures newfound respectability, the Supreme Court ruling heralded a new era in which conservative watchdog organizations such as the Legion of Decency would find it more difficult to suppress controversial films (although many of the Legion's descendants still attempt to ban films they consider unsavory). Unfortunately, many commentators overlook the film that sparked all of the fuss – a work that, according to critic Peter Brunette, is both unconventionally reverent and intensely critical of "conventional religion."

Richard Porton

Date May 26, 1952

Why It's Key This pivotal case helped to erode the rigid censorship of films in the United States.

Key Scene **Georgia takes a drive**
The Bad and the Beautiful

Georgia Lorrison (Turner), the alcoholic daughter of a dead matinee idol, has been rescued from her screwed-up existence and transformed into a movie star with her debut performance. She owes her success to visionary producer Jonathan Shields (Douglas), with whom she's fallen in love. Leaving the after-the-premiere party with a magnum of champagne, she traces Shields to his luxury retreat. He has gone home, he tells her, because he wants to be alone with his post-film depression. Georgia learns the truth after she senses, moving across her face, the Murnau-esque shadow of the magazine-cover model (Stewart) who's been cooling her heels in Jonathan's upstairs bedroom. Now it's not enough for Jonathan that Georgia feels betrayed and stunned: he has to berate her for feeling sorry for herself, finding her vulnerability an all-too-hittable target for the projection of his own self-loathing. She runs out, gets in her car, and drives onto the road. Minnelli's camera is in the car with her, and –

astonishingly – he keeps it rolling steadily as she gets more hysterical. Horns beep, and oncoming headlights surge through the car interior, but Georgia – sobbing and also terrified – can't control herself any more than she can control her vehicle. The most perfect freak-out in cinema, no less great for being obviously done on a soundstage, with the car a set that's being rocked back and forth, and for being performed by the most Hollywood of all Hollywood stars, an actress usually known for cool self-possession.
Chris Fujiwara

Date 1952

Nationality USA

Director Vincente Minnelli

Cast Lana Turner, Kirk Douglas, Elaine Stewart

Why It's Key It's the most perfect freak-out in cinema.

Opposite *The Bad and the Beautiful*

1950–1959

219

Key Event **3-D – Cinema moves (briefly) into the third dimension**

Hollywood's first 3-D production, the 1952 adventure *Bwana Devil*, was a hit despite terrible reviews. The reason wasn't so much the story, about man-eating African lions, as the excitement of a new experience: motion pictures in depth, with visual elements seeming to leap out of the screen. Studios scrambled to capitalize on the craze, led by Columbia with *Man in the Dark* and Warner Bros. with *House of Wax*, both premiering in April 1953.

People see in depth thanks to the visual cortex, which interprets the two-dimensional images imprinted on the eyes – each slightly different from the other – as a single three-dimensional image. Flat images reproduce this effect when the viewer's two retinas see near-identical pictures that mimic the normal displacement of the eyes. Experiments with 3-D movies began in the 1890s, but things got serious in the early 1950s, when competition from television made Hollywood eager for spectacles that the humble TV

tube couldn't provide. Three-projector Cinerama, wide-screen CinemaScope, and stereophonic soundtracks debuted around the same time.

3-D's golden age ended roughly a year after it began. It's a cumbersome format – in its early phase, two precisely synched projectors were needed – and you have to wear those silly glasses. Few art-minded filmmakers have found much aesthetic value in it, aside from Alfred Hitchcock, whose 1954 thriller *Dial "M" for Murder* uses it ingeniously. 3-D's legacy survives in giant-screen IMAX 3-D, occasional novelty releases, and the work of avant-gardists like Ken Jacobs, whose "Nervous System" offers the seemingly impossible: one-eye 3-D vision.
David Sterritt

Date November 26, 1952

Why It's Key Hollywood's brief enthusiasm for three-dimensional effects produced movies as different as the1953 musical *Kiss Me Kate* and the 1954 shocker *Creature From the Black Lagoon*, exemplifying the film industry's desire to regain its dwindling audience with spectacles TV couldn't offer.

Key Scene **A few steps link past and present in quiet sunlight** *Life of Oharu*

Saikaku's picaresque novel of a woman's reversals of fortune through the many events of her life is transformed into something spiritual in Mizoguchi's film. One sequence reveals this with a rare and special effectiveness. It is late in the narrative, and Oharu (Tanaka) has been reduced to playing the samisen and begging. We see her sitting in front of a gate, and in a closer shot, she gets up, reacting to something, and moves left to right, ascending a small slope; we then see what she saw and reacted to: the retinue of her son (whom she bore for a lord when young before being sent away from court). She sees her son only fleetingly, and then the camera reverses direction to track with her back to her place by the gate. There are only nine shots from the first of these images to the last, in a sequence running over five minutes, and the last of these (over two minutes) is especially beautiful, as the camera follows her movement back for half the take, then is still as she settles in place and cries, in an

exquisitely sustained moment. The quiet, unexpected materialization of Oharu's past within her present is magical, and brought to perfection by Mizoguchi's command of both camera movement and fixed composition, subtlety of light and shadow, sound (there is no dialogue), and the expressions and movements of Tanaka, while at the same time, the thorough eloquence of all these elements makes the heroine a transcendent figure.

Blake Lucas

Date 1952

Nationality Japan

Director Kenji Mizoguchi

Cast Kinuyo Tanaka

Original Title *Saikaku ichidai onna*

Why It's Key The elaborately detailed narrative journey of a memorable heroine is elevated in a privileged moment that reveals with special acuity the consummate artistry and long-take mastery of Mizoguchi.

1950–1959

Key Scene **Don sings and dances in the rain** *Singin' in the Rain*

Don Lockwood (Kelly) kisses Cathy (Debbie Reynolds) good night at her door. He's so glad that he doesn't care if it's pouring, so he needs neither the taxi he dismisses, nor the umbrella he plays with to almost any but its intended purpose. The scene, actually edited out of ten shots, gives such an illusion of continuity that it is experienced and felt as a single mobile take, thanks to the "invisible" cuts induced by shot size and camerawork, music and rhythm, movements and grand gestures of the actor-dancer-singer, who, oblivious to reality, seems to inhabit a dreamlike bubble of expansive, contagious, communicative happiness as he trots on the street, plays with street lamps, passes a variety of shop windows, and crosses hurried, wet passers-by, including a policeman who, no doubt, wonders about Don's sanity.

This crazy explosion of elation, happiness, and joy is one of the summits of the classical MGM musical of

the '50s, which meant a short-lived revolution in the genre: rather than in a show-business stage number, the characters expressed their feelings within their everyday surroundings through seemingly spontaneous song and dance, at first only slightly stylized, then more and more exaggerated until they flew out of reality into the most glorious ecstasy.

Miguel Marías

Date 1952

Nationality USA

Directors Gene Kelly and Stanley Donen

Cast Gene Kelly

Why It's Key This musical number embodies the "natural" style developed by the Arthur Freed unit at MGM and represents the highest expression of joy in the movies.

Opposite *Singin' in the Rain*

THOSE WEDDING BELLS ARE RINGING FOR THAT "BORN YESTERDAY" GIRL!

COLUMBIA PICTURES presents

JUDY HOLLIDAY

in

The Marrying Kind

ALDO RAY

introducing

Written by RUTH GORDON and GARSON KANIN

Produced by BERT GRANET · Directed by GEORGE CUKOR

Key Scene **The puppet show**
Totò a colori

What if the greatest poet on earth wrote in an obscure language, spoken by a tiny minority of people? The question – provocatively raised by Jorge Luis Borges – may well apply to the films of Totò (Antonio de Curtis), who brought his experience as a vaudeville comedian onto the screen in over a hundred titles made between 1937 and 1967. His appeal defies generational boundaries: Italian television still broadcasts his films on a regular basis; many of his jokes have become part of everyday language, and there are many who regard him as the greatest comedy actor in the history of cinema (yes, even above Chaplin and Keaton). Of course there is no way to prove the claim, as his gags can be fully understood only in their native language; some are just impossible to translate. Pier Paolo Pasolini, the first *auteur* who understood the universal appeal of Totò's genius, featured him in *Uccellacci e uccellini* (1966) and in the sublime short *La terra vista dalla luna* (1967).

Totò a colori is widely regarded as Totò's masterpiece, a dazzling and surreal exercise in body language. Film directors who worked with him used to say that they didn't need to do much beyond letting the camera roll; he would do all the rest. We see him here in a chase scene where he hides from his pursuers by disguising himself as a wooden marionette on stage. Once the show is over, his body collapses just like a dead puppet: it's a touching, self-reflective statement on the nature of acting.

Paolo Cherchi Usai

Date 1952

Nationality Italy

Director Steno (Stefano Vanzina)

Cast Totò, Isa Barzizza, Franca Valeri

Why It's Key Vernacular art transcends the boundaries of language.

1950-1959

223

Key Scene **The most painful memory**
The Marrying Kind

SPOILER

In a peak period of his career, Cukor collaborated on a number of films with writers Garson Kanin and Ruth Gordon, including this insightful, beautifully constructed one about a couple, Chet (Ray) and Florence Keefer (Holliday), who remember events of their marriage, prompted by a sympathetic divorce court judge (Kennedy). For an hour, the story, while essentially serious and realistic, is played for warm comedy, then tragedy strikes at a Decoration Day picnic when their young son accidentally drowns. There is nothing more impressive in cinema than this kind of change of mood, done here to telling effect and in a way that is brilliantly deliberated in Cukor's direction. Joey's death is powerfully evoked in seven fairly brief shots, and on either side are two very long takes, each close to two minutes. The first seals the mood of the first hour, Chet and Florence at their most happy and relaxed, physically close for a few moments before he lies back and she sits over him playing the ukelele and singing "Dolores." On the other side is a fast dissolve back to the courtroom and Florence breaking into sudden anguished crying, after which we see Chet also as a man seemingly destroyed, as he talks while first moving away from the seated women, then moving back. It's not simply the great acting or staging or feeling for the couple that makes this transition great, but the durations and distances of these two shots, which measure how quickly and how cruelly life can change.

Blake Lucas

Date 1952

Nationality USA

Director George Cukor

Cast Judy Holliday, Aldo Ray, Madge Kennedy

Why It's Key Cukor provides one of the most masterful examples ever of shifting the mood of a film from light to dark while preserving the sense of a formal whole.

Opposite *The Marrying Kind*

Key Scene **Crusoe's solitude**
The Adventures of Robinson Crusoe

The director later remarked of his Defoe adaptation that "what most interested me about Robinson was his complete human solitude." In the same compressed and almost brutally direct style that marks the whole film, Buñuel stages the castaway's fall into despair (precipitated by the death of his dog, his only companion, after years of survival on his island) in three sequences linked by voice-over. "Now truly alone" – Dan O'Herlihy's sonorous narrating voice almost keens – he rushes to the valley of the echo to stand on a hilltop shouting out the 23rd Psalm for the consolation of hearing his own voice sound back. The reverential effect that might conventionally be suggested by the Biblical passage is undercut by Crusoe's visible rage and despair as he repeats the phrase "my soul" in a hoarse bellow. That the echoed words confirm rather than alleviate his solitary imprisonment is underscored by the next brief scene in which he reads the Bible, again repeating the 23rd Psalm, but finds that the words – "green pastures" – have become babble. Now he is reduced to racing at night toward the water's edge, the limit of his prison, waving a torch and crying out "Help!" In an extraordinarily simple and powerful long shot he is framed, back to the camera, standing in the surf against a beautiful and in the context utterly disheartening seascape. His torch extinguished in the waves, he turns around and marches grimly straight into the camera, the screen going black as if he had walked through the camera
Geoffrey O'Brien

Date 1952

Nationality Mexico/USA

Director Luis Buñuel

Cast Dan O'Herlihy

Why It's Key In a movie that was marketed as an entertainment for children – featuring "The Most Fabulous Hero in All Adventure History!" – Luis Buñuel evoked the horror of solitude as piercingly and unrelentingly as any film has done.

Opposite *The Adventures of Robinson Crusoe*

224

Key Person **Robert Mitchum**
Jeff goes home *The Lusty Men*

One of the most beautiful openings of any film introduces the character of rodeo cowboy Jeff McCloud (Mitchum). Unusually, he is first established in a documentary evocation of a rodeo, without dialogue or interaction with other characters. Injured by a bull, Jeff leaves the rodeo grounds alone and hitches a ride to a place that we come to realize was his childhood home; for awhile, he is by himself there, then his solitude ends. In tone and texture, Ray's images are highly evocative: Jeff's limping walk across the arena at dusk amid papers blowing in the dimming light, the morning glow over the countryside as he walks toward the ranch, his look at the house from the gate, his crawl under the house to find some things he left there years before. So is the soundtrack: Roy Webb's score begins discreetly when Jeff gets out of the truck, its wistful main melody first appearing when he is at the gate. The most important element, though, is Mitchum, who has the rare gift of knowing how much emotion the camera will pick up and how much it is up to him to convey, in his body as well as his face. People express emotion more quietly when they are alone, and the emotion here is profound, especially Jeff's first look at the house from the gate, and his expression, almost like that of a little boy, as he looks at his things. As these scenes end, a rich drama will begin, but we have already seen what the film most deeply is – a meditation on one man's sense of the circle of his life.
Blake Lucas

Date 1952

Nationality USA

Director Nicholas Ray

Cast Robert Mitchum

Why It's Key In a memorably reflective opening, one of cinema's greatest directors works with one of its greatest actors to create a complex character in the most gracefully restrained way.

Key Film
Ikiru

One might plausibly claim that Akira Kurosawa's *Ikiru* contains two key "moments": the first half and the second half. Although there are numerous outstanding scenes, images, and gestures in Kurosawa's oeuvre, what is often most striking about his films is the audacity of their overall design. Banal messages and crude schemata are frequently stated baldly before being either lost sight of or directly contradicted as the full scale of the structure emerges. Both *Ikiru* and *High and Low* are divided into two parts of unequal length, initially focusing on men who find themselves acting on previously suppressed humanist impulses, then abruptly relegating them to the background as control of the narrative is assumed by a new (and significantly larger) set of characters. The first part of *Ikiru* follows minor official Kanji Watanabe (Takashi Shimura) as he discovers that he is dying of cancer, and ends with him deciding to fight alongside those who are demanding that a piece of wasteland be transformed into a playground, a socially useful act that he hopes will give his life some meaning. The second, much shorter part takes place after Watanabe's death and depicts the differing responses to his successful campaign. The simplistic morality of Watanabe's decision seems less clear-cut once it has been situated in a wider context, *Ikiru*'s final scenes suggesting that the well-intentioned protagonist has made little impact on a culture whose problems are too deep-rooted to be solved by liberal reforms and the actions of decently motivated individuals.

Brad Stevens

Date 1952

Nationality Japan

Director Akira Kurosawa

Cast Takashi Shimura

Aka *Living*

Why It's Key This film provides the best evidence of Kurosawa's ability to communicate challenging ideas through audacious large-scale structures.

Opposite *Ikiru*

1950–1959

Key Scene **The final spin of the wheel**
Rancho Notorious

SPOILER

An unusual Western, but at the same time unpretentious, realized in the apparently simple but highly refined style of late Lang, *Rancho Notorious* is supremely representative of this artist, especially as its concerns cohere within a few images in the denouement. Seeking revenge for the rape and murder of his fiancee, working cowboy Vern Haskell (Kennedy) becomes involved with the gunman Frenchy Fairmont (Ferrer) and the latter's lover, legendary Altar Keane (Dietrich), who runs the Chuck-a-Luck hideaway. After the unraveling of several interrelated threads, the three wind up on the same side in a final gunfight against other outlaws, in which Altar takes a bullet for Frenchy. As she dies, close-ups of each of the three are expressive, but a brief three-shot, composed with an extraordinary beauty, is even more so: in their looks and postures, the characters reveal a profound change in Lang's philosophy, which he explained late in life. He had once believed (in his early German films and first American ones) that man was ruled by fate, but he came to believe that character was fate. Altar, Vern, and Frenchy know this about themselves as the film ends, and that is the key to why the two men will die also, willingly, as the recurrent song "The Legend of Chuck-a-Luck" reveals over a final image that follows. Brilliantly, Lang has used that song, with its line "listen to the wheel of fate," to interrogate his own earlier understanding of life and set it against this mature vision.

Blake Lucas

Date 1952

Nationality USA

Director Fritz Lang

Cast Marlene Dietrich, Arthur Kennedy, Mel Ferrer

Why It's Key A timeless story of "hate, murder, and revenge" becomes an uncommonly moving meditation on the eternal question of fate versus free will.

Key Scene **Diane wanders through the empty house** *Angel Face*

It's a familiar motif in *film noir*. An attractive, compelling woman comes into the life of a basically moral, if unsettled and imperfect, man, and destroys both him and herself – and usually others as well. Here it's Diane Tremayne (Simmons), a kind of Electra-like child-woman, and not so conventional a figure, even if the script follows a predictable enough, though highly absorbing, course. Preminger, while his style is characteristically sharp and attentive, seems not so intent on highly elaborate camera movement, beautiful for its own sake, as in, say, *Fallen Angel* (1945), but as the film draws near to its close, a remarkable four-minute sequence occurs. Diane is now all alone in the big house where she has lived. She wanders from room to room, then outside, then into the quarters where her ex-lover Frank (Robert Mitchum) had stayed. A repeated camera movement, following her from a hall into a room, or out of one, becomes a motif of the sequence, which is entirely without dialogue, sustained by the superb performance of Simmons, the haunting music of Dimitri Tiomkin, and the visual grace of Preminger, and brought to a plaintive final note as she awakes in the morning, huddled in a chair, wrapped in Frank's coat. The sequence transforms Diane, showing the viewer not a murderess but simply a troubled young woman who commands a profound sympathy. In this transformation, the film becomes a deeper mystery than its narrative even begins to suggest.

Blake Lucas

Date 1953

Nationality USA

Director Otto Preminger

Cast Jean Simmons

Why It's Key In finding the space for a character to become something more and other than what she has been defined as, Preminger affords a rare vision of what aesthetic and moral nuance can attain together.

228

Key Scene **The Pompeii ruins discovery** *Voyage in Italy*

An English couple journeying in Italy to clear up the affairs related to a recently deceased uncle's estate have, while forced to stay together in a strange environment, wandered apart, realizing what they had so far avoided to admit through each living his or her own lives. They have just said the words "let's get a divorce," when they have to accept an invitation to see new archeological discoveries in the ruins of Pompeii, an ancient city buried in lava and ashes after a cataclysmic volcanic eruption. The people working on the ongoing excavation slowly and carefully unearth what seems at first an arm, then two legs, then a skull from which, delicately, the earth is brushed off to reveal the plaster cast of a disintegrated head. Finally, there appear – much like photographed images appearing on a film as it is developed – the full bodies of a man and a woman who died suddenly in their sleep as they lay together in bed and who now look like the sculpture of a couple. We make these discoveries gradually and at precisely the same time as do the two characters, Katherine (Ingrid Bergman) and Alex Joyce (George Sanders), so that we can fully share or at least understand their reaction; both are impressed, and Katherine is affected so deeply that she wants to leave the place. As Alex escorts her out of the ruins towards their car, he admits, "I was pretty moved myself" – a first step towards mutual understanding, which prepares us to accept as (barely) feasible the almost miraculous reconciliation of the couple.

Miguel Marías

Date 1953

Nationality Italy/France

Director Roberto Rossellini

Cast Ingrid Bergman, George Sanders

Original Title *Viaggio in Italia* (aka *Journey to Italy; Voyage to Italy; Strangers*)

Why It's Key It reveals how the imprint of something from the past can move and affect, in a mirror-like way, people in the present.

Key Event
Zanuck backs CinemaScope

In the early 1950s, Hollywood's major studios faced competition from TV and decreasing box-office revenues. Among the devices with which the studios tried to shore up their position, the one that had the biggest impact on how the cinema would look for years to come was CinemaScope. Devised by Henri Chrétien and purchased by 20th Century-Fox in 1952, the process used an anamorphic lens that, mounted on an ordinary camera, photographed images that were horizontally squeezed; unsqueezing during projection yielded an image wider than the film frame.

On March 12, 1953, after viewing rushes for the first two CinemaScope productions (*The Robe* and *How To Marry a Millionaire*), production chief Darryl F. Zanuck sent a memo to all his producers, announcing that henceforth "Twentieth Century-Fox will concentrate exclusively on subjects suitable for CinemaScope." It soon became clear, as the new format caught on, that a wider screen required no sacrifice in intimacy. Hollywood directors like Nicholas Ray, Vincente Minnelli, Otto Preminger, and Richard Fleischer made complex, dynamic, and personal films in 'Scope.

Standardized at an aspect ratio of 2.35:1, anamorphic widescreen spread around the world under various brand names (in the United States, Panavision lenses proved more popular than those that bore the CinemaScope mark). When used by a brilliant, or sometimes even just a competent, director, 'Scope can bring a heightened emphasis on composition and space that still justifies the enthusiasm that Jacques Rivette expressed when, writing in *Cahiers du cinéma* in 1954, he predicted that "ours will be the generation of CinemaScope."

Chris Fujiwara

Date March 12, 1953

Why It's Key When it adopted the anamorphic widescreen format for all its productions, 20th Century-Fox changed the look of cinema.

Key Film
El

Under the guise of a melodrama about a pathologically jealous husband and his long-suffering wife, *El* is a fiercely sardonic indictment of bourgeois mentality and of religion's oppressive, nefarious influence on the human psyche. Francesco (de Cordova), the protagonist, is a wealthy, devoutly religious 45-year-old bachelor. The brilliant opening sequence, set in a church during a Holy Thursday mass, shows religious rituals to be ambiguously linked to erotic fetishism, as the camera follows a priest who washes and kisses the feet of choir boys. Francesco, who participates in the ceremony (he carries the basin of water), looks at the crowd. The camera pans along the feet of the first row of people, glides past a pair of woman's shoes, continues on, then pans back to the woman and tilts up to reveal first her shapely legs, then the rest of her. Francesco is smitten. Later he will marry Gloria (Garcés), but only to torment her with his jealousy, to the point of physically torturing her in a chilling scene in which she is heard screaming in pain behind closed doors. In another scene he is shown gathering needle and thread and ropes, apparently with the intention of tying up his wife and sewing up her vagina (a Sadean reference). Gloria will eventually escape as he sinks into madness (his hallucinations in a church provide Buñuel with an opportunity for some "sacrilegious" imagery). Francesco ends up in a monastery where, despite his claim of being cured, he proves to be still crazy in a memorable zig-zagging closing shot.

Jean-Pierre Coursodon

Date 1953

Nationality Mexico

Director Luis Buñuel

Cast Arturo de Cordova, Delia Garcés, Luis Beristáin

Why It's Key One of the most striking and personal films of Buñuel's Mexican period, and the link between his early surrealist masterpiece, *L'Age d'or*, and the daring French films of his late period.

Key Scene **Dancing in the dark**
The Band Wagon

Can Tony Hunter (Astaire) and Gaby Gerard (Charisse) overcome their mutual distrust and disregard, can the old hoofer relinquish some of his pizzazz and the ballerina drop some of her polish, and can they, for the benefit of the show they have been cast in as leading man and woman, dance together? The two meet one night in his suite at the Plaza. He walks her out for an evening and they decide to take a hack ride into the Park. On benches all around, in the soft twilight, are lovers caught in the dream of romance. "Look," says Tony, disparaging their workaholic lives in the theater, "People!"

In a clearing they find space to be alone together. The tune in their heads is Arthur Schwartz and Howard Dietz's "Dancing in the Dark." She extends her foot as she walks beside him, does a little turn; watching carefully, he gracefully matches her. They begin to dance, she in a white dress, he in a white suit, their moves complementing each other in a "natural,"

effortless, waking dream of sensitivity and simplicity. The dance is talent, professionalism, sacrifice, abandonment of the self, love. But central to the enchantment of this supreme moment in the careers of Astaire and Charisse, and in the history of the American movie musical, is the setting by E. Preston Ames and Cedric Gibbons. This Central Park is realistic enough to make us believe Tony and Gaby are of the real world, working together against a real problem; yet at the same time palpably false, a movie set, so that, as we watch, our delirious belief is continually reflected to us as a construction, a piece of magic.
Murray Pomerance

Date 1953

Nationality USA

Director Vincente Minnelli

Cast Fred Astaire, Cyd Charisse

Why It's Key It's musical dance onscreen at its very best.

Opposite *The Band Wagon*

230

Key Film
I Love Melvin

One of the most delightful musicals ever to come out of MGM or any other studio, *I Love Melvin* is also one of the lesser known and most underrated, even though it boasts two of the three stars of the triumphal *Singin' in the Rain*, Donald O'Connor and Debbie Reynolds, whose rapport both in straight comedy scenes and song-and-dance numbers is just terrific. The bumpy romance between an aspiring Broadway musical actress and the lowly assistant to a grumpy *Look* magazine photographer (their boy-meets-girl moment is when they actually bump into each other in Central Park – as they will again in the film's closing gag – and Melvin's enthusiastic kisses never fail to almost knock the girl down) is directed by Don Weis with a zest that keeps you grinning with glee throughout most of the proceedings.

The film – which revolves around Melvin's mounting troubles after he unwisely boasts that he can arrange to have his girl's photograph featured on the

cover of *Look* – opens with an elaborate musical number featuring Reynolds, a scene from a film being shot. After the take, everybody on the set from director to stagehands wildly compliments the star. Then, when her mother shakes her awake, it all turns out to have been just Debbie's dream. Other highlights include a wonderful tongue-in-cheek duet by O'Connor and Reynolds, a charming rollerskate number by O'Connor with his girlfriend's little sister, a choreographed football game on stage (with Reynolds as the football!) and a mad solo romp through the *Look* photography studios by O'Connor as a lightning-fast quick-change artist. Who could ask for anything more?
Jean-Pierre Coursodon

Date 1953

Nationality USA

Director Don Weis

Cast Donald O'Connor, Debbie Reynolds, Jim Backus

Why It's Key It's an unfairly neglected gem from the greatest era of the Hollywood musical.

Key Event **United Artists releases *The Moon Is Blue* without a Production Code Seal**

In 1951, Otto Preminger had a Broadway hit with F. Hugh Herbert's comedy *The Moon Is Blue*, and he and Herbert decided to make it into a film. Preminger set up a deal with United Artists to finance and distribute the picture, which would star William Holden as an architect, Maggie McNamara as the slightly kooky girl he picks up one evening on the observation deck of the Empire State Building, and David Niven as the architect's playboy neighbor. An old pro at dealing with Joseph Breen's Production Code Administration (Hollywood's self-censorship agency), Preminger probably knew from the start that *The Moon Is Blue*, with its non-stop chatter about sexual matters, would be refused the Breen office's Seal, which was then considered almost necessary to ensure widespread exhibition for a film. When, on January 2, 1953, Breen advised him that the script for the film could not be approved, Preminger was probably not surprised, no more than he could have been when, on April 10,

Breen deemed the finished film unapprovable. The problem was "an unacceptably light attitude towards seduction, illicit sex, chastity and virginity." United Artists decided to distribute the film anyway. Not only did the film get bookings throughout the country (starting on June 22 in Chicago, where it was shown to "adults only"), but it became a hit – thanks in no small part to the notoriety that the denial of the Seal engendered. This success was a highly visible blow both to the major studios' monopoly on film distribution and to the censorship they exercised over filmmaking in the attempt to enforce this monopoly.
Chris Fujiwara

Date June 22, 1953

Why It's Key The success of *The Moon Is Blue* struck a blow against film censorship and against the major studios' attempts to shut out competition from independents.

Key Speech **Moe's deathbed monologue** *Pickup on South Street*

Thelma Ritter got an Oscar nomination for her supporting role as Moe, a police informer who sells neckties as a front. This is the only time Samuel Fuller's unfashionable working-class cinema has ever been honored in such a fashion. Fuller had a special feeling for feisty old ladies – most of whom seem to be based to varying degrees on his mother – and none of these is more memorable than Ritter. A figure of some pathos, she only cares about making enough money to be buried in a decent cemetery.

The curious thing about Moe is that Skip (Richard Widmark) – the closest thing this movie has to a hero, and he's an unapologetic pickpocket – doesn't resent her at all because he reasons she's just making a living the best way she can. He likes her more than he likes the cops who employ her, and his loyalty is reciprocated. She eventually gets shot by a Commie hitman (Kiley) for refusing to reveal the address of Skip, who inadvertently filched some microfilm containing

Commie secrets; a 78 rpm record of "Mam'selle" is playing in the background. She's so tired – run down like an old clock, as she puts it – and so afraid that she says if he blew her head off he'd be doing her a favor.

Fuller was a liberal, but this was at the height of the Red Scare, when Commies were generic villains. His heart is with the outcasts, not the cops – so it isn't surprising that J. Edgar Hoover hated this movie.
Jonathan Rosenbaum

Date 1953

Nationality USA

Director Samuel Fuller

Cast Thelma Ritter, Richard Kiley

Why It's Key A tired old stool-pigeon sacrifices her life in order to defy the Commies, and breaks our hearts.

Key Speech **The narrator asks the audience to make up the story** *The End*

Christopher Maclaine's shattered and shattering masterpiece tells six stories of people in San Francisco on the last day of their lives – the planet is about to be destroyed in a nuclear holocaust. The editing is profoundly disturbed; cuts often separate images from each other rather than fusing them. Mixing black and white and color and intercutting many disjointed images, Maclaine's narration provides what little continuity there is; this is in part a film about storytelling, laced with dark humor. The narration is often heard over a completely black screen, calling attention both to his own awkwardness and to the film-viewing situation – is this a film, or a storyteller performing in a darkened room? And in a variety of ways the narration seeks to break through the passivity of the customary film viewing situation to engage the audience with each other, themselves, and the larger world – a necessary move for a film about the world's possible annihilation. Late in the film, for example, Maclaine announces, "The person next to you is a leper." But the truly sublime moment in the narration comes at the beginning of the fifth section: "Ladies and gentlemen. We have asked you to insert yourself into the cast. Now we ask you to write the story. Here is a character. Here is the most beautiful music on earth. Here are some pictures. *What* is happening?"
Fred Camper

Date 1953

Nationality USA

Director Christopher Maclaine

Why It's Key The narration is one of several elements that makes this a profoundly transgressive, boundary-destroying film.

1950–1959

233

Key Scene **The mother falters** *Tokyo Story*

The middle-aged woman, who has been sitting outdoors with her husband, hesitates for half a second while rising to her feet. That's all. You see no camera movement, no cut to a close-up, no reaction shot. And why would you? Tomi (Higashiyama) has neither fainted nor failed, and her husband, Shukichi (Ryu), has no cause for alarm. Two ordinary people, viewed in long shot against a clear sky, have merely stood up following an ordinary conversation. It's just that one did it a little more easily than the other.

That's all. That's everything.

As in life itself, a passing moment foretells enormous changes for an entire family: the aging couple from the provinces, their grown children in Tokyo, their widowed daughter-in-law. But in life, with so much flowing around you, it's difficult to catch the fleeting detail and feel everything that it means. To achieve that level of exquisite alertness, you need the art of Yasujiro Ozu. He gets his effects by subtraction rather than addition, helping you notice things by removing the distractions. When people speak of the unsurpassed subtlety of his art, this is what they mean: that his cinematic world is complete, that the emotions he evokes are full, but that events in his films happen only a little more emphatically than they would in your daily experience.

This is what people have in mind when they speak of Ozu: Tomi's knees bend very slightly, and your heart plummets.
Stuart Klawans

Date 1953

Nationality Japan

Director Yasujiro Ozu

Cast Chishu Ryu, Chieko Higashiyama

Original Title *Tokyo monogatari*

Why It's Key A small but critical scene, beautifully understated and deeply moving, sums up the art of Yasujiro Ozu.

Key Scene **Lust in the surf**
From Here to Eternity

On a Honolulu beach, just before the Pearl Harbor attack brings the U.S. into war, the adulterous flirtation between neglected and frustrated army wife Karen (Kerr) and ramrod sergeant Warden (Lancaster) turns physical in a horizontal embrace and kiss at water's edge, timed so that the surf washes voluptuously over the contoured bodies of the two stars. According to Zinnemann, the Breen Office objected not to the conventional bathing suits or the clinch but, ostensibly, to the water, and indeed, despite lasting only 12 seconds, the shot did send a sexual frisson around the world, with nature's surf forthrightly embodying the elemental force of the lovers' erotic urges. Catching two adults at the very moment of consenting, it portrayed directly a negotiation of needs and personal morality that American films usually mitigated with disguises, displacements, or starry-eyed romantic ideals. This affront to Hollywood's schoolmarm moral posturing almost atoned for the compromises necessary to bring James Jones's gritty best-seller, with its anti-heroic critique of military careerism, to the screen, such as turning G.I.s frequenting brothels into wholesome innocents booking "conversation" time with "hostesses." Nevertheless, the genie was out of the bottle, and this carnal moment on the beach now seems to foreshadow the tide of sexual frankness that would soon sweep away the Production Code restrictions.
Robert Keser

Date 1953

Nationality USA

Director Fred Zinnemann

Cast Burt Lancaster, Deborah Kerr

Why It's Key It was the most widely disseminated (and parodied) erotic image from 1950s cinema.

Opposite *From Here to Eternity*

235

Key Scene **Ghostly picnic with the princess** *Ugetsu*

Princess Wakasa (Kyo) helps ceramist Genjuro (Mori) bathe in a garden pool; she moves out of frame and undresses out of sight, and as he moves right to join her, the camera flies to the left, almost caressing the grass. The shot dissolves to a new image of the lawn, as the camera discovers, at the lakeshore, the couple picnicking in radiant sunshine. He chases her, she playfully flees from his advances, he embraces air, until finally she surrenders. The important things are precisely what we don't actually see, although we can imagine them so vividly that we think we saw them and remember them. Within a long shot, there is an spatial ellipse because one of the characters, watched by the other, remains out of our field of vision. Then there's a temporal ellipse, although the place seems nearby.

Later we learn something we had somehow vaguely suspected but dismissed as too far-fetched, too fantastic an idea: that the princess is a long-dead errant ghost, wandering in the world of men because she died without knowing the pleasures of love.
Miguel Marías

Date 1953

Nationality Japan

Director Kenji Mizoguchi

Cast Machiko Kyo, Masayuki Mori

Original Title *Ugetsu monogatari*

Why It's Key It shows how editing and ellipses are all-important even in a film based on long takes and continuity.

Key Scene **The explosion**
The Big Heat

SPOILER

When the title phrase is uttered near the end of the film, it refers to the dragnet that closes in on the crime syndicate which police lieutenant Dave Bannion (Ford) spends the film investigating. But the words could also refer to this earlier scene in which Bannion acquires, tragically, the personal motive that will enable him to fight the gangsters with so much vindictiveness. Bannion prepares his young daughter (Bennett) for bed while his wife, Katie (Brando), leaves the house to go for a drive. As Bannion tells the little girl her favorite story, we hear a car engine starting, then a big explosion. Bannion rushes outside to find the car in flames. Desperately trying to save his wife, he smashes the window to open the locked car door; but we learn later that Katie has been killed by the bomb that the gangsters planted in the car in an attempt to deter Bannion's investigation.

The relentless precision of Lang's direction makes this scene gripping and suspenseful no matter how many times one watches it. The logic of the "key moment," as Lang practices it in a film that (like all his films) is constructed as a cycle of linked moments, is such that the inevitability of each event is more important than its quality of happening as if for the first time. We watch *The Big Heat* again and again, not even hoping that, for once, Katie will, this time, *not* go out to start the car, or that Dave will *fail*, for once, to find the car keys (which – in a bitter Langian irony, *he* gives to her). What we watch, in hopelessness, is inevitability itself, coming to claim its victim.

Chris Fujiwara

Date 1953

Nationality USA

Director Fritz Lang

Cast Glenn Ford, Jocelyn Brando, Linda Bennett

Why It's Key This pitiless scene reveals the logic of the Langian key moment.

Key Scene **The release**
The Naked Spur

SPOILER

The catharsis of *The Naked Spur* begins in its stunningly realized climactic sequence of rocks, river and death, but it is most fully felt in the aftermath, when the bitter past of Howard Kemp (Stewart) dissolves inside him as he grasps Lina (Leigh) by the shoulders and cries – the moment that signals his self-renewal. The outlaw Ben (Robert Ryan) is dead, as are Howard's unwanted partners Roy (Ralph Meeker) and Jesse (Millard Mitchell), and death has been cruel and violent for all three men. Now there is only the bounty which will buy back the ranch a faithless woman had sold. Howard drags Ben's body to his horse in a final paroxysm of fury, but then turns to Lina and sees in her face the light of unconditional love and a new beginning, and at last relents. The tears and cracking voice of Stewart in close shot are a high moment of this great actor's career, perfectly complemented by the softer yet no less vibrant playing of Leigh. It is Mann, though, whose artistry is most movingly felt.

His sense of space, forceful compositions, and use of Rocky Mountain landscapes have throughout worked hand in glove with the characterizations to carry every level of the drama, and as the camera moves up into the sky, then follows a dissolve to come back to the two characters moving through dead trees within an open expanse, one sees in these images that there is a spiritual rhythm within life, and that "choosing a way to live" can happen even in the roughest passage.

Blake Lucas

Date 1953

Nationality USA

Director Anthony Mann

Cast James Stewart, Janet Leigh

Why It's Key Working from a brilliant original screenplay by Sam Rolfe and Harold Jack Bloom, Mann brings into play all his gifts as a filmmaker and carries one of the greatest of all Westerns to an apotheosis of moral and spiritual beauty.

Opposite *The Naked Spur*

Key Scene **The encounter**
The Barefoot Contessa

In cinema, an *encounter* – the initial chance meeting between two people who are fated to be together, either rapturously or tragically – can be magical. In *The Barefoot Contessa*, characters unquestioningly follow the cue of omens or a "sixth sense," intoning "what will be, will be." One special encounter is exquisitely stretched by Mankiewicz over ten minutes and three scenes. It concerns the meeting of Maria (Gardner) with her future Count (Brazzi). In the first scene Maria has stolen away, secretly, to dance with gypsies in a field; she realizes that the Count (who, by chance, interrupted his melancholic travel at this spot) is gazing at her. No words pass between them; he has no idea that she is a movie star. In the second scene, at a casino on the Riviera, Maria, now playing her public role as the companion of a boorish billionaire, is surprised to see the Count appear once again. Then she breaks up with the billionaire, in the middle of one of his petulant fits, simply by taking the hand of this handsome stranger and leaving with him. The third scene occurs in the Count's car. "What are you doing here, besides having come for me?", she asks, laconically. "There is no other reason," he replies solemnly. "When did you know that you had come for me?", she asks. "You did, too," he answers. "You knew as well as I." This encounter binds two lives forever in a shared destiny, a mood for love.

Adrian Martin

Date 1954

Nationality USA

Director Joseph L. Mankiewicz

Cast Ava Gardner, Rossano Brazzi

Why It's Key Mankiewicz stretches the time of a fateful meeting over three exquisite scenes.

Opposite *The Barefoot Contessa*

Key Event **Publication of Truffaut's "A Certain Tendency of the French Cinema"**

The first major critical piece by the then little-known, 21-year-old François Truffaut, "A Certain Tendency of the French Cinema," required a year of revisions to mute its incendiary tone before *Cahiers du cinéma* published it with an introductory disclaimer. The precautions were to no avail: Truffaut's attack on the "Tradition of Quality" instantly sent the French film community into convulsions and heralded the ascendancy of Truffaut's young circle of iconoclasts at *Cahiers*. A dazzling stylist who wrote in short, slang-laden paragraphs, Truffaut focused his ire on the celebrated screenwriting team Jean Aurenche and Pierre Bost, whose success had established an anti-bourgeois, anti-clerical, anti-military tone for the post-war cinema: "A film is no longer made in France without the authors believing they are remaking *Madame Bovary*." Truffaut's religious bias and distaste for profanity identified the *politique des auteurs* as a right-wing movement in the eyes of its many adversaries. But, in disputing the idea that scenes from great novels were intrinsically unfilmable, Truffaut linked himself to Bazin's groundbreaking studies of mixed art forms; in his discussion of the literary underpinnings of Aurenche and Bost's adaptations, he integrated Rohmer's Bazin-influenced ideas on the presentation of space; and by championing a new array of French filmmakers, he started a process of canon reform that would have a rapid and lasting effect. In a few years, Truffaut would be embarrassed by the aggressive tone of his manifesto – but "A Certain Tendency" still stirs the blood of modern readers with a taste for polemics.

Dan Sallitt

Date January 1954

Why It's Key It was an influential polemic that marked the advent of the *politique des auteurs*.

Key Scene **Attempt at separation**
The Crucified Lovers

Kenji Mizoguchi's *The Crucified Lovers* is one of the great films on the unconditionality of absolute love – an emotion that renders a tragic end inevitable, since sublime love is always in conflict with society. Based on a 17th-century *bunraku* (puppet-theater) play by Monzaemon Chikamatsu, *The Crucified Lovers* tells the story of two lovers of different classes. Osan (Kagawa), the much younger wife of a miserly Kyoto scroll maker, becomes suspected, falsely, of having an affair with Mohei (Hasegawa), one of her husband's clerks. Osan and Mohei flee together and, during their escape, fall passionately in love.

They take refuge in the hut of an old woman in a forest. While Osan and the woman talk inside the house, Mohei, who knows that without him, Osan still stands a chance of being accepted back by her husband, sneaks away. Realizing that he has gone, Osan runs out after him. As she does so, Mizoguchi – one of the cinema's great masters of camera movement – devises an exceptional shot that cranes up to get a better view of the steep slope below her, down which, in the background of the shot, we see Mohei running. Osan runs after him, calling his name, and the camera remains suspended in the sky. Breathtaking in its sweep and expansiveness, irresistible in its emotional pull, the shot gives urgent expression to Osan's tragic need for her lover at the same time as it distances us from them both, revealing their story as a sublime spectacle.
Chris Fujiwara

Date 1954

Nationality Japan

Director Kenji Mizoguchi

Cast Kazuo Hasegawa, Kyoko Kagawa

Original Title *Chikamatsu monogatari*

Why It's Key In a single crane shot, Mizoguchi affirms the tragic significance of his worldview.

Key Scene **"Little Brown Jug"**
The Glenn Miller Story

The notion that bandleader Glenn Miller long resisted his wife's desire for him to do a swing arrangement of the immemorial folk tune "Little Brown Jug" and that Miller's version of the song, which became a hit, did not surface until after his disappearance and presumed death in Europe in 1944, was a pure invention by the writers (Valentine Davies and Oscar Brodney) of this largely fictional biopic starring James Stewart. In any case, this idea made it possible for a bland, amiable exercise in nostalgia to close on an unusual and moving note. Having learned of her husband's fate, Helen Miller (Allyson) is advised to tune in the last recorded broadcast of his Army Air Force Band. She does so, and is surprised to hear that, as a Christmas present, Glenn at long last acceded to her request and performed "Little Brown Jug." In a lengthy close-up, Helen, eyes wet with tears, listens to the song. Over the course of the shot, her emotions fan out from grief to a complex mixture of pleasure, sorrow, bravery, and pensive uncertainty: she seems, before our eyes, to change from someone grieving to someone who is both remembering and facing a future of remembering. Allyson, who often appeared in lightweight ingenue roles in second-tier musical-comedies, can take her seat in the Pantheon of screen acting on the basis of this one beautiful shot.
Chris Fujiwara

Date 1954

Nationality USA

Director Anthony Mann

Cast June Allyson, Harry Morgan

Why It's Key This coda turns sheer grief into a delicate mix of feeling.

Key Film *Salt of the Earth* The struggle for social justice within and behind the image

In the wake of HUAC and the Hollywood blacklist, this film – based on a real strike of mostly Hispanic zinc miners in New Mexico – was made by a number of blacklisted industry veterans (Biberman, writer Michael Wilson, and producer Paul Jarrico, most notably) and with the International Union of Mine, Mill and Smelter Workers as a partner. It holds a unique place in cinema history as the only theatrical film made openly by blacklistees, and for itself being "blacklisted" by ruthless interference at every stage of both production and distribution (especially, in both phases, by Roy Brewer, powerful leader of IATSE, the film technicians' union); finally completed, it managed only a limited American release at the time before going on to greater reputation. That uniqueness has perhaps obscured the film's real merit as a work both politically and artistically effective, as Biberman blends actors with non-actors and script with historical reality to create images that capture a hopeful moment in a

troubled time. Rather than a simplistic vision in which the striking miners are unambiguous heroes, the film achieves complexity by subjecting their own patriarchal attitudes to critique, and it is the women taking center stage in the struggle, and redefining it, who carry the film's most inspired ideas, with an especially resonant expressiveness in the luminous face of narrating heroine Esperanza (Revueltas). The bridge from an earlier tradition of socially-conscious American cinema to a later one of an independent cinema outside the mainstream, *Salt of the Earth* holds that place with its own special character and dignity.
Blake Lucas

Date 1954

Nationality USA

Director Herbert J. Biberman

Cast Rosaura Revueltas, Juan Chacón, Will Geer, Clinton Jencks, Virginia Jencks, Henrietta Williams, Ángela Sánchez, Joe T. Morales

Why It's Key Out of one of America's darkest political realities, the Communist witch hunts of the postwar years, came this celebrated response – a positive cinematic statement by blacklisted filmmakers about the America that is and the one that could be.

1950–1959

241

Key Scene **A mother's mournful call echoes across space and time** *Sansho the Bailiff*

In one of the most devastatingly moving of films, a searing drama of a family torn apart by medieval brutality, it is perhaps a fragment of sound rather than any one image that echoes most hauntingly. Two children kidnapped and sold into slavery on the Japanese mainland are now grown, and we first learn that their mother (Tanaka) is still alive in a scene when, atop a hill, she looks off toward the mainland calling their names: "Anzu... Zushio..." That they have had to take other names in the meantime only adds to the moment's poignancy, and at least to this non-Japanese speaker, there is something about the specific sound of the mother's call to them that, partly in the way she seems to extend the vowels a bit in time, seems to evoke the vast space and years of time that separate all three. Indeed, Mizoguchi's feeling for the way spaces between objects can evoke history, for the vastness of ways in which things can be connected, is a hallmark of his style, and in *Sansho the Bailiff* the sound

fragment of the mother's call resonates beautifully with his imagery: the vast expanse of sea that separates mother and children seems at once filled with her invocation of her children's names and too impossibly vast to be bridged by any human's words. Later, a new slave in the children's compound sings the mother's song, which had become popular in the mother's region, and this provides the children their first news that their mother is alive, propelling the rest of the narrative forward.
Fred Camper

Date 1954

Nationality Japan

Director Kenji Mizoguchi

Cast Kinuyo Tanaka

Original Title *Sanshô dayû*

Why It's Key Mizoguchi's use of a near-infinite space to suggest the affecting transience of individual lives in the face of history here resonates with perhaps the most emotionally wrenching sound fragment in all cinema.

Key Scene **Down Main Street**
Silver Lode

By the 1950s, the Western as political allegory had become a staple on all levels of production, with Fred Zinnemann's *High Noon* (1952) the classic highbrow example. Its template – a man threatened by gangsters trying to find allies – became quite popular, but no film has made better, richer use of it than *Silver Lode*, the supreme masterpiece in the cheapie twilight years of veteran director Allan Dwan. Featuring a chief villain named McCarthy posing as honorable U.S. Marshal to discredit a reformed ex-gang-member turned "respected" citizen (John Payne), its allegory can hardly be called subtle – but the surrounding, morally layered, barbed study of democracy and its abuse certainly is. Dwan has modestly called this "the story of a man who is condemned and redeemed for the wrong reasons," but it's really one of the great satirical portraits of society, a dark suspense comedy about the foundations and the erosion of civilization. The B-picture technique of avoiding close-ups in favor of economical long takes proves ingenious, insisting on interaction among characters. Most impressive is the execution of the film's centerpiece, a clever riff on the typical showdown on Main Street: Payne's by-now-outcast antihero runs down the street alone, miraculously pursued all the way by a relentlessly tracking camera, through decorations for the celebration of Independence Day. Of course independence has been abandoned by the town along with the protagonist, but that was only the ironic starting point of the film's multi-faceted take on the dialectics of freedom.

Christoph Huber

Date 1954

Nationality USA

Director Allan Dwan

Cast John Payne

Why it's Key Allan Dwan's cheap, late, masterful western is one of the great satirical studies of society. Its centerpiece moment – a jaw-dropping camera track down Main Street – is both the logical extreme of Dwan's *mise en scène* and a barbed reversal of genre conventions.

Key Speech **"I'm a stranger here myself"**
Johnny Guitar

Some films seem like they're on drugs, their emotions heightened by something we cannot see. *Johnny Guitar*, a Western about a saloon owner, Vienna (Crawford), who has built her hostelry in an isolated spot and is waiting for the railroad to be built to bring her customers, is one such film. The sets are too arranged, the dialogue written and performed in a state of shock or hysteria whose cause we can only surmise, and, as so often in her career, the film's dramatic excess is reflected in Joan Crawford's glassy, staring eyes.

This intensity flowed from the people who made the film. Crawford and co-star Mercedes McCambridge hated each other bitterly. Quixotic director Nick Ray, who studied with Frank Lloyd Wright, was interested in the architecture of the film as much as its story. Its liberal screenwriter, Philip Yordan (together with uncredited blacklistee Ben Maddow), salted the movie with a furious anti-fascism. Their dialogue – "How many men have you forgotten?" "As many women as you remember" – is a flood of aphorisms, inspired by Howard Hawks films like *To Have and Have Not*. In one scene the title character (Hayden), who's blown into town and is an old flame of Vienna's, says the famous line "I'm a stranger here myself," which became Ray's catchphrase, his expression of dismissive existentialism. It could have been the tagline of the whole Western genre.

Johnny Guitar's intensity is reflected in critical responses to it. François Truffaut wrote that anyone who rejected it "will never recognise inspiration, poetic intuition, or a framed picture, a shot, an idea, a good film, or even cinema itself." Hear hear.

Mark Cousins

Date 1954

Nationality USA

Director Nicholas Ray

Cast Joan Crawford, Sterling Hayden, Scott Brady

Why It's Key Master director Nicholas Ray said that all his films could have been called "I'm a stranger here myself."

Opposite *Johnny Guitar*

Key Scene **The killer sees Jefferies**
Rear Window

Up to this point in the film, Thorwald (Burr) has been the unsuspecting (but suspected) object of photographer Jefferies's (Stewart's) scrutiny from his apartment across the yard. From the beginning, the man has been viewed from a distance, framed by the window of his apartment that suggests a movie screen (it has often been noted that Jefferies in his wheelchair, watching the outside world from his window, is like a spectator watching a movie in a theater). When Thorwald finally notices he is being watched, the tables are suddenly turned: *he* becomes the watcher, and Jefferies the helpless object.

Although Thorwald has been a menace before, in the scene where Lisa (Kelly) searches his apartment, and he is seen coming back home, then confronting her, he was still kept at a distance, the whole scene viewed from afar by the now frantic but helpless Jefferies. Now he is about to become dangerously active, invading Jefferies's privacy and threatening his very life. Private spaces are violated on both sides of the yard, Thorwald's breaking into Jefferies's place echoing Lisa's earlier entering of Thorwald's apartment through the window, and Jefferies' defenestration by Thorwald providing a kind of "poetic justice" counterpart to Lisa's own break-in. The Hitchcockian ambivalence and irony become even greater if one accepts the interpretation, suggested by some critics (e.g. Robin Wood), of the Thorwald character as Jefferies's alter ego.

Jean-Pierre Coursodon

Date 1954

Nationality USA

Director Alfred Hitchcock

Cast James Stewart, Grace Kelly, Thelma Ritter, Raymond Burr

Why It's Key This is the climax and most suspenseful moment of one of Hitchcock's major masterpieces.

Opposite *Rear Window*

Key Scene **"The Man That Got Away"**
A Star Is Born

Early in *A Star Is Born*, Norman Maine (Mason) tracks Esther Blodgett (Garland) to the joint on Sunset Boulevard where, after finishing their club gig, Esther and her band go for their private pleasure. The musicians are practicing their arrangement of "The Man That Got Away" (by Harold Arlen and Ira Gershwin), and the pianist (Noonan) invites Esther to join in. Cukor films her performance in a single take lasting three and a half minutes. The *mise en scène* is simple: the narrow and well-lit space within which Esther performs is bounded at the back by the piano, on the sides by two groups of musicians in shadow, and in front by the table where she sits at the end of the number. The camera tracks slightly backward and forward, opening up or restricting the space so that wherever she goes, she constantly remains within a structure of womb-like snugness; a pervasive mood of warmth and reassurance (despite the bleakness of Gershwin's lyrics) is constantly expressed through the looks, smiles, and gestures with which Esther makes contact with her accompanists. The song is a transcendent moment of pure enjoyment within what will become a lacerating melodrama, and the song – in Garland's great rendition – already anticipates the film's resolution in affirming the triumph of creative brilliance over loss and suffering.

Chris Fujiwara

Date 1954

Nationality USA

Director George Cukor

Cast Judy Garland, Tommy Noonan, James Mason

Why It's Key Garland's electrifying performance is beautifully complemented by Cukor's *mise en scène* and camera movement.

Key Scene **The glove**
On the Waterfront

Marlon Brando's performance in *On the Waterfront* is arguably the most influential acting performance of all time. Generations of actors would be inspired by his performance for his phrasing and unexpected choices and the way he always seemed in the moment. When it won the Oscar, it signified mainstream Hollywood's acceptance of the Method. Although the scene with Rod Steiger in the back of the taxi would be the one that every young actor would practice in front of a mirror, the scene that most perfectly illustrates how the Method changed film acting is surprisingly low-key. Terry Malloy (Brando) is walking through a park with Edie Doyle (Eva Marie Saint), whose brother, unbeknownst to her, he helped set up to be killed. During a rehearsal for the scene, Saint accidentally dropped her glove. Staying in character, Brando picked it up. But instead of giving it back to her he tried it on and then held on to it, teasing her, forcing her to follow him nervously as she tried in vain to get it back. What might have been a fairly pedestrian scene illuminated their characters. The sensitivity underneath Malloy's tough-guy bluster, the eroticism and sexual interplay of their flirtation, Edie's Catholic guilt all radiate from that purloined glove. Brando and Saint showed it to Kazan, and he put it in the film, where it would be studied by young actors for years to come.

Al Weisel

Date 1954

Nationality USA

Director Elia Kazan

Cast Marlon Brando, Eva Marie Saint

Why It's Key A rehearsal accident became one of the most famous moments in movies.

Opposite *On the Waterfront*

Key Scene **The hero burns a page of poetry to stay alive** *Track of the Cat*

John Wayne produced this strange art film as a favor to William A. Wellman, who'd recently directed him in the highly successful *The High and the Mighty*. What Wayne actually thought of this curiosity – adapted by ace screenwriter A. I. Bezzerides from an allegorical novel by Walter Van Tilburg Clark – is apparently unrecorded. Sometimes it suggests an American version of Carl Dreyer's *Ordet* in its portrait of a dysfunctional, mainly male rural family in the middle of nowhere.

The action mainly unfolds in a house where family members quarrel and bicker, but we periodically cut away to a nearby snow-covered mountain where first Arthur (William Hopper), then his brother Curt (Robert Mitchum), hunt for a black panther that we hear but never see. The film's in CinemaScope and color, but virtually all of it's designed in black-and-white, apart from Curt's red and black coat. Then, after Arthur is killed by the panther, and Curt finds his body, he switches his own coat with Arthur's black and white one before sending Arthur's body back home on his horse. He holes up in a cave when a storm starts up, and, reaching into Arthur's coat pocket, finds a volume of John Keats's poetry. Still later, while trying to keep from freezing to death outside, he feeds a fire with the Keats poem that begins, "When I have fears that I will cease to be…." Addressing his dead brother, he says, "The only time any good came from your moanin', Boy."

Jonathan Rosenbaum

Date 1954

Nationality USA

Director William A. Wellman

Cast Robert Mitchum

Why It's Key John Wayne's only art movie as a producer suddenly turns literary.

Key Scene **The opening shot**
A Generation

The opening shot in Wajda's first major film is a technical tour de force that announced very clearly that a substantial talent was in control. Credit for the extraordinarily complex shot must be shared with Wajda's director of photography, the gifted Jerzy Lipman, with whom Wajda collaborated on many films. In a single take lasting two minutes, the camera pans and then tracks across the desolate wasteland of war-torn Warsaw and gradually closes in on a community of humble dwellings as people go about their daily business – the camera moves past children playing, women chattering, old men playing cards, into a close-up of a dangerous game with a knife being played by a group of young men. In one masterful progression, one sees and feels the authentic bleakness of the location and becomes involved in the reckless exploits of the youths at the centre of the story. It's a beautifully choreographed exposition that begins a bold story about the wartime resistance against the German invasion of Poland. Not only was *A Generation* Wajda's first feature after a number of short films, and the first of his trilogy about the war (followed by *Kanal* and *Ashes and Diamonds*), but it revealed to the world that Polish cinema was being reinvented and reinvigorated by a new generation of young filmmakers – not only Wajda and his cameraman, but also his cast, including the young Roman Polanski, and two young actors who became significant stars in Polish cinema – Tadeusz Lomnicki and Zbigniew Cybulski.

Andrew Pike

Date 1955

Nationality Poland

Director Andrzej Wajda

Cast Tadeusz Lomnicki, Roman Polanski, Zbigniew Cybulski

Original Title *Pokolenie*

Why It's Key This is the first scene in the first major film by the leading light in the renaissance of Polish cinema in the 1950s.

Key Scene **The delivery of the television**
All That Heaven Allows

Of all Sirk's glossily subversive melodramas, this is arguably his greatest, as deliriously emotion-fuelled as *Written on the Wind* (1956) yet as openly disenchanted with the compromises, injustices, and lies underpinning the American Dream as *The Tarnished Angels* (1958). Chronicling the troubled romance of middle-class widow Cary (Wyman) and her slightly younger, faintly bohemian back-to-nature gardener Ron (Rock Hudson), the film measures and bemoans the class snobbery, gender inequality, and downright pettiness that define and delimit the aspirations of Eisenhower's America: Cary is deemed country-club material, Ron too down-market partly because of a refusal to conform.

Cary's grown kids, Ned (Reynolds) and Kay (Talbott), purportedly concerned with her happiness and the dead dad's memory, reject Ron outright as unsuitable; then, having ensured that she ditch him and having determined their own futures, they arrive for a "last Christmas" together: Ned's selling the family home and heading to Paris, Kay's getting married. Amazed, their hitherto devoted mother puts her hands to her temples, stares despairingly at the carpet and tells Kay, "the whole thing's been so pointless." Still, the ungrateful brats have bought her a gift, and a TV deliveryman (Lewis) enters with his patter: "Turn that dial and you have all the company you want right there on the screen… drama, comedy, life's parade at your fingertips." As the camera moves in to show Cary's dismal gaze reflected on the dull monochrome screen, the hollow reality behind the much-vaunted ideals of familial love, female emancipation, and widespread postwar well-being could not be more painfully evident.

Geoff Andrew

Date 1955

Nationality USA

Director Douglas Sirk

Cast Jane Wyman, Gloria Talbott, William Reynolds, Forrest Lewis

Why It's Key This is the darkest moment in Sirk's magnificently meticulous melodrama.

Key Film
Blinkity Blank

A stunning five-minute-and-14-second experimental film, made without a camera by etching directly on opaque, unframed film stock, *Blinkity Blank* assails the viewer's eyes with a bombardment of intermittent bursts of abstract or semi-abstract apparitions that often occupy the screen for a mere split second. In-between the blanks, one may briefly notice (provided one doesn't blink) a flurry of feathers, a parachute, a bird cage, a pineapple, an umbrella that turns into a hen-like figure, as well as many undescribable doodles that keep bouncing all over the screen. "This is not a film you *see*," wrote French critic André Martin in 1955, "it's a film you *think* you see." You do hear, however, and not just think you hear, Maurice Blackburn's dodecaphonistic score (played by a great-sounding quintet of clarinet, bassoon, flute, cello, and oboe) with strikingly percusive synthetic-sound punctuations added throughout like so many punches by McLaren's scratchings on the soundtrack.

Unlike most avant-garde films, *Blinkity Blank* is full of humor – e.g. the fight between a big bad bird and a much smaller but very pugnacious worm-like creature. The film even "tells a story" – no matter how elusive. Two fierce, fantastic birds fight, court, mate, and ultimately produce a multicolored egg, whence emerges a tiny, anthropomorphic "bird" that sort of takes a bow as the word "end" pops up. Should you wish to wax philosophical you might say that the film is about procreation, birth, the struggle for survival – in a word: life.

Jean-Pierre Coursodon

Date 1955

Nationality Canada

Director Norman McLaren

Why It's Key McLaren's masterpiece is the culmination of his groundbreaking investigation of the aesthetic possibilities of camera-less animation.

Key Scene **Paro and Chandramukhi see each other** *Devdas*

Villager Paro (Sen) and city courtesan Chandramukhi (Vyjantimala) love Devdas (Kumar), a man caught between village and city and between feudalism and modernity. Unable to cope, he dissipates himself in drink. Paro decides to visit Devdas in his village and leaves in a hurry, neglecting important household duties, only to find that Devdas has left for Calcutta. In a parallel scene, Chandramukhi also leaves to look for Devdas in the village.

This is the occasion for a song: Paro, a simple village girl, going back to her rich husband's house in a palanquin; Chandramukhi, well-versed in sensuality, who has now renounced everything, her love leading her to a devotional spirituality, walking across fields to the village in search of Devdas. The song, "Kahin ghani chav hai, kahin dhoop hai" ('There is dense shade somewhere, elsewhere, hot sun'), unfolds now, comparing and contrasting the differing destinies of the two women. The women see each other – and pass

each other by. In the fleeting glance there is a hint of recognition of who the other could be, a recognition of their bond of love for Devdas, and also a distancing, as each moves away to the different social sphere she lives in. This philosophical song on contrary ways of life, each of which has to be affirmed, is syncretic in a unique way: the stanzas are set to a complex tune with East Indian orchestration (which the great composer Sachin Dev Burman used often in his songs), but sung by the versatile film singer Mohammad Rafi in a very North-Indian mode against the chorus, which has the feel of folk music, sung by the men who are carrying the palanquin.

Rashmi Doraiswamy

Date 1955

Nationality India

Director Bimal Roy

Cast Dilip Kumar, Vyjantimala, Suchitra Sen

Why It's Key This scene – two women's intuitive recognition of each other and their common destiny of being dispossessed in love – creates an opening into a higher order of perception.

Key Scene **The resurrection**
Ordet (The Word)

SPOILER

The first person we see in this unique film is Johannes (Rye), a demented man convinced he is Jesus, much to the consternation of his older brother (Christensen), who rejects religion, and their father (Henrik Malberg), an old Lutheran having a crisis of faith. But the most important character is the older brother's wife, Inger (Federspiel), who represents a golden mean between Johannes's craziness and her husband's materialism.

Inger eventually dies while delivering a stillborn baby, upsetting Johannes so much that he flees in distress. When he returns for her funeral, he appears to have recovered his sanity. Yet he remains the most devout believer in the family, asking the mourners why they haven't prayed for Inger's life to be restored. Nobody has a good answer, and Johannes suggests that their lack of spirituality is sealing Inger's fate: "You must rot," he says to her corpse, "because the times are rotten." Then he takes action. After asking Inger's daughter whether she thinks his faith can raise the dead – the little girl answers yes – he prays. Inger's hands unclasp, her eyes open, her husband lifts her from the coffin, and they exchange a life-affirming kiss.

In mainstream treatments of the supernatural, filmmakers use artificial effects of ever-growing sophistication to create a sense of spectacle and fantasy. The genius of Dreyer's approach lies in its forthright refusal of such tricks. Inger's resurrection is as physically and psychologically real as the austere *mise en scène* and unadorned cinematography with which it's depicted. Few moments in film history equal its transcendent power.
David Sterritt

Date 1955

Nationality Denmark

Director Carl Theodor Dreyer

Cast Preben Lerdorff Rye, Birgitte Federspiel, Emil Hass Christensen, Ann Elisabeth Rud

Why It's Key A resurrection scene demonstrates that cinema can evoke a metaphysical dimension through the straightforward depiction of physical reality.

Opposite *Ordet*

1950–1959

251

Key Person **Hideko Takamine**
The first look at the heroine *Floating Clouds*

The reach of *Floating Clouds* is great, and such is Naruse's gift of concise expressiveness that it is all intimated within this single brief shot of Yukiko (Takamine), who will be not only a memorably vibrant character within the film but a figure emblematic of the history of Japan as its culture quietly evolves through the years immediately following World War II. After some establishing shots to indicate the end of the war and the repatriation of those who had served in other countries, the first staged shot briefly tracks Yukiko moving with the crowd of others who have come back. It lasts only a few seconds, but we see a young woman autonomous in space, her face and posture revealing of her intention to do all she can to control her own destiny even in the face of difficult times and an implacable world. Through Naruse's direction, pared to the essential, and Takamine's superb acting, which has the character fully created in this initial view of her, the idea of a movingly human journey takes hold immediately. It is a journey complete with a complex relationship, never resolved in a conventional sense, with Kengo (Masayuki Mori), the man with whom Yukiko enjoyed a never-forgotten love in French Indochina during the war – a journey of two. But it begins with her, in this moment, in that soulful gaze ahead; out of that seeming simplicity, cinematic sublimity is born.
Blake Lucas

Date 1955

Nationality Japan

Director Mikio Naruse

Cast Hideko Takamine

Original Title *Ukigumo*

Why It's Key Naruse's direction and Takamine's acting show how a simple introductory shot of a character can intimate the beauty and meaning of a whole film.

Key Scene **"There's Nothing Like Love"**
My Sister Eileen

One of the most underrated (and one of the last) of the great Hollywood musicals of the fifties, *My Sister Eileen* – a remake of a 1942 non-musical movie of the same title – is a cornucopia of great songs and dances, anchored by a witty, ebullient, and flawlessly structured screenplay (written by the director and Blake Edwards).

In this five-minute scene, Eileen (Leigh) and Ruth (Garrett), two sisters from Ohio recently arrived in New York with dreams of success, are in their dingy Greenwich Village basement apartment, talking about what they expect from life. (As an earlier scene, a solo sung by Ruth, has established, Eileen is the charmingly sexy sister whom all men pursue, while they ignore the borderline bluestocking Ruth.) Eileen starts praising the wonders of love to a sardonically dejected Ruth. Gradually the talk drifts into a semi-recitative (Ruth about dating: "It might interfere/With my career/ And from what I hear/ Men are not sincere."

Eileen: "They're only big bad boys") that leads into the song proper, sung by Leigh. After Leigh's chorus, the scene returns briefly to spoken dialogue, then Leigh dons a football helmet and shoes that a neighbor has dropped in their apartment, now playfully impersonating a gentleman and asking her sister for a dance – the music starts up again, in a minuet-like reworking of the original tune. After their little number, it's Ruth's turn to pick up the tune as she cooks some spaghetti, and the scene ends up in a duet reprising the song.

Jean-Pierre Coursodon

Date 1955

Nationality USA

Director Richard Quine

Cast Janet Leigh, Betty Garrett

Why It's Key This exquisite duet on a fine Jule Styne-Leo Robin song is a consummate example of inventive narrative, sly choreography, and fluid direction. It shows how plot and characterization can be integrated into an apparently conventional song-and-dance sequence.

Opposite *My Sister Eileen*

252

Key Scene **The staircase**
Rebel without a Cause

In Nicholas Ray's classic film, an unusual camera movement occurs when Jim (Dean) comes home late at night from the "chickie run" in which his opponent, Buzz (Corey Allen), has ended his life in flames. Finding his father (Backus) asleep in front of a static-emitting TV, Jim lies on a nearby couch and slowly inverts his body so that his head is upside-down. The offscreen voice of his mother (Doran), calling Jim's name, is heard before Ray cuts to her body, rapidly descending the stairs – and the shot, adopting Jim's point of view, is upside-down! The camera tilts around 180 degrees, uprighting itself, as the mother reaches the foot of the stairs and approaches the camera.

In a film filled with crisis and anxiety, the inversion of the camera stands as a peak of disorientation. This is because the gesture is so extreme and because the viewer feels the match between the camera and Jim's perspective to be wrong: when I see the world with my head upside-down, my brain can somehow right the

image, so that I am still placed "correctly" in the world; but with Ray's image I must wait till the camera turns around. All at once, the image is wrong, Jim is wrong, his mother is wrong, Nicholas Ray is wrong, I am wrong. Later in the scene, the camera tilts again, but to a lesser degree, when the mother confronts her son on the staircase. This smaller movement is the high point of the film. It threatens to reopen the wound that, earlier, the more extreme shot made in the relationship between image and perception.

Chris Fujiwara

Date 1955

Nationality USA

Director Nicholas Ray

Cast James Dean, Ann Doran, Jim Backus

Why It's Key Nicholas Ray's choice of an unusual camera movement throws into question the relationship between spectator and image.

Key Scene **A car speeds through isolating darkness** *Kiss Me Deadly*

The ultimate *film noir* and the ultimate paean to sex, violence, and the bomb in 1950s America, Robert Aldrich's masterpiece begins with a lonely highway rushing toward us, seen from a car. A pretty woman wearing only a trenchcoat (Leachman) steps out of the shadows, forcing the driver, Mike Hammer (Meeker), to stop. All around there is only night, and the white dashes in the road's center, initiating a violence of light itself, the clashes between white and black that will animate much of the film – as when Mike Hammer defends himself at night by throwing a bag of popcorn into the air to distract his pursuer. In Hollywood's more classical style, the camera is anchored securely to the rooms or the landscapes it films. That we learn that Uncle Charlie is guilty in Hitchcock's *Shadow of a Doubt* (1943) not through any plot information but through an intensely claustrophobic tilted shot of him alone in his bedroom is possible only because the camera is normally level. Not so in *Kiss Me Deadly*. The Cartesian coordinates of the universe have been consumed by speed, violence, and nihilistic pursuit of "the great whatsit": this is truly a world without ground. A cut twists and reshapes the space, or breaks it apart; objects suddenly transform themselves; the machine-like violence on the soundtrack provides an added drone that fills the film with its untamable energies. All these are appropriate to a film whose "hero" has no values except "what's in it for him," and all this stems from the opening scene, from the ability of a car to consume space, replacing the actual world with the driver's pure movement.

Fred Camper

Date 1955

Nationality USA

Director Robert Aldrich

Cast Ralph Meeker, Cloris Leachman

Why It's Key The obliteration of space in the opening scene resonates throughout the film; without firm ground, threats can emerge everywhere, and morality is impossible to maintain.

1950-1959

Key Scene **The river** *The Night of the Hunter*

Next to *Citizen Kane*, the greatest debut in American cinema is the work of another actor, Charles Laughton, and though Welles was able to make more films (albeit with difficulty), Laughton was never given the opportunity. In adapting Davis Grubb's short novel, *The Night of the Hunter*, to the screen, Laughton employed James Agee as writer and Stanley Cortez as cinematographer – two bold, innovative choices. Laughton was fascinated by the films of D.W. Griffith, and watched many of them before he started shooting the film. He told Griffith's former leading lady, Lillian Gish, whom he cast as the Good Woman, that he wanted to make audiences sit up in their seats again, the way they did at Griffith films.

The film starts out as a particularly inventive Depression-era thriller, with Robert Mitchum, in one of his finest roles, as serial killer Harry Powell, who kills widows and steals their modest savings. For a tense hour or so we watch him home in on the tragic Willa (Shelley Winters), marry and murder her, and then terrorise her children, John (Chapin) and Pearl (Bruce), who know the whereabouts of stolen money their dead father has hidden. When the children escape his clutches and embark in a small boat down the river, the film suddenly, brilliantly changes gears: the depiction of the river creatures – frog, rabbits, owl, tortoise, sheep, a spider's web – coupled with the star-filled sky and a soundtrack of eerie lullabies, transforms a thriller into the grimmest of fairy tales.

David Stratton

Date 1955

Nationality USA

Director Charles Laughton

Cast Robert Mitchum, Billy Chapin, Sally Jane Bruce

Why It's Key This scene is the audacious turning point of Laughton's masterpiece.

Opposite *The Night of the Hunter*

Key Scene **Group on the beach**
Le Amiche

Freely based on a novella, *Among Women Only*, by Cesare Pavese, Antonioni's fourth feature follows the lives of five young women in the upper-middle-class milieu of Turin through the eyes of Clelia (Rossi Drago). She is returning to her hometown having risen from her working-class origins to success in the world of fashion in Rome. A Sunday outing which includes the five girlfriends and two of the main male characters occurs one-quarter of the way into the film, the first of three key scenes involving the group. Antonioni's placement and movement of the group in the windswept beachscape not only foreshadows the scenes on the deserted island in *L'avventura*, it exceeds them in Antonioni's deployment of the camera in choreographing the ensemble in real time. The vitality of movement and gesture in this scene masks a personal malaise that develops into separate but linked stories involving three couples in varying states of emotional crisis. The synthesis of precisely controlled observation with a feeling of contingency is here free of the overwhelming sense of ennui that at times threatens to dissolve the narrative in *Il Grido*, the succeeding "trilogy," and *Red Desert*.

Bruce Hodsdon

Date 1955

Nationality Italy

Director Michelangelo Antonioni

Cast Eleanora Rossi Drago, Valentina Cortese, Yvonne Furneaux, Gabriele Ferzetti, Madeleine Fischer, Franco Fabrizi, Annamaria Pancani

Why It's Key In a scene like this, Antonioni's path-breaking synthesis of subjectivity and objectivity appears fully formed.

256

Key Event
The death of James Dean

On September 30, 1955, 24-year-old James Dean was killed on the road outside Cholame, California, when his Porsche Spyder collided with another car, driven by Donald Turnupseed. Though Dean was known for his love of fast cars and took part in the iconic "chickie run" scene of *Rebel without a Cause*, he was not breaking the speed limit at the time of the accident. Turnupseed survived the crash, about which he never spoke in public.

Movie stars had died young before, exciting outpourings of fan grief (notably, Rudolph Valentino in 1926), but Dean's death – after starring in only three movies, two unreleased at the time – stands as the most significant, and ranks along with the deaths of John F. Kennedy, Martin Luther King, and Princess Diana among the most discussed, mourned, mythologised, and commemorated tragedies of the 20th century. Though Elia Kazan's *East of Eden* had made Dean a major star in the 1950s sensitive-tormented Method mould of Montgomery Clift and Marlon Brando, it was Nicholas Ray's *Rebel without a Cause*, released a month after Dean's death, that cemented his position as *the* archetypal teenage martyr of the 1950s. Dean's death gives the film's tragic finish – in which it is the character played by *Sal Mineo* who dies, though many audiences misremember Dean's Jim Stark being gunned down by the cops – an extra resonance that elevates it to classic status. Hot debate continues as to whether, if he had lived, Dean could have sustained his career at such a level – would he have become Marlon Brando or Paul Newman or Vic Morrow or Cameron Mitchell? But that's beside the point – death freezes him as one of the screen greats, but also as one of the faces of the century.

Kim Newman

Date September 30, 1955

Why It's Key This moment of tragedy became a key memory for a generation of teenagers and established Dean's martyr image forever.

Opposite James Dean

Key Scene **The bathtub**
Diabolique

SPOILER

1950–1959

Arguably the twisty thriller from which all twisty thrillers spring, Henri-Georges Clouzot's classic blindsided viewers by violating expectations of fair play. Based on the novel by Pierre Boileau and Thomas Narcejac, the plot finds a miserly and sadistic boys' school headmaster, Michel (Meurisse), being targeted for murder by his abused wife, Christina (Véra Clouzot, the director's wife), and his mistress, Nicole (Simone Signoret). The scheme requires the women to lure Michel to Nicole's country home and drown him in the bathtub, then dump it into the school's swimming pool and make it look like an accident or suicide. But this is all a prelude to a super-deluxe double cross by the mistress and the headmaster, whose corpse disappears, then ultimately reappears in his wife's bathtub, then rises up, zombie-like, the payoff of an elaborate fakeout that scares Christina so badly that her weak heart (established but not emphasized in the script) gives out, allowing the conspirators to live happily ever after. Although the twist was arguably dependent on withheld or glossed-over information, and improbable on its face (Michel must have had astounding breath control), viewers loved it; their ranks included Alfred Hitchcock, who intended *Psycho* partly as an act of one-upsmanship. The list of subsequent thrillers that aped Clouzot in letter or spirit include *Witness for the Prosecution*, *The Usual Suspects*, *The Sixth Sense*, and *Fight Club*, plus an inferior 1996 remake starring Isabelle Adjani, Sharon Stone and Chazz Palminteri. The bathtub scene itself was referenced in *The Shining*, *Fatal Attraction*, and *What Lies Beneath*. The crowd-pleasing secondary character of police inspector Fichet (Charles Vanel), a cigar-smoking eccentric, inspired Peter Falk's long-running TV sleuth *Columbo*.
Matt Zoller Seitz

Date 1955

Nationality France

Director Henri-Georges Clouzot

Cast Paul Meurisse, Véra Clouzot

Original Title *Les Diaboliques*

Why It's Key It's the most memorable moment from one of the most widely imitated of all screen thrillers.

258

Key Film
Les maîtres fous (*The Mad Masters*)

Les maîtres fous is the extraordinary, wild document of a remarkable social reality of African life in the mid '50s: construction workers on the colonial Gold Coast who, on weekends, go into the bush and abandon themselves to the frenzies of the Hauka cult. Rouch, a radical ethnographer with a hand-held camera, shows this ritual of trance possession in intimate detail: music is played, drugs are ingested, the throat of a chicken is cut and its blood spread around. At the trance's height, the men, mouths foaming, imitate the manners of their British colonial masters, becoming majors, generals, or the doctor's wife, and they play-act roundtable conferences and military marches. (A cut-away, mid-film, to the real thing looks no less surreal.) They also submit their bodies (painlessly, it seems) to fire from torches, and cook up a dog to eat. An abrupt coda shows these men, smiling, back digging ditches on Monday morning; Rouch wonders on the soundtrack: "Looking at these excellent workers, one wonders – have they found a panacea for mental illness, have they found a way to absorb the inequalities of society?" In his book *The Cinematic Griot*, Paul Stoller describes the well-developed resistances of present-day viewers to the film: some vomit, some seek rational explanations for the trance behavior, others are insulted and dismiss the film as racist. Anthropologist George DeVos explains: "The spectator is ill at ease, but at the same time he must take in what he has been given to see."
Adrian Martin

Date 1955

Nationality France

Director Jean Rouch

Why It's Key It's an extraordinary work of ethnographic cinema.

Key Scene **The opening circus scene**
Lola Montès

*L*ola Montès is the supreme exploration of Max Ophuls's fascination with femininity as a form of spectacle. The film's theme is embodied in its structure, which presents Lola (Carol) as the main attraction in a circus where key events from her "scandalous" life are enacted before a paying audience. The opening two-minute sequence shot shows the circus's owner/ringmaster (Ustinov) directly addressing Ophuls's camera, simultaneously introducing Lola to both the audience watching the film and the audience portrayed onscreen: "And now, ladies and gentlemen, the moment you have all been waiting for! The most sensational act of the century! Spectacle! Emotion! Action! History! A creature a hundred times more wild than any beast in our menagerie! A monster of cruelty... with the eyes of an angel!" By having Ustinov use such language as might be found in a film's trailer, Ophuls implicates the mechanisms of cinema in his critique of the process by which woman is reduced

from subject to object, becoming less an autonomous individual than an image offered to the voyeuristic gaze. This idea is brilliantly illustrated by the shot of Ustinov, positioned at frame left, circling his seated star, the camera retreating before him as he promises that Lola will answer "the most indelicate questions, the most intimate questions, the most indiscreet questions." The ringmaster here functions as a stand-in for the director in more ways than one, controlling the *mise en scène* while emphasizing the powerlessness of Lola, who remains motionless at frame right while the camera moves around her. We will never comprehend *Lola Montès* if we insist on speaking of "style" and "meaning": for Ophuls, style *is* meaning.
Brad Stevens

Date 1955

Nationality France/West Germany

Director Max Ophuls

Cast Martine Carol, Peter Ustinov

Why It's Key This scene shows how style and meaning are inseparable in Max Ophuls's work.

1950-1959

259

Key Scene **A bullet through the hand at point-blank range** *The Man from Laramie*

*L*ockhart (Stewart) is a stranger on a mission to find the gun runners whom he holds responsible for his brother's death in a Cavalry detachment's encounter with Apaches armed with repeating rifles. He soon encounters two sons of the local cattle baron (Donald Crisp): Dave (Nicol), the real son, is weak and psychopathic; Vic (Arthur Kennedy), the responsible "adopted son," is employed as ranch foreman with the brief to keep Dave out of trouble in return for an implied stake in the cattle empire. Lockhart, in conflict with all of them, increasingly assumes the role of the old man's idealized son. The extremity of Dave's vengeance on Lockhart, the malevolent stranger in his father's dreams, lies in the manner of its portrayal. The expanses of desolate landscape that Mann integrates into the widescreen drama are suddenly punctuated by searing close-ups allied with carefully calculated camera movement. What had previously been relatively inconsequential in the matinee Western – a bullet

wound to the hand – becomes a seminal event in this film's archetypal revenge plot. It's as if Stewart, the country boy of thirties movies, now made self-sufficient and tarnished by life's disappointments, has at least momentarily been caught up in some kind of end game. His pain and outrage are palpable.
Bruce Hodsdon

Date 1955

Nationality USA

Director Anthony Mann

Cast James Stewart, Alex Nicol

Why It's Key This scene marks an important transition in the presentation of violence, not only in the Western but in Hollywood films in general.

Key Scene **The animated credits**
The Man with the Golden Arm

Bronx-born design pioneer Saul Bass single-handedly lifted credit titles into a zone of artistic experimentation, employing paper cut-outs, optical effects, and animation to craft a bridge into a film's world. From his debut work for Otto Preminger's *Carmen Jones* (1954), with its symbolic flame and rose motifs that succinctly embodied the story's consuming passions, Bass advanced, with *The Man with the Golden Arm*, to boldly non-representational titles that electrified the motion picture industry. To Elmer Bernstein's pounding brass-driven jazz theme, abstract white bars enter from all four directions, grouping and dispersing unpredictably even as they press at the minimally rendered names, until the central logo emerges: the jagged arm of the drug-addicted poker-dealer hero. Unifying the production with a coordinated poster, Bass dared to ignore the stars, instead surrounding the stark arm design with thick bars in black and two shades of purple. His unique artistic signature, part Bauhaus economy and part Constructivist graphics, was instantly recognizable to the public, and proved in great demand in over 50 unforgettable film sequences, including the segmented torso for Preminger's *Anatomy of a Murder* (1959), the slashing ribbons of Hitchcock's *Psycho* (1960), and the slinking black alley cat prowling across the wide screen in Edward Dmytryk's *A Walk On the Wild Side* (1961). After a two-decade hiatus spent working on corporate logos and his own film projects, Bass returned for late-autumn collaborations with Stanley Kubrick (*The Shining* [1980]) and Martin Scorsese (*Casino* [1995]).
Robert Keser

Date 1955

Nationality USA

Director Otto Preminger

Why It's Key Saul Bass made credits design into an artistic expression of a movie's themes.

Key Person **Rod Steiger**
The studio chief's visit *The Big Knife*

SPOILER

Rod Steiger, as magnetic as fellow Method-actor Marlon Brando, wasn't handsome like Brando. In the 1950s he didn't get leads in prestige pictures like Brando did. Bitter or not, in *The Big Knife* Steiger unleashed all the contempt he could muster for "profession: movie star." As studio head Stanley Hoff he slides like an anaconda into the Bel-Air pad of star actor Charlie Castle (Palance) and squeezes him to death.

Steiger, who was 31 when Aldrich filmed this Clifford Odets adaptation, plays an older man. He's hardened with a Mabuse-like armor: sunglasses, hearing aid, black suit, white crew cut. The air fills with Hoff disparagement before he shows up. We're told he's crass, that he's not one of the producers who make movies with "guts and meaning" like Stanley Kramer. By the time he arrives to blackmail Charlie into renewing his contract, talk like that has won him our sympathy. Steiger's great philistine totally dominates his two long scenes. Even cowering like a turtle before Charlie's manliness he turns himself in an X that blots out everything. Then he explodes like a neutron bomb, leaving the set standing but obliterating the people.

"Who *are* you?" he howls at Charlie. "Some kind of special aristocracy because the female public wants to make love with you? I built the studio! I ripped it out of the world with *my* brains and *my* hands and *who are you*?" He exits exulting in himself like he's holding a shell to his ear to catch echoes of his greatness.
A. S. Hamrah

Date 1955

Nationality USA

Director Robert Aldrich

Cast Jack Palance, Rod Steiger, Ida Lupino, Wendell Corey, Everett Sloane, Nick Dennis

Why It's Key It's a Steiger tour de force.

Opposite **Rod Steiger**

Key Scene **The final shot**
I Live in Fear (aka *Record of a Living Being*)

I Live in Fear focuses on the moral dilemma faced by Dr Harada (Shimura), a Family Court arbitrator who must judge the mental competence of Kiichi Nakajima (Toshiro Mifune), a foundry owner determined to leave Japan before what he sees as the inevitable nuclear holocaust. As the representative of a typical bourgeois institution, Harada is incapable of understanding that this problem cannot be resolved in terms (sanity/insanity) that, far from being ideologically neutral, are precisely those proposed by the system responsible for it. Nakajima may be described as "born to take everything too far," but his protest fails because he does not take it far enough, retaining his position of patriarchal privilege even as he struggles to escape patriarchy's more obviously undesirable excesses. The necessity of rejecting all conventional methods of comprehending reality is implied by the devastating final image: on the left we see Harada walking down a staircase as he leaves the asylum to which Nakajima has been committed; on the right we see Nakajima's mistress, Asako (Negishi), walking along a corridor (but framed so that she appears to be moving towards the top of the screen) with a baby strapped to her back. An old man (visualized as descending) incapable of change is here juxtaposed with, but separated from, a young woman (visualized as ascending) who has consistently redefined familial, sexual, and financial relationships (she gives Nakajima money, and she is uninterested in having him acknowledge that he is the father of her child). As the only character (aside from Nakajima's youngest daughter, Sue), motivated by something other than self-interest, it is Asako, not Nakajima, who is the "Living Being" of the original Japanese title, the one truly "born to take everything too far."

Brad Stevens

Date 1955

Nationality Japan

Director Akira Kurosawa

Cast Akemi Negishi, Takashi Shimura

Original Title *Ikimono no kiroku*

Why It's Key This shot demonstrates Kurosawa's ability to sum up the overall themes of his films in individual images of great resonance.

262

Key Scene **Harihar Ray returns home**
Pather Panchali

Harihar Ray (Kanu Bannerjee), an impoverished priest, returns home to his native village from Rana Ghat where he has finally managed to make ends meet. On arrival, he sees that his modest little home has been decimated by a storm. Staring through a gap in the outer wall, he mumbles to himself, "couldn't this have waited?", and exits to the right of screen. The camera remains static on the family cow in the foreground and the destroyed hut in the background for more than a moment, magically drawing attention to itself and to Harihar's return. Harihar re-enters the frame, and as he does so also enters another enclosure, that of his house. Sharbajaya (Karuna Bannerjee), his wife, appears out of nowhere, as if her husband's long-overdue return were commonplace enough. In absolute silence, she brings a pail of water for him to wash with, not responding to the flow of talk he brings forth in his excitement at being back with something to show for his long absence. He produces the gifts he has brought for the family – a board and rolling pin and a picture of the Goddess Lakshmi for Sharbajaya, and a sari for their little daughter Durga. There is a close-up of Sharbajaya, her back to Harihar, clutching the sari and then breaking down. The music rises as we see her back in a medium-long shot as she sinks to the ground. Harihar kneels down beside her, and we see from his expression that he has understood that Durga has died. No word is spoken. The eloquence lies in the image. Satyajit Ray's first feature film remains his most timeless.

Aruna Vasudev

Date 1955

Nationality India

Director Satyajit Ray

Cast Kanu Bannerjee, Karuna Bannerjee, Subir Bannerjee

Aka *Song of the Road*

Why It's Key Quite simply, it's the greatest Indian film of all time.

Key Person **Dead body on the lawn**
The Phenix City Story

Nearly every account of Phil Karlson's work contains the word "hysteria" – which is rather odd when one thinks about it, because so many suspense films show excitable behavior that could be called hysteria, and even exhibit hysteria themselves in their pacing and sense of emphasis. Why should Karlson be singled out? *The Phenix City Story*, a docudrama that is perhaps Karlson's strongest work, gives us a clue. Early in the story, the gangsters who control Phenix City, Alabama, issue a grim warning to returning vet John Patterson (Kiley), who has shown signs of resisting the mob's dominance: they kill a young black girl and throw her body on the Pattersons' lawn. The family dissolves into screeching terror for long minutes of screen time, crying and quivering through their discussions of whether to resist or surrender. Their reactions are not excessive for people who have had a body dumped in front of their house. But Karlson is breaking a time-honored law of fiction that links ramped-up emotion to

the buildup of suspense before an event that the audience fears. By contrast, the aftermath of calamity is usually muted, transformed into melancholy to match the audience's more restrained response as it restores its equilibrium. By opting for emotionality after something bad happens, Karlson shoves us out of this regulated pattern of identification. His brand of hysteria is oddly uncomfortable because it issues an invitation for us to abandon the secure role of spectator and take on the insecure role of participant.
Dan Sallitt

Date 1955

Nationality USA

Director Phil Karlson

Cast Richard Kiley, Lenka Peterson

Why It's Key It's possibly the most hysterical scene in the career of America's poet of hysteria, Karlson.

Key Event
RKO sells its film library to TV

Though initially the Hollywood studios saw television as a threat, soon they recognized the revenue potential of supplying the new medium with programming – first by producing shows for TV, then by leasing or selling old theatrical films for broadcast. The first studio to take the latter course was RKO, which was bought by a subsidiary of General Tire and Rubber Company in July 1955. In December, RKO's new owner sold the studio's library of 740 films for $15.2 million to another conglomerate, C&C Super Corporation, which proceeded to distribute the films to TV stations via a new subsidiary, C&C Television Corporation. The success of the deal encouraged the other studios, which by 1958 had sold or leased some 3,700 features, mostly pre-1948, to TV. These films constituted an important part of TV programming (and, therefore, advertising revenue).

The regular availability of works from what is now considered the classical period of American cinema

had an enormous impact on American culture. Commercial TV became a vast repertory cinema, where generations of cinephiles – including many who would become filmmakers – educated themselves in the auteurs, stars, and genres of the past. Long after it had ceased production, RKO, which started the ball rolling, remained one of the most stable sources of this education, with films such as *King Kong*, the Astaire and Rogers musicals, Orson Welles's *Citizen Kane* and *The Magnificent Ambersons*, and Val Lewton's works showing constantly on WOR-TV in New York. In the 1980s, deregulation and the rise of home video caused a decline in TV's importance as a purveyor of film history.
Chris Fujiwara

Date December 1955

Why It's Key For a quarter of a century, broadcast TV became a film-history school.

Key Event
Janus Films founded

J anus Films, founded in March 1956 by Harvard classmates Bryant Halliday and Cyrus Harvey Jr., was for years the most prestigious distributor of foreign films in the United States. Halliday and Harvey cut their teeth in the film business running repertory cinemas. They are perhaps most fondly remembered for launching the Brattle Theatre in Cambridge, Massachusetts – an emblematic cinema associated with the so-called "golden age of cinema" ushered in during the post-World War II era; the team subsequently branched out and opened a similar venue, the 55th Street Playhouse, in New York City. It's not surprising, therefore, that it's difficult to separate nostalgia for the repertory cinemas that once flourished in major American cities (but have now, because of video and high rents, become nearly defunct) from the distinguished roster of films (by, among others, Truffaut, Antonioni, Kurosawa, and Fellini) that Janus introduced to American audiences.

The Janus imprimatur lives on in the Criterion Collection, the DVD outpost run by Peter Becker and Jonathan Turell, the sons of two men, William Becker and Saul Turell, who succeeded Harvey and Halliday as Janus executives. When Criterion released a boxed set of 50 noteworthy films from the Janus library in 2006, *The New York Times*'s Dave Kehr compared the hefty assortment of discs to the 51 volumes of world literary classics assembled by Dr. Charles W. Eliot of Harvard (and commonly known as "Dr. Eliot's Five-Foot Shelf" or the "Harvard Classics") in 1909. This comparison underlines the extent to which the Janus library continues to be linked with, however imprecisely, a semi-official cinematic "canon."
Richard Porton

Date March 1956

Why It's Key Janus Films, founded by two Boston-based entrepreneurs, is almost synonymous with the heyday of the American repertory cinema in the Fifties and Sixties.

Key Speech **"You're next!"**
Invasion of the Body Snatchers

SPOILER

I n the climax of *Invasion of the Body Snatchers*, Dr Miles Bennell (Kevin McCarthy) – the sole survivor of a small town taken over by seedpod-grown imitation humans from outer space – stumbles out onto a busy, nighttime highway, ranting that "they're taking over" and babbling like a madman. In one of the great black-and-white widescreen close-ups, the bug-eyed Bennell turns directly to the audience and shrieks: "You're next!" Originally, director Don Siegel intended to end his film of Jack Finney's novel *The Body Snatchers* with this image and this line, but the studio insisted on a frame story that allowed for at least some hope that the invasion would be thwarted. Nevertheless, it's a defining moment in 1950s film paranoia – a wake-up call for an affluent but disaffected America.
Kim Newman

Date 1956

Nationality USA

Director Don Siegel

Cast Kevin McCarthy

Why It's Key The fear never goes away.

Opposite *Invasion of the Body Snatchers*

he had to find her... he had to find her...

WARNER BROS. PRESENT THE C.V. WHITNEY PICTURE STARRING

JOHN WAYNE IN
THE SEARCHERS.

VISTA**VISION** JEFFREY HUNTER · VERA MILES · WARD BOND · NATALIE WOOD · JOHN FORD
MOTION PICTURE High Fidelity
COLOUR BY TECHNICOLOR   SCREEN PLAY BY FRANK S NUGENT · EXECUTIVE PRODUCER MERIAN C. COOPER · ASSOCIATE PRODUCER PATRICK FORD · PRESENTED BY WARNER BROS.

ETHAN
Whatever it
took—he'd
find her!

DEBBIE
Somewhere
out there
— she was
captive!

LAURIE
Her heart
wanted to
wait—and
couldn't!

MARTIN
He started the
search as a boy,
and ended it
a man!

CLAYTON
The Good Book
in one hand
—and a gun
in the other!

Key Scene **The end of all our exploring**
The Searchers

Recognized universally as one of the greatest film westerns, *The Searchers* is the saga of Civil War veteran Ethan Edwards (Wayne) who, returning to his sister's home after a Comanche raid, finds most of his family butchered and his niece Debbie (Wood) kidnapped. With Martin Pawley (Hunter), a half-breed who has been living with the family, at his side, he sets out to track the renegade Scar (Henry Brandon) and his band, and to recover Debbie. But the search takes years. Ethan and Martin encounter numerous obstacles, meet many strangers, and burn with tension – Ethan is an incorrigible Indian-hater. When they finally find him, Scar has taken Debbie as his squaw. Ethan is mortified, and his heart turns cold toward the girl. Violated, she must die. Martin tries to protect Debbie, sneaking into her teepee, waking her, and whispering that he will take her home. But Scar comes in, and Martin must shoot him. As cavalry forces raid the Indian encampment, Ethan rides into Debbie's teepee, ostensibly to kill her. She is gone. But he sees Debbie in flight, and races after her on horseback, Martin scampering after him, screaming "No, no, Ethan!" Debbie flees over a hilltop and into a cave, with Ethan right behind her and Martin following up, gun in hand. "No, Ethan. No!" Debbie tries to crawl into the ground, but Ethan is upon her, towering, imperturbable. He drags her up forcefully, but in a single fluid motion, now gentle and protective, lifts her into his arms. "Let's go home, Debbie." In this moment is the quintessence of Wayne's two-sided screen persona, unyieldingly stalwart but also tender and compassionate.

Murray Pomerance

Date 1956

Nationality USA

Director John Ford

Cast John Wayne, Natalie Wood, Jeffrey Hunter

Why It's Key It's a supreme example of John Wayne's two-sided masculinity.

Opposite *The Searchers*

Key Speech **An audacious three-word statement** *Bigger Than Life*

Ed Avery, played by James Mason, is a family man who lives in a friendly town, teaches school for a living, and dotes on Lou (Rush), his pretty wife, and Richie (Olsen), their likable young son. A painful ailment puts him on cortisone pills – a new medication that's been hailed as a wonder drug, but causes serious side effects in some patients.

Before long Ed starts exceeding his proper dosage, and his mental health takes a sharp downward turn. Full of manic energy, he tells parents their kids are barbarians, subjects his own son to unsparing discipline, and concludes that God has a special interest in his activities. The crisis comes when Richie disappoints him once too often and Ed, consumed by Bible-quoting dementia, decides God wants him to emulate Abraham and sacrifice the boy. Desperate to protect her child, Lou reminds Ed that God saved Isaac at the last minute, telling Abraham not to kill him after all. Ed's reply: "God was wrong."

As megalomaniacal as those words are, they're spoken with a sense of profound conviction and terrifying self-righteousness that only a master actor like Mason could have brought to them. They concisely crystallize the story's three thematic threads, all relating to middle-class obsessions of the 1950s era – education, childrearing, and religion. And they give an injection of bone-chilling audacity to a screenplay that dares to be irreverent toward some of the period's most sensitive, not to say sacred, subjects. The result is an exceptional moment in mid-century American cinema.

David Sterritt

Date 1956

Nationality USA

Director Nicholas Ray

Cast James Mason, Barbara Rush, Christopher Olsen

Why It's Key In the 1950s, when melodrama offered a rare outlet for strong emotional expression, this succinct sentence pushed narrative audacity to its outer limit.

Key Scene **The scream that changed the narrative world** *The Man Who Knew Too Much*

Day is Jo McKenna, an internationally celebrated singing star who has given up her career, married Ben (James Stewart), a doctor, and now traveled with him and their son (Christopher Olsen) to Morocco, where, in the midst of an intrigue involving the murder of a strange Frenchman (Daniel Gélin), the boy is kidnapped. To find him, the McKennas travel to London. Ben is trapped by the criminals, but Jo heads off to find the police, who are protecting a foreign dignitary during a concert at the Royal Albert Hall. In an extended sequence here – one which has typified Hitchcock's reputation for the artfully dramatic use of setting – she must listen to Arthur Benjamin's "Storm Clouds" Cantata in its entirety, all the while agonizing about her missing child and caught with foreboding because she knows that a man is to be assassinated somehow in this city. As the music unfolds, in rolling majestic phrases, Jo, who is at heart not only a mother but also a singer, is caught up with it quite as much as with her

fear for the boy, and at the climactic moment (the instant – we know, but Jo does not – at which the assassin has been trained to shoot, here, in this very hall), she cannot restrain herself any longer and breaks the spell of the music with a horrendous shriek.

In one vocal gesture, then, Hitchcock arranges for the classy decorum of the concert hall to collapse; for the assassination attempt to be foiled; for the woman to exercise power; for the singer tearfully to sing; and ultimately for the kidnapped child to be saved. This is a masterly moment in the exercise of cinematic economy, where a tremendous number of forces are brought together for an instant of overwhelming tension and release.

Murray Pomerance

Date 1956

Nationality USA

Director Alfred Hitchcock

Cast Doris Day, Reggie Nalder

Why It's Key One of the key iconic moments in Hitchcock's work, it shows why the woman's voice has more power than the assassin's bullet.

268

Key Scene **Dance of death** *Written on the Wind*

Like all rich families in 1950s cinema, the Hadleys have everything but happiness. Old Jasper Hadley (Keith) sits atop an oil fortune, but must live with the fact that his wife is gone, his son Kyle (Stack) is an alcoholic wastrel, and his daughter Marylee (Malone) is a nymphomaniac. To make things worse, Kyle's oldest and best friend, Mitch (Hudson), a boy from the other side of the tracks, cares more about the oil business than Kyle does by a long shot, and has the same warmth of concern for Kyle's new wife, Lucy (Bacall). The self-hating, suicidal, near-sterile Kyle is more than Lucy can handle, a constant failure who has to be redeemed by the devotions of his friend. But Marylee hints to Kyle that Lucy is pregnant by Mitch. This film gives what is perhaps the most eloquent and economic expression to the problematic family of film melodrama: torn within by contradictions and impossible passions, pressured from without by a relentlessly watchful society. At a critical moment the

fault lines of the fractured melodramatic family come to the surface in this film:

Marylee is in her bedroom, in an orchid pink negligee, dancing masturbatorily to hot jazz. The camera swings around with her, frequently at hip level, as she abandons herself to the sexual rhythms and loud harmonies. Downstairs in his study, her father has come to the end of his tether. As he gropes his way up the curved plantation staircase, he suffers a heart attack. He buckles and falls all the way back down, with Marylee's dancing music blaring away as though all the world were only a carnival.

Murray Pomerance

Date 1956

Nationality USA

Director Douglas Sirk

Cast Robert Keith, Robert Stack, Dorothy Malone, Rock Hudson, Lauren Bacall

Why It's Key It's a fine example of how film melodrama exteriorizes family strains.

Key Scene **First escape attempt**
A Man Escaped

A prisoner is driven in the back seat of a car, part of a caravan after a dragnet. He looks intently to his front, to his left at the car door's handle, and to his right, past another, injured captive, handcuffed to someone we almost cannot see, probably another caught Resistance fighter. With one of the fingers of his left hand he tries the handle slightly, to see if it's locked. As a cart forces the driver to slow, we realize the man (on whose face we remain), Lt. Fontaine (future filmmaker Leterrier), is tempted to make a try at opening the door, but he desists. Then a tramway provides a better occasion, and he jumps out of the car and the frame. Shots and cries in German are heard while the camera stays inside the car, as he's returned to it, handcuffed, and hit with a pistol butt; the image dissolves into the next scene, his arrival in prison.

Swifter or simpler it could not be – at first sight at least, since it has a lot of shots and camera movements, almost as many as a contemporary (and related) Hitchcock film, *The Wrong Man*. Without any dialogue as yet, with minimal elements, Bresson manages both to build a suspense that could be called "impersonal" (since we don't know anything about Fontaine, not even his name) and to present to us a stubborn, obstinate character. The film starts in mid-action, and the tension comes precisely from the camera's impassibility, the way the actor gazes and moves. We have to guess what we don't see or are not told, but we easily understand who he is and why he's been caught by the Gestapo, because we can see what he looks at and read his thoughts, in this sublest of developments of Kuleshov's theories.

Miguel Marias

Date 1956

Nationality France

Director Robert Bresson

Cast François Leterrier

Original Title *Un condamné à mort s'est échappé ou Le Vent souffle où il veut*

Why It's Key This scene, one of the most impressive and elliptical beginnings in cinema, not only sets the mood and announces what is coming, but teaches how to look at a film of its kind.

269

Key Scene **"Cry Me a River"**
The Girl Can't Help It

The Girl Can't Help It is full of cameo appearances by contemporary rock acts, but its most strangely beautiful – and least comic – scene pits Tom Ewell's alcoholic press agent against the ghostly presence of his former client (and rejected lover), torch singer Julie London "as herself." London had just become a major recording star, helped greatly by the sexy covers of such albums as *Julie Is Her Name* and *Calendar Girl*. Ewell, returning drunk to his bachelor pad, contemplates those album covers, drops "Cry Me a River" (London's signature hit) on the turntable, and proceeds to pour himself another drink before registering the transparent form of Julie herself singing the song at his kitchen table. He goes from room to room to find her in a series of suggestive poses and exotic outfits – toreador pants and espadrilles in the living room, frilly nightgown in his bed – her image gradually becoming more corporeal as she continues to sing her song of bitter recrimination against the man who abandoned her. He escapes to the stairway, and she's there, staring up at him accusingly, until her voice subsides into echo effect just as her body thins out into superimposition before vanishing altogether. Ewell – in a shot that might have come from a 1956 drama about the perils of alcoholism – buries his face despairingly in his arms. This little ghost story about a man haunted by the covers of pop albums is a movie in itself, and its unexpected emotional force and sheer oddness seep into everything that follows, giving farce a bittersweet aftertaste.

Geoffrey O'Brien

Date 1956

Nationality USA

Director Frank Tashlin

Cast Tom Ewell, Julie London

Why It's Key The power of pop culture to spill out of its own context is dramatically illustrated by a scene in Tashlin's rock and roll comedy.

Key Scene **The parting of the Red Sea**
The Ten Commandments

Cecil B. DeMille built his reputation on half sleazy, half moralistic spectacles, including his 1923 silent version of *The Ten Commandments*, but his four-hour, widescreen, Technicolor remake of the Old Testament story trumped every gaudy splendor he'd showcased up to then. The centerpiece was, to put it blasphemously, Hollywood's ultimate money shot: a massive (and massively expensive) visualization of Moses (Heston) parting the Red Sea to help the Israelites escape Egypt, then closing the waters on Pharoah's pursuing minions. In the original, DeMille's technicians visualized God's wrath by cutting a swath through a tank of hardened gelatin, then heating the top until it liquefied again, pouring over the edges and filling up the gap. For the remake, DeMille's effects team combined several planes' worth of matte paintings (including "parted sea" elements composed of ribbon-like material simulating wave walls), reversed footage of thousands of gallons of water being poured into a tank, and footage of ant-like Israelites and doomed Egyptian charioteers on the sea floor. The sequence was credited with making a hit of the Biblical epic (some repeat viewers bought tickets, then popped in after the intermission and left after the Big Scene). Steven Spielberg, no stranger to spectacle, once called the parting of the Red Sea "the best special effects sequence of all time" and spent much of his career trying to equal it – most notably in 1977's quasi-religious UFO epic *Close Encounters of the Third Kind*, which includes a scene where Richard Dreyfuss's unhinged hero lets his kids stay up late watching DeMille's film on ABC, then makes them go to bed after the waters close.

Matt Zoller Seitz

Date 1956

Nationality USA

Director Cecil B. DeMille

Cast Charlton Heston

Why It's Key It's Hollywood's ultimate money shot.

Opposite *The Ten Commandments*

270

Key Speech **The villain tells a story**
Seven Men from Now

Elegant in style and masterly in cinematic storytelling from its first frames, the first film of what is now known as the Ranown cycle (six Westerns directed by Boetticher, starring Scott, mostly written by Burt Kennedy, and mostly produced by Ranown, Scott's own company with Harry Joe Brown) hits the heights during a midpoint nocturnal rain, when the villain, Masters (Marvin), tells a story in close quarters inside a wagon while sharing coffee with ex-sheriff Stride (Scott) and John and Annie Greer (Reed and Russell) as they all travel to Flora Vista. In his story, a wife left a soft man for a tougher one, and Masters sees some parallels. As he has observed, Annie and Stride, though both decent and respectful, have been drawn to each other (for the revenge-seeking Stride, in the wake of the killing of his wife by outlaws). Knowing he hits a nerve in each of the others, the flamboyant Masters – always ostentatious in his bright green scarf – savors his phrases: "Been that way ever since ever I guess...."

"Ain't you interested in what she up and did, Sheriff?" "Yeah, she looked a lot like you ma'am, but not near as pretty." And as much as he enjoys it, so do we. A whole extra level of complex response to the Ranowns has its first flowering here. The villain can be the villain and yet fascinating, even likeable, and tell some hard truth. This great sequence is due equally to Kennedy's wonderful writing, Boetticher's inspired staging and shot breakdown, and Marvin's playing, never more brilliant than here, as he poses, dominates, takes his time – a Mephistopheles of the range.

Blake Lucas

Date 1956

Nationality USA

Director Budd Boetticher

Cast Randolph Scott, Gail Russell, Lee Marvin, Walter Reed

Why It's Key The much-lauded Ranown cycle hits an early peak in this great sequence, as one of the genre's most mesmerizing villains takes center stage.

Key Scene **The falsely accused man prays**
The Wrong Man

Manny (Fonda), a musician, is arrested for a series of robberies he didn't commit. He's exonerated when another man is caught red-handed in a similar crime, but by this time his family has shattered.

The climax takes place when Manny follows the advice of his mother (Esther Minciotti) to pray for strength. He walks into another room, where his eye is caught by a picture of Jesus on the wall. Hitchcock cuts to the portrait with Manny's shadow to its left, giving a subliminal sense of Manny as less solid and material than before. While he prays we see a close-up of his face, which becomes transparent (losing another degree of physicality) as Hitchcock superimposes a shot of the "real criminal," whose face grows larger as it approaches the camera. This effect turns Manny's head into a vessel that's filled before our eyes with the form and face of his supposedly evil twin.

What pours into Manny after his prayer, then, is not a spirit of goodness but a specter of the badness that's been plaguing him, suggesting Hitchcock's perennial theme of spiritual kinship between "right" and "wrong" sides of human nature, especially since it remains unclear that the new "criminal" is any guiltier of the earlier crimes than Manny was. The film's paradoxes can't be logically resolved. All we can definitively say of Hitchcock here is what T.S. Eliot said of John Webster, the 17th-century playwright: He was "much possessed by death/And saw the skull beneath the skin."

David Sterritt

Date 1956

Nationality USA

Director Alfred Hitchcock

Cast Henry Fonda

Why It's Key The ordeal of a falsely accused man comes to its climax with a prayer. Some critics have dismissed this as a *deus ex machina* device, but it's actually a subtle expression of the spiritual kinship between good and evil sides of human nature.

1950–1959

273

Key Film
The Pajama Game

Stanley Donen directed, or co-directed, a dozen Hollywood musicals, most of them outstanding. *The Pajama Game* was his only adaptation of a Broadway musical, since *Funny Face* retained nothing from the 1927 show except for the title, the Gershwin songs, and a much older Fred Astaire in the lead. Actually, the comparison between the two movies, released within a few months of each other, shows the striking diversity of Donen's talents within the genre. The sophisticated view of the world of high fashion and the location shooting in Paris of the former contrasts sharply with the good-naturedly plebeian atmosphere and backlot filming of the latter.

The success of *The Pajama Game* is due partly, of course, to the originality and freshness of the Broadway hit, but also to a wise decision to trust the show and stay as close to it as possible. The cast, with the exception of Doris Day, was imported from the stage, no new songs were added and only a very few were dropped, no attempt was made to "open up" the action, which, except for the big Fourth of July picnic sequence, takes place entirely in the factory's workshop and offices, or in the modest house by the railroad track where Day lives with her stamp-collecting father. And yet the movie, made on a relatively small budget and filmed in a few weeks, doesn't look stagey at all and comes through, in its modest fashion, as almost as full of *joie de vivre* as the legendary *Singin' in the Rain*.

Jean-Pierre Coursodon

Date 1957

Nationality USA

Directors Stanley Donen and George Abbott

Cast Doris Day, John Raitt, Carol Haney

Why It's Key A rare example of a Broadway show faithfully and thoroughly successfully adapted to the screen.

Opposite *The Pajama Game*

Key Scene **Radha challenges the money lender** *Mother India*

Ten years after India gained Independence and the subcontinent was torn apart by the Partition of British India into India and Pakistan, there was not much euphoria left about freedom. It was then that one of the old-style movie moghuls, Mehboob Khan, decided to remake his 1940 hit, *Aurat* (*Woman*). This time he cast Nargis as Radha, the woman who would epitomise India.

Radha begins the film as an old woman, who is asked to inaugurate a dam. As we are already aware from the title that she is the presiding deity of the film, this request fits in with the belief of the first Prime Minister, Jawaharlal Nehru, that big dams were the temples of modern India. The rest of the film is told in an extended flashback, which begins when Radha marries Shamu (Raj Kumar). An accident takes away Shamu's arms, and, unable to work, he vanishes into the night. Radha is left to manage, and this she does, pulling the plough when the cow dies – another iconic moment – and bringing up her sons. Then comes a flood, and her children have nothing to eat. Radha goes to Sukhilal the moneylender (Kanhaiyalal), but he wants sex in exchange for food. She is tempted to ease her children's hunger pangs, but when she finally and dramatically refuses the food, the theater audience explodes in a crescendo of shouts and whistles of approval. (*Mother India* continues to be shown at a theater in India every day, and the response is still as vigorous as when the film was first shown.)

Jerry Pinto

Date 1957

Nationality India

Director Mehboob Khan

Cast Nargis, Kanhaiyalal

Why It's Key In refusing to barter sex for food for her starving children, Radha establishes the moral superiority of the Indian woman.

274

Key Person **Timothy Carey**
Killing a cockroach *Paths of Glory*

To cover up his vain blunders, a French general (George Macready) in World War I orders three of his soldiers (Meeker, Carey, Joe Turkel), chosen almost at random, to be court-martialed and then shot by a firing squad for dereliction of duty, as an example to their fellow soldiers. When their last meal is brought to them, they can mainly only talk desperately about futile plans for escape and the hopelessness of their plight. Then Corporal Paris (Meeker) looks down at a cockroach crawling across the table and says, "See that cockroach? Tomorrow morning, we'll be dead and it'll be alive. It'll have more contact with my wife and child than I will. I'll be nothing, and it'll be alive." Ferrol (Carey) smashes the cockroach with his fist and says, almost dreamily, "Now you got the edge on him."

We're apt to laugh at the absurdism and grotesquerie of the moment – especially Timothy Carey's deadpan delivery, as if he had a mouthful of mush and was soft-pedaling the phrase like Lester Young on his tenor sax. One of the creepiest character actors in movies, he doesn't fit the period; even if we accept him as a French soldier, accepting him as one in World War I is more of a stretch, because he registers like a contemporary beatnik. That's also how he comes across in *East of Eden*, *One-Eyed Jacks*, *The Killing*, or *The Killing of Chinese Bookie*. But for precisely that reason, he gives the line the existential ring it deserves.

Jonathan Rosenbaum

Date 1957

Nationality USA

Director Stanley Kubrick

Cast Ralph Meeker, Timothy Carey

Why It's Key A quintessential character actor achieves his apotheosis when his character kills a bug.

Key Scene "Where are those to claim to be proud of this land?" *Pyaasa*

Released ten years after independence and partition, *Pyaasa* was the first in a series of films addressing critically the state of the nation by confronting explicitly the contradictions of nationalist "modernization" against a then still pervasive, condescending sense of accomplishment. Guru Dutt did so within a medium and an industry, Hindi cinema, which was crucially implicated in those tensions, by trying to graft the personal, emotive layers of the story onto the economic, social, and cultural dimensions of modernization. In so doing, *Pyaasa* pushed the conventions of the Hindi melodrama to their limit.

The question the film addresses is: how to speak subjectively within a medium which is sustained by power blocs that resist many aspects of modernization, including notions of civil rights and freedom of speech for all? In this scene, Vijay (Guru Dutt), a poet, staggers through the lanes of the red-light district. As he stops to sit on the ground, we cut to a close-up of Vijay's face. His eyes are closed. This close-up and a musical cue introduce a subjective perspective on the misery of the district's inhabitants. Vijay starts singing, but his subjective point of view is never fully taken up by the camera. Throughout, the scene is characterized by a discrepancy between objective and subjective layers of narration – between what the camera shows in the background, in a reportage style, and what Vijay sees. The tension between these two addresses produces a third narrative layer, Vijay's song, as a direct address that presents the deprivation of "these lanes" as a manifestation of the state of the nation. In this way, an originally pre-industrial and highly codified mode of address, the song, is adapted to the visual, industrial conventions of cinema in order to create a space from which the betrayal of nationalist modernization could be voiced, subjectively, to the collectivity responsible for its failure.

Valentina Vitali

Date 1957

Nationality India

Director Guru Dutt

Cast Guru Dutt

Aka *Eternal Thirst*

Why It's Key In this scene converge many of the stylistic, narrative conventions of the Hindi melodrama.

Key Scene **Quixote attempts to save a damsel in distress** *Don Quixote*

The greatest sequence I've seen from Orson Welles's unfinished, independently produced *Don Quixote* has no sound and isn't included in the boring and ugly version of Welles's *Quixote* assembled posthumously by Jesús Franco. Welles shot this sequence in Mexico City in 1957, when he was in flight from the postproduction hassles he encountered on his last Hollywood studio picture, *Touch of Evil*.

There's some evidence that the sequence in question, which has no dialogue, was intended as a flashback narrated by Dulcie (McCormack), a contemporary American girl staying in the same Spanish or Mexican hotel as Welles (playing himself), who's been telling her the story of Quixote in installments in the hotel patio. Apparently, between installments, she's been encountering both Quixote (Reiguera) and Sancho Panza (Tamiroff) in the flesh, in the garb of their own period, and she's telling Welles about one such encounter.

In a movie audience, she's joined by Sancho, who apparently has never seen a movie before. The same seems to be the case with Quixote, whom they see seated a few rows ahead of them. But the doleful knight becomes so upset that he strides down the aisle in his armor and starts puncturing the screen with his lance and tearing it to shreds. Onscreen we see some sword-and-sandal epic. He's clearly coming to the aid of one of the maidens, and the crowd goes wild, cruelly cheering him on. Eventually they storm out, and he's left alone with Dulcie and Sancho, barely aware of what he's done.

Jonathan Rosenbaum

Date 1957

Nationality Mexico

Director Orson Welles

Cast Patty McCormack, Akim Tamiroff, Francisco Reiguera

Why It's Key Orson Welles captures the essence of Cervantes' novel inside a movie theater.

Key Event
The death of Humphrey Bogart

In 1957, two years after Bill Haley had rocked around his clock, as Elvis was doing that famous Ed Sullivan show, Humphrey Bogart, a great smoker in the movies, a great drinker in real life, was wasting away of cancer in his home in L.A. For decades Bogart had embodied the kind of slow-to-anger masculinity that Hollywood admired. American cinema was emotional, romantic, and melodramatic from the start; slow-burn stars like Bogart were its counterpoint. His late conversions to the cause in *Casablanca* (1942) and his hints at caring in *The Maltese Falcon* (1941) and *To Have and Have Not* (1944) were all the more moving because they were so hard won. Within a few years Tyrone Power (1958), Errol Flynn (1959), Clark Gable (1960), and Gary Cooper (1961) would die too, and this kind of Hollywood maleness, part fake, would go with them.

Bogart wasn't the greatest actor of his generation (James Cagney and Bette Davis were more talented); and, by the time of his death, performers like Marlon Brando, Rod Steiger, Montgomery Clift, and Shelley Winters had begun to make his acting style look narrow or repetitive. But he was lionised by the French as the Sartre of *film noir*, an existential in a trench coat. For people as diverse as Frank Sinatra and Judy Garland, Bogart was a man of principle who steered through the fluff and tinsel of the industry. He had evolved a way of reconciling celebrity with the philistinism of the studio honchos, and said no when he hated something. Actors like Steve McQueen, James Coburn, and Sean Connery were in the same mould and learnt from him. His huge circle of Hollywood friends – the Rat Pack – admired his independence, though it was his young wife, Lauren Bacall, who tuned him to the Democratic, anti-McCarthy cause. Read *By Myself*, her memoir about his illness and death, and weep.

Mark Cousins

Date January 14, 1957

Why It's Key It was the beginning of the end of the golden age of Hollywood acting.

Opposite Humphrey Bogart

Key Scene **Death in the desert**
Bitter Victory

To cross the desert and perpetrate a raid in search of German documents, the introverted and poetic Captain Leith (Burton) has been put under the command of the gauche and brutal Major Brand (Jurgens). Brand is one of those arrogants who revel in, and also hide behind, the dictates of military procedure; Leith is one of those thinkers who see a ruin and dream back into prehistory to breathe a different sort of time. The raid is a failure, the platoon divided in the desert. One of the German soldiers has been wounded, as has a member of Leith's group, but as Brand and the others determine to move onward, Leith must stay behind with the two victims, alone in the desert.

In the crisp black-and-white cinematography, the sands are bleached and the sky is brilliant. Black beetles crawl around the dying German. Leith points his pistol and the soldier says, "*Nein!*", showing a photograph of his wife and child. "We were so happy before the war. Help me." Leith shoots. Then, as his mate is begging for death, he points the gun a second time, his hand trembling. But when he pulls the trigger, there are no bullets left. He bends and collects the agonized soldier in his arms, carrying him into the desert although the man is damning him for cowardice. On a dune crest, white as magnesium in the glare, he meets his Arab guide (Pellegrin), who pronounces the soldier dead. Burton puts the body down and laughs dementedly, silently. "I kill the living... and save the dead!"

Murray Pomerance

Date 1957

Nationality France/USA

Director Nicholas Ray

Cast Richard Burton, Raymond Pellegrin

Aka *Amère victoire*

Why It's Key Here is a maverick director's explicit anti-war statement, rare in 1950s film.

Key Scene **Christmas Day** *An Affair to Remember*

In Leo McCarey's color and CinemaScope remake of his 1939 *Love Affair*, Cary Grant and Deborah Kerr take over Charles Boyer and Irene Dunne's roles of a painter and a singer who meet and fall in love on a trans-Atlantic crossing and are then separated by fate. The premise of the final scene – a highlight of both films – is that the woman, Terry, doesn't want the man (called Nickie in the second version) to learn about the car accident that has left her a paraplegic. Nickie tracks her down and visits her on Christmas Day, which she's spending alone on her sofa. She still refuses to reveal her plight, but the man has a sudden insight and realizes the truth.

A director whose trademark was his liberating charm with actors, McCarey wasn't known for flourishes of *mise en scène*, but the manner in which Nickie confirms his suspicion is a visual climax of *An Affair to Remember*. He crosses the vast CinemaScope living room, the camera following him, and opens the door to Terry's bedroom. McCarey cuts to a close shot inside the bedroom, where Nickie sees his painting on the wall – proof that Terry was the wheelchair-bound buyer of whom he was told by his gallery owner. Because the camera is on him as he enters the room, we first see his face as understanding dawns on it, and only then does McCarey pan slightly to frame the painting reflected in a mirror. This simple camera movement is a heart-wrenching double-whammy moment of pure cinema: Nickie's reaction (which Grant plays with characteristic understatement) already tells us what he sees; but then the camera movement lets us share his reaction by restaging his discovery for us.
Chris Fujiwara

Date 1957

Nationality USA

Director Leo McCarey

Cast Cary Grant, Deborah Kerr

Why It's Key A director's delicacy and restraint create a sublime moment of cinema.

Key Scene **The knight and his squire visit a church** *The Seventh Seal*

A knight (von Sydow) and his squire (Björnstrand) return battle-weary and disillusioned from the Crusades to discover that their native land is ravaged by the plague. The knight is plunged in metaphysical despair and questions the existence of God. He is paid a visit by Death (Ekerot) but manages to ward Death off and buy time by engaging him in a game of chess. On their way back to the knight's castle, the knight and his squire stop off at a rural church, where an artist (Olsson) is painting a series of frescos of the plague. While the squire converses with the painter, the knight enters the chapel and confesses his deepest misgivings and doubts to the shrouded monk in the confessional. He questions the presence of God, begs for a sign of His existence, and expresses his ardent desire to perform a significant deed of charity before Death ultimately takes him away. In the process he confesses his chess strategy to the monk, who reveals that he is Death himself. The scene epitomizes the individual's need to believe in a higher power, especially in troubled times (which seems all the more relevant in today's world), and the two-facedness of organized religion and its inability to provide spiritual sustenance to those in despair.
Aruna Vasudev

Date 1957

Nationality Sweden

Director Ingmar Bergman

Cast Max von Sydow, Gunnar Björnstrand, Bengt Ekerot, Anders Ek, Gunnar Olsson

Original Title *Det Sjunde inseglet*

Why It's Key It poses essential, eternal questions of human existence in a haunting and allegorical cinematic context.

Opposite On the set of *The Seventh Seal*

Key Person **Victor Sjöström**
Final leave-takings *Wild Strawberries*

One of the finest road-movies ever made, Bergman's masterpiece charts the spiritual and geographical odyssey undertaken by elderly medical professor Isak Borg (Sjöström, himself a director of importance who greatly influenced Bergman) as he leaves Stockholm for his *alma mater* in Lund to collect an honorary award. Making the trip with daughter-in-law Marianne (Thulin) – on the brink of leaving a husband (Björnstrand) who's even cooler emotionally than his father – Borg has numerous encounters en route, including one with Sara (Andersson), an ebullient young hitchhiker who reminds him of his first (lost) love of the same name, while revisiting/reinterpreting his life through remembrance, dreams, and conversations.

As the trip proceeds, Borg begins to realise that his self-defensive rectitude and devotion to work have not only limited his experiences and hurt others but influenced his son's attitude to life and to Marianne. Bergman maps Borg's journey towards self-knowledge by a variety of means – expressionist nightmares, lyrical reminiscence, gentle satire, and naturalistic drama – without ever lapsing into sentimentality. Crucial to his creation and maintenance of a coherent mood is Sjöström's robust performance, which never elicits gratuitous sympathy. Consequently, as he's bid goodnight first by Miss Agda (Kindahl), his starchy housekeeper, then by a serenading Sara, and finally by his son and Marianne (who have now decided to stay together), and then attains a modicum of tranquility at the end of a taxing day by thinking back to an idyllic childhood moment involving his parents, we feel Borg's redemptive serenity is fully deserved. And Sjöström's radiant expression makes it wholly credible.
Geoff Andrew

Date 1957

Nationality Sweden

Director Ingmar Bergman

Cast Victor Sjöström, Ingrid Thulin, Gunnar Björnstrand, Bibi Andersson, Julian Kindahl

Original Title *Smultronstället*

Why It's Key The most emotionally affecting scene in Bergman's warmest film, illuminated by a superb lead performance.

Key Scene **"Mr. Successful, You've Got It Made"** *Will Success Spoil Rock Hunter?*

Madison Avenue adman Rockwell P. Hunter (Randall) signs movie star Rita Marlowe (Jayne Mansfield) to endorse Stay-Put lipstick, thereby making his company a fortune and eventually turning him into first a vice president at the ad agency, with a key to the executive washroom, then the new president. Before long, even though his alienated fiancée (Betsy Drake) has broken off with him in disgust, he's clearly "got it made" – a phrase that he and this movie keep repeating so many times, in so many different ways, like a desperate mantra, that it begins to sound increasingly sinister. Perhaps the most pertinent gloss on this is provided by the company's former president (John Williams), who has meanwhile happily left advertising for horticulture and offers his words as a kind of warning: "Success will fit you like a shroud."

The climax of Frank Tashlin's definitive satire of 50s America, aptly filmed in expansive CinemaScope, spells this out in glitzy neon. After Hunter says goodnight to the office cleaning ladies, the scene segues into a solipsistic musical number played out to an unseen chorus chanting "You've got it made," as he literally sees his name in lights, dancing deliriously through the empty executive boardroom under various shifting forms of expressionistic lighting. Tashlin, a former animator, makes it all look like a crazed cartoon. But by the sequence's end, Hunter also discovers that he can't keep his pipe lit. In the movie's Freudian shorthand, this means that he doesn't really feel successful after all.
Jonathan Rosenbaum

Date 1957

Nationality USA

Director Frank Tashlin

Cast Tony Randall

Why It's Key In a key satire of the 50s, a Hollywood dream overtly springs to life inside a Hollywood dream.

Key Scene **Tension at 21**
Sweet Smell of Success

For the first 20 minutes of Alexander Mackendrick's corrosive *Sweet Smell of Success*, the Clifford Odets-Ernest Lehman screenplay takes the viewer into the small, sad world of Sidney Falco (Curtis, never better), a seedy, desperately ambitious New York press agent. After it's been established just what kind of a grub Falco is, we meet an even bigger grub: J.J. Hunsecker (Lancaster), the all-powerful newspaper columnist and television star whose acidic pen can make or break celebrities of every type. J.J. isn't eager to see Falco when the latter tries to talk to him at the 21 Club ("You're dead, son – get yourself buried"), but Falco weasels his way into the great man's presence anyway. Also at J.J.'s table are, according to the seen-it-all maître d', "a Senator, an agent, and a thing with blonde, wavy hair." A few caustic lines of dialogue later, the film establishes just what J.J. thinks about press agents in general and Falco in particular ("fully up to all the tricks of his very slimy trade"). Falco's defence of

his profession doesn't ring entirely true, and then J.J. starts quizzing the blonde bimbo (Russell) whose sleazy agent (Adler) has brought her to meet the Senator (Forrest), his seemingly harmless questions dripping with acid ("Why is it that everything you say sounds like a threat?", the Senator wonders). This is the great scene in which the arrogant J.J., unlit cigarette in mouth, orders Falco to "Match me," and the turning worm nervously declines. Mackendrick's dazzlingly successful segue from the charms of Ealing comedy to the horrors of McCarthy-era New York has been justly commended; few films have captured this glittering, empty, glamorous, dangerous world so adroitly.
David Stratton

Date 1957

Nationality USA

Director Alexander Mackendrick

Cast Burt Lancaster, Tony Curtis, William Forrest, Jay Adler, Autumn Russell

Why It's Key This scene shows the world of media glamour at its most rancid.

Key Scene **The children's party**
Night of the Demon

American scientist Holden (Andrews), on a mission in England to debunk belief in the supernatural, pays an unannounced visit to the vast country estate of Dr. Karswell (McGinnis), the leader of a black-magic cult. Holden finds Karswell made up and dressed as a shabby clown, entertaining local children at his annual Halloween party. As the two men walk together, Karswell, goaded by Holden's ironies about things supernatural, assumes a businesslike air that only makes his words more sinister: "How can we differentiate between the powers of darkness and the powers of the mind?" The tension is broken by the shock intrusion of two masked boys, whom Karswell dismisses with candy before returning to the business at hand: convincing Holden that magic is no joke. He takes off his hat, lowers his head, pinches his brow, and "There: it's done." In moments the calm afternoon is disrupted by a violent storm: lightning snaps off a tree branch behind Holden's head; wind sends rattan

chairs hurtling across the lawn, as adults scurry to collect the terrified children.

Unimpressed by the electric fans the producer had provided for the sequence, Tourneur called for plane engines to create a suitably ferocious wind – an insistence that proves he wasn't one to shrink from grand effects, however much he loved suggestion. This love shows in the way Tourneur builds the sequence, whose rapid turns from teasing lightness to seriousness are mirrored in the simple, precise cuts from two-shots of the men to tensely complementing close shots.
Chris Fujiwara

Date 1957

Nationality UK

Director Jacques Tourneur

Cast Dana Andrews, Niall McGinnis, Peggy Cummins, Athene Seyler

Aka *Curse of the Demon*

Why It's Key The exquisite subtlety and the boldness of construction Jacques Tourneur brought to his films are illustrated in this classic sequence.

Key Event **John Cassavetes appears on the radio show *Night People***

One Sunday evening in February 1957, John Cassavetes appeared on Jean Shepherd's radio show *Night People*, discussed a theatre piece he had been directing, and casually remarked that it might provide the basis for a good film. When Shepherd asked if it would be possible to finance such a project, Cassavetes (at least as he later recalled it) replied, "If people really want to see a movie about *people*, they should just contribute money." Approximately $2,500 trickled in during the following week, and shooting soon began on what would eventually be known as *Shadows* (first version 1958, final version 1959). No recording was kept of this edition of *Night People*, and nobody can recall the exact date on which it was broadcast. Much of its remembered content might be more myth than fact. Yet the story is too resonant to be easily dismissed. Even the show's name would have made a wonderful title for one of Cassavetes' films, which usually focused on individuals marginalized by the daylight world. Cassavetes had not actually planned to appeal for money, his announcement being made in that improvisational spirit which would become the distinguishing characteristic of both his future work and the filmmaking school it inspired: traditional methods of raising money for motion pictures were here being rejected and transformed, in much the same way that the resulting films would reject and transform narrative structures. If Cassavetes is (as he has often been described) the godfather of America's independent cinema, then this is surely the moment when that cinema was born.

Brad Stevens

Date February 1957

Why It's Key America's independent cinema can be traced to this moment.

Opposite *Shadows*

Key Scene **The final shot, a rainbow over the city** *The Man Who Invented Gold*

Christopher Maclaine's other masterpiece, a bit less well-known than *The End* (1953), centers on "Madman," a would-be alchemist mocked by his neighbors who wants to become the "gold man," and thus find his way to the "world of light." This protagonist is played by three different actors, Maclaine himself among them, which can make the film quite confusing on first viewing. Once again Maclaine mixes black and white and color and cuts in a highly disjointed manner, but this film is much more of a light poem than *The End*, with light streaming through windows and a spectacular moment when multiple colored pigments are thrown atop each other to make an abstract design. There's a whiff of Gnosticism at the film's core: the madman's quest is not so much for riches as for freeing objects of their materiality to release their light – the only thing worth believing in. Near the end a "poet" appears with the words "It's hard to believe" written in multiple colors on a sheet of paper, the colors recalling the earlier scattered pigments in yet another anticipation of the final image. Madman's attempts don't succeed, which is why the final image is so important and so moving even though it lasts only one-third of a second: the camera moves along the length of a rainbow in the sky, making a dark hanging garment to the left appear to rise along it to the top of the frame. With this movement, Maclaine connects the most ordinary of objects, clothing on a line, with the rainbow, which stands outside of materiality as an icon of pure light. The brevity of the shot is important too: the daily world is full of miracles that might make alchemy unnecessary – if we're quick enough to notice.

Fred Camper

Date 1957

Nationality USA

Director Christopher Maclaine

Why It's Key In a film about alchemy, Maclaine finds the real miracle in an ordinary rainbow.

Key Scene **The hero's final epiphany**
The Incredible Shrinking Man

Much science-fiction in the classics of the 1950s has imagination, charm, and a measure of profundity, but it's rare to find a work in any genre with the courage of its convictions to the extent this haunting, singular work can claim. Its epiphany emerges in a final sequence that those who love this film know like a prayer. The odyssey of Scott Carey (Williams) ends after he has been shrinking in size throughout the film, has spent the second half of it isolated in his own cellar, and done violent battle for food with a spider. Exhausted, he collapses on the dirt below the grate, and seems to briefly sleep within a shaft of light, a dark shadow passing over him like a wave and then giving way to a renewal of light as he awakes and moves to the grate to step out into an ever-expanding world, not restored to what he was (as convention gave us every right to expect) but instead accepting himself existentially in relation to the universe. The transformative effect of that shadow/shaft of light release is for us as well, to feel the effect of Carey's final eloquent narration ("...to God there is no zero... I still exist") in harmony with Arnold's beautiful concluding images, which resonate so deeply with the hero's newly-found serenity and the film's own spirituality.

Blake Lucas

Date 1957

Nationality USA

Director Jack Arnold

Cast Grant Williams

Why It's Key The one-of-a kind science fiction classic of the 1950s steps away from convention to transcendence in a sublime ending.

Opposite *The Incredible Shrinking Man*

Key Scene **Night crossings of the border**
Touch of Evil

The first shot of Orson Welles's last Hollywood picture was one of the most impressive openings in the cinema, immersing the spectator with its crane movements and its rhythmically paced double-action in an uninterruptedly dynamic narrative movement. Part of its power came from the unique combination of sharp deep-focus black-and-white night photography, the breathtaking continuity of a single take registering different movements, and Henry Mancini's music, apparently added in disregard for Welles's more realistic ambient-music plans. I regret to say that the only version available today, a 1998 "restoration" that purportedly follows the author's requested changes to the production company's cut – doesn't work at all for me and lowers the tension for the whole film, seriously impairing its effect.

The four-minute shot begins with someone connecting the timer of a bomb and planting it in a parked car, and it shows simultaneously a planned action – the bombing – and two random criss-crossing movements across the Los Robles U.S.-Mexican border: that of top Mexican police official Mike Vargas (Heston) and his newly-wed American wife, Susan (Leigh), on foot, and that of the car carrying an old local businessman and his girlfriend (Lansing). The filming contrasts a carefully planned action (the single crane shot elaborately designed by Welles) with the surprise of its sudden violent end (accompanied by a cut), unexpected for characters and audience alike. This contrast was subliminally suggested by Mancini's combination of a Latin-like percussion undercurrent and a diegetical-seeming jazzy melody, whose absence now diminishes the rhythm and unity of that most complex long take.

Miguel Marías

Date 1958

Nationality USA

Director Orson Welles

Cast Charlton Heston, Janet Leigh, Joi Lansing

Why It's Key This famous shot is one of the greatest manifestations of the powers of cinema to build an intensified "reality" of its own.

Key Scene **A masked figure disrupts a budding romance** *The Tarnished Angels*

SPOILER

A central visual motif of this black-and-white 'Scope masterpiece is the intrusion of elements from the background into the foreground, a foreground typically occupied by the characters. This occurs from the very opening scene, in which the movements, structures, and visual "noise" of a carnival tend to dominate the action, almost as if pressing forward. It's given narrative force when a flyer's coffin suddenly emerges from a previously nondescript tent. And it acquires chilling force when a young son is trapped in a circular plane ride as the smoking plane of his plane-racing father (Stack) is seen directly behind him. The effect of all of these compositions is to deny the characters flesh-and-blood autonomy and freedom. As happens so often in Sirk, objects, or other characters, create intrusive tensions, threatening to flatten out the space and draining the protagonists of wholeness. While newspaper reporter Burke Devlin (Hudson) is romancing the beautiful LaVerne (Malone), the

neglected wife of the pilot, Sirk frequently cuts to a party just outside, mostly dancing torsos whose anonymity gives them a spooky, almost extra-human presence. Then the motif of background intrusion is given its most dramatic and literal realization, as a character in a death mask bursts in on them. This moment is not only great in itself; it gains its full power and meaning from the way it echoes related visual patterns throughout, infusing its terrible life-denying meanings into those other intrusive moments as well.
Fred Camper

Date 1958

Nationality USA

Director Douglas Sirk

Cast Rock Hudson, Dorothy Malone

Why It's Key In perhaps Sirk's most terrifying moment, a character, functioning almost as an object, destroys two characters' attempt not only at authenticity but also at simple physical contact, reflecting the great theme of most of his work.

286

Key Scene **The burning of the Golden Pavilion** *Conflagration*

The novel *The Temple of the Golden Pavilion* was first published in 1956 and became one of Yukio Mishima's most successful works, both in Japan and internationally. Ichikawa's film adaptation, co-authored with his frequent collaborators, Natto Wada and Keiji Hasebe, overshadows most other screen versions of Mishima novels. Ichikawa extracted performances of great intensity from his two leading actors: Ichikawa as the young novitiate in a temple, tortured by family betrayals and a compulsive speech impediment, and Nakadai as the crippled cynic who both befriends and torments him. The final destruction of the temple's famous golden pavilion is an expression of long-suppressed emotion that provides a cathartic climax to a story of obsession, desperation, and spiritual crisis. Filmed in eerie darkness until the sudden eruption of fire, the sequence is a tour de force, with its visual impact matched by emotional release. All of Ichikawa's major films look magnificent, and this is no exception.

The cinematography by Kazuo Miyagawa (who photographed films by Kurosawa, Ozu, and Mizoguchi, as well as others by Ichikawa) is masterful in its dynamic camera movements, evocative lighting, and beautiful use of the widescreen format. The film helped to establish Ichikawa as a director of real substance: after a prolific period of development, making some 30 films in the decade after the end of the war, he had attracted international attention with *The Harp of Burma* in 1956. *Conflagration* confirmed his status, and rarely was Mishima served so well by filmmakers.
Andrew Pike

Date 1958

Nationality Japan

Director Kon Ichikawa

Cast Raizo Ichikawa, Tatsuya Nakadai

Original Title *Enjo*

Why It's Key This is the climactic scene of one of the best screen adaptations of a Mishima novel.

Key Scene **In the last shot, space opens up for the first time** *Some Came Running*

Dave (Sinatra) arrives in his midwestern hometown with Ginny (Shirley MacLaine) following him. Ginny loves him, but he loves Gwen (Hyer), a somewhat repressed teacher, and becomes friends with the gambler Bama (Martin). Like most of Minnelli's great late 50s 'Scope and color melodramas, this is about cycles of entrapment, characters caught in entanglements they cannot break free of: Gwen is stuck in her straight-lacedness, Dave in his lust(s), Ginny in her unblinking love for Dave, and as for Bama, he never takes his hat off. Basing his color scheme on the inside of a jukebox, Minnelli creates tightly wound compositions whose multiple surface planes function as ensnaring matrices: in Dave's last scene with Gwen, the symmetrical decor of her bedroom links lamp to lamp and curtain to curtain. When a hoodlum pursues Dave at a carnival, tracking shots follow the characters in a way that multiplies objects, piling color on color. When Ginny dies to protect Dave, we dissolve to her

funeral, a two-minute scene in a cemetery high above the Ohio River that literally reverses the film's vision. In three short shots, Gwen emerges from her car, a final close-up of her signaling that Ginny's selflessness has transformed her. The rest of the scene is filmed in a single take of more than a minute in length, stopping on Dave and then on Bama – who, in one of the most unaccountably moving gestures in all cinema, removes his hat. The camera then tracks past Bama to look directly down the river, into almost infinite distance. This most liberating composition of the film signals that more than one character has found freedom.
Fred Camper

Date 1958

Nationality USA

Director Vincente Minnelli

Cast Frank Sinatra, Dean Martin, Martha Hyer

Why It's Key At the film's very end, the characters in this multi-character melodrama find their way out of Minnelli's characteristic entrapments, as the camera offers a vision of freedom.

Key Person **Helen** *Howrah Bridge*

When *noir* came to India, it acquired melodramatic and moral overtones. The hero could be a product of the city, but the female lead was always a virginal village belle who was perpetually in distress. As her foil, a naughty girl was called for, someone who could be at home in a gang's den or a nightclub. Enter Helen Richardson (screen name: Helen) in beads, sequins, tassels, feathers, veils, scarves, rhinestones, and gold-flecked make-up. Helen's dances usually aimed at seducing the hero and with him the audience.

Howrah Bridge begins with a young man who has fallen into bad company. He sells a family heirloom to pay his gambling debts but is murdered and the money taken from him. His brother (Kumar) comes to the city to uncover the truth about the death and is taken to a nightclub. There, Helen dances her first hit solo, "Mera Naam Chin Chin Choo" ("My Name is Chin Chin Choo") lip-synching to Geeta Dutt's singing.

After this, Helen became a marker of the underbelly of the city in Hindi cinema, the bad girl who danced, smoked, had a good time and died in the hero's arms if she had any lines to speak. (In most of her 700-odd films, she didn't. She danced and disappeared.) She worked in most of the other Indian-language cinemas, too, and was still gamely hoofing it, without a shred of irony, as late as 1981. She redefined what feminine sensuousness meant in Bollywood and acquired a huge, devoted fan following.
Jerry Pinto

Date 1958

Nationality India

Director Shakti Samanta

Cast Ashok Kumar, Madhubala, Helen

Why It's Key The Anglo-Chinese danseuse Helen begins the career that will redefine femininity in Bollywood.

Key Person **Chhabi Biswas**
A monumental performance *The Music Room*

Structured like a classical Indian raga, *The Music Room* is an ironic study of a melancholic aristocrat, Biswambhar Roy (Biswas), immured in a desolate mansion by a placid river that can turn treacherous. Roy's wife and young son had drowned four years ago, on the night he was hosting a soiree in his prized music room. Roy is stirred from his habitual apathy when the upstart moneylender Ganguli (Gangapada Basu) aspires to become a patron of arts. Roy believes that only noble blood and cultured breeding can bestow this status; to prove it, he wastes the last of his gold coins to host a last grand soiree – a proud man imprisoned in past glory, oblivious to the changes in rural Bengal of the 1920s.

    With delicate inflections and bursts of flamboyance, Biswas' monumental performance complements the film. He uses changes in body language, from swagger to ambling stoop, and (despite being, in real life, tone-deaf) conveys a music connoisseur's spontaneous appreciation with subtle gestures and fleeting facial expressions. As the candles flicker and die in the magnificent gloom of the salon, Roy's final triumph is followed by a *Lear*-like passage of rage, despair and mortal fear. After a boastful toast – in English, linking the aristocrat to the colonial rulers – to his noble ancestors, he dissolves in inchoate terror on seeing a spider crawl up the leg of his own portrait. Biswas creates sympathy for the music lover and yet leaves room for the director's ambivalent view of his protagonist and the class he represents.

Maithili Rao

Date 1958

Nationality India

Director Satyajit Ray

Cast Chhabi Biswas

Original Title *Jalsaghar*

Why It's Key A famous stage actor, Biswas incorporates a calculated theatricality into his acting for the camera.

Key Scene **Kenaoui listens to his beloved having sex** *Cairo Station*

SPOILER

Films had been made in Egypt since the 1920s, but they were mostly formulaic musicals and comedies. Youssef Chahine, who studied cinema and theatre in America and loved the musicals of Fred Astaire and Gene Kelly, made his first feature in Cairo in 1950, aged 24. Four years later, in *The Blazing Sky*, he gave Omar Sharif his first part, but it was his twelfth feature, *Cairo Station*, that became a landmark. Prefiguring Alfred Hitchcock's *Psycho* by two years, it charted the mental decline of Kenaoui (played by Chahine himself), a crippled newspaper seller in Cairo, whose sexual frustrations become murderously warped. In one remarkable scene, the object of his affections, Hanouma (the voluptuous Rostom), is having sex in a railway barn. Kenaoui is outside. The camera tracks in on his anguished face, then goes close on a railway track as it is bent by a train, then tracks closer onto Kenaoui and a bottle of Coca Cola he's holding, then back to the bending track, then to Kenaoui as he smashes the bottle, then dollies away from him, as if in disgust. The bending track is Chahine's metaphor for Kenaoui's mental tensions. The director's cutting and framing, his rhythm and contrast between static close-up and gliding tracking were reminiscent of Sergei Eisenstein's films. No Arab or African filmmaker had rendered thought so cinematically. Years later, Chahine said, "Freedom of expression is not given, it is taken." This film marked the first moment when he really took this freedom.

Mark Cousins

Date 1958

Nationality Egypt

Director Youssef Chahine

Cast Youssef Chahine, Hind Rostom

Original Title *Bab el hadid*

Why It's Key Chahine's breakthrough is the first great Arab film and the first great African film.

Opposite *Cairo Station*

Key Scene **The coffin is in the cellar!**
Dracula (Horror of Dracula)

Vampire hunter Van Helsing (Cushing) has learned that Count Dracula (Christopher Lee) has visited well-to-do Mina Holmwood (Melissa Stribling), drunk her blood, and put her under his spell. The question that baffles Van Helsing and Mina's alarmed husband (Gough): how did Dracula get into the house, which the two men have spent the whole previous night guarding? To revive their spirits while they ponder this problem, Holmwood asks his maid (Olga Dickie) to fetch them a bottle of wine. "Oh, sir, I don't like to," the woman replies hesitantly; "Madam told me the other day that I must on no account go down to the cellar." Here Fisher cuts to a shot of Van Helsing, who, for about three seconds, stares in silence, as the significance of what has just been said sinks in. Then he leaps up and dashes to the cellar, where, sure enough, he finds the earth-filled coffin where Dracula rests during the day.

The moment in which understanding dawns on Van Helsing is a great acting moment. It depends, of course, on staging, composition, and cutting – elements under Fisher's control – but it exists, essentially, because of Cushing: his appealing combination of the cerebral and the athletic, the exquisite skill with which he paces his performance. It's a small moment from a film with many big ones, but such small moments deserve attention, too: they provide the reason for the audience to believe in the big ones.
Chris Fujiwara

Date 1958

Nationality UK

Director Terence Fisher

Cast Peter Cushing, Michael Gough, Olga Dickie

Why It's Key A great acting moment becomes, here, a great moment of cinema.

Opposite *Dracula*

Key Speech **"Here I was born, and there I died"** *Vertigo*

SPOILER

Visiting the giant redwoods in a Northern California national park, Madeleine (Novak), a mysterious and haunted blonde, and Scottie (Stewart), the detective who has become obsessed with her while investigating on behalf of her concerned husband, look at a cross-section of one of the long-lived trees, its rings marking the passing of many centuries. "Their true name is *sequoia semper virens*," Scottie tells her, "always green, always ever-living." Madeleine, who believes herself the reincarnation of an ancestor named Carlotta and thus doomed, puts her fingers on two rings, which are only marginally separated. "Here I was born, and there I died," she says. "It was only a moment for you; you took no notice." Then she wanders off and disappears among the trees, momentarily convincing the troubled Scottie that she really has disappeared; he finds her and starts pressing her about who she is and her recent suicide attempt ("what was there inside that drove you to jump") but, being neither Madeleine nor Carlotta, she evades his queries and asks to be taken somewhere into the light. Like so much of their relationship – which later turns out to be a sham that disguises several stranger truths before it almost becomes real again – their cross-purposes conversations and Madeleine's half-revelations haunt Scottie after he believes Madeleine has died. In this most fairy-tale-like of mysteries, the hero and heroine are literally lost in the woods, surrounded by ancient magic – the solid, thick, tall trees are an inverse of the dizzying towers, ledges, and precipices that unnerve Scottie, and represent a world in which the elusive heroine is ultimately doomed to be reduced to another cut-down tree, tagged like a tourist attraction, preserved by a love which is also a living death. In another context, but with almost as much poignance and meaning, the scene is excerpted in Terry Gilliam's *Twelve Monkeys* (1995), where Madeleine's fatalism seems to apply to human civilization.
Kim Newman

Date 1958

Nationality USA

Director Alfred Hitchcock

Cast James Stewart, Kim Novak

Why It's Key It's the most eerily romantic scene in cinema.

Key Film *A Movie* A collage artist conquers cinema the first time out

Throughout much of his career, Conner has been a filmmaker without a movie camera. He turned to cinema after mastering collage and assemblage art, extending the central act of collage – juxtaposing bits of material on a surface – to juxtaposing bits of celluloid on a motion-picture reel. Most of his movies are "found footage" films, made from fragments of preexisting pictures located in archives, second-hand shops, and refuse piles.

Deciding that chase scenes are cinema's most popular trademark, Conner began his first movie, *A Movie*, by editing a great number of these into an uproarious sequence that begins with galloping cowboys and moves to stampeding animals, a freakish bicycle race, and other incongruous variations on the movie-chase motif. This ever-startling montage has the forthright (il)logic of a dream, reflecting Conner's roots in the Dadaist and Surrealist traditions. Ditto for the film's other segments, which may look haphazard on first viewing but are carefully organized around specific visual themes.

The soundtrack music is *The Pines of Rome* by Ottorino Resphigi, which suits the antic mood of the early segments. When darker, more despairing images ensue – a slaughtered animal, an air disaster, a starving child – the music grows more celebratory and triumphant, suggesting that modern humanity's sheer shamelessness leads us to take perverse pride in our sociopolitical sins. Guilt and contrition would be more appropriate feelings, but such unsettling emotions are exactly what ordinary movies are designed to distract us from. Conner's rigorously moral work is an unsparing antidote to the poison of mass-media mindlessness.
David Sterritt

Date 1958
Nationality USA
Director Bruce Conner
Why It's Key After honing his skill as a maker of collages and assemblages, Beat Generation artist Conner crafted a cinematic look at the dark sides of modernity, giving new life to "found footage" film in the process.

Key Scene **The spectacular amusement park scene** *Anticipation of the Night*

Perhaps because Brakhage expressed interest in the pre-linguistic seeing of babies, perhaps because this is his first major masterpiece, this film is often misunderstood as celebrating the freedom of children's seeing. Quite the contrary. It opens with a man's shadow falling across the frame, and it is through this unseen protagonist's eyes that we observe his travels as he tries to establish some connection to the world. But except for some brief bursts of light poetry, such as flickering shadows on the wall, the film is largely a depiction of abject failure. Whether observing landscapes from a moving car, or spiraling around a baby in a field, or moving his camera back and forth across an illuminated temple-like structure at night, Brakhage seems trapped in his own pathways much more than "dancing" with his subjects, though he was to do much of the latter in later work. His alienation is perhaps clearest in the amusement park scene. Kids on circular rides that rocket toward the camera just as quickly rocket away. Groups whirl by on a turning circular platform that keeps them locked in their own world. The people on a Ferris wheel are seen moving away from the camera. The alluring blaze of lights that form the background only heighten the shadow man's alienation from these fleeting human glimpses, and the mechanical movements of the rides are the severest versions of the almost mechanical repeating motions through which the camera depicts most of the film's world, trapping all in the kinds of fixed movements and mechanical rhythms that Brakhage's later work largely overcame.
Fred Camper

Date 1958
Nationality USA
Director Stan Brakhage
Why It's Key The protagonist's alienation from the world he travels in is made incisively clear here.

Key Scene **The failed director meets his creation** *Kaagaz Ke Phool*

It is now accepted that Guru Dutt is one of the greatest Indian film directors, but *Kaagaz Ke Phool*, the first Indian film in CinemaScope, divides his followers into those who think it's a pessimistic, self-indulgent portrait of the career of a film director and those who think it is his finest work ever. But few would argue about the work of his regular cinematographer, the autodidact V. K. Murthy, in this film. Suresh Sinha (Dutt) is a brilliant film director who falls in love with Shanti (Rehman), a star he creates. As she begins to succeed, he begins to fail, and in one of the key sequences in the film, they meet in an abandoned studio. During production of *Kaagaz Ke Phool*, Murthy pointed out to Dutt a beam of sunlight with dust motes playing in it, and the director gave him ten days to replicate it for this scene. Murthy tried many stratagems to produce the shaft of light but failed. Then he saw a technician playing with a mirror, focusing a shaft of sunlight on the wall, and thought,

"Damn everything, I will use sunlight and mirrors." A huge mirror was placed outside the studio to bounce light into it. This was caught by another mirror placed on the catwalk and reflected down on to the floor, creating the sunbeam. The scene is scored with one of the many superb songs (music director: S. D. Burman; lyricist: Sahir Ludhianvi) heard in the film. This one, "Waqt ne kiya kya haseen situm" ("What an exquisite trick time has played on us"), has become one of the all-time classics of the genre called the Hindi film song.

Jerry Pinto

Date 1959

Nationality India

Director Guru Dutt

Cast Guru Dutt, Waheeda Rehman, Johnny Walker

Aka *Paper Flowers*

Why It's Key Cinematographer V. K. Murthy gets sunlight to play sunlight inside a studio in an auteur's film about his own career.

Key Scene **The final shot** *The 400 Blows*

SPOILER

At the end of *The 400 Blows*, after various misadventures, 12-year-old Antoine Doinel (Léaud) is sent to a reform school by the authorities. He manages to escape during a football game and runs toward the sea; when he finally reaches it, he turns and looks into the camera: the last image suddenly zooms in and freezes. The shot shows that, if Antoine appears to be temporarily free, he can't in fact go anywhere else: he has to look back at what he has left behind in order to confront it sooner or later. François Truffaut's first feature film tackles the problem of juvenile delinquency with the desire to adopt from start to finish the troubled teenager's point of view, unlike movies such as Jean Delannoy's *Chiens perdus sans collier* (*Lost Dogs without Collars*, 1955). Truffaut's film brings to the fore the complete failure of society: the family circle, the education system, and the state have all been unable, at one point or another, to solve the issue in a convincing way. The very last shot

can also be interpreted, therefore, as a call for help, a questioning aimed at the spectators who are comfortably sitting in the cinema and who are, contrary to all expectations, taken to task by Antoine's direct and harsh look at the camera lens. This aesthetic disruption of the filmic spectacle, one of the many attacks on the cinema institution made by the French New Wave directors, is obviously as much a social stand as a political one.

Frank Lafond

Date 1959

Nationality France

Director François Truffaut

Cast Jean-Pierre Léaud

Original Title *Les Quatre cents coups*

Why It's Key It's the most famous freeze frame in cinema history.

Key Scene **Bidding for life**
North by Northwest

Roger O. Thornhill (Grant) has been chased across America, an inadvertent pawn of U.S. Intelligence and the unwilling target of a foreign intrigue. In the cornfields of Indiana, he has been attacked by a cropduster and has now returned to Chicago, soiled, outraged, and disappointed in Eve Kendall (Saint), a girl he met on a train, who seems just a little too surprised to see him alive again. He trails her to an auction gallery for a confrontation and finds her ensconced contentedly with the archvillain and his factotum. But the villain (Mason) also has thugs, and after he makes his exit with Eve, one of these (Williams), dagger in hand, blocks the exit. How can Roger get out alive?

Hitchcock delighted in exploiting his settings for dramatic effect, and the auction scene forms a perfect background in which he can arrange for Thornhill to display social acumen as a tactical weapon. This is one of the most delicate and complex interweavings of *mise en scène* and dramatic structuring in all of Hitchcock. As the auctioneer (Tremayne) flogs off item after item, Thornhill systematically begins to bid, thus keeping intact the decorum of the soiree and blocking his would-be assassin from creeping too near through the audience of Chicago aristocrats. But then he starts breaking the unwritten rules of the event, those invisible threads that keep social structure from flying apart at the seams. He offers far too little, he insults the quality and value of the objects on the stage (thus implicating his stuffy neighbors in the room as idiots), and finally provokes a man to scuffle, at which point the room explodes in disorder and the police are called. Roger is escorted out between two patrolmen, happy as a clam.

Murray Pomerance

Date 1959

Nationality USA

Director Alfred Hitchcock

Cast Cary Grant, Eva Marie Saint, James Mason, Martin Landau, Adam Williams, Les Tremayne

Why It's Key This scene is an excellent example of Hitchcock's use of narrative setting for establishing dramatic tension.

Opposite *North by Northwest*

Key Film *Hiroshima mon amour*
The twitching hand of a lover

It's almost 20 minutes into Alain Resnais's mesmerizing first feature, after an extended depiction of a night of lovemaking and conversation between a French film actress (Riva) and a Japanese architect (Okada), both married to other people, who've just met in contemporary Hiroshima. Their night is conveyed impressionistically, unfolding like a piece of music. She describes her visit to the Peace Museum, which documents in excruciating detail the effects of the atomic bomb dropped on Hiroshima on August 6, 1945, and he replies, "You know nothing of Hiroshima." We discover that she lives in Paris, and before that lived in Nevers, but we still know nothing about her past there. In the morning, dressed in a kimono and holding a cup of tea or coffee, she stands on a broad terrace, looking down at bicyclists far below, then returns to the bedroom where her lover still lies sleeping, his outstretched right hand twitching slightly. There's a sudden cut to a close-up of the twitching hand of her dying German lover in Nevers almost 15 years earlier, the camera quickly panning up to his blood-streaked face as she kisses him, although at this point we don't know who he is or where they are or anything else about them apart from the jolt of this traumatic moment. This may be the first such "subliminal" flashback in film history, a shock cut rendering an involuntary memory-flash of Proustian intensity, and much of the remainder of this remarkable feature will be devoted to unpacking it.

Jonathan Rosenbaum

Date 1959

Nationality France/Japan

Director Alain Resnais

Cast Emmanuelle Riva, Eiji Okada

Why It's Key It's probably the first Proustian shock cut in cinema.

Key Scene **Outing on the hillside** *Dil Deke Dekho* (*Give Away Your Heart and Then See*)

Nasir Husain's non-conflictual attitude towards tradition and modernity is best expressed in the music of *Dil Deke Dekho*. Neeta (Parekh) and her group of friends are on an outing in the hills. Raja (Kapoor), in an attempt to impress her, tells her that he is a reincarnation of the legendary singer Tansen, and Neeta challenges him to sing. He sings "Megha re boley" ("The clouds, they say…"), using the traditional imagery of the elements and the call to the beloved; the women of the hillside immediately respond to the call and come dancing to the hilltop where Kapoor is singing. The song is imbued with an exquisite and subtle sense of irony – evident to the women of the hills – brought about by the "modern" Shammi Kapoor, with his distinctive body-language, singing a song about nature.

In a smooth take-over from this mood, a rock 'n' roll band suddenly emerges, and Neeta sings "Meri jaan wah wah" ("My beloved, how great!...") in a duet with Raja, with her friends and the tribals doing their respective dance steps to the song. The lyrics of this second song, in contrast to the first, are completely situational and relate to the girl's coquettish assessment of Raja. This is one of the most benign juxtapositions of two modes of being and two modes of music, with playfulness towards both, in the realm of popular Hindi cinema. It is also symptomatic of Nasir Husain's vision of modernity and gender positioning, that the man playfully sings the "traditional" song "Megha re boley" and the woman a more westernized "Meri jaan wah, wah."

Rashmi Doraiswamy

Date 1959

Nationality India

Director Nasir Husain

Cast Asha Parekh, Shammi Kapoor

Why It's Key This multiple song sequence signals the future style of an important Hindi film director.

Key Scene **The punchline** *Some Like It Hot*

Whether it's true or not that *Some Like It Hot* is the funniest of all American comedies, it unquestionably has the most memorable ending. For most of the film, jazz musicians Tony Curtis and Jack Lemmon, unwilling witnesses of the St. Valentine's Day Massacre, have been hiding out in an all-girl band dressed in drag. Curtis has spent much of his time ringing the quick changes to romance delectable songstress Marilyn Monroe by doing a Cary Grant impersonation, while Lemmon has been fending off the advances of amorous, elderly millionaire Osgood Fielding, played, in a casting coup, by veteran comic Joe E. Brown. In 1959, older audiences would have remembered Brown as a former vaudevillian who enjoyed a brief career as a lead in comedy films made after the advent of sound.

When, in the boat at the end, Lemmon's "Daphne" tries to break the news gently, Osgood simply isn't having any. "We can't get married." "Why not?" "I'm not a natural blonde." "Doesn't matter." "I smoke." "I don't care." "For three years I've been living with a saxophone player." "I forgive you." "I can never have children." "We can adopt some." Finally, Lemmon removes his wig as he clinches the argument: "I'm a man!" And the philosophical Osgood, a silly smile on his face, returns with the immortal line, "Nobody's perfect," to which Lemmon can only end the film on a sublime double-take. Perfection!

David Stratton

Date 1959

Nationality USA

Director Billy Wilder

Cast Jack Lemmon, Joe E. Brown

Why It's Key The funniest last line of any comedy, ever.

Key Scene **An alcoholic cures his shakes in a hand close-up** *Rio Bravo*

Dude (Martin), the best friend of Sheriff John T. Chance (Wayne), has lost his friend's respect by turning into a drunk. Defending a jail besieged by a land baron whose "no good" brother is in prison for murder, the men hear a nasty melody, "the cutthroat's song," played by someone the land baron has hired. And suddenly Dude, who has had the shakes so bad he cannot hold his hands steady, perfectly pours his liquor back into the bottle without spilling a drop, responding to the felt pressure of the melody. Hawks's cinema grows outward from the smallest details and gestures of his performances. He builds his compositions and their flow organically, based in part on the appearances and body rhythms of his characters. Hawks is the opposite of a cinema formalist such as the Murnau of *Tabu* (1931), in which an inescapable fatalism rules the universe through compositions that seem to have existed since the dawn of time, or Lang, in which an extra-human machine can vitally alter the course of the narrative. In Hawks, every patch of light in the frame seems to grow out of his characters' faces, hands, and bodies; every cut seems to grow from their movements. It makes perfect sense that a key turning point in one of his greatest films would be expressed through a hand gesture, and one feels that the remainder of the film grows out of that close-up of Dude's hands: hand movements somehow become entire compositions.
Fred Camper

Date 1959

Nationality USA

Director Howard Hawks

Cast John Wayne, Dean Martin

Why It's Key Hawks's cinema builds on, and pivots around, the gestures of his characters, and this moment is one of the pivotal points of the film.

Key Scene **A horse called Tears** *The Wonderful Country*

The odyssey of Martin Brady (Mitchum), who has made a life in Mexico after a dark early event in his life, is as much internal as worked out in the action, and he does not wear his feelings too openly, though Mitchum's subtle acting lets us see them. When he does smile, it will likely be because of his beloved horse, Lágrimas (Spanish for Tears), a name profoundly meaningful for what the horse represents in his life if at odds with the measure of happiness their close companionship has brought him. Late in the film, after Brady has crossed the border to America and then recrossed to Mexico in a series of events that seem to have diminished his options to be at home anywhere, he rests at the home of Santiago Santos (Caruso) while Lágrimas recovers from a slight injury. A brief scene following the convalescence begins with a beautiful close shot of the horse, the camera then moving to Martin astride him; and Martin's joy in riding his horse once more, being with him, is touchingly evident (to Santos and his family, too, who watch with evident pleasure). *The Wonderful Country* is characteristically low-key and lyrical like this, and perhaps that is why it has not been widely recognized as the masterpiece it is, and as one of the greatest Westerns. In the context of the whole, under Parrish's brilliant, sensitive direction throughout, this is a moment imbued with deep emotion.
Blake Lucas

Date 1959

Nationality USA

Director Robert Parrish

Cast Robert Mitchum, Anthony Caruso

Why It's Key Parrish and his collaborators show how sensitive and reflective a mature Western can be, as the traditional bonding of a man and his horse is taken to a whole new level of affective meaning.

Key Speech "I *beg* the court"
Anatomy of a Murder

An important item in dramaturgical theory is the notion that a scene should have *steps*: separate phases that are clearly marked in the staging, building in some meaningful or pleasing way. Preminger is among cinema's most theatrical directors, in the best sense; for him, social life is always a theatre, a performance pitched to persuade or mislead. You can intuit the moments of calculation in his ever-acting characters precisely when they pause: calmly, for public effect; or quickly, during the fleeting off-beat in which they think up their next improvisation. In a crucial scene 86 minutes into *Anatomy of a Murder*, where lawyer Biegler (Stewart) manages to finally introduce evidence of a rape into his defense of a soldier (Ben Gazzara), you can gauge prosecution attorney Lodwick (West) and Biegler both playing to the crowd (the jury) in their different ways. Preminger literally lays out, in a wide-angle one-minute take, the steps: first Lodwick and Biegler draw level with each other before Judge Weaver (Welch); then Biegler moves a step forward to deliver a monologue that ends with the line "I *beg* the court …"; then he takes another step – now positioned quite close to the camera – and lowers his voice into a dramatic whisper to repeat, "I *beg* the court … to let me cut into the apple." After the Judge deliberates for a few agonising shots – another kind of Premingerian pause – the tension breaks; Biegler has won this point and the trial can continue.

Adrian Martin

Date 1959

Nationality USA

Director Otto Preminger

Cast James Stewart, Joseph N. Welch, Brooks West

Why It's Key It's a striking example of the importance of the calculated pause in Preminger's theatrical cinema.

Opposite *Anatomy of a Murder*

Key Scene **The theft on the train**
Pickpocket

Often called one of Robert Bresson's most accessible films, perhaps because of the concluding glimmer of redemption, *Pickpocket* is in fact one of the densest and strangest manifestations of the French master's indelible style. An enigmatic variation on Dostoevsky's *Crime and Punishment*, it's the story of a petty thief, a disaffected young Parisian named Michel (Lasalle) who picks pockets for a living, fancies himself beyond common morality, and pursues his vocation with an opaque obsessiveness.

In the curious opening titles, Bresson cautions, "The style of the film is not that of a thriller." And yet, distilled and elliptical as it is, *Pickpocket* promotes a kind of metaphysical suspense and even, during the brilliantly orchestrated scenes of theft in broad daylight, the excitement of a conventional thriller. Michel himself notes that his heart quickens in these moments. From the start, Bresson emphasizes the eroticism of pickpocketing: the physical proximity, the violation and penetration, even (in many cases here) the seemingly complicit glance between perpetrator and victim.

The muted delight of these encounters erupts into something like ecstasy in the film's best-known set piece. It begins at the Gare de Lyon, as a shadowy throng of thieves forms an assembly line at the ticket counter while the camera fixes on wallets, bags, and suitcases. The pickpockets then move on to a stationary train, pulling off a stealthy, delicate dance of removal and exchange within a compartment's narrow corridor. The choreography of the theft is breathtaking, but the precise framing and rhythmic montage are equally dazzling and hard to apprehend on a single viewing – feats of legerdemain worthy of the movie's master thieves.

Dennis Lim

Date 1959

Nationality France

Director Robert Bresson

Cast Martin Lasalle, Kassagi

Why It's Key This remarkable feat of choreography and montage is the greatest technical tour de force in a Bresson film.

Key Scene **Seetha's dance with a fake cobra** *The Indian Tomb*

There are two erotic temple dances performed inside a cave by Seetha (Paget) – the betrothed of the Maharajah of Eschnapur (Reyer), the hero's employer – in Fritz Lang's two-part 1959 remake of an exotic fantasy he coscripted with Thea von Harbou back in 1920. Thirty-odd minutes into *The Tiger of Eschnapur*, she performs at the foot of a huge statue of a goddess, briefly writhing within the palm of the statue's outstretched hand. And 40-odd minutes into *The Indian Tomb*, long after Seetha has fallen into a romantic relationship with the hero (Paul Hubschmid), she has to prove her innocence to the temple priests by dancing with a cobra. The cobra rises and then lunges to strike her, but the Maharajah kills it first, offending the priests by violating their sacred rites.

This has all the earmarks of high camp because the cobra, clearly a tawdry prop, is being pulled around with wires, and Paget is wearing a silver-colored bikini that's fit for a Las Vegas showgirl. But for all its kitschiness, this scene isn't camp at all because Lang believes in what he's showing on some level, and gives the scene the hypnotic intensity of a private obsession. In Seetha's first dance, both the Maharajah and the hero (more briefly) figure as the voyeurs of her performance, but the second time, even though the Maharajah is present, Lang's *mise en scène* implies that the only voyeurs who matter are neither the Maharajah nor the priests, just Lang and us – the only gods who really matter.

Jonathan Rosenbaum

Date 1959

Nationality West Germany/France/Italy

Director Fritz Lang

Cast Debra Paget, Walter Reyer

Original Title *Das indische Grabmal*

Why It's Key It's unabashed erotic kitsch from a visionary filmmaker.

Key Event
Fire at the Cinémathèque française

Film is fragile, subject to many insults, from poor processing to chemical decomposition to mold damage and even, in the case of nitrate stock, combustion when exposed to high temperatures or direct sunlight. As a result, tragedies abound in film history, starting on 4 May 1897 at the very dawn of film exhibition, when nitrate-based film ignited in the projector during a Lumière showing in Paris, killing 180 people. The majority of Fox Film's silent film inventory perished forever in 1937 when a storehouse in Little Ferry, New Jersey, exploded, raining burning celluloid onto bystanders. Even in a temple of international cinema like the Cinémathèque française, a still unexplained fire on 10 July 1959 destroyed 50 feature films, including some lent by the Polish archives, as well as the last complete print of Jean Renoir's *Le Tournoi dans la cité* and the only known print of the second part of Erich von Stroheim's *The Wedding March* (known as *The Honeymoon*), which had never been released in America. Some blamed the improvisational management style of the brilliant and contentious Henri Langlois, but later administrations presided over still more fires, not least one at the Rambouillet warehouse on 3 August 1980, when 300-foot high flames engulfed 20,000 films – half the film holdings of the Cinémathèque. Sadly, cellulose triacetate has not proven a reliable alternative to volatile nitrate, since this so-called "safety film" also decomposes, but in a different manner, so film archives continually seek funds to store their flammable collections in repurposed military fortresses and facilities built as bomb arsenals.

Robert Keser

Date July 10, 1959

Why It's Key The destruction of priceless films at the very place created to safeguard them demonstrated the need for funds to preserve the film heritage properly.

Key Scene **Hang tree**
Ride Lonesome

The characters in *Ride Lonesome* cross the desert toward a dead tree that's ghostlike, the destination of a bounty hunter named Ben Brigade (Scott). Brigade insists he's taking the killer he has in custody to a town called Santa Cruz, then the tree appears. Boone (Roberts), an outlaw competing with Brigade for his captive, knows this tree, a "hang tree" with a "jury limb," and so does Brigade. Night falls (an indigo day-for-night), and the men make camp near the tree with Mrs. Lane (Steele), a young widow they've saved from marauding Apaches.

If *Ride Lonesome* is the best of the seven westerns Boetticher made with Scott, it has a lot to do with this night scene, a dark idyll before the film's showdown. The tree looms in the background as the woman they've rescued crosses between the two men. While Boone stares at her, Brigade's gaze is fixed on the dead tree, which Boetticher contrasts with the blonde's shapely form. For Boone Mrs. Lane represents the possibility of a new life. For Brigade she embodies a past he's come to avenge. And for both men the tree is a death they may not escape.

Nothing is wasted in the stripped-down clarity of *Ride Lonesome*'s 80 minutes. This is the apotheosis of the classical western, which ends with Boetticher. The hang tree burns in the film's last shot, taking the genre with it.

A. S. Hamrah

Date 1959

Nationality USA

Director Budd Boetticher

Cast Randolph Scott, Karen Steele, Pernell Roberts

Why It's Key It's a definitive Western's defining image.

301

1950–1959

Key Scene **The mother's farewell to her daughter** *Imitation of Life*

The ostensible star of Sirk's greatest film is Lana Turner, playing an actress who neglects her loved ones for the sake of her career. But the most emotionally wrenching scenes usually center on Annie (Moore), the actress's African-American maid, and Annie's daughter, Sarah Jane (Kohner), a light-skinned young adult who's been passing as white.

Sarah Jane's decision to hide her racial background has caused grave conflict with her mother, whose pride in being black is rooted in personal dignity and loyalty to tradition. Annie's distress about her daughter's self-hatred starts when Sarah Jane is still a child, and grows almost unbearable when the young woman abruptly leaves home.

Desperate to see her just once more, Annie tracks her down to the nightclub where she works, finally promising to accept her wishes and bow out of her life. It's an anguished and humiliating moment for Annie, especially when Sarah Jane covers for her presence by pretending she's a former nanny. Annie goes along with the deception, since it allows her to bid Sarah Jane farewell for what will probably be the last time. Her grief is so palpable that even her daughter is moved, but since Sarah Jane can't say a proper farewell without revealing that Annie is her mother, she only says "Goodbye," then mouths the word "Mama" in silence.

That silence speaks more than any words could – about family heartache, about 1950s racism, and about America's inability to articulate the social and psychological schisms that threaten to ruin it.

David Sterritt

Date 1959

Nationality USA

Director Douglas Sirk

Cast Juanita Moore, Susan Kohner

Why It's Key This is among the most moving scenes in one of the few 1950s films to confront racism as a source of dysfunction in American family life.

Key Scene **The attack of the seat-buzzers** *The Tingler*

The greatest moment in the screen oeuvre of gimmick-meister William Castle comes in the climax of his insane horror film *The Tingler*, as a murderous crustacean purportedly created at the base of the human spine during moments of terror escapes from scientist Vincent Price and gets loose in a movie theater. Castle's *coup de cinéma* involved wiring up certain seats with devices that simulated the effect of the Tingler on selected patrons, and then setting them off as the onscreen monster rampages in the dark and Price seems to be addressing the audience directly. "Ladies and gentlemen, please do not panic, but *scream*! … Scream for your lives!" So much attention has been paid to the buzzing-seat gimmick – which was used in only a few theaters even during the original release – that film fans too rarely notice what an astonishing picture *The Tingler* is in every other way.

Kim Newman

Date 1959

Nationality USA

Director William Castle

Cast Vincent Price

Why It's Key This was the greatest single "gimmick" in the history of ballyhoo.

Opposite *The Tingler*

1950–1959

302

Key Scene **The hoodlum's girlfriend bids farewell to the camera** *Breathless*

SPOILER

Breathless is a good title for Godard's debut film, which races to the rhythm of its antihero's on-the-run lifestyle. But the original title, *À bout de souffle*, also points to other meanings – being winded, exhausted, or literally "at the end of breath," as the protagonist is when he dies. This ambiguity is appropriate, since the film foregrounds Godard's view of human nature as ambiguous, ambivalent, and inescapably enigmatic.

The plot centers on Michel (Belmondo), a Parisian crook who woos Patricia (Seberg), his American girlfriend, while waiting to flee the country. Late in the movie, Patricia picks up a phone and betrays Michel to the police, for reasons that remain obscure, even to her. When the cops arrive, a brief shootout ends with wounded Michel staggering grotesquely down the street, as if trying to escape – or catch? – his imminent death. Patricia can't understand his last words, "*C'est vraiment dégueulasse*," but a bystander translates them as "You are really a little bitch." A more accurate

translation would say "disgusting" or "sickening," with a hint of the "nausea" that Jean-Paul Sartre famously invoked. Speaking into the camera, Patricia says she still doesn't understand; then she turns her pertly coiffed head away from us, the filmmakers, and everything that's happened.

Few films offer a more richly ironic view of the unsolvable conundrums at the heart of the human condition. It might have seemed more cynical with Godard's original ending: he wanted Patricia to rifle through Michel's pockets; but Seberg, clearly in tune with Patricia's ornery spirit, refused.

David Sterritt

Date 1960

Nationality France

Director Jean-Luc Godard

Cast Jean-Paul Belmondo, Jean Seberg

Original Title *À bout de souffle*

Why It's Key The final ambiguous moments of Godard's first feature crystallize his existentialist views of society, human nature, and cinema itself.

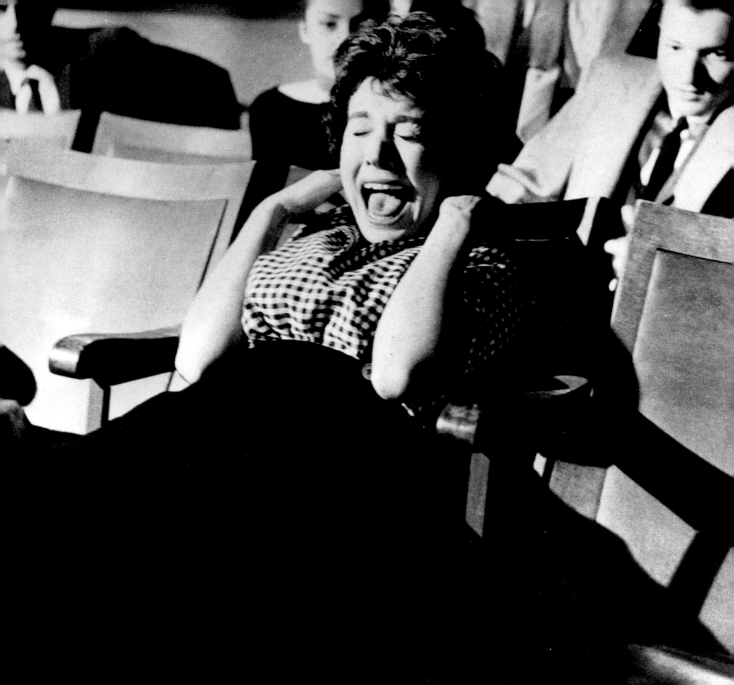

Key Scene **Proclaimed a goddess, Doyamoyee receives the sick Devi** *Devi*

Satyajit Ray made his mark in 1955 with *Pather Panchali*. Five years later, for *Devi*, he cast 18-year-old Sharmila Tagore as Doyamoyee, a young woman in an upper-class family whose father-in-law dreams that she is a goddess, whereupon, regardless of her will, she is treated as if she had spiritual powers. Cinematographer Subrata Mitra, one of the world's greatest, gives the whole picture a kohl-black, linear look. The story is classically told, and what fascinates is that although *Devi* seems to be fuelled by rage at the naïve theism of India, at the time its acting and filming could hardly be more restrained. In one remarkable scene, Doyamoyee sits on a platform, utterly still, as local peasants present their sick children to be cured by her. Her eyelids move just once, and then a tiny, momentary, startled look flashes in her eyes as she sees her husband (Chatterjee), who has just arrived to discover that she has been transformed into a deity. Much of mainstream Indian cinema is overacted or underdetailed. This is the opposite.

Mark Cousins

Date 1960

Nationality India

Director Satyajit Ray

Cast Sharmila Tagore, Soumitra Chatterjee

Why It's Key This is one of the stillest, most beautiful moments in Indian cinema.

Key Person **Roger Corman** A low-budget genie *House of Usher*

Corman has produced almost 400 movies as of early 2007, and directed more than 50. He was almost ridiculously prolific in his early career – in 1957 he made at least eight features – and swung easily from horror and science fiction to western, comedy, satire, sexploitation, and beyond. For many years American International Pictures provided an open-minded base of operations for his nonstop creativity and willingness to go against the grain – often portraying strong female characters, for instance.

He entered a new phase in 1960 with *House of Usher*, produced with a relatively high budget. Its success sparked a cycle of Edgar Allan Poe adaptations praised for their florid screenplays, kinetic camera work, and expressive color designs. Breaking with AIP in 1967 after a marketing dispute, Corman decided to concentrate on producing rather than directing. He founded New World Pictures in 1971, and in coming years the company gave formative opportunities to such fledgling auteurs as Martin Scorsese, Jonathan Demme, Ron Howard, Joe Dante, Jerry Zucker, and James Cameron, who were encouraged to embed political comments in their pictures. Corman also distributed major European art films in the United States market.

The decline of traditional B movies led Corman to establish Concorde-New Horizons in the middle 1980s, using more lurid content in an appeal to cable-TV and home-video audiences. Since then TV production has remained his primary focus. His influence has diminished in a changing media world, but his earlier contributions place him among the most intrepid American independents.

David Sterritt

Date 1960

Nationality USA

Director Roger Corman

Cast Vincent Price, Mark Damon, Myrna Fahey

Aka *The Fall of the House of Usher*

Why He's Key Ever resourceful and intelligent, Corman charted an influential course for low-budget moviemaking.

Opposite *House of Usher*

Key Event **Otto Preminger names Dalton Trumbo as screenwriter for *Exodus***

On January 19, 1960, Otto Preminger told the *The New York Times* that Dalton Trumbo, a member of the Hollywood Ten, was writing the screenplay for his upcoming production of *Exodus*, based on Leon Uris's best-seller about the formation of the modern state of Israel. What's more, Preminger said, Trumbo would receive credit on the film. The story broke on the front page the next day. On the one hand, Preminger assumed the role of a hard-nosed businessman, claiming that the decision to hire Trumbo was "simply realistic and practical and not political." On the other hand, he cited an ethical obligation to the public: "I think that to employ Trumbo and hide that fact under a fictitious name would constitute cheating the public," Preminger said. Finally, Preminger took aim at the Blacklist, in which all the major studios had taken part, without publicly acknowledging the fact, for the past 12 years. "I am not an authority on the Hollywood blacklist," Preminger said. "But assuming that such a

thing exists, I will not participate in it. In my opinion, it is illegal and immoral." Preminger's announcement was the beginning of the end of the practice. In subsequent years, the names of formerly blacklisted writers turned up on more films, and the Writers Guild of America has worked to give credit to writers for their uncredited work during the Blacklist.

Chris Fujiwara

Date January 19, 1960

Why It's Key For the first time, a Hollywood producer announced that he was using the services of a writer who was known to be blacklisted.

Key Event **Jerry Lewis uses the video assist for the first time**

For *The Bellboy*, the first professional film on which he would receive credit as director, Jerry Lewis faced a problem: since he would also star in the film, appearing in almost every scene, how would he be able to judge a take he had just shot? Past actor-directors had relied on co-directors, crew members, or their fellow actors for advice. Lewis needed a different solution – and found it in a system (which he had devised as early as 1956) that attached a closed-circuit TV camera to the film camera. The TV camera sent an image to a monitor that, placed in Lewis's sightline, showed him what he was getting on film, at the same time as he was getting it. He also found the system helpful in rehearsing actors and setting up shots.

The system caught on in Hollywood under the name "video assist." Lewis himself is in the forefront of directors who have made it a necessary part of their aesthetic and process, solidifying the conquest of time that cinema represents. To directors who lack the

knowledge and skill to use it as a creative tool, video assist offers just redundant gadgetry, a psychological crutch, and the illusion of an achievable perfection. The expanding hegemony of digital-video production may render the video assist redundant, but at this moment it remains a standard filmmaking option.

Chris Fujiwara

Date February 1960

Why It's Key Lewis's technological breakthrough enhanced filmmakers' options and extended cinema's dominion over time.

Opposite *The Bellboy*

Key Scene **Beginning to tunnel**
Le Trou

Five cellmates in La Sante prison have created the tools they will need to implement their escape plan. A sentry is posted to monitor the corridor with a tiny periscope made from a toothbrush and a fragment of mirror. The most experienced prisoner (Keraudy) takes a makeshift hammer to the layer of concrete that must be passed to dig a tunnel – and the soundtrack is shattered by the unconcealable, repeated crash of steel into stone. The audience's senses and nerves are jangled: how can this din be hidden from the guards? Are these men crazy? But the digging continues, and we realize that calculated risk is the rule in this environment. We are greatly accustomed to the dramatic convention whereby the form of the film is manipulated to support the audience's emotional investment: the scene is about concealment, so we expect the movie to take on the qualities of concealment by giving us the muffled sounds of digging, perhaps punctuated by a single,

teasing loud noise that is hastily suppressed. Jacques Becker's innovation here is nothing more than his willingness to show an event that is true to the characters' world rather than to the audience's dramatic expectations. We might recall that, in Becker's *Rendezvous in July* (1949), we heard for the only time in movies the sound of loud music bouncing jarringly off the stone walls of a small jazz club. There again, the price of originality was simply to set up a microphone and leave it at that.

Dan Sallitt

Date 1960

Nationality France

Director Jacques Becker

Cast Marc Michel, Raymond Meunier, Michel Constantin, Jean Keraudy, Philippe Leroy

Why It's Key The most suspenseful of all prison escape scenes is also the most plausible.

1960–1969

309

Key Scene **The dialogue-free central sequence** *Psycho*

SPOILER

At roughly the halfway point of this brilliant thriller, Marion Crane (Leigh) leaves the office of motel manager Norman Bates (Perkins) and goes to her room. There she calculates some figures on a slip of paper, indicating her resolution to return the money she's stolen, and steps into the bathtub for a shower while Norman spies on her through a secret hole in the wall.

The camera spies on her as well, and we see a blurry figure appear beyond the shower curtain, which is ripped aside as a mysterious murderer slashes Marion to death. Her dead eye stares sightlessly as blood and water wash together down the drain. From the house on the hill where Norman lives with his mother, we hear the scene's only words: "Oh God, Mother! Blood! Blood!" Norman then runs to Marion's room, cleans up the horrific carnage, stows her body and belongings in her car, and sinks the evidence in a nearby swamp.

This sequence's overwhelming force has many sources, including the visual rhymes linking a flushing toilet, the wasting of a life, the camera's voyeuristic gaze, and the swamp as an existential dumping ground for forbidden waste. But all such elements are enhanced by Hitchcock's decision to present the action without dialogue, giving it a primal imagistic power that bypasses word-based logic, plugging into the visual imaginary with terrifying ease. The master of suspense was also a master of silent cinema, and of its ability to touch the mind's most elemental emotional levels.

David Sterritt

Date 1960

Nationality USA

Director Alfred Hitchcock

Cast Anthony Perkins, Janet Leigh

Why It's Key By unfolding one of his most gripping, unsettling sequences without dialogue, Hitchcock demonstrates the power of pure cinema to evade the mind's usual emotional defenses.

Opposite *Psycho*

Key Event **See it from the beginning!**
Psycho

The phrase "this is where we came in" is still in common parlance, used whenever a tiresome situation recurs or someone repeats themselves – and yet it hasn't been applicable in its original usage for half a century. Before 1960, theatres rarely bothered to advertise start times and had a policy of continuous programming whereby an A feature, a supporting film, a short subject, trailers, a cartoon, and a newsreel played on a loop. Audiences turned up at cinemas whenever they felt like it and sat through all the attractions until they reached the point in a program when they had taken their seats, then left – often watching the end of a film hours before they got to the opening reels. Alfred Hitchcock can't have been the first filmmaker to be appalled by this practice, which implied an alarmingly casual attitude to his work and a fundamental disrespect for the director's position as a storyteller and an artist. But he was the first to do something about it. In *Psycho*, Hitch had a film with a

carefully contrived twist ending and a strategy of canny misdirection to point away from the revelation. On the film's first release, Hitchcock insisted cinemas not allow patrons to be seated once the picture had started – and then made this policy part of an ingenious, witty publicity campaign that stressed the terrifying secrets of the film. Posters insisted "No one ... BUT NO ONE ... will be admitted to the theatre after the start of each performance of Alfred Hitchcock's *Psycho*" or "it is required that you see *Psycho* from the very beginning!" and Hitchcock himself was shown pleading (perhaps in echo of the scripted curtain speech of Agatha Christie's play *The Mousetrap*): "Don't give away the ending – it's the only one we have!" All this made audiences all the more eager to find out the answers even if they had to wait two hours after buying their tickets before they could enter the auditorium.

Kim Newman

Date June 1960

Why It's Key Alfred Hitchcock changed the filmgoing habits of the world.

Opposite Alfred Hitchcock

Key Scene **Bare trees**
Eyes without a Face

Images of trees define Franju's black-and-white horror film, which is saying a lot considering a girl's face is surgically removed in it. Trees are white on black or black on white in *Eyes without a Face*. Lit by the headlights of a car, they emerge from the inky night like bioluminescent coral. During the day they are silhouettes against the cloudless late-autumn sky.

White trees are the first things we see in the film, and the last. A dead girl's white legs remind us of them; they stick out from behind the shiny black raincoat of the woman (Valli) dumping her body in the Seine. Cinematographer Eugen Shuftan is careful to get the reflections of trees on the hood of the surgeon's (Brasseur's) sedan whenever he pulls up – black on black. At a funeral bare trees point above the crosses stuck in the ground. The surgeon and his assistant lure a young woman (Mayniel) to the clinic in his suburban villa by mentioning trees: "You'll love it there, it's surrounded by trees." The film is matter-of-fact about

everything, but the word starts to sound ominous: "I'll show you your room, it looks out over... the trees."

Franju and Shuftan denature their trees. Without leaves they are skeletal, bodies without flesh. The sounds of nonmigratory birds and chained dogs barking dot the soundtrack like the trees line the picture. In *Eyes without a Face*, the natural doesn't exist anymore, but it hasn't been replaced by anything.

A. S. Hamrah

Date 1960

Nationality France

Director Georges Franju

Cast Pierre Brasseur, Alida Valli, Juliette Mayniel, Edith Scob

Original Title *Les Yeux sans visage*

Why It's Key Franju photographs nature in an unnatural world.

Key Scene **The feather scene**
Mughal-e-Azam (The Great Mughal)

1960–1969

Mughal-e-Azam was 14 years in the making, its cast changing several times and its budget expanding beyond the producer's worst nightmares to make it one of the most expensive Indian films of all time. When seeing the film, mostly shot in black and white, but with some songs in color, it is hard to imagine that this was anything other than a flawlessly smooth production. Ostensibly the story of the Great Mughal, Akbar (Prithviraj Kapoor), driven to fighting his rebellious son (Kumar) for the love of a slave girl (Madhubala), this popular fiction uses a historical narrative to show that India's Muslims are models of secularism, at a time when their loyalty was questioned after the creation by partition of the Muslim state of Pakistan.

Rumors abound about affairs between Hindi film stars, but Dilip Kumar declared his love for Madhubala in a court case over a film contract. This avowal added excitement to the scenes of the lovers' meeting, in which the passion of the prince is elaborated through music, as the great classical musician, Bade Ghulam Ali, sings as the lovers are shot in close-up. Madhubala's beautiful and iconic face is motionless in ecstasy, as Dilip Kumar watches in adoration. From time to time they tease the audience by hiding their faces from the camera with a white feather, forbidding the audience's look but inviting their speculation and showing that Hindi cinema has its own ways of showing eroticism.

Rachel Dwyer

Date 1960

Nationality India

Director K. Asif

Cast Dilip Kumar, Madhubala

Why It's Key Although the sequence in the Mirror Palace is exquisite, this moment is perhaps the most erotic moment in the history of Indian film.

Key Scene **The stairs**
The Housemaid

SPOILER

The Housemaid begins quietly enough: a middle-class family of four moves into a two-story house, a symbol of wealth in postwar Korea. However, the new housemaid they have contracted (Lee) behaves in strange and unpredictable ways, taunting the children, catching rodents with her bare hands, and showing an unhealthy interest in a bottle of rat poison. When she seduces the husband (Kim) and becomes pregnant, the stage is set for the housemaid to overturn the Confucian hierarchies of the household.

Director Kim Ki-young, nicknamed "Mr. Monster" for the perverse energy that runs through his work, gradually ratchets up the tension in this film to a level that few of his contemporaries outside of Hitchcock could match. The penultimate scene takes place on the stairway, which has already been the site of the miscarriage of a fetus and the death of a young boy. Having fallen completely under the housemaid's influence, the husband drinks poison with her in an act of double suicide. However, moments short of death, he decides to go to his wife. From the second floor he sets off down the stairs, with the housemaid begging him not to, hugging his left leg and staring up into his eyes. With each downward step he takes, her head slams into the stair below.

There is much that is unforgettable in *The Housemaid*, from the jaw-dropping performance of Lee Eun-shim to the film's stunning reversal in its final moments, but somehow the "thump, thump, thump" of the housemaid's head stands out as the crowning touch.

Darcy Paquet

Date 1960

Nationality South Korea

Director Kim Ki-young

Cast Lee Eun-shim, Kim Jin-gyu

Original Title *Hanyeo*

Why It's Key This is the emotional climax of an overlooked masterpiece.

Key Scene **The protagonist finds a camera store shaped like a camera** *The Flower Thief*

Taylor Mead takes a beatnik-like, picaresque romp through San Francisco. A childlike innocent, he steals a flower, finds a large teddy bear that he makes his companion, rides a cart downhill, and hangs out with a variety of characters. There are chases through the streets that recall silent comedies, as do the film's improvisatory rhythms and Mead's performance, with his sometimes exaggerated expressions. The old Army film stock Rice shot this feature on produces washed-out, sometimes indistinct images that suit the work's fugitive spirit. Trying to connect with people and objects, Mead often seems to succeed. He finds a closed camera store that's shaped like a camera, and, standing in front of it, purports to turn one of its large "dials." This single image encapsulates his approach: the world is, or should be, his plaything. At the same time Rice's compositions are surprisingly formal, and the contrast between his film's block-like images and free spirit gives this wonderful work its animating tension. Stark black-and-white images often resemble sketches in which dark and light forms collide, paralleling the fixed urban structures and the city's dramatic topography that Mead's antics seek to transform into toys.

Fred Camper

Date 1960

Nationality USA

Director Ron Rice

Cast Taylor Mead

Why It's Key Playing with the oversized dial on the camera front as if it's a real control, Mead exemplifies this film's playful approach to the world.

Key Scene **Rafe lifts his shovel over his shoulders** *Home from the Hill*

Once a year Texans in this film's small town clean their family graves. Town matriarch Hannah Honeycutt (Parker) finds Rafe Copely (Peppard) digging weeds from his mother's plot in neglected Reprobate's Field. "Perhaps you remember her," says Rafe.

She does. Rafe is the bastard spawn of a liaison between her husband, Wade (Robert Mitchum), and Ann Copley, a "sandhill tacky," as Wade will ungallantly put it. Rafe is both philosophical and ever so slightly bitter about his status as Wade's unacknowledged son. Rafe's query starts a chain reaction that destroys what's left of the Honeycutt marriage, but also begins his own healing.

Hannah walks away. Minnelli dissolves to a shot of Rafe walking alongside a river. He carries the shovel over his shoulders, his arms over it, his hands reaching out as if he were a prisoner in stocks. Bronislau Kaper's music swells. He's passed from the stark world of the graveyard to a green world of renewal and there he encounters his half-brother, Theron (Hamilton), having a picnic with his girlfriend Libby (Patten).

Rafe had been instrumental in bringing Libby and the shy Theron together. He's attracted to Libby too. The future of all three characters is determined this very day in this splendid melodrama, which, with Minnelli's *Some Came Running* (1958), completes a diptych of mid-century life in small-town America, films where gentler dreams are crushed by rough, rampaging male sexuality, personified here by Mitchum's man's man, whose macho code poisons the life of everyone around him. Rafe's tender work clearing his mother's grave is a prisoner's protest against that code, and the beginning of its downfall.

Gregg Rickman

Date 1960

Nationality USA

Director Vincente Minnelli

Cast George Peppard, Eleanor Parker, George Hamilton, Luana Patten

Why It's Key Minnelli creates a key emotional moment with a simple gesture.

Key Scene **Nita's song**
The Cloud-Capped Star

The face of a man, Shankar (Chatterjee), is in profile on the extreme-left of the frame, singing into the darkness. Halfway through the shot, the camera moves to starkly reframe the scene: we are suddenly aware that Shankar and his melancholic sister, Nita (Choudhury), sit close, side by side, but turned completely away from each other; now, at the pan's end, we see Nita, in profile on the extreme-right of the frame, singing into the darkness… It would be hard to find, beyond an iconoclast like Godard, such a perfect demonstration of the difference between what critic-filmmaker Alain Bergala calls the *arrangement* of a shot (situating the figures in a set) and the *attack* upon it chosen by the camerawork. Who but Ghatak, a proto-modernist working here within the traditional genre of melodrama, would have filmed this *mise en scène* in such a strange, disconcerting way? The whole of this bleak scene – in which the ever-sacrificial Nita begs her brother (who is soon to depart) to teach her a Tagore song – is marked by breaks, ellipses, "unmotivated" camera movements, unrealistic pools and speckles of light in a painfully obscure darkness, and above all a wild sound mix that passes from ambient noise through song to the echoing lash of a whip that expressionistically conveys Nita's increasingly manic despair. Every cut, every sound cue, is an event in Ghatak: rather than simply "establish" a scene, he restlessly withdraws and redraws it, according to the turbulent pressure of the emotions within it.
Adrian Martin

Date 1960

Nationality India

Director Ritwik Ghatak

Cast Supriya Choudhury, Anil Chatterjee

Original Title *Meghe Dhaka Tara*

Why It's Key No one but Ghatak would have filmed this bleak scene in such a restless, disconcerting way.

Key Scene **The brick wall**
Village of the Damned

SPOILER

In the final scene of this adaptation of John Wyndham's novel *The Midwich Cuckoos*, the alien children gather in their classroom to hear a lecture on atomic energy from their human teacher (Sanders). Planning to save the Earth from the children's designs of conquest at the cost of his own life, he's brought a time bomb concealed in his briefcase. Since he knows the children can read his mind, the teacher must try to think about something – anything – else until the bomb goes off. The leader of the children (Stephens) announces, puzzled: "You're not thinking of atomic energy – you're thinking of a brick wall." Indeed he is, as the film shows by superimposing, over huge closeups of his eyes and the eyes of the children as they penetrate his thoughts, a shot of a brick wall that slowly crumbles. Eventually his will relents, and the children turn to look at the briefcase – which at that moment blows up.

Why is this scene so memorable? The answer is clear. If the filmmakers' goal were merely to show the object of the character's thought, a shot of a simple brick wall would have been enough. But the scene also shows the process of thought – the gradual erosion of the man's concentration – through the metaphor of the wall crumbling. If I were now to encounter *Village of the Damned* for the first time, I might find this metaphor academic and literary. Having seen the film as a child, the idea seemed wonderful to me, and it still does.
Chris Fujiwara

Date 1960

Nationality UK

Director Wolf Rilla

Cast George Sanders, Martin Stephens

Why It's Key It remains a powerful cinematic metaphor.

Opposite *Village of the Damned*

Key Scene **Keiko feels the world turn**
When a Woman Ascends the Stairs

The staircase of the title is as narrow as a coffin, and not much better lighted. Every time that Keiko (Hideko Takamine) trudges up its steps, she feels boxed in, even before she reaches the top riser and the Ginza bar where she works. She has become "Mama" to her colleagues – not a desirable status, when you're a bar girl – and knows she cannot go on much longer charming the men. But she has debts to pay, and family members to support in other, equally cramped interiors. She must keep smiling at the customers while she tries to figure a way out.

In scene after scene, Mikio Naruse emphasizes the physical constraints on Keiko. So it feels all the more devastating when the turning point in her story, the moment when she knows hope is lost, happens outdoors. Once again, she has gone up, ascending not a staircase but a hill in the Tokyo suburbs. Here, at the top, she learns that her supposed escape route has come to a dead end.

But the camera does not stop. It moves with Keiko, surveying the vistas that have been absent from the film until now. For the first time, a landscape fills the CinemaScope frame, as Keiko turns and looks out over her city. A world of endless lives, endless possibilities, seems to unfold before her. None of them is hers.
Stuart Klawans

Date 1960

Nationality Japan

Director Mikio Naruse

Cast Hideko Takamine

Original Title *Onna ga kaidan wo agaru toki*

Why It's Key In a moment of stunning expressive power at the climax of Naruse's masterpiece, character, plot, setting, and camera movement all become one.

Key Scene **The screening of *Metropolis***
Paris Belongs to Us

Exactly two hours into Jacques Rivette's ambitious, 141-minute first feature, a complex and paranoid intrigue about Paris bohemians, we suddenly, and without warning, see the great "Tower of Babel" sequence from Fritz Lang's *Metropolis*. As this visionary sequence concludes with the hands of rebels reaching up towards Heaven, the film breaks, exposing a blank white screen. We find ourselves in a living room, where Rivette's heroine, Anne (Schneider), her brother, Pierre (Maistre), and many others have been watching the film.

It's a perfect symbolic representation of the tormented Parisian world Anne has encountered over the course of the plot – populated by a struggling theater group rehearsing *Pericles* and such exiles as a recently suicided Spanish composer and a victim of American McCarthyism, and characterized by intimations of a real or imagined worldwide conspiracy that Anne has stumbled upon. In short, it's a chaotic Tower of Babel that hovers over a frightening void. And

just as the jumble of languages produces incoherence, the mix of all colors produces white, yielding a blank screen.

The epigraph of Rivette's haunting feature is "Paris belongs to no one," and just as Betty's perception shifts back and forth between a surfeit and an absence of information, and Paris figures as either a comforting possession or a threat, Rivette's metaphysics alternates between a paranoid universe where everything signifies and an absurdist universe where nothing has meaning. In this film by a film critic, *Metropolis*'s Babel becomes the clinching cross-reference that clarifies the starkness of Rivette's design.
Jonathan Rosenbaum

Date 1960

Nationality France

Director Jacques Rivette

Cast Betty Schneider, François Maistre

Original Title *Paris nous appartient*

Why It's Key It's the first film quotation in a New Wave feature, and a far-from-gratuitous one.

Key Scene **The gangster's mother drops dead** *Shoot the Piano Player*

Like Godard's *Band of Outsiders* four years later, Truffaut's second feature flopped commercially and then became universally cherished, for similar reasons – a confounding of genre expectations that alternates laughs with shocks in a noirish context with adorable characters. One of the hero's brothers, a mischievous kid named Fido (Kanayan), gets kidnapped by two childish thugs who proceed to boast to him about their various possessions as they drive him away: Ernest (Boulanger) brags about his musical lighter (which plays the theme from *Lola Montès*), a fancy American pen, a suit from London, and "vented shoes of Egyptian leather," while Momo (Mansard) insists his supposedly silk scarf is actually made of metal and is Japanese. Fido refuses to believe it's either one, and when Momo swears, "If I'm lying, may my mother drop dead this instant," Truffaut cuts to an oval-shaped silent-film insert of a lady keeling over, kicking up her heels as she hits the floor.

In fact, there are a couple of other ladies who die in this movie, both lovers of the title hero (Charles Aznavour), and it isn't at all funny when they do. But part of Truffaut's methodology throughout is to keep pulling the rug out from under our feet. Gangsters are usually figures of menace, but these two are like the kids proudly showing off their toys to one another in the first scene of *Zero for Conduct* (1933), while Fido plays the somewhat patronizing but ultimately skeptical grownup. And Truffaut validates his skepticism with a breezy cutaway.

Jonathan Rosenbaum

Date 1960

Nationality France

Director François Truffaut

Cast Richard Kanayan, Claude Mansard, Daniel Boulanger

Original Title *Tirez sur la pianiste*

Why It's Key Truffaut proves conclusively that you can do anything in a movie.

Key Person **Melina Mercouri** *Never on Sunday*

Melina Mercouri's infinite energy was felt in every area she ventured. Tall and angular, with long arms and large mouth, she did not exactly meet the beauty benchmark. When on stage, however, playing Medea in Euripides' tragedy, her presence filled the theatre. Similarly, in cinema, her arresting charisma overpowered everything else onscreen.

Mercouri's fiery performance in *Stella* (1955) impressed the Cannes festival's jury, which nominated her for the best actress award. During festival parties Mercouri displayed the same sizzling energy and acquired quite a reputation for cheerful drinking and dancing. She attracted the attention of American émigré Jules Dassin, whose muse she was soon to become. Dassin immortalised her exuberance in his 1960 hit, *Never on Sunday*, in which she played a lively prostitute who challenges and subverts the stiff Puritanism of Westerners. So popular was the film that it was credited with single-handedly jump-starting the

Greek tourist boom of the period. Later on, during a period of exile from the Greek junta, Mercouri played in a Broadway stage version of the film, always with the same energy and to a great acclaim.

After her return to Greece she was elected member of the Parliament in 1977 and eventually served as Greece's cultural minister. In her political career, she displayed the same vigour and energy as in her acting; her outspoken campaign for the return of the Elgin marbles to Greece is still remembered as one of the most daring (albeit unsuccessful) episodes in the field of cultural diplomacy.

Dina Iordanova

Date 1960

Nationality Greece

Director Jules Dassin

Cast Melina Mercouri, Jules Dassin

Original Title *Pote tin Kyriaki*

Why It's Key The endless energy and charismatic presence of the Greek actress transcended the artistic profession and leaves durable traces in areas beyond cinema.

Key Film
L'Avventura The final gesture

The mystery and beauty of *L'Avventura* are only deepened by a modernity of style, thought, feeling, and detail that one might have thought would risk becoming "dated" but which, instead, becomes fresher and more poignant at each viewing. Antonioni's art has no difficulty surviving the negatives that have been hurled at it, all the complaints of "pretentiousness" and "trendiness." Jeered at and booed by the audience that first saw it at Cannes, *L'Avventura* was defended by its director as an analysis of its time: "Whenever something bothers him, man reacts, but he reacts badly, only on erotic impulse, and he is unhappy.... Starting out from this point of fear and frustration, his adventure can only end in a stalemate."

The great last shot of *L'Avventura* presents such a stalemate. Claudia (Vitti) discovers that her lover, Sandro (Ferzetti), has engaged in a random infidelity during a party at a hotel. She runs outside in a panic of emotion. Sandro follows and sits dejectedly on a bench, weeping. For a moment each is trapped in solitude: then, standing behind the bench, Claudia puts her hand on the back of Sandro's head. More than a sign of forgiveness, her gesture is, like many gestures in this film (which is so much about landscapes, urban and rural), a response to environment and mood – an exact acknowledgment of the uncertainty and disappointment that oppress both lovers and that find concrete depiction in Antonioni's concluding image of a man and a woman, seen from behind, on a plaza in 20th-century Italy, at dawn.

Chris Fujiwara

Date 1960

Nationality Italy/France

Director Michelangelo Antonioni

Cast Monica Vitti, Gabriele Ferzetti

Why It's Key *L'Avventura*, a breakthrough in European cinema, remains indelible for its depiction of modernity and mood.

Opposite *L'Avventura*

Key Person **Yukio Mishima**
Afraid to Die

Mishima plays a yakuza in prison. Another gang tries to kill him, but Mishima switches places with an unfortunate fellow and escapes. From then on, this strange yakuza will go on to escape from being the new leader of his gang, from his singer girlfriend, and from a girl he raped and who has become pregnant. Like a wounded beast, he tries to survive – until the girl convinces him to keep the baby. The result: he's killed while buying a toy for the future baby.

Masumura and Mishima were students together. Masumura and others were shooting films showing young rebels, sexually free and politically incorrect. Mishima was a successful and scandalous writer who preached for the renewal of the Japanese nation. The two creators shared an instinct for the domination of flesh and a passionate, tragic sense of life as something trans-human.

In this film, under his black leather jacket, the skinny body of Mishima suggests a Pasolinian androgynous hero, and the modernist camera catches the tragic feeling rising from Mishima's state of mind. He's burning from inside, looking for something greater than life that he can't find in the yakuza's rules, or in justice or social utopia or a woman's love. A heroic death is the only noble issue in this world: that's the meaning of the last sequence, in which Mishima dies on an escalator, spending his last energy climbing it in the opposite direction – a metaphor of a vain resistance to destiny.

Antoine Coppola

Date 1960

Nationality Japan

Director Yasuzo Masumura

Cast Yukio Mishima

Original Title *Karakkaze yarô*

Why It's Key Two giants of Japanese modernity meet: subversive writer Mishima and director Masumura.

FEDERICO FELLINI
LA DOLCE VITA
CINERIZ
MARCELLO MASTROIANNI · ANITA EKBERG
ANOUK AIMEE · YVONNE FURNEAUX · ALAIN CUNY · ANNIBALE NINCHI
MAGALI NOEL · JACQUES SERNAS ... NADIA GRAY
TOTALSCOPE
MARCHIO DEPOSITATO DALL'A.T.C.
GIUSEPPE AMATO

Key Scene **The Bassano di Sutri sequence**
La dolce vita

The climactic sequence of Federico Fellini's grand tour of Roman high and low life, this segment of the episodic epic begins in a café on the Via Veneto where the film's journalist anti-hero Marcello (Marcello Mastroianni) hangs out, the better to cull stories for the gossip sheet he writes for. He spies Nico, the German-born model, who announces she has just given up modelling – as she had at that point in real life. This folding of the actual over the fictional marks the ensuing sequence, which features both people "playing themselves" (actual counts and princes) and Fellini renditions of society "types" (a member of the aristocracy played by a Roman restaurant headwaiter). Hitching a ride in a friend's car, Nico takes Marcello to Bassano di Sutri, an ancient Roman villa where the dregs of what were once the "nobility" are in the midst of a rather dissolute party that no one seems to enjoy. But Fellini finds enjoyment, as a bean-thin dissolute princeling (Prunas) shows Marcello around a smoky living room filled with half-passed-out guests. Among them he finds someone he knows – Maddalena (Aimée) a sexually restless rich girl Marcello imagines he could "really" love. But she's spirited away by another guest for a tryst in one of the castle's many rooms while Marcello is taken off to an impromptu seance that turns into an orgy. Forgetting Maddalena, Marcello finds himself in the arms of a sharp-tongued Englishwoman (McDonald). At dawn the desiccated celibrants watch as their hosts join their maternal grandmother on her way to morning mass. The magisterial beauty of the sequence stems from Fellini's uncanny ability at tonal shift from elegant to louche. The result is a sequence that's satirical, lyrical, and oddly moving, quite unique in cinema.
David Ehrenstein

Date 1960

Nationality Italy

Director Federico Fellini

Cast Marcello Mastorianni, Anouk Aimée, Nico, Audrey McDonald, Oliviero Prunas

Why It's Key The best way to describe this scene is as a ghost story in which all the participants are still alive.

Opposite *La dolce vita*

Key Scene **By the quays**
Cruel Story of Youth

The rebel-lovers are looking for their friends. Members of leftist organizations, they are walking and screaming in a middle of a rally protesting the Japan/U.S. Security Pact. Looking at the red flags everywhere, the lovers seem to be fascinated but afraid of all this, too. They finally prefer to take a walk and lay down near the sea under the setting sun. The woman (Kuwano) falls in the water, but the man (Kawazu) refuses to help her reach the quay. They play this cruel game until they fall in each other's arms sweating, while sounds from the rally go by.

We can see that the lovers are aware of the sacrifices political activism will force them to make, and they are not sure of success in their bid for political utopia. Political frustration drives them to spend their energy in self-destruction by sex. Oshima's directorial choices lead us deeper into the scene: the unexpected locations near the quays, a sunny dark red coloration that makes the actors' skins shine strangely, and the irrational attitude of the characters force the spectator to focus only on the sensuality of the images. Then we can understand and, at the same time, feel what the young rebels are protesting: both within the society, and within political activism, they are losing the simple feeling of being alive.
Antoine Coppola

Date 1960

Nationality Japan

Director Nagisa Oshima

Cast Yusuke Kawazu, Miyuki Kuwano

Original Title *Seishun zankoku monogatari*

Why it's Key This sequence is a manifesto of the power of images to carry both rational ideas and emotional vibrations.

Key Scene **Christmas Day at the Sheldrake home** *The Apartment*

For once, the Academy of Motion Picture Arts and Sciences voters, who awarded six Oscars in 1960 to Billy Wilder's *The Apartment* – including Best Film, Direction, and Screenplay – got it right; this wasn't just the best picture of the year, it's one of the best of all American movies. The ever-cynical Wilder had been snapping at the heels of American society in the films he scripted and the films he directed prior to this, but never before, or since, was he able to mount such a full-frontal attack on the American Establishment. Jack Lemmon's C.C. Baxter is a pathetic cog in the wheel, a humble employee of a gigantic New York company who is given promotion solely because, as a bachelor, he is able to loan his apartment to married company executives who want to spend secret time with their secretaries. Baxter is hopelessly in love with Shirley MacLaine's sweet Fran Kubelik, an elevator operator who happens to be the mistress of big boss J. J. Sheldrake (Fred MacMurray at his most loathsome),

and the film's key sequence takes place on Christmas Day when, after a tryst with Sheldrake, Fran has attempted suicide. From his dreary, dark apartment, Baxter phones his boss in his elegant, spacious home in White Plains, where Sheldrake, wearing a new dressing gown with the price tag still in place, is embarrassed to take the call in front of the Christmas tree where his sons are opening gifts and his wife wants to know who's on the line. And back in the apartment, Fran recovers enough to realise that her lover wants nothing to do with her, at least not on Christmas Day. The scene is truly devastating.

David Stratton

Date 1960

Nationality USA

Director Billy Wilder

Cast Jack Lemmon, Shirley MacLaine, Fred MacMurray

Why It's Key This is Wilder's most caustic attack on American corruption and greed – and it's funny, too.

Opposite *The Apartment*

Key Speech **"Manners reflect one's descent"** *Seniman Bujang Lapok*

Ramli (P. Ramlee), Ajiz (Aziz Sattar), and Sudin (S. Shamsuddin), apply to be film actors. Sudin is told off by a non-Malay guard at the studio for his rough language. Ramli admonishes Sudin, saying that "manners reflect one's descent." However, this line is really aimed less at Sudin than, indirectly, at three other people: the studio manager (Kemat Hassan), a film director (Ahmad Nisfu), and a doctor (Ahmad Mahmud), who, using language unworthy of their status and position, have only harsh words for the three youths and others that they confront. Sudin may be forgiven for his rudeness as he is not highly educated, but what about these men who are older and should be wiser?

The phrase "manners reflect one's descent" is frequently used in Malay society to admonish without antagonizing. It has been appropriated in a number of films, including Yasmin Ahmad's *Gubra* (2005) and Din

C. J.'s *Ayahku* (2007). With numerous showings of *Seniman Bujang Lapok* on television, this line continues to resonate with new generations of viewers.

Hassan Abd. Muthalib

Date 1961

Nationality Malaysia

Director P. Ramlee

Cast P Ramlee, Aziz Sattar, S. Shamsuddin

Aka *The Nitwit Movie Stars*

Why It's Key This line of dialogue has entered the collective memory and is often repeated in everyday conversation and appropriated by contemporary filmmakers.

Key Scene **The parody of "The Last Supper"** *Viridiana*

The first film that Buñuel made in Spain upon his return from a period of more than 20 years in exile following the 1936-39 Civil War, *Viridiana* is best known for the controversy that surrounded its alleged blasphemy (a crown of thorns tossed into a bonfire, a cross disguised as a switchblade, among other moments), which led to the Spanish dictatorship's banning its distribution, with the backing of the Vatican. It is, however, a film that adheres to a long carnivalesque tradition of the popular grotesque (which includes religion) – one that has a particular resonance in the cultural legacy of Spain, from Quevedo to Goya, Valle Inclán, and Almodóvar.

The unforgettable climactic sequence of *Viridiana* commences shortly after former novice Viridiana (Silvia Pinal) and her rakish cousin Jorge (Francisco Rabal) leave the family estate to formalize ownership of their inherited property before a notary. In their absence, the group of beggars that the charitable Viridiana has sheltered invade the house and prepare a burlesque banquet, at which the assembled gathering pose for a mock group-portrait in a direct low-life parody of Leonardo's "The Last Supper." After metaphorically taking the beggars' picture by raising her skirts, the "photographer," played by actress Lola Gaos (whose distinctive features have graced many Spanish films), issues a cackle of laughter that signals the onset of riotous festivity involving cross dressing, food fights, dancing, ribaldry, violent encounters between deformed bodies – to the thunderous soundtrack of Handel's Messiah. This mixture of high and low culture generates a mesmerizing sense of the uncanny; the scene is uncanny, too, in the sense of *Unheimliche* (unhomeliness) that Freud identifies, in his reading of ghost stories, as the bourgeois anxiety produced by the perception of unruly strangers lurking within consciousness.
Steven Marsh

Date 1961

Nationality Spain

Director Luis Buñuel

Cast Lola Gaos, José Calvo

Why It's Key This famous sequence – a medieval feast of fools in which the order of things is inverted – is fundamental to forging the film's relentless black humor.

Opposite *Viridiana*

325

Key Scene **Shammi Kapoor's triumphant "Yahoo!"** *Junglee*

Often called the Elvis Presley of India, Shammi Kapoor was to twist, shake, jerk, and jive into the hearts of millions of young people. In the romantic comedy *Junglee*, Kapoor plays Chandrashekhar, an aristocrat who denies emotion and keeps himself under excessive self-control. On a visit to Kashmir, he meets a beautiful girl, Rajkumari (Banu). Chandrashekhar's love for Rajkumari transforms him, and he surrenders all inhibition to break into the song "Yahoo – Chahe koi mujhe junglee kahe…" ("Even if they call me wild"). His wild dance of freedom while descending the snow-covered slopes became a clarion call for the young in the 1960s.

This film heralded a new age of fun and romance in Indian cinema. Central to the universe of the Hindi film had been the unfolding of a moral or spiritual crisis, which needs to be resolved at the end of the film. With the liberatory cry of "Yahoo," a "Western" lifestyle, based on tourism and a consumerist modernity, became the new idiom of Indian cinema. Many films in the 1960s developed a tourist aesthetic of sights and outdoor action, taking their cue from the skiing and horse riding depicted in *Junglee*. Mimicking a colonial lifestyle, the new Western-style tourist-hero unapologetically endorsed a regime of fun. "Yahoo" is the moment of the birth of this hero and that regime.
Meenu Gaur

Date 1961

Nationality India

Director Subodh Mukherji

Cast Shammi Kapoor, Saira Banu

Why It's Key Shammi Kapoor's ecstatic call to freedom liberated an entire Indian generation from a cinema of restraint.

Key Scene **The girl, the sailor, and the ride at the fair** *Lola*

In his first feature, Demy taps deep into a dreamy and wistful romantic spirit while returning to the seaside town where he grew up. Here, a group of appealing characters cross paths in encounters at once fated and unexpected, none more magical than the visit to a fair by the 14-year-old Cécile (Duperoux) and the white-suited sailor Frankie (Scott), who have met once before and now meet again. In two rides they share, there is an exuberance and innocent eroticism, seen most of all in Cècile's face as she leans her head against his arm. Then, as they come off the second ride to Bach's first prelude from *The Well-Tempered Clavier*, the director hits one of the great lyric peaks of cinema, throwing a sequence of seven shots over about 30 seconds into slow motion – long a much-abused cliché in later years, but completely fresh and spontaneous here. In the slowed action, one sees the scene's choreography in all its beauty: the movements of the sailor's body as he lifts the girl, her look of ecstatic happiness as her hair whirls, their exhilaration as they run through the crowd. As if this were not enough, the scene doubles as evocation in the vivid present of a precious memory of the film's heroine (Anouk Aimée) – but that is its reflective aspect, only a ripple of why it stands on its own as a privileged moment that manages guilelessly to intimate, at the same time, both present happiness and sadness to come.

Blake Lucas

Date 1961

Nationality France/Italy

Director Jacques Demy

Cast Annie Duperoux, Alan Scott

Why It's Key As the New Wave breaks on the Nantes seashore, Demy's romanticism hits an early peak in a hallucinatory memory image occurring in a vivid present.

Key Scene **The bank robbery and subsequent chase** *Aimless Bullet*

Yu Hyun-mok's *Aimless Bullet* (as the title, *Obaltan*, is usually translated) is South Korea's best application of the cinematic approach pioneered by the Italian Neorealists. Set in Seoul after the Korean War, the film focuses on an extended family of seven living in a crudely-built shack, grappling with joblessness and despair. Made during a brief window of relaxed censorship between a student-led revolution in 1960 and a military coup in 1961, *Aimless Bullet* is a forceful indictment of the social system of its day. Nonetheless, coming 16 years after Rossellini's *Open City* (1945), the film is stylistically more in tune with later modernist work, with unusual camera angles and creative use of sound. Although little known abroad, *Aimless Bullet* has been named the best Korean film in history by local critics on multiple occasions.

One sequence in particular showcases the film's cinematic strengths, while referencing many of its political concerns as well. Unemployed veteran Yong-ho (Choi) is running from the police after having robbed a bank. The pursuit through real-life locations in downtown Seoul brings him past multiple signs of economic and social decay: an abandoned construction site, a row of poor fortune tellers, a labor demonstration, and a cavernous underground stream where a woman has hanged herself, with a crying baby still strapped to her back. Finally he is cornered in an empty factory; realizing he is lost, he throws the money into the faces of his pursuers, fires his gun in the air, and breaks into sobs. Another soul has slipped through the cracks.

Darcy Paquet

Date 1961

Nationality South Korea

Director Yu Hyun-mok

Cast Choi Mu-ryong, Kim Hye-jeong

Original Title *Obaltan*

Why It's Key This is the most haunting and politically-charged sequence in this early Korean masterwork.

Key Scene **The final reunion**
Splendor in the Grass

A film of harrowing, melodramatic intensity for most of its two hours and four minutes (which include violent conflicts of generations, frustrated romantic passion, youthful rebellion, a mental breakdown, a suicide, a fatal car crash), *Splendor in the Grass* quiets down for this beautifully low-key closing sequence in which Wilma Dean (Wood) – after a long stay in a mental institution following her breakdown – is taken by her friends to visit her former boyfriend, Bud (Beatty), now a farmer married to a nice Italian girl, Angelina (played with moving simplicity by Lampert). Bud and Angelina have a young child, and she is again pregnant. The somewhat awkward encounter of the three is so moving precisely because it is so devoid of pathos and because so much is left unsaid. The sequence, the exact opposite of the kind of hysterical "Method" acting for which Kazan's films are famous, is the visual equivalent of the lines from Wordsworth's "Ode" that give the film its title: "Though nothing can bring back the hour/Of splendor in the grass, of glory in the flower/We will grieve not, rather find/Strength in what is left behind" – and the poem, which, in an early scene, was somewhat childishly "discussed" by a stock old-maidish schoolteacher with a classroom of bored teenagers, suddenly illuminates one of the deepest truths that only "growing up" reveals.

Jean-Pierre Coursodon

Date 1961

Nationality USA

Director Elia Kazan

Cast Warren Beatty, Natalie Wood, Zohra Lampert

Why It's Key A melancholy ending to a tumultuous story of adolescent love brings closure to one of Kazan's major masterpieces.

1960–1969

327

Key Speech **Loridan's Place de la Concorde monologue** *Chronicle of a Summer*

As Marceline Loridan walks through the Place de la Concorde and into the beginning of the vast market space of Les Halles, Michel Brault's camera, mounted to the back of a small car, seems to float away from her. She speaks into the microphone of the Nagra recorder she carries with her, maintaining a powerful and disconcerting intimacy while her image recedes. "I was almost happy to be deported with you, I loved you so much…" Loridan's speech is mundanely poetic, delivered in a hushed tone as if in confidence – an effect that contrasts sharply with her public surroundings. She recounts her memories of deportation to the camps, her humiliation when an SS guard struck her in front of her father, and her difficult return to the rest of the family. "I saw everyone on the station platform: mom, everyone. They hugged me… I had a heart of stone. It was Michel who moved me. I said, 'Don't you recognize me?' He said, 'Yes, I think… I think you are… Marceline.' Oh… papa…"

This powerful moment is further complicated by Loridan's admission, later in this extraordinarily layered and self-critical film, that although the words were deeply felt, she was conscious of what she was doing, and hence "acting." The speech also drew the attention of director Jean Rouch's friend, filmmaker Joris Ivens, who asked Rouch after a preview screening: "Who was that beautiful girl?" Ivens and Loridan would become partners in film and life, together producing some of the most ambitious and challenging work in the history of documentary cinema.

Travis Miles

Date 1961

Nationality France

Directors Jean Rouch and Edgar Morin

Cast Marceline Loridan

Original Title *Chronique d'un été*

Why It's Key One of the most moving passages in documentary cinema, this sequence also illustrates the fluid mobility of the hand-held 16mm camera that would have such an indelible effect on the French New Wave.

Key Scene **The camera rushes repeatedly into Seyrig's arms** *Last Year at Marienbad*

Alain Resnais' most radical departure from Alain Robbe-Grillet's published screenplay for *Last Year at Marienbad* is his elimination of what Robbe-Grillet calls a "rather swift and brutal rape scene." In this ravishing puzzle film about an unnamed man (Albertazzi) in a swank, old-style hotel trying to persuade another guest (Seyrig), also unnamed, that they met and had sex there the previous year (illustrated throughout by subjective imaginings that might be either his or hers), Resnais includes only the beginning of such a scene, when the man enters the woman's bedroom and she moves back in fear. As in much of the film, Resnais makes the moment campy and melodramatic, as if dimly remembered from an old Hollywood movie. It occurs 70-odd minutes into a 94-minute film.

While the man's offscreen commentary insists, "No, no no! That's wrong – it wasn't by force...," Resnais retains only one of the scripted shots – "A long,

deserted corridor down which the camera advances quite rapidly" in which "the lighting is strange: very weak on the whole, with certain lines and details violently emphasized." But Resnais places this shot before rather than after the imagined physical contact. This weirdly overexposed, hallucinatory track ends with the camera turning down a separate corridor and then speeding repeatedly, in separate takes, into the welcoming arms of the woman, each time in a slightly different manner. An overheated sexual fantasy in a film chock full of erotic reveries, it marks a voluptuous climax to Resnais' masterpiece about imagination and longing.

Jonathan Rosenbaum

Date 1961

Nationality France/Italy

Director Alain Resnais

Cast Delphine Seyrig, Giorgio Albertazzi

Original Title *L'année dernière à Marienbad*

Why It's Key A climax of erotic reverie in a film of erotic reveries.

Opposite *Last Year at Marienbad*

Key Scene **Leper and church tower** *Touch Me Not*

Crisostomo Ibarra (del Mar) and Maria Clara (Vital) are walking down the street when they see a leper. Maria Clara, pitying the leper, gives him her rosary; the leper, grateful, prostrates himself. Then Sisa (Carino), driven mad by the loss of her son, approaches the leper and points to the church tower above them, saying her children are trapped there. Soldiers of the Guardia Civil drive the leper away.

It's a throwaway scene, one the viewer can easily miss, but the shot is Philippine colonial society crystallized in a single image: standing at ground level, the bourgeoisie; near ground level are the derelict and outcast; towering above all, aloof and unperturbed, the almighty Catholic Church's bell tower. Life flows along the roadway, represented by town folk making their way to church; they are halted by the spectacle of the leper, begging for alms. The shot at first glance presents the status quo – the underclass on his haunches, the middle class upright above him – but de Leon's camera

(which is itself at ground level) is angled just so that the leper, sitting closer to the lens than anyone else, appears to be the same height as the more respectable citizens. The Guardia Civil, on horseback, ride up and loom over everyone on foot – they represent the third power in the country, the secular government, with which the church sometimes competes for power over the people. Against a police force on horseback, and the bell tower above all, both middle and underclass are powerless.

Noel Vera

Date 1961

Nationality Philippines

Director Gerardo de Leon

Cast Eddie del Mar, Edita Vital, Lina Carino

Original Title *Noli Me Tangere*

Why It's Key This scene is a supreme example of Gerardo de Leon's *mise en scène* and the way his compositions can sum up themes, characters, relationships.

Key Scene **By the river**
Two Rode Together

One of John Ford's favorite tricks was getting actors to run through scenes and then printing the rehearsal as a final take. In *Two Rode Together*, a Western that Ford himself had little good to say about, he used this method to let a completely immobile camera film Richard Widmark and James Stewart hunkered down on a log by a river, variously washing their faces, lighting cigars, or trying out head movements and hand gestures as they carry on a desultory conversation about money, corruption, marriage, and the stiletto that Stewart's would-be fiancée carries in her garter belt. *Two Rode Together* is a busily plotted movie, crowded with characters and their respective back stories, so condensed that there is room for little beyond the most rapid exposition; it demonstrates how casually Ford could, at this late stage of his career, pack a scene's worth of plotting into a single shot. To summarize the film as a whole would involve talking about Indian-white relations, murder, lynching, sexual hypocrisy; but the little scene in which Widmark and Stewart pause a moment by the riverbank makes the rest of the movie simply that – a movie – as if in this scene we were privileged to share a moment of actual reality with actors who don't know they're acting. There is absolutely nothing major about the scene except for Ford's obsessive desire to capture such moments. Here he realizes almost perfectly – with a camera setup worthy of the earliest cinema – a relaxation of tension that makes the actors part of a space we share with them, going nowhere in particular but totally alive. Then Andy Devine pipes up and we're back in the movie.

Geoffrey O'Brien

Date 1961

Nationality USA

Director John Ford

Cast James Stewart, Richard Widmark

Why It's Key Three minutes and 51 seconds of inconsequential chitchat turn a cowboy movie into cinema verite.

1960-1969

331

Key Person **Marilyn Monroe**
The Misfits

SPOILER

Roslyn (Monroe) came to Reno to get divorced, but instead of returning home she falls in with cowboy Gay Langland (Gable) and his crowd. When he invites her to come "mustanging" with the boys, it sounds like a good time – until she learns it means buzzing wild horses with a biplane, then lassoing the confused and exhausted animals. Roslyn can't stand these beautiful creatures being reduced to "six cents a pound" dog chow, so she begs and pleads with Gay to stop, even offering to buy the animals from him. When he refuses and ropes a mare still with her calf, Roslyn can't take it anymore. She runs into the ruined flatlands, a serrated animal howl escaping her throat and cutting into the audience like a buzzsaw blade. In that agonized keen it all comes spilling out of the Method actress – the foster homes, the sexual abuse, the divorces, the beatings, the miscarriages, the hospitalizations, the abandonments, the drugs: the ever-widening chasm between her damaged self and the pliant, ethereal blonde batting her mascaraed eyes at the faceless patrons huddled in the dark. In less than two years after shooting this scene Monroe would be dead. *The Misfits* is her legacy, and this scene her condemnation of the public who stared and stared but never really saw how capable an actress she was. "You're only happy when you see something die!" she howls into the scorched desert, her words plucking at our guilty complicity in her demise. "I pity you!"

Violet Glaze

Date 1961

Nationality USA

Director John Huston

Cast Marilyn Monroe, Clark Gable, Eli Wallach, Montgomery Clift

Why It's Key Monroe foreshadows her epitaph in a wrenching scene from her final film.

Opposite *The Misfits*

Key Scene **The doll house**
The Ladies Man

Many of the pioneers of cinema – artists and theorists alike – dreamed of a total, Wagnerian synaesthesia, a synchronous fusion of all possible elements: color, movement, sound, architecture. In an explosion of '60s Pop Art design that gleefully transcends the kitsch barrier, Jerry Lewis gave us one immortal realisation of this ancient dream in *The Ladies Man*. Over three and a half minutes, we are introduced to the strange, surreal word of a girls' dormitory – starting with a sole student practising the trombone, and ending with dozens assembling in the dining room for breakfast. Every element begins with restraint and ends in excess: primary colors multiply (red, white, blue, green), the music builds to big-band swing, walls and even the glass in make-up mirrors disappear as the camera swoops across, up, down to take in all these interweaving morning actions of hair brushing, exercising, record sorting … And the entirety choreographed to the beat, girls bouncing and marching, like a musical sequence without an obvious "number." The scene is a dazzling declaration of the power and elegance of artifice, and a manifesto for Lewis's virtuosic control and freedom as a director (publicity materials proudly show him riding an enormous crane before the cut-out set). But its smooth "perfection" is deliberately undercut by discordant notes: the booming thud that accompanies frumpy Kathleen Freeman whenever she enters, and especially the perfectly still shots of Jerry himself asleep, ass in the air – oblivious to all this spectacle until an alarm clock wakes him up.

Adrian Martin

Date 1961

Nationality USA

Director Jerry Lewis

Cast Jerry Lewis, Kathleen Freeman, Helen Traubel

Why It's Key A dazzling declaration of the power and elegance of artifice, this scene is also a manifesto for Lewis's virtuosic control and freedom as a director.

332

Key Scene **Holly's party**
Breakfast at Tiffany's

The party in Holly Golightly's (Hepburn's) one-bedroom Manhattan apartment starts out slowly with Holly's agent (Balsam) telling stories about her to her new neighbor, Paul (Peppard). Is she a fake phony or a real phony? It's better to be a real phony. She's a real phony, they decide. The place begins to get crowded. Somebody's hat catches fire. Mag Wildwood (Whitney), a loud model, shows up with a couple of rich guys (Villalonga and Adams). Mag gets trashed and collapses. Nobody cares. When the booze runs out a delivery boy brings more. Oh yeah, lots of smoking. The mambo music is loud and the upstairs neighbor (Rooney, in an infamous performance) calls to complain. The phone is hard to get to – it's in a closed suitcase. The place is wall-to-wall people, well dressed but not stiffs. You can't move. People are making out in the shower. This is what people move to New York for and what they want out of a party once they're there: proximity!

The party scene is slapstick relief after all a lot of talking and setting up, which is what a party's supposed to be. Edwards doesn't cut it into pieces. It's all easy, loping group shots following people from place to place. Before this scene, Paul was a writer-schnook, now he starts to seem decent. Not so Holly, who exits on the arm of a fat, giggling millionaire and directs the cops upstairs to her apartment.

A. S. Hamrah

Date 1961

Nationality USA

Director Blake Edwards

Cast Audrey Hepburn, George Peppard, Martin Balsam, Dorothy Whitney, José Luis de Villalonga, Stanley Adams, Mickey Rooney

Why It's Key It might be the best party scene in movies.

Opposite *Breakfast at Tiffany's*

Key Scene **The woman goes behind the screen** *The Chapman Report*

This takeoff on the Kinsey Report includes several sequences in which interviewers ask suburban women about their sex lives. The interviewers are situated behind a screen, so that the women can remain anonymous, but one interviewer, Paul (Zimbalist), intrigued by one of his more troubled subjects, who leaves her purse behind, breaks confidentiality by bringing it to her home. She's upset when she recognizes his voice – but they start a romance. This transgression is echoed in the film's finest sequence, Paul's seven-minute interview with Naomi (Bloom). It's presented mostly in three long takes of two to three minutes; in the first of these, Naomi says, "I like to face the man I'm talking to," and suddenly walks to the other side of the screen. But she also walks back behind it, and then back again; in the last of the long takes, she remains completely behind it. What's at issue here, and in much of Cukor, is what characters think of themselves, and of each other, and

of their shifting interconnections, which are articulated through the ways the characters are placed in relation to each other and to the camera. Here, Naomi's boundary-crossing and ever-changing relationship to her interviewer connotes a severely unstable self. Bloom's superb performance as a "nympho" evokes that instability beautifully, with her nervous mannerisms and halting rhythms.

Fred Camper

Date 1962

Nationality USA

Director George Cukor

Cast Claire Bloom, Efrem Zimbalist, Jr.

Why It's Key In one of the greatest scenes in all of Cukor's work, his interest in the shifting relationships between characters, and between characters and the camera, is made explicit.

Key Scene **The image moves** *La Jetée*

Despite its unorthodox story and style, the 28-minute *La Jetée* has become Marker's best-known work. Its plot inspired Terry Gilliam's fantasy *Twelve Monkeys*.

The action takes place after nuclear holocaust has destroyed the world's surface. Working underground, surviving scientists pursue time-travel research, hoping to rescue their own era through appeals to the past and the future. Their experimental subject is a volunteer (Négroni) deemed suitable because since childhood he's been haunted by a mysterious memory: the face of a woman (Chatelain) struck with horror as a man falls dead before her on an airport jetty. Dispatched into the past, the traveler (never named) finds and falls in love with the woman. Later he visits the future, where shadowy beings provide the aid he asks for. Afraid of being discarded when he's no longer useful, he escapes into the past, where his loved one lives – only to discover that he himself is the dying man whose fate has haunted him.

La Jetée unfolds almost entirely in still photographs, which heighten the film's sense of barely grasped reality. This device also conveys Marker's conviction that photos are like memories, and vice versa – discontinuous images that must be reassembled by the one remembering (or viewing) if they're to form a meaningful pattern. Yet at one moment the movie does move, slipping into normal cinematography as the woman opens her eyes after sleep. Movement makes this the film's most memorable image – and its most stirring, since it's an image born of love.

David Sterritt

Date 1962

Nationality France

Director Chris Marker

Cast Hélène Chatelain, Jean Négroni

Why It's Key In a movie that doesn't move, telling its story through narration and still photographs, a single moving image takes on extraordinary emotional power.

SPOILER

Key Scene **Bringing down the house**
The Mad Fox

Until recently Japanese director Tomu Uchida wasn't really known in the West, probably because he used such a different range of styles – with remarkable results – that he was impossible to pigeonhole. Ironically, whoever has seen his 1962 masterpiece *The Mad Fox* will confirm that its most overwhelming aspect is its singular style. A widescreen period piece about love and betrayal, it heightens artificiality with intoxicating results. It is both a culmination of Uchida's interest in theatrical forms and his reflection on filmic representation. The actors walk over revolving stages into fields shining in Van Gogh yellow and through papier-mâché decor. A female character is tripled, her other incarnations being her twin sister and a vixen in human form, with the fairytale's foxes usually represented by actors holding up masks, though once even as animated flames. No wonder the hero (Okawa) goes insane (on the plot level it also has to do with his defamation and the deadly torture of his love).

Constantly changing from one mode of representation to the next, the film is jaw-dropping enough for most of its running time, but for the finale, Uchida pulls out all the stops. As the tragic hero realizes that his dreams of happiness and marriage have been an illusion, they collapse, quite literally: the stage-scenery-house in which he lived them, pulled by strings, topples in on itself. The world around him remains a stage, though, and in conclusion the narrator warns: "Love is just impossible, after all."

Christoph Huber

Date 1962

Nationality Japan

Director Tomu Uchida

Cast Hashizo Okawa, Michiko Saga

Original Title *Koya koi nasuna koi*

Why it's Key In this eye-popping, exhilaratingly artificial color fantasy, director Uchida achieves a singular fusion of film and theatre to delve into the mad protagonist's mind, then tops it off with a literal breakdown.

Key Scene **The slow-motion action sequence** *Confessions of an Opium Eater*

The casting of Vincent Price, by this time established in morbidly sensitive Roderick Usher-type roles, as an athletic adventurer who intervenes in a San Francisco tong war, is the least strange feature of this remarkable film by the producer of *Written on the Wind*, *The Tarnished Angels*, *The Incredible Shrinking Man*, and *Touch of Evil*. No mere cardboard exotic thriller, *Confessions of an Opium Eater* is the self-undoing of the cardboard exotic thriller, a free-floating, end-of-an-era pastiche in which what remains of the Hollywood tradition of the backlot Chinatown B-movie, here mixed with sub-Hollywood exploitation elements, comes out in its tattered finery for a grimy and poetic last hurrah before being sold off to the highest bidder. No sequence better reveals the film's determination to disintegrate before our eyes than the one that begins when the hero awakens in an opium den, where he has sought a respite from being interminably chased, only to realize his enemies have found him and

consider the chase still on. Still in the thrall of the opium he smoked, he runs away and crashes through a window – but he and his pursuers are in slow motion, and the soundtrack is completely silent. The sequence continues in slow motion across a succession of sets for several minutes. Action and narrative are paralyzed; Price, Zugsmith, and the audience spiral together through a bottomless dream of cinema. "Was I dead, or was I only beginning to live?" the hero wonders, and each viewer of this film must ask the same question.

Chris Fujiwara

Date 1962

Nationality USA

Director Albert Zugsmith

Cast Vincent Price

Aka *Souls for Sale*

Why It's Key Cinema disintegrates before our eyes.

Key Scene **The characters vanish as night falls on the city** *Eclipse*

SPOILER

Antonioni earned renown as a poet of the "empty frame" at least as early as 1960, when *L'Avventura* introduced a new cinematic idiom capable of expressing modern manifestations of anomie, alienation, and angst with unprecedented subtlety. Yet while this points to important aspects of Antonioni's art, the fact remains that his "empty" frames are emphatically not empty. They exclude major characters and narrative elements, but what they do include – significant objects, environmental features, and the like – have extraordinary resonance.

The final "scene" of *Eclipse* exemplifies this. The film's protagonist is a restless Roman woman (Monica Vitti) who gets romantically involved with a stockbroker (Alain Delon) despite misgivings about their compatibility. Parting after a tryst in the man's office, they agree to get together again that evening.

Neither of them arrives for the appointment, but Antonioni's camera does. For more than seven minutes, it peers into locations where the lovers have traveled – or might have traveled, or could have traveled – during the story, which we gradually realize has ended, even though the movie still continues. The characters are absent, but the city that contains them is more present than ever. The final image, of a shining streetlight in close-up, provides the crowning touch – an emblem of the dark, compelling beauty that emerges when pellucid day fades into lonely, mysterious night. Making a brave leap beyond psychology and individuality, Antonioni brings us to the realm of the eclipse – relinquishing his characters' identities, but gaining a vision of their world's larger, more enduring soul.

David Sterritt

Date 1962

Nationality Italy/France

Director Michelangelo Antonioni

Original Title *L'Eclisse*

Why It's Key Concluding his story of ungratified romance with a sequence devoid of characters and dialogue, the great Italian director makes one of his most profound statements on isolation and absence as defining conditions of modern life.

Key Scene **The circular shot** *The Manchurian Candidate*

Eleven minutes into the film, Captain Marko (Sinatra) experiences a nightmare where he's seated with other soldiers on a dais at a ladies' garden society meeting (called "Fun With Hydrangeas"). As the camera begins circling past the matronly speaker, the G.I.s bemusedly watch the audience of ladies in floral hats, but then when the camera completes its circle, the platform now sports huge blow-ups of Stalin and Mao, while a Chinese mind-control expert (Dheigh) explains that the American soldiers are subjects of brainwashing. Unsettling discontinuities ensue, as the lecturing dowager mouths the communist villain's words, and the audience alternates between horticulturalists and ominous-looking Asians gazing from amphitheater perches as if observing a surgery. Rather than merely recounting mind control, this hallucinatory six-minute sequence visualizes it, ending with the ultimate horror of a Congressional Medal of Honor winner (Harvey) obeying his programming to strangle a soldier. Some later cryptic repartee ("Are you Arabic?"), lifted directly from Richard Condon's source novel, sustains this introduction of a absurdist streak into mainstream cinema, which would inspire Kubrick's black comedy *Dr. Strangelove* (1964). The film's plot of a lone sniper's assassination attempt anticipated the Kennedy slaying in Dallas a year later, while inaugurating America's long run of paranoid thrillers from *The Parallax View* (1974) to *Syriana* (2005).

Robert Keser

Date 1962

Nationality USA

Director John Frankenheimer

Cast Frank Sinatra, Laurence Harvey, Khigh Dheigh

Why It's Key This forerunner of conspiracy thrillers uses a surreal 360-degree shot to embody the paranoid fear of mind control.

Opposite *The Manchurian Candidate*

Key Scene **A church with no God**
Winter Light

The middle panel of Bergman's "Absence of God" trilogy – which includes *Through a Glass Darkly* (1961) and *The Silence* (1963) – strikes to the heart of the matter immediately, in a lengthy opening sequence set during a midday Sunday service in a Lutheran church in bleak winter. A grim pastor, Tomas (Björnstrand), conducts the service, attentive to every detail of the church's rituals, the prayers and communion and music, although they seem only rituals, and ones in which he is not truly engaged. The very small congregation – most importantly Tomas's unhappy mistress, Marta (Thulin); a fisherman, Jonas (von Sydow); his wife, Karin (Lindblom); and the devout sexton Algot (Edwall) – dutifully listen and participate. It's only a small country village, but the church is impressively spacious and elaborate. Everything is there – except God. And that emptiness is resounding in the beautiful sequence, so precisely filmed and played, so evocatively suffused in Sven Nykvist's cinematography with the chill of that eponymous light. To find in the film that follows that Tomas has lost his faith, that one of the characters will commit suicide after Tomas cannot help him, that Tomas and Marta are in a crisis together as well, is no surprise. Yet in the paradox which pervades the entire trilogy, Bergman's *mise en scène* and the entire tone and texture of his realization suggest that even if nothing happens to dispel God's silence, God may in truth be profoundly present after all.

Blake Lucas

Date 1962

Nationality Sweden

Director Ingmar Bergman

Cast Gunnar Björnstrand, Ingrid Thulin, Max von Sydow, Gunnel Lindblom, Allan Edwall

Original Title *Nattvardsgästerna*

Why It's Key Bergman begins the second film of his great trilogy, which poses challenging questions about religious faith and the concept of God in a way no other filmmaker has, with an especially imposing and provocative sequence.

Key Scene **Humbert Humbert murders Clare Quilty** *Lolita*

Stanley Kubrick's *Lolita* begins with Humbert Humbert encountering Clare Quilty. Yet we might just as easily describe this film as beginning with James Mason (who plays Humbert) encountering Peter Sellers (who plays Quilty). In his book *Charles Laughton: A Difficult Actor*, Simon Callow discusses the clash of acting styles in Kubrick's *Spartacus* (1960), comparing Laurence Olivier's Crassus – "every point... cleanly and sharply indicated... as if there were a thin black line around the role" – with Laughton's Gracchus, who "has no such boundaries, no such definition." A similar point could be made about Mason/Humbert and Sellers/Quilty. Humbert sees his identity as comprehensible and of a piece: even when he behaves uncharacteristically by falling in love with a teenage girl, he does so as a deviation from a norm which itself remains unquestioned. With Quilty there is no norm from which to deviate, his impersonation of a psychiatrist being neither more nor less plausible than the "real" Quilty, with his blatantly fake American accent.

Lolita's opening confronts a methodical role-player with an anarchic improviser: Humbert has clearly written this "scene" in his head, but his attitude is mocked by a collaborator who refuses to go along with the plan, instead using Humbert's script as the basis for an extended comic riff in which identities are adopted and abandoned with bewildering rapidity. Ultimately, we must describe *Lolita* as beginning with Humbert failing to confront Quilty. Because, in Humbert's terms, Quilty is not there to be confronted. There is no *there* there, nothing but an abstract notion of performance which turns even the act of pleading for one's life into merely the last in a series of comic turns. Humbert can only kill Quilty by shooting at the painting behind which his nemesis has crawled, directing his anger towards that surface image which is all he has access to.

Brad Stevens

Date 1962

Nationality UK

Director Stanley Kubrick

Cast James Mason, Peter Sellers

Why It's Key This scene focuses, in a particularly revealing way, on notions of performance that are evident in all of Stanley Kubrick's films.

Opposite Lolita

Key Scene **Jules attends the funeral**
Jules and Jim

SPOILER

Set in the World War I era, this French New Wave masterpiece chronicles the deep friendship between Jules (Werner) and Jim (Serre), two energetic young intellectuals, and their shared affection for Catherine (Moreau), a freewheeling beauty who vacillates between them. She eventually marries Jules, but her regard for Jim never diminishes, and Jules would rather tolerate their infidelity than lose either one of them.

As much as one sympathizes with all three, it's clear this situation can't go on indefinitely without reaching some sort of crisis. Catherine herself comes to realize this, and one ordinary day she shows up with her new motorcar, inviting Jim to take a ride and telling Jules to watch them. Turning onto an unfinished bridge, she drives straight off the edge, killing herself and Jim in a catastrophic plunge.

What follows is even more extraordinary: We look on as their bodies slide into a crematorium furnace, what's left of their bones is ground into powder, and the remains are poured into urns for interment – all of which is a staunch reminder, in keeping with Truffaut's spiritual skepticism, that human beings are nothing but material in body and mind. Then, just when we might expect Jules to be most miserable, he leaves the cemetery with a spring in his step as the soundtrack plays a high-spirited tune. He has lost the people most precious to him in the world; but his existential ordeals are over, and he's entitled to a deep-seated sigh of relief.

David Sterritt

Date 1962

Nationality France

Director François Truffaut

Cast Oskar Werner, Jeanne Moreau, Henri Serre

Original Title *Jules et Jim*

Why It's Key The ending of this romantic drama brings tragedy and transcendence into a seamless whole.

Key Scene **The ghostly introduction to the long flashback** *Sahib Bibi aur Ghulam*

To those familiar only with Bollywood's cheery romantic optimism, this melancholic epic about the decline of an aristocratic family will come as quite a shock. It stars Guru Dutt as the lower class Bhoothnath, who arrives in colonial Calcutta and lodges in the mansion of the Choudhury family. Through his eyes we see their decadence and laziness. As an actor, Dutt was India's John Garfield; as a director, his baroque camerawork and fascination with social and psychological decline bring to mind Orson Welles. Though *Sahib Bibi aur Ghulam*'s credited director is screenwriter Abrar Alvi, its *mise en scène* and worldview are those of its producer and star, Dutt. Trained as a dancer and choreographer, he found commercial and critical success behind the camera in the 1950s until his very personal, *Citizen Kane*-like *Kaagaz Ke Phool* (*Paper Flowers* [1959]) proved too sombre for popular taste and flopped. The rejection shook Dutt's confidence, which explains why he didn't take a director's credit here. In retrospect, however, it's hard not to see *Sahib Bibi aur Ghulam* as his *The Magnificent Ambersons*.

In the famous opening sequence, Bhoothnath (Dutt) is a works director overseeing the demolition of the Choudhury mansion. Lunch arrives, and the workers disappear, leaving him alone, in the ruins, with his memories. The camera prowls through the dark building and past its cobwebs. Bhoothnath hears ghostly voices calling him back into the past, when the mansion was grand, when he was still learning about life. As they do so, images of those days flood the screen, and the film's back story begins. Indian cinema is full of flashbacks; this is amongst its greatest.

Mark Cousins

Date 1962

Nationality India

Directors Abrar Alvi and Guru Dutt

Cast Guru Dutt

Why It's Key This is one of the most elegiac moments in Dutt's career and in Indian cinema.

Key Scene **Cleo sings a song**
Cleo from 5 to 7

Cleo from 5 to 7 supposedly charts the two hours during which the eponymous heroine (Marchand), a pop singer, waits to learn if she has terminal cancer. But it's characteristic of Varda's playful shifts between objectivity and subjectivity that the film only lasts 90 minutes. Despite chapter headings that claim almost scientific precision ("Chapter VII, Cleo from 5:38 to 5:45 pm"), there are plenty of ruses for changing the registers of reality, sometimes even in the middle of shots.

The preceding chapter, "Bob from 5:31 to 5:38," half an hour into the film, charted the arrival at Cleo's Paris digs of her pianist-composer Bob (played by Legrand, the film's pianist-composer) and lyricist (Korber). They carry on like clowns while running through a lovely repertory of possible songs for her – including a catchy waltz in which Varda's camera keeps time by swinging back and forth between the characters. Then Chapter VII ushers in "Sans toi," a tragic torch song Cleo sings with sheet music while the camera slowly traces a crescent shape around her. But midway through the shot, the piano's replaced by an unseen orchestra, the lighting shifts to theatrical, and she's no longer reading the lyrics. By the time the song's over, Cleo's mood has darkened considerably, and she promptly shifts her wardrobe from white to black and sheds her wig. According to Varda, this sequence is "the hinge of the story," and "the circular movement which isolates Cleo is like a huge wave carrying her off."

Jonathan Rosenbaum

Date 1962

Nationality France/Italy

Director Agnes Varda

Cast Corinne Marchand, Michel Legrand, Serge Korber

Original Title *Cléo de 5 à 7*

Why It's Key All of a sudden, the heroine sees her life anew, and the film changes key.

Key Event **Oberhausen Manifesto**
The beginning of New German Cinema

Declaring that "the future of the German film lies in the hands of those who have proven that they speak a new film language," the 26 signers of the Oberhausen Manifesto in 1962 paved the way for a revitalized German cinema that would have lasting impact on world film.

Named after the Oberhausen International Short Film Festival, the manifesto came not a moment too soon. German movies of the post-Nazi period had no real agenda beyond bland entertainment; quality sank so low that in 1961 not one German picture was accepted by the Venice Film Festival; and ticket sales were headed toward the record low they reached in 1963. The only hope, according to filmmaker Alexander Kluge and his fellow Oberhausen activists, was to carve out a new conception of motion-picture creativity, transferring to feature-length productions the audacity and experimentation being displayed in low-budget shorts. More specifically, the group demanded "freedom" from three oppressive forces: the formulas of the entrenched film industry, the sway of special-interest groups, and the "outside influence of commercial partners." In sum, filmmakers should be allowed to create without hindrance, interference, or exploitation.

Subsequent events traceable to the manifesto include the founding of the Board of Young German Film in 1965 and the signing of the Film and Television Agreement in 1974, which provided money from TV networks to adventurous projects by Volker Schlöndorff, Rainer Werner Fassbinder, Werner Herzog, Wim Wenders, and other *Neue Kino* auteurs. Together they replaced "papa's cinema" with the filmmaking of the future.

David Sterritt

Date February 28, 1962

Why It's Key This statement of purpose by West Germany's boldest young filmmakers led to a German cinema liberated from encrustations of the past.

Key Scene **Cracking the conundrum**
The Exterminating Angel

This pitch-dark comedy is surrealistic from the start, when a brief but important moment – servants leaving their employer's house just before a big dinner party, for no reason they can pinpoint – happens twice, seen from two different camera angles. Why? For no reason you can pinpoint.

Many more repetitions take place during the course of the story, but they're no more striking than the strangeness of the story itself. Preparing to leave when the dinner party ends, the guests find various reasons to hang around a little longer, and gradually realize that nobody can leave the room, even though the door is wide open. Days pass; water and food supplies wane; nauseating stenches waft from a closet used as a toilet and another where a dead man is immured; outsiders prove as unable to enter the house as the occupants are to exit it; the once-dapper guests become frustrated, then outraged, then positively maddened by their plight. And suddenly a woman notices that all the room's inhabitants are in the exact places they occupied at the first moment of their dilemma – an insight that allows them to rush out the door, ending their entrapment. Until a few days later, when Sunday mass concludes, and even the priests seem stuck inside the church....

True to Bunuel's surrealistic sensibility, *The Exterminating Angel* is both wholly consistent – repetition is a guiding principle throughout – and wholly disorienting, for characters and spectators alike. All that's certain is that nothing is certain. And there's no reason you can pinpoint.
David Sterritt

Date 1962

Nationality Mexico

Director Luis Buñuel

Cast Silvia Pinal, Enrique Rambal, Augusto Benedico, Nadia Haro Oliva, Tito Junco, Patricia de Morelos

Original Title *El Ángel exterminador*

Why It's Key The last major work of Buñuel's great Mexican period expresses his irrepressibly surrealistic spirit through pitch-dark comedy, reminding moviegoers that aesthetic anarchy can be as funny as it is provocative.

Key Person **John Wayne B**urning down the house *The Man Who Shot Liberty Valance*

Notorious bandit Liberty Valance (Lee Marvin) is dead. Tom Doniphon (Wayne), the man who shot him, had built an addition to his house, to which he hoped to take as his bride the woman (Vera Miles) he had loved in silence. Ransom Stoddard (James Stewart), who will take the glory of the shooting, will also take the woman. After he realizes this, Doniphon gets drunk and staggers home. Seeing the room that must remain untenanted, he hurls an oil lamp into it, setting the house afire. It's up to Pompey (Strode), his helper/protector, to carry him out to safety and free the terrified horses.

The ferocious, exhausted grace of Wayne's performance stamps this scene indelibly. Lurching home across a crepuscular long shot, struggling with the size and weight of his own body: this is how Wayne, through Doniphon, conveys deep sadness and hopelessness, while the impassiveness, tenderness, and respect contained in Ford's view of him as he self-destructs are delegated to Pompey, the scene's heroic on-screen witness. In Doniphon's belated concern for his horses, Wayne conjures up the character's whole future (which will largely lie offscreen): a semi-conscious attempt to manage whatever can be saved from his wreckage.
Chris Fujiwara

Date 1962

Nationality USA

Director John Ford

Cast John Wayne, Woody Strode

Why It's Key John Wayne and John Ford prove themselves poets of despair.

Opposite *The Man Who Shot Liberty Valance*

SPOILER

Key Scene **Old friends advance against gunfire** *Ride the High Country*

Two former lawmen meet again after years of poverty. Steve Judd (McCrea) wishfully thinks he's still able to earn a decent retirement; Gil Westrum (Scott) is full of resentment and ready to deceive his old friend, stealing the gold they have to escort from mining camp to town. Honest Steve is bitterly disappointed by Gil's treachery and puts him under surveillance. Pursued and ambushed by young miners, the unruly Hammond brothers, the oldtimers have to join forces. Armed only with revolvers against their adversaries' rifles, they challenge the remaining three brothers, who fall into the trap and allow them to get closer. The two old friends advance together, and go on forward under fire till they kill the three. Fatally wounded, Steve asks Gil to keep away the young couple they have been protecting from the miners. "So long, partner." Gil rises, accompanied by the camera in a sort of shared salute, leaving Steve beneath the frame. Then a new shot returns to the dying man, also framing Gil's legs – "I'll see you later" – as he reluctantly turns away, leaving Steve to die privately. As Peckinpah himself does, when Steve looks up at the faraway mountains, then lies down out of frame forever, to die unwatched. The simplest, most logical dramatic buildup, told with easygoing discretion and respect for his characters by a filmmaker later famed for his slow-motion impact-edited bloodbaths.

Miguel Marías

Date 1962

Nationality USA

Director Sam Peckinpah

Cast Randolph Scott, Joel McCrea, Mariette Hartley, Ron Starr, James Drury, John Anderson, Warren Oates

Aka *Guns in the Afternoon*

Why It's Key The right distance and rhythm are arguably more effective than impressive dynamics, both in a gunfight and when shooting a scene.

Opposite *Ride the High Country*

Key Scene **Lawrence disappears behind the windshield** *Lawrence of Arabia*

Despite its superficial focus on battles and the mass movements of men, *Lawrence of Arabia* remains a curiously withdrawn film, an epic whose protagonist, T. E. Lawrence (O'Toole), dies in a motorcycle crash before the narrative is properly under way. Lawrence's intense involvement with events taking place on a wider historical stage is simply a way of avoiding interior problems by setting them within the context of a larger struggle: how insignificant is the pain caused by a burning match when that match can be transformed, in the space of a single cut, into the far more extreme heat of a blazing desert sun. Yet David Lean is primarily concerned with the collapse of Lawrence's project. Our final view of Lawrence is also Lawrence's final view: while being driven away in a jeep, he stands to look at some Arabs riding by; sitting down again, his face disappears behind the jeep's dirty windshield. Ejected from that arena in which he had hoped to be revealed as "extraordinary," Lawrence is rendered almost literally invisible. "Goodbye, Dolly. I must leave you. Though it breaks my heart to go" sing some soldiers who drive past at this point, and it is indeed as if, in leaving Arabia, Lawrence were saying farewell to a lover: to the "clean" landscape wherein he tried (but failed) to lose himself, but which ultimately revealed to him precisely those "dirty" masochistic and homoerotic aspects of his sexuality he wished to deny. "Well, sir. Going home" observes Lawrence's driver; but, as the anonymous motorcyclist who overtakes the jeep reminds us, "home" for Lawrence means only death.

Brad Stevens

Date 1962

Nationality UK

Director David Lean

Cast Peter O'Toole

Why It's Key This scene perfectly sums up the interior nature of this epic film.

Key Event **Elizabeth Taylor breaks $1 million for *Cleopatra***

She was supposedly kidding when she told the film's (first) producer, Walter Wanger, that she'd do it for a million dollars, but Wanger – who was eager to start production and had lost his original star, Joan Collins, to scheduling problems – said yes, and it was all gravy from then on. Taylor's contract specified 10 percent of the film's gross (a type of deal first negotiated by James Stewart for 1950's *Winchester '73* that tipped Hollywood's balance-of-power in favor of actors) plus $125,000 for 16 shooting days and another $50,000 for each additional week. Thanks to a troubled two-year production that was initiated in London in 1960, then aborted when Taylor fell ill, then restarted in Rome the following year, Taylor – who costarred opposite future fifth husband Richard Burton as Mark Antony – ultimately made $2 million for her acting services alone. And that wasn't counting the fee she collected as the owner of Todd-AO, an anamorphic widescreen process developed by Taylor's late third husband,

producer Michael Todd, that Taylor insisted be used on *Cleopatra*. In 1963, 20th Century-Fox filed a lawsuit against Taylor and Burton accusing them of causing production delays; Taylor countersued, and the resulting settlement added another $5 million to her take. It was all a drop in the bucket of the film's $44 million budget – which, inflation-adjusted to $295 million (in 2007 dollars), marks it the most expensive film ever made. But the affair still illustrates the extent to which post-World War II Hollywood is held hostage to movie stars, particularly on megaproductions built on glamorous names.
Matt Zoller Seitz

Date 1963

Why It's Key Taylor's then-unheard-of $1 million for starring in 20th Century-Fox's *Cleopatra* was the most buzzed-about payday of its time, but she ended up making a lot more than that.

Opposite *Cleopatra*

Key Scene **Tancredi and Angelica are absorbed into the dancers** *The Leopard*

Despite its apparent focus on the patriarchal figure of Prince Fabrizio Salina (Burt Lancaster), Luchino Visconti's *The Leopard* is primarily concerned with those changes undergone by Italian society as power passes from the older to the younger generation. The main representatives of the latter are Salina's nephew Tancredi Falconeri (Delon) and Tancredi's bride-to-be, Angelica Sedara (Cardinale). Although they are initially presented as positive individuals, being associated with a breaking down of rigid class barriers, Tancredi and Angelica are ultimately shown to embody that spirit of conformity which is sweeping the country and will render all of the proudly individualistic Prince's values superfluous. As so often in Visconti, this idea is communicated not through dialogue, but rather through eloquently expressive visual imagery. As Tancredi and Angelica embrace during the party sequence that occupies most of the film's final hour, a line of dancers is seen assembling elsewhere in the

palace. In one astonishing shot (to which Bernardo Bertolucci paid homage in *The Conformist*), a distant view of Tancredi and Angelica kissing is suddenly invaded, from the bottom-right-hand corner of the frame, by the line of dancers, which first approaches, then moves past the lovers, who are easily tempted to join it. The contrast between that simple joy and sense of community expressed by the dance and the pessimistically regarded forces of conformity with which it is linked gives the film in general, and this scene in particular, that melancholy quality one finds in much of Visconti's best work.
Brad Stevens

Date 1963

Nationality Italy/USA

Director Luchino Visconti

Cast Alain Delon, Claudia Cardinale

Original Title *Il Gattopardo*

Why It's Key This scene demonstrates Luchino Visconti's ability to express complex ideas through visual imagery.

Key Scene **The woman applies her eyeliner** *The House Is Black*

Iran is the only country in the world whose first great film was directed by a woman. In most countries in the world, cinema was an entertainment for the working classes, but in Iran, the Shah was the first movie buff. Until the 1960s, Iranian directors made formulaic comedies and musicals. In 1963, 28-year-old Forugh Farrokhzad, widely regarded as the country's greatest 20th-century poet, wrote, directed, and edited *The House Is Black* and set Iranian film on a new course. The 20-minute-long documentary takes place in a leper colony. Brilliantly photographed and cut with the staccato of Eisenstein's *October*, it creates a gripping dance out of the lives of the sufferers. Voiced-over by Forugh's poetry, it is much a prayer as a poem – one of cinema's greatest works of metaphysics. The significance of *The House Is Black* for world film has emerged slowly in subsequent decades. It inspired subsequent Iranian directors like Dariush Mehrjui and, in particular, Samira Makhmalbaf, who says that one

scene, in which a woman applies kohl eyeliner to her eyes, which roll as she does so, made her want to make movies. More generally, *The House Is Black* set the tone for poetic realism that would dominate Iran's art cinema for decades to come. Farrokhzad was killed in a car crash in 1967, aged just 32.

Mark Cousins

Date 1963

Nationality Iran

Director Forugh Farrokhzad

Original Title *Khaneh siah ast*

Why It's Key This is the most memorable moment in the first great Iranian film.

Key Scene **Silver Cine audition** *Contempt*

SPOILER

Earlier in *Contempt* Fritz Lang (playing himself) asks translator Francesca Vanini (Moll) the Italian word for "strange." The word lingers over unhappy husband and wife Paul (Piccoli) and Camille (Bardot) as they arrive at a movie theater where Paul is meeting Lang and an American film producer (Palance) to discuss their adaptation of *The Odyssey*.

They enter under a poster for *Rome Adventure* and leave under a marquee announcing *Voyage in Italy*. This is the transition scene between their stay at Cinecittà and their departure for Capri. Auditioning a girl singer to play a role in *The Odyssey* provides an excuse for the movie-theater setting. Italian pop blares as they take their seats across the aisle from each other, Camille next to Lang, Paul next to the producer. Francesca, translating their conversation, and a photographer taking flash pictures divide the space between them. The camera dollies back and forth as the singer dances across the stage mouthing the

song's lyrics out-of-sync in front of the movie screen. As the foursome talk the camera dollies across the aisle, too, but Godard cuts out the music so we can hear them speaking. It's simple, but jarring in the way it's "wrong."

This veiled criticism of dubbed sound in Italian movies, along with Lang's explanation of unity in Homer, mirrors the couple's break. Everything is separation: between image and sound in dubbed movies, between mankind today and in *The Odyssey*, between wholeness and Godardian fragmentation, between integrity and corruption, between lovers drifting apart.

A. S. Hamrah

Date 1963

Nationality France

Director Jean-Luc Godard

Cast Brigitte Bardot, Michel Piccoli, Jack Palance, Fritz Lang, Giorgia Moll

Original Title *Le mépris*

Why It's Key Abrupt shifts reflect a couple's separation.

Key Scene **Twisting at the spa**
8½

A chic elderly chanteuse has just finished singing a German ballad of the sort that made Zarah Leander famous, when the mood radically changes. The orchestra strikes up a twist, and we cut to a mass of black hair covering a woman's face. She whips back her head to reveal a triumphant smile, and as the camera pulls back, we see she's dancing with a white-haired older gentleman whose huffing and puffing shows he can't quite keep up with her. He smiles as she breaks away and continues to dance on her own. We've met this pair before: Gloria Morin (Steele), a "student" who has just completed her thesis on "The Solitude of Man in Contemporary Theater," and Mario Mezzabotta (Pisu), an old friend of the film's filmmaker hero, Guido Anselmi (Mastroianni). Ordinarily we'd cluck our tongues and cite the adage "There's no fool like an old fool." But Fellini is generous with both his "old fool" and the latter's young paramour. The contrast between 1930s "lesbian chic" (the singer is there to entertain the many sapphic spa-goers "of a certain age") and the youthful polymorphous perverse sexuality of Steele makes this movie moment unique.

David Ehrenstein

Date 1963

Nationality Italy

Director Federico Fellini

Cast Marcello Mastroianni, Barbara Steele, Mario Pisu

Original Title *Otto e mezzo*

Why It's Key Moving from the white aged singer to the dark young dancer, the scene folds one form of eroticism over another.

Key Scene **The former Auschwitz guard spots the former inmate** *Passenger*

Lisa (Slaska) is returning home to Germany after many years. Minutes before her boat departs she sees Martha (Ciepielewska) board. She recognises her at once as a Jewish POW from Auschwitz where she, Lisa, was a senior guard. Shocked, she tells her husband a version of what happened. Then, in an interior monologue, she tells herself the truth, which is more disturbing and horrific.

Passenger's Auschwitz scenes are staged with the hush and otherwordliness of a nightmare, and, for these alone, the film qualifies as a landmark. But something else is extraordinary about the film. Director Munk died in a road accident in 1961, aged 39, leaving most of the present tense of his film – the scenes on the boat – unshot. His assistant Witold Lesiewicz spent years completing it but decided to use only still images for the unshot scenes. So, when Lisa sees Martha walking up the boat's gangway, each is frozen in time. The subsequent scenes on deck, with Lisa and her husband, are too. As a result, only the past, its iniquities, and the wartime power struggle between the two women are alive, in moving imagery. Just as the director died, so it feels that the women did back then, too, and their meeting years later is a bad dream. Chris Marker famously used still images to great effect in *La Jetée*, made at exactly the same time as *Passenger* was completed. The effect here is just as striking.

Mark Cousins

Date 1963

Nationality Poland

Director Andrzej Munk

Cast Aleksandra Slaska, Anna Ciepielewska

Original Title *Pasazerka*

Why It's Key One of the best films about the Holocaust, *Passenger* benefits from being incomplete.

Key Film *Blonde Cobra*
The systematic derangement of the cinema

Sometimes he's a child, and sometimes he's a nun named Madame Nescience, and sometimes he's a "man of imagination suffering pre-fashionable Lower East Side deprivation and consumed with American 1950s, '40s, '30s disgust," as filmmaker Jacobs describes the hero of this almost indescribable movie. He's played by Jack Smith, director of the 1963 underground classic *Flaming Creatures* and an actor who embodied the anti-art exuberance of unfettered Dadaism as unstintingly as anyone ever has.

Smith's performance in *Blonde Cobra* was originally shot by filmmaker Bob Fleischner for a pair of underground monster-movie comedies he was directing. Fleischner abandoned the project and gave the footage to Jacobs, whose editing made it even more anarchic, including long passages of sound without picture. Jacobs also recorded a soundtrack of songs and monologues, setting the mood for Smith by playing ancient 78-rpm records from his collection. In a

particularly bold maneuver, Jacobs wrote screening instructions calling for a radio to be turned on – playing talk rather than music – at two precise points during the movie. This injects another element of aleatory disorder, adding to the liberating chaos of the experience and making every exhibition of the film unique.

Blonde Cobra has been called the masterpiece of Baudelairean cinema, a subgenre of which Jacobs and Smith have been the reigning, and arguably the only, practitioners. But it's equally appropriate to invoke another French poet, Arthur Rimbaud, whose call for a "systematic derangement of the senses" finds its cinematic apogee in the collaborations of these mad improvisational wizards.
David Sterritt

Date 1963

Nationality USA

Director Ken Jacobs

Cast Jack Smith

Why It's Key The tragicomic antics of performance artist Jack Smith, edited with Dadaist panache and juxtaposed with the sound of live radio, are a rollicking example of the Baudelairean cinema he and Jacobs pioneered.

Key Scene **McQueen soars the barbed wire on his motorbike** *The Great Escape*

P.O.W. escapee Virgil Hilts (McQueen) is fleeing on a motorcycle, Nazis in hot pursuit. After so many minutes of camp prisoners tunneling toward freedom, the open countryside offers exhilarating hope. But high barbed wire fences keep thwarting Hilts's (and our) narrative of escape. Then, the miracle: in a merging of the character with the so-cool actor playing him, Hilts pauses, guns his bike's engine, and effortlessly zooms up over the barrier. In any packed movie theater, the crowd will gasp audibly as the feat happens. This is the magic of movies, so often linked – from Méliès on – to the marvel of flight. It's easy to understand why *The Great Escape* is a venerated object of action cinema.

But the moment of flight is fleeting indeed. Hilts surmounts the barrier only to confront another that, when he tries to soar again, defeats him. Crashing into the barbed wire, he is recaptured. Despite its title's rah-rah promise, *The Great Escape* refuses the uplifting pleasures of classic Hollywood adventure to hint

instead at a downbeat fatalism that increasingly represents the darker side of the 1960s, a decade caught between a buoyant Age of Aquarius and undertones of "sympathy for the devil." From *Punishment Park* to *The Prisoner* to *Cool Hand Luke* and to *The Great Escape*, imprisonment becomes an apt metaphor for the decade.

The Great Escape signals a last gasp of the old Hollywood machinery trying to tell rousing tales of simple heroism even as times have changed. Virgil's flight – and its dismal aftermath – capture a fraught moment in both social and cinematic history. It remains perhaps in memory both because it is so magical and also because we know it didn't last. History is there to remind us of that.
Dana Polan

Date 1963

Nationality USA

Director John Sturges

Cast Steve McQueen

Why It's Key It's a great moment in the history of action cinema, all the more thrilling because so wondrous and unexpected.

Opposite *The Great Escape*

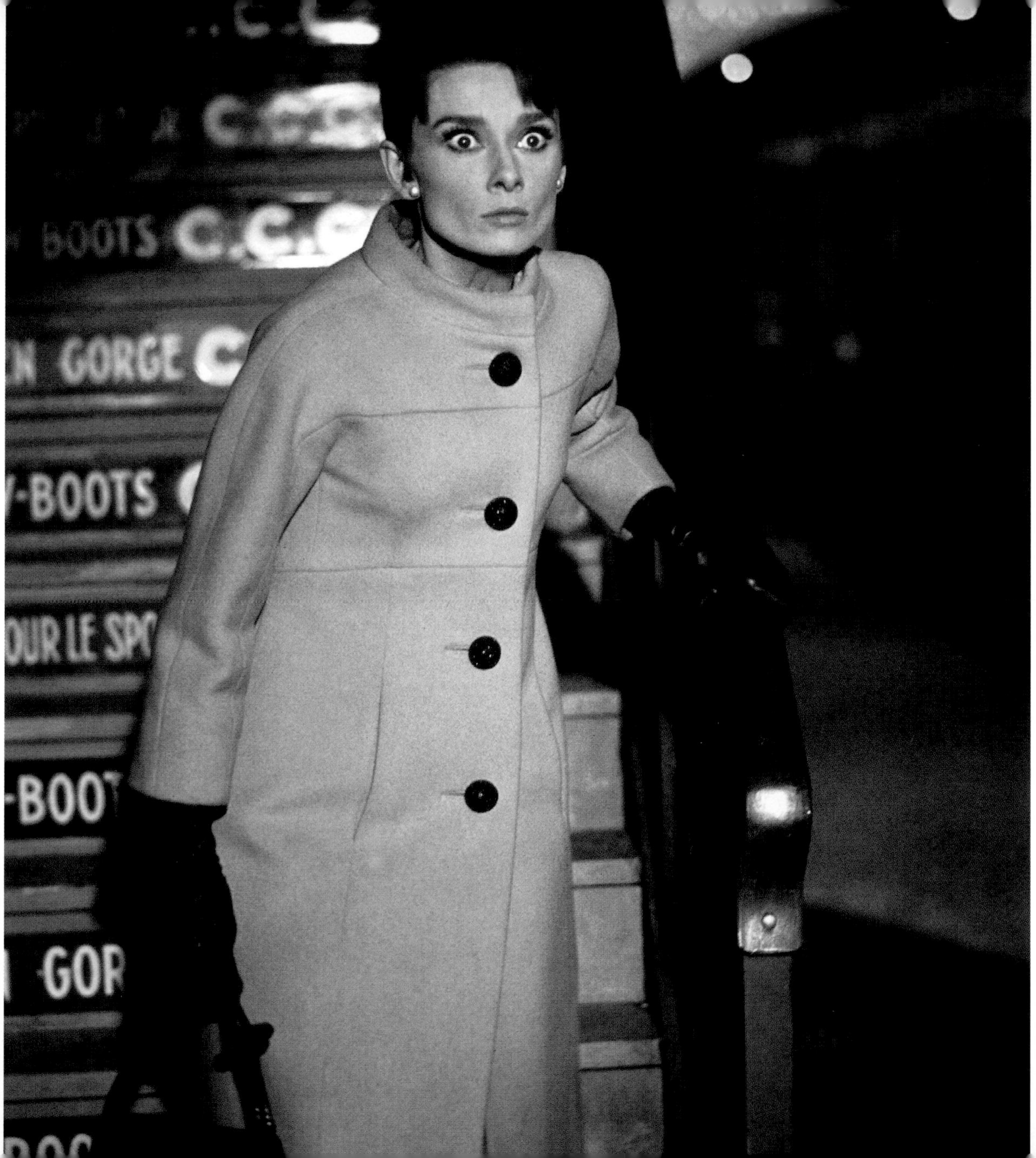

BOOTS C.C.
N GORGE
-BOOTS
OUR LE SPO
-BOOT
N GOR

Key Scene **The long journey home** *The Love Eterne*

Long before Bruce Lee brought Hong Kong cinema to world attention, the territory had a thriving commercial film industry, specialising in quite feminine melodramas and musicals influenced by mainland opera traditions. The Shaw Brothers were the biggest producers in town, but not even their canny sense of what the market wanted prepared them for the success of *The Love Eterne*. It was received with fanaticism across Asia. One woman saw it 100 times on its release. It made Ang Lee cry and inspired him to make films.

The story is a centuries-old Chinese legend, not unlike *Mulan*: Chu Ying-tai (Le Di, credited as Betty Loh Tih in the West), a teenage girl from a rich family, dresses up as a male in order to get to go to school. On her journey there, she meets Liang Shan-bo, a working class boy, played by the actress Ling Po (credited as Ivy Ling in the West). Ying-tai falls for Shan-bo but, as she's pretending to be a boy, can't show her feelings. After

three years of schooling, they begin a long, musical, and symbolic journey home, during which their passion for each other is expressed.

The scenario itself obviously plays with sexual norms, but casting an actress as the boy doubles the playfulness. As if this wasn't enough, legendary director Li stages his tale in some of the most stylised sets in movie history. Every scene seems to take place by a fantasy bridge or to be overhung with cherry blossom. Every composition looks like a scroll. Every costume, every hand move, every knowing look is artfully planned. *The Love Eterne* is a high-water mark of cinematic sumptuousness.

Mark Cousins

Date 1963

Nationality Hong Kong

Director Li Han Hsiang

Cast Le Di, Ling Po

Original Title *Liang Shan Bo yu Zhu Ying Tai*

Why It's Key One of the most famous Chinese-language films made since 1949, it's one of the most stylised musicals ever made and an early landmark in gay cinema.

Key Scene **The mystery of ever-changing identities** *Charade*

SPOILER

Despite Donen's suspect insistence on disconnecting *Charade* from Hitchcock's cinema, much as he admits to admiring him, this is the closest any other filmmaker – including Truffaut and De Palma – ever got to the spirit, feeling, and flavor of several of Hitchcock's apparently "lighter" films, such as *To Catch a Thief* (1955) and *North by Northwest* (1959), thanks also to Cary Grant. Donen proved even more successful than Hitchcock (even in the serious *Suspicion* [1941] and *Notorious* [1946]) at making the audience doubt Grant's innocence.

Most of *Charade*, after Grant's first appearance, deals with the question that, unconsciously at first, desperately at the ending, torments Reggie (Hepburn): who is he really, and is he to be trusted, this elegant man who is certainly fun and whom she likes despite his lies? The scene in question is placed in the column square before the Palais Royal theatre in Paris, at night. She's trying to get a Mr. Bartholomew from the U.S.

Embassy to help her and has been pursued in the subway by Grant, who has turned out not to be Mr. Bartholomew, as he was not really any other of the different names he gave her since they met. Another man (Matthau), gun in hand, pretends to be Bartholomew and warns her against Grant, who also wants from her the stamps for which her husband was killed. "That man is Carson Doyle," warns Grant. Reggie exclaims, "Oh, I don't know who anybody is!" "Trust me," insists Grant. "Why should I?" The situation is both a very funny one and a real source of anxiety for characters and audience – as in Hitchcock at his best.

Miguel Marías

Date 1963

Nationality UK/USA

Director Stanley Donen

Cast Audrey Hepburn, Cary Grant, Walter Matthau

Why It's Key This climactic scene offers a further turn of the screw on the issue of love vs. trust – a theme as important in comedy as in the thriller.

Opposite *Charade*

Key Film
Vidas Secas (Barren Lives)

Nelson Pereira dos Santos' *Vidas Secas* is recognized as the film that initiated Brazil's Cinema Nôvo, a composite cinematic movement meant to reform Brazilian society through films capable of awakening the political conscience of audiences. Exemplary in these terms, *Vidas Secas* opens on a quote calling for awareness of the poverty of millions in the Brazilian Northeast, and the film deploys consistent aesthetic choices (use of non-professional actors, plain dialogue, unfiltered black-and-white cinematography) to testify to the deprived life of the people of the drought-stricken sertão.

Taken from a literary work by Graciliano Ramos, *Vidas Secas* chronicles a season in the life of Fabiano (Iório) and his family. Displaced, they wander the drought-plagued backlands, finally finding shelter in a farmhouse, where Fabiano gets an ill-paid job as cowhand. In a memorable sequence, dos Santos depicts how Fabiano's eldest son acquires the conscience of living in an earthly version of hell. After hearing the word "hell" from a shaman, the boy asks his parents about its meaning. The mother (Ribeiro) evasively describes it as "an ugly place." Fabiano makes no comment. Returning to his mother, the kid gets further explanation: "It's the place where condemned souls go, it's full of fire and tongues of flames." "Have you been there?" he naively asks, receiving a ladle blow on the head as answer. He runs outside crying and starts observing the surrounding landscape. Repeating his mother's words, the boy looks at the house, the dry lands, the meager cattle. "Hell, hell, hell," he recites like a mantra.

Paolo Bertolin

Date 1963

Nationality Brazil

Director Nelson Pereira dos Santos

Cast Átila Iório, Maria Ribeiro

Why It's Key In line with the principles of Cinema Nôvo, of which it is regarded as the starting point, *Vidas Secas* advocates the awakening of conscience.

Key Film *The Zapruder Film* Abraham Zapruder records the Kennedy assassination

The most financially successful film of all time (by ratio of cost to revenue) ran a paltry and shaky 486 frames and eventually sold for $16 million. But Abraham Zapruder, a garment magnate from Dallas, Texas, could have done without his success. The traumatized maker of the film that would bear his name screamed "They killed him! They killed him!" to the bewildered crowd who hadn't seen the president's head open like a gory firework through the unblinking lens of a Bell & Howell 8mm camera. Knowing he had something significant, he turned the film over to the Secret Service and, later, sold the rights to *Life*, the magazine in whose pages the world first saw what a lone gunman had wrought upon the President of the United States. (The $16 million was the National Archives' price, paid to Zapruder's survivors in 1998.) The Zapruder film is seductive not only because of what it answers, but what it doesn't answer: conspiracy theorists 40 years later still gnash their teeth over the "back and to the left" jerk of Kennedy's head, a sticking point seized upon by Oliver Stone in *JFK* (1991). But what it records is heartbreaking and catastrophic; a powerful and healthy man reduced to brain matter and skull fragments in broad daylight, his pretty wife mouthing "Oh my God" and clambering away from her beloved's body in hysterical flight. The Zapruder film is terrifying because the unflinching camera reveals our nakedness in the face of death. Somewhere there's a frame 313 waiting for all of us.

Violet Glaze

Date November 22, 1963

Nationality USA

Cameraman Abraham Zapruder

Why It's Key An amateur filmmaker preserves the best evidence of a cataclysmic event.

Opposite Showing the Zapruder film

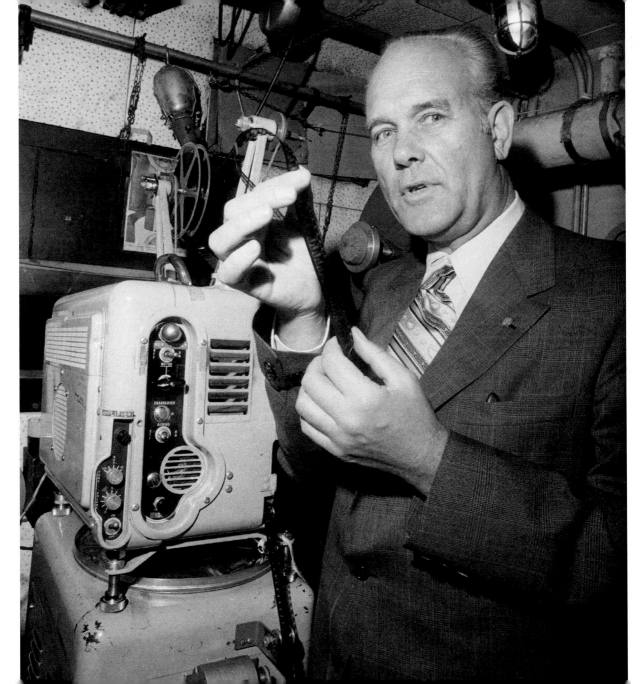

Key Scene **Buddy Love's début at the Purple Pit** *The Nutty Professor*

Midway through *The Nutty Professor*, shy, bumbling chemist Julius Kelp (Lewis) drinks a portion he has invented in order to build himself a more acceptable masculine image. In the ensuing sequence in the Purple Pit, a hangout for local college students, it becomes clear that his attempt has succeeded all too well. Director Lewis zooms in on a shot of actor Lewis in the guise of Kelp's new alter ego, snazzy in a powder-blue suit, hair slicked back, puffing on a cigarette as he surveys the scene. The newcomer – who will call himself Buddy Love – proceeds to put his stamp on the place by talking the bartender (Lester) through the complicated recipe for the Alaskan Polar Bear Heater, a mere taste of which paralyzes the man who just mixed it, though Love downs the rest of the large glass with no visible effects. He then puts the moves on gorgeous Stella (Stevens), taking her on the dance floor and serving her a series of preposterous lines (starting with "I know what you're thinking: where

has he been all my life?"). Finally, he takes over the bandstand for a rendition of "That Old Black Magic."

Lewis does all he can to make Buddy Love as repellent as possible. In doing so, he can't help investing Love with traits that are human (like his discomfort from his own cigarette smoke and his striking, awkward phrasing of the song). Nor does he allow us to ignore an uncomfortable dual truth – that we, the viewers, all *want* Love to pinch-hit aggressively for the emasculated Kelp, and that Love's egomania, contempt for others, and sub-Rat Pack fakeness are only exaggerated versions of traits American culture holds up as admirable.

Chris Fujiwara

Date 1963

Nationality USA

Director Jerry Lewis

Cast Jerry Lewis, Stella Stevens, Buddy Lester

Why It's Key It's a legendary and revealing sequence from an American classic.

1960–1969

357

Key Scene **The insane mute** *Shock Corridor*

SPOILER

"Whom God Wishes To Destroy He First Makes Mad." Few movies begin with quotations from Euripides, but Fuller was no ordinary auteur. He belonged to the small company of American filmmakers who have created genuine art in Hollywood's poverty row, making B pictures so meagerly financed and free of movie stars that producers didn't mind experimentation as long as the budget and schedule held firm. In the deliciously lurid *Shock Corridor* he crafted a seamless blend of visual and verbal elements, shooting a no-nonsense screenplay with a camera that seems on the verge of assaulting the characters, or the audience, or both.

The hero, Johnny (Breck), is a reporter investigating a mysterious murder in a mental hospital. To gain access, he talks his girlfriend (Towers) into posing as his sister (!) and claiming he tried to rape her (!!) so he'll be remanded to the institution. Hunting for clues there, he meets three patients who embody – in

suitably demented ways – three of America's great fixations of the post-World War II period: a commie-hater (James Best) who became a communist, a black civil-rights pioneer (Hari Rhodes) who thinks he runs the KKK, and an A-bomb expert (Gene Evans) who's regressed to childhood.

Johnny solves the case, but his exposure to American madness has made him a mad American, diagnosed with catatonic schizophrenia. "What a tragedy," says his psychiatrist (Matthews). "An insane mute will win the Pulitzer Prize." It appears God wished to destroy him. *Why* is a mystery we have to sort out for ourselves.

David Sterritt

Date 1963

Nationality USA

Director Samuel Fuller

Cast Peter Breck, Constance Towers, John Matthews

Why It's Key Fuller's films tap into the rawest levels of the American unconscious, and here he plumbs their depths as powerfully as at any other point in his career.

Opposite *Shock Corridor*

Key Scene **Helicopters rule the Earth**
The Damned

Often awkward, and dotted with flaws, *The Damned* nonetheless increasingly seems like the summation and high point of director Joseph Losey's career in the entertainment industry, before *Eve* (made after *The Damned*, though released before) and *The Servant* gave him a second life as an international art-filmmaker. Perhaps *The Damned* seems privileged because its story structure embodies Losey's dominant motif: the extinction of anguished, sympathetic humanity, leaving behind only a barren deep-focus world, photographed as if the filmmaker were in collaboration with the forces of destruction. Once the film's heroes, Simon (Carey) and Joan (Field), make contact with the radioactive children whom the British government is grooming to inherit a post-apocalypse Earth, the pair begin fading from the center of the narrative, both physically weakened by radiation sickness and fictionally deprived of the hero's prerogative to alter the story's outcome. In the end,

after their attempt to free the children is crushed, they are allowed to depart on their boat, while a helicopter hovers overhead to destroy their bodies after their inevitable death from contamination. Still ignorant of their fate, the couple play out a final, abortive love scene under the beating of the helicopter's rotor. Losey leaves them for a crescendo of images of the bleak crags of Portland Bill and the town of Weymouth, juxtaposed with the disembodied cries of the captive children on the soundtrack. Then he delivers a final ghostly tableau under the end credits: the helicopter in foreground, the boat cruising in the background, its occupants, our heroes, likely dead by now.
Dan Sallitt

Date 1963
Nationality UK
Director Joseph Losey
Cast Macdonald Carey, Shirley Anne Field, Alexander Knox, Viveca Lindfors
Aka *These Are the Damned*
Why It's Key This scene is the bleakest expression of Losey's anguished worldview.

Key Scene **Outside the schoolhouse**
The Birds

In Bodega Bay, which has already suffered several individual attacks by apparently crazed birds, Melanie Daniels (Hedren) agrees to fetch young Cathy (Veronica Cartwright) from school. She arrives before the end of class and sits in the playground, elegantly smoking a cigarette, while the kids chant "The Wee Cooper o' Fife," a repetitive and mind-numbing Scots folk song. Melanie has a lot to think of, and doesn't notice the birds landing in ones and twos on the climbing frame behind her. Then, a fluttering catches her attention and – from Melanie's point of view – the camera swivels, following a bird as it flaps through the air and lands on the frame, which is now completely covered with menacing birds. We know they'll attack, but for the moment they're just waiting and watching, not even squawking much. Given that *The Birds* is an early example of "high concept" filmmaking, Alfred Hitchcock chooses to tantalize us: we know we're here for a film in which birds attack humanity, but he takes his time

before the expected mass assault. Every minor incident or passing bird is a feint, revving up suspense as the film seems to be concerned with trivial Melanie and her doings; the playground scene, which sets up the first truly terrifying sequence in the film, is the final calm before the storm, as the next hour will consist of non-stop action and horror. Broken down, it's as unsettling and ambiguous a sequence as the park incident in *Blowup* (1967), making us pay attention to a woman not doing anything much as the calm images (only that last POV shot is at all tricky) and layered soundtrack (the children's monotone; small bird-sounds) set us up for the horror to come.
Kim Newman

Date 1963
Nationality USA
Director Alfred Hitchcock
Cast Tippi Hedren
Why It's Key It's a textbook example of building suspense in an apparent narrative dead spot.

Opposite *The Birds*

Key Film *Flaming Creatures*
The birth of camp, the death of Jack

These 43 minutes of black-and-white footage – shot on discarded reversal film stock, sometimes so washed out that it creates a surreal effect of white-on-white – would change American media forever. Underneath a totally off-sync soundtrack that goes from eerie silence to Latin pop, rock 'n' roll, music lifted from Maria Montez's exotic B-movies, and desultory, hilarious dialogue about how to take lipstick off one's cock – the film unfolds fractured, decentered tableaux, some static, some frantic. Bodies of uncertain gender (drag queens; muscular guys with hairy armpits, beards, and lipstick; real women even) are wittily intermingled among white lilies, roses, fake jewelry, Arabian garb, gauze, lace – it's like a still life turned mad, like an echo of Sternberg's most baroque *mise en scène*. Close-ups of flaccid penises being stroked, of a luscious breast being fondled, of female genitals being exposed during a mock orgy/gang rape scene, alternate with pseudo-narrative moments: the morning-after of a bacchanal followed by an earthquake (!), the seductive dance of a Spanish woman (Montez in drag), a Marilyn-Monroe-like drag-queen vampire rising from a coffin…

The film was rooted in the queer extravaganzas of Lower Manhattan in the 1960s – a time of innocence when you could dance your life away; and Jack Smith wanted his audiences to have "fun." Hailed by Susan Sontag as the birth of camp, *Flaming Creatures* was brutally censored, in both the U.S. and Europe. Smith withdrew it from circulation, never released another film, and locked himself in the paranoid/mad-genius mode that eventually killed him.

Bérénice Reynaud

Date 1963

Nationality USA

Director Jack Smith

Cast Frances Francine, Sheila Bick, Dolores Flores/Mario Montez, Judith Malina

Why It's Key Directed by an underground genius, this film had a lasting influence on Andy Warhol, Werner Schroeter, Nan Goldin, Mike Kelley, and others.

Key Scene **The skeleton fight**
Jason and the Argonauts

In *The 7th Voyage of Sinbad* (1958), animator Ray Harryhausen pit the heroic sailor against a swordfighting skeleton. Because this was the best-remembered scene in a picture full of wonders, Harryhausen took the opportunity to reprise the effect on an even bigger scale in his next mythical adventure as Jason (Armstrong) and a few surviving Argonauts face off against a whole band of skeleton warriors grown from teeth seeded in the ground by a wicked king. It's a tour de force, perfectly matching live stuntmen to modelwork, essentially co-directed by the credited Don Chaffey and Harryhausen himself, backed by Bernard Herrmann's memorable xylophone-based music. Kids have always loved animated bones (as in several classic Disney shorts), and skeletons are ideal for dimensional animation, since they are basically stripped-down armatures of the sort found inside King Kong and his many successors. In *Sinbad*, the fight takes place indoors in a dark cave where shadows and a controllable set allow for effects shortcuts. Showing great confidence, Harryhausen sets the skeleton battle of *Jason* out of doors, atop a cliff, in broad daylight.

Kim Newman

Date 1963

Nationality UK

Director Don Chaffey

Cast Todd Armstrong

Why It's Key It's magical excitement at its best.

Opposite *Jason and the Argonauts*

Key Scene **The executioner as condemned man** *El Verdugo* (*The Executioner*)

In the year preceding the release of *El verdugo*, Luis García Berlanga's bleak and largely unrecognized comic masterpiece, Spain's military dictatorship executed three political opponents: Communist Party member Julián Grimau and anarchists Francisco Granados and Joaquín Delgado (the latter two were garrotted). This film chronicles how the hapless José Luis (Manfredi) is propelled unwillingly into assuming the hereditary role of state executioner. Summoned to Mallorca from Madrid with his new wife and father-in-law, in a grim parody of a honeymoon, José Luis is called upon to garrotte a convict. Desperately hoping that the victim will be pardoned, the reluctant executioner is attended to first by a priest and then the gluttonous prison governor (who offers him champagne) before being obliged to wear a tie, forced upon him by a guard as if it itself were the cords of the garrotte.

The film's penultimate sequence, one long (and seemingly endless) take, shot with a static camera, sees José Luis, his legs buckling beneath him, forced to cross a white-painted anteroom to the room in the distance where the execution is to be performed. All extradiegetic noise is evacuated from the sequence; the soundtrack is reduced to the scraping of shoes as the resistant José Luis is dragged squirming and vomiting across the white hall. Two groups slowly make their way across the room: in the lead the convict, surrounded by guards and reconciled to his fate, followed by another group of warders propping up the wretched José Luis, the priest ferrying between the two, administering prayers to both condemned men. Finally, still struggling, José Luis disappears, squeezed through the diminutive black door at the far end of the white chamber. Rarely in the history of cinema has there been a more powerful indictment of the monstrosity that is the death penalty.

Steven Marsh

Date 1963

Nationality Spain

Director Luis García Berlanga

Cast Nino Manfredi

Why It's Key This scene from a great Spanish comedy is one of the most powerful indictments of the death penalty ever filmed.

Key Scene **The whipping** *Youth of the Beast*

One of the mistresses (Kazuki) of a yakuza boss (Kobayashi) has tried to seduce his new henchman, Jo (Shishido), into killing another of his mistresses. The chief punishes her in front of Jo in his modern living room. Jo is just a spectator of all this, as he is a spectator of yakuza life (he's in fact looking for revenge). The chief whips his mistress, first in the living room and then outside. There the sky is in fire, and the land looks like a yellow desert on the moon: everything looks strange and fantastic.

Suzuki wants to remind us of myth. The characters are seeking to express their primary feelings, instincts behind the masquerades of modernity. The American-style apartments, the bourgeois costumes of the yakuza, the fashionable look of the mistress are all fakes: men are still searching desperately for the great legends that structure their destiny. So they act irrationally in a supposedly well-organized world, losing their minds for a moment. At the end, the chief drops his whip and embraces his crying mistress. The film-studio set appears as a fake modernity, too, and may be the synthesis of it: Suzuki has begun with this sequence a process of deconstruction inside what was supposed to be a simple yakuza B movie.

Antoine Coppola

Date 1963

Nationality Japan

Director Seijun Suzuki

Cast Jo Shishido, Akiji Kobayashi, Minako Kazuki

Original Title *Yaju no seishun*

Why It's Key Old and new mythologies are revisited by a genius of cinema: the roots of modernity in the Japanese cinema are here.

Key Film *Mothlight*
A high point in abstract cinema

Brakhage regarded the camera's eye as an extension of his own. His works capture the world not as Hollywood movies do – with their artificial lights, steady tripods, and neat storytelling – but as humans do in everyday living, where vision is never fixed or stable, and sight is always impinged upon and modified by mind.

Mothlight is a departure for Brakhage, since instead of tapping into human sight it evokes "what a moth might see from birth to death if black were white and white were black." He made it without a camera, gluing moths' wings, twigs, and leaves between strips of transparent Mylar tape, then printing the assemblage directly onto film. The result is a four-minute dance of light, shadow, and shade, skipping across the screen as lightly as a feather escaping gravity on a momentary breeze.

The theme of birth, death, and rebirth underpins all of *Mothlight*, starting with the fact that it conjures a sense of vigorous life with materials that are not only dead but caught in an unchanging pattern on film. At the same time, the passage of the film strip past the projector lamp – like the flight of a moth attracted to a lightbulb or candle flame – reanimates the elements fixed upon it, restoring the semblance, and perhaps in some magical way the substance, of the life formerly owned by these fragments of organic matter. In creating one of the greatest abstract movies, Brakhage plumbed the real world to depths rarely reached by the "realism" of ordinary films.
David Sterritt

Date 1963

Nationality USA

Director Stan Brakhage

Why It's Key Gluing moths' wings, leaves, and twigs between strips of transparent tape and printing the results on film, Brakhage created one of the greatest and most influential American abstract movies.

Key Film *21-87*
The rapturous end credits

Using a combination of stock footage discarded by his National Film Board of Canada colleagues and original footage shot in Toronto and New York, *21-87* is Lipsett's abstract meditation on the alienation and declining spirituality of industrial life. A film based explicitly on the contrapuntal relationship of sound and image, *21-87* is replete with moments when the two elements spark off each other in startling and poignant ways. (As with his other early films, Lipsett composed the audio tracks before assembling the images.) An autopsy is performed to the sounds of clattering machinery, a church choir sings over shots of the circus, teenagers dance like mannequins and mannequins speak the word of god, people gaze up in reverence at a trained monkey.

The most powerful sequence of the film, however, and one of the most powerful in all avant-garde cinema, is its closing, which departs from the poetic, observational visual quality of the rest of the film and approaches a kinetic abstraction that is more akin to the rapid-fire montages of Bruce Conner than NFB documentaries. The drifting, poetic quality of the film is accelerated so that its sadness becomes desperation, its weariness, exhaustion. Images of lights begin to cluster, and we see a blurred reflection of Lipsett and a mysterious shot of a man raising his hands as if in supplication to a glaring light bulb. A few repetitions of this apparition, interspersed with credits, wind down to the title card. By implicating himself in this catalogue of dislocation, Lipsett converts a seemingly whimsical film into a personal revelation: a postcard from hell.
Travis Miles

Date 1964

Nationality Canada

Director Arthur Lipsett

Why It's Key This somber portrait of a soulless world is made indelible by a powerful and disjunctive ending that serves as a despairing directorial signature.

Key Scene **The yellow bag, the empty safe, the luggage, the hair** *Marnie*

The quiet, orderly, neat, and very simple way that Hitchcock uses to start *Marnie* is a model of pacing, guiding the spectator's gaze and supplying information in a careful, selective way. It takes about eight minutes and really begins with the credits: 19 visiting cards, black on white with a touch of gold, presented in a kind of slide show. Then come three brief sequences, the first and the last without any dialogue. The first "live" image is the close-up of a yellowish handbag under the arm of a walking woman, the camera following her for an instant, then stopping to let her go on, then following her a bit more, from a distance, to halt again and let her diminishing figure recede in a deserted railway station.

Cut to a close-up of a fat, short, middle-aged man with glasses (Gabel). "Robbed!" he claims indignantly, as we see his empty safe, and he describes in delectable detail – to the merriment of a couple of cops and his secretary – the thief, a pretty woman without references who has disappeared with almost ten thousand dollars. A visiting client (Connery) suggests she could be summed up as "resourceful."

The third sequence starts on the same bag as before, though now looking rather white (an effect of the lighting, or the absence of a filter), in an hotel corridor. The brunette woman (her back to the camera) packs two pieces of baggage, selects another of her four Social Security cards under different names, and undoes her hair, which then emerges ash-blond from a water-filled sink, as Tippi Hedren's wet face, with an expression of release and cleansing, is seen for the first time in the film in a memorable close-up.

Miguel Marías

Date 1964

Nationality USA

Director Alfred Hitchcock

Cast Tippi Hedren, Sean Connery, Martin Gabel

Why It's Key It's a textbook example of how to begin a mystery movie and tell what is already an elaborate story with the utmost economy.

Opposite *Marnie*

Key Scene **The cast does the Madison** *Band of Outsiders*

Naïve young Odile Monod (Karina) is a happy girl as she lines up and dances "the Madison" in partnership with her two prospective lovers, opportunistic Arthur (Brasseur) and melancholy Franz (Frey). The Madison was one of a number of post-Twist non-contact dances popular in the mid-1960s – dancers stand in line and move more or less in synch. In Leibniz's philosophy, a "monad" (from the Greek word for "unit") is an isolated individual who contains his or her own past, present, and future. Everyone we see dancing here is isolated, listening to the music, and dancing a private number.

Band of Outsiders is one of Godard's most musical films, in which he introduces the dance with a lengthy scene of choreographed movement, as the three characters change chairs, jockeying for position around the café table. "One minute of silence" (actually 36 seconds) follows as these loquacious Parisians try to be quiet for a while, Godard turning off the soundtrack to prepare our ears for a trip to the café's basement, where we hear snatches of two songs from composer Michel Legrand's score for a much more obviously romantic love tale than this, *The Umbrellas of Cherbourg* (1964). The Madison follows, Godard's voice-over telling us what each of the dancers is thinking: Arthur about Odile's sexuality, Odile about her own, and Franz wondering if the world is a dream, or the dream a world. The dance is over, but the monad/Monod lingers on.

Gregg Rickman

Date 1964

Nationality France

Director Jean-Luc Godard

Cast Anna Karina, Claude Brasseur, Sami Frey

Original Title *Bande à part*

Why It's Key Cinephiles love privileged moments, and few moments in film history are more privileged than this dance in a Parisian café, filmed by the ultimate cinephile, Godard.

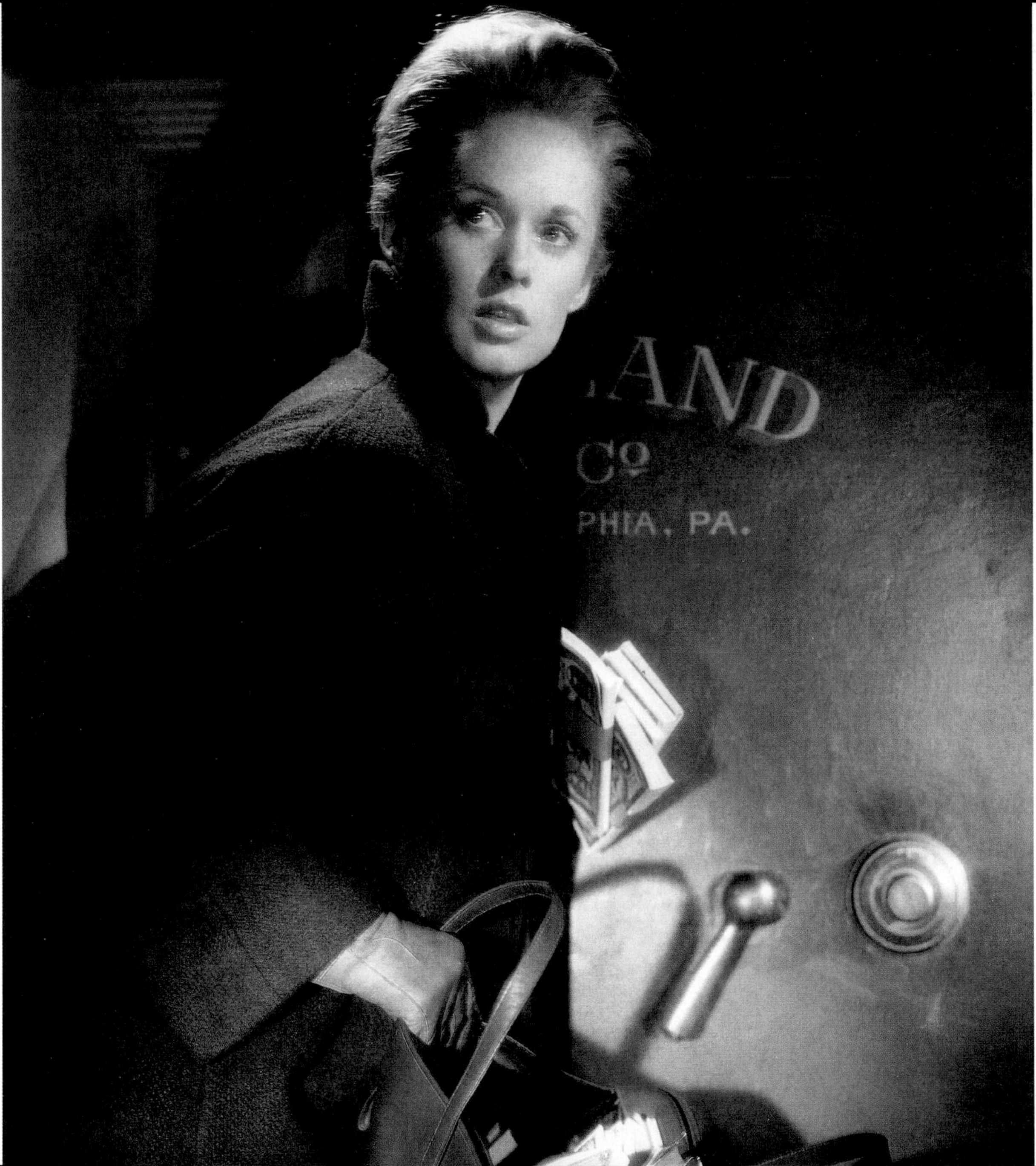
AND
Co
PHIA, PA.

Key Scene **The preacher**
Black God, White Devil

In the 1960s, Latin American cinema created the manifesto for, and template of, filmmaking in the so-called Third World. Among its groundbreaking works was *Black God, White Devil*, Glauber Rocha's second feature, made when he was just 25. About a cowhand, Manuel (Del Rey), who kills a cheating landlord and then becomes a fugitive, the film rages against the obliteration of indigenous Brazilian culture and the marginalisation of the poor. Tracked by the semi-mythic Antonio das Mortes (do Valle), Manuel and his wife encounter the black prophet-preacher Sebastião (Silva), who preaches social upheaval, saying that the rich must become poor and the sea must become desert. Forty minutes into the film, Manuel hauls a huge rock onto his head and slowly, agonisingly, climbs a mystical mountain accompanied by Sebastião, the Black God of the film's title. Rocha cuts to an ecstatic scene, perhaps during an eclipse, when someone shouts "The sun is made of gold." Manuel's wife writhes as if possessed, and the Black God kills their child silently, with a knife, and makes the sign of the cross with her blood on her head.

Political cinema is often bland, something of which Rocha was incapable, as scenes such as this one show. His was an Old Testament rage. Marry it to real filmmaking talent and you get something like Ford's *The Searchers* crossed with Eisenstein's *Ivan the Terrible*.

Mark Cousins

Date 1964

Nationality Brazil

Director Glauber Rocha

Cast Geraldo Del Rey, Maurício do Valle, Lidio Silva

Original Title *Deus e o Diabo na Terra do Sol*

Why It's Key This is the most striking scene in the most influential Brazilian film ever made.

Key Person **Lee Marvin**
The Killers

SPOILER

When Siegel made this adaptation-remake of Hemingway's short story, Lee Marvin was starring on TV, but in movies he specialized in playing violent, sarcastic men for directors who valued his ability to smash people in the mouth. His understated acting style and silver-gray hair conferred intelligence and authority on the rash, amoral hoods he played. These contradictory impulses came together in Charlie Strom, a middle-aged hit man looking to answer a question, then cash out.

We first see Strom reflected in his associate hit man's (Gulager's) sunglasses as the two men, both in shades and tailored suits, march into a school for the blind. The poised, angular Strom listens with his head up but cocked, an arched eyebrow, slit-like eyes. He looks like he's staring with his lower teeth.

Small signals he makes control the film, directing the other characters so he doesn't have to raise his voice. Seating himself across from Sheila (Dickinson), an untrustworthy mob wife, he crosses his legs, removes his hat, shoots his cuffs and crosses his arms. "What do you want?" she asks. "The money," he answers, giving the definitive interpretation of those two words but sounding like he's ordering lunch.

We leave Strom clutching a briefcase, bleeding on a suburban lawn. Lee Marvin is the un-McQueen. Not handsome, unconcerned with the audience and therefore compelling, he is distant and takes things personally. He's too smart to be monumental like other movie stars, but when he falls it's like a world got killed.

A. S. Hamrah

Date 1964

Nationality USA

Director Don Siegel

Cast Lee Marvin, Angie Dickinson, John Cassavetes, Ronald Reagan, Clu Gulager

Why It's Key It's Marvin's career-defining performance

Opposite *The Killers*

Key Scene **Ann-Margret dances with Elvis**
Viva Las Vegas

The post-Army film career of Elvis Presley was sadly disastrous – as his manager Colonel Parker turned down projects like *West Side Story* (1961) in order to stick him in a succession of mild, danger-free musicals that effectively neutered the dangerous rock 'n' roller into a children's entertainer. One thing that kept Elvis small-time in the movies was a refusal to pair him either with romantic partners who could match him for charisma or dance partners who could match his moves … except *once*, in George Sidney's widescreen-and-color ode to America's trashy desert fun palace, *Viva Las Vegas*. Ann-Margret followed her star-making turn in *Bye Bye Birdie* (1963) – which was a satire on Elvis – by striding into the film in short shorts, viewed from under a hot-rod. She paces the King every step of the way. Their stand-out musical moment together comes not in the title song, which Elvis does solo, but in a gymnasium scene in which Elvis performs "C'mon Everybody," and Ann-Margret steams up the screen with her frenzied, hyper-sexualized dance style – it's perhaps the only instance of an Elvis musical number in which the audience is fixated on *someone else's* hips.

Kim Newman

Date 1964

Nationality USA

Director George Sidney

Cast Elvis Presley, Ann-Margret

Why It's Key Just once, Elvis met his match.

Opposite *Viva Las Vegas*

Key Film
Diamonds of the Night

Set during World War II and based on the prose of Czech writer and Holocaust survivor Arnost Lustig, the film focuses on the flight of two teenage boys (Jánsky and Kumbera) from a convoy headed toward a concentration camp. The boys spend most of the time running through forests and hills. Even though they are in the open, the masterful camerawork creates a feeling of claustrophobia. Most of the film is shot with a hand-held camera that follows the protagonists at close range. There is almost no dialogue; the surrealistic, trancelike flashbacks of empty city streets bathed in sunlight and silent women in windows add to the bewilderment of the chase.

The importance of the film is in the masterful way in which the means of cinematic language are used to convey subjective experiences like terror, fear, hunger, anxiety. Nemec skilfully deploys close-ups; the sound of breathing and the rapid montage of subjective views are juxtaposed with tableau-like representations of an outside world that remains alienated and unattainable. Nemec is mostly known for his interest in surrealistic representation and is responsible for such key works of 1960s Czech surrealism as *Report on the Party and the Guests* (1966) and *Martyrs of Love* (1966); his early masterpiece is of key importance in the annals of Holocaust cinema.

Dina Iordanova

Date 1964

Nationality Czechoslovakia

Director Jan Nemec

Cast Ladislav Jánsky, Antonín Kumbera

Original Title *Démanty noci*

Why It's Key It's a masterful rendering of subjective Holocaust experience.

Key Person **Mary Astor**
Ruined finery *Hush...Hush, Sweet Charlotte*

For this follow-up to his hit *Whatever Happened to Baby Jane?* (1962), a horror film that united aging stars (and off-screen enemies) Joan Crawford and Bette Davis, Robert Aldrich pulled off an even greater casting coup. Not only did he talk Olivia de Havilland into co-starring opposite Davis when Crawford dropped out, he got Mary Astor to fly to Louisiana to do a cameo as Jewel Mayhew, the reclusive, ailing widow on whom the plot of this rich slice of Southern Gothic proves to hinge. The second of Jewel's two scenes takes place on the veranda of her decaying plantation house, where her guest for tea is a visiting Englishman (Kellaway) who's been poking around town for information about the decades-old decapitation murder of Jewel's husband – a crime that has gone unsolved, though it's widely assumed the guilty party was batty Charlotte (Davis), who had been having an affair with the victim. In a few minutes of screen time, bathed in cinematographer Joseph Biroc's sluggish sunlight,

Astor delineates a chilling and moving portrait of a woman who long ago accepted her fate as a haunted prisoner of the past and who now says she thinks she's glad her end is about to come. Her whole performance is like a long, slow fade-out in which, finally, nothing is seen except a hard glint of light in the pupils of the eyes. It was Astor's last screen appearance.

Chris Fujiwara

Date 1964

Nationality USA

Director Robert Aldrich

Cast Mary Astor, Cecil Kellaway

Why It's Key Film acting has rarely come so close to death.

Key Scene **Crazed formalist propaganda**
I Am Cuba

This misguided yet awesome Soviet-Cuban tribute to the Cuban Revolution, comparable in some ways to the Latin American adventures of Sergei Eisenstein (the unfinished *Que Viva Mexico!*) and Orson Welles (the unfinished *It's All True*), contains many stretches of virtuoso filmmaking from cinematographer Sergei Urusevsky. Among the more spectacular instances of camera movement is a delirious, breathtaking two-and-a-half minute shot. Like an earlier shot that moves several floors down a hotel exterior to approach and enter a swimming pool before going underwater, it's a kind of shot that could only have been realized through teamwork and a relay of camera operators – collective artistry in action.

The coffin of a radical student slain by Batista's police during a mass uprising is carried by his comrades through downtown Havana, surrounded by a huge crowd. The camera moves ahead of a young woman and past a young man – catching him in close-

up as he turns around, hoists the front of the coffin onto his right shoulder, and walks away with the other pallbearers – then cranes up the five floors of a building, past people watching from balconies and parapets. The camera moves to the right across the street and through a window into a cigar-rolling factory, where it follows workers as they hand a Cuban flag one to another, eventually unfurling it from a window. The camera moves out that window and over the flag, then follows the funeral cortege from above for what seems like a quarter of a mile.

Jonathan Rosenbaum

Date 1964

Nationality USSR/Cuba

Director Mikhail Kalatozov

Cast uncredited

Original Titles *Soy Cuba/ Ya Kuba*

Why It's Key One of the most spectacular camera movements in the history of cinema transcends its apparent motivation.

Key Scene **The horseback tournament** *Lilith*

A gorgeous sunny day, full of light and magic. Lilith (Seberg at her prettiest, most feminine) looks free and happy, more childish than ever before, more beguiling, too. She seems to know very well how to lead Vince (Beatty) on and then swiftly set him off-balance, not once or twice but as many times as she wishes, playfully but without joy. She reveals how twisted her mind is when she teases, tempts, frightens, and almost seduces little boys, whispering in their ear things we cannot hear and they probably don't understand. Mediaeval-style knights and fair ladies, a sort of tournament, with lances and horses, the lady's colors – Lilith's scarf – as a pennant, with Vince proving himself very able. The troubling quality both of Rossen's second unexpected masterpiece in a row (after *The Hustler*) and of its eponymous heroine stems from their attractiveness and their ensnaring mystery, which repel and draw at the same time, producing a feeling akin to vertigo. The film does it with light, music, rhythm, acting, editing. It captures, bewitches, then frightens and worries the entrapped, almost entranced viewer, very softly and delicately, like poison ivy. And this bright, holiday-like day outside of the sanatorium is perhaps the knot of the film.

Miguel Marías

Date 1964

Nationality USA

Director Robert Rossen

Cast Jean Seberg, Warren Beatty

Why It's Key It captures the disquieting duplicity of beauty and the seeming innocence and happiness of childlike playing in a fairytale fantasy, together with the raw grim madness behind the faces of people who are no longer children and are no longer really playing.

Key Scene **A ferocious fight before the opening credits** *The Naked Kiss*

Few films have such a slam-bang beginning as this one. The soundtrack throbs with wailing jazz, and the screen fills with belligerent close-ups of a woman, Kelly (Towers), and a man, Farlunde (Mansfield), locked in furious battle: She's pelting him savagely with her handbag, he's whining for mercy and stumbling into furniture.

Seconds later there's a new surprise – the man grabs Kelly's hair and pulls it clean off, revealing a totally bald scalp above her attractive face. Falling to the floor, he's knocked unconscious. Kelly kneels over him and wrestles his wallet out of his pants; it contains $800, but she declares that she's only taking the $75 he owes her. She stuffs the bills into her bodice and strides away. The movie's credits then commence, superimposed over a leisurely shot of Kelly replacing her wig and fixing her makeup.

Fuller eventually supplies the information we need to make sense of all this: Farlunde is a pimp, and Kelly is a hooker fed up with the indignities he's heaped on her, such as punishing her by shaving her head. Her story continues to surprise as she moves to a new town, quits prostitution, takes a job caring for hospitalized kids, and gets romantically involved with a revered citizen who's also a child molester. This is rich and strange material, and the fierce opening scene – partly filmed with cameras hanging around the actors' necks – sets the sensational mood with a brio that only Fuller could have generated.

David Sterritt

Date 1964

Nationality USA

Director Samuel Fuller

Cast Constance Towers, Monte Mansfield

Why It's Key The first scene of this daring melodrama, with in-your-face images of jarring intensity, crystallizes the raw, rude power that makes Fuller a major figure in B-movie history.

Key Scene **Gertrud meets her lover in a park** *Gertrud*

"She awoke at last to find herself getting laid; she'd come in on a sexual crescendo in progress, like a cut to a scene where the camera's already moving." Curiously, this sentence by Thomas Pynchon in *The Crying of Lot 49* (1966) comes only two years after the release of Carl Dreyer's final feature. This isn't to suggest any influence – only a striking congruence with a cut to a scene where the camera's already moving as it follows Gertrud's (Rode's) determined stride across a park to keep her rendezvous with Erland Jansson (Owe), the much younger composer she's fallen in love with. In the previous scene – ponderously paced, in a claustrophobic flat – she has just told her stuffy middle-aged husband at some length that she no longer loves him and is leaving him. And Dreyer's sudden cut *in media res* to her moving towards Erland expresses infatuation and orgasmic passion like few other camera movements in cinema – as if to replicate both her impatience and her ecstatic anticipation. The startling

wrench of the cut is accentuated by a plaintive phrase played by a flute in the score that lasts only as long as her steps, the first music we hear after the film's credits.

They meet at a bench beside a placid pond that seems to glisten with Gertrud's happy rapture. Much later in the film, when Erland breaks her heart in the same setting, the same pond is ruffled by quiet turbulence, but here it shines with joy.

Jonathan Rosenbaum

Date 1964

Nationality Denmark

Director Carl Dreyer

Cast Nina Pens Rode, Baard Owe

Why It's Key It's only the second scene in a film about love, and Dreyer expresses in a single cut everything we need to know about passion.

Opposite *Gertrud*

1960–1969

373

Key Scene **A trashy pop icon sings for charity in an empty stadium** *Pajarito Gómez*

The scene plays like a music video. A pop star known as Pajarito Gómez (Pellegrini) sings a tune in the middle of an empty stadium. While the camera travels around him, some documentary footage is intercut. At first these seem to be typical images of any poor Latin American quarter, but gradually we realize that the people depicted are in fact mental patients of some public sanitarium, who survive in appalling conditions. The overlapping of the tender pop song with those documentary images is quite disturbing.

Pajarito Gómez is a ruthless satire on artificial pop idols who are tailor-made by music corporations. The film has an episodic structure that allows some scenes to assume the different formats of a TV show, a concert film, a commercial spot, and even a photo-novel. The stadium scene illustrates the very public efforts that Gómez makes for charity causes, in this case "to help the poor demented." The simple juxtaposition of him singing and the documentary

footage points at many levels: it underlines the contradiction between his world of trashy fiction and the most unbearable of realities, but also, as a part of Pajarito's shameless public life, it hits the hypocrisy implicit in the kind of charity that needs publicity to justify itself. Finally, it also illustrates the total lack of rapport between Pajarito and his social context: the song does not allude in any form to the "poor demented's" plight; far from it, its lyrics are composed with the verses of prayer that children use to recite at night before going to sleep. Nobody attacked the darker myths of Argentine society (which at the time were more or less those of any society with a healthy middle class) with greater force than Rodolfo Kuhn.

Fernando Martín Peña

Date 1964

Nationality Argentina

Director Rodolfo Kuhn

Cast Héctor Pellegrini

Why It's Key By confronting the simple-minded lyrics with terrible images of the poor people the singer is presumably helping with the tune, Kuhn creates a complex piece of satire.

Key Speech **The dog joke**
The Patsy

In the last half of *The Patsy* a team of show-biz handlers teaches a bellboy named Stanley (Lewis) a simple joke to tell on stage. The joke concerns a dog chasing a car who catches and buries it. Stanley rushes it backwards, yelling "I got a car that chases dogs!" "Slower!" instruct the handlers. He tries it slower: "I... got... a dog... that..."

At a try-out, Stanley offers, "Like, my dog chased a car a lot." The handlers record another appearance at the nightclub and listen to the tape later. "Remember about my dog who was always chasing cars?" Stanley asks. "He finally caught one, a Mustang. And he buried it in the backyard." It still doesn't work. Stanley can't grasp the rudiments of stand-up.

Why does the movie harp on this lame joke? The handlers train Stanley to replace a famous comedian who died as the film began. The dead comic, a version of Jerry Lewis, is like the car in the joke Stanley can't tell: the handlers can't bury the comedian any more than Stanley can get the dog to bury the car. Nor can Stanley lip-sync in the record act Lewis resurrects from earlier in his career. In the movies Lewis directed he struggles not to conform to playback, and comedy is so exasperating it makes people watching it break things, the way his handlers drop cups and overturn bottles watching him in disbelief.

A. S. Hamrah

Date 1964

Nationality USA

Director Jerry Lewis

Cast Jerry Lewis, Keenan Wynn, Phil Harris, Everett Sloane, Ina Balin, Peter Lorre, John Carradine

Why It's Key A joke Lewis can't tell exposes *The Patsy*'s unconscious.

Key Event
Warhol shoots *Empire*

On the night of July 25, 1964, from 8 pm till dawn, Andy Warhol aimed his new Auricon 16mm direct-sound camera out a window on the 41st floor of the Time-Life building at the Empire State Building. Jonas Mekas, who was present, wrote about the event in his *Village Voice* column the following Thursday and permitted himself this speculation: "My guess is that *Empire* will become the *Birth of a Nation* of the New Bag cinema." Indeed, like *Birth of a Nation*, *Empire* deals with black/white issues, almost the only movement during the eight hours of its running time being the change of light in the static monochrome composition. *Empire* also resembles Griffith's film in its power to arouse violent emotions, as was proved the following March, when Warhol's film was first shown at the Film-Makers' Cinematheque. Mekas reported: "Ten minutes after the film started, a crowd of 30 or 40 people stormed out of the theatre into the lobby, surrounded the box office, Bob Brown, and myself, and threatened to beat us up and destroy the theatre unless their money was returned." The ranks of those who have walked out of *Empire* increases every time the film is shown, though given the rarity of those screenings, the number of walk-outs may not yet be out of the triple digits. As Stephen Koch wrote, "If ever a film was devised to be discussed and not seen, *Empire* is surely that film." It remains a landmark of Pop Art and a fundamental work of conceptual cinema.

Chris Fujiwara

Date July 25, 1964

Why It's Key Warhol's eight-hour epic is as much of a monument as the building that is its star.

Key Scene **Christ walks on water**
The Gospel According to St. Matthew

*T*he Gospel According to St. Matthew is unique for many reasons. It recreates the New Testament using an entirely non-professional cast, rugged and utterly believable locations, and almost documentary black-and-white cinematography, after the fashion of neorealism, which greatly influenced Pasolini in the early stages of his career. Despite being a non-believer, the radical and nonconformist Pasolini was perhaps attracted to the notion of Christ as a firebrand revolutionary who commands respect and is nothing short of being a demagogue. But the true victory of this masterpiece lies in Pasolini's casting of a young student of Spanish literature, Enrique Irazoqui, as Christ.

In the Miracle of the Loaves and Fish, when Christ multiplies five loaves of bread and two fish into an inexhaustible supply for the gathered multitude, he asks his followers to take a boat to the other side of the water, where he will meet them. While crossing the channel, the followers see a distant spectre approaching them across the waters. All becomes quiet, the wind fades away, the waves lash no more, sparkles of light play on the water. And you see Christ performing another miracle. The beauty and starkness of the long shot of Christ in silhouette walking on water are revelatory. Not only because it rivals any CGI special effect in any number of films today, but also because it draws attention to itself in a film otherwise entirely neorealistic in treatment. It is a sublime moment.

Aruna Vasudev

Date 1964

Nationality Italy

Director Pier Paolo Pasolini

Cast Enrique Irazoqui, Margherita Caruso

Original Title *Il Vangelo secondo Matteo*

Why It's Key Pasolini, iconoclast and avowed atheist, brings the Gospel to life in a manner that even the most ardent of believers can only aspire to.

Key Scene **The sinister photo**
Repulsion

SPOILER

*C*arole (Deneuve), a manicurist at a London beauty parlor, is severely disturbed. What brings out her psychosis most alarmingly is sex, which she's repressed to an extreme and damaging degree. Left alone in the apartment she shares with her sister (Yvonne Furneaux), she ultimately loses her mind altogether. Ordinary rooms become ominous death traps, everyday noises resonate like inscrutable threats, and finally the very walls come alive, sprouting disembodied arms that grope for her.

In the end Carole is catatonic, lying helpless and almost lifeless as her sister's lover (Hendry) carries her away from the carnage she's caused in the last stages of her decline. As the film moves toward its final fade-out, the camera glides purposefully through the flat's wrecked living room, singling out small details – a ticking clock, a crumbled cracker – and suggesting that some privileged image may unlock Carole's unconscious for us at the last moment.

This seems imminent as the screen fills with a photograph showing Carole as a child with her parents. The older folks look cheerful, but as the camera closes in on Carole's face, we see that she's gazing distractedly into the distance; moving still closer, we see the glint of unmistakable madness in her eyes. That's all the explanation the film has to offer, and it's to Polanski's credit that he doesn't pretend to know more about the mind's mysteries. This isn't an exercise in psychological theory. It's a work of art, and one of the most truly frightening the screen has given us.

David Sterritt

Date 1965

Nationality UK

Director Roman Polanski

Cast Catherine Deneuve, Ian Hendry

Why It's Key As the story moves toward its conclusion, a moving-camera shot suggests that an explanation for the main character's madness is about to be revealed – which it is or isn't, depending on how you take the last enigmatic image.

Key Film *The Hundred Horsemen*
Playing with narration

Vittorio Cottafavi was the master of the peplum, Italy's low-budget sword-and-sandal epics popular in the early 1960s. At the time, he was rightfully championed as an auteur by *Cahiers du cinéma*; nowadays he's rarely mentioned (his films are mostly not available on DVD) – outranking Sergio Sollima, brilliant director of political spaghetti westerns, as the most disconcerting case of auteurist amnesia concerning Italy's popular sixties cinema. Cottafavi's magnificent blend of colorful popular spectacle, complex humanism, and Brechtian storytelling shines in his masterpiece *The Hundred Horsemen*, an epic about the Moorish occupation of a Spanish community during a period of truce in the 11th century. Even cut versions (like the English dub *Son of El Cid*) cannot help but hint at the richness of Cottafavi's vision, ideologically (patriotic sentiments and prejudices are acknowledged, but ultimately superseded by pacifism) and aesthetically. Full of picaresque mood swings and startling directorial ideas – not least about narration itself – the film opens with a painter relating events directly to the camera while finishing a fresco of the outcome, which doubles for Cottafavi's canvas, especially since parts have yet to be filled in. Which the painter also does as intermittent offscreen narrator, until the final battle, during which the film suddenly switches to black-and-white, not just to appease censors (like Tarantino's *Kill Bill Vol. I*, 38 years later), rather making a pertinent point about the bleakness of war. Only then does our painter-narrator return, playfully inserting himself into the happy end, thus enabling closure on several levels.

Christoph Huber

Date 1965

Nationality Italy/Spain/West Germany

Director Vittorio Cottafavi

Cast Mark Damon, Antonella Lualdi, Arnoldo Foà

Original Title *I cento cavalieri*

Why It's Key The masterpiece of nearly forgotten peplum king Vittorio Cottafavi brilliantly combines popular spectacle and Brechtian experiments in storytelling.

Key Scene **The first fight scene**
Faster Pussycat! Kill! Kill!

"Ladies and gentlemen – welcome to violence!" Go-go dancers Varla (Satana), Billie (Williams), and Rosie (Haji) are racing cars in the desert for kicks when they're interrupted by "safety first Clyde" Tommy (Barlow) and his nasal girlfriend Linda (Bernard). The big drip's all excited about breaking his personal best for a land speed record, but Varla isn't impressed. "I don't beat clocks," she sneers. "Just people." The trio shames Tommy into a race that ends in Varla running her puny opponent off the road, cackling in sadistic delight. When Tommy rushes to retrieve his stopwatch from the buxom bully, Varla karate-chops his hand and shoves him to the dust. Exotic dancer and martial-artist-turned-actress Satana gained her cult following after appearing as the stacked and satanic Varla, a masochist's wet dream with bad-girl bangs, cat's-eye makeup, and a killer hourglass packed into tight black denim. While the top-grossing film of 1965 espoused a saintly femininity in *The Sound Of Music*, Satana was kicking ass in the California desert and pioneering future female-led action films like *Kill Bill* (2003), *Alien* (1979), and *The Terminator* (1984). Varla's an unstoppable wolverine of a woman – when a desperate Tommy punches her in the gut, she judo-flips him to the ground, and, in a scene that's still nakedly shocking, pulls his wrists back, presses the heel of her boot to his neck, and snaps his spine with an audible crack. Eat that, Maria von Trapp.

Violet Glaze

Date 1965

Nationality USA

Director Russ Meyer

Cast Tura Satana, Lori Williams, Haji, Ray Barlow, Susan Bernard

Why It's Key Varla's assault on Tommy changes the rules about women and action in films.

Opposite *Faster Pussycat! Kill! Kill!*

Key Film *Chemmeen (The Wrath of The Sea)* The storm

Arguably the most important Malayalam film ever made, certainly the most famous, *Chemmeen* set new standards and broke new ground when it was released. Based on a 1956 novel by Thakazhi Sivasankara Pillai, who also wrote the film's script, it was one of the first Malayalam films made in color and the first South Indian film to win a National Award. In drawing on literary sources and quietly, realistically capturing a slice of Kerala life, this simple, tragic tale of forbidden love in a small fishing village gently epitomises the features of mainstream Malayalam cinema.

The best Indian films are often built on memorable music scores, and *Chemmeen* is no exception. Famed Bollywood music composer Salil Choudhury made his first foray into Malayalam cinema here; his tunes became instant classics and are played from tinny radios in local tea shops and sung with great gusto at high-school talent competitions to this day. The most famous sequence of *Chemmeen* is its final one, in which hapless fishermen struggle against a terrifying storm that has stirred up a whirlpool – both a metaphor for, and a terrific technical achievement by, a fledgling film industry. Like all the greatest films, *Chemmeen* not only helped define an industry but also defined a people; it has passed into local legend and become an intrinsic, indelible part of popular culture. The next time you are on a Kerala beach, ask someone to hum a tune: the response will probably be the musical ode to the lowly fishermen in *Chemmeen*, "Kadalinakkare ponnore!" ("Oh you who cross the seas!").

Sonia Benjamin

Date 1965

Nationality India

Director Ramu Kariat

Cast Sathyan, Sheela, Madhu

Why It's Key This film is to Malayalam cinema what *Citizen Kane*, *Gone with the Wind*, and *Casablanca* combined are to Hollywood.

Key Film *Alphaville* The escape from Alphaville

SPOILER

The escape of secret agent Lemmy Caution (Constantine) and new love Natasha von Braun (Karina) from the future city of Alphaville, and the death of ruling computer Alpha 60 at the same time, find the gathering threads of numerous literary and cinematic antecedents (Eluard, Feuillade, Cocteau, Hawks, Aldrich) woven together in Godard's poetic vision. Though his film is science-fiction, Godard's city somewhere in intergalactic space far from Earth is actually the real Paris of the present day (1965), its familiar landscape transformed in the black-and-white images created by Godard and brilliant cinematographer Raoul Coutard into a world of cold, luminous surfaces, of abstract glass and neon patterns, of blinking lights that suggest an endless nocturnal vigil. At the same time, the droning, gravelly voice of Alpha 60, with just an edge of pathos, is that of a real man, not an electronic one. Though Caution is as tough as they come, his philosophical and moral perspective, as well as his humanism, provide him with the riddle that finally destroys Alpha 60. The escape and the ending are movingly signalled in an image of Lemmy in negative as he comes to rescue Natasha, then addresses the computer with the answer in a memorable emblematic image from behind a pane of glass, with Natasha at his side. The final image, as the couple glides through the night along the intergalactic highway, is one of serenity; and enslaving technocracy, which *Alphaville* intimates with such prescience, for once recedes in the face of tenderness.

Blake Lucas

Date 1965

Nationality France

Director Jean-Luc Godard

Cast Eddie Constantine, Anna Karina, Akim Tamiroff, Howard Vernon

Original Title *Alphaville, une étrange aventure de Lemmy Caution*

Why It's Key Cinematic poetry turns darkness into light, as ethics and emotion traverse the galaxies to defeat malevolent technology.

Opposite *Alphaville*

Key Scene **The unexpected transition from black and white to color** *Quixote*

Taking the form of a transcontinental journey ending with an anti-war demonstration in New York City, Bruce Baillie's 45-minute "epic" is a dense assemblage of farm workers, road signs, people of all types, bridges, machinery, continually re-juxtaposing peaceful and violent sections. Conceiving of the U.S. landscape as a collision of forms, Baillie also imagines something else, a rootless, placeless meditative space from which all objects can be experienced as transitory illusions. Superimpositions, rapid cutting, and a dream-like sensibility that smoothly layers a woman's face over a demonstration all express the idea of an unending quest for resolution that can never fully succeed. About a third of the way into the film, which has so far been in black and white, there's a dark image of a field worker's hand in a leaf-filled close-up with only the faintest whistling sound, and we cut to what seems to be a similar angle of the same subject, also very dark, but with a tiny hint of color. The color is so faint that the first-time viewer does a double-take – is this a hallucination? The brighter colors in the next few images reveal that it's not, and a long lyrical section, which includes sheep on a hill at sunset, ensues before louder sections follow. The transition is more than a dazzling effect: by causing us to wonder what we're seeing, it calls every image of the film into question, revealing that each is a product of its maker's and viewer's subjectivity, but also perching each on the brink of some possible transformation.

Fred Camper

Date 1965

Nationality USA

Director Bruce Baillie

Why It's Key This surprise causes viewers to question what they are seeing at every moment in the film.

Key Scene **Edie Sedgwick is seriously out of focus** *Poor Little Rich Girl*

In this period of Andy Warhol's filmmaking, when he was still in control of his output, he was shooting mostly sync-sound films on two 33-minute reels, each a continuous take. He shot this Edie Sedgwick portrait that way, but due to a technical problem both reels were almost completely out of focus. He reshot them, but then, in a decision that reveals him as a far more calculating artist than most assume, he paired one out-of-focus reel with an in-focus one. So the film begins with 33 minutes of blur, in which things become sharp for only the briefest of instants. The camera and Edie are together in her apartment, eventually with an offscreen male, whose presence only adds to the already-present voyeuristic element: as we see this scantily-clad beauty apply makeup, chat on the phone, or try on clothes, many of us are subconsciously waiting, like a peeping Tom, for something else to happen. But "it" never does, and as is generally the case in Warhol voyeurism is frustrated in favor of static compositions, a celebration of appearances, and in this film, a "celebration" of the ultimate film surface, the textures of out-of-focus black and white. What's striking is how little is added by the in-focus reel; it feels like just a different version of the first. When Sedwick tries on clothes, nothing is revealed. When she chats, only the most superficial of interests emerge. Her parading of her appearance hides her real soul – or perhaps, her lack of one. In this sense, her performance perfectly matches the out-of-focus "style" of the first reel: both evoke the void.

Fred Camper

Date 1965

Nationality USA

Director Andy Warhol

Cast Edie Sedgwick

Why It's Key In this audacious pairing of in and out of focus, Warhol, often misunderstood as interested primarily in glamour and celebrity, reveals an aesthetic of surfaces and emptiness.

Key Scene **The dance**
Loves of a Blonde

This hilarious sequence consists of several shot/reverse shots following the timid glances exchanged among three young women and three middle-aged army reservists. They are seated around white-cloth-covered tables at the opposite ends of a large dancehall; the orchestra plays a frolic polka, and the dance is about to kick off. There is no audible dialogue: all the interaction is in the exchange of glances among the three women (who lean toward one another to whisper inaudible comments) and the men (who do the same, evidently giving tips on how to overcome anxiety). The more time passes, the more comical and awkward the inaction. One of the men is so fretful that he drops his wedding ring under the table; the camera follows it as it rolls down the floor.

The women may have come to the dance ready to be seduced, but by the end of the scene, when the dancing starts, the awkwardness of the situation has grown so overwhelming that the momentum is lost.

Women and men have looked at each other, have measured and weighed each other, and already know that nothing will come out of it – all without a single word exchanged, against the background of the cheerful tune. The whole affair, which was initiated by the director of a provincial factory who is desperate to find spouses for his female workers, has been doomed from the onset. So much for the centralised running of people's lives under state socialism.

Dina Iordanova

Date 1965

Nationality Czechoslovakia

Director Milos Forman

Cast Hana Brejchová, Vladimír Pucholt, Vladimír Mensík

Original Title *Lásky jedné plavovlásky*

Why It's Key This scene best conveys the awkwardness of the mating game: girls look at men and are being looked at.

Key Event **The BBC bans its own production, *The War Game***

Seeking to break media silence about Britain's nuclear weapons buildup, groundbreaking BBC documentarian Peter Watkins applied his you-are-there newsreel techniques to a speculative portrayal of what could happen if three hydrogen bombs were detonated in southeastern England. The resultant stark horrors – failure of electricity and water sources, massive food and medicine shortages, dead-eyed children blinded by the nuclear flash, desperate adults with radiation lesions and psychological "shell-shock," and police shooting violent rioters – were dramatized with such blistering immediacy that the BBC secretly screened the film for government officials and then banned it as "too horrifying for the medium of broadcasting." Ignoring widespread support for disarmament, Harold Wilson's freshly elected Labour government proved understandably nervous about this filmic proof that it was ignoring the public will. Watkins viewed the ban as supporting his hypothesis – that policy was being

formed behind closed doors and far from public scrutiny – and conducted an unprecedented defense, resigning from the BBC within days, then marshalling an extensive press campaign, and even offering to buy the film outright. After a six-month firestorm of controversy that reached Parliament, the BBC finally released the film to cinemas in Britain and abroad in March 1966 (whereupon it won the U.S. Academy Award as Best Documentary), but still refused permission for television broadcasts in any country. The embattled director moved on to blazingly ambitious works in Norway (*Edvard Munch* [1974]) and France (*La Commune*, [2000]) but as his vision of the future *The War Game* remains enduringly topical for its red-alert warning about weapons of mass destruction.

Robert Keser

Date November 26, 1965

Why It's Key The incident, which exposed media's subservience to political interests, resulted in a cinema release as a means to undermine TV censorship.

Key Film
Now

Santiago Álvarez was born in Havana in 1919, studied in New York, and was radicalised in the coal mines of Pennsylvania in the 1940s. Back home in Cuba in the 1950s, he opposed Batista and, after the Revolution in 1959 and despite almost no film experience, he was appointed head of the newsreel division of the Cuban Film Institute, ICAIC. By the time of his death in 1998 he had directed an estimated 700 films, many of short and medium length.

Over forty years after it was made, Álvarez's short film *Now* can still reduce audiences to tears. The Lena Horne song calling for an end to racial segregation that gives the film its title was banned on many radio stations in the U.S. Álvarez supplied it with an image track and, at the film's end, to drive home its imperative, had the word "now" written in a hail of machine gun bullets. He once said, "give me two photos, music, and a moviola… and I'll give you a movie," which explains his technique in *Now* but not

its power. Álvarez chose still photographs of white-on-black beatings and brutal treatment meted out by U.S. police during civil-rights marches and skirmishes. He filmed these images in close-up and with rostrum moves. He intercut them with newsreel footage – some bootlegged – of more beatings. After a slow intro, Horne's first verse is sung to a dance beat. Álvarez cut on the beat, echoing the energy and defiance in Horne's voice. The beauty of the latter combined with the anguish in the imagery to create an enraged, experimental montage of sobering effect. As the song builds, Álvarez shows images of hangings too, and Nazi imagery of Horst Wessel. Didactic, yes, but *Now* makes most music videos of the 1980s and since seem lifeless indeed.

Mark Cousins

Date 1965

Nationality Cuba

Director Santiago Álvarez

Cast Lena Horne (voice)

Why It's Key The forerunner of the modern music video is a powerful attack on racism in the U.S.

Key Scene **Alessandro drives his mother to the graveyard, literally...** *Fists in the Pocket*

Alessandro (Castel) is driving his blind mother (Gerace) to the cemetery. They're on the mountain route connecting their isolated villa to the town, when the mother asks Alessandro to lower the windshield. He proposes to stop for a break and parks the car in a small rest area. Alessandro inspects the vista of the gorge underneath, while the mother, left momentarily stranded, asks where she could sit. Alessandro tells her to walk on, and then he pushes her off the edge. The camera tracks to a close-up of Alessandro, who mumbles a prayer over Ennio Morricone's disquieting score.

When released in 1965, Marco Bellocchio's debut stirred great controversy in conservative Italy. Deputies from the ruling Christian Democratic party demanded its banning, on account of its attack on family values and its irony toward Catholicism. The sequence of Alessandro killing his defenseless mother was at the center of the dispute. Sharply breaking with the

tradition of neorealism, Bellocchio's masterwork also goes far beyond an assault on the bourgeoisie, as it depicts a moral wasteland where traditional values have lost significance: they're mere corpses, waiting to be buried. As the most acute commentators have observed, more than serving as a prelude to the youth protests of 1968, this portrayal of a thoroughly dysfunctional family represents the most vivid indictment of the Fascist remnants in the Italian collective psyche. That might be the reason why *Fists in the Pocket* still stays so provocative and disturbing.

Paolo Bertolin

Date 1965

Nationality Italy

Director Marco Bellocchio

Cast Lou Castel, Liliana Gerace

Original Title *I Pugni in tasca*

Why It's Key This shocking scene is the central provocation in Bellocchio's landmark of Italian cinema.

Opposite *Fists in the Pocket*

Key Scene **Raju pledges his love to Rosie**
Guide

Known for his song picturisation, Vijay Anand deserves to be equally known for his distinctive framing and deframing of movement and for his long takes, unusual in commercial cinema. His close-ups are not moments of stasis in which the frame and face are held: what engages him are cinematic lines, which are simultaneously lines of thought and emotion, that can be drawn from face to face and other objects.

In *Guide* (adapted from R K Narayan's novel), Rosie (Rehman) runs away from her husband and comes to Raju (Dev Anand) for help. Raju commits himself to her, and the song "Tere Mere Sapne" ("Your dreams, my dreams, are now one") begins. This sequence is a study in three long takes that dovetail with Raju's avowal of love. The space is charged with the movings-away and drawing-together of the protagonists, caught in the fluidity of the emotions of love and hesitation. The refrain is covered in one take. The instrumental music that follows, then a stanza,

and then a repetition of the refrain are all filmed in a second shot that begins with the full figure of Rosie moving away in doubt and hesitation; the shot continues with mid-shots and close-ups of both of them and is choreographed in movings-out-of-frame, entries-into-frame, and semicircular movements within the frame. The last two stanzas and the final refrain are taken in one shot, during which she finally responds to his outstretched hand and goes into his arms: a cut would be redundant.

Rashmi Doraiswamy

Date 1965

Nationality India

Director Vijay Anand

Cast Waheeda Rehman, Dev Anand

Why It's Key This sequence is a superb example of Vijay Anand's long-take mastery.

384

Key Scene **The German's revelation**
The Flight of the Phoenix

The men are exhausted. Their plane fell in the middle of the Sahara desert, and they've been working night after night trying to build another plane from the wreckage, following the directions of a German (Kruger) who claims to be a plane designer. After many nights of hardship, clinging to that weak hope, the guilt-ridden pilot (Stewart) and his copilot (Attenborough) learn, in a very casual chat with the German, that he has designed only model planes. Which, in their situation, is as if they've been following God – after trying very hard to believe in Him – only to find out He has made only clay dummies.

At that point there is an unforgettable piece of acting by Attenborough, who bursts into laughter as he realizes the implications of what the German has revealed. His laughter gets more and more hysterical (finely counterpointed by shots of a quietly devastated Stewart), and then it gradually turns into a long a desperate cry, while his whole body becomes a figure

of almost child-like helplessness. The figure of a man who has lost it.

There are similar moments of despair in the several films that Aldrich devoted to groups of men thrown into borderline scenarios (*Ten Seconds to Hell, Attack!, Too Late the Hero, The Dirty Dozen*, etc.). But none of them gets deeper into the maddening anguish of the situation. At the opposite pole from Hawksian professional camaraderie, not only do these men battle among themselves, fail miserably at their crafts, and face the risk or the reality of dying without honor nor glory: they basically crack up, and then have a very hard time putting together some of the pieces.

Fernando Martín Peña

Date 1965

Nationality USA

Director Robert Aldrich

Cast James Stewart, Richard Attenborough, Hardy Kruger

Why It's Key Richard Attenborough provides one of the most memorable moments of cracking up in Aldrich's work.

Key Scene **The ending**
Black Girl...

Senegal. Black governess Diouana (Diop) travels to France with the white family that employs her. She is excited by this move to the country that she has heard so much about and gives her employers a wooden mask that she got from a Senegalese boy (Boy), as a present. When they get to France, they hang the mask with other examples of African art. Over time, Diouana's role changes. She is required to clean and cook and becomes a maid. She gets to wear the latest fashions but is lonely and demeaned. She disputes her relegation and, in a heated argument, tries to pull the mask away from Madame (Jelinek). Eventually, exasperated and despairing, Diouana commits suicide.

The white bathroom, near-black blood, and black-and-white '60s dress gives the suicide scene the graphic intensity of a lino print, but it is the film's ending that really shows that Sembene is already, in his first featurette, a state-of-the-continent director. After Diouana's death, Monsieur (Fontaine) takes the mask back to Senegal and gives it to the boy. The latter wears it with some menace and then, in the film's final moment, removes it to reveal that he is crying. A great symbolic ending to one of Africa's first films.
Mark Cousins

Date 1966

Nationality Senegal

Director Ousmane Sembene

Cast Mbissine Thérèse Diop, Anne-Marie Jelinek, Robert Fontaine, Ibrahima Boy

Original Title *La Noire de...*

Why It's Key This is the most striking scene in the first black African feature film.

Key Scene **The food orgy**
Daisies

In an avant-garde feminist farce full of giggles and outrages, the ultimate jolt, which reportedly got its director into the most trouble, is an extravagant food orgy. Prior to this, the countless antics of two 17-year-old girls, both named Marie, nearly all involve food and/or drink, some of it served in posh restaurants, as well as the promise of sexual favors to dirty old men that are never delivered. Sometimes the transgressions are mainly formal; sometimes they involve both food and sex, such as when phallic bananas are compulsively sliced.

Eventually, the heroines' plotless wanderings bring them via a dumbwaiter to a huge banquet hall filled with delicacies. After tentatively sampling a few dishes, they start sinking their hands into the sauces, devouring chickens, swilling diverse kinds of liquor, mixing together different dishes, gorging on pastries, and finally engaging in a food fight worthy of Laurel and Hardy – much of this done to the strains of the Austrian national anthem. Then they start dancing on the table, swinging from an ornate chandelier, and smashing plates and glasses. Finally, to make matters even worse, they pretend to clean up the carnage – reassembling plates like jigsaw puzzles and scraping food off the floor to heap it back onto trays. Indignant Czech citizens who decried the waste and self-indulgence were only rising to the bait. The film ends with newsreel shots of aerial bombardment, over which a title appears: "This film is dedicated to those whose only reason for outrage is mutilated lettuce."
Jonathan Rosenbaum

Date 1966

Nationality Czechoslovakia

Director Vera Chytilová

Cast Jitka Cerhová, Ivana Karbanová

Original Title *Sedmikrasky*

Why It's Key The climactic shock in this avant-garde farce is connected to food, not sex.

Key Scene **Miss 19**
Masculine-Feminine

What untold depths will Miss 19 reveal to us now? Winner of a teen-magazine beauty contest, Elsa Leroy stands before Godard's camera with her back to the light like her hands are nailed to the windowsill and answers offscreen questions about socialism and birth control in an unbroken take six-and-a-half minutes long. Often regarded as an indictment of plasticity or misogynist cruelty, Godard's "Interview with a Consumer Product" is one of the things that stops *Masculine-Feminine* from being the yé-yé movie some music buffs would prefer.

Miss 19 is nice to Paul (Léaud), "a pollster for the IFOP." She seems a little nervous but not defensive, and aware she's being punked. She admits she doesn't know much about politics. When she expresses admiration for American women, Paul cuts her off: "Does the word reactionary mean anything to you?" When he sees his questions about love are going nowhere he asks her if she can name a place where a war is going on. "No," she laughs. "But I don't care."

We sense Paul asks Miss 19 questions he wishes he could ask Madeleine (Chantal Goya), the girl he loves. Earlier in the film he shouted "I want to live with you!" into a recording he never gave her. Over shots of Paris street life, Paul reflects on his work: "Polls quickly veer from their true goal, the observation of behavior, and instead insidiously go for value judgments." His exposé of Miss 19 was as much about him as her.
A. S. Hamrah

Date 1966

Nationality France

Director Jean-Luc Godard

Cast Elsa Leroy, Jean-Pierre Léaud

Original Title *Masculin féminin*

Why It's Key An insidious interview turns back on itself.

Opposite *Masculine-Feminine*

Key Scene **Balthazar's end**
Au hasard Balthazar

For some critics, Bresson's movies are examples of transcendental style, using the physicality of film as a paradoxical means for evoking spiritual essences. Others argue that religiosity gives way in his later films to a materialist philosophy more aligned with modern pragmatism and pessimism. *Au hasard Balthazar*, the tale of a (commonplace) donkey who might well be a (holy) saint, is a central film for both schools of thought.

In outline it's a sort of biopic with two main characters: Balthazar, named for one of the biblical magi, and Marie (Anne Wiazemsky), a young woman who (like the donkey) moves from one male master to another while sinking into subordination and sadness. At the end Balthazar is owned by smugglers, who abandon him when they're fired on and forced to flee. A close-up shows that Balthazar is wounded – nothing fatal from the look of it, but enough to cause bleeding and pain. He walks into a meadow, and a flock of sheep approaches from the distance, urged along by barking sheepdogs. Soon he's surrounded by the milling sheep, whose pale fleeces contrast with his darker coloring. In the final shot he's dead and alone, as if the snow-white sheep had carried off his soul.

This image lays bare life's ineluctably material foundation. Yet with equal force it suggests the possibility that Balthazar has reached a state of mystical grace, and the serenity of his appearance bears this out. If the meek shall inherit the earth, Balthazar is surely a blessed innocent.
David Sterritt

Date 1966

Nationality France/Sweden

Director Robert Bresson

Why It's Key Purity of expression merges with purity of purpose to produce an indelible vision of serenity born from suffering.

Key Scene **Unsaved by the cavalry**
The Good, the Bad and the Ugly

Tuco (Wallach) and the man he calls Blondie (Eastwood) pursue gold across the Texas desert in a stolen Confederate coach. Disguised in the gray uniforms of dead Rebels, they know the blue-clad Union Army is chasing a Confederate regiment across the same terrain. Tuco rouses the napping Blondie to tell him he's spotted a cavalry platoon moving in their direction. "Blue or gray?" Blondie asks.

Tuco lifts the eye patch he's wearing to get a better look. "They're gray like us!" he shouts. "Hurrah for the Confederacy! God is with us because he hates the Yanks too!"

Blondie pushes back his hat and squints. "God's not on our side because he hates idiots also," he informs Tuco as the soldiers approach covered in the desert's gray dust. They watch as the officer leading the troops beats the dust off his jacket with a pair of gloves, revealing his blue uniform underneath. By yelling about which side God was on, Tuco invalidated the special protection granted men who pursue their own goals during wartime. Cut to Blondie and Tuco chained in a prison camp.

The film insists there are two kinds of people in the world. Leone's penchant for contrasting two kinds of shots, close-ups and long shots, finds its corollary in the gray or blue of the two kinds of soldiers who move toward Blondie and Tuco from afar. Leone turns gray soldiers blue the simplest way possible. Movies were invented for ideas like that.
A. S. Hamrah

Date 1966

Nationality Italy

Director Sergio Leone

Cast Clint Eastwood, Eli Wallach

Original Title *Il buono, il brutto, il cattivo*

Why It's Key It's a visual idea that only works in movies.

Opposite *The Good, the Bad and the Ugly*

Key Scene **Tetsu walks down the narrow hall before the battle** *Tokyo Drifter*

Tetsu (Watari) walks down an incredibly narrow hallway before the final battle in *Tokyo Drifter*, the gangster masterpiece by Seijun Suzuki (commonly known as "Seijun" in Japan). Its triangular shape is emblematic of the geometric spaces art director Takeo Kimura made for the film, but it also contrasts with Tetsu as a creature of space. He earlier counts out the steps he must run on a rail line before shooting a fatal shot; in the climax he throws his gun several paces in front of him so he can run and fire as he catches it. He needs room to move, but he is confined by gangster obligations to a boss he realizes is betraying him. Emerging from that restricted hallway into the nightclub gives him space to both throw his pistol and confront his boss. But it also foreshadows Seijun's own emergence from the tight paths of genre filmmaking with *Branded to Kill* (1967), a work so narratively daring that it was branded "incomprehensible" by Nikkatsu president Kyusaku Hori, and Seijun was out of a job.

The resulting fan protests crystallized trends in Japanese cinephilia and ideas about the image that would proliferate after the end of the studio era, concepts that themselves were later embodied in Seijun's freely artistic productions (like *Zigeunerweisen* [1980]), made after a ten-year hiatus. Yet Tetsu, who rejects the girl because a yakuza must walk alone, returns to the hallway after the last battle. While yearning for room to move, Seijun also continued to keep one foot in genre.
Aaron Gerow

Date 1966

Nationality Japan

Director Seijun Suzuki

Cast Tetsuya Watari, Chieko Matsubara

Original Title *Tokyo nagaremono*

Why It's Key This image symbolizes Seijun's career shift and his struggle between genre and art.

Key Scene **Ondine goes berserk**
Chelsea Girls

The speed-addicted extrovert called Ondine appeared in several Warhol productions, including the epic named after Manhattan's fabled Chelsea Hotel, where it was shot. The film comprises more than six hours of material, but Warhol cut that in half by showing it two reels at a time, projected side by side. As usual in his movies, Warhol is less interested in story or characters than in the real-life personalities of the people in front of his proudly voyeuristic camera. Here a number of his "superstars" are on display, from the relatively well-behaved Gerard Malanga and Marie Menken to the flamboyantly colorful Mario Montez and Brigid Polk, among many others.

If one performer can be said to steal the show, it has to be Ondine, who dubs himself (or his character – there's no clear distinction) the Pope of Greenwich Village, a hyperbolic title he treats with mingled arrogance, irreverence, and contempt. Playing father confessor for Ingrid Superstar, another Warhol regular,

he charges her with lesbianism (hardly a crime in Warhol's world) and berates her with increasing force, until you wonder who's in charge of this performance – himself, his character, or nobody at all. When another performer (Davis) arrives, calling Ondine a phony, he runs genuinely amok, striking her and hollering for Warhol to stop the camera, which Warhol of course won't do.

Ondine later claimed his *Chelsea Girls* performance had moments of "genius." But the real creative credit belongs to Warhol, whose cinematic style reveals undreamed-of new dimensions in the age-old art of "acting."

David Sterritt

Date 1966

Nationality USA

Directors Andy Warhol, Paul Morrissey

Cast Ondine (Robert Olivo), Angelina "Pepper" Davis

Why It's Key Warhol's inspired voyeurism pays chilling dividends when a "superstar" forgets he's playing a role and acts out his real-life instability.

Key Scene **Spoken credits**
Fahrenheit 451

SPOILER

A simple idea motivates Truffaut's credits sequence: Reading is banned in the world of *Fahrenheit 451*, so the titles are spoken, not printed. We listen to the credits the way the characters in the film receive the programs they watch on TV, and we see a series of photos like the picture-comics they look at instead of reading newspapers.

Truffaut brought more cinematic acumen to this minute-long sequence than many filmmakers deploy in an entire feature. Washed-out pastels overlay 17 black-and-white stills of TV antennas as the camera zooms in on each. Offscreen, Alex Scott (who also plays one of the book people) announces the film's title and the principals' names in the clipped tones of British radio, accompanied by Bernard Herrmann's ethereal score.

Truffaut turns the spoken credits from *The Magnificent Ambersons* (and *Contempt*) into a kind of Hitchcockian intro reminiscent of Chris Marker's *La Jetée*, science-fiction dealing in memory. The

sequence follows the film's path: The first 13 shots show suburban roofs cut off from nature, the last four set the houses among trees; the film's protagonist flees suburban emptiness by escaping to the wintry forest of the book people. Even before the credits, Herrmann's music imparts a mystery and romance denied the turning globe of the Universal Studios logo-snipe in other Universal films. This is music of the spheres broadcast through a swirling aurora into homes only dimly aware of the cosmos.

A. S. Hamrah

Date 1966

Nationality UK

Director François Truffaut

Cast Alex Scott (voice)

Why It's Key Truffaut thematically integrates the opening credits sequence into his adaptation of Ray Bradbury's novel.

Opposite *Fahrenheit 451*

Key Film *All My Life*
The cosmos in a camera movement

The type of cinema labeled "structural film" puts apparatus in the foreground; these movies don't just *use* lighting designs, zoom lenses, tracking shots, and so forth, but are *about* those things. Some such pictures are formalistic and technical. But the best are full of vibrant life, proving that the *stuff* of cinema can also be the *subject* of cinema.

This three-minute masterpiece is a sublime example. The camera sits in a garden surrounded by a wooden fence, and Baillie turns it through a slow 360-degree pan. On the soundtrack Ella Fitzgerald sings "All My Life," signaling the movie's deeper meaning: in keeping with his Buddhist philosophy, Baillie sees life as a cycle, "real" and "unreal" at the same time. A film is like that, too – especially this one, which takes us through a literal circle, punctuated by bursts of color from roses embodying life's natural beauty.

Near the end, the camera starts the single variation in its movement, tilting gradually up toward the clear blue sky. A telephone wire runs diagonally across the area, and for a moment it seems a regrettably artificial intrusion on the scene. But just as the lens is about to pass completely beyond it, the camera hesitates for just an instant – and in that instant you realize the pesky man-made artifact represents the last earthly substance to be dealt with before spiritual transcendence can be called complete. That moment arrives as the song ends, the camera passes into uninterrupted sky, and the movie glides to its perfect conclusion.

David Sterritt

Date 1966

Nationality USA

Director Bruce Baillie

Why It's Key The camera presents a 360-degree pan of a flower-filled garden while Ella Fitzgerald and Teddy Wilson's band perform the title song, creating a philosophical statement on the finitude and infinitude of earthly life.

Key Scene **The Battle of Shrewsbury**
Chimes at Midnight

In 1941, with *Citizen Kane*, Orson Welles established himself as American cinema's greatest innovator. It and his subsequent films as director showed that power and its dissipation were his themes. He was a "king" actor whose larger-than-life characters were hubristic and illiberal, but he was also a "king" director in that his filming style had an epic sweep and grandeur, even on a small budget.

Shakespeare's *Henriad* (*Henry IV* parts 1 and 2, *Henry V*) was therefore natural material for Welles, but its portrait of Prince Hal becoming King Henry V and assuming "the port of Mars" was too conservative for Welles. He could not endorse Henry V when he compared himself to the sun hidden by a cloud that will seem more glorious for being previously dimmed. Far more attractive to the filmmaker was the corpulent, bumbling, foolish, but good-hearted Sir John Falstaff, who warns Hal "banish me and you banish laughter."

Given this re-reading, it's no surprise that the film's staging of the Battle of Shrewsbury of 1403, which in Shakespeare is a treasonous one in which Hotspur takes up arms against Henry IV, is full of mockery. It begins with massed armies and chivalric pageantry, but soon it becomes unclear who's fighting who. Falstaff (Welles) scurries back and forth trying to avoid combat, screen direction gets confused, the Shropshire mud covers knights and infantrymen alike as they hack at each other, and Welles slips into slow-motion to emphasise how elephantine is the whole pointless, tragic mess. The scene is wordless, touched by the anarchic schoolboy retribution of Laurel and Hardy, and so brilliantly designed that by the end it looks like a frieze drawn in grey clay.

Mark Cousins

Date 1966

Nationality France/Spain/Switzerland

Director Orson Welles

Cast Orson Welles

Aka *Falstaff*

Why It's Key An inspiration for many subsequent films, it is rightly considered among the greatest battle scenes in cinema.

Opposite *Chimes at Midnight*

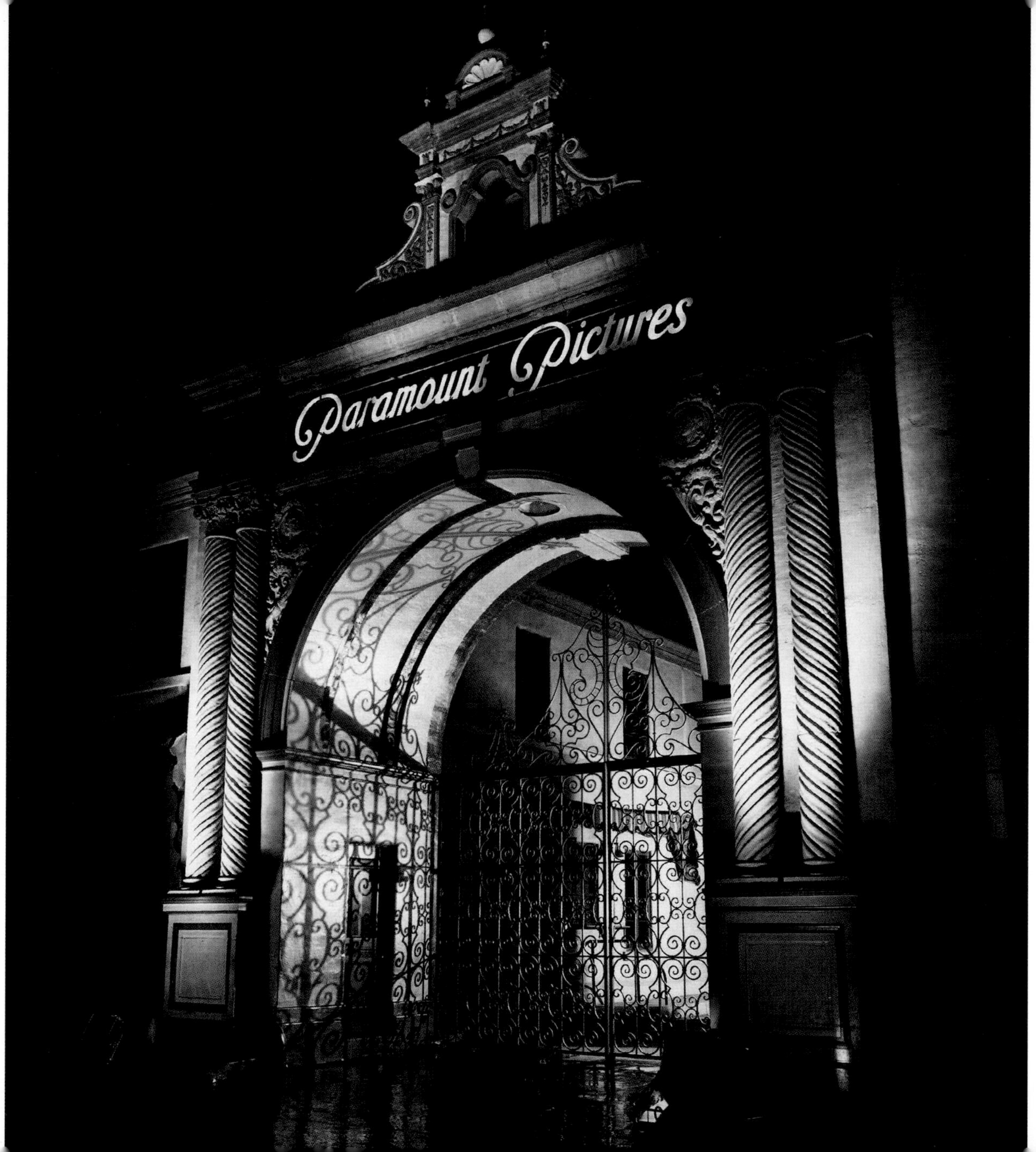
Paramount Pictures

Key Film **A hat is blown off in the wind as a gunshot is heard** *Unsere Afrikareise*

In 1961, Peter Kubelka was commissioned to make a "documentary" on the African hunting trip of a group of his fellow Austrians. He shot many hours of footage and sound – and then took five years to edit his materials into this 13-minute masterpiece, first cataloguing his footage and sounds into various categories, then assembling all the image and sound fragments into what is in effect a giant matrix of multiple meanings. An animal writhing in its death throes is accompanied by annoying popular music, their rhythms matching almost perfectly; a white man shakes a black man's hand to the sound of thunder, commenting on the white's self-importance.

Very early in the film, the hat that's blown off to a gunshot, the first stunning instance of strong asynchronicity, signals to the viewer that an awareness of each instant is crucial, that the film will be charged with electricity and unpredictability. Part of Kubelka's statement concerns the way the hunters relate to the

place – the sublimated eroticism of their views through gun sights, the way that for them killing substitutes for touching. Shots, crackling fires, and loud music on the sound track all impose a grid of violence over the natural world we see. Each asynchronous sound/image pair builds on the last, and the next, until the film becomes a labyrinth of sensed interconnections – an image doesn't just connect with its accompanying sound, but with every other image and sound in the film. The film has the quality of a monument, a massive multi-sided document of civilizations.

Fred Camper

Date 1966

Nationality Austria

Director Peter Kubelka

Aka *Our Trip to Africa*

Why It's Key In Kubelka's greatest essay in the use of asynchronous sound, his pairings of sound and image comment on the values of a European hunting party in Africa.

Key Event **Paramount Pictures acquired by Gulf and Western**

The Hollywood "studio system," which had been remarkably successful through the thirties and forties, began to crumble in the fifties, but, as in the case of the Roman Empire, its decline and fall took a long time. The most prestigious major studio, along with MGM, and the most successful financially in the mid-to-late forties, Paramount was badly hit by the 1947 Consent Decree that forced the studios to divest themselves of their lucrative theater chains (the studio was the first of the majors to comply, in 1949). By 1966, Paramount's profits had been mediocre for at least a dozen years, and the displeasure of a number of top executives and directors led to the acceptance of a purchase offer from Gulf and Western Industries (for $83 a share, considerably more than the market value at the time). A widely diversified conglomerate founded by Charles Bluhdorn in 1957, G&W ventured into entertainment for the first time with the acquisition

of Paramount. Acquisitions of motion-picture studios by conglomerates would soon become the rule rather than the exception in the new Hollywood.

Jean-Pierre Coursodon

Date October 19, 1966

Why It's Key Not counting General Tire and Rubber's 1955 purchase of moribund RKO, this was the first major purchase of a Hollywood studio by a conglomerate.

Opposite *Paramount Pictures*

Key Scene **The stereo closet**
Zontar the Thing from Venus

*Z*ontar, which endures as a thing of ridicule, started life as a remake of Roger Corman's *It Conquered the World* (1956). AIP needed filler to complete a TV sales package and contracted Buchanan, a Texas filmmaker known for ambitious if substandard exploitation fare, to quickly remake several of its '50s sci-fi monster movies in color and 16mm for about $30,000 each. Shown on late-night TV for years, the films are remembered by insomniacs as cheesy and boring. They're also more than that.

If, as Godard said, "the definition of the human condition should be in the *mise en scène* itself," then *Zontar*, which plays like an industrial documentary on Dallas living rooms and shopping centers, puts it there in negative. A dead-watch-battery miasma pervades the film, a three in the afternoon of the soul.

Much of the film consists of an embittered scientist (Houston) speaking into a radio wall-unit he's installed behind a checked sliding door in a closet in his den. That's how he communicates with Zontar, a Venusian invader hiding in a nearby cave. We don't hear Zontar respond, though, just static and a low hum. "Yes, it's true," the scientist says to Zontar with his back to the camera. "I *am* your only friend."

The inadequacy of the film's world seems normal and accurate, snapshots of the time as it was. In the end it's a valid document of a place that did survive some kind of attack, but kept on going the same dull way, learning nothing.

A. S. Hamrah

Date 1966

Nationality USA

Director Larry Buchanan

Cast John Agar, Anthony Houston, Susan Bjurman, Patricia De Laney

Why It's Key It's a "bad" film that reveals truths "good" films can't.

Key Scene **Catching sight of reality**
Blowup

*A*rrogant, self-important, a narcissist to end narcissists, the photographer protagonist of this film (Hemmings) creeps through an East London park, merrily snapping photographs of pigeons, a refuse collector, the breezy trees, and velvety green swards. He comes upon a pair of lovers and photographs them at length, but later, blowing up his images, finds in the dark shadows of the park border a lone gunman. By being there with his camera, he has saved a man's life! But now two girls interrupt him and they have sex. Deflated, emptied of all hope, he looks at the pictures again, then blows up a blow-up of a spot on the ground, making a photograph that is all grain, all ambiguity. There beneath a bush is . . . a body? It is night now in swinging London, and he takes himself back to the scene of the "crime."

The park, save for the swish of the wind in the trees, is silent, and is empty. A massive advertising sign – turquoise neon, an incomprehensible glyph – casts eerie illumination, a kind of high-tech moonlight. He treads the soft grass, wearing his dark green velvet sports coat and white trousers, approaching the bush where he thinks he may have spied the corpse, and suddenly he comes upon it. It lies, as in state, in a sumptuous puddle of tranquility, the gray suit, the gray complexion, the gray hair, the open eyes like a child's marbles. This is Antonioni's manifesto on seeing and filmmaking: instead of witnessing the world and then making an image, one commits oneself to making images and *afterward*, viewing what one has done, one sees.

Murray Pomerance

Date 1966

Nationality UK/Italy

Director Michelangelo Antonioni

Cast David Hemmings

Why It's Key Antonioni makes an important philosophical statement about pictures and the act of looking.

Opposite *Blowup*

Key Scene **Alma's monologue about two boys on the beach** *Persona*

If film is foremost a visual medium, why does the most indelible moment in *Persona* spring from spoken words? Alma (Andersson) is a nurse assigned to the care of Elisabet (Ullmann), an actress who's elected to never speak again. As part of Elisabet's therapy, Alma accompanies the troubled woman to a seaside vacation home for recuperation. "People tell me that I'm a good listener," chatters Alma to the silent Elizabet. "Isn't that strange? Nobody ever bothered to listen to me. Not the way you do now." Elizabet's implicit permission to speak is emboldening for Alma, prompting her to spill the details of an experience she'd held secret – how, one June afternoon, both she and a female friend ended up having public sex with two curious adolescents who had been spying on their sunbathing. Alma recounts this sequence of events with a tinge of disbelief, as if she's still not certain it was she who called to the boy mounting her friend: "Aren't you coming to me, too?" What's audacious is

not Alma's confession but the way Bergman achieves an out-of-body experience by framing this monologue in minimalist close-up. Something about the blankness of this shot combined with Alma's alternately tormented and joyous confession allows the audience to leave the screen and privately cavort in a sweaty and sunlit visualization ripe with the tang of seawater and the crumble of sand on hot skin. Bergman proves that film is always a visual medium, even when its images aren't visible.
Violet Glaze

Date 1966

Nationality Sweden

Director Ingmar Bergman

Cast Liv Ullmann, Bibi Andersson

Why It's Key Bergman's restraint in staging this scene makes the scenario described ineffably vivid.

Key Scene **The rubber-stamped tryst** *Closely Watched Trains*

In the autumn of 1944, young apprentice trainman Milos Hrma (Václav Neckár) is more concerned with losing his virginity than with the war going on around him and the German supply trains that roar through the rural Moravian station at which he works. Though he is smitten with conductress Masa (Jitka Bendova), Milos's failure with the opposite sex is even more galling when compared with the success of womanising train dispatcher Hubicka (Somr). Perhaps the film's most memorable scene is that in which Hubicka frolics with his latest conquest, Zdenka (Zelenohorská, who subsequently co-starred in Menzel's long-banned *Larks on a String*). In a sequence that manages to be both funny and erotic, Hubicka slowly and tenderly presses his bureaucratic rubber stamps on her thighs and buttocks.

Adapted from the autobiographical novel by Czech favorite son Bohumil Hrabal, *Closely Watched Trains* won the Academy Award for Best Foreign Language

Film in 1968 and remains among the most well-known and best-loved films of the Czech New Wave that was cut short by the 1968 Soviet invasion. Unlike many of his countrymen and fellow filmmakers, including Milos Forman and Ivan Passer, director Jirí Menzel (who mischievously cameos as a doctor in *Closely Watched Trains*) stayed to work in his homeland. Among his subsequent films were two additional Hrabal adaptations, *Cutting It Short* (1976) and *I Served the King of England* (2006); interestingly, both come from novels initially banned in Czechoslovakia. The deft handling of politically-charged metaphor and sexually-charged humanity render *Closely Watched Trains* an ingratiating triumph.
David Stratton

Date 1966

Nationality Czechoslovakia

Director Jirí Menzel

Cast Josef Somr, Jitka Zelenohorská

Original Title *Ostre sledované vlaky*

Why It's Key Czech director Menzel's fine adaptation of Bohumil Hrabal's much-loved novel deftly walks a tightrope between political satire and endearingly eccentric human behavior.

Opposite *Closely Watched Trains*

Key Scene **The king alone**
The Rise of Louis XIV

SPOILER

Rossellini ends his examination of the Sun King's rise with a three-minute shot following Louis (Patte) through his bedroom as he removes the trappings of his power. The camera pans with the king as he crosses to a table in high-water pantaloons, black stockings, and gold shoes. He removes his black gloves, hat, wig, medallion, sash, and frilly jacket. By convincing the aristocracy to dress in this finery he has diverted its attention from the matters of state he now controls. By inventing a fashion he's instituted a reign of what Rossellini biographer Tag Gallagher calls "totalitarianism via consumerism."

Alone in his room, he reads aloud from La Rochefoucauld's *Maxims*: "There is a loftiness that does not depend on fortune. It is a certain air of superiority that seems to destine one for great things.... This quality enables us to usurp other men's deference and places us further above them than birth, rank, and merit itself." He sits behind his desk and continues:

"Neither the sun nor death can be faced steadily." He puts the book down and repeats the last line. Fade to black.

The scene has melancholy, even morbid finality; the quotation is an epitaph. The book is like a mirror. Louis has made himself like the sun and like death. He can't be faced or challenged. Yet the scene isn't exactly heavy. Rossellini's moving camera keeps it lively even as he criticizes the kind of spectacle Louis uses to rule, the kind movies make of history.
A. S. Hamrah

Date 1966

Nationality France

Director Roberto Rossellini

Cast Jean-Marie Patte

Original Title *La prise de pouvoir par Louis XIV*

Why It's Key The film's concise dénouement movingly examines the nature of spectacle.

1960–1969

Key Speech **Declaration of principles**
The Wild Angels

The quintessential 1960s guilty pleasure, Roger Corman's *The Wild Angels* stars Peter Fonda as Heavenly Blues, leader of a California chapter of the Hell's Angels motorcycle club. When gangmate Loser (Bruce Dern) is killed, the crew drapes his coffin with a swastika and goes on a rampage of rape and destruction in and around a small-town church. Directors Peter Bogdanovich and Monte Hellman labored on the harmlessly transgressive script, and the film's interesting cast includes Diane Ladd (she and Dern are the parents of actress Laura Dern, who was conceived during the shoot), Dick Miller, Michael J. Pollard, and Nancy Sinatra as Blues's woman, Mike. In a climactic funeral service showdown with tight-lipped minister Norman Alden, the conflicted hero explains the bikers' rebellious nature with an inarticulateness bordering on the poetic: "We don't want nobody telling us what to do, we don't want nobody pushing us around.... We want to be *free*, we want to be free to *do*

what we want to *do*. We want to be free to *ride*, we want to be free to *ride* our *machines* without being *hassled* by *The Man!* And we want to get loaded, and we want to have a good time!" In 1967, much the same creative team – plus Jack Nicholson – made *The Trip*; less than two years after that, Fonda and Nicholson teamed with Dennis Hopper to make the genre sensation *Easy Rider*. But *The Wild Angels*, with its quaint nihilism and 26-cents-a-gallon gas, remains the touchstone.
David Stratton

Date 1966

Nationality USA

Director Roger Corman

Cast Peter Fonda, Nancy Sinatra, Diane Ladd, Norman Alden, Michael J. Pollard

Why It's Key It's a memorable moment from the film that kickstarted the low-budget biker movie craze a full three years before *Easy Rider*.

Opposite *The Wild Angels*

6660-85

Key Scene **Chasing yourself**
Kill, Baby...Kill!

This gothic horror is genuinely forbidding. Bava's vivid camerawork, with its emphatic zooms and rich '60s color, creates a shut-off atmosphere suited to the movie's Carpathian town, a blighted place dominated by a ruined villa. The story spirals around the ghost of a little girl whose appearance, announced by a bouncing white ball, predicts the deaths of those who see her. The little girl is a manipulable symbol the villa's baroness, her mother, uses to instill fear in the villagers who caused her daughter's death.

Bava analyzes the way fear breeds violence. When the villagers see the little girl they become so afraid they commit suicide. Science enters this world in the form of a coroner (Rossi-Stuart) sent to perform an autopsy, but his self-assured, enlightened attitude increases the death toll. Lured into the villa, his psyche begins to crumble like everything around him.

Responding to a woman calling his name from offscreen, the coroner bursts into a room where a painting of the villa covers one wall. He runs through the room to another door and bursts through that one – back into the same room. He continues this circuit eight times, getting closer to himself with each pass, until he grabs the shoulder of a figure running ahead of him and spins him around to find he's staring himself in the face. Bava does this through editing and pace, with two actors dressed alike. It's utterly convincing, a reminder cinema had all the tools it needed before computers.

A. S. Hamrah

Date 1966

Nationality Italy

Director Mario Bava

Cast Giacomo Rossi-Stuart

Original Title *Operazione paura*

Why It's Key Bava's penetrating gothic horror is psychologically resonant and unexpectedly avant-garde.

Key Scene **Last gesture of defiance**
7 Women

Completed in 1965 and belatedly and cursorily released, this unexpectedly woman-centered Ford film, his last feature, tells the story of a group of missionaries in China during the thirties and ends with the self-sacrifice of the unwelcome American doctor whom most regarded as a "black sheep." True to her oath, like all Ford's doctors, Dr. Cartwright (Bancroft in her greatest role), in order to save lives, agrees to be the concubine of the bandit chieftain Tunga Khan (Mazurki). She's cursed for that by the repressed and puritanical principal (Margaret Leighton) and is understood only by the latter's now rebellious assistant (Mildred Dunnock), who tries to dissuade their savior from commiting suicide ("It's a sin!"). Once the other women (and a newborn baby) are safely on their way, Dr. Cartwright, strikingly dressed like a Chinese courtesan in sharp contrast to her usual men's clothing, goes through the mission's corridors with a lamp to the Khan's room – in elegant, gliding movements accompanied by the subtlest and most caressing camerawork in Ford's career, and with a lighting that conjures what Sternberg's *Shanghai Express* or Capra's *The Bitter Tea of General Yen* could have been, had they been filmed in color and wide screen. She serves drinks, pouring poison into both cups, and, bowing in mock submission, she toasts him – "So long, you bastard!" – waits a moment while Tunga drops dead out of frame, then empties her cup and throws it with anger to the ground, as Ford's final work fades to black, in one of the most poignant moments in the history of film.

Miguel Marías

Date 1966

Nationality USA

Director John Ford

Cast Anne Bancroft, Mike Mazurki

Why It's Key With an almost Mizoguchian purity, this scene shows Ford's themes of sacrifice and glory in defeat, as a fitting end to his career.

Opposite *7 Women*

Key Scene **Mouchette's suicide**
Mouchette

If ever a director needed to be rescued from his admirers (and, indeed, from those attitudes encouraged by the director himself in his public statements), that director is Robert Bresson. The assumption that Bresson is essentially a Christian filmmaker whose work expresses his rigid religious beliefs has led to numerous misreadings and outright distortions. The most obvious victim of this tendency is *Mouchette*, which ends with a young girl, the eponymous Mouchette (Nortier), deciding to escape a brutal world of patriarchal violence and seemingly endless misery by drowning herself. Bresson specialists claim to find redemption here, even going so far as to link Bresson with a radical wing of Christianity that views suicide as a positive act. An unbiased look at *Mouchette*, however, reveals it to be an impassioned protest against an intolerable (but socially specific) situation, a protest many commentators simply ignore in order to render their religious interpretations more plausible. The forces of religion, though unquestionably present, are shown to be part of, rather than a solution to, the protagonist's problems, either signifiers of a transcendence notable only for its absence (the church, where Mouchette's father brutally pushes her into some holy water), or justifications for yet another ordeal (the prayer she is forced to sing). Mouchette's suicide, preceded (and in some ways foreshadowed) by a scene in which she watches several male hunters killing a helpless rabbit, is portrayed as inevitable, yet completely unredeemed. We can only sentimentalize this masterpiece by seeing its climax as transcendent.
Brad Stevens

Date 1967

Nationality France

Director Robert Bresson

Cast Nadine Nortier

Why It's Key This scene shows how Bresson's stylistic minimalism can be used to create a specific social protest.

Key Scene **The dance at Puerto del Fuego**
Face to Face

Although such critical attention as *Face to Face* has received tends to focus on the relationship between intellectual professor Brad Fletcher (Volonté) and uneducated outlaw Beauregard Bennet (Milian), the heart of Sergio Sollima's magnificent spaghetti western can be found in its depiction of Puerto del Fuego, a community of equals existing between civilization and savagery, which, as in many American Westerns, is defined by a dance sequence. But whereas the dance in *My Darling Clementine* (1946) emphasizes formality, *Face to Face*'s is neither entirely formal nor entirely informal: that energy expressed elsewhere in acts of aggression is not repressed by the dance, but rather accommodated within it, Bennet's solitary jig on a table co-existing harmoniously with the circle simultaneously formed by several other celebrants. Even Fletcher is moved, rejecting the claim of Maximilian (Ángel del Pozo) that Puerto del Fuego's inhabitants are "ghosts of the past... the dregs of the old romantic frontier who were not able to accept the coming of the telegraph, the railroad, or reality, for that matter" by insisting, "I've never seen anyone more real." Here is the midpoint where Fletcher's "mind" meets Bennet's "heart," where the violence of both men is dissipated in communal activity, and various conflicts (East/West, intelligence/strength, individual/group, book/gun, garden/wilderness) are resolved. Yet it is the combined presence of the professor and the outlaw that ultimately leads to Puerto del Fuego's destruction in a massacre rendered all the more unendurable by the fact that we witness only its aftermath. As in Michael Cimino's *Heaven's Gate* (1980), the values celebrated are felt to be already lost, crushed by the civilized savagery of a modern America that Fletcher and Bennet, in their opposed but complementary ways, represent.
Brad Stevens

Date 1967

Nationality Italy/Spain

Director Sergio Sollima

Cast Gian Maria Volonté, Tomas Milian

Original Titles *Faccia a Faccia / Cara a Cara*

Why It's Key This is among the finest Western dance sequences.

Key Scene **Striking the set** *A Man Vanishes*

SPOILER

In his 1973 film *F For Fake*, Orson Welles announced that he would tell the truth for one hour. When the hour is up, he slips into magic and lies. *A Man Vanishes*, made six years previously, undergoes a similar shape-shift in relation to the truth. It starts as a documentary. Yoshie Hayakawa's husband has disappeared. New-wave filmmaker Shohei Imamura offers to film her as she tries to find him. Using conventional observational techniques, he shows how she tracks down her husband's colleagues and friends and the people who saw him last. Gradually she pieces together the puzzle of his disappearance.

Towards the end of the movie, there is a scene in a tea-house. Yoshie is quizzing more people. One of them suggests that her husband was last seen with a woman. The scene is tense; then, strangely, we see Imamura in the shot. Then a voice refers to Imamura directly. Then he says "OK, strike the set." We cut to a very wide shot; stage hands knock down hardboard walls, and we see that we are in fact on a set. Somewhere along the course of the movie, Yoshie lost interest in finding her husband and transferred her affections to Imamura. The reason for the film had disappeared, and so the director turned it into a disquisition on reality and artifice. In the '60s, '70s and '80s, Japan produced some of the greatest documentaries ever made. Few are more gripping or revealing than *A Man Vanishes*.

Mark Cousins

Date 1967

Nationality Japan

Director Shohei Imamura

Cast Yoshie Hayakawa, Shohei Imamura

Original Title *Ningen johatsu*

Why It's Key This is the shocking moment when we realise that what we are watching is no longer a documentary.

Key Scene **A cup of coffee becomes the cosmos** *2 or 3 Things I Know About Her*

In some ways, *2 or 3 Things I Know About Her* is the color and 'Scope climax of Godard's "research" before 1968, and its personal importance can be felt in how he narrates the film in a kind of urgent whisper. Following the day in the life of Juliette (Vlady), a suburban housewife who works part-time as a prostitute in order to buy clothes, he follows her into a Paris café, where she drinks a Coke. Then he cuts to other people and objects in her immediate vicinity while delivering a poetic monologue about his difficulties in coming to terms with the modern world. Midway through his rap, he settles on a gigantic close-up of a cup of coffee.

Between pauses and cutaways, he ponders the swirling black liquid as if it were the solar system, turning metaphysical: "Since I can't extricate myself from the objectivity that crushes me or the subjectivity that isolates me, I have to listen, I have to look around myself more than ever. The world – *mon semblable, mon frère*."

He cuts to closer and closer views of the coffee as a sugar cube drops in and dissolves: "The world alone today, where revolutions are impossible, where bloody wars menace me, where capitalism is no longer sure of its rights and the working class is in retreat, where the overwhelming progress of science gives future centuries an oppressive presence, where the future is more present than the present, where far-off galaxies are at my door... *mon semblable, mon frère*."

Jonathan Rosenbaum

Date 1967

Nationality France

Director Jean-Luc Godard

Cast Marina Vlady

Original Title *2 ou 3 Choses que je sais d'elle*

Why It's Key Godard finds the universe in a grain of sand – or, more precisely, in a cup of coffee and a sugar cube.

Key Scene **The deportation**
Commissar

During the civil war in Russia, a female Soviet commissar (played by the remarkable Mordukova) realises that she is pregnant. It is too late to get rid of the baby. Her comrades send her to give birth in the care of the large family of a Jewish shoemaker (Bykov). The time that the Commissar spends with the family gradually changes her take on issues such as violence and historical justice. Soon after she has given birth, the town is attacked by the Whites; the very presence of the Commissar puts the shoemaker's family at risk.

It is with this important realisation that a disturbing flash-forward occurs. As Yiddish music (composed by Alfred Schnittke) plays on the sound track, the whole Jewish population of a town, marked with yellow stars sewn on their clothes, are being deported through the foggy streets to an unknown destination. The film takes place in 1920, but, as if in astonishing anticipation of the Holocaust, the deportees progress through a dark passageway and arrive at a murky place where they are met by others like them, wearing the uniforms of prisoners of a Nazi concentration camp. The camera rises into the air, following the smoke from the camp's chimney.

Reportedly, the film was shelved because of its avant-garde approach and particularly because of this scene. In Soviet cinema it was legitimate to highlight other aspects of suffering, but not the Jewish Holocaust.

Dina Iordanova

Date 1967

Nationality USSR

Director Alexandr Askoldov

Cast Nonna Mordukova, Rolan Bykov

Original Title *Komissar*

Why It's Key A traumatic flash forward into history anticipates the Holocaust.

Key Scene **When Françoise met Kelly**
The Young Girls of Rochefort

Nothing, arguably, rivals the musical in its ability to externalise emotions like love, longing, and ecstatic *joie de vivre*, and Demy's second foray into the genre outdoes even his wholly sung *The Umbrellas of Cherbourg* by adding dance to the equation. Repainting the titular coastal town in an array of summery hues to match the characters' bright garb also contributed to an upbeat mood of romantic infatuation, while Michel Legrand's jazzy score – probably his finest – and the casting of sisters Catherine Deneuve and Françoise Dorléac opposite American musical stars like Gene Kelly and George Chakiris enhanced the fairytale theme of a near-universal quest for a dream type.

And when the soulmates played by Kelly and Dorléac first meet – he helping her pick up the contents of a bag dropped in the street – it's as if the encounter were fated. Legrand's "piano concerto" theme soars as their eyes meet, and though she walks off home saying she's unsure they'll meet again, he feels otherwise, and as the symphonic melody shifts tempo to an increasingly racy, jazzy fugue, he saunters off down the street, expressing his joy at having found his ideal woman through words and ever more energetic dance. It's here the scene really takes off, Demy's use of both professional dancers and local townsfolk (including two young twin brothers) as witnesses to his hero's happiness serving to ground his fantasy of romantic destiny in the kind of milieu familiar from the audience's own lives. In short, the mundane becomes magical; for Demy's lovers, there really is heaven on earth.

Geoff Andrew

Date 1967

Nationality France

Director Jacques Demy

Cast Françoise Dorléac, Gene Kelly

Original Title *Les Demoiselles de Rochefort*

Why It's Key It's the most vibrantly joyous scene in perhaps the most exuberantly energetic film in a genre renowned for its vitality.

Opposite *The Young Girls of Rochefort*

Key Scene **There goes the bride**
The Graduate

Benjamin Braddock (Hoffman) is adrift after college, not wanting a conventional career – such as "plastics," to quote the film's most famous word – but lacking an alternative. Then a family friend named Mrs. Robinson (Anne Bancroft) lures him into having an affair. Ben isn't sure this is a good idea, or even that he's having a good time, especially since his parents want him to date Mrs. Robinson's daughter, Elaine (Ross), who happens to be his age.

Ben and Elaine do get together, and soon they fall in love. Then she discovers his affair with her mom, and she takes revenge by getting engaged to another man. Learning that her wedding is imminent, heartbroken Ben leaps into his car, drives frantically toward the faraway church, runs out of gas just before he gets there, and continues his agonizing race on foot. Finally he arrives, peers through a window at the ceremony, and in a stunning twist on movie-wedding conventions, he sees the minister close his book, signifying that the knot has already been tied. All he can do is yowl "Elaine!!!" like a desolate animal in a plate-glass cage.

But she hears him, and better yet, she answers in kind: "Ben!!!" And suddenly she's fleeing the altar, as Ben holds off the outraged congregation by swinging a huge cross as if it were a medieval weapon. Boarding a city bus, they head toward an unknown future, their faces alternating between glee and thoughtfulness. Their lives will never be the same. And neither will the movies.

David Sterritt

Date 1967

Nationality USA

Director Mike Nichols

Cast Dustin Hoffman, Katharine Ross

Why It's Key This audacious comedy helped define an era, and no scene was more important than the climax, which breaks one of Hollywood's most sacred rules by declaring that love and marriage don't necessarily go together, and that love is way more important.

Opposite *The Graduate*

1960–1969

409

Key Scene **Perry Smith's final monologue**
In Cold Blood

The script called for a monologue spoken against the backdrop of a rainy night, as convicted murderer Perry Smith (Blake) reminisced about a pivotal instant in his relationship with his father. One desperate evening, the old man pulled a gun on his little boy, setting in motion a chain of events that led the adult Smith to where he now stood dressed in prison blues, shackled, and awaiting the hangman for his role in the massacre of the blameless Clutter family. But in setting up the semi-routine shot, cinematographer Conrad Hall realized that if Blake stepped close to the window during his soliloquy, the melting spatters of rain projected onto his face from the backlit window resembled shadowy tears. In the final print, Smith recounts his childhood trauma dispassionately. "I guess the only thing I'm gonna miss in this world is that poor old man and his hopeless dreams," he concludes, his inflection devoid of emotion. But the cascading water reflected rolling down his cheeks tells another story.

Hall went on to win three Oscars for his work on *Butch Cassidy and the Sundance Kid* (1969), *American Beauty* (1999), and *Road to Perdition* (2002), but in his storied career he never surpassed the serendipitous elegance of that masterful shot in *In Cold Blood*. As he himself described it in the cinematography documentary *Visions Of Light* (1992), Blake could allow his character an appropriate restraint without sacrificing deeper meaning because "the visuals were crying for him."

Violet Glaze

Date 1967

Nationality USA

Director Richard Brooks

Cast Robert Blake, Scott Wilson, John Forsythe

Why It's Key Cinematographer Conrad Hall finds a poetic substitute for real tears.

Key Scene **Chris's rampage**
Point Blank

Walker (Marvin) brings Chris (Dickinson) to an ultramodern desert house that belongs to the powerful crime syndicate against which he's been waging a one-man war. Pissed off at him for his one-track murderousness, Chris beats Walker repeatedly with both hands for about a minute. Frustrated by the result (he barely totters, but she crumbles to the floor, exhausted), she goes on an invisible rampage through the house, first turning on all the electric appliances in the kitchen (forcing Walker to shut them off one by one), then playing cool Johnny Mandel jazz on the hi-fi real loud (unable to find the right button on the elaborate control panel, Walker simply tears apart the reel-to-reel tape), finally commandeering the house's public-address system to deliver Walker a message in the tones of a smooth-jazz disk jockey ("Why don't you just lie down and die?"). In Boorman's remarkably self-conscious thriller, Chris's rampage is not only an ironic revenge (by means of signifiers of femininity) on the male destructiveness that the genre conventionally celebrates; it's also a unique piece of time-based mixed-media environmental art, whose strategies reproduce those of the film itself: to bring into play the trappings and devices of late capitalism in order to expose the emptiness of the motives and requirements of the old *film noir* game.
Chris Fujiwara

Date 1967

Nationality USA

Director John Boorman

Cast Lee Marvin, Angie Dickinson

Why It's Key The heroine, with the support of the film, launches an all-out attack on the privilege of male destructiveness.

Opposite *Point Blank*

Key Scene **The fourth shot**
The Red and the White

Hungary, 1919. In the aftermath of the Russian Revolution, the influence of which is spreading westwards, Hungarian Communist volunteers side with the Bolshevik "Reds" in a civil war against their Czarist "White" countrymen. In the film's fourth shot, staged by a river, a Red soldier hides as another is interrogated, then shot, by a White officer. Some of the action begins in the extreme distance, but Jancsó and his cinematographer Tamás Somló film this and the foreground without cutting. The camera tracks, then stops, ten times during their three-minute shot. The moves are edgy, they capture the anxiety of the hiding soldier, yet the film never seems to sympathise, or become complicit, with the agonies of the civil war it depicts. We see a series of humiliating undressings and appalling fratricides, yet remain detached because there are few close-ups and no character-centred scenes. Everything is camera-centred, beautifully choreographed but as disturbing as and, apparently, as uncaring as Pasolini's *Salo*. The killings are arbitrary. The control enjoyed by the officers seems uncomfortably related to the control with which Jancsó stages this remarkable war film. Such an approach is far from the Manichean certainties of socialist realism, so no wonder *The Red and the White* was banned in the USSR. Its elegance and *froideur* are unforgettable and influenced filmmakers like Béla Tarr and Fred Kelemen in subsequent decades.
Mark Cousins

Date 1967

Nationality Hungary

Director Miklós Jancsó

Cast József Madaras, Tibor Molnár

Original Title *Csillagosok, katonák*

Why It's Key This is a great example of Jancsó's long-held shot-sequences.

501-99

Key Scene **Birds and bullets fly**
Bonnie and Clyde

As a teenager, I was narrator in a school play about the glamorous Australian "bushranger" outlaw/rebel, Ned Kelly. As Kelly lay dead, mowed down by police, I came on stage to declaim: "The sad, lonely life, and the lonely ending... " *Bonnie and Clyde* also ends with the murder of its beyond-the-law heroes. "Birds and bullets fly" is the apt DVD chapter title for this finale: before the bullets, Bonnie Parker (Dunaway) and Clyde Barrow (Beatty), euphorically happy, are alive to everything happening around them in the natural world, like that flock of birds. Little do they realise that this burst of disturbed nature is a last-second omen, and that they have been lured to their death, at the roadside, by an innocent-looking bystander. Many viewers misremember the murder as a more protracted and extravagant spectacle than it actually is; the volleys of fire, and the slow-motion that captures the strangely lyrical paroxysms of Bonnie's and Clyde's bodies, are quite restrained compared to many later films. Due to Penn's careful play of contrasts – the quick change in mood, the movement from quiet to loud – this finale is certainly sudden and shocking. But what really clinches the scene is the mute, disquieting ballet that follows. The cops slowly approach the corpses (which are no longer seen) and, in the final shot, a car window's looming bullet-hole seems to fracture the image itself. The film cuts to black before the chief cop can speak: no comforting "sad, lonely life" wrap-up here.

Adrian Martin

Date 1967

Nationality USA

Director Arthur Penn

Cast Warren Beatty, Faye Dunaway, Denver Pyle, Dub Taylor.

Why It's Key The shocking climax closes the film with no comforting wrap-up.

Opposite *Bonnie and Clyde*

1960–1969

413

Key Scene **Doorway to nowhere**
Playtime

What Tati always manages to bring to the screen is an entire universe, to some degree mirroring the world in which we live and to some degree extending that world into a ballet. *Playtime* follows the adventures of Tati's regular character, Hulot, stuck this time in the suburbs of Paris with local citizens and a crowd of American tourists. In Tati, every shot is composed with the rigor of a Mondrian and choreographed as though by Massine. The movements of fingers, walking sticks, dogs, pipes, elevators, office chairs, airplanes, cashiers, pipes, dripping water... all possible objects, living and not, are intertwined in a picture at once gloriously abstract and hilariously contingent. This film, Tati's undisputed masterpiece, and one of the great examples of both comic filmmaking and mime, highlights a scene in a brand new nightclub – so new, indeed, the workers are still gluing floor tiles and fixing the ceiling as the first-night guests, in their gowns and tuxedos, blithely arrive. One of Tati's central issues has to do with the irony of putting up appearances, maintaining a good "front" to cover for weaknesses or improprieties, even for vacuity, underneath. No moment in Tati, or in comedy, more brilliantly or more simply conveys this irony than the broken-door sequence at the club. The plate-glass door has accidentally been smashed to smithereens. Hulot oversees the quick sweeping up of the glass, then takes the brass door handle and stands at attention, moving the invisible "door" open and closed for an arriving guest. Soon, the doorman picks up his cue and continues this insanity. Everyone's perfectly delighted with the grace and efficiency, and not a soul sees that the emperor's door has no real close.

Murray Pomerance

Date 1967

Nationality France/Italy

Director Jacques Tati

Cast Tati, Léon Doyen

Why It's Key Tati offers a brilliant demonstration of the irony of appearance, which is central to film.

Key Scene **In a film built on stillness, something finally happens** *Wavelength*

Wavelength is often described as an unbroken zoom across an empty room. But the room isn't empty: It has furniture, people enter a few times, and the zoom's final goal is a photograph tacked on the opposite wall. And the zoom isn't uninterrupted – indeed, the cinematography is action-packed in a minimalist way, with splices, superimpositions, changing color filters, and slight hitches and pauses as the zoom proceeds.

One of the movie's aims is to foreground the richly artificial nature of cinema, always a product of culturally conditioned minds and hands. Its other, related aim is to suggest cinema's capacity for simulating – and stimulating – human thought on its most contemplative, meditative levels. The film as a whole accomplishes this by asking its viewers to watch, wait, and wax very, very patient as the zoom's 45-minute trajectory gradually unfolds. Within this, a key moment occurs when a man (played by Hollis Frampton, a great avant-garde filmmaker) walks into the room and drops dead.

It's an event worthy of melodrama, but the camera doesn't acknowledge that anything has happened – the zoom simply continues, excluding the corpse from view as the lens's field of vision grows ever narrower. Ultimately the screen is filled with a tight close-up of the photograph on the far wall: a picture of ocean waves, at once boundlessly vast and as modest as a snapshot. Snow's camera has unveiled the power of Zen-like focus and deliberation, and the ability of filmic artifice to transcend the human world it replicates.
David Sterritt

Date 1967

Nationality Canada/USA

Director Michael Snow

Cast Hollis Frampton, Amy Taubin, Joyce Wieland

Why It's Key The camera's quiet concentration offers an unsurpassed instance of cinema as contemplation.

Key Scene **Antoine has coffee with Fabienne Tabard** *Stolen Kisses*

This endearingly sweet comedy, the third in the five-episode Antoine Doinel cycle, opened in Paris in September 1968, after months of quasi-revolutionary national turmoil, and seemed irrelevant to many younger viewers and critics at the time. Antoine (Léaud), after a less than honorable discharge from the army, is seen drifting from job to odd job (including a long stretch as a would-be private eye), courting and quarelling with the prim and proper Christine (Claude Jade), whom he will ultimately marry, and mooning over Fabienne Tabard, his boss's wife, played by the exquisite Delphine Seyrig ("She is not a woman, she's an apparition," he enthuses when asked to describe her.) The Fabienne-Antoine relationship, typical of Truffaut's recurring theme of women as "magical," takes a comical turn when he is having coffee with her at the Tabards' after her rather obnoxious husband (Lonsdale) has left on some errand. In a fixed two-shot she pours coffee for an obviously flustered Antoine, neither of them saying a word. After a while Fabienne gets up, goes to the record player, and asks: "Do you like music, Antoine?" to which he answers: "Yes, sir" (this recycles an anecdote related by Anatole France in a book of childhood memories, an example of Truffaut's frequent borrowings). After his blunder, a nervous, embarrassed Antoine spills his coffee and flees in shame. His fiasco will have a fairy-tale happy ending, however, when his idol visits him in his room the next morning and delivers a quite remarkable monologue ("I am not an apparition, I am a woman, it's just the opposite") before joining him in bed (off-screen – the scene is left to our imagination).
Jean-Pierre Coursodon

Date 1968

Nationality France

Director François Truffaut

Cast Jean-Pierre Léaud, Delphine Seyrig, Michel Lonsdale

Original Title *Baisers volés*

Why It's Key It's one of many delightful scenes in Truffaut's sunniest picture.

Key Film
Innocence Unprotected

Makavejev takes footage from the first Serbian talkie – an outrageously silly and amateurish melodrama from 1942 directed by and starring body-builder Dragoljub Aleksić – and mixes it with other documentary and found footage. (Such a technique was pioneered in Makavejev's 1967 *Love Affair; or The Case of the Missing Switchboard Operator* and successfully continued in his controversial *WR: Mysteries of the Organism* [1971] and *Sweet Movie* [1975].) The backbone of *Innocence Unprotected* is Aleksić's film, which concerns his amorous pursuit of a modest Belgrade girl and is punctuated by scenes showing off the muscles of his chest and upper arms. This footage is intercut with stunts performed in the 1940s (including Aleksić's flight over Belgrade, hanging from an airplane by his teeth) and with footage of the war-time political situation. Extensive use is made of present-day interviews with Aleksić, who, after suffering serious health setbacks, has reinvented himself as a Titoist hero and celebrates a glorious comeback in the new Yugoslavia of the 1960s.

Through the audacious and imaginative use of associative montage, ranging from music collages to the intrepid intercutting of documentary and feature material, Makavejev investigates the relationship of personal manoeuvring, volatile politics, and historical memory, bringing together clashing accounts and challenging the viewer into subverting and questioning official narratives. The film is an avant-garde work that plays with stereotypes and exposes bigotry, while treading the fine line between political and personal referencing, between mockery and splendor.
Dina Iordanova

Date 1968
Nationality Yugoslavia
Director Dusan Makavejev
Cast Dragoljub Aleksić
Original Title *Nevinost bez zastite*
Why It's Key This bizarre masterpiece combines collage techniques and associative montage.

Key Person **Bulle Ogier**
Gigi la Folle *Les Idoles*

For over 35 years, *Les Idoles* was effectively a lost film. It resurfaced briefly in French cinemas in 2004, but today exists on a Japanese-release DVD; front, back, inside, and even printed on the disc itself, is one member of the cast: Bulle Ogier. She had appeared in several shorts before 1967, but *Les Idoles* marked her feature debut. And what a debut it is: as Gigi la Folle ("crazy Gigi"), Ogier channels the *yé-yé* pop-starlet phenomenon into something magnificently monstrous. She hops, struts, squeals, twirls an umbrella – and her ensemble numbers with the other "idols," Charly (Clémenti) and Simon (Kalfon), are even wilder. But this film was no one-off, freak occurrence: for seven years, Ogier had honed her craft as an experimental actor in the troupe led by a legendary figure, Marc'O, whose trajectory runs from '50s Lettrism to the creation of a new stage form which he called "music-theatre." *Les Idoles* is music-theatre from a politically radical, Situationist viewpoint: these idol-celebrities are a grotesque exaggeration of tendencies within the "society of the spectacle" (the film is remarkably prophetic), poised between narcissistic splendor, artistic burn-out, and ruthless exploitation by sinister back-stage Svengalis of the pop-rock music industry. Alternating performance scenes, a press conference, and vignettes of the twisted personal lives of the stars, the film is a document both of its time and of the heady avant-garde culture that allowed Ogier to become a singularly "non-psychological" actor in subsequent films by Rivette, Buñuel, Tanner, Oliveira, and Ruiz.
Adrian Martin

Date 1968
Nationality France
Director Marc'O
Cast Ogier, Pierre Clémenti, Jean-Pierre Kalfon, Valérie Lagrange, Michèle Moretti
Why It's Key Ogier channels the *yé-yé* pop-starlet phenomenon into something magnificently monstrous.

Key Speech **Child's play**
Night of the Living Dead

Johnny (Streiner) is having a real day of it today: he is forced to accompany his sister Barbara (O'Dea) to their father's grave, although he doesn't even remember him. He begins to joke, saying in a sepulchral voice: "They're coming to get you, Barbara! … They're coming for you!" Stiffly moving toward the young girl, Johnny revives a game they both played in the cemetery when they were children. The two are in very different states of mind: whereas he has surmounted the usual childhood fears, Barbara takes the teasing very seriously and remains afraid of what was frightening to her as a kid. She believes that inanimate things can suddenly come to life in spite of all appearances: she is the one who hasn't grown up yet. Aren't horror films supposed to play with our fears? Obviously, her beliefs can explain the state of shock in which Barbara will remain during most of the film. Johnny's prank also sports an ironic undertone since it announces what will soon happen to them, and, although *Night of the Living Dead* is rightly regarded as a film that made the horror genre enter its modern age, it also anticipates the trend in much more recent horror films toward a sustained use of self-reflexivity. More than 20 years later, Romero will himself hint at this moment in *Two Evil Eyes* (1990), when a living-dead character declares: "They are coming for you, Jessica!" Unfortunately, to far lesser effect.

Frank Lafond

Date 1968

Nationality USA

Director George A. Romero

Cast Judith O'Dea, Russell Streiner

Why It's Key It's one of the most famous lines in horror cinema.

Opposite *Night of the Living Dead*

1960–1969

Key Scene **Smash-up**
Just for the Hell of It

SPOILER

Just for the Hell of It is a juvenile-delinquent shocker the director of *Blood Feast* slapped together in Florida the same year he made four other films. It is unconcerned with quality, but within its context of indifference its destructiveness is triumphant. The film is a blur of flailing. Long, desultory group fights filmed indifferently through a dirty lens alternate with scenes of absurd rampage where the cast puts a baby in a trash can or tears up magazines in a waiting room.

The violence begins before the credits. A prank at a house party triggers a dozen post-teenagers to break mirrors, rip up sofas with knives, smash tables and lamps, and chop a piano to bits. They smear the walls with red paint in this pseudo-happening that would shame an Action artist, and which predates the Manson murders by a year. The scene plays without music; Lewis fades out on it coldly.

Lewis was a literature professor who switched to advertising before making nudie and gore movies. Currently he's a big shot in direct marketing who has said his fondest wish is to conduct a symphony orchestra. No filmmaker has insisted he is not an artist and that film is not an art like Lewis has. He says it in every interview; his films shout it in the streets, from Ozark mountaintops and Florida motel signs. *Just for the Hell of It* is cheap and ugly, but if isn't art, nothing is. Which is exactly Lewis's point.

A. S. Hamrah

Date 1968

Nationality USA

Director Herschell Gordon Lewis

Cast Ray Sager, Nancy Lee Noble

Why It's Key This nihilistic exploitation film defies categorization.

Key Scene **Stuck needle**
Les Biches

Scenes of people listening to records have a special quality. Maybe it's because the black disc spins like a film reel. (Bowling is like that, too.) In *Les Biches* Chabrol makes that quality unnerving. The characters may want to hear the record they're playing, but instead of enjoying it with them we watch and listen like the only person not drinking at their party.

By the time they ask the curiously-named Why (Sassard) to put on a record, it's already clear Frédérique (Audran) and Paul (Trintignant) have made her their servant. They ask her for things all the time: *Get me a beer, Why, bring me the butter, pour me some cognac.* The music she puts on is what they already have on the turntable, easy listening music for rich perverts, a cross between Poulenc and Les Baxter featuring a high-pitched, wordless vocal. As the three of them drink and fondle each other, the record gets stuck in a groove, and they ask Why to get up and fix it. The music follows them as they stagger to Frédérique's bedroom, where Frédérique shuts the door on Why, who loved Paul first.

Les Biches, a clearing of the decks for Chabrol, ushered in six years of great filmmaking. Chabrol used it to push himself past the nouvelle vague. Its ménage is *Jules and Jim* gone sour in 1968. In *Les Biches*, those who have are given more, while what little the homeless street artist Why has is taken away.
A. S. Hamrah

Date 1968

Nationality France

Director Claude Chabrol

Cast Jacqueline Sassard, Stéphane Audran, Jean-Louis Trintignant

Why It's Key Chabrol inaugurates a peak period in his career with this curdled ménage à trois.

Key Event **Jean-Luc Godard punches Iain Quarrier**

Cinema's history is littered with evidence of those struggles that so frequently take place between artists and their sources of finance: Erich von Stroheim's *Greed* (1924) and Orson Welles's *The Magnificent Ambersons* (1942) are perhaps the most obvious examples, existing today only as a series of disjointed fragments. By contrast with these ruined masterpieces, the interference to which Jean-Luc Godard's *One Plus One* (1968) was subjected seems almost insignificant: producer Iain Quarrier changed the film's title to *Sympathy for the Devil* and added the final version of that now-eponymous Rolling Stones song (which Godard had shown being rehearsed) to the closing sequence's soundtrack. In order to accommodate this song in its entirety, Quarrier also extended the ending through the use of a still-frame. These alterations, though small, wreaked havoc with the director's concept, which was to show groups (consisting of musicians and revolutionaries) incapable of bringing their various projects to a state of completion: as Godard (quoted in Richard Roud's *Jean-Luc Godard*) pointed out, "'one plus one' does not mean 'one plus one equals two'. It means what it says." When the producer's cut premiered at 1968's London Film Festival, Godard's response was direct and to the point: before leaving the screening, he punched Quarrier in the face. Godard, in both his films and his public activities and pronouncements, often makes us confront those ideological and financial realities which determine the shape of cultural works, but are usually rendered invisible in the interests of bourgeois good taste. By turning the battle between art and commerce into a genuine battle in which actual blows are exchanged, Godard's attack on Quarrier serves as a quintessentially Godardian "moment."
Brad Stevens

Date November 29, 1968

Why It's Key This event renders explicit those usually hidden conflicts between art and commerce.

Opposite Jean-Luc Godard

Key Film
The Colour of Pomegranates

In *The Colour of Pomegranates*, the Armenian poet-troubadour Sayat Nova grows up soaked in a culture in which pre-Christian, Christian, and Islamic elements are intertwined inextricably. The film reflects this intertwining with its imagery of pagan sculptures, drawings on Biblical themes (with floral motifs that belong to Islamic traditions), carpets, jars, pomegranates... St. George – the patron saint of many countries, including Armenia – figures in the film. A *hamam* (or "Turkish bath"; it exists in various forms from Russia to Turkey to Rome) serves as a setting.

The film is semi-autobiographical in its delineation of the struggles of the artist and his suffering. It is a testament, as are his other films, to Paradjanov's thinking-out the complex interrelationships between core (the metropolises of the USSR) and periphery (Ukraine, Transcaucasus, and Central Asia), Europe and Asia. Paradjanov's films celebrate homelessness: not residing in one home, one culture, one nation.

Paradjanov uses the frontality of theatre in the cinematic frame. Frontality ruptures the perspectival look. It is an affront to a gaze that wishes to enter and subjugate. He also refuses the continuum of diegetic time in favour of a succession of tableaux bound together by sound bridges or by repetitions-in-difference. The sound, too, raises itself from mere ambient sound to the level of metaphor: the rustling of paper, or the sounds of a baby crying mingled with muted voices in a bathhouse, seem to reach us by travelling through a tunnel in time. The stylised actions of the actors only serve to underline the break with realistic delineation of character. The Brechtian notion of gest – the gesture that takes on historical meaning – is employed very effectively by Paradjanov. This also explains his minimal reliance on the realistic effects of dialogue in his films.
Rashmi Doraiswamy

Date 1968

Nationality USSR

Director Sergei Paradjanov

Cast Sofiko Chiaureli, Melkon Aleksanyan

Original Title *Sayat Nova*

Why It's Key Paradjanov's unique film style challenges not just socialist realism, but all forms of realism and modernism.

Key Scene **The gymnastics scene**
If...

Towards the midway mark of this Vigo-inspired semi-surrealist study of British schoolboys in revolt is a scene in which our trio of heroes goes to the gym. Wallace (Warwick) prepares to do his gymnastics routine, and as he does so, he looks up at the balcony, where a group of younger boys is preparing to leave. Bobby Phillips (Webster), much prized by the "Whips" (a select group of seniors who virtually run the enitre school), is pulling his sweater up over his head. As he does so, Wallace grabs the exercise bar. In his BFI book on the film, Mark Sinker describes the scene as "Phillips puts on his sweater, tidies his tousled fringe, watches Wallace from the balcony, ever aware he radiates allure. Wallace gives Phillips a het-coquette over-shoulder glance and grin, then leaps into his beautiful slow-motion gymnastic dance in the air – and the music shifts from soft pulse-blood drumming to poised chords defying gravity." How much Phillips may be aware of his allure is open to question, but not the

intense romanticism of the scene. Wallace is offering up his body as an act of love. Though we later see these lovers asleep in bed, no sexual act is ever shown taking place between them – and that's what this scene is for. Like the dance duets in Astaire-Rogers musicals, it's better than sex.
David Ehrenstein

Date 1968

Nationality UK

Director Lindsay Anderson

Cast Richard Warwick, Rupert Webster

Why It's Key It's one of the most beautiful expressions of homoerotic love the cinema has yet given us.

Opposite *If...*

Key Scene **Welcome home!**
Planet of the Apes

When an astronaut is stranded on a planet ruled by evolved races of apes, he can never be sure of anything. That's what George Taylor (Heston) learns in the last scene of *Planet of the Apes*, when he discovers a half-buried Statue of Liberty on a beach and realizes that all this time he was still on Earth. This visually striking use of America's greatest symbol does not figure in Pierre Boulle's novel and was suggested by screenwriter Rod Serling, who, as the creator of *The Twilight Zone*, was most familiar with such narrative reversals. At first, only huge fragments of an unknown shape are visible in the foreground, as the film cleverly postpones the shock revelation until the very last shot. The absence of music at that point and during the following end credits (we hear only the rumble of the waves) emphasizes the hopelessness of the situation and helps us to stand back from the fiction. Though its visual value can't be disregarded, this climactic twist also conveys the film's anti-militarist message and lets us consider the hypothetical consequences of the nuclear menace that pervaded the Cold War era – something that various remarks about the warmongering nature of human beings long foreshadowed. "We finally really did it. You maniacs! You blew it up!", Taylor can rightly complain. The ending of the film forces the spectators to put everything they have seen before into a new perspective – a trick that contemporary horror and science-fiction films, including M. Night Shyamalan's *Sixth Sense* (1999), will often rely upon.

Frank Lafond

Date 1968

Nationality USA

Director Franklin J. Schaffner

Cast Charlton Heston

Why It's Key It's one of the most famous endings in cinema history.

Opposite *Planet of the Apes*

423

Key Scene **Chet and the women**
Faces

Unfolding largely over the course of one long night, *Faces* is in essence a collection of seemingly endless, shapeless scenes, almost all of which feature a startling moment of rupture, an instant when the mood turns ugly on a dime. In the first extended sequence, grizzled businessman Dickie (John Marley) and his friend Freddie (Fred Draper) are drunkenly carousing with Jeannie (Gena Rowlands), a woman they've just met at a bar. The unraveling moment happens when a suddenly jealous Freddie asks Jeannie how much she charges. Later in the film, another such moment – a canny mirror image of the earlier one – occurs when Chet (Cassel), the focal point of an impromptu ladies' night out, abruptly informs his new acquaintances, "We're making fools of ourselves."

In response to her husband's walking out, Maria (Carlin) and three friends have ventured out to a club and impulsively picked up Chet, a fresh-faced, uninhibited contrast to their ossified husbands. Back at Maria's, Chet loosens up the ladies with alcohol-fueled dancing and flirtation. The mood is awkward but tinged with excitement – until his matter-of-fact statement lands with a thud, provoking obvious humiliation and compensatory tantrums from the two most uptight women, who leave in a huff. Florence (Gulliver), the oldest, not only stays but flings herself at Chet, pleading for a kiss with a desperate abandon that is almost mortifying. If the viewer is spared embarrassment, it's because Chet doesn't find Florence embarrassing. He kisses her full on the mouth. His generosity may seem heroic, but as the impact of the scene sinks in, it's clear that the true bravery lies in Dorothy's ostensibly pathetic actions. What Cassavetes is celebrating here is the desire for upheaval, the appetite for risk, the fight to feel alive.

Dennis Lim

Date 1968

Nationality USA

Director John Cassavetes

Cast Seymour Cassel, Lynn Carlin, Dorothy Gulliver

Why It's Key This extended sequence is a perfect example of the thrilling tonal unpredictability and emotional intensity that characterize John Cassavetes' best work.

Key Scene **Moo**
The Killing of Sister George

The success of *The Dirty Dozen* in 1967 allowed Robert Aldrich to found his own company, inaugurating one of the most intriguing, deeply personal phases of any Hollywood career, expressing his uncompromising, tough-as-nails worldview in a series of fascinating films combining the aggressive pessimism of his earlier noirs with a discomfitingly honest vulgarity. They included Aldrich's personal favorite, *The Killing of Sister George*, a black comedy about lesbians that was commercially killed by the newly installed X rating, which caused its suppression on many theater circuits. Which ironically mirrors the fate of its heroine, played by Beryl Reid as an unrepenting butch dyke afraid that "Sister George," the smalltown do-gooder she plays in an impossibly idyllic BBC TV series, may be killed off as her alcohol-fueled private escapades cause the station public embarrassment. Two of Aldrich's favorite themes – abuse of power and fakery threatening to overwhelm

reality – get a particularly claustrophobic workout, as Reid's character is increasingly stifled, by lies (on TV and in private) she alone rebels against, and oppressive *mise en scène*. With characteristic merciless ambivalence Aldrich had introduced her as abusive, but she turns out to be the victim, gaining in tragic humanity as she is gradually stripped of personal certainties. The ending is bleak, heartbreaking and supremely sarcastic: after her demise as George, she destroys the set (including George's fake coffin) in a futile fit, then sinks down and lets out three desperate moos, in preparation for her next job, voice artist for Clarabell, the "flawed, credible cow."

Christoph Huber

Date 1968

Nationality USA

Director Robert Aldrich

Cast Beryl Reid

Why It's Key Aldrich's personal favorite among his films is a high point of his most uncompromising period. And the heartbreaking ending nails his peculiar blend of vulgarity, honesty, pessimism, and anger.

Key Scene **The traffic jam**
Week-end

Cinephiles can easily become disenchanted at the glimpse of a behind-the-scenes production still: did that magnificent camera movement, so lyrical and sweeping in one's memory, really require only that miserable little piece of tracking rail? It is a curious, almost magical property of cinema. *Week-end* – which is in every respect a militantly anti-magic, anti-illusion film – allows itself one virtuoso touch: the 7-minute, 40-second sequence that Godard modestly trumpeted as "the longest tracking shot in cinema history"; it seems (in the viewer's mind) to stretch for kilometres, but is, in fact, 300 metres. The content of the scene is a traffic jam along a stretch of suburban road, and Godard structures it as an escalating slow-burn gag, with an apocalyptic punchline (a bunch of dead bodies). This sequence-shot – like a J.G. Ballard story in miniature – moves implacably from the banal through the surreal to the horrific; the noise-music of car horns gets denser and louder, as the inventory of sights and

activities gets weirder: at least 60 stalled vehicles (including farm trucks, a bus, horse-and-carriage, and motor bike), games played by commuters bored out of their minds, random flare-ups of road rage. (Godard's wife, Anne Wiazemsky, contributed the idea for one car to be inexplicably trapped in the queue facing in the wrong direction.) Jean-Pierre Gorin, who would soon become Godard's closest collaborator, later remarked: "Jean-Luc makes his films for the sake of a particular 10 minutes in them"; those 300 metres of *Week-end* more than justify the whole.

Adrian Martin

Date 1968

Nationality France

Director Jean-Luc Godard

Why It's Key This famous shot progresses from the banal through the surreal to the horrific.

Key Scene **"Springtime for Hitler"**
The Producers

Having "picked the wrong play, the wrong director, the wrong cast," Max Bialystock (Mostel) and Leo Bloom (Wilder) turn up at the theatre on opening night, eager for their overfinanced Broadway musical, *Springtime for Hitler*, to flop. To cinch the scheme, Max crassly tries to bribe the theatre critic for the New York Times in the lobby. The curtain goes up, and a first-night audience are astonished – though with that title, what did they expect? – by Mel Brooks's inspired parody of old-fashioned musical production numbers (complete with Busby Berkeley overhead shot of a dancing swastika) and appalling bad taste ("Springtime for Hitler and Germany/Winter for Poland and France"). Of course, the dumbstruck crowds soon realise – as did audiences for *The Producers* – that the saving grace of this potential disaster is that it's hilarious. Unmatched by the more elaborate staging of the number in the 2005 musical remake, this "Springtime" may be the most painfully funny few minutes in movie history.

Mel Brooks, who, uncharacteristically, does not appear in the film, dubs the dancer who raps "don't be stupid, be a smartie, come and join the Nazi Party"; he would do the same line for the Broadway show and the later film.

Kim Newman

Date 1968

Nationality USA

Director Mel Brooks

Cast Zero Mostel, Gene Wilder

Why It's Key Bad taste can be funny.

Key Scene **The last shot**
The Bridegroom, the Actress, and the Pimp

SPOILER

Newly married, ex-prostitute Lilith (Ungerer) and James (Powell) enter a modern apartment building. A cut to an interior shot shows Lilith's pimp (Fassbinder) looking up from an armchair and saying, "It's not so easy to escape from our family." As he talks, the camera pans to the right to show Lilith and James looking down at him. She walks forward slowly, the camera panning with her. Then she reaches down and picks up a revolver from the arm of his chair, takes a few steps back – the camera panning right and up with her again – and fires at the pimp. Now looking up, she recites lines from St. John of the Cross – "If from my lowly state the flame of my love were so strong as to absorb death" – and walks past the armchair, the camera panning with her (and angled so that the pimp and the chair are underneath the frame line), to a large open window in which are framed a tall tree and several smaller ones, backlit by dazzling sunlight. Leaning against the jamb, she continues to speak, and

the camera slowly tracks forward to reframe and refocus on the view outside, to which, finally, is joined the orchestral conclusion of Bach's Ascension Oratorio. The complicated shot is brought off with the utmost simplicity in performance and direction. Against the starkness and spareness, in themselves so eloquent, of the action and the apartment set, the beauty of the final image – heightened by the firmness of the forward camera movement – makes an overpowering lyrical statement.

Chris Fujiwara

Date 1968

Nationality West Germany

Director Jean-Marie Straub

Cast Lilith Ungerer, Rainer Werner Fassbinder, James Powell

Original Title *Der Bräutigam, die Komödiantin und der Zuhälter*

Aka *The Bridegroom, the Comedienne, and the Pimp*

Why It's Key The movement from starkness to lyricism within a single shot is one of the most memorable in the work of Straub and his collaborator, Danièle Huillet.

Key Event
The Langlois affair

On February 9, 1968, the French Ministry of Culture, through the Centre National du Cinéma (CNC), the governmental agency that oversees and funds the Cinémathèque française, unexpectedly announced the dismissal of Henri Langlois, who had founded the Cinémathèque in 1936 and had been its legendary director ever since, rescuing countless old films from destruction and introducing a whole generation of film buffs, critics, and future filmmakers to the richness of motion-picture history through daily screenings of rare films. "Without Langlois, *Cahiers* and the New Wave wouldn't have existed," wrote *Cahiers du cinéma* in their April-May 1968 double issue, whose cover sported a Magritte-like etching of Langlois holding Marey's "photographic gun," one of the historic items in the Cinémathèque's Museum.

The uproar triggered by the decision was tremendous. Letters of protest poured in. Langlois supporters, including most film critics and filmmakers, organized defense committees and demonstrated in the streets of Paris. They clashed with the police, some blood was spilled, and Jean-Luc Godard famously lost his glasses in the scuffle. While the government's decision had been wrong and careless, Langlois' supporters were, to a certain extent, in denial: their idol was really responsible for some serious mismanagement; but he was more than anything else a symbol, and as such had to be protected. The intensity of the protest (which led to Langlois' being reinstated) was indicative of a more general state of unrest which would erupt three months later in the country-wide upheaval of May '68.

Jean-Pierre Coursodon

Date February 1968

Why It's Key The firing of the director of the Cinémathèque française caused a furor and was the harbinger of the May 1968 revolutionary events, which brought about a sea change in French society and French cinema.

Key Scene **The final shot**
Once upon a Time in the West

The final shot takes a long time to arrive, after 155 minutes or so of Leone at his best – highly choreographed gunfights, glowering close-ups, and Morricone's magical music – but it's worth waiting for: a single shot that is a magnificent culmination of a great Western epic. Finally, the railroad is being built, a township being constructed, and hordes of laborers crowd the widescreen frame. A steam train puffs and screeches up to the end of the line, laden with yet another crowd of workers. After the death of the villain and the departure of the man she loves, Cardinale turns her face away from tragedy towards the future. From her house overlooking the bustling construction site, she strides confidently down to the crowd of workers, carrying water casks for them; they crowd around her, and the camera slowly pans away, as the end credits roll; and we see in the distance the departing heroes – one living and the other dead, slumped across his horse. In a single sweeping shot, the camera captures the way of the future, embodied in Cardinale's triumphant stride, and sees the way of the past dwindling slowly into the distance. Morricone's score changes as the shot proceeds – from exultant orchestra and chorus over Cardinale's walk to a fading harmonica theme for the passing of the Old West. It's a tour de force involving a cast of hundreds, complex action, and flawless timing. Tonino Delli Colli was the cinematographer.

Andrew Pike

Date 1968

Nationality Italy

Director Sergio Leone

Cast Claudia Cardinale

Original Title *C'era una volta il West*

Why It's Key This is the brilliant resolution to, arguably, Sergio Leone's greatest Western.

Opposite *Once upon a Time in the West*

Key Event
MPAA rating system goes into effect

Starting in the early 1950s, many of the strictures imposed by the Hollywood Production Code of the 1930s began to erode. The unprecedented flowering of sexual freedom in the 1960s affected the film industry and the tastes of the filmgoing public. When several American studios flouted the Production Code by releasing films without the usual certificates of approval in 1966 (MGM's *Blowup* and Warner Bros.' *Who's Afraid of Virginia Woolf*), the Motion Picture Association of America conceded that the old system needed to be scrapped and instituted the ratings system, which continues to inspire controversy among both conservatives who consider the MPAA's ratings too lenient and liberals who condemn them as de facto censorship.

In 2006, Kirby Dick's documentary *This Film Is Not Yet Rated* launched an all-out critical assault on the MPAA Ratings Board. Accepted by even many liberals as a legitimate form of self-regulation and parental guidance, the MPAA ratings – G, PG, PG-13, R, and NC-17 – were denounced by Dick as outmoded and hypocritical. Despite Dick's claims that the MPAA is more hostile to explicit sexual content than extreme violence – and stigmatizes gay sex more severely than on-screen heterosexual coupling – it seems unlikely that these biases will be corrected in the future. On the other hand, as of this writing (January 2007), the MPAA announced that it would make an effort to rectify the lack of transparency in the board's decision-making process, thereby addressing another major structural flaw emphasized by Dick in his film.

Richard Porton

Date November 1968

Why It's Key The Motion Picture Association of America's ratings system marked the death of the old Production Code – and the birth of a new regime of self-regulation.

Key Scene A capitalist adjusts to Communism *Memories of Underdevelopment*

Tomás Gutiérrez Alea (1927-1996) was a founder of the Instituto Cubano del Arte e Industrias Cinematograficos (ICAIC); as a young man, he'd studied cinema in Rome, and he brought a sophisticated, European sensibility to his work, which, in 1966, had produced *Death of a Bureaucrat*, one of the funniest films of the decade. The somewhat gloomily-titled *Memories of Underdevelopment*, which is set in 1961, two years after Castro took power in Cuba, is a fiction film with significant documentary elements, and tells the story of Sergio (Sergio Corrieri), a well-to-do Havana businessman who stays behind in Havana after his parents and his wife depart for Miami – not so much because he believes in Communism as because he's too damn lazy to leave. In a key sequence, set in his well-appointed apartment, with its harbor views, he plays a tape recording he made of his wife prior to her departure, in which she complains bitterly about the heat and the sweat of this "backward country." As his wife's voice fills the room, he pokes around in her things, checking out her make-up and her underwear and finally pulling a pair of pantyhose over his head so that he looks like a bank-robber, an alien. During the course of the film, Alea charts the gradual connection Sergio makes with the New Cuba so that by the conclusion of this witty, elegant movie, when we see the Cuban side of the Missile Crisis, our understanding of his journey is complete.

David Stratton

Date 1968

Nationality Cuba

Director Tomás Gutiérrez Alea

Cast Sergio Corrieri

Original Title *Memorias del subdesarrollo*

Why It's Key This film provides an ironically detached view of a society in the process of major change.

Opposite *Memories of Underdevelopment*

Key Scene **Rats captive in the U.S. escape to Canada** *Rat Life and Diet in North America*

Made at the height of the Vietnam War, when the Canadian Wieland was living in New York while American draft resisters were fleeing to Canada, this film begins with rats being held captive by cats in what one of the film's many titles identifies as "political prison," complete with repeating alarm sounds. Towering cats in silhouette seem menacing as the rats scurry about. The grid of their screened-in cage and occasional views of rectilinear New York buildings out a window make a geometrical trap that clashes with the rats' movements, as do the superimposed red crosshairs in following scenes. After escaping, the rats are seen among cluttered plates on a table as they dine in a "millionaires [sic] house." When they finally reach Canada "to take up organic gardening," we get a short but glorious burst of landscape images, a few long shots and many closeups of leaves. Later the rats also play among flowers. These images break out of the cluttered traps of the earlier portions of the film with openness not dependent on showy grandeur. Wieland's little montage captures the detached calm and feeling of free space that characterizes much of the Canadian landscape, at least for Americans, and is more fully explored in Wieland's masterpiece, the feature-length landscape film *La Raison avant la passion*, which shows a trip across Canada.

Fred Camper

Date 1968

Nationality USA

Director Joyce Wieland

Why It's Key Wieland's little montage captures a sense of calm and free space.

Key Event
Interruption of the Cannes Festival

The 21st Cannes Festival opens on May 10, trying to ignore the country's situation: riots and strikes increasing all over. Despite the rapid progression of the political events, most of the Cannes community pretends to continue as always, until the 18th. On that day, at a press conference, a delegation of filmmakers including François Truffaut, Jean-Luc Godard, Claude Lelouch, and Claude Berri asks for the interruption of the Festival, as an act of solidarity with the workers' and students' struggle. The audience supports the idea; Alain Resnais, Richard Lester, and Carlos Saura withdraw their films from competition; Louis Malle resigns from his jury-member function, followed by Monica Vitti, Roman Polanski, Terence Young… But the Festival organizers and most of the industry participants want Cannes to continue, they have business to do. To interrupt the total confusion, which is starting to escalate into a physical fight, Robert Favre Le Bret, then head of the Festival, tries to begin a screening. Godard, Truffaut, and a few others string up the curtains to prevent them from opening, while Geraldine Chaplin hits a few faces on her way to reach the mike and ask that the movie she stars in not be projected. The next day, the Festival is prematurely closed. The leading figures of the "Cannes insurrection" leave for Paris, where cinema's "Etats généraux" (Estates-General, or general assembly) are organized in an attempt to invent a new model for film production and distribution. In a way, this will be the turning point of the French New Wave generation. After the decline of the May '68 movement, each of them will go his own way, quite alone.

Jean-Michel Frodon

Date May 18, 1968

Why It's Key May '68 burst into the film festival, showing the complex relations inside the movie world and between that world and real social life.

Key Scene **The closing shot of the boy staring out to sea** *Le Révélateur*

Most of his admirers would probably describe Philippe Garrel as the precise opposite of a cinephile, insisting that his work is, for better or worse, informed entirely by personal experience. But Garrel's *Le Révélateur* both begins and ends with overt cinematic references. The opening scene shows a man and a woman sharing an unusually long cigarette: the reference here is to a famous image of displaced sexuality from Irving Rapper's *Now, Voyager* (1942), in which Paul Henreid lights two cigarettes and passes one to Bette Davis. *Le Révélateur's* final shot shows a young boy (Robiolles) staring out over a large body of water, clearly evoking the ending of François Truffaut's *The 400 Blows* (1959), in which Antoine Doinel runs up to the sea, turns around, and is suddenly frozen in a still frame. But unlike those acts of homage associated with the Nouvelle vague, these references are systematically critical. If *Le Révélateur* is concerned with the difficult passage into adulthood, then *Now,*

Voyager represents that classical cinema, the cinema of childhood, Garrel is trying to move beyond. *The 400 Blows* reference, on the other hand, suggests a rejection of Truffaut's pessimistic implication that Doinel's youthful rebellion has gone as far as it can possibly go, giving him no option except to turn back and become integrated into society. In contrast with the still frame that traps Doinel, Garrel leaves his youthful protagonist confronting that unexplored region which exists outside society, contemplating new freedoms, new possibilities of resistance.

Brad Stevens

Date 1968

Nationality France

Director Philippe Garrel

Cast Stanislas Robiolles

Why It's Key This scene shows how an experimental film can define itself by referring to more mainstream works.

Key Scene **A cartoon starts to move** *The Film That Rises to the Surface of Clarified Butter*

One of the stranger films in cinema history begins with a figure drawing a cartoon at a table. First we see the line-drawing process over her shoulder, and then cut to a head-on view of the figure on paper. Then the figure starts to move in a relatively crude animation that recalls the origins of film animation. This comes quite unexpectedly: one had thought the drawing was finished. And while the drawing process was revealed, the animation process is not, almost in a joke on the early animation *Gertie the Dinosaur* (1914), which does display its individual drawings. Then the cartoonist is seen showing off the drawing in negative, though the drawings are still in positive. This other surprising moment underlines the artificiality of both the drawing and the film image itself. The whole process, drawing and drawing coming to life and then the drawing being "shown off," is repeated four more times, some of them with slightly different drawings of the same figure and the last two without the "showing off" part. Part of what

is so fascinating about Landow's work is its extreme hermeticism, which the repetitions add to. The strange reference to a film very different from celluloid in the title, and the contradiction between the on-screen "magic" and the film's acknowledgement of its own artifice, give it the status of a sui generis object for which thematic interpretations will not take one very far.

Fred Camper

Date 1968

Nationality USA

Director George Landow (now known as Owen Land)

Why It's Key This surprising moment underlines both the magic and the artificiality of cinema.

Key Scene **The cut from flying bone to soaring spaceship** *2001: A Space Odyssey*

The premise of Kubrick's masterpiece is that some unknown breed of being has been observing life on Earth from the beginning, and intervening on rare occasions to spur the evolution of human intelligence. The sign of such an occasion is the appearance of a mysterious black monolith that plays some inscrutable role in the process.

Our first view of the monolith comes during the story's first portion, subtitled "The dawn of man." Bands of pre-human primates are fighting over a waterhole, and after the monolith makes itself visible to one of the packs, a humanoid has an unprecedented thought – conceptualizing the idea of tools, and more specifically, the idea that bones can be used as weapons. This primate's pack wins the next battle for the waterhole, using bones as clubs, and the realization follows that these implements can also be used to kill animals. In a burst of inchoate triumph, a humanoid flings a bone into the air, where its flight against the blue sky fills the screen until the movie cuts abruptly to a long spacecraft – its shape articulated in ways that resemble a human spine – floating silently in the blackness of space.

The implication is clear: The highest technologies of today (and tomorrow) are on the same intellectual continuum as the first bone raised to bash in the brains of a pre-human foe. Equally clear is the lesson that all tools, however crude or sophisticated, can be used for good and evil. The choice is up to the user.

David Sterritt

Date 1968

Nationality UK/USA

Director Stanley Kubrick

Cast Keir Dullea, Douglas Rain

Why It's Key One of the most legendary cuts in modern cinema makes a comment on the possibilities of human evolution that's as concise as a biblical injunction, as awesomely condensed as a singularity in deepest space.

Opposite *2001: A Space Odyssey*

Key Event
Andrew Sarris's *The American Cinema*

In the Spring 1963 issue of *Film Culture*, Andrew Sarris had published a director-oriented guide to American film history that was committed to memory by a cadre of hardcore film buffs. Sarris had fallen under the influence of the *Cahiers du cinéma* writers who had promulgated the *politique des auteurs*, and, thanks to a celebrated attack by Pauline Kael, was the best known of the critics importing this foreign doctrine to American shores. In 1968, Sarris expanded the *Film Culture* article to book form, and the auteur theory, as Sarris had renamed the *politique*, acquired its Bible. Presenting American film history as a collection of director filmographies, *The American Cinema* provocatively grouped directors in humorously named categories – from "The Pantheon" and "The Far Side of Paradise" to "Strained Seriousness" and "Less Than Meets the Eye" – that by no means reflected the filmmakers' current status in the eyes of the Motion Picture Academy and the mainstream press. The combination of list-oriented geekiness, iconoclasm, and sheer quantity of films seen was a cocktail that few cinephiles could resist. Though he was not immune to the polemical brio that emanated from *Cahiers*, Sarris was essentially an open-minded, pragmatic thinker who brought a welcome tone of geniality and intellectual prudence to auteurism. "The transcendental view of the auteur theory considers itself the first step rather than the last stop in a total history of the cinema," he wrote. "Eventually we must talk of everything if there is enough time and space and printer's ink."

Dan Sallitt

Date 1968

Why It's Key It heralded the mainstreaming of auteurism in American film culture.

Key Scene **Jackie Raynal pisses on the floor**
Deux fois (Twice)

Raynal's mysterious and confounding film cannot be easily reduced to description. Made after her stint as an editor for Eric Rohmer, and while she was involved with the dandified cine-intellectuals of the Zanzibar Group, the film is composed predominantly of distinct passages wherein Raynal performs repetitious gestures and phrases (we see three versions of her purchasing soap) or striking tableaux and modest documentary observations akin to the early films of Andy Warhol. Both crude and lyrical, the visual style is shot through with a diffuse, gauzy ambience generated by high contrast black-and-white cinematography.

The punctuating declaration that is the urination sequence occurs roughly two-thirds of the way through *Deux fois*. Raynal, topless and wearing only black panties and nylons, leans against the wall at the back of an empty studio space. A man crouches to the right of her, suddenly approaching the camera and breaking into menacing but comic grimaces. As he ducks away and out of sight, Raynal drops to her knees, looking increasingly distraught before finally relaxing her face, dropping her arms and pissing on the floor through her tights. The act combines a singular mix of transgression (this is not what we expect to see), humor, and tenderness: her expression as she urinates seems to implore the audience for a reaction. It is a remarkable gambit, elevating the viewers out of the dreamy quietude of the other sequences and restoring them to bodies and sensations.

Raynal herself would later lampoon the startling and singular nature of the act in her autobiographical film *Hotel New York* (1984), in which, after a screening of *Deux fois*, an audience member (documentary filmmaker Errol Morris) asks incredulously if the girl on screen actually urinated or if she had "a squirting device under her tights."
Travis Miles

Date 1968

Nationality France

Director Jackie Raynal

Cast Jackie Raynal

Why It's Key In one aggressive, vulnerable, and unexpected moment, Raynal combines Warholian portraiture with surrealist transgression.

Key Scene **The ocean at sunset**
The Profound Desire of the Gods

Legend has it that Japanese civilisation began on Kurage Island, as the result of incest between sibling gods. In modern times, Kariya (Kitamura), an engineer from Tokyo, goes there to well for water. He encounters the Futori family, who still practice incest, and gets embroiled in the anthropologically complex, irrational lives of the family and their fellow islanders. Soon Kariya starts having sex with Toriko (Okiyama), the family's uninhibited, mentally handicapped daughter. As he brings western goods and Coca Cola, the islanders treat him as a god.

Suggesting what *Local Hero* might be like if it had been directed by Werner Herzog, *The Profound Desire of the Gods* has to be seen to be believed. Its landscape photography is astonishingly lush, yet it was cinematographer Masao Tochizawa's first major film. The film glories in primitivism and base sexual desires and is wildly politically incorrect. Like many of master director Imamura's films, it seems to taunt polite Japanese society, its etiquette and niceties. Just when it seems that the film can astonish no more, its lovers take to the open sea in a boat. Golden sunlight sweeps across the surface of the water, Tochizawa's camera seems to float above it, then roll with the waves. The sense of space and light takes the breath away. No wonder the film is among the favorites of Bertrand Tavernier and Jonathan Demme.
Mark Cousins

Date 1968

Nationality Japan

Director Shohei Imamura

Cast Kazuo Kitamura, Hideko Okiyama

Original Title *Kamigami no fukaki yokubo*

Aka *Legends from a Southern Island*

Why It's Key This scene is among the most beautifully lit and shot in film history.

Key Scene **The strangling**
Army of Shadows

The director, himself a veteran of the Resistance, pared down his eleventh feature into a steely succession of fact-based episodes set in Nazi-occupied France. In the film's most traumatic demonstration of how life-and-death gravity consumes routine heroics, Melville's anonymous Resistance members gather in a grimy abandoned house to carry out the death penalty. It's the first execution for hesitant novice Le Masque (Mann), but rugged chief Gerbier (Ventura) insists that the young traitor (Libolt) "has to die and you're going to help." Densely lit in muddy blues and moody grays, they dispassionately discuss how to proceed as the condemned youth trembles with foreboding. Should they stab him? Strangle him? Bash his head in? As they cannot risk making noise, they first gag him and then improvise a silent strangling with a towel and a twisting wooden stick. Melville positions his camera low, with Le Masque holding the traitor's thrashing legs and Gerbier securing his arms as he promises the boy that "you won't suffer." In a series of close-ups that study the killers rather than the killed, we look up at heavy-hearted Félix (Crauchet) behind the boy as he constricts the makeshift noose around the victim's neck until the tear-stained head falls forward lifelessly. Withholding bloodshed and exciting gunplay, this seven-minute set piece conveys the full weight of death and drives home both the emotional consequences of war and the brutal cost of patriotism, which demands more than brandishing flags and dutifully marching to the ballot-booth.

Robert Keser

Date 1969

Nationality France

Director Jean-Pierre Melville

Cast Lino Ventura, Claude Mann, Paul Crauchet, Alain Libolt

Original Title *L'Armée des ombres*

Why It's Key In a war movie that withholds the excitement of violence, this harrowing scene instead dramatizes the gravity of killing a human being.

Key Scene **The bed scene**
My Night with Maud

The finest of Rohmer's "Six Moral Tales" is inspired by Pascal's wager – basically, that it's wiser to believe in God than not, since if you're right you go to heaven and if not you've lost nothing – and centres on a slightly smug Catholic engineer (Trintignant) who sees a girl at Mass he then rather rashly decides he'll marry (without their even having had a proper conversation), only to be introduced by a friend to an extremely attractive free-thinking divorcée (Fabian). The crunch comes when a sudden snowfall means he has to sleep over at her appartment, and the cold impels him to forsake an armchair for the bed in which, beneath the coverlet, Maud sleeps naked. Will he or won't he succumb to temptation?

This question seamlessly conjoins the physical and the metaphysical, as the indecisive but stubborn protagonist struggles to balance his strongest natural impulses against a far more cerebral – but, thanks to Rohmer's refusal to patronise, no less important – determination to live according to the principles of religious faith. The conflict between fate and freedom of choice is made superbly manifest in the beautifully observed moves of the emotionally divided engineer as he wavers to and fro on the bed; Nestor Almendros' black-and-white camerawork, designed to highlight the special qualities of a wintry Clermont-Ferrand (Pascal's birthplace), merely enhances the sensual intensity of the moment when the engineer is forced to make a choice. Trintignant and Fabian, true to Rohmer's expertise with eliciting subtly nuanced naturalistic performances from his actors, are terrific.

Geoff Andrew

Date 1969

Nationality France

Director Eric Rohmer

Cast Jean-Louis Trintignant, Françoise Fabian

Original Title *Ma nuit chez Maud*

Why It's Key It's a rare – and very witty and sexy – example of complex, abstract philosophical ideas being dealt with successfully in a materialistic, two-dimensional medium.

CAC-EK

Key Scene **Thornton sitting in the dust, rises to join old Sykes** *The Wild Bunch*

Deke Thornton (Ryan), forced to become the reluctant pursuer of his old partners in crime, arrives to see the aftermath of the most celebrated massacre in the cinema. He sits in the dust, defeated and sad, wholly a character out of Faulkner's *The Unvanquished* or *Flags in the Dust*, and lets his despicable posse of carrion-hunters go collect the reward. He sees injured survivors leave the remnants of their town in silence; he hears the bounty hunters' merry singing, then shots, then the wind blowing; he smiles bitterly, almost chuckles. The stench of death is suddenly forgotten as old Sykes (O'Brien) and several Mexican horsemen, led by Don José (Urueta), approach. Thornton and Sykes exchange looks; the old man tells Deke the crows didn't get far. "I figured," retorts Deke, who then says he plans vaguely to "drift around down here." Sykes mutters ruefully, "Me and the boys… Want to come along? It ain't like it used to be, but…" Both men laugh, Thornton rises and turns to mount gracefully on his horse, and they all ride towards the horizon to go on fighting elsewhere, searching for a new excuse to stay alive, a remnant of the frontier, a reminder of the taste of adventure, while the soundtrack repeats the nostalgic Mexican farewell song "La Golondrina," and the laughing faces of the five killed members of the Bunch reappear as ghosts from "the lost region" that its poignant lyrics mention.

Miguel Marías

Date 1969

Nationality USA

Director Sam Peckinpah

Cast Robert Ryan, Edmond O'Brien, Chano Urueta, William Holden, Ernest Borgnine, Warren Oates, Ben Johnson, Jaime Sánchez

Why It's Key It's an epic farewell to the Western genre, rejecting oblivion and surrender.

1960–1969

437

Key Film
Easy Rider

The times they were a-changin'. After the box-office and Oscar success of *The Sound of Music* (1965), major studios invested in a glut of super-expensive, old-fashioned musicals – *Doctor Dolittle* (1967), *Star!* (1968), *Hello Dolly!* (1969) – that proceeded to rack up enormous losses. Meanwhile, Raybert Productions – a partnership between Bob Rafelson and Bert Schneider, with a releasing deal at Columbia – picked up a biker project directed by Dennis Hopper and starring Peter Fonda that even exploitation-savvy American International Pictures had passed on. *Easy Rider*, a monumental hit with the counterculture crowds who had been staying away from the cinemas, shook up Hollywood. Suddenly, suits realised there was an audience that could make a low-budget picture into a top-grosser and that could not be reached by conventional pictures. In the wake of *Easy Rider*, studios hired long-haired filmmakers and greenlit movies the executives frankly didn't understand.

Financially, this policy often proved disastrous, as when Hopper headed down to South America for the extended, drug-fuelled production of *The Last Movie* (1971). Artistically, the policy meant a brief window when the majors made and released films like Haskell Wexler's *Medium Cool* (1969), Russ Meyer's *Beyond the Valley of the Dolls* (1969), Rafelson's *Five Easy Pieces* (1970), Robert Altman's *M*A*S*H* (1970), Arthur Penn's *Alice's Restaurant* (1970), Michelangelo Antonioni's *Zabriskie Point* (1970) and Monte Hellman's *Two-Lane Blacktop* (1971). Some, like *M*A*S*H*, were even hits. In the long run, this policy saved Hollywood – letting the likes of George Lucas, Steven Spielberg, Brian De Palma, and John Landis in through the door.

Kim Newman

Date 1969

Nationality USA

Director Dennis Hopper

Cast Peter Fonda, Dennis Hopper, Jack Nicholson, Karen Black, Luana Anders

Why It's Key The success of this film persuaded studios to take a chance on new ideas, new filmmakers, and new audiences.

Opposite *Easy Rider*

Key Speech **"I'm walkin' here!"**
Midnight Cowboy

Lowlife con artist Ratso Rizzo (Hoffman), all wracking cough and nasal whine, hobbles onto a Manhattan street just as a taxi edges in front of him, inciting him to slam his fist on the hood with such force that his cigarette drops from his lips, as he asserts his right to existence: "I'm walkin' here!" Hoffman has consistently claimed he improvised this line spontaneously, but producer Jerome Hellman swears that the moment was both scripted and rehearsed with a paid cab driver. Still, the public took up the line as a rallying cry, imitating the X-rated film's espousal of lower-class protagonists long ignored in mainstream film. Joe Buck (Voight in a star-making part), the soft-hearted Texas naïf planning to service Gotham's neglected womenfolk (because "the men are mostly tutti-fruttis"), becomes first victim and then protector of the feisty and thin-skinned outcast Rizzo in his economic sinkhole at the seedy end of 42nd Street. Though he ends up servicing his own sex, the big city fails to curdle Joe's sunny optimism, as

director Schlesinger envelops gritty realities in a romantic aura, much as Blake Edwards applied gloss to *Breakfast at Tiffany's* (1961), while simultaneously modeling Hollywood's newfound attention to the economic and sexual frankness that would surge through underclass provocations like John Huston's *Fat City* (1972), Hal Ashby's *The Last Detail* (1973), Martin Scorsese's *Taxi Driver* (1976), and Barbet Schroeder's *Barfly* (1987).

Robert Keser

Date 1969

Nationality USA

Director John Schlesinger

Cast Dustin Hoffman, Jon Voight

Why It's Key A petty criminal of the lower depths demands respect despite his social disrepute.

Opposite *Midnight Cowboy*

438

Key Film *L'Amour fou*
Coming together, falling apart

Rivette made three films in the 1960s, fewer than other major figures of the French New Wave. The third, *L'Amour fou*, came out in 1969 and can stand as an end-of-the-decade summation of the *Nouvelle vague* aesthetic in a time of confusion and change. It's also the film in which Rivette's previously murky aspirations as a filmmaker coalesced, revealing his true direction.

The film is recognizably New Wave, but in a broken way. Shot in black-and-white in 1967 and '68, it takes place in Parisian cafés and apartments that belong to the mid-'60s more than the post-'68 world of Rivette's later films. It seems to balance on the exact point between two eras, and serves as a record of the transition between them.

In *L'Amour fou* the relationship between a theater director, Sébastien (Kalfon), and his girlfriend, Claire (Ogier), disintegrates during rehearsals for his production of Racine's *Andromache*, which are being

recorded by a documentary film crew. The boundaries between life and art and film and theater are not the only ones broken down. In one amazing scene Sébastien and Claire prove you can spend the whole day in bed and methodically destroy your apartment at the same time.

A stark shot of two folding chairs on the play's white stage goes out of focus and then back in, breaking this four-and-a-quarter hour film in half. Somehow the film is anchored by these two empty chairs, which represent Sébastien and Claire and seem lost and otherworldly in their absence.

A. S. Hamrah

Date 1969

Nationality France

Director Jacques Rivette

Cast Jean-Pierre Kalfon, Bulle Ogier

Why It's Key Rivette sought a new way to make films and found it in *L'Amour fou*.

Key Film **The rupture of the master/slave dialectic** *Burn!*

*B*urn! is a theorized meditation on the North-South antinomy during the transition from colonialism to neo-colonialism on a fictional Caribbean island. The protagonists, José Dolores (Márquez), a free black, and Sir William Walker (Brando), English agent provocateur, tentatively collaborate to prosecute a popular revolt against Portuguese rule. Walker's raison d'être, however, is to advance England's economic and strategic interests in the Caribbean during a period of intense rivalry between European imperial states for markets and raw materials. In this island setting, Dolores and Walker personify the global struggle between capital and labor, upon which pivots North-South relations and the dispossessed of humanity.

Having robbed the Bank of Queimada, Dolores and Walker, along with their accomplices, withdraw to a village where they intoxicate the inhabitants to distract the Portuguese and, thereby, facilitate escape. As they depart and are challenged by a Portuguese soldier, who

discovers the gold bullion hidden among sacks borne by a pack mule, Dolores impales the soldier on the bayonet of his rifle. With a calculating gaze, Walker asserts that "Well, Portuguese die too," revealing the psychology of bondage that is the master-slave relationship. Moments later, Dolores's fear of the Portuguese "master" is transcended in the soldier's death.

In this fateful act and revelatory moment, Dolores comprehends that the source of the master's mortality is himself. In his doing so, the relationship between master and slave is demystified, and the conditions, however inchoate and rudimentary, for self-consciousness and agency are realized. Pontecorvo's depiction of this emancipatory moment evokes Frantz Fanon, who wrote in *Black Skin, White Masks*: "He who is reluctant to recognize me opposes me. In a savage struggle I am willing to accept convulsions of death, invincible dissolution, but also the possibility of the impossible."
Michael T. Martin

Date 1969

Nationality Italy/France

Director Gillo Pontecorvo

Cast Marlon Brando, Evaristo Márquez, Renato Salvatori

Original Title *Queimada!*

Why It's Key The scene depicts and theorizes the first utterances of "self-consciousness," the necessary basis for agency and revolutionary change in the film.

Key Scene **The casting of the bell** *Andrei Rublev*

In response to the savagery of war-torn Russia in the early 15th century, artist Andrei Rublev (Solonitsyn) takes a vow of silence and refuses to paint any more of the inspirational religious icons for which he has become renowned. As he wanders the countryside, he witnesses the casting of a huge bell, supervised by a young teenager who is the son of a deceased master of bell-casting. The boy, Boriska (played brilliantly by Nikolai Burlyayev, who had acted before for Tarkovsky in *Ivan's Childhood* [1962] and who became a prolific actor in Russian cinema), volunteers for the task saying that before his father died, he had passed the secret of casting on to him. In a long extended sequence, we (and Rublev) observe the work – the digging of the enormous pit, the search for the right clay, the pouring of the molten metal, and the eventual emergence of the huge bell from its clay mould. As the bell rings for the first time, the boy collapses in tears in the mud, in relief, exhaustion, and happiness, and confesses to

Rublev that his father had told him nothing. Rublev, inspired by the boy's act of faith and by his all-consuming creative drive, abandons his silence and returns to painting, to use the gift that his God has given him to bring joy to people. Tarkovsky's acknowledged debt to Kurosawa is evident in the rain and mud and the visceral urgency of the sequence: It is a magnificent and eloquent finale to a spectacular epic of medieval Russia, resolving the horrors of the period in a grand moment of spiritual epiphany for the film's tormented hero.
Andrew Pike

Date 1969

Nationality USSR

Director Andrei Tarkovsky

Cast Anatoli Solonitsyn, Nikolai Burlyayev

Original Title *Andrey Rublyov*

Why It's Key This is the spectacular resolution to a great Russian epic.

Key Scene **Making dinner while listening to the radio** *Dillinger Is Dead*

The exposition of *Dillinger Is Dead* feels a lot like other expositions: Glauco (Piccoli) drives home from his job as a manufacturer of industrial masks, greets his wife who is in bed with a headache, sits down to a prepared meal, then decides that he'd rather eat something special. As we follow Glauco around his house and watch him play idly with objects or make small decisions about what to do next, we wait for the event that will get the narrative ball rolling. But the event is slow in coming, and we start to wonder how long director/co-writer Marco Ferreri plans to stretch out this meandering introduction. Glauco browses in a cookbook and begins making a late-night gourmet dinner, listening to the radio while he cooks – and as the film chains little causes and effects together and teases our story expectations, three songs play from beginning to end, complete with disc-jockey chatter. This use of commercial music as wallpaper – naturalistic, yet in violation of movie conventions –

makes time seem to stand still, and shifts us to an indeterminate state of spectatorship. We now know that Ferreri is capable of leaving the film on this mundane level forever; but he continues to open new storytelling doors. In fact, while looking for a spice, Glauco opens an actual closet door, rummages around, and finds… a gun. Does this time-honored Chekhovian signifier mean that a suspense film is finally beginning? Perhaps, but Glauco still has a meal on the stove to attend to….

Dan Sallitt

Date 1969

Nationality Italy

Director Marco Ferreri

Cast Michel Piccoli

Original Title *Dillinger è morto*

Why It's Key It's still one of the cinema's most daring experiments in deferring story expectations.

Key Event **"Cinema/Ideology/Criticism"**

The events of May 1968 precipitated a massive shift in film culture that was nowhere more clearly defined, or longer-lasting in influence, than in the changing editorial policy of *Cahiers du cinéma*, as signalled by the publication of Jean-Louis Comolli and Jean Narboni's "Cinema/Ideology/Criticism" in the magazine's October 1969 issue. Calling for "a critical theory of the cinema… in direct reference to the method of dialectical materialism," Comolli and Narboni overturned André Bazin, one of the magazine's founders: while agreeing with Bazin that cinema reproduced reality, they claimed that reality itself expressed the dominant ideology and that the crucial difference between films lay in whether they unthinkingly reflected this ideology or sought "to disrupt or possibly even sever the connection between the cinema and its ideological function." For this disruption or severing to happen, Comolli and Narboni write, the filmmaker must not only "deal with an

explicitly political subject" but also challenge "the traditional way of depicting reality." Falling short of this double action are fiction films and documentaries that depict "political" content in conventional forms; to that group, Comolli and Narboni prefer films that though apparently innocuous in content are radical in form. "Cinema/Ideology/Criticism" not only led to a crisis at *Cahiers*, whose publisher locked out the editors from their offices before selling its interests in the publication to a consortium including François Truffaut, but led directly to a line of ideological film criticism that was pursued for years thereafter at *Cahiers* and other journals, including the British *Screen*.

Chris Fujiwara

Date October 1969

Why It's Key This text has become a touchstone for politically engaged criticism of cinema.

Key Scene **The balloon scene**
Badou Boy

Born in 1945 in Dakar, Djibril Diop Mambety was expelled from Senegal's National Theatre, became the country's and the continent's most baroque filmmaker, and died of lung cancer in 1998, having completed just two feature films. His legend, which *Ecrans Afrique* ascribed to "his iconoclasm, his poetry, his alcoholism, his wanderings, his arrogance and his lucidity," rests on the satirical, Wellesian inventiveness of his two features, *Touki Bouki* (1973) and *Hyenas* (1992), but *Badou Boy*, his second, medium-length film, shows that he arrived fully formed in cinema and didn't ramp up to *Touki Bouki's* daring stylistics and tone. Its story, about the street boy of the title (Ba) being chased by a fat policeman, has more than a touch of Chaplin about it: the mockery is there, the affinity for excluded people. Ten minutes in, a guy is smoking. Balloons fly past his face. Badou Boy and another man saddle a horse, standing and crouching again and again, saying "*Ça va bien? Ça va?*" again and again, their repetitions

creating the rhythm and absurdity of the sequence. These events have no particular social meaning but, visually, they beautifully staged. A satirical master – Brechtian, Buñuelian, Eisensteinian – is clearly at work.
Mark Cousins

Date 1970

Nationality Senegal

Director Djibril Diop Mambety

Cast Lamine Ba

Why It's Key The *mise en scène* of this early Mambety film shows that Africa's greatest filmmaker had found his remarkable style before his feature debut, *Touki Bouki*.

Key Scene **Don Lope and his wife at home**
Tristana

As a movement, Surrealism was long finished by 1970, but Buñuel was still thriving and had become by this point not only a man unique in sensibility but also one of the most assured masters of film directing in all ways and in all aspects. In addition to its fascinating characters and striking story (from a novel by Benito Pérez Galdós), *Tristana* shows Buñuel's gifts for the expressiveness of a location (the beautiful old city of Toledo), of color, of subtle camera movement and composition. All of this comes together near the end of the film, when the symbiotic relationship of Tristana (Deneuve) and her guardian/lover Don Lope (Rey) completes its reversal. She has returned to him, her affair with the artist Horacio (Franco Nero) whimpering to an end after a tumor requires that she have a leg amputated. Finally, they are married, and the patriarchal Lope, formerly disdainful of the Church, sits drinking coffee with three priests on a snowy winter evening, while a now hard and bitter Tristana – in a

series of counterpoised, beautifully calibrated images – walks forward and back on her crutches in the hall outside. Beneath the simple action are whispers of Spain's changing political fortunes, and the scene's surface has a dreamlike vibrancy while also being fully believable for all its perversity. It takes a special mind and artistic hand to hold so many internal contradictions and complexities in so graceful a balance and with such seeming ease.
Blake Lucas

Date 1970

Nationality Spain

Director Luis Buñuel

Cast Catherine Deneuve, Fernando Rey

Why It's Key The one enduring Surrealist genius brings all the subtle beauty of his mature style to a seemingly straightforward story, raising it to an expressive peak in one of his most indelible scenes.

Key Scene **The opening scene**
The Music Lovers

The scene is a winter carnival in Moscow. Tchaikovsky (Chamberlain) and his lover, Count Chiluvsky (Gable), are there enjoying themselves, and so are all the major characters in the story to follow. We see Tchaikovsky's wife-to-be, Nina (Jackson), his benefactor, Madame Von Meck (Telezynska), even the young lieutenant (Aris) Nina fancied before she met Tchaikovsky. But while the scene introduces them to us, they don't make contact with the film's central character. They operate in separate spheres – even as we're invited to sense the connections that will be made later. Scored to the "Dance of the Clowns" from *The Nutcracker*, it's easily the most impressive opening scene since *Touch of Evil*. But Russell isn't the same kind of bravura filmmaker. Whereas Welles locks the spectator into his use of the single take with a steady, stealthily moving camera (following Charlton Heston and Janet Leigh at a Mexican-border crossing where a car carrying a bomb is about to explode), Russell

swerves his camera around constantly and cuts at will. It all begins with a moment most viewers may not catch unless they're very alert. The camera is at the top of a toboggan slide, and a sled jumps right over it. Our camera, attached to another sled, then goes down that same toboggan slide and meets the characters just mentioned. This sense of hurtling through space to music is key to the mood of the entire film – a kind of restless, reckless exhilaration expressive of the way the characters have allowed music to take over their lives. And this is why the full and proper title is *Ken Russell's Film on Tchaikovsky and the Music Lovers*.

David Ehrenstein

Date 1970

Nationality UK

Director Ken Russell

Cast: Richard Chamberlain, Glenda Jackson, Christopher Gable, Kenneth Colley, Max Adrian, Izabella Telezynska, Ben Aris

Why It's Key The scene commences the narrative and introduces the characters in a unique mode of pure display.

Key Scene **The capture of Australia's most notorious outlaw** *Ned Kelly*

Ned Kelly was an Australian "bushranger" or outlaw whose exploits in the 1870s were the subject of many films. Tony Richardson's production, co-written by Richardson with an Australian Kelly expert, Ian Jones, was an attempt to re-tell the Kelly story as a folk legend, accompanied by a ballad (sung by Waylon Jennings) that linked the various episodes of his life. The film made much of Kelly's rebellion against social injustice arising from the conflict between poor Irish Catholic settlers and powerful British colonialists. In the leading role, Richardson cast a modern-day rebel in the form of Mick Jagger to enhance the theme. Accompanied by a media frenzy and much amusement at the extravagant ways of "foreign" film production, the film was shot in rural New South Wales and completed in London. The climactic scene shows Ned's final shootout with the police, in which he wore a massive suit of homemade armour. Barely able to move under the weight of the metal plating, he was

easily captured. Richardson's staging of the scene never escapes a sense of absurdity and carries minimal dramatic tension, with Jagger's persona completely buried beneath the layer of metal. Although Richardson's film dealt with a subject close to Australian hearts, it made little impact when it was released in 1970: a well-publicized premiere in "Kelly country" in Victoria won little favor, and local critics and audiences remained unmoved. Jagger was dismissed as a "puny Pom" who should never have been allowed to play "our Ned."

Andrew Pike

Date 1970

Nationality UK/Australia

Director Tony Richardson

Cast Mick Jagger, Allen Bickford, Geoff Gilmour, Mark McManus

Why it's Key It's an iconic moment in Australian popular culture.

ANTONIONI's ZABRISKIE POINT

Key Scene "Whistling in the Dark"
Darling Lili

"Whistling in the Dark," the exceptionally haunting song by the great team of Henry Mancini and Johnny Mercer that is so affectingly performed by Andrews (in the role of beloved music-hall star/German spy Lili Smith), opens *Darling Lili* in one long, highly elaborate take. The music begins over a dark screen, then her face is illuminated as she begins to sing, and the camera begins a series of sweeping virtuoso turns as it moves with her around the stage, catching the color of the stage lights and intimating Lili's relationship to her audience out in the auditorium, before at last coming to rest as her figure becomes still once more, the darkness again surrounding her face, then the screen returning to blackness. At once musical, comedy, romance, and World War I adventure (and the American cinema has always reveled in mixed genres, though not always with commercial success), the film ends as it began, with the same song seemingly staged and filmed in the same way, but this time corrupted by cuts to subjective shots, which correspond to a forgiven Lili's feelings and suggest that the phrase in the lyric "...sing the shadows away" now has personal meaning for her. In the same way, the purity of that opening long take would soon be displaced in Hollywood cinema, as musical numbers in later films tend to use far more cutting, though they generally lack the kind of grace note Edwards provides with that poignant "Whistling in the Dark" reprise.

Blake Lucas

Date 1970

Nationality USA

Director Blake Edwards

Cast Julie Andrews

Why It's Key In 1970, what this beautiful song and its cinematic realization represented in Hollywood musicals was ending, but at the same time was never more gloriously alive.

1970–1979

445

Key Scene **The explosion**
Zabriskie Point

SPOILER

As wish-fulfilments go, the finale of *Zabriskie Point* is hard to beat. Every rotten thing about the modern, industrialised world – its coldness, alienation, exploitation, lack of freedom, destruction of nature – is concentrated in the ultra-modern, maze-like house where Daria (Halprin) works under an attorney (Rod Taylor) who is sewing up a real-estate development. Daria, disgusted, drives away from the house, parks, gets out; then her hard, hateful gaze back seems to bring on an almighty explosion: one big bang repeated and stretched over five glorious minutes. The main action of the house exploding is covered from at least a dozen different angles; then Antonioni goes in (as the Pink Floyd score swells) for surreal close-up details: clothes, packaged bread, newspapers, spines of books, all cascading in slow-motion, becoming increasingly abstract and lyrical… It is an odd, excessive spectacle: the film enjoys channelling its hippie eco-message into this ultimate act of anarchic destruction; but, at the same time, finds a way to appreciate all the design and architectural fads and fixtures of 1970 just as they are at the point of disappearing into the void. Finally, there is an abrupt cut of both image and sound: Daria, beaming, drives away. Antonioni seems unwilling to settle the classic art-film question: was it real or just a dream? It hardly matters, for the scene captures what is most essential about Antonioni's cinema: the sovereign dialectic of the artist who both builds and tears down what he has built, deriving ecstasy from both gestures.

Adrian Martin

Date 1970

Nationality USA

Director Michelangelo Antonioni

Cast Daria Halprin

Why It's Key The scene captures the essence of Antonioni.

Opposite *Zabriskie Point*

Key Scene **Mick fails to control the crowd**
Gimme Shelter

The Maysles brothers' hallucinatory record of the disaster at the Altamont Speedway on December 6,1969, during a free concert by the Rolling Stones, is the very definition of a bummer. History records that the organisers hired a local chapter of the Hells Angels to provide security – and perhaps some brand of diabolic authenticity – for the event, and that the ensuing day-long face-off between a few dozen unforgiving bikers and 300,000 jittery hippies climaxed in the fatal stabbing of a young man called Meredith Hunter by the Angel Alan Passaro. The triumph of *Gimme Shelter* is its transfiguration of these squalid and depressing circumstances into a single, continuous act of perception – rendering them, in fact, beautiful.

Early in the day the vibe kinks and plummets – heads in the crowd keep turning, as at the silent circulation of bad news – and by nightfall the situation is well out of hand; the hippies are rattled, having bad trips, the Hells Angels scowling and defensive, circling their bikes. As the Stones take the stage the Angels are laying about them with their customized leaded pool-cues, and there are pleading, crying faces in the front row. A particularly violent scuffle interrupts "Sympathy For The Devil" and Mick Jagger makes some hapless attempts at crowd control: "Oh, babies. There's so many of you! Just be cool down the front there, don't push around..." Filming Jagger in profile, the Maysles' camera captures the expression of one rat-faced Angel who is steadily contemplating Jagger from stage-right: an expression of supreme distaste and near-loathing.
James Parker

Date 1970

Nationality USA

Directors Albert and David Maysles, Charlotte Zwerin

Cast The Rolling Stones, The Hells Angels

Why It's Key Having summoned the forces of darkness at Altamont, the Rolling Stones prove unable to control them. *Gimme Shelter* is one of the greatest documentaries ever made.

Opposite *Gimme Shelter*

Key Scene **Chas shoots Turner**
Performance

In Marco Ferreri's *Tales of Ordinary Madness* (1981), poet Charles Serking (Ben Gazzara) observes that "When Hemingway put his brains to the wall with a shotgun, that was style." In our Postmodern age, an artist's suicide is frequently seen as the one act that cannot be interpreted as ironic or insincere. This explains why Donald Cammell's gunshot suicide on April 24, 1996, created a level of interest in the director's work vastly exceeding that which existed when he was alive. Several other transformations were brought about by this event, including an almost universal abandonment of the assumption that credited co-director Nicolas Roeg was *Performance*'s primary author. *Performance*'s key scene shows Chas (Fox) killing Turner (Mick Jagger), a gangster's murder of an artist which is "transformed" into a suicide by the latter's acceptance of death. Interviews reveal that Cammell regarded death itself as a point of transformation, an end rather than a beginning, an attitude clear enough from *Performance*, in which the camera follows Chas's bullet as it penetrates Turner's skull, encountering a photograph of Jorge Luis Borges (which shatters) before emerging into a street, where we discover that Chas has "turned" into Turner. It was obviously this sequence that several writers had in mind when they later claimed that Cammell took 45 minutes to die, observing his final moments in a mirror before asking his wife: "Do you see the picture of Borges?" Rebecca and Sam Umland's book *Donald Cammell: A Life on the Wild Side* records the dull truth that Cammell died instantly. But the claims themselves suggest the nature of those needs addressed by Cammell's life and work (two things now inseparable); the desire for artistic authenticity in a culture dominated by inauthentic gestures.
Brad Stevens

Date 1970

Nationality UK

Directors Donald Cammell and Nicolas Roeg

Cast James Fox, Mick Jagger

Why It's Key This scene shows how closely Donald Cammell's work was connected with his life (and death).

Key Event **President Nixon views *Patton* twice, then decides to invade Cambodia**

Press reports at the time, confirmed by later historians, have Nixon watching Franklin J. Schaffner's *Patton* (1970) twice before making a move that President Johnson had refused, expanding the Vietnam War into Cambodia. Claims were made at the time of a multi-story headquarters from which the Vietnam war was directed by the U.S.'s opponents – which only served to show how badly the administration misunderstood the nature of the guerrilla conflict they were fighting. Even if, as seems likely, *Patton* merely supported a decision Nixon would have made anyway, his application of his admiration for the general himself and for George C. Scott's bravura portrayal to Vietnam and Cambodia offers yet another example of the classic mistake of "fighting the last war." This was a mistake that shouldn't have been made: in the movie, Patton himself is an acknowledged anachronism, "a sixteenth century man" and "a romantic warrior lost in contemporary times." It's suspected that Nixon may have also loved the movie for its portrayal of Eisenhower as a force holding Patton back; Nixon had had his own antagonisms with Ike.

Patton is seen winning territory and killing the enemy, which is how World War II was won but how Vietnam could never have been won; movie fantasies can only lead to a gross misunderstanding of the ever-changing present. Sadly, U.S. leaders have utterly failed to learn from Nixon's mistake, as they now appear to believe that the fight against terrorists can also be won by conquering territory – though as of this writing (January 2007) they have failed even at that.
Fred Camper

Date April 1970

Why It's Key The viewing of a movie is here connected to a disastrous military decision that ultimately cost untold lives and arguably led to the genocide of Pol Pot, while failing to achieve its goal of helping to win the Vietnam War.

Opposite *Patton*

Key Scene **An epiphanous conclusion** *Zorns Lemma*

The central section of this celebrated avant-garde film consists of a series of cycles of 24 shots, each one second long. Each shot represents a different letter of the alphabet (two pairs of letters are merged) by showing a different New York City street sign beginning with that letter, but, what is more, all the signs are alphabetized – not only is an "A" followed by a "B," but all the "A"s (and the other letters too) appear in alphabetical order from one cycle to the next. As these repetitions continue, the shots with lettered signs are gradually replaced with wordless images – a hand painting a wall, a fire, the sea. These replacement images are richly sensual, supple, and full of mystery, and the gradual replacement process creates a growing expectation, in the viewer, as to how it will conclude. Frampton was a still photographer before he began making films, and his debt to Edward Weston is apparent in the complex light and color patterns of each image. When in the very last cycle the very last sign is replaced by an image, the transition from text to cinema, from names to images, from stories to light, is completed, and that one and only completely wordless cycle has a strange, visionary power, partly because the viewer has waited so long for it, wondering if in fact it would come, and yet this longed-for moment of completion is over so soon.
Fred Camper

Date 1970

Nationality USA

Director Hollis Frampton

Why It's Key Frampton answers the myth that so-called "structural" films are preplanned and academic with a predictable conclusion that nonetheless has the power of poetic epiphany.

Key Speech **"I want you to hold it between your knees."** *Five Easy Pieces*

Hot on the heels of *Easy Rider*, Jack Nicholson defined the middle-class restlessness of the then-dawning 1970s as selfish, insecure pianist-turned-oil-rigger Bobby Dupea in director Bob Rafelson's supremely assured *Five Easy Pieces*. With Tammy Wynette-obsessed girlfriend Rayette (Black) in tow, Bobby heads north to visit his dying father, picking up hitchhikers Palm and Terry (Kallianiotes, Basil) along the way. The quartet stops at a roadside diner, setting the stage for one of the cinema's most iconoclastic scenes as Bobby attempts to order a chicken salad sandwich from an inflexible waitress (Thayer). Though it's justifiably famous for Bobby sneering "I want you to hold it between your knees" before sweeping water glasses and cutlery to the floor, it's the sequence's throwaway coda that cuts deepest: later, in the car, deflecting Palm's praise for his defiance, Bobby wearily points out: "I didn't get it [the sandwich], did I?" "No, but it was very clever," says Palm, unwittingly nailing

Bobby's futile struggle to fit in; "I would have just punched her out." Though often criticized as misogynist, the film was scripted by a woman, Carole Eastman (1934-2004), writing as Adrien Joyce, "who knew me very well," Nicholson reveals. "I was playing it as an allegory of my own career." Thirty-two years later, in a deleted scene from Alexander Payne's *About Schmidt* that surfaced on the DVD, Nicholson's Warren Schmidt meekly accepts an eatery's "no substitution" rule. Thus is the anxiety of youth deadened into complacency by the passage of time, and thus does a great actor inhabit difficult, complex characters.
David Stratton

Date 1970

Nationality USA

Director Bob Rafelson

Cast Jack Nicholson, Karen Black, Helena Kallianiotes, Toni Basil, Lorna Thayer

Why It's Key It's a classic moment from one of the most piercing character studies in all American cinema.

Opposite *Five Easy Pieces*

Key Film **The swordswoman, the ghosts, and the monks** *A Touch of Zen*

A scholar (Shi), unable to fight but expert in military tactics, meets the enigmatic Miss Yang (Xu), who lives in a supposedly haunted house. As in a traditional Chinese horror tale, scholar and beauty steal one night together. Appearances prove deceiving. A seemingly generous stranger (Tin Peng) turns out to be an agent of the eunuch persecuting the beauty, the blind fortune-teller (Bai) is a general protecting her, Miss Yang herself learnt martial arts with a saintly Abbot (Chiao). Only the latter's deadly palm ("the touch") and his spiritual powers can offset the formidable skills of the evil commander (Han, also one of the martial arts choreographers).

Taking three years to complete the film, Hu got in trouble with his Taiwanese producers. Back in Hong Kong, he secured the international rights to the film, re-edited it, and brought it to Cannes – putting a new style of *wuxia pian* (martial arts film) on the cinephilic map.

A Touch revolves on the notion of in-betweenness, symbolized by the alliance between the scholar and the *xia nü* (female warrior), enacted through a couple of virtuoso sequences – one in the alluring labyrinth of a bamboo forest, the other in the darkness of the "haunted house" – that are turned by Hu into a profound meditation on the mystery of life. Bodies are moving, ambling, running, jumping, flying across several levels of illusion and reality; between trees, mountains and houses; light, fog, and darkness; superstition and strategy; the spiritual realm and the forces of evil. Hu's martial arts oeuvre reveals itself as a *mise en scène* of the gaze, with bodies transcending their earthly weight at the speed of the light impressing our retina.
Bérénice Reynaud

Date 1971

Nationality Taiwan/Hong Kong

Director King Hu

Cast Xu Feng, Shi Jun, Bai Ying, Roy Chiao, Han Yin-jie

Original Title *Xia nü*

Why It's Key It was the first Chinese film to win a price (for technical achievement) at Cannes.

Key Scene **The wedding without the bride** *The Ceremony*

The famous wedding scene in *The Ceremony* is just one of countless highlights from a body of work rich in provocative and memorable moments. In this scene, a traditional arranged marriage is organized for a young man. On the day of the wedding, however, the bride announces that she will not be taking part, and the conservative patriarch of the family insists that the ceremony proceed regardless – with the young man marrying effectively an empty space. Tradition must be respected at any price. It's a sequence of deadpan absurdity filmed by Oshima and his director of photography, Tsutomu Narushima, in brilliant wide-screen compositions and rich color, powerfully driving home the appalling emptiness of the ritual, despite its elaborate and expensive trappings. By this time, Oshima had a substantial body of work behind him in which he persistently confronted Japanese tradition, xenophobia, and political conservatism: films like *Death by Hanging* and *Diary of a Shinjuku Thief* (both 1968)

were as stylistically challenging as they were politically radical. *The Ceremony* is one of his most mature works, observing a family over several decades as they meet on ritual occasions – weddings, anniversaries and deaths. Co-written with two of Oshima's frequent collaborators, Mamoru Sasaki and Takeshi Tamura, it is flawlessly executed and devastating in its measured attack on a claustrophobic, spiritually bankrupt Japan.
Andrew Pike

Date 1971

Nationality Japan

Director Nagisa Oshima

Cast Kenzo Kawarazaki, Atsuko Kaku, Akiko Koyama

Original Title *Gishiki*

Why It's Key It's a great moment of surrealism in a devastating satire on Japanese society.

Key Scene **Family reunion** *Twitch of the Death Nerve* (aka *Bay of Blood*)

SPOILER

American slasher movies like *Halloween* and *Friday the 13th* imitated this bloody thriller set around a bay, the first film of its kind. Bava's European original includes youthful characters killed in the woods, but its interest lies elsewhere, and its multiple victims come from several classes and age groups. Two of them, Renata (Auger) and Albert (Pistilli), tow their young children (Cestié and Elmi) to the bay in pursuit of an inheritance.

Today mechanical plot twists and pointless reversals pad the last reels of thrillers long after they've meaningfully ended. Bava's shock ending, however, is an exclamation point that throws the whole film into relief. As the murderous couple Renata and Albert smile and hug, congratulating each other for achieving their goal ("It's the least I could do for my family," says Albert), Bava's camera zooms out and a double-barreled shotgun enters the frame from the right. *Blam blam*.

Cut to their eight-year old son holding the shotgun, his younger sister beside him. "They're good at playing dead," she observes, then the children skip off like they're in a soap commercial as a happy chorus of yeah-yeahs fills the soundtrack.

"Children should stay with their parents," Albert told Renata before they left them alone in their camper. A shot of the kids breaking a ceramic head links them to the film's mayhem, then Bava deserts them, too, and we worry about them. Where are they? Are they in danger? This *Week-end*-like movie's harsh ending somehow recalls the sunny domestic horror that finishes Varda's *Le Bonheur*. It's just as radical and surprising.
A. S. Hamrah

Date 1971

Nationality Italy

Director Mario Bava

Cast Renato Cestiè, Nicoletta Elmi, Claudine Auger, Luigi Pistilli

Original Title *Ecologia del delitto*

Why It's Key Bava puts a final twist on the genre he'd inadvertently invented.

Key Scene **The opening montage**
Szindbád

Szindbád, often promoted by Hungarian film critics as the most significant film produced in the country, is based on the writings of Gyula Krúdy, a *fin-de-siècle* aristocratic author and notorious *bon vivant* of Budapest's café culture. Krúdy's prose style displays a remarkable proto-modernist regard for synaesthetic experience, with his romantic protagonists slipping between times and places in a fashion strongly reminiscent of Proust and Woolf. *Szindbád* itself is based on Krúdy's most celebrated work, *The Travels of Sindbad*, centering on the amorous adventures of the eponymous ladies' man.

Huszárik, a painter and product of the Béla Balázs Studio in Budapest (known for its aesthetic experimentation), does not so much adapt Krúdy as transcribe the poetic and emotional tone of his sensuous writing into visual analogues. This technique is most dramatically employed in the film's opening montage, a 90-second parade of stunning and immaculately composed shots (filmed by the brilliant Hungarian cinematographer Sándor Sára) that serve to induct the viewer into the nostalgic and timeless world of Sindbad.

In rapid, cyclical procession, we see brilliantly colored oil in water, flaring coals, a flower in bloom, lace, smoke rising from a forest, rain dripping from a slate roof, a lock of hair, a woman's antique portrait. Reading more like a shot list from an abstract film-poem by Stan Brakhage or Bruce Baillie than the inception of a European "quality picture," this passage exemplifies the power of cinema to create pure moods through rhythmic visual cues. Through the autumnal, tender work that follows, we are drawn into a world of deathless dreaming, where the past exists as trains of imagery, crowding the mind like too-strong perfume.
Travis Miles

Date 1971

Nationality Hungary

Director Zoltán Huszárik

Cast Zoltán Latinovits

Why It's Key A rhapsodic cluster of images effortlessly introduces the viewer to the world of the declining Austro-Hungarian Empire, employing editing and composition that extravagantly combine costume drama with the avant-garde.

Key Scene **A man touches a tree**
Land of Silence and Darkness

The Institute for the Blind in Milan, Italy, has a permanent exhibition called "Dialogues in the Dark." The gallery displays objects of all sorts, but there is no light whatsoever to see them. The touring guides are blind people who introduce the visitors to a world where all perception is part of an unfamiliar galaxy of sounds, smells, and tactile experiences. One leaves the venue in a state of wonder and exhilaration, as if the body had learned again what it really means to see things, and how much the other senses can achieve without the eyes, allegedly the most important bridge between ourselves and the outside world. But is it really the most important? *Land of Silence and Darkness* overturns this assumption by showing men and women who cannot see, hear, or talk. Try to imagine this. You can't express yourself in words; you can't listen to what's going on around you; you don't know the meaning of colors, profiles, shadows. If you think this is a universe of nothingness, you have forgotten the most important thing: the sense of touch. In the most overwhelming scene of the film, a man clings to a tree, feels its rough surface, presses his body against it, almost as if two living entities were trying to communicate something to each other in a way we can't even begin to understand. Werner Herzog has always used cinema to seek the ultimate ecstatic experience. He found it here, where cinema does not exist.
Paolo Cherchi Usai

Date 1971

Nationality West Germany

Director Werner Herzog

Cast Fini Straubinger

Original Title *Land des Schweigens und der Dunkelheit*

Why It's Key Touch is the ultimate visual experience.

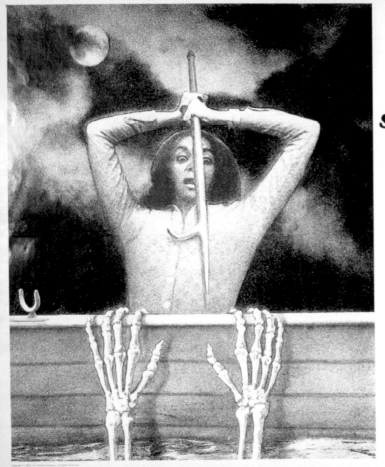

Something is after Jessica. Something very cold, very wet...

and very dead.

Paramount Pictures Presents A Charles B. Moss. Jr. Production

"LET'S SCARE Jessica To Death"

Starring Zohra Lampert · Barton Heyman · Kevin O'Connor
Gretchen Corbett · Alan Manson and Mariclare Costello
Written by Norman Jonas and Ralph Rose
Produced by Charles B. Moss. Jr. Directed by John Hancock

GP ··· Color A Paramount Picture

Key Speech **Paean to sexual liberation** *WR: Mysteries of the Organism*

Milena (Dravič), a newly emancipated Yugoslav assistant-beautician, comes home after work to find her roommate (Kaloper) engaged in vigorous sexual intercourse. After smoking a cigar and perusing the new issue of *Communist*, Milena, a follower of Frankfurt School psychologist Wilhelm Reich, walks out onto the courtyard-balcony of her third-floor communal dwelling and delivers a radical speech, praising the marvels of healthy orgasmic liberation and the importance of enlightened sexuality for true revolutionary society. The male comrades who gather to listen to her speech are enthusiastic; led by Milena, they form a line and dance across the communal terrace, repeating her words in song. At this moment, the sequence jumps to display documentary footage of ecstatic masses cheering Mao across Tiananmen square, and then to a scene from Mikhail Chiaureli's *The Vow* (1946), featuring Stalin and other Soviet leaders triumphantly marching at the end of World War II, a scene that plays to the tune of "Lili Marlene." This is followed by footage of mental patients who are force-fed and subjected to electro shocks.

Dusan Makavejev's subversive revolutionary-sexual treatise *WR: Mysteries of the Organism* uses unconventional narrative techniques to interweave a range of subplots traversing continents and contexts while dealing with sexuality, sanity, and socialism. The free flow of associations in the sequence of interlinked images at the end of Milena's speech is a daring example of the symbolic pastiche that Makavejev is best known for in the history of cinema.

Dina Iordanova

Date 1971

Nationality Yugoslavia/ West Germany

Director Dusan Makavejev

Cast Milena Dravić, Jagoda Kaloper

Original Title *W.R. – Misterije organizma*

Why It's Key A speech praising the revolutionizing potential of orgasmic sexuality is reinforced by an imaginative associative collage sequence.

Key Scene **The vampire in the lake** *Let's Scare Jessica to Death*

SPOILER

One of the most purely terrifying sequences in American horror cinema comes towards the end of John Hancock's still-underrated *Let's Scare Jessica to Death* – it's a rare horror film sequence that depends on building sustained dread and terror rather than a sudden, sharp shock. Jessica (Lampert), the emotionally fragile heroine, goes swimming in the cove behind her isolated farm, dragged in by Emily (Costello), an ambiguous hippie girl found sleeping rough on the property. It has been suggested that Emily looks a lot like Abigail Bishop, a 19th-century girl who drowned in the lake and is rumoured to live on as a vampire. The girl playfully pushes Jessica under the water, creepily alternating malice with apology, then disappears. Jessica, shivering, fears Emily has drowned – but she pops up again, face unnaturally pale, and walks out of the lake. But now Emily is Abigail: when she went under, she was wearing a crimson bathing costume; when she comes out of the lake, she's wearing a soaked Victorian wedding dress. From then on, the film is an escalating series of shocks and horrors, but the waterlogged vampire bride is the movie's most striking, and lasting, image.

Kim Newman

Date 1971

Nationality USA

Director John Hancock

Cast Zohra Lampert, Mariclare Costello

Why It's Key This is the creepiest scene of the 1970s.

Opposite *Let's Scare Jessica to Death*

Key Person **Bruce Lee**
Bruce Lee becomes a superstar *The Big Boss*

Like many overnight successes, Bruce Lee toiled for decades before becoming a star. The San Francisco native (and son of Chinese opera star Lee Hoi-Chuen) made his debut as an infant in the lost Cantonese-language film *Golden Gate Girl* (1941). Small roles as a child actor in Hong Kong films gave way to parts in American TV shows like *The Green Hornet* and *Longstreet*, but Lee was continually frustrated with the common Hollywood practices of limiting Asian roles to slanty-eyed fiends or bucktoothed idiots and, even more galling, casting Caucasians in sallow makeup. When Lee, a kung fu expert in his private life, was passed over for a lead role on the TV series *Kung Fu*, he headed back to Hong Kong in disgust and brokered a deal with Golden Harvest films. Their first effort, *The Big Boss* (1971), was shot in Thailand with all the campy splendor a rock-bottom budget can provide, but when the final product was released the box-office response was electric. Audiences had never seen someone like

Lee – insolent, charismatic, fast like a panther and effortlessly cool, with a physique like high-tension steel. His whipcrack kicks and punches into the lens seemed aimed not only at his character's enemies but at Charlie Chan, Fu Manchu, and every sexless, inscrutable, lisping, and squinty Oriental stereotype. When Lee dispatched the bad guys in the final showdown with the springloaded perfection of a striking cobra, it put the world on notice that Asians were matinee-idol material.

Violet Glaze

Date 1971

Nationality Hong Kong

Director Lo Wei

Cast Bruce Lee, Maria Yi, James Tien

Original Title *Tang shan da xiong*

Why It's Key Bruce Lee destroys Asian stereotypes with a few well-aimed punches.

Opposite *The Big Boss*

Key Scene **"Ode to a Screw"**
Taking Off

Amidst the tumult of the downtown New York hippie scene at the dawn of the 1970s, suburban teenager Jeannie Tyne (Linnea Heacock) wanders through a huge audition for singer-songwriters. Meanwhile, back in the comfort of their huge rural house, her parents, Larry and Lynn (Buck Henry, Lynn Carlin) talk to other adults in similar circumstances, attempting, without much success, to understand why kids are taking off and dropping out. Working with veteran screenwriter Jean-Claude Carrière and playwright John Guare (*Six Degrees of Separation*), then-recent Czech émigré Milos Forman announced himself to U.S. audiences with this engaging, warm-hearted satire of American mores and artistic freedom. Like all Forman films, *Taking Off* adroitly mixed scenes of hilarity with scenes of pain, and as always he's fascinated by the plain beauty of average faces. One by one, guileless young women – including then-unknowns Carly Simon and Kathy Bates – punctuate

the episodic story with earnest performances of self-penned songs. Most memorably, Mary Mitchell's "Ode to a Screw" includes such naughtily liberating couplets as "you can fuck the moon and June and the sea/But before you fuck them you must first fuck me." In January 2005, *Taking Off* finally premiered in Prague – 35 years after it was made. "I wanted to make it the same way we made films in Czechoslovakia," Forman said in his taped introduction. "We would look around, see what's happening, and put together a story from that." Mysteriously, *Taking Off* has yet to see official release on DVD, which only seems to cement its legendary status.

David Stratton

Date 1971

Nationality USA

Director Milos Forman

Cast Mary Mitchell

Why It's Key Forman's first American film casts a fresh eye on middle-class suburbia's struggle to understand the youth movement.

Key Scene **The photographer's final, most mysterious picture** *(nostalgia)*

At first glance, this 36-minute short seems like a modest autobiographical movie. On the screen, we see 12 photographs, each visible for about three minutes. On the soundtrack, we hear a first-person account of when, where, and under what circumstances the pictures were taken.

But oddities soon become apparent. Each photo is positioned on the coils of an electric hotplate, whose heat causes the picture to darken, curl, and burst into flame. Just as noticeably, the images and voiceovers don't match – the narrator is always discussing the *next* picture in the series, which we haven't seen yet. As a final paradox, viewers who've done their homework will realize that the first-person narration isn't being spoken by filmmaker Frampton but by his friend Michael Snow, another great avant-garde director.

All these devices serve the film's central theme, which is the complexity and slipperiness of memory,

and the unreliability of the technical means we use to mummify and preserve the ever-elusive past. We think of film and photography as repositories of truth, Frampton tells us, but their products are actually as fragile and uncertain as the evanescent images in the mind's eye.

In the last sequence, the narrator describes a photo containing a chance detail that filled him with overwhelming dread – but instead of presenting this picture, Frampton's film abruptly ends. His message is plain: The past can't be grasped, the future can't be seen, and the present is slipping into the void at the rate of 24 frames per second.

David Sterritt

Date 1971

Nationality USA

Director Hollis Frampton

Cast Michael Snow

Why It's Key The concluding section of this enigmatic film casts richly productive doubt on the "truth" of photography and film.

Key Scene **Enter the "Little Dragon"** *The Big Boss*

In the U.S., Bruce Lee had developed the *Jet Kune Do* ("art of the intercepting fist"), combining Chinese *Wing Chun*, Korean *taekwondo*, and Western boxing and wrestling. Returning to Hong Kong, where he had started as a child and teenage actor, Lee put his mastery to good use. In his first vehicle, this formulaic kung fu flick, the charismatic, joyful physicality of the "Little Dragon" (Lee's Chinese nickname) illuminates every frame. A romantic, good-natured mama's boy, he can be led astray by good wine and loose women, becoming all the more endearing. In his first fight, it takes him just one minute to dispose of nine of Big Boss's knife-wielding thugs: two kicks from the right foot for one, one single kick for the second, a kick from each foot for the third, a counter-attack with the right fist for the fourth…. Lee gathers energy by swiveling around, turning his back to his opponent, and then kicking him by throwing his leg behind or using his other leg after completing the move. This is just for

starters. The fights become increasingly deadly until the spectacular showdown with Big Boss (master Han Yingjie, who also served as action choreographer on the film), who had ordered the slaughter of his factory co-workers. Lee gets mad, rips his T-shirt off his muscular torso, kills his nemesis, then repeatedly punches his face and collapses on his body. The legend was born… and lives on.

Bérénice Reynaud

Date 1971

Nationality Hong Kong

Director Lo Wei

Cast Bruce Lee, Han Yingjie

Original Title *Tang shan da xiong*

Why It's Key Back in Hong Kong after 12 years in the U.S., Bruce Lee stars in the first Chinese Martial Arts film to cross over to Western audiences.

Opposite *The Big Boss*

Key Scene **The introduction of Cassavius** *Malpertuis*

Kümel's work presents a catalogue of potent atmospheres and environments, and *Malpertuis* constitutes his finest organization of these materials. Most of the film takes place inside and on the grounds of the titular house (the word is difficult to translate, meaning both "evil house" and "fox's den"), alternating between stifling enclosure and unexpected artificial grandeur.

After the young sailor Jan (Carrière) is shanghaied and brought back into the fold of his decrepit and sinister family, the key reunion is between him and the family patriarch, Cassavius (Welles). Ensconced in an upstairs suite, Cassavius's presence is heralded by his shouting and pounding on the floor for food. The enfeebled kitchen servants respond with fear and awe. "He's hungry again!"

Cassavius himself is introduced in a wide shot that locates his massive body at the center of an enormous crimson bed; the bed itself vastly extended and framed by curtains that suggest both a throne and a makeshift stage. As Jan gawks, servants enter and place an entire feast at the foot of the bed before retiring. Cassavius is a typical late Welles portrayal, combining threatening authority with an unhealthy physique that is ideal for the character. His situation as an impotent but commanding force, trapped in the belly of an enormous cinematic construction, clearly and cleverly mirrors elements of Welles's personal biography. Intelligent, decadent, and suggestive, the scene reveals some of the aesthetic pleasures to be found in works often and absurdly maligned as "Euro-trash."

Travis Miles

Date 1971

Nationality Belgium

Director Harry Kümel

Cast Orson Welles, Mathieu Carrière, Susan Hampshire, Michel Bouquet

Why It's Key A master of atmosphere and symbolic design, Kümel outdoes himself with the introduction of the imposing Cassavius, a god-like figure in an outlandish set.

Key Speech **Sam the Lion's monologue by the fishing hole** *The Last Picture Show*

Critic-turned-filmmaker Peter Bogdanovich's second film, *The Last Picture Show*, about the dying Texas town of Anarene circa 1951, was not just a depiction of rural life before TV, cheap long distance phone service, and the Interstate Highway System; it was also an elegy for the circumspect storytelling and stately rhythms of pre-1960s Hollywood, which Bogdanovich honored visually, with monochrome photography and elegant camerawork, even as his script's sexual frankness pushed in the other direction. These elements converge in one of the great screen monologues, delivered by Johnson's elderly Sam the Lion, owner of the town's doomed movie theater, in a scene where he visits a local fishing tank with Sonny (Bottoms). Sam talks about how, decades earlier, after his sons died and his wife went insane, he fell in love with a beautiful young woman and often took her here to skinny-dip. Sonny asks what happened to the girl, and Sam reveals that she got married and lived unhappily ever after. But Sam says he has no regrets. "She was here I'd probably be just as crazy now as I was then in about five minutes. Ain't that ridiculous? No, it ain't really. Because being crazy about a woman like her is always the right thing to do." As critic Roger Ebert has pointed out, the scene seems inspired by the moment in *Citizen Kane* when the accountant Bernstein remembers glimpsing a woman on a Staten Island ferry for a fleeting moment, and still thinks of her years later as (in Ebert's words) "a beacon of what could have been."

Matt Zoller Seitz

Date 1971

Nationality USA

Director Peter Bogdanovich

Cast Ben Johnson, Timothy Bottoms

Why It's Key The elegiac mood and the sexual frankness of Bogdanovich's film converge in this monologue.

Opposite *The Last Picture Show*

Key Event **Dolby noise reduction used on the soundtrack of *A Clockwork Orange***

In 1966, Dolby Laboratories revolutionized the record business by introducing noise reduction technology to audio recording. Five years later, Stanley Kubrick's *A Clockwork Orange* became the first film to use Dolby's technology in mixing its soundtrack. Up until then, both Hollywood sound mixers and theater sound systems emphasized high-frequency sounds, to obscure unwanted background noise and make dialogue as intelligible as possible; this resulted in tinny distortion and ensured that sound would always be cruder than picture. But when Dolby noise reduction came to theatrical films, it freed filmmakers and their sound designers to make soundtracks richer, more subtle, and more daring, without requiring exhibitors to give up the mono format. One notable beneficiary was Robert Altman, a fan of overlapping dialogue who pushed the technique to new extremes in such films as *Thieves Like Us* (1974) and *Nashville* (1975).

Dolby kicked sound design up another notch in 1975 with Dolby Stereo, which took the space on the film strip allotted to the usual mono soundtrack and split it to allow left and right channels, a center screen channel, and a fourth channel for ambient sound and special sound effects; depending on the theater, the soundtrack could be read as four channels (for a surround-sound effect) or as the traditional one channel. When coupled with Dolby recording technology, the upshot was a flowering of dense, clean, boldly visceral sound design that kicked off in 1977 (with the release of *Star Wars* and *Close Encounters of the Third Kind*) and continued through 1992 (with the introduction of even more nuanced Dolby Digital) and up through the present day (with Dolby home theater equipment).

Matt Zoller Seitz

Date 1971

Why It's Key It led to a revolution in film sound design.

Opposite *A Clockwork Orange*

Key Scene **The hair dye runs** *Death in Venice*

SPOILER

A Venetian hairdresser opens a pot of blackening and brushes the paint onto the graying locks of visiting composer Gustav von Aschenbach (Bogarde), flattering him that "You are much too important a person to be a slave to conventions about nature and artifice" as he adds lip rouge, mascara, and a final dusting of powder. But the corpse-like makeup makes the musician look even older, and he shrinks in discomfort when strangers crowd him in an elevator, or strolling musicians mockingly surround his chair. In the throes of his newfound obsession with the smolderingly angelic Tadzio (Andresen), this idealist who abstracts sensual emotions into cerebral notions remains closed in, unable to speak to the boy even while following him through the cholera-plagued city. Finally, stricken and near collapse, he's helped to a beach chair, where he despairingly feasts on the visual eroticism of Tadzio wrestling an Italian youth, when suddenly the first trickle of hair dye, black as death,

creeps out from under Aschenbach's straw hat and runs down his fevered cheek, like mortality marking him for extinction. Tadzio enigmatically points out to the pink sea, then looks back at the dying man, now tragically alone as his foolish vanity melts. Embracing his mortality and forsaking unruly desire, Aschenbach finally succumbs as workers bear his body away in a hauntingly elegiac yet pitiless long shot.

Robert Keser

Date 1971

Nationality Italy/France

Director Luchino Visconti

Cast Dirk Bogarde, Bjorn Andresen

Original Title *Morte a Venezia*

Why It's Key It visualizes the moment when artifice fails and mortality can no longer be denied.

Key Speech **The Girl's final line: "No good"**
Two-Lane Blacktop

Date 1971

Nationality USA

Director Monte Hellman

Cast Laurie Bird, Warren Oates, James Taylor, Dennis Wilson

Why It's Key This scene shows how the finest cinematic dialogue is that which works in harmony with other filmic elements, rather than being outstanding in itself.

If asked what I believed to be the finest dialogue in cinema history, I would nominate Laurie Bird's final line from Monte Hellman's *Two-Lane Blacktop* (written by Rudolph Wurlitzer), a line which consists of only two words: "No good." This is obviously not great writing in the generally accepted sense, yet, like Noriko's "Life is disappointing" from Yasujiro Ozu's *Tokyo Story* (1953), it represents that point towards which the entire film has been moving. The line is delivered in a roadside diner where The Driver (James Taylor), The Mechanic (Dennis Wilson), and G.T.O. (Warren Oates) are indirectly (but quite unambiguously) trying to convince Bird's character (referred to only as The Girl) that she should finally make a choice, rather than continuing to relate sexually with all three of them (a dilemma also faced by many of Jean Renoir's heroines, who were frequently asked to choose between three lovers). Although they see themselves as having rejected bourgeois society and everything it represents, these men are all, in their different ways, incapable of engaging in relationships not rooted in concepts of ownership and sexual exclusivity. In this context, the line "No good" has the force of a radical protest against an intolerable situation, a rejection not merely of the trappings of middle-class life, but of all those inherited assumptions with which it is associated. In contrast to those "liberal" filmmakers who imply that patriarchy can be redeemed by a few individual reforms, Hellman, like Jean-Luc Godard, suggests that the only solution is to dismiss the entire mess and start again from zero.

Brad Stevens

Key Scene **"Theme from Shaft"**
Shaft

Date 1971

Nationality USA

Director Gordon Parks

Cast Richard Roundtree

Why It's Key At last, black audiences had their own Bogart, Cagney, or Alan Ladd.

"Who's the black private dick that's a sex machine with all the chicks?" The era of the "blaxploitation" film truly arrived in the opening sequence of *Shaft*, as Isaac Hayes's Oscar-winning theme tune thrumms on the soundtrack for what seems like many minutes, and John Shaft (Richard Roundtree), stylish in brown midi-coat and snappy threads, strides through Times Square like he owns the whole of New York City. It's an iconic image of black empowerment – the dude who takes no shit from the Man and isn't too sold on being hassled by brothers either – and also an up-to-the-moment reimagining of the classic *film-noir* figure of the private eye. As Raymond Chandler wrote, "down these mean streets a man must go who is not himself mean, who is neither tarnished nor afraid. He is the hero, he is everything. He must be a complete man and a common man and yet an unusual man... He must be the best man in his world and a good enough man for any world." Can you dig it? Following Shaft came a parade of iconically-dressed and coiffeured, blatantly-named cool bloods, mean muthas and tough mamas: Ron O'Neal's Youngblood Priest (*Superfly* [1972]), Jim Brown's *Slaughter* (1972), Fred Williamson's *Black Caesar* (1973), Tamara Dobson's *Cleopatra Jones* (1973), Pam Grier's *Foxy Brown* (1974), Isaac Hayes's *Truck Turner* (1974), Roscoe Orman's *Willie Dynamite* (1974), Jim Kelly's *Black Belt Jones* (1974), Jeannie Bell's *T.N.T. Jackson* (1975), Rudy Ray Moore's *Dolemite* (1975), and even William Marshall's *Blacula* (1972).

Kim Newman

Opposite *Shaft*

Key Scene **The swordsman gives his girlfriend his sleeve** *The New One-Armed Swordsman*

Much has been written about the virile bonding between Chang Cheh's characters. Though they may pursue (or be pursued by) a female love interest, male friendship usually remains their main source of motivation, not only for taking physical action against a given enemy but also to morally uplift themselves from disgrace, emotional turmoil, or extreme self-punishment. I think this particular treatment of virile friendship is best represented by a happy interlude of *The New One-Armed Swordsman*, in which the title character (Chiang) offers his only hand to his male friend (Ti Lung) and his loose sleeve to his girlfriend (Li Ching). It is a scene that may be played for laughs (or not), but in any case it perfectly establishes the different roles that those relationships perform in the development of the main character: while the female cannot get to the core of the One-Armed Swordsman's plight after his mutilation, the male friend quickly manages to give him back his self-confidence and a

reason to live. Also, it is to avenge his friend's brutal murder that, in the end, the swordsman sets off to confront single-handedly (no pun intended) a whole army of enemy warriors.

Fernando Martin Peña

Date 1971

Nationality Hong Kong

Director Chang Cheh

Cast David Chiang, Ti Lung, Li Ching

Original Title *Shin du bei dao*

Why It's Key It reveals a lot about the different places male-male and male-female relationships occupy in Chang Cheh's films.

Key Scene **Chasing the train** *The French Connection*

The breathtaking chase sequence in Peter Yates's *Bullitt* (1968) was eclipsed by the rightly-celebrated urban pursuit in William Friedkin's breakthrough film, *The French Connection*. Stories abound over the construction of this harrowing sequence, in which hard-charging Detective Jimmy "Popeye" Doyle (Hackman) commandeers a civilian's car to chase an elevated subway train carrying hit man Pierre (Bozzuffi). Filmed out of chronological order over five weeks almost entirely on the Stillwell Avenue subway line in Brooklyn, it required numerous street closings to achieve a convincing illusion of a man, and a machine, out of control. Friedkin edited the sequence to Carlos Santana's rhythmic "Black Magic Woman," which enhances the percussive effect of the crashes and near-misses along the way. The real star of the sequence is stunt driver Bill Hickman, who drove the black car Steve McQueen was chasing in *Bullitt* and was a good friend of James Dean – the first person, in

fact, to arrive on the scene of the accident that killed him. To see more of Hickman's work, check *The Seven-Ups* (1973), made in large part to cash in on *Connection*'s success. Hackman, who took the role only after it was turned down by McQueen, Jackie Gleason, James Caan, Peter Boyle, and even columnist Jimmy Breslin, won the Oscar for Best Actor, and the film itself became the first R-rated movie to win the Academy Award for Best Picture. Though it may be primitive by today's somehow dishonest CGI standards, still evident are the skill and the sweat brought by Friedkin, Hackman, and Hickman to an incalculably influential stunt sequence.

David Stratton

Date 1971

Nationality USA

Director William Friedkin

Cast Gene Hackman, Marcel Bozzuffi, Bill Hickman

Why It's Key This is a famous action setpiece from a visceral cop movie that improbably won the Best Picture Oscar.

Opposite *The French Connection*

Key Film **Wanda**
East of Palookaville

Always described as Elia Kazan's wife who played the wild sister in *Splendor in the Grass*, Barbara Loden should be remembered as the director of *Wanda*. This bleak film follows a lower-class woman named Wanda Goransky (Loden) through a series of numbing encounters in narrow bars serving quarter beers, downtown hotels where the sink is next to the bed, and all-night restaurants where people eat spaghetti while smoking. The film hurts. Its plodding grimness reduces life to getting money and eating.

Shot by a documentary cameraman in 16mm color in Pennsylvania coalfields and in Waterbury, Connecticut, *Wanda* has the brute intensity of *Harlan County U.S.A.* Wanda is disconnected. She loses her family in divorce court and can't hold a job. After she's pickpocketed in a movie theater she wanders into a bar during a robbery and leaves with the thief, a Mr. Dennis (Higgins), who calls her "Hey, stupid" and slaps her in the face.

Subsumed by the broken people they're playing, Loden and Higgins don't appear to be acting any more than the non-professionals in the film's other roles. Wanda tells Mr. Dennis she's never had anything and never will. "You don't have anything, you're nothing," he explains. "You're not even a citizen of the United States." Then he gets on the roof of his car with a bottle of bourbon and swipes at radio-controlled airplanes like King Kong. Loden deglamorizes his bank robbery scheme into a series of pathetic incidents, denying her heroine a movie ending.

A. S. Hamrah

Date 1971

Nationality USA

Director Barbara Loden

Cast Barbara Loden, Michael Higgins

Why It's Key Loden's great first film should not have been her last.

Key Scene **"Did he fire six shots, or only five?"** *Dirty Harry*

By the time they collaborated on *Dirty Harry* in 1971, director Siegel and star Clint Eastwood had already begun their revisionism of cop movies with *Coogan's Bluff* (1968). It was, in fact, Eastwood who insisted on Siegel as director if he were to consider a script that had gone through some five revisions and two previous potential leading men, Paul Newman and Frank Sinatra. Whereas Coogan was a polite but shrewd country cop learning the ropes in the big city, Inspector Harry Callahan is something very different, a single-minded enforcer not afraid to bend – or even snap – the rules when they stood in the way of justice. Before beginning his determined pursuit of a crazed killer called Scorpio, Callahan wanders into his regular greasy spoon. "The usual lunch or the usual dinner?" asks the counterman, Mr. Jaffe (played by veteran character actor and Siegel/Eastwood regular Woodrow Parfrey). "What difference does it make?" asks Harry, neatly summing up the character's jaded lifestyle. When a bank robbery across the street interrupts his hot dog – "Aw, shit!", Harry mumbles through meat and bun – out comes the legendary .44 Magnum handgun for the face-off with an unnamed wounded felon (Albert Popwell, who went on to supporting roles in the subsequent three films in the franchise), whom Harry taunts by giving him a last chance to go for his gun. This meting out of frontier justice in an urban setting proved a flash point in the America of 1971, as the film was called a "fascist classic" by Pauline Kael but nevertheless became a mainstream hit. Cop movies would never be the same.

David Stratton

Date 1971

Nationality USA

Director Don Siegel

Cast Clint Eastwood, Woodrow Parfrey, Albert Popwell

Why It's Key It's the most famous scene from a film that became the template for all modern-day conflicted cop movies.

Opposite *Dirty Harry*

Key Scene **The first dance of the courtesan** *Pakeezah*

High-class Shahabuddin (Ashok Kumar) learns that he has a daughter by a courtesan who has been dead for 17 years. He comes to the red-light area to meet the courtesan's sister. The sister, who has brought up the daughter, first taunts him for abandoning her sister and then tells him that since the daughter, Sahibjan (Kumari), has already "sat down" for the *mujra* (a dance), he can come back to take her the next day.

The topography of the *kotha* (place of residence and performance), where Sahibjan and her aunt live, is unique. The street, with anonymous men milling around, is seen in many films, but few directors are able to create the street as "character." In *Pakeezah*, the street not only has snatches of song and dance and a multitude of men, seeking pleasure. Amrohi creates a sumptuous, complex set of many-storeyed buildings where all around, one can see girls dancing, a visual complement to the snatches of different songs that can be heard. Sahibjan's aunt's *kothi* (mansion) is

at the head of the street, at a prime spot. From here the whole street is visible. The song "Inhi logon ne" ("These very people…") is set here, in an open lobby, with the entire street of pleasure stretching out in the background. The exquisite CinemaScope *mise en scène* has Sahibjan dancing in the foreground, enticing her clients, along with the worried aunt, who is obviously planning their escape from Shahabuddin. This centring on the figure of Sahibjan is paradoxically decentred by the spreading-out of performances at various levels all across the street.

Rashmi Doraiswamy

Date 1971

Nationality India

Director Kamal Amrohi

Cast Ashok Kumar, Meena Kumari, Raj Kumar

Why It's Key The topography of the red-light street is brilliantly realized in this scene.

Key Scene **Sealed with a kiss** *Intimate Confessions of a Chinese Courtesan*

What's palpable in *Intimate Confessions of a Chinese Courtesan* is the jubilation experienced by two beautiful women over acting together and being each other's partners in crime, love, and hate – all at the expense of men who are turned into patsies and murder victims. Both born in Taiwan, Lili Ho and Betty Pei Ti signed contracts with the prestigious Shaw Brothers Studio in Hong Kong and effortlessly reached the status of screen goddesses. Casting the pair in a martial-arts-cum-soft porn movie was an inspired coup. In *Intimate Confessions*, Ai Nu (Ho) is captured, brought into a brothel, and forced into submission by the lesbian Madam Chun (Pei Ti). Chun, who has a fondness for licking the blood of her victims and whipping the soft skin of her slaves, falls hard for the girl (after a bit of off-screen lesbian rape). The latter plays ball, and we are treated to sumptuous shots of the beauties in bed together, playfully testing their kung fu against each other, flirting and jostling, and dazzling

their patrons. Ai Nu masters the exquisite art of toying with men – and making them beg for more. This helps her when the young chief of police half-heartedly tries to arrest her after a series of murders.

Ai Nu wants nothing less than the total destruction of the brothel. "I never loved you," she tells Chun at the end of the carnage, before slicing her arm off. Chun has one last weapon left – her soft, inviting mouth. Lesbian sex was never so sensual, wicked, and campy. Hey – it was the first time!

Bérénice Reynaud

Date 1972

Nationality Hong Kong

Director Chor Yuen (Chu Yuan)

Cast Lily Ho, Betty Pei Ti

Original Title *Ai Nu*

Why It's Key A seasoned martial-arts director offers the first images of lesbian eroticism in Chinese cinema.

Key Event
When Buñuel met Hitchcock

Art history is full of speculations about which great painters may have crossed paths when they happened to be in the same general area at the same time. Film history, however, has no need to invent the meeting of Alfred Hitchcock and Luis Buñuel: it happened, over dinner in Hollywood in the early '70s. Critics have delved into the uncanny affinities between these two artists: both dealt with morbid states of (usually masculine) obsession, and the powers of "the gaze"; they were touched by the legacy of Surrealism, having both collaborated with Salvador Dalí. Buñuel was well aware of Hitchcock's œuvre – and it turns out that Hitchcock was equally aware of Buñuel's, not only from the London film clubs of his youth, but also in the period when he began to draw inspiration from European art cinema of the '60s. But it was during this meeting that the most profound commonality between Hitchcock and Buñuel revealed itself. Buñuel's *Tristana* (1970) – a cold, relentless tale of innocence betrayed

and revenge taken – had recently appeared. In the course of the film, the young woman played by Catherine Deneuve has a leg amputated; at one point, the camera wanders over from her playing the piano to frame the sight of her replacement leg lying about, detached. This was the specific detail Hitchcock loved; indeed, he was reduced to murmuring, rapt, over and over: "Ah, that leg … that leg!" For these two great auteurs, that leg embodied fetishism, raised to the finest art.
Adrian Martin

Date 1972

Why It's Key The meeting of two great directors confirmed the profound commonality between them.

Key Film *Out 1: Spectre*
Swinging the Eiffel Tower

The original *Out 1* (1971), a comic TV serial, was almost 13 hours long. The actors invented their own characters and improvised their dialogue while Rivette's deliberately artificial story circulates around the notion of two solitary 1970 eccentrics in Paris who never meet – a dropout pretending to be a deaf-mute (Léaud as Colin) and a café con-artist out for money (Berto as Frédérique). Both stumble upon evidence of a secret organization made up of 13 disparate individuals hoping to control society – a concept derived from novellas by Balzac. Apparently this organization was never more than a utopian, pre-1968 idea of 13 friends that never congealed. But for Colin its existence is a puzzle to be solved, and for Frédérique it's an occasion for blackmail.

After French TV rejected his serial, Rivette spent a year editing it down to the 255-minute *Spectre* – telling roughly the same plot in a much more disturbing, enigmatic, and paranoid fashion while changing the

meaning and resonance of many shots. Colin's efforts to get an Eiffel Tower trinket to swing back and forth 13 times – a minor gag in the midst of the original that parodies his manic efforts to impose meaning where there is none, to convert chance into destiny – becomes the final shot. Now it's an ironic metaphor for the viewer's frustration in trying to make sense out of *Out 1: Spectre*. After repeated efforts, Colin finally concludes, "It doesn't work," speaking now for Rivette as well as the spectator: the physical act becomes metaphysical.
Jonathan Rosenbaum

Date 1972

Nationality France

Director Jacques Rivette

Cast Jean-Pierre Léaud, Juliet Berto, Michel Lonsdale, Bulle Ogier, Michèle Moretti, Bernadette Lafont

Why It's Key The last shot of a very long puzzle film offers an ironic metaphor for the experience of watching it.

MARLON BRANDO

Last Tango in Paris

X

A Film by BERNARDO BERTOLUCCI
with MARIA SCHNEIDER · MARIA MICHI · GIOVANNA GALLETTI and with JEAN-PIERRE LEAUD also starring MASSIMO GIROTTI
Produced by ALBERTO GRIMALDI   Directed by BERNARDO BERTOLUCCI   A COPRODUCTION PEA PRODUZIONI EUROPEE ASSOCIATE S A S · ROME · LES PRODUCTIONS ARTISTES ASSOCIES S A · PARIS   United Artists
Original Motion Picture Soundtrack Available on United Artists Records and Tapes

Key Scene **The invitation to and release from temptation** *Chloe in the Afternoon*

Very early in *Chloe in the Afternoon*, we know that Frédéric (Verley), a personable if at times quietly anxious married man, can be seduced into buying a shirt by an attractive female sales clerk. Can he also be seduced into something more serious, like an extra-marital affair with the provocative, unattached Chloé (Zouzou)? In that question lies the suspense, which recalls Alfred Hitchcock, of the last of Rohmer's "Six Moral Tales." The dénouement of this highly sophisticated, always absorbing drama finds Chloé asking Frédéric to towel off her naked body, which he does in a tasteful, yet highly erotic shot in which we see his face from behind her. Ready to capitulate to his desire, he begins to pull his turtleneck over his head but sees his face in the mirror, in a reminder of a moment with his family – wife (Francoise Verley), daughter, and newborn son – and resists temptation, leaving to run down a winding flight of stairs in masterly overhead shot, the clattering sound of his footsteps expressing both his panic and release from it, in the only truly great homage to *Vertigo* (1958). It is the moment that affirms that cinematic suspense has less to do with genres and situations than with how the style and form of a film are approached, and with tension and release – the release here returning Frédéric to his wife and a single-take final scene in which Rohmer's trademark irony is suffused with a profound melancholy.

Blake Lucas

Date 1972

Nationality France

Director Eric Rohmer

Cast Bernard Verley, Zouzou

Original Title *L'Amour, l'après-midi*

Why It's Key Eric Rohmer provides the finest example of Hitchcockian suspense outside the master's own work, while creating the ironies and melancholy contours of his own world with a special sophistication and grace.

Key Scene **Strangers meet** *Last Tango in Paris*

Grief-stricken over the suicide of his French wife, middle-aged American businessman Paul (Brando, at the height of his powers) wanders Paris aimlessly, so numb to what's going on around him he can barely function. After crossing paths at random with an attractive younger woman, Jeanne (Schneider), Paul sort-of follows her to an empty apartment she's inspecting as a future home for herself and her husband-to-be, a self-absorbed filmmaker (Jean-Pierre Léaud). Paul and Jeanne will eventually form a strong bond built on anonymous sex; at Paul's insistence, they don't even exchange first names. As Roger Ebert perceptively noted, physical intimacy becomes "an elemental force… the medium of exchange" between the emotionally devastated Paul and the compliantly curious Jeanne. It's during their first encounter that director Bertolucci sets the mysterious, restless mood: as the soon-to-be-lovers pace around the flat, Vittorio Storaro's camera wanders from them to unrelated objects, curious about the surroundings in a way the principal characters aren't. Their first, volcanic coupling has been called rape; defining it thus is a slippery slope, but there's little doubt of the physical force – and mutual need – of the participants. Later films in which sex is a crucial part of the plot, such as Michael Winterbottom's *9 Songs* (2004) and John Cameron Mitchell's *Shortbus* (2006), owe a debt to *Last Tango in Paris*, the first mainstream feature to equate physical intimacy with human communication.

David Stratton

Date 1972

Nationality Italy/France

Director Bernardo Bertolucci

Cast Marlon Brando, Maria Schneider

Original Title *Ultimo tango a Parigi; Le dernier tango à Paris*

Why It's Key It's a highlight of an emotionally devastating treatise on loneliness, despair, sex, and need.

Opposite *Last Tango in Paris*

Key Scene **Divine eats dog shit**
Pink Flamingos

Why does everyone only remember the shit-eating? In *Pink Flamingo's* 107 minutes, we're treated to mother-son fellatio, insemination with a turkey baster, a man flinging his legs over his head so we can see him open and close his anus in time to the music, two people having sex with a beheaded chicken wedged between them, a pretty girl suddenly waggling her penis at the camera, a shoplifter shoving raw meat between her legs, a married couple bringing each other to orgasm by sucking on each other's toes, and simulated cannibalism, castration and arson. (The only "depravity" that's been semi-defused by time is a lesbian couple adopting a baby.) But nothing tops the glamorously grotesque Babs Johnson (Divine) settling her bulk on the sidewalk next to a squatting dog and, after a moment's hesitation, scooping up the turd like a girl playing jacks and shoving the whole ungodly mess in her mouth, alternating between involuntary gagging and Jayne Mansfield vamping as she displays a genuine shit-eating grin. While the gross-out genre Waters innovated would eventually discard a queer art-house sensibility (think Douglas Sirk melodrama via Buñuel and nitrous oxide) for the relentless bully-boy heterosexuality of *Animal House* (1978) or *Porky's* (1982), there would be no semen hair gel in *There's Something About Mary* (1998) or violated confectionary in *American Pie* (1999) without Divine and her cast-iron taste buds. The film's braying narrator, Mr. J, even taunts all future challengers: "The filthiest people alive? Well, you think you know somebody filthier?"

Violet Glaze

Date 1972

Nationality USA

Director John Waters

Cast Divine

Why It's Key John Waters invents the gross-out film.

474

Key Scene **The villagers face the corporation**
Minamata: The Victims and Their World

A law-school graduate and student activist, Noriaki Tsuchimoto began working in film with a clear socio-political vision of the role that media should play in effecting change. Tsuchimoto is best known for his work documenting the effects of mercury poisoning on the fishing community of Minamata on the west coast of the Japanese island of Kyushu, and he has made at least 15 films in the community over the course of several decades. *Minamata: The Victims and Their World* is a troubling and vital work. Intent on documenting (often lyrically) the daily lives of people devastated by exposure to industrial waste, the film refuses to gloss over the banality and quietude of their lives but also points toward their gradual radicalization.

Mercury poisoning in Minamata was caused by the negligence of the Chisso Corporation, who were producing acetaldehyde in a local factory and expelling mercury as a waste product. In order to provide a platform for redressing their grievances, many of the Minamata victims and their families bought single shares in the corporation, an act that would enable them to speak at annual shareholders' meetings. The inevitable confrontation is an extraordinary and harrowing event to watch. As the victims desperately plead for a response of any kind to their situation, the implacable corporate representatives carry through their business without responding, effectively and publicly ignoring the death and disfiguration they directly caused. Watching, we feel the sadness and indignation of an accumulated human resistance not only to corporate irresponsibility but faceless, indiscriminate murder.

Travis Miles

Date 1972

Nationality Japan

Director Noriaki Tsuchimoto

Original Title *Minamata: Kanja-san to sono sekai*

Why It's Key An emotionally and politically redemptive act, the documentation of this charged protest embodies the notion of filmic activism.

Key Film *River Yar*
The spring and autumn equinoxes synch

The filmmakers conceived of the 35-minute-work as an attempt to fuse the technological foundation of cinema with the vast forces controlling the natural world – in this case, the tilting of the earth toward and away from the sun. To display this phenomenon, Welsby and Raban decided to represent on screen the variable duration of daylight in the weeks leading up to and following the spring and autumn equinoxes. A location was selected overlooking a tidal estuary, so that the swell and recess of water would also demonstrate the passage of time and the effect of the moon. While the camera remained stationary, one frame of film was exposed every minute, all day and night, for two six-week periods, three weeks before and three weeks after each equinox. Wild sound was recorded at increments throughout the day.

The effect of the film is tremendous. Each filming period is represented on a separate screen, projected side by side. Because of technical problems, the filmmakers were unable to film a successful time-lapse for every day, so they made the inspired decision to begin the film with a real-time sunrise on the right screen and conclude it with a real-time sunset on the left. The binocular effect of seeing days whirl by on one side while the sun slowly illuminates or darkens the landscape on the other is one of the most singular in non-narrative cinema. At the midpoint of this vertiginous experience, the conceptual tack of the film becomes clear when the speeding days synch up for a few cycles, and the equinoxes pass.

Travis Miles

Date 1972

Nationality UK

Directors Chris Welsby and William Raban

Why It's Key The natural world has seldom been more cleverly and rapturously represented on film than in this definitive moment of the British school of process- and structure-oriented filmmaking.

Key Scene **Weightlessness**
Solaris

Originally seen by critics as the Soviet answer to Stanley Kubrick's *2001: A Space Odyssey* (1968), Andrei Tarkovsky's *Solaris* is strangely earthbound and mired in the past for a science-fiction film set mostly on another planet in the future. Tarkovsky did not share Kubrick's fascination with technology – or his misanthropy. And unlike Stanislaw Lem, who wrote the book on which *Solaris* was based, he was not concerned so much with Man confronting the Cosmos as he was with the humanity he brought with him. Kris Kelvin (Banionis) has been sent to find out what happened to the mission on the planet Solaris, whose ocean, he discovers, has the power to make people's most traumatic memories come to life. Kelvin awakes one day to discover his wife, Hari (Bondarchuk), who committed suicide years before, sitting beside him, forcing him to relive their troubled relationship over again. At first Kelvin approaches the situation as an intellectual problem to be solved. He and his fellow scientists, those who haven't been driven completely mad from being haunted by their own pasts, have a dry discussion on the nature of humanity and love in the space station's library, surrounded by books and artwork from the past. Is Hari human? Is she capable of love or being loved? Then suddenly, in a moment of breathtaking beauty, Kelvin and Hari begin floating through the air, as a candelabra and books glide by them. It is moment of transcendence that illustrates the power of love and art to take us to another level. It's moment that seems to come out of nowhere and that transports us the way a piece of music or a painting can.

Al Weisel

Date 1972

Nationality USSR

Director Andrei Tarkovsky

Cast Natalya Bondarchuk, Donatas Banionis

Why It's Key Tarkovsky spent his career proving that cinema was an art form as important as every other art – a message that this scene brings home unmistakably.

Key Film
Dies irae

The story of Petr Skala is one of the most astonishing in film history. Since the late 1960s, in a time of relentless stifling of intellectual freedom in Czechoslovakia, he made experimental films at home with virtually nothing: discarded blank or exposed 16mm film strips, a magnifying glass or a microscope, crude engraving tools such as needles and manicure sets, the few color dyes commercially available at the time. There was no question of showing them in public: as a result, Skala has never seen his films projected in a cinema. His technique turns celluloid film into something between a sculpture and an engraving, a plastic surface to be scratched, blotted, burnt, and treated with the most ingenious range of methods. Dishwashing sand, egg white, cigarette lighter liquid, acetone, sugar, and honey are combined with glues and hairsprays, then applied to the film emulsion and carved upon with tiny needles – a process that elevates surgical tools such as a scalpel for eye

operations to the status of filmmaking equipment. This looks like making art from the relics of a post-apocalyptic world; it is, in fact, the product of a vision that found its shape in a society where vision itself was a forbidden word. Beneath a superficial resemblance to Stan Brakhage's work, *Dies irae* reveals a more complex structure, owing to mathematics, alchemy, and music. It is a shifting miniature of spiritual radiance, a miracle of craftsmanship achieving visual ecstasy, like sunlight coming through the Rothko-like stained glass of an imaginary church.

Paolo Cherchi Usai

Date 1972

Nationality Czechoslovakia

Director Petr Skala

Why It's Key A no-budget film achieves metaphysical power.

Key Scene **The lobster dinner**
The Heartbreak Kid

SPOILER

This restaurant scene opens with a shot of a waiter's finger tapping a live lobster on a plate, prodding it to show it's alive before it's boiled and served. May does the same thing to the couple about to eat it, Lennie (Grodin) and Lila (Berlin), newlyweds from New York honeymooning in Miami Beach. Lila is unaware Lennie wants to dump her for Kelly (Cybill Shepherd), a blonde co-ed from the Midwest he met on the beach while Lila recovered from a sunburn in their hotel room. Lennie is determined to tell Lila their marriage is over, finish the meal with a piece of the restaurant's famous "Florida pecan pie" and no hard feelings, and get to Minnesota to claim Kelly

This may be the only scene in an American comedy that really qualifies as brutally funny; it's like a punch in the stomach. Lila's humiliation, as unbearable as it is, is worsened by our perception of her as a slob whose abandonment is inevitable, and by Grodin's feigned deflective ire at a waiter (Preminger) who tells

him the restaurant is out of pie. This is screwball comedy without redemption, an underdog comedy where the underdog is a jerk.

Neil Simon's screenplay, from a Bruce Jay Friedman story, must be given credit along with May's direction and the film's priceless performances, including Eddie Albert's as Kelly's father, a man who (in another dinner scene) doesn't buy Lennie's talk of beef that doesn't lie, sincere potatoes, and undeceitful cauliflower.

A. S. Hamrah

Date 1972

Nationality USA

Director Elaine May

Cast Charles Grodin, Jeannie Berlin, Erik Lee Preminger

Why It's Key May exposes deceitful masculinity and female obliviousness while pushing romantic comedy to its limit.

Opposite *The Heartbreak Kid*

Key Scene **Tea with poisoned milk**
The Discreet Charm of the Bourgeoisie

Triggered by minor annoyances, the dreams and memories of civil servants invade the lives of Buñuel's upper-class characters whenever they sit down to eat. Bloody anecdotes, related by the people who maintain order in their world, animate their unease.

Simone (Seyrig), her sister Florence (Ogier), and their friend Alice (Audran) go to a café for tea. Florence, annoyed by the presence of a cellist, makes Simone change seats with her so she won't have to look at him. As Alice notices a soldier (Robard) staring at them, a waiter (Musson) arrives with news the café is out of tea. They switch their order to coffee with milk. The soldier joins them. He relates a macabre story, which we see in flashback: As a child his dead parents appeared to him and convinced him to murder his stepfather with poisoned milk. The waiter returns. The café is also out of coffee – and milk.

Florence, who is single and seems to prefer alcohol to sex, can't stand to look at a cello. Alice, whom we've seen cavorting in the bushes of her estate, is the first to notice the soldier. Simone, off to an assignation, allows him to hold the door for her as she leaves. Yet the soldier's confession makes less of an impression on them than the café's lack of tea and coffee. Protected by haute couture and polite smiles, these unflappable women have an uncanny ability to ignore the poetic. Eventually it opens fire.
A. S. Hamrah

Date 1972

Nationality France

Director Luis Buñuel

Cast Delphine Seyrig, Bulle Ogier, Stéphane Audran, Bernard Musson, Gerald Robard

Original Title *Le charme discret de la bourgeoisie*

Why It's Key Buñuel profiles a class through the interplay of dream life and daily life.

Key Scene **Horse's head in the bed**
The Godfather

Jack Woltz (Marley), a Hollywood studio head, doesn't want to give mobbed-up singer Johnny Fontane (Al Martino) a key role in an upcoming war picture. "Let me lay it on the line for you and your boss, whoever he is," Woltz tells the Corleone consigliori, Tom Hagen (Robert Duvall). "Johnny Fontane will never get that movie. I don't care how many dago guinea wop greaseball goombahs come out of the woodwork." Woltz wakes up in bed with blood all over the silk sheets and discovers the severed head of his beloved racehorse, Khartoum, and Johnny Fontane gets the picture. Though the circumstances are clearly based on Columbia boss Harry Cohn's decision to cast Frank Sinatra in *From Here to Eternity* (1954), the dead horse seems to be writer Mario Puzo's invention – perhaps inspired by the moment in *The Public Enemy* (1931) where Cagney and pals troop into a stable with machine-guns and "rub out" the horse that threw and killed a gang boss. A real horse's head, fresh from a dogfood factory, plays the luckless Khartoum.
Kim Newman

Date 1972

Nationality USA

Director Francis Ford Coppola

Cast John Marley

Why It's Key Now we know what you get if you defy the Godfather.

Key Scene **César tells David that Rosalie is pregnant** *César and Rosalie (César et Rosalie)*

Although *César et Rosalie* boasts – in true Sautet style – a multitude of supporting players (siblings, relatives, children, friends, co-workers, often convivially gathered around a dinner table), the film's focus is Yves Montand's stunning performance as César, arguably his best ever and one of the greatest in French film history.

The film is the story of the often painful, sometimes comical evolution of a triangle formed by César, a working-class self-made man who made his fortune in salvaged material, Rosalie (Romy Schneider), his lover and unofficial girl Friday (she is his translator and interpreter with foreign clients), and David (Frey), a low-key, quiet, rather passive artist specializing in comic strips, who was once Rosalie's lover and has returned to France after years in the United States. César, who is deeply insecure underneath his constantly bragging, self-assured macho façade, realizes that Rosalie is still attracted to David and he to her. After he spends a night looking for Rosalie, who visited David and his colleagues in their workshop, César (who has previously befriended David) meets David in a café and tells him that Rosalie is pregnant and that they are getting married within a few days. This is an absolute lie, showing César at his most convincing yet transparent, and the starting point of an increasingly complex and ambiguous relationship between three characters who never seem to be able to live either together or apart.

Jean-Pierre Coursodon

Date 1972

Nationality France/Italy/Germany

Director Claude Sautet

Cast Yves Montand, Sami Frey

Why It's Key Central to the narrative, this scene reveals fascinating aspects of a complex character.

Key Scene **The self-mutilation** *Cries and Whispers*

The self-mutilation of Karin (Thulin) in this film is one of the more memorable horror scenes in movie history. The character has been properly introduced as someone very strong but emotionally closed, whose only warm moment, with her sister Maria (Liv Ullmann), ends in painful rejection. She is married to a man (Georg Årlin) who is even colder that she is, so it is only appropriate that she decides to deny him her body as well as her heart, as she proceeds to do – using a broken glass, with gory results. Though her motivations are clear enough, the scene comes quite unexpectedly and, since there seem to be no consequences to her action, it may very well be just a horrible fantasy. In any case, it only matters as a means to convey the level of self-damage she's ready to endure in order to keep herself unreachable by others. For Bergman this was the first of a few graphically violent scenes that he filmed in the seventies, a trend that climaxed in *From the Life of the Marionettes* (1980) and that he decided to abandon in his later films.

Fernando Martín Peña

Date 1972

Nationality Sweden

Director Ingmar Bergman

Cast Ingrid Thulin

Original Title *Viskningar och rop*

Why It's Key This memorable moment of horror shows how far someone will go to stay out of reach.

Key Scene **The conquistador isolated on his raft** *Aguirre, the Wrath of God*

Aguirre (Kinski), a 16th-century explorer, breaks away from a Spanish expedition to lead his own party up the Amazon, lusting for wealth and power. Much adversity comes their way, but he'll sacrifice anything – including lives – to achieve his goals, however impossible they obviously are.

Herzog launched his career in West Germany's bold Neue Kino movement, which included Wim Wenders and Rainer Werner Fassbinder, among others. While these filmmakers had different aims and agendas, they all wanted to put German cinema back in touch with realities it had largely spurned. Herzog's method has been to work against reality's grain – devising visionary, often delirious imagery meant to defamiliarize the world so we can begin to understand it in radically fresh ways.

Aguirre can be interpreted as an allegory of authoritarianism, with its deranged hero standing for the Hitlers of all eras. But to read this movie through an intellectual lens is to undervalue its sensory appeal, which carries its ultimate meaning. In the end, Aguirre doesn't so much represent as embody the dementia of rulers who would "stage history as other men stage plays," to quote him in the final scene. There stands the conquistador of conquistadors – on a waterlogged raft, surrounded by corpses and marmosets, still declaiming his plans for future feats ("…and I will marry my own daughter…") as the camera swirls around him in circles going nowhere. This is history as nightmare. It's almost a relief when the film loosens its grip and allows us back into the light of day.

David Sterritt

Date 1972

Nationality West Germany

Director Werner Herzog

Cast Klaus Kinski

Original Title *Aguirre, der Zorn Gottes*

Why It's Key In his finest film with his quintessential star, Herzog provides a consummate example of his desire to picture the world as it's never been viewed or imagined before.

481

Key Scene **"I'm XXing!"** *The World of Geisha*

An intertitle appears on screen: "I'm XXing!" It is a scene of passion in Tatsumi Kumashiro's soft porn or "pink" film *The World of Geisha*, so most spectators can fill in the XXs. Yet they are significant. The major studio Nikkatsu shifted production towards "Roman Porno" films only to see several directors arrested on obscenity charges in 1972. It was during this tense time that Kumashiro audaciously decided to adapt a banned story to film. *The World of Geisha* comments on all this by making visible what usually tries to remain invisible: censorship. Not only does the film cite famous censorship incidents in Japanese history, such as the blanking out of newspaper articles on rice riots in 1919, it also "censors" itself in a way that can only make the viewer conscious of the abuse of power. Large black rectangles invade the screen to cover up the naughty bits, and XXs cover up "obscene " dialogue, using the exact same techniques as fascist-era Japan. That this battle over censorship marvelously overlaps with the narrative's own battle of the sexes and succeeds in reflecting on cinema within a history of political expression is testimony to Kumashiro's genius, but it also represents how important "pink film" was to Japanese film history, becoming not only the training ground for great directors of the 1980s and 1990s like Masayuki Suo (*Shall We Dance?* [1996]) and Kiyoshi Kurosawa (*Cure* [1997]), but also the focal point for rethinking cinema and politics in Japan after the 1960s.

Aaron Gerow

Date 1973

Nationality Japan

Director Tatsumi Kumashiro

Cast Junko Miyashita, Hideaki Esumi

Original Title *Yojohan fusuma no urabari*

Why It's Key This intertitle symbolizes pink film's political struggle against censorship.

Key Scene **Garrett shoots his reflection**
Pat Garrett and Billy the Kid

The story is one of the most told in cinema: Pat Garrett, now a sheriff, shoots and kills Billy the Kid, who has become an outlaw. That what lies within this story is more than the familiar event of legend is crystallized in Peckinpah's film when Garrett (Coburn) shoots Billy (Kristofferson), then sees and fires upon his own reflection in a mirror. The concise action has piercing effect: Billy smiles to see his old friend unexpectedly, just before a grim-visaged Pat fires; Pat sees his reflection; cut back to him firing again and the sound of the shattering glass, and as Billy lies dead, a rueful Pat stares into the broken mirror. The mortality that here imposes itself as the soul of the story is that of Pat, whose own violent death years later provides a frame for the action, and makes that action a meditation. So, in an act of modernism for the Western, and more moving because it is one enacted by a director with deep ties to the Western ethos, a circularity, built on measured alternations of violence

and reflection, leads to a climactic moment in which philosophical self-awareness echoes like gunfire. The drama is one of Pat's own consciousness, expressed with a marvelously projected inwardness by an actor more commonly thought of as extroverted. For mortality, seen as in a mirror, reflects back on the complexities of relationships, the emotions that can float through them, darkening and changing as a man's life evolves, as his betrayals become his self-betrayals, and what was true remains even as it is destroyed.
Blake Lucas

Date 1973

Nationality USA

Director Sam Peckinpah

Cast James Coburn, Kris Kristofferson

Why It's Key The spiritual concerns of the classical Western are affectingly validated within a modernist work by a director who is linked to both phases of the genre.

Key Event
Political upset at the Oscars

It wasn't the first Oscar protest but it is certainly the most remembered and, also, the most revealing. Marlon Brando sent 26-year-old part-Apache Sacheen Littlefeather to refuse his second Oscar, for *The Godfather* (1972), and read out a 15-page speech on his behalf. Given only 45 seconds to speak, Littlefeather made her points about the portrayal of Native Americans in film and TV at the time with courtesy and succinctness. There were audience gasps and cheers. Charlton Heston thought "It was childish," Jane Fonda said that what Brando did "was wonderful." Afterwards it was discovered that Littlefeather was actually a Mexican actress, born Maria Cruz, but in any case the iniquities of history had finally caught up with America's dream factory. Brando was one of the country's discrepant rebels. In the previous decade, Hollywood had belatedly stopped wearing blinkers about America's past and social change. New directors were making films with grown-up themes and stories. The

high-profile nature of the Academy Award ceremony, its glitz and expense, its whiff of kitsch and celebrity, seemed dated. The Brando-Cruz protest, though only partially successful, brought a welcome moment of moral seriousness to Hollywood's shop window, a seriousness that would be echoed in the occasional Oscar protests thereafter.
Mark Cousins

Date March 27, 1973

Why It's Key American cinema's annual PR event is used by Marlon Brando to highlight the unjust treatment of Native Americans.

Opposite **Marlon Brando**

Key Scene **A walk into the Pacific**
The Long Goodbye

In Robert Altman's adaptation of Raymond Chandler's novel, detective Philip Marlowe (Gould) is hired by Eileen (Van Pallandt), the wife of alcoholic writer Roger Wade (Hayden), to retrieve her missing husband. Having finished this task, Marlowe continues his visits to the Wades' Malibu house, suspecting that they are involved in the apparent suicide of his best friend, Terry. One night, Eileen serves Marlowe a homemade dinner while her husband is asleep. After dinner, Marlowe questions her about Terry. As they talk, Vilmos Zsigmond's camera (adrift constantly throughout the film) becomes interested in the distant figure of Roger Wade, who, unseen by the other two, has left the house and is marching across the beach toward the ocean.

At first, Wade is seen through a large window behind Marlowe and Eileen. During the conversation, Altman cuts to a shot from outside the house: Marlowe and Eileen now stand on the opposite side of the window from the camera, and Wade is an improbably,

jarringly bright reflection in the glass (one of the many miracles Zsigmond works in *The Long Goodbye*) as he walks into the Pacific, bent on suicide. Altman's staging of the scene, while heightening its suspense (will the other two see Wade in time?), makes of Wade's act the occasion for both an exceptionally stylized statement, and a muted critique, of the hazy, glassy, hallucinatory L.A. look that dominates the whole film.

Chris Fujiwara

Date 1973

Nationality USA

Director Robert Altman

Cast Elliott Gould, Sterling Hayden, Nina Van Pallandt

Why It's Key Robert Altman's direction and Vilmos Zsigmond's cinematography make a powerful visual statement.

1970–1979

485

Key Event
Lucas hangs on to the "garbage" rights

When *American Graffiti* (1973) became a runaway hit, writer-director George Lucas had the opportunity to renegotiate his deal at 20th Century-Fox to make a science-fiction film. The suits were surprised when Lucas didn't ask for more money upfront but instead insisted on retaining the merchandising rights of the film – including but not limited to income from any soundtrack album, tie-in book, or range of toys. This far-sighted decision, along with control of the sequel rights, eventually made Lucas financially independent of the studio system in a way his mentor, Francis Ford Coppola, could only dream of. Hitherto – except at Disney, where Mickey Mouse watches have been ticking since the '30s – merchandising rights were considered the "garbage" of any contract. When *Star Wars* (1977) became the highest-grossing film of all time, and anything bearing its logo – action figures (i.e., dolls, but not for sissies), lunchboxes, underwear – began to shift like gangbusters, there was a seismic

shift in the entertainment industry. The Lucasfilm empire rose not just on ticket sales, but on toys, posters (advertising materials soon became recategorized as collectibles), a novelisation signed by Lucas (but ghosted by Alan Dean Foster), and all manner of tie-in product – an industry that continues to this day. Thereafter, studios would look not just for films but franchises, and associated products (especially toys) would become almost paramount.

Kim Newman

Date August 20, 1973

Why It's Key Lucas's success with the merchandising of *Star Wars* changed the ways movies were made, sold, promoted, and profited from.

Opposite *Star Wars*

Key Scene **Dream of a funeral**
The Traitors (Los traidores)

Roberto Barrera (Proncet), a corrupt union leader, dreams his own funeral. At first we are not aware that it is a dream, so we don't know how to decode the growing weirdness of the scene. Barrera is, at the same time, in the coffin and among the mourners. Though all go through the movements as expected in such a situation, the visual context reveals the mockery: one man cannot stop laughing, two others play cards on Barrera's coffin, Barrera's wife flirts with the President, another union leader finishes his solemn speech and proceeds to eat an oversized sandwich.

Though it has been called a fiction film, *The Traitors* is more of a "reconstructed documentary," since nothing was invented for the script. Even the dream sequence has its roots in newspaper reports of actual events (many prominent union leaders, most of them corrupt, were killed by the so-called "Peronist left" between 1969 and 1973). In Argentine cinema, this film stands alone in dealing successfully with the clashing forces that defined Argentina's political history between 1955 and 1973.

Hardly known outside Argentina, *The Traitors* should be remembered for having suffered one of the most extreme examples of censorship in the history of film. Most of its cast could no longer work after the 1976 military coup; one of its scriptwriters and part of the crew had to exile themselves; and its director, Raymundo Gleyzer, was murdered by the dictatorship after being "disappeared" on May 1976. All known prints of the film were confiscated or destroyed by the military. It was only after ten years of democracy that the film resurfaced, because the head of a film society managed to keep a print hidden in mislabeled cans. Since then, *The Traitors* has been acknowledged as a major work and has inspired dozens of new filmmakers.

Fernando Martín Peña

Date 1973

Nationality Argentina

Director Raymundo Gleyzer

Cast Víctor Proncet

Why It's Key With a wild sense of humor rare in political films, this sequence plays like Winsor McKay's *Dream of a Rarebit Fiend*.

486

Key Scene **Nasser announces that Israel has captured the Sinai** *The Sparrow*

After the international success of *Cairo Station* (1958), Youssef Chahine became an impassioned spokesman on film's role in liberation movements. At first he welcomed Gamal Abdel Nasser's pan-Arab Nationalism, but by the early 1970s, he was enraged by state corruption and devised *The Sparrow* to denounce it. The film follows a journalist and a young policeman who are investigating wrongdoing in high places. They and others meet in the house of Bahiyya (Tewfik), a left-wing hangout. The film climaxes with Nasser's announcement on national television of Egypt's defeat in the Six-Day War. Chahine brilliantly captures the shock of this announcement, the instant national wound it inflicted, as dramatic as the death of JFK for Americans. As the news unfolds, Bahiyya becomes enraged. She runs onto the street and shouts: "No! We must fight. We won't accept defeat!" Chahine tracks backwards as she runs, and a crowd gathers behind her. Tewfik's performance is remarkable at this moment. Chahine was always a master of screen movement: here the mobility, her flight, the sense of people flooding onto the streets like a tidal wave, together combine to render the urgency of the moment unforgettable, like a scene directed by Dziga Vertov. *The Sparrow* was banned in Egypt for two years.

Mark Cousins

Date 1973

Nationality Egypt/Algeria

Director Youssef Chahine

Cast Mohsena Tewfik

Original Title Al Asfour

Why It's Key The greatest film about the Six-Day War is also one of the bravest Arab films ever made.

Key Scene **Dennis walks off-screen in protest** *Speaking Directly*

Speaking Directly is, among other things, an experiment in materialist autobiography: an attempt both to lay bare the device of cinema itself and to fully expose the relative privilege of the filmmaker. Though Jost is, in economic terms, about as marginal a figure as the cinema has ever seen, in *Speaking Directly* he acknowledges his position as a heterosexual white male with access to the cinematic apparatus. What's more, Jost reminds us, "I am able to make a film largely because… somewhere other people work in factories and mines."

In the section of the film marked "People I Know (Directly)," Jost films his neighbor Dennis, who explains that Jost has attempted to make a film about the inability of a filmmaker to communicate with his audience, given all the corrupt social institutions that intercede in the filmmaking process. This effort, Dennis claims, makes Jost a fraud. He refuses to take any further part in the project, and walks off-camera. But

first, he suggests that the film's audience should repeat his protest from our side of the equation, by ripping the print from the projector and destroying it. Barring such direct revolt, Dennis suggests we simply walk out. No doubt perceiving some degree of truth in Dennis's statement, or at least a problem needing to be more fully explored, Jost leaves Dennis in. As a result, every viewer of *Speaking Directly* is forced to make an ethical decision that most cinema refuses to so much as countenance.

Michael Sicinski

Date 1973

Nationality USA

Director Jon Jost

Cast Dennis (surname withheld)

Why It's Key In a pivotal moment in Marxist self-criticism, Jost's film allows space for the spectator's frustration with him and his film on-screen. Destructive audience participation is sincerely proposed.

487

Key Scene **The forest floor suddenly seems to move** *The Wold-Shadow*

The Wold-Shadow opens with a static, tripod-mounted shot of a forest, repeated across several fade-outs and fade-ins – already something very unusual for Brakhage, who rarely repeats shots and usually shoots hand-held. The whole ethos of his work is to reject the givens of the world, to reject "ordinary" or shared seeing, and so the repetitions create a curious tension, an expectation of transformation. Then, suddenly, the forest floor seems to move rapidly. Apparently it's a brief time-lapse image, but the effect is extraordinary, even for Brakhage, in that the visionary moment is not located in his, or the viewer's, eyesight, so much as in the forest itself. Confirmation comes in the very next image, in which paint seems to congeal over the forest floor. Then we cut to a sheet of white plastic. In a characteristic move, Brakhage here reveals the source of his artifice: he has mounted plastic in front of his lens, and is painting on it. A series of spectacular, brightly colored compositions follow, many

of them abstracted versions of the forest composition. Indeed, one gets the impression that every image was taken with the lens pointed at the forest, even though in many it's impossible to tell, but a relationship to Georges Méliès's fixed camera-angle films suggests itself. Even with the artifice revealed, one still feels it is the forest itself that is magically changing, and that sense gives the film a terrifying power.

Fred Camper

Date 1973

Nationality USA

Director Stan Brakhage

Why It's Key By suggesting that the forest is itself changing, rather than that our eyes are altering the forest, Brakhage breaks with his usual celebration of individual subjectivity to create a world alive with magical, transformative energy.

Key Speech **The unwritten note**
The Mother and the Whore

Alexandre (Léaud), the protagonist of Eustache's semi-autobiographical film, is usually less sincere than any of the three women in his life – ex-girlfriend Gilberte (Isabelle Weingarten), present lover Marie (Bernadette Lafont), or girlfriend-in-waiting Veronika (Lebrun). He is often an intellectual poseur, says many things for effect, keeps emotions at a distance through words. So it is unexpected when he does reveal himself to Veronika, relating the end of his relationship with Gilberte and her subsequent abortion of their child with a heartbreaking honesty, echoed in Eustache's *mise en scène*, which evokes early filmmaking in its simple, elegant images (most of the long scene, set in a cafe, consists of alternating close-ups of Alexandre and, at certain moments, Veronika). "I wish she had left just with a note… 'Goodbye, I'm leaving,'" he begins, and poetically reiterates this later – that one should always leave a note. That simple assertion is deepened by a steady eloquence of expressed feeling ("I don't think

life can be like these strange worlds which bar reentry once the doors close"), and given life in Léaud's great performance (the actor's voice almost imperceptibly softens, and there is visible pain in his eyes). Behind Alexandre is Eustache himself, a magisterial artistic talent who would die a suicide less than ten years later. In his beautiful writing here, can we hear something even beyond post-1968 malaise, the failure of love, and the sense that life is harrowing and in some way incomprehensible?

Blake Lucas

Date 1973

Nationality France

Director Jean Eustache

Cast Jean-Pierre Léaud, Françoise Lebrun

Original Title *La Maman et la putain*

Why It's Key In a haunting scene of this towering end-of-the-line New Wave masterpiece, Jean Eustache gives profound and highly personal meaning to Alexandre Astruc's influential phrase "*le caméra-stylo.*"

Key Scene **The *Frankenstein* screening**
The Spirit of the Beehive

Erice creeps up on his leading character, Ana (Torrent), in *The Spirit of the Beehive*, over the course of an exquisite prologue lasting 18 minutes. He starts with the general, the "mass": a crowd of kids and adults gathering in a town hall that has been unfussily converted into a cinema (it is Castilian Spain, under Franco, circa 1940) for a screening of James Whale's 1931 *Frankenstein*, starring Boris Karloff. Gradually, we are guided to pay attention to two particular children (Ana and her sister, Isabel [Tellería]); and then, subtly, to focus on Ana. Of the various spectator responses in that cinema – intrigued, distracted, disapproving, amused, bored – hers is the most rapt. Only well-chosen fragments of *Frankenstein* are given to us, alternated with or overlaid upon scenes introducing the girls' lonely parents: a solemn warning at the start ("It might shock you"), a snatch of dialogue that carries all over town ("What if we never went beyond what's known?"). Erice's boldest stroke in the arrangement of

this cinema-going scene is the way he deliberately omits the specific moment in *Frankenstein* which most disturbs Ana – the creature's inadvertent, "innocent" murder of a young girl as he plays with her by the water ("Isabel, why did he kill her?", she asks twice). We see this tragic incident's aftermath: a man carrying the child's corpse in his arms through a village street. Yet that death is precisely the traumatic moment around which the core, dreamlike logic of Erice's film will turn.

Adrian Martin

Date 1973

Nationality Spain

Director Victor Erice

Cast Ana Torrent, Isabel Tellería

Original Title *El Espíritu de la colmena*

Why It's Key The dreamlike logic of Erice's film turns on a missing scene.

Opposite *The Spirit of the Beehive*

Key Scene **The flyswatter**
Essene

The work of master documentarist Frederick Wiseman is arguably the richest portrait of American life in the last decades of the 20th century (and the beginning of the 21st); transcending the notion of mere "documentation" with increasingly essayistic structures, Wiseman's oeuvre of "reality fictions" is actually the closest thing to a great American novel of recent times – no wonder the filmmaker himself has pointed out that you might as well see it as one big long film. Yet Wiseman is still simplifyingly tagged a "critical chronicler" for his method of tackling one "institution" after another. Both "institution" and "criticism" are far too narrow ideas for Wiseman's complex canvas, constantly dialectically expanding (cf. his remarkable revisions, examining other high schools, hospitals, or army bases years later). *Essene*, Wiseman's portrait of a monastery and one of his most moving films (as well as one of the best on religion overall), proves the point just as well, showing the religious institution with a deep, tender respect for the spiritual quest of its inhabitants – but Wiseman's keen eye for ironies is ever intact. One of the most priceless moments of vérité capturing occurs when the abbot has a talk with ever-contrarian troublemaker Brother Wilfred, who cantankerously wields a flyswatter. As the abbot offers a bit of salient advise, Wilfred pauses as if to answer – then with an unexpected, hilarious quick-as-lightning-movement swats a fly, folds his arms before his chest again, and remains triumphantly silent. Wiseman later remarked: "That moment I knew God loved me."

Christoph Huber

Date 1973

Nationality USA

Director Frederick Wiseman

Why it's Key America's master documentarist captures a moment of hilariously contrarian monk action.

Key Scene **A radical course of treatment**
The Exorcist

While making a film in the cozy fall chill of Washington, D.C.'s Georgetown neighborhood, actress Chris MacNeil (Burstyn) is renting a house with her 12-year-old daughter, Regan (Linda Blair). When the young girl is seemingly possessed by the devil, veteran priest Father Merrin (Max von Sydow) teams with younger, doubting cleric Damien Karras (Jason Miller) to rid her of the demon. Director William Friedkin's sensationally successful follow-up to *The French Connection* is a textbook adaptation of a novel by William Peter Blatty (who also scripted), neatly balancing the temporal and spiritual aspects of the incendiary story. As harrowing as many of the effects-laden confrontations with the possessed Regan are, Friedkin understands that the processes of modern medicine can be just as terrifying. Thus, after the weeping Regan is subjected to a series of intrusive tests – which, of course, reveal nothing physically wrong with her – audiences share Chris's confusion and anger: "Christ, 88 doctors and all you can tell me with all of your bullshit…." It's only then, well into the film, that the title is explained: "There is one outside chance of a cure. I think of it as shock treatment," says clinic head Barringer (Masterson), as treating doctor Klein (Heyman) looks on. "Have you ever heard of exorcism?" It's a powerful moment for Burstyn, who, as audience surrogate, protests with "You're telling me that I should take my daughter to a witch doctor? Is that it?" Without this legitimate skepticism, it's doubtful the climactic showdown between Karras and the demon would have such a cathartic effect.

David Stratton

Date 1973

Nationality USA

Director William Friedkin

Cast Ellen Burstyn, Peter Masterson, Barton Heyman

Why It's Key This is a crucial moment from one of the most popular – and unsettling – mainstream horror films ever made.

Opposite *The Exorcist*

Key Scene **Amitabh Bachchan lands his first punch** *Zanjeer (The Chain)*

Before Amitabh Bachchan exploded into violence, the Bollywood hero was marked by his ability to love. He might raise his fists once or twice during the course of the film, but those were perfunctory fight scenes, often inflected with humor.

Then *Zanjeer* happened. It tells the story of Vijay (Bachchan), whose parents are killed because his father refuses to be silent about his master's manufacturing spurious pharmaceuticals. Vijay is adopted by a police officer and grows up to be one. He then takes on everyone with his fists flying. The first fight in the film happens when he is sent to clean up the illegal businesses of one Sher Khan (Pran). It ends in a draw, but it must have become immediately apparent to viewers that someone had changed the rules. Although the sound of the punches falling continued to be "dishoom dishoom" – the onomatopoeia that defines fight scenes in popular parlance – the young actor was making it new. He was throwing himself into the fight. His face was murderous with rage and covered in sweat. He looked convincing even when he was slinging his entire rangy six feet against four men, all of whom would fall down obligingly. *Zanjeer* was a hit, and the definition of the "hero" changed forever. He would now be a warrior, and he would be marked by his ability to challenge the status quo and defend his rights. This Angry Young Man avatar went on to dominate the next 20 years at the box office. As did Amitabh Bachchan, who became a superstar.

Jerry Pinto

Date 1973
Nationality India
Director Prakash Mehra
Cast Amitabh Bachchan, Jaya Bhaduri, Pran, Bindu
Why It's Key Amitabh Bachchan redefines masculinity, the notion of violence, and the definition of anger in Hindi cinema.

Key Event
Marin Karmitz founds MK2

Born in 1938 to a Romanian Jewish family, Paris-based Marin Karmitz can rightfully claim that he is the man behind "world cinema." Arriving in France as a child after living through anti-Semitic pogroms in Romania, Karmitz entered filmmaking in the 1960s, directing several films associated with the leftist movement of 1968. Toward the end of the decade, however, he switched to producing; he has since been involved with underwriting most of the films of Claude Chabrol.

Karmitz is committed to the idea of vertical integration of the film industry. His company, MK2, is a conglomerate that has a production arm (MK2 Productions), a distribution branch (MK2 Diffusion, mostly engaged in distributing highbrow and foreign cinema), and a chain of art-house cinemas across Paris and suburbia. The MK2 enterprise integrates all aspects of the film cycle in a profitable economic venture, giving Karmitz substantial leverage in promoting non-commercial cinema to wider audiences.

Since the 1980s Karmitz has been primarily engaged with a number of international cineastes whose work he has systematically backed and sustained. He introduced to Western audiences directors such as Yilmaz Güney (Turkey) and Lucian Pintilie (Romania). Karmitz is partly responsible for the phenomenal international success of the Iranian Abbas Kiarostami, the Pole Krzysztof Kieslowski, and the Austrian Michael Haneke.

Karmitz's contribution to promoting world cinema is twofold: discovering and bringing to world fame talent from smaller nations; and creating a vertically-integrated operation that supports the production, distribution, and exhibition of alternative, noncommercial films.

Dina Iordanova

Date 1973
Why It's Key Combining the roles of producer, distributor, and exhibitor, Karmitz is one of the main figures behind "world cinema."

Key Scene **A snippet of home-movie footage has a transformative impact** *Fuji*

In mid-career, animator Robert Breer, whose photographed and abstract films revealed a debt to his early master as a painter, Piet Mondrian, began rotoscoping. This technique of tracing a photographed film frame by frame was used by Hollywood animators in the service of greater realism, but Breer, an avant-garde filmmaker interested in revealing rather than concealing artifice, made no attempt at smooth or "realistic" drawings. Instead, he used rotoscoping to create tensions between "realistic" seeing and the graphic elements – color, line, flatness, flicker – of pure cinema.

Fuji begins with a short home movie taken on a train ride in Japan, poorly focused and exposed, but showing a bit of Mount Fuji through a window. Breer then unfolds an almost infinite set of variations, some occasioned by the film footage, some not. For example, the snow-capped peak of Mount Fuji becomes a triangle that rotates and morphs into pure line. That triangle acquires a variety of colors as well. Seeing is exploded into all its imaginative possibilities – look at the world creatively, Breer seems to be saying, and you will find there an explosion of color, line, and movement. When the home movie returns at the film's end, now one feels it has come to life with an infinity of newer possibilities, seeming to vibrate with all the colors and lines we have seen within it, and more. In this respect, Breer has come close to the aesthetic of Stan Brakhage, whose films argue for a renewal of original, inventive seeing.
Fred Camper

Date 1974

Nationality USA

Director Robert Breer

Why It's Key The ending of *Fuji* is one of the great moments in that strain of avant-garde or experimental film whose effect is to enrich – even, to make visionary – daily seeing.

Key Scene **"An Emotional Accretion in 48 Steps"** *Film about a Woman Who...*

In 1972, Yvonne Rainer, one of the most brilliant exponents of the Judson Church movement of postmodern dance, switched to film with *Lives of Performers*. She eventually directed seven 16mm features, until dance claimed her back in the late 1990s. Her second cinematic venture, *Film about a Woman Who...*, masterfully illustrates why "dancing could no longer… 'express' the new content of [her] work, i.e. the emotions." Unabashedly autobiographical, pre-feminist yet playfully anchored in some unsuspected corners of the "dark continent" of female subjectivity, the film explores a woman's ambivalent desires, her complex sense of self, her emotional "faux pas," and, more importantly, her rage.

Having translated bodies into motion, then learnt how camera movement and depth of field could turn motion into pure light, Rainer returns to early cinema – montage, shallow focus, extreme close-ups – to articulate what Lacan termed "the sexual impasse." In the 7-minute "Emotional Accretion" sequence – a woman (Neff) realizes that she has "betrayed herself" when attempting to drown her irritation against her lover (Leech) by cuddling in his arms. Her awakening is staged through 48 takes – typed intertitles alternate with fragmented, diffracted, reframed actions, shot in different angles, modes, and styles, from *film noir* contrasted lighting to post-Godardian disruption between image, sound (synch or not), and music – that incisively deconstruct the lures of melodrama as well as the tropes of the avant-garde. And she ends on an operatic bang: "She hadn't wanted to be held…. She had wanted to bash his fucking face in."
Bérénice Reynaud

Date 1974

Nationality USA

Director Yvonne Rainer

Cast Dempster Leech, Renfreu Neff

Why It's Key An elegant transition from dance to film, this seminal text of the ebullient New York art scene of the 1970s posits *woman* as the privileged subject of the avant-garde.

Key Scene **The suicide attempt**
A Woman under the Influence

Mabel (Rowlands) is under the influence of many things, including her family, her working-class milieu, the instability of her mercurial mind, and just possibly the moon. Her offbeat thought processes lend her a quirky charm that help explain why Nick (Falk), her husband, fell in love with her.

But sometimes her internal conflicts veer out of control, derailing the improvisational openness with which she faces life. One day she reaches a crisis so disorienting that she starts slashing at her wrists. Nick's first job is to get their little children out of the room, which isn't easy, since they're distraught with fear. Then he has to bring Mabel back to her senses, which he finally does by striking her.

This has angered critics who feel the movie gives Nick a free pass for egregious male-chauvinist behavior. But that position misses the point: Mabel isn't a deeply troubled woman married to a psychoanalyst, she's a deeply troubled woman married to a working-class guy who simply doesn't know what else to do. Like her, he's improvising his way through life, making a nonstop stream of existential choices that prove to be right or wrong or both or neither.

What makes us care for them is that they truly love each other. Beneath all the upheaval they're something the movies don't show us very often: a *functional* family grounded in trust, affection, and mutual respect for one another's lunacies – which, properly perceived, are what make life interesting in the first place.

David Sterritt

Date 1974

Nationality USA

Director John Cassaveles

Cast Gena Rowlands, Peter Falk

Why It's Key Working at the peak of their powers, a towering writer-director and a brilliant actress (also his wife) depict the dynamics of mental illness in a family that has little but instinct and intuition to guide its actions.

Key Scene **The wife takes her leave**
Reason, Argument, and Story

On paper it sounds a recipe for self-indulgent tedium: An alcoholic filmmaker, way past his prime and presumably operating with depleted brain cells, makes one last stab at a masterpiece – an autobiographical and experimental work about how he has frittered away his own genius. And the opening scene – men in black body stockings dancing in a kitsch Hollywood-musical way – doesn't bode well. But then you slide into the altered state of this film, with its unplugged honesty and moving self-disclosure. In the second scene, Ghatak, playing himself, is slumped on the floor, by a window. His low-angle framing emphasises the slump. His wife arrives and announces she is leaving. He cares more about the bottle and his fading artistic self than her. Camera placement and eye-line mismatching at first look amateurish, but quickly it becomes clear that Ghatak knows what he is doing. This goodbye scene disorients us, just as as it disorients him. The film style is dissociated. And then, for those who have followed Ghatak's work, there is the familiar otherworldly sound mix. At one point the voices of man and wife echo and, so, overlap. At other times in the film, we feel that we are, sonically, in a 50s sci-fi movie. This is not perhaps the first of Ghatak's films to watch but, like Orson Welles's *Othello*, which it resembles in eccentricity, it is pure cinema. It's one of India's most memorable films.

Mark Cousins

Date 1974

Nationality India

Director Ritwik Ghatak

Cast Ritwik Ghatak, Saugata Burman

Original Title *Jukti, Takko Aar Gappo*

Why It's Key Ghatak is one of India's most individualistic filmmakers, and this is his most honest scene.

Key Scene **The helicopter**
Elektra, My Love

SPOILER

Jancsó's adaptation of the Greek tragedy of *Elektra* sets the action in a timeless but rustic setting on the Hungarian plain. It is a world of human bodies, horses, and rudimentary buildings, where every interaction involves participation in ritualistic movement and gesture.

The helicopter or aircraft is a persistent symbol in Jancsó's work, often standing in for the oppressive "everywhere-at-once" nature of the state. In *Elektra, My Love*, he inverts its negative connotation and employs it as a true *deus ex machina*, liberating his actors from the flat, limitless plain and placing them, momentarily, in the heavens. The aircraft appears in the film's rapturous, single-take denouement, after the protagonists have overthrown the tyrant Aegisthus and taken their own lives. Resurrected and warmly embracing, as if finally free, Orestes (Cserhalmi) and Elektra (Töröcsik) move toward and board a bright red helicopter, which lifts slowly from the ground. The accompanying voiceover (spoken by Töröcsik) tells the fable of a firebird that gives hope and strength to the oppressed but that dies every evening, only to be born again, more wondrous, the following day. As the fable is related, the brilliant-colored helicopter flies into and out of the camera's view, in spiral patterns that mirror the pageantry of the horsemen below. The name of the firebird is finally revealed as the helicopter descends again and Orestes and Elektra alight and take their place at the head of a dancing chain of beautiful young men and women. "Blessed be your name: revolution."
Travis Miles

Date 1974

Nationality Hungary

Director Miklós Jancsó

Cast György Cserhalmi, Mari Töröcsik

Original Title *Szerelmem, Elektra*

Why It's Key Unexpected and ecstatic, the arrival of the helicopter at the film's conclusion exemplifies Jancsó's willingness to create pageantry and visual symbolism with little regard for narrative or temporal logic.

Key Scene **Two kids play with circus props**
Parade

The final sequence in Jacques Tati's last and least-known feature – a performance shot mainly on video in Stockholm's Circus Theatre for Swedish television, but also a passionate manifesto – is almost four minutes of improvisation by two kids: a three-year-old girl (Dandenell) and a six-year-old boy (Jägerstedt), playing with stage props after the show is over and mainly trying to imitate the professionals they've just seen. According to Tati's biographer David Bellos, these tots, recruited from a nursery, were selected not just for their looks but also because they were the least obedient in following orders. Their restless activities – hitting bells with hammers, painting, trying to juggle with paintbrushes, letting air out of balloons, trying to play musical instruments, and rocking back and forth inside huge bowls – look strictly unsupervised.

Parade is Tati's ultimate assertion that ordinary people and spectators can be as interesting and as enlightening to watch as professional entertainers, himself included. (He's the emcee, and he also performs his most famous pantomimes, but he takes care to show how bored one little girl is when he makes his first appearance.) This is also part of the message of his masterpiece *Playtime*, but Tati radicalizes the notion even further here by going out into the lobby and focusing on latecomers just as the show's getting started. And after he focuses on these two kids performing their own show at the end, and doing it strictly for themselves, he pans upward past a couple of adult spectators in the otherwise empty front bleachers.
Jonathan Rosenbaum

Date 1974

Nationality France/Sweden

Director Jacques Tati

Actors Anna-Karin Dandenell, Juri Jägerstedt

Why it's Key Tati ends his career by asserting that we, not he, are the greatest show on earth.

Key Speech **Define reality** *F for Fake*

"That's her real name, you know. Oja. Oja Kodar." Welles pronounces these syllables like they're hard facts. Why? We already know his costar's name. But it isn't her real name. He doesn't tell us it's a name he gave her long before they made *F for Fake*. Welles uses her name to introduce a confession: Everything he said in the film's last 17 minutes was a lie. "My job," he says, "was to try to make it real."

"Not that reality had anything to do with it." He utters these words over a shot of a man we know as Oja's grandfather. More precisely, over a shot of her grandfather's legs floating in the air over a grassy field, the rest of his body out of frame. "Reality?" asks Welles. "It's the toothbrush waiting at home for you in its glass. A bus ticket, a paycheck, and the grave."

The grandfather winks and nods at Welles on the word "paycheck" as Welles passes his black cloak over the levitating old man like he's dead. The grandfather, Welles reveals, never existed. He was a fiction, too, an actor. The old man disappears in mid-air; before he's gone we just glimpse a chicken-wire figure under the sheet where the grandfather was supposed to be.

Did Welles write those marvelous lines about reality himself? He must have. Yet after seeing *F for Fake* who would be surprised to pick up a book someday and find them there? And would it make any difference?

A. S. Hamrah

Date 1974

Nationality France

Director Orson Welles

Cast Welles, Oja Kodar

Why It's Key Welles reveals the truth behind art's lie, and vice versa, in this first essay film.

Key Scene **The opening game of hide-and-seek** *To Die in the Country*

Shuji Terayama's *To Die in the Country* begins with an image referenced in the film's UK release title, *Pastoral Hide-and-Seek*. Six children, three girls and three boys, are playing "*kakurenbo*" ("hide-and-seek") in a cemetery: one of the girls covers her face with her hands and shouts "*Mou iikai?*" ("Are you ready?"); "*Maa dada yo!*" ("Not yet!") reply her five playmates while concealing themselves behind tombstones. As in a ritual, the question "*Mou iikai?*" is repeated, now meeting with the response "*Mou ii yo!*" ("Ready!"). The girl, who is facing the camera, lowers her hands without turning around as her friends emerge from their hiding places in the background, revealing that they have been transformed into older versions of themselves, their neutral clothing replaced with gender-specific costumes: school/military uniforms and a suit for the males, a motherly kimono and an overtly sexual outfit for the females. Despite having no direct connection with the ensuing narrative, this opening shot anticipates that breaking-down of generational barriers which will allow Terayama's nameless filmmaker protagonist (Kantaro Suga) to interact with his adolescent self. Childhood is defined as both a time of freedom and the source of all our discontents, that formative period we spend our adult lives futilely trying to evade, as in a game of hide-and-seek. Maturity creeps up on us unexpectedly, springing a gender-based trap which the opening's cemetery setting imbricates with the inescapable fact of our ultimate demise. Yet *To Die in the Country* is far from pessimistic: if the process depicted is unavoidable, it is nonetheless shown to be the product of a specific social mechanism (which can be subjected to criticism and analysis) rather than a vague metaphysical principle (which can't).

Brad Stevens

Date 1974

Nationality Japan

Director Shuji Terayama

Original Title *Den-en ni Shisu*

Why It's Key This shot reveals Terayama to be one of Japan's most stylistically audacious filmmakers.

Key Scene **A low-caste boy throws a stone at a great house** *Ankur (The Seedling)*

When Shyam Benegal, nephew of Guru Dutt, decided to stop making advertising films, he made *Ankur* and launched art-house cinema as an antidote to the glorious, glossy excesses of Bollywood in the 1970s.

Surya (Nag), a landlord's son, returns to his village and begins an affair with a lower-caste woman, Lakshmi (Azmi). When the time comes for him to marry, he cannot stand up to the weight of tradition, and although Lakshmi is pregnant with his child, he drives her from his house. Lakshmi explodes in a spectacular outburst – a scene after which, it seems, nothing more can happen in the film to cap it. But then Benegal shows a little boy throwing a stone at the landlord's house. It is a small gesture, a futile gesture, and one that perhaps suggests that there is no way out of the endless cycle of rural poverty, exploitation, and impotent rage detailed in the film – or perhaps it's the revolution, or an augury of it? It's uncertain, and

Benegal has consistently refused to explain the point in interviews. But the shattering glass and the explosion of birds, the little boy running in the parched landscape of interior India were new and terrifying in Hindi film, simply because they were so multivalent. The film also launched Shabana Azmi, who went on to become one of the cornerstones of what came to be called parallel cinema.

Jerry Pinto

Date 1974

Nationality India

Director Shyam Benegal

Cast Shabana Azmi, Anant Nag, Sadhu Meher

Why It's Key The futile gesture said much about caste politics in India and inaugurated art-house cinema in India.

Key Scene **Arlette suddenly turns her head** *Stavisky...*

It's part of a flashback early in Alain Resnais' *Stavisky...*, when successful con-artist Serge Alexandre Stavisky (Belmondo) steps into the back of a limo in 1933 Paris with the dapper Baron Raoul (Boyer), asking his friend to tell him about the social "triumph" of Stavisky's wife, Arlette (Duperey), whom the Baron has just seen in Biarritz. While the Baron assures him it was magnificent and describes the lovely weather, we see the Baron approach a palatial resort hotel, walking to the strains of Stephen Sondheim's first movie score.

This is clearly Resnais' homage to Ernst Lubitsch, master of '30s glamor and elegance: after we see the Baron enter the hotel and take the elevator, there's one of Lubitsch's signature shots – a crane moving horizontally across the building's façade, charting the Baron's progress through French windows in long shot as he crosses Arlette's sumptuous suite, a flurry of crisscrossing maids marking his path until we see, through the last of the many windows, Arlette getting

dressed in her bedroom. A closer, stationary shot shows him knocking at her door, and then – in one of the most breathtakingly gorgeous, exquisitely-timed cuts in all of cinema – Arlette in close-up suddenly turns and smiles in response to his knock. It's a beautiful instant, yet one that carries a creepy foreboding, more Resnais than Lubitsch. And Serge's concurrent dialogue with the Baron confirms this foreboding: "Nightmare, what nightmare?" – asking the Baron about the troubling dream he reports that Arlette had.

Jonathan Rosenbaum

Date 1974

Nationality France

Director Alain Resnais

Cast Jean-Paul Belmondo, Charles Boyer, Anny Duperey

Why It's Key An exquisite homage to Ernst Lubitsch suddenly dovetails into something more perturbing.

Key Event **Sony Betamax VCR goes on sale in the U.S.**

Looking at photographs of the Sony Betamax, the first home videocassette recorder, it's hard to imagine that the device was once considered high-tech. The original model, the LV-1901, retailed for $2,295, was a monstrosity that included a 19-inch color TV and an SL-6300 VCR, and its tapes could hold just 30 or 60 minutes of recorded material. But the device still created a new showbiz revenue stream, home video, which would eventually account for half the movie business's total revenue. It sparked a lengthy copyright battle over the right of citizens to tape TV broadcasts for home use (resolved by the Supreme Court, in the citizens' favor). And it proved a case study in how superior marketing and consumer friendliness could beat superior technology. Rival JVC's home video format, VHS, was introduced in 1976, and it ultimately supplanted Betamax, a slightly better format; VHS won because JVC made a cheaper product, licensed its technology to more manufacturers, and made tapes

that held two hours of recorded material (a gambit matched, to no avail, by Sony's two-hour X-2 format). Another possibly pivotal factor: where Sony fought the porn industry's attempts to use Betamax, JVC encouraged it. By the late 1980s, Betamax was a niche format and a synonym for "obsolete"; sales were discontinued in the U.S. in 1993, and Sony produced its last Betamax machine in 2002, the first year when all videocassette formats were outsold by a new medium, DVD.
Matt Zoller Seitz

Date November 1975

Why It's Key The first video recorder for the general public, it led to the creation of a new channel for film distribution.

Key Scene **The killing of the john** *Jeanne Dielman, 23 Quai du Commerce, 1080 Bruxelles*

SPOILER

The dryly fastidious title of Chantal Akerman's three-hour-plus domestic epic mirrors its methodology. In this formal tour de force and feminist touchstone, the Belgian filmmaker uses Warholian strategies of duration and repetition to create a monumental, obsessively detailed portrait of its titular subject (Seyrig), a middle-class Brussels widow who happens to be both mother and whore.

Covering 48 hours over three days, the film immerses itself in the ritualized minutiae of Jeanne's household chores. These mundane events are captured with a static camera, often in real time. The viewer is compelled to experience the full monotony of each task as Jeanne does the dishes, shines her teenage son's shoes, goes shopping, cooks dinner, eats a meal. Into her regimented schedule, she also fits in one paying gentleman caller an afternoon.

Akerman so firmly establishes Jeanne's routine that when the tiniest cracks start to emerge –

overcooked potatoes, a dropped spoon – they play like major events. The low-level dread and slow-motion suspense erupt on the third afternoon (and after three hours of film time), with the arrival of the third "john." While the two earlier encounters were marked by discreet ellipses, this time the camera follows Jeanne and her client into the bedroom. They have sex, both apparently reaching orgasm. She then reaches for a pair of scissors and stabs the man in the neck.

Rife with metaphoric implications, the murder is commonly interpreted as Jeanne's attempt to regain control (and suppress desire). A stark break from the naturalistic trance that preceded it, Akerman's conclusion ruptures the spell of the movie and redefines its meaning. It's a stunning moment, a literal climax, at once sensational and ambiguous, logical and inexplicable.
Dennis Lim

Date 1975

Nationality Belgium

Director Chantal Akerman

Cast Delphine Seyrig

Why It's Key This concluding provocation radically alters the tone and meaning of this masterpiece of experimental and feminist cinema.

Key Scene **The fight in the warehouse**
Deewaar (The Wall)

Deewaar is one of the films that established Amitabh Bachchan as India's superstar, a position he still holds. The film has elements of *Mother India* and *On the Waterfront*, with its central theme of a family whose father leaves in shame, and which survives by moving to Mumbai and living on the streets. The older son, Vijay (Bachchan), works in the docks before becoming a gangster, while the younger brother (Shashi Kapoor) becomes a policeman, and the family is divided.

Vijay resents the extortion money that the dockworkers pay the gangsters for their "protection." He lies in wait for the thugs in a warehouse. Dressed in a dark blue shirt, stretching his iconic long legs, clothed in white flares, across a table top, Bachchan epitomises cool. Moving slowly, speaking deeply, he locks the door, then throws the gangsters' leader the keys, telling him to put them in his pocket until he will retrieve them. A choreographed brawl ensues, featuring kung-fu kicks and fighting with shovels, as barrels burst and sacks of flour explode. The one-man fighting machine grabs a flick-knife and with a disapproving "tsk-tsk," throws it away, single-handedly thrashing the baddies while barely breaking a sweat. He removes the keys from the unconscious baddy and exits the warehouse to the cheering of crowds.

This scene shows Bachchan as the strong, silent man seeking his own idea of justice in a corrupt world. It changed the model of Indian masculinity and made him a superstar.

Rachel Dwyer

Date 1975

Nationality India

Director Yash Chopra

Cast Amitabh Bachchan, Shashi Kapoor, Nirupa Roy, Neetu Singh, Parveen Babi

Why It's Key this scene establishes Bachchan as a superstar, fighter against injustice, and king of cool.

Key Scene **Flashback: loss of family and loss of hands** *Sholay (Flames)*

Hindi cinema's first "curry Western," released in 1975, doffs its hat to Sergio Leone's moody frontier dramas, in particular, *Once upon a Time in the West* (1968). Ramesh Sippy's *Sholay* places the mythic figure of the Indian *dacoit* against a landscape typical of the Western genre. The film concerns the hunt by former policeman Thakur Baldev Singh (Kumar) for the dreaded *dacoit* Gabbar Singh (Khan). The origins of the enmity between the two men are revealed in the lengthy flashback sequence that explains why Baldev, who's always seen with his arms covered by the shawl he wears around his shoulders, is unable to lend a hand to his accomplices during a gun battle with Gabbar's henchmen.

In the flashback, Gabbar arrives at Baldev's house and shoots and kills various members of his family one by one. He remains perched atop a hill and finally descends to the house below to find the sole survivor, Baldev's grandson. In a direct reference to *Once upon a Time in the West*, Gabbar kills the child off-screen: the implication of a gory death is more horrific than its depiction. He also captures Baldev and slices off his hands with a sword after uttering a line of dialogue that endures in popularity: "*Yeh haath mujhe de de, Thakur*" ("Give me your hands, Thakur").

Though scenes of violence and vendetta are not new to 1970s Hindi cinema, *Sholay*'s clinical approach, which depends heavily on Hollywood-style rapid cuts and spare use of emotions, raises the benchmark. The flashback sequence comprises a series of widescreen long shots tightly strung together. Dialogue is kept minimal, and melodrama is nearly absent – even though a family, the most important social unit in Hindi cinema, is slaughtered.

Nandini Ramnath

Date 1975

Nationality India

Director Ramesh Sippy

Cast Sanjeev Kumar, Amitabh Bachchan, Dharmendra, Hema Malini, Jaya Bachchan, Amjad Khan

Why It's Key Technical finesse combines with taut storytelling to create a sense of dread.

Key Film
Dersu Uzala

In the wake of the commercial failure of *Dodeskaden* (1970), a project very dear to Kurosawa's heart, the director had difficulty finding backing for his work and attempted suicide. It took him several years to find financial support for another film. Eventually, with funding from the Soviet Union, Kurosawa embarked on *Dersu Uzala*, his first film made outside Japan and his first in another language (Russian). It went on to become one of his most successful films, attracting huge audiences internationally and winning several major awards including the 1975 Oscar for Best Foreign Language Film. Its success led directly to backing from the USA and two large-scale productions, *Kagemusha* (1980) and *Ran* (1985).

Dersu Uzala was filmed on location in the Ussuri region of eastern Siberia. Based on fact, the film is set in the first decade of the 1900s and tells of the friendship between an indigenous hunter, Dersu (Munzuk), and a Russian surveyor and explorer, Vladimir Arsenyev (Solomin). At first the Russians regard Dersu as ignorant and uncouth, but he soon earns Arsenyev's respect and becomes his mentor about the wilderness, survival, and life itself. Arsenyev wrote two books about his experiences with Dersu, and an earlier film had been made in 1961. Apart from his frequent collaborator, Asakazu Nakai, as one of his directors of photography, Kurosawa worked with a largely Russian crew. The resulting film is a genuine epic, creating an awe-inspiring vision of the Siberian forests and bringing the character of Dersu magnificently to life.
Andrew Pike

Date 1975

Nationality Japan/USSR

Director Akira Kurosawa

Cast Maksim Munzuk, Yuri Solomin, Svetlana Danilchenko

Why It's Key It was Kurosawa's comeback film after commercial failure and attempted suicide.

Opposite Akira Kurosawa

Key Scene **The protagonist is spat on by his fellow villagers** *Xala*

A group of African villagers, some in ritualistic costumes, have congregated in a room; a man stands in the centre naked from the waist up. The men get closer and spit on his naked torso. White saliva slowly slithers down the chocolate skin. The overstated diegetic sound of the spitting reverberates with hostility; the frame freezes.

Ousmane Sembene, who started off as a writer, switched to cinema when he realised that he could more effectively reach his fellow Africans, the majority of whom may be illiterate, through the medium of film. The protagonist of his classic *Xala* is a black businessman, Hadji (Leye), who, immediately after the national emancipation of the country, is made a member of the administration. While the white colonisers appear to have withdrawn, they are still in charge via the crooked black puppet government. Hadji is scorned by members of his family not only because he refuses to speak his native Wolof and prefers to drink imported Evian water, but also because he decides to take a young third wife. Cursed by the people he has betrayed, he turns impotent and cannot consummate the marriage. *Xala* chronicles Hadji's failing attempts to cure the demeaning condition. Soon he is no longer in favor with the rulers, and his business goes astray. In order to recover, he will need to restore the link with his community. So he returns to the village, letting himself being spat on in disdain. This final scene epitomises the contempt in which native Africans hold corrupt black elites.
Dina Iordanova

Date 1975

Nationality Senegal

Director Ousmane Sembene

Cast Thierno Leye

Why It's Key This scene epitomises the film's critical view of the post-colonial black administration of Africa.

Key Scene **The assassination**
Nashville

This is one of Altman's large-canvas movies, portraying 24 characters against the backdrop of the country-music business, which dominates the city of the title. The film's diverse elements are held together by various narrative threads, including the ups and downs of the mental health of a singer (Blakley), the monologues of a visiting reporter (Geraldine Chaplin), and a political campaign being waged across the area. The overall impression is of a quintessentially American scene marked by a vitality that's robust but not always healthy, since a number of elements – jingoistic songs, self-serving attitudes, peculiar political slogans – seem products of unsophisticated, if not downright fatuous, minds.

Everything in the teeming movie builds toward a mass political rally that unites all the characters we met during the opening airport scene. The rally is rolling along when catastrophe strikes – the singers onstage are thrown into confusion, and we realize they've been shot at by someone in the audience. After the American political assassinations of the 1960s, including those of John and Robert Kennedy and Martin Luther King Jr., even the assassination of a show-biz figure is a believable event at a political rally; but it's shocking anyway, and Altman is canny enough to leave its causes and effects uncertain. Another entertainer on the scene (Harris) launches into a big number – "You may say that I'm not free/But it don't worry meeee" – and the crowd comforts itself by joining in.

Is singing these lyrics an act of healing? Or evasion? Or denial? Altman's resonant moment lets us ponder and decide for ourselves.

David Sterritt

Date 1975

Nationality USA

Director Robert Altman

Cast Barbara Harris, David Hayward, Michael Murphy, Henry Gibson, Ronee Blakley

Why It's Key A panoramic portrayal of a music-crazy American city ends with a song, conveying social implications as provocative as they are ambiguous.

Opposite Nashville

1970–1979

503

Key Scene **The end of it all**
Graveyard of Honor

Kinji Fukasaku is rightfully considered a unique voice of Japanese genre cinema. Some cult items – like the campy Mishima adaptation *Black Lizard* (1968) or the slightly atpyical swan-song success *Battle Royale* (2000) – have tilted his admirers' perspective, but admittedly even Fukasaku's main body of work, a series of hard-hitting yakuza films, including the *Battles without Honor and Humanity* series from 1973 onward, do invite *auteur brut* appreciation with their often hysterical stylistic innovations (the topsy-turvy chaos of handheld-camera CinemaScope, intensified by flash/freeze-frame exclamation marks) and consistent tone (nearly nihilist, yet also strangely alive in wild, wounded despair). But Fukasaku is nothing less than the voice of a betrayed postwar generation, his films teeming with underdog anger about all the broken promises of collective prosperity. No wonder the furious war indictment *Under the Flag of the Rising Sun* (1972) and the prototypically titled lost-youth ballad *If You Were Young: Rage* (1970) sit comfortably amidst the gangster mayhem following another lost battle of the left, the 1960 protest against the renewal of the U.S.-Japan Security Treaty. Fukasaku's most potent expression of the perceived spiritual and political void is *Graveyard of Honor*, the pitch-black postwar saga of an unruly mob member. The film builds inexorably to his shocking suicide leap in prison, a wave of blood spilling towards the nearby camera on impact. An ever-so-brief epilogue contextualizes the violence by wondering about the inscription left on his gravestone by this "postwar gangster stereotype": "humanity and justice."

Christoph Huber

Date 1975

Nationality Japan

Director Kinji Fukasaku

Cast Tetsuya Watari

Original Title *Jingi no hakaba*

Why it's Key Few directors channelled anger and despair about social betrayals into wild genre cinema as Kinji Fukasaku did. Even on Fukasaku's terms, the finale of his masterpiece *Graveyard of Honor* is unparalleled.

Key Scene **The Vice-Consul approaches, screams, and is ejected** *India Song*

A renowned author of fiction and occasional screenwriter (most famously of Resnais' *Hiroshima mon amour*) in the fifties and sixties, Duras switched to writing and directing films almost exclusively throughout the seventies, turning out a dozen of them between 1969 and 1981. *India Song*, which recycles material from three interrelated books by Duras, is a truly "experimental" film even though it does have a plot of sorts. "Primarily based on sound," as Duras pointed out, the film eschews traditional dialogue, replacing it with an almost whispered commentary by exquisitely delicate, diaphanous feminine voices. Words, names – a person's (Anne-Marie Stretter) or a place's (Lahore, Savannahkhet) – take on an incantatory quality. Action, sometimes hinted at by the voices, is never shown. The characters move about slowly, as in a trance, or dance endlessly, mostly confined to one bare room with a huge mirror, suggesting memories or a dream of long-past events

more than actual people in a real environment. Throughout the film a haunting piano melody keeps returning, becoming inseparable from the spell of the voices and the slow-motion, underwater-like look of the non-action.

Central to the narrative is the scene in which the Vice-Consul of Lahore (Lonsdale), now in disgrace in Calcutta for his weird behavior (such as shooting at beggars), comes to a party at the Embassy and tells the Ambassador's wife (Seyrig) of his hopeless love for her. Although this is the only moment with any "action," all of it takes place offscreen: the Vice-Consul makes a scene, demanding to be "accepted" and screaming, and is taken away. His screams somehow echo the screams of the mad Indian woman who is repeatedly mentioned throughout the film.

Jean-Pierre Coursodon

Date 1975

Nationality France

Director Marguerite Duras

Cast Delphine Seyrig, Michel Lonsdale, Matthieu Carrière

Why It's Key It's the pivotal scene in Duras' most radical and successful filmic transposition of her literary universe – a unique, mesmerizing voice come to life on the screen.

Opposite *India Song*

Key Scene **The camera goes through the window** *The Passenger*

SPOILER

Most directors who want to stage a lengthy single-take set piece start their films with these virtuoso sequences, like Orson Welles with *Touch of Evil* (1958) or Robert Altman with *The Player* (1992). In *The Passenger*, Michelangelo Antonioni chooses to climax his film with an astonishing seven-minute take. He claimed that he made this decision simply because he didn't want to shoot a conventional death scene for Locke (Nicholson), the journalist who has switched identities with a gun-runner and comes to an end in a hotel room in a dusty Spanish town. Showing the influence of Michael Snow's underground film *Wavelength* (1967), which spends a slow 45 minutes crossing a single room, Antonioni begins with what seems to be a long-held static shot from inside the hotel room, as Locke lies on the bed (essentially, Nicholson, the star, disappears from the finale of the film) out of shot, and the camera tracks slowly towards (and through) the barred windows into the piazza. Cars

arrive, key characters – killers, a mystery girl (Schneider), Locke's wife (Runacre), cops – come and go in the space between the hotel and a bullring, and even passing extras (an old man, a playing boy) take on significance, as the camera executes a 360-degree turn and comes to look back through the bars at a now-unidentifiable dead man on the bed. A policeman asks the wife if the corpse is her husband, and she ambiguously murmurs, "I never knew my husband." The film has one more shot – at dusk, with people leaving town and the credits appearing. It took over a week to stage this sequence, which depended on the bars of the window (and also, according to Nicholson, the entire facade of the hotel!) being moved apart as the camera crossed and then coming together again before our gaze returns to the window.

Kim Newman

Date 1975

Nationality Italy/France/Spain/USA

Director Michelangelo Antonioni

Cast Jack Nicholson, Maria Schneider, Jenny Runacre

Original Title *Profession reporter*

Why It's Key A perfect match of technological innovation and artistic intent, this is a crowning moment in the career of one of the cinema's great artists.

Key Scene **The far point of obsession**
The Story of Adele H.

SPOILER

Many artists are empathic to passion, far fewer to obsession. Obsession is forbidding, without happy rewards, most often held away as something to witness, like spectacle. Truffaut stands out as one who could effectively shape a film around it without holding himself at a distance. The story of Victor Hugo's younger daughter, Adèle (Adjani), who becomes obsessed with the officer Lieutenant Pinson (Robinson), who had been her lover and then disengaged, becomes his most moving statement on the subject – the director honors her subjective experience for its rich intensity and sees it as no less valid than any other. Following her as she goes first to Halifax and descends through stages of disillusionment about Pinson to pretense and eventually madness, Truffaut is always close to her, capturing all the nuances of her feelings, especially through Adjani's remarkable performance. In the last ten minutes, the story climaxes in an evocatively visualized sequence in Barbados, the light of day pouring down as Pinson goes to find her and she walks past him on the street, with no one else in view, not seeing or knowing him. Her disappearance around a corner as he looks after her is haunting. The scene reveals, with great insight, that obsession is not about the object of obsession but what is sought within oneself, no matter where it takes one. Adèle had written "That a girl shall walk over the sea into the new world to join her lover, this I shall accomplish." Perhaps her journey has been more heroic than that.

Blake Lucas

Date 1975

Nationality France

Director François Truffaut

Cast Isabelle Adjani, Bruce Robinson

Original Title *L'Histoire d'Adèle H.*

Why It's Key A true story of a young woman's amazing journey – across the ocean and within herself – becomes a masterly meditation on the complexity of being human, climaxing in a moment of powerful revelation.

1970–1979

506

Key Person **Saskia**
The original passeur

The legendary ticket-taker was a middle-aged Eastern European woman called Saskia. I was 19 and had just arrived in Paris, checked the listings, and rushed to the Cinémathèque. From the Latin Quarter, you'd take the bus 63, leave at the Albert de Mun stop, walk down the boulevard and enter the Palais de Chaillot Gardens. In this residential neighborhood the streets were quiet and empty at night, and there was no sign to indicate the place. I erred, retraced my steps, entered the garden the wrong way and got lost. Finally I found the entrance. Saskia scolded me: "This is a masterpiece; you're late; you can't enter once the screening has started!" I was in tears: "Madam, I'm coming from Marseille. All my life I have wanted to see Erich von Stroheim's *Greed*!" My life so far had been short, but during a good third of it Georges Sadoul's *Dictionnaire du cinéma* had been my bible – making me long for unavailable cinephilic treasures. The dragon lady looked at me, half-scoffing half-dismayed, took my money, and gave me a ticket. I entered the Temple. I had missed the sequence with the bird. On the screen McTeague was unsuccessfully resisting the evil impulse to kiss an unconscious Trina. Confronting what I had read about *Greed* to the film itself was an earth-shattering moment, as it had been for generations before and after me – and Saskia had ushered us all in.

Bérénice Reynaud

Date 1975

Why It's Key The Dragon Lady who guarded the entrance at the Cinémathèque française had a heart of gold and ushered many generations into the reality of cinephilia.

Key Scene **Sonny dictates his will**
Dog Day Afternoon

On August 22, 1972 – the same day Nixon was nominated for a second term – a man named John Wojtowicz walked into a Brooklyn, New York, branch of the Chase Manhattan Bank and declared a hold-up. When it was revealed he needed the money for a gay lover's sex-change operation, the day-long standoff with police attracted a crowd of thousands and the attention of the entire city. Warner Bros., traditionally the studio of social-problem films, snapped up the rights to a *Life* magazine story on the heist, signed Al Pacino – hot off *Godfather II* – to play the lead (now called Sonny Wortzik), and hired veteran New York director Sidney Lumet for the requisite authenticity. The film's emotional core is reached some 97 minutes in, as Sonny, convinced he'll be gunned down, dictates a will. He declares his love, "more than a man has ever loved any other man in all eternity," as his bank-manager hostage, Mulvaney (Boyar), impassively sips coffee. Only in New York. Wojtowicz, who loved that scene but hated the movie as a whole, used the $7,500 he was paid by Warners to fund the operation; served seven of the 20 years to which he was sentenced; lived on welfare after his release – in Brooklyn; and died of cancer in early January 2006. Through the fragile alignment of Frank Pierson's Oscar-winning script, a perfect performance, and shrewd directing, a sad episode in this sad life has been transformed into enduring art.

David Stratton

Date 1975

Nationality USA

Director Sidney Lumet

Cast Al Pacino, Sully Boyar

Why It's Key Warner Bros. updates its social problem film to 1970s New York, harnessing a fearless Al Pacino performance in the process.

1970–1979

507

Key Event
The murder of Pier Paolo Pasolini

The Italian harbor city of Ostia, near Rome: in his *Caro Diario* (1994), Nanni Moretti rides a long way on his Vespa, to arrive at the very spot in Ostia where writer-director Pier Paolo Pasolini was murdered on 2 November 1975. Later that day in '75, a 17-year-old boy, Giuseppe Pelosi, was arrested, claiming that he had beaten Pasolini to death after the latter had sodomized him with a large piece of wood. Immediately, numerous theories of conspiracy and cover-up were floated, kept alive in the public's mind by figures such as Pasolini's former star, Laura Betti, and his future biographer, Enzo Siciliano. There have been documentaries, dramatic reconstructions, and heated polemics – because no one stoked the contradictory forces in Italian society like Pasolini. Was he murdered by some far-right, anti-communist, homophobic cabal? Why were there so many holes in the official police investigation? Was the Mafia involved? Remember that Pasolini pilloried the Left in his newspaper columns almost as much as the Right, and that the final film he completed, *Salò*, was received in most quarters as an unbearably nihilistic provocation. Almost 30 years later, in May 2005, Pelosi recanted his original confession and proposed a different version of events: Pasolini had indeed been murdered by a gang of three middle-aged men who yelled remarks about his politics and sexuality – and who, afterwards, threatened Pelosi and his family to silence him. The case was reopened in '05 but remains unresolved, as judges considered the new information "insufficient to continue."

Adrian Martin

Date November 2, 1975

Why It's Key The death of a central figure of Italian culture remains an open case.

Key Scene **The final duel**
Barry Lyndon

This is a film about history as loss. The camera rarely moves – its frames resemble paintings of a vanished time – and its chief stylistic signature is the reverse zoom, allowing a scene to begin with a close-up and then carry our gaze gently but firmly into the distance, as if the 18th-century milieu were fading from reality before our eyes. Kubrick sustains a sense of contemplative distance even when the camera zooms toward rather than away from its subject, since zooming lets a director change the visible field without physically moving the camera (and, vicariously, the viewer) any closer to what it's photographing. Some critics find too much detachment in Kubrick's approach, but *Barry Lyndon* contains many profoundly touching moments that refute this.

The climactic duel is a fine example. Although zooming is absent here, the episode begins with a tight close-up of hands loading a pistol, and the most striking subsequent images are usually caught in medium-distance shots or moody long shots that connect the characters to their environment, a spooky old barn where death seems almost palpable. The soundtrack further enhances the atmosphere, with unseen pigeons cooing and fragments from the film's main musical theme (a Handel sarabande) played almost subliminally on low strings and timpani. It's a keenly important scene, marking the moment when the self-seeking hero (O'Neal) belatedly shows he has the makings of a gentleman after all. And it's as suspenseful as a moviegoer could ask – an ideal combination of style, story, and feeling.

David Sterritt

Date 1975

Nationality UK

Director Stanley Kubrick

Cast Ryan O'Neal, Leon Vitali, Peter Cellier

Why It's Key A dueling scene, shot and edited with the stately rhythms of a baroque air, leavens a consummately thoughtful drama with humanizing warmth and keen suspense.

Opposite *Barry Lyndon*

Key Film *Winstanley*
The cows

Since Kevin Brownlow is an established film historian, it seems appropriate that his two early films with military historian/production designer Andrew Mollo are like gateways to an alternate universe of films about history. Both *It Happened Here* (1966) and *Winstanley* are basically years-in-the-making no-budget efforts, displaying fanatical attention to detail and a stridently independent vision: less dramatic than immersive, these films acquire a quasi-documentary quality all their own, lending uncanny credibility to their worlds, while their rapt contemplation also adds an aura of mystery. Fittingly, *It Happened Here* is an alternate-universe tale, science-fiction-history: a portrayal of England in 1944 after four years of Nazi occupation. Remarkable as the film is, its confrontational subject matter at times overwhelms its one-of-a-kind achievements – an anti-Semitic rant by a Nazi (played, in accordance with directorial principles, by a real fascist) caused protest and had to be cut on initial release. *Winstanley* charts the failed effort of a nonviolent sect to establish a commune during the English Civil War, but the plot just seems to drift by in waves, hardly distracting from the obsessive gaze (Brownlow's love for silents shows) at this mysterious past. One cannot help but notice details like the slightly unusual cows (or pigs): Brownlow and Mollo searched all over England after advice from animal-husbandry experts to find specimens most likely to resemble those in 17th-century Surrey.

Christoph Huber

Date 1975

Nationality UK

Directors Kevin Brownlow, Andrew Mollo

Why it's Key Respected film historian Kevin Brownlow made two early, fascinating no-budget films with Andrew Mollo that achieve a unique level of immersion in historical worlds, not least thanks to an unparallelled fanaticism in the attention to detail: You can see it by just studying the animals.

Key Scene **The ballet scene**
The Story of Joanna

Gerard Damiano's *The Story of Joanna* is perhaps the most ambitious American hardcore porn film of the 1970s, boasting a rich *mise en scène* and a meticulously thought out structure: notice how Jason (Gillis), who maintains an image of suave sophistication to protect himself from exposure, is introduced as a mirror reflection, and how the repeated sexual penetration of Joanna (Hall) is reversed when she finally penetrates her "impenetrable" lover's body by shooting him in the mouth. The film includes two moments that might have been specifically designed to frustrate and alienate its target audience (and were actually removed from certain prints): one of the few explicit portrayals of male homosexuality to be found in a "mainstream" pornographic work, and a five-minute dance sequence. The latter, which shows Gillis looking on as Hall and Steven Lark perform a pas-de-deux to the accompaniment of Tomaso Albinoni's "Adagio in G Minor," was improvised by Damiano when he

discovered that his lead actress had formerly been a member of the Stuttgart Ballet Company. This sequence offers a compressed version of the surrounding narrative: the male dancer appears to dominate the female (much as Jason appears to dominate Joanna), lifting her from the ground, controlling her movements, manipulating her body, mimicking sexual intercourse; the female even appears to be dying in the male's arms at one point (foreshadowing Joanna's threat to shoot herself); but the dance ends with the female standing over the male, who, in anticipation of Jason's fate, lies motionless on the floor, defeated by an irresistible feminine force. This is clearly filmmaking of a high order, neatly encapsulating *The Story of Joanna*'s view of heterosexuality as an arena in which death-obsessed masculinity ritualistically erases itself.
Brad Stevens

Date 1975

Nationality USA

Director Gerard Damiano

Cast Terri Hall, Steven Lark, Jamie Gillis

Why It's Key This scene shows what can be achieved in a generally despised genre.

Key Scene **The printing office sequence**
Mirror

The fear of having made a proofing error in a prestigious state literature publication makes Maria Nikolaevna (Terekhova) run to the printing press in pouring rain. The sequence brings out in fine detail a psychological portrait of people who lived in fear under the cult of personality. There is no mention of Stalin; only a poster of him is on the wall in the office. Yet everyone in the printing room is under a pressure that only the possibility of political repression can evoke. The nervousness of the new recruit, the extreme mood swings of Maria and her friend, Lisa (Demidova), the detachment of another colleague (Grinko) during their hysteric outbursts (he's probably been witness to many such scenes, and pragmatically says that some people should work, while others should do the worrying), the way Maria continues to turn pages even after she has found that the mistake she feared had not, in fact, been made (so that no one will realise what word she was looking for), the worried workers who crowd around

her, the announcement by one of them, in barely hidden panic, that even if there is a mistake, the printing has already been done, Lisa's little dance in the corridor - all delineate the character of the protagonists in a "novelistic" manner, but Tarkovsky tops off the sequence with a poem by his father on mood and atmosphere change, recited on the soundtrack as Maria walks back to her office from the printing room.
Rashmi Doraiswamy

Date 1975

Nationality USSR

Director Andrei Tarkovsky

Cast Margarita Terekhova, Nikolai Grinko, Alla Demidova

Original Title *Zerkalo*

Why It's Key It's a psychological portrait of Terror.

Opposite *Mirror*

The birth of the blockbuster

With the acclaimed TV movie *Duel* (1971) and the epic road film *Sugarland Express* (1974) under his belt, 28-year-old director Steven Spielberg was already considered a wunderkind; but *Jaws* made him a cultural force, revising the definition of a blockbuster, redefining the process by which one was promoted, and forever marking the summer as the center of Hollywood's accounting year. Adapted from Peter Benchley's 1974 novel, a bloody page-turner that was sold to Universal while it was still in galleys, Spielberg's movie might have been a success anyway, since it preserved Benchley's visceral shocks while adding warmth, well-drawn characters, and a playful cruelty reminiscent of Hitchcock in thumbscrews mode. But after successful previews, Universal's marketing department amplified the movie's impact by booking the movie onto a then-extravagant 400 screens and stoking audience awareness with a massive TV ad campaign. The film grossed $100 million in the U.S. and Canada in a matter of weeks, and thanks to superb word-of-mouth and a high percentage of repeat viewers, maxed out at $260 million – a haul that (not adjusted for inflation) bested even *Gone With The Wind*, which made just about $189 million. Before *Jaws*, studios assumed they'd move incrementally into the black each year, thanks to one or two big hits and a few modest ones; after *Jaws*, a jackpot mentality took hold, with studios spending fortunes to will megahits into creation. The legacy includes everything from George Lucas's *Star Wars* trilogy and Spielberg and Lucas's *Indiana Jones* films through *Top Gun, Terminator 2, Titanic,* the *Lord of the Rings* and *Harry Potter* franchises, and such nonstarters as *Last Action Hero* and *Waterworld* – all of which make the relative intimacy of *Jaws* seem quaint.
Matt Zoller Seitz

Date 1975

Why It's Key *Jaws* changed the rules for Hollywood.

Opposite *Jaws*

Key Scene **A newsreel cameraman films his own murder** *The Battle of Chile*

This epic documentary trilogy by Guzmán traces the complex political processes that brought Salvador Allende to power in Chile and ended with the military coup d'état in 1973. The whole film is carefully structured, and most of its footage is quite amazing. One moment stands out. While filming the first military actions against Allende, on June 29, 1973, Argentine newsreel cameraman Leonardo Henrichsen caught his own death on film. A group of soldiers get down from a truck, one of them looks directly at Henrichsen's lens, takes out his gun, and shoots. The camera trembles, and Henrichsen, fatally wounded, decides that he will do his work until the very end and keeps pointing the camera at his murderer. A few seconds later, Henrichsen, still rolling film, falls to the ground and dies.

One of the most celebrated American documentaries is *Harlan County U.S.A.* (1976) by Barbara Kopple; there is a famous scene in that film in which a man waves his gun at one of the cameramen. At the same period, in Latin America, they used to shoot filmmakers, but very few people ever have the chance to see the films they died for.
Fernando Martín Peña

Date 1975

Nationality Venezuela

Director Patricio Guzmán

Original Title *La Batalla de Chile*

Why It's Key A man died to make this film.

Key Scene **Mr. Sophistication sings**
The Killing of a Chinese Bookie

If you pay them off you'll lose some more; if you build it they will come to take it. This lesson, learned at the hands of gangsters, sinks in for strip-club owner Cosmo Vitelli (Gazzara) as he returns, bleeding, to his cabaret. Why try at all? When Mr. Sophistication (Roberts), the club's bedraggled emcee, begins his goodnight version of "I Can't Give You Anything but Love," Cassavetes provides an answer

Instead of violence, *The Killing of a Chinese Bookie* ends with a musical number. Mr. Sophistication throws fake money into an audience that's shouting "take it off!" at the half-naked De-Lovelies on stage. He snappishly changes the song's lyrics to reflect petty demands: "Happiness, great success/All the things you always *whined* for." As his song grows triumphant, he exclaims "Love, love, love – *hot love!*"

Then one of the De-Lovelies (Haji) needles him by lighting a novelty explosive on his shoulder. He sighs and heads backstage, where a hand is extended in comfort or congratulation; his singing resumes over the end credits. Sometimes the message of love – *hot love!* – can be delivered by a pissed-off little fat man in sweaty whiteface. We leave Cosmo bleeding on the sidewalk, hurt but on his feet. His bullet hole rhymes with Mr. Sophistication's shoulder explosion. In Mr. Sophistication (aka Teddy), Meade Roberts, a screenwriter Cassavetes tapped to act, created an unforgettable figure. He is the humiliated professor of *The Blue Angel* on stage with ex-ultravixens, consigned to awkward grandeur in L.A.

A. S. Hamrah

Date 1976

Nationality USA

Director John Cassavetes

Cast Meade Roberts, Ben Gazzara, Haji, Alice Friedland, Donna Marie Gordon

Why It's Key Cassavetes goes from the ridiculous to the sublime.

Key Scene **The sex competition at the court of the Pope** *Fellini's Casanova*

There is a vocal minority of people who believe that *Casanova* is the best film Fellini ever made. It may not be as iconic as *La dolce vita* or *8½*, and its cold appearance may baffle those who had been seduced by the romantic nostalgia of *Amarcord*, but it is hard to argue with the fact that no other of his works has the same degree of sheer abstraction and earthy physicality. *Casanova* is also a feast for the eyes and the ears; long before digital stereo, Fellini has created a soundscape of unparalleled intricacy where Nino Rota's music is mingled with the poems of Andrea Zanzotto and with the director's own genius for the spoken word. Like all great poetry, some of the lines in the film cannot be adequately translated. One in particular stands out for its flamboyant multilingualism: Casanova has been invited to compete with a Roman nobleman in having as many orgasms as possible in a single sexual encounter, and claims the right to choose his partner for the trial. The offscreen voice of an old

female aristocrat agrees with him: "*il a raison, 'a donna s'à deve scéjjer lui.*" The literal translation is "he's right, the woman is his choice"; however, the sentence is uttered in such an inextricable blend of French and Roman dialect that the atmosphere of cultivated vulgarity at the court of the Pope becomes an almost tactile feeling. James Joyce would have stood up in applause.

Paolo Cherchi Usai

Date 1976

Nationality Italy

Director Federico Fellini

Cast Donald Sutherland, Tina Aumont, Leda Lojodice

Original Title *Il Casanova di Federico Fellini*

Why It's Key Its intricate soundtrack is a microcosm of the director's world.

Opposite *Fellini's Casanova*

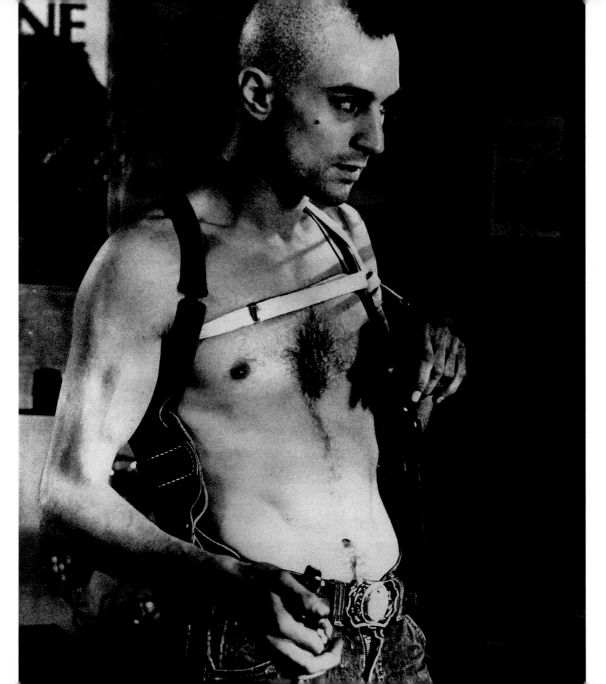

Key Scene **The camera lifts to Travis's Mohawk as he pops his pills** *Taxi Driver*

When do we first know for certain that Travis Bickle (De Niro) is terrifyingly psychotic? It could be when he reads his diary entries about New York's meanest streets. Or when he makes a quick-draw contraption to strap on his arm, or when he gives his famous "You talkin' to me?" monologue. Yet at such moments, it's just possible he's still driven by the puritanism ("Here is a man…who stood up against the scum…") that occupies one part of his fragmented mind. At the rally for Senator Palatine (Leonard Harris) all doubts dissolve.

We see only Travis's body as he arrives. Then we see Palatine declaiming words that scream with irony: "We meet at a crossroads…." Travis's hand shakes a couple of pills from a bottle, and as the hand moves to his mouth, the camera moves abruptly with it, showing his head for the first time since we saw him preparing for violence in his apartment. Gone is his habitual trim haircut. In its place is a bizarre Mohawk – a ragged ridge of hair flanked by stretches of ill-shaven skull that Travis's fevered brain seems about to burst through, like the plumes of steam escaping from the city's manholes.

The haircut's Indian name is appropriate – the rally is at Columbus Circle, named after the explorer who started Europe's devastation of America's natives – and this is one "savage" whose rage has reached explosive force. "All the animals come out at night," he said earlier. Now he's one of them. And in broad daylight.

David Sterritt

Date 1976

Nationality USA

Director Martin Scorsese

Cast Robert De Niro

Why It's Key Camera work, acting, and hairstyle (!) combine in one of American film's most jolting revelations of unleashed evil.

Opposite *Taxi Driver*

517

1970–1979

Key Scene **Tonya urinating** *Insiang*

Insiang (Koronel) has just come home with groceries and is frying new-bought eggs over a tiny stove for her and her mother, Tonya (Mona Lisa), when behind her a man draped only in a towel suddenly steps out of their bathing stall (a curtained-off corner of the house): it's Dado (Vernal), Tonya's brand-new boyfriend, who has spent the night there without Insiang knowing. He stops, smiles; he tightens the towel round his waist and walks past Insiang (who is staring at the floor) into Tonya's bedroom (yet another curtained-off corner), where we hear him tease her awake. She runs laughing out of her room to find Insiang staring at her. She stops; without a word she goes quietly to the corner behind Insiang, squats. Brocka cuts to a shot of Insiang listening (despite herself) to the hiss of urine, and a shot of Tonya shifting uncomfortably on her heels. Tonya stands up, picks up a ladle, pours water down the sides of the drain.

Other than the opening shot (of Dado in a slaughterhouse, plunging his knife into a pig's throat), this scene provokes the strongest reaction, mostly from foreign viewers. Brocka has already shown the squalor of Tondo slums with earlier, documentary-like footage but this detail drives home the fact that Filipino squatters live in conditions other countries can barely even imagine – in houses so cramped and crude that rooms are partitioned by hanging cloth, a bathroom is a cement hole, and privacy is an agreement between people not to look at each other while performing basic body functions.

Noel Vera

Date 1976

Nationality Philippines

Director Lino Brocka

Cast Hilda Koronel, Mona Lisa, Ruel Vernal

Why it's key This scene shows one of Lino Brocka's most inimitable gifts: the singling out of a detail or image that captures the misery of the Filipino poor.

Key Scene **The dissonance of civilizations**
Xica da Silva

In the 18th century, a special Portuguese envoy (Wilker) has come all the way to the Brazilian colony of Minas Gerais to investigate rumours about the unholy liaison of a white man and a black slave, who seems to have acquired unprecedented standing because of her legendary sexual powers. The envoy is told that he will be treated to a special African meal. Soon a host of black slaves come and serve a range of colorful dishes. A group of musicians perform African rhythms while female slaves dance. Xica da Silva (Motta), the black slave famous for conquering countless men, appears naked and performs a sexually inviting dance. At the end she offers her sexual favors, quite confident that by now the envoy must be overwhelmed by her daring display of sexual freedom.

Xica's well-tested technique, however, does not work in this case. The Portuguese man is more attracted to the gold and other riches of the province, and the favors of the black seductress are not of much interest. Her past experiences have led her to believe (wrongly) that the untamed boldness she displays would always overpower the reticent Europeans and their customs. In fact, however, she has been fooling herself – a revelation that gives the scene symbolic status in relation to Brazil's colonial history. It's true that the inhibitions of the European cannot withstand the feral supremacy of tropicalism. Brazil's bitter lesson is, however, that the imperial rule of rationality and the consistency of underlying economic interests nonetheless overpower any temporary infatuation with the carnal and the sensual.

Dina Iordanova

Date 1976

Nationality Brazil

Director Carlos Diegues

Cast Zezé Motta, Walmor Chagas, José Wilker

Why It's Key European repression is challenged by the untamed sensuality of Afro-Brazilian rituals – unsuccessfully.

518

Key Scene **The distant horizon**
The Desert of the Tartars

Drogo (Perrin) comes to the isolated Fort Bastiani in a remote corner of the frontier as a young man, open and expectant about his life; years later, his purpose – to wait with his comrades for the enemy Tartars who have never come and may not even exist – has exhausted him, and he is ill and near death at what may be a crucial moment. Cruelly, his friend Simeon (Griem), who has shared the years with him since they were both young lieutenants, orders his departure in an unhappy final parting. The final four shots (lasting two minutes) resolve the action – the slow track along the outpost wall as the soldiers wait in readiness, the breathtaking appearance of two parallel lines of Tartars filling the horizon, the overhead view of the coach that carries Drogo leaving the fort, the close-up of a now accepting Drogo as he drifts into sleep. That is the ending of this existential adventure film, more muted and ambiguous but at the same time more thrilling and dramatic than that of any other. The end, like the whole, suggests a range of allegorical and philosophical readings, but deserves equally to be appreciated for the beauty of the cinematic qualities so pervasively instilled in Zurlini's realization: color – in shades of beige, gray, blue amid the sand and mountains; sound – of horse's hooves, whistling wind, silence; the location – striking, imposing, eternal. Out of such elements the director forges a vision that is metaphysical, but one that also sees vividly the physical world in which life plays out.

Blake Lucas

Date 1976

Nationality Italy

Director Valerio Zurlini

Cast Jacques Perrin, Helmut Griem

Original Title *Il deserto dei tartari*

Why It's Key The end of Zurlini's last film quietly brings the adventure genre to an apotheosis.

Key Event
Steadicam

In the early 1970s, cameraman Garrett Brown and engineers from Cinema Products, Inc., developed the Steadicam system, which mounts the camera on a mobile, spring-leaded arm attached to a weight-bearing harness, giving hand-held camerawork the smoothness of a conventional dolly. In 1976, Brown first used the Steadicam in three major films: *Rocky, Bound for Glory*, and *Marathon Man*. In 1978, the Academy of Motion Picture Arts and Sciences (which rarely remembers the "sciences" part of its remit) gave him a special technical Oscar in honour of the invention. Its first great showcase was Stanley Kubrick's *The Shining* (1980), in which Brown rushed around the corridors of the Overlook Hotel set, keeping up with a child on a tricycle. Another iconic early use of the Steadicam was for the point-of-view shots that represent a prowling monster in John Landis's *An American Werewolf in London* (1981). The gyroscopic arm-handle of the Steadicam inspired the similarly-mounted machine guns of the Space Marines in *Aliens* (1986).

Kim Newman

Date 1976

Why It's Key The invention of this device enabled the camera to roam as freely as the eye.

Key Scene **Abandoned checkpoint**
Kings of the Road (In the Course of Time)

Bruno (Vogler), who lives on the road as a movie projector repairman in a van wired for sound, forms a taciturn friendship with Robert (Zischler) after the latter, recently separated from his wife, attempts suicide by driving his Volkswagen into the Elbe River in a gesture of despair that seems more absurd than potentially tragic. The legacy of Nazism and the division of Germany are ever present in the bleak border provinces through which the two travel in a series of disconnected journeys. Their relationship comes to a head in an abandoned border checkpoint that the wall graffiti indicates has been manned by Americans. This gives rise to Robert's musing that "the Yanks have colonised our subconscious" – a recurring theme in the film. With the aid of a bottle of bourbon, the two men open up to each other for the first time. The scene, which speaks of male bonding displaced by heterosexual yearning, seems unforced when compared with the repression endemic in the Hollywood buddy movie (which is tailored to meet the demands of popular entertainment).

In a way that is seemingly casual (the story was made up as they went along) but incisive (Wenders had a clear itinerary), the film sets up personal, political, and cultural implications that resonate beyond the particular historical moment, as documentary-like workings of chance blend with what Wenders called "feature texture."

Bruce Hodsdon

Date 1976

Nationality West Germany

Director Wim Wenders

Cast Rüdiger Vogler, Hanns Zischler

Original Title *Im Lauf der Zeit*

Why It's Key In this scene, the links between motion and emotion, memory and desire are deeply implicated in the need to communicate.

Key Scene **The hand from the grave**
Carrie

After the school has burned down and the bodies are carted away, Brian De Palma's film of Stephen King's novel *Carrie* seems to be over – but, in a languidly sunstruck sequence (filmed in reverse), Susan Snell (Irving) wanders towards the rubble where telekinetic Carrie (Spacek) used to live to lay flowers at a grave-marker-like real-estate sign. As Pino Donaggio's romantic score swells, Carrie's hand shockingly erupts out of the ground to grab Sue, who then wakes up screaming. It's the textbook definition of a gratuitous shock, delivered when audiences were already reaching for their coats, and it set a fashion that persisted for decades. Among the most blatant reuses of the gimmick are John Cassavetes' detonation at the end of De Palma's telekinetic follow-up, *The Fury* (1978), in which Irving gets to wield the power, and Jason's leap out of Crystal Lake at the finish of *Friday the 13th* (1980). The *Carrie* scene may be the single biggest jolt in the history of horror movies. Spacek insisted that she be allowed to do the shot rather than use a hand double, realising that no one could match her distinctively freckled wrists.

Kim Newman

Date 1976

Nationality USA

Director Brian De Palma

Cast Amy Irving, Sissy Spacek

Why It's Key It made us all jump.

Opposite *Carrie*

520

Key Person **Chor Yuen (Chu Yuan)**
Labyrinth of allegiances *Killer Clans*

Overshadowed far too long by the martial arts films of King Hu and Chang Cheh, the series of gaudy, baroque, and frequently mind-boggling swordplay melodramas Chor Yuen directed for Shaw Brothers have been a major (re)discovery since the Hong Kong studio finally opened its archive vaults. Coincidentally, at the very same time, a new-millennium series of highbrow martial art-house films along the lines of Zhang Yimou's *Hero* has testified to the influence of Chor's lush and lurid genre films with their carefully colored, drapery-framed compositions and elaborately plotted storylines, usually lifted from novels by renowned martial arts writer Ku Lung. The first of these adaptations was *Killer Clans*, whose exquisite *mise en scène* and labyrinthine storyline – it concerns a clan feud so convoluted that some of the warring "societies" have unkowingly harbored sleeper assasins for "three generations" – are like a masterful preview of coming attractions: Chor, a veteran director versatile in many genres, embarked on more than a dozen Ku Lung adaptations, not to mention similarly stylized efforts based on other sources. Although after a few years some wear began to show, the uniformly fine first films in this martial-arts cycle suggest an endless world of inscrutable conspiracies, hidden identities, and treacherous trap-doors: a pulp universe worthy of Borges. The showdown of *Killer Clans* expresses this most elegantly in purely visual terms. Mere glances between the main characters ultimately reveal their hidden allegiances and assignments before necessitating the final battle.

Christoph Huber

Date 1976

Nationality Hong Kong

Director Chor Yuen (Chu Yuan)

Cast Ku Feng, Yueh Hua

Original Title *Liu xing hu die jian*

Why it's Key Chor Yuen's labyrinthine martial-arts melodramas conjure a pulp universe worthy of Borges. The most elegant expression of their convoluted conspiracies comes at the end of the masterful inauguration of Chor's cycle of Ku Lung adaptations.

Key Film *In The Realm of the Senses*
One of the few hardcore art films

Japanese film, as seen through the disdainful eyes of Nagisa Oshima, was a yawn-inducing wasteland of samurai epics, wan parlor dramas, and the occasional latex monster. "My hatred for Japanese cinema includes absolutely all of it," he famously declared, and then set about making fiercely iconoclastic movies packed with all the vim, passion, and petty cruelties of a less anemic culture. When censorship laws relaxed enough in the '70s to decriminalize pornography, Oshima jumped at the chance to finally treat sex on screen with the unrestrained realism it deserved. He adapted the true story of former prostitute Sada Abe (who, in 1936, was arrested while wandering down the street carrying the severed genitals of her lover tucked in her kimono) into a hardcore allegory about obsession, sadomasochism, and the beauty inherent in death and bloodshed. Not content to simply titillate, Oshima's film is one big middle finger aimed at mainstream culture's taboos on the eroticism of menstruation and the sexuality of elderly people and children. Then there's the knee-clenchingly graphic finale. It's hard to remember the world was once abuzz with the prospect of "porno chic" cinema, building on the promise of films like *Behind The Green Door* (1972), when the promise of a new and dignified stag-film aesthetic never really materialized. *In The Realm of the Senses* is a rare bloom of a film, the kind of artifact that could have flowered only for a few fleeting months in the thin and sandy divide between art and porn.

Violet Glaze

Date 1976

Nationality Japan/France

Director Nagisa Oshima

Cast Tatsuya Fuji, Eiko Matsuda

Original Title *Ai no corrida*

Why It's Key Erotic obsession gets the uncensored treatment it deserves.

Opposite *In The Realm of the Senses*

1970–1979

523

Key Speech **Kebebe speaks the dream of the film** *Harvest: 3,000 Years*

Most of the great African films were made on the Francophone West coast, but travel eastward, in the decade when Ousmane Sembene came to the fore, and you discover this epic masterpiece. Written and directed by Ethiopia-born Haile Gerima, who studied in America and who now teaches film at Howard University, *Harvest: 3,000 Years* is performed in the Amharic language and shot by Elliot Davis, who went on to work with Spike Lee. The first thing you notice is the look of the picture – telephoto lenses, low-contrast black-and-white imagery, everything shot from far away. Then there's the pace, rigorous and slow, like Godard's *Week-end*. The film starts with a prayer for a nice day, but, as the title suggests, its timeframe is millennial. Over its two and a half hours the film introduces us to a peasant family and shows how they are timelessly subordinated to a cruel landlord. The great seer of the film is its madman, Kebebe (Gebru Kassa), who asks the angriest question in African cinema, if not world cinema. He lost his land to the colonials and, in a conversation with a boy, enquires: "Is there any place where there are no flies and no Europeans?" The question cuts to the bone, as does the film. Visually, *Harvest: 3,000 Years* might be detached from its characters, but ideologically it is right inside their minds.

Mark Cousins

Date 1976

Nationality Ethiopia

Director Haile Gerima

Cast Gebru Kassa

Original Title *Mirt Sost Shi Amit*

Why It's Key This scene, better than any other, expresses the rage in African cinema.

Key Speech **"Retards like the zoo"**
Rocky

Few Hollywood franchises are as widely known as the *Rocky* series, yet the original film remains strangely unexplored. Fans retain vague recollections of Stallone jumping up and down at the Philadelphia Museum of Art, Bill Conti's seminal score, and Carl Weathers (pound for pound America's most patriotic actor) working the crowd in a bizarro Uncle Sam outfit. The movie's improbable inspirational tale (based on a fight between Muhammad Ali and Chuck "The Bayonne Bleeder" Wepner) is a byword for a certain kind of 100-proof schmaltz.

Less recognized is the atmosphere of petty, prideless hustling and relentless Philadelphia meanness that sells Stallone's Cinderella story. The script is shot through with a kind of spiteful wit that was (and to some extent still is) the lingua franca of the City of Brotherly Love, a town that devours all its heroes. Rocky, known the world over as an inarticulate mumbler, is actually a tireless raconteur, a spinner of puns and tall tales who stands out for the comparative gentleness of his speech.

(A characteristic exchange with Burt Young as a prospective brother-in-law: "Pushin' thirty friggin' years old! She's gonna die alone if she don't wise up." Rocky: "I'm thirty myself." Paulie: "And you're dyin' alone, too." Rocky: "I don't see no crowd around you, neither.")

The movie's atmosphere of ball-breaking reaches its zenith in a throwaway exchange between Rocky and a mob bodyguard (Sorbello) who doesn't like him. The mobster sets out to insult Rocky's girlfriend:

Bodyguard: I hear she's retarded.

Rocky: She ain't retarded, she's shy.

Bodyguard: Take her to the zoo. Retards like the zoo.

It's a pure insult line, unleavened by insight or originality, maddeningly funny in the delivery. *Rocky* takes a large portion of such hard, dead-end speech and crafts an atmosphere of hopelessness and urban decay that neither the movie's false happy ending nor its legacy of countless sequels fully conceals.

Tim Cavanaugh

Date 1976

Nationality USA

Director John G. Avildsen

Cast Sylvester Stallone, Joe Sorbello, Joe Spinell

Why It's Key *Rocky* is not a feel-good picture.

Key Scene **The last scene**
The Marquise of O

Rohmer follows Heinrich von Kleist's novella quite closely, obtaining a strangely detached tone that stays there even during the emotional scenes. A woman (Clever) is saved by a Russian officer (Ganz) from a fate worse than death at the hands of a group of aroused soldiers. She faints in the arms of her saviour, who returns her home; then, a few weeks later, she appears to be pregnant. Since she has not had sexual relations with any man, she is understandably puzzled. It is soon quite clear that the Russian officer has taken her while she was unconscious, but nobody seems to consider that possibility. Full of remorse, the officer asks for her hand in marriage, but she and her family delay the answer, while the pregnancy becomes more and more apparent. During the following months, the officer insists on his proposal of marriage in every possible way and gets rejected as many times. Eventually, she has the baby on her own and keeps rejecting the officer.

Finally, the officer confesses his trespass to her family and shows his remorse. The tension between the officer and the woman becomes unbearable. And then, in the very last scene, Rohmer – and Kleist – decide to relieve it: in spite of everything, she accepts her feelings for him, and they embrace. The End. That last scene couldn't possibly have worked if Rohmer had decided to update the plot with contemporary feelings and reactions. Instead, he keeps it close to Kleist, as if the film were some sort of documentary on everyday life in the past. Thanks to that, the end of the story works on its own weird terms.

Fernando Martín Peña

Date 1976

Nationality West Germany/France

Director Eric Rohmer

Cast Edith Clever, Bruno Ganz

Original Title *Die Marquise von O...*

Why It's Key Rohmer's stylistic choices and fidelity to his literary source work a cinematic miracle.

Key Scene **The final scene**
Mikey and Nicky

SPOILER

Elaine May's *Mikey and Nicky* ends much as it began, with the eponymous protagonists positioned on different sides of locked doors: the opening scene shows Mike (Falk) trying to enter a hotel room in which his best friend, Nick (Cassavetes), has locked himself; the closing scene shows Nick frantically knocking on the front door of Mike's home while the hitman (Beatty) to whom Mike has betrayed him moves into position. Although the intervening sequences may look like undisciplined exercises in improvisation, the classical perfection of the overall structure suggests this masterpiece's ambitions. Everything is tightly contained: the narrative occurs during a single night and follows two characters as they journey through a few blocks of an American city. Yet this concentration of detail allows a complex thematic mesh to emerge naturally from, rather than being imposed upon, the dramatic situation, taking in mortality, the existence of God, the difficulty men have relating to women, the inability to break with patterns of behavior established during childhood, the homoerotic undertones of heterosexual male friendships, and the way those on the lower rungs of power structures avoid confronting the moral implications of their acts. Connecting all this is an emphasis on the barriers individuals place between themselves as protection against intimacy. The door that ends the film thus bears a heavy symbolic weight, not in the way such externally imposed symbols as Sergei Eisenstein's stone lions in *Battleship Potemkin* (1925) do, but rather as a consequence of those meanings it has accrued from the events preceding its appearance.
Brad Stevens

Date 1976

Nationality USA

Director Elaine May

Cast John Cassavetes, Peter Falk, Ned Beatty

Why It's Key This scene is among the most complex and powerful in American cinema.

Key Scene **Elsa and the baby**
Three Years Without God

Elsa (Aunor) has given birth to a girl, the result of her rape by Masugi (de Leon). She has resisted Masugi's offers of conciliation and marriage, has demonstrated the iron will and rage of a Filipina cruelly wronged by the Japanese Occupation.

O'Hara's camera is trained on Elsa's impassive expression, but quick inserts of Masugi's face – eyes tight shut and panting; eyes open and asking "Was it good?", "Did it hurt?" – betray her thoughts. A handheld camera follows as she leaves her house with the child and walks onto a bridge, a visual metaphor for her state of mind: she's in a transition state, between two diametrically opposing sentiments (this in fact is the film's turning point); a pan from the bridge down to the rocky creek far below suggests the depth of the chasm inside of her. She raises the wrapped babe (you see a chubby arm move) high above her head; cut to a close-up of her face, of her horror at the act she is contemplating, then fade to a setting sun….

The anger of Asian countries against the wartime Japanese was and is unforgivingly intense (see, for example, Zhang Yimou's *Red Sorghum* [1987]); O'Hara was playing with emotional dynamite when he made this film, which was vehemently criticized for dealing complexly with the issue. By binding us to Elsa's viewpoint, O'Hara shows how such attitudes can feel wrong in the face of all we know is right: a point made more relevant by these times of exacerbated nationalism and ethnic hatred.
Noel Vera

Date 1976

Nationality Philippines

Director Mario O'Hara

Cast Nora Aunor, Christopher de Leon

Original Title *Tatlong Taong Walang Diyos*

Why It's Key It's one of the most vivid demonstrations on film of two powerful ideas in mortal conflict with each other: first, that the wartime Japanese are to be hated and opposed; second, that all human beings are to be cherished.

Key Event **The death of Henri Langlois –**
The eagle folds his wings

Henri Langlois died in 1977, at 63, almost ten years after a mass protest prevented the Culture Ministry to remove him from the Chaillot Cinémathèque he had founded in 1936. Inhabiting the space with his spectacular bulk, Langlois was surrounded by the "four musketeers." The German historian Lotte Eisner worked there for 30 years, after her release from concentration camps in 1945. Eisner, Langlois, and the filmmaker Marie Epstein, who was "director of technical services" till 1977, were the only ones to know where some prints were stored. During the Occupation, Langlois had hidden prints away from the Germans all throughout France, and the Cinémathèque, cruelly lacking money, was performing miracles with makeshift solutions. Restoration was the job of Renée Lichtig, born in 1912 in Shanghai in a White Russian family.

Running the Cinémathèque with Langlois, with a somewhat unorthodox management style, was his companion, Mary Meerson, a former beauty queen with a mysterious Eastern European past. She had fallen in love with and married the famous designer Lazare Meerson. Upon his death in 1938, she met Langlois, who was a shy yet visionary young man, ten years younger than her. They grew old together – overweight, cantankerous, infuriatingly disorganized, and consumed by a shared passion for cinema and film preservation. Their only child was the Cinémathèque, and their relationship was intimate, enigmatic, boisterous. She survived him 17 years. He had been her lover, her child and her creation. "I gave him the wings of an eagle," she said.

Bérénice Reynaud

Date January 13 1977

Why It's Key With the disappearance of the man who had dreamt and founded the Cinémathèque française starts the less poetic era of the "cultural managers."

Key Scene **Lobsters for dinner**
Annie Hall

If the directorial career of Woody Allen is motivated by a sequence of love affairs – with European cinema, with Kierkegaard, with various women, with the possibilities of his own self-reflexiveness onscreen – *Annie Hall* represents its apotheosis, with his persona as a screen schlemiel consolidated fully for the first time as he bonds with Diane Keaton. No moment in Allen's cinema is more pregnantly evocative of this connection and this anxious love and self-reflexiveness than the "lobster scene." Having retreated to the Hamptons for a weekend cavort, Annie (Keaton) and Alvy (Allen) are celebrating their new friendship with a self-made lobster dinner. But Alvy, Jewish as they come, knows gornisht from lobsters; and Annie, the pristine princess from the Midwest, doesn't want to touch anything that crawls. Picking the creatures up with arms outstretched, as though handling dynamite, and mortified at the idea of dropping them into the boiling pot, the two mince around the kitchen in paroxysmal squeals of fear and excitement, their lobsters like threatening aliens in a 1950s Saturday-afternoon serial.

This sequence, filmed in one day in Amagansett, Long Island, is an interesting example of how location shooting can be problematic. The red-brick floor tiles of the kitchen prevented the crawling crustaceans (painted red, because their green tinge seemed unappealing) from being seen on film. Plywood had quickly to be laid down and whitewashed to make a contrasting background. The result is a screen moment that is deliciously homey and at the same time psychologically creepy: how will these two delicate and neurotic souls ever manage to come together in loving repose?

Murray Pomerance

Date 1977

Nationality USA

Director Woody Allen

Cast Woody Allen, Diane Keaton

Why It's Key It shows how problematic location filming can be.

Opposite *Annie Hall*

Key Scene **Alien spacecraft form the Big Dipper** *Close Encounters of the Third Kind*

After the hostile example set by aliens in *The War of the Worlds* (1953), *Earth vs. the Flying Saucers* (1956), and *Invasion of the Body Snatchers* (1956), you wonder why Roy Neary (Dreyfuss) is so gung-ho on reacquainting with the unearthly visitors who buzzed his truck late one night, especially after his encounter left him sunburned only on the right side of his face. But he pursues his obsession with hypnotic obstinacy, alienating his wife (Garr) and young children while constructing a model of a mysterious geological formation in his living room. His fixation takes him to Wyoming and a secret platform on the far side of Devil's Tower where scientists are confirming what he already knew – aliens are here, and they're ready to meet us. Director Steven Spielberg's vision of peace-loving extraterrestrials destroyed the warlike paradigm for movie aliens and paved the way for other non-violent species in *Cocoon* (1985), *The Abyss* (1989), and Spielberg's own *E.T. The Extra-Terrestrial* (1982). But

more importantly, *Close Encounters* marked the beginning of Spielberg uncovering his true voice. His previous films *Duel* (1971), *The Sugarland Express* (1974), and *Jaws* (1975) showed a mastery of craft but lacked the auteur touches – a luminous *mise en scène*, abandonment succored with reunion, an all-encompassing childlike wonder – now recognized as archetypically Spielbergian. When the first wave of the alien fleet hails the Earth by aligning their incandescent ships in friendly replica of the Big Dipper, it's the first of many awe-inspiring – and career-defining – moments of enchantment.

Violet Glaze

Date 1977

Nationality USA

Director Steven Spielberg

Cast Richard Dreyfuss, Teri Garr, François Truffaut, Melinda Dillon, Bob Balaban

Why It's Key The magic moment when the spaceships form the constellation in the sky marks the beginning of Spielberg's auteurship.

Opposite *Close Encounters of the Third Kind*

529

Key Scene **The dream within the dream** *Eraserhead*

Surrealism and cinema are an odd couple. Surrealism thrives on images from the world of dreams, but cameras can only film physical objects, and even digital techniques are usually deployed to make the unreal look as real as possible. Aside from a handful of pioneers in the field – Luis Buñuel, Maya Deren – no filmmaker better exemplifies the Surrealist spirit than Lynch, who accurately described his first feature as "a dream of dark and disturbing things."

The hero is Henry (Nance), a young man whose new wife (Charlotte Stewart) gives birth to a monstrous baby, then leaves him to care for the noisy, demanding creature. Every aspect of the film, from its acting and dialogue to its grim cinematography and nerve-jangling sound design, contributes to its otherworldly atmosphere. And just when you thought it couldn't get more delirious, Henry has a dream. In it he's visiting the Lady in the Radiator (Near), an apple-cheeked songstress who lives in a dark cranny of his room, and

suddenly a bizarre stalk shoots out of his neck, knocking off his head, which falls to the street below. There it's grabbed by a street urchin (Coulson), who sells it to a factory that uses the brain as raw material for pencil erasers. Only then does Henry awaken, more perplexed and dissatisfied than ever.

The movie's title now makes sense. Or does it? For the viewer, this scene marks the transition from watching somebody's dream to feeling trapped in somebody's nightmare. Few moments match it for pure hallucinatory power.

David Sterritt

Date 1977

Nationality USA

Director David Lynch

Cast John Nance, Laurel Near, Thomas Coulson, Darwin Joston, Neil Moran, Hal Landon Jr.

Why It's Key By nesting a dream sequence within a dreamlike movie, Lynch carries film surrealism to dizzying heights.

Key Scene **Chato deflowered**
Burlesque Queen

Chato (Santos) has gotten a job at Mr. Fernando's burlesque theater without her father knowing; Mr. Fernando has hit upon the brilliant idea of having her dance with a mask on – she'll be known as the mysterious "Tsarina." Chato brings her boyfriend, Jessie (Quizon), to the theater; they snatch kisses in a stairwell. In her dressing room, Celso's camera follows Chato as she and Jessie sit on a bench, sliding backwards, both unbuttoning their clothes.

Celso uses Jessie's smooth back as both veil and metaphor for Chato's nudity, the clothes dropping from overhead hangers as metaphor for her failing inhibitions; what makes the scene erotic and nakedly emotional is Chato's face, glimpsed over Jessie's left shoulder as terror (the widened eyes), greed (the remote expression, as if she were a starving man wolfing down a steak), pain (the startled look of one who has been kicked in the crotch), guilt (the tears) and finally pleasure (the bit lower lip) flit across and mingle

in her eyes. Celso goes wild here, free-associating with a series of images deftly inserted into the sequence: of an audience applauding wildly in approval; of a male acrobat tossing and balancing four or five women; of Canuplin (the "Charlie Chaplin of the Philippines") pulling pink undergarments from a man's pants; of a performer nailing a spike up his nose, nailing another through the bridge of his nose, then swallowing a sword (this being the penultimate moment before Chato's penetration). All rendered piercingly poignant by a sad little ballad strummed out on a guitar.

Noel Vera

Date 1977

Nationality Philippines

Director Celso Ad. Castillo

Cast Vilma Santos, Rolly Quizon

Original Title *Burlesk Queen*

Why It's Key "The Celso Kid" does what few other filmmakers can do: transform a sordid moment into lyricism, tenderness, beauty.

530

Key Scene **Nude murder victim on display**
The Pyjama Girl Case

The mutilated body of a brutally murdered girl is found on a beach in Sydney. A retired police inspector (Milland) becomes interested in the case, but his investigation is hampered by the difficulty of identifying the victim. The inspector arranges for the victim's nude body to be preserved and put on public display, hoping that someone will come and identify her.

Many aficionados of the Italian giallo seem to consider this film a lesser entry in the genre. No doubt 40 other gialli contain moments at least as worthy of notice as the scene in *The Pyjama Girl Case* in which the inspector visits the morgue to see the results of the preparation of the victim's body. But this moment possesses several qualities that make it distinctive. First, obviously, the very premise is not only a revealing baring-of-the-device (all gialli play on the attractions of violent death and mortified flesh) but also a cynical attack on the psychology of the spectator (what kind of

crazed people would turn out to look at the girl's body? The same people who would see *The Pyjama Girl Case*) and even a mordant critique of the police (how many real investigations are conducted today using techniques even more desperate and ridiculous than this?). Second, there is the performance of 72-year-old, bald, but crisply authoritative and attractively aware-of-his-limitations Ray Milland, who brings a stunned, rueful irony to the inspector's reaction to the low-budget science-fiction-porn tableau his plan has called into being. Staring at the naked corpse and shaking his head, he takes leave of his colleagues with a wry "Good luck," packing into the line a bland, appalled, almost affectionate contempt that takes in the whole project, including the film itself.

Chris Fujiwara

Date 1977

Nationality Italy/Spain

Director Flavio Mogherini

Cast Ray Milland

Original Title *La ragazza dal pigiama giallo*

Why It's Key A star in the twilight of his career reaches mainstream commercial cinema's heart of darkness: the Italian giallo.

Key Scene **The man with two penises**
Casotto

Aformer collaborator of Pier Paolo Pasolini, Sergio Citti has offered a more accessible interpretation of his mentor's aesthetics: his style is a lively variation on neorealism, but owes much to the canon of the *commedia all'italiana*. A brilliantly twisted version of this formula is to be found in *Casotto*, almost an experimental film in its visual abstraction and unconventional narrative premise (plus a Hare Krishna jingle as the only music soundtrack). The entire story is told from within a beach cabin on a hot summer day, with all sorts of people coming in to change clothes. Well, that's the theory; in fact, they also come in to eat, drink, make love. Aside from one shot at the beginning, the camera never leaves the cabin; we can look outside the door, but never get out. There's plenty to see inside, a microcosm of human existence where flesh, sweat, and bodily functions are exposed in a tour de force of unbridled voyeurism. Indeed, we do what many people would: we take a peek at naked bodies, share the latest gossip between friends, enjoy being the invisible witnesses of other people's lives. There's even a drama unfolding between two dogs, and a dream sequence with Biblical symbology turned into surreal comedy. Speaking of which, one of our casual encounters in the film is with a man who gets in and prepares for a swim. A frontal shot of his crotch reveals that he has two penises. Cut to the man's face. He looks very, very sad. He is a priest.

Paolo Cherchi Usai

Date 1977

Nationality Italy

Director Sergio Citti

Cast Franco Citti, Gigi Proietti, Jodie Foster

Why It's Key Extreme realism and extreme surrealism are one and the same thing.

Key Scene **They won't let my people go**
Killer of Sheep

In the depressed neighborhood of Watts, Los Angeles, Stan (Sanders), tries to keep his family together by having a "decent" job and avoiding the temptations of "easy" crime – but the drab conditions of his existence take a toll on him. He is sullen, insomniac, and unable to communicate with his wife (Moore). *Killer of Sheep* is the first feature directed by Charles Burnett, who, while at UCLA, was part of a group of young African American filmmakers (including Julie Dash and Billy Woodberry), sometimes called "the L.A. Rebellion": influenced by Italian neorealism and Latin American Third Cinema, they wanted to change the way their community was being represented.

The five scenes showing Stan at work in a slaughterhouse trigger memories of genocide and slavery, creating a sense of historical impasse and social desperation. In one scene, in the foreground, two sheep are standing; in the background, on the left, several more are ushered, in silhouette; they turn around to line up after the first two, then look off-screen and start panicking, trying to escape – to the warm voice of Paul Robeson… Another shot displays their bodies dangling on hooks, the men splitting the carcasses open, skinning, cutting, washing them. Cut to another arrival of sheep, half-heartedly bleating, confused and desperate…

The last sequence starts on Stan's upper body framed by two carcasses hanging; later we see him herding the sheep who, frightened, end up in a narrow funnel that leads to their death. Sadly, ironically, (hopefully?), Dinah Washington sings "Unforgettable."

Bérénice Reynaud

Date 1977

Nationality USA

Director Charles Burnett

Cast Henry Gayle Sanders, Kaycee Moore

Why It's Key Eventually acquired by the Library of Congress, the film heralded a new era in the representation of African American life.

Key Scene **The necrophilia scene**
Iodo

The films of the brilliant and eccentric Kim Ki-young are often built around obsessions. In *The Housemaid* (1960) a family's obsession with middle-class respectability allows the title character to tear apart their home. *Iodo*, set on a remote island, centers around themes of procreation. A local shaman (Park) extorts money by keeping the only purebred male pig on the island. A supposedly cursed islander stakes his livelihood on breeding abalone through artificial means of fertilization.

Years later, the entrepreneur is dead, having vanished from the deck of a tourist ship. However, the shaman boasts that she can bring him back from the sea and claims, moreover, that the seed within his corpse is still viable, so he can impregnate his childless widow. Sure enough, after an elaborate ritual, his corpse washes up on the beach, but soon a local barmaid (Lee) claims ownership of the corpse for herself. A contest breaks out between the two women.

The film's climax is shocking by today's standards, let alone those of 1970s Korea. The man's corpse is laid out and a slender stick is inserted into his phallus to make it stand. To the rattle of the shaman's bells, and with intense red lighting permeating the scene, the barmaid disrobes and climbs onto the man. The movements of the bodies and the camera are measured and rhythmic, but not in a way we normally associate with sex. Suddenly the shaman is stabbed from behind. The woman, oblivious, cranes her face up towards the sky, and then down again. The intensity of Lee Hwa-shi's acting, and Kim's inspired camera, lend a surreal edge to this startling and yet unexpectedly tender scene.

Darcy Paquet

Date 1977

Nationality South Korea

Director Kim Ki-young

Cast Lee Hwa-shi, Park Jeong-ja

Original Title *I-eodo*

Why It's Key Still sensational today, this scene functions as the perfect conclusion to a complex, breathtaking work.

532

Key Scene **The first (double) murder sequence** *Suspiria*

When Dario Argento shot his first horror film in 1977, he probably remembered very well the lesson he had learnt during the years he was making gialli: murder scenes should be original set pieces that leave the spectator breathless. In *Suspiria*, the introduction of the main character (Harper) is quickly followed by a scene showing two girls being brutally murdered by an (almost) invisible force. The first girl (Axen) is repeatedly stabbed, pushed through a glass roof, and hung from the ceiling, while the second (Javicoli) is impaled by the fall of the glass fragments. It is a complicated double-murder sequence, whose unrestrained gruesomeness (e.g., the close-up of the knifed heart), symptomatic of the genre during the seventies, is transcended by the director's carefully calculated but audacious aesthetic choices. The vast and empty Art Deco scenery gives an impression of theatricality. The artificial lighting and color patterns that also run through the film, combined with a

saturated soundtrack by Goblin, provide an impressive visual and sound assault. However, the excessiveness and unrealism of the scene are a sign that violence per se is not Argento's main goal. The last shot, showing the second girl's body lying on the ground, is quite revealing. The image is exquisitely framed; a red stain and yellow glass pieces are harmoniously arranged on the mostly black and white geometrical floor. Murder can be an art, wrote Thomas De Quincey, who was the principal source of inspiration for *Suspiria*, and the horror director can be a painter.

Frank Lafond

Date 1977

Nationality Italy

Director Dario Argento

Cast Jessica Harper, Eva Axen, Susanna Javicoli

Why It's Key This moment is a great example of Dario Argento's aestheticization of violence.

Key Scene **Ed Lachman forgets his sunglasses** *La Soufrière*

The somewhat legendary status of director Werner Herzog has much to do with the supposedly insane risks he's willing to take (although it is worth noting that he insists, in most cases quite believably, that the hazards have been hugely exaggerated). The most famous instance is undoubtedly when Herzog actually had a huge boat pulled over a jungle mountain for *Fitzcarraldo* (1983), but really this has nothing on the folly of his 1977 decision to visit the deserted island of Guadeloupe. There was a good reason why the island was deserted: All experts expected it to be destroyed in an imminent massive volcanic eruption. The German version of Herzog's 30-minute film about the mad trip even carries the subtitle "Waiting for an Inevitable Catastrophe," but the disaster did not happen, and there is due disappointment in Herzog's voice-over narration. There is something deeply disturbing in the film's craving for the apocalypse, not least when mid-film Herzog embarks on a lovingly detailed detour

elaborating on the effects of an earlier eruption nearby. But in typical Herzogian fashion the intimdating quality of this paean to love of death is balanced by a sense for its comical absurdity. It peaks in a moment that must count both as cinema's ultimate representation of human hubris and a satire on it. Returning from a climb up to the perilously smoking volcano, Ed Lachman, one of the two cameramen accompanying Herzog, notes that he has forgotten his sunglasses – but quickly it's decided that's not much of a problem, really: "We will just get them tomorrow."

Christoph Huber

Date 1977

Nationality West Germany

Director Werner Herzog

Original Title *La Soufrière - Warten auf eine unausweichliche Katastrophe*

Why It's Key Man's hubris and love of death have never been so convincing. Or so funny.

1970–1979

Key Film *37/78 Tree Again*
Time out of joint

Few filmmakers have produced a body of work that holds up as well in its entirety as that of Austrian avant-garde master Kurt Kren. Partly because he constantly pushed the cinematic boundaries of seeing the world like no other. Significantly, Kren insisted that his experiments also surprise himself – and with characteristic modesty acknowledged that he had to see his works repeatedly before he started to figure them out for himself, while allowing for any other reaction as equally valid. Humility always was key to his oeuvre, both in production (his visual poems would use, amongst other things, a sad cactus, the structure of a children's rhyme, or broken beer bottles) and interpretation (no cine-autobiography is as unobtrusive as his, adding up with every stoic number/year title-preamble glistening shards of outsider-artist Bohemian life, decade-long expat ordeal, and late return home, not one frame pathetic). Nothing illustrates this humility better than the story behind his most monumental

time-space-exploration (along with *31/75 Asyl*), *37/78 Tree Again*. For months Kren returned daily to the same spot in Vermont to shoot a tree, rewinding the film according to a prearranged plan – a roll of expired infrared film, to be precise. It might have been just a blur, but instead Kren left us a beaming, endlessly rewatchable enigma: three minutes and 48 seconds of time out of joint, every frame a rush of changing seasons and leaf colors, of moving clouds and animals, of decay and renewal, of a tree – and the world – paradoxically caught in perpetual flux.

Christoph Huber

Date 1978

Nationality Austria

Director Kurt Kren

Why It's Key Director Kurt Kren pushed the boundaries of seeing like no other. In this supreme masterpiece he shows just a tree – and through it nothing less than the entire world in flux.

Key Scene **A musician asks a young woman to join him on the road** *Renaldo & Clara*

Bob Dylan's *Renaldo & Clara* seems destined to never achieve the recognition it so richly deserves. Mocked by Dylan fans, who regard it as a shapeless mess, this masterpiece has mostly escaped the notice of discriminating cinephiles, who would undoubtedly be more receptive to its ambitions. Dylan's film can be seen as a companion piece to Jacques Rivette's *Out 1* (1972), with which it shares an emphasis on the relationship between narrative and identity, demonstrating how freeing the former from its traditional moorings results in a fragmentation of the latter. Take the scene in which Ronnie Hawkins plays a musician trying to convince a young woman that she should leave her father's farm and join him on the road. Dylan presumably instructed Hawkins to keep asking this woman to join him until she finally agreed, while instructing the woman to keep resisting Hawkins' demands. The result is less a conversation than a pair of loosely related monologues delivered by two individuals locked into their own points of view, trapped within their one-dimensional identities. The scene ends with neither character having progressed (or shown any ability to progress) from the positions they occupied when it began. Yet this rigidity is implicitly mocked by the overall structure of Dylan's film, in which identities are infinitely malleable, taken up and abandoned as swiftly as the various narrative fragments, rarely consistent from one sequence to the next. An element of improvisational give and take is shown to be a prerequisite for the achievement of full humanity.
Brad Stevens

Date 1978

Nationality USA

Director Bob Dylan

Cast Ronnie Hawkins

Why It's Key This scene demonstrates how formal structures can accommodate improvisational elements.

Key Film *Drunken Master*
Jackie Chan finds his niche

Wong Fei-Hung (Chan) is every kung fu master's nightmare – a mischievous boy who'd rather flirt with pretty girls and con diners out of their restaurant meals than practice his martial arts. But under the tutelage of eccentric dipsomaniac Su Hua Chi (Yuen) he learns "Eight Drunken Immortals" style, an esoteric fighting technique that requires getting completely sloshed before facing your opponent. Chan, a veteran since childhood of the ultra-disciplined Peking Opera School, sought employment in Hong Kong's mushrooming movie industry as an actor and stunt man (that's him getting pulled by the hair for a brief instant in *Enter the Dragon* [1973]), but found it hard to distinguish himself from the hundreds of equally athletic and acrobatic Bruce Lee wannabes glutting the industry. He broke out of the pack by capitalizing on his natural good humor and excellent comic timing, injecting a much needed dose of levity into the often overgrim genre. When Fei-Hung battles opponents with silly fighting techniques like "iron head," endures ridiculous training more appropriate for the Three Stooges, or balks at learning the effeminate fighting style of the eighth female immortal "Miss Ho, the drunken woman flaunting her body," Chan continues the work of silent comedians like Buster Keaton who combined sight gags with physical daring and expertise. Chan's good humor uniquely elevates *Drunken Master's* many combative *pas de deux* into something closer to a crowd-pleasing dance movie, turning what could have been a forgettable chop-socky flick into an effortlessly fun cult favorite.
Violet Glaze

Date 1978

Nationality Hong Kong

Director Yuen Woo-Ping

Cast Jackie Chan, Siu Tien Yuen, Jang Lee Hwang

Original Title *Jui kuen*

Why It's Key Jackie Chan continues Buster Keaton's proof that humor and action are not incompatible

Opposite *Drunken Master*

Key Scene **Meet Pearl!**
Interiors

Maureen Stapleton's entrance in *Interiors* marks one of the most striking uses of color in contemporary cinema. The story is about Eve (Page), a mother who is stifling her husband and children, and her family's liberation after she suicides. Allen spends considerable time setting up the swankly interior-decorated prison Eve has fashioned, in which husband Arthur (Marshall), and daughters Renata (Keaton), Joey (Hurt), and Flyn (Griffith) are trapped by the hypercreative matriarch's utterly relentless exercise of tastefulness and restraint. She is committed to the principle of understatement, and everything in her world is either beige or pale gray. The home, its furnishings, its draperies, its dried flowers – all beige. Eve's clothing, the clothing of her daughters: beige. Arthur's neckties – subdued to match his pale gray suits. The movements: all measured and quiet and assured. The arrangements of vases, chairs, bowls: perfectly Grecian and perfectly – painfully – neutralized. The jostling world of New York City brings Eve nothing but agony. As she prepares to gas herself, she uses tape to seal off the windows of her room, but meticulously, as though for aesthetic effect. In a long gray robe she poses herself on a divan – David's Madame Recamier – converting herself to a sculpture even in death. Later, Arthur begins dating again, and one evening, with his family gathered to celebrate Thanksgiving in the overwhelmingly beige apartment that is Eve's legacy, he plans to present his new friend to his children. Sedate music is playing. Quietly, the girls are conversing with their boyfriends, all immaculately groomed and dressed with the sort of taste that Eve would have silently applauded. There is a ring at the door. When it is opened, there stands Pearl (Stapleton), smiling nervously, but in fire-engine red. As she enters, everyone loses composure, their world seems to disintegrate, their past to vanish, their perspective to shift. The dead garden has come alive.
Murray Pomerance

Date 1978

Nationality USA

Director Woody Allen

Cast Geraldine Page, E. G. Marshall, Diane Keaton, Mary Beth Hurt, Kristin Griffith, Maureen Stapleton

Why It's Key It's one of the most striking uses of color in contemporary cinema.

Key Scene **Locking down the mall**
Dawn of the Dead

A monster plagues the horror genre: the monster of cheating the angles. From one point of view, the fleeing heroine has stumbled to her knees and is inches from mutilation at the hands of Freddy or one of the Boogens; from another, she is half a city block ahead of her pursuer, with a full head of go-girl steam. The vampire hunters and vampires appear to be squared off for a complex battle, when suddenly the angle-cutting monster bursts onto the set in a fog of jump cutting and shakycam.

The human integrity of George Romero's zombies precludes this artistic crime. Romero's films, and especially his living dead cycle, pulsate with life and deliver rank, fleshy mortality. The slow, absurd logic of frailty triumphs always over the delusion of strength. The possibility of transcendence is mocked, tossed, and gored. In zombie war, geography is destiny. Dawn of the Dead, the second episode in Romero's zombie series, begins as a de-urbanization nightmare set in inner-city Philadelphia, but fatefully relocates the action to a suburban Pittsburgh shopping mall. Many celebrate the film's anti-consumerist satire; few note its physical heft, its truth to the reality of tactics and terrain.

This extended sequence, in which the heroes lock down and sweep the zombie-infested shopping center, hits its marks as well as any war or heist movie. The shape of the fighting zone is carefully detailed: the mall's maneuverable atrium; the two-level department store with its locking safety-glass doors; the ghoul-strewn exit ramp and parking lot, etc. The action – a complicated victory and its eventual undoing – unfolds with care and precision. Among many other things, it is one of the greatest action sequences ever filmed. Fans have responded by making the film's Monroeville Mall location a site of pilgrimage.
Tim Cavanaugh

Date 1978

Nationality USA

Director George A. Romero

Cast David Emge, Ken Foree, Scott H. Reiniger, Gaylen Ross

Why It's Key Romero's careful detailing of tactics and terrain makes this one of the greatest action sequences ever filmed.

Opposite *Dawn of the Dead*

Key Film *The Tree of Wooden Clogs*
The day of the slaughtering of the pig

On a rainy winter day, there's great excitement at the farmhouse. The butcher comes; the pig is going to be slaughtered. Children curiously stare from afar as the butcher slits the animal's throat. The farmers collect the spilling blood, wash the hog's skin, shave the hair, then hang the animal and scorch it. As the butcher starts cutting the meat, local priest Don Carlo (Silva) comes along to meet the Widow Runk (Brescianini). Despite the heavy rain, the laundress is at the ditch, washing clothes. The priest tells the widow that, in order to ease her burden, the nuns at the orphanage can take in two of her six offspring.

In *The Tree of Wooden Clogs*, the line between documentary and fiction looks extremely fine. Although Ermanno Olmi's labor of love (he scripted, directed, photographed, and edited the film) is set in a rural tenement in the countryside of Bergamo, Northern Italy, around 1898, the everyday routines and rituals he depicts were still very familiar to the cast of real-life

farmers he recruited. The passing of seasons, the hardships of work in the fields, the communal fraternity among farmers are presented by Olmi in vignettes in which the strings of fictional manipulation are hardly perceivable. The simple dislocation from one space to another can mark a shift from documentation of peasants' practices to fictional plot – as in the sequence described above. And in the compassionate character of Don Carlo, one can appreciate Olmi's sincerely Catholic worldview.

Paolo Bertolin

Date 1978

Nationality Italy

Director Ermanno Olmi

Cast Teresa Brescianini, Carmelo Silva

Original Title *L'Albero degli zoccoli*

Why It's Key In two back-to-back sequences, Olmi shifts from ethnographic documentation to fictional storyline.

Opposite *The Tree of Wooden Clogs*

Key Event **The Beijing Film Academy reopens after the Cultural Revolution**

The rebirth of contemporary Chinese cinema is often traced to the international premiere, at the 1985 Hong Kong Film Festival, of *Yellow Earth*, a subtly political debut feature about the encounter between a Red Army soldier and a peasant family in rural 1930s China. Directed by Chen Kaige and photographed by Zhang Yimou, it represented a stunning break in both content and style from the Maoist propaganda films of the previous decades (and the earlier Shanghai-centered "golden ages" of Chinese cinema), and it propelled the so-called Fifth Generation of mainland Chinese filmmakers onto the world stage.

This movement was incubated at the Beijing Film Academy, which reopened in September 1978 after being closed for more than a decade during the Cultural Revolution. Chen and Zhang, who made his directing debut in 1987 with *Red Sorghum*, were among the first post-Mao graduating class, along with Tian Zhuangzhuang, director of 1986's *Horse Thief*. A sense

of shared experience gave this new wave both a cohesiveness and a political subtext. Many Fifth Generation filmmakers were born in the early '50s, not long after the inception of the People's Republic, and were "sent down" to the countryside for re-education in the late '60s.

Zhang and Chen went on to become the chief exporters of mainland Chinese cinema. Tian has been less prolific, largely due to a ban imposed after 1993's *The Blue Kite*, a family drama highly critical of Maoist policies, but he has assumed the role of mentor for younger filmmakers, many of whom began their careers underground, outside the official system. The Academy remains one of the most competitive film schools in the world. More recent alumni include Jia Zhangke, Lou Ye, and Wang Xiaoshuai, members of a new generation whose films grapple with the contradictions of a post-Tiananmen, rapidly modernizing China.

Dennis Lim

Date September 1978

Why It's Key The Academy's first post-Mao graduating class included the key members of the Fifth Generation that put Chinese cinema on the international map.

Key Film *In girum imus nocte et consumimur igni*

A slow traveling shot along the Laguna of Venice…. The black-and-white tones playing with the setting sun's shadows on the palazzi fronts make them look like human faces, old and proud faces… like the deep water of the Laguna which seems darker than Chinese ink… while a calm and lost voice-over is telling its truth about life, history, and the endless changes of times. It is the voice of Debord himself. Amid the Venetian images appear images from old Soviet films, Westerns, and old French dramas, punctuated by TV commercials. The voice explains how corrupted our "spectacular" society is, how life as an adventure is finished, how the avant-gardes are dead. And then we recognize the Situationists (members of the avant-garde artistic and political movement of which Debord was the most prominent figure) in the images of a cavalry surrounded by Indians, and Debord himself behind the character of the Devil in a film by Marcel Carné.

During 20 years, Debord's films were invisible. They became a legend – as did the Situationist group itself after the 1968 insurrection. *In girum imus nocte* (like such previous Debord films as 1961's *Critique of Separation* and 1973's *The Society of the Spectacle*) uses "*détournement*" (displacing sentences or images to change the meaning of a work) and parody to identify a self-destructive critique inside the whole production of the culture industry. "*Détournement*" is also a way to write an epitaph to the old cinema and a nostalgic poem for a lost future. Cinema is dead because the revolution failed: only nostalgia remains in *In girum imus nocte* as an epitaph to the missing social revolution.

Antoine Coppola

Date 1978

Nationality France

Director Guy Debord

Why It's Key This film is an epitaph to cinema and an epitaph to the social revolution.

Key Film *All That Jazz*
The fear of death

Fosse, a famous choreographer with the most distinctive style in the profession (and formerly a brilliant dancer, as in *My Sister Eileen* [1955]) endeavored to transcend or ignore the musical-comedy genre in all five of his films as a director. To call *All That Jazz* a musical (as it is routinely labelled) is about as accurate as calling *Oedipus Rex* a comedy. Two major themes are inextricably intertwined in *All That Jazz*: death and show business (death is also a prominent theme in *Lenny* [1974] and Fosse's last film, *Star 80* [1983]). A Lenny Bruce monologue about the fear of death, used by the protagonist, Fosse's alter ego Joseph Gideon (Scheider), for his film *Standup* (actually, Fosse's own *Lenny*), is run again and again throughout *All That Jazz*. Gideon, plagued by heart attacks in the middle of the rehearsals for a new Broadway musical, ultimately turns his own dying into a flamboyant spectacle – a glossy, vulgar, Las-Vegas-ish show. The entire film is a series of variations on Gideon's love-hate relationship with show business, his constant efforts to turn Broadway-style dross into gold.

Fosse's strikingly daring approach deals with death romantically (the film is structured as a dialogue between Gideon and his "angel of death"), comically (the Bruce monologue), clinically (the hospital scenes with the open-heart surgery) and ironically (the climactic song-and-dance staging). Dazzlingly directed and edited, *All That Jazz* deserved the Academy Award for Best Film that went to a much lesser effort (Robert Benton's *Kramer vs. Kramer*).

Jean-Pierre Coursodon

Date 1979

Nationality USA

Director Bob Fosse

Cast Roy Scheider, Jessica Lange

Why It's Key The autobiographical testament of a major choreographer turned major film director, this is one of the most personal, most original films to come out of Hollywood.

Opposite *All That Jazz*

Key Scene **The on-screen guide falls asleep** *The Hypothesis of the Stolen Painting*

Many cinephiles recognise Ruiz's signature visual games: the bizarre compositions, ornate lighting patterns, disorienting split-lenses. But the thick, Cocteau-like mood of *The Hypothesis of the Stolen Painting* depends just as much on the soundtrack's Wellesian weave of memorable voices. One of these voices belongs to an old, on-screen narrator (Jean Rougeul from Fellini's *8½* [1963]) who leads us through his unusual art collection (and speculates, hypothetically, on the painting missing from a series); while another, younger voice belongs to an off-screen presence (Gabriel Gascon) who variously guides, prompts, and comments on events. These voices seem not to dwell in the same time, space, or even the same aural universe – the old man's words are "live," surrounded by air and atmosphere, while the young man's voice is studio-recorded, airless, close and intimate in our ears. But, in one matter-of-factly droll gag, they form a relay of sorts. The old man is speaking but, tired out, falls asleep before our eyes. The other narrator picks up the trail of words – but, out of politeness, whispers, as if (in perfect unreality) in earshot of his elder. Eventually, the old man awakes and recommences his narration – picking up exactly where the younger man stopped. In part a send-up of the sort of solemn, highbrow documentaries on art that appear on "quality" TV channels everywhere, *Hypothesis* (a free variation on motifs from the novels and paintings of Pierre Klossowski) lulls the viewer into a false assumption of security, before subtly deranging our senses.

Adrian Martin

Date 1979

Nationality France

Director Raoul Ruiz

Cast Jean Rougeul

Original Title *L'Hypothèse du tableau volé*

Why It's Key Ruiz sends up the authority of narrating voices with a brilliant joke.

Key Scene **Emergence of the beast** *Alien*

SPOILER

Alien in many ways set a standard for gruesome and terrifying science-fiction effects, this in the wake of a long tradition in which alien forms had typically been depicted as humanoid: frightening intention was usually signaled and readable prior to frightening action. Now, the horrifying could be organic, slimy, toothed, and smart all at once, and action could be swifter than a bullet (a quantum leap beyond what had been seen in *The Blob* [1958]). The film tells of the crew of the Nostromo, adrift in space on a commercial salvage mission. Answering what seems like an S.O.S., they encounter a vast field of incubating "eggs" on a strange planet. As Kane (Hurt) bends over to examine one of these, it explodes in his face and a tentacled creature attaches itself to the outside of his space mask. He is immediately dragged back into the ship and confined in sick bay.

After days in quarantine, with the gray, octopus-like creature attached to his face, Kane is suddenly freed; the entity is dead. But soon later, in a scene that is second only to the *Psycho* shower in shocking timing, Kane takes ill in the wardroom as the team is eating. He seems to be having digestive trouble, and to be trying to vomit upon the table. Everyone clears back. Suddenly he is on his back, his white t-shirt throbbing and a look of excruciating agony twisting his face. With no warning his chest explodes outward as a huge moist dagger-toothed wormlike creature, which has been gestating in his heart, lifts its hideous head, scans the territory, and springs out with a screech to race for safety in the paneling of the ship. Kane is a goner, but where is the alien? Soon, and then soon again, and again and again, it will reappear, no longer so small, no longer so sociable.

Murray Pomerance

Date 1979

Nationality UK

Director Ridley Scott

Cast John Hurt

Why It's Key This moment provides a paramount early example of the union of horror cinema and advanced body make-up.

Opposite *Alien*

Key Scene **Hugging the atomic bomb**
The Man Who Stole the Sun

Kazuhiko Hasegawa is somewhat legendary for making two absolutely astounding, but underseen features in the '70s. The second and even more ambitious was called *The Man Who Stole the Sun* and, for purposes of classification, does fit best into the popular genre of the epic action thriller. But it utilizes the template in unique and constantly suprising ways. Its unsettling mixture of comedy and suspense could be compared to John Frankenheimer's original 1962 version of *The Manchurian Candidate* just for sheer, ballsy weirdness, but that's where the similarities end. Hasegawa's anti-hero (Sawada) is a high-school science teacher who manages to build an atomic bomb and demands... well, what exactly? While a classical cat-and-mouse game with a police inspector (played by action icon Bunta Sugawara) ensues, the film's counter-culture-fueled satire mercilessly elaborates its punchline: that the supposedly revolutionary protest of its suitably long-haired outsider protagonist turns out to be an end in itself – stumped, at some point he simply asks for a cancelled Rolling Stones concert to take place after all! Hasegawa generally uses genre tropes in complex ways, and his image for his antihero's newfound attraction to (atomic) power is characteristic. The usual procedure – used to exemplary effect in Irving Lerner's fine 1959 B-picture *City of Fear* – is to have an unwitting nuclear thief hug his deadly loot for creepy effect. In Hasegawa's film it is both disconcerting and touching when the teacher knowingly cuddles up with his nuclear ball for a good night's sleep.

Christoph Huber

Date 1979

Nationality Japan

Director Kazuhiko Hasegawa

Cast Kenji Sawada

Original Title *Taiyo o nusunda otoko*

Why it's Key A lot of things are unusual about this dazzling, provocative action epic by mythic director Kazuhiko Hasegawa: especially its handling of nuclear fear, as the anti-hero learns to stop worrying and embrace the bomb.

Key Scene **The tiger**
Apocalypse Now

"It's a fucking tiger!" Chef (Forrest) goes walking in the jungle in search of mangoes and is startled by the sudden appearance of a hissing big cat, which jolts Francis Ford Coppola's *Apocalypse Now* briefly into horror-movie territory. Chef learns an important lesson: "Never get out of the boat!" This is a textbook example of the Val Lewton "bus" – but in the context of Coppola's acid-and-napalm-drenched Vietnam, a man-eating tiger (a bigger version of the pussycats that often startle heroines in slasher movies) is almost harmless set beside the other spiritual and physical perils that lurk deeper in the jungle. Subversive underground filmmaker "T. Graham" assembled *Apocalypse Pooh*, which lays Coppola's soundtrack over images from Walt Disney's Winnie the Pooh films and perfectly matches Chef's cry to the first appearance of Tigger!

Kim Newman

Date 1979

Nationality USA

Director Francis Ford Coppola

Cast Frederic Forrest

Why It's Key Because of the scare, and the lesson. "Never get out of the boat."

Key Film *Stalker*
The miracle in the final shot

Few films resist synopsis more than *Stalker*, but the emotions and the decrepit settings are never in doubt. The story concerns the title hero (Aleksandr Kaidanovsky) being hired by a writer (Anatoli Solonitsyn) and a scientist (Nikolai Grinko) to guide them into the supposedly miraculous Zone, where their innermost wishes are supposed to be fulfilled. But an absence of miracles is all they encounter, and the three men come back beaten, the Stalker most of all. Greeted by his wife (Alisa Freindlikh) and crippled daughter (Abramova), he declares himself a failure, the world a desolate place devoid of faith.

However reluctant Tarkovsky may have been to discuss the story's allegorical meanings, he was outspoken about its main theme, "human dignity," and the redemptive power of love shown by the Stalker's wife – calling it a "final miracle to set against the unbelief, cynicism, moral vacuum poisoning the modern world" as exemplified by the writer and scientist. But in fact the film concludes with another miracle concerning the daughter. Seated alone – after reading a poem that we hear her recite in voiceover while dandelion fluff drifts around her – she idly, telekinetically, and rather sadly makes two glasses and a jar slide across the table in front of her as the camera moves back. Then, as the camera moves forward again, the loud rattle of an approaching train is briefly accompanied by Beethoven's "Ode to Joy" before the image fades out on her placid face. The sounds of the train and Beethoven seem equally matched against this quiet, unseen moment of ecstatic revelation.
Jonathan Rosenbaum

Date 1979

Nationality USSR/West Germany

Director Andrei Tarkovsky

Actor Natasha Abramova

Why It's Key After all hope is lost, a moment of ecstatic revelation.

Key Scene **The guru's footsteps**
Shankarabharanam (Jewel of Shiva)

Setting a trend that lasted over a decade, not only in Telugu films but the other three South-Indian-language cinemas (Tamil, Kannada, and Malayalam), this landmark film celebrates the classical music of South India, fusing well-known compositions and new libretti into an accessible score for the ordinary music lover. J. V. Somayajulu, in his film debut (he went on to carve out a niche playing dignified and humane patriarchs), plays Shankara Shastri, an austere, highly respected musician whose fortunes decline when public taste shifts to Western pop and Bollywood hits. A devout Brahmin, the widowed Shastri flouts public opinion in a conservative small town when he shelters Tulasi (Bhargavi), a dancer from a hereditary courtesan community, whose mother has sold her to the local landlord and who has run away.

The film, which unfolds in an extended flashback, opens with Tulasi's return to the town, after an absence of 12 years, with her young, musically gifted son, Shankaram (Tulasi). She sees Shastri's footprints by the river where he bathes after ritual worship. (Earlier, the camera has followed his bare feet on the steps, every footfall resonating with notes of the musical scale.) Shankaram sees his mother kneel and worshipfully touch the wet footprints. "He is father and mother, guru and god," Tulasi tells Shankaram, and he repeats the reverential act. The gesture of salute to the tradition of preserving the classical heritage shows the silent communion between Shastri and Tulasi, united by devotion to art. The scene recalls the moment in Debaki Bose's Bengali classic *Vidyapati* (1937) in which a queen lays flowers on the footsteps of the poet she loves, claiming she sees in him the god she worships.
Maithili Rao

Date 1979

Nationality India

Director K. Vishwanath

Cast J. V. Somayajulu, Manju Bhargavi, Tulasi

Why It's Key It reveals the spiritual dimension of the guru-disciple relationship, while transcending the usual clichés.

Key Speech **Inspiring words for a daughter** *November 1828*

Resistance fighter Kromoludiro (Sitompul) is held captive by the Dutch colonizers. His daughter, Laras (Rachman), is sent to procure information about the resistance movement. Kromoludiro, tied to a pillar, speaks eloquently, knowing that his end is near. He first speaks as a father, then a teacher, finally as a leader. Forbidding Laras to marry the son of the traitorous village headman, he says, "it is far better that Java sink into the sea" than for such a man to sire children of a sovereign nation. He speaks not only to the on-screen character but also to the Indonesian audience.

In a nation that fought fiercely against Dutch and Japanese colonizers, this scene in *November 1828* resonated with audiences not only because of its patriotic dialogue but because of its staging and Sitompul's performance. Though tied to the main pillar of the house (a site of spiritual significance in Indonesian society), Kromoludiro appears to be in control. For powerfully depicting strength in adversity, the jury of the 1979 Indonesian Film Festival gave Sitompul the A. K. Gani Award for acting, alongside El Manik who received the Best Supporting Actor award.
Hassan Abd. Muthalib

Date 1979

Nationality Indonesia

Director Teguh Karya

Cast Maruli Sitompul, Jenny Rachman

Why It's Key This powerful scene gives voice to a people's pride and longing for self-determination.

Key Scene **The pierced eye** *Zombie* (aka *Zombie Flesh Eaters, Zombi 2*)

On the zombie-blighted Caribbean island of Matool, Paola Menard (Karlatos) is besieged in her home by the flesh-eating walking dead. She ventures too near a window, and a hand crashes through, grabs her head, and pulls her towards a jagged shard of the shutter – which slowly pierces her eyeball. Lucio Fulci's *Zombi 2* – released in America as *Zombie* and the UK as *Zombie Flesh Eaters* – is a cheeky cash-in on George Romero's *Dawn of the Dead* (known as *Zombi* in Italy), but this moment of eye-abuse is one of the great gruesome bits of business in splatter-film history. Fulci would try to top himself by blowing a grapefruit-sized bullet hole through a little girl's head in *The Beyond* (1982), but the universal neurosis about any threat to the eye makes the earlier scene an easy winner in the "ugh" department. The business was trimmed on its first release in Britain, but censors perhaps made it more unpleasant – keeping the agonising set-up but abbreviating the squelchy pay-off so that audiences don't get the relief of spotting slightly rubbery make-up effects. It is distantly reminiscent, of course, of the razor-across-the-eyeball moment in Luis Buñuel's *Un chien andalou* (1929).
Kim Newman

Date 1979

Nationality Italy

Director Lucio Fulci

Cast Olga Karlatos

Why It's Key You might not like it, but you won't ever forget it. Like the onscreen victim, you can't look away.

Opposite *Zombie*

Key Scene **The *xia nü* invades the screen**
Raining in the Mountain

Words seem too heavy to describe the exhilarating weightlessness, the movement of the light, the exchange of gazes, the dazzling speed, the elegance of the stunts that grace *Raining in the Mountain*. In a remote monastery, a precious scroll is coveted by unscrupulous individuals. One of them, wealthy Master Wen (Sun), has hired a female thief, White Fox (Xu), and her accomplice, Gold Lock (Wu). When they grab the scroll, a chase ensues. Lock is killed; Wen and Fox cross the river, but, when they arrive on the other bank, from every surrounding rock, beautiful women dressed in saffron, orange, and white jump on them: they are the retinue of Master Wu Wai, the holy man advising the Abbot.

The pair flee and hide in the nearby woods, where the noise of clothes flapping in the air attracts their attention. Now hidden in the trees, the women attack them from above, displaying, along with their lithe bodies, the alluring expanse of their clothing. Hu offers ten sumptuous shots of the women jumping/flying, seen from different angles, creating one of the most exquisite choreographies of the *wuxia* (martial arts) genre. As Wen escapes, Fox, clad in black and red, faces them alone, to be finally captured in a web of saffron-and-orange ribbons.

In *Come Drink with Me* (1966), King Hu already placed a *xia nü* (female warrior) at the center of the fiction. Here he literally saturates the screen with them – both visually and narratively. The *xia nü* is no longer an outsider; she becomes, as in the origins of the genre, the main element of the story.

Bérénice Reynaud

Date 1979

Nationality Hong Kong

Director King Hu

Cast Xu Feng, Sun Yue, Wu Mingcai

Original Title *Kongshan Lingyu*

Why It's Key The Chinese martial-arts film reaches a new aesthetic maturity.

Key Speech **Ray Winstone takes over**
Scum

Ray Winstone is as solid a lump of England as can be found. Londoner, schoolboy boxing champion, ex-skinhead, lifelong supporter of West Ham United Football Club, he brings to every scene in which he appears the possibility of tenderness and the possibility of violence. In *Scum*, Winstone plays the young offender Carlin, suffering in juvenile detention (or Borstal, as it was known in 70s Britain) and resolving to live by William Blake's First Rule for the institutionalized: "I must Create a System, or be enslav'd by another man's...."

Unable to live without molestation under the regime of the inmate Banks (Blundell), the 'daddy' of his wing, Carlin must take over. He must destroy the authority of Banks and instantly establish his own. He achieves this inside two minutes, first by taking out one of Banks's lieutenants (Phil Daniels) with two pool balls in a sock, and then by decisively battering Banks while he is shaving. Winstone is at his finest in these two minutes; the efficiency with which he scoops the pool balls off the table and loads them into a black sock, casually instructing the startled players to "Carry on!"; the suddenness and completeness of his attack. As Banks's lieutenant goes down a known stool pigeon (Burdis) scrambles for the door to alert the staff. "Back, grass!" commands Carlin. His control is total, almost telekinetic: the boy comes back into the room as if reeled on an invisible spool. Carlin then heads upstairs, with a strut so refined in its intimation of brutality that it is almost feminine, to find Banks. Fifteen seconds later, the great line: "I'm the daddy now!"

James Parker

Date 1979

Nationality UK

Director Alan Clarke

Cast Ray Winstone, John Blundell, Mick Ford, Phil Daniels, Ray Burdis

Why It's Key Ray Winstone's knack for expressive violence became a benchmark of British film realism.

Key Scene **Jack Torrance's job interview**
The Shining

Like so much of Stanley Kubrick's work, *The Shining* is essentially about communication: communication between a husband and wife; between the living and the dead; between the present and the past; communication by radio, telephone and several forms of media; and, crucially, that privileged method of communication, the eponymous "shining," which links Hallorann (Scatman Crothers) with Danny (Danny Lloyd). But the film begins with a scene – Jack Torrance (Nicholson) being interviewed by the Overlook Hotel's manager, Stuart Ullman (Nelson) – which reduces communication to the blandest level imaginable. Torrance's conversation with Ullman is conducted in a manner that suggests they are both reading from a script: the interview is nothing more than a formality (Torrance already has the job), its participants required only to maneuver themselves into position like chess pieces in a game whose outcome is already known. Which, once the film's climax has been reached, proves to be exactly what was happening on a much larger scale, with Torrance, manipulated by supernatural forces, enacting a pre-determined role he must continuously repeat for reasons he will never comprehend. This juxtaposition of banal dialogue and cosmic mystery, already familiar from *2001: A Space Odyssey* (1968), connects with Kubrick's interest in the various ways identity is expressed, the two extremes represented in *Lolita* (1961) by Humbert's disciplined role-playing and Quilty's wild improvisations. For Kubrick, identity can be either crudely limited or endlessly expansive – two possibilites that the films, with their frequent emphasis on doubling and doppelgangers, imply may, when seen in the widest of all possible contexts, be merely different sides of the same coin.
Brad Stevens

Date 1980

Nationality UK/USA

Director Stanley Kubrick

Cast Jack Nicholson, Barry Nelson

Why It's Key This scene shows how Stanley Kubrick's films address philosophical questions of identity and communication.

Key Film ***Berlin Alexanderplatz***
The paradox of freedom

Fassbinder reiterated many times that Alfred Döblin's 1929 novel was his crucial formative influence: emotionally, psychologically, intellectually, sexually, artistically; and the 15-½ hour television miniseries he made from it is a monumental creative achievement as well as his testament. It may be challenging to find that the story of Franz Biberkopf (Lamprecht) is a disturbing one of petty criminals and prostitutes, in which men abuse women, sometimes to the point of murder, and are destructive of each other as well, while the world they live in is that of a Germany between the wars that is hurtling toward Nazism. Even so, this is a cinematic space fully humanized, from which one does not want to turn away, so liberatingly truthful and at the same time artful is the director in facing and understanding the world that made him. Fassbinder's interest is more in his ideas about the story than the story itself (which is resolved in only a muted way in the two-hour epilogue), but his command of all aspects of drama – and crucially, melodrama – makes the narrative and all its characters and relationships steadily and powerfully absorbing in their own right. At the same time, the layering-over of a more experimental kind of film, one in which often his own narrating voice runs counter to or in some way interrogates the images, lifts the film to an unaccustomed level of tough-minded, courageous thought. There is tenderness in that voice, its inflections at one with the compassion and poetry with which Fassbinder is prepared to illuminate the darkest corners.
Blake Lucas

Date 1980

Nationality West Germany

Director Rainer Werner Fassbinder

Cast Günter Lamprecht, Hanna Schygulla, Barbara Sukowa, Gottfried John, Elisabeth Trissenaar, Franz Buchreiser, Brigitte Mira, Ivan Desny, Roger Fritz, Barbara Valentin, Claus Holm, Annemarie Düringer

Why It's Key One of the defining artistic figures of his time peaks in a work that joins mastery of classical forms with bracingly modern ideas.

Key Person **Thelma Schoonmaker joins the Scorsese fold** *Raging Bull*

The marriage between directors and actors is as dicey as a mail-order betrothal, but every once in a star-crossed while a director finds an actor who's an effortless medium for their vision, and an actor finds a director who can create a seamless habitat for their soul. It happened for Jimmy Stewart and Frank Capra, it happened for Toshiro Mifune and Akira Kurosawa, and it happened for Robert De Niro and Martin Scorsese. But there's an invisible flying buttress holding together the unassailable architecture of the Scorsese-De Niro collaboration, and that's editor Thelma Schoonmaker. Scorsese had been wooing Schoonmaker to edit his films ever since the two met during a summer class at NYU, but her lack of a union membership hindered their collaboration. 1980's *Raging Bull* was their first Hollywood partnership, and Schoonmaker quickly proved her talent was equal to the job. Her deft cutting revealed the vulnerability and brutality expressed in the athleticism of self-loathing prize fighter Jake La Motta (De Niro), a tormented thug who takes out his masculine insecurities on his blameless wife (Moriarty) and atones for his sins by allowing himself to be battered in the ring – yet another Scorsese character finding purification in bloodshed. The matches pieced together by Schoonmaker are rhythmic, fluid, and exhilarating, a passion play told in 15 rounds, punctuated by the white-hot crackle of flashbulbs and the spray of stigmata. Schoonmaker rightly won an Oscar for her exhilarating work and went on to edit every movie Scorsese made afterwards.
Violet Glaze

Date 1980

Nationality USA

Director Martin Scorsese

Cast Robert De Niro, Cathy Moriarty, Joe Pesci

Why It's Key Scorsese finds his perfect collaborator in the uniquely talented editor Thelma Schoonmaker.

Opposite *Raging Bull*

Key Event *Close Encounters of the Third Kind: The Special Edition*

Three years after *Close Encounters of the Third Kind* (1977) was released to critical acclaim and box-office success, director Steven Spielberg persuaded Columbia to let him rework the film and re-release it as *Close Encounters of the Third Kind: The Special Edition*. The studio gave the go-ahead on the condition that the climax be extended – giving the new version a marketing hook ("Now There Is More"), since the studio felt customers would come back only if they were promised a look inside the alien spaceship. Though he reinstated a few sequences originally dropped and shot new scenes with the principal cast, Spielberg actually trimmed the mid-section of the film, which some critics had condemned as overlong. At 132 minutes, the *Special Edition* runs three minutes shorter than the original. The fact that a slightly altered three-year-old film could be a box-office attraction on a par with a new release paved the way for the "director's cut" industry, notably with alternate versions of Ridley Scott's *Blade Runner* (1982) and James Cameron's *Aliens* (1986), George Lucas's revisions of his original *Star Wars* trilogy with "improved" special effects and other tweaks in the late 1990s, and Francis Ford Coppola's *Apocalypse Now Redux* (2001). Now, thanks to DVD, a theatrical-release film is often the equivalent of a rough cut or a précis, with an ever-increasing multiplicity of slightly variant editions making their way onto the marketplace. (Case in point: in 1998, Spielberg assembled a 137-minute "Collector's Edition" of *Close Encounters*, which is essentially the 1977 theatrical cut augmented by the extra footage used in the 1980 *Special Edition*.) With pictures as old as Orson Welles's *Touch of Evil* (1958) and Sam Peckinpah's *Major Dundee* (1965) appearing on DVD in "director's cut" versions assembled after the deaths of the directors by disciples purportedly following their instructions, any release of any film must be counted as provisional.
Kim Newman

Date 1980

Why It's Key From now on, every version of every film is just provisional.

Key Speech **"What's our vector, Victor?"**
Airplane!

Three pilots are sitting in a cockpit: Captain Clarence Oveur (pronounced "Over"), his co-pilot Roger Murdock, and flight engineer Victor Basta. As they prepare for takeoff they are in radio communication with the airport control tower, and with each other.

Control tower: LA departure frequency 123 point-niner.
Capt. Oveur: Roger.
Roger: Huh?
Victor: Request vector, over.
Capt. Oveur: What?
Control tower: Flight two-zero-niner clear for vector 324.
Roger: We have clearance, Clarence.
Capt. Oveur: Roger, Roger. What's our vector, Victor?
Victor: Tower's radio'd clearance, over.
Capt. Oveur: That's Clarence Oveur. Over.
Victor: Roger.
Control tower: Roger, over.

Roger: Huh?
Capt. Oveur: What?

Nonsense needs no justification, but in the event that any were required I would submit, from the above scene, three things: the bustling, affable seriousness of Peter Graves as Captain Clarence Oveur; the clangingly bad acting of Kareem Abdul-Jabbar as Roger Murdock; and the hearty efficiency of Victor Basta, played by the talented Frank Ashmore.
James Parker

Date 1980

Nationality USA

Director Jim Abrams, David Zucker, Jerry Zucker

Cast Peter Graves, Kareem Abdul-Jabbar, Frank Ashmore

Why It's Key In this '70s comedy behemoth, an empyrean of nonsense is attained that would have flattered Lewis Carroll.

Opposite *Airplane!*

1980–1989

553

Key Scene **The lift**
Dressed To Kill

SPOILER

De Palma caught the bug from *Psycho* (1960): the seeming star of the show is killed off early, so the plot pursues another tangent, some passer-by perhaps… Which is exactly what happens in *Dressed to Kill*, when Kate (Dickinson) is knifed to death in an elevator by an odd-looking blonde (Caine), and Liz (Allen), a hooker who happens to be waiting at the floor where the lift stops, becomes the new heroine. Yet where Hitchcock multiplied plot-threads with a clear, tidy end in sight, De Palma embraces the modern, chaotic absurdism of a narrative shooting off in all directions, as if hallucinating itself. He cherishes outrageous juxtapositions, like the cutting between the sing-song drawl of Liz's voice and the full-on intensity of Pino Donaggio's score as Kate is slashed. There is a wealth of visual and aural invention: the grain of the image in the blown-up reflection of Caine's face in the elevator security mirror; the disquieting flutter of the women's hands in slow motion – until Liz snatches up

the knife, and the film smartly snaps back to normal speed. De Palma mixes up everything: speeds, textures, points-of-view, private guilt (Kate retrieving her wedding ring) and public shame (a rude little girl's insistent stare). Even the film's "ideology" gets a merry salad-toss treatment: what begins as dark moral tale (bad girls will be punished) ends as macabre screwball comedy, with Liz holding the incriminating knife, imploring tenants to believe that she is not the killer.
Adrian Martin

Date 1980

Nationality USA

Director Brian De Palma

Cast Angie Dickinson, Michael Caine, Nancy Allen

Why It's Key De Palma embraces the chaos of a narrative that seems to hallucinate itself.

Key Scene **Alex assaulted by his mother**
Manila by Night

When Virgie (Solis) confronts her son, Alex (Martinez), about his drug taking, Alex denies it, but Virgie doesn't believe him. What follows is a storm of maternal fury, unmatched by any other in an already turbulent film. She slaps him, mauls him, rains blows on his back and head; she throws things – knickknacks, heavy objects, anything and everything detachable and ready at hand. In glorious slow motion, she smashes a drawer on his skull, wood splinters flying like exploded shrapnel. The scene feels like it has gone too long, or gone past any conventional point it was meant to make; suddenly you're reminded of a Buster Keaton comedy where everything is flying around in a tornado, and Keaton is the still, rooted center in the storm. The film has pushed past the point of drama into absurdity, is well on its way past absurdity into appalling comic horror.

Bernal dots his films with odd moments like this that throw you straight out of the story, then somehow bring you boomeranging back, from a different perspective and with added power. We know that Bernal took drugs recreationally, that he had a mortal fear of his mother; Virgie's horrific response seems to be Bernal's nightmare version of what his mother might do to him should she find out about his drug use (or, perhaps, what she has done to him already). More, the scene is a brief but potent encapsulation of Bernal's vision of the middle class – of the chaotic, amoral turmoil that seethes beneath the Filipino bourgeoisie's respectability and, on occasion, breaks through.

Noel Vera

Date 1980

Nationality Philippines

Director Ishmael Bernal

Cast William Martinez, Charito Solis

Original Title *City after Dark*

Why It's Key The image, emblematic of the chaos and corruption in the middle class, is captured by Bernal as visual poetry.

Key Film

Heaven's Gate

A severely flawed yet fascinating would-be masterpiece, this three-hour-and-40-minute Western epic of breathtaking scope and challenging complexity was sorely misunderstood and mercilessly panned by critics who seemed intent on seeing Cimino "get his comeuppance" for his admittedly monumental hubris. Although it was not an easy film to follow, many of the defects, obscurities, and alleged absurdities reviewers were quick to point out became clear and meaningful upon a second viewing (or even an attentive first one). To take only one example, the Harvard prologue, judged "irrelevant" and incomprehensible by most reviewers at the time, actually introduces some of the film's main themes. Unfortunately, no critic bothered to give the film a second chance (there were no press previews until the opening day). The consequences were dire not only for Cimino and his film's career (it hardly had any – United Artists withdrew it after just a few days in one New York theater), but for the studio (which found itself on the verge of bankruptcy and was bought by MGM in 1981) and the future of auteur cinema, as Hollywood studio executives started drastically cutting costs and limiting filmmakers' creative autonomy.

A much shorter, re-edited version of *Heaven's Gate* was released in 1981 and met with very little critical or commercial success. More recently the full version has become available on DVD.

Jean-Pierre Coursodon

Date 1980

Nationality USA

Director Michael Cimino

Cast Kris Kristofferson, Christopher Walken, Isabelle Huppert, John Hurt, Jeff Bridges

Why It's Key The critical and commercial failure of this hugely ambitious production by Cimino changed the course of Hollywood filmmaking in the eighties.

Opposite *Heaven's Gate*

★REAGAN

FOR PRESIDENT
Let's make America great again.

Key Event **Ronald Reagan is elected President of the United States**

In 1980, Ronald Reagan landed his greatest role: playing the leader of the free world. Like no American president before him, this one-time B-actor and TV personality understood the power of media spectacle and mass entertainment. His years in office represented what the subtitle of a Reagan biography calls "the triumph of imagination." No less than a Hollywood production or a theme park (he co-hosted the TV coverage of the opening of Disneyland in 1955), Reagan's America was founded on a shared fantasy.

The Great Communicator was not a great actor, though he made for a servicably stolid leading man in the B movies that launched his Hollywood career. He presided over the Screen Actors Guild and fingered suspected communists during the McCarthy witch hunt before going on to the governorship of California in 1966.

Reagan's was a feel-good, narcotizing regime, and the blockbuster movies of the period (not least those by Steven Spielberg, poet laureate of Reaganland) correspondingly promoted a sentimental optimism and detachment from reality. The presidency itself was a triumph of stage management, a performance that recognized the importance of the big moment and the well-timed line. Many of his famous one-liners ("Where's the rest of me?" "You ain't seen nothing yet," and, post-assassination attempt, "Honey, I forgot to duck") were in fact direct movie quotes.

Hardly a Method actor, he was – to quote *The New Yorker*'s obituary headline – a Method president, who sometimes went so far as to invent vivid backstory, most notoriously claiming to have witnessed the liberation of Nazi concentration camps when he had never left American soil during the war. His immortal quote was a Freudian slip, but it serves as a motto for the post-Reagan world in which politics and show business are forever entangled: "Facts are stupid things."
Dennis Lim

Date November 4, 1980

Why It's Key The Reagan presidency redefined the relationship between entertainment and politics.

Opposite *Heaven's Gate*

1980–1989

557

Key Speech **Alex's monologue about an old mansion** *Bad Timing*

SPOILER

Approximately halfway through *Bad Timing*, Alex Linden (Garfunkel) tells Milena Flaherty (Russell) about an old mansion he remembers living near: "It made me feel good knowing something so beautiful was so close.... At night, as a kid, I would use it to guide me.... One day I had to go to Boston. That was Friday. When I got back on Tuesday, it was gone. Gone. Like *that*." This dialogue defines Alex as someone obsessed with images of lost innocence, which he associates with the certainties of childhood. But it comes across as a self-consciously "written" piece of character psychology: and its "author" is neither director Nicolas Roeg (though there is an obvious connection with Mary-Lou's "trains" monologue in Roeg's *The Man Who Fell to Earth*) nor screenwriter Yale Udoff, but rather Alex Linden himself. As a professional psychoanalyst, Alex is quite capable of reminiscing in a manner specifically calculated to imply that he is a deeply sensitive individual. Yet Milena's response is highly ambiguous: she simply stares at Alex, apparently disturbed by suspicions she is unable to express. For what is most striking about Alex's speech is its total lack of spontaneity, the very quality Milena reveals with every word and gesture: the quality that both attracts and repels Alex, and which he eventually tries to eliminate by reducing Milena to a catatonic state (thus turning her into another "lost" object he can continue to desire). Although *Bad Timing* appears to be concerned with the mystery of femininity, the manner in which Roeg's camera tracks past mirrors in which Alex appears and disappears as he discusses the mansion suggests that masculinity is the real enigma being explored here.
Brad Stevens

Date 1980

Nationality UK

Director Nicolas Roeg

Cast Art Garfunkel, Theresa Russell

Why It's Key This scene shows how dialogue can be used to reveal character in a way that is totally cinematic.

Key Scene **Harold Shand's last ride**
The Long Good Friday

SPOILER

Harold Shand, gangland king of the East End, is being assaulted by powers beyond his ken. Attempting to cement a massive deal for the redevelopment of London's Docklands with a visiting American moneyman, he finds that his top men are being knocked off and his pubs blown up, and he has no idea why. 'Who's having a GO at me?' he snarls, with a harassed, cornered urgency that in another age would signify the avenging presence of the Furies. In fact, the entity that seeks Shand's destruction has another name: The Irish Republican Army.

Francis Monkman's theme tune to *The Long Good Friday*, in the seedy pulse of its synthesizers and the gauche flaring of its saxophones, captures everything about the movie. We hear this music when Bob Hoskins, as Shand, makes his entrance, striding with Caesarian grandeur through an airport, and we hear it when he makes his exit. This latter event comprises the last minute and a half of the film. Shand is in the back seat of his limousine; his attempt to take out the local IRA leadership has failed, his own driver has been abducted, and as the man in the passenger seat (Brosnan) turns round, grins, and trains a gun on him, Shand realises he he is being driven to his death. He hisses; his jaw juts, exposing shining lower incisors. The camera stays on him. Fear, rage, and even a kind of brutal acceptance – as of an animal who knows its time has come – are all contending in his face. He looks close to laughter.

James Parker

Date 1980

Nationality UK

Director John Mackenzie

Cast Bob Hoskins, Pierce Brosnan

Why It's Key In one minute of non-verbal acting, Bob Hoskins is at the height (or the depth) of his powers.

Opposite *The Long Good Friday*

558

Key Scene **A soldier discovers evil**
The Big Red One

The wily old sergeant (Marvin) has been leading his platoon of raw young fighters through the sun-bleached, labyrinthine streets of Europe. Since landing at Normandy, most of the boys have been giving vent to their frustrations, fears, and fantasies under the unrelenting pressure of German shelling and sniping. But in the face of traumatizing bloodshed, cacophonous noise, disorientation, and mounting tension among the band – one boy has a testicle blown off by a mine while another learns that his writing is to be published back home – a cloud of repressive silence seems to have settled over Griff (Hamill), a sweet-looking, utterly silent Midwesterner for whom the battles have seemed displaced, unreal. "Action... without clear purpose" the film seems to suggest war is, for those who are caught in its vortex. Bodies drop, are torn, voices cry out in the darkness, but the evil against which one has set one's purpose is always absent, over the next hill, drifting with the smoke.

The platoon comes to a concentration camp from which the Germans have fled. Griff and the sergeant are stepping cautiously among the still warm ovens, under a blue sun-baked sky. With his rifle, Griff pries open an oven and peers inside. A single German soldier has hidden himself there, among the bones. In close-up we see Griff's face harden, his steel blue eyes go cold with vision. He shoots. He shoots again. He shoots again. He shoots again and again. He shoots again, and again, and again, and again, and again. He keeps shooting. "I think you got him," the sergeant whispers gently, in an ultimate acknowledgment of understanding and humanity.

Murray Pomerance

Date 1980

Nationality USA

Director Samuel Fuller

Cast Lee Marvin, Mark Hamill

Why It's Key It's an important case of cinematic frankness about the Holocaust.

Key Film
Diva

Was there ever a more potent setting of information-age unease than the underground parking garage? A nightmare location going back at least to the 1929 St. Valentine's Day Massacre, the indoor (and later multilevel) parking structure appeared in movies as early as *Scarface* (1932) but really flourished in post-modernity, as films probed the car-park's horrifying silence, its paradoxical combination of limited visibility and panoptic lack of privacy. The parking structure provides quiet menace in *All the President's Men* (1976), Philip K. Dick-style comedy in *Petulia* (1968), suspense in *Telefon* (1977), and absurdist futility in *The Conversation* (1974), among many others.

Back in 1981, *Diva* came encoded with various hopes and delusions – chief among them that Beineix would lead a *nouvelle-Nouvelle vague* of flashy, self-conscious, insouciant, genre-inverting pictures. That proved to be a false promise. Beineix hit the jackpot again with 1986's *Betty Blue* before sinking into obscurity. *Diva* stands up today for qualities unnoticed at the time: the stately pace, strenuous bohemian posturing, and use of familiar movie types (good types though, including Luu's shoplifting pixie and a young Pinon as a hit man known only as The Vicar). In its way, the movie is all parking garages, providing catnip for loft fetishists, freight elevator groupies, and other fans of large enclosed industrial spaces. *Diva* plays both to and against the rules of sixties-seventies parking garage cinema, setting suspense scenes, artfully meandering conversations, and even a car bombing in its parking spaces. While the parking garage lives on as a favorite movie setting, *Diva*'s postmodern reflexivity makes it unlikely any new levels of meaning, or of parking, will be found in it.

Tim Cavanaugh

Date 1981

Nationality France

Director Jean-Jacques Beineix

Cast Frédéric Andréi, Roland Bertin, Wilhelmenia Fernandez, Gérard Darmon, Chantal Deruaz, Thuy An Luu, Dominique Pinon

Why it's Key It sums up underground parking garage paranoia.

Key Scene **Wez and the Golden Youth in medium shot** *Mad Max 2 The Road Warrior*

What a world of trouble Mel Gibson might have saved himself had he let us know from the beginning that he is an artist of the id, a creator transforming his own ugly depths into our beautiful nightmares. The first appearance of Wez (Wells), *The Road Warrior*'s subsidiary villain, is not, of course, directed by Mel himself, but it's no coincidence that the scene overlaps one of Gibson's most important psychic sources: the terror of homosexuality that drove his magnificent performance in *What Women Want* (2000), the standout scene in *Braveheart* (1995) in which the king defenestrates his feckless son's boyfriend, and other gems of Gibsonia.

It's not Wez's bright eyes, thick prison muscle, or cardinal-colored Mohawk. It's his lover, a handsome young man with long bleached hair and a pet's docile manner. The Golden Youth (Brown), led by Wez on a dainty leash, dressed in a skimpy biker-slut outfit, surveys everything with Olympian detachment. The barely verbal Wez communicates mainly by howling; the Golden Youth says nothing at all. His devotion to Wez hints at deep and perverse love. Most unsettlingly of all, he's the only character in the film who seems completely satisfied with his situation. Wez himself is merely a pumped-up movie threat; Wez and the Golden Youth are something more dangerous: an invitation.

Pointedly, Wez's mania only takes full flower after he loses his catamite to a hilariously lethal boomerang. After that he's a killer haunted by lost love, and he achieves a tragic radiance granted to no other characters in the picture. How fortunate that Mel Gibson survived intact this encounter with gay lethality. No wonder he dismisses the Mad Max films as youthful trash.

Tim Cavanaugh

Date 1981

Nationality Australia

Director George Miller

Cast Vernon Wells, Jimmy Brown

Why It's Key Gay bikers are here.

Key Scene **White face/white mask**
Mephisto

Mephisto, based on Klaus Mann's 1936 novel of the same title, concerns a consummate opportunist, Hendrik Höfgen (Brandauer), modelled after the great German theatrical actor Gustav Gründgens. So many adjustments and opportunistic compromises are made by Höfgen in his desire to accommodate his Nazi patrons that by the end of the film, the overarching question becomes: is there an end to the downward trajectory that the protagonist has been following? His moral decline begins when he gives up his leftist ideas and continues with a series of betrayals. Höfgen's acceptance of the leadership of the national theater in Berlin associates him with morally ambiguous figures like Nazi apologist Leni Riefenstahl. Played unforgettably by Brandauer, Höfgen is the epitome of the spineless artist who is ready to compromise everything for the sake of transitory glory.

At the end of *Mephisto*, one of Höfgen's Nazi patrons (Hoppe) takes him, in the middle of the night, to the grandiose Olympic Stadium in Berlin. He puts him in the middle of the field and has him tracked by blinding spotlights. Höfgen makes a few steps in one direction, and then in another, then attempts to shield his eyes, but the shining light follows him around relentlessly. Höfgen soon stops resisting, faces the light, and gazes straight into the camera, his face pale and his eyes fixed: he is a mask, and it is clear that there is no longer a real person behind it.

Dina Iordanova

Date 1981

Nationality Hungary/West Germany/Austria

Director István Szabó

Cast Klaus-Maria Brandauer, Rolf Hoppe

Why It's Key This scene reveals the ultimate extreme of opportunism: the "mask" has taken over the essence.

1980–1989

561

Key Scene **Dr. Jekyll changes into Mr. Hyde**
Dr. Jekyll et les Femmes

Like every other adaptation of Robert Louis Stevenson's *The Strange Case of Dr. Jekyll and Mr. Hyde*, Walerian Borowczyk's *Dr. Jekyll et les Femmes* shows Jekyll turning into Hyde. What makes Borowczyk's version of this scene unusual, though not unique, is that Jekyll and Hyde are played by different actors, respectively Udo Kier and Gérard Zalcberg; what makes Borowczyk's scene absolutely unique is that rather than drinking the formula that brings about his transformation, Jekyll pours it into a bathtub in which he subsequently immerses himself. In the space of a single shot, Jekyll disappears beneath the bath water's surface; approximately 20 seconds later, a figure emerges from the water, and we discover that Hyde/Zalcberg has replaced Jekyll/Kier. How was this done? The camera could have been temporarily stopped while one man was substituted for the other, but the constantly lapping water would have made any cut obvious. The trick is worthy of Méliès: I have no

idea how Borowczyk achieved it, and am quite happy to remain in a state of ignorance. It is precisely our capacity for "innocent" child-like wonder that Borowczyk must reawaken before proceeding to his film's audacious climax, in which Jekyll's fiancée, Fanny Osbourne (Marina Pierro), bathes in the transforming formula and joins Hyde, the two of them casting off all traces of adult repression and retreating to a pre-socialized state in which they lash out at respectable bourgeois society, destroying Vermeer's *Woman in Blue Reading a Letter*, burning Jekyll's books, crucifying a priest, stabbing Fanny's mother, and finally devouring each other in a cannibalistic frenzy, an ending made all the more astonishing by its gleeful tone.

Brad Stevens

Date 1981

Nationality France

Director Walerian Borowczyk

Cast Udo Kier, Gérard Zalcberg

Original Titles *Dr. Jekyll and His Women; The Blood of Doctor Jekyll*

Aka *The Strange Case of Dr. Jekyll and Miss Osbourne*

Why It's Key This scene shows how cinematic special effects can be used to reinforce a radical project.

Key Person **Chow Yun-fat** A haircut, a gun, and a smile *The Story of Woo Viet*

Before John Woo cast Chow Yun-fat in *A Better Tomorrow* (1986), a major Hong Kong director had already brought out the most radiant traits of his persona. In *The Story of Woo Viet*, 26-year old Chow plays a tired killer, who has to kill again, yet retains his honor and dignity. A former South Vietnamese soldier, he ends up in a Hong Kong refugee camp, where he witnesses a murder and disposes of the assailant. Then he tries to emigrate to the U.S. via Manila.

First, Hui shows him with longish hair – in a low-key-cool-cat avatar (revisited by Johnnie To in 1989's *All about Ah-long*). To get a fake passport and pass for Japanese, Chow gets a haircut and a white-tailored suit – voilà! Later, on a mission to kill for a Manila Chinatown boss, he sports stylish sunshades. The main difference between the characters in *The Story of Woo Viet* and *A Better Tomorrow* is that Woo's hero is a man's man, whereas Hui's sensitivity uncovers the sensual romanticism that was to make Chow a

heartthrob of Asia. He charmingly breaks the heart of a social worker (Miao) but falls hard for a girl met by chance in the smugglers' office (Chung). To buy her back from a prostitution ring, he forfeits his chances of going to the U.S. and becomes a hired killer. Hui will return to Chow-the-seducer in 1984's *Love in a Fallen City*, where the star plays a complex playboy. In *The Story of Woo Viet*, she also explores heroic male bonding: moments of friendship with a killing partner (Lo) herald Woo's *The Killer* (1989). A star was born.

Bérénice Reynaud

Date 1981

Nationality Hong Kong

Director Ann Hui

Cast Chow Yun-fat, Cora Miao, Cherie Chung, Lo Lieh

Original Title *Woo yuet dik goo si*

Why It's Key In a taut action thriller, Hong Kong New Wave director Ann Hui reveals Chow Yun-fat's star quality.

Key Scene **"The peasants will revolt"** *Too Early, Too Late*

The first part of this two-part film is set in France. Over shots of countryside, the voice of co-director Huillet reads a text by Friedrich Engels about conditions of French peasant life in the 19th century. This section ends with a lengthy shot of a small concrete structure on the edge of a farm. On the wall that faces the camera, a red graffito shouts mutely, "*Les paysans se révolteront*" ("The peasants will revolt"). After the phrase is a date, "197-": the last digit, maybe "6" or possibly "0," is obscured from our view by a picket of the wire fence that runs across the foreground of the shot.

Engels's text analyzes the failure of radical social movements to reach fruition during the French Revolution: "As the [Paris] Commune with its aspirations to brotherhood came too early, so [Communist precursor François-Noël] Babeuf came too late." Too early, too late: we are somewhere in history, but where? The effacement of that last digit in the graffito is, of course, deliberate, and it may remind

us of the difficulty of being sure when a shot in a film, or any photographic image, was taken – even though the link between a photograph and its time remains absolute. Or it may remind us that at any given moment in late-capitalist history (a period of which Straub and Huillet are among the great cinematic chroniclers), it's both too early – the peasants have yet to revolt – and too late: the drunken boat has sailed.

Chris Fujiwara

Date 1981

Nationality France/Egypt

Directors Jean-Marie Straub, Danièle Huillet

Original Title *Trop tôt, trop tard*

Why It's Key In this shot, Straub and Huillet give us time to think about where we are in history.

Key Scene **Noel shut out of his in-laws' house** *In the Blink of an Eye*

Mila (Charo Santos) and Noel (Ilagan) marry despite the wishes of Mila's father, Mang Dadong (Vic Silayan), who persuades the newlyweds to stay with him. Annoyed by the situation, Noel talks it out with his best friend over a bottle of beer after work. The sequence in question starts with a long shot of Mang Dadong's house, where Noel's friend drops him off by taxi late at night. Cut to the camera peering over the gate at Noel, through strands of barbed wire. Noel looks up; cut to what he sees: the lit window of Mang Dadong's bedroom. Cut back to Noel, waiting. Sudden cut to the long shot of Mang Dadong's house; the bedroom light goes out. Cut back to Noel, the growing anger on his face. He kicks the gate hard; it shivers. He turns and walks away. Cut back to the long shot, as Noel walks out of the camera frame.

With seven brief shots of a man interacting with a bedroom window, de Leon has sketched Noel's precise status in Mila's family, the father's sum feelings regarding him, and Noel's utter impotence at doing anything about any of it. The audience, Filipino or foreign, reacts identically, with uneasy laughter. The film – de Leon's masterpiece, and arguably the most perfect Filipino film ever made – is basically a comedy with the soul of gothic horror, provoking gasps through the sharply observed humor and the tightening sense of claustrophobia that surrounds the characters.
Noel Vera

Date 1981

Nationality Philippines

Director Mike de Leon

Cast Jay Ilagan

Original Title *Kisapmata*

Why It's Key A fine sample of de Leon's understated style of storytelling, this moment is also an eloquent example of the kind of painful humiliation and mental cruelty his characters can inflict upon one another.

Key Person **Yilmaz Güney** *Yol (The Way)*

The most outstanding figure of Turkish cinema, actor-director Yilmaz Güney can be compared to John Cassavetes in that he acted in popular cinema and used his income to fund socially committed directorial projects, in that he pioneered a specific kind of socially critical cinema, and in that he died prematurely. In the 1960s Güney became a key figure of the popular Yesilçam cinema, starring in a wide range of cheaply made action-adventures and becoming Turkey's hottest screen icon. Despite this he was regularly in trouble with the authorities for his leftist beliefs and for the neorealist-type films he directed. He stood for the urban poor and criticized the westernization of Turkey, which led to the abandonment of identity roots and the countryside.

Güney endured a series of prison terms for his commitment to socialist causes, culminating in 1976 in an 18-year sentence for the murder of a judge. Imprisoned did not mean silent in his case, however.

Preparing extended storyboards, he set up arrangements that allowed him to direct films by proxy. His most famous film, the Cannes-winner *Yol*, was made by Serif Gören, who worked under Güney's guidance. In this haunting story of prisoners who go on a short leave to visit with their despondent village families in the Kurdish South of Turkey, Güney addressed the silent plight of his fellow Kurds.

After a daring escape from prison (featured in Erden Kiral's 2005 *Yolda*), Güney ended up exiled in Paris where he worked on his final film, *Duvar* (*The Wall*), exposing the severity of the Turkish teenage-prison system. Güney died from cancer at 47 in 1984.
Dina Iordanova

Date 1982

Nationality Turkey

Director Serif Gören (acting as proxy for Yilmaz Güney)

Cast Tarik Akan, Halil Ergün

Why It's Key He made his best film by sending guidelines out of prison to his proxy.

Key Scene **Dragging the boat over the hill**
Fitzcarraldo

He may have put his talent into his films, but Herzog's real genius is his ability to make other people look even more insane and horrible than he does. Kinski is now enshrined as the scourge of the Wernerverse, largely on the strength of his off-camera antics on the set of this film (the back story being one of many areas where *Fitzcarraldo* exceeds *Apocalypse Now*, to which it is a counterpart). With time, however, it's becoming clear that Kinski's instability was just a minor personality quirk next to Herzog's mesmeric, misanthropic lunacy.

With *Fitzcarraldo* Herzog manages to project his madness onto the personage who inspired the film – the semi-legendary Peruvian rubber baron Carlos Fermín Fitzcarrald López, who reportedly attempted to open up an unexplored trade route by having a boat dismantled and carried over a narrow isthmus between two rivers. This story of delusional striving wasn't quite delusional enough for Herzog, however, who knew that to make a movie about moving a boat over a hill, you

have to drag an *actual* boat, in one piece, over an *actual* hill, endangering the lives and limbs of as many crew members as possible. The act of making the movie was even crazier than the action of the movie.

The result is a bit like the theoretical perfectly detailed map of the world (which of course would be the same size as the world). The sequence is drab, beautiful, laborious, and transcendently idiotic, but it places the film at the opposite end of the continuum from a studio aesthetic in which artificiality is generally the goal. *Fitzcarraldo*'s signature scene is money up on the screen in the truest sense, and it makes no effort to draw metaphoric meaning from the spectacle of a steamboat being dragged through acres of mud. The slow, wheezy ungainliness of the project is the project's attraction, and knowing how they did the trick – or rather, didn't do a trick – makes the very exercises of making and seeing films seem vaguely pointless.
Tim Cavanaugh

Date 1982

Nationality West Germany

Director Werner Herzog

Cast Klaus Kinski, Claudia Cardinale

Why It's Key That's no special effect; it's a real boat they're dragging over a hill.

Opposite *Fitzcarraldo*

Key Scene **Field work**
On Top of the Whale

The polyglot cast of *On Top of the Whale* delivers its lines like they learned them phonetically. They speak six European languages and one made-up for the two surviving members of an indigenous Patagonian tribe (Mora and Navarro). Beginning in a near-future Netherlands Soviet Republic, the film follows an anthropologist (Badin) and his family to a house in Tierra del Fuego (actually Holland), which cinematographer Henri Alekan photographs like a landscape in Murnau. By the end of this "film about survival" it's unclear whether Ruiz means the survival of Indians facing extinction or Europeans who betray their own past.

The Indians believe "one is an even number" and speak a language of 60 words whose meanings vary with inflection and change daily. At first the anthropologist is excited to be studying these men, but his enthusiasm wanes as they repeat the same word to him whether they're shown a tape recorder or

binoculars. Isolated in this lonely spot where the Indians bury mirrors, the family loses itself in "metaphoric images" of Lacanian psychoanalysis becoming a religion.

In this moody, hilarious film's last scene the anthropologist approaches the two Indians in long shot as they back across a gully. They sit opposite each other talking about the future, Ruiz cutting between them in shot-reverse shot. When the anthropologist gets up to leave, Ruiz cuts back to the long shot and we remember how far apart they are. The strange effect of this simple, unexpected cut reverberates as the scene fades and the film ends.
A. S. Hamrah

Date 1982

Nationality Netherlands

Director Raoul Ruiz

Cast Luis Mora, Jean Badin, Ernie Navarro

Original Titles *Het Dak van de Walvis*; *Le Toit de la baleine*

Why It's Key Basic film grammar reverses Western assumptions.

Key Film *Tron*
The first substantially computer-animated film

There are only 15 minutes of purely computer-generated imagery in *Tron*, but what's astounding is that the digital imaging crew produced any footage at all. Forget that it took four monolithic computers two hours to render just a half-second of film. Even worse, the still embryonic software could synthesize only still pictures, not moving images. Animators made a good guess at each object's trajectory and speed, worked out the calculations on reams of graph paper, and then laboriously hand-typed the coordinates for each frame. But all the work was worth it. *Tron* was a gorgeous electronic fantasy, a neon-veined vista of "cyberspace" released only three months after science-fiction author William Gibson coined the term. But after being severely trounced in the public imagination that summer by *E.T. The Extraterrestrial*, *Tron* faded into cult obscurity. Its real legacy, however, can be measured in the technicians, programmers, and animators who were enthralled by the possibilities hinted at in its pixel-gilded majesty. Pixar head John Lasseter indelibly remembered seeing *Tron* test footage while working as an animator at Disney Studios. Thirteen years later, his company's innovative *Toy Story* (1995) earned a Special Achievement Oscar "for the development and inspired application of techniques that have made possible the first feature-length computer-animated film." Unfortunately, that honor wasn't extended to director Steven Lisberger in 1982, as the Academy of Motion Picture Arts and Sciences blocked *Tron* from entering the Best Special Effects category. Using computers to make a movie, they contended, was cheating.
Violet Glaze

Date 1982

Nationality USA

Director Steven Lisberger

Cast Jeff Bridges, Bruce Boxleitner, David Warner, Cindy Morgan

Why It's Key Innovations presented in this movie irrevocably changed the special effects industry.

Opposite *Tron*

Key Speech **Tootsie unsexes herself**
Tootsie

SPOILER

In one of Nicholson Baker's books we find a character who reads eighteenth-century English novels as a matter of "neurological necessity." For a certain period in the early '90s I found myself in a similar position with regard to Sydney Pollack's *Tootsie*. I watched it at least twice a month, on a steady dose. The intervening years have not clarified this for me: certainly I was depressed at the time, but my depression seemed to have little to do with the theme or themes of *Tootsie*. Dustin Hoffman plays Michael Dorsey, a down-at-heel but furiously uppity New York actor looking for work. Despairing of his limited prospects, Dorsey dresses up in women's clothes and succesfully auditions for the role of a female doctor on the popular TV soap *Southwest General*.

Bill Murray plays Dorsey's roommate Jeff, a failed playwright, watching the proceedings with laconic awe. His lines are few, but they anchor the film. Murray at his best can give the impression of a man whose credulity was strained a long time ago and is not expected to recover; in *Tootsie* his slab-like masculinity is a foil to the twittering and fieriness of the rouged, protean Hoffman. At the film's wild denouement, as Dorsey dramatically de-wigs and unmasks himself during a live broadcast of *Southwest General*, and jaws drop around the studio, it is somehow Jeff's reaction in which we are most interested. He is at home, in front of the TV, exhibiting his usual doughy bohemian calm. "That is one nutty hospital," he observes. To himself.
James Parker

Date 1982

Nationality USA

Director Sydney Pollack

Cast Dustin Hoffman, Bill Murray

Why It's Key Bill Murray's downbeat one-liners were never more effective than in this sentimental romp.

Key Film
The Thing

The late seventies and early eighties can be thought of as the era of Rob Bottin, Rick Baker, Chris Walas, and assorted other special makeup effects pioneers who collectively created, and satisfied, a boom market for melting, expanding, contorting, wilting, and generally transforming bodies. We need not puzzle over the complex structures of time-lapse, animal parts, heaters, and latex skin required to do the bubbling-flesh effects in *Alien* (1979), *An American Werewolf In London* (1981), *Raiders of the Lost Ark* (1981), *The Incredible Melting Man* (1977), and countless others.

Requiring the services of 34 special makeup effects staffers, among them luminaries like Bottin and Stan Winston, *The Thing*, an ostensible remake of the Howard Hawks-produced 1951 *The Thing from Another World*, towers above all other entries in the field of bubbling flesh. The snout of a Siberian Husky explodes like a blooming flower; a man's head rolls off his shoulders, sprouts alien tentacles, and walks across a room spider-style; the Thing in its ultimate form is a mass of dogs, men, aliens, bone, and sinew. Late in the film one character gets a load of a particularly bizarro effect and simply mutters, "You've gotta be fuckin' kidding me."

If this were the extent of the achievement, *The Thing* would be a technical curiosity. But Carpenter, working with *Bad News Bears* screenwriter Bill Lancaster, constructs a literary entertainment. The film does full justice to John W. Campbell's classic short story "Who Goes There?", about an alien that reproduces by consuming body, soul, and mind, creating a perfect replica of its victim. This is an original text of science-fiction paranoia and assimilation horror, and Carpenter mines it greedily. The all-male cast fully expresses the director's cockeyed machismo. Although there's one hokey computer-explains-it-all scene, the visual strategies – including a gruesome improvised blood test – are as pleasingly analogue as the special effects.

Tim Cavanaugh

Date 1982

Nationality USA

Director John Carpenter

Cast Kurt Russell, Donald Moffat, T. K. Carter, Wilford Brimley, Keith David

Why It's Key It's the greatest technical and artistic use of the bubbling-flesh effect.

Opposite *The Thing*

1980–1989

569

Key People **Bappi Lahiri and Mithun Chakraborty** *Disco Dancer*

With *Disco Dancer*, composer Bappi Lahiri and actor Mithun Chakraborty, the "Disco Kings," became icons of 1980s India. Bappi's eclectic mix of Western pop, rock, and disco made Western-style dance into a Bollywood attraction, while Mithun became a dancing sensation. Songs from *Disco Dancer* such as "Jimmy Jimmy" and "I Am a Disco Dancer" became cult hits.

The success of the Bappi-Mithun duo owed much to the aspiration in middle-class India for a wider but as yet inaccessible modernity, mastery of the apparatus of which enables the underprivileged dancing hero of 1980s Bollywood films to fight against injustice and corruption. In *Disco Dancer*, the wealthy Mr. Oberoi (Om Shivpuri) falsely accuses young Anil (Mithun) and his mother of theft. Anil lives in rage and humiliation until he defeats Oberoi's son, Sam (Karan Razdan), in a dance competition to become a disco star. The rage, anger, and chutzpah of the Mithun hero are inexpressible without the self-confidence of Bappi's music. Subverting "Western" music as a site of privilege in middle-class India (his adaptations of hits by ABBA or Michael Jackson often led to accusations of plagiarism), Bappi articulated a hybrid modernity – a mix of the pre-colonial old and the postcolonial new – that combines both Indian and Western musical influences. Often relegated to the category of B-grade films produced for distribution outside large metropolitan centres and shunned by critics, the films of the Bappi-Mithun duo were huge hits and set new trends that were later incorporated by the A-grade industry.

Meenu Gaur

Date 1982

Nationality India

Director Babbar Subhash

Cast Mithun Chakraborty, Kim

Why It's Key The phenomenal success of *Disco Dancer* anticipated Bappi Lahiri's dominance of film music in the '80s and propelled Chakraborty to stardom.

Key Scene **The coffin-car**
Who Pays the Piper (aka *Let it Be, Buddies*)

A Mumbai police commissioner has been murdered. Two budding photographers (Naseeruddin Shah and Ravi Vaswani) find his missing body buried under a newly-constructed bridge. The vibrations of the local train cause the coffin to slide away and land on the footpath under the bridge, where the impact causes the body (played by a live actor, Satish Shah) to assume a sitting position and makes the wreath he's holding look like a steering wheel. A drunken construction executive (Om Puri) comes along, finds the body blocking the road, and thinks that the dead man is another drunkard who has taken a vow of silence and that the coffin is a sports car with a punctured tyre. He proceeds to tow the coffin away.

On the walls of the bridge in the background of this hilarious sequence are posters of Indian New Wave films, including Mani Kaul's *Uski Roti* (1969), Kumar Shahani's *Maya Darpan* (1972), and Muzzafar Ali's *Gaman* (1978). By the time *Who Pays the Piper* was made, the Indian New Wave was a dying phenomenon. The posters could represent the wishful thinking that one day the New Wave's posters would adorn every wall in the city. They could also be hard-hitting realism: the New Wave is dead, with its body being towed away by a maverick builder who does not even realise the worth of what he has. Whatever the connotations of this sequence, it remains a rare, laughter-inducing commentary by the New Wave on itself.
Rashmi Doraiswamy

Date 1983

Nationality India

Director Kundan Shah

Cast Naseeruddin Shah, Ravi Vaswani, Satish Shah, Om Puri

Original Title *Jaane Bhi do Yaaron*

Why It's Key It shows a black humor rarely seen in the Indian New Wave Cinema.

Key Scene **Defanging the wolves**
The Eight Diagram Pole Fighter

SPOILER

Lau Kar Leung, himself a martial-arts master with renowned roots, started as Shaw Brothers' (very influential) fight choreographer in the mid-sixties, becoming a preeminent director of kung-fu films the following decade. His works, the most popular being probably the martial-arts training classic *The 36th Chamber of Shaolin* (1978), possess a distinctive blend of action and comedy, a deep spiritual respect for the traditions they both question and honor, and a singular transparency in rendering movements and confrontations. Except for the comedy, this also applies to his dark masterpiece, *The Eight Diagram Pole Fighter*, which ushered in Shaw's last year of cinema production with a blistering critique of the revenge plot so central to the martial-arts genre, as Lau aggressively pushed the studio style to an unusually intense level of operatic stylization. Only two brothers survive a clan feud; one (Alexander Fu Sheng) recedes into madness, the other (Liu) into a Shaolin temple, where the monks are training with wooden wolves. A magisterially handled sequence shows how they are taught to defang them with a dexterous series of movements, while the hero argues for the kill. The finale, a wild, virtuosic ten-minute assault of non-stop martial arts, pivots around a drastic restaging: The monks' method effectively causes a horrifying sputtering of blood and teeth; the brother's succesful quest for vengeance effects only a sense of futility. In the process he has become an eternal wanderer and outcast, like Ethan Edwards in *The Searchers* (1956): All that remains for him is to turn his back and walk away.
Christoph Huber

Date 1983

Nationality Hong Kong

Director Lau Kar Leung

Cast Gordon Liu

Original Title *Wu lang ba gua gun*

Why it's Key It's the pivotal moment in the most intensely stylized film of Lau Kar Leung, master of martial arts and their filmic representation.

Key Scene **The introduction to Paul Snider's apartment** *Star 80*

Like Nicolas Roeg's *Bad Timing* (1980), Bob Fosse's *Star 80* appears to be concerned with definitions of femininity but is actually an investigation into masculinity. For all its emphasis on women as objects for the male gaze, the body most frequently on display here is that of Paul Snider (Roberts). Snider expresses his maleness by demonstrating the ability to control Dorothy Stratten (Mariel Hemingway), an ability meaningless unless publicly acknowledged by other men, and it is the underlying homoeroticism of Snider's project that causes him to be rejected by "successful" males (notably Hugh Hefner) unwilling to confront those impulses upon whose repression *Playboy*'s "world within a world" was built. One key early shot begins by focusing on a portrait of Telly Savalas (an actor Snider claims to be on friendly terms with) smoking a cigarette and striking a stereotypically "cool" pose. Fosse's camera pans away from this portrait, past the pictures of nude women, an expensive car, and the

Playboy mansion that decorate Snider's wall, and finally discovers Snider working out with weights, shaping his own body much as he will later shape Stratten's. Snider subsequently examines his torso in a mirror before introducing himself to his own reflection, rehearsing that calculated charm he intends to use during social encounters. This sequence both establishes the masculine ideal Snider aspires towards and suggests the sheer artificiality of his relationship with it: he could almost be an actor preparing for a part, creating a "character" by reproducing all those external details of attitude and behaviour vital to a believable performance. This neglected masterpiece subjects the ways in which our culture defines identity and gender to the most scathing critique imaginable.
Brad Stevens

Date 1983

Nationality USA

Director Bob Fosse

Cast Eric Roberts

Why It's Key This moment reveals the artificiality of masculinity as defined by our culture.

Key Scene **Rupert arrives for the weekend** *The King of Comedy*

SPOILER

Pretending he's scheduled a working weekend, Rupert Pupkin (De Niro), an amateur comic desperate for fame, takes Rita (Abbott), a girl he knew in high school, to the home of Jerry Langford (Lewis). The nighttime talk-show host is Rupert's idol; Rupert is his stalker. Langford has definitely not invited him over.

Rupert's hostile disregard for other people pours out in this scene, aggravated by joking and wheedling. His refusal to acknowledge the gap between his own life and what he knows from TV humiliates Rita, infuriates Langford, and unnerves Langford's butler, Jonno (Chan). Rupert makes it worse by using Rita as a shield. When she insists they leave, he begs Langford to correct her: "She's a girl who works in a bar. Tell her she's wrong, Jerry, please."

Langford's patience reaches its limit when Rupert admits he's made a mistake. "*So did Hitler!*" Langford yells back, golf club in hand. Rupert, flinchy and petulant, rears back, making even more of a spectacle

of himself. "I'm gonna be 50 times more famous than you!" he yells at Langford, confusing talent with fame.

There's something epic in the confrontation between De Niro and Lewis. The modern sculptures it takes place around lend it a Greek quality. Langford, dressed in shorts and sneakers, is stoic and regal. Rupert, with his little mustache and two-toned shoes, is a jester heralding a new regime of shamelessness. Rita's peach chiffon dress and Jonno's white coat further isolate Rupert in this living room where there's no TV.
A. S. Hamrah

Date 1983

Nationality USA

Director Martin Scorsese

Cast Robert De Niro, Jerry Lewis, Diahnne Abbott, Kim Chan

Why It's Key Hunger for fame becomes invasion of privacy in Scorsese's dark satire.

Key Scene **Andrei's mystical walk**
Nostalghia

SPOILER

Andrei (Yankovsky) is a Soviet poet visiting Italy to research the life of an 18th-century serf who traveled to Italy for musical studies, then returned to Russia and committed suicide. Like that composer, and perhaps like the filmmaker who shares his own first name, Andrei is caught in various binds – between East and West, loyalty to the past and hopes for the future, conscious logic and subconscious intuition. Beset by sadness, memory, and desire, he seems more attuned to his inner landscape than to the countryside he's moving through.

Yet he's fascinated when he meets Domenico (Erland Josephson), a peculiar old character who once incarcerated his family for seven years, thinking – with a hubris he now sees as ridiculous – that he could shield them from a coming apocalypse. Domenico dies in an act of purgative sacrifice, and Andrei decides to fulfill an odd request the old man made – that he walk the length of a medieval pool, once thought to have healing powers, with a lighted candle. Andrei traverses the old stone structure, now drained and coated with mud, shielding a candle's feeble flame with his hands and coat. It takes three tries to reach the end, and each time the camera ventures closer to him; when he finally succeeds, an off-screen sound suggests that the effort has fatally strained his weak heart. Shot in a single take, Andrei's walk is among the most suspenseful scenes ever filmed, and one of the most sublime efforts to bridge the cinematic gap between physical action and metaphysical vision.

David Sterritt

Date 1983

Nationality Italy/USSR

Director Andrei Tarkovsky

Cast Oleg Yankovsky

Why It's Key A simple walk through a moldy old structure, presented as a single shot, blurs the boundaries between fiction and reality to riveting effect.

Key Film *Zelig*
Insertions into history

Thanks to innovative optical technology expressly designed for *Zelig* by Joel Hynek and his associates, filmmakers could for the first time insert actors seamlessly into existing historical footage. This breakthrough enabled Allen's proto-mockumentary to form a bridge between the invented newsreel of Orson Welles's *Citizen Kane* (1941) and the blurring of fact and fiction in Robert Zemeckis's *Forrest Gump* (1994). Advancing his conceit of a man so desperate to assimilate that he assumes the characteristics, physical appearance, and even racial features of others, Woody Allen mats himself (playing Zelig) into archival film: this man without qualities turns up alongside such Jazz Age and Great Depression luminaries as Scott Fitzgerald, Al Capone, Babe Ruth, and Hitler. Allen's premise makes a compelling metaphor for depersonalization in the face of America's societal drive to consensus, while also addressing the culture of celebrity, a theme Allen would pursue from *Stardust Memories* (1980) to *Deconstructing Harry* (1997). With spoof op-ed cartoons and commissioned songs, as well as commentary from intellectuals like Susan Sontag and Saul Bellow, not to mention the cultural cachet of a British-accented narrator, Allen applies a cinematic sophistication lacking in later documentary lampoons, including Rob Reiner's *This Is Spinal Tap* (1984), Larry Charles's *Borat* (2006), or even Allen's own *Sweet and Lowdown* (1999). For his part, Hynek continued to advance technological special effects by placing actors within paintings in Vincent Ward's *What Dreams May Come* (1998) and crafting the widely influential "bullet time" sequences in Andy and Larry Wachowski's *The Matrix* (1999).

Robert Keser

Date 1983

Nationality USA

Director Woody Allen

Cast Woody Allen, Mia Farrow

Why It's Key A new technology stimulated the development of the mockumentary.

Opposite *Zelig*

Key Event The publication of Shigehiko Hasumi's *Director Yasujiro Ozu*

It is rare for a critical study of a film director to have a significant influence on not only the way movies are discussed, but also how they are made. This was the case with *Director Yasujiro Ozu*, a 1983 work penned by Shigehiko Hasumi, a scholar of French literature at the University of Tokyo who devoted much of his writing to film. In the book he countered conceptions of Ozu as either a minimalist or the "most Japanese" of directors by returning to Ozu's basis in cinema, arguing that anything Japanese was less a reflection of Japan than a product of film and Ozu's unique manipulation of motifs. Ozu, he asserted, did not reduce cinematic devices to a minimum, but rather remained true to those devices that acknowledged the limits of the medium, his peculiar eyeline (mis)matches, for instance, recognizing cinema's inability to show two sets of eyes looking at each other in one shot. Hasumi thus distanced Ozu from tricks like montage that attempted to fictionally transcend such limitations. These views of Ozu and of cinema came to fundamentally shape film criticism of the 1980s and 1990s, and such filmmakers as Masayuki Suo and Naoto Takenaka were inspired to emulate Hasumi's version of Ozu. Many post-eighties directors, such as Suo, Kiyoshi Kurosawa, Shinji Aoyama, Makoto Shinozaki, Akihiko Shiota, and Kunitoshi Manda were students of Hasumi when he taught at Rikkyo University, and their films still evince the influence of his Ozu – even when utilizing long takes.

Aaron Gerow

Date 1983

Why It's Key This is arguably the book that has most influenced Japanese cinema.

Key Scene Max Renn absorbed by the television *Videodrome*

Max Renn (Woods) likes weird. As president of a bottom-feeder sleaze cable station, he seeks out kinky, revolting, and bizarre video for a living. But ever since he discovered the scrambled signal of an S&M snuff broadcast called "Videodrome," things have gotten too weird even for him. "Your reality is already half video hallucination," warns media prophet Brian O'Blivion (Creley) in a videotaped message. "If you're not careful, it will become total hallucination. You'll have to learn to live in a very strange new world." Max's television set begins to respirate, panting "Come to me" through the luxurious pout of Nicki Brand (Harry). Soon, in an indelibly freaky visualization of TV as the "great glass tit," Max succumbs to the pulsating console's siren call and buries his face in the soft and throbbing screen. Director David Cronenberg's oeuvre hovers around the primal horror of our body's revolt against us, but this time the revolution has already taken place. Our video-augmented eyes and ears have traveled the globe or – as the moon landing poster in Max's apartment reminds us – into the universe. Media, just as McLuhan predicted, has saturated our being so completely there's no line between what we've lived and what we've screened. When Max fulfills the self-immolating wish of every kid who was warned not to sit so close to the TV, his onanistic merging with the moving image hits uncomfortably close to the bone for every film fanatic who's gladly given over their brain to cinematic hallucinations.

Violet Glaze

Date 1983

Nationality Canada/USA

Director David Cronenberg

Cast James Woods, Debbie Harry, Jack Creley

Why It's Key Cronenberg disquietingly depicts our uneasy symbiosis with the moving image.

Opposite *Videodrome*

Key Person **Maurice Pialat** Suzanne's missing dimple *A nos amours* (*To Our Loves*)

Suzanne (Bonnaire) is in love with her schoolmate Luc but loses him when she inexplicably gives her virginity to a summer-camp one-night stand. The trauma launches Suzanne on a turbulent adolescence: she develops a taste for rebellion and promiscuity that alienates her from her disintegrating family, who respond with ineffectual physical violence. Gradually we understand that Suzanne may not be capable of happiness: "It's as if my heart is dry," she tells a lover. Director Maurice Pialat throws away important chunks of Suzanne's life between scenes, so that her diverse moods and actions jostle together in a continuous present tense without conventional dramatic development. But Pialat makes time stop for one scene that becomes the emotional center of the film: Suzanne's candid 1 a.m. chat with her beloved father (Pialat), largely shot in over-the-shoulder extreme closeups. Having struck Suzanne in anger that evening, the father seems on his way to a rueful acceptance of

her rampaging sex life; he in turn obliges Suzanne to accept that he will leave his family soon, an event from which Suzanne will never completely recover. Pialat ends the scene by providing documentation for the image before our eyes: "You have only one now. You used to have two dimples," says the father to his embarrassed, smiling daughter. Bonnaire as well as Suzanne has only one dimple, and the observation comes from Bonnaire's director as well as Suzanne's father. As always, Pialat distrusts fiction, and therefore tricks reality into making an appearance before his camera.

Dan Sallitt

Date 1983

Nationality France

Director Maurice Pialat

Cast Sandrine Bonnaire, Maurice Pialat

Why It's Key It's not only the centerpiece of Pialat's greatest film, but it also typifies the fusion of fiction and personal reportage at the heart of Pialat's style.

Key Scene **The kiss of innocence** *Merry Christmas, Mr. Lawrence*

We are in a torrid, shadowy Japanese prison camp in World War II, where peaceable long-time prisoner Lawrence (Conti) has learned to speak Japanese and come to appreciate the Japanese culture. The commandant is Yonoi (Sakamoto), young, effete, highly educated, meditative, rigidly fey. Into this steamy and overgrown scene of confinement comes the poetic South African Jack Celliers (Bowie), with shocking red hair, misty eyes, a taste of the otherworldly lingering about him. He is a rebel, to be sure, the sort who gallivants into the jungle to collect pink orchids, and has no patience for the charming Lawrence or respect for the uptight, yet somehow vulnerable Yonoi. Yonoi has been punishing his prisoners, especially the sick ones, and one hot day insists they line up in the parade ground under the scorching sun. Celliers breaks rank, calmly marches up to him as Yonoi grasps the hilt of his long shiny sword. A plantation hat covering his flaming hair, Celliers

leans forward, ever so gently, and makes to whisper something in the commandant's ear.

We see the lips pressing near Yonoi's smooth neck in a close shot which is slightly slowed down. Is he kissing Yonoi? The commandant is as hard as stone for a moment, a cabinet locked within a cabinet, and then he explodes. Celliers, stockaded, is finally put to death by being buried up to his neck in sand. By blue moonlight, Yonoi comes near the end to clip a handful of the hair, which now looks as white as snow: passion married to form. This is an avatar of the cinematic rendition of homoerotic love in wartime.

Murray Pomerance

Date 1983

Nationality UK/Japan

Director Nagisa Oshima

Cast Tom Conti, Ryuichi Sakamoto, David Bowie

Original Title *Senjou no merii kurisumasu*

Why It's Key It's an unique combination of militarism, masculinity, eros, and beauty.

Key Scene **Train commuters dream the ultimate film** *Sans Soleil*

Chris Marker's fictional documentary combines globe-trotting images (purportedly the footage of a nomadic cinematographer) with a digressive torrent of words (the cameraman's letters, read aloud by the female recipient). A testament to the invigorating properties of alienation, the film roams from Iceland to Guinea-Bissau to San Francisco but mostly lingers in and around Tokyo, which sparks Marker's richest musings on the nature of memory and the recorded image.

At one point the Marker alter-ego reveals that his dreams are increasingly set in the subterranean department stores of Tokyo. He wonders if these dreams are fragments from "a giant collective dream of which the entire city may be the projection." The underground labyrinth leads to train stations, prompting the remark that trains act as repositories for the dreams of its dozing passengers, making "a single film of them – the ultimate film."

We see a stream of commuters passing through turnstiles, handing in tickets for this "ultimate film." Then the show begins. In a long, wordless passage, set to a burbling Moog-synthesizer score, Marker shows us commuters gradually lulled to sleep and guesses at the content of their "dreams," cutting in snatches of sci-fi, horror, and softcore TV detritus. The reverie continues until one woman blinks awake. Outside the train, eyes on a billboard look back at her.

Beautifully shot and edited, it's the most haunting sequence in the film. In a few endlessly suggestive minutes, Marker evokes the ambiguous potency of images, the mysterious essence of dreams, and the anonymous community common to both urban life and movie watching.
Dennis Lim

Date 1983

Nationality France

Director Chris Marker

Why It's Key The associative poetry of Chris Marker's montage-driven filmmaking is at its most potent in this haunting, wordless passage.

1980–1989

577

Key Film **"Sword gods" become rays of light** *Zu: Warriors from the Magic Mountain*

Tsui Hark directed *Zu* for Golden Harvest, which supplied him with unprecedented means of production to adapt the fantastic world of martial-arts novelist Huanzhu Louzhu via special effects never used in Hong Kong before. He hired *Star Wars* technicians Robert Blalack and Peter Kuran, along with Tama Takahashi, matte photographer on *Blade Runner*. For *Zu*, they mobilized blue screens, models, optical effects, matte painting, stop motion, and 1,500 shots of computer-generated effects. Tsui combined imported technology with the talents of his local team: martial arts directors Yuen Biao and Corey Yuen. Wires (used for the first time in 1966 for *The Jade Bow*) were thoroughly revamped, as Tsui wanted the fighters to "bounce up and down or spin around" rather than flying in a straight line – which he achieved in one-take shots combining stop motion and wire work through computer. On the other hand, he developed a rapid editing style, rather than shooting fight scenes in long takes.

Zu plunges into the mythology of the "sword gods" (*jian xia*) who will only be able to defeat demons once they become united. To convey his mystic conception of the swords (*jian*), Tsui designed them not as actual objects but as "computer-generated powers" – using a special program, Network Shader. The ever-changing shape of the monster Insomnia was brought to life through RenderMan program. The results are dazzling, revealing the full magic of Tsui's golden touch and the things that made him tick: sword, sorcery, modern technology, ancient mysticism, a passion for Chinese culture.
Bérénice Reynaud

Date 1983

Nationality Hong Kong

Director Tsui Hark

Cast Adam Cheng, Brigitte Lin, Damian Lau, Yuen Biao, Moon Lee, Sammo Hung, Mang Hoi

Original Title *Suk san: Sun Suk san geen hap*

Why It's Key *Star Wars* technicians meet Hong Kong wire masters to create an exhilarating new form of martial-arts film.

Key Scene **The final massacre**
Scarface

In *Scarface*, De Palma takes to a melodramatic, even operatic, extreme a classic theme of gangster cinema: the hero's obsession with territorial control, and the inexorable loss of this power. Tony Montana (Al Pacino), Cuban refugee, dreams of absolute command: over his own body, over the hearts and minds of those close to him, and over the turf of his criminal empire – this is his American Dream, after all. But, at the end of his extravagant rise and fall, after snorting a mountain of cocaine, he cannot even see, on his own security cameras, those who come to kill him. The big action finale in *Scarface* is outrageously hyperbolic: dozens of snipers scurry in like insects, pumping Tony full of bullets that he seems able to supernaturally withstand – at least long enough to utter his oft-quoted line, "Say hello to my little friend!" This is the gangster's fantasy of invincibility, but it won't save Tony from being blown to pieces, ultimately, by a dark Angel of Death at his back, where his panoptic vision no longer extends.

Scarface was decried by many on its initial release as a vulgar, nasty, politically insensitive work. Indeed: which is why it is among the great movies of the '80s. More than any subsequent disaster film, De Palma's epic gives us the subversive thrill of seeing a social microcosm explode into a thousand fragments – with, all the while, a blimp flying above, heralding a bitterly mocking slogan in neon: "The World Is Yours."

Adrian Martin

Date 1983

Nationality USA

Director Brian De Palma

Cast Al Pacino

Why It's Key This legendary action set piece caps one of the great movies of the '80s with a subversive thrill.

Key Scene **The final shot**
L'Enfant secret (*The Secret Child*)

In his *The Time-Image*, philosopher Gilles Deleuze describes the final, virtuosic sequence-shot in *L'Enfant secret*: "We see the café window, the man with his back turned, and, in the window, the image of the woman also from the back crossing the street and going to meet the [drug] dealer." Garrel commented respectfully but matter-of-factly on this analysis: "Objectively the reason for this was the poverty of resources: I had to film through a window to avoid yet more camera noise," adding, "always, when I shoot, I'm solely preoccupied with technical problems." He is too modest: this is among cinema's most shattering endings, its fusion of emotional intensity with formal rigor total. It is a scene of utter betrayal: Elli (Wiazemsky) has been found out as a hopeless addict, and rejects the "lecture" offered compassionately by her lover Jean-Baptiste (de Maublanc); she collapses onto his hand, kissing it sweetly but desperately, as he strokes her hair, obsessively, in brutal silence. A perfect impasse. Finally, the lights go up; there are no end credits, not even a black screen. This film, which was scraped together bit by bit, which spent years in the lab before Garrel could afford to rescue it, bears every mark of its difficult passage into the world, and reflects the scars of its maker's personal life (an addiction shared with singer Nico, electro-shock therapy). It is a painfully fragile film – one in which we feel the cinema being born, and even dying in this final scene.

Adrian Martin

Date 1983

Nationality France

Director Philippe Garrel

Cast Anne Wiazemsky, Henri de Maublanc

Why It's Key It's one of the most shattering endings in cinema.

Key Event
The UK Video Recordings Act

The explosive growth of home video in the early 1980s took place in the United Kingdom in a state of non-regulation, and movies that would never have been passed for theatrical release by the British Board of Film Censors were available to rent on every high street. The press, eager to indulge in a moral frenzy while going into salacious detail, ran campaigns about the obscenities and horrors to which British children – let alone the majority of adult renters – were being exposed, and made famous films like *SS Experiment Camp* (1976), *I Spit On Your Grave* (1978), *The Driller Killer* (1979), *Cannibal Holocaust* (1979), and *The Evil Dead* (1983). The Department of Public Prosecutions issued a list of "video nasties" as a guideline to the video-rental-shop proprietor who wished to avoid prosecution under obscenity laws. This satisfied no one, since a few especially gross titles (*Mark of the Devil* [1970]) failed to make the list while other very mild items (*Frozen Scream* [1975]) somehow qualified.

Furthermore, a simple list of titles led inevitably to mistakes – Tobe Hooper's *Death Trap* (1976) and Sidney Lumet's *Deathtrap* (1982) are easy to get mixed up – and was in constant flux, as private or public prosecutions under the Obscene Publications Act often failed to secure the desired outcome. The eventual blanket solution was the Video Recordings Act, which simply made all previous video releases illegal – whether of Italian zombie cannibal pictures or children's cartoons – and entrusted the BBFC with the task of rating a backlog of many thousands of video releases as suitable for home viewing, on the tacit assumption that the nasties would be refused a certificate. A trade in bootlegged or formerly legal tapes sprang up, with some prized items fetching enormous sums. Two decades on, almost all the so-called "video nasties" are legally available uncut on DVD in the UK.
Kim Newman

Date 1984

Why It's Key Britain had its first taste of state-imposed film censorship (the BBFC was previously an industry-sanctioned body), and film fans were deprived of a flood of hard-to-see material.

Key Scene **Embrace in a taxi**
Love Streams

SPOILER

It is impossible to cleanly segment a Cassavetes film, especially *Love Streams*: incidents overlap and blur, characters ceaselessly move indoors, outdoors, into cars, off planes; it is a film of open doorways through which people (and animals) pour in every direction. Nonetheless, a slice of three shots for the memory: Robert (Cassavetes) walks out his front door and approaches two cabs that have mysteriously arrived in his driveway, with the intention of sending them away. The next shot sets up a "reveal": a driver tells Robert, "I have a lady in the cab," and the camera shifts around to show not her but Robert's double take at the taxi door. Cut to Sarah (Rowlands) inside; "Paris," she says, gesturing to her many shopping bags. Then Robert *dives* in, and if ever emotion compelled motion (one definition of cinema), it's in this zoom that follows Robert's ungainly arc into the most beautiful, most real embrace in all cinema. Cassavetes the director gives this moment its expansive time; but, soon enough,

there's an off-screen voice and a pan – nothing goes uninterrupted in this film – and there we see, at the cab's front window, Robert's distraught son, Albie (Jakob Shaw), mumbling "Dad…" Later he will ask his father, accusingly: "Who was that? Do you love her? Do you kiss her?", and twice Robert will sternly reply: "Not the way *you* mean." But he won't bother explaining – as the film itself also scarcely bothers to do – that Sarah is Robert's beloved sister.
Adrian Martin

Date 1984

Nationality USA

Director John Cassavetes

Cast Cassavetes, Gena Rowlands

Why It's Key It's the most beautiful greeting in cinema.

Key Scene **Lake Erie**
Stranger Than Paradise

Jarmusch's mournful examination of emptiness renews a longing for emptiness in a world stuffed with crap. *Stranger Than Paradise* captures what in retrospect turned out to be a last moment of unbranded American reality. It was the end of the non-branded American film, too, and arrived just before Sundance-ification engulfed non-studio filmmaking in the USA. Jarmusch looked at the world and noticed there was nothing instead of something. Today we wonder why there's everything instead of nothing.

The Lake Erie scene comes near the end of the film's second third. The shady hipsters Willie (Lurie) and Eddie (Edson) leave New York to visit Willie's teenage cousin Eva (Balint) in dead-of-winter Cleveland. When Eva, newly arrived from Hungary, told Eddie back in New York she'd come to America to move there, he assured her she'd love Cleveland, a beautiful city with a big beautiful lake. "Have you been there?" she asked. "No," he answered.

The film's black-and-white Cleveland is a dead-end America of train tracks and old-man bars, the hot-dog stand where Eva works, the interior of a movie theater showing a kung-fu flick to practically no one, not much different from the trio's New York. Eva takes Willie and Eddie to see the big lake. The three of them stand there with their backs to the camera. It holds on these black figures shivering in hats and coats, whipped by the snow and wind. The lake is a white void, a blank, the horizon erased. "It's not always frozen," says Eva.

A. S. Hamrah

Date 1984

Nationality USA

Director Jim Jarmusch

Cast John Lurie, Eszter Balint, Richard Edson

Why It's Key It was lonely, not indie.

Opposite *Stranger Than Paradise*

Key Person **Harry Dean Stanton**
Always intense *Repo Man*

In *Repo Man* Harry Dean Stanton, existential journeyman of marginal movies, became a father figure for the deadbeat-dad generation, a mentor for people who hated teachers and bosses. We meet his character, Bud, a wiry man in a brown suit driving a blue Impala through a "bad area," conning an aimless punk, Otto (Estevez), into helping him repossess a car.

Stanton's battered soul and haggard face found their verbal equivalent in the cracked speeches Cox wrote for Bud. "Not many people got a code to live by anymore," Bud tells Otto. They speed through the L.A. River while Bud explicates from the driver's seat. "Ordinary fuckin' people. I hate 'em. An ordinary person spends his life avoiding tense situations. A repo man spends his life getting *into* tense situations." As Bud frays, his sentiments devolve: "If there was just some way to find out how much the motherfuckers owe and make them pay." Stanton plays against Cox's sarcasm, making Bud affecting

when Otto irks him: "Not happy in your job? I feel like we're not *communicating* anymore."

Desperate, Bud violates his code. Unceremoniously shot by cops, he asks for a cigarette, dying amid great confusion next to an irradiated Chevy Malibu, the film's grail. Otto gets into the car with another denizen of the repo yard and takes off. We recall Bud's words from an earlier speech: "All these people, man, they all have one person in each car. The city wants us to carpool. Nobody gives a shit."

A. S. Hamrah

Date 1984

Nationality USA

Director Alex Cox

Cast Harry Dean Stanton, Emilio Estevez

Why It's Key After acting for thirty years, Stanton finally got his due.

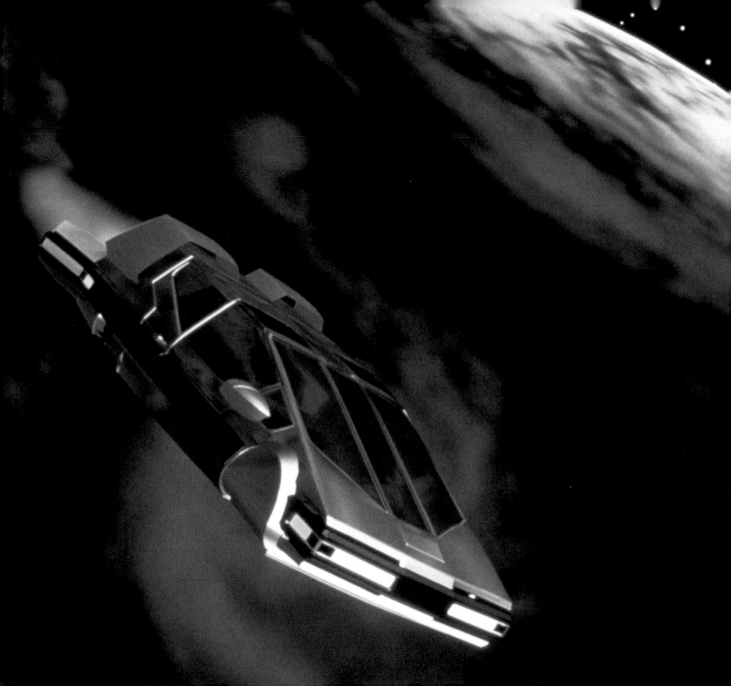

Key Event **The rebirth of Chinese cinema with *Yellow Earth***

Spring 1939, a Northern province of China. A soldier (Wang) who is collecting folk songs arrives at a desperately poor village, where he moves into the cave-like home of a family whose 13-year-old daughter (Xue) goes to the Yellow River each day and yearns for a new life. *Yellow Earth*'s opening sequence alone created a unique visual experience. Shot with very long lenses by Zhang Yimou and influenced by Chinese scroll painting from the early 20th century, it captures the timelessness of the mountain landscape, the luminosity of the river, the smallness of the walking soldier. The horizon is often at the very top or very bottom of the frame. The daughter's song – "suffering is forever, sweetness is short-lived" – expresses her isolation and that of the whole nation. Locked in a Confucian world of traditional family values, she is amazed, for example, when the soldier does his own sewing. Seeing him do so makes her believe that, after an eternity of stasis, Communism might bring change

and freedom. History records that it delivered the former but not the latter, which makes her hope desperately sad, but what was thrilling about *Yellow Earth* was its refusal to indulge in any certainties – Confucian or Maoist. Instead, its unforced melancholy and its interest in absence (we do not see the mother or the girl's eventual wedding) give it a rare delicacy, almost a Buddhist-meditative quality. After the barrenness of the Cultural Revolution, Chinese cinema was remarkable again. Cinematographer Zhang would go on to become one of the greatest pictorialists in movie history.

Mark Cousins

Date 1984

Nationality China

Director Chen Kaige

Cast Wang Xueqi, Xue Bai

Original Title *Huang tu di*

Why It's Key This film signaled the return of Chinese cinema.

Key Film
The Last Starfighter

The invincible lousiness of this Reagan-era space opera has succeeded in preventing *The Last Starfighter* from getting its due as a genuine movie breakthrough: It is the first film to do virtually all its effects, except makeup and explosions, on a computer. A fractured Walter Mitty plot has never-popular star Lance Guest getting recruited by a group of galactic good guys for a sub-*Star Wars* battle in fighter spacecraft. Robert Preston rounds out both his life and career with a rehash of his *Music Man* huckster character.

None of which mattered back in 1984, when the special effects – courtesy of a Cray X-MP computer – provided a chilling, exhilarating glimpse of the future. This milestone is almost impossible to recollect now, when the movie's effects look more primitive than what's available in a cheap video game. But the level of detail Castle's team managed to pull off – a decent illusion of depth, shadows on the hulls of spaceships,

and so on – clearly signaled the eclipse of model-based movie magic.

Like *The Last Starfighter* itself, the CG universe must be viewed with very mixed feelings. More than two decades into the era of digital effects, Hollywood has yet to learn that CG is an essentially charmless tool, capable of doing anything except imparting any style or personality to an uninspired premise. Still, the range of expression that was once tied to a laborious industrial production model is now essentially limitless. It's oddly fitting that this forgotten picture provided the first hint of what was coming.

Tim Cavanaugh

Date 1984

Nationality USA

Director Nick Castle

Cast Lance Guest, Robert Preston, Dan O'Herlihy, Barbara Bosson, Marc Alaimo

Why It's Key It was the proof-of-concept for computer graphic effects.

Opposite *The Last Starfighter*

Key Scene **Opium smile**
Once upon a Time in America

The final shot of Sergio Leone's final film has David "Noodles" Aaronson (De Niro) lying on a cot in an opium den, face upside-down on screen. After nearly four hours in which the uptight Noodles has barely cracked a smile, he grins broadly. This takes place in the early 1930s, just before the scenes which opened the picture; in the context of the narrative, Noodles has just betrayed his best friends to the police – ostensibly for their own good, but actually leading to their deaths – and is sought by killers who intend to murder him. So why is he smiling? Has the drug allowed him to be overwhelmed by the childhood memories that take up the first third of the film? Or are all the scenes which take place in 1968, where Max (James Woods) is alive and the real architect of their downfall, merely a guilty man's wish-fulfilment dream? Is Noodles relieved to be free of his controlling, dangerous friend, or does he really know that the burned corpse after the shoot-out isn't Max? Or is Noodles, like us, simply awed and delighted by the cinematic mastery of the whole endeavour?

Kim Newman

Date 1984

Nationality USA

Director Sergio Leone

Cast Robert De Niro

Why It's Key We'll *never* know what he's really thinking.

Opposite *Once Upon a Time in America*

584

Key Scene **The red slipper in the yellow landscape** *Yellow Earth*

The soldier (Wang) advances, alone, in a deserted landscape; the yellow earth of the title is a vast expanse of aridity that almost fills out the entire screen. Until then, the post-1949 Chinese earth was a blank page on which the heroic deeds of the Communist Party could be written. Here the *mise en scène* displays it as the site of resistance: the land resists the peasants' pitiful toiling; society resists change. Chen Kaige and his DP, Zhang Yimou, reframe their protagonist in a medium shot as he transcribes the song of an unseen peasant, whose humble voice, mixed with the bitter screams of the birds and the sound of the wind, inhabits this desolation.

Shrill, high-pitched instrumental music replaces these melancholy tones. A panning shot moves up to the top of the cliff, where a wedding procession advances in single file, profiled in contre-jour against the pale sky, almost like the abstract design of ideograms. The first close-ups of the film show details of the procession; finally, we see two red-clad little feet coming out of the palanquin: the bride is a child.

Reverse-angle shot: another little girl (Xue) looks, in horrified fascination, at the red slipper. The soldier sees the procession *from the outside, in long shots*, as the survival of ethnomusical practices he is supposed to record. The girl sees it *in close-ups; she's already inside*. She knows that she is fated to become a child bride. The soldier won't save the girl.

Bérénice Reynaud

Date 1984

Nationality China

Director Chen Kaige

Cast Wang Xueqi, Xue Bai

Original Title *Huang tu di*

Why It's Key It's a complex, telling scene from the film that put the Fifth Generation on the international map and heralded a new film language in Chinese cinema.

ONCE UPON A TIME
IN AMERICA

ARNON MILCHAN Presents A SERGIO LEONE Film
Starring ROBERT De Niro "ONCE UPON A TIME IN AMERICA"
Also Starring JAMES WOODS   ELIZABETH McGOVERN   JOE PESCI
BURT YOUNG as "Joe"   TUESDAY WELD   and TREAT WILLIAMS as "Jimmy O'Donnell"

Music by ENNIO MORRICONE   Photographed by CLAUDIO TONDELLI   Screenplay by SERGIO LEONE
LEONARDO BENVENUTI   PIERO DE BERNARDI   ENRICO MEDIOLI   FRANCO ARCALLI   FRANCO FERRINI

Produced by ARNON MILCHAN   Directed by SERGIO LEONE

TREBLINKA

Key Scene **Gag apotheosis**
Barres

Luc Moullet's gag-comedies, exhibiting a stunning economy of means, owe something to Jacques Tati – but they have a harsher, more political undertone. All the neurotic eccentricities of the people in his films (some of the most memorable incarnated by Moullet himself), all the minute, daily, compulsive obsessions with counting, collecting, ordering, or figuring out a routine, arise in response to the same, monumental object: a near-fascistic "society of control" that places prison-like constraints around every aspect of work and leisure in Western countries. *Barres* is literally about this society's "bars": those that appear at entranceways in the French metro system to regulate and police customer traffic. Moullet's way is thus clear: he will list (in charmingly handwritten titles), and demonstrate in rapid comic vignettes, the dozens of ways in which wily citizens manage to sneak through this ever-renewed, ever-more-complex system of state-enforced "discipline and punishment" without paying.

Everything proves useful in this solemn mission: chewing gum, string, auto spare parts, leaping and kicking skills. There is no plot in *Barres*, only a parade of subversive gestures, performed alike by young and old, hippies and professionals… occasionally interrupted by the corporate billboards devised to discourage people from such "stupidities." Against this view, Moullet posits a counter-image of the French nation and its culture: cheating the "bar" reconciles classes, promotes better health, and – in a glorious comic apotheosis – constitutes a veritable Olympic sports event, as seemingly dozens of bodies cram together at once through the turnstiles to circumvent the system.
Adrian Martin

Date 1984

Nationality France

Director Luc Moullet

Why It's Key Moullet posits a counter-image of the French nation and its culture.

Key Scene **The train ride to Treblinka**
Shoah

The Nazis' attempted genocide of European Jewry was, as we know, hardly filmed or photographed. Many movies attempted to recreate it, or use it as a backdrop, but the atrocity seemed un-photographable, or resistant to film. As a result, when Claude Lanzmann came to make *Shoah*, which runs for nine and a half hours and took him eleven years, he decided to use not a frame of archival footage and not a single photograph. Instead, he painstakingly visits the sites of the massacres, meets eyewitnesses or participants, and interviews them in forensic detail. One editing decision he makes is remarkable. Though the interviews are usually conducted through interpreters, he does not edit out the interpretation. He lets the shots run long, the questions and answers transformed again and again as they move between the three people. It's as if to edit, to shorten, to remove the middle person would be an unforgivable ellipsis in a film about the most appalling ellipsis of the 20th century.

This decision makes *Shoah* a great work of cinema as well as history, as does the following: when Lanzmann approaches one of the concentration or death camps, he sometimes films from the front of a train. The resulting tracking shot travels forward through space. If we could not hear the train or see the track, we would feel as if we were gliding. Such shots were invented in the earliest years of cinema. The British director G. A. Smith used one in 1898, filming from the front of a train. For his audiences, such moments were entirely new visual experiences. They later became known as "phantom rides." Lanzmann's use of them, almost 90 years later, movingly restores their phantom quality. To see them in *Shoah* is to think of the millions who were murdered.
Mark Cousins

Date 1985

Nationality France

Director Claude Lanzmann

Why It's Key This film is one of the greatest films ever made, and this scene has the elemental power of the earliest films.

Opposite *Shoah*

Key Scene **The dystopian-dream finale**
Brazil

Gilliam's greatest film got off to a shaky start when its American distributor, Universal Pictures, declared it a dud and refused to release it. Gilliam arranged press screenings anyway, and when the Los Angeles film critics named it best picture of the year, Universal relented.

It's easy to understand the studio's nervousness, since *Brazil* evades the usual commercial categories, starting with its title, which refers not to the nation but to escapist fantasies nurtured by Sam, the hero (Pryce). He's a bureaucrat of the future, serving a society that could be called totalitarian if it didn't sabotage itself with nonstop glitches and blunders. When one of these gets an innocent man arrested, Sam's effort to set things right touches off a string of uproarious errors, and eventually he's branded with a false terrorism charge. Tracked down by the authorities, he finds himself in the hands of his old friend Jack (Palin), who's ordered to torture a confession out of him.

Ignoring his pleas for mercy, Jack aims a lethal-looking instrument at Sam's eye – when a shot rings out, a bullet strikes Jack, and Sam is sprung by the real terrorists! He scampers away, and several close shaves later he's safe in the countryside with the woman of his dreams (Greist). But suddenly the faces of Jack and his boss (Vaughan) intrude on the bucolic scene, and we realize the breathless escape was nothing but a hallucination. Sam has succumbed to the most exquisite torture of all – the torture of hope.

David Sterritt

Date 1985

Nationality UK

Director Terry Gilliam

Cast Jonathan Pryce, Michael Palin, Kim Greist, Peter Vaughan

Why It's Key The term "dark comedy" takes on its deepest shades at the end of this raging science-fiction fantasy about a future gone horribly awry.

Opposite *Brazil*

588

Key Film *Come and See*
The experience of war

Based on documentary writings by Ales Adamovich, *Come and See* presents a shocking chronicle of atrocities committed by German occupiers against ordinary Byelorussian peasants during World War II. The story is told from the point of view of teenage boy Flyora (Kravchenko). At the beginning of the film, he is just a child playing with others, but by the end of the picture he has lived through so much pain and suffering that he has matured into a white-haired wrinkled adult.

Flyora's ordeal begins in his native village, where a German raid leaves his mother and sisters dead along with most of the other villagers. Flyora joins the partisans and participates in several actions, during which he witnesses further atrocities in nearby locations. The most shocking is the terrifying extermination of an entire village, as people are herded into a barn, locked in, and set on fire (a fate that historically befell hundreds of Byelorussian villages).

The experience of war is shown through a combination of naturalistic scenes and surrealistic elements (a lost peacock appearing amidst the smoke, a haunting image of a reconnaissance plane, a Nazi woman eating a lobster, a Nazi man cuddling a little exotic animal). One of the film's final scenes – raising issues of guilt and responsibility – shows the Germans responsible for the massacre eagerly arguing their innocence. In a symbolic ending, it is revealed that Flyora, who has survived all the terror and has nearly lost his mind, is unwilling to pursue revenge, as this would mean engaging in similarly indiscriminate annihilation and destruction.

Dina Iordanova

Date 1985

Nationality USSR

Director Elem Klimov

Cast Aleksei Kravchenko

Original Title *Idi i smotri*

Why It's Key It's the most powerful Soviet film about World War II.

Key Film *The Time to Live and the Time to Die* Ah-Ha and his grandmother

An intensely personal story, narrated by the director in the first person, *The Time to Live and the Time to Die* is the story of a Cantonese family living in Taiwan since 1948, cut off from their "home" in mainland China and unable ever to return there. The main character, a child called Ah-Ha by his grandmother, pays no heed to the news broadcasts and letters from home, and as he grows older drifts into delinquency. The film movingly depicts the growing gap between the generations – the older tied spiritually to the past in China, and the younger gradually caught up in the social changes occurring in Taiwan. The film is the second part of a trilogy of "coming of age" stories that Hou directed – the first, *A Summer at Grandpa's* (1984) based on the experiences of co-screenwriter T'ien-wen Chu, and the third, *Dust in the Wind* (1986) with screenwriter Nien-Jen Wu. All of Hou's films are distinguished by their intimacy and the extraordinary naturalism of the action – as though real life is being quietly observed. The actors hardly seem to be acting at all, but rather reacting spontaneously to what is happening around them. And yet, the films are always purposeful and complex and achieve strong emotional impact. *The Time to Live and the Time to Die* is rich with many memorable sequences, especially those detailing the young Ah-Ha's relationship with his progressively demented grandmother. It is without doubt one of Hou's best films and deservedly attracted wide international attention including a major award at the Berlin International Film Festival.

Andrew Pike

Date 1985

Nationality Taiwan

Director Hou Hsiao-hsien

Cast Mei-Feng, Yu-Yuen Tang, Feng Tien

Original Title *Tong nien wang shi*

Why It's Key This is a major film by one of the most important Taiwanese directors.

Key Scene **The lovers say farewell** *The Satin Slipper*

At the end of this searingly beautiful, seven-hour masterpiece, the two would-be lovers (Cintra and Barzyk), who hardly ever meet and who never touch, know they must part. They say their farewells on a ship's deck off the coast of Africa, in a very long take against the background of a rust-red sky. That their longest scene together is also their parting makes perfect sense in a film about Spanish imperialism's 16th-century conquests – based on Paul Claudel's nine-hour play of the same title. Throughout its length, the film piles on layers and layers of ambitions and illusions. Discussions about the attempt to conquer the world for Christ are set against brightly-colored, obviously fake theatrical backdrops of rolling waves and leaping fish. The momentous news of the defeat of the Spanish Armada is presented in an understated, low-key fashion. By the film's latter portions it is clear that the hopes of the lovers and the imperialists' hopes of uniting the world are parallel delusions, both bound to fail less because of specific causes than because of metaphysical ones: the whole world is itself a brightly colored, glorious illusion.

This tension, between the beauty of illusions in the plot and in the image and one's foreboding that they must crumble, is what animates the film, but when the long-take farewell came, its distended temporality and the obvious sincerity of the lovers somehow removed it from the film's delirious dreamworld. These were real lovers, whose real chance at happiness was being denied – and I collapsed in tears.

Fred Camper

Date 1985

Nationality Portugal/France/West Germany/Switzerland

Director Manoel de Oliveira

Cast Luís Miguel Cintra, Patricia Barzyk

Original Title *Le Soulier de satin*

Why It's Key The emotional climax to this drama movingly sums up its larger theme of human strivings and their failures.

Key Scene **The meta-shock**
The Purple Rose of Cairo

Date 1985

Nationality USA

Director Woody Allen

Cast Mia Farrow,
Jeff Daniels

Why It's Key Woody Allen
breaches the wall between
film and audience.

Rarely credited as a formal innovator, Woody Allen here arguably laid the groundwork for meta-fictions, films that are aware of their own narratives, like Charlie Kaufman's *Adaptation* (2002), Michel Gondry's *The Science of Sleep* (2006), and Marc Forster's *Stranger Than Fiction* (2006), while also anticipating video-game-like interactivity between audience and spectacle. At the depth of the Great Depression, downtrodden waitress Cecilia (Farrow) escapes an abusive husband and financial troubles by compulsive moviegoing at her local Bijou, viewing and re-viewing a brittle pre-Code comedy set in Art Deco penthouses and nightclubs. The shock of awareness begins when one character, pith-helmeted African explorer Tom Baxter (Daniels), glances out from the screen and addresses Cecilia directly, saying: "You must love this picture!" Then, climbing down from the silver screen, he leaves with her, as the remaining performers argue about how to proceed and movie patrons upbraid them for allowing the plot to fall apart. A further complication arises when beleaguered producers enlist Gil Shepherd (also Daniels), the career-conscious actor who plays Baxter, to charm Cecilia into disclosing the whereabouts of their fugitive leading man, thus dramatizing the distinction between role and actor. In the poignant resolution, Cecilia loses both men, but at least her dream life provides refuge, as she watches Astaire and Rogers dancing cheek to cheek in *Top Hat*. Should we pity Cecilia's withdrawal into escapism or envy her immersion in that movie's glittering celebration of music and romance? Is it a sad ending or a happy one?

Robert Keser

Key Scene **The double suicide**
A Zed & Two Noughts

Date 1985

Nationality UK/
Netherlands

Director Peter Greenaway

Cast Brian Deacon,
Eric Deacon

Why It's Key Greenaway's
love for patterns is
ingeniously worked out in a
grimly logical way that ends
the main characters as well
as the movie.

Greenaway organizes his films in terms of games, numbers, and patterns, which he finds endlessly fascinating. But he's not uncritical of them – and in his world, the only thing more pervasive than patterns is the *breakdown* of patterns, including the ones we choose to organize our lives.

The main characters of this movie are identical twins (played by the Deacon brothers) whose wives have died in a freak accident; consumed with grief, they want to know how this incongruous tragedy barged into their once-orderly lives. Since they're zoologists, they embark on a systematic study of decay, photographing cadavers with a time-lapse camera that makes decomposition visible. They also get sexually involved with the driver of the car in which their wives died; she eventually gives birth to twins, sired (she believes) by both men.

The film's progress roughly parallels the brothers' research into the decay of ever-more-sophisticated creatures, and it seems inevitable that they'll culminate their project with a record of human death. Using themselves as specimens, they set up a table in a discreet patch of woods, aim their time-lapse camera at it, start "The Teddy Bears' Picnic" playing on a phonograph, and inject each other with a lethal drug. But the plan refuses to hold – snails live in this forest, and a zillion of them climb their slimy way onto the camera and the phonograph, causing the whole set-up to break flamboyantly down. There's only one pattern Greenaway trusts, and that's a pattern that can't be trusted.

David Sterritt

Key Speech **Henry's evil gets "explained"**
Henry: Portrait of a Serial Killer

Henry (Rooker) is mean and murderous enough to scare most other villains off the screen. His homicides are horrifically violent, making it clear that he finds killing very pleasurable. And they're terrifyingly random, since he knows that the more unpredictable he is, the less likely it is the cops will track him down.

Although he's a loner, Henry takes a roommate – a drifter named Otis (Tom Towles) who quickly gets the hang of serial killing, becoming Henry's protégé and partner. Otis's sister Becky (Arnold) also moves in, winning Henry's heart, or whatever passes for one in his cold-blooded breast. (Otis already lusts after her – for a serial killer, incest is small change.)

Becky's been told that Henry killed his mother, and one day she asks him about this. Henry opens up: "I stabbed her," he says. With pain in his voice, he goes on to describe how she abused and humiliated him as a child. It's a classic scene, providing the psychoanalytic facts we need to understand – and feel in control of –

the roots of Henry's evil. "I shot her dead," he concludes. But a moment ago he said he'd stabbed her, and when Becky mentions this, Henry smoothly backpedals: "Oh yeah… I stabbed her."

And instantly we realize that the whole monologue was a product of Henry's sheer insanity, no more revealing than the brand of beer he drinks. There's no explanation for malevolence this profound. It just *is*. And we have to live with it – if people like him don't get us first.

David Sterritt

Date 1986

Nationality USA

Director John McNaughton

Cast Michael Rooker, Tracy Arnold

Why It's Key In an ingenious maneuver, McNaughton makes a disturbing film even more so by offering a Freudian explanation for the title character's evil ways, then pulling the rug out from under us.

Opposite *Henry: Portrait of a Serial Killer*

1980-1989

593

Key Scene **"In Dreams"**
Blue Velvet

In David Lynch's *Blue Velvet*, Ben (Stockwell), hailed by the sinister Frank (Hopper) as "one suave fucker," takes down a mobile mechanic's light and gestures as if were a lounge singer's microphone, then mimes to Roy Orbison's hit "In Dreams." A whole strand of Lynch's film picks up "easy listening" tunes – like Bobby Vinton's title number and Ketty Lester's "Love Letters (Straight From the Heart)" – and presents them in a manner that exposes the fetishism, obsession, and oneiric delirium lurking behind their taken-for-granted golden-oldie familiarity. The effeminate but lethal Ben, face masked with white kabuki make-up and clad in a Claude Rains smoking jacket, seems to attack Orbison's song, projecting his whole rotten soul into its desperate, elusive, twisted lyrics. Later, the song is reprised as Jeffrey (MacLachlan) is brutally beaten by Frank's goons – but it's the mime sequence, perhaps inspired by Dennis Potter's use of dubbed standards in

Pennies From Heaven, that remains inextricably lodged in the mind.

Kim Newman

Date 1986

Nationality USA

Director David Lynch

Cast Dean Stockwell, Dennis Hopper, Kyle MacLachlan, Isabella Rossellini

Why It's Key This sums up David Lynch's mastery of the bizarre juxtaposition.

Key Scene **Art-gallery impressionism**
Ferris Bueller's Day Off

Ferris Bueller (Broderick) is an odd kind of hero, at least for a screen genre like the teen movie that so so often prizes anti-social rebellion. Although he contrives a "day off" school for himself, girlfriend Sloane (Sara), and severely repressed pal Cameron (Ruck), Ferris is no juvenile delinquent. He is a self-proclaimed guru of self-improvement, living life to the full – indeed, given the adulation accorded him by the entire student body, this supremely narcissistic lad resembles a cult leader. Ferris's fun-filled sight-seeing tour around his home town includes not the teen movie staples of sex, drugs, booze, and property destruction, but a very instructive trip to the Art Institute of Chicago to take in masterworks by Picasso, Modigliani, Kandinsky… The scene is a smooth blend of MTV music clip (a wacky montage set to The Dream Academy's instrumental version of The Smiths' "Please, Please, Please, Let Me Get What I Want"), feel-good pedagogy (Great Art is good for you), and the fresh,

giddy invention that, for a few action-packed years, Hughes brought to pop cinema: especially the actors' postures, gestures, and movements, a hundred delightful bits of business that ceaselessly threaten to overturn the plot. The highlight of this gallery scene is a vertiginous few seconds at the end, where Cameron stares neurotically at a Seurat, his ever-deeper gaze translated into successive inserts of a child's face, the colors and lines of which it is composed, and finally the material surface of the canvas itself.

Adrian Martin

Date 1986

Nationality USA

Director John Hughes

Cast Matthew Broderick, Mia Sara, Alan Ruck

Why It's Key It's a great example of the inventiveness Hughes brought to pop cinema for a few years in the '80s.

Opposite *Ferris Bueller's Day Off*

Key Scene **The banquet room**
A Better Tomorrow

In the most famous shot of *A Better Tomorrow*, the dashing gangster Mark (Chow) lights his cigarette with a (counterfeit) $100 bill. Yet the true mythological dimension of the hero intervenes later, in a two-minute, three-part sequence suffused with Woo's obsessions about heroism and religion. Mark enters a restaurant where a traitor is entertaining his gang. In the first part, directed like a musical, Chow's body is as light as Fred Astaire's. While playfully flirting with the hostesses, Mark hides guns in the flower pots adorning the corridor. Then, at his most heroic, he enters the banquet room. A series of reverse-angle shots articulates the duel between Mark and the evil godfather. A second series alternates Mark shooting with the bodies of his adversaries falling. The last series contrasts iconic shots of Mark shooting two guns at the same time with images of the gangsters dying or trying to shoot back. Throwing his empty guns, Mark exits the

room, then retrieves the weapons he had hidden and shoots his pursuers.

Looking thoughtful, Mark throws his gun away, and starts munching on a match (his trademark gesture). A wounded gangster, crawling in his own blood, shoots him in the knee. Mark falls on yet another flower pot, grabs the last gun, and shoots at the man – killing him after an exchange of gunfire, with an expression of sadness, pain, and rage: the Passion of St Mark has started. His body has become heavy, and he will spend the rest of the film as a cripple, first in self-inflicted abjection, then redeeming himself through friendship, before dying alone for his "faith."

Bérénice Reynaud

Date 1986

Nationality Hong Kong

Director John Woo

Cast Chow Yun-fat

Original Title *Yingxiong bense*

Why It's Key In his breakthrough film John Woo coins an elegant film language that revamps the Hong Kong gangster genre and propels Chow Yun-fat to international fame.

Key Scene **A Tibetan thief mourns his child** *The Horse Thief*

To eschew censorship, Tian Zhuangzhuang set the action in 1923 "pre-liberated" Tibet. Exiled from his tribe for stealing horses, Norbu (Tseshang) flees with his wife, Dolma (Dan), and their little boy, Tashi (Jayang), across visually stunning yet inhospitable landscapes. When Tashi becomes sick, Norbu brings a pitiful, tiny dish to a temple to gather the holy water that falls from the roof. Tian shoots him in a low angle, turning him into a heroic figure. Then he places the camera obliquely *above* Norbu's face, which, combined with the effects of CinemaScope, decenters and dwarfs him. Finally, a close-up frames Norbu's legs, while, in the background, a man enters the temple courtyard – leaving a big jar behind as an act of anonymous kindness.

Yet the child dies – a tragedy left off-screen. Tian shows the burial rites performed by the parents on the snow-covered tundra. The same repetitive actions (raising their arms to the sky, prostrating themselves, lying down on the frozen ground), shot from different angles and distances, are superimposed in transparency – creating the impression of a boundless, eternal grief. On the soundtrack, the lament of a lonely female voice is gradually complemented with instrumental music and bells tinkling – until a chorus of monks replaces the woman. At the end, a single male voice emerges, singing what seems to be a prayer. Tian recorded these songs in the Tibetan plains. For the first time since 1949, spirituality is treated with intimacy and respect as a key element in the psychology of the characters in their narrative drift.

Bérénice Reynaud

Date 1986

Nationality China

Director Tian Zhuangzhuang

Cast Dan Jiji, Tseshang Rigzin, Jayang Jamco

Original Title *Dao ma zei*

Why It's Key With the visionary gaze of a painter and the loving care of an ethnographer, a Fifth Generation director films a Tibet deeply imbued with forbidden spirituality.

Key Scene **Spyros watches The Girl dancing** *The Beekeeper*

All of Theo Angelopoulos's films deal with the relationship between onscreen and offscreen space: and if a pessimistic view of Greek history is usually their main "onscreen" concern, this may be merely the overt expression of a far deeper "offscreen" pessimism. One of *The Beekeeper*'s most haunting moments shows Spyros (Mastroianni) approaching a roadside cafe where a young female hitchhiker known (as in *Two-Lane Blacktop*) simply as The Girl (Mourouzi) is dancing alone next to a juke-box. We observe The Girl from what is essentially Spyros's viewpoint, seeing only her back as she dances to a song with the English-language lyric "All by myself, I'm bound to make it." This image is recalled when Spyros visits a dying French friend (Serge Reggiani) who performs a similarly solitary dance before the ocean, and Angelopoulos reinforces the connection by again focusing on the dancer's back. These lonely dances ostensibly stand in marked contrast to that communal dance which takes place at the wedding of Spyros's younger daughter. Yet if The Girl's energetic dance seems strangely joyless, the one that occurs during the wedding lacks both energy and joy. The Girl lives totally in the present ("I don't remember anything," she insists), while Spyros (whom she dubs "Mr. 'I Remember'") is weighed down by the past, both extremes being presented as equally unattractive. For Angelopoulos, community/memory and isolation/amnesia are less opposed terms than variations on the same dilemma: as Spyros' opening voiceover reminds us, that beehive which provides the film's central metaphor contains not a communal ideal, but rather a "waxed prison" whose captives "all together... dance high up in the air."

Brad Stevens

Date 1986

Nationality Greece/France

Director Theo Angelopoulos

Cast Marcello Mastroianni, Nadia Mourouzi

Original Title *O Melissokomos*

Why It's Key This scene shows how an image can be poetically resonant both in itself and as part of a larger pattern.

Key Scene **The closing sequence**
Swan Song

In the mid-1980s, Chinese cinema burst forth with new directors and new ideas that attracted worldwide attention. In the North, directors like Chen Kaige and Zhang Yimou emerged. In the South, based in Guangzhou at the old Pearl River Studios, the young Zhang Zeming suddenly attracted attention with his remarkable first feature, *Swan Song*. Filmed entirely on location in the back streets of old Guangzhuo, *Swan Song* is the story of a musician who finds his inspiration in the sounds of the street. His son returns after many years spent in hardship during the Cultural Revolution and has little sympathy for his father's work. Gradually, however, the son learns to value his father's music and realizes that both he and his father have been damaged in China's ruthless stampede towards materialism. The son finally finds his own spiritual home in the bustling life of the back alleyways of the old city. In the final scene, his reconciliation with his home-place is observed without dialogue, yet with great eloquence. It is a hot evening, and after turning off a bowdlerised performance of his father's music on television, the son quietly smokes a cigarette in his doorway and for the first time really hears the sounds of the street that had once inspired his father. The understatement of the closing scene makes it all the more powerful and brilliantly concludes a bleak view of modern China and its betrayal of traditional culture and social values. Not unexpectedly, the film was not widely seen within China itself, but it won applause from international critics and festivals.

Andrew Pike

Date 1986

Nationality China

Director Zhang Zeming

Cast Chen Rui, Diqing Feng

Original Title *Juexiang*

Why it's Key This scene is the culmination of a story that takes a withering look at the materialism of modern China.

Key Event
The Taiwanese New Wave Manifesto

This evening, big party at 69 T'sinan Road in Taipei. It's the 40th birthday of the inhabitant, who happens to be a preeminent figure of the young Taiwanese cinema: Edward Yang. With his friends, he is celebrating the surge of a new way to make cinema, directly connected to the change of the political regime, after decades of Kuomintang dictatorship. Young directors, producers, technicians, actors, critics, and scholars, some of them raised in Western countries (Yang has a Ph.D. in electronics from UCLA), others deeply rooted in Chinese culture, have put together an array of films that have received more and more audience and international recognition, starting with the two omnibus films that launched the movement and showcased two of its leaders, *In Our Time* (1982), which included an episode by Edward Yang, and *Sandwich Man* (1983), which featured one by Hou Hsiao-hsien. The moment has now come for the new filmmakers to address the local film industry and media and demand the attention and support that have until now been denied to them. Similar to the Oberhausen Manifesto that launched the German New Wave 20 years before, the document cosigned by 54 cinema persons on November 6, 1986, has a larger meaning. It emphasizes the "spring of Asian cinema" and will serve as a reference for other young filmmakers of the area.

Jean-Michel Frodon

Date November 6, 1986

Why It's Key It's the first peak of the surge of the new Asian cinemas which, from Beijing and Seoul to Tehran, reshape the map of world cinema at the turn of the century.

Key Scene **The house burning**
The Sacrifice

The last film of the most enigmatic of filmmakers centers on an enigma that refuses to be clarified. The film's climax may or may not be the Apocalypse, the world may or may not have ended (if it did, it wasn't with a bang but in a Tarkovsky whimper of tinkling glasses and spilled milk), a prayer may or may not have been answered, a "miracle" performed or not. Maybe it was all in the eye and mind of the beholder, Alexander (Josephson), the protagonist. To him, however, there is no ambiguity. To save the world he has promised to sacrifice his house, a locus of happiness. The sacrifice has the shocking absurdity of all biblical sacrifices, and like them cannot be questioned.

Having set fire to a kind of pyre he built up, Alexander sits on the grass, amidst the puddles, watching his house start burning. Throughout the sequence, a six-minute long take in extreme long shot with the characters far away from us, the camera, on a 150-foot-long dolly track, will move right, then left, then right again, endlessly following the erratic motions of Alexander, then of his panicked family, then of two ambulance men, all trying to catch Alexander. (Note: A first take of the sequence aborted because of a camera malfunction, and the burned-down house had to be rebuilt for a new take, the one seen in the film.) This distancing of an action whose pathos almost veers into slapstick comedy proves to be incomparably more gripping than any conventional dramatic use of close shots, editing, music, etc. In its back and forth movement, the camera now shows the house burning, now moves away from it, until finally the burnt-out frame collapses. This just had to be shown in real time. Seldom has a long take been so stylistically justified.

Jean-Pierre Coursodon

Date 1986

Nationality Sweden/France

Director Andrei Tarkovsky

Cast Erland Josephson, Susan Fleetwood, Valérie Mairesse, Sven Wolter

Original Title *Offret*

Why It's Key An unforgettable climactic scene in what proved to be Tarkovsky's testament (he died soon after the film's release).

Opposite *The Sacrifice*

Key Scene **The silent scenes with Frida in her wheelchair** *Frida*

Biopics are among the hardest films to get right. A whole life squeezed into a two-hour slot often seems forced, and expository lines of the "Look, here comes Oliver Cromwell" variety are clunky indeed. A film on the life of Mexican painter Frida Kahlo seems, on paper, particularly prone to such problems (since she knew, for example, Leon Trotsky). All credit then to Jewish Mexican director Paul Leduc, who avoids the pitfalls of the genre but suggests the tone of Kahlo's life in a series of engrossing, mostly wordless vignettes.

Right from the start, the camera of DP Ángel Goded prowls Kahlo's Coyoacan house, finding actress Ofelia Medina in bed, or in the bath, surrounded by surrealist clutter and her paintings, then drifts onwards to another detail. She hums to herself, nuzzles Diego Rivera (Gurrola), paints, or daydreams. We've seen this visual style before, in the films of Robert Altman, but one key element makes Leduc's treatment of it remarkable: Kahlo is in a wheelchair for much of the picture, so the slow prowling shots inevitably feel as if they are shot from her point of view. In other words, the film enacts Kahlo's memories (there are numerous flashbacks to her childhood) and, as a result, captures her subjectivity far better than Julie Taymor's 2002 film, in which Salma Hayek plays Kahlo.

Mark Cousins

Date 1986

Nationality Mexico

Director Paul Leduc

Cast Ofelia Medina, Juan José Gurrola

Original Title *Frida, naturaleza viva*

Why It's Key This great film by an undervalued filmmaker features a unique use of the tracking shot.

Key Scene **The camera circles the three major characters in the first act** *Mélo*

Is Resnais' adaptation of Henry Bernstein's 1929 melodrama filmed theater? Yes and no. A personal filmmaker who loves to hide behind his writers, Resnais always has secondary agendas up his sleeve. Here, during the first act of a play about a romantic triangle of classical musicians – a married couple named Pierre and Romaine (Arditi and Azéma) and their friend Marcel (Dussollier) – the three are in a patio after dinner, and Marcel, seated across from his host and hostess, is explaining why he gave up hoping for a love of total trust. He recounts playing a Bach sonata in a concert years ago, playing it especially for and to his mistress in the audience, and then discovering her exchanging glances with a stranger in the same audience, something she lied about afterwards.

Resnais films Marcel's monologue in one take. A slow camera movement that begins behind the couple and ends on a close up of Marcel subtly traces the adulterous story that will follow from his own viewpoint,

through the onscreen groupings of characters: Marcel seen alongside the couple, then between them, then with Romaine, and finally alone. And the same camera movement conveys both the flow of the Bach he's playing and him scanning the audience looking for his mistress. In short, Resnais – a master of mixing tenses in his early features like *Hiroshima mon amour* and *Last Year at Marienbad* – is showing here how to convey the effects of flash-forwards and flashbacks without leaving the present.

Jonathan Rosenbaum

Date 1986

Nationality France

Director Alain Resnais

Cast Pierre Arditi, Sabine Azéma, André Dussollier

Why It's Key A flashback and flash-forward are both implicit in one sustained camera movement.

1980–1989

600

Key Scene **Hwa-young refuses to recognize her son** *Gilsotteum*

SPOILER

With 100 films to his credit, Korean director Im Kwon-taek boasts several highlights to his long career, including the Buddhist-themed *Mandala* (1981); his now-legendary *Sopyonje* (1993); and the folk opera adaptation *Chunhyang* (2000). Im is best known for ravishing period dramas; however, one of his most powerful scenes appears in a drab-looking, contemporary-set work from 1986.

Gilsotteum takes place during a real-life television campaign in 1983 to reunite families separated in the Korean War, who may have unknowingly settled in different parts of South Korea. Min Hwa-young (Kim) is an upper-class woman, now remarried, who receives word from a man named Seok-cheol, who may be her long-lost son of 33 years. Together with her former boyfriend, she travels to a rural village to meet him, but the hesitant mood of reconciliation (they aren't sure if they have the right person) is frequently broken by Seok-cheol's rough manners and cruelty towards his

wife. Finally, Hwa-young is told at a maternity test that Seok-cheol is almost certainly her son. However, she refuses to accept the results, citing the small chance of a false positive. She then leaves the stunned Seok-cheol to go back to her family.

The symbolic reference to a nation that has been divided since 1945 may be obvious, but *Gilsotteum* also raises issues about blood ties, identity, class, and the idea of a "singular Korean people." The scene could also be considered prescient: in polls, younger South Koreans say that, if given the choice, they would prefer not to reunify with the North.

Darcy Paquet

Date 1986

Nationality South Korea

Director Im Kwon-taek

Cast Kim Ji-mi, Shin Sung-il, Han Ji-il

Why It's Key It's a symbolic moment that provides an unusually honest assessment of Korea as a divided nation.

Key People **Zhang Yimou and Gong Li**
The bride wore red *Red Sorghum*

A bride is carried in a traditional red palanquin. Aware that the groom is a leper, the young porters jolt and make fun of her. The procession is stopped by a highwayman, who robs the porters and musicians and lifts the red veil that covers the bride. The unexpected, lustful smile of the heroine illuminates the screen. Thus 22-year-old Gong Li became an overnight star. And, so did, more significantly, her director/lover, Zhang Yimou.

It is rare for a director to be mobbed by autograph-hungry crowds, but that happened to Zhang – and not (only) because he had starred in *The Old Well* by Wu Tianming (the "godfather" of the Fifth Generation). As much as the lush, sensual imagery he designed for *Red Sorghum*, as much as the role he had played in the genesis of the Fifth Generation (as the DP for Chen Kaige's *Yellow Earth*), it was Zhang's good looks and his romance with Gong that made him famous. As his wife noisily refused a divorce, the scandal sheets from Beijing to Hong Kong had a ball. Reunited with his glamorous star only when they made movies, Zhang obsessively cast her in melodramatic situations (*Ju Dou, Raise the Red Lantern*) in which the camera lingered on her exquisite beauty. The international success of these first three films turned the couple into celebrities abroad as well – ushering a new star system *à la chinoise* that could be successfully exported to the West.

Bérénice Reynaud

Date 1987

Nationality China

Director Zhang Yimou

Cast Gong Li

Original Title *Hong gaoliang*

Why It's Key The international success of Zhang Yimou's first film as a director cast the couple he formed with Gong Li as the heroes of a new star system.

Key Speech **Billy Crystal gets a headache in his eye** *Throw Momma From The Train*

Throw Momma From The Train is a coarsely brilliant study of writer's block and writer's envy, a "black comedy" not in the usual oxymoronic sense of that term – in which the blackness is feebly illuminated by the comedy and the comedy lost in the blackness – but in the sense that it treats serious themes with a corrosive, and finally redemptive, wit. Billy Crystal plays Larry Donner, teacher of creative writing at a community college, stalled on the first line of his novel: "The night was HOT...", "The night was DAMP...", "The night was DRY, yet it was RAINING..." etc. Crystal's sour backchat and compulsive wisecracking are perfectly suited to the condition of a man failed by words. Larry Donner's problem has a single root cause: the blockbusting success of his ex-wife Margaret, who lives in Hawaii and writes books with titles like *Hot Fire*.

Nestling keenly in Donner's creative writing class is Owen (DeVito). Not exactly the star pupil, Owen is more of a white dwarf – a zone of no talent, radiating entropy. He is largely ignored by his teacher, but when Donner looks down mid-class at the pile of writing assignments handed him by his pupils, and happens to see that the top one is Owen's, and that Owen's first line is "The night was humid," he can ignore him no longer. Donner looks up with pure horror in his face, and manages the immortally surreal line: "Class dismissed. I have an enormous headache in my eye."

James Parker

Date 1987

Nationality USA

Director Danny DeVito

Cast Billy Crystal, Danny DeVito, Kim Greist

Why It's Key An extreme of literary panic is beautifully caught in this movie.

Key Scene **Velu Naicker avenges his wife's murder** *Nayakan*

The movie's centerpiece is a vendetta sequence that references *The Godfather* but also establishes Ratnam's mastery of composition, shot breakdown, and narrative rhythm. The wife of up-and-coming smuggler Velu Naicker (Hassan) has been gunned down by his rivals, the Naidu brothers. Naicker swears revenge before his wife's cremation rites have been completed. Thus begins *Nayakan*'s most chilling sequence, in which Naicker consolidates his position in the underworld. Through a series of cuts, edited to a rhythm similar to the sequence in *The Godfather* when Michael Corleone avenges his brother Sonny's killing, the Naidu brothers die one by one. The sequence seamlessly weaves together several gorgeously composed shots that depict Naicker's goons killing one brother at the barber and another while cavorting with two prostitutes. Naicker takes the third brother himself by shooting him in the eye. The sequence lasts a few minutes but lingers in the mind long after the film is over.

One of India's best-known directors, Ratnam makes movies in his native tongue, Tamil, and, more recently, in Hindi, the language of Bollywood. Ratnam's movies have always been removed from the bombast and bluster of Tamil cinema. They display precision and poise and replace the declamatory dialogue dear to Tamil movies with meaningful pauses and crisp dialogue. *Nayakan* is one of the best examples of Ratnam's cinema and a welcome addition to the post-*Godfather* gangster-film tradition.

Nandini Ramnath

Date 1987

Nationality India

Director Mani Ratnam

Cast Kamal Hassan, Janakraj, Saranya, Nasser, Nizhalgal Ravi, Delhi Ganesh, Tinnu Anand

Why It's Key Ratnam's *Nayakan* isn't just a splendid homage to Coppola's *The Godfather*. It's also one of the best examples of how mainstream Indian filmmakers effortlessly synthesise diverse influences to produce a hybrid form that nods both to East and West.

Key Speech **The forms of swearing** *Withnail and I*

Obscenity, far from being a blunt instrument, in the right hands is the very nib of a poet's quill, and Bruce Robinson's *Withnail and I* contains some of the most poetic swearing in English cinema. As the film's nameless narrator (McGann) and his friend/roommate Withnail (Grant) – two jobless actors who appear to be failing even at an undemanding bohemianism – negotiate the downward-tending currents of late-'60s London, their swearing reaches a pitch of hysterical perfection. "Monty, you terrible cunt!" is the line that will live forever.

The two men swear differently. Withnail, a fallen aristocrat, drapes his curses in an air of seigneurial privilege and scorn. "What FUCKER said that?" he enquires languidly, in a smouldering North London pub, after being informed that someone has called the narrator a "ponce." The narrator, on the other hand, still has the traces of a working-class upbringing in his accent, and when he calls Withnail a "fucking

BASTARD" he is, as it were, swearing upwards, asserting ancient rights of class grievance. (This is different from when he calls his friend a "silly tool," which bespeaks affection and concern.)

Everybody's swearing nowadays, and on television too. When I interviewed Robinson in 1997 he gleefully envisaged a time when the weatherman would stand grinning in front of his luminous graphic and say "There's a right cunt of a cold front coming in and it's going to fuck the lot of you..." Under such circumstances, with the words losing their magic by the hour, *Withnail and I* will be considered an archive of romantic profanity.

James Parker

Date 1987

Nationality UK

Director Bruce Robinson

Cast Paul McGann, Richard E. Grant, Richard Griffiths

Why It's Key Swearing is an art, like everything else, and nowhere is it done better than here.

Opposite *Withnail and I*

IN VIETNAM
THE WIND DOES IT BLOW
IT SUCKS

BORN TO KILL

Stanley Kubrick's
FULL METAL JACKET

Key Scene **The assault**
The Emperor's Naked Army Marches On

In 1956, Kenzo Okuzaki murdered a real-estate broker. In 1969, he shot at and tried to kill the Emperor. A decade later, he hired filmmaker Kazuo Hara to document his attempt to discover the mysterious circumstances in which several Japanese soldiers died in Papua New Guinea after the end of World War II. The result, a crusade fuelled by Okuzaki's rage and righteousness, is one of the most ethically challenging films ever made.

Okuzaki tracks down the officers who were in charge at the time of the soldiers' deaths. Old men now, they are reluctant to speak to him and argue that the past should be forgotten. So strongly does Okuzaki disagree with this that he starts to attack them, saying "please pardon my violence" as he does. At no point does cameraman-director Hara seem to intervene to protect the old officers. Towards the end of the film, Hara hires an actor to pretend to be the brother of one of the soldiers, then brings him to another

confrontation with an officer, hoping that the presence of the "brother" will force the officer to confess what really happened – that the soldiers were murdered and eaten by their superiors. The ailing officer is unmoved by the brother, so Okuzaki starts to berate him, then kick him, then calls the police to have himself arrested.

Such scenes are astonishing and superficially like the confrontations on Jerry Springer's television show, until you realise that for Okuzaki, the crimes are so terrible, and history matters so much, that anything is permissible, including lying to and beating up old men. Japanese documentary in the '60s, '70s and '80s was amongst the best anywhere in the world. This is among its greatest, most discomforting achievements.

Mark Cousins

Date 1987

Nationality Japan

Director Kazuo Hara

Cast Kenzo Okuzaki

Original Title *Yuki yukite shingun*

Why It's Key This powerful film breaks most of the rules of documentary.

Key Scene **The closeup of a dying Vietcong woman** *Full Metal Jacket*

I had the rare privilege of seeing Stanley Kubrick's last war picture – an adaptation of Gustav Hasford novel's *The Short Timers*, about his experiences during the war in Vietnam – with war specialist Samuel Fuller, shortly after the film came out. He didn't much care for the picture, he said afterwards, because he didn't much like films about training, and besides, this movie wasn't antiwar enough for his taste; he thought it might even encourage some teenage boys to enlist in future wars. Of course, Fuller had extensive war experience and Kubrick had none, which might have also played some role in forming his bias.

But one thing in the film that he loved without qualification was the close-up of the wounded Vietcong sniper (Le) at the end while she's begging for Joker (Modine) to finish her off – above all, for the look of absolute hatred in her eyes. "How did Kubrick do that?" he said with admiration.

It's a powerful scene in many ways. For one thing, it's a moment when the Feminine Other that's been haunting all the grunts throughout the picture is finally confronted head-on – an obsession that comes to the fore repeatedly in the opening sequence in training camp. It also creates a truly upsetting rhyme effect with the close-up of the insanely grinning "Gomer Pyle" just before he shoots Sgt. Hartman at the end of that opening sequence – a rhyme conveyed almost subliminally through a hum on the soundtrack over both close-ups.

Jonathan Rosenbaum

Date 1987

Nationality USA

Director Stanley Kubrick

Cast Matthew Modine, Ngoc Le

Why It's Key It condenses the film's power into an intense, mysterious moment.

Opposite *Full Metal Jacket*

Key Scene **The final shot**
The Sicilian

SPOILER

Michael Cimino's *The Sicilian* ends with the funeral of Salvatore Giuliano (Lambert), completing a circle which began with our initial glimpse of Giuliano, who was introduced standing behind a coffin. If *The Sicilian* has a somewhat more straightforward narrative than Cimino's masterpiece *Heaven's Gate*, it nonetheless shares that film's focus on a divided protagonist, an egotist committed to socialist ideals, existing among yet above the poor, exercising a charismatic authority which is regarded as magnificent even while it is being exposed as an insurmountable flaw. The final shot (cut from the truncated version initially shown in American cinemas) neatly sums up these opposed views of Giuliano. As various mourners depart the funeral, we see Giuliano on horseback, rising up as if attempting to reach the sun overhead. This ghostly image is positioned at the exact centre of the widescreen frame: a tree can be seen at the frame's extreme left, a gravestone topped by a cross at the extreme right. The evocation of Giuliano's glory is thus juxtaposed with a positive image of natural growth on the one hand, a negative image of unyielding tradition, associated with religion and death, on the other. In his ability to convey complex ideas purely through the arrangement of such elements as might naturally exist within the dramatic world he has created, Cimino proves himself to be among the worthiest modern practitioners of that classical *mise en scène* we usually associate with such filmmakers as Anthony Mann, Otto Preminger, Alfred Hitchcock, and John Ford.
Brad Stevens

Date 1987
Nationality USA
Director Michael Cimino
Cast Christopher Lambert
Why It's Key This shot reveals how cinematic imagery can convey complex meanings.

606

Key Scene **"Me and Dot are swingers, as in 'to swing'"** *Raising Arizona*

The mid-film curveball in *Raising Arizona* comes during a picnic in a dreary desert campground, where Cage and Hunter, playing a childless couple who have kidnapped the eponymous quintuplet "Nathan Arizona Jr." to raise as their own, do a stressful meet-and-greet with Cage's boss and his wife (McMurray and McDormand). The sequence hangs suspense from multiple angles: the threat that their crime will be discovered, the bigotry and obnoxiousness of the other couple, the risk that the frazzled Cage might give himself away during an attempted heart-to-heart with his employer. But the boss leads the conversation down a path it's safe to say no viewer sees coming: He and his vapid wife are swingers, looking to end the day with a little wife-swapping. That proposition ends with Cage beating up his boss, the irony being that the film teems with alternative family arrangements (Cage and Hunter's parenting-by-kidnap, a couple of escaped cons who want to become Nathan Jr.'s two dads, a bounty hunter who brags of having been sold on the black market as a baby), compared to which open marriage looks benign.

What seemed bizarre at the time – that the Republican crescent in the Southwest could be the center of polyamory in the U.S. – has since become conventional wisdom. The Coens have pulled similar tricks in other films, finding hyper-urbane speech patterns among the seemingly inarticulate, powerful flavors in bland geography, and weird richness in communities where being strait-laced is a point of pride. Because of their status as rootless cosmopolitans touring Texas, the Midwest, or the Mississippi Delta, the brothers' fascination with America's slangy, multihued strangeness is taken – or mistaken – for ironic condescension. Maybe that's what it is, but nobody else making movies today has compiled a body of work that is more alive with the craziness and regional variety of the United States.
Tim Cavanaugh

Date 1987
Nationality USA
Director Joel Coen
Cast Nicolas Cage, Holly Hunter, Sam McMurray, Frances McDormand
Why It's Key It blew the lid off Sun-belt swinging and revealed a richer, weirder America.

Key Scene **Desire**
Law of Desire

In 1987, twelve years after the death of Spanish dictator Francisco Franco ended almost four decades of grim, traditionalist, Catholic-inspired denial of pleasure, Pedro Almodóvar's international breakthrough came with a paean to the utopian freedom afforded by the body and sexual diversity. *Law of Desire*, like the work of Almodóvar's predecessor Luis Buñuel, offers an explosive and precipitously poised celebration of sensuality.

In 30 seconds of theatrical intensity in central Madrid, amid the oppressiveness of a sweltering summer night, a group of three people – a woman, a man, and a young girl riding piggy-back on his shoulders – are caught in a high shot as they pass beneath a rising arc of spouting water in the blue light of the street. Tina (Maura), a voluptuous and flamboyant transsexual, in a tight-fitting orange dress and crimped shoulder-length red hair, dashes to the end of the water jet: "Hose me down! Don't hold back," she cries out to the road cleaner. "Hose me down!" she gasps, with rapturous delight. The urban erotic of scaffolded buildings and groaning sexual ecstasy is Almodóvar's signature territory: a cityscape of desire (not dissimilar to the steamy Louisiana of Tennessee Williams – another major influence on this director).

Watching are Tina's gay brother, Pablo (Poncela), a film and theater director, and Tina's adoptive daughter, Ada (Velasco): an alternative family caught in the flow of water that connects and divides them. In a film often concerned with the thwarting of desire – in which heterosexuality and the conventional nuclear family conspire with the strictures of tradition – this emblematic moment marks a spontaneous release of repression. Part of a family romance upended and reworked, the scene is potently ambiguous in its mixing of the private and the public spheres. There is nothing more public than the city street, the heat coming off the stone buildings, the shock of cool water drenching warm flesh.
Steven Marsh

Date 1987

Nationality Spain

Director Pedro Almodóvar

Cast Carmen Maura, Eusebio Poncela, Manuela Velasco

Original Title *La ley de deseo*

Why It's Key This emblematic scene celebrates the spontaneous release of repression in a public space.

Key Scene **Niankoro talks to the hyena**
Yeelen

Indigenous black African cinema was born in the late 1960s. Through most of the 1970s, its vanguard talents – Ousmane Sembene, Djibril Diop Mambety, Med Hondo, and others – made films about contemporary African life as it shook off its colonial past. They raged against or satirised the retreating European power structures and mores. The result was adrenalysed cine-journalism.

Then, around 1980, black African cinema underwent one of the most fascinating thematic shifts in movie history. The here-and-now, the decolonial moment, was largely abandoned as a subject for cinema and replaced by "the time before." Films like Gaston Kabaoré's *Wend Kunni* (1982) and Med Hondo's *Sarraounia* (1986) were set in periods before Euro-Christianity or Arab-Islam arrived on the continent. The most beautiful of these dream-time films was Souleymane Cissé's *Yeelen*, a luminous work set in the 1500s CE, whose title means Brightness. *Yeelen* is an Oedipal story in which a young magician, Niankoro, sets out to fend off the arrival of his evil father and in so doing encounters the cosmology of his tribe. Early in this journey Cissé mounts a simple scene: Niankoro is walking barefoot on baking, cracked ground. He sits for a moment under a tree. Laughter startles him. He looks up and sees a hyena, who tells him that his life will be radiant. There is indeed radiance in what follows, but one night the magician's blind uncle says "it is possible to die without ceasing to exist" – a heartbreaking premonition of colonialism. African cinema in the 1980s was about mythic time. *Yeelen* was its masterwork.
Mark Cousins

Date 1987

Nationality Mali/Burkina Faso

Director Souleymane Cissé

Cast Issiaka Kane

Why It's Key This is a key scene in the mythic African cinema of the 1980s.

Key Scene **The showdown at the train station** *The Untouchables*

Government agent Eliot Ness (Costner) and his partner (Garcia) want to apprehend Al Capone's bookkeeper. In the original screenplay by David Mamet, they caught the accountant as his train was pulling out of Chicago's famous Union Station, but Paramount balked at the cost, asking De Palma to shoot it all inside the building.

De Palma is one of cinema's great borrowers, regarding himself as a visual stylist who doesn't care where his plots come from. To solve the Union Station problem he took his cue from a silent-movie classic: *Battleship Potemkin*, directed by Sergei M. Eisenstein in 1925. In its gripping "Odessa Steps" sequence, cinema's first great montage theorist used split-second editing to create an intense situation – soldiers massacring people in a park – and to build a series of mini-dramas within it, including the plight of a mother whose baby carriage goes careening helter-skelter down the steps.

In the *Untouchables* update, the lawmen are in the station to greet the bookkeeper. Using montage (and slow motion) to stretch out time, De Palma cuts among different viewpoints and angles as they wait, heightening suspense. As the showdown approaches, a woman starts struggling up the station's steps with a baby carriage, exactly where the shooting is about to erupt. Ness has to help her, but the bookkeeper is arriving…. The hero's two tasks, helping the stranger and catching the villain, symbolize the conflicts he faces as a violent peace officer. De Palma's brilliant filmmaking shows the enduring power of creative artistic thievery.

David Sterritt

Date 1987

Nationality USA

Director Brian De Palma

Cast Kevin Costner, Andy Garcia

Why It's Key De Palma's update of a legendary silent-film sequence demonstrates the perennial vitality of pure visual storytelling.

Opposite The Untouchables

Key Scene **A clean getaway in the first scene** *The Stepfather*

A boy on a bike tosses a newspaper toward a comfy house on a suburban street. The camera gets a bit jittery as it moves closer to the home, then cuts to close-ups when it gets inside. In the bathroom we see a bearded man (O'Quinn) wearing jeans and a work shirt. He looks ordinary at first, but when his face appears in the mirror, it's streaked with blood-red blotches. He strips off his clothes and steps into the shower. Then he shaves his beard and dresses in a new outfit – crisp shirt, jacket, tie.

Is he a bad guy? Or a good guy? Or is that ketchup on his face, making the whole scene a (literally) red herring? Picking up the suitcase with his discarded clothes, he walks down a hallway, pausing to tuck a child's plaything in a toy chest. Then he walks downstairs, the camera moving with him. Something is slightly wrong – on the wall behind him, one of the pictures has been knocked askew. Then something is very wrong – near the bottom of the stairs, the wall is covered with bloody smears. The man reaches the ground floor and barely glances at what we see through the living-room entrance: a whole family lying slaughtered on the floor. He walks out the front door, picking up the newspaper before strolling on down the street.

Now we know: This is a very, very bad guy. And whatever the reasons for this atrocity, he's making a frighteningly clean getaway.

David Sterritt

Date 1987

Nationality USA

Director Joseph Ruben

Cast Terry O'Quinn

Why It's key Building mystery and suspense through step-by-step revelation of details, the opening sequence is one of the most effective in thriller history.

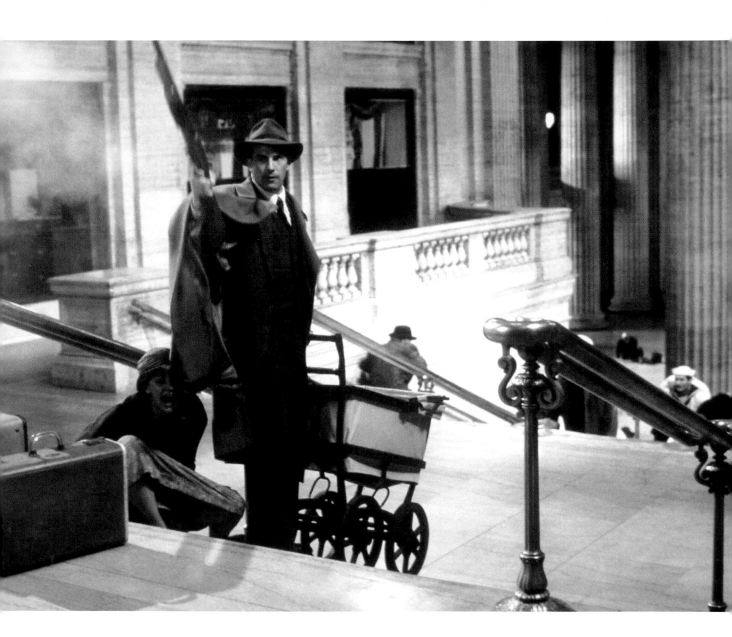

Key Event
Hubert Bals Fund founded

In 1988, the International Film Festival Rotterdam launched the Hubert Bals Fund, named in honor of the festival's founding director. The fund supports feature films and feature-length documentaries by independent filmmakers in developing countries with grants for script and project development, production, postproduction, and distribution. The guidelines for the grant application form state: "The prime consideration of the panel that considers all the projects will be the artistic qualities of an application."

To date, the Hubert Bals Fund has supported more than 600 projects. Viewers who attend international film festivals and venues that boast adventurous programming have seen the fund's credit on such films as Nuri Bilge Ceylan's *Distant* (2002) and *Climates* (2006), Elia Suleiman's *Divine Intervention* (2002), Garin Nugroho's *Opera Jawa* (2006), Lucretia Martel's *The Holy Girl* (2004), and Abderrahmane Sissako's *Waiting*

for Happiness (2002) – to name just a few of the most distinguished titles.

It's impossible to doubt that the biggest proportion of the most exciting filmmaking of the past 30 years has come from Asia, the Middle East, Latin America, and Africa. Given the variable reliability of government support for challenging films, the disastrous effects of globalization on local cultures, and the totalizing and hegemonic policies of Hollywood, the role played by the Hubert Bals Fund in world cinema becomes more important each year.

Chris Fujiwara

Date 1988

Why It's Key The fund provides crucial support for filmmakers in developing countries.

Key Film *Akira*
Anime invades the West

It's fitting that *Akira* begins with an explosion. On June 16, 1988, according to the prologue, a white-hot fireball mysteriously engulfed Tokyo. Now, in 2019, the rebuilt Neo Tokyo is a cyberpunk slum inhabited by pill-poppers, religious fanatics, terrorists, and teenage motorcycle hoodlums like Kaneda (voiced by Iwata) and Tetsuo (Sasaki). Tetsuo is injured in a fiery bike crash with a grotesquely aged child (Nakamura) and is spirited away to a secret lab, where his recuperation is marked by the emergence of strange new psychic abilities. Now Kaneda and anti-government revolutionary Kei (Koyama) must join forces to rescue Tetsuo and uncover the secret of "Akira" and its connection to the devastating blast 31 years ago. Before *Akira*, most Westerners thought Japanese animation meant TV cartoons like *Speed Racer*, kiddie fare full of technical shortcuts and campy overdubs. But director Katsuhiro Otomo (who previously wrote and drew the encyclopedic comic book of the same

name) instead gave his dystopian epic a convoluted plot, graphic violence, hallucinatory visuals, black humor, a hypnotic percussive score, an artisan attention to detail, and precisely synched dialogue peppered with deeper meditations on evolution, enlightenment, and mass annihilation. When Akira exploded, civilization crumbled – but when *Akira* exploded (also on June 16, 1988, the date of its premiere) its shockwaves not only cleared the path for films like *Spirited Away* (2001) and *Ghost In The Shell* (1995) but sharply defined a new high water mark for the art of animation.

Violet Glaze

Date 1988

Nationality Japan

Director Katsuhiro Otomo

Cast Mitsuo Iwata, Nozomu Sasaki, Tatsuhiko Nakamura, Mami Koyama

Why It's Key This movie's release marks the beginning of Japanese animation's ascending influence.

Opposite *Akira*

Key Scene **Sequence in a movie theater**
Distant Voices, Still Lives

This scene is far from being the only epiphany in Terence Davies' work, or even the only one tied autobiographically to his childhood in Liverpool and to his experience of movies. (There's another one in *The Long Day Closes*, synchronized to the theme song of *Tammy and the Bachelor*.) But this is only one set at a movie theater, and Davies starts it off with an image he's described as an homage to *Singin' in the Rain*: raindrops splashing on a sea of black umbrellas, then a slow crane upwards to one-sheet posters for *Love Is a Many Splendored Thing* and *Guys and Dolls*. Cut to a slow camera movement left and forward, through an auditorium's crowd of spectators spotted with wisps of cigarette smoke, to the figures of Eileen (Walsh) and Maisie (Ashbourne), both sobbing their eyes out in response to what they're watching, none of which we see.

It's a stirring indication of the emotional catharsis that movies can bring, Davies' movies included. And then he concludes with one of those irrational yet powerful moments that only he can come up with: over the final strains of "Love Is a Many Splendored Thing," a diptych uncannily shows us the character George (Vincent Maguire) falling from a height through a glass skylight in two separate takes at once. It's a tribute to Davies' genius that he can make such an anomalous dovetailing of cinematic ecstasy into industrial accident seem like the most logical thing in the world.

Jonathan Rosenbaum

Date 1988

Nationality UK

Director Terence Davies

Cast Angela Walsh, Lorraine Ashbourne, Vincent Maguire

Why It's Key Davies regards moviegoing as a religious experience, and this scene's an epiphany.

Key Scene **Special sunglasses allow a man to see the world as it is** *They Live*

John Carpenter emerged from the same California milieu in the 1970s as George Lucas and Steven Spielberg. He has worked in the same Hollywood they have, in the same genres, but in many ways he is the anti-Spielberg and the anti-Lucas. *They Live* is the most extreme example of this. It criticizes not only spectacular entertainment but commercial image-making in general. That it does this in a cheap, blunt sci-fi flick starring a professional wrestler is nothing to sneeze at. Here Carpenter reveals himself as an enemy of what one of this film's villains calls "our ongoing quest for multi-dimensional expansion."

They Live addresses what another character in it calls "the annihilation of consciousness." Carpenter means class consciousness, too. Roddy Piper plays an out-of-work construction worker who finds sunglasses that expose what billboards, magazines, and product labels really say – OBEY; MARRY AND REPRODUCE; CONSUME; WATCH TV – and what the overlords who put them there really look like (they look like metal skulls wearing toupees).

When Piper wears the sunglasses, he sees the OBEY world in black-and-white. Carpenter cuts between two ordinary views, one in color and filled with signs, the other in black-and-white and also filled with signs. He keeps them separate and makes no attempt to optically integrate them. This radical simplicity is meat-and-potatoes semiotics as arresting as anything in Cronenberg. After seeing *They Live* it will be hard to forget what it says on the black-and-white dollar bill: THIS IS YOUR GOD.

A. S. Hamrah

Date 1988

Nationality USA

Director John Carpenter

Cast Roddy Piper

Why It's Key A highlight of 1980s American cinema, it is the last Hollywood sci-fi movie to meaningfully indict contemporary reality.

Opposite *They Live*

Key Scene **Kiss in the phone booth**
As Tears Go By

Many Hong Kong films are unofficial reworkings of successful European or American films. For his feature debut, Wong Kar-wai took Scorsese's *Mean Streets* as a model, but he added a deep romantic level that his later films confirmed as very much his own. *As Tears Go By* is a contemporary gangster film in which a man (Lau) tries to take care of his younger brother (Jacky Cheung). A beautiful but somewhat sad girl (Maggie Cheung) comes into the scene, and gradually it becomes obvious that she is in love with the Lau character, but neither of them is willing to commit yet. Well into the film, however, when Wong has played to the hilt the tension between these two characters, he puts them in a phone booth, where they are finally too close to each other to resist: in an scene that is both exhilarating and erotic, they embrace and kiss each other passionately. And Wong goes along with their climax, moving the camera closer to them and fading gradually to white.

The scene is memorable enough to have been chosen not only for the cover of the DVD but also (in a series of three stills) for the front cover of David Bordwell's book *Planet Hong Kong*. It also anticipates the kind of old-fashioned romanticism that permeates most of Wong's best work.

Fernando Martín Peña

Date 1988

Nationality Hong Kong

Director Wong Kar-wai

Cast Andy Lau, Maggie Cheung

Original Title *Wong gok ka moon*

Why It's Key It defines the romanticism of Wong's cinema.

1980–1989

614

Key Scene **The killer's tape-recorded confession** *The Thin Blue Line*

Errol Morris hadn't intended to save a life. The unemployed filmmaker and private detective was curious about James Grigson, a forensic psychiatrist nicknamed "Dr. Death" because of his reputation as a star witness in capital murder cases. After interviewing Grigson and some of the felons he'd put on death row, Morris was struck by the resoluteness with which convicted murderer Randall Adams maintained his innocence. But after meeting David Harris, the teenage runaway who swore he'd seen Adams pull the trigger, Morris knew they'd got the wrong man. For three years Morris deconstructed Dallas County's corrupt case against Adams, patiently discrediting the testimony of untrustworthy "witnesses" and uncovering the truth of police officer Robert Wood's 1976 murder. Morris's result, the "non-fiction *film noir*" *The Thin Blue Line*, was universally lauded as a masterpiece of unconventional documentary, combining talking-head interviews, reenactments, photographic evidence, and

a narcotic score by Philip Glass into a tone poem of slowly surfacing evil. The most powerful moment is the unforgettable, brazenly static coda of Harris's final interview unreeling on a mini tape recorder. Far from an intentional stab at minimalism – Morris's only film camera broke that day – the unlikely technique of filming the pocket-sized machine replaying Harris's garbled confession sucks us down like a whirlpool to the unassailable truth. Is Randall Adams innocent? "I'm sure he is," hisses Harris's disembodied and tinny voice from the recorder's tiny speaker. "Because I'm the one who knows." Because of evidence presented in this film, Adams was released from jail in 1989.

Violet Glaze

Date 1988

Nationality USA

Director Errol Morris

Cast David Harris, Randall Adams

Why It's Key A movie saves an innocent man from prison.

Key Scene **The wedding**
Stars in Broad Daylight

A double wedding in a Syrian village becomes the occasion for the members of an extended family to celebrate their reunion and flaunt their wealth before a vast number of guests. The wedding takes place outdoors in early evening under garlands of lightbulbs. On tables filled with food and drink, TV monitors provide, disorientingly, different angles of the event: the arrival of a popular singer (in white tuxedo and shades) appears on a monitor as if it were part of a TV special (no doubt his natural habitat). The contrast between the participants' formulaic effusions ("I swear to God, I won't move before I kiss your hand"; "God will punish anyone who leaves without filling his stomach") and the gangster-like ruthlessness with which the event has been arranged becomes both funnier and more frightening as night falls and the event gets farther under way: this is the spectacle of patriarchy at its most well-oiled and gaudiest. Mohammad's camera glides about smoothly, but

servants, carrying the tables with the TV monitors, thus give a handheld unsteadiness to the video shots of a deaf-mute bridegroom, grinning uncertainly, and the increasingly restive bride at his side. The men make deliriously excessive speeches; two small boys sing a paean to the military. Then, as the popular singer finishes his song, the bride silently rises from her chair and strides away across a field into a waiting minibus, which promptly whisks her away. *Stars in Broad Daylight* was banned in Syria, presumably for its sardonic social criticism, of which this scene is a terrific example at the same time as it is a complex, mysterious, exciting piece of cinema.

Chris Fujiwara

Date 1988

Nationality Syria

Director Oussama Mohammad

Cast Abdullatif Abdul-Hamid, Zuhair Ramadan, Sabah As-Salem

Original Title *Nujum al-Nahar*

Why It's Key Patriarchy and ceremony get skewered in this brilliant and hilarious sequence.

1980–1989

615

Key Scene **Greenwald denounces Keefer**
The Caine Mutiny Court-Martial

Herman Wouk's 1953 play *The Caine Mutiny Court-Martial* (based on his 1951 novel *The Caine Mutiny*) ends with a party at which naval lawyer Barney Greenwald denounces both Lt. Stephen Maryk, the man he successfully defended on a charge of mutiny, and Maryk's intellectual fellow officer, Lt. Thomas Keefer. In his 1954 film adaptation of the novel, Edward Dmytryk has Jose Ferrer, cast as Greenwald, upbraid Keefer (Fred MacMurray) in a manner that implies moral certainty: despite being drunk, Ferrer's Greenwald remains lucid and coherent, with Dmytryk's staging suggesting that all those present acknowledge the validity of Greenwald's praise for the tradition represented by such authority figures as Captain Queeg. Although textually faithful to Wouk's play (which was actually allowed to substitute for a screenplay), Robert Altman's 1988 film has Eric Bogosian deliver Greenwald's dialogue as a drunken rant, much of which is lost in the multi-layered soundtrack. Whereas

Dmytryk's *mise en scène* remained tightly focused on Ferrer, Altman renders Bogosian almost invisible, frequently having him stagger out of the frame or obscured from view by partygoers engaging in unrelated conversations. When Greenwald throws a drink in Keefer's face, Dmytryk inserts a closeup of the humiliated MacMurray, but Altman stays in long shot, allowing us to see that Bogosian has accidentally soaked an extra (who contemptuously mutters the word "missed") standing behind Kevin J. O'Connor (the actor playing Keefer). By making stylistic choices which render a right-wing speech inaudible and privilege group interactions over individual scene-hogging, Altman presents a devastating critique of his source material's authoritarianism.

Brad Stevens

Date 1988

Nationality USA

Director Robert Altman

Cast Eric Bogosian, Kevin J. O'Connor

Why It's Key This scene shows how *mise en scène* creates meaning.

Key Scene **Ruprecht the monkey boy**
Dirty Rotten Scoundrels

To select the "Ruprecht the monkey boy" sequence as the great moment in *Dirty Rotten Scoundrels* might seem at first to insult the immaculate contrivances of the rest of the film: the prolonged impersonation by the Steve Martin character, for example, of a Navy officer wheelchair-bound by "emotional trauma." But Ruprecht, in all his base comedy, is the heart of *Dirty Rotten Scoundrels*. Small-time hustler Freddy (Martin) crudely imposes himself upon Lawrence Jamieson (Caine), master con man of the Franco-Italian Riviera, and demands that the old dog teach him some of his tricks. As part of his ensuing apprenticeship in the art of fleecing rich women, Freddy must play the part of Ruprecht – the "special" younger brother of a deposed and financially distressed European monarch. Jamieson, naturally, plays the king, seducing funds from the ladies with promises of marriage and tales of his own imminent restoration and then – at the crucial moment –

introducing them to Ruprecht, whose weirdness is guaranteed to scare them off.

In a too-tight suit, his hair slicked down into oily bangs and a patch over one eye, Ruprecht sits at the dinner table and unnerves the ladies. "Now Diana," coaxes the affable Jamieson, "as you were saying, you don't think the poor should be allowed in museums...?" But Diana cannot speak. Ruprecht is stabbing at his eyepatch with a fork. Later he will trap another lady in an eel-like embrace, and his brother the king will be forced to threaten him – but lovingly, lovingly – with the "genital cuff."
James Parker

Date 1988

Nationality USA

Director Frank Oz

Cast Steve Martin, Michael Caine, Frances Conroy

Why It's Key Steve Martin's ludicrous physical comedy is the perfect foil to Caine's immaculate poise.

Key Film
Heshang (River Elegy)

In the 1980s, as a result of Deng Xiaoping's post-Maoist "market-Leninism," Chinese civil society, its intellectuals, historians, politicians, media, and citizens were rethinking the country's relationship to modernity, history, Enlightenment, and the West. The very different certainties of Confucism and Communism were, in some quarters, being challenged. Unlikely as it seems, in 1988 a massive six-part, Chris Marker-esque essayistic documentary entered the fray. *Heshang* was made for Chinese state television, broadcast twice in 1988, watched by over 200 million people, and made front-page news, and extracts from its commentary were pinned up on public notice boards. Its aim, says Su Xiaokang, was to "bring intellectual issues to the general public." Played over rapidly edited footage of every aspect of Chinese life, its densely argued commentary deconstructed many assumptions about the symbols of Chinese culture. "There is a blind spot in our national psyche," the commentary argued; "by the

middle of the 15th century, when the Ming Dynasty reconstructed the Great Wall, it had become an act altogether of failure and of retreat." To turn the Great Wall from a symbol of pride to one of retreat was brave, and *Heshang* continued in this vein, like a vast scroll painting, re-picturing Chinese history. It was called "propaganda for bourgeois liberalism" by the authorities, and banned. Its filmmakers fled China or were arrested and harassed. It has been argued that the documentary's electrifying effect scared the authorities and, in part, led to the crackdown that culminated in the Tiananmen Square massacre. If this is so, *Heshang* had a greater social and political impact than almost any other film.
Mark Cousins

Date 1988

Nationality China

Director Xia Jun

Why It's Key This epic documentary electrified political debate in China.

Key Event
The first megaplex

The growth of the multiplex was so closely connected to the rise of crappy moviegoing experiences that it seemed the two trends were organically related. Through the 1970s, going to the movies was an increasingly less rewarding experience, as single-screen theaters were brutally chopped into two- or four-screen houses, with "low-pitched" floors, staggered rows, lousy sound, and screens that often seemed to be smaller than the lobby cards for the films. Gimmicks like "Sensurround" merely pointed up the declining standards of what appeared by almost every measure to be a dying form of entertainment.

That began to change as a better class of massive multiplexes grew up around the world, featuring stadium seating, stereo sound systems, and a newly discovered logic of theater construction. Kinepolis Brussels, which opened in 1988 with 25 screens and a seating capacity of 7,500, is generally considered the first of the "megaplexes." The debut of the megaplex demonstrated that there's nothing inherently bad about a movie house with many different theaters, that it is possible to realize both efficiencies of scale and a decent level of exhibition. The houses in a modern multiplex are not always palatial, or even particularly sizable, but they're movie paradises compared to the Soviet-style screening rooms that followed the demise of the single-screen movie palace. For anybody who can remember the stench of death that permeated the chopped-up multiscreen houses of the past, it is hard to argue that the experience of seeing a movie hasn't improved markedly since the 1980s. Not bad for a medium that is both long-lived and perpetually on its last legs.
Tim Cavanaugh

Date September 1988

Why It's Key It signaled the end of the multiplex dark ages.

Key Event
Avid introduces digital nonlinear editing

From the corporate historical timeline on Avid Technology's Web site: in 1989, "Avid introduces the industry to digital nonlinear editing with the Avid/1 Media Composer system, the company's flagship editing solution. The Media Composer system revolutionizes the postproduction process by providing editors with a faster, more intuitive, and more creative way to work than was possible with traditional analog linear methods. This development helps pave the way for a digital revolution within the film, video, and broadcast industries."

Contrary to what might be believed, digital nonlinear editing is not merely a technological improvement that makes it possible to do, conveniently and quickly, the same kind of thing that used to be done in a somewhat more cumbersome way. It could have been this (and, of course, can still be this if that's what the filmmaker wants to use it for), but instead it has changed the way people think about film editing and changed the way films look. Digital editing confirms the status of image and sound as data, freeing them from their material support and also alienating them from the filmmaker, who no longer works with time lengths materialized on strips of film and tape. Duration has become an infinitely variable relativity of time values. All cuts become virtual, reversible, "non-destructive." Despite the name of the popular editing program Final Cut Pro (introduced by Apple in 1999), digital editing takes the "final" out of "final cut."

This is just a note on a cinema that is as yet obscurely known: the digitalized cinema that has become increasingly prevalent since around the year 2000.
Chris Fujiwara

Date April 1989

Why It's Key By freeing image and sound from any standard of time, digital editing changes how filmmakers and viewers perceive time in film.

Key Event *Batman* perfects the blockbuster-as-product

*B*atman was greenlit not just because some guys in suits thought it might be a box-office hit, but because its conception ensured that it would employ talents and promote properties from every corner of Time-Warner's far-flung media empire. The source material – Bob Kane's cowled vigilante – came from DC Comics, a wholly owned subsidiary, and was considered a "pre-sold" property (meaning one with an enthusiastic core audience). The inevitable Warner Home Video cassette – scheduled in advance for November of the same year as the film's release to theaters, locking the film into a theatrical window that would once have been thought too brief – was to be propelled by summer buzz and positioned as a perfect Christmas stocking stuffer. Prince, a Time-Warner music artist, was commissioned to record a pop soundtrack "inspired by" the film and to appear in music videos that could simultaneously sell both the soundtrack and the movie. The director, Tim Burton, was a pop auteur who was then being positioned as a future one-man brand, à la Walt Disney or Steven Spielberg. The villain, the Joker, was to be played by Jack Nicholson, a onetime '70s antihero who'd made a mint in the '80s playing a lovable cartoon facsimile of his movie-star persona.

Though cynically conceived, *Batman* was a smash, spawning five sequels, a new animated series, an animated movie, and a couple billion dollars' worth of bat-emblazoned consumer goods. It all made the success of *Star Wars* – a labor of geek love that found its audience organically, and became a merchandising phenomenon many months after its box-office triumph – seem quaint in comparison. As Lucas's film was to the feather-haired, analog '70s, Burton's was to the buzz-cut, synthesized '80s: an iconic distillation of its era. When *Rolling Stone* critic Peter Travers hopped on the hype bandwagon by blurbing *Batman* as "the film of the decade," he had no idea how right he was.
Matt Zoller Seitz

Date 1989

Why It's Key More than a mere comic book tie-in, *Batman* was the first fully vertically-integrated corporate blockbuster.

Opposite *Batman*

Key Scene **The flying fork**
Time of the Gypsies

*D*irector Kusturica does not like using special effects and prefers choreographing scenes, rather than relying on editing tricks. Thus, in *Time of the Gypsies*, the fantastic landmark scene in which the long-suffering protagonist Perhan (Dujmović) finally takes revenge by directing a flying fork into the neck of his oppressor, the crime lord Ahmed (Todorović), is realised in one complex long take. The scene takes place in a large tent, amid a wedding in full swing. Perhan pretends to beg Ahmed for forgiveness and is invited to join in the celebration. Seated at the end of the wedding table, he uses his telekinetic powers to kill Ahmed by raising a fork from the table and accelerating it in a deadly flight into the latter's neck. The surrounding crowd of dancing guests adds to the feel of a multi-layered, complex event.

In a shot that lasts more than two minutes, the camera (operated by Kusturica himself) makes five sweeping movements, linked with a complex choreography of the moves of objects and people in the background. The flying fork is, in fact, held by invisible threads and moved by a puppeteer hidden under the wedding table, but the camera moves create a *trompe-l'oeil* effect by diverting the viewer's attention to the frantic events in the background.
Dina Iordanova

Date 1989

Nationality Yugoslavia/UK

Director Emir Kusturica

Cast Davor Dujmović, Bora Todorović

Original Title *Dom za vesanje*

Why It's Key This single-take scene achieves its richness and intricacy thanks to the masterfully planned and rehearsed coordination of actors, extras, and camerawork, rather than relying on special effects.

Key Film *The Asthenic Syndrome*
The shift from one film to another

The sole film banned during Gorbachov's *glasnost* era, Kira Muratova's *The Asthenic Syndrome* is a landmark of late Soviet cinema. Abstaining from political assessments, Muratova paints the most poignant and disarming fresco of life in the Soviet Union, circa 1989. Fascinated with the absurd and the ugly, built on a centrifugal structure, and filled with bizarre digressions and non-naturalistic performances, *The Asthenic Syndrome* captures the outer and inner chaos of the times, exposing the decay of the material landscape and the disarray of the souls inhabiting it.

The film itself is plagued by the eponymous syndrome, an ailment that induces alternate states of fretful aggressiveness and inane passivity. Muratova initially trails the peculiarly fidgety mourning of a woman (Antonova) who, inconsolable after the loss of her husband, assaults anyone crossing her path. Unexpectedly, the black-and-white images are revealed as projections on a movie screen, as Muratova shifts to the color presentation of a theater screening of the film. As a host introduces the main actress, who is said to have played in films by Sokurov, Klimov, and Muratova, audiences get up and leave, scornfully insulting the film. "Life's already so harsh and bleak, I want to be entertained at the movies," says one man. The last remaining viewer is fast-asleep Nikolai (Popov), the narcoleptic professor who will be the vague focus of the film's second, longer act. Providing a zestful meta-comment on viewers' responses to her films, Muratova here epitomizes the ever-unpredictable, protean nature of her filmmaking.

Paolo Bertolin

Date 1989

Nationality USSR

Director Kira Muratova

Cast Olga Antonova, Sergei Popov

Original Title *Astenicheskiy sindrom*

Why It's Key This surprising moment is a symptom of the ailment that affects both the film itself and the reality it depicts.

Key Scene **Buck punches the clown**
Uncle Buck

Loveability, so much more mysterious than sexiness, was John Candy's stock-in-trade: the couch-like comforts of his person, his bemused smile, his laugh that seemed to echo with loneliness. In *Uncle Buck* Candy, playing the title role, is brought in – as a last resort, in a family emergency – to babysit his brother's three kids: wreathed in cigarsmoke and awkward bonhomie he rolls up at their suburban palace, clueless but willing.

The film's great moment arrives, like a bus, when Buck meets Pooter the Clown (Starr), who has been hired as entertainment for a party hosted by one of the younger children (Macaulay Culkin). Pooter is late, and when he finally appears, mounting the groomed verge in his mouse-car (a VW Beetle tricked out with enormous ears and whiskers) and staggering out towards the house, we know something is amiss. Muttering and belching, he rings the doorbell. Buck answers, cardigan-clad, chuckling gamely, but a whiff of the clown's breath puts him on alert. He closes the door behind him. "What, did you have a few drinks this morning?" says Buck, eyes narrowing. "Huh? Yeah, I think you did." Pooter reacts badly to this, begins to reel off profanities, and Buck punches him in the face. Twice. At the first impact we hear Pooter's clown-nose parp its sad horn, at the second the lights-out crunch of bone on bone. How right, how fit: to see Candy's muffin-like softness converted for a necessary instant into the hardness of a closed fist, to smite a drunken clown, gives us a sensation of elementary justice.

James Parker

Date 1989

Nationality USA

Director John Hughes

Cast John Candy, Mike Starr

Why It's Key It is a rare treat to watch the gentle Candy turn violent. And he does it so well.

Key Scene **Salim's consciousness of himself** *Don't Cry for Salim the Lame*

Don't Cry for Salim the Lame begins with the protagonist (Pavan Malhotra) walking down a busy Mumbai street, talking about himself and his name in a humorous fashion. He is immediately established as a new 'type' in the Hindi cinema (a cinema that rarely has lead heroes from minority communities), a marginal Muslim, talking in a typical Mumbai style of language, belonging to the migrant, working, semi-lumpenised or lumpenised classes, with a consciousness of himself and his place in the scheme of this world. This first-person narration, particularly at the beginning of the film, links the film to the French New Wave and even the Hong Kong New Wave.

The film establishes the community in the Muslim neighborhood and different "types" of people very effectively. Salim is drawn into nefarious activities, but the horror of riots between religious communities transforms him, as does the influence of a progressive Muslim, to whom he declares (having refused to participate in the gang-orchestrated killing of a Hindu) that he has moved from darkness into light. This shout of joy that he repeats on the street, with his insistence that he is an "Indian," links this scene to a self-reflexive key moment earlier in the film, when Salim and his two friends discuss their pasts (they had to leave their studies early in their lives) and the lifestyles they would like to lead. They shout in youthful energy to the unseen people in the highrise buildings near the beach: "We live in style! We are no less than anybody!" – references to the titles of popular Hindi films. Then they break into a dance that epitomises the body language of their class.

Rashmi Doraiswamy

Date 1989

Nationality India

Director Saeed Mirza

Cast Pavan Malhotra, Makarand Deshpande, Ashutosh Gowarikar, Surekha Sikri, Neelima Azim

Original Title *Salim Langde Pe Mat Ro*

Aka *Waste No Tears on Salim the Lame*

Why It's Key It's a representative moment from a Hindi New Wave film about marginal Muslims and the dawn of a secular, progressive self-consciousness.

1980–1989

621

Key Scene **The CGI water tentacle** *The Abyss*

The one moment that everyone remembers from James Cameron's waterlogged science fiction film *The Abyss* is the water tentacle – a serpentine liquid shape that rises from a pool to probe an undersea base and, confronted with human beings, briefly mirrors their faces in 3-D Computer-generated imagery had been a part of the cinema special effects arsenal since the early 1980s – featuring in *Tron* (1982), *The Last Starfighter* (1984) and others – but this set-piece, showcasing an organic rather than a mechanical creation, was the CGI equivalent of Al Jolson's "you ain't heard nothin' yet!" Within months, ambitious pictures were in development – notably Cameron's *Terminator 2: Judgment Day* (1991) and Steven Spielberg's *Jurassic Park* (1993) – built entirely around CGI creations, but when the scene was shot no one knew if the effect would work The sequence was written in such a way that it could be painlessly snipped from the story without audiences noticing if the computer programmers weren't able to realise the effect properly: in the event, the results exceeded expectations, and the CGI era dawned.

Kim Newman

Date 1989

Nationality USA

Director James Cameron

Cast Ed Harris, Mary Elizabeth Mastrantonio, Michael Biehn

Why It's Key This first tentative toe in the water would lead to the incorporation of CGI as the paramount form of film special effects.

Key Film *Do the Right Thing*
Mookie makes up his mind

Produced, written, and directed by Spike Lee, with Spike Lee leading its ensemble cast, *Do the Right Thing* conformed to the do-it-yourself model of African American cinema, as practiced by everyone from Oscar Micheaux in the 1920s to Melvin Van Peebles in the 1970s. But this was black auteurism with a difference. By the time Lee made *Do the Right Thing*, he'd released a surprise hit (1986's *She's Gotta Have It*), become a successful advertising director (co-starring in TV spots with Michael Jordan), and signed a distribution deal with Universal. This was a new moment in cinema history. No African American filmmaker had ever before won such a public platform.

What did Lee decide to put onto it? A boiling-hot drama about American racial animosity, as experienced right then in his beloved Brooklyn.

Some viewers responded primarily to the movie's pop-off-the-screen style and hip-hop rhythms; others, to its outspoken contemporaneity (which Lee's dimmer critics called inflammatory). But there was structure, too, as contained in the opposing lines of dialogue spoken to Lee's character, Mookie. From Mookie's neighbor Da Mayor (Ossie Davis) came the advice "Always do the right thing." From Mookie's employer Sal (Danny Aiello) came the excuse "You do what you have to."

At the climax, with all of the movie's forces converging on him, Mookie does both. He walks across the screen to a row of garbage cans, picks one up and walks back again, toward a waiting storefront window. No moment in film history is more resonant than the shattering release.

Stuart Klawans

Date 1989

Nationality USA

Director Spike Lee

Cast Spike Lee

Why It's Key At the defining moment for an incipient New Black Cinema, Spike Lee made the nervy choice, behind the camera and on the screen.

Opposite *Do The Right Thing*

Key Film
Siddeshwari

Mani Kaul studied with the eccentric Indian master director Ritwik Ghatak and came to the fore in 1970 with one of India's greatest experimental features, *Uski Roti* (*Our Daily Bread*). Undervalued in the Northern hemisphere, he released eleven films between it and *Siddeshwari*, a biographical quasi-documentary about the legendary classical singer of the title. Its soundtrack is full of Siddeshwari's soaring music and, as if to find a visual analogue, Kaul's camera cranes around saffron-stained shrines, through casements and past vermillion walls, or is locked onto the cerulean edge of a boat as it floats along the bank of a river. Not even Visconti's *Senso* (1954) is more operatic. The lustre of these images, their color palette and textures, are unforgettable. Like Shohei Imamura's *A Man Vanishes* (1967), Orson Welles' *F for Fake* (1974), Chris Marker's *Sans Soleil* (1983), and Alexandr Sokurov's *Confession* (1998), *Siddeshwari* introduces imagined elements to documentary, with the effect, as in each of those films, of enriching the film philosophically.

Mark Cousins

Date 1989

Nationality India

Director Mani Kaul

Why It's Key This is one of the most beautiful films ever made.

Key Scene **The filmmaker's song**
Sink or Swim

Friedrich's masterpiece unfolds in 26 segments. Its autobiographical narration, eloquently read by young Jessica Meyerson, centers on the filmmaker's childhood, when her parents were splitting up and her father, a professor with an authoritarian streak, dished out discipline that crossed the line into abuse.

Instead of trying to illustrate this emotionally charged material in a literal way, Friedrich fills the screen with allusive images, including archival footage and shots she photographed as an adult. The result is an intensely revealing document that might seem too personal for comfort if the circumspection of its imagery didn't so perfectly balance the intimate content of its spoken words. Another distancing device is the film's overall configuration, marking the story's progress by labeling the episodes with letters of the alphabet in reverse order.

One expects the movie to finish with the segment tagged A, but instead Friedrich offers a profoundly moving coda: home-movie footage of herself as a girl, printed multiple times in overlapping layers that mimic the structure of the accompanying soundtrack, on which Friedrich sings "The Alphabet Song" as a round, dubbed from multiple tapes of her present-day voice. At the very end, the screen returns to a single picture and the soundtrack to a single voice, leaving us with a faded image of Friedrich as a child and the unadorned cadence of the song's last line: "Tell me what you think of me." The viewer wants to reply: "I think you are one of cinema's most courageous avant-garde artists."
David Sterritt

Date 1990

Nationality USA

Director Su Friedrich

Cast Su Friedrich

Why It's Key In a daring act of cinematic self-exposure, the filmmaker inserts her own voice and picture into a deeply personal film during its last moments, making an intimate and revealing portrait even more so.

Key Scene **Henry takes Karen to the Copacabana** *Goodfellas*

When *Goodfellas* was first released, in the days before *Pulp Fiction* (1994), reviewers appeared to be most struck by its hardcore violence and its flurries of expletives. A decade and a half later its full-frontal violence may still shock, but what now comes more clearly into view is Scorsese's masterful use of the mobile camera and the long take, apparent everywhere in the film but perhaps nowhere more than in the entry of Henry (Liotta) and Karen (Bracco), on a date, into the Copacabana.

Accompanied throughout by the pounding rhythm of The Crystals' "Then He Kissed Me," and without ever cutting, the camera eagerly follows the couple as they leave their car, cross the street, and descend, via the service entrance, into the club's very entrails, passing Gino the bouncer, eating his hamburger, past the couple habitually making out in the shadows, through the endless labyrinth of one crowded kitchen opening up into another to emerge finally into the red glow of the club itself. And even then the camera refuses to let its gaze go, continuing to pan and follow as the new table is set up, the couple is seated, greetings are exchanged with other wiseguys, and the comedian launches into his routine of one-liners. Three exhilarating minutes of screen travel, from street to stage, gloriously uninterrupted by a single cut!

The most illustrious precedent for such a long take is, of course, the opening of Orson Welles' *Touch of Evil* (1958) and there's no doubt a wink from one Hollywood wunderkind to another. But Scorsese's purpose, ultimately, is to move us rather than to quote, and it works, of course. Like Karen, the viewer is also excited by Henry's world and, for better or for worse, we, too, have been drawn in.
Gino Moliterno

Date 1990

Nationality USA

Director Martin Scorsese

Cast Ray Liotta, Lorraine Bracco

Why It's Key This long take is a piece of virtuoso filmmaking, Scorsese at his very best.

Opposite *Goodfellas*

Key Scene **How to end on the right note**
To Sleep with Anger

Film is a visual medium; so everyone says. So how does Charles Burnett symbolize the return of peace, order, and rightness at the end of *To Sleep With Anger*? He does it with sound.

In one of the most ingenious summings-up in film history – a moment that is as seemingly effortless as it is magical – Burnett literally leaves the last notes to a small boy, who throughout the movie has been tormenting the other characters with his trumpet. Arhythmic blats, squeals, bleats, and quavers have issued relentlessly from the boy's window, making kids in his South Central Los Angeles neighborhood cover their ears. This comical torture (known as "practicing") provides a background for the main action, which takes place not in the boy's house but next door. There, a family is being undone by the arrival of Harry Mention (Danny Glover): an old friend from the South, or maybe someone who's just pretending to be a friend.

The film's dramatic discord emanates from Harry: an unruly, uncanny force from a past that won't stay buried. But the aura of cracked trumpet notes reminds you that *To Sleep with Anger* is about more than the one family that Harry disrupts. It's about a history and a community. Images can show a family coming together again. But to suggest a restoration of community, Burnett needs music. The kid next door finally learns to play his horn – not gradually, as in life, but all at once – so that *To Sleep With Anger* concludes with a moment of magical harmony.

Stuart Klawans

Date 1990

Nationality USA

Director Charles Burnett

Why It's Key One of the most ingenious summings-up in film history is also an exceptional case of movie sound winning out over image.

Key Scene **The motorbike ride of Makhmalbaf and Sabzian** *Close Up*

Hossein Sabzian, a bookbinder, emerges from a jail sentence for having impersonated famous filmmaker Mohsen Makhmalbaf in order to ingratiate himself with the well-to-do Ahankhah family, pretending he was planning a movie about them. He's greeted by the real Makhmalbaf, arriving on his motorbike to take him to visit the Ahankhahs, and filmmaker Abbas Kiarostami and his crew, who have arranged this meeting, are filming the entire encounter from a distance. We hear them saying that Makhmalbaf's lapel mike is faulty, and notice that the dialogue between Makhmalbaf and Sabzian ("Do you prefer being Makhmalbaf or being Sabzian? I'm tried of being me") periodically becomes inaudible – on the street, after Sabzian climbs on the back of the motorbike, and when they stop briefly for Sabzian to buy flowers for the Ahankhahs.

But is this faulty sound the truth, a half-truth, or an outright lie? Is it an accident or a contrivance? What we've previously seen in this film has been a restaging of events, including the trial, by all the participants. And the sound was deliberately and overtly suppressed during part of the final sequence in Kiarostami's previous "non-fiction" feature, *Homework* (1988). During the latter part of the motorbike ride here, we hear no dialogue at all, but a very effective reprise of the theme music from Kiarostami's very first feature, *The Traveler* (1974), suggesting that this apparent accident is very helpful to Kiarostami's dramaturgy. Is it possible, then, that he is himself guilty here of impersonating a documentary filmmaker?

Jonathan Rosenbaum

Date 1990

Nationality Iran

Director Abbas Kiarostami

Cast Mohsen Makhmalbaf, Hossein Sabzian

Original Title *Namay-e nazdik*

Why It's Key A convicted imposter finally meets the man he's been impersonating, and they set off together to visit the family that was fooled.

Key Scene **"I will break your fall"**
Trust

Maria (Shelly) is a pregnant high-school dropout, thrown out of her house when her father keels over dead after an argument with her. Matthew (Donovan) is a reform-school graduate with a police record, whose violent temper prevents him from participating in society. Because *Trust* is a Hal Hartley film, Maria and Matthew are also talented amateur philosophers and poets, and the instant love between them is interrogated ceaselessly, by themselves and everyone around them. In the film's central scene, Maria unexpectedly lets herself topple backwards off an embankment under the Long Island Rail Road. Satisfied when the startled Matthew catches her, she then demands that he duplicate her act of trust. "Maria, I'm twice your size," he says. "If I fall on you from that height, I'll kill you!" "Matthew, go up," Maria says with utter serenity. "I will break your fall, I promise." Matthew contemplates the situation, then resigns himself and climbs the embankment to submit to his young love's request. But another plot thread crops up, and the test is left uncompleted. What could Maria have done to break Matthew's fall? Not the right question: she clearly would have been helpless. We might rather ask: why would Hartley create such a brutal conflict between the mythology of romantic love and the laws of physics, and then slip out the back door? Perhaps he doesn't want us to trust his power to provide closure. As the tag line from another Hartley film goes: "The world is a dangerous and uncertain place."

Dan Sallitt

Date 1990

Nationality USA

Director Hal Hartley

Cast Adrienne Shelly, Martin Donovan

Why It's Key The scene that gives Hal Hartley's greatest film its title manages to celebrate true love and undermine it at the same time.

Key Speech **The madness of Zhang Xiaping**
The Last Dreamers *Bumming in Beijing*

You will not find these words in the English-subtitled version. The young American woman translating the dialogue lost her bearings – for good reasons. The sequence was recorded in Beijing, in early 1990 Wu had been documenting the lives of five of his friends, art-school graduates who had opted to stay illegally (and precariously) in Beijing rather than take the faraway jobs they were assigned to. When he was able to resume shooting after the June 4 massacre, one woman has married the first available American man and fled the country. Those remaining are in a state of depression. The spirited Zhang Xiaping has her first exhibition. Wu visits her as she's hanging her paintings, but what his camera captures is a spectacular breakdown.

Pointing at a self-portrait, she cries out "Is it a man or a woman?" Then, rolling on the floor, she utters a series of repetitive sentences: "God, can you hear me? Hi, motherfucker, who am I?.. I'm telling all of you in this world. My last name is wrong... Motherfucker, where do I get my last name from? This is really painful... I don't even know my last name!"

Shattering the rules of Confucian propriety, Zhang Xiaping screamingly questions sexual difference, as well as patriarchal rule. She reclaims the heritage of the first mad goddess in Chinese mythology, yet mourns the violence done to her generation, the turning of Chinese femininity into a commodity for sale to foreigners. And, yes – she will lose her name – and become a *hausfrau* in Austria.

Bérénice Reynaud

Date 1990

Nationality China

Director Wu Wenguang

Cast Zhang Ci, Mu Sen, Zhang Xiaping, Zhang Dali, Gao Bo

Original Title *Liuliang Beijing – Zuihou De Mengxiangzhe*

Why It's Key The tape that marked the birth of the "New Chinese Documentary" documents the emotional collapse of the post-Tiananmen generation.

Key Event **Creation of the Network for the Promotion of Asian Cinema**

Since the Fifties, when outstanding works like Akira Kurosawa's *Rashomon* (1950) and Satyajit Ray's *Pather Panchali* (1955) won prizes at international film festivals, films from Asia have steadily held world attention. For many years, however, this recognition benefited only those films that made it to the international film-festival circuit and to arthouses that traded in the exotic appeal of Asian films to Western audiences. Focusing on a small group of auteurs, Western film connoisseurs generally showed little interest in the history and scope of Asian cinema.

The surge in Asian cinemas at the start of the Nineties, coupled with the economic power of many Asian economies at the time, coincided with a conscious effort by Asians to define their own culture and cultural practices. In New Delhi in 1990, a conference was organized by *Cinemaya*, an Asian-cinema magazine founded by Indian critic Aruna Vasudev, to address the need for an organization to promote Asian interests in film. The conference led to the establishment of Asian film centers in several countries and, in 1994, to the founding of NETPAC, an international organization whose members now include filmmakers, critics, festival organizers, distributors, exhibitors, and educators. NETPAC sponsors juries of Asian-film competitions at both major and young film festivals, and the NETPAC prize has helped advance individual careers and widen the renown of Asian cinema in general.

Nick Deocampo

Date 1990

Why It's Key NETPAC has been instrumental in advancing the widespread recognition of Asian cinema in Asian and international film festivals.

Key Speech **Frank White explains that he has been reformed** *King of New York*

Everyone seems to agree that it is difficult to discuss Abel Ferrara's work without using the word "improvisation." But what do we mean when we talk about improvisation in this context? Who does the improvising? And to what end? At one point in *King of New York*, Frank White (Walken), the protagonist, visits a restaurant where he enters into conversation with columnist (Hamill) and a woman identified only as "British Female" (Angel). The following exchange appears in Nicholas St John's screenplay:

Female: Frank White; I've heard a lot about you; (Pregnant pause) it was all bad.
Frank: Don't believe everything they put in the papers. I been reformed.

In the film, Vanessa Angel essentially delivers the line written for her, but Christopher Walken replies: "Don't believe everything that Pete writes in the columns, because... well... anyway, I... I've been reformed." He seems about to offer an explanation ("because"), momentarily loses track ("well") and dismisses his attempted digression ("anyway") before hesitantly ("I... I've") coming to the "point."

If Vanessa Angel and her screen character are dull role-players incapable of breaking with convention or conceiving of identities as anything other than solid and immutable, Christopher Walken and Frank White are vibrant improvisers who see identity as a work in process and use the raw material of social interaction as a theme on which to play a series of variations. To be fully alive is to be constantly in motion, continually guarding against the danger of allowing one's identity to define itself, to become a rigid theory rather than a fluid process. For Ferrara, as for Max Ophuls' *Lola Montès*, life is movement.

Brad Stevens

Date 1990

Nationality USA/Italy

Director Abel Ferrara

Cast Christopher Walken, Pete Hamill, Vanessa Angel

Why It's Key This scene reveals how important improvisation is in Abel Ferrara's films.

Opposite *King of New York*

Key Scene **Saga's return to the village**
Tilai (The Law)

A man riding his donkey traverses the barren lands of Sahel. The main theme from Abdullah Ibrahim's score induces a soothing atmosphere. Coming home after two years of absence, the man, Saga (Rasmane Ouedraogo), serenely observes his native village from a cliff, then blows his horn to announce his arrival. Suddenly, at the village, everyone stands still. "Don't worry, he'll understand," says Kougri (Assane Ouedraogo), Saga's younger brother, to Nogma (Cissé), who was Saga's bride-to-be. Everyone gathers at the doors of the village, as Kougri advances to greet Saga and tell him the awful news: their father has taken his rights over Nogma, and turned her into their mother. Feeling betrayed, Saga abruptly departs.

Idrissa Ouedraogo's Tilai provides a primary example of the African cinema that in the late Eighties and early Nineties knew a brief season of exposure in international art houses. Set in pre-colonial Africa, and often ridden with references to ancestral traditions,

films like Tilai earned criticism from some who thought them tailored to satisfy Western audiences' yearning for exoticism. Regardless of such allegations, Tilai presents Ouedraogo's pristine cinematic skills at their height, as perfectly typified by the stunning overture. In just a few minutes Ouedraogo handles a dramatic shift in tone with an economy of means and a dryness comparable to the surrounding landscape of African savannah. Tight editing, naturalistic performances, and a masterful orchestration of spatiality conjure up the lapidary set-up for a tragedy of Shakespearean proportions, in which the reasons of tradition, blood, and honor collide without possibility of reconciliation.
Paolo Bertolin

Date 1990

Nationality Burkina Faso/France/Switzerland/Italy/UK/Germany

Director Idrissa Ouedraogo

Cast Rasmane Ouedraogo, Ina Cissé, Assane Ouedraogo

Why It's Key This opening sequence displays Ouedraogo's command over cinematic language in providing a concise yet powerful start to this tragedy of the savannah.

Key Scene **Daybreak**
Night on Earth

E xpanding on the tripartite structures of his three previous features, Jarmusch here made his own portmanteau film; each of the five chapters – located in L.A., New York, Paris, Rome, and Helsinki – is set during the same 20 minutes (i.e., at a different hour of the night, depending on the time zone), and concerns an encounter between a taxi-driver and one or more passengers. Each is prefaced by a brief, impressionistic montage of the city's architecture and is marked to some degree by its cultural and cinematic history. Hence the opening episode in L.A. has an agent automatically (and wrongly) assuming her driver is keen to get into the movies, while the Roman segment features broad comedy involving crazy driving, sex, and religion.

The final (and most moving) episode in Finland pays tribute to the famously miserabilist but humane films of Jarmusch's friend Aki Kaurismäki, whose regular actors play the dead-drunk passengers and – in the case of Kaurismäki's then *acteur fétiche* Pellonpää

– the driver, who calmly quietens his clients' boastful claims to hardship with his own tale of terrible family misfortune. Given the snowy, small-hours setting, it's an appropriately melancholy coda to the predominantly light-hearted preceding encounters, but Jarmusch never wallows in sentiment. The film ends with one of the drunks dropped off outside his home. Seated blearily on the kerb, he attracts the notice of a neighbor leaving for work, who, as the sun begins to color the winter sky, simply says "Morning," as if this were a daily sight. One word in the right light, and Jarmusch evokes friendship, hope, and life's eternal cycle.
Geoff Andrew

Date 1991

Nationality USA

Director Jim Jarmusch

Cast Matti Pellonpää, Kari Vaananen

Why It's Key Here is the supremely light-touched conclusion to a wise, warm, deceptively inconsequential film.

Opposite *Night on Earth*

Key Film *Thelma and Louise*
Thelma and Louise go off a cliff

Ridley Scott's film, a conversation piece during the early 1990s, is, in some respects, a conventional road movie. But, since the eponymous heroines (or perhaps anti-heroines) are women, a fairly modest genre film moved to the center of debates surrounding the representation of female characters in popular culture and Hollywood's appropriation of feminist motifs.

Like many road narratives, *Thelma and Louise* features a crime spree and gun-toting protagonists. Unlike, say, Joseph H. Lewis's *Gun Crazy* (1950) or Nicholas Ray's *They Live by Night* (1949), the focus is not on a romantic couple on the run for either hedonistic or avaricious reasons. These working-class women from Arkansas decide to hit the road after confronting, and killing, a brutal, would-be rapist. Fearing the legal consequences, they set out on a bumpy journey across the American West, taking time out for brief romantic encounters and small-time robberies.

Thelma and Louise's abrupt decision to commit suicide at the end of the film by driving their car off a cliff baffled many ordinary filmgoers and annoyed academic and feminist commentators. On the other hand, many of these commentators admired the movie's tentative attempt to deal with questions such as rape and spousal abuse from a female perspective. (The script was written by a woman, Callie Khouri, who claimed the film marked an effort to counteract Hollywood's propensity to depict women as brainless bimbos.) Even if they found the film's conclusion a clichéd cop-out, most serious viewers were willing to acknowledge the groundbreaking aspects of Scott's movie and overlook its flawed ending.

Richard Porton

Date 1991

Nationality USA

Director Ridley Scott

Cast Susan Sarandon, Geena Davis

Why It's Key The abrupt conclusion of Scott's road movie sparked controversy and consternation among critics and moviegoers.

Opposite *Thelma and Louise*

Key Scene **Killing her softly**
A Woman's Tale

Dutch-born, Melbourne-based Paul Cox has, in 30 years of filmmaking, created a body of work that is almost unique. Throughout his career Cox has told intimate stories about ordinary people, and if they often seem obsessed with things sexual, well that's the way it is in his world. His collaborators have been more than just fellow workers; they've been friends and family, and actor Sheila Florance was one of the closest members of his group, having appeared in his first feature, *Illuminations* (1975), and in cameo roles in several of his other films (though in Australia she was better known for her role in the long-running television series, *Prisoner*). In 1991, Florance was dying of cancer, but Cox decided to give her the leading role in *A Woman's Tale*, which is about an elderly woman (Florance was 75 years old) dying of cancer and looking back on a well-lived life. Because the old woman is determined to die at home among her possessions, a young nurse

(Dobrowolska), who has grown to love her, decides to give her a lethal injection.

The sequence is handled like a love scene. The nurse lays the old lady tenderly down on her bed, where bright light from a nearby window illuminates her lined face. We see the hypodermic syringe, but not the moment of the fatal injection. "I'm not afraid," Florance says in her husky voice. "Life is so beautiful. Remember – keep love alive"; and as the nurse lies down beside her dying patient, Cox dissolves to a waterfall, a symbol of eternal life and renewal. It's a death scene like no other.

David Stratton

Date 1991

Nationality Australia

Director Paul Cox

Cast Sheila Florance, Gosia Dobrowolska

Why It's Key This is the apotheosis of one of cinema's most singular auteurs.

Key Film *A Brighter Summer Day*
The murder on Guling Street

SPOILER

Xiao Si'r (Chang) is waiting at the exit of a night-school building. He intends to take his vengeance on the person he thought was his best friend, but who ended up stealing his dream girl, Ming (Yang). Si'r stumbles instead on Ming herself, who fathoms what's on his mind. He says he wants to stand by her always and help her change, but Ming rebuffs the offer. "You're hopeless," Si'r concludes, "shameless and hopeless," and stabs the girl. Then, as Ming lies lifeless on the ground, Si'r implores her to get up.

A Brighter Summer Day represents a summit in the career of Taiwanese New Wave spearhead Edward Yang. This 239-minute (185 in the abridged version) chronicle of Sixties' Taiwan portrays youths fascinated by American culture and forming street gangs, while their elders, caught up in a climate of political repression, surrender their delusion of returning to the mainland. Multiple narrative strands create a novelistic density that finds its unity in Yang's admirable *mise en scène*. While Si'r and Ming converse, Yang's camera follows their movements in medium shot. When Si'r stabs Ming, he reemerges from outside the frame, his shoulders to the camera – a composition that amplifies the unexpectedness of the gesture while concealing the naked violence. Cutting immediately thereafter to a long shot to discreetly frame Si'r's despair, Yang magnifies the emotional resonance of the scene.

Paolo Bertolin

Date 1991

Nationality Taiwan

Director Edward Yang

Cast Chang Chen, Lisa Yang

Original Title *Guling jie shaonian sha ren shijian*

Why It's Key The dramatic climax of the film highlights the subtlety of Yang's touch.

Key Scene **"Look deep within yourself, Clarice."** *The Silence of the Lambs*

As a particularly imaginative serial killer nicknamed Buffalo Bill skins his female victims at will, a young FBI recruit, Clarice Starling (Foster), is dispatched to interview incarcerated sociopath Hannibal Lecter (Hopkins), who may or may not have information on the killer and his current victim, a politician's daughter. Having come from Roger Corman's B-movie stable, director Jonathan Demme seemed a natural for the sensationalist material in Thomas Harris's second novel, after *Red Dragon*, to feature Lecter (Brian Cox had played him in the 1986 movie of the first book, retitled *Manhunter*). But few expected a movie of such deliberate rigor, perfectly matching the precision of Ted Tally's faithful screenplay. Nowhere is this more evident than in the first meeting between Starling and Lecter, who face off at his dank subterranean cell, separated by a thick acrylic glass wall that comes to seem quite frail by the encounter's end. It's a magnificently balanced sequence: Foster wide-eyed with terror yet stubbornly determined not to wilt in the heat of pure evil, Hopkins reeking of oily charm even as the character's profound psychosis leaks through. Note the Lynchian use of industrial white noise on the soundtrack, and Howard Shore's foreboding score. It's this scene that features the "liver with some fava beans and a nice chianti" line, but the sequence as a whole is far more complex, and chilling, than that memorable line suggests. "Look deep within yourself," Lecter counsels, and that's more like it.

David Stratton

Date 1991

Nationality USA

Director Jonathan Demme

Cast Jodie Foster, Anthony Hopkins

Why It's Key This sinister and complex sequence exemplifies the rigor of Jonathan Demme's thinking man's thriller.

Opposite *The Silence of the Lambs*

Key Event **$100 million spent on** *Terminator 2: Judgment Day*

The main difference between the 1984 science fiction thriller *The Terminator* and its 1991 sequel was the disparity in budget: about $93 million and change. The director of both movies, James Cameron, started out as a special effects man for Roger Corman, then broke through with his second movie as writer-director, *The Terminator*, about a cyborg (Arnold Schwarzenegger) sent from a machine-dominated future to kill waitress Sarah Connor (Linda Hamilton), who's fated to birth humanity's future savior. It cost $6.4 million, (half of Hollywood's 1984 norm), starred below-the-radar actors (the most famous of whom was Schwarzenegger), featured small-scale action scenes, and relied on charmingly old-school analog effects (including rear projection, miniatures, and stop motion puppets à la Ray Harryhausen). The sequel – arguably a remake on steroids – found Schwarzenegger's time-traveling android reprogrammed to protect Connor and her son, John (Edward Furlong), against a shape-shifting bad Terminator (Robert Patrick). The film's Brobdingnagian action highlights included the detonation of an actual office building and vehicle chases that required shutting down parts of L.A.'s canal system and the Long Beach freeway. The bad cyborg's shape-shifting was conveyed via "morphing,"an pricey new digital effect that Cameron had first tried in his 1989 nautical thriller *The Abyss*. Those elements – plus the $15 million required to re-hire Schwarzenegger, who had become a worldwide superstar in the interim – swelled the budget to $100 million, prompting entertainment columnists to re-ask the age-old question, "Have budgets gotten out of hand?" According to the film's worldwide box office to date – more than half a billion dollars – the answer was no.
Matt Zoller Seitz

Date 1991

Why It's Key It was the most expensive film ever made to its date.

Opposite *Terminator 2: Judgment Day*

Key Scene **Tejo revolts** *Kasba (Small Town)*

Kasba, based on Anton Chekhov's short story "In the Hollow," is one of the most intelligent adaptations in the Indian New Wave of a literary text. Tejo (Vashisht), married to the retarded second son of a merchant, helps run the family business, which consists in the main of adulterating food grains, in a small town in the hills. The elder son's wife gives birth to a child by another man, but the merchant, assuming the child is his grandson, wills all his property to him. This enrages childless Tejo, whose energy and drive have kept the family business going. She lashes out bitterly against her father-in-law, pulls drying clothes down from a line and tramples on a sari, and even pours boiling water on her sister-in-law's child. In the next sequence, we see Tejo looking pensively out a window. The camera draws away from her, and the rest of the sequence is held together by instrumental music that creates a distance from which the tragedies can be viewed. The scene continues with the distraught sister-in-law, Tara (Hansra), walking with her dead baby to the river. She sits on the rocks in the river. The light that infuses the landscape is unusual and quietly benign. A small boy tries to make a horse drink water. The faint sound of the bell on the horse's neck is heard. Tara, almost as if intoning poetry, punctuates the music with "It will not drink. It is not thirsty. Will not drink." This is a unique case where spoken words fit into the music in cinema rather than the other way round.
Rashmi Doraiswamy

Date 1991

Nationality India

Director Kumar Shahani

Cast Mita Vashisht, Navjot Hansra

Why It's Key Shahani privileges melody over drama in this portrait of suffocation in a small town.

Key Film
A Year along the Abandoned Road

In 1990, when digital effects were still young, director Morten Skallerud decided to make a short film on a Norwegian fjord. The camera would be mounted on the top of a vehicle along a deserted road at the edge of the sea; at every minute or so he would shoot just one frame, then move the vehicle a few feet ahead, then shoot another frame. This meticulous procedure was followed for an entire year, day and night. As the fjord is so close to the Arctic Circle, "day" and "night" have a different meaning: there's light for the entire duration of the summer, and sheer darkness throughout the winter. If this project doesn't seem strange enough so far, the filmmaker also decided that the camera should use 70mm film, thus making the whole endeavor all the more demanding. But the result is a spectacle to behold. Within twelve minutes, the entire cycle of seasons flows in front of our eyes with images of pure, unmediated poetry. The hills turn green, then are sprinkled with vast constellations of flowers, then fade into brown and grey until they are gradually covered in snow. The sky is a lively mosaic of clouds, endless shades of blue, yellow, and orange, stars running in elegant circles. The ocean dances back and forth with the rhythm of tides. Every now and then a few human figures briefly appear, just long enough to be detected. Jan Garbarek's evocative score does the rest. We have seen nature breathing.

Paolo Cherchi Usai

Date 1991

Nationality Norway

Director Morten Skallerud

Original Title *Året gjennom Børfjord*

Why It's Key We can breathe in unison with nature (without special effects).

Key Scene **Two painters singing** *The Dream of Light* (aka *Quince Tree of the Sun*)

This documentary (almost day-by-day) chronicle of real-life artist Antonio López trying to get on a canvas a quince tree before its fruits rot includes bits from his everyday life with family and friends, or listening to music and news on the radio while he stands alone at work. His Art Academy companion and friend Enrique Gran comes to Madrid and pays him a couple of visits. On the second, dated precisely November 23, 1990, while the visitor holds some leaves from a branch of the tree to help his colleague get an unobstructed view of the quince fruit he's painting, he suggests he might sing a bit, and starts an amateurish, out-of-key rendition of a folk song which Antonio also remembers and starts to sing in duet. Unsatisfied, both call for a new start, until they get it right enough, Antonio intent on painting and Enrique still holding the branch. This outstanding scene, both funny and moving, and obviously completely unscripted, was shot mainly in frontal shots from behind the canvas, and slightly to one side, so as not to hinder the painter's work, and somehow recalls the feeling conjured by John Ford when he shot old-time friends James Stewart and Richard Widmark sitting by the riverside in *Two Rode Together* (1961).

Miguel Marías

Date 1992

Nationality Spain

Director Víctor Erice

Cast Antonio López, Enrique Gran

Original Title *El sol del membrillo*

Why It's Key This scene gives insight into what a long-standing friendship means, as part of a unique document on the everyday life and work of an artist.

Key Scene **The cautionary prologue**
Careful

"Careful, children!" says the narrator, and he's speaking to old and young alike. The characters of this pitch-dark comedy live in a mountain-bound village where the slightest sound can trigger a deadly avalanche – burying the living, and sometimes unburying the dead by sweeping away their graves.

The ever-present danger makes everyone as cautious as can be, stifling their sneezes and severing animals' vocal cords so an ill-timed bleat won't wipe out everything in sight. And even this isn't enough, because nature makes noises no human can control – one flock of migrating geese can bring catastrophe. Fortunately for the townspeople, the slopes provide isolated spots where freak acoustics keep sounds from escaping, so youngsters can frolic and dads can spank naughty kids without fear. But outside these havens, vigilance reigns around the clock.

The facts of life in this "Canadian Alpine" locale are laid out in the opening narration by Herr Trota (Cowie), a wise elder whose breathlessly voiced warnings ("Think twice!" "Peril awaits the incautious wayfarer!") are illustrated by sepia-toned shots of properly careful acts and rashly impulsive ones. As usual in Maddin's work, everything in this scene is arranged to mimic the look and sound of an archaic German Expressionist film that's been improperly stored for the past several decades. Ditto for the rest of the movie, which amounts to a surreal infomercial for repression, telling a grimly hilarious story of villagers obsessed with incestuous desires that lead to madness, mutilation, and suicide. Didn't anyone tell these people to be careful?!?
David Sterritt

Date 1992

Nationality Canada

Director Guy Maddin

Cast Victor Cowie

Why It's Key Using eccentric montage and suitably daft narration, Maddin crystallizes his approach to filmmaking as an artful combination of high camp, cinematic self-reference, and nostalgia minus the schmaltz and sentiment.

1990–1999

639

Key Scene **Wanted: a woman who can fly**
The Dark Side of the Heart

Oliverio (Grandinetti), an impoverished poet who wanders the streets of Buenos Aires trading poems for steaks and selling verse to passing motorists, seduces and abandons a multitude of beautiful women in search of a soul mate. In an early scene that sets the tone for the film's erotic surrealism, it's easy to see why she's proving elusive: "I don't give a damn if a woman's breasts are like magnolias or figs, if her skin feels like peach or sandpaper," he explains to his most recent bedmate, but "on no account whatsoever will I forgive a woman who cannot fly." And with that, he presses a button on the nightstand, and his partner is swallowed by a trapdoor into a windy, bottomless void.

The sequence is a tidy introduction to the erotically-charged world of admired Argentine filmmaker Eliseo Subiela (b. 1944). First noticed internationally via his moody 1987 sci-fi fable *Man Facing Southeast,* which won the FIPRESCI prize in Toronto (and was feebly remade as *K-Pax* in 2001), Subiela's unabashedly carnal love of women and his fondness for striking visual and melodramatic metaphor have made him a success at home and a cult figure abroad. Subsequent features by Subiela worth seeking out include the beguiling cinema-centric 1995 romantic fantasy *Don't Die without Telling Me Where You're Going*, the millennial manifesto *The Adventures of God*, and a charming 2001 sequel, *Dark Side of the Heart 2*.
David Stratton

Date 1992

Nationality Argentina

Director Eliseo Subiela

Cast Dario Grandinetti

Original Title *El Lado oscuro del corazón*

Why It's Key Here is contemporary magic realism from an unheralded master of the form.

Key Scene **Mimi's death**
La Vie de bohème

Kaurismäki's screenplay is based on the Henri Murger novel that inspired Giacomo Puccini's opera *La Bohème*, about Rodolfo and Mimi, a penniless painter and the woman he loves. But here similarities with Puccini end. Grand opera is – well, grand. Kaurismäki, by contrast, is one of cinema's great minimalists, building absorbing stories with concise dialogue, understated acting, and no-frills camerawork.

This movie begins with marvelous comic flair as we meet the main characters. Rodolfo (Pellonpää) is an Albanian émigré with no visa, Marcel (André Wilms) is failing as a dramatist because he won't trim his 21-act play, and Schaunard (Kari Vaananen) is a composer whose avant-garde opus turns out to be uproariously awful. They do their best to sustain a sense of dignity, playing down their poverty while following the rules of starving-artist etiquette. But as the plot grows bleaker, the dialogue loses its witty flourishes.

In the final scene, tubercular Mimi (Didi) is in the hospital with Rodolfo at her bedside. He goes outside to pick her some flowers, and she's dead when he returns. Without a word, he drops the flowers on the floor, stepping on them as he leaves the room. After telling his friends he wants to be alone, he takes his faithful dog by the leash and walks down a shadowy corridor, vanishing in the distance as the movie ends. Kaurismäki respects his privacy. There's nothing to be said or shown that could relieve Rodolfo, or us, of the despair at the heart of living.
David Sterritt

Date 1992

Nationality France/Italy/Sweden/Finland

Director Aki Kaurismäki

Cast Matti Pellonpää, Evelyne Didi

Why It's Key Using minimalist acting and austere cinematography, Finland's greatest filmmaker creates one of cinema's purest expressions of despair.

Key Scene **Hawkeye running**
The Last Of The Mohicans

There's running and there's running. Tom Cruise has powered through movie after movie, chasing or being chased, his hands slapping at the air in a pantomime of urgency but his legs rotating with the calmness of pistons. His running has a vigorous, contained thespianism – the notion that he might trip or be obstructed does not occur. Harrison Ford, on the other hand, is anything but compact: he is always tumbling away from explosions, scrambling for cover, sprawling massively on rough ground. He runs with a reeling, bandy-legged, near-Falstaffian gait, his face rumpled with affront: the fact that he is running at all seems something of a trespass on his dignity. And then of course there is the fierce, inelegant stomp of Franka Potente in *Run, Lola, Run*, pounding the streets of Berlin, her punk-rock red hair blazing like an Olympian torch.

But the cream of filmic running is to be found in Michael Mann's adaptation of *Last Of The Mohicans*, in which Daniel Day-Lewis plays the Mohican brave Hawkeye. Burning with love for the kidnapped Cora (Madeleine Stowe), Hawkeye spends much of the movie in high-speed pursuit of her. Day-Lewis is at his leanest and most intense here – light-footed, low-shouldered, with a sort of feral slouch in the curve of his spine as he sprints across the forest floor. Opposing braves and soldiers who rise up before him are dispatched *en passant* with tomahawk, knife, or pistol: he doesn't even look to see where they fall.
James Parker

Date 1992

Nationality USA

Director Michael Mann

Cast Daniel Day-Lewis

Why It's Key Day-Lewis is fleeter of foot than any action hero before or since.

Opposite *The Last Of The Mohicans*

Key Scene **Carl serves up "Good Morning America"** *Twin Peaks: Fire Walk with Me*

"I've already seen places," says Carl Rodd, manager of the Fat Trout Trailer Park and early-morning host to a pair of FBI agents. "I just want to stay where I am." Carl stares into space. Unshaven, bandaged, dressed in a tattered bathrobe, he is, in Harry Dean Stanton's mournful performance, the very picture of a man in hiding from life.

Carl has just served the agents cups of "Good Morning America" – coffee with "the sting of the 48-hour blend," as Agent Chester Desmond (Isaak) puts it. Desmond had objected to two-day old coffee from the rude local sheriff's pot in a preceding scene, but accepts it from Carl, perhaps understanding that it's the best someone like Carl can offer. After all, the agents have come calling at an early hour, violating the handwritten plea on his door: "DO NOT *EVER* DISTURB BEFORE 9 A.M. – EVER." "It's late," say Desmond and his coroner colleague Sam Stanley (Sutherland) to each other. They'd been up all night at an autopsy. "It's early, it's really early."

"We could use a good wake-me-up call" says the naïve Stanley, and he says it twice. He's right. Ominous things are about to happen in Carl's trailer park, despite his best efforts to hide from a world that has taken him places he didn't want to go. A strange old woman (Lynch in drag) is about to appear. Agent Desmond is about to disappear. And Agent Dale Cooper (Kyle MacLachlan) will turn up later and wake Carl up again. "It's OK," he'll say, "I was having a bad dream."

Gregg Rickman

Date 1992

Nationality USA

Director David Lynch

Cast Harry Dean Stanton, Chris Isaak, Kiefer Sutherland

Why It's Key Lynch's nightmare world is grounded in very everyday life.

642

Key Speech **"Get with the program!"** *Bad Lieutenant*

A nun (Thorn), who has been brutally raped by a gang of street kids, kneels before a church altar in pious supplication. Beside her is LT, the bad lieutenant (Keitel) – bloated, shambling, incoherent, drugged out of his mind, unable to remain in the correct kneeling position, but nonetheless respectful enough of the faith to avoid saying "motherfucker." They engage in a philosophical dialogue. LT promises her "real justice": he vows to bypass the law and personally track down and kill her attackers. His rap is persuasive: wouldn't this act prevent a repetition of such evil? But her response is firm: "I've already forgiven them." LT takes in the nun's Christian discourse and offers this exasperated advice: "*Get with the program*!" It is a scene, like many in *Bad Lieutenant*, that teeters between psychodrama and hilarity, and which is impossible to "place" in terms of its reality-status. The two-shot forces together stark incommensurables: two ways of life (sacred and profane), two logics (ethereal and emotive), two acting styles (stiff and Method). Is the nun really saying these things? Is LT perhaps imagining, projecting the whole thing from his tormented, guilt-ridden consciousness? We shall never know, because Ferrara's direct, unadorned style equates the apparent reality of this story and its tawdry New York milieu with the inner visions (sordid and sublime) of its supreme anti-hero. After all, only a moment after the nun hands LT a set of rosary beads, he will turn to see (and likewise berate) Jesus Christ himself.

Adrian Martin

Date 1992

Nationality USA

Director Abel Ferrara

Cast Harvey Keitel, Frankie Thorn

Why It's Key Teetering between psychodrama and hilarity, this moment demonstrates the force of Ferrara's direct style.

Opposite *Bad Lieutenant*

Key Film
Roja

Acclaimed regional director Mani Ratnam burst onto the national stage with this critically lauded and commercially successful tale of a young wife's frantic struggle to free her kidnapped husband from the hands of Kashmiri terrorists. With its focus on nationally relevant issues like the Kashmir crisis, its cogent ideas of Indian nationhood, its catchy music, and its casual jingoism, *Roja*, made in Tamil, was ideal for consumption by a wide audience and was dubbed into Hindi, Malayalam, Marathi, and Telugu. *Roja*'s main cast and crew became national celebrities, especially music director A. R. Rahman, whose musical virtuosity has led to his being branded the "Mozart from Madras."

In the 14 years since its release, the little Tamil film with big ideas has been appreciated for its unabashed patriotism and condemned for its xenophobia, consumed whole by mass audiences and picked apart by critics, telecast on Indian television annually for Independence Day and recently re-released for international audiences looking for cinematic solutions to the problems of terrorism. *Roja* enraged academics, including Tejaswini Niranjana and Rustam Bharucha, who tore into its uneasy blend of poetics, polemics, and politics. The scholarly debate the film engendered created the space for the organised study of cinema in India, and *Roja* remains the film most often investigated in Indian-cinema studies. By crossing language barriers and addressing a national audience in a way no regional film had done before or has done since, *Roja* has, for better or worse, become part of India's colorful cinematic imagination.

Sonia Benjamin

Date 1992

Nationality India

Director Mani Ratnam

Cast Madhoo, Arvind Swamy, Pankaj Kapoor, Nasser

Why It's Key This film introduced India to one of its best filmmakers, smashing linguistic and geographical barriers as well as box-office records in the process. As a bonus, it heralded the debut of musical genius A. R. Rahman!

Key Scene **Johnny talks religion**
Naked

Johnny (Thewlis), the antihero of Leigh's scorching drama, has appealing traits of energy and imagination, and repellent ones of sexual rapacity and aimless animosity. The movie follows his adventures during a long night in London, where he's fled from Manchester with enemies at his heels.

Seeking shelter from the cold, he strikes up a conversation with a security guard named Brian (Wight), who lets him inside to warm up. Johnny commiserates with Brian for having "the most tedious fucking job in England," but Brian claims his all-night vigils give him a respite from "the hoi polloi" so he can ponder the future, which he finds a "very interesting" pastime. Brian's optimism marks him as a worthy conversational opponent for Johnny, who sketches a series of contradictory notions that almost cohere thanks to his fluid articulation – that humanity is doomed to extinction, that evolution will make people equivalent to God, and that the imminence of the Apocalypse is clear from Scripture, astronomy, and current events.

Johnny's knowledge of the Bible is surprising in such a scruffy and belligerent person, although his statement that he believes in God is qualified by his subsequent remark that, given the proliferation of evil in the world, the only possible God is one of hate. Brian does his best in the debate, but like the rest of the movie, this is Johnny's show. *Naked* is a searing portrait of England in the Thatcher years, and Johnny's spiel on religion helps it become far more than a merely political portrait.

David Sterritt

Date 1993

Nationality UK

Director Mike Leigh

Cast David Thewlis, Peter Wight

Why It's Key The protagonist's late-night conversation with a security guard reveals multiple layers of reverence and irreverence in his personality, lending real complexity to a character who might been a one-dimensional metaphor for dystopian England under Margaret Thatcher's rule.

Key Scene **The visit to the site of Pasolini's murder** *Caro Diario (Dear Diary)*

Moretti's engagingly eccentric three-part film – an amusing, insightful, and often touching blend of autbiographical reminiscence, ruminative essay, and low-key fiction – is a highly distinctive and distinguished contribution to the realist tradition of Italian filmmaking. As such, it's wholly appropriate that the final minutes of the film's first chapter – which consists mainly of the director-star riding around Rome on his scooter, commenting on the architecture and quality of life in the city as he does so – are an homage to another profoundly politicised auteur who preceded him: Pier Paolo Pasolini, who was murdered in mysterious, perhaps politically sinister circumstances in 1975.

Strangely but crucially, Moretti never discusses the controversial questions surrounding Pasolini's brutal death. Assuming that if we have heard of Pasolini, we will also know a little about his demise, Moretti simply announces that he's going to visit the place where he was killed, and travels there on his Vespa. For several minutes, long travelling shots accompany him as he rides from the suburbs towards the coast; on the soundtrack, a lyrical and meditative piano piece by Keith Jarrett. Finally, when he arrives, the camera simply peers, at a distance and through a fence, at the desolate wasteland where Pasolini met his end. Stark, straighforward, wholly unsentimental, Moretti's tribute benefits from being largely wordless; its simple poetry, rooted in the reality of the Italian landscape, is a subtle yet extremely effective acknowledgement of Pasolini's enduring influence and importance, both as an artist and as a political commentator.
Geoff Andrew

Date 1993

Nationality Italy/France

Director Nanni Moretti

Cast Nanni Moretti

Why It's Key It's a marvellously understated and wholly cinematic tribute from one filmmaker to another.

1990-1999

645

Key Scene **Ganga becomes Nagavalli through dance** *Manichithrathazhu*

SPOILER

This scene is a fantastically choreographed dance sequence, a clever set-up for an ingenious climax, and an inventive insight into the world of the psychotic all at once. Up until now, the tautly directed thriller has hinted that the strange happenings in the ancient Madambi house could be the work of avenging ghosts or jealous relatives, or merely the delusions of its superstitious inhabitants. Dr. Sunny (Mohanlal) reveals to Nakulan (Gopi) that the cause of all the eerie events is the latter's beloved wife, Ganga (Shobana), whose overactive imagination and history of schizophrenia have led to her falling under the influence of the house's bloody history and becoming Nagavalli, a beautiful dancer who was imprisoned, then murdered in the house centuries ago. The two men hear a drum beating. Drawn by the rhythm to the courtyard, they see Ganga, now lost completely to her grandiose hallucination, dancing with manic abandon, rotting flowers in her unkempt hair, kohl smeared across her crazed eyes. Her dance of desperation as seen by her stupefied audience is intercut with scenes of how she sees herself: as the graceful Nagavalli, dancing in front of an ancient court of admirers. The scene also incorporates the seeds of Dr. Sunny's creative cure, which will form the film's climax. Shobana as Ganga exhibits both her considerable acting prowess and her renowned dancing ability in a role that won her a National Award, in a scene that remains one of the finest examples of Indian cinema's superior ability to tell a tale through dance.
Sonia Benjamin

Date 1993

Nationality India

Director Fazil

Cast Shobana, Mohanlal, Suresh Gopi

Why It's Key This complex dance sequence delicately balances Indian cinema's most vital ingredients – music, dance, and melodrama – with a flair unmatched in the four times the film has been remade since its original release.

Key Film
Blue

After sitting in the dark for the first half hour my retina began reacting in a strange way to the color saturation of Yves Klein's blue, uniformly displayed on the screen. The space surrounding the rectangle of the frame slowly became fluorescent, with shades of green and ochre yellow. A few more minutes elapsed before my brain began to register the blue as a drifting cloud of grey, intermittently almost white. Since then, I have seen Derek Jarman's last feature film more than a dozen times (always on a big screen, with the Dolby Surround at full blast). Every time, the monochrome surface would interact differently with the music, the voices, the noises, the artificial night of the theater. I often paid attention to what I was thinking while staring at the film; I sometimes wept. Critical detachment – whatever that means – only came much later. I read Jarman's book *Chroma*: "I've placed no color photos in this book, as that would be a futile attempt to imprison them. How could I be certain that the shade I wanted

could be reproduced by the printer? I prefer that the colors should float and take flight in your minds." I then discovered that *Blue* is a film without a negative: each print is made with a complex technique allowing for the direct application of color onto the projection copy, meaning that no two prints are absolutely identical to each other. I could watch *Blue* over and over again and be certain that I had never seen it before.

Paolo Cherchi Usai

Date 1993

Nationality UK

Director Derek Jarman

Cast (voiceover) Derek Jarman, John Quentin, Nigel Terry, Tilda Swinton

Why It's Key It is a meditation on the act of seeing.

1990-1999

647

Key Scene **Cinema exploits postmodernity** *Arizona Dream*

The cropduster attack sequence in Hitchcock's *North by Northwest* (1959) is one of the grand set pieces of 20th-century cinema, grandiosely elaborating Hitchcock's fondness for dramatic exploitation of setting yet at the same time offering a profoundly comic predicament for Cary Grant, by that time a major star of the silver screen. Grant's Roger Thornhill is dressed in an expensive suit and city shoes, but to save himself he must race through dusty fields, jumping onto the ground and burrowing into a stand of corn. *Arizona Dream* presents a barroom talent contest in which a goofy cinephile, Paul (Gallo), shows off the ultimate in postmodern "talents," namely, the ability to have so devotedly absorbed a beloved motion picture that one can mime an entire sequence in a kind of living, silent homage. He announces that he is going to "perform" Grant in the cropdusting sequence of *North by Northwest*.

With four stalks of corn as props behind him, he stands alone on a pathetic little stage, precisely as

Thornhill does in the Hitchcock film. Shot by shot he does an exact reconstruction, with no sound track behind him. We are left to imagine each buzz of the passing aircraft, each change of Paul's posture as a new "shot," and to marvel at the precision of the reconstruction even to the point where, his act collapsing around him as the uncomprehending audience boos, Paul dives into the shabby-looking corn. The sequence requires us to see two films at once, of course, overlapped, and offers chuckles as we recognize how Paul doesn't look like Cary/Roger any more than this bar looks like a cornfield. Film allows for the overlapping and interchanging of spaces, for the imagination to bounce from anywhere to anywhere.

Murray Pomerance

Date 1993

Nationality USA/France

Director Emir Kusturica

Cast Vincent Gallo

Why It's Key It's a brilliant example of cinematic postmodernity.

Opposite *Arizona Dream*

Key Scene **Poor Valto, left alone with a woman** *Take Care of Your Scarf, Tatjana*

Finnish maestro Kaurismäki specialises in deadpan comedy dramas of an unusually morose nature, which, one suspects, he attributes specifically to the Finnish temperament. His films are packed with male characters who are praeternaturally taciturn, gloomy, and given to negotiating their long dark nights of the soul with not a little help from alcohol. This, his most perfectly realised comedy (at 65 minutes, there's not an ounce of narrative fat on it), boasts two such "heroes" – vodka-guzzling garage mechanic Reino (Pellonpää) and his client, coffee-addicted tailor Valto (Valtonen), who despite their pretensions to rock 'n' roll hipsterdom are men of ludicrously few words, particularly in the company of women. So they are mightily uncomfortable when Estonian Tatjana (Outinen) and Byelorussian Klavdia (Tykkyläinen) more or less force the terminally taciturn duo to give them a lift in their car.

Many moments derive priceless comedy from the men's discomfiture and absurd social ineptitude (the one time they seem animated is when they enthuse about some spanners they've spotted in a shop window!), but the most discreetly revealing is in a bar, when Reino, now lovelorn, accompanies Tatjana back to their hotel, leaving the even shyer Valto seated alone opposite Klavdia. Mortified by a development that might foreshadow intimacy, incapable of conversation but too polite to get up and leave, Valto suddenly – and altogether needlessly – turns his attention to adjusting the thermostat tap on a radiator next to their table. The gesture takes only a few seconds but speaks volumes about this heartrendingly sad paradigm of pathological masculine reserve.

Geoff Andrew

Date 1993

Nationality Finland

Director Aki Kaurismäki

Cast Mato Valtonen, Kirsi Tykkyläinen, Kati Outinen, Matti Pellonpää

Original Title *Pidä huivista kiinni, Tatjana*

Why It's Key A telling detail so small and subtle it might go unnoticed, in the most expertly judged of all Kaurismäki's distinctively melancholy comedies of Finnish manners.

Key Scene **Wrestling time** *Sonatine*

Japanese actor-director Takeshi Kitano is a true all-rounder – comedian turned TV celebrity, painter, writer, you name it – so it's no surprise his attitude to cinema can be described as playful, to put it mildly. Still, his acceptance as world-class filmmaker in the West mostly hinges on traditional values of appreciation: He gets points for stylistic idiosyncracies in genre films, even more so if he imbues them with melodramatic gravitas, as in his (fine) 1997 Venice winner *Fireworks*. Still, Takeshi seems at his most personal when he is at his most freewheeling – as in 1995's malignantly misunderstood vulgar farce *Getting Any?* or 2005's endearingly demented self-refraction *Takeshis'*. But actually he gave it all away as early as 1993 in *Sonatine*, whose art-house gangster surface adheres to a more agreeable pattern of contemplative serenity but is shot through with brutal bursts of experimentation. And it is not just a film about men playing – centering on a submerged, useless group of yakuza (naturally led by master prankster Takeshi himself) idling away their time inventing games on a beach – it is all about the opportunities cinema affords to play with that "biggest train set" of Orson Welles. Takeshi illustrates this perfectly with wrestlers, starting with cut-paper models of fighters moved by fingers drumming on a table, then extending to human size, the designated full-scale-paper-fighter-impersonators similarly made to hop in the sand, thanks to the wonder of time-lapse photography and an awe-inspiring dedication to bring the most ridiculous visions to life.

Christoph Huber

Date 1993

Nationality Japan

Director Takeshi Kitano

Cast Takeshi Kitano, Aya Kokumai

Why it's Key Orson Welles called cinema "the biggest electric train set a boy ever had." Takeshi Kitano plays with it.

Key Scene **Bubby has become a father**
Bad Boy Bubby

The first part of the film is so grim that it makes one wonder how it will be possible to sustain its horrors throughout the end. A 35-year old man (Hope) is confined since birth in a room where his mother (Claire Benito) treats him as a sexual object. There's no way out: if he opens the door, she says, the poisoned air of the outside world will suffocate him. When he inquires about the meaning of the word "suffocating," the mother wraps his face with cellophane until he almost chokes to death. Intrigued by the experience, Bubby tries the same experiment on a cat, then on the parents themselves during sleep. They all get killed, and Bubby is now alone, terrified by what awaits him behind that door. When he eventually manages to overcome his fears, *Bad Boy Bubby* becomes a ravishingly dark comedy, an unlikely rite of passage in an unknown and mostly hostile environment. It is at this point that the film takes an amazing turn. After a casual encounter in a park, Bubby discovers that he can talk with paraplegics: they not only understand him, but they also find in him a friend. The astonished nurse (Johnson) falls in love with him, and it's a true, reciprocated love. While the credits roll, we see Bubby and his wife playing with their child in the garden of their home in the suburbs. Within less than two hours, the starkest view of family abuse has become a celebration of life and hope.

Paolo Cherchi Usai

Date 1993

Nationality Italy/Australia

Director Rolf de Heer

Cast Nicholas Hope, Carmel Johnson

Why It's Key A story of horror and abuse turns into a moving fairy tale.

Key Scene **The resurrection in the cemetery** *The Lovers*

Two lovers have been separated by death. The woman's funeral has just ended. The desperate young man (Wu) stands alone in front of the tomb. Suddenly clouds turn grey, wind blows stronger and stronger. A tempest begins, coming from nowhere, from out of time. The dead young woman (Young) comes out from deepest and darkest limbo. Pale but alive, she catches her lover and brings him back with her into the ground. The tempest is over. Two butterflies suddenly emerge from the tomb, play together awhile, and, finally, go straight to the sky.

This scene takes place within an Asian Romeo-and-Juliet story. The lovers are from different social classes. They have been trying to break the rules of neo-Confucianist Chinese society without success. This story is traditional and tries to justify social hierarchy as a fatality that only death can help to escape.

But Tsui Hark enforces an alternate reading of the story through his treatment of this sequence. After one hour of traditional romantic comedy, the tempest, the opening of the ground, and the ghost create a tragic dimension. Visually, we are close to the great visions of directors like Gance or Murnau. Cinema can break the rules of ordinary vision of reality and reveal the rhizomatic relationships between things. The message has changed: beyond human, beyond good or bad, the order of human society is in contact with the order of all nature.

Antoine Coppola

Date 1994

Nationality Hong Kong

Director Tsui Hark

Cast Charlie Young, Nicky Wu

Original Title *Leung juk*

Why It's Key Fresh and free imagination without limits – as in the visionary era of Abel Gance and F. W. Murnau – returns to the screen in a legendary sequence.

Key Scene **Dance of revenge**
Anjaam

Not long before becoming a superstar beloved by housewives around the globe, Shahrukh Khan starred in this Hindi musical extravaganza as a rich mama's boy obsessed with a beautiful stewardess (Dixit) and trying to win her over by all means necessary, including murder and scarring his own face. It may sound like your average Bollywood stalker melodrama and for about an hour also may feel like it – until Dixit suddenly caresses snakes and dances amid giant burning crystals in a trippy song set piece. Another hour of escalating humiliations follows, before the last third truly delivers on the promise of insanity. Innocently incarcerated in a prison-brothel and having lost her unborn child because of a beating, Dixit's character turns into nothing less than the Wrath of God (more precisely, as ensuing near-nonstop incentive background singing reminds us, the goddess Durga). In a series of stylish set pieces she hangs the warden, bites out her brother-in-law's veins, and so on, as the camera circles ever more furiously through color-coordinated, hellish landscapes. And only then she tracks down Khan's playboy, moves in with a scythe – and finds him quadriplegic. For proper revenge she nurses him towards rehabilitation, then does a love dance by the pool, while he watches longingly, wheelchair-bound – until she pushes him in, so he can pull himself out for the appropriately perverse finale.
Christoph Huber

Date 1994
Nationality India
Director Rahul Rawail
Cast Madhuri Dixit, Shahrukh Khan
Why It's Key Many films promise murderous madness – this Bollywood extravaganza delivers it in spades. And, of course, with song and dance.

Key Scene **The fall and rise of the Hula Hoop** *The Hudsucker Proxy*

Joel and Ethan Coen's underrated satire on the postwar American Dream repays repeat viewings for its subtle, resonant use of circular/cyclical motifs; it also boasts one virtuoso sequence as sustained in its invention and wit as anything in the modern American cinema. It's the late '50s, and hick-from-the-sticks Norville Baines (Robbins) has been appointed – absurdly, by plotting vice-chairman Mussburger (Newman) – boss of Hudsucker Industries; Norville's one idea is pencilled as a circle, his explanation, "You know… for kids!" But Mussburger, needing Norville to fail, gets the board to greenlight the project, whereupon to music by Aram Khachaturian, a magnificent montage sequence depicts the development, the manufacturing, the first dismal efforts to sell and the sudden upturn in fortunes of Norville's invention: the Hula Hoop.

Deploying editing and imagery often reminiscent of Soviet classics by Eisenstein et al., the Coens envisage Eisenhower's USA as a gargantuan bureaucracy greedily devoted to the pursuit of money, power, and fame, and predicated on near-totalitarian conformism. Hence the initial failure of the hoop – nobody has the nous to see what it's for – until one unit, tossed out by an angry shopkeeper, rolls as if destined down several streets to stop at the feet of a small boy. Curious, this anonymous infant visionary raises the thing around his waist, flicks his hips, and changes the course of history: a flock of kids eventually dig what he's doing, and stampede sheeplike back to the store, first subscribers to a nationwide fad that soon makes the newsreels. History was never taught so flamboyantly – or, indeed, so funnily or cinematically – as here.
Geoff Andrew

Date 1994
Nationality USA
Director Joel Coen
Cast Tim Robbins, Paul Newman, Jennifer Jason Leigh
Why It's Key A dazzlingly inventive tour de force of comedy, utterly cinematic in terms of technique and creative vision.

Opposite *The Hudsucker Proxy*

Key Scene **Jackie reads her children's book to Michael** *What Happened Was...*

Sadly underappreciated since its 1994 Sundance debut, *What Happened Was...* is a delicate, subtle film whose sensitivity to its deeply flawed characters shines like a beacon in a media environment dominated by cruel humiliation of the weak, especially the lower classes. The film depicts an awkward first date between Jackie (Sillas), an administrative assistant, and Michael (Noonan), a paralegal, both of whom work at the same New York firm. The film is punctuated with tense silences, misunderstood questions and overtures, and eventually with bracing honesty, as this anti-meet-cute evolves into a long, dark night of two souls.

Michael is a Harvard alum, while Jackie is a hard-scrabble working-class woman from the outer boroughs. In the scene, Jackie informs Michael that she is a published author and offers to read him some of her work. He is naturally hesitant, since if her fiction is embarrassing it will increase his discomfort exponentially. Instead, Jackie reveals herself to be a somewhat naïve but bracingly honest children's-book-author/performance artist, turning out the lights and delivering a tale of incest, abuse, and eventual escape. Like a female Charles Bukowski (imagine!) or some demon spawn of Sam Fuller and Judy Blume, Jackie has crafted a steely-eyed tale of innocence despoiled. (The ambiguity as to just how autobiographical it is only adds to the frisson, and Michael's dumbstruck awe.) Although this scene is followed by a disclosure that, in another context, could belittle Jackie, Michael – and the audience – instead respond with protective tenderness.

Michael Sicinski

Date 1994

Nationality USA

Director Tom Noonan

Cast Tom Noonan, Karen Sillas

Why It's Key In the context of Noonan's examination of self-deception and class difference, this scene affords its female character a heartbreaking moment of dignity and pride. Not all depictions of awkwardness or embarrassment end in cruelty.

1990–1999

653

Key Event
Turner Classic Movies debuts

Turner Classic Movies began as a low-concept cable premise: both a showcase channel for a media bazillionaire's back catalogue and a competitor for the then-dominant (and since much-deteriorated) American Movie Classics. Yet it almost immediately turned Ted Turner – until then the tribune of hideously colorized, pan-and-scan home video – from a film villain into a friend to all cinephiles. And let's not even get started on what it did for the peppy movie raconteur Robert Osborne, whose intro-and-outro tips on the station's film offerings have introduced countless channel surfers to the idea that film is a topic worth thinking about.

This isn't to say that TCM is a hub of revolutionary film criticism. The channel's selection – as implied in its name – leans heavily toward an institutional, film-of-quality approach, and Osborne's commentary is mainly of the gossipy Hollywood stamp. But the high standards of the network, along with the demands of a 24-hour schedule, make for a broad selection, including silents, foreign-language pictures, and historical curios.

More than anything else, the station was instrumental in pushing letterboxing, uninterrupted showings, and other exhibition standards that at the time were considered far too challenging for casual viewers. Some milestone was reached in 2003, when even home-video dinosaur Blockbuster announced a new preference for letterboxing over full-screen rentals. TCM may not have been the deciding factor in the upping of audience expectations for home viewing of film, but its constant (and occasionally self-congratulatory) advocacy for better viewing and more participation in entertainment was an important step in the unexpected popularization of serious movie viewing. Anybody who is serious about movie culture should be grateful to Ted Turner.

Tim Cavanaugh

Date 1994

Why It's Key It mainstreamed cinephilia.

Opposite The launching of Turner Classic Movies

Key Film *Satantango*
The doctor drinking himself into a stupor

Around 75 minutes into *Satantango* – a 450-minute, black-and-white black comedy set in rural Hungary in which everyone's a scoundrel, everything is monstrous, and it never stops raining – the film spends about an hour with a burly doctor (Berling), and for most of that time he's alone. During the first half of this protracted stretch, filmed in very few takes, he's seated in his shack, drinking himself into a stupor with fruit brandy when he isn't spying on his neighbors through binoculars, pointlessly recording their precise movements in copious detail in a journal he's keeping, or snapping at a woman who briefly stops by to deliver his food. We even see him nod off and start snoring at one point, and stumble to the floor and pass out at another. Otherwise he just keeps drinking, pouring out more fruit brandy, and mumbling to himself. Somehow, director Béla Tarr and screenwriter László Krasznahorkai, adapting his own novel, keep us mesmerized throughout this unholy spectacle.

By contrast, the second half of this sequence – when the doctor runs out of brandy and has to trudge out into the rain and mud to get some more – is action-packed. Yet what's so hilarious about the first half, especially as it's performed by Berling (an actor best known for his work with Rainer Werner Fassbinder), is its demonstration of how much exertion is required simply for this overweight man to get himself drunker and drunker. This project becomes an almost heroic effort, worthy of Samuel Beckett.

Jonathan Rosenbaum

Date 1994

Nationality Hungary/Germany/Switzerland

Director Béla Tarr

Actor Peter Berling

Original Title *Sátántangó*

Why it's Key In a long, virtuoso sequence where practically nothing happens, we see how much work getting drunk can be.

654

Key Speech **The watch monologue**
Pulp Fiction

At one point in Quentin Tarantino's *Pulp Fiction*, Captain Koons (Walken) delivers a watch to Butch, a child who will grow up to become the boxer played by Bruce Willis. Koons explains that the watch belonged to Butch's father, and that it was purchased "during the First World War… in a little general store in Knoxville, Tennessee…. This was your great-grandfather's war watch." The watch, we are informed, was later worn by Butch's grandfather, who was killed fighting in World War II, then by Butch's father, who died in a Vietnamese prison camp where Koons was also being held. In our culture, the watch a son inherits from his father is an item of great significance, representing the phallus being passed from one generation of patriarchal males to another. The history of this particular watch is also the history of 20th-century America, from WWI to Vietnam. Yet, however much symbolic value we invest in it, the phallus is neither more nor less than a penis, that anatomical appendage seen by the male as

embodying his superiority to the female. Drawing on those undercurrents of homoeroticism which emerge so frequently in his work, Tarantino has Koons expose the true nature of this symbolism by revealing that Butch's father hid the watch "in the one place he knew he could hide somethin', his ass. Five long years he wore this watch up his ass. Then he died of dysentery, he gave me the watch. I hid this uncomfortable hunk of metal up my ass two years…And now, little man, I give the watch to you." For Tarantino, patriarchy is best represented by the image of several men placing penis substitutes up their asses.

Brad Stevens

Date 1994

Nationality USA

Director Quentin Tarantino

Cast Christopher Walken

Why It's Key This scene represents Quentin Tarantino at his best.

Opposite *Pulp Fiction*

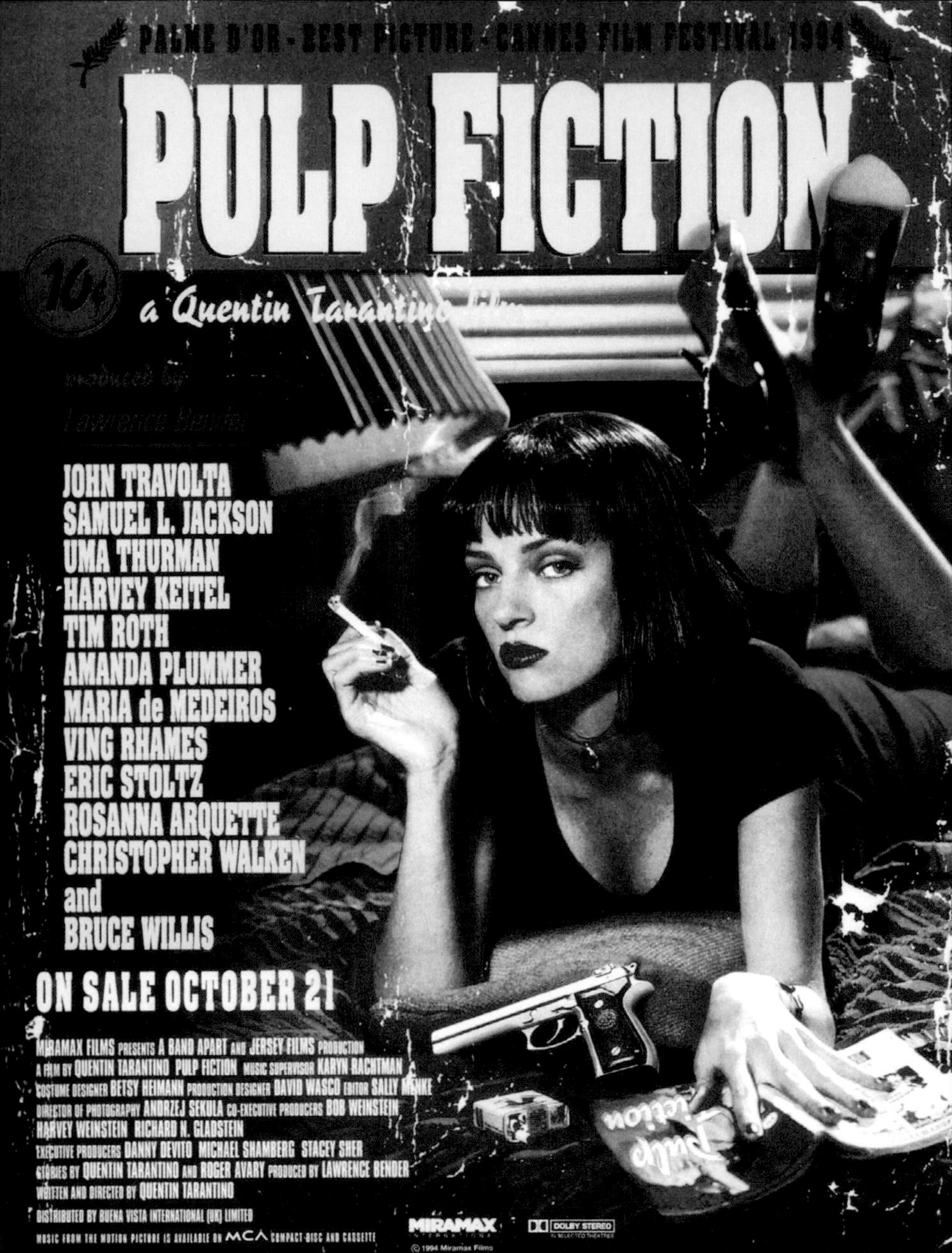
PALME D'OR - BEST PICTURE - CANNES FILM FESTIVAL 1994
PULP FICTION
10¢
a Quentin Tarantino
JOHN TRAVOLTA
SAMUEL L. JACKSON
UMA THURMAN
HARVEY KEITEL
TIM ROTH
AMANDA PLUMMER
MARIA de MEDEIROS
VING RHAMES
ERIC STOLTZ
ROSANNA ARQUETTE
CHRISTOPHER WALKEN
and
BRUCE WILLIS
ON SALE OCTOBER 21
MIRAMAX FILMS PRESENTS A BAND APART AND JERSEY FILMS PRODUCTION
A FILM BY QUENTIN TARANTINO PULP FICTION MUSIC SUPERVISOR KARYN RACHTMAN
COSTUME DESIGNER BETSY HEIMANN PRODUCTION DESIGNER DAVID WASCO EDITOR SALLY MENKE
DIRECTOR OF PHOTOGRAPHY ANDRZEJ SEKULA CO-EXECUTIVE PRODUCERS BOB WEINSTEIN
HARVEY WEINSTEIN RICHARD N. GLADSTEIN
EXECUTIVE PRODUCERS DANNY DEVITO MICHAEL SHAMBERG STACEY SHER
STORIES BY QUENTIN TARANTINO AND ROGER AVARY PRODUCED BY LAWRENCE BENDER
WRITTEN AND DIRECTED BY QUENTIN TARANTINO
DISTRIBUTED BY BUENA VISTA INTERNATIONAL (UK) LIMITED
MUSIC FROM THE MOTION PICTURE IS AVAILABLE ON MCA COMPACT DISC AND CASSETTE
MIRAMAX
© 1994 Miramax Films
DOLBY STEREO

Key Scene **May Lin walks through a park**
Vive L'Amour

Tsai Ming-liang's *Vive L'Amour* ends with an 11-minute sequence showing May Lin (Yang) entering a public park that is still under construction, sitting on a bench and, in a closing image that lasts a full six minutes, crying. The reasons for May's tears, though never explicitly spelled out, are made clear enough by those shots of her walking through the park. As with many other ambitious films – such as Jacques Tati's *Playtime* (1967) and Michelangelo Antonioni's *L'avventura* (1960) – that ask us to accept an unfamiliar narrative approach, what initially seems sparse and dull can, once the director's "language" has been grasped, start to look plentiful and thrilling, an embarrassment of riches suddenly visible where we had previously perceived only poverty. The more often one watches this sequence, the more obvious it becomes how every aspect of Tsai's *mise en scène* relates to May's emotional state: the solitary floating balloon; the leafless trees (some surrounded by protective

scaffolding); the taped-off areas; the apartment blocks at the frame's rear; the muddy water; the piles of earth; the sound of the wind accompanied by the clacking of May's shoes; the almost total absence of grass (visible only in the extreme background), bright colors, or other pedestrians. All these details combine to give us a fuller and more vibrant portrait of what is going on inside May's head than any explanatory dialogue could hope to achieve, the landscape functioning as both an externalization of and a context for the character's isolation and alienation.

Brad Stevens

Date 1994

Nationality Taiwan

Director Tsai Ming-liang

Cast Yang Kuei-mei

Original Title *Aiqing wansui*

Why It's Key This scene shows how visual imagery can reveal emotional states.

657

Key Person **Brigitte Lin**
Chungking Express

When Wong Kar-wai cast Brigitte Lin in *Chungking Express*, she was internationally famous for her transgender role as Master Asia in Tsui Hark's *Swordsman* series. Here she embodies another masquerade, caught between East and West: a Chinese woman wearing a blonde wig, dark sunglasses way into the unforgiving night, a tan raincoat belted at the waist, and high-heel shoes.

Lin becomes a signifier of the improbable space created by the film (both the real city and a state of mind). With the blonde wig Wong borrows one of the most predictable Western tropes, and turns it into a pure cinematic icon. When Lin draws her gun, her right arm extended, she conjures up classical Hollywood images: *Gun Crazy* (1950), *Bonnie and Clyde* (1967)…; when she walks away after one last killing, her silhouette echoes a famous shot of *The Big Combo* (1955). Deadly is the female, it's Marilyn, Madonna, and Barbara Stanwyck wrapped into one seductive menace.

Yet, as a fetish she's a disposable commodity; while she's running in the streets, her Caucasian drug boss/lover has sex with *another* Chinese woman donning a wig.

Wong creates a new mythology – that will resurface in his own *Fallen Angels* and other neo-Chinese films as well: Lou Ye's *Suzhou River* (2000) or Quentin Lee and Justin Lin's *Shopping for Fangs* (1997). Lin's presence is defined by its contours, as she continually eludes protagonists and spectators. Once the wig is finally discarded, another tantalizing cinematic artifact is revealed, a mane of "real" black Asian hair that flows in slow motion with the alluring grace of Master Asia's paraphernalia.

Bérénice Reynaud

Date 1994

Nationality Hong Kong

Director Wong Kar-wai

Original Title *Chung hing sam lam*

Why It's Key A blonde woman running for her life becomes the symbol of China's collision with post-modernity.

Opposite *Chungking Express*

Key Scene **The final gallery of staring faces** *Animals and More Animals*

Best known for *To Be and To Have* (2002), Philibert is arguably French cinema's best-kept secret and one of contemporary film's undiscovered masters. A documentarist adept at achieving extraordinary trust and intimacy with his subjects – be they schoolchildren, parents and teachers, the inmates and staff of a psychiatric hospital, or the deaf – he makes movies that are at once humane, poetic, and profoundly yet playfully philosophical. A companion-piece to *La Ville Louvre*, this hour-long masterpiece chronicles the three-year renovation of the zoology gallery in the National Natural History Museum in Paris, closed for almost 30 years and now being transformed into a bizarre ark of all (dead) creatures great and small.

Without commentary, Philibert simply observes – the term, given his careful framing and editing, is deceptive – staff as they investigate, repair, transport, and arrange the stuffed bestiary prior to the Museum's reopening. He has a surrealist's eye for a strange, telling moment, from when a demotion machine's claw pecks at a wall to scenes of parakeets' feathers tweaked, crocodiles brushed, badgers bashed, sealskins emptied, fish balanced, hippos hoovered, and elephants, giraffes, and rhinos wrapped protectively in polythene and clingfilm. The experts, meanwhile, speak their arcane lingo, asking how many heliconius butterflies might fill a vitrine, or ordering vultures by phone. But it's the last montage, of various stuffed fauna, from an owl to a tiger, returning our gaze with a glazed stare, that really brings home the message that life, finally, is just meat moving of its own accord; all else might be mere illusion.

Geoff Andrew

Date 1994

Nationality France

Director Nicolas Philibert

Original Title *Un Animal, des animaux*

Why It's Key It's an amusing, enlightening, incisive coda to one of the very rare films that really make us think about what it actually means to be alive.

658

Key Scene **The ending** *Through the Olive Trees*

SPOILER

There are not many films that make you actively peer at the screen to decipher what is happening in the depth of the image. But that is what Kiarostami does at the conclusion of *Through the Olive Trees*, as we watch, further and further in the distance, Hossein (Rezai) race through a line of trees and catch up to Tahereh (Ladanian) – to ask (we assume) for her hand in marriage. But we hear nothing of what they say to each other, and cannot know exactly why Hossein returns alone to his starting-point. All we have to go on is the evidence that, right throughout the making of the film-within-the-film, Tahereh has refused to acknowledge him. So does this ending confirm the pessimism of the given (the past) or affirm the optimism of surprise (the future)? Kiarostami's work is often assimilated to a neorealist aesthetic, an unadorned "window on the world," a seizing of ordinary things as they present themselves to the naked eye. But this ending (like all his endings) is more like a grand apparition, a true event, than mere reportage. And this visionary aspect is underlined for us: in the lead-up to that three-and three-quarter minute closing shot "through the trees," Hossein exits the frame and the film director (Ali Keshavarz), takes his place. He looks out, to survey the scene, to bear witness to it – but also, in a sense, to conjure it into being through the magic of his wish.

Adrian Martin

Date 1994

Nationality Iran

Director Abbas Kiarostami

Cast Hossein Rezai, Tahereh Ladanian, Mohammad Ali Keshavarz

Original Title *Zir-e darakhtan-e zeyton*

Why It's Key This scene underlines the visionary aspect of Kiarostami's work.

Opposite *Through the Olive Trees*

Key Scene **In the second section, symmetrical forms emerge** *Chartres Series*

Inspired by a visit to Chartres cathedral, this film magnificently captures the shards of colored light that traverse the actual cathedral's terrifyingly vast darkness from the stained-glass windows high above. Contrary to the clinical but false objectivity of the art documentary, with its sterile close-ups, Brakhage's vision finds a metaphor for the idea of light crossing space and impinging in consciousness in fields of rapidly changing and organically irregular colored forms. They are like other forms in his other handpainted films – and nowhere near as regular as the cathedral itself. So in the second section, there's a series of Rorschach-like organic forms, a bit to the left of center, but exactly symmetrical left-to-right (the symmetry was achieved through optical printing). This sequence ultimately leads to larger symmetries in the fourth, in which parallel band-like columns are seen side by side. A balance is achieved across the film between Brakhage's organic vision, which stresses unpredictability and changes, and the repetitive patterns of Gothic architecture. Brakhage himself hated symmetry, he once said; it represented for him all those fixed and predetermined structures that trapped light and interrupted the natural flow of his vision. And in his film, it is almost frightening to see organic shapes being mirrored so precisely, made into cathedral-like forms.

Fred Camper

Date 1994

Nationality USA

Director Stan Brakhage

Why It's Key Symmetry represents the fixed structures that Brakhage always struggled against, as he does here.

Key Scene **Hiring a housekeeper** *La Cérémonie*

SPOILER

Something telling, something vital to the film, happens in *La Cérémonie*'s first few seconds. But it's the kind of fleeting moment that doesn't register, and can't register, until the film is over. By then it will probably have been forgotten.

A woman (Bonnaire), a tiny figure seen in long shot, stops in front of a bar, looks at the door, and turns to ask a passerby for directions. He points across the street. The woman proceeds in that direction and enters a café, where another woman (Bisset) is waiting for her. We've been watching this scene from inside the café, from the second woman's point of view. Our point of view is hers. It's a viewpoint *La Cérémonie* will come to indict. But that's not the telling detail.

The woman in the café is Catherine Lelièvre, a bourgeois housewife and art-gallery owner waiting to interview Sophie Bonhomme for the position of housekeeper. Catherine is friendly, Sophie all business, but the two women, dressed professionally, seem on equal footing. They're not. The plot of this thriller hinges on the consequences of Sophie's illiteracy. She had to ask directions because she couldn't read the signs: she couldn't tell the bar from the café.

Chabrol undermines the concept of "the reveal" by getting it out of the way before he does anything else. It's the first sneaky move in a subtly radical film.

A. S. Hamrah

Date 1995

Nationality France

Director Claude Chabrol

Cast Sandrine Bonnaire, Jacqueline Bisset

Why It's Key Chabrol discloses the film's secret in its first five seconds.

Key Scene **Crossing the line**
Wild Side

For quite some time Scottish-born filmmaker Donald Cammell was just considered a tragic footnote in cinema history, as Nicolas Roeg's co-director on the cult classic *Perfomance*, released to much controversy in 1970. Since Roeg's subsequent work, using similar elliptical montage techniques, caught attention, while the remainder of Cammell's "career" consisted of three underrated films, the latter's contribution was long neglected. At first glance Cammell's films do seem more conventional, but weirdness lurks at every corner in 1977's visionary and ridiculous computer-rape fantasy *Demon Seed* and 1987's *The White of the Eye*, an early entry in the soon-sprawling serial-killer genre that's unlike anything that followed: chilly and feverish, uneven and all the more unsettling for that. This irritating instability reached its apotheosis in *Wild Side*, which was cut down in 1995 by its producers, Nu Image, to fit the erotic-thriller cable-sales mold (undoubtedly contributing to Cammell's suicide one year later), but was restored by friend and cutter Frank Mazzola in 2000. In this longer version the peculiar tension between madness, hilarity, and lyricism is breathtaking throughout, not least because of Christopher Walken's tour de force as threatening financier Bruno Buckingham – a performance that transcends mere acting. At one point in an argument he fiercely bellows something that sounds like "You've crossed the Bruno-line," but the justified fear on his opponent's face suggests that it's Walken himself who has crossed a line and become one with his character, thus seeming capable of anything: dangerous or worse.
Christoph Huber

Date 1995

Nationality UK/USA

Director Donald Cammell

Cast Christopher Walken, Steven Bauer

Why It's Key Donald Cammell has long been underrated as "just" the co-director of the cult film *Performance*, yet his small oeuvre is intriguing throughout. Its unsettling qualities peak with Cammell's last film, in which Walken transcends acting and his threats seem real.

Key Scene **Charlene warns Chris away**
Heat

In Mann's films, the camera set-ups are more crucial than the individual shots. Because Mann is fond of "master shots" – covering the whole or a large part of a scene in one (usually mobile) flow – and then breaks this master up with various detailed inserts. But if such "intensified continuity" and abundant "coverage" sounds like the TV-derived norm of contemporary Hollywood, what Mann does with it is special. In effect, he creates starkly separate spaces or zones in a scene – thus multiplying the master shots required, and the possibilities for their editing combination. A key scene in *Heat* – when Charlene (Judd), set up by the cops to nab her partner-in-crime Chris (Kilmer), uses the one moment in her power to warn him away with a hard look and a tiny hand gesture – would seem simple on paper. But, on screen, its effect is monumental. Surrounding Charlene are figures present in the room and (as so often in Mann) on the end of an open phone: each one waits anxiously, in his pocket of space, for Charlene's decision to head out to the balcony and identify Chris. It is this pervasive fishbowl effect – which the film reinforces with numerous reflective surfaces – that lends such gravity to the wordless, close-up insert of her hand, a truly decisive moment in the plot. Almost united, Charlene and Chris must split apart again, their only link thereafter being a soulful duet of inter-cut close-ups.
Adrian Martin

Date 1995

Nationality USA

Director Michael Mann

Cast Ashley Judd, Val Kilmer

Why It's Key Mann's special use of space makes a crucial gesture monumental.

Key Event
Publication of *Unthinking Eurocentrism*

Ella Shohat and Robert Stam's *Unthinking Eurocentrism: Multiculturalism and the Media* exposes the power play in North-South and West-East constructs of "otherness." Focusing on issues of representation, the book shows how, by validating certain narratives and suppressing others, Western art and ideology have stifled cultural pluralism.

Bringing together massive and wide-ranging evidence from the history of Western cinema, *Unthinking Eurocentrism* offers a systematic critique of the biased representation of non-Western cultures and argues for a new, more diverse media pedagogy. New York-based international-film scholars Shohat and Stam insist that the entrenched Eurocentric construct should be defeated by critically dissecting mainstream Western representations of the exotic and the foreign. Only in this way is it possible to overturn the unshakable vision of the world as consisting of one superior and many inferior cultures ("the West and the Rest," in cultural theorist Stuart Hall's expression) and offer instead a new, progressive understanding of the world as consisting of multiple, equally significant cultural entities that co-exist without being hierarchically ordered.
Dina Iordanova

Date 1994

Why It's Key This landmark film-studies work criticized the biased representation of non-Western cultures and argued in favor of a new, multicultural media pedagogy.

Key Scene **The soon-to-become lovers dance** *The Bridges of Madison County*

This really magical moment comes unexpectedly about mid-movie, after the second meeting of Mrs. Francesca Johnson (Streep) and Robert Kincaid (Eastwood). They've been together in the countryside, while he was taking photographs of covered bridges, and now they've finished dining at her home, when a nosy and gossipy neighbor called Madge phones Francesca, and while she talks (about him, a photographer whose presence has aroused some curiosity; "A hippy? No, I don't think he looks like one," answers Francesca to some comment we cannot hear), she casually strokes his shoulder affectionately (he's sitting at the table, with his back to her). He takes her hand lightly and retains it on his shoulder, and when she finally hangs up the phone, he gets up and they dance to Johnny Hartman singing Dietz and Schwartz's "I See Your Face Before Me." They seem suspended in time, almost floating weightlessly, encapsulated together in space, as if isolated in a shared bubble of warmth from the rest of the world. At a certain point, he whispers "If you want me to stop, tell me now," as a series of dissolves – quite infrequent in modern cinema, apart from Víctor Erice's films – continue to show them slowly and pleasantly dancing, the camera circling around them closer and closer, and they get increasingly close to each other, looking, smiling, kissing, embracing each other, already a couple, for much longer than the song (supposedly coming from the radio) really lasts.
Miguel Marías

Date 1995

Nationality USA

Director Clint Eastwood

Cast Clint Eastwood, Meryl Streep

Why It's Key It captures like few other film scenes what falling in love can mean.

Opposite *The Bridges of Madison County*

Key Scene **Hole in the head**
The Quick and the Dead

The Quick and the Dead, with its gun-toting heroine (Sharon Stone), is somewhat in the tradition of *Johnny Guitar* (1954), but it relates far more intimately to the Sergio Leone legacy of Italian Westerns. It is pure, almost abstract, juggling a high-ball mixture of corny camp humor, intense generic emotion, and a severe, majestic sense of film form. It hardly touches upon complexities of law and morality common to the genre; basically, it comprises a bunch of gunfights in the main street of a spindly little Western town, strung together as a contest progressively waged among the assembled hotheads and opportunists. And once the fighting revs up, things rapidly become stylized: the camera angles get exponentially weirder, the editing quickens, the soundtrack amplifies every little breath, movement of clothing, and insect buzz. Raimi's creativity is concentrated not in the various characters and their emotional dramas, but in the sudden, outrageous moments of violent gore, the accelerated

rushes of melodramatic action, the grotesque comedy of bodies slouching, spitting, falling, or being knocked flying to the ground by an almighty, slow-motion bullet. He is one of those directors for whom the cinema is essentially a game, an exhibitionistic display. And his wildest effect comes when the capitalist villain Herod (Hackman) interrupts his overlord spiel ("I'm in charge of everything! I decide who lives and dies!") to kill Clay (David): he blows a large (and bloodless) hole clear through his skull, allowing Raimi to frame this sadistic baddie through the opening.

Adrian Martin

Date 1995

Nationality USA

Director Sam Raimi

Cast Gene Hackman, Keith David

Why It's Key It's the wildest effect in a wildly creative display of stylized action.

Opposite *The Quick and the Dead*

Key Scene **On the verge of developing the legendary film footage** *Ulysses' Gaze*

World-weary film director "A." (Keitel) travels through the troubled Balkans of the 1990s in an attempt to restore some long-lost film footage shot by the Manaki brothers, the cinema pioneers of the region. The meandering journey takes him to war-ravaged Sarajevo, where the Jewish curator of the local cinematheque, Ivo Levi (Josephson), holds the secret to unveiling the content of these sacred reels. Amid apocalyptic devastation, the two men gather in a basement room in anticipation of the moment when they will relive the lives of those whose lost images will be momentarily restored on the screen. It is a moment of sublime tranquillity: having finally found each other, the two men are both relaxed because now, it seems, they have all the time on earth for each other and for an all-embracing conversation. But the scene raises doubts about the possibility to use past records meaningfully for present-day intellectual needs.

Within the next hour, the Jewish curator is killed on the lawless streets, and A. remains alone, staring into the glimmering images of innocent peaceful togetherness that flash on the screen. The revered footage no longer matters. The old curator has managed to bring back the memory of happy multicultural coexistence recorded on the missing reels. But now, amid all this war and destruction, the happy memory is irretrievably lost, just as those to whom it mattered have been destroyed. Recovering the lost footage that asserts past conviviality cannot heal the present-day intolerance.

Dina Iordanova

Date 1995

Nationality Greece/ Germany/UK/France/Italy

Director Theo Angelopoulos

Cast Harvey Keitel, Erland Josephson, Maia Morgenstern

Original Title *To vlemma tou Odyssea*

Why It's Key This scene encapsulates both the longing for, and the futility of, reaching back into history via recorded moving image.

Key Scene **Warm bodies on a motorcycle at dawn** *Fallen Angels*

The avant-pop romanticism of Wong Kar-wai's urban-youth period reached new heights of abstract eloquence in this brashly stylized gangster nocturne, an action painting in rain and neon. Set entirely at night and shot mainly in wide angle by Christopher Doyle, *Fallen Angels* is a kinetic reverie, a dream of light and motion that blinks awake in a final moment of bittersweet transcendence.

In the penultimate scene, two lovelorn strangers are thrown together in a noodle shop on a cold winter's night. A hitman's agent (Reis) is nervily smoking and forking down her dinner. Takeshi Kaneshiro's mute goofball emerges bloodied from a brawl that mysteriously erupts behind her. They sit with their backs to each other, registering their mutual presence.

Wong elides the moment of contact, and as the first, trembling a cappella notes of the Flying Pickets' "Only You" come on, he cuts to an image we've seen a couple of times before: Kaneshiro's motorcycle zipping through traffic and into an underpass, as the dividing line and tunnel lights whiz by. This time, the shot is slowed down. He's with Reis, her body slumped close and her head on his shoulder. In voice-over, she reveals that she hasn't been so close to a man in a while. "The road wasn't that long," she muses, "and I knew I'd be getting off soon. But at that moment I felt such warmth."

This achingly beautiful scene is suffused with the melancholy of transience that courses through all of Wong's work. It's a perfect moment – and a fleeting one, mourned even before it's over. Further emphasizing its impermanence, Kaneshiro exhales a puff of cigarette smoke, which floats up and evaporates. The camera pans skyward: dawn is breaking over the skyscrapers of Hong Kong. It's the final shot of the film and the first glimpse of daylight.
Dennis Lim

Date 1995

Nationality Hong Kong

Director Wong Kar-wai

Cast Takeshi Kaneshiro, Michele Reis

Original Title *Duo luo tian shi*

Why It's Key This lovely ending perfectly illustrates the paradox at the heart of Wong Kar-wai's melancholic worldview: The more beautiful the moment, the sadder it is.

Opposite *Fallen Angels*

Key Scene **The heroine finds isolation at the end** *Safe*

"Fine… I'm fine…. That's fine…. " The blandly affirmative "fine" is a favorite word of Carol White (Moore), an upper-middle-class homemaker who seems ideally situated in the comfort and security of her suburban home. But things become less fine when she contracts a mysterious ailment that puzzles her physicians even as its symptoms grow more severe.

The most interesting guess is that she has "environmental illness" caused by the brew of toxins and contaminants swirling ubiquitously through modern cities. Is this a real disease? The movie's tone suggests that the answer doesn't matter – it's real for Carol, and in today's self-obsessed climate the boundaries between reality and fantasy are irredeemably blurred.

Hope reawakens when Carol learns of a new-age health center that promises ultra-hygienic (and ultra-spiritless) surroundings for its residents. Soon after moving there, she sees an odd figure in the distance – a man whose flight from impurities has led him to view the world through a gas mask and dwell in a sterilized shelter. The moment we see this high-tech igloo we can predict that Carol will end up there, since it marks the logical end of her self-isolating quest. Instead of seeking wholeness by expanding her range of experiences and insights, she has chosen to eliminate ever more from her life, starting with the home and husband she once prized. At the end she's gazing into a mirror and affirming her love for herself, signaling that her solipsism is complete. It's one of the truest, most terrifying love scenes ever filmed.
David Sterritt

Date 1995

Nationality UK/USA

Director Todd Haynes

Cast Julianne Moore

Why It's Key The conclusion of this unsettling story is inevitable in narrative terms, chilling in emotional terms, and courageously unsparing in its critique of so-called individualism as an excuse for narcissism and self-absorption.

Key Scene **Cut Stephen Chow in half**
Out of the Dark

Before Hong Kong comedy superstar Stephen Chow became his own director and won international acclaim, he enjoyed a formidable partnership with eternally underrated filmmaker Jeff Lau. The Chow-Lau connection peaked in 1995 with the release of both their two-part masterpiece *A Chinese Odyssey* and their film maudit: *Out of the Dark*, a horror comedy hated at home and hardly exported. Being on the brink of comprehensibilty, it is the most outrageous application of Chow's characteristic "*mo lei tau*" (literally: "makes no sense") comedy style of impossible juxtapositions and (de)constructive punning. In retrospect it is the one film that really tackles handover fears, then supposedly referenced in every other HK release, head-on. Beneath its stark-raving-mad turns and mercilessly dark jokes about an asylum inmate and self-declared *Leon, The Professional*-style ghostbuster (Chow), magical flying paper hats, and multiple dynamite mishaps, *Out of the Dark* is a lucid and rigorous film about overcoming the fear of separation. The story kicks into high gear with a ghost's head disconnected from his body, then takes its crucial turn with a woman prevented from joining in on her husband's suicide attempt. From there it's only a small step to the separation of all kinds of body parts, while the key theme is separation from reality. Consequently, the happy end comes with an ultimate divorce from sanity. But this turns out to be premature: Of course, the happy end is only possible (and with *Caligari*-style doubts at that) after Chow's protagonist finally convinces his love interest that he has to be chainsawed in half.

Christoph Huber

Date 1995

Nationality Hong Kong

Director Jeff Lau

Cast Stephen Chow, Karen Mok

Original Title *Wui wan yeh*

Why it's Key A comedy so dark it was golden boy Stephen Chow's singular flop at home, *Out of the Dark* is not only the most extreme example of his brand of humor, but also takes the perceived themes of Hong Kong cinema before the handover to their logical conclusion.

Key Scene **"It didn't snow that year."**
The Neon Bible

Few moments in movies reveal the power of imagination more succinctly than the opening of Terence Davies' CinemaScope adaptation of John Kennedy Toole's first novel, written when the southern author was only 16. It opens with 15-year-old David (Tierney) alone on a train at night, the camera moving past him to the darkness glimpsed outside. Then David at ten (Bell) is seen peering out a rain-streaked window in his rural home to the strains of "Perfidia," circa 1948, while narrating offscreen, "People came to see us that Christmas. They were *nas*, those people – they brought me things..."

A moment later, we cut to a diptych: on screen left, an empty porch topped by icicles framing an enchanted snowfall, as decorous as a neatly filled box by the surrealist artist Joseph Cornell. On screen right, young David is seated on the floor inside, now looking out the same window in profile, while narrating offscreen, "There was no snow – no, not that year."

When the next shot shows us his aunt (Rowlands) in full frame greeting him through the window, the icicles are still lining the top of the frame. But a shot later, when David comes out on the porch to greet her, it's raining again.

Davies, who once compared filling a CinemaScope frame to settling down in Canada, also knows the period like the back of his hand. And the power of snow to briefly supplant rain in a ten-year-old's mind has the force of an epiphany.

Jonathan Rosenbaum

Date 1995

Nationality UK

Director Terence Davies

Cast Drake Bell, Jacob Tierney, Gena Rowlands

Why It's Key It reveals the power of imagination in a flash.

Key Event
The Dogme 95 Manifesto

In March, Danish filmmakers Lars von Trier and Thomas Vinterberg issued the Dogme 95 manifesto, a list of "rules" they promised to obey in their next projects. Soon, fellow directors Kristian Levring and Søren Kragh-Jacobsen took the Dogme 95 "vow of chastity" and joined the Brotherhood. "It was easy," Vinterberg said. "We asked ourselves what we most hated about film today, and then we drew up a list banning it all. It took half an hour and it was a great laugh." The Manifesto consists of ten rules, including "the camera must be hand-held," "the film must not contain superficial action (murders, weapons, etc. must not occur)," "optical work and filters are forbidden," "genre movies are not acceptable," and "the director must not be credited." *Dogme #1* was Vinterberg's *Festen* (1998), and #2 von Trier's *The Idiots* (1998). Subsequently, more than 150 films have supposedly adhered to the manifesto and borne the official numbering – though the originators have long since lost interest. The first non-Danish Dogme was #5, Jean-Marc Barr's *Lovers* (1999), and the first American entry was #6, Harmony Korine's *Julien Donkey-Boy* (1999). At once a joke, a canny promotional device, and a genuine attempt to speak up for a homemade, engaged, grass-roots level of filmmaking, Dogme 95 attracted a great deal of attention – quite a bit hostile (the British critic Alexander Walker was especially splenetic), though it certainly suggests a viable alternative to, say, the Jerry Bruckheimer school of filmmaking. It may be impossible to adhere to every single tenet of the manifesto (directors found the stricture against being credited a tough pill to swallow), and the bar on genre movies was broken at least as early as *Dogme #3*, Kragh-Jacobsen's *Mifune* (1999), a romantic comedy.

Kim Newman

Date March 13, 1995

Why It's Key This was the cinema's "back to basics" movement.

Key Scene **The healing snowfall**
Maborosi

Leaving behind the big city and troubling memories of her first husband's apparent suicide, a young widow (Esumi) remarries and rebuilds her life in a remote seaside town, yet cannot shake recurrent guilty dreams that press at her like the winter wind pressing at her windows. Documentarist Kore-eda's debut feature began his investigations of human fragility when faced with the bottomless emptiness of loss (1998's *After Life* and 2004's *Nobody Knows* followed). Exploiting off-screen space, he holds shots even after people have left the frame, asserting the space's reality independent of players. The indirect narrative immerses us in the heroine's consoling absorption with everyday tasks, but the plainspoken dialogue tells less than the asymmetrical, unpredictable images that translate surges of feeling into light, even visualizing the end of a tunnel rushing closer. The heroine's inward disturbances resolve when chiming bells announce a funeral procession as mourners move single-file down a winding path along the open sea. As the shot continues, snowflakes begin to waft down and gradually thicken and swirl, glinting into the lens, with the camera so elevated that the snowfall could not have been faked. Did Kore-eda miraculously catch nature at the exact right moment? Then, the dark figures exiting the frame one by one seem to free the heroine to rebalance her existence. Later, released from her conflicts by the healing snowfall, she finally voices her fears to her husband (Takashi Naito) in an unremitting long shot, ready to begin accepting the serenely impartial and uncontrollable universe.

Robert Keser

Date 1995

Nationality Japan

Director Hirokazu Kore-eda

Cast Makiko Esumi

Original Title *Maborosi no hikari*

Why It's Key It captures a record of nature's spontaneous bounty that perfectly resolves the film's theme of loss.

Key Scene **The first glimpse of Iceland**
Cold Fever

Fridrik Thor Fridriksson is a one-man movie industry, whose hand is in many of Iceland's films. This gorgeous road movie deadpans its way across wintry landscapes and past a gallery of eccentrics; certainly as visually crisp as his other films, it's also unexpectedly mystical. The story of Hirata (Nagase), a Japanese man who visits the place of his parents' death seven years after it happened to perform a ritual for them, partly makes it so, but what adds to the otherworldliness are the little explosions of visual magic that Fridriksson plants along the way, like the moment when a car, long frozen to the ground, rises from the cracking ice as if about to levitate. The first visual coup is even more significant. Hirata's life in Japan with his grandfather (played by veteran director Seijun Suzuki) is framed in a 1.66:1 aspect ratio – compact and claustrophobic. But when he first glimpses Iceland, the screen bursts open horizontally, to a 2.35:1 ratio. Not only is the effect delicious for cinephiles – as if we've cut from Ozu to Leone – but it makes us acutely aware that Hirata has entered a spatially and philosophically different world. It is a moment that deserves to be as well known as the switch from monochrome to color in *The Wizard of Oz*.

Mark Cousins

Date 1995

Nationality Iceland

Director Fridrik Thor Fridriksson

Cast Masatoshi Nagase

Original Title *Á köldum klaka*

Why It's Key This moment from a high point of Icelandic cinema offers one of the all-time great uses of screen ratio.

Key Scene **The first number**
Haut bas fragile (Up, Down, Fragile)

Something is up in the *mise en scène* of this seemingly ordinary meeting between Ninon (Richard) and Roland (Marcon). In the airy studio where décors for film and theatre are constructed – a space pregnant with fiction, artifice, and magic – the bodies of these characters slowly become possessed: they take formal steps and strike poses, mention how "close and distant" they are from each other, and their dialogue takes on an incantatory rhythm, stuck on the repetition of odd words like *perturbé* ('disturbed'). Then, with an amorous clinch and a perfectly timed cut closer-in, music begins – and singing and dancing, too. Almost an hour into this typical Rivette film about Parisian wanderings and conspiracies, and suddenly we are into a musical? You can describe the punning song ("Ni oui Ninon") as a whimsical piece of fluff, and you might find the dance a touch awkward or amateurish, but Rivette and his performers embrace it all: *Haut bas fragile* is about the dream of everyday life metamorphosing – via only the slightest nudges of stylisation – into the idealised realm of art, and specifically popular-musical art. Rivette's films, with their obsessive walkers and mannered talkers, have frequently circled this moment of ignition, but here he goes all the way: love expresses itself in ironic, playful postures and swooning falls. But *Haut bas fragile* always keeps a charming margin of reality: the singing is 'live' (thus prone to imperfection), and a shower of sparks to accompany the rapture come from a welder's tool.

Adrian Martin

Date 1995

Nationality France

Director Jacques Rivette

Cast Nathalie Richard, André Marcon.

Why It's Key Suddenly, everyday life metamorphoses into art.

Key Film *Floating Life*
Life on the move

Floating Life is one of the most important films to capture the feel of life on the move, without a permanent base or firmly determined ethnic and home identities. It is one of the first films to recognize that, in an age when migration and life in diaspora have become basic modes of existence, the theme of constant displacement is increasingly important.

Clara Law, a Macau-born Hong Kong director whose entire work is preoccupied with issues of migration, made *Floating Life*, the first non-English-language film made in Australia, shortly after she migrated to Australia. The film is set in the last years of Hong Kong's existence as a British colony. Members of three generations of the Chan family, driven by the uncertainty and anxieties associated with the 1997 takeover from China, are shown leaving Hong Kong and dispersing to various geographic locations – Australia, Canada, and Germany – where they engage in setting up new homes and new lives. Moving around

necessarily brings disquieting experiences, but staying in one place is no longer possible. In this dispersed mode of existence, it is difficult for the family to remain as close as they once were, and they gradually drift apart. The terminally-ill Hong Kong imaginary rendered by Law generates a sense of urgency; the protagonists come across as lonely and insecure, clinging to a bag of fragrant tea or a photograph of a village house as they take on the challenges of adjusting to their new "floating" identities and soon rejoin their extended families, gathering in cyberspace.

Dina Iordanova

Date 1996

Nationality Australia

Director Clara Law

Cast Annette Shun Wah, Annie Yip, Anthony Wong

Original Title *Fu Sheng*

Why It's Key It's an atmospheric film about floating identities, contemporary migrations, and life in diaspora.

1990-1999

671

Key Scene **The Czech and Russian flags**
Kolya

SPOILER

The middle-aged protagonist, Louka (Sverák), lives in Prague at the end of the 1980s. His career has been adversely affected by the defection of his brother; he has to make ends meet in various inventive ways. Louka genuinely hates the Russians, who have occupied his country since 1968, but agrees to pocket a fee and enter a marriage of convenience to a Russian woman (Irina Livanova). However, things take an unexpected turn and Louka finds himself stuck with his new wife's five-year-old son, Kolya (Chalimon), of whom he must reluctantly take care.

In the key scene of the film, Louka arrives at his attic apartment with the boy. Having been ordered by the landlady to display the Czech and Soviet flags to celebrate the victory holiday, Louka grudgingly complies. This triggers a dialogue between Louka and Kolya (conducted in Czech and Russian and relying on word-play mischief) about which of the flags they prefer. The exchange takes place while Louka has

kneeled down to untie the boy's shoes – symbolically bending in front of the little Russian colonizer.

Normally, the things Louka says would only be whispered and could put him in serious danger. But since the comments are made in front of a boy one cannot take them seriously: the fearsome colonizing power is now represented by a diminutive innocuous lad. The fearsome Homo Sovieticus is no longer dreaded but mocked, and the fear with which people in the Soviet Bloc lived for decades is derided.

Dina Iordanova

Date 1996

Nationality Czech Republic

Director Jan Sverák

Cast Zdenek Sverák, Andrei Chalimon

Why It's Key The scene symbolically represents the end of the Soviet occupation of Eastern Europe.

Key Scene **The opening scene**
A Moment of Innocence

In the 1970s, a teenage revolutionary, Mohsen Makhmalbaf, was imprisoned for attempting to stab a policeman. He educated himself in jail and, after he was released, became a novelist and, eventually, one of Iran's best-known filmmakers. As he often works with non-professional actors, in the mid-1990s he put a casting advertisement in a Tehran newspaper to cast a new film. One of the people who turned up was Tayebi, the policeman whom Makhmalbaf had stabbed. Fascinated, the director abandoned the planned film and asked the policeman if he himself would direct a film of his version of the stabbing; Makhmalbaf would tell it from his own point of view, and they'd intercut the two.

The result, which played at 47 film festivals around the world, was like the *Rashomon* of the 1990s, a brilliant, intense, genre-bending disquisition on the relativity of truth and the innate ambiguity of a filmed scene. In *A Moment of Innocence*, Tayebi walks to Makhmalbaf's real house, rings the bell, talks to his real daughter Hana (who would become an acclaimed director), and says who he is: a documentary moment, but restaged (and hilarious). For much of its length the film seems to continue in this mode, filming both directors as they stage their versions of events. But some scenes appear to be non-fiction, but staged, and by its end, the film has transcended such distinctions.
Mark Cousins

Date 1996

Nationality Iran

Director Mohsen Makhmalbaf

Cast Mirhadi Tayebi, Hana Makhmalbaf

Original Title *Nun va Goldoon*

Why It's Key The opening minutes of this film sets the scene for one of the most fascinating story lines in 1990s cinema.

Key Person **Lili Taylor** "I dedicate this play to me" *I Shot Andy Warhol*

SPOILER

In this compelling portrait of Warhol's would-be assassin, Lili Taylor plays Valerie Solanas, author of the *SCUM Manifesto*, like she's a newsboy from a '30s movie looking for someone to talk to. With her choppy haircut and black cap, looking sideways and smoking, she hangs around a New York newsstand and hustles "finks." That's how she meets her publisher, Maurice Girodias of the Olympia Press (Bluteau). "Give me 15 cents and I'll give you a dirty word," she tells him. "What's the word?" he asks. "Men," she says. Girodias promptly offers to buy her a drink.

Taylor's voice prevails over the tragedy of Solanas's life. Harron wisely allows her to recite passages from the *Manifesto* in black-and-white monologues meant to evoke Warhol screen tests. No matter how nutty Valerie's ideas, Taylor's delivery lends them credence.

Her voice cuts through the complacency of Warhol's entourage. Her asides are memorable. "An exquisite mosaic!" she remarks to a john showing her the scabs on his chest.

After Valerie dolls herself up in a red dress to sign a book contract with Girodias over dinner (the film's most affecting scene), she begins to unravel. She doubts herself and reverts to the angry student who answered a letter about corsages for her college newspaper by scrawling FUCK YOU on it.

"All I know is I want a piece of the groovy world myself." She never gets one. "Where do you live?" a cop asks her after her arrest. "Nowhere," she answers.
A. S. Hamrah

Date 1996

Nationality USA

Director Mary Harron

Cast Lili Taylor, Lothaire Bluteau, Jared Harris

Why It's Key It's a consummate portrait of artistic honesty gone mad.

Opposite *I Shot Andy Warhol*

Key Scene **Use of the Underworld track "Born Slippy"** *Trainspotting*

Trainspotting was a film mainly about the squalors and fitful glories of heroin use, but the timing of its release and the raffish, dayglo energy of its direction, and above all its use of the Underworld track "Born Slippy", placed it squarely within the emerging culture of Generation Ecstasy. "Drive boy dog boy dirty numb angel boy/ In the doorway boy she was a lipstick boy..." The distorted voice of Underworld lyricist/frontman Karl Hyde, chanting out what sounded like a hallucinated, transgendered picaresque set in the more vicious areas of London's West End, was a call, if not to action, then to experience. In the context of Danny Boyle's movie, "Born Slippy" was deployed to connote mounting adrenalin, certainty, and ruthlessness as Mark "Rent Boy" Renton (McGregor) – the film's hero/narrator – decides to steal from his three hapless Edinburgh drug buddies the money they all just made in a large heroin deal. The money is in a briefcase, the drug buddies are all unconscious after a celebratory bender, and as

Renton gingerly carries the swag past the snoring forms of his co-conspirators the enormous percussion of "Born Slippy" begins to pound. The scene is morally inert – we do not care about Renton's friends sufficiently to worry about the fact that he is ripping them off – and the sense of danger is rudimentary, child-like (will they wake up and discover him?). And yet the music imparts a cold immediacy to the action, a truly drug-like vitality.

James Parker

Date 1996

Nationality UK

Director Danny Boyle

Cast Ewan McGregor, Ewen Bremner, Jonny Lee Miller, Robert Carlyle

Why It's Key: Here is music used not as soundtrack or comment, but as pure stimulant – very Nineties.

Opposite *Trainspotting*

Key Film *The Day a Pig Fell into the Well* Hyo-sub and Po-kyong at the love motel

Hong Sang-soo's 1996 debut, *The Day a Pig Fell into the Well*, was not only the first chapter in the career of an outstanding filmmaker but also the first blossoming of a new generation of Korean auteurs who attracted international attention in the following years. *The Day...* already put into place three main elements of Hong's cinema. First and foremost: the obsession with structure. *The Day...* is articulated in four segments depicting four interconnected characters (Hong had each segment written by a different scriptwriter), each introduced on a day when everything turns wrong (that's what the title refers to). Second: a detached and objectifying gaze that refuses to endorse the characters' points of view and insists on often incongruous and bizarre details, so that the coincidences, rhymes, and repetitions that punctuate Hong's films alternatively bloom into magic symmetries or crystallize into unfathomable riddles. Third: narratives that focus on never-mutually-accommodating

relationships between men and women, unmasking both the immaturity of the male characters and the passiveness of their female counterparts.

One of Hong's trademarks is the love scene set in a love motel, where men-women relations are unveiled in their barest dynamics. Hong's very first love-motel sequence in *The Day...* has writer Hyo-sub (Kim) and the adulterous Po-kyong (Lee) making love after Hyo-sub has revealed his egotistic insecurity and jealousy by asking Po-kyong if she still has sex with her husband; not satisfied, during the intercourse, Hyo-sub demands that Po-kyong tell him she belongs to him. It's a remarkable page from Hong's manual of human ethology.

Paolo Bertolin

Date 1996

Nationality South Korea

Director Hong Sang-soo

Cast Kim Eui-sung, Lee Eung-kyung

Original Title *Twaeji ka umul e ppajin nal*

Why It's Key A trademark of Hong Sang-soo, sex scenes in love motels reveal the bare essence of men-women relationships.

Key Scene **The trampoline sequence**
Shine

Geoffrey Rush was highly respected in Australia as a stage actor before he was cast in the leading role in *Shine*. Although he had played supporting roles in a few films, this was his first major screen appearance: It deservedly won him the Oscar for Best Actor and led to a prolific career in international cinema. In *Shine*, Rush played a real character, the pianist David Helfgott, who emerged from a tough childhood, the appalling pressures of the competitive music world, and years of mental institutions and psychotherapy to become an eccentric genius happily married to an astrologer, Gillian. One of Gillian's first encounters with David is a scene in which he dances exuberantly and almost naked on a trampoline, responding to classical music playing through a Walkman. The scene, beautifully performed by Rush and by Lynn Redgrave as Gillian, became frozen as an image on the posters for the film's American release. Rush's observation of Helfgott's eccentricities in speech and behavior provide a strong

center for a moving and well-crafted drama. As well as the Oscar for Rush, the film won many international awards and screened successfully in many countries; the director, Scott Hicks, went on to direct in the USA with films like *Snow Falling on Cedars* and *Hearts in Atlantis*; and the success of the film dramatically expanded the real Helfgott's concert career both in Australia and overseas.

Andrew Pike

Date 1996

Nationality Australia

Director Scott Hicks

Cast Geoffrey Rush, Noah Taylor, Googie Withers, Armin Mueller-Stahl, Lynn Redgrave

Why It's Key It's an exuberant moment in an Australian film that was an international success.

Opposite *Shine*

Key Scene **The flashback to the Gwangju Massacre** *A Petal*

SPOILER

The Gwangju Massacre of 1980, which might briefly be described as Korea's Tiananmen Square, sent shock waves through Korean society and politics. Among the films that would later depict that horror-filled week, Jang Sun-woo's *A Petal* remains the strongest and most controversial. Mostly set after the massacre, the direct depiction of the event comes in flashback towards the end, when the psychologically damaged, sexually abused protagonist (played by future pop star Lee Jung-hyun) visits her older brother's grave to explain how their mother died.

The sequence begins at the girl's home, where she ignores her mother's warnings and follows her to the city center. Demonstrators crowd the streets, furious at shootings by the military in previous days (the bodies are pulled through the crowd in protest). At last the protesters gather into a giant mob, screaming at armed soldiers lined up opposite them. When shots ring out and bodies begin to fall, chaos ensues.

In the rush to get away, the girl trips and falls, and her mother runs back to her. As they get up again, the mother is shot in the back and slides to the ground. The girl screams in grief, but also glances back at the oncoming soldiers. The most traumatic event for the young girl, presented twice on the screen, is when she tries to pull her hand from her mother's clenched death grip. She is not strong enough; she steps on her mother's hand and pulls, finally breaking free and running off, leaving her dead mother behind.

Darcy Paquet

Date 1996

Nationality South Korea

Director Jang Sun-woo

Cast Lee Jung-hyun, Lee Young-ran, Moon Sung-keun

Original Title *Kkotnip*

Why It's Key This extended black-and-white flashback is the most emotionally wrenching portrayal on film of modern-day Korea's single most traumatic event.

"A TERRIFIC TWISTED COMEDY A DAZZLING MIX OF MIRTH AND MALICE"

PETER TRAVERS — ROLLING STONE

A FILM BY JOEL AND ETHAN COEN

FARGO

18

SMALL TOWN

BIG CRIME

DEAD COLD

FRANCES McDORMAND   **WILLIAM H. MACY**   **STEVE BUSCEMI**

POLYGRAM FILMED ENTERTAINMENT PRESENTS IN ASSOCIATION WITH WORKING TITLE FILMS 'FARGO' FRANCES McDORMAND WILLIAM H. MACY STEVE BUSCEMI HARVE PRESNELL PETER STORMARE MUSIC BY CARTER BURWELL PRODUCTION DESIGNER RICK HEINRICHS
DIRECTOR OF PHOTOGRAPHY ROGER A. DEAKINS, A.S.C. LINE PRODUCER JOHN CAMERON EXECUTIVE PRODUCERS TIM BEVAN ERIC FELLNER PRODUCED BY ETHAN COEN WRITTEN BY JOEL COEN AND ETHAN COEN DIRECTED BY JOEL COEN
ORIGINAL SCREENPLAY PUBLISHED BY FABER & FABER ¦¦ ©1996 POLYGRAM FILM PRODUCTIONS B.V.

PolyGram

Key Event
First DVD players go on sale in Japan

The advent of digital video disks or digital versatile disks (DVDs) was a case study in the way simple marketplace competition can make for a wealthier culture. Studios were faced with the challenge of getting skeptical home viewers to upgrade from their trusted VHS cassettes to a new and strange format. (It's hard to believe that this was ever a problem, but it's true.) The solution came in two ringing truths. First, that the VHS format was garbage and the rental-store economy that supported it insane; second, that by increasing the home-video value proposition, you could turn DVD into a sell-through rather than a rental product. This second revelation served an aesthetic explosion of commentary tracks, outtakes, supporting documentaries, storyboard galleries, script comparisons, alternate versions, critical histories, primary-source collections for movies based on true events, and on and on.

If this were graduate school, such documentation would seem like scholarship, like work. It was the genius of the DVD to reveal that this was something normal people can find interesting. By luck, the format hit at a time when the culture was beginning to resemble graduate school in a variety of ways – book clubs, boxed-set CDs with liner notes, whole cable channels parsing the levels of meaning in the entertainment industry – that smashed the studio ideal of the passive viewer. (Ironically, read-only media like DVD vastly expanded the participatory element of entertainment.) Most DVD extras may be crap; but enough of them are not, and the culture of engagement the format has created was one of the twentieth century's final gifts.
Tim Cavanaugh

Date November 1, 1996

Why It's Key The DVD turned home viewing into film school.

Key Scene **The scene of the crime**
Fargo

"THIS IS A TRUE STORY," proclaims the very first title card in *Fargo*, but in fact this skewed crime caper is a complete fabrication from the febrile imaginations of brothers Joel and Ethan Coen. Tightly-wrapped car dealer Jerry Lundegaard (William H. Macy) hatches a plan in mid-1980s Minnesota to have his wife kidnapped for ransom. Since the audience has already seen three innocent people shot along a deserted, snow-bound road in the wake of the abduction, the offbeat joy of this investigation scene comes from watching down-to-earth, pregnant police chief Marge Gunderson (McDormand) reconstruct the events in a distinctively deadpan local patois. "Okay," she muses, "so we got a trooper pulls someone over, we got a shooting, these folks drive by, there's a high-speed pursuit, ends here and then this execution-type deal." She then gently guides her low-wattage subordinate, Lou (first-time actor Bohne), through a howlingly funny gaffe involving dealer tags. "I'm not sure I agree with you a hundred per cent on your police work, there, Lou," she says gently, receiving from him the film's favorite all-purpose expression: "Oh. Geez." But ever the generous boss, she defuses the situation with a joke: "Did you hear the one about the guy who couldn't afford personalized plates, so he changed his name to J3L2404?" The most perfectly balanced Coen film to date, *Fargo* is at once a grimly economic comedy of place and a gruff love letter to the practicality of blue collar America.
David Stratton

Date 1996

Nationality USA

Director Joel Coen

Cast Frances McDormand, Bruce Bohne

Why It's Key Oscar-winning script and lead performance combine in a genre-defying crime comedy.

Opposite *Fargo*

Key Scene **The demise of the father in the post-Tiananmen era** *Sons*

Li Maojie and his wife were famous ballet dancers. During the Cultural Revolution, they were probably exiled in a faraway countryside. Now he's old, out of shape, an alcoholic. His wife, Fu Derong, supports him by giving dance lessons. His sons, Touzi and Xiao Wei, are two young good-for-nothings who are vaguely involved in Beijing's nascent rock underground, who puke in the street and beat up their girlfriends. One day Li Maojie drags his wife to the divorce bureau. Yet, because of the shortage of housing, they keep on living together, in a drab apartment building. She still cares for him and cooks for the entire family. In drunken anguish, he screams her name in the collective courtyard.

The brothers convinced their neighbor, Zhang Yuan, one of the first exponents of China's "Sixth Generation," to make a film about the family, in which each member would play his or her own role. Mixing documentary and fiction, *Sons* captures an acute moment of crisis. One night, Fu Derong agrees to stay in her ex-husband's room. He makes her drunk. Touzi comes home, and, furious at seeing what Li Maojie has done, breaks a stool over his head. Zhang cuts to an extreme close-up of the old man's bloody face; looking sad and suddenly sobered up, he says twice: "I thank you, my good boy." Then he adds: "A son who beats his old man. The gods will be mad. An impious son is the father's fault."

Bérénice Reynaud

Date 1996

Nationality China

Director Zhang Yuan

Cast Li Maojie, Fu Derong, Li Ji (Touzi), Li Wei (Xiao Wei)

Original Title *Erzi*

Why It's Key Here cinema acts as a precise X-ray of the societal unease that swept China in the early 1990s.

Key People **The Farrelly brothers** Forgiveness through fighting *Kingpin*

The brothers Bobby and Peter Farrelly are Hollywood's last great humanists. Beneath the gross-out veneer of their fabulous comedies they conduct deeply moving investigations into the interconnectedness of mankind's ignorance and innocence. Their work is the most noble expression of a particular, admirable streak of lowbrow comedy, with frequent bowel failures and similar gags not in the service of easy ridicule, but rather helping to express existential ordeals: the weaknesses of the body mirroring those of the mind. And the bigger their character's weaknesses, the more the Farrellys seem to love them, as evidenced by their most underrated film, the bowling saga *Kingpin*, which was mostly trashed upon its 1996 release, probably since its dirty humor wasn't mitigated by any hipness factor (like Jim Carrey's star turn in 1994's predecessor *Dumb and Dumber*). Yet in its satirical treatment of pop culture (and breast fetishism) it is clearly a worthy successor,

exactly four decades later, to another comedic road movie, Frank Tashlin's Lewis-Martin classic *Hollywood or Bust*. But whereas Tashlin's exuberant satires thrive on approximating the objects of their caricatures, the Farrellys emphasize hope and forgiveness for their characters in characteristic grace notes, although there is certainly nothing graceful about their delivery. What must count as the turning point in the film's designated romance between Harrelson's handless ("not handsome") bowler and Angel's busty bimbo plays out as a nasty parking-lot fight (punching breasts and kicking not just in the groin, but also when down) to the "Theme from Love Story."

Christoph Huber

Date 1996

Nationality USA

Directors Bobby Farrelly, Peter Farrelly

Cast Woody Harrelson, Vanessa Angel

Why It's Key The Farrelly brothers, defiantly emphasizing hope for their characters, express romance through a nasty parking-lot brawl.

Opposite *Kingpin*

Key Scene **The "post card" interludes**
Breaking the Waves

All through the 1980s and into the 1990s, Danish director Lars von Trier seemed stuck in a rut of unfeeling formalism. His movies looked as remarkable as Fritz Lang's *Metropolis* but were so heartless that they could have been directed by that film's robot. Then came a *volte face*. From almost ignoring his actors, he went to worshipping them, in his TV series *The Kingdom* (1994) and, even more so, in *Breaking the Waves*: following their every move with a swishing, swooning hand-held camera, lighting 360 degrees so they could go wherever they wanted, jump cutting in mid-sentence because a facial expression in another take was more authentic. Cinematically, he was born again.

The first of what von Trier retroactively called his Golden Heart Trilogy, *Breaking the Waves* is one of the most unexpectedly moving films of its era, because it traces the changing feelings of its main character, Bess (Emily Watson), obsessively and close-up. Her goodness is absolute, her self sacrifice is like that of a character from the New Testament. A further surprise is that von Trier drops into his ferocious melodrama – perhaps as respite from its harrowing emotions – wide, static, idealised landscape shots – Chapter Headings – each about a minute long and accompanied by pop songs from the 1970s, and somewhat augmented by an intensely colored rainbow or something equally kitsch. There's little precedent for such moments in cinema; they are closer to variety theater or children's fairy tales, but that is the point. By this stage, von Trier was looking much wider than cinema for ideas. In the coming years, Brecht, Marx, Minnelli, Catholicism, and British TV drama would all be grist to his mill. He has become the most significant stylistic researcher in cinema of his era, bar none.
Mark Cousins

Date 1996

Nationality Denmark

Director Lars von Trier

Why It's Key These punctuating scenes are among the most stylistically unexpected moments in '90s cinema.

Key Scene **Maggie Cheung steals Arsinée Khanjian's jewels** *Irma Vep*

Costumed in a tight black latex suit, Maggie Cheung, playing herself, is in Paris to play the title role in a remake of Louis Feuillade's 1916 crime serial, *Les vampires*. She also seems to be the object of the sexual fantasies of everyone working on the film – most noticeably the director (Jean-Pierre Léaud) and the woman handling costumes (Nathalie Richard).

After what seems like a restless, sleepless evening in her hotel room, Cheung goes out into the hallway, still in her suit, stealthily climbs the stairs, and, after spying a maid delivering a tray to a room and leaving, sneaks into the room herself. Still hidden, she sees a nude woman (Khanjian, wife and lead actress of Atom Egoyan) describing her lonely boredom on the phone to someone named Fred, then glimpses the woman's jewels in another room, which she promptly steals. Running to a fire escape and climbing to the roof in a driving rain, she briefly fondles the jewels, then tosses them down to the street in slow-motion.

When we see Maggie next, she's being woken in her room, still in costume. Then we see her body double film a take where Irma climbs to a roof. We never learn whether Maggie's theft was a dream or a real act performed as a kind of rehearsal. Khanjian is another kind of body double, her nudity implicitly replacing Cheung's in our own sexual fantasies. Both women are plainly bored and lonely, looking for excitement, and so are we.
Jonathan Rosenbaum

Date 1996

Nationality France

Director Olivier Assayas

Cast Maggie Cheung, Arsinée Khanjian

Why It's Key If a movie can be said to have an unconscious, here's where this one's secret is buried.

Key Scene **The coda**
Taste of Cherry

A man (Ershadi) drives around the slag-heap outskirts of Tehran in a Range Rover propositioning laborers and soldiers. He wants to pay someone to check on him after a suicide attempt to make sure he's dead, then fill his grave with dirt. The man, Mr. Badii, never divulges his reason but finds someone to accept his offer, a taxidermist (Bagheri) who understands melancholy and knows that "what you get is a matter of luck. Birds don't fall into the net to make you happy."

As *Taste of Cherry* ends, Badii swallows sleeping pills and lies down in the hole he's dug to await his death. It is night. Thunder rumbles in the distance. A couple of lightning flashes illuminate Badii in medium close-up, but the screen is otherwise black. We hear rain falling. It appears the film is done.

It isn't. Kiarostami fades-in to video footage of soldiers marching up a hill in long shot, accompanied by a Louis Armstrong recording of "St. James Infirmary" (no vocals). He cuts to scenes of the crew at work, including Ershadi, who smokes and offers Kiarostami a cigarette. This unexpected break in the narrative deepens the film's ambiguous ending and makes it more powerful. There is no definitive explanation for why it's there. It is several things at once: a scene of mournful tranquility, contemplation of the happiness of being alive, relief from the film's tension, rejection of sentimentality, a scene of rebirth, and an invitation to leave the theater.

A. S. Hamrah

Date 1997

Nationality Iran

Director Abbas Kiarostami

Cast Homayoun Ershadi, Abdolhossein Bagheri

Why It's Key Kiarostami won't provide closure.

Key Scene **The hypnotic opening**
Moonspins between Land and Sea

Giuseppe M. Gaudino's *Moonspins between Land and Sea* is a one-of-a-kind movie that ambitiously attempts to evoke the *genius loci* of Pozzuoli, a town in the Gulf of Naples boasting Roman origins and plagued by seismic instability throughout its history. By means of what Gaudino himself has tagged as "visual lumps" – clusters of fragmentary and undefined images superimposed on one another – *Moonspins between Land and Sea* coalesces fiction and documentary, blurs the edges of epochs, and reconciles popular cinema with avant-garde techniques. In the exploded spatial and temporal construction he creates, Gaudino both charts a visionary geography and compiles a history based upon archetypes.

Gaudino establishes his formal procedures while the opening credits are still rolling. A first "visual lump" matches snippets of natural and human landscapes to Epsilon Indi's mesmerizing score. We see the film's narrator, Gennaro (Grasso), the youngest son in a family of fishermen, in the back seat of a car. His voice-off introduces the "very special and bizarre" city of Pozzuoli and lists the many historical celebrities who have trodden this land – a list ending with himself, symptomatically leveling any hierarchy and temporal distance. Archive footage showing people displaced by earthquakes leads to the fictional sequence of Gennaro's family leaving its abode. Over accelerated images of the gulf at nighttime, Gennaro's voice then relates a dinner between the emperor Nero and Nero's mother, Agrippina; scratchy images of characters speaking Latin follow, visualizing the event.

Paolo Bertolin

Date 1997

Nationality Italy/Germany

Director Giuseppe M. Gaudino

Cast Olimpia Carlisi, Salvatore Grasso

Original Title *Giro di lune tra terra e mare*

Aka *Round the Moons between Earth and Sea*

Why It's Key The opening establishes the spellbinding combination of narrative cinema and avant-garde filmmaking achieved by this unique film.

Key Person **Pam Grier**
Overture *Jackie Brown*

Every film Quentin Tarantino has made showcases why he's the king of pop-culture pastiche, but only one has a heart. *Jackie Brown* is Tarantino's masterpiece, simply because he manages to conceive of two characters who actually resemble human beings with a believable emotional life. The love story between the titular stewardess and a bailbondsman makes this more than the announced meeting of two styles of medium cool – 1970s blaxploitation (as represented by Pam Grier) and TV-rejuvenated 1960s thriller (Robert Forster) – and serves as moving counterpoint to the ironic detachment surrounding Tarantino's usual meta-character-creations (although Samuel L. Jackson as this film's main example of them clearly relishes representing an eccentric, vampiric gangster, especially one who gets to utter Tarantino's carefully modulated patented speeches). Grier is treated with uncommon respect by Tarantino, with two remarkable shots of her bracketing the film. The opening is particularly clever,

encapsulating what follows: the camera tracks sideways along with Jackie Brown, gliding – as if by hovercraft – on an airport conveyor, past a mosaic (announcing the film's eclectic patchwork style), until she starts to move, getting ever faster, finally running for the exit. Tarantino scores this for maximum elegance with Bobby Womack's wonderful soul ballad "Across 110th Street" (and scores another reference: it's the title song of Barry Shear's fine 1972 crime film of the same name), but the real elegance comes quite naturally from Grier, her mature beauty, and her aura of self-respect, captured with admiring tenderness.

Christoph Huber

Date 1997

Nationality USA

Director Quentin Tarantino

Cast Pam Grier

Why It's Key Tarantino's greatest film is the one with believable human characters. The magnificent opening alone gives the titular heroine (and the actress who plays her) what the director rarely allows for: natural respect.

Opposite *Jackie Brown*

1990–1999

Key Scene **Mamiya asking the police "Who are you?"** *Cure*

Mamiya (Hagiwara), an amnesiac who may also be the mesmerist who has prompted a number of murders, is seated in front of a room of police officials by Takabe (Yakusho), the detective who arrested him. When a police chief (Osugi) asks him if he is aware of the charges against him, the young man responds with the question he has repeated throughout *Cure*: "Who are you?" His query may be necessitated by his extreme amnesia, which makes him unable to remember what was said a minute before, but it is more insistent this time: "Police Chief Fujiwara, who are *you*?" Mamiya's inquiry probes into the basis of identity, questioning the social definitions of who we are. As such, it exemplifies a prominent motif in 1990s Japanese cinema, as both fiction and non-fiction films often featured figures searching for their identity in a post-Cold War, post-economic-bubble Japan that was unsure of itself. But the fact Mamiya remembers Fujiwara's name and also seems to proselytize the lack

of identity (the "cure" of the title) indicates Kiyoshi Kurosawa is less seeking a pre-existing identity than pursuing a critical ambiguity that shakes the foundations of not only Japanese society – its morality and notions of identity – but also existence itself. His horror cinema is disturbing because it renders indefinite the borders between bodies and shadows, people and their images on screen, life and death, and even between film and its various genres. "Who are you?" is then directed as much at us and at cinema as against Police Chief Fujiwara.

Aaron Gerow

Date 1997

Nationality Japan

Director Kiyoshi Kurosawa

Cast Masato Hagiwara, Koji Yakusho, Ren Osugi

Original Title *Kyua*

Why It's Key This moment exemplifies 1990s Japanese cinema's complicated focus on identity.

Key Film **The life of an hourly** *American Job*

Chris Smith made his debut film in the Midwest for $14,000 with writer Russell playing a version of himself, a guy drifting in a perpetual fog of lousy minimum-wage jobs. The gangly, bespectacled Russell looks like Kevin, the nerdy stock clerk from *Repo Man*, but his performance is self-effacing, not unctuous. *American Job* was barely released and got little support from critics. Shot in 16mm in the fading colors of a Wisconsin autumn, it's a real achievement in independent filmmaking, socially conscious, formally daring, and unpretentious.

The film moves steadily among low-paying jobs where conversations with co-workers mostly turn to what you'd do if you won the lottery. Russell starts the film as a lever puller in a factory, ends up as a telemarketer, and in-between tries washing dishes in a chicken joint, housekeeping in a motel, and third-shift warehouse inventory. Private time is almost nil. At one job, Russell's lunch is a slice of meat wolfed down in a men's room he's supposed to be cleaning.

Non-professional actors make up the rest of the cast, picked because they had experience as hourlies or managers in the film's workplace settings. Uniformly excellent, they help Smith blur the line between shambling indie and vérité documentary, crafting a low-key tragicomedy that's like a working-class *Office Space* with less hope and no plot. At the chicken place they hose down the day-old rolls before they throw them out. It's a fitting image for the forgotten level of American life the film explores.
A. S. Hamrah

Date 1997

Nationality USA

Director Chris Smith

Cast Randy Russell

Why It's Key It's a unique, genuinely independent examination of minimum-wage work in mid-'90s America.

Key Scene **The wife supports her husband's crippled body** *Funny Games*

Haneke has explored the disorienting, dehumanizing aspects of media-saturated culture in most of his movies, from the 1992 melodrama *Benny's Video* through the 2005 political drama *Caché*. The ironically titled *Funny Games* ranks with the most disturbing – and therefore the most effective – since it confronts the "entertainment value" that violence so effortlessly carries for contemporary audiences, including the audiences for Haneke's own work.

The plot centers on a mother, father, and child (Lothar, Mühe, and Stefan Clapczynski) whose vacation home is invaded by two murderous thugs who amuse themselves by torturing and killing helpless victims. The twist is that the sadists occasionally smile, wink, and speak directly to the camera, forcing us to acknowledge that we're choosing to watch – and on some level enjoying – the horrific "games" they're playing on the screen.

In one of the film's most harrowing moments, the husband's body has been broken by a horrific beating, and his wife prevents him from collapsing by bearing his full weight on her slender frame. Haneke presents this in a long, unbroken shot that serves as both a continuation of the story and a documentary of a real woman, actress Lothar, struggling with a burden that strains her physical strength to the breaking point. This moment transforms a film that could have seemed didactic or tricky into an indelibly real commentary on the unstable boundary between "real" and "fantasy" violence. Rarely has film fiction overlapped so powerfully with the actual world in which we live, communicate, and consume untold hours of movie mayhem.
David Sterritt

Date 1997

Nationality Austria

Director Michael Haneke

Cast Susanne Lothar, Ulrich Mühe

Why It's Key This relentlessly long take transforms a potentially abstract film into a devastatingly vivid commentary on the effects of violence in the real physical world.

Opposite *Funny Games*

HANEKE: 'FUNNY GAMES'

A film by MICHAEL HANEKE

with SUSANNE LOTHAR · ULRICH MÜHE · ARNO FRISCH · FRANK GIERING · STEFAN CLAPCZYNSKI and others

Director of Photography JÜRGEN JÜRGES · Editor ANDREAS PROCHASKA · Sound WALTER AMANN · Production Designer CHRISTOPH KANTER · Costume Designer LISY CHRISTL

A WEGA-FILM production · Producer VEIT HEIDUSCHKA © WEGA FILM 1997

Key Scene **The sinking school bus and the spider-bite story** *The Sweet Hereafter*

Egoyan's greatest film centers on a lawyer (Holm) who visits a rural Canadian town, hoping to organize parents in a lawsuit for damages after a school-bus accident that killed several children. His visits to grieving households take place against the background of his own grief over his young daughter (Caerthan Banks), whose occasional phone calls reveal that drug abuse is leading her life toward tragedy.

Egoyan lets us discover the lawyer's mission and form impressions of the families – some of whom are highly suspicious of his motives – before depicting the accident, which happens when the bus skids onto a frozen lake and the ice grimly cracks beneath its weight. This somber sight is intercut with a conversation the lawyer has during a plane journey. Meeting a former acquaintance of his family, he tells her about an incident from his daughter's childhood – when she was bitten by spiders and he rushed her to a hospital with a knife held against her throat in case she

needed a tracheotomy before they arrived.

This long-ago event mirrors his present situation: Again he's on an errand of mercy, and again the errand requires him to stifle emotion and be morally dispassionate – to the point of seeming cold and callous, if this is needed to achieve the necessary end. Although he sees himself as a good and capable person, he could also be like the Pied Piper of Hamelin, who used a village's children for his own cold purposes. Holm's brilliant acting makes both possibilities visible at once.
David Sterritt

Date 1997

Nationality Canada

Director Atom Egoyan

Cast Ian Holm

Why It's Key In a superb example of parallel montage, Egoyan cuts between the film's central traumatic event and a monologue by the main character that's both metaphorical and moving.

Key Scene **The lost honor of a small town pickpocket** *Xiao Wu*

The brilliant revelation of the second wave of post-1989 filmmakers, *Xiao Wu* follows the wanderings of the title character (Wang) through the streets, construction sites, karaoke bars, bathhouses, and farms of his dusty hometown of Fenyang, Shanxi Province. Petty criminal and master pickpocket, cool, bespectacled, and strangely old-fashioned, Xiao Wu – like a scaled-down John Woo hero – believes in honor among thieves, but his plight reveals the moral crisis of an entire generation. Jia shoots in cinéma vérité-style, in the crude light of post-socialism, with a paucity of means and non-professional actors, producing moments of raw poetic truth – such as the uneasy, low-key, yet tender courtship between Xiao Wu and a slightly mythomaniac karaoke hostess; or the scene in which the homeless protagonist, seeking shelter in a deserted public bathhouse, strips and then starts singing.

The 2½ minute shot that ends the film marks out Jia as a major *auteur* in world cinema. Xiao Wu and the

policeman who has arrested him walk through the town's main drag; having an errand to run, the cop handcuffs him to a suspension cable; Xiao Wu waits, squatting old-style, casting nervous glances, then stands up, as the camera, following his gaze, pans to the right and scrolls slowly. On bicycles or motorbikes, or simply standing, men, a few women, and some children stare at the protagonist (who is now a vanishing point absent from the image, since the imaginary reverse angle is missing) and gossip with idle curiosity, unaware they are witnessing their own alienation.
Bérénice Reynaud

Date 1997

Nationality China

Director Jia Zhangke

Cast Wang Hongwei

Why It's Key With a hand-held pan, the Chinese Sixth Generation enters a post-socialist phase of the "society of the spectacle."

Key Scene **Crying into the tape recorder**
Happy Together

Made on the eve of Hong Kong's reversion to Chinese sovereignty, *Happy Together* is itself a movie about separation and renewal. Set on the other side of the world – in Argentina, where its on-off gay couple has relocated in an umpteenth attempt at a new beginning – it's also a meditation on perspective and the distance required for it. Its first line, "We could start over," is repeated throughout like a mantra, albeit one that neither the speaker nor the listener fully believes.

Yiu-fai (Leung) is the adult in this relationship, the patient, long-suffering one, bristling at the martyr role to which he's been consigned. Po-wing (Leslie Cheung) is alternately callous and needy, fully aware of his own beauty and the hold he has on his lover. After several rounds of breaking up and making up, Wing storms out, and this time, both men realize, it's really over.

Meanwhile, Fai has grown close to Chang (Chang Chen), a young Taiwanese co-worker. But the kid, with whom Fai shares an easy, slightly flirtatious rapport, is leaving town. At a bar on their last night out, Chang produces a tape recorder and asks Fai to speak into it – as a souvenir, he explains. He doesn't like pictures and he believes the voice is a more accurate barometer of emotion than facial expression.

As Chang gets up to dance, Fai holds the tape recorder up to cover his face – his eyes tell us he's crying. Christopher Doyle's camera stops in its tracks and the shot is held for over half a minute. Fai composes himself, silently, but is overcome again, and finally lets out a choked sob. (Later, playing back the tape at the southern tip of Argentina, that's all Chang hears.) In this piercing thumbnail sketch of a man unhappy alone, words are not enough, and they may not be necessary.
Dennis Lim

Date 1997

Nationality Hong Kong

Director Wong Kar-wai

Cast Tony Leung, Chang Chen

Original Title *Cheun gwong tsa sit*

Why It's Key Releasing a dam of pent-up emotion, this wordless scene is a turning point in Wong Kar-wai's evolution from insouciant stylist to grown-up grand romantic.

Key Scene **Sandii smiles at the end of the film** *New Rose Hotel*

The overwhelming majority of "serious" critics primarily value cultural objects which present meaning as a secret message buried within the code of style. Little surprise then that the films of Abel Ferrara, whose surfaces stubbornly resist penetration, are so unfashionable. Consider *New Rose Hotel*'s final shot: X (Dafoe) climbs into bed with Sandii (Argento), telling her that "If you really want to, we'll walk away"; Sandii smiles at X's half-hearted invitation to abandon the dangerous scheme with which they are involved. This is the last of those flashback memories which make up the final 20 minutes, as X, having withdrawn to the eponymous hotel, attempts to work out if, how, and why Sandii betrayed him. Ferrara refuses to offer us a solution to this mystery, to imply that Sandii smiles because she is amused at X's tentativeness, delighted by the offer, contemplating her betrayal, or thinking about something else entirely. Since she is facing away from X, she may even be acknowledging her complicity with the film's viewer, asserting that – despite her involvement with two men who believed her to be a pawn in their game, an object for their gaze – she was always the one controlling the look. The question which obsesses X will never be answered, simply because it cannot be answered in the terms in which it is posed. In Ferrara's masterpieces, as in those of Jean Renoir, there are no short-cuts to understanding, no easily interpretable gestures, no conclusions to be drawn. There is only the experience of being constantly alive and responsive to everything.
Brad Stevens

Date 1998

Nationality USA

Director Abel Ferrara

Cast Willem Dafoe, Asia Argento

Why It's Key This scene reveals that complex ambiguity which typifies Ferrara's mature work.

Key Scene **The incredibly long and complex opening shot** *Snake Eyes*

Few films ever started like *Snake Eyes*. The first shot, so extraordinarily long, so full of characters and anonymous moving crowds, with so many movements in so many directions you are not really conscious of its being only one continuous tracking, panning, craning shot all along, follows the main character, Atlantic City's police chief (Cage), during the preliminaries and the start of a championship fight and actually tells most of what happens in the whole movie. The impression of seeing and embracing everything just as it's happening, reinforced the second time you see the film as you realize it is really a single shot (even where you thought there had to be some trick masking the editing together of several shots), is finally revealed illusory, as in several other De Palma films. The author of *Dressed to Kill* (1980), *Blow Out* (1981), and *Body Double* (1984) seems recurrently obsessed with telling the audience: look harder, look better, look twice; you think you have understood more than you did, while you are unable to see much of what is shown to you, which you either underestimate or overlook or forget or, on the contrary, take for granted as the truth, jumping to conclusions or overinterpreting details. So don't trust your eyes, your ears, your mind. A good portion of the film will be dedicated to looking at the opening shot again at varying speeds (since the events have been recorded by surveillance videos and TV cameras) and from diverging points of view (since witnesses' memories make it possible to reconstruct some parts of what happened).

Miguel Marías

Date 1998

Nationality USA

Director Brian De Palma

Cast Nicolas Cage, Gary Sinise, Carla Gugino

Why It's Key This tour de force is one of the longest and most difficult shots in the history of cinema.

Opposite *Snake Eyes*

Key Scene **The ending** *Dil Se.. (From the Heart)*

SPOILER

Meghna (Koirala) is setting out on her terrible mission. Loaded with explosives, she is on her way to kill the Prime Minister in a kamikaze attack. Radio-executive Amar (superstar Khan) suddenly appears in front of her; there he is once again, proclaiming his unfailing love. As Meghna tries to leave, he grabs her shawl, and in one swift move wraps it around his arm, taking her into his embrace. "You don't have to come with me, but please take me with you," he whispers. Amar asks Meghna to tell him she loves him, at least this once. As they both cry, they hold each other tight – and explode in a ball of fire.

Mani Ratnam is one of the great innovators in Bollywood. A regional filmmaker (coming from the Tamil industry) who successfully handled the transition to the all-India market, Ratnam helped introduce the notion of auteur to Bollywood and enchanted audiences with lavish music numbers, influenced by the style of commercials and music videos. *Dil Se..* is the third installment in a trilogy about terrorism, also including *Roja* (1992) and *Bombay* (1995), and although it flopped at the Indian box office, it features some of the most entrancing music sequences ever tailored in Bollywood ("Chal Chaiyya Chaiyya," "Dil Se Re"), sumptuously photographed by Santosh Sivan. The virtuoso climax of the unusually straightforward (by Bollywood standards) narrative represents the utmost infringement of Bollywood commandments: a heart-wrenching unhappy ending.

Paolo Bertolin

Date 1998

Nationality India

Director Mani Ratnam

Cast Shahrukh Khan, Manisha Koirala

Why It's Key The one Bollywood grand finale you shouldn't miss!

Key Speech **Eternity, not property**
The Thin Red Line

In retrospect no big-budget Hollywood production of the 1990s seems as noble as the comeback of philosopher-cum-director and supreme visual stylist Terrence Malick. Not so much for proving that big money and big vision do still come together on occasion, more for the sincerity with which the film continued and expanded the startling and divisive experiments with narration Malick had begun in *Badlands* (1973) and mastered in *Days of Heaven* (1978). Fittingly enough for a visual-aural poem about man's transience contrasted with unchanging nature, in the context of Malick's career *The Thin Red Line* seems both return and restart, as well as continuum. The war-film setting, with U.S. troops attacking at Guadalcanal, is just backdrop for an undulating meditation about light and death. The star cast is dispersed into a polyphony of overlapping voices, whispering thoughts floating over the battlefields like souls, as if they were the actual protagonists, while the moribund bodies are torn by grenades and bullets. Human tragedy is both meaningless and all the more harrowing in view of indifferent nature: The play of sunlight and surges of wind leave exquisite traces on the sea of grass, a small leaf timidly folds in on itself upon the touch of a soldier, while nearby people die, driven crazy by their categories so useless in the face of the cosmos. "Property," a soldier (Penn) concludes at some point, "the whole thing is about property." But, Malick's images ask, what price eternity?

Christoph Huber

Date 1998

Nationality USA

Director Terrence Malick

Cast Sean Penn

Why it's Key Malick's comeback after decades offers a crystallization of his key themes.

Opposite *The Thin Red Line*

1990–1999

Key Scene **Giovanni hiding from a street protest** *The Way We Laughed*

The Golden Lion it won aroused much controversy, but *The Way We Laughed* deploys the distinctive features of Gianni Amelio's style in their utmost maturity. His inclination towards elliptical narratives is mirrored by the crystallization of the story (involving two brothers who emigrate from Sicily to the industrial North of Italy in the late Fifties) into a cluster of vignettes, each accounting for one single day of a different year, while the long sequences, unhurried camerawork, and pictorial cinematography wrap the slow-burning drama in an arresting visual form.

A moment encapsulating the complexity of Amelio's film shows Giovanni (Lo Verso) carrying the school textbooks of his brother, Pietro. On the main avenue, laborers march, brandishing red flags and singing the Communist hymn "Bandiera Rossa" (red flag). When protesters pass by him, Giovanni skirts the wall, bending over the books to protect them. After a red flag flaps over him, extra-diegetic music silences the chants from the crowd, and Giovanni addresses the books, reciting a letter to his brother he cannot write, because he doesn't know where Pietro is and because he is illiterate. Besides emphasizing the bond between Giovanni and Pietro and the relevance of education as a means of emancipation, this touching sequence recapitulates the film's recurring motif of hiding – both physically and metaphorically – as the brotherly relationship is punctuated by lies, secrets, and mutual feelings of inadequacy. In this case, however, the motif acquires further resonance, since Giovanni also shies away from the political and the public.

Paolo Bertolin

Date 1998

Nationality Italy

Director Gianni Amelio

Cast Enrico Lo Verso, Francesco Giuffrida

Original Title *Così ridevano*

Why It's Key A deceptively simple sequence shows Amelio's ability to blend thematic and stylistic density.

Key Scene **A gangster ponders his humiliation** *Satya* (*Truth*)

*S*atya redefined the notion of violence for Hindi cinema. It contains few fight sequences in the old style, where all the men dropped their weapons and went at it with bare hands. Here power flows out of the barrels of revolvers, and it's never vengeance or vigilanteism; it's about doing a job. The film inaugurated a new kind of hero for Hindi film: the professional criminal. The script by Anurag Kashyap and Saurabh Shukla uses language that might be overheard at one of the sleazier dance bars (where women perform for men) in the northern reaches of the city of Mumbai. The film is also audacious enough to poke fun at Bollywood's underworld funding (a year earlier, the daylight murder of a film producer, Gulshan Kumar, was said to be proof of what the real goons could do when you stopped playing ball).

Satya (Chakravarthi), whose name means truth in Sanskrit, comes to Mumbai in search of work, joins the gang of a politician (Govind Namdeo), and finds a friend in Bhiku Mhatre (Manoj Bajpai), who makes one of the most convincing young thugs ever. In a key scene, Bhiku tells Satya of his shame at having to endure being reined in by his boss. He curses and rants as they watch the Arabian Sea break in front of them. Bhiku talks of abstractions – of honor and masculinity and hierarchy. And yet, he speaks *tapori*, the argot of Mumbai's streets, which until this point had been used in Hindi film only for comic effect. It's a brilliant tightrope walk, and Bajpai executes it brilliantly. He is so charismatic in the film that when his character dies, the film sags – but only slightly.

Jerry Pinto

Date 1998

Nationality India

Director Ram Gopal Varma

Cast J. D. Chakravarthi, Manoj Bajpai

Why It's Key A startling debut performance by a powerful actor brings together *tapori* – Mumbai's street argot – and high drama.

Key Film *Histoire(s) du cinéma*
Godard's tribute to Italian neorealism

*G*odard's *magnum opus* to date, at least of his late period, is an eight-part video, though film is its main subject – a critical reverie comprised of multiple clips, commentary, and many general allusions to art and history. More precisely, it's the history of the 20th century as perceived by cinema, and the history of cinema as perceived or at least witnessed by the 20th century. In terms of Godard's adopted mythology, moreover, the cinema and the 20th century are characterized by two key countries (France and the U.S.), two decisive falls from cinematic innocence (the end of silent films that came with talkies and the presumed end of talkies that came with video), two decisive falls from worldly innocence (the two world wars), and two collective cinematic resurgences that took place in Europe, affecting the consciousness of the rest of the world – Italian neorealism and the French New Wave.

For me, the work's climax comes at the end of the fifth episode, *Currency of the Absolute*, when Godard accompanies a passionate montage of emotional highpoints from Italian neorealist films with a tender Italian song about the Italian language. There's a Godardian theory behind this, of course, involving his conviction that "with *Rome, Open City*, Italy simply reconquered the right of a nation to look itself in the eye, and there followed the astonishing harvest of great Italian cinema." But whatever the occasion or pretext, the outpouring of pure emotion at the end of this chapter has few precedents in his work.

Jonathan Rosenbaum

Date 1998

Nationality France

Director Jean-Luc Godard

Cast uncredited

Why It's Key The major thinker of the French New Wave shows that he also has a heart.

Key Scene **"The Last Goodbye"**
Those Who Love Me Can Take the Train

It begins, as does everything in this amazing film, *in media res*. Sami (Cogan) has just been showing Jean-Marie (Berling) a picture of the latter's late mother taken many years before, and Jean-Marie – who mourns her as much as he does Jean-Baptiste (Trintignant), the uncle whose funeral the the film revolves around – says he doesn't want to keep the picture. Then Elodie (Schiltz), daughter of Thierry (Zem), the thuggish drug-addicted male nurse (and boytoy) entrusted with Jean-Baptiste's care, grabs the picture and runs off giggling. Suddenly she stops and points out the train window. "There's Poppa!" she screams, pointing at a station wagon swiftly moving on a road alongside the train. The driver is Thierry, and his passenger is the encoffined corpse of Jean-Baptiste. The mourners on the train rush to the window for a look as "The Last Goodbye" by the then just-deceased singer-songwriter Jeff Buckley lets loose on the soundtrack. At the same time we hear a snippet of the

last interview Jean-Baptiste made about his life and work, in which he talks about sex and love. "Loving someone means putting up with their shit," he says – neatly encapsulating the theme of Chéreau's entire film, in which life and death, young and old, gay and straight commingle with abandon in a handheld vision of seeming chaos that's delineated with the cool clear hand of an absolute moviemaking master.

David Ehrenstein

Date 1998

Nationality France

Director Patrice Chéreau

Cast Charles Berling, Delphine Schiltz, Nathan Cogan, Roschdy Zem, Dominique Blanc, Valeria Bruni Tedeschi, Bruno Todeschini, Chantal Neuwirth, Jean-Louis Trintignant, Thierry de Peretti, Marie Daëms

Original Title *Ceux qui m'aiment prendront le train*

Why It's Key It offers one of the purest cinematic expressions of loss and regret.

695

Key Scene **The opening sequence**
Confession

Aleksandr Sokurov was born in 1951, the son of an army officer. He studied at Moscow's famous VGIK film school, and, after graduating, benefited from the mentorship of Andrei Tarkovsky, who befriended him and called him "a cinematic genius." In 1980, Sokurov embarked on career that would become the most funerary in movie history. *Mother and Son* (1986), a threnodic tone poem about a dying mother was, said Paul Schrader, "73 heart-aching, luminescent minutes of pure cinema." In that it featured a woman, its subject was, however, atypical of Sokurov. Closer to the core of Sokurov's mournful art was this film, *Confession*, originally made as a television series. Like much of his work, it is about isolated men. The opening scenes situate us in the dark, frozen Russian North. Snow blows through the Arctic night. Young sailors chip at a ship with metal rods. The sound clangs out into the sky. A Chekhovian voice-over begins, that of the ship's

captain. He wonders about that night, about his life, and about his sailors.

As with many of Sokurov's movies, this looks so green, and the sound is so muffled, that it is as if were taking place on the ocean bed. The men are like sea horses – slow-moving and otherworldly. None of the action is staged, but the captain and his confessions are entirely imaginary. The music of Mahler and Tchaikovsky drifts semi-audibly through the film. The effect is monastic, at times homoerotic, certainly not journalistic or Griersonian (traps into which documentary has too often fallen).

Mark Cousins

Date 1998

Nationality Russia

Director Aleksandr Sokurov

Original Title *Povinnost*

Why It's Key This is one of the most meditative documentary films ever made.

Key Film *The Last Big Thing*
Geist has fallen

Shot in 1995 but unreleased until 1998, *The Last Big Thing* follows alienated anti-hipster Simon Geist (Zukovic) as he drives his purposefully damaged car to fake interviews for a nonexistent magazine called *The Next Big Thing*.

Geist has an agenda. His dedication to exposing the "L.A. fame need" infecting his city attracts the attention of an unhappy trust-funder named Darla (Heimbinder). The two move into a "personality-less, non-individualistic" house near the desert, where they drink beer in their backyard over the *Los Angeles Times* and plot Geist's forays into town. In their spare time they bark monosyllables at a nightclub comic or sit in a movie theater glowering at blockbusters. As Geist's aphoristic confrontations begin to backfire, he becomes increasingly megalomaniac. Soon a crisis is upon him – he's asked to direct a music video.

Few satires really blister; this one does. Geist's clipped, controlled rants, often delivered into a tape recorder as he drives, are incisive monologues filled with unrivaled hatred for the vacuous. Punctuated by fender benders and the whine of car alarms, Geist's indictment of a "culture finally going down on itself" where "all meaning has been neutered" and "all mediums are pointless" is an analog yawp of despair poised on a digital abyss. Heimbinder's red-haired Darla, in her olive-drab jumpsuit, drags the pop-culture detritus of a loveless world heroically behind her. The two of them are strangely resilient, and so is the film, a gem from an era of manufactured cult items.
A. S. Hamrah

Date 1998

Nationality USA

Director Dan Zukovic

Cast Dan Zukovic, Susan Heimbinder

Why It's Key This satire is the best unknown American movie of the 1990s.

1990–1999

697

Key Speech **Joe is reclaimed by alcohol**
My Name Is Joe

Joe (Peter Mullan) is an unemployed, Glaswegian, recently reformed alcoholic in his late thirties, living with precarious dignity on the chemical hair-trigger between sobriety and relapse. There is a survivor's twinkle in his eye and, in his heart, a terrier-like determination to do the right thing: he helps people, he protects people, he coaches an amateur football team. But the anxiety of his condition is hardwired into his grizzled little frame: Peter Mullan's bouncy, chippy street-strut displays the competing energies of the man, all at equal strength. Chaos walks beside him. One of his football players falls foul of a local drug lord, conciliation doesn't work, and Joe goes to war.

"...And I am an alcoholic": this is the unspoken coda to the film's title. Joe's addiction is the dark side of the moon, the enthralling shadow of his past. "All right, Joe," says a Glasgow thug, confronted by Joe in a pub, "Last time you were in here you had piss running down your leg." Ken Loach's political commitments – his commitment to reality, as it were – make him the least supernatural of directors, but when the booze gets a grip on Joe and begins to talk, in its own voice, in vile, croaking words dredged up from some unseen depth of rottenness, the presence of an evil spirit is palpably felt. If that is not a testament to Loach's gifts as a filmmaker, I don't know what is.
James Parker

Date 1998

Nationality UK

Director Ken Loach

Cast Peter Mullan

Why It's Key Loach, a diehard realist, becomes a black magician in this scene.

Opposite *My Name Is Joe*

Key Scene **The repentant father and the grace of God** *The Colour of Paradise*

Mohammad (Ramezani), the blind boy, has been sent away by his father (Mahjoub) who wishes to remarry and to learn the trade of carpentry. In the last sequence, the father, his engagement having been broken off, comes to take his son back home. The dense and lonely forest they pass through reverberates with the Satanic sounds that the father always hears. The bridge on the tumultuous mountain river breaks as they cross it, and child and horse fall into the river. The father jumps into the river after his son; carried by the rushing waves, he loses consciousness.

When he comes to, he is in an uninhabited landscape with huge, bare uprooted tree trunks dotting the landscape like installations. White birds fly. The father spots his son, who seems to be dead, lying in the distance. He picks him up and cries. The camera, which craned upward as the father ran to Mohammad, returns to zero in on the lifeless hand of the child, as it gets infused with a warm light. A bird with its distinctive chirp calls once again – and the hand begins to move again. Is this another world, or is it in this world that God touches Mohammad with light?

The use of the crane as bird's-eye view and as God's-eye view, as grace that envelops those who seek Him, is in stark contrast in spirit, significance, and genre to the other great use of the bird's-eye view – in Hitchcock's *The Birds* (1963). The whole of *The Colour of Paradise*, and this sequence in particular, put into focus the paradox of the cinema's relationship to the seen and unseen, to blindness and sight, to representation and unrepresentability.

Rashmi Doraiswamy

Date 1999

Nationality Iran

Director Majid Majidi

Cast Hossein Mahjoub, Mohsen Ramezani

Original Title *Rang-e khoda*

Why It's Key It's one of the greatest – and most paradoxical – uses of the bird's-eye view in cinema.

Key Scene **Murder on the Mediterranean** *The Talented Mr. Ripley*

The smug, rich, profligate Dickie Greenleaf (Law) is hardly delighted to meet nervous, pallid Tom Ripley (Damon) on the Italian beach, but as the summer days pass he becomes enchanted with Tom's goofiness and ability to imitate, intrigued at Tom's belief they knew one another at Princeton, and then tickled to discover that Tom has been sent as a secret emissary by Dickie's father, a man to whose household in New York the son has no desire to return. They bond, although Tom has more in mind than just friendship and living off the Greenleaf millions; he finds Dickie slightly more than admirable, indeed an object of affection. One day they are out on the sapphire Mediterranean when a frank conversation begins. Tom chides Dickie for "following his penis around" and bedding any girl he can find; chuffed, Dickie takes a cold look at Tom and pronounces him tedious, presumptuous, and unbearable. A fight breaks out, Dickie smacking Tom and Tom responding now with all the humiliated heat of unrequited love. He cudgels Dickie with an oar. Dickie bleeds out in the bottom of the boat, and Tom rolls him into the sea.

In this scene, Anthony Minghella displays a superb portrait of class distinction and masculine violence, slowly building from a subtle disagreement through a presentation of Dickie's arrogant superiority and Tom's mortified self-negation in the face of it, to an instant of uncontrollable release. Tom does not hate Dickie, he worships him, and his god has pronounced him unfit. Is the killing murder, or a form of suicide? Tom, the supreme actor and imitator, will now take Dickie's passport and transform himself into what he has most admired, the beautiful man who is above Tom Ripley's head.

Murray Pomerance

Date 1999

Nationality USA

Director Anthony Minghella

Cast Jude Law, Matt Damon

Why It's Key It's a fascinating case of violence flowing from unrequited love.

Opposite *The Talented Mr. Ripley*

Key Scene **The hero asks if the boy thinks he's a bad man** *The Wind Will Carry Us*

An engineer named Behzad Dorani arrives with a small camera crew in a very remote Kurdish village, waiting for a 100-year-old woman to die so he can shoot a documentary about the funeral ceremony. (Coincidentally or not, this 1999 film qualifies as a sort of millennial statement in more ways than one.) A local boy named Farzad Sohrabi serves as his guide, and Behzad often exploits and abuses him shamefully, especially when he's frustrated about the old woman not dying quickly enough.

Behzad is plainly Kiarostami's critical self-portrait – a skeptical look at the kind of power he wields over the non-professional and poor actors he often works with. And he proves how skeptical he is in the way he films some of the dialogues between Behzad and Farzad, firing his own questions at the boy and then subsequently intercutting his responses with shots of Behzad that were filmed later. In one of the most telling of these exchanges, Behzad asks the boy to tell him frankly, "Do you think I'm bad?" The boy blushes as he says no, and one has the impression that he's simply being polite.

Kiarostami confirmed this impression when I asked him about it in an interview: "I had to ask him that question because he didn't like me very much, in contrast to the actor who was playing the main character," he said, laughing. "So that's why he wasn't very convincing when he called me a good man!"
Jonathan Rosenbaum

Date 1999

Nationality Iran/France

Director Abbas Kiarostami

Cast Behzad Dorani, Farzad Sohrabi

Original Title *Bad ma ra khahad bord*

Why It's Key Kiarostami exposes what's questionable about his own tactics as a filmmaker.

1990–1999

701

Key Event
Eyes Wide Shut drubbed

When it was released its mere existence was an affront to the audience and, therefore, in those days when Americans weren't supposed to stop cheering the Dow, to the pocketbook of Warner Bros., the studio that paid for it. Bad for business, it was bad, period. *Eyes Wide Shut* has survived the opprobrium of the bubble era that was a sign of its distinction. It's a reminder of that dumbed-down audience, eager to congratulate itself for being bored.

Is that classical music? They're putting on evening clothes – where are their guns? She's dancing with a middle-aged Hungarian. What the... I don't... You can't... *zzzzz*.

It was knockout in the first round. Kubrick's fluid camerawork lulled them. The modulated performances of Tom Cruise and Nicole Kidman seemed to waste the stars of *Days of Thunder*. The film's evocation of Christmastime New York as a lonely city of sexual conspirators seemed fake in a world of yet-to-be-indicted CEOs. When *Eyes Wide Shut* was released on over 2,400 screens in the summer of 1999 it was guaranteed to tank, almost as if a major studio had wanted to prove it could kill the auteur film for good and make it look like a marketing accident. Was it meant as a sacrifice, like the one the drug-addicted girl makes for Bill Harford at the orgy?

LUCKY TO BE ALIVE reads a newspaper headline in *Eyes Wide Shut*. Kubrick died four months before it came out.
A. S. Hamrah

Date Summer 1999

Why It's Key The lack of critical and commercial support for Stanley Kubrick's last film revealed how low the cineplex had sunk.

Opposite *Eyes Wide Shut*

Key Scene **Rosetta almost lets her friend drown** *Rosetta*

1990–1999

Luc and Jean-Pierre Dardenne are avid readers of the philosopher Emmanuel Levinas for two reasons, both of which are evident in *Rosetta*. Firstly, for what he says about our perception of a person: that a face must be seen, not for its banal stereotype, but in its irreducible "nudity." From that, the Dardennes invented a way of filming, thus of seeing: far from simple "you are there" realism (for which it is sometimes mistaken), it stares and stares until all masks are stripped. Secondly, for the moral drama that Levinas evokes: you can only truly internalise the lesson "thou shalt not kill" if you have gone to the brink of the desire to kill, and turned back. That is exactly what Rosetta (Dequenne) does in the scene where her moped-riding friend, Riquet (Rongione), inadvertently falls into the swampy water near the trailer-park where she lives – and, for a few agonizing seconds, Rosetta (without verbalizing it) clearly contemplates letting him drown for the sake of taking his job. This is a woman of a kind we have never before seen on screen: what drives her (to insane extremes) is not love or maternity or ambition, but the most basic determination to claim the dignity of work, to hold onto even the most menial paying job. It is this that makes her a monster, and also offers the crucible that defines her humanity. Filmed from every side, Rosetta remains a mysterious creature of pure becoming – a cinematic character *par excellence*.

Adrian Martin

Date 1999

Nationality France/Belgium

Directors: Luc and Jean-Pierre Dardenne

Cast Emilie Dequenne, Fabrizio Rongione

Why It's Key This moment of moral crisis reveals the Dardennes' conception of cinema.

Key Scene **Best lightsaber duel in any Star Wars movie** *The Phantom Menace*

Of all the things George Lucas chose to correct in *Star Wars*'s much-ballyhooed 1997 special edition, the anemic lightsaber "duel" between Obi-Wan Kenobi (Sir Alec Guinness) and Darth Vader (David Prowse) is strangely neglected. In a scene sloppily assembled from a grab bag of mid shots and close-ups, Obi-Wan and Vader circle each other like overmedicated samurai, making halfhearted jabs at each other until Obi-Wan dissolves into a pile of burlap. If these two were fighting in someone's living room, it's doubtful they could even knock over a lamp accidentally. But the final Jedi showdown in *The Phantom Menace* (1999), thanks to the triangulated synergy of stunt coordinator Nick Gillard, assistant Andreas Petrides, and actor/stuntman/martial arts champion Ray Park, not only gave the lightsaber duel the treatment it deserved, but created the most invigorating example of swordsmanship in Western cinema since the days of Douglas Fairbanks and Errol Flynn. John Williams's nervous score filigrees the adrenaline rush when young Obi-Wan (McGregor) and his master Qui-Gonn Jinn (Neeson) meet the unyielding glare of Sith lord Darth Maul (Park). Lightsabers ignite with an ozoned ZORCH, and the men fly at each other with a ferocity underscored by Maul's acrobatic lethality as he lands vicious kicks, twirls his double-bladed weapon, and snarls. This time, Lucas wisely frames the action in long shots like a dance movie, ratcheting up the exhilaration until the cataclysmic final thrust. We won't divulge what happens, but it's the only time in the entire film Darth Maul blinks.

Violet Glaze

Date 1999

Nationality USA

Director George Lucas

Cast Ewan McGregor, Liam Neeson, Natalie Portman, Jake Lloyd, Ray Park

Aka *Star Wars: Episode I – The Phantom Menace*

Why It's Key The lightsaber duel is finally done right.

Opposite *The Phantom Menace*

Key Scene **The son climbs a wall and into a motorboat** *Adieu, plancher des vaches!*

At one point in *Adieu, plancher des vaches!*, a nameless young man (Tarielashvili), wearing a respectable suit but carrying a battered backpack, climbs over the wall separating his family's luxurious estate from the outside world, descends a conveniently positioned ladder, walks towards the nearby river, jumps into a waiting motorboat, and sails away while changing into casual clothes. All the key elements of Iosseliani's cinema are contained in this shot. Everything in this Keatonesque world without close-ups has been arranged to facilitate constant movement, its inhabitants traversing the fluid space on or in boats, motorbikes, cars, buses, trains, horses, skates, luggage transporters, and helicopters, pushing, dragging, or carrying backpacks, baskets, trays, dogs, prams, toilets, and dustbins. All potential barriers to movement (including class barriers) are nimbly surmounted, with identities cast off as easily as clothes, and immobile structures (such as walls and bookcases) existing solely to be climbed: the motorcyclist (Philippe Bas) must clamber up into his tiny living space, while a maid (Mirabelle Kirkland) cleans windows using a roof rig, enters a house by scaling its walls, and is last glimpsed on the side of a cliff. Even the local tramps manage to climb a building with the help of some scaffolding (though they perversely use a staircase, theoretically an area of transition, as a place to sit and drink). Iosseliani, himself an incorrigible barrier-jumper who divides his time between Georgia and France, is one of the cinema's greatest optimists. *Adieu, plancher des vaches!* may have a Renoiresque quality, but it is less a film from the director of *Boudu sauvé des eaux* than a film by Boudu himself.

Brad Stevens

Date 1999

Nationality France/Switzerland/Italy

Director Otar Iosseliani

Cast Nico Tarielashvili

Aka *Farewell, Home Sweet Home*

Why It's Key This scene contains all the key elements of Iosseliani's cinema.

1990–1999

705

Key Scene **"Uncle F*cka!"** *South Park: Bigger, Longer & Uncut*

"Shut your fucking face, Uncle F*cka!" A few minutes into Trey Parker and Matt Stone's *South Park: Bigger, Longer & Uncut*, the four kids from the TV cartoon troop merrily into a cinema to see Terrance and Phillip, their Canadian comedy idols, in their movie vehicle, *Asses of Fire*. The onscreen bickering between Terrance and Phillip escalates, and they launch into an explosively hilarious, hideously profane song – in three short minutes, Parker and Stone add a new insult to the language, shock many audiences as silent as the *South Park* grown-ups around the ecstatic kids, and deftly parody Rodgers and Hammerstein. "You don't eat or sleep or mow the lawn, you just fuck your uncle, all day long!" It should have taken the Best Original Song Oscar… but the studio entered "Blame Canada!" instead, only to lose (as did Aimee Mann and Randy Newman) to an unmemorable Phil Collins song from *Tarzan* (1999), whereupon Parker and Stone vindictively had Collins burned at the stake in a *South Park* episode.

Kim Newman

Date 1999

Nationality USA

Directors Trey Parker, Matt Stone

Why It's Key If you thought "Springtime for Hitler" was tasteless…

Opposite *South Park: Bigger, Longer & Uncut*

Key Event **http://www.blairwitch.com/**
The Blair Witch Project

In 1823, James Hogg published a "news item" in *Blackwood's Magazine* alleging that a century-old corpse had been discovered in a Scots peat bog, clutching a manuscript that an editor was preparing for publication. A year later, Hogg's terrifying and fantastical *The Private Memoirs and Confessions of a Justfied Sinner* appeared, purporting to be that discovered manuscript. It doesn't matter whether Hogg's readers genuinely believed his novel was the authentic memoir of a puritan who had sold his soul to the Devil, any more than it matters whether the crowds who flocked 176 years later to *The Blair Witch Project* believed that the film consisted of documentary footage left behind by three young filmmakers who had disappeared after an encounter with something nebulous and supernatural in the woods. The genius, in the 19th and the 20th centuries, was in the marketing – taking the hackneyed "this is really honestly a true story" gambit used on everything from *Plan 9 From Outer Space* (1959) to *The Texas Chain Saw Massacre* (1974) and putting it over. Daniel Myrick and Eduardo Sanchez, creators of the Blair Witch phenomenon, took advantage of what was then a new tool by setting up an Internet site at http://www.blairwitch.com/ (still active) that purported to be about the "real" legend (completely invented) of the Blair Witch and listed the cast of the film (as did the Internet Movie Database) as "missing, presumed dead." In addition to being a canny way of stirring up interest in the film, the site (like the *Curse of the Blair Witch* tie-in pseudo-documentary that was aired on cable TV and included as a DVD extra) added value to the story with historical background and extra-textual business not included in the film itself.

Kim Newman

Date 1999

Why It's Key The movies discovered a new cousin, as much an adjunct as a marketing tool: the Internet.

Opposite *The Blair Witch Project*

706

Key Scene **Choose your steps**
The Mission

Prolific Hong Kong director Johnnie To started his career in television, whose tight schedules (presumably even tighter than those of Hong Kong film production!) probably endowed him with a sense for economy in the face of necessities. This must help in maintaining an output that is as profuse as it is consistent. To has rarely made a bad film, especially since the inception of his production company Milky Way in 1996, although three directorial efforts a year are for him the rule rather than the exception. To employs a remarkable range of styles with great acuity, as evidenced by the trio of films that secured his international recognition in 1999: on one end, the fast-moving thriller-comedy *Running Out of Time*; on the other *The Mission*, an astonishing exercise in poised choreography (in between: the introverted Macau crime drama *Where a Good Man Goes*). *The Mission* opens with a seemingly ordinary scene: Lam Suet, Hong Kong cinema's Peter Lorre, hopping away on one of those do-the-right-step dance slot-machines. In retrospect it encapsulates the entire movie, testifying to a self-conscious, flawless construction. It's the story of five bodyguards (Lam Suet plays one) killing time and killing men in superbly choreographed, almost abstract bits of step-by-step movement: sweepingly elegant successions of static tableaux. The first scene also introduces one of the film's rhythmic hallmarks: an endlessly reprised three-chord riff that must be the catchiest music ever played on a cheap, cheesy synthesizer.

Christoph Huber

Date 1999

Nationality Hong Kong

Director Johnnie To

Cast Lam Suet

Original Title *Cheung fo*

Why It's Key A seemingly ordinary opening for an exceptionally stylized thriller, it actually demonstrates director Johnnie To's characteristic economy and elegant construction.

Key Film *Outer Space*
Battle of the films

Decades of found-footage filmmaking using Hollywood source material prepare one only insufficiently for the onslaught of Peter Tscherkassky's mature work. The Austrian experimental filmmaker's "CinemaScope Trilogy," consisting of *L'Arrivée* (1998), *Outer Space* (1999), and *Dream Work* (2002), is a singularly potent fusion of his earlier film-theoretical and psychoanalytical preoccupations with a kind of direct material ecstasy achieved by extensive reworking via loving manual operations and meticulous exposure in the darkroom. The most overwhelming expression of this ecstatic rush is probably the centerpiece, *Outer Space*, which uses Sidney J. Furie's 1982 horror film *The Entity* as basis for another kind of horror film. In Furie's somewhat dubious fiction, the heroine (Barbara Hershey) was psychically and sexually assaulted by an invisible force. In Tscherkassky's astonishing collage, the woman is attacked by elements of the film strip itself: the jagged light of the soundtrack or the perforation holes. Rampage and fragmentation intensify (also on the soundscape, a dazzling and unsettling collision of noises, words, music cues); the woman finds her image reproduced, then caught in the standstill of time, then gone. But she returns, and by the end, uneasy equilibrum is achieved, as the woman keeps her eyes on her reflections, awaiting another intrusion. In its impact – going from a hypnotic, eerie buildup to a near-chaotic climax and back – *Outer Space* is as powerful as any illusionist film would be, but its beauty hinges on the expert destruction of illusion: a decidedly more productive, if almost paradoxical, equilibrium.

Christoph Huber

Date 1999

Nationality Austria

Director Peter Tscherkassky

Why It's Key A masterpiece of found-footage filmmaking, Tscherkassky's ecstatic onslaught pits a horror film against itself, with productive results.

Key Film *The Matrix*
"Bullet time"

Computer-generated imagery made its movie debut in 1973's *Westworld*, but it took nearly a decade before the smooth-lathed look of virtual forms entered the public consciousness in *Tron* (1982). Before long, demand waned for craftspeople trained in old-school disciplines like matte painting and model building, as the all-powerful computer now created eye-poppers like the rampaging stained-glass knight in *Young Sherlock Holmes* (1985), the personified tendril of water in *The Abyss* (1989), or the photorealistic velociraptors in *Jurassic Park* (1993). So in 1999 it seemed brazenly atavistic for visual-effects designer John Gaeta to begin work on the *The Matrix*'s money shot by attaching hundreds of still cameras to a snaky metal rig. Each camera generated a single frame when fired in sequence, à la Muybridge-motion-study, around a flailing or leaping actor. When the images were stacked like a flipbook in the computer, the result – Neo (Reeves) dodging bullets in slow motion as we swirl around him like the eye of God – was revolutionary. Before "bullet time," filmmakers viewed computers as fancy model makers, able to sculpt objects from algorithms rather than balsa and latex. Gaeta discarded that hoary paradigm and instead envisioned a boundless cinematic space unhampered by the limits of physics, time, or human vision. Almost a century ago Picasso and Braque shattered the idea of a single viewpoint by depicting objects simultaneously from many points of reference. When Neo twists away from those bullets in slow motion, film finally enters its Cubist period.

Violet Glaze

Date 1999

Nationality USA

Directors Andy Wachowski, Larry Wachowski

Cast Keanu Reeves, Carrie-Anne Moss, Laurence Fishburne, Hugo Weaving

Why It's Key "Bullet time" made the unrealized potential of digital effects a reality.

Opposite *The Matrix*

Key Scene **The opening scene**
La Commune (Paris 1871)

Like his previous benchmarks, *The War Game* (1965), *Privilege* (1967), *Punishment Park* (1971), *Edward Munch* (1974), and *The Journey* (1987), Peter Watkins' *La Commune* is a radical reconfiguration of the cinema, not merely as an art form but as a means of conveying information, challenging audiences to be something other than passive receivers of emotional effects. Shot on black-and-white digital video, this five-and-a-half-hour production recreates a episode barely mentioned in most histories – that brief moment during the Franco-Prussian War when the ordinary citizens of Paris forged a *de facto* socialist government and ruled themselves in defiance of the monarchist status quo. It was of course doomed from the start. The Communards (men, women, and children) were in short order slaughtered and buried in an unmarked mass grave. (The Straub/Huillet short *Every Revolution Is a Throw of the Dice* was shot on that unmarked grave.) As is his wont, Watkins utilizes a film-within-a-

film format, here one in which two competing television networks – Commune TV and Versailles TV – offer different accounts of the events. In the film's opening sequence, we meet the two Commune TV reporters (Aurélia Petit and Watkins' son, Gérard), standing on the film set as they introduce what has for them already happened. In effect it has already happened twice. Once in actual history and the second time before Watkins's cameras as the world of the Commune is recreated in a factory that once housed Georges Méliès's studios. In that sense the actors we see before us are ghosts who are at the same time very much alive.

David Ehrenstein

Date 2000

Nationality France

Director Peter Watkins

Cast Gérard Watkins, Aurélia Petit

Why It's Key Conveying two senses of the past in one, the scene signifies the multifarious ways the cinema can deal with Time.

Key Scene **The girl carrying her boyfriend on her back** *Work in Progress*

This is the abrupt ending of an extraordinarily perceptive, affectionate, and generous documentary on the effects of a rehabilitation project on urban landscape and the inhabitants of a central, marginalized old quarter in Barcelona, shot for more than three years by Guerín and a small team of young students, writing with the camera and building up the structure in the editing process, also very long. This swiftly back-tracking shot precedes for almost four minutes the march forward (we don't see where to) of a very young couple of junkies we have met before on several occasions, with Juana (a prostitute) carrying Iván on her back, talking as they advance between the houses of a narrow street – some in ruins, some newly rebuilt. They may seem rude and cynical, but the action captured by Guerín, the rhythm of their movement, her out-of-breath jests show how deeply they care for each other and how far she's ready to go to encourage and help him. No actors, they are not playing roles; she

runs, and he slips, and she heaves him up again. The long take was unavoidable in order to show – respecting time and space – the real effort, the resilience, the burden she carries without complaining, even proudly, because she's strong and cares for him enough to suffer his failings good-humoredly, almost joking about his idleness. This epic shot represents a new attitude, which seems to be a belated answer to the kind of self-pity that James Dean movies embodied in the fifties, in which youngsters blamed everybody else for their problems.

Miguel Marías

Date 2000

Nationality Spain/France

Director José Luis Guerín

Cast Juana Rodríguez, Iván Guzmán

Original Title *En construcción*

Why It's Key This scene shows love in an unsentimental and matter-of-fact way, no matter how lost the lovers may be.

Key Scene **The hero's suicide in the opening scene** *Peppermint Candy*

By the side of a river in 1999, a group of middle-aged men and women are having a 20-year reunion. Soon a former co-worker named Young-ho (Sol) arrives, but he starts to act strangely: dressed in a crumpled business suit, he shouts into the karaoke machine, runs into the water and screams, curses up at the sky. When he finally moves off and climbs up onto one of two railway bridges crossing the river, a sense of relief moves through the group. Only one man becomes concerned for Young-ho's safety and calls for him to come down. The sound of an impending train causes initial panic, but when it passes, they realize it was running on the other bridge, and that Young-ho is safe. That will not be true of the second train to pass a few minutes later.

Young-ho dies screaming the words, "I want to go back," and in a sense the film grants him his wish. The suicide follows 20 years of personal and historical trauma, but as viewers we have witnessed it without any background knowledge. Similar to Jane Campion's 1986 TV film *Two Friends*, the narrative then sets off backwards in time to reveal the roots of Young-ho's action: to three days earlier, to 1994, to 1987, to 1984, to 1980, and to a picnic at this same spot in 1979. Along the way, Young-ho will gradually become less traumatized, less corrupt, and less complicit in some of the worst horrors of late 20th-century Korean history.

Darcy Paquet

Date 2000

Nationality South Korea

Director Lee Chang-dong

Cast Sol Kyung-gu

Original Title *Bakha satang*

Why It's Key The image of a man about to be killed by a train is the starting point for an ingeniously structured story, told in reverse, about a psyche crushed by historical events.

Key Scene **Nena teaching Jose how to dance** *Demons*

Nena (de Leon), teenage daughter of the Negros Islands upper class, has invited her poor childhood friend Jose (Alano), whom she hasn't seen for years, to a party at her mansion; Jose arrives, too shy to pass the barred gates. O'Hara shoots Jose through bars, Nena behind him. She asks if he dances; Jose cannot. Cut to a shot behind the two as Nena turns, walks towards us, asks Jose to come closer. Quick inserts of Nena's hands taking Jose's; of Jose's face, startled; Nena's smiling, dimpled. They begin to sway. Time passes in a series of dissolves, to a softly played folk melody; a frog burping (O'Hara started out and continues to work in radio) suggests how lost they are to everything except each other. Jose stops; holds Nena back at arm's length; turns; runs; the melody reprises at a more urgent pace. Jose sprints through the jungle (from left to right, in a series of shots), to jump into a beautiful waterfall-fed pool. When Jose's friend asks what's wrong, Jose replies, "I got an erection! A real live erection!"

The love story develops from pity (the girl staring at the boy's crumbling pants), to recognition (the young woman realizing that the young man is not embarrassed but angry), to these first stirrings of sexual attraction. The rest of the film is a wild mix of war atrocities, no-budget special effects, and Filipino poetry, but this – the heart of the film – is as simple and moving as the folk song that accompanies the story.

Noel Vera

Date 2000

Nationality Philippines

Director Mario O'Hara

Cast Matet de Leon, Alex Alano

Original Title *Pangarap ng Puso*

Why It's Key This scene is a wonderful example of O'Hara's ability to sketch out a scene simply, quietly, effectively.

Key Scene **The helicopter ride before the crash** *Kippur*

There are no anti-war speeches in *Kippur*; instead, there is an unprecedentedly vivid reconstruction of combat situations lived 17 years before by the filmmaker. Sound and image, the naturalness of the actors, everything contributes to show what war is, from the unusual point of view of soldiers who don't shoot, but who act as stretcher-bearers and retrievers of wounded fighters.

Under fire, the paramedics carry an injured tank-soldier, trying not to be shot while keeping the stretcher balanced even while their feet stick in the mud, but the wounded man dies before they can bring him to the evacuation chopper. They all are beaten, dog-tired, and sad as the helicopter finally takes off. Flying near the ground, they see a mud battlefield turned into a tank graveyard, while the haunting funereal music mixes on the soundrack with the nerve-racking noise of the propellers. Suddenly, as they seem to be on their way to safety, and the landscape seems almost sunny and peaceful, the helicopter is hit by a missile and two gun blasts, the doctor and most of the orderlies are severely injured, and they have to make an emergency landing that is almost a crash.

There are no effects, no hemoglobin showers, no disembodied hands or feet, no enemy, no heroism, no patriotic speeches. Only (mostly young) people under stress doing their job the best they can manage.
Miguel Marías

Date 2000

Nationality Israel/France

Director Amos Gitai

Cast Liron Levo, Tomer Ruso, Uri Ran Klauzner, Yoram Hattab, Juliano Merr, Ran Kauchinsky

Why It's Key This scene makes the viewer share the sudden crisis inside a helicopter that is attacked while its pilots and passengers are tired and demoralized.

Key Scene **After the factory burns down** *Songs from the Second Floor*

A man has just torched his factory. He stands on a grim subway train covered in ashes. Suddenly, everyone on the train starts to sing. Then we are in a café. Outside, a night-time city street plunges to a vanishing point. The ashes man arrives, in a daze, and talks absurdly of what he has done. On the street again, an apocalyptic event has caused the city to come to a halt. Rats scuttle to and from the vanishing point. Then the ashes man is in his insurance company talking about the fire, but we are distracted by events outside the company's window. Cars are still in gridlock. We can hear wailing. Slowly, a procession of people emerges from the background. They are thrashing each other with whips.

Songs from the Second Floor is as physically astonishing as silent epics like *Cabiria*. Mostly filmed on massive sets built to force perspective and scale, it is a master class in production design and *mise en scène*. In terms of color, puce green dominates. The camera seldom moves, and shots run for many minutes, the key piece of staging often emerging from the background, some way into the action. Like late Jacques Tati films, such as *Trafic*, Andersson's film revels in immensely complex staging. Again like silent cinema, each scene is a tableau, and there is little or no reverse-angle cutting. In the era of CGI and hand-held, low-cost, digital shooting, *Songs from the Second Floor* seemed from another world. It cost a fortune to make, and was funded by Andersson's own lucrative career in advertising. It paints a picture of urban life where everyone is a zombie and human interaction is absurd. Not even in the films of Luis Buñuel is cinematic surrealism so brilliantly rendered.
Mark Cousins

Date 2000

Nationality Sweden

Director Roy Andersson

Original Title *Sånger från andra våningen*

Why It's Key This is modern cinema's most striking surrealist sequence.

Key Scene **Bath and shower**
The Captive

Simon (Merhar), after stalking and marrying Ariane (Testud), keeps her a prisoner after making the discovery that he is not the one to whom a particularly fond smile of hers, captured by chance in a home movie shot on the beach with some other friends, was directed. That he regards her mostly from an aesthetic point of view, as he would a beautiful flowerpot, an elegant table, or a valuable sculpture – while she, despite being his prisoner, remains aloof, elusive, and isolated from him – can be gathered, upon a little reflection, from the image that was chosen as the film's poster: Simon sitting in the bathtub, while, on the other side of a blurred glass panel (so that he sees her, but not clearly), Ariane dries her body with a towel. Thus they live in crystal cages separated by translucent walls, in theory within each other's sight and reach, but, in reality, apart.

Miguel Marías

Date 2000

Nationality Belgium/France

Director Chantal Akerman

Cast Stanislas Merhar, Sylvie Testud

Original Title *La Captive*

Why It's Key This scene crystallizes into a fleeting single everyday image the lack of straightforwardness in the couple of Simon and Ariane.

2000–

713

Key Film
In absentia

From the short *Street of Crocodiles* (1986) to the feature-length *Institute Benjamenta* (1995), the Quay Brothers have given us some of the most exquisite works in the art of cinema animation. While sometimes arcane to the average viewer, the alchemy of their visuals redefines the notion of sensorial overload: such is the case with *The Piano Tuner of Earthquakes* (2005), whose texture makes each shot look like a dynamic painting of mysterious beauty. *In absentia* pushes this kind of experience to the extremes, as it matches the elegance and craftsmanship that are the trademarks of the Quays' style with a percussive emotional urgency not to be found in any other of their films. The subject matter is simple enough: a mentally deranged woman is writing a letter to an absent lover who may or may not exist; we see the protagonist's hand frantically filling pages upon pages with a pencil whose tip often breaks under the pressure of her fingers. Visions of time, remembrance, hope and desire are thrown upon us with unbridled, anguished force, as in the worst imaginable nightmare of an abandoned heart. What makes *In absentia* an assault on the senses, however, is its powerful blend of visions and sounds. The music for the film was composed by Karlheinz Stockhausen, whose electronic score brings the mental state of the protagonist to the level of a psychological storm. When the music abruptly ends and the screen becomes dark, only twenty minutes have elapsed, but we won't need to see another film for a while. Our soul is shaken.

Paolo Cherchi Usai

Date 2000

Nationality UK

Director Stephen and Timothy Quay

Why It's Key Music and film join for an assault on the senses.

Key Scene **Two lovers are threatened by the melting of their image** *La flamme*

Ron Dyens' very short films are playful tributes to the art of silent cinema – with an edge. The subject of *La flamme* is an experience that was not uncommon in movie theaters: when a projector does not work properly, the image can freeze and then literally melt in front of the viewer. In technical terms, this happens when the film remains trapped in the sprockets of the machine; only one image at a time is meant to be projected for a tiny fraction of a second, and any single frame stuck in front of a powerful light source will quickly burn. In practical terms, the damage is limited to a tiny portion of the print, like the hole left by a cigarette on a piece of fabric. On the screen, however, the burning of the film is magnified to epic proportions. In the nitrate-film era (before 1951), the accident could set fire to an entire theater; with digital projection, the effect is obviously impossible. The point made by *La flamme* is that the melting of an image can actually be quite gorgeous to watch (I still remember looking at a

film where this occurred precisely at the moment when a stunningly beautiful lady was staring at the camera). Ron Dyens goes even further: the melting film threatens a late 19th-century romance on the beach, like a monster in a science fiction film. All the lovers can do is run away while their world dissolves around them.

Paolo Cherchi Usai

Date 2000

Nationality France

Director Ron Dyens

Cast Lucie Duchêne, Régis Romele

Why It's Key The destruction of film is the story itself.

Key Scene **Fight in the bamboo forest** *Crouching Tiger, Hidden Dragon*

Li Mu Bai (Chow) is a man at the crossroads of history, a Master at a time when social hierarchies are in flux and all the ethics associated with his knowledge are changing. His encounter with Jen (Zhang) convinces him she is a student worth having, but she lacks the attitude of receptive humility towards knowledge: completely fascinated by the world of *jiang hu*, she wants to belong to this world of excitement, without accepting its codes of behavior.

Each fight scene in *Crouching Tiger, Hidden Dragon* reveals a different emotion. The bamboo-grove fight sequence between Li Mu Bai and Jen is preceded by two fight sequences that highlight its mood through contrast. The first, pitting Jen against warriors in a teahouse, is a source of much generic mirth. The passionate fight that follows between Yu Shu Lien (Michelle Yeoh) and Jen over the Green Destiny Sword is choreographed with immense dignity, showing them as professionals equal to men,

employing a wide range of moves and, in Yu Shu Lien's case, a variety of knives.

In the bamboo grove fight sequence, a number of elements – the rhythmic cutting, the music, the affective close-ups, the coming together in a move and drawing away, Li Mu Bai's immense tenderness and Jen's rebelliousness – turn the encounter of fighting skills into a love scene. Li Mu Bai's playfulness as a teacher, who sets a task for the overconfident student and watches while she copes with it or fails, is unforgettable.

Rashmi Doraiswamy

Date 2000

Nationality Taiwan/ Hong Kong/China/USA

Director Ang Lee

Cast Chow Yun-fat, Zhang Ziyi

Original Title *Wo hu cang long*

Why It's Key It's the fight sequence as love scene.

Opposite *Crouching Tiger, Hidden Dragon*

Key Scene **Making a leap**
Vanilla Sky

Date 2001

Nationality USA

Director Cameron Crowe

Cast Tom Cruise, Noah Taylor, Penelope Cruz

Why It's Key Cruise's awakening is a monument to hubris.

If *The Matrix*'s "welcome to the desert of the real" ended the 1990s, Tom Cruise's plunge from a New York skyscraper began the 21st century with a hyperreal splat. Released three months after the Twin Towers fell, *Vanilla Sky* is both the last pre-9/11 and the first post-9/11 Hollywood movie. It posits a world where the disfigurement of Cruise's face is a global catastrophe and his coming to consciousness an act of lifesaving suicide. "Things are very different now," as tech-support avatar Edmund Ventura (Taylor) tells Cruise's narcissist publisher David Aames. "Forgive me, I'm blowing your mind."

Crowe's baby-boomer fantasy tinkles with notions like a jostled perfume counter. By the film's end, when Aames ascends in an elevator with Ventura like he's Lon Chaney starring in *The Fountainhead*, the viewer is prepared to have his mind blown in the worst way. After a bittersweet parting with Penelope Cruz as love-object Sofia ("wisdom") Serrano ("mountain"), a woman who lives every moment to the fullest even though she's dead, Aames jumps from the roof and plummets through the Monet-inspired CGI clouds into the canyon of Manhattan.

While comparison to Wile E. Coyote is as apt as to the victims of 9/11, Ventura describes this (everything in *Vanilla Sky* is described by its characters at least four times) as "a brilliant journey of self-awakening." A montage of rock-era imagery accompanies Aames as he descends like one of the parade balloons we'd seen pass his apartment window, only this time made of lead.
A. S. Hamrah

Opposite *Vanilla Sky*

Key Scene **Xiao Bo's father or mother**
Enter the Clowns

Date 2001

Nationality China

Director Cui Zi'en

Cast Cui Zi'en, Yu Bo

Original Title *Choujue Dengchang*

Why It's Key Starting his first digital feature with an insolent 9-minute take, trouble-maker and *enfant terrible* Cui Zi'en ushers in a new era for Chinese queer cinema.

The camera follows a young man in red tartan pajamas, Xiao Bo (Yu), as he looks, alternatively, at the off-screen space on the left, then away from it, tears filling his eyes. "Dad, have a drink." Off-screen, a soft voice answers, "Call me Mom," then emits a series of requests: "Help me with my earrings… with my lipstick." Xiao Bo complies, his hand disappears, making the necessary motions to apply the lipstick on someone lying in bed; another hand, a tad plump, with manicured nails, appears behind his, holding the make-up case.

The voice now offers to breast-feed her son, to be "a real mother, for once." Xiao Bo's face disappears off-screen; the camera follows him as he's suckling on a nipple, then as he stands up and turns his head away. The off-screen voice talks about dying, and asks for one last favor: "See me off with your milk." Xiao Bo turns his back to the camera, his right arm moving slightly; a tilt down reveals that his pants are unfastened. He is now leaning against the face of the person in bed, who is burrowing in his crotch, gently holding his thigh, then after a few seconds, reclining back in bed. Xiao Bo withdraws, puts his pants back on. Cut. Back to a close-up of Xiao Bo, looking left. A camera movement finally reveals the face of the person lying in bed: an effeminate man with short hair and tastefully applied make-up – the director Cui Zi'en himself.
Bérénice Reynaud

Key Scene **The brother-sister incest**
To the Left of the Father

Through a hole in a barn-window shutter, adolescent André (Mello) intently observes his sister, Ana (Spoladore), dressed in white. Through that same spyhole, an infant André watches a white dove approaching the snare he set. Undistinguishable details of pupils equate André's anxiety and expectation at different ages. André opens the window: Ana has vanished. The camera wanders about the abandoned barn, finally stopping on Ana, on the porch. The hands of child André hold the rope attached to the snare. As adolescent André closes the door, infant André snares the dove. Holding Ana's hand, André begs the Lord for a miracle to allow him to go on living his incestuous passion, while child André's hand caresses the dove's wing. André promises God the sacrifice of a lamb, as brief images of Ana herding sheep emerge. "Together we'll set the world on fire," says adolescent André. "She's mine, she's mine," exults child André, as he runs through the countryside; finally he sets the dove free.

A rereading of the prodigal-son parable, recast with a family of Lebanese immigrants dominated by an oppressive patriarch, *To the Left of the Father* is a 170-minute baroque cavalcade through Proustian layers of temporality, guided by the sweeping images of master cinematographer Walter Carvalho. The stunning sequence here described is just one of many intoxicating moments in Luiz Fernando Carvalho's sensuous rendition of Raduan Nassar's *Lavoura Arcaica*, a lyrical tragedy that had been deemed inadaptable to film. The director's daring debut has been hailed by critics as Brazil's most visionary and incandescent film since Glauber Rocha.

Paolo Bertolin

Date 2001

Nationality Brazil

Director Luiz Fernando Carvalho

Cast Selton Mello, Simone Spoladore

Original Title *Lavoura Arcaica*

Why It's Key This spellbinding sequence speaks for the savage and sensuous beauty of this visual poem.

Key Speech **Royal speaks of his illness**
The Royal Tenenbaums

Has anybody, anywhere, ever talked like Royal Tenenbaum? Almost certainly not. And yet the language given to the disgraceful patriarch and namesake of Wes Anderson's third movie seems to be the realest thing in it. As performed by Gene Hackman at his gruffest and funniest, Royal's stately use of slang, his hip pomposity ("Of course I've missed you like hell, my darlings," says the pomaded old fraud to his children) evoke a twinkling Fifties underlife of elegant rascal-hood and strange, scandalous dignity: in fiction, his brother would be Saul Bellow's Henderson. "You're true blue, Ethel!" "Let's shag ass…" "That's a hell of a hound dog you got there. What's he go by?" Royal's talk is both an affront and a tonic to the disappointed Tenenbaum children, all mouldering poetically through their various crises. He instructs his estranged grandsons to call him "Pappy." Of his many great lines I would select the following, spoken early in the film when Royal's masquerade of terminal illness – a ruse to reinsert himself in his family's affections – is yet to be uncovered. "What have you got?" asks his son Richie (Luke Wilson), full of concern. Stoically, Royal gives the answer: "I've got a pretty bad case of cancer." Later, in a fit of pique, his faithful manservant will harmlessly stick a small knife in his side. Nothing can touch him, until he comes down with a bad case of death.

James Parker

Date 2001

Nationality USA

Director Wes Anderson

Cast Gene Hackman, Luke Wilson, Ben Stiller, Gwyneth Paltrow

Why It's Key Reacting against Anderson's quaintness gave Hackman the chance to be funnier than ever before.

Opposite *The Royal Tenenbaums*

BRAD RENFRO WITH ILLEANA DOUGLAS AND STEVE BUSCEMI

THORA BIRCH   SCARLETT JOHANSSON

A TERRY ZWIGOFF FILM

GHOST WORLD

Key Scene **Enid dances to a Bollywood musical** *Ghost World*

It's nighttime in suburbia, and the camera tracks past the windows of several very ordinary people, all of them evidently watching television. It stops at a teenager's bedroom, where the source of the music we've been hearing becomes evident – it's a dance hall, where Indian men and women wearing cat's-eye masks vigorously dance to a 1960s-style pop tune. Their movements are frenzied, comic, angular – particularly those of a vivacious brunette who throws herself into the tune without reserve. The teenage girl in red flannel pajamas extends her arms, shaking them to join the brunette in musical ecstasy.

Ghost World is all about how this young woman, Enid (Birch), grows up in a series of detachments, from father, childhood, girlhood chum, and from her culture. Already she's begun detaching herself from the latter – seeking out Bollywood musicals on videotape. (This particular musical number, "Jaan Pehechaan Ho," comes from Raja Nawathe's 1965 film *Gumnaam*, and

is included in its entirety on the *Ghost World* DVD.) Enid rejects the fast-food world of retro-1950s diners she's been born into, trying out different alternate cultures as the film proceeds, finding a soul mate in the alienated record collector Seymour (Steve Buscemi), who has bizarre Mexican film posters on his wall and turns her on to obscure blues musicians. *Ghost World* speaks to our modern alienation from our crummy commercialized world and demonstrates just how novelty-seeking buffs like Enid and Seymour continually revitalize it by seeking out authentic lost voices from other worlds. They stand in for the movie buffs who like films like *Ghost World*… and seek out their own special moments in films old and new… the project of this entire book.

Gregg Rickman

Date 2001
Nationality USA
Director Terry Zwigoff
Cast Thora Birch
Why It's Key The way outsiders seek their identity in cultures other than their own is wittily shown.

Opposite *Ghost World*

Key Scene **The two young men kiss** *Y tu mamá también*

SPOILER

There had been great directors in Mexico since the 1930s. In the 1940s, the work Emilio Fernández and Fernando de Fuentes represented a golden age. Luis Buñuel's arrival in 1946 inspired a distinctly Mexican art cinema that struggled against the odds in subsequent decades. In the late 1990s, unexpectedly, such art cinema found a world audience. To some in Mexico and abroad *Y tu mamá también*, Alfonso Cuarón's first Mexican film after his sojourn in Hollywood directing *A Little Princess* (1995) and *Great Expectations* (1998), looked too like an American teen road movie. Certainly its story – about two young men taking a pretty woman on a road trip to find a dream beach – sounds overfamiliar, but Cuarón's critics ignore his social acuity. The director and his brother and co-writer, Carlos Cuarón, bluntly intrude on their sexual adventure story with voiceovers that draw attention to class difference and deprivation. At one point, Julio (Bernal), who comes from a much richer family than his friend, Tenoch

(Luna), says that when he is at Tenoch's house he lifts the toilet seat with his foot. Such hints at class revulsion play into the climax of the film where, drunk, the boys each kiss Ana (Mercado) and then, tentatively, each other. Next day they are repelled by the memory of this last kiss, and, as a result, their friendship falls apart. The scene certainly takes a dig at Mexican machismo and homophobia, but in a country so completely divided by class, where social mobility is extremely limited, the fall-out from the kiss seems powered by class anxiety, too. The young men's friendship bridges an economic chasm in Mexican society and so cannot survive. Seen in this light *Y tu mamá tambien*, far from being an Americanisation of Mexican cinema, is one of the most revealing Mexican films ever made.

Mark Cousins

Date 2001
Nationality Mexico
Director Alfonso Cuarón
Cast Gael García Bernal, Diego Luna, Ana López Mercado
Why It's Key This is a great symbolic moment in the revival of Mexican cinema.

Key Film *A.I. Artificial Intelligence*
The last day with his mother

The last major film project of Stanley Kubrick, realized posthumously by his friend Steven Spielberg, can easily be read as an allegory about cinema that also becomes a parable about the delusions of mankind. A boy robot named David (Osment) has been programmed to love Monica, his adopted mother (O'Connor), even after she abandons him, believing that she'll reciprocate his love if, like Pinocchio, he becomes a "real boy." Many centuries after mankind has perished, David is found by future beings who intercept his memories and tell him that they can resurrect both Monica (using a preserved lock of her hair to clone her) and the suburban home where she once lived with David, but only for one day, after which she must vanish forever. So they spend a blissful day together, his seventh birthday, and then go to bed together, where he falls asleep for the first and only time, becoming a "real boy" at the same moment that he and Monica and the rest of humanity essentially breathe their last gasp.

The bleakness is quintessential Kubrick, the suburban bliss quintessential Spielberg, and the triumph and desolation of this terminal Oedipal quest seem to belong to the personal visions of both filmmakers. The Blue Fairy who grants David his last wish by giving him his erotic idyll with Monica oddly resurrects both the mysterious black monolith of Kubrick's *2001: A Space Odyssey* and the benign extraterrestrials of Spielberg's *Close Encounters of the Third Kind*, melding them together into the same ecstatic yet despairing vision.
Jonathan Rosenbaum

Date 2001

Nationality USA

Director Steven Spielberg

Actors Haley Joel Osment, Frances O'Connor

Why it's Key Humanity ends with a screwed-up android spending an idyllic day with the clone of his adopted mother and then going to bed with her.

Opposite *A.I. Artificial Intelligence*

2000–

722

Key Scene **The shooting of a costume ball to a Them song** *Wild Innocence*

A young filmmaker, François Mauge (Kacem), has accepted a shady deal with his producer (Subor), in order to film his script about heroin addiction with an aspiring actress he has just met and fallen in love with, Lucie (Faure). After they cross the border with a load of heroin, the filming starts with a costume ball in Amsterdam, where young, sophisticated-looking "beautiful people" in 18th-century three-cornered hats, robes, cassocks, embroidered cuffs, and ruffled shirts dance to Them's "Friday's Child," making baroque gestures in a sort of crazily convulsive choreography that exhales sadness and despair behind its affected elegance and dreamlike lightness. It is a moment of extreme beauty, gracefulness, and poignancy, shot in black-and-white widescreen, which culminates when the beautiful Lucie goes outdoors and sits alone snorting drugs on the bank of a moonlit channel.
Miguel Marías

Date 2001

Nationality France/ Netherlands

Director Philippe Garrel

Cast Julia Faure, Mehdi Belhaj Kacem, Michel Subor

Original Title *Sauvage Innocence*

Why It's Key A magic moment of bliss and beauty is revealed as a fragile staged illusion.

Key Scene **The scattered family's reconciliation** *Kabhi Khushi Kabhie Gham...*

Karan Johar's *Kabhi Khushi Kabhie Gham...* exemplifies the trends that dominate the Bollywood industry at the dawn of the third millennium. Aiming at the pounds and dollars of the NRI (Non-Resident Indians) whose currencies have increasingly become more coveted than rupees, products such as *K3G* (as it's known among Bollywood aficionados) rely on star-studded casts (*K3G* reunites three generations of Bollywood stardom: Amitabh Bachchan and real-life spouse Jaya Bhaduri, Shahrukh Khan and Kajol, Hrithik Roshan and Kareena Kapoor), exotic locations (in *K3G*, Egypt), exuberant production values, and imaginative music numbers to embellish conservative narratives about love and family, meant to uphold traditional Indian values in the globalized world.

There are so many insulting sides to a film like *K3G* – the articulation of gender politics, the shameless exaltation of brand-consumerism (a slap in the face of poverty), the silly India-*über-alles* nationalism – that one

should, rationally, end up hating oneself for succumbing to the film's irresponsible charm and old-fashioned emotional core. But that's Bollywood's magic – a magic that makes it possible to reconcile the deepest emotional strains in the very last five minutes of a 210-minute film. Amid a deluge of overwrought emotions, Rahul (Khan) returns to his parents' mansion after ten years of absence, to meet his father (Bachchan), who had repudiated him after his love-marriage with low-class Anjali (Kajol). Suddenly, everybody's ready to admit their faults, to cry without restraint, and hug one another in the name of the ties that bind. It's difficult to hold back tears. But don't ever tell Naomi Klein.

Paolo Bertolin

Date 2001

Nationality India

Director Karan Johar

Cast Amitabh Bachchan, Shahrukh Khan, Kajol

Aka *Happiness and Tears; Sometimes Happiness, Sometimes Sorrow*

Why It's Key The new Bollywood is still capable of finding its redemption in the emotional floods of its inescapable happy endings.

2000–

724

Key Speech **Bickering over the editing table** *Où gît votre sourire enfoui?*

Despite a small circle of cinephiles championing their intransigent work, the films of longtime partners Danièle Huillet and Jean-Marie Straub are often treated as inaccessible or at least deliberately difficult. Their extreme materialism, rejecting common notions about acting, storytelling, even *mise en scène*, has caused controversy and marginalization throughout their career. Already, their feature debut, *Not Reconciled*, finished back in 1965, when only Straub was credited as director, was ridiculed until Godard and others stepped in. The final collaboration, *Quei loro incontri*, still drew massive walkouts (especially by the press) at its Venice competition screening in September 2006, only one month before Huillet's death. If it weren't so criminally underseen itself, Pedro Costa's magnificent document about Straub/Huillet preparing the third cut of their 1999 film *Sicilia!* would be a perfect antidote to many misguided preconceptions about the couple. Not only does their

agonizing over the right edit – with sound naturally given equal weight – illustrate that their extreme precision is not pedantic, but passionate, and that their aesthetics develop from their ethics. But the film is also a great screwball comedy about love for, and with, cinema. "Somebody who pole-vaults with you would fall on his face every time," from back at the editing table Huillet interrupts one of Straub's long foreground monologues about film. "It is hard not to talk nonsense," Straub replies. "You can always shut up," Huillet counters. "That is the radical solution," Straub muses. "Can you finish your monologue, Straub? I have to work."

Christoph Huber

Date 2001

Nationality France/ Portugal

Director Pedro Costa

Why it's Key Radical filmmakers Danièle Huillet and Jean-Marie Straub are mostly famous for being intransigent. They are indeed, but they're also extremely passionate and funny, which is why this documentary portrait of them is among the best films about filmmaking.

Key Scene **The narrator coughs**
Dogtown and Z-Boys

Among the sweetest experiences in cinema, at least for viewers, is when the most basic codes of professional filmmaking – the things that usually run so smoothly we hardly even notice them – suddenly misfire and leave the rails. Although many savvy narrative filmmakers, from John Waters to Raúl Ruiz, have cultivated these transgressive "mistakes," such derangement is far less common in documentary, where the conventions dictating a "well-made film" are lamentably close to the mainstream television standard. Chief among these conventions is the role of voice-over narration. Sean Penn may not exactly be the "voice of God" in the upbeat skateboarding doco *Dogtown and Z-Boys*, but, for the most part, his mellifluous tone is the glue that holds together the collage of still photos, interviews, archival footage, and graphics. That is, until one priceless gaffe takes place. It occurs 20 minutes in, and happens so fast that it's easy to miss. Penn, relating the history of skateboard design,

evokes "the new…," then stops, clears his throat, and re-begins correctly: "…the manoeuvres performed on the boards…." Not only is this inadvertent bit of business left in; it also becomes the basis for some jazzy image-and-sound riffing that is worthy of Orson Welles's *F for Fake* (1974). On the erroneous "new," the image (of a skateboard) "shudders" slightly, is if registering the glitch; and as Penn coughs, we see a fast zoom-out. Next shot: amateur footage of riders, smooth voice-over; *Dogtown* is back on the rails, as if nothing ever happened…

Adrian Martin

Date 2001

Nationality USA

Director Stacy Peralta

Cast Sean Penn

Why It's Key An inadvertent glitch in the narration gets registered in the image.

2000–

725

Key Scene **Back in time**
Millennium Mambo

A mystifyingly underrated film by Taiwanese master Hou Hsiao-hsien, *Millennium Mambo* opens on such an ecstatically ethereal note that what follows inevitably suggests an extended hangover in selected hangouts of Taipei's electronic scene, following the often quite bored life of a narcissistic girl (Shu Qi) as if she were a Warhol superstar – although Warhol might have been aghast at the sensational lighting and elaborate long takes by cameraman Mark Ping-bin Lee. Furthermore, the proceedings are put in perspective by a third-person voice-over (probably the heroine speaking in hindsight) announcing and sometimes contradicting events. The volatile mid-film image of a face pressed in snow memorably encapsulates Hou's fascination with passing time and hazy memory, but even more impressive is the beginning, in which the camera tracks behind Shu running in slow motion through a sordid neon-lit underpass, as a techno beat swells and a harmonious melody chimes in (the song

reappears repeatedly at crucial moments that are often only in retrospect recognizable as such). The voice-over starts by revealing its future perspective, looking back ten years at what happened in 2001. Shu slowly turns around, her searching look at the camera an invitation to follow her back in time. But at the end of this hypnotic, weightless sequence the camera stops helplessly at the top of the exit stairs, while Shu runs off into the city, reminding us that there'll be only so much we can grasp of her and the memories of that year of heavy snow.

Christoph Huber

Date 2001

Nationality Taiwan/France

Director Hou Hsiao-hsien

Cast Shu Qi

Original Title *Qianxi mambo*

Why It's Key The opening for Hou's ravishing, underrated film establishes his interest in time and memory in one hypnotic long take.

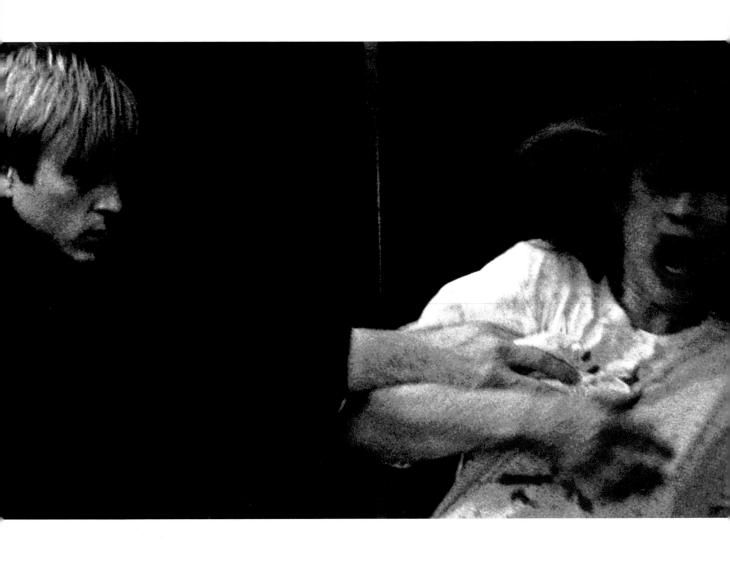

Key Person **Isabelle Huppert** Erika's face as she stabs herself *The Piano Teacher*

There are many extraordinary scenes in Haneke's multi-award-winning adaptation of Elfriede Jelinek's harrowing study of a woman so affected by a domineering mother and the rigours of a Viennese education in classical music that she is pathologically unable to engage in any "normal" kind of emotional or sexual communication. At once profoundly and unsettlingly transgressive (like much of Haneke's work) and admirably restrained in its refusal to exploit or sensationalise, the film remains memorable for the tissue-sniffing visit of music-academy professor Erika Kohut (Huppert) to a peep-show parlor; for Erika's sadomasochistic encounters with initially adoring student Walter (Magimel) in a public toilet and later in her own barricaded bedroom; and for her desperate attempts to show some kind of love for the detested mother (Annie Girardot) with whom, bizarrely, she still shares a bed.

Huppert's performance throughout is courageous and enormously eloquent, a miracle of suggestive restraint and subtle, almost miniaturist detail attaining great depth and intensity. But nothing quite matches the fleeting expression caught on her face in Bergmanesque close-up as – in a perversely ironic attempt, perhaps, to free herself from the masochistic obsession for Walter now gripping her – Erika plunges a knife into her own shoulder. Anguished, agonised, horrified, yet strangely triumpant, it is a look that reminds one less of the movies than of certain paintings: Munch's *The Scream* comes to mind. If only for these few seconds (but in truth for many others), Huppert and Haneke both deserve a prominent position in the cinematic hall of fame.
Geoff Andrew

Date 2001

Nationality France/Austria

Director Michael Haneke

Cast Isabelle Huppert, Benoît Magimel

Original Title *La Pianiste*

Why It's Key The most remarkable few seconds of one of the very finest film performances in years

Opposite *The Piano Teacher*

2000–

727

Key Film
My Sassy Girl

SPOILER

For decades most of Asia paid little attention to Korean pop culture, and Korean cinema was an insular world put on display only rarely at international film festivals. As Korea grew richer and its commercial film industry blossomed, however, that began to change. *Christmas in August* (1998) and *Shiri* (1999) received successful releases in Hong Kong and Japan, but it was the romantic comedy *My Sassy Girl* from 2001 that truly broke into mainstream consciousness throughout Asia. No Korean film since has matched its success. Young Chinese citizens polled in 2006 about ten things that remind them of Korea cited *My Sassy Girl* alongside kimchi and taekwondo.

Based on a serial novel published on the Internet, the film charts the travails of university student Kyun-woo (Cha) in his budding romance with a sultry beauty (Jun) who shows a propensity for bizarre behavior, heavy drinking, and playing rough. They first meet on a late-night subway car where, drunk, she pukes on an

old man's head before calling Kyun-woo (a complete stranger) "honey" and passing out. Things go downhill from there, but soon Kyun-woo is in love, an obedient puppy at her heels. Actress Jun Ji-hyun, who was launched to superstardom with this performance, shatters numerous stereotypes of the demure Asian woman – at least until the latter reels, when her eccentricities are explained away and she takes on a more traditionally feminine role. Nonetheless the film adequately captures a sense of shifting gender roles in Asian society, while tapping into more universal anxieties about dating.
Darcy Paquet

Date 2001

Nationality South Korea

Director Kwak Jae-yong

Cast Jun Ji-hyun, Cha Tae-hyun

Original Title *Yeopgi-jeogin geunyeo*

Why It's Key This romantic comedy from Korea became a strong commercial hit throughout Asia, helping to kick off the so-called "Korean Wave" or craze for Korean pop culture.

Key Scene **The empty windows in the Science Institute** *Conjugation*

In a cold night of 1989, a lateral tracking shot pans over rows of empty buses. A young couple on bicycle appear. Guo Song (Qiang) tries to pry the doors of a bus open. Then he and his girlfriend, Xiao Qing (Zhao), sneak in, grab each other in their padded jackets, and make hurried, passionate love. Having met when demonstrating in Tiananmen Square, they are now without a place to call their own. Guo Song has been assigned to work in a factory; Xiao Qing studies French and moonlights as a waitress. Instead of reconstructing the Beijing of ten years before, Tang insightfully focuses on intimate, domestic scenes.

Illegally (for they are not married), the couple rent a hovel in a hidden *hutong* (back alley) and work hard at their dream of personal happiness, with the memory of "missing" friends lingering on. One evening, warned by the landlord that the police are going to check on the tenants, they clear out, kill time in a video club, and end up in one of the buses… Another night, Xiao Qing notices a building where windows are always dark. It's the dormitory of the Science Institute. The students were probably killed in the spring. Yet, what she is thinking about is that there are *empty apartments*, and they should be allowed to move in. The dead mark the site of an unspoken *absence* – the living are homeless… *Conjugation* subtly explores these cracks between China and its citizens, laying the map for the social malaise of an entire generation.

Bérénice Reynaud

Date 2001

Nationality China

Director Emily Tang

Cast Qiang Yu, Zhao Hong

Original Title *Dong ci bian wei*

Why It's Key The first underground Chinese film about the aftermath of the Tiananmen Square massacre, *Conjugation* is also the first feature directed by a female director of the Sixth Generation.

Key Scene **The airport scene** *Water and Salt*

To what extent are our ideas about the cinematic canon determined by the whims of distributors, the limitations of critics, the size of publicity budgets, or just plain chance? Villaverde's *Water and Salt* poses this question in a particularly acute form. It is, in my opinion, among the finest films of the 21st century. Yet it remains almost totally unknown, hardly screened outside the festival circuit, unavailable on DVD (though an unsubtitled VHS edition was released in Portugal). Since it is impossible to demonstrate the qualities of this masterpiece in a short paragraph, one moment must represent the whole: a sequence shot showing the film's protagonist, Ana (Ranzi, playing an artist clearly modelled on Villaverde), meeting her husband, Marido (de Almeida), at an airport. Ana is accompanied by her daughter, Criança (Villaverde's daughter, Clara Jost), and the shot begins with a close-up of their linked hands, from which Villaverde's camera pulls back as Marido arrives and greets his family. But the resulting image is composed in such a way that a woman speaking into a public telephone at the right of the frame is granted the same visual prominence as those individuals with whom the narrative is more directly concerned. By refusing to use devices which might separate the "important" characters from those "unimportant" people surrounding them, Villaverde provides a superlative example of that cinematic humanism best represented by Jean Renoir, Hou Hsiao-Hsien, and Abel Ferrara: a humanism conveyed not through rhetorical assertions, but rather by a stylistic approach which embodies the humanist position in a living form.

Brad Stevens

Date 2001

Nationality Portugal

Director Teresa Villaverde

Cast Galatea Ranzi, Joaquim de Almeida, Clara Jost

Original Title *Água e Sal*

Why It's Key This scene demonstrates the qualities of an unknown masterpiece.

Key Event **Publication of Hamid Naficy's** *Accented Cinema*

Hamid Naficy's *An Accented Cinema: Exilic and Diasporic Filmmaking*, the first methodical study of the work of migrant filmmakers, highlighted the fact that this work is closely defined by specific production conditions that are often restrictive and in any case different from the conditions available to native filmmakers. Naficy calls the work of migrant filmmakers "accented cinema," explaining: "If the dominant cinema is considered universal and without accent, the films that diasporic and exilic subjects make are accented.... The accent emanates not so much from the accented speech of the diegetic characters as from the displacement of the filmmakers and their artisanal production modes." Across various cultures, accented cinema often displays analogous patterns of storylines and recycles specific artistic tropes of displacement, epistolary motifs, and biographical narratives.

Naficy's work is particularly influential for bringing about the understanding that the study of film, and especially its transcultural dimension, needs to take into account the various symbolic practices that relate to production and consumption patterns (alongside the more traditional approaches of textual analysis and psychoanalysis). Naficy acknowledges the importance of exploring patterns of representation but insists that production conditions and distribution modes should be seen as equally important factors in the creation and the reception of cinematic texts, especially in the contemporary world where diasporic filmmaking is gaining such importance and prevalence.
Dina Iordanova

Date 2001

Why It's Key This book was the first systematic study of diasporic and exilic filmmakers, their production circumstances, and their specific forms of expression.

Key Scene **The opening credits** *Pistol Opera*

In 1967, Japanese cult director Seijun Suzuki so enraged the president of the Nikkatsu studio – where he'd already made about 40 quickie features over the past nine years – with his baroque hit man thriller *Branded to Kill* that he was fired for making "incomprehensible" films. Over 30 years would pass before Suzuki made a sequel, *Pistol Opera*, with few theatrical features in between, and one can't exactly conclude from the results that he learned any lessons about clarity or restraint.

Even the pre-credits sequence about a hit man killing or not killing another hit man with a carefully aimed rifle – we see someone's body in extreme long shot fall from a rooftop and dangle at the end of a rope before the supposed victim, located somewhere else, flashes a knowing grin – prepares us for something pretty abstract. What we get, though, is even loonier: to the sounds of raucous rock tinged with a hint of brassy Dixieland, punctuated periodically by shouts and punchy Japanese lyrics, dazzling graphics of eyes appear in successive strips, then sliding silhouettes and overlapping gels of pistols, vaguely human figures, and loud wallpaper designs. All these indulge in rapid crisscrossing patterns, followed by flurries of snow and the eyes of a cat. Most of this bears some relation to the action that follows, much of it having to do with a gorgeous hit woman named Stray Cat (Makiko Esumi) killing or not killing various designated victims. But the hallucinogenic free-form colors of Disney's 1944 *The Three Caballeros* may seem closer to the mark.
Jonathan Rosenbaum

Date 2001

Nationality Japan

Director Seijun Suzuki

Original Title *Pisutoru opera*

Why It's Key We're alerted to this movie's formalist hijinks at the outset.

Key Scene **The elephant wore pink**
Fish and Elephant

Non-acting their own parts à la Warhol and captured with a *vérité* camera, two young women elbow their way through the crowded streets of Beijing, fending off boorish boyfriends, inadequate suitors, obnoxious customers, psychotic ex-girlfriends, and marriage-minded moms. One, Xiaoqun (Pan), is gay; the other, Xiaoling (Shitou), is not. Or so it seems. They meet in Xiaoling's clothes stall; Xiaoqun, the keeper of a (female) elephant, invites her new friend to visit the Zoo; after a sweet, shy courtship, they're in bed together. Xiaoling's boyfriend experiences a sorry, drunken bout of identity crisis and is soon out of the picture. Xiaoqun's mother (Zhang) is more intrusive: determined to marry off her 30-year old daughter, she moves from her hometown to the little love nest, blissfully unaware of what is really going on.

Then Mom, stuck in her role of divorced-woman-as-victim, meets a nice widower and has to revise her morality standards. In a static shot almost five minutes long, she meets with her daughter in a noisy restaurant; in the foreground, two young men drink huge glasses of beer. As her mother has violated Confucian propriety by confessing her desire to remarry, Xiaoqun dares to break her code of silence, revealing she likes girls and Xiaoling is her lover… Former documentarist Li Yu switched to fiction to better protect her subjects; mixing several levels of reality, her affectionate depiction of the life of a lesbian couple reveals the complexity of interaction among women, gay or straight, in a changing China.

Bérénice Reynaud

Date 2001

Nationality China

Director Li Yu

Cast Pan Yi, Shitou, Zhang Jilian

Original Title *Jinnian xiatian*

Why It's Key The first Chinese lesbian underground feature made a splash on the international circuit and launched the career of a young female Sixth Generation director.

Key Scene **The death of old Maata**
Waiting for Happiness

After a night spent drinking tea and smoking to bid farewell to a friend who has resolved to depart for Europe, old Maata (Abeid) exits into the desert, holding an alight bulb in his hand. This man who hates travels, departures, and goodbyes is setting out for the biggest journey. Maata sits in the dunes as the bulb's glow increases. At the first rosy lights of dawn, little Khatra (Kader), Maata's apprentice electrician, joins the old man, to discover he's dead. Khatra sings a French song the old man hated, hoping Maata will wake up to scold him. Eventually, Khatra disengages the bulb, taking the symbolic legacy with him.

The films of Mauritanian *auteur* Abderrahmane Sissako eschew conventional plotting and rely upon a sparse dramaturgy devoid of predictable dramatic punctuation. Sissako's understated adherence to the places and people he portrays veers towards the sensitivity of documentary, yet *Waiting for Happiness* also encompasses instances of sheer magic and lyricism. Depicting the people, colors, and sounds of Nouhadhibou, a town on the West coast of Africa where people gather to embark on journeys of hope to Europe, Sissako reflects on the theme of exile and mulls over the ever-problematic underdevelopment of the continent and the crippling post-colonial bonds with Europe. The character of the old electrician Maata is symbolic of those who stubbornly stay and work for progress; his serene death, and the hand-off of the light bulb to little Khatra, delicately convey a message of undying hope.

Paolo Bertolin

Date 2002

Nationality France/Mauritania

Director Abderrahmane Sissako

Cast Khatra Ould Abder Kader, Maata Ould Mohamed Abeid

Original Titles *Heremakono; En attendant le bonheur*

Why It's Key This serene representation of death embodies the understated magic of Sissako's film.

Key Film
Russian Ark

As he was filming his meditative documentary *Confession* (1998), Aleksandr Sokurov conceived of an even more daring film, which he came to think of as a movie in "a single breath." In the past, directors like Hitchcock, Mizoguchi, Minnelli, and Welles had experimented with sustained shots, but technology had moved on since their day. It was possible, in the digital era, to film – on a hard disk – for much longer than celluloid or videotape allowed, so Sokurov planned a single-shot film in which a European travels through the Hermitage Museum in St Petersburg, debating the nature of 19th-century Russian culture. The shot would cover 1,300 metres of ground, travel through 33 galleries, and encounter hundreds of actors and extras and three live orchestras. Sokurov rehearsed for six months. He had 22 assistant directors. Tilman Büttner operated the Steadicam. Filming took place on 23 December, when the city has only four hours of daylight, so only two takes were possible.

The first was abandoned. Take two had to work, and it did. As if to repudiate Soviet cinema and politics, not only was there no montage, but the European traveller's journey stopped short of the Revolutions themselves, ending on a bleak image of the future as a brooding sea. *Russian Ark* is perhaps reactionary, a whispered fantasy about Tsarist Russia, but it is also a masterpiece of *mise en scène*. Watching it is like seeing cinema reborn.
Mark Cousins

Date 2002

Nationality Russia

Director Aleksandr Sokurov

Cast Sergei Dontsov, Mariya Kuznetsova

Original Title *Russkiy kovcheg*

Why It's Key This landmark in cinema history is the first feature-length film composed of one continuous shot.

Opposite Russian Ark

Key Scene **The montage that spans America** *25th Hour*

SPOILER

The protagonist is Monty (Norton), a young New Yorker spending his last night with friends and family before starting a prison stretch for drug dealing. When morning finally arrives, his father, James (Cox), comes to drive him to the penitentiary. Battered and exhausted from experiences of the preceding hours, Monty dozes in the passenger seat. Then, as they head up the first stretch of highway, James unexpectedly offers to turn west and keep on going, bringing his son to some distant destination where he can start a new, anonymous life.

The screen fills with this fantasy as his monologue spins on, envisioning a utopia untarnished by past errors and rich with the possibilities America offers to the free, unfettered spirit. Bygone mistakes recede, races commingle in domestic harmony, and new generations build ways of living untainted by wrong decisions of their predecessors. At one breathtaking moment, as the screen is mostly occupied by a large

bus in the main street of some little town, James suggests that maybe, just maybe, Monty's beloved girlfriend (Rosario Dawson) might someday be able to join him – and just as he says this the bus pulls away, revealing her as she walks to Monty's side, filling the last gap in James's reverie.

The film's final shot, showing the car still headed for the upstate prison, confirms the daydream's phantasmal nature. But it renders the sequence no less resonant – one of cinema's most eloquent expressions of the potential for transcendence cradled in the everyday conditions that all people share.
David Sterritt

Date 2002

Nationality USA

Director Spike Lee

Cast Edward Norton, Brian Cox

Why It's Key Taking off from the sadness of its main characters, this film's conclusion builds a vision of sociocultural utopia that's as compelling as it is, regrettably, unreal.

Key Scene **The dance**
La Vie nouvelle (New Life)

Grandrieux's films are severely mutated musicals. Their trance-dance music is driven, anguished; a robotic techno-beat overlaid by cries, slurs, growls, murmurs. Boyan (Nagy) in *La Vie nouvelle* is a sinister Lord of the Dance, and Mélania (Mouglalis) his puppet. Mélania seeks more than ecstasy; she wants to escape her miserable lot as prostitute and sex-slave in Sarajevo, to violently tear herself out of her skin. In the five-minute near-psychedelic dance scene near the end of the film, there is no space between bodies, jammed together in a difficult, fraught intimacy; they meet not in Dionysian abandon but on fearful alert. *Mise en scène* – the art of bodies in space – is here a dance of death, the living death of everyday power relations. The sequence develops in stages, closely tied to the layering of tracks in the music mix. Boyan resembles a Nosferatu. Mélania's spinning reaches a frenzied crescendo, accompanied by an eerie whip-like sound. Her face in close-up is flattened, stretched, lost and found from one frame to the next. For a few magical seconds, Mélania seems weightless, detached from time and space – freed at last. But there is no escape for her: suddenly we hear a crowd, and this woman under the influence is no longer in a rehearsal space, but a nightclub. Again a prisoner, always on show and for sale… *La Vie nouvelle*: this "immense video clip" of a film (as Raymond Bellour called it), bound together by rhythms, pulsations, and screams of horror.

Adrian Martin

Date 2002

Nationality France

Director Philippe Grandrieux

Cast Zsolt Nagy, Anna Mouglalis

Why It's Key Grandrieux proposes *mise en scène* as dance of death.

Key Scene **Bathtub**
Femme Fatale

There is a picture book called *Movie Stars in Bathtubs*, but there aren't enough movies with movie stars in bathtubs. De Palma's *Femme Fatale*, which stars Rebecca Romijn, does much to correct that.

Romijn plays Laure Ash, a jewel thief thrown from a hotel balcony by her accomplices. When the parents of a missing girl named Lily find Laure unconscious on the hotel floor they whisk her home and put her to bed in their daughter's room. In a typical De Palma touch, Laure is a blonde disguised as a brunette, making her Lily's double. (Romijn plays her, too.) Laure awakens, sees Lily's photograph, and realizes she can use her look-alike's passport to escape the men she's double-crossed. Before she leaves she decides to take a bath.

Laure's bath frames at least half the film's action. Drinking tequila and smoking, Laure drifts off as the tub begins to overflow. Thunder strikes outside, waking her up (again) as Lily returns, loads a gun, and puts it to her head to commit suicide. A fish tank overflows as Lily pulls the trigger. Now Laure can take Lily's place for good.

De Palma brings a lifetime's contemplation of cinematic trickery to this, his most abstract and satisfying thriller. When Laure is thrown from a bridge into the Seine she finds herself suddenly without her clothes and awakens in the overflowing bathtub again. Again Lily returns and puts a gun to her head, and for once De Palma denies himself a victim.

A. S. Hamrah

Date 2002

Nationality France

Director Brian De Palma

Cast Rebecca Romijn, Antonio Banderas

Why It's Key It's De Palma at his best.

Opposite *Femme Fatale*

Key Scene **The birth of a calf**
(A)torsion

Films about the Balkan conflicts following the breakdown of Yugoslavia in the 1990s have become a subgenre of the war movie. Though set in the same period and location, *(A)torsion* takes us by surprise in the simple story of a farmer whose main problem has only a tangential connection with the ethnic strife in the region. His very pregnant cow (with a severely twisted foetus) is so scared by the noise of the bombs falling around the shed that she screams and kicks around as if she is about to have an epileptic seizure. Amidst people seeking shelter and the rattle of machine guns, the members of a Renaissance choir are ready to escape the (unnamed) country with the excuse of a concert to be held in Paris. They have bribed an army officer and are about to enter the tunnel which will lead them to safety, when a boy stumbles upon the group and begs them to help prevent the poor cow from going totally crazy. But how can they be of any assistance? They are musicians, not veterinarians. And so they do the only thing they know well: once inside the barn, they start singing *a cappella* in front of the mad cow; the music slowly heals her anxiety; a calf is born, right in front of the camera. The choir leaves while the boy cuddles the newborn calf: "don't be afraid," he whispers, "I will sing another song for you." Fade out. We can still hear the crackling sound of the guns, out in the darkness.

Paolo Cherchi Usai

Date 2002

Nationality Slovenia

Director Stefan Arsenijević

Cast Admir Glamočak, Davor Janjić

Original Title *(A)torzija*

Why It's Key A fairy tale can blossom in the Balkan wars (with no hint of saccharine).

2000–

Key Scene **The unveiling**
10

Kiarostami's experiment in low-budget filmmaking consists of ten chapters shot in a car driven around Tehran by a divorcee (Mania Akbari); each comprises a conversation with a passenger – several with her argumentative son, the rest with various women. What makes *10* remarkable is that (with one brief exception) every shot was filmed by a video camera fixed on the dashboard and trained either on the driver's seat or the passenger's; mostly, Kiarostami wasn't in the car as the scenes were recorded. The conversations were partly inspired by the real-life experiences of the driver and her son, partly the fruits of Kiarostami's imagination; the result is as vividly suggestive of raw, unfiltered reality as anything in documentary.

Hence the power of the moment when one passenger removes her scarf to reveal a shorn head; she cut off her hair after being jilted by her boyfriend, We see her, however, not as a victim but as someone strong enough to insist on her own worth – to the point of exposing her head in public, an act forbidden in the Islamic Republic. Her defiant courage – real, since the non-professional actors were filmed travelling the streets of Tehran – is profoundly moving not only because of what it says about her as an individual and about the predicament of women in Iran, but because it sets an encouraging example to the driver… whose hand, in one of just three instances when both passenger and driver are simultaneously visible on screen, suddenly appears from the right of the frame to wipe a tear from her friend's face. A small gesture, with enormous resonance.

Geoff Andrew

Date 2002

Nationality Iran/France

Director Abbas Kiarostami

Cast Mania Akbari

Why It's Key The climax of an audaciously minimalist film, it illustrates that small can be not only beautiful but emotionally, psychologically, and even politically very significant.

Key Scene **The Mackerel**
Resurrection of the Little Match Girl

Iconoclast Jang Sun-Woo is arguably the greatest of contemporary South Korean directors this side of living legend Im Kwon-Taek, yet unlike national brand names Kim Ki-Duk or Park Chan-Wook he has remained an outsider, thanks to his unpredictability. Which is on ample display in one of the great film follies of the early 21st century: *Resurrection of the Little Match Girl*, a visionary virtual-reality action satire next to which the *Matrix* sequels, released only months later, looked like the ridiculous waste of time and money they were. The outrageous premise of Jang's film is a prime example of his penchant for black humor and his interest in social outcasts: A humiliated delivery boy (Kim) flees into the world of a game loosely based on Andersen's "Little Match Girl" tale – to win you have to make her think of you as she dies! The satire is sharp throughout, riffing not just on gaming worlds, but on what movies have become under their influence, expertly deconstructing while delivering. Awesome action setpieces are scored operatically, revealing themselves as the musical numbers of the blockbuster era. Still, the co(s)mic pessimism about virtual realities and real inequalities is balanced by Taoist philosophy as a way of engaging with the world. The dialectics culminate with the introduction of the most powerful and legendary of weapons, a mentally controlled toy gun called The Mackerel. The punchline is delicious: To really control The Mackerel, you have to accept that it is – a mackerel.

Christoph Huber

Date 2002

Nationality South Korea

Director Jang Sun-Woo

Cast Kim Hyun-Sung

Original Title *Sungnyangpali sonyeoui jaerim*

Why it's Key Because it's The Mackerel. You do not question the legendary Mackerel.

Key Scene **Disintegration of reality**
demonlover

SPOILER

"Just another hero, riding through the night," announces a Krautrock hymn at the beginning of *demonlover*, and indeed this ingenious anti-thriller chronicles the disappearence of its increasingly insignificant heroine (icy Connie Nielsen). Roundly booed at its Cannes competition premiere in 2002 – often a good sign (cf. *The Brown Bunny*) – this dark, stylish, and complex film takes a headlong plunge into a virtual nowhere. Olivier Assayas neatly sets up the fall by using the trademark style of his earlier, remarkable melodramas (frequent collaborator Denis Lanoir contributes distinctive, mobile handheld-camera takes), but the story edges towards big-business thriller. Yet the bidding wars of multinational corporations for profitable Japanese Internet porn remain as sketchy as the globalized settings – conference rooms, hotels – are anonymous. Then, as if infected by a computer virus, the plot disintegrates, its associative jumps much like clicking oneself through the Internet via hyperlinks, until the *film* resembles a sinister, hallucinatory role-playing game. *demonlover* finally transports the themes and televisionary transformations of David Cronenberg's 1983 masterpiece *Videodrome* to the Internet era, Assayas slyly acknowledging his predecessor. Reality begins to fall apart in a Japanese hotel, TV running, conjuring the earlier film's medium of mutation, even its Japanese sex-film-within-the-film "Samurai Dreams," which points back (or rather: forward) to *demonlover*'s story developments – adding another ingenious meta-twist to its many circular structures. And might that bitterly ironic final image of a DNA sequence be the key to the code of Cronenberg's much-quoted "new flesh"?

Christoph Huber

Date 2002

Nationality France

Director Olivier Assayas

Cast Connie Nielsen

Why It's Key Finally updating Cronenberg's masterpiece *Videodrome* for the Internet era, Assayas's complex anti-thriller tips the hat to its predececessor in particularly sly ways.

Key Scene **The transcendent, vertiginous finale** *Irréversible*

Noé stirred controversy with his 1998 debut feature, *I Stand Alone*, about a dissolute butcher contemplating mayhem and suicide. But nothing prepared cinephiles for *Irréversible*, a picture so caustic that moviegoers have been known to race for the exits in disgust. The film contains horrific material, to be sure, including a savage murder and a vicious anal rape, filmed in agonizingly long takes that are almost unbearable to watch. Adding to the viewer's disorientation, the story unfolds backward, each scene revealing what happened *before* the one we've just witnessed.

But anyone who thinks shock value is the film's main purpose has missed its deeper meanings. On one level, *Irréversible* is a thoughtful examination of the animalistic urges dwelling beneath the shallow surfaces of contemporary life. On another, it's an intricately structured essay on the interrelated natures of time, causality, cognition, and intuition. And

ultimately it's an artfully ambivalent statement about the possibility of finding peace and happiness in the degraded modern world.

This becomes clear in the final scene, when the heroine (Bellucci) – pregnant, although she doesn't know it yet, and unaware of the brutal rape awaiting her – is lying in a park, reading and resting as children play around her. The camera, which has been swooping and diving almost continuously throughout the film, soars to the sky for a gorgeous overhead view, then starts spinning in a literally dizzying display of ecstatic visual pyrotechnics. Fallen though it is, the world can be beautiful. And so can this one-of-a-kind movie.
David Sterritt

Date 2002

Nationality France

Director Gaspar Noé

Cast Monica Bellucci

Why It's Key With a hand-held camera and a low budget, an innovative filmmaker creates a moment of rapturous beauty in a film otherwise marked by horror and dread.

Opposite *Irréversible*

Key Scene **Even Hong Kong dikes get the blues** *Ho Yuk, Let's Love Hong Kong*

Born and raised in Hong Kong, but with a pattern of scholarship and teaching that brought her to New York, Michigan, London, and Taiwan, videomaker/writer/educator/activist Yau Ching shoots her city as only those who have lost their homeland know how. As queer culture is both present and invisible in Hong Kong, gay subjects experience a simultaneous sense of ownership and dispossession. Yau translates these feelings by casting a doubt on the reality of what we see, injecting the tropes of the erotic lesbian sci-fi fantasy into an acutely realistic depiction of Hong Kong. Drenched in post-colonial melancholia, and haunted by postmodern ghosts, the city bears the marks of Ackbar Abbas's *déjà disparu*. Yau's lens turns it into a utopia, fueled by the hidden energy of lesbian desire.

Emotionally remote Chan (Wong) lives with her mom and dreams of buying a house for her – but uses the money she earns as a stripper/performer in an erotic video game to buy the services of a mainland

prostitute. Businesswoman Nicole (Koo) swoons over Chan's neatly packaged and multifarious video image, while cute little Zero (Lam), who sells sex toys and cell phones in the street, is hot for the real Chan, who's not interested. In the last sequence, Nicole accidentally runs into Chan one night, without recognizing her. She casually asks for a light, smokes by her side in silence, and then walks off, as Zero enthusiastically enters the other side of the frame; but Chan, once more, pushes her away.
Bérénice Reynaud

Date 2002

Nationality Hong Kong

Director Yau Ching

Cast Wong Chung Ching, Erica Lam, Colette Koo

Original Title *Hao Yu*

Why It's Key This is the first movie made in Hong Kong by a woman about women in love with each other.

Key Film *Infernal Affairs* Ming decides to seal his secret identity with bloodshed

SPOILER

It makes sense that Martin Scorsese, maestro of Catholic guilt, would want to remake *Infernal Affairs* as *The Departed* (2006), as the Hong Kong original begins with a recitation from the Buddhist Nirvana Sutra: "The worst of the Eight Hells is called Continuous Hell. It has the meaning of continuous suffering." Continuous suffering is something that both Yan (Tony Leung) and Ming (Andy Lau) understand too well. Yan, a cop, has spent the last decade pretending to be a Triad member, reluctantly indulging in the drugs, violence, and mayhem expected of a gangster in order to insure his deep cover, while Ming nervously wonders when the police officers in his department will realize he's a mole planted by Triad boss Sam (Eric Tsang). The two men play a shadowy cat and mouse game against the starkly saturated vista of urban Hong Kong, each walking a tightrope of fear while paying the psychological price for a life lived in lies. The shocking denouement has a momentarily triumphant

Yan finally taking his shadow nemesis hostage in a high rise elevator, only to be shot and killed by another cop secretly on the take. Ming thanks his lucky stars and then slaughters his surprise benefactor, a move that destroys his humanity but leaves him secure in the knowledge that three can keep a secret if two are dead. *Infernal Affairs* concludes on an uncomfortably existential note, defying the action genre's laws of payback to prove we're not punished for our sins, but by them.
Violet Glaze

Date 2002

Nationality Hong Kong

Director Wai Keung Lau, Siu Fai Mak

Cast Andy Lau, Tony Leung

Original Title *Mou gaan dou*

Why It's Key It's a crucial scene in an existential action film riddled equally with bullet holes and guilt.

Opposite *Infernal Affairs*

Key Film *West of the Tracks (Tiexi District)* The violent beauty of ruins to come

Wang Bing spent two years documenting the slow death of factories and working-class housing compounds in Shenyang. Yet his images, alternating between the intimate (a man naked in a factory shower; a grandmother under the light of an oil-lamp; a young man collapsing in tears) and the grandiose (the huge spaces of derelict factories as the sun seeps through broken windows) are about *us*. And this is not only because Wang shoots first-person with a small DV camera, taking the spectator in his wake – walking along the narrow catwalks of the steel mill; climbing the metal stairs of the copper smelting plant, his footsteps resonating in the hollow vastness around; sitting by the *khan* where a mother is dying of cancer; projecting his shadow on the snow-covered streets. It is because the grand tragedy he minutely documents reflects *our* condition. All over the world factories are closing; for China the transition between pre- and post-

industrial age is just more abrupt, violent, and cruel than in First World countries.

First and last, there is the train, the iron horse, once the harbinger of industrial progress – now increasingly obsolete, noisy, polluting. Trains cut across Tiexi District; they carry freight between factories even as they close one after the other; they pass by rows of shabby shacks, as they are forcefully evacuated by developers (the working poor who refuse to move spending a winter without heat, electricity, or water). Trains remain in the gutted landscape, they keep on running their dead-end course, offering the last jobs, the last paradoxical mode of survival.
Bérénice Reynaud

Date 2003

Nationality China

Director Wang Bing

Original Title *Tiexi Qu*

Why It's Key A nine-hour monumental trilogy on the dismantling of an industrial complex in Northeast China becomes a cinematic landmark.

Key Scene **Stopover embrace**
The Brown Bunny

Bud Clay (Gallo), a jealous and unsatisfied motorcycle racer, travels across the U.S. in his van from the East Coast to Los Angeles. At a highway rest stop, he notices a blonde woman (Tiegs) sitting alone at a table outdoors, drinking coffee and smoking. As he passes through to get a Coke from a vending machine, she looks at him: they make eye contact, feeling each other's loneliness. The woman, though not in her prime, a bit jaded or blurred, is still attractive, and she seems interested in Bud. Almost at his van, he looks back at her, then goes to the table and sits at her side; we see her name – Lilly – on her handbag, which she puts away. Bud caresses her, holds her head, asks "You OK?" and they embrace with gratitude, feeling mutually comforted. While they kiss, the camera stays on Lilly's face, Bud's head being seen from the back, almost out of frame. They hug, and her face comes into focus, while he seems suddenly to collapse into desolation, and it's her turn to kiss him and comfort him. He rises, gets into his van's driving seat, starts the motor, and departs, as she (now photographed from behind) watches her go away.

Silence, physical contact, tenderness, compassion, and mutual consolation are briefly exchanged between two strangers in a very moving sequence which lasts more than six minutes and gets much of its delicate force from the way director-writer-cinematographer Gallo stages and frames each shot, unsymmetrically composed, off-centered, so that everything feels unrehearsed and looks casual, caught on the spot.

Miguel Marías

Date 2003

Nationality USA

Director Vincent Gallo

Cast Vincent Gallo, Cheryl Tiegs

Why It's Key This almost wordless sequence conveys through unusual compositions and acting the mutual kindness of strangers.

Opposite *The Brown Bunny*

2000–

743

Key Speech **The young girl reads her dead mother's last letter** *Saraband*

Of the eleven parts into which *Saraband* is divided, the seventh, "Letter from Anna" is probably the longest and one of the strongest. It takes about eight minutes and shows Karin (Dufvenius), the young grandchild of the long-ago divorced husband of Marianne (Ullmann), confiding to the older woman (who might have been, but isn't, her grandmother) the letter she has found, addressed to her father, Henrik, by her mother, Anna, just a week before the writer's death, when she learned how little time she had left. It is a very hard letter, Karin warns Marianne, too much for her to re-read, but Marianne proves unable to decipher Anna's handwriting, so Karin has to read it aloud. Bergman fragments the scene in four main, close, simple, almost conventional set-ups: one showing both characters in profile, one centered on each with the other's shoulder in frame, another with Karin in close-up; he knows the situation needs no dramatization, no reinforcing effects. The letter, which Karin cannot read in full, shows Anna to have been a very sensitive, loving, and intelligent woman, who feared Henrik would, after her death, take possession of Karin – as has in fact happened despite her very earnest admonitions. That her father could not be unaware of what he's doing to her, and that he never mentioned the letter, increase Karin's anger while, at the same time, she fears for Henrik's life if she goes away to live independently and pursue her own career as a cellist.

Miguel Marías

Date 2003

Nationality Sweden

Director Ingmar Bergman

Cast Liv Ullmann, Julia Dufvenius

Why It's Key Rarely has the cinema ever made so alive and present a character never seen (except in a black-and-white photograph) and already dead when the film starts – and without even using her voice.

Key Scene **Concluding musical number**
Down with Love

*D*own with Love tries to spoof three comedies I couldn't care less about – *Pillow Talk* (1959), *Lover Come Back* (1961), and *Send Me No Flowers* (1964). I'm delighted that the filmmakers, too young to have experienced this era first-hand, got it all wrong, from studio logo to palatial Manhattan penthouse apartments (as in *How to Marry a Millionaire* and *The Tender Trap*) to "think-pink" advertising décor (as in *Funny Face* and *Will Success Spoil Rock Hunter?*), all of which date from 1953-1957. And the visual and verbal double entendres, antismoking gags, and overt references to feminism and homosexuality, no matter how hilarious, all clearly come from post-1964.

But this collapsing of the '50s, '60s, '70s, and '80s into a hyperbolic dream of a dream speaks volumes about who we are today, expressing a yearning for what's wrongly perceived as a less cynical and more innocently romantic period. Preoccupied with a trio of hypocritical comedies as if they contained awesome and precious secrets, *Down With Love* offers a surprising number of creative and poetic insights into some of the more tender aspirations of today.

The payoff is the wonderfully executed and exuberant concluding musical number, "Here's to Love," where Renée Zellweger and Ewan McGregor, the two stars in evening drag, bump and grind their way through lurid colors and tacky TV set designs as if they were frolicking through some version of paradise regained. However ironically pitched, their euphoria seems genuine enough to renew one's faith in the possibility of a reinvented present.

Jonathan Rosenbaum

Date 2003

Nationality USA/Germany

Director Peyton Reed

Cast Renée Zellweger, Ewan McGregor

Why It's Key Maybe it gets the early '60s wrong, but it gets 2003 exactly right.

Opposite *Down with Love*

2000–

Key Scene **Soulmates are born**
The Dreamers

*P*oetry, said William Wordsworth, is emotion recollected in tranquility. What a profoundly poetic moment is to be found early in *The Dreamers*, as the blossoming frisson of adolescent excitement in the presence of strangeness and possibility is brought to the screen. An American youth away from home for the first time in the Paris of 1968, Matthew (Pitt) fixes every vista as legendary, finds every breath intoxicating, crossing the Pont d'Iéna toward the Cinémathèque française. His religion, his art, his philosophy, his nourishment, his raison d'être: film. He tumbles into a crowd of students protesting the ouster of Henri Langlois, winding his way through them with increasing anticipation until he comes to the doors of the sacred temple, which have been locked. Pinioned there with symbolic chains is a pretty girl, Isabelle (Green), whose eyes catch onto his and seize him in a close-up. Her twin brother, Theo (Garrel), arrives a moment later, tousle-headed and bubbling over with enthusiasm. "Do you know what Godard says?" asks Theo, urgently, "He says, 'Nicholas Ray is the cinema!'" Isabelle glows; Matthew is all innocence, hunger, breathlessness. The twins lead him off by the river, his first new friends in France, his guides on a journey where he will discover love, truth, art, politics, and the gap that separates what he is from what he is not. Theo offers part of the sandwich he is sharing with Isabelle; Matthew politely refuses; Theo absolutely insists. Instantly now, as they stroll beneath the trees of the Port de Passy with the magical river by their side, they have become one flesh.

Murray Pomerance

Date 2003

Nationality Italy/France/UK

Director Bernardo Bertolucci

Cast Michael Pitt, Eva Green, Louis Garrel

Original Title *Les Innocents*

Why It's Key It shows how eroticism doesn't necessarily depend on sexuality.

Key Scene **The pas de deux to "My Funny Valentine"** *The Company*

Altman's ballet film was seen by few and liked by fewer. Yet it's arguable that it's one of the all-time great dance movies – almost everyone in the cast was a member of the Joffrey Ballet of Chicago – and a truly radical American film, in that it foregoes the contrivances of a conventional plot. The narrative – focused loosely on the wholly ordinary experiences of young dancer Ry (Campbell) – simply observes the troupe as they prepare for the first public performance of the fantasy *The Blue Snake*. From the choreographer pitching his idea for that ballet to the far from climactic scene of its première, we see rehearsals, negotiations, some socialising, and a few other dances being performed; in short, life goes on, as the film straddles fiction and documentary.

The pas de deux in which Campbell – a competent if unremarkable dancer – partners one of the Joffrey dancers to "My Funny Valentine" is merely the most memorable example of Altman's refusal to play by

generic rules. Ry gets her break after a dancer designated for the number suffers an injury, but it's no big deal: in contrast to all those showbiz sagas prior to *The Company*, the girl is congratulated on her performance but doesn't attain stardom. But the *mise en scène* is superb. Altman used several high-definition cameras to film the dance sequences, achieving great spontaneity and authenticity, and for this number – performed on an outdoor stage – he whipped up a storm; as the cameras prowl at a characteristically elegant pace, observing the two dancers persevering against the odds even as the audience abandon their seats, the grace, skill, strength, and dedication required of ballet folk are made gloriously visible.

Geoff Andrew

Date 2003

Nationality USA/UK/ Germany

Director Robert Altman

Cast Neve Campbell

Why It's Key Sheer beauty of execution combined with a refusal to conform to narrative rules make this typical of Altman's late work at its best.

Key Scene **The DNA test results arrive from the U.S.** *Memories of Murder*

Korean director Bong Joon-ho based his stunning sophomore work on a string of real-life serial rape-murders that took place in rural Korea during the 1980s. By close to the film's end, the police – who have grown more and more desperate with each new body – believe they have identified the killer. Hyun-gyu (Park) is a thin, cold-eyed man who arrived in town shortly before the murders began. Although they lack proof, the police have found a drop of the killer's semen, and they hope to link it to Hyun-gyu through DNA testing, carried out in the U.S.

In driving rain next to a railroad tunnel, Tae-yoon (Kim), the Seoul detective who once prided himself on logic-centered technique, is trying to beat a confession out of Hyun-gyu. His partner runs up a with the envelope from the U.S. Desperate, they tear it open, but are shocked to read that "since the DNA fingerprint does not correspond exactly to the semen sample, it cannot be said conclusively that the suspect is the murderer."

The wording of the letter is vague, but the moment operates on several levels: an affirmation that even the most guilty-looking suspect may be innocent; a failure of science to deliver ultimate truth or understanding; and perhaps even, on a symbolic level, a failure on the part of the U.S. Throughout the period of South Korea's military dictatorship, many pro-democracy activists hoped the U.S. would intervene to support their cause. Nonetheless, South Korea ranked as a key ally in the Cold War, so the demonstrators ultimately had to wage their fight alone.

Darcy Paquet

Date 2003

Nationality South Korea

Director Bong Joon-ho

Cast Song Kang-ho, Kim Sang-kyung, Park Hae-il

Original Title *Sarin-ui chueok*

Why It's Key A film that at first seems to resemble a standard police thriller reveals added complexity in this penultimate scene.

Key Scene **The shot of the empty auditorium near the end** *Goodbye, Dragon Inn*

One singular aspect of Tsai Ming-liang's masterpiece is how well it plays. I've seen it twice with packed film-festival audiences, and both times, during a shot of an empty cinema auditorium, where nothing happens for over two minutes, you could hear a pin drop. Tsai makes it a climactic epic moment.

Indeed, for all its minimalism, *Goodbye, Dragon Inn* fulfills many agendas. It's a failed heterosexual love story, a gay cruising saga, a Taiwanese *Last Picture Show*, a creepy ghost story, a melancholy tone poem, and a wry comedy. A cavernous Taipei movie palace on its last legs is showing King Hu's 1966 hit *Dragon Gate Inn* to a tiny audience – including a couple of the film's stars (Miao Tien and Shih Chun), who linger like ghosts after everyone else has left – while a rainstorm rages outside. As the martial-arts classic unfolds on the screen, we follow various elliptical intrigues in the theater, such as the limping cashier (Chen Shiang-chyi) pining after the projectionist (Lee Kang-sheng), whom she never sees. Tsai has a flair for imparting a commanding presence to seemingly empty pockets of space and time.

With the cashier, we peer at the end title on the screen. Then, in a shot lasting well over five minutes, the camera faces the empty auditorium as the lights flicker on and she enters with a broom on the right – recording her slow passage up one aisle, across the middle row, and down the other aisle until she exits on the left. Then we linger for two minutes more, communing with silence and eternity.

Jonathan Rosenbaum

Date 2003

Nationality Taiwan

Director Tsai Ming-liang

Original Title *Bu san*

Why it's Key A minimalist master shows what can be done with an empty movie-theater auditorium.

Key Scene **New Year's celebrations** *The Best of Youth*

SPOILER

New Year's Eve. The Carati family is celebrating together. Matteo (Boni) unexpectedly shows up. As everybody plays board games, Matteo feels increasingly estranged. He tries to call Mirella (Sansa) on the phone: she's at home, but intentionally doesn't respond. Matteo sneaks out, noticed only by brother Nicola (Lo Cascio). At home, he tries to call Mirella again; she finally picks up, but Matteo has already hung up. On TV, host Gianni Morandi invites audiences to join him in a New Year's toast. At Carati's home, everybody rejoices. "Happy New Year," Matteo says to the TV; he then turns away, opens the window, and jumps from the terrace. The camera slowly tracks towards the terrace.

The unanticipated suicide of the tortured and sensitive Matteo comes as the major shock in Marco Tullio Giordana's *The Best of Youth*. Conceived originally as a TV miniseries in four parts, Giordana's six-hour epic (whose original title comes from a collection of poems by Pasolini) tracks the fate of an Italian family over four decades, from the Sixties till the year 2000. Matteo's suicide, occurring in the mid-Eighties, marks a turning point in the saga, a gradual withdrawal from the political towards the personal. Despite this reticence, Giordana's film suffered from a bad case of self-censorship by its producers: the Italian TV network RAI cancelled its broadcasting, afraid (under the conservative Berlusconi regime) of its somewhat leftist content. Luckily, *The Best of Youth* was rescued from oblivion by success at Cannes, where it won the Un Certain Regard section, and garnered worldwide theatrical exposure.

Paolo Bertolin

Date 2003

Nationality Italy

Director Marco Tullio Giordana

Cast Luigi Lo Cascio, Alessio Boni, Maya Sansa

Original Title *La Meglio gioventù*

Why It's Key This emotionally shocking sequence marks an eminently symbolic turning point in Giordana's sprawling familial saga.

Key Scene **The hero jumps into the millionaire's swimming pool** *Crimson Gold*

The action of Jafar Panahi's fourth feature – the second one to have been scripted by his mentor Abbas Kiarostami, who based the story on a true incident – is bracketed by a pizza delivery man's pathetic, abortive efforts to hold up a jewelry store. And the night before this happens, at the end of a long day full of everyday humiliations, Hussein delivers a pizza to a millionaire in a swank penthouse whose female companion has just walked out on him. The neurotic and talkative rich man invites Hussein to share his pizza with him, and it's the only time in the movie when we see the hero relaxing. He spends the remainder of the evening wandering around the palatial digs, supposedly like a kid in a candy store. But Hussein is played by a nonprofessional actor   an overweight, medicated paranoid schizophrenic – and his deadpan responses to his surroundings are never more incongruous than when he spontaneously dives, fully dressed, into the millionaire's indoor pool.

Should we conclude that Hussein's seeming idyll in the penthouse partially motivates his criminal behavior the next morning by showing him what he can't have? The film won't say, though perhaps we could conclude that the rich man's friendliness only underlines the impossibility of Hussein's ever joining any class above his own. The film takes care not to motivate him with any facile psychologizing, yet the diffidence of the actor's performance offers a glancing clue that he can't even be convincingly carefree when he wants to break loose.

Jonathan Rosenbaum

Date 2003

Nationality Iran

Director Jafar Panahi

Cast Hussein Emadeddin

Original Title *Talaye sorkh*

Why It's Key A pizza delivery driver who's always made to feel out of place tries to go with the flow.

Opposite *Crimson Gold*

Key Scene **Chase through the Louvre** *Looney Tunes: Back in Action*

You could say that film aficionado Joe Dante was born to make *Looney Tunes: Back in Action*, a mix of live-action and cartoon characters that, for once, registers as a true tribute to the anarchic spirit of the great, original Warner Bros. cartoons with Daffy Duck, Bugs Bunny, and other timeless animation creations. In an era of (really) downsized "Baby Looney Tunes" and generally emasculated cartoon revivals, Dante's achievement stood out as special, despite occasionally noticeable studio interference. The cramming of every madcap frame with hilarious in-jokes, funny non-sequiturs, and freewheeling gags testifies to a real pop-culture-lover's fascination, which is why Dante even gets Daffy's hysterical working-class antagonism exactly right, amid the onslaught of references to personal favorites ranging from Robbie, the robot of 1956's Shakespeare-in-space marvel *Forbidden Planet*, to the satirical live-action comedies former Looney Tunes cartoonist Frank Tashlin made around the same

time. Dante's related (and updated) satire of corporate entertainment is an auteurist trademark, and here it finds memorable expression in the demented evil plan of the ACME CEO (played as a human toon by Steve Martin) to turn all humans into monkeys (for profit). But the film's masterstroke – and not just in its impressive technical execution – is a chase through the Louvre. When Elmer Fudd hunts Bugs and Daffy literally *through* famous paintings (and they mutate accordingly: melting in Dali, disintegrating into dots in pointillist Georges Seurat), it's not only hilarious, it also attests to their true status in cultural history.

Christoph Huber

Date 2003

Nationality USA

Director Joe Dante

Why It's Key A true fan, Joe Dante got the update of Bugs and Daffy right. And then he showed where they truly belong in cultural history.

Key Scene **The last image: a legacy**
Come and Go

Among the things that account for the shocking beauty of the cut to the last scene in João César Monteiro's final film, *Come and Go*, is the stylistic unexpectedness. The sudden, giant close-up of an eye comes as an extreme break from the Portuguese director's signature style of long shots, to which the previous three hours of the film have adhered; thus it gathers a sudden emotional heft, like the similar close-up at the end of Jacques Tati's *Mon Oncle* (1958), but stronger. Yet this film is not only formally characteristic of its eccentric, genial Portuguese auteur, with its impeccable, mostly symmetric static takes glowing in what seems to be incredibly beautiful natural light. It is typical of Monteiro in every other respect as well, not least in casting himself as the lead, an elderly man clearly enjoying exchanging sexually outspoken dialogue with younger ladies and inevitably destined to be a marginal outlaw. The typical, deadpan humor of the proceedings does not betray that the almost septuagenarian Monteiro knew that he was dying from cancer when he made this, but that knowledge is another reason why that final shot seems so magnificent. As Monteiro's own eye towers on screen, so huge that the retina reflects the park where much of *Come and Go* took place, this not just, simply and movingly, says "This is how I saw the world." It also asks us to contemplate the vastness of this statement.
Christoph Huber

Date 2003
Nationality Portugal
Director João César Monteiro
Cast João César Monteiro
Original Title *Vai e vem*
Why It's Key It may well be the most brilliantly conceived goodbye shot in cinema. It certainly is one of the most moving.

Key Scene **The hallway fight scene**
Oldboy

At the start of the most famous scene from Park Chan-wook's *Oldboy*, protagonist Oh Dae-soo (Choi) stands at one end of a hallway holding a knife to another man's throat. Between him and the elevator at the end of the hall are at least 15 thuggish-looking men carrying large sticks. Oh could probably use the hostage to extricate himself from the situation, but something in him needs to fight. After sending the hostage away, and dropping the more lethal knife in favor of a hammer, he attacks the crowd.

The film's original storyboard called for a large number of individual shots, but late in the process Park changed his mind. Onscreen we see an artfully-choreographed chaos: bodies shoved and thrown left and right, tumbling to the ground; actor Choi Min-shik swinging his hammer or punching like a rangy boxer (no martial arts on display here); a knife (rendered with CGI) thrust into Oh's back (it proves incapable of slowing him down); and finally the signs of hesitation and fear creeping into the eyes of the 15 men, who realize they won't be able to beat him. In contrast to the jumbled mass of bodies onscreen, the camerawork itself is a model of simplicity: shot straight-on, with no swiveling or turning, the camera tracks slowly to the left or right, keeping Oh in the center of the screen. This single shot, which reportedly took 17 tries to get just right, goes on for an incredible two minutes and 40 seconds.
Darcy Paquet

Date 2003
Nationality South Korea
Director Park Chan-wook
Cast Choi Min-shik, Oh Dae-soo
Why It's Key This one-man-vs.-fifteen brawl shot in a single take in a narrow hallway is one of the most memorable fight scenes ever filmed.

Opposite *Oldboy*

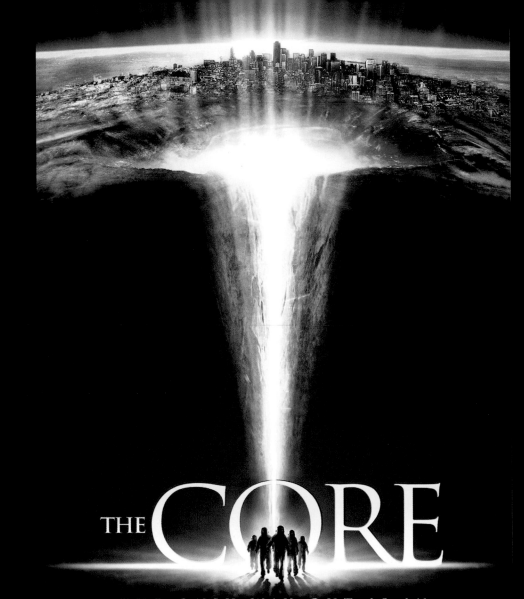

Key Scene **Ducks walking on the seashore**
Five (5 Long Takes Dedicated to Yasujiro Ozu)

As its subtitle explains, this 75-minute feature, shot on DV at the San Lorenzo Beach while Kiarostami was visiting the Gijón Film Festival in Asturias, Spain, is made of five very long stationary shots. This is the fourth and shortest of the five. The camera, on a tripod, looks at the shoreline, framed so that one sixth is beach, three sixths sea, and the remainder cloudy gray sky.

A duck appears – an unusual sight at the seashore – walking in a leisurely manner from left to right. Then another, and another, then a group. Some that look rather like geese. Quite a parade, in fact. White, black and white, brownish, or simply dirty-white ducks, some quacking noisily, most of them silent. Some cross the frame slowly, or with some difficulty, others seem quite purposeful and steadily increase their pace. Occasionally, one seems bent on outrunning the others, which seem to crowd the stretch of sand Kiarostami has focused on. Each has its own peculiar style, pace, gait. This goes on for five very funny and

intriguing minutes, while you begin to wonder how it will end. Suddenly and unexpectedly (probably blocked out of sight, out of the framed space, by Kiarostami; I can imagine him waving his hands to make them go back), the ducks change direction and begin to cross our field of vision from right to left, running or walking for the remaining minute. More Tatiesque than Ozu-like.
Miguel Marías

Date 2003

Nationality Iran/France/Japan

Director Abbas Kiarostami

Why It's Key It's a practical demonstration of how funny and interesting even the simplest things can be, with minimal means, without actors, dialogue, or plot.

Key Scene **The L.A. River's last run**
The Core

Residents of Los Angeles are accustomed to associating the city's painful traffic congestion with the various numbered highways that crisscross Southern California. Moviegoers know better and recognize that America's movie capital hosts a thoroughfare busier than the 405, the 101, and the 10 put together. It's the dried-up concrete basin of the Los Angeles River, and in its time it has provided emergency access to the giant ants in *Them!* (1954), a chopper-flying Roy Scheider in *Blue Thunder* (1983), John Travolta in *Grease* (1978), Arnold Schwarzenegger and the morphing terminator in *Terminator 2: Judgment Day* (1991), Lee Marvin in *Point Blank* (1967), the Rodriguez brothers in *Repo Man* (1984), Mark Wahlberg in the remake of *The Italian Job* (2003), and the casts of several dozen other films, TV shows, and commercials.

The science-fiction disaster film *The Core* has few claims to movie immortality, featuring a goofy premise, corny writing, incredibly stupid science, and a cast that

should be doing better things. But the opening scene, in which astronaut Hilary Swank must emergency-land a Space Shuttle in the city of the angels, is the *summa* of L.A. River traffic films. Of all the vehicles taken through the river, the shuttle is undoubtedly the largest and the least probable. Even viewers sanguine about the prospect of a *Challenger/Columbia* tragedy will sweat bullets imagining the generations of movie talent that seem certain to be wiped out as NASA's wheezing white elephant runs over all of them. Fear not: Swank, as close as the space age is likely to come to an Amelia Earhart figure, handles the challenge with aplomb.
Tim Cavanaugh

Date 2003

Nationality USA

Director Jon Amiel

Cast Hilary Swank, Bruce Greenwood

Why It's Key It narrowly avoided shutting down L.A.'s busiest freeway.

Opposite *The Core*

Key Scene **The last warning**
Greendale

Surprisingly, two of the most political American films of 2003 were brainchilds of Rock 'n' Roll superstars. *Masked and Anonymous*, directed by Larry Charles, but overwhelmed by his co-writer and star Bob Dylan, was an episodic dystopian fantasy about corporate greed and private mythology, with Dylan's hilariously deadpan poker-face performance setting the tone – in equal measures cryptic and caustic. Part of the idea may have been to disguise some of the more naive (however poignant) sentiments of the aging protest rocker. Not surprisingly, Neil Young couldn't care less about such discretion. Thus, his 2003 polit-musical extravaganza *Greendale*, based on his eponymous concept album, may wear its bleeding eco-libertarian heart on its anti-Bush sleeve, but nobody could mistake it for pretentious rock opera. Shot in proudly grainy Super-8, with amateurish actors lip-synching the lyrics of the director-writer-cameraman-composer, the film has the aura of a guerrilla home movie. Cinematic folly

doesn't get more personal than this, but for all his concern with individual freedom, Young recognizes the necessity of communal protest. The grand finale takes place on a stage reassembling the whole cast, captivated by the energetic mantra of the three-chord garage-rock song. There's something defiantly triumphant about this sentimental final call to save the planet (and, yes, "Be the Rain"), not least because everybody joins in: It's quite a sight when the activists are accompanied by firemen, cops, and FBI agents waving their fists along to the lyrics of a song that warns "Don't believe what the government says."
Christoph Huber

Date 2003

Nationality USA

Director Neil Young (as Bernard Shakey)

Cast Sarah White, Eric Johnson, Ben Keith

Why It's Key Young's guerrilla-style home movie seeks to invigorate protest rock by all means – including the memorable and singular sight of fist-waving FBI agents joining in the final pro-Earth, anti-government song.

Key Scene **Bush in the schoolroom**
Fahrenheit 9/11

Most moviegoers have strong opinions about Moore, pro or con. But one can applaud his filmmaking savvy and the overall thrust of his politics while also recognizing his weakness for tendentious argument and first-person showboating.

All these qualities are on display in his documentary about the Bush administration's responses to the assaults of September 11, 2001, on the World Trade Center and other targets. No scene is more powerful than the depiction of President Bush proceeding with a photo-op visit to a Florida school after being informed of the first plane hitting the Twin Towers, and staying in the classroom after being told a second plane had struck and the U.S. was under attack. Showing footage of Bush in the schoolroom, with a book in his lap and a preoccupied expression on his face, Moore gives the shot his own polemical slant via narration: "Not knowing what to do… Mr. Bush just sat there and continued to read *My Pet Goat* with the children."

Noting that Bush's failure to do anything – even leave the room for information – lasted for almost seven long minutes, Moore goes on to wonder if the vacation-loving president were wishing he'd shown up at work more often, or had a conference with his counterterrorism chief, or refrained from cutting the FBI's terrorism funding. By the time this part of Moore's monologue is over, the image of Bush's paralysis has become indelible. It's unlikely to lose its ghastly strength even when the Bush government is (literally) history.
David Sterritt

Date 2004

Nationality USA

Director Michael Moore

Cast George W. Bush

Why It's Key Moore offers a prime example of how to inject a piece of deceptively bland footage with a potent ideological charge.

Opposite *Fahrenheit 9/11*

Key Scene **The closing close-up of Grandma Emilia's face** *Familia Rodante*

In the late 1990s, Argentina suddenly and rather improbably emerged as one of the world's more rewarding film-making nations; by the middle of the next decade, notwithstanding its economic crisis, it had established itself as a significant force in terms of the imaginative and artistic vitality of the films it fielded at international festivals. While a number of directors – Lucrecia Martel, Lisandro Alonso, Carlos Sorin included – attracted attention as figures to watch, none proved more prolific or consistently entertaining than Trapero, whose finest film yet remains this at first apparently ramshackle road movie about an extended family's odyssey from Buenos Aires to the Brazilian border in a camper van.

The cantankerous clan take the 1000-kilometre trip after their octogenarian matriarch Emilia (Chironi) announces at her birthday party that she intends to serve as matron of honour at a niece's wedding. As the jam-packed, far from dependable vehicle makes its faltering way to its destination, allegiances shift, tempers fray and arguments erupt, until the wedding is reached and drunkenly enjoyed. The wayward narrative feels as messily out of control – and as fundamentally meaningless – as everyday reality… until, after the party, Emilia takes a well-earned rest from the journey and the celebrations. The long, still, deeply compassionate close-up of her weary lined face, resigned yet resilient to everything life has thrown at her, speaks volumes of her strength, patience, experience and the wisdom derived over time; echoing the (shorter) opening shot, it also finally makes sense of everything in the film that precedes it.
Geoff Andrew

Date 2004

Nationality Argentina/ Spain/Brazil/UK

Director Pablo Trapero

Cast Graciana Chironi, Liliana Capurro, Ruth Dobel

Why It's Key It's a wise and wonderfully becalmed conclusion to an exuberantly chaotic vision of family life.

Opposite *Familia Rodante*

2000–

Key Scene **An animated sequence over the theme park** *The World*

Jia Zhangke's masterpiece – mainly set in and around a theme park called The World outside Beijing that features simulacra of such sights as the Taj Mahal, the leaning tower of Pisa, the Parthenon, and even lower Manhattan with the twin towers still intact – concentrates on alienated employees who work there, whose intimate communications with one another are expressed mainly through furtive text messaging. In particular, we follow the shaky romance of Tao (Zhao), a dancer who doubles as hostess at various attractions, wearing matching costumes, and Taisheng (Chen Taisheng), a security guard who's been going with her ever since they both lived in Shanxi province, though lately they've been drifting apart.

In this scene, she's dressed as an airline hostess inside a stationary airplane that's one of the park's attractions – an exotic curiosity for tourists who've never been on a plane – and sitting in Taisheng's lap during a break from work when he receives a call on his mobile. Then he reports that he has to go see a mutual friend of theirs, but he discourages her when she asks if she can come along.

The film suddenly shifts to an animated fantasy – as it periodically does when characters receive text messages and we're allowed to catch glimpses of their secret fantasies. In this one, we move from a cartoon version of Taisheng's mobile to Tao in her costume flying outside the plane, high over the park and city – experiencing a freedom and exhilaration she can never find in her life.
Jonathan Rosenbaum

Date 2004

Nationality China

Director Jia Zhangke

Cast Zhao Tao

Original Title *Shijie*

Why It's Key Even alienated employees working at a Chinese theme park can dream along with the customers.

Key Scene **Field of flowers talking**
Izo

There are filmmakers whose fans and advocates can be their worst enemies. Such is the case with Takashi Miike, not only one of the most prolific directors on earth, but also one of the most cultishly revered. Alas, this cult – and thus Miike's reputation – focuses not on his apparent stylistic originality but rather on his recurrent use of violent imagery, placing him squarely in that "Asia Extreme" section usually accompanied by much gushing about gore and little thought. (This is also why some of Miike's weaker works, like 2001's excessive comic adaptation *Ichi the Killer*, are inexplicably hyped.) Yet clearly Miike is a fierce humanist, as is proven by his overlooked sweet comedies, and – more strikingly – by his most confrontational film: *Izo*, a 128-minute bloodbath about a disgruntled avenging samurai demon single-mindedly hacking his way through Japanese society. It's a decidedly spiritual slasher movie, full of rich religious and historical imagery, straightforward in its view of

violence as the human tragedy. Its defiantly repetitious structure suggests a punk song (desperately screaming acid-folk singer Kazuki Tomokawa appears) as well as a prayer mantra. The murderous anti-hero (Nakayama) is described as the personification of absurdity ("a soul without a soul"), which leads to all kinds of unexpected scenes, the most staggering showing this poor deluded man ridiculed by the flowers in a surrounding field. But after a mystical climax suggesting rebirth and redemption, Miike, ever the humanist, ends on the close-up of one flower, suggesting forgiveness.
Christoph Huber

Date 2004

Nationality Japan

Director Takashi Miike

Cast Kazuya Nakayama, Kazuki Tomokawa

Why It's Key It proves that Takashi Miike, revered as the most prolific extremist among Asian "cult" filmmakers, is actually a humanist. And yes, it is a field of flowers talking.

Key Event **Publication of Chris Anderson's "The Long Tail"**

The Long Tail, a term coined by *Wire* editor Chris Anderson in his 2004 article (and subsequent 2006 book) of that title, describes an Internet age in which new technologies profoundly change the manner of cultural consumption, allowing for a much wider scope of narrowcasting alongside mass distribution of a few select smash hits. In the new mode of distribution, a vast number of products, while not available at store-based locations, can be obtained from Internet-based distributors that command huge on-demand inventories and that can both expand existing markets and cater to niche consumer interests. Markets become liberated from the "tyranny of geography": the new distribution set-ups enable unlimited availability of specific products, and the remote village is as adequately supplied with cultural goods as the most central metropolitan locations. For the first time in history, blockbusters and specialist products are just as worthy of being carried from a distributor's point of

view, because a very big number of niche products multiplied by a small number of sales results in an economic figure comparable to blockbuster-type revenues.

The implications for film distribution are enormous. Marketing strategies change profoundly, as, in the Long Tail, free word-of-mouth recommendations in Internet chat rooms are as powerful as million-dollar TV ads for new Hollywood blockbusters. The age of the blockbuster is drawing to an end, as latent demand for relatively uncommercial cultural products is growing. Globalizing comes hand-in-hand with narrowcasting and niche marketing; the movement is not toward a more homogenous world but to one of individual consumer choices, where catering to niche interests can result in major commercial success.
Dina Iordanova

Date 2004

Why It's Key This article is the definitive announcement of the end of blockbuster culture and the arrival of the thriving Internet-enabled trade of niche products.

Key Scene **Nina Simone impression**
Before Sunset

"We have all kinds of time." That is what a character says at the end of the deadline-driven *Cleo from 5 to 7* (1962), suddenly suspending the story (as the critic Roger Tailleur wrote) "in a moment of serene silence, finally out of time." Something similar occurs at the end of *Before Sunset*, which is, like its predecessor *Before Sunrise* (1995), so tensely fixed on the fleeting hours, minutes and seconds before Jesse (Ethan Hawke) and Celine (Julie Delpy) must end their "brief encounter." In the earlier film, Jesse and Celine were both in a foreign place, Vienna; now he is in her hometown of Paris, on a publicity tour for a book that fictionalises their previous experience. In its final 15 minutes, *Before Sunset* becomes especially tense: a cab scene re-finds the exquisite tension between private intimacy and public display that characterised *Before Sunrise*, but adds to it nine years of accumulated doubt, pain, and regret. But the finale, in Celine's apartment, manages to reverse this gloomy atmosphere. The cab is waiting and a plane will soon be boarding, but Jesse shows no sign of getting off Celine's couch: instead, he enjoys the homely sight of her affectionately mimicking a performance by Nina Simone, a show in which the singer took (as Celine explains) "all the time in the world." Suddenly, in this sovereign suspension of a looming deadline, Jesse and Celine have, it seems, all kinds of time – and the future is, once again, free and open to them.

Adrian Martin

Date 2004

Nationality USA

Director Richard Linklater

Cast Ethan Hawke, Julie Delpy

Why It's Key Suddenly, the characters have "all the time in the world."

Key Scene **The final scene**
10 on Ten

In 1948, Alexandre Astruc argued that the camera should be as directly expressive as a pen. In 1966, François Truffaut published his book-length interview with Alfred Hitchcock. In 1975, Gallimard published director Robert Bresson's *Notes on Cinematography*. The following year, Martin Scorsese completed his film of Paul Schrader's screenplay *Taxi Driver*, in which Robert De Niro drove around in what Schrader called an "iron coffin." Somehow, this documentary film combines all four. It is a confident assertion of cine-authorship. It is an incisive and personal insight into a filmmaker's art, and it is a film about the inwardness of driving in which its director-presenter Abbas Kiarostami calls an "iron cell."

For most of its running length, *10 on Ten* is a monologue spoken by Kiarostami in his car as he drives around the hills of Tehran where he shot *The Taste of Cherry*. He describes how scripts must be minimal and open, equipment must be unobtrusive, situations must be unforced, special effects must not be used, and cinema must be an art of the real. He speaks without inflection, but his opinions are deeply felt. At one point he even claims that American cinema is more dangerous than the American military.

For 80 minutes the film stays in this mode, but then, at its end, Kiarostami unclips the camera, takes it around the side of the car, and frames a cedar tree. This shift is striking, but solitary trees feature often in his films and stills. Then he tilts down and zooms in to reveal, slowly, an anthill in a crack in the road. This second haiku creates a rush of feeling, as if a dry lecture had turned rapturous, like Thoreau's *Walden*. Immediately we feel that Kiarostami can't have just been lucky in finding the anthill as he zoomed. He must have scouted the site, found the spot, and planned this little metaphysical fillip. If so, how? A mysterious ending to the mother of all making-ofs.

Mark Cousins

Date 2004

Nationality Iran

Director Abbas Kiarostami

Cast Abbas Kiarostami

Why It's Key This film is a "making of" as a work of art; its ending elevates it.

Key Scene **The pre-credits scene**
Café Lumière

Café Lumière begins with a pre-credits scene that reveals the complexity of which Hou Hsiao-hsien is capable. The protagonist, Yôko Inoue (Hitoto), is introduced in a three-and-a-half minute sequence shot showing her in her Tokyo apartment. The camera pans slightly left and right, but essentially remains in the same position: when Yôko moves behind a partition to address her landlady, we see only the space she has just vacated. The effect is both detached and warm: none of those stylistic devices which tell us that we should regard a character as good or bad, major or minor, crude or complex are in operation here. The dream about an unhappy mother that Yôko recounts is of neither more nor less importance than the pineapple cakes she gives to the landlady or the washing she is hanging up. For Hou, "shallow" practical concerns are inseparable from "deep" inner lives. The autonomy of the viewer is respected alongside that of the character, and if we are to "understand" Yôko, we must do so by paying attention to every movement and gesture instead of futilely attempting to establish which details are the most "significant." "I felt like I was looking at a day in the life in a living room next door," observed a Japanese friend to whom I showed the film: indeed, we will surely find Yôko (and *Café Lumière*) literally incomprehensible until we stop trying to fit her into a neat psychological/sociological/thematic box, and start treating her with the same respect we would routinely give to flesh-and-blood individuals.

Brad Stevens

Date 2004

Nationality Japan/Taiwan

Director Hou Hsiao-hsien

Cast Yo Hitoto

Original Title *Kôhî jikô*

Why It's Key This scene is a perfect example of cinematic humanism.

Key Scene **Meeting on the bridge**
Le Pont des Arts

SPOILER

The most intriguing filmography in recent French cinema comes courtesy of an American in Paris. In the 1970s, U.S.-born Eugène Green founded a theater company in the capital of France "with a twofold aim: to rediscover the modernity of Baroque theater and to bring about a renewal in contemporary theater." By 1999 those renewal efforts (in the meantime encompassing music and literature as well) extended to cinema with the magnificent Flaubert adaptation *Toutes les nuits*, which showcased a fully developed style, close to Robert Bresson, but with a pronounced, if deadpan sense of humor. The 2003 follow-up *Le monde vivant* was a no-budget fairy-tale with knights in jeans and a dog roaring like a lion (he belongs to the lion knight). But there is no doubting the deeply heartfelt nature of Green's explorations of love, art, the power of words, and baroque ideas. Most movingly, this is proven in the "impossible" climax of his 2004 masterpiece *Le Pont des Arts*: On the titular bridge, a student (Michaux) meets the singer (Régnier) whose voice (thanks to Monteverdi) he has fallen for – even though she had jumped to her death here earlier in the film. As they approach each other, Green cuts to their shadows merging on the bridge, which is flooded in the exquisite light of the morning sun. An indelible moment, both for its assertion that love and true art can transcend material reality and for its implicit demonstration that cinema, the art of light and shadows, can do the same.

Christoph Huber

Date 2004

Nationality France

Director Eugène Green

Cast Adrien Michaux, Natacha Régnier

Why It's Key An American in Paris, Eugène Green makes the most original films of contemporary French cinema. They are very funny, but the indelible climax of this masterpiece also proves they are just as serious.

Key Scene **Having a baby** *Sideways*

Sideways is an exquisitely perceptive film about the tenuous bonds of friendship and the quicksilver vagaries of love, deftly written by director Payne and his long-time writing partner, Jim Taylor (after Rex Pickett's novel), and lustily played by the perfectly balanced quartet of Paul Giamatti, Thomas Haden Church, Virginia Madsen, and Sandra Oh. Memorable quips abound, but beneath the hilarity is a strong strain of yearning and loss, nowhere more affecting than late in the film, when Miles (Giamatti), having survived an adventurous, ultimately disastrous bachelor trip to California wine country with pal Jack (Church), is best man at Jack's wedding and runs into his newly-remarried ex-wife, Victoria (Hecht), whom he's struggled to forget. Already melancholy over the misunderstanding with Jack that's torpedoed a promising new relationship with waitress Maya (Madsen), as well as the most recent rejection of his new novel, Jack is stunned to learn that Victoria's pregnant with corporate-looking new husband Ken

(Brooks). Jack's line is "Oh. Huh… Well. Congratulations, Vicki. That's wonderful news"; Giamatti finesses the moment with perfection: flickering across his face are grief and loss, barely contained by reflexive good manners and a previously untapped well of emotional strength. It's a breathtaking moment, made all the more powerful by the hundreds of wedding extras milling behind him. Giamatti's Miles is a performance for the ages: part milquetoast, part malcontent, and all mensch.

David Stratton

Date 2004

Nationality USA

Director Alexander Payne

Cast Paul Giamatti, Jessica Hecht, Lee Brooks

Why It's Key It's a revealing moment from an intelligent movie that's perceptive, benevolent, yet scathing in its portrayal of mid-life crises.

Key Scene **Sandaled feet going down a flight of stairs** *Notre Musique*

This short moving shot – an island in the midst of the film – affects not only the sequence in which it is suddenly inserted, like a breath of air, but everything we watch afterwards. Probably because of its unrelatedness, it may be the most musical and only truly peaceful moment in *Notre Musique* (a further meditation of Godard on death, war, and cinema, set in pacified but devastated Sarajevo), since even the third and last segment, though titled "Paradise" (after "Hell" and "Purgatory"), is rather mournful. This striking shot of a young woman's sandaled feet descending a flight of stairs in a quiet and stately manner bears no narrative connection to the shot preceding it, and its relation to the next is rather mystifying: one may wonder – whose feet are these? Those of either of the two main female characters? It seems, rather, that the sandaled feet (which appear in the film's poster and trailer, so they are important to Godard) are those of another character, the Native American woman played

by Leticia Gutierrez: although she's never framed in full-body, we assume the feet are hers because her quiet, smiling face is shown in the next shot.

Whereas most filmmakers have always edited shots in a significant way, to make a point, Godard has long used "montage" to question our assumptions and our ways of seeing. The effect is rhythmically exhilarating and deeply moving, as these feet become fleeting signs of serenity and self-confidence. In the context of Sarajevo, almost intimations of hope. And also of something Godard (re)discovered around 1979 and has not ceased to search for since: Beauty, natural or created by man, which may or not be self-revealing. That's what the camera should be for: to capture, enlarge, connect, and make visible what may be hidden. That's revelation, one of the powers of cinema that most filmmakers are forgetting.

Miguel Marías

Date 2004

Nationality France/Switzerland

Director Jean-Luc Godard

Cast Leticia Gutierrez

Why It's Key This fleeting moment shows how an isolated, "meaningless" detail can affect a whole film.

Key Speech **Terrible words from father to daughter** *Kings & Queen*

This comes, as unexpectedly to Nora (the impressive Devos) as to the audience, near the ending of a long, complex, segmented film in which funny and tragic events alternate disturbingly, as Desplechin looks compassionately at several characters on the verge of hysteria or nervous breakdown, often obsessed with parenthood and unable to reach a mature, balanced relationship. Nora's father (Garrel) has recently died while revising the publisher's proofs of his latest book, a sort of personal journal. She finds a handwritten text addressed to her – his favorite, cherished daughter – which turns out to be a terribly harsh indictment of how she turned out, confessing that he has come to hate her and feels anger at the idea of dying before she does, wishing that she should be suffering the pains of cancer in his place. She's aghast, while she reads and visualizes her father quietly but fiercely uttering the very words she's reading, like a ghost come to torment her with the painful truth, so she tears the pages off and hides them. It is certainly the most terrible scene of recrimination between two persons since Ingmar Bergman dared film the letters exchanged between former lovers in *Winter Light* and the confession of daughter to mother in *Autumn Sonata*, not to mention the recent *Saraband*, and it reminds us of the cinema's unique power, well above the novel or the stage, to convey how much even written words can hurt, because in films they are usually also heard, and we can watch how they hit the people at whom they are aimed and, often, feel the hardness with which they are pronounced, as in *Kings & Queen*.

Miguel Marías

Date 2004

Nationality France

Director Arnaud Desplechin

Cast Emmanuelle Devos, Maurice Garrel

Original Title *Rois et reine*

Why It's Key This scene shows how powerful words are as weapons, and how forcefully the cinema can convey their destructive impact.

2000–

762

Key Scene **Scraps sees Frankie leaving the hospital** *Million Dollar Baby*

SPOILER

With pain and a weight in his heart, which can be seen in his face and movements, and very much against his convictions and wishes (as the two previous scenes have made quite clear), out of love for Maggie (Swank), the girl who persuaded him to train her as a boxer, with successful but but ultimately tragic results, Frankie (Eastwood) has just put an end to her suffering and her terrible prospects of a future, were she to survive.

Frankie has sneaked into her hospital room, told her he's going to do as she wanted, kissed her, and performed painfully but efficiently the requested task. He kisses her dead lips lightly and leaves, thinking he's been unobserved. But we guess, and then see, that his partner Scraps (Freeman) is hidden, watching, suffering for (and understanding) both of them. The way Eastwood shows their faces in half shadow, then Frankie in long shot and disappearing – while Freeman's voice states: "Then he walked out. I don't think he had anything left" – gives soberly the director's generously understanding vision of the three main characters in the film. And the voice reveals itself as part of the letter Scraps is writing to Dunn's estranged daughter ("You should know what kind of a man your father really was").

Miguel Marías

Date 2004

Nationality USA

Director Clint Eastwood

Cast Clint Eastwood, Morgan Freeman, Hilary Swank

Why It's Key It uses voice-over sparingly to give, simultaneously, three different points of view on a keyed-down, highly dramatic event.

Opposite *Million Dollar Baby*

Key Speech **A just universe**
Harold & Kumar Go to White Castle

The Academy Awards will always favor portentous handwringing like Paul Haggis's *Crash* when it comes to Important Issues (and they did), but no studio film in recent years offered a vision of a multicultural society as hopeful and diverse as that of Danny Leiner's excellent stoner comedy *Harold & Kumar Go to White Castle*. Even better than Leiner's previous stoner comedy, *Dude, Where's My Car?* (which was maybe less of a sociological achievement, but still the finest surreal pop-culture-skewering offered in any 2000 Hollywood production), this quest for the American Dream, as exemplified by the munchies-induced craving for fast-food-chain burgers, makes for an exceedingly clever film that only the most prejudiced could mistake for unchallenging. Just witness the faux-unremarkable opening (typically over-edited and -scored) apparently focusing on those white jocks who usually star in lowbrow comedy – only to discard them in favor of the true heroes: a Korean- and an Indian-American (Cho as Harold and Kal Penn as Kumar), whose long, (cannabis-)digressive, and unpretentiously multiracial journey through the night exemplifies self-empowerment. As the black police-prejudice victim (Williams) they meet in prison says, the book *Essays on Civil Obedience* in hand: "In the end the universe tends to unfold as it should." The genius of Leiner's film is that it makes this come true without compromising its attitude, which is satirical of both political correctness and overused racial stereotypes.

Christoph Huber

Date 2004

Nationality USA

Director Danny Leiner

Cast Gary Anthony Williams, John Cho

Why It's Key Hollywood's finest portrait of multicultural society is this stoner comedy. Its unforced humanist philosophy is summed up in this speech.

Opposite *Harold & Kumar Go to White Castle*

Key Scene **The blind Korean masseuse and Trebor's scar** *The Intruder*

This happens around the middle of a story that takes us from the French-Swiss border to Korea and then Tahiti as we follow Trebor (Subor), a most mysterious middle-aged man, undoubtedly a shady character, who has had an illicit heart transplant and tries to recover a neglected son when it seems already too late for almost anything. A short, squat Korean woman (Jang) we instantly realize is blind enters the darkened hotel room where Trebor rests after the operation. She opens the window curtains, letting in some grey cloudy light (one may wonder why), sets her bag on an armchair, and addresses him in Korean; then she silently massages him and finally uncovers his chest-long heart-surgery scar. She puts her shoes on, recovers her bag, gets paid in banknotes, and goes out, gently guided to the door by her patient. They exchange just a few words, probably without understanding each other; their contact is merely physical, and professionally impersonal at that. Yet there is some strange sort of relationship, even a kind of silent intimacy between them, unexplained like almost everything else in Claire Denis' film: at first we don't quite grasp what may be happening, but soon our forced attention to everything we can see or hear allows us to guess. It is one of the most naked, simple, and fascinating ways of telling a story, counting on the cooperation of the wondering viewer, who is never quite sure of what is happening.

Miguel Marías

Date 2004

Nationality France

Director Claire Denis

Cast Michel Subor, Jang Young-sook

Original Title *L'Intrus*

Why It's Key This fleeting scene summarizes the mysterious, anguished structure of meetings in this elliptical film.

Key Scene **A gay romance is reshaped into a tiger hunt** *Tropical Malady*

It is morning, and Tong (Kaewbuadee) is sleeping. He wakes up and looks at the greenery outside the window. Soldier Keng (Lomnoi) enters the room, but Tong is no longer there. Keng sits on Tong's bed and pats the bedclothes. On the radio, a villager recounts the vanishing of cattle, blaming a monster from the jungle. Keng browses an album of pictures and lingers on a photo of Tong with another guy. Suddenly, the image is swallowed by black, as if something has gone wrong with the projector. In a fade-in from black, the drawing of a tiger surfaces, as the opening credits of a new film roll: *A Spirit's Path*. The film moves to the jungle, introducing the story of a Khmer shaman trapped in the body of a tiger.

Mysterious Object at Noon (2000) and *Blissfully Yours* (2002) established Apichatpong Weerasethakul's niche fame as a filmmaker renewing cinematic language with playful inventiveness. Winning a Jury Prize at Cannes 2004, *Tropical Malady* made him the first Thai *auteur* to benefit from worldwide critical recognition. The tender chronicle of the flirtation between a country boy and a soldier in the first half of the film is transposed, in the second, into the ominous courting between a tiger spirit and a soldier hunting it, played by the same pair of actors. Weerasethakul denies explanations, leaving audiences full freedom of interpretation. There can be no doubt, however, that the simulation of a projection dysfunction at the break between the two halves is a vertiginous touch of genius.
Paolo Bertolin

Date 2004

Nationality Thailand/France/Italy/Germany

Director Apichatpong Weerasethakul

Cast Banlop Lomnoi, Sakda Kaewbuadee

Original Title *Sud Pralad*

Why It's Key This brilliant caesura parts the film in two and reveals Weerasethakul's playful cinematic sensibility.

766

Key Film *East of Paradise*
Changing points of view

An elegant old lady, Maria Werla, walks into a room in New York and tells a story from her childhood. At the start of World War II, she fled eastward from Poland, suffered appalling hardships at the hands of the Red Army, and ended up in a Soviet work camp in Siberia. She speaks for over an hour, in close-up, getting more tearful as she goes, seeming to relive the horrors of those times. No archive or photographs illustrate her story. She is filmed as a talking head, TV-style, so that her unrelenting account almost becomes unbearable.

Then, after an hour, we see still images of New York in the 1950s. Why? Perhaps they represent the woman's view of the New World when she emigrated there. Then, equally mysteriously, we cut to 1970s footage of a guy getting out of the shower, drying his dyed blonde hair, preparing heroin, and injecting it. In voice-over he tells us about himself. We watch him get dressed. He skateboards around New York, speaking to us in voice-over as he does. How could his Dionysian 1970s tale relate to Werla's 1940s one? He keeps narrating. Then we see him sick in bed and then dead from AIDS, and still the voice-over continues, still in the first person. Only then do we realise that all the time we have been hearing "I" as we watched him, it was not he who was speaking. Gradually we conclude that the "I" is the filmmaker Kowalski himself.

Point of view in documentary is one of its key structuring devices, but never before have I seen the "I" in a documentary emerge only in its final stages, after or "from behind" two characters – Werla and the 1970s guy – who seem to be our protagonists. *East of Paradise* undergoes a torque halfway through. It is a broke-back film, and the result is electrifying.
Mark Cousins

Date 2005

Nationality USA

Director Lech Kowalski

Why It's Key This film is one of the most remarkably structured documentaries ever made.

Key Scene **"This Time Tomorrow"**
Regular Lovers

If you look up Philippe Garrel on YouTube, you will see a dazzling series of music clips: a long take of driving set to Nico; glimpses of a movie-shoot cut to Them. Such music is, in truth, sparingly used in the generally minimalist cinema of Garrel. But the pop summit of Garrel's career is undoubtedly the scene of young people dancing in *Regular Lovers*. As usual, Garrel scarcely "fills in" the location: some people on a couch and a few walls defining an open space are all that is needed to signify a nightclub (no bar, no DJ visible). The song, perfectly chosen for this chiselled, black-and-white memoir of the 1968 Paris revolt, is The Kinks' "This Time Tomorrow" (although Garrel allows himself, as always, the luxury of anachronism: the *Lola versus Powerman and The Moneyground* LP didn't appear until 1970) – capturing the sense that these youths are living through an intense but precarious Utopia, that everything may dissolve (as it does) a day or month or year hence. The interlinked choreography of bodies and camera is relatively straightforward but, in the context of a film so preoccupied with states of blockage and melancholy, it explodes off the screen: exuberant dancers cross the space, solo moves blend into trio-formation steps, couples form and split. It is a moment of pure joy. And how rare it is, in contemporary cinema, to hear an entire song respected in its integrity, rather than merely "sampled" for a quick mood-injection or peppy transition.

Adrian Martin

Date 2005

Nationality France

Director Philippe Garrel

Original Title *Les Amants réguliers*

Why It's Key It's the peak of Garrel's use of pop music in film.

Key Scene **The pain of a people**
Evolution of a Filipino Family

SPOILER

The ambition, form, and scope of Lav Diaz's 12-hour epic would be remarkable in any context, but coming from the Philippines, whose film scene is governed by formulaic commercial product, they are all the more impressive. Furthermore, the film's challenging length corresponds to the provocative subject matter, which is treated with staggering complexity. Ultimately, this is nothing less than a work about the nation's refusal to come to terms with its troubled past. A family chronicle, spanning 16 years – beginning shortly before dictator Marcos declared martial law in 1972 and ending after he had to relinquish presidency in 1987 – *Evolution* restages the oppressive experience in a near-documentary manner, detailing daily struggles like farm work in large chunks of real-time, long-shot, long-take scenes. Shot over a period of twelve years, whenever there was money available, the film, by necessity, takes *arte povera* to extremes. The shoddy texture (cheap video and even worse transfers of the 16mm-material Diaz began with) only adds to the experience, whose believability is further enhanced by the fact that you actually *see* the child actors growing up. Only as *Evolution* unfolds does it become clear that its hyperrealistic scenes are part of a complicated larger mosaic representing a troubled relationship to history, as modern, even Brechtian devices intrude. Yet the film's greatest power rests in the unbroken take. Accordingly, its epiphanic "moment" is a 20-minute scene in which a mortally wounded family member stumbles through the capital's empty backstreets, his slow suffering encompassing the pain of a people, as if to realize the experience of a nation in agony for centuries – first under foreign powers, and finally under one of their own.

Christoph Huber

Date 1994-2005

Nationality Philippines

Director Lav Diaz

Cast Pen Medina

Original Title *Ebolusyon ng isang pamilyang Pilipino*

Why It's Key A nation's suffering epitomized in the fate of a character has long been turned into a cliché. This one-of-a-kind epic restores the concept's dignity and power.

Key Scene **The fireworks no longer work**
Land of the Dead

With *Land of the Dead*, George A. Romero continued his classic zombie cycle inaugurated in 1968 by the Vietnam-era cult phenomenon *Night of the Living Dead* and made his studio comeback after a disappointed departure over a decade earlier. Indeed, *Land of the Dead* may have cost as much as all earlier Romero films put together and is designed in a more accessible manner than even its closest relation in the film series, the 1978 shopping-mall splatter epic *Dawn of the Dead*. But it's no less heartfelt a statement on the repressed and oppressed of contemporary American society. Some 21 years after the bloody philosophizing of the chamber endgame *Day of the Dead*, Occam's razor is dropped in favor of a blunt instrument to produce the kind of political satire the U.S. deserves: times are horrible enough to make supernatural horrors unnecessary. Romero envisions a fenced-in Pittsburgh "civilization" with the rich-poor divide taken to extremes: a corrupt mogul presides over an elite tower surrounded by dwellings for an underclass kept in good spirits by Abu Ghraib-style games to hold off the zombie "other." At first fireworks serve as distraction for the undead, but they are developing their own consciousness. In a radical gesture, Romero then proposes that the barriers between oppressed men and zombies are the ones that really must be overcome. Ultimately this leads to an indelible image: Big fireworks to which the "enlightened" zombies no longer respond fill the sky, heralding an Independence Day of the Dead.
Christoph Huber

Date 2005

Nationality USA

Director George A. Romero

Why It's Key For decades, Romero's zombie pictures have been just what the U.S. deserves. In its most radical proposition, the fourth film in the cycle suggests that the differences between (oppressed) humans and zombies have become moot.

Opposite *Land of the Dead*

2000–

Key Scene **The slaughterhouse**
Workingman's Death

Once confined to the margins of mainstream production, documentary has been the object of a worldwide resurgence at the dawn of the 21st century. Not surprisingly, the phenomenon has taken a variety of forms, ranging from updated and often incoherent variations on *cinema vérité* to raw populism, talking heads, and minimalist abstraction. *Workingman's Death* defies all these categories: it has no voiceover, but its political message can be heard loud and clear; it was made in prohibitive conditions, and yet it maintains a firm control over style and technique; it is epic in scale without losing sight of individual drama. Each of its five episodes (plus an epilogue) deals with an aspect of manual work within a hostile environment: an abandoned mine in Ukraine, a sulphur spring in Indonesia, a seaside ship cemetery in India where migrants risk their lives by disassembling rusty oil cargos with their bare hands. But the most harrowing sequence takes place in an open-air slaughterhouse in Port Harcourt, Nigeria, a vision matching Dante's descriptions of Hell. Hundreds of people take their cattle and goats to a specialist butcher who kills his victims with savage precision amidst a frightening mix of mud, blood, and smoke, all drenched in a chilling symphony of human voices and animal screams. How the film crew managed to stay cool in this overwhelming landscape is beyond comprehension; even from the distance of a theater seat, we become first-hand witnesses of the apocalypse in the form of the purest cinematic ecstasy.
Paolo Cherchi Usai

Date 2005

Nationality Austria/ Germany

Director Michael Glawogger

Why It's Key Hell on Earth becomes an ecstatic visual experience.

Key Speech **"I sold him"**
L'Enfant (*The Child*)

Basically homeless in Belgium's postindustrial landscape, sleeping in boxes under bridges, purse-snatcher and small-time fence Bruno (Renier) and welfare mother Sonia (François) romp and rub heads together like two puppies, until the teenaged father sets off pushing a pram carrying their newborn son while casually panhandling passersby. When he returns with the carriage empty, Sonia asks, "Where's the baby?" He guilelessly replies, "I sold him." With these three blood-chilling words (four in French: *Je l'ai vendu*), Bruno's carefree, unmoored existence comes to an abrupt halt, as the sudden glimpse into her partner's monstrous moral black hole sends Sonia to the hospital in shock. We've already witnessed his clandestine trading of his bundled baby for a stack of Euros, but his words make the act worse ("We'll have another baby"). His need to regain Sonia's respect, even her attention, drives him as he sheds a boy's thoughtless self-involvement and gropes his way toward an adult's conscious human commitment. With the Dardennes' camera riding shotgun alongside him as he accelerates his borrowed motorcycle down highways in his effort to redeem himself, *L'Enfant* acutely puts a face on faceless economics, reflecting a society where everything's for sale and money measures worth, where Bruno's precious cell phone encourages him to act unthinkingly on every raw impulse – even as the filmmakers grant this most deadbeat of dads their clear-eyed compassion.

Robert Keser

Date 2005

Nationality Belgium

Directors Jean-Pierre and Luc Dardenne

Cast Jérémie Renier, Déborah François

Why It's Key These three words indict modern consumerist society where everything's for sale and instant gratification leads youth to betray their own humanity.

Opposite *L'Enfant*

2000–

771

Key Scene **The blow job**
The Wayward Cloud

SPOILER

If, a few minutes before the end of a film, Tsai Ming-liang's normally static camera begins slowly, implacably moving forward, you know something scary is coming down the pike. Scary, confronting, mind-boggling – but also sublime, since it dares us to transcend conventional moral-ethical assumptions. The encounter between father and son in a gay steam bath works this way in *The River* (1997), and so does the finale of *The Wayward Cloud*. The tentative love story between Chen (Chen Shiang-chyi) and Lee (Lee Kang-sheng) remains sweet so long as they gaze at each other on a kids' swing, or playfully make dinner – and so long as Lee keeps his tawdry job as a porno actor secret. But this degree of compartmentalisation – which finds its perfect analogy in Tsai's geometric, segmented framings and locations – ultimately adds up to a repression, a wall that must be breached for real intimacy to occur. This is what the finale enacts. What Chen sees through a grill, after the camera tracks in on her, is the shooting of a porno scene involving a comatose or possibly dead Japanese actress (Sumomo Yozakura), ceaselessly propped up as sex-doll/partner for Lee. As Chen and Lee lock eyes, she begins – in encouragement, identification, madness? – to mime the sound of an orgasm; and just before he comes he leaps to the grill and puts his cock in her mouth. Is this transgressive *amour fou* or the ultimate in alienated objectification? That lonely, wayward cloud of the end-credits song is not telling…

Adrian Martin

Date 2005

Nationality Taiwan/France

Director Tsai Ming-liang

Cast Chen Shang-chyi, Lee Kang-sheng, Sumomo Yozakura

Original Title *Tian bian yi duo yun*

Why It's Key Is it transgressive *amour fou* or the ultimate in alienated objectification?

Key Scene **Americans take photographs of the Chaplin-like emperor of Japan** *The Sun*

Unlike the other 20th-century absolute leaders depicted before by Sokurov (late Hitler in *Moloch*, early Stalin and dying Lenin in *Taurus*), Japanese emperor Hirohito (Ogata) is more or less pleaded not guilty (and then one recalls the fact that he was sole among the defeated not only to survive, but to remain in office, albeit powerless) and presented as a somehow unlikely majesty (majesty is precisely what he lacks), uneasy as a god (he eagerly renounces that insulating condition), a rather charmingly eccentric fellow, a frail, shy, modest human being, the least imposing figure one can imagine.

His modesty helps make him into an image that will actually help save his life, when he allows a group of American photographers to do a session in his palace's garden. He walks out unnoticed at first, and, when they see him, the press people immediately link him to Charlie Chaplin, an universally beloved if outdated figure, while he smells roses and salutes, hat in hand.

The subtle, delicate comedy of the scene reveals a hitherto unsuspected ability and penchant in Sokurov, a transcendent, serious, ever-growing filmmaker.
Miguel Marías

Date 2005

Nationality Russia/Japan/Italy

Director Alexander Sokurov

Cast Issey Ogata

Original Title *Solntse*

Why It's Key Sokurov introduces in this scene a new conception of historical film.

Opposite *The Sun*

772

Key Scene **Car springs** *Hat Wolff von Amerongen Konkursdelikte begangen?*

The first feature of Austrian-born director Gerhard Benedikt Friedl is strikingly original in conception and execution, its form being not just the expression of a social crisis (and, more pointedly, a crisis of representation). Rather, its ingenious design invites viewer engagement with a complex problem in ways both humorous and frightening: It's a serious cinematic puzzle. Although the scope is vast, the means used are simple: Visually, there's an anonymous succesion of meticulously framed pans and tracking shots through European centres of finance, rural landscapes, and production facilities (the deep-focus photography is simply astonishing throughout). This is accompanied by a deadpan voice-over relating a history of German economic dynasties, especially their crimes and foibles, in the 20th century. As details pile up in a labyrinthine manner, it becomes increasingly impossible to separate the "relevant" from the distracting – a difficulty that mirrors the contemporary impossibility of following the

intricacies of modern economics in a tangled mass of information. Paranoia and irony are conjured, the feeling of insecurity heightened by the fact that sound and image seem aligned on some occasions, completely unrelated at others, and ever so slightly out-of-synch in between. A particularly hilarious instance is near the end, when we're told about some shady, yet official business with "car springs," while for once the camera-car bounces relentlessly on shaky ground after so much steady-going. This could not just be comic relief – or could it? Promptly the dubiously "objective"-sounding voice-over and coldly executed camera movements resume.
Christoph Huber

Date 2005

Nationality Germany/Austria

Director Gerhard Benedikt Friedl

Aka *Did Wolff von Amerongen Commit Bankruptcy Offences?*

Why It's Key Friedl's strikingly orignal debut feature derives a lot of its power from the fact that the viewer can never be quite sure how sound and image align, exactly. This is the most hilarious instance of simple correspondence – or is it?

Key Scene **Pocahontas runs around a maze** *The New World*

In a *Film Comment* (March/April 2006) article about Terrence Malick, Kent Jones complained that several of the actors in *The Thin Red Line* (1998) hardly seemed to be inhabiting the same film. Though intended negatively, this observation hints at something central to Malick's work: his characters' insistence on behaving as if they are the protagonists of fictional narratives, viewing the world as a stage and other people as merely supporting players. *Badlands* (1973), narrated by Holly (Sissy Spacek) in the style of a romantic novel, is particularly clear on this point, but *The New World* – in which both white settlers and fellow Native Americans see Pocahontas (Kilcher) not as an individual, but rather as the embodiment of whatever desires they wish to project onto her – is this theme's supreme exploration. For Captain John Smith (Colin Farrell), Pocahontas is an innocent child of nature, representing a new world in which he can abandon his imperialist heritage and start again from

zero ("Here the blessings of the earth are bestowed upon all. None need grow poor"). Pocahontas is later received at the court of King James with a poem whose tone is virtually a parody of Smith's declarations ("The New World's Princess new life brings, and swells our joys upon this day"). The key image here is a garden maze introduced towards the film's climax. For Malick, Pocahontas is too complex, too irreducible to be defined as the living incarnation of this or that ideal: she is as mysterious and impenetrable as the maze she circles while playing with her son, and into which she eventually disappears.

Brad Stevens

Date 2005

Nationality USA

Director Terrence Malick

Cast Q'Orianka Kilcher

Why It's Key This scene sums up the theme of Malick's masterpiece.

Opposite *The New World*

Key Scene **Cinephile suicide** *Cigarette Burns*

SPOILER

In the 21st century much has been made of television's superiority to mainstream Hollywood cinema, and not without reason: The best TV is ostensibly allowed to deal with subjects that no longer pass corporate-movie clearance, from complex treatment of hot political issues to simply showing someone smoking (and not being the designated villain). The latter sight is on ample display in the episodes of *Masters of Horror*, a TV series conceived to make use of those greater freedoms (and there was even formidable political satire, with Joe Dante's clever contribution, *Homecoming*) and giving some veterans of the genre a chance to flex their muscles outside Hollywood's teen/slasher norms. Despite a certain nerdiness in the script, John Carpenter's episode, *Cigarette Burns*, is just outrageous enough to evoke a deserved nostalgia for the cinematic experience, even if one senses an ironic acknowledgment of its disappearance just by looking at the title: Like all the

Masters of Horror episodes, *Cigarette Burns* was shot on HD video, so its own cigarette burns are digitally conjured artifacts. Still, the story of the search for a mysterious film that drives all its viewers to insanity has a punchline as gory as it is exquisite: an appalling, yet truly human, ending to cinema. After decades of waiting, a film collector (played by Udo Kier, who justifiably calls this his "favorite onscreen death") finally lays eyes on the mad movie – then puts his own bowels into the projector and lets it roll.

Christoph Huber

Date 2005

Nationality USA

Director John Carpenter

Cast Udo Kier

Original Title *Masters of Horror: Cigarette Burns*

Why It's Key It took a television series to present the apotheosis of film-loving self-disembodiment. If this is the end of cinema, so be it.

Key Scene **The sick woman is confronted by tanks** *Avenge but One of My Two Eyes*

In cold blue morning light, "birthright tourists" – American teenagers and many others – are on top of the Masada cliffs in Israel, being told the first century story of the 900 Jewish zealots who killed themselves there rather than submit to the Romans. In this setting, the story is haunting. Avi Mograbi films fly-on-the-wall style.

Later he shows Israeli children learning the story of Samson. His film's title is taken from Samson's entreaty to god – to let him avenge one of his eyes against the Philistines. Just as the teenagers absorb the sense that their forebears performed a heroic suicide, so, now, these younger people absorb a far older myth about killing oneself for a lofty principle. In a third scene, a sick Palestinian woman is prevented from getting into an ambulance by two Israeli tanks, which corral her and her family like sheep dogs. Interviewed moments later, she says that what just happened was humiliating.

Mograbi uses no commentary, but these three scenes marshal his argument in an essayistic way. The proposition "death is preferable to domination" is clearly the message of the Masada story. Samson's self-sacrifice is born of the same principle. Yet add the scene with the sick woman, and the similarity between such founding myths and the humiliation that leads to suicide bombing becomes clear. The Israeli state has long argued that suicide bombing is incognisable, yet through montage, Mograbi suggests that Samson was the first suicide bomber. Two ideas, when brought together, produce a third. *Avenge but One of My Two Eyes* is one of the great essayistic films of modern times.

Mark Cousins

Date 2005

Nationality Israel

Director Avi Mograbi

Original Title *Nekam Achat Mishtey Eynay*

Why It's Key This great essayistic documentary is one of the best films ever made in Israel.

Key Scene **The opening scene** *Three Times*

Where master Japanese director Yasujiro Ozu's low-key domestic dramas seldom registered the profound upheaval his country underwent in the first half of the 20th century, the films of his admirer Hou Hsiao-hsien always seem to reverberate with social and political change. Taiwan, Hou's home country, was shunted around in the same century from the Japanese to the Chinese Kuomintang Nationalists, who, in 1949, imposed a martial law that lasted until 1987. Historic events are seldom on-screen in Hou films, and their protagonists often live far from the centre of the action, so the reverberations are often subtle, like vibrations on the surface of a bowl of tea.

Three Times is a masterpiece made of such vibrations. A triptych, set in 1966 ("A Time for Love"), 1911 ("A Time for Freedom"), and 2005 ("A Time for Youth"), it pictures how three couples, each played by Shu and Chang, register the changes in society around them. In the second section, set during

Taiwan's Japanese period, Shu plays a singer in a brothel, who would like to escape. Space is confined, the imagery is golden, and, exquisitely, the dialogue is intertitled, as in silent cinema. The third section's contemporary setting sees the couple drowning in a sea of text messaging, sexual libertarianism, and soulless urban development. The first section is an elegy for '60s romance and aesthetics, set in a pool hall, shot in Hou's long-lensed, drifting signature style and accompanied by The Platters' "Smoke Gets in Your Eyes." Chang has been drafted. In his final few days before service he meets Shu and asks if he can write to her. The timid delicacy of their meeting, the click of billiard balls, and the song's yearning together define the beauty and balance of a relationship that, in the subsequent sections of the film, will seem too knotted, then too loose.

Mark Cousins

Date 2005

Nationality Taiwan

Director Hou Hsiao-hsien

Cast Shu Qi, Chang Chen

Original Title *Zui hao de shi guang*

Why It's Key This is one of the most evocative and subtle opening scenes in Asian cinema.

Key Scene **Too close**
Climates

During a tense holiday, university professor Isa (Nuri Bilge Ceylan) breaks up with his girlfriend, Bahar, a TV art director (Ebru Ceylan, the director's real-life wife). Months later, Isa learns that Bahar is working on a shoot in eastern Turkey. He decides to follow her there to win her back, and the two reunite. The hotel-room scene that ensues between them, devoid of dialogue, is filmed in an extraordinary collage of too-close shots: his head, her hair, his hand holding a cigarette. Each person's body becomes, in turn, a barrier in the image. Throughout *Climates*, Ceylan switches back and forth between the implied viewpoints of Isa and Bahar, reflecting how the desires and expectations of each fail to match up with those of the other. His film deals with the radical isolation of subjectivity. Yet by constantly juxtaposing Bahar's consciousness with Isa's, Ceylan shows in concrete terms of cinema that the solitude of one is only the momentary obliteration of the other.

Afterwards, Bahar tells him about a dream she had during the night that made her happy. His only response is to ask what time she has to be on set for work. As she registers his inability (or refusal?) to share her experience, her mood subtly, visibly darkens. There are few performances like this in cinema, and few directors who have the penetration and the patience to film them.

Chris Fujiwara

Date 2006

Nationality Turkey

Director Nuri Bilge Ceylan

Cast Nuri Bilge Ceylan, Ebru Ceylan

Original Title *Iklimler*

Why It's Key Ceylan reveals himself a master of mood and a cinematic philosopher.

Key Scene **The testimony song**
Bamako

Malian filmmaker Sissako has continued to refine his unique style of patient, observational cinema, preferring to eschew individual protagonists and conventional character psychology in favor of wide-ranging portraits of different West African communities. This approach achieves its apex in *Bamako*, a film centered on a makeshift trial in which representatives of the African population bring charges against the World Trade Organization and the World Bank. These people claim that Mali and other African nations have been held hostage by crippling debt as a result of mandatory capitulation to Westernized neo-liberal economics. As one woman testifies, "Africa is not a poor continent. It is a victim of its wealth."

Some have criticized *Bamako* for being a simplistic anti-globalization screed, one that bandies about words like "neo-colonialism" and "debt forgiveness" without adequately defining the parameters of the debate. However, Sissako's most powerful statements in this film actually call the entire trial into question, disrupting the very idea that Western ideals of jurisprudence and economic policy-making could ever adequately redress, or even express, the daily struggles of Africans in the developing world. After patiently waiting to be called to the stand, an elderly villager (Bamba) finally steps forward and testifies. Instead of recounting facts or spouting ideology, the man delivers a passionate, plangent folk song, his eyes closed, swaying with barely contained agitation. His untranslated, unsubtitled song speaks volumes, not only about what is at stake in the trial itself, but about those experiential truths that fall between the cracks of rationalized discourse.

Michael Sicinski

Date 2006

Nationality Mali/France

Director Abderrahmane Sissako

Cast Zegué Bamba

Why It's Key This showstopper conveys the limitations of traditional concepts of evidence and testimony, as well as Western jurisprudence itself.

Key Scene "Doing our jobs"
A Prairie Home Companion

The seeming slightness of Altman's final film is in keeping with its source, Garrison Keillor's popular radio show – though the main subject of the film is death. The premise is that Keillor's show is about to be shut down by the conglomerate that has bought both it and the St. Paul, Minnesota, theater from where it is broadcast. During the last show, one of its regular performers, an aged singer named Chuck (L. Q. Jones), dies peacefully in his dressing room, and Keillor (a heavy-set, pleasantly glum-looking Midwesterner with glasses) is asked backstage if he wants to acknowledge Chuck's passing on the air. "I don't do eulogies; I just don't," he replies. When singer Yolanda (Streep) suggests "a moment of silence," Keillor says: "Silence on the radio? I don't know how that works…. We don't look back in radio, that's the beauty of it. Nobody gets old, nobody dies. We just keep on going." Yolanda's teenage daughter, Lola (Lohan), steps forward, outraged and stunned: "What if you died?" "I

will!", says Keillor. "You don't want people to remember you?" Lola exclaims. He replies, "I don't want them to be *told* to remember me." As the camera zooms in slowly on Lola, she persists, outraged: "Somebody died down there. And we're not even paying attention? And you're not even going to say anything?" Keillor, now offscreen, says flatly: "We pay attention by doing our jobs." Then he's called back to the stage. In a piece of filmmaking that, characteristically, seems casual and understated, Altman lets Keillor articulate an ethic of casualness and understatedness and to make a statement that softly vindicates the delicacy, warmth, and underlying seriousness of the director's triumphant valedictory work.

Chris Fujiwara

Date 2006

Nationality USA

Director Robert Altman

Cast Garrison Keillor, Lindsay Lohan, Meryl Streep, Lily Tomlin, Tim Russell

Why It's Key In a quiet and offhanded moment, Altman and Keillor articulate a philosophy of art.

Opposite *A Prairie Home Companion*

Key Scene Marhab finally visits Khatoun and knocks on her door *It's Winter*

In bleakest midwinter, Mokhtar leaves his young wife, Khatoun (Hadjar), to find work. As he does so, Marhab (Nicksolat), a younger motor mechanic who could have walked out of an Italian neorealist film by Vittorio de Sica, arrives. Marhab is an economic migrant, too, but can't concentrate on the casual work he finds, especially once he spies Khatoun. He watches her from a distance and, slowly, builds up the courage to knock on her door. The scene in which he finally does so is a master class in acting and editing. We stay on Nicksolat's fox-like face as he expresses the anxiety and eroticism of the moment, looking screen-left constantly, though Hadjar is off screen-right. Pitts and cinematographer Mohammad Davudi film Nicksolat square-on, as Pasolini often did with his actors. As Nicksolat grows in confidence in the scene, we see him preparing to look at Hadjar. At last, with a flick of his eyes, he does so – and only then does Pitts cut to Hadjar. This simplest of visual ideas reaps electrifying

results because of the authenticity of the performances and the deferment of feeling that the film has depicted. By the law of averages, Iran could not produce yet another master director, but *It's Winter* suggests that it has done so again. The trick, says actor-director Mania Akbari, is to make cinema that is "poor on the outside, rich on the inside."

Mark Cousins

Date 2006

Nationality Iran

Director Rafi Pitts

Cast Ali Nicksolat, Mitra Hadjar

Original Title *Zemestan*

Why It's Key This scene shows why Iranian filmmakers continue to be at the forefront of film art.

Key Scene **Setting Meera free**
Dor (*Thread*)

In a desert region of the Indian state of Rajasthan, Meera (Takia), a vulnerable teenage girl whose spirit has been crushed by her husband's recent death, accepts her submissive role in his patriarchal Hindu family. She has befriended Zeenat, a Muslim (Panang), unaware that the latter is the wife of the man who stands accused in Saudi Arabia of killing her husband. Zeenat's friendship has brought laughter and a sense of self-worth into Meera's arid existence, but when Meera learns that Zeenat has befriended her in order to get Meera's letter of pardon for her husband, Meera feels betrayed. Then her authoritative father-in-law (Karnad), who has been planning to "lease" her as a temporary concubine to his rich tenant, locks Meera in her room.

A hand picks up the keys tucked under the pillow of the father-in-law, who is sleeping outside Meera's room, and unlocks the door: Dadi, Meera's grandmother-in-law (Baokar), has come to free Meera and to urge her to make her own decision. Meera cries out: "Must I be forced into being an angel instead of a human being craving revenge?" The hitherto harsh Dadi turns wise and tender: "Listen to your heart," she says; "it's only given to human beings to be able to forgive." The massive doors open, and the camera frames Meera in the gap, the dull blue of her widow's garb now subtly brighter against seasoned wood and dusty walls. She runs out into the lane, towards the temple in the sands where she used to meet Zeenat. The dramatic scene is a prelude to Meera's final freedom. When the widowed old matriarch, who would be normally expected to support orthodoxy, sets the young woman free, the moment resonates with emotion without belabouring a feminist credo.
Maithili Rao

Date 2006

Nationality India

Director Nagesh Kukunoor

Cast Ayesha Takia, Gul Panang, Girish Karnad, Shreyas Talpade, Uttara Baokar

Why It's Key A quietly paced film, with exquisite tonal shades, reaches its moment of decision.

Key Scene **Dedication**
A Scanner Darkly

Philip K. Dick is usally called a science-fiction author, but it would be more accurate to call him a writer of ideas: it is quite striking how little futuristic padding accompanies his philosophically fantastic conceits. Thus, it is legitimate to ask whether there has ever been an apt cinematic adaptation of Dick before Richard Linklater's congenial 2006 animation *A Scanner Darkly* (based on the eponymous, autobiographically inspired 1977 novel). The list of previous contenders contains classics like 1982's *Blade Runner*, but that visually incredibly influential film is just as guilty as most others of distracting from the core of Dick's philosophical quandaries with all kinds of "visionary" visual embellishments. Linklater's decision to use rotoscopy seems at first glance a similar kind of betrayal, but it is justified both by the source's only futuristic element – a constantly shape-shifting camouflage suit that is ideally rendered by the animation technique – and by providing a sensation of alienated perception, in accordance with the film's themes. It represents drugged as well as administered sensual experience, for in the diabolical dialectics of both source novel and film, drug abuse also refers to the (capitalist) system responsible for addiction. By sticking as close as possible to the original, Linklater highlights the increased topicality of Dick's novel, but retains its lived-in sadness (despite much spot-on humor) about the toll of addiction. The last "shot" is devastating, all the more for its simplicity: the book's final dedication to friends damaged by drugs scrolls by, proving both the sincerity and effectiveness of Linklater's dedication to the material.
Christoph Huber

Date 2006

Nationality USA

Director Richard Linklater

Why It's Key By sticking to the source, Linklater's animation finally did cinematic justice to Philip K. Dick. Proof lies in the simple, devastating final shot.

Opposite *A Scanner Darkly*

Key Scene **The mysterious little buzzing box** *Belle toujours*

If you saw Luis Buñuel's *Belle de jour* (1967), you'll remember something that you'll wonder about again on being reminded of it. An Asian client of occasional, vocational daytime prostitute Séverine (Catherine Deneuve), in the evenings a high-society married lady, comes to visit her with a queer wooden box, whose content and use are not even hinted at. The only clue is a sort of insect buzz that it emits as he opens it slightly for Séverine to see inside. Everyone being curious, we all have wondered now and then what was in the box and for what purpose he brought it.

Almost 40 years later, her old acquaintance (Piccoli) reencounters Séverine (now played by Bulle Ogier, a not unlikely aging option), pursues her, and at last persuades her to accept a dinner invitation at a luxurious restaurant. He aspires to conquer her with a gift: the Asian's expensive box, which he found at an antiques pawnshop. That she's not happy at all with the idea and immediately leaves the restaurant

doesn't quite come as a surprise. The surprise lies elsewhere: we do not get the slightest idea or hint about the box's contents. Which shows how well de Oliveira has understood Buñuel's sense of humor and narrative strategies in this most elegant and beautifully serene of films.

Miguel Marías

Date 2006

Nationality France/ Portugal

Director Manoel de Oliveira

Cast Michel Piccoli, Bulle Ogier

Why It's Key Taking as a starting point a film by a different, though related filmmaker, this scene shows it's possible to understand the mystery and recapture the spirit of another author and keep being oneself.

Key Scene **The singing of the Iranian national anthem** *Offside*

It's near the end of this raucous and pointed Iranian comedy. A bunch of young girls, who disguised themselves as boys in order to sneak into a Tehran soccer match where girls are strictly forbidden, have been caught and arrested by reluctant cops and taken off in a kind of paddy wagon. Then the news suddenly breaks that the home team has won, meaning that Iran qualifies for the World Cup, and girls and cops alike are so overcome with joy that the girls are temporarily set free, celebratory sparklers and sweets are passed around, and the strains of the national anthem are heard on the soundtrack.

What does one make of this final detail? Up until now, this deft fusion of laughter and suspense, documentary and fiction, has functioned a bit like a comic and highly commercial remake of Panahi's earlier (and banned) *The Circle* (2000) – a much artier work of protest against the oppression of women in Iran. Could the anthem be viewed as some sort of

concession to the mullahs, who wound up banning this movie anyway – even though it may conceivably have helped inspire the president, Mahmoud Ahmadinejad, to try to revise the law and admit girls into sporting events, at least until the mullahs overruled him? Not at all. Because the version of the national anthem being sung here is an older, pre-Revolutionary one, deliberately stirring the sort of nationalistic feelings that the mullahs have been suppressing in favor of promoting pan-Islamic identity.

Jonathan Rosenbaum

Date 2006

Nationality Iran

Director Jafar Panahi

Why It's Key Panahi shows how he can be a populist without compromising his politics.

Opposite *Offside*

Key Scene **A helping hand**
Little Miss Sunshine

How do you pull a character out of the depths? The question occurs along the road in *Little Miss Sunshine*, well before the Hoover family has reached its destination but long after its pattern of falterings has been set. Though driven onward by a paterfamilias (Greg Kinnear) whose motto is "Refuse to lose," the Hoovers have spent the whole movie stumbling and flailing. Now they may never reach the site of the beauty pageant that their seven-year-old daughter Olive (Breslin) is determined to win. Another emotional pothole has been struck, and Olive's teenage brother Dwayne (Dano), the mute and brooding, has jumped out of the family van. While the vehicle sits on the road's shoulder, Dwayne crouches below, at the foot of a steep hill, inconsolable and unmovable.

Words are useless. (Dwayne rejected them long ago.) But after the elders have pleaded and failed, little Olive simply walks up and touches Dwayne on the shoulder, and he rises, ready to do for her what he won't do for his parents or himself.

She has brought him back up – and so, in an act that completes and surpasses this moment of trust, he does the same for her. When the slope proves difficult for Olive, Dwayne silently picks up his sister and carries her uphill, as you'd carry a dangling cat. There's a sweet momentum to the gesture: he lifts her without breaking stride, as the camera tracks them, so that she swings upward easily. Her utter lack of surprise tells you she's where she belongs.

Stuart Klawans

Date 2006

Nationality USA

Directors Jonathan Dayton and Valerie Faris

Cast Paul Dano, Abigail Breslin

Why It's Key An offhand gesture gives a lift to the spirit, and to one of contemporary America's rare character-driven comedies.

Opposite *Little Miss Sunshine*

Key Scene **Love in smoke**
I Don't Want To Sleep Alone

A homeless man (Lee) and the waitress (Chen) of a dismal Kuala Lumpur coffee shop attract each other over a series of chance meetings. One night she follows him into the half-finished, abandoned, and partly flooded concrete palace that represents for the film a site of illusion and escape. Ensconced on an upper floor, the pair try to make love in this bizarre and inhospitable environment, but their attempt is hampered by the omnipresent haze (reportedly the effect of a forest fire in Indonesia) that has overtaken the city. Fits of coughing and gasping interrupt the couple's long, passionate kisses – at one point, she has to cover her mouth with the plastic bowl she uses as a gas mask. At the end of the smoke-suffused scene, the man improvises an air-filtration-device-for-two, using the legs of the jeans he's stripped off.

Funny, alarming, and mysterious, this scene is prime Tsai. The two characters are transported out of the world by their lust for each other and by the unearthly nature of their trysting place. At the same time, they must adjust to the world's altered atmosphere, using for unfamiliar purposes the objects of their ordinary lives. Their resourcefulness allows the lovers to invent a poetic and concrete language to express the intensity of their need for each other, despite the economic, political, and environmental devastations that affect them.

Chris Fujiwara

Date 2007

Nationality Taiwan/France/Austria

Director Tsai Ming-liang

Cast Lee Kang-sheng, Chen Shiang-chyi

Original Title *Hei yan quan*

Why It's Key Once again in Tsai Ming-liang's films, people stay human under the most hostile conditions.

"THE FUNNIEST LAUGH-OUT-LOUD AUDIENCE PLEASER
AT THE SUNDANCE FILM FESTIVAL."
ROGER EBERT CHICAGO SUN-TIMES

"THE ROAD IS TWISTED AND SO ARE THE LAUGHS.
THIS ONE IS A WINNER."
PETER TRAVERS Rolling Stone

"A HILARIOUS TALE ABOUT WINNING, LOSING
AND THAT NETHER STATE IN BETWEEN WHERE
MOST OF US MUST LEARN TO LIVE."
DAVID GERMAIN AP Associated Press

"A MAGICAL EXPERIENCE."
RUTHE STEIN San Francisco Chronicle

OFFICIAL SELECTION
SUNDANCE
FILM FESTIVAL

LITTLE MISS SUNSHINE
A FAMILY ON THE VERGE OF A BREAKDOWN

IN THEATRES THIS SUMMER

MOVIE TITLE INDEX

DIRECTOR INDEX

793

PEOPLE INDEX

EVENT INDEX

799

ACKNOWLEGMENTS

Indices compiled by
Ann Barrett

Picture Credits
Corbis
Bettmann/CORBIS 4, 5, 10, 15, 22, 35, 38, 50, 56, 62, 82, 89, 90, 93, 97, 104, 109, 112, 117, 118, 132, 137, 138, 159, 178, 200, 221, 260, 277, 308, 355, 389, 436, 451, 490, 501, 573; Bureau L.A. Collection/CORBIS 640; CinemaPhoto/Corbis 123,124, 283; CORBIS 94; CORBIS SYGMA 673, 684, 693, 708; David J. & Janice L. Frent Collection/CORBIS 556; Georges Pierre/Sygma/ Corbis 378; Hulton-Deutsch Collection/CORBIS 311, 394, 418; John Springer Collection/CORBIS 9, 13, 21, 27, 30, 65, 74, 129, 150, 153, 165, 170, 190, 199, 204, 207, 215, 218, 243, 247, 254, 265, 284, 298, 307, 356, 401, 412, 421, 439, 465; MAIMAN RICK/CORBIS SYGMA 652; Merie W. Wallace/ Warner Bros/Bureau L.A. Collection/Corbis 763; MGM/Corbis 351, 633, 634; Michael Gibson/Universal Pictures/ZUMA /Corbis 769; Michael Nicholson/CORBIS 55; Mitchell Gerber/CORBIS 716; PARIS CLAUDE/CORBIS SYGMA 16; Reuters/CORBIS 755; Roger Ressmeyer/CORBIS 484; Steve Sands/New York Newswire/ Corbis 719; Sunset Boulevard/ Corbis 143, 257, 512; Swim Ink 2, LLC/CORBIS 44, 49; Underwood & Underwood/CORBIS 79, 100, 103, 169, 182, 187; Warner_Bros_Italy/ epa/Corbis 700.

Picture Credits
Kobal
20th Century Fox / The Kobal Collection 146, 346, 422, 448, 466; 20th Century Fox/Columbia / The Kobal Collection 540; 20th Century Fox/Fox Searchlight Pictures / The Kobal Collection 785; 20th Century Fox/ Regency / The Kobal Collection 745; A.I.P. / The Kobal Collection 304; AKIRA / The Kobal Collection 610; AMBLIN/DREAMWORKS/WB / The Kobal Collection / JAMES, DAVID 723; ANGLO ENTERPRISE/ VINEYARD / The Kobal Collection 390; ANOUCHKA/ARGOS/SANDREWS / The Kobal Collection 386; ARGOS/OSHIMA / The Kobal Collection 522; ARGOS/SVENSK FILMINSTITUT/FILM 4 INT / The Kobal Collection 598; ARTISAN PICS / The Kobal Collection 707; BASIC PICTURES/MEDIA ASIA FILMS LTD / The Kobal Collection 741; BERIT FILMS / The Kobal Collection 203; BUNUEL-DALI / The Kobal Collection 68; CALENDAR PRODS / The Kobal Collection 559; CANAL+ / SONY / The Kobal Collection 770; CAPITOL/GRANADA/JERSEY/UA / The Kobal Collection 720; CAROLCO / The Kobal Collection 637; CESKOSLOVENSKY FILM / The Kobal Collection 398; CINETHESIA-GROKENBERGER/ZDF / The Kobal Collection 581; CINO DEL DUCA/PCE/LYRE / The Kobal Collection 319; Columbia / The Kobal Collection 166, 222, 234, 253, 303, 360, 461, 516, 528; Columbia/SONY/The Kobal Collection/CHUEN, CHAN KAM 715; CONSTALLATION/HACHETTE ET CIE / The Kobal Collection 646; CUBAN STATE FILM / The Kobal Collection 428; DUO FILMS/ATRE FRANCE CINEMA / The Kobal Collection 731; EDWARD R. PRESSMAN PRODS / The Kobal Collection 643; EGG FILMS/SHOW EAST / The Kobal Collection 751; ELIAS QUEREJETA PRODS / The Kobal Collection 489; EMBASSY / The Kobal Collection 408; ENDGAME/KINGSGATE FILMS/SENATOR INTERNATIONAL / The Kobal Collection / GIRAUD, SOPHIE 764; EVE PRODUCTION INC / The Kobal Collection 377; EXCELSA/MAYER-BURSTYN / The Kobal Collection 156; FARABI CINEMA/KIAROSTAMI / The Kobal Collection 659; FIGMENT/NOEL GAY/CHANNEL 4 / The Kobal Collection 674; FILMS 59/ALATRISTE/ UNINCI / The Kobal Collection 324; FILMS ALEPH/HISTORIA / The Kobal Collection 586; FORA FILM/ HERMITAGE BRIDGE STUDIO / The Kobal Collection 732; Fox FILMS / The Kobal Collection 71; GOLDEN HARVEST / The Kobal Collection 457; 458; HAMMER / The Kobal Collection 290; HANDMADE FILMS / The Kobal Collection 603; HERZOG/FILMVERLAG DER AUTOREN/ZDF / The Kobal Collection 564; HORSEPOWER FILMS / The Kobal Collection 752; IMAGE TEN / The Kobal Collection 417; INTERNATIONAL FILMS ESPANOLA/

ALPINE PRODUCTIONS / The Kobal Collection 393; JAFAR PANAHI FILM PRODUCTIONS / The Kobal Collection 748; 782; JET TONE / The Kobal Collection 656; JET TONE PRODNS / The Kobal Collection 666; LADD CO/WARNER BROTHERS / The Kobal Collection 585; LENFILM/NIKOLA FILM / The Kobal Collection 773; LORIMAR/UNIVERSAL / The Kobal Collection 582; LUCASFILM/20th Century Fox / The Kobal Collection 703; MALJACK PRODS / The Kobal Collection 592; MAYSLES/20th Century Fox / The Kobal Collection 447; MGM / The Kobal Collection 196, 231, 237, 238, 295, 314, 339, 345, 369, 402, 411, 433, 444; MGM / The Kobal Collection / DAVE DAL 397; MIRAMAX/ BUENA VISTA / The Kobal Collection 655; MOMENTUM FILMS / The Kobal Collection 677; MOSFILM / The Kobal Collection 511; NEW LINE / The Kobal Collection / WALLACE, MERIE W. 774; P.E.A / The Kobal Collection 515; PALLADIUM / The Kobal Collection 250; 372; PALOMAR / The Kobal Collection 477; PANDORA/ LUMINA FILMS / The Kobal Collection 756; PARALLAX/ROAD MOVIES / The Kobal Collection 696; PARAMOUNT / The Kobal Collection 244, 271, 333, 342, 479, 483, 502, 595, 609, 704; PARAMOUNT/MIRAMAX / The Kobal Collection / BRAY, PHIL 699; PARAMOUNT/RAFRAN / The Kobal Collection 427; PARC FILMS/MADELEINE FILMS / The Kobal Collection / JEANBRAU, HELENE 407; PICTUREHOUSE / The Kobal Collection / GORDON, MELINDA SUE 778; POLYGRAM/WARNERS/SILVER PICTURES / The Kobal Collection 651; PROD EUROPEE ASSO/PRODS ARTISTES ASSOC / The Kobal Collection 472; PROD TEPEYAC/ULTRAMAR / The Kobal Collection 225; PRODUCERS' RELEASING CORPORATION / The Kobal Collection 161; PRODUZIONE DE SICA / The Kobal Collection 181; QUINTA COMM. / The Kobal Collection / GEORGE, ETIENNE 735; RAI/IC/GPC / The Kobal Collection 539; RETEITALIA/SCENA FILM / The Kobal Collection 629; RIAMA-PATHE / The Kobal Collection 320; RYSHER ENTERTAINMENT / The Kobal Collection / SHELDON, JIM 681; SEASONAL FILM CORPORATION/The Kobal Collection 535; STUDIO CANAL+ / The Kobal Collection 738; STUDIO CANAL+/CENTRE NATIONAL DE LA CINEMATOGRAPHIE / The Kobal Collection 726; SUNCHILD PRODS/ FILMS ARMORIAL / The Kobal Collection 505; SVENSK FILMINDUSTRI / The Kobal Collection 41; 278; TERRA/TAMARA/CORMORAN / The Kobal Collection 329; The Kobal Collection 289; 383; 543; 662; TOHO / The Kobal Collection 226; TOUCHSTONE/PARAMOUNT / The Kobal Collection / DORY, ATTILA 690; TRI STAR / The Kobal Collection / CLOSE, MURRAY 665; UNITED ARTISTS / The Kobal Collection 195, 323, 336, 521, 527, 551, 555; UNITED ARTISTS/SEVEN ARTS / The Kobal Collection 330; UNITED FILM / The Kobal Collection 536; UNIVERSAL / The Kobal Collection 352, 359, 365, 366, 454, 568, 574, 613, 623; UNIVERSAL/ EMBASSY/The Kobal Collection 589; VARIETY / The Kobal Collection 546; VICTOR/PYRAMIDE/ CANAL +/PANDORA / The Kobal Collection 742; VINCENT GALLO PRODS. / The Kobal Collection 630; WALT DISNEY PICTURES / The Kobal Collection 567; WARNER BROS / The Kobal Collection 149, 175, 212, 266, 272, 462, 469, 508, 552, 604, 624; WARNER BROS/DC COMICS / The Kobal Collection 618; WARNER INDEPENDENT PICTURES / The Kobal Collection 781; WEGA FILM / The Kobal Collection 687; WORKING TITLE/POLYGRAM / The Kobal Collection 678